M000034983

DogFriendly.com's

Campground and RV Park Guide

by
Tara Kain and Len Kain
DogFriendly.com, Inc.

DogFriendly.com's Campground and RV Park Guide
by Tara Kain and Len Kain

DogFriendly.com, Inc.
6454 Pony Express Trail #33-233
Pollock Pines, CA 95726 USA
1-877-475-2275
email: email@dogfriendly.com
http://www.dogfriendly.com

PLEASE NOTE
Although the authors and publisher have tried to make the information as accurate as possible, they do not assume, and hereby disclaim, any liability for any loss or damage caused by errors, omissions, misleading information or potential travel problems caused by this book, even if such errors or omissions result from negligence, accident or any other cause.

CHECK AHEAD
We remind you, as always, to call ahead and confirm that the applicable establishment is still "dog-friendly" and that it will accommodate your pet.

DOGS OF ALL SIZES
If your dog is over 75-80 pounds, then please call the individual establishment to make sure that they allow your dog. Please be aware that establishments and local governments may also not allow particular breeds.

OTHER PARTIES DESCRIPTIONS
Some of the descriptions have been provided to us by our web site advertisers, paid researchers or other parties.

ISBN 13 – 978-0-9718742-6-8
ISBN 10 – 0-9718742-6-3

Printed in the United States of America

Table of Contents

2. Dog-Friendly Camping Cabins.. **283**

UNITED STATES – State Guides

CANADA – Province Guides

Introduction

DogFriendly.com's guides have helped over one million dog lovers plan vacations and trips with their dogs. This book is a guide for people who want to camp with dogs in tents, RVs, and motor homes. With this book, it is our goal to help you not only find campgrounds for you and your pet but also parks to visit, trails to hike, beaches and other places to enjoy together. We have researched campgrounds and RV parks, U.S. and Canadian Parks, State Parks and Provincial Parks for their detailed pet policies. This goes beyond a statement such as "Pets Allowed, with Restrictions" or "Pets allowed – on leash". These are the types of descriptions most campground guides have regarding pets. People who travel with pets know, however, that this is not the real pet policy. There are many other questions such as

- What additional fees are there for my pet?
- How many dogs may I have in my campsite?
- Are some breeds not allowed at the campground?
- Are there size restrictions on dogs at the campground?
- How many dogs may I have at my campsite?
- Dogs may be allowed in my RV but are they allowed if I camp in a tent? Or in the camping cabins?
- Is there a place to walk my dog? Am I allowed to walk my dog throughout the campground?
- Is there a place to let my dog off-leash? Are there any other pet amenities at the campground?
- If the campground is in a park are dogs allowed on the trails in the park? What other areas of the park are they allowed in?

The book also has highway guides for major highways throughout the U.S. and Canada listing campgrounds in cities along these highways. This will make it easier to find a place for the night. It also has a listing of off-leash dog parks and dog-friendly beaches and a guide to the U.S. National Parks. If you also plan on staying at hotels and other lodging during your travels you might also consider our book "DogFriendly.com's United States and Canada Dog Travel Guide" which looks at these accommodations as well as attractions, stores and outdoor restaurants that allow dogs.

Thank you for selecting DogFriendly.com's Camping and RV Park Guide and we hope you spend less time researching and more time actually going places with your dog. Enjoy your dog-friendly camping.

About Authors Tara and Len Kain

Tara and Len Kain have traveled over 150,000 miles across the U.S. and Canada with their family and dogs in search of some of the best dog-friendly places around. They founded DogFriendly.com in 1998 and have been traveling together with dogs since 1990. Currently, over 1 million people annually visit DogFriendly.com. Tara and Len, along with DogFriendly.com, have been featured in many newspaper articles, on radio and on TV. Tara, Len and their family reside in the California foothills near Sacramento.

Your Comments and Feedback

We value and appreciate your feedback and comments. If you want to recommend a dog-friendly place or establishment, let us know. If you find a place that is no longer dog-friendly, allows small dogs only or allows dogs in smoking rooms only, please let us know. You can contact us using the following information.

Mailing Address and Contact Information:
DogFriendly.com, Inc.
6454 Pony Express Trail #33-233
Pollock Pines, CA 95726 USA
Toll free phone: 1-877-475-2275
email: email@ dogfriendly.com
http://www.dogfriendly.com

How To Use This Guide

General Guidelines

1. Please only travel with a well-behaved dog that is comfortable around other people and especially children. Dogs should also be potty trained and not bark excessively.

2. Always keep your dog leashed unless management specifically tells you otherwise.

3. Campgrounds listed do not allow dogs to be left alone in your campsite unless specified by management. If the establishment does not allow pets to be left alone, try hiring a local pet sitter to watch your dog in the room.

4. Pet policies and management change often. Please always call ahead to make sure an establishment still exists and is still dog-friendly.

5. After purchasing your book, please visit http://www.dogfriendly.com/updates for FREE book updates. We will do our best to let you know which places may no longer be dog-friendly.

Preparation for a Road Trip

A Month Before

If you don't already have one, get a pet identification tag for your dog. It should have your dog's name, your name and phone number. Consider using a cell phone number, a home number and, if possible, the number of where you will be staying.

Get a first aid kit for your dog. It comes in very handy if you need to remove any ticks. The kits are usually available at a pet store, a veterinary office or on the Internet.

If you do not already have a dog harness for riding in the car or motor home, consider purchasing one for your dog's and your own safety. A loose dog can fly into the windshield or into you and injure you or cause you to lose control of the vehicle. Dog harnesses are usually sold at pet stores or on the Internet.

Make a trip to the vet if necessary for the following:

- A current rabies tag for your dog's collar. Also get paperwork with proof of the rabies vaccine.
- Dogs can possibly get heartworm from mosquitoes in the mountains, rural areas or on hikes. Research or talk to your vet and ask him or her if the area you are traveling to has a high risk of heartworm disease. The vet may suggest placing your dog on a monthly heartworm preventative medicine.
- Consider using some type of flea preventative for your dog.
- Make sure your dog is in good health.

Several Days Before

Make sure you have enough dog food for the duration of the trip.

If your dog is on any medication, remember to bring it along.

Some dog owners will also purchase bottled water for the trip, because some dogs can get sick from drinking water they are not used to. Talk to your vet for more information.

If you are visting the desert or another hot envionment be aware that your dogs paws may burn if it is very hot. You may consider boots for your dog if you are planning to spend much time in these environments.

The Day Before

Do not forget to review DogFriendly.com's Etiquette for the Traveling Dog!

Road Trip Day

Remember to pack all of your dog's necessities: food, water, dog dishes, leash, snacks and goodies, several favorite toys, brush, towels for dirty paws, plastic bags for cleaning up after your dog, doggie first aid kit, possibly dog booties if you are venturing to an especially cold or hot region, and bring any medicine your dog might be taking.

Before you head out, put on that doggie seat belt harness.

On The Road

Keep it cool and well ventilated in the vehicle for your dog.

Stop at least every 2-3 hours so your dog can relieve him or herself. Also offer him or her water during the stops.

Never leave your pet alone in a parked car - even in the shade with the window cracked open. According to the Los Angeles SPCA, on a hot day, a car can heat up to 160 degrees in minutes, potentially causing your pet (or child) heat stroke, brain damage, and even death. If you leave your pet in an RV make sure that the windows are open, there is sufficient air flow or you are running fans or A/C.

If your dog needs medical attention during your trip, check the yellow pages phone book in the area and look under Veterinarians. If you do not see an emergency vet listed, call any local vet even   during the evening hours and they can usually inform you of the closest emergency vet.

Etiquette for the Traveling Dog

So you have found the perfect getaway spot that allows dogs, but maybe you have never traveled with your dog. Or maybe you are a seasoned dog traveler. But do you know all of your doggie etiquette? Basic courtesy rules, like your dog should be leashed unless a place specifically allows your dog to be leash-free. And do you ask for a paper bowl or cup for your thirsty pooch at an outdoor restaurant instead of letting him or her drink from your water glass?

There are many do's and don'ts when traveling with your best friend. We encourage all dog owners to follow a basic code of doggie etiquette, so places will continue to allow and welcome our best friends. Unfortunately all it takes is one bad experience for an establishment to stop allowing dogs. Let's all try to be on our best behavior to keep and even encourage new places to allow our pooches.

Everywhere...

- Well-Behaved Dogs. Only travel or go around town with a well-behaved dog that is friendly to people and especially children. If your dog is not comfortable around other people, you might consider taking your dog to obedience classes or hiring a professional trainer. Your well-behaved dog should also be potty trained and not bark excessively. We believe that dogs should be kept on leash. If a dog is on leash, he or she is easier to bring under control. Also, many establishments require that dogs be on leash and many people around you will feel more comfortable as well. And last, please never leave your dog alone at a campground, hotel or other establishment unless it is permitted by the management.

- Leashed Dogs. Please always keep your dog leashed, unless management specifically states otherwise. Most establishments (including lodging, outdoor restaurants, attractions, parks, beaches, stores and festivals) require that your dog be on leash. Plus most cities and counties have an official leash law that requires pets to be leashed at all times when not on your property. Keeping your dog on leash will also prevent any unwanted contact with other people that are afraid of dogs, people that do not appreciate strange dogs coming up to them, and even other dog owners who have a leashed dog. Even when on leash, do not let your pooch visit with other people or dogs unless welcomed. Keeping dogs on leash will also protect them from running into traffic, running away, or getting injured by wildlife or other dogs. Even the most well-behaved and trained dogs can be startled by something, especially in a new environment.

- Be Considerate. Always clean up after your dog. Pet stores sell pooper scooper bags. You can also buy sandwich bags from your local grocery store. They work quite well and are cheap!

At Campgrounds or RV Parks...

- Although most RV Parks and many campgrounds allow dogs each has different rules, restrictions and types of dogs that are allowed. Be aware of these rules when you check in and respect them.

- Always assume that a dog must be on leash in a campground. If there is an off-leash area then use that area for your pets off-leash activity.

- Always assume that your dog is not allowed in common areas such as swimming pools, game rooms and general stores unless it is specifically allowed by management.

- Be respectful of your neighbors. Don't assume that they will want to have your dog barking at them or visiting with them. Only leave your dog outside of your vehicle if it is chained or otherwise restrained and you are there to supervise.

- Many campgrounds have designated specific dog walk areas. Walk your dog in the designated areas. Always clean up after your dog.

In Parks...

- Respect the park's leash laws and always clean up after your pet. Those parks that ban dogs cite these two reasons in most cases as to why dogs are not allowed in the park.

- Always assume that another park visitor is not interested in a visit from your dog unless they specifically invite your dog over to them. This is especially true of children.

At Hotels or Other Types of Lodging...

- Unless it is obvious, ask the hotel clerk if dogs are allowed in the hotel lobby. Also, because of health codes, dogs are usually not allowed into a lobby area while it is being used for serving food like continental breakfast. Dogs may be allowed into the area once there is no food being served, but check with management first.

- Never leave your dog alone in the hotel room. The number one reason hotel management does not allow dogs is because some people leave them in the room alone. Some dogs, no matter how well-trained, can cause damage, bark continuously or scare the housekeepers. Unless the hotel management allows it, please make sure your dog is never left alone in the room. If you need to leave your dog in the room, consider hiring a local pet sitter.

- While you are in the room with your dog, place the Do Not Disturb sign on the door or keep the deadbolt locked. Many housekeepers have been surprised or scared by dogs when entering a room.

- In general, do not let your pet on the bed or chairs, especially if your dog sheds easily and might leave pet hair on the furniture. Some very pet-friendly accommodations will actually give you a sheet to lay over the bed so your pet can join you. If your pet cannot resist coming hopping onto the furniture with you, bring your own sheet.

- When your dog needs to go to the bathroom, take him or her away from the hotel rooms and the bushes located right next to the rooms. Try to find some dirt or bushes near the parking lot. Some hotels have a designated pet walk area.

At Outdoor Restaurants...

- Tie your dog to your chair, not the table (unless the table is secured to the ground). If your dog decides to get up and move away from the table, he or she will not take the entire table.

- If you want to give your dog some water, please ask the waiter/waitress to bring a paper cup or bowl of water for your dog. Do not use your own water glass. Many restaurants and even other guests frown upon this.

- Your pooch should lay or sit next to your table. At restaurants, dogs are not allowed to sit on the chairs or tables, or eat off the tables. This type of activity could make a restaurant owner or manager ban dogs. And do not let your pooch beg from other customers. Unfortunately, not everyone loves dogs!

At Retail Stores...

- Keep a close eye on your dog and make sure he or she does not go to the bathroom in the store. Store owners that allow dogs inside assume that responsible dog owners will be entering their store. Before entering a dog-friendly store, visit your local pet store first. They are by far the most forgiving. If your dog does not go to the bathroom there, then you are off to a great start! If your dog does make a mistake in any store, clean it up. Ask the store clerk for paper towels or something similar so you can clean up any mess.

At Festivals and Outdoor Events...

Make sure your dog has relieved himself or herself before entering a festival or event area. The number one reason that most festival coordinators do not allow dogs is because some dogs go to the bathroom on a vendor's booth or in areas where people might sit.

Breed Specific Laws and the Effect of These Laws on Travel With Dogs

There has been a trend in cities, counties, states and provinces towards what is known as Breed-Specific Laws (BSL) in which a municipality bans or restricts the freedoms of dog owners with specific breeds of dogs. These laws vary from place to place and are affecting a greater number of dog owners every year. Most people may think that these laws affect only the "Pit Bull" but this is not always the case. Although the majority of dogs affected are pit-bulls other breeds of dogs as well as mixed breeds that include targeted breeds are also named in the various laws in North America. These laws range from registration requirements and leash or muzzle requirements to extreme laws in which the breed is banned from the municipality outright. Some places may even be permitted to confiscate a visitors dog who unknowingly enters the region with a banned breed.

As of August 29, 2005 the province of Ontario, Canada (including Toronto, Niagara Falls, and Ottawa) passed a very broad breed-specific law banning Pit Bulls and "similar" dogs from the province. The law allows for confiscation of visiting dogs as well as dogs living in Ontario. It is extremely important that people visiting Ontario make sure that they are able to prove that their dog is not a Pit Bull with other documentation. Various cities throughout the U.S. and Canada have muzzle requirements for Pit Bulls and other restrictions on targeted breeds as well. Breed-specific laws do get repealed as well. In October, 2005 the city of Vancouver, BC removed its requirement that Pit Bulls be muzzled in public and now only requires dogs with a known history of aggressiveness to be muzzled.

The breed specific laws usually effect pit bull type dogs but are often vaguely written and may also effect mixed breed dogs that resemble the targeted breeds. These laws are always changing and can be passed by cities, counties and even states and provinces. We recommend that travelers with dogs check into whether they are affected by such laws. You may check www.DogFriendly.com/bsl for links to further information on BSL.

DogFriendly.com does not support breed-specific laws. Most people who take their dogs out in public are responsible and those that choose to train a dog to be viscous will simply choose another breed, causing other breeds to be banned or regulated in the future.

Customs Information for Traveling Between the United States and Canada

If you will be traveling between the United States and Canada, identification for Customs and Immigration is required. U.S. and Canadian citizens traveling across the border need the following:

People

- Proof of citizenship such as your passport or a certified copy of your birth certificate issued by the city, county or state/province where you were born.

- Photo identification such as a current valid driver's license.

- People with children need to bring their child's birth certificate. Single parents, grandparents or guardians traveling with children often need proof or notarized letters from the other parent authorizing travel.

Dogs

- Dogs must be free of evidence of diseases communicable to humans when possibly examined at the port of entry.

- Valid rabies vaccination certificate (including an expiration date usually up to 3 years from the actual vaccine date and a veterinarian's signature). If no expiration date is specified on the certificate, then the certificate is acceptable if the date of the vaccination is not more than 12 months before the date of arrival. The certificate must show that the dog had the rabies vaccine at least 30 days prior to entry.

- Young puppies must be confined at a place of the owner's choosing until they are three months old, then they must be vaccinated. They must remain in confinement for 30 days after the vaccination.

Chapter 1

Dog-Friendly Campgrounds and RV Parks

United States Listings

Alabama Listings

Alexander City

Wind Creek State Park
4325 H 128
Alexander City, AL
256-329-0845
This park of 1,445 acres, along the shores of a 41,000 acre clear-water reservoir, provides a marina, trails, various habitats, and a variety of land and water activities and recreation. Dogs of all sizes are allowed at no additional fee. Dogs may not be left unattended, and they must be leashed and cleaned up after in camp areas. Dogs are not allowed in or around the cabins, in park buildings, or on the beaches. Dogs are allowed on the trails. The camping and tent areas also allow dogs. There is a dog walk area at the campground. Multiple dogs may be allowed.

Auburn

Leisure Time Campground
2670 S College Street
Auburn, AL
334-821-2267
Dogs of all sizes are allowed. There are no additional pet fees. Dogs must be leashed and cleaned up after. The camping and tent areas also allow dogs. There is a dog walk area at the campground. Multiple dogs may be allowed.

Birmingham

Cherokee Campground
2800 H 93
Helena, AL
205-428-8339
Dogs of all sizes are allowed. There are no additional pet fees. Dogs must be quiet, leashed, and cleaned up after. There is a dog walk area at the campground. Multiple dogs may be allowed.

Birmingham South Campground
222 H 33

Pelham, AL
205-664-8832
Dogs of all sizes are allowed. There are no additional pet fees. Dogs must be leashed and cleaned up after. The camping and tent areas also allow dogs. There is a dog walk area at the campground. Dogs are allowed in the camping cabins. Multiple dogs may be allowed.

Cullman

Good Hope Campground
330 Super Saver Road
Cullman, AL
256-739-1319
Dogs of all sizes are allowed. There are no additional pet fees. Dogs must be leashed and cleaned up after. The camping and tent areas also allow dogs. There is a dog walk area at the campground. Multiple dogs may be allowed.

Dauphin Island

Dauphin Island Campground
109 Bienville Blvd
Dauphin Island, AL
251-861-2742
Dogs of all sizes are allowed. There are no additional pet fees. Dogs must be quiet, leashed, and cleaned up after. The camping and tent areas also allow dogs. There is a dog walk area at the campground. Multiple dogs may be allowed.

Decatur

Point Mallard Campground
2600-C Point Mallard Drive
Decatur, AL
256-351-7772
Dogs of all sizes are allowed. There are no additional pet fees. Dogs must be leashed and cleaned up after. The camping and tent areas also allow dogs. There is a dog walk area at the campground. Multiple dogs may be allowed.

Delta

Cheaha Resort State Park
19644 H 281S
Delta, AL
256-488-5111
This park is at the highest peak in the state and is surrounded by national forest. It offers spectacular scenery, provides 6 hiking trails and a variety of land and water activities

and recreation. Dogs of all sizes are allowed at no additional fee for the camp area. There is a $10 per night per pet additional fee for the cabin or chalets. Dogs may not be left unattended, and they must be leashed at all times, and cleaned up after. Dogs are not allowed on the beaches or in buildings. Dogs are allowed on the trails. The camping and tent areas also allow dogs. There is a dog walk area at the campground. Dogs are allowed in the camping cabins. Multiple dogs may be allowed.

Double Springs

Bankhead National Forest
1070 H 33N
Double Springs, AL
205-489-5111
This forest provides a variety of camping areas, trails, recreation, and diverse ecosystems that support a large variety of plants, fish, mammals, and bird species. Dogs are allowed at no additional fee. Dogs may not be left unattended, and they must be leashed and cleaned up after in the camp areas. Dogs are allowed on the trails. This campground is closed during the off-season. The camping and tent areas also allow dogs. There is a dog walk area at the campground. Multiple dogs may be allowed.

Eufaula

Lakepoint Resort State Park
104 Lakepoint Drive
Eufaula, AL
334-687-8011
This scenic 1,220 acre park along the 45,000 acre Lake Eufaula offers a convention center, an 18-hole golf course, and a variety of land and water recreation. Dogs of all sizes are allowed at no additional fee. Dogs may not be left unattended, and they must be leashed and cleaned up after. Dogs are not allowed in park buildings, at the lodge, or on the trails. The camping and tent areas also allow dogs. There is a dog walk area at the campground. Multiple dogs may be allowed.

Fort Payne

Desoto State Park
13883 County Road 89
Fort Payne, AL

256-845-5075
Rushing waterfalls and fragrant wildflowers greet visitors at this 3,502-acre park that offers a nature center, hiking trails, and a variety of land and water activities and recreation. Dogs of all sizes are allowed at no additional fee. Dogs may not be left unattended, and they must be leashed and cleaned up after. Dogs are not allowed in public swim areas, in park buildings, or at the lodge. Dogs are allowed on the trails. The camping and tent areas also allow dogs. There is a dog walk area at the campground. Multiple dogs may be allowed.

Gadsden

Noccalula Falls Park and Campground
1600 Noccalula Road
Gadsden, AL
256-543-7412
Dogs of all sizes are allowed. There are no additional pet fees. Dogs may not be left unattended, and they must be quiet, leashed, and cleaned up after. There are some breed restrictions. The camping and tent areas also allow dogs. There is a dog walk area at the campground. Multiple dogs may be allowed.

River Country Campground
1 River Road
Gadsden, AL
256-543-7111
Dogs of all sizes are allowed. There are no additional pet fees. Dogs must be leashed and cleaned up after. The camping and tent areas also allow dogs. There is a dog walk area at the campground. 2 dogs may be allowed.

Gulf Shores

Gulf Breeze Resort
19800 Oak Road W
Gulf Shores, AL
251-968-8884
Dogs of all sizes are allowed. There are no additional pet fees. Dogs may not be tied to camp property and they may not be left unattended outside. Dogs must be leashed and cleaned up after, and they are not allowed in the buildings, pavilion, bathrooms, or at the pool. The camping and tent areas also allow dogs. There is a dog walk area at the campground. Multiple dogs may be allowed.

Gulf State Park
22050 Campground Road
Gulf Shores, AL
251-948-6353
This 6,150 acre park offers a 900 acre lake with white sandy beaches, nature programs, miles of various trails, and a variety of land and water recreational pursuits. Dogs of all sizes are allowed at no additional fee. Dogs may not be left unattended, and they must be leashed and cleaned up after. Dogs are not allowed on the beaches or in buildings. Dogs are allowed on the trails. The camping and tent areas also allow dogs. There is a dog walk area at the campground. Multiple dogs may be allowed.

Luxury RV Resort
590 Gulf Shores Parkway
Gulf Shores, AL
251-948-5444
Dogs of all sizes are allowed. There are no additional pet fees. Dogs may not be left unattended, and they must be leashed and cleaned up after. This is an RV only park. There is a dog walk area at the campground. Multiple dogs may be allowed.

Southport Campground
108 W 28th Avenue
Gulf Shores, AL
251-968-6220
Dogs up to 25 pounds are allowed. There are no additional pet fees. Dogs may not be left unattended outside, and they must be leashed and cleaned up after. There are some breed restrictions. The camping and tent areas also allow dogs. There is a dog walk area at the campground. Multiple dogs may be allowed.

Huntsville

Monte Sano State Park
5105 Nolen
Huntsville, AL
256-534-3757
This serene 2,400 acre park provides 14 miles of hiking trails and a variety of outdoor recreational pursuits. Dogs of all sizes are allowed at no additional fee. Dogs may not be left unattended outside, and they must be leashed at all times, and cleaned up after. Dogs are not allowed on the beaches anywhere, or in buildings. Dogs are allowed on the trails. The camping

and tent areas also allow dogs. There is a dog walk area at the campground. Multiple dogs may be allowed.

Knoxville

Knox Hill RV Park
252 Old Patton Road
Knoxville, AL
205-372-3911
Dogs of all sizes are allowed. There are no additional pet fees. Dogs may not be left unattended, and they must be leashed and cleaned up after. The camping and tent areas also allow dogs. There is a dog walk area at the campground. Multiple dogs may be allowed.

Langston

Little Mountain Marina
1001 Murphy Hills Road
Langston, AL
256-582-8211
Dogs of all sizes are allowed. There are no additional pet fees. Dogs may not be left unattended, and they must be quiet, leashed, and cleaned up after. There are some breed restrictions. The camping and tent areas also allow dogs. There is a dog walk area at the campground. 2 dogs may be allowed.

South Sauty Creek Resort
6845 S Sauty Road
Langston, AL
256-582-3367
Dogs of all sizes are allowed. There are no additional pet fees. Dogs may not be left unattended, and they must be leashed and cleaned up after. This RV park is closed during the off-season. The camping and tent areas also allow dogs. Multiple dogs may be allowed.

Mobile

Magnolia Springs RV Hideaway
10831 Magnolia Springs H
Foley, AL
800-981-0981
Dogs of all sizes are allowed. There are no additional pet fees. Dogs may not be left unattended outside, and they must be quiet, well behaved, leashed, and cleaned up after. This is an RV only park. There is a dog walk area at the campground. Multiple dogs may be allowed.

Palm Lake Resort
15810 H 59
Foley, AL
251-970-3773
Dogs of all sizes are allowed. There are no additional pet fees. Dogs may not be left unattended outside, and they must be quiet, well behaved, leashed, and cleaned up after. This is an RV only park. There is a dog walk area at the campground. Multiple dogs may be allowed.

Shady Acres Campground
2500 Old Military Road
Mobile, AL
251-478-0013
Dogs of all sizes are allowed. There are no additional pet fees. Dogs may not be left unattended outside, and they must be leashed and cleaned up after. There is a dog walk area at the campground. Multiple dogs may be allowed.

Montgomery

Capital City RV Park
4655 Old Wetumpka H (H 231N)
Montgomery, AL
877-271-8026
Dogs of all sizes are allowed. There are no additional pet fees. Dogs may not be left unattended outside, and they must be leashed and cleaned up after. This is an RV only park. There is a dog walk area at the campground. Multiple dogs may be allowed.

Ozark

Ozark Travel Park
2414 N H 231
Ozark, AL
334-774-3219
Dogs of all sizes are allowed. There are no additional pet fees. Dogs may not be left unattended outside, and they must be leashed and cleaned up after. There is a fenced in dog run for off lead. The camping and tent areas also allow dogs. There is a dog walk area at the campground. Multiple dogs may be allowed.

Pelham

Oak Mountain State Park
200 Terrace Drive
Pelham, AL
205-620-2527
The state's largest park at 9,940 acres is home to the Wildlife Center, the largest wildlife rehabilitation center in Alabama, and also to the unique Treetop Nature Trail. They also provide a wide variety of recreational pursuits. Dogs of all sizes are allowed at no additional fee. Dogs may not be left unattended except for short periods, and they must be on no more than a 6 foot leash, and cleaned up after. Dogs are not allowed in buildings. The camping and tent areas also allow dogs. There is a dog walk area at the campground. Multiple dogs may be allowed.

Silver Hill

Wales West
13670 Smiley Street
Silver Hill, AL
888-569-5337
Dogs of all sizes are allowed. There are no additional pet fees. Dogs must be leashed and cleaned up after. There are some breed restrictions. There is a dog walk area at the campground. Multiple dogs may be allowed.

Talladega

Talladega National Forest
1001 North Street
Talladega, AL
256-362-2909
This forest provides a variety of camping areas, trails, recreation, and diverse ecosystems that support a large variety of plants, fish, mammals, and bird species. Dogs are allowed at no additional fee. Dogs may not be left unattended outside, and they must be leashed and cleaned up after in the camp areas. Dogs are allowed on the trails. This campground is closed during the off-season. The camping and tent areas also allow dogs. There is a dog walk area at the campground. There are no water hookups at the campground. Multiple dogs may be allowed.

Troy

Deer Run RV Park
25629 H 231N
Troy, AL
334-566-6517
Dogs of all sizes are allowed. There are no additional pet fees. Dogs may not be left unattended outside, and please clean up after your pet. They may be off lead only if they are under voice control and will not chase other animals. Dogs are allowed on the trails that wind through the 72 acre park. This is an RV park only. There is a dog walk area at the campground. Multiple dogs may be allowed.

Tuskegee

Tuskegee National Forest
125 National Forest Road, Bldg 949
Tuskegee, AL
334-727-2652
This forest provides a variety of camping areas, trails, recreation, and diverse ecosystems that support a large variety of plants, fish, mammals, and bird species. Dogs are allowed at no additional fee. Dogs may not be left unattended, and they must be leashed and cleaned up after in the camp areas. Dogs may be off lead in the forest only if they will not chase and are under voice control. The camping and tent areas also allow dogs. There is a dog walk area at the campground. There are no water hookups at the campground. Multiple dogs may be allowed.

Wing

Conecuh National Forest
H 137
Wing, AL
334-222-2555
This forest provides a variety of camping areas, trails, recreation, and diverse ecosystems that support a large variety of plants, fish, mammals, and bird species. Dogs are allowed at no additional fee. Dogs may not be left unattended, and they must be quiet, well behaved, leashed and cleaned up after in the camp areas. Dogs are allowed on the trails. The camping and tent areas also allow dogs. There is a dog walk area at the campground. There are no water hookups at the campground. Multiple dogs may be allowed.

Alaska Listings

Anchorage

Golden Nugget Camper Park

4100 DeBarr Road
Anchorage, AK
907-333-2012
Dogs of all sizes are allowed. There are no additional pet fees. Dogs may not be left unattended, must be leashed, and cleaned up after. The camping and tent areas also allow dogs. There is a dog walk area at the campground. Multiple dogs may be allowed.

Ship Creek Landing's RV Park
150 N Ingra
Anchorage, AK
907-277-0877
Dogs of all sizes are allowed. There are no additional pet fees. Dogs must be leashed and cleaned up after. This RV park is closed during the off-season. The camping and tent areas also allow dogs. There is a dog walk area at the campground. Multiple dogs may be allowed.

Denali

Denali Rainbow Village
M.P. 238.6 George Parks H
Denali, AK
907-683-7777
Dogs of all sizes are allowed. There are no additional pet fees. Dogs must be leashed and cleaned up after. This RV park is closed during the off-season. There is a dog walk area at the campground. Multiple dogs may be allowed.

Denali Riverside RV Park
M.P. 240 George Parks H
Denali, AK
907-388-1748
Dogs of all sizes are allowed. There are no additional pet fees. Dogs must be leashed and cleaned up after. This RV park is closed during the off-season. There is a dog walk area at the campground. Multiple dogs may be allowed.

Denali Park

Denali National Park and Preserve
PO Box 9
Denali Park, AK
907-683-2294
Dogs must be on leash and must be cleaned up after in Denali National Park. Dogs are only allowed on the paved roads and dirt roads. One place to walk is on the road to Savage after mile 15, which is a dirt road and only the park buses are allowed. Access is by car depending on weather. Dogs on leash are

allowed in the Denali National Park campgrounds, but they may not be left unattended in the campgrounds. The park features auto touring, camping, and scenery.

Glenallen

Tolsona Campground
M.P. 173 Glenn H
Glenallen, AK
907-822-3865
Dogs of all sizes are allowed. There are no additional pet fees. Dogs must be leashed and cleaned up after. This RV park is closed during the off-season. The camping and tent areas also allow dogs. There is a dog walk area at the campground. Multiple dogs may be allowed.

Glennallen

Northern Lights RV Campground
18 H.7 Glen Highway
Glennallen, AK
907-822-3199
Dogs of all sizes are allowed. There are no additional pet fees. Dogs may not be left unattended, must be leashed, and cleaned up after. This RV park is closed during the off-season. There is a dog walk area at the campground. Multiple dogs may be allowed.

Healy

McKinley RV and Campground
248.5 M.P. George Parks H
Healy, AK
907-683-2379
Dogs of all sizes are allowed. There are no additional pet fees. Dogs are not to be left unattended except for short periods, and only if the the dog will be quiet and well behaved. Dogs must be leashed and cleaned up after. The camping and tent areas also allow dogs. There is a dog walk area at the campground. Multiple dogs may be allowed.

Kenai

Beluga Lookout Lodge and RV Park
929 Mission Avenue
Kenai, AK
800-745-5999
Dogs of all sizes are allowed. There are no additional pet fees. Dogs must be leashed and cleaned up after. Dogs may not be tied up

outside unattended. This RV park is closed during the off-season. The camping and tent areas also allow dogs. There is a dog walk area at the campground. Multiple dogs may be allowed.

North Pole

Riverview RV Park
1316 Badger Road
North Pole, AK
888-488-6392
Dogs of all sizes are allowed. There are no additional pet fees. Dogs may not be left unattended or tied up outside alone. Dogs must be leashed and cleaned up after. This RV park is closed during the off-season. There is a dog walk area at the campground. Multiple dogs may be allowed.

Santaland RV Park
125 St Nicholas Drive
North Pole, AK
907-488-9123
Dogs of all sizes are allowed. There are no additional pet fees. Dogs must be leashed and cleaned up after. This RV park is closed during the off-season. The camping and tent areas also allow dogs. There is a dog walk area at the campground. Multiple dogs may be allowed.

Palmer

Mountain View RV Park
1405 N Smith Road
Palmer, AK
800-264-4582
Dogs of all sizes are allowed. There are no additional pet fees. Dogs may not be left unattended at any time, must be leashed, and cleaned up after. Dogs must not be near the neighbors' trees that edge some of the property. This RV park is closed during the off-season. The camping and tent areas also allow dogs. There is a dog walk area at the campground. Multiple dogs may be allowed.

Seward

Bear Creek RV Park
33508 Lincoln
Seward, AK
907-224-5725
Dogs of all sizes are allowed. There are no additional pet fees. Dogs must be leashed and cleaned up after. There is a dog walk area at the

campground. Multiple dogs may be allowed.

Skagway

Garden City RV Park
15th and State Streets
Skagway, AK
907-983-2378
Dogs of all sizes are allowed. There are no additional pet fees. Dogs may not be left unattended, must be leashed, and cleaned up after. This RV park is closed during the off-season. There is a dog walk area at the campground. Multiple dogs may be allowed.

Skagway Mountain View RV Park
12th and Broadway
Skagway, AK
907-983-3333
Dogs of all sizes are allowed. There are no additional pet fees. Dogs must be leashed and cleaned up after. This RV park is closed during the off-season. The camping and tent areas also allow dogs. There is a dog walk area at the campground.

Sterling

Alaska Canoe and Campground
35292 Sterling H (M.P.84)
Sterling, AK
907-262-2331
Dogs of all sizes are allowed. Dogs may not be left unattended, must be leashed, and cleaned up after. Dogs are also allowed to go on the canoe trips. This RV park is closed during the off-season. The camping and tent areas also allow dogs. There is a dog walk area at the campground. Multiple dogs may be allowed.

Tok

Tundra Lodge and RV Park
M.P. 1315 Alaska H
Tok, AK
907-883-7875
Dogs of all sizes are allowed. There are no additional pet fees. Dogs may not be left unattended, must be leashed, and cleaned up after. This RV park is closed during the off-season. The camping and tent areas also allow dogs. There is a dog walk area at the campground. Multiple dogs may be allowed.

Valdez

Bear Paw RV and Tent Park
101 N Harbor Drive
Valdez, AK
907-835-2530
Dogs of all sizes are allowed. There are no additional pet fees. Dogs must be leashed and cleaned up after This RV park is closed during the off-season. The camping and tent areas also allow dogs. There is a dog walk area at the campground. Multiple dogs may be allowed.

Arizona Listings

Amando

Mountain View RV Ranch
2843 E Frontage Road
Amando, AZ
520-398-9401
Dogs of all sizes are allowed. There are no additional pet fees. Dogs must be quiet, well behaved, leashed, and cleaned up after. The camping and tent areas also allow dogs. There is a dog walk area at the campground. Dogs are allowed in the camping cabins. Multiple dogs may be allowed.

Apache Junction

La Hacienda RV Resort
1797 W 28th Avenue
Apache Junction, AZ
480-982-2808
One dog up to 60 pounds, or 2 dogs up to 10 pounds each are allowed. There are no additional pet fees. Dogs may not be left unattended outside, and they must be quiet, well behaved, leashed, and cleaned up after. There are some breed restrictions. There is a dog walk area at the campground.

Lost Dutchman State Park
6109 N. Apache Trail
Apache Junction, AZ
480-982-4485
This park is located at the base of the Superstition Mountains, and there are many year round recreational activities and trails to explore. Dogs are allowed at no additional fee. Dogs may not be left unattended, and they must be leashed and cleaned up after. The camping and tent areas also allow

dogs. There is a dog walk area at the campground. There are no electric or water hookups at the campground. Multiple dogs may be allowed.

Mesa/Apache Junction KOA
1540 S Tomahawk Road
Apache Junction, AZ
480-982-4015
Dogs of all sizes are allowed, and there are no additional pet fees for tent or RV sites. There is a $25 refundable deposit for the cabins and only 2 dogs are allowed. Dogs may not be left unattended, and they must be leashed and cleaned up after. There are some breed restrictions. The camping and tent areas also allow dogs. There is a dog walk area at the campground. Dogs are allowed in the camping cabins. Multiple dogs may be allowed.

Superstition Sunrise
702 S Meridian
Apache Junction, AZ
480-986-4524
This park is mostly close to 55 or older, no children. Dogs of all sizes are allowed. There are no additional pet fees. Dogs must be leashed and cleaned up after. There is a fenced in area for off lead. Dogs must be walked in the designated pet areas only, and not to the office or other non-pet areas. There is a dog walk area at the campground. Multiple dogs may be allowed.

Weaver's Needle Travel Trailor Resort
250 S Tomahawk Road
Apache Junction, AZ
480-982-3683
Dogs of all sizes are allowed. There are no additional pet fees. Dogs must be leashed and cleaned up after, and there is a fenced in dog park on site. Dogs must be walked in designated areas for pets only and not in the rest of the park where campers do not have dogs. There is a dog walk area at the campground.

Benson

Benson KOA
180 W Four Feathers
Benson, AZ
520-586-3977
Dogs of all sizes are allowed, and there are no additional pet fees for tent or RV sites. There is a $5 one time fee per pet for the cabins. Dogs

may not be left unattended outside, and they must be leashed and cleaned up after. The camping and tent areas also allow dogs. There is a dog walk area at the campground. Dogs are allowed in the camping cabins. 2 dogs may be allowed.

Butterfield RV Resort and Observatory
251 S Ocotillo
Benson, AZ
520-586-4400
Dogs of all sizes are allowed. There are no additional pet fees. Dogs must be leashed and cleaned up after. There is a fenced in area for dogs where they can be off lead. There is a dog walk area at the campground. Multiple dogs may be allowed.

Kartchner Caverns State Park
2980 S H 90
Benson, AZ
520-586-2283
The guided cave tours are a main attraction at this park and reservations for the caves are suggested. Other attractions at this park include the Discovery Center, interactive displays, an amphitheater, and a variety of hiking trails. Dogs are allowed at no additional fee. Dogs must be leashed and cleaned up after. Dogs are not allowed in the Discovery Center or other park buildings. The camping and tent areas also allow dogs. There is a dog walk area at the campground. There are no water hookups at the campground. Multiple dogs may be allowed.

Black Canyon City

Black Canyon City KOA
19600 E St Joseph Road
Black Canyon City, AZ
623-374-5318
Dogs of all sizes are allowed. There are no additional pet fees. Dogs may not be left unattended, and they must be quiet, leashed, and cleaned up after. There are some breed restrictions. The camping and tent areas also allow dogs. There is a dog walk area at the campground. Multiple dogs may be allowed.

Bullhead City

Silver Creek RV Park
1515 Gold Rush Road
Bullhead City, AZ
928-763-2444

Dogs up to 50 pounds are allowed. There are no additional pet fees. Dogs may not be left unattended, and they must be well behaved, leashed, and cleaned up after. There is a dog walk area at the campground. 2 dogs may be allowed.

Camp Verde

Trails End RV Park
983 Finney Flat Road
Camp Verde, AZ
928-567-0100
Dogs of all sizes are allowed. There are no additional pet fees. Dogs must be leashed and cleaned up after. There is a dog walk area at the campground. 2 dogs may be allowed.

Zane Grey RV Park
4500 E H 260
Camp Verde, AZ
928-567-4320
This beautifully landscaped RV park is close to several attractions in the area, and they offer large clean restrooms, showers, spa, laundry facilities, and propane. Dogs of all sizes are allowed for no additional fee. Dogs may not be left alone at any time, and they must be leashed and cleaned up after. There is a dog walk area at the campground. Multiple dogs may be allowed.

Zane Grey RV Park
4500 E H 260
Camp Verde, AZ
928-567-4320
One dog up to 25 pounds is allowed at this adult RV park. There are no additional pet fees. Dogs must be leashed and cleaned up after, and they are not allowed on the grass. There is a dog walk area at the campground.

Casa Grande

Buena Tierra RV Park and Campground
1995 S Cox Road
Casa Grande, AZ
520-836-3500
Dogs of all sizes are allowed. There are no additional pet fees. Dogs may not be left unattended outside or left out at night. Dogs must be quiet, well behaved, leashed, and cleaned up after. The camping and tent areas also allow dogs. There is

a dog walk area at the campground. Multiple dogs may be allowed.

Palm Creek Golf and RV Resort
1110 N Hennes Road
Casa Grande, AZ
800-421-7004
Dogs up to 55 pounds are allowed. There are no additional pet fees. This is a 55 or over park, and one person can be 41 or over. There is a pet section where dogs are allowed, and they are allowed in the park model rentals. Dogs must be on no more than a 6 foot leash, except in the dog runs, and they must be cleaned up after. There is a dog walk area at the campground. 2 dogs may be allowed.

Val Vista Winter Village
16680 W Val Vista Blvd
Casa Grande, AZ
520-836-7800
Dogs up to 25 pounds are allowed. There are no additional pet fees. At least one person must be 55 or over. There is a pet section in the park, and dogs must be walked in that designated area. Dogs must be leashed and cleaned up after. There are some breed restrictions. There is a dog walk area at the campground. Dogs are allowed in the camping cabins. Multiple dogs may be allowed.

Cornville

Lo Lo Mai Springs
11505 Lo Lo Mai Road
Cornville, AZ
928-634-4700
Dogs of all sizes are allowed. There is a $3 per night per pet additional fee for tent and RV sites, and there is a $5 per night per pet additional fee for cabins. Dogs may not be left unattended at any time, and they must be leashed and cleaned up after. The camping and tent areas also allow dogs. There is a dog walk area at the campground. Dogs are allowed in the camping cabins. 2 dogs may be allowed.

Lo Lo Mai Springs Outdoor Resort
11505 Lo Lo Mai Road
Cornville, AZ
928-634-4700
Abundant springs in this area provides lush foliage creating a rich oasis for recreation in the high desert. Amenities offered at this campground include hot showers, a spring fed pond, clean restrooms, a

heated swimming pool, Jacuzzi, convenience store, club house, children's playground, ball and game courts, and a variety of recreational pursuits. Dogs of all sizes are allowed. There is a $3 per night per pet additional fee for the campground or the cabins. Dogs are not allowed in the cottages. Dogs must be leashed and cleaned up after. Dogs are allowed throughout the park, but not at the pool or in buildings. The camping and tent areas also allow dogs. There is a dog walk area at the campground. Dogs are allowed in the camping cabins. 2 dogs may be allowed.

Cottonwood

Dead Horse Ranch State Park
675 Dead Horse Ranch Road
Cottonwood, AZ
928-634-5283
This park along the Verde River Greenway, shares a unique ecosystem, in that their Cottonwood/Willowriparian gallery forest is one of less than 20 riparian type zones in the world. There are also many trails to explore. Dogs are allowed at no additional fee. Dogs may not be left unattended, and they must be leashed and cleaned up after. Dogs are not allowed in park buildings or ramadas. The camping and tent areas also allow dogs. There is a dog walk area at the campground. Multiple dogs may be allowed.

Flagstaff

Coconino National Forest
1824 S Thompson Street
Flagstaff, AZ
928-527-3600
This diverse forest, of 1,821,495 acres, offers alpine tundra, pine forest, high mountain desert and a variety of land and water recreation. Dogs of all sizes are allowed at no additional fee. Dogs may not be left unattended, and they must be leashed at all times, and cleaned up after in camp areas. The camping and tent areas also allow dogs. There is a dog walk area at the campground. There are no electric or water hookups at the campground. Multiple dogs may be allowed.

Flagstaff KOA
5803 N H 89
Flagstaff, AZ
928-526-9926

Dogs of all sizes are allowed. There are no additional pet fees. Dogs may not be left unattended outside, and they must be leashed and cleaned up after. The camping and tent areas also allow dogs. There is a dog walk area at the campground. Dogs are allowed in the camping cabins. Multiple dogs may be allowed.

Woody Mountain Campground and RV Park
2727 W H 66
Flagstaff, AZ
928-774-7727
Dogs of all sizes are allowed. There are no additional pet fees. Dogs may not be left unattended, and they must be quiet, leashed, and cleaned up after. This RV park is closed during the off-season. The camping and tent areas also allow dogs. There is a dog walk area at the campground. 2 dogs may be allowed.

Fort McDowell

Eagle View RV Resort
9605 N Fort McDowell Road
Fort McDowell, AZ
480-836-5310
Dogs of all sizes are allowed. There are no additional pet fees. Dogs must be leashed and cleaned up after. There is a dog walk area at the campground. Multiple dogs may be allowed.

Grand Canyon

Ash Fork RV Park
783 W Old Route 66
Ash Fork, AZ
928-637-2521
Dogs of all sizes are allowed. There are no additional pet fees. Dogs must be leashed and cleaned up after. The camping and tent areas also allow dogs. There is a dog walk area at the campground. Multiple dogs may be allowed.

Flintstones Bedrock City
Junction 64 and 180
Williams, AZ
928-635-2600
Dogs of all sizes are allowed. There are no additional pet fees. Dogs may be off leash at the site if the dog is well behaved and will stay on the site regardless of what passes by. They must be on leashed when walked and dogs must be cleaned

up after. The camping and tent areas also allow dogs. There is a dog walk area at the campground. Multiple dogs may be allowed.

Grand Canyon/Williams KOA
5333 H 64
Williams, AZ
928-635-2307
Dogs of all sizes are allowed. There are no additional pet fees. Dogs may not be left unattended, and they must be quiet, leashed, and cleaned up after. There are some breed restrictions. This RV park is closed during the off-season. The camping and tent areas also allow dogs. There is a dog walk area at the campground. Dogs are allowed in the camping cabins. Multiple dogs may be allowed.

Kaibab National Forest
Railroad Blvd
Williams, AZ
928-635-8200
This picturesque forest of 1.6 million acres borders both the north and south rims of the Grand Canyon. It is the largest contiguous ponderosa pine forest in US and its diverse ecosystems support a large variety of plants, fish, mammals, bird species, and recreation. Dogs of all sizes are allowed at no additional fee. Dogs may not be left unattended except for shore periods, and they must be leashed and cleaned up after in camp areas. Dogs may be off lead on the trails if no one is around, they will not chase wildlife, and are under strict voice command. The camping and tent areas also allow dogs. There is a dog walk area at the campground. Dogs are allowed in the camping cabins. There are no electric or water hookups at the campground. Multiple dogs may be allowed.

Williams/Circle Pines KOA
1000 Circle Pines Road
Williams, AZ
928-635-2626
Dogs of all sizes are allowed. There are no additional pet fees. Dogs may not be left unattended outside, and they must be leashed and cleaned up after. Dogs must be crated when left in a cabin. There are some breed restrictions. The camping and tent areas also allow dogs. There is a dog walk area at the campground. Dogs are allowed in the camping cabins. Multiple dogs may be allowed.

Holbrook

Holbrook/Petrified Forest KOA
102 Hermosa Drive
Holbrook, AZ
928-524-6689
Dogs of all sizes are allowed. There are no additional pet fees. Dogs must be leashed and cleaned up after. The camping and tent areas also allow dogs. There is a dog walk area at the campground. Multiple dogs may be allowed.

Huachuca

Mountain View RV Park
99 W Vista Lane
Huachuca, AZ
800-772-4103
Dogs of all sizes are allowed. There are no additional pet fees. Dogs may not be left unattended outside, and they must be leashed and cleaned up after. There are some breed restrictions. The camping and tent areas also allow dogs. There is a dog walk area at the campground. Multiple dogs may be allowed.

Jacob Lake

Kaibab Campervillage
Forest Road #461
Jacob Lake, AZ
928-643-7804
Dogs of all sizes are allowed. There are no additional pet fees. Dogs may not be left unattended, and they must be leashed and cleaned up after. This RV park is closed during the off-season. The camping and tent areas also allow dogs. There is a dog walk area at the campground. Multiple dogs may be allowed.

Kingman

Kingman KOA
3820 N Roosevelt
Kingman, AZ
928-757-4397
Dogs of all sizes are allowed. There is, however, a $20 refundable deposit for the cabins. Dogs must be leashed and cleaned up after. There are some breed restrictions. The camping and tent areas also allow dogs. There is a dog walk area at the campground. Dogs are allowed in the camping cabins. Multiple dogs may be allowed.

Lake Havasu City

Cattail Cove State Park
P. O. Box 1990
Lake Havasu City, AZ
928-855-1223
This 2,000 acre park offers a beach, boat ramp, an amphitheater, 61 campsites, and a variety of year around land and water recreation. If you have your own watercraft, there are an additional 28 campsites along the water's edge. Dogs of all sizes are allowed at no additional fee. Dogs must be leashed at all times, and cleaned up after. Dogs may not be left unattended at any time. The camping and tent areas also allow dogs. There is a dog walk area at the campground. Multiple dogs may be allowed.

Islander RV Resort
751 Beachcomer Blvd
Lake Havasu City, AZ
928-680-2000
Dogs of all sizes are allowed. There is a $1 per night per pet additional fee. Dogs are not allowed to be left unattended outside, and they must be leashed and cleaned up after. This is an adult only park. There are some breed restrictions. There is a dog walk area at the campground. 2 dogs may be allowed.

Lake Havasu State Park
699 London Bridge Road
Lake Havasu City, AZ
928-855-2784
This park is home to the Mohave Sunset Walking Trail and the Arroyo-Camino Interpretive Garden that showcases the variety of life in and around the park. Dogs are allowed at no additional fee. Dogs must be leashed, cleaned up after, and water and shade must be provided. The camping and tent areas also allow dogs. There is a dog walk area at the campground. Multiple dogs may be allowed.

McNeal

Double Adobe
5057 W Double Adobe Road
McNeal, AZ
520-364-4000
Dogs of all sizes are allowed. There are no additional pet fees. Dogs must be well behaved, leashed, and cleaned up after. The camping and tent areas also allow dogs. There is a dog walk area at the campground. Multiple dogs may be allowed.

Munds Park

Munds Park RV Resort
17550 Munds Ranch Road
Munds Park, AZ
928-286-1309
Dogs of all sizes are allowed. There are no additional pet fees. Dog may be off lead on the trails with voice command, and be leashed and cleaned up after when in the park. This RV park is closed during the off-season. The camping and tent areas also allow dogs. There is a dog walk area at the campground. Multiple dogs may be allowed.

Page - Lake Powell

Page-Lake Powell Campground
849 S Copper Mine Road
Page, AZ
928-645-3374
Dogs of all sizes are allowed. There are no additional pet fees. Dogs may not be left unattended, and they must stay off the grass, be leashed and cleaned up after. The camping and tent areas also allow dogs. There is a dog walk area at the campground. Multiple dogs may be allowed.

Wahweap RV Park and Campground
100 S Lake Shore Drive
Page, AZ
888-486-4679
Dogs of all sizes are allowed. There are no additional pet fees. Dogs may not be left unattended, and they must be leashed and cleaned up after. There is also a lodge on site where pets are allowed in the standard rooms. There is a dog walk area at the campground. Multiple dogs may be allowed.

Parker

Buckskin Mountain State Park
5476 H 95
Parker, AZ
928-667-3231
This scenic campground sits along an 18-mile stretch of the Colorado River between Parker Dam and Headgate Dam. The park has different activities planned throughout the year. There are ranger led hikes, weekly speakers, ice cream socials, boating safety classes, and campfire programs. They also offer basketball and volleyball courts, a playground,

clothing boutique, restaurant, camp store, arcade, restrooms, and a gas dock. Dogs of all sizes are allowed for no additional fee. They may not be left unattended at any time, and they must be leashed at all times, and cleaned up after. Dogs are not allowed in the cabaña area or on the beach from the day use area to the cabañas. At the River Island area, dogs are allowed in the water, but must be kept on right side of boat ramp. Well behaved dogs on lead are allowed on the variety of trails and throughout the rest of the park. The camping and tent areas also allow dogs. There is a dog walk area at the campground. Multiple dogs may be allowed.

Patagonia

Patagonia Lake State Park
400 Patagonia Lake Road
Patagonia, AZ
520-287-6965
This park has a variety of water and land recreation, trails, and the Sonoita Creek State Natural Area is now open to the public. Dogs are allowed at no additional fee. Dogs may not be left unattended, they must be on no more than a 6 foot leash, and be cleaned up after. Dogs are not allowed in the public swim areas. The camping and tent areas also allow dogs. There is a dog walk area at the campground. Multiple dogs may be allowed.

Phoenix

Cotton Lane RV
17506 W Van Buren Avenue
Phoenix, AZ
623-853-4000
Dogs up to 40 pounds are allowed. There are no additional pet fees. Dogs must be quiet, well behaved, leashed and cleaned up after. This is a 55 plus park, so at least one person must be 55 or older. There is a dog walk area at the campground. 2 dogs may be allowed.

Covered Wagon RV Park
6540 N Black Canyon H
Phoenix, AZ
602-242-2500
Dogs of all sizes are allowed. There is a $1 per night per pet additional fee. Dogs may not be left unattended, and they must be leashed and cleaned up after. There are some breed restrictions. The camping and tent areas also allow

dogs. There is a dog walk area at the campground. Multiple dogs may be allowed.

Desert Sands RV Park
22036 N 27th Avenue
Phoenix, AZ
623-869-8186
Dogs of all sizes are allowed. There are no additional pet fees. Dogs may not be left unattended, and they must be leashed and cleaned up after. There are some breed restrictions. There is a dog walk area at the campground. Multiple dogs may be allowed.

Desert Shadows RV Resort
19203 N 29th Avenue
Phoenix, AZ
623-869-8178
Dogs of all sizes are allowed. There are no additional pet fees. Dogs are to be walked along the path just outside the front gate, and they must be leashed and cleaned up after. This is an adult resort and at least one person must be 55 or older. Dogs are not allowed in the park models. There are some breed restrictions. There is a dog walk area at the campground. 2 dogs may be allowed.

Destiny RV Resort
416 N Citrus Road
Phoenix, AZ
623-853-0537
Dogs of all sizes are allowed, but there can only be 2 average sized dogs or 3 if all small. There are no additional pet fees. Dogs are not allowed to be tied to the trees or tables, and may not be left unattended outside. Dogs must be on no more than a 6 foot leash and cleaned up after. There is a fenced in area for off lead, and there is a Bark Park about 4 miles from the resort. There are some breed restrictions. There is a dog walk area at the campground.

Pioneer RV Resort
36408 N Black Canyon H
Phoenix, AZ
800-658-5895
Dogs of all sizes are allowed. There are no additional pet fees. Dogs must be leashed and cleaned up after. There are some breed restrictions. There is a dog walk area at the campground. This is a 55 plus park so one person must be 55 or older. 2 dogs may be allowed.

Tonto National Forest
2324 E. McDowell Road
Phoenix, AZ
602-225-5200
The fifth largest forest in the US with almost 3 million acres offers a wide range of ecosystems, habitats and spectacular scenery. It also supports a large variety of plants, animals, and recreation. Dogs of all sizes are allowed at no additional fee. Dogs may not be left unattended, and they must have current rabies, shot records, and license. Dogs must be leashed at all times and cleaned up after in camp areas. Dogs are allowed on the trails. The camping and tent areas also allow dogs. There is a dog walk area at the campground. There are no electric or water hookups at the campground. Multiple dogs may be allowed.

Phoenix Area

Mesa Spirit
3020 E Main Street
Mesa, AZ
480-832-1770
Dogs of all sizes are allowed. There are no additional pet fees. Dogs must be quiet, well behaved, leashed and cleaned up after. Dogs must remain in the pet section of the campground. At least one person must be 55 years or older to stay at this resort. There is a dog walk area at the campground. 2 dogs may be allowed.

Silveridge RV Resort
8265 E Southern
Mesa, AZ
480-373-7000
Dogs of all sizes are allowed. There are no additional pet fees. Dogs must be leashed and cleaned up after, and they must stay in the pet section of the campground. At least one person must be 55 or older to stay at this resort. There is a dog walk area at the campground. Multiple dogs may be allowed.

Picacho

Picacho Peak State Park
Picacho Peak Road
Picacho, AZ
520-466-3183
This park has a variety of trails varying in length and difficulty. The trails are open from 8 am to sunset. Dogs are allowed at no additional

fee. Dogs may not be left unattended, they must be on no more than a 6 foot leash, and be cleaned up after. Dogs are not allowed on the advanced trails. The camping and tent areas also allow dogs. There is a dog walk area at the campground. There are no water hookups at the campground. Multiple dogs may be allowed.

Prescott

Prescott National Forest
344 S Cortez Street
Prescott, AZ
928-443-8000
This forest of over a million acres provides spectacular scenery, a rich cultural history, and diverse ecosystems that support a large variety of plants, animals, and recreation. Dogs of all sizes are allowed at no additional fee. Dogs may not be left unattended, and they must be leashed and cleaned up after. Dogs are allowed on the trails. This campground is closed during the off-season. The camping and tent areas also allow dogs. There is a dog walk area at the campground. Multiple dogs may be allowed.

Willow Lake RV and Camping Park
1617 Heritage Park Road
Prescott, AZ
928-445-6311
Dogs of all sizes are allowed. There are no additional pet fees. Dogs must be leashed and cleaned up after. The camping and tent areas also allow dogs. There is a dog walk area at the campground. Multiple dogs may be allowed.

Quartzsite

B-10 Campground
615 Main
Quartzsite, AZ
928-927-4393
Dogs of all sizes are allowed. There are no additional pet fees. Dogs must be leashed and cleaned up after. There are some breed restrictions. This RV park is closed during the off-season. There is a dog walk area at the campground. Multiple dogs may be allowed.

Safford

Roper Lake State Park
101 E. Roper Lake Road
Safford, AZ

928-428-6760
This park has 2 camping sections, and offers a model Indian village, land and water recreation, and a natural hot spring. Dogs are allowed at no additional fee. Dogs may not be left unattended, and they must be leashed and cleaned up after. Dogs are not allowed in park buildings or on the beach, but they are allowed on the trails. The camping and tent areas also allow dogs. There is a dog walk area at the campground. Dogs are allowed in the camping cabins. Multiple dogs may be allowed.

Sedona

Rancho Sedona RV Park
135 Bear Wallow Lane
Sedona, AZ
928-282-7255
Dogs of all sizes are allowed. There is a $1 per night per pet additional fee, and there are discounts for AAA or Good Sam members. Dogs may not be left unattended outside, and they must be quiet, leashed, and cleaned up after. There is a dog walk area at the campground. Multiple dogs may be allowed.

Seligman

Seligman/Route 66 KOA
801 E H 66
Seligman, AZ
928-422-3358
Dogs up to 25 pounds are allowed. There are no additional pet fees. Dogs must be leashed and cleaned up after. There are some breed restrictions. The camping and tent areas also allow dogs. There is a dog walk area at the campground. Multiple dogs may be allowed.

Show Low

Fool Hollow Lake Rec Area
1500 N Fool Hollow Lake Road
Show Low, AZ
928-537-3680
Nestled among 100 foot pine trees along a lake at 6300 feet, this rec area offers an impressive list of weekend activities May through September such as parades, car shows, festivals, concerts, rodeos, and more, in addition to a variety of land and water recreation. Dogs are allowed throughout the park for no additional fee, and on the trails, as long as they are on lead at all times,

and cleaned up after. The campground offers 123 camping sites, a dump station, fish cleaning station, boat ramps, picnic tables, picnic ramadas, grills, playgrounds, private showers and restrooms. The camping and tent areas also allow dogs. There is a dog walk area at the campground. Multiple dogs may be allowed.

Fool Hollow Lake Recreation Area
1500 N Fool Hollow Lake
Show Low, AZ
928-537-3680
This park offers 100 foot pine trees and a large mountain lake. The lake is at 6,300 feet altitude and also provides a home for Great Blue Herons. Dogs of all sizes are allowed. There are no additional pet fees. Dogs may not be left unattended, they must be on no more than a 6 foot leash, and be cleaned up after. Dogs must be quiet and well behaved. Dogs are not allowed in any of the buildings. The camping and tent areas also allow dogs. There is a dog walk area at the campground. Multiple dogs may be allowed.

Springerville

Apache-Sitgreaves National Forest
309 S Mountain Avenue
Springerville, AZ
928-333-4301
Two forests were combined creating over 2 million acres of spectacular scenery, hundreds of miles of trails, a variety of recreational pursuits, and more areas of water than any other Southwestern National Forest. Dogs of all sizes are allowed at no additional fee. Dogs may not be left unattended, and they must be leashed and cleaned up after. Dogs are allowed on the trails. The camping and tent areas also allow dogs. There is a dog walk area at the campground. There are no electric or water hookups at the campground. Multiple dogs may be allowed.

St Johns

Lyman Lake State Park
On H 180/191 11 miles E of St Johns
St Johns, AZ
928-337-4441
This park shares the ancient historic Pueblo Trail, and offers many sites of interest and villages of the Hopi people. Dogs of all sizes are allowed, and there are no additional pet fees

for tent or RV sites. There is a $5 one time additional pet fee for the cabins. Dogs must be leashed and cleaned up after. The camping and tent areas also allow dogs. There is a dog walk area at the campground. Dogs are allowed in the camping cabins. Multiple dogs may be allowed.

Tombstone

Picacho Peak RV Resort
17065 E Peak Lane
Picacho, AZ
520-466-7841
Dogs of all sizes are allowed. There are no additional pet fees. Dogs may not be left unattended outside, and they must have up to date shots, and be leashed and cleaned up after. This is an adults only park. There are some breed restrictions. There is a dog walk area at the campground. 2 dogs may be allowed.

Tombstone RV Park
MM 315 H 80
Tombstone, AZ
800-348-3829
Dogs of all sizes are allowed. There are no additional pet fees. Dogs may be walked in the park, but they must be taken to the dog walk areas to do their business, and cleaned up after. There is a dog walk area at the campground. Multiple dogs may be allowed.

Tucson

Green Valley RV Resort
19001 S Richfield Avenue
Green Valley, AZ
520-625-3900
Dogs up to 50 pounds are allowed. There are no additional pet fees. Dogs must be leashed and cleaned up after. There is a dog walk area at the campground. 2 dogs may be allowed.

Catalina State Park
11570 N Oracle Road
Tucson, AZ
520-628-5798
This scenic desert recreational park has a variety of attractions plus an archaeological site to explore and there are 8 trails of varying length and difficulty. Dogs are allowed at no additional fee. Dogs must be leashed and cleaned up after. Dogs are not allowed at the Pusch Ridge Wilderness area, but they are

allowed on trails. The camping and tent areas also allow dogs. There is a dog walk area at the campground. Multiple dogs may be allowed.

Coronado National Forest
5700 N Sabino Canyon Road
Tucson, AZ
520-388-8300
This forest, with elevations ranging from 3000 feet to 10,720 feet, covers more than 1.7 million acres over twelve widely scattered mountain ranges. The rugged mountains rise from the desert floor, and are known as the "sky islands". There is recreation during all seasons. Dogs of all sizes are allowed at no additional fee. Dogs may not be left unattended, and they must be leashed and cleaned up after. Dogs are allowed on the trails, but they are not allowed in the Push Ridge Wilderness Area. The camping and tent areas also allow dogs. There is a dog walk area at the campground. There are no electric or water hookups at the campground. Multiple dogs may be allowed.

Crazy Horse RV Park
6660 S Craycroft
Tucson, AZ
520-574-0157
Dogs of all sizes are allowed. There is $1 per night per pet additional fee for daily rates; $5 by the week, and $15 by the month. Dogs must be walked in designated areas only, and they must be leashed and cleaned up after. Dogs may be left in the RV only if air conditioned. Tucson pet ordinance prohibits dogs from being left in an auto or tied up at any time. There is a dog walk area at the campground. 2 dogs may be allowed.

Prince of Tucson RV Park
3501 N Freeway
Tucson, AZ
520-887-3501
Dogs of all sizes are allowed. There are no additional pet fees for the first two dogs, thereafter the fee is $2 per night per pet. Dogs may not be left unattended outside, and they must be leashed and cleaned up after. Tucson pet ordinance prohibits dogs from being left in an auto or tied up at any time. There are some breed restrictions. There is a dog walk area at the campground. Multiple dogs may be allowed.

Alamo Lake State Park
Alamo Road
Wenden, AZ
928-669-2088
This recreational park has one of Arizona's best fishing holes, and there is more than enough to interest nature lovers also with a wide variety of flora and fauna. Dogs are allowed at no additional fee. Dogs may not be left unattended, and they must be leashed and cleaned up after. Dogs are allowed on the trails. The camping and tent areas also allow dogs. There is a dog walk area at the campground. Multiple dogs may be allowed.

Winslow

Homolovi Ruins State Park
Honahanie Road
Winslow, AZ
928-289-4106
This archeological recreational park explores the rich Native American history. There is a book store as well as the exhibits, and several trails. Dogs are allowed at no additional fee. Dogs must be leashed and cleaned up after. Dogs are not allowed in any of the buildings. The camping and tent areas also allow dogs. There is a dog walk area at the campground. Multiple dogs may be allowed.

Yuma

Cocopah RV & Golf Resort
6800 Strand Avenue
Yuma, AZ
928-343-9300
Dogs of all sizes are allowed. There are no additional pet fees. Dogs must be walked in designated pet areas only, and they must be leashed and cleaned up after. Dogs are not allowed in the golf course area. This is an adult only resort. There is a dog walk area at the campground. 2 dogs may be allowed.

Shangri-la RV Resort
10498 N Frontage Road
Yuma, AZ
877-742-6474
Dogs of all sizes are allowed. There are no additional pet fees. Dogs must be walked in the designated pet areas only, and they must be leashed and cleaned up after. There are some breed restrictions. There is a dog walk area at the campground.

2 dogs may be allowed.

Westwind RV and Golf Resort
9797 E 32nd Street
Yuma, AZ
928-342-2992
Dogs of all sizes are allowed. There are no additional pet fees. Dogs are also allowed in the park models in the pet section only. Dogs must stay in the designated pet areas only to be walked, and are not allowed at the office or other non-pet areas. Dogs may not be left unattended, and they must be leashed and cleaned up after. There are some breed restrictions. There is a dog walk area at the campground. 2 dogs may be allowed.

Arkansas Listings

Alma

Fort Smith/Alma KOA
3539 N H 71
Alma, AR
479-632-2704
Dogs of all sizes are allowed. There are no additional pet fees. Dogs must be leashed and cleaned up after, and they may not be on the playground. There is only 1 pet friendly cabin. There are some breed restrictions. The camping and tent areas also allow dogs. There is a dog walk area at the campground. Dogs are allowed in the camping cabins.

Batesville

Speedway RV Park
1005 Heber Springs (H 14W/H 25S)
Batesville, AR
870-251-1008
Dogs of all sizes are allowed. There are no additional pet fees. Dogs must be leashed and cleaned up after. The camping and tent areas also allow dogs. There is a dog walk area at the campground. 2 dogs may be allowed.

Benton

I 30 Travel Park
19719 I-30
Benton, AR
501-778-1244

Dogs of all sizes are allowed. There are no additional pet fees. Dogs may not be left unattended, and they must be leashed and cleaned up after. There is a dog walk area at the campground. Multiple dogs may be allowed.

Cotter

Denton Ferry RV Park
740 Denton Ferry Road
Cotter, AR
800-275-5611
Dogs of all sizes are allowed. There are no additional pet fees. Dogs must be leashed, and cleaned up after. There is a dog walk area at the campground.

Eureka Springs

Eureka Springs KOA
15020 H 187S
Eureka Springs, AR
479-253-8036
Dogs of all sizes are allowed. There are no additional pet fees. Dogs must be leashed and cleaned up after. This RV park is closed during the off-season. The camping and tent areas also allow dogs. There is a dog walk area at the campground. Multiple dogs may be allowed.

Eureka Springs Kettle Campground
4119 E Van Buren (H 62)
Eureka Springs, AR
479-253-9100
Up to 3 dogs of all sizes are allowed, and there are no additional pet fees for the tent or RV sites. There is a $10 one time additional pet fee for the cabins, and only 2 dogs are allowed up to 50 pounds. Dogs may not be left unattended outside, and left in your RV only (not in cabins at all) if they will be quiet, well behaved, and comfortable. Dogs must be leashed and cleaned up after. Dogs are not allowed in buildings or in the pool area. The camping and tent areas also allow dogs. There is a dog walk area at the campground. Dogs are allowed in the camping cabins.

Wanderlust RV Park
468 Passion Play Road
Eureka Springs, AR
479-253-7385
Dogs of all sizes are allowed. There are no additional pet fees. Dogs must be leashed and cleaned up

after. This RV park is closed during the off-season. The camping and tent areas also allow dogs. There is a dog walk area at the campground. Multiple dogs may be allowed.

Flippin

Cedar Hollow RV Park
76 MC Road 8110
Flippin, AR
870-453-8643
Dogs of all sizes are allowed. There are no additional pet fees. Dogs must be leashed and cleaned up after. There is a dog walk area at the campground. Multiple dogs may be allowed.

Hot Springs

Cloud Nine RV Park
136 Cloud Nine Drive
Hot Springs, AR
501-262-1996
Dogs of all sizes are allowed. There are no additional pet fees. Dogs must be leashed and cleaned up after. There are some breed restrictions. The camping and tent areas also allow dogs. There is a dog walk area at the campground. Multiple dogs may be allowed.

Hot Springs National Park KOA
838 McClendon Road
Hot Springs, AR
501-624-5912
Dogs of all sizes are allowed. There are no additional pet fees. Dogs must be leashed and cleaned up after. The camping and tent areas also allow dogs. There is a dog walk area at the campground. Dogs are allowed in the camping cabins. Multiple dogs may be allowed.

Lake Catherine State Park
1200 Catherine Park Road
Hot Springs, AR
501-844-4176
Almost 2,000 acres of lakes add to the recreation at this state park. There are a variety of activities, recreation, and trails to explore. Dogs of all sizes are allowed at no additional fee. Dogs may not be left unattended, and they must be leashed and cleaned up after. Dogs are not allowed in buildings or on the beaches, but they are allowed on the trails. The camping and tent areas also allow dogs. There is a dog walk area at the campground. Multiple dogs may be allowed.

Lake Hamilton RV Resort
3027 Albert Pike
Hot Springs, AR
501-767-4400
Dogs of all sizes are allowed. There are no additional pet fees. Dogs may not be left unattended, and they must be leashed and cleaned up after. Outside pens or kennels are not allowed, and dogs must be walked in designated pet areas only. There is a dog walk area at the campground. Multiple dogs may be allowed.

Ouachita National Forest
100 Reserve Street, Federal Bldg
Hot Springs, AR
501-321-5202
This working forest of nearly 2 million acres provides diverse ecosystems that support a large variety of plants, animals, and recreation. Dogs of all sizes are allowed at no additional fee. Dogs may not be left unattended, and they must be quiet, leashed at all times when in the camping areas, and be cleaned up after. The camping and tent areas also allow dogs. There is a dog walk area at the campground. There are no electric or water hookups at the campground. Multiple dogs may be allowed.

Jacksonport

Jacksonport State Park
205 Avenue Street
Jacksonport, AR
870-523-2143
Located along the White River, this park is home to the Tunstall Riverwalk Trail, and a variety of water and land recreation. Dogs of all sizes are allowed at no additional fee. Dogs may not be left unattended, and they must be leashed and cleaned up after. Dogs are allowed on the trails. The camping and tent areas also allow dogs. There is a dog walk area at the campground. Multiple dogs may be allowed.

Jasper

Dogwood Springs Jasper Resort
P.O. Box 157/On H 7 one mile N
Jasper, AR
870-446-2163
Well behaved dogs of all sizes are allowed at no additional fee for the tent or RV sites. There is a $10 per night per pet additional fee for the

cabins, plus a $50 refundable deposit that is refundable by mail 7 days after checkout. Dogs may not be left unattended at any time, and they must be quiet, leashed at all times, and cleaned up after. Your visitors may not have a dog on the property or in their vehicle on the property, for any reason, at anytime. The camping and tent areas also allow dogs. There is a dog walk area at the campground. Dogs are allowed in the camping cabins. Multiple dogs may be allowed.

Jersey

Moro Bay State Park
6071 H 600
Jersey, AR
870-463-8555
This park is one of the most popular fishing and water sport areas in the state and offers a variety of land and water recreational opportunities. Well behaved, quiet, dogs of all sizes are allowed at no additional fee. Dogs must be leashed and cleaned up after. Dogs are not allowed in the buildings, but they are allowed on the trails. The camping and tent areas also allow dogs. There is a dog walk area at the campground. Multiple dogs may be allowed.

Lake Village

Pecan Grove RV Park
1518 Barton Springs Road
Lake Village, AR
512-472-1067
Dogs of all sizes are allowed. There are no additional pet fees. Dogs must be leashed and cleaned up after. Long term guests are allowed one dog up to 15 pounds. There is a dog walk area at the campground. 2 dogs may be allowed.

Little Rock

Little Rock North/Jct I 40 KOA
7820 Crystal Hill Road
N Little Rock, AR
501-758-4598
Dogs of all sizes are allowed. There are no additional pet fees. Dogs may not be left unattended outside, and they must be leashed and cleaned up after. There is a fenced dog area. There is only 1 pet friendly cabin. The camping and tent areas also allow dogs. There is

a dog walk area at the campground. Dogs are allowed in the camping cabins. Multiple dogs may be allowed.

Burns Park Campground
4101 Arlene Laman Drive
North Little Rock, AR
501-771-0702
Dogs of all sizes are allowed. There are no additional pet fees. Dogs must have up to date shot records, and be cleaned up after. Dogs must be leashed while in the park, but there is a dog park with large fenced in areas about a mile and a half away. The camping and tent areas also allow dogs. There is a dog walk area at the campground. Multiple dogs may be allowed.

Marion

America's Best Campground
7037 I 55
Marion, AR
870-739-4801
Dogs of all sizes are allowed. There are no additional pet fees. Dogs must be leashed and cleaned up after. The camping and tent areas also allow dogs. There is a dog walk area at the campground. Multiple dogs may be allowed.

Morrilton

Morrilton/Conway KOA
30 Kamper Lane
Morrilton, AR
501-354-8262
Dogs of all sizes are allowed. There are no additional pet fees. Dogs may not be left unattended outside, and they must be leashed and cleaned up after. This RV park is closed during the off-season. The camping and tent areas also allow dogs. There is a dog walk area at the campground. Dogs are allowed in the camping cabins. Multiple dogs may be allowed.

Petit Jean State Park
1285 Petit Jean Mountain Road
Morrilton, AR
501-727-5441
In addition to a variety of recreation, this park offers a 95 foot waterfall, a 170 acre lake, its own airport, and is home to an impressive array of trails. Dogs of all sizes are allowed at no additional fee. Dogs must be leashed and cleaned up after. Dogs are not allowed in the lodge or at the pool, but they are allowed on the trials.

The camping and tent areas also allow dogs. There is a dog walk area at the campground. Multiple dogs may be allowed.

Mountain Home

White Buffalo Resort
418 White Buffalo Trail
Mountain Home, AR
870-425-8555
Dogs of all sizes are allowed at no additional fee for the tent or RV sites. There is a $10 per night per pet additional fee for the cabins. Dogs may not be left unattended outside or in the cabins or tents. Dogs are not allowed on the furniture in the cabins. Dogs may only be left in an RV if they will be quiet and well behaved. The camping and tent areas also allow dogs. There is a dog walk area at the campground. Dogs are allowed in the camping cabins. 2 dogs may be allowed.

Mountain View

Fiddler's Valley RV Resort
234 Oak Avenue
Mountain View, AR
870-269-5700
Dogs of all sizes are allowed. There are no additional pet fees. Dogs may not be left unattended outside, and they must be quiet, leashed, and cleaned up after. There is a dog walk area at the campground. Multiple dogs may be allowed.

Ozark RV Park
1022 Park Avenue
Mountain View, AR
870-269-2542
Dogs of all sizes are allowed. There are no additional pet fees. Dogs must be leashed and cleaned up after. This RV park is closed during the off-season. The camping and tent areas also allow dogs. There is a dog walk area at the campground. Multiple dogs may be allowed.

Ozarks

Harrison Village Campground
2364 H 65S
Harrison, AR
870-743-3388
Dogs of all sizes are allowed. There are no additional pet fees. Dogs must be leashed and cleaned up after. There are some breed restrictions. The camping and tent areas also allow dogs. There is a

dog walk area at the campground. Multiple dogs may be allowed.

Paragould

Crowley's Ridge State Park
2092 H 168N
Paragould, AR
870-573-6751
Sitting atop forested hills, this park offers interpretive programs throughout the year as well as a variety of land and water recreation. Dogs of all sizes are allowed at no additional fee. Dogs may not be left unattended, and they must be leashed and cleaned up after. Dogs are not allowed in buildings or at the group facilities, but they are allowed on the trails. The camping and tent areas also allow dogs. There is a dog walk area at the campground. Multiple dogs may be allowed.

Pocohontas

Old Davidson State Park
7953 H 166S
Pocohontas, AR
870-892-4708
This historical park offers exhibits, interpretive tours, and a variety of land and water recreation. Well behaved, quiet dogs of all sizes are allowed at no additional fee. Dogs must be leashed at all times, and be cleaned up after. Dogs are not allowed in buildings or in the lake, but they may wade by the edge on leash. Dogs are allowed on the trails. The camping and tent areas also allow dogs. There is a dog walk area at the campground. Multiple dogs may be allowed.

Russellville

Ozark-St. Francis National Forest
605 W Main Street
Russellville, AR
479-964-7200
These are two separate forest areas have their own unique qualities, but they both offer a wide variety of land and water recreation. Ouachita also has the tallest mountain in the state, and an incredible living underground cave. Dogs of all sizes are allowed at no additional fee. Dogs may not be left unattended, and they must be leashed and cleaned up after. Dogs are not allowed in the swim areas, but they are allowed on the trails. This campground is closed during

the off-season. The camping and tent areas also allow dogs. There is a dog walk area at the campground. There are no water hookups at the campground. Multiple dogs may be allowed.

West Fork

Devil's Den State Park
11333 W H 74
West Fork, AR
479-761-3325
This park provides an impressive array of caves, crevices, and trails to explore, in addition to a variety of land and water recreation. Dogs of all sizes are allowed at no additional fee. Dogs must be leashed and cleaned up after. Dogs are allowed on the trails. The camping and tent areas also allow dogs. There is a dog walk area at the campground. Multiple dogs may be allowed.

West Memphis

Tom Sawyer's Mississippi River RV Park
1286 S 8th Street
West Memphis, AR
870-735-9770
Dogs of all sizes are allowed. There are no additional pet fees. Dogs must be quiet, well behaved, leashed, and cleaned up after. Dogs are also welcome to swim at the river. The camping and tent areas also allow dogs. There is a dog walk area at the campground. Multiple dogs may be allowed.

Wynne

Village Creek State Park
201 County Road 754
Wynne, AR
870-238-9406
Interpretive programs and exhibits inform visitors of the natural and cultural heritage of this unique park. There are several miles of trails, and a variety of land and water recreation. Dogs of all sizes are allowed at no additional fee. Dogs may only be left unattended for short periods, and only if they will be quiet and well behaved. Dogs must be cleaned up after. Dogs are not allowed in the water or in buildings, but they are allowed on the trails. The camping and tent areas also allow dogs. There is a dog walk area at the campground. Multiple dogs may be allowed.

Yellville

Sherwood Forest RV Park & Campground
216 MC Road 5042
Yellville, AR
870-449-3452
Dogs of all sizes are allowed. There are no additional pet fees. Dogs may not be left unattended, and they must be leashed and cleaned up after. The camping and tent areas also allow dogs. There is a dog walk area at the campground. Dogs are allowed in the camping cabins. Multiple dogs may be allowed.

California Listings

Alturas - Modoc National Forest

Blue Lake Campground
Forest Service Road 64
Likely, CA
530-233-5811
This campground is located along Blue Lake at a 6,000 foot elevation in the Modoc National Forest. There are 48 RV and tent sites, several of which are located directly on the lake. RVs up to 32 feet are allowed. There is a $7 per vehicle fee. Amenities include picnic tables, fire pits, vault toilets and piped water. A boat ramp is located near the campground. Rowboats, canoes and low powered boats are allowed on the lake. The 1.5 mile Blue Lake National Recreation Trail begins at this campsite. Dogs on leash are allowed at the campgrounds, on trails and in the water. There are no additional pet fees. Please clean up after your pets. This campground is closed during the off-season. The camping and tent areas also allow dogs. There is a dog walk area at the campground. There are no electric or water hookups at the campgrounds. Multiple dogs may be allowed.

Mill Creek Falls Campground
Mill Creek Road
Likely, CA
530-233-5811
This campground is located in the Modoc National Forest at an elevation of 5,700 feet. There are 19 RV and tent sites. There is a $6 per night fee. Amenities include picnic tables, fire pits, vault toilets and

drinking water. The Clear Lake Trail begins here and provides access into the South Warner Wilderness. Dogs on leash are allowed at the campgrounds, on trails and in the water. Please clean up after your pets. To get there from the town of Likely, go 9 miles east on Co. Rd. #64. Then go northeast on West Warner Road for 2.5 miles. Go east on Mill Creek access road for 2 more miles. This campground is closed during the off-season. The camping and tent areas also allow dogs. There is a dog walk area at the campground. There are no electric or water hookups at the campgrounds. Multiple dogs may be allowed.

Anaheim Resort Area

Anaheim Resort RV Park
200 W Midway Drive
Anaheim, CA
714-774-3860
This popular park near Anaheim's resort area offers many amenities such as tours to many popular attractions, a heated pool and spa, and a well kept environment. Dogs up to 50 pounds are allowed at no additional fee. Dogs may not be left unattended outside, and they must be leashed and cleaned up after. Dogs are not allowed in buildings or the pool area. This is an RV only park. There is a dog walk area at the campground. 2 dogs may be allowed.

Canyon RV Park at Featherly
24001 Santa Ana Canyon Road
Anaheim, CA
714-637-0210
This RV only park is situated on the Santa Ana River surrounded by mature cottonwood and sycamore trees. They have 140 RV hookup sites. Other amenities include a pool, playground, laundry, acres of wilderness and trees, bike trails, and an amphitheater. This park is about 14 miles from Disneyland. Well-behaved leashed dogs are welcome for an additional $1 per day. Please clean up after your pets. There are some breed restrictions. There is a dog walk area at the campground. Multiple dogs may be allowed.

Orangeland RV Park
1600 W Struck Avenue
Orange, CA
714-633-0414

Set among Valencia orange orchards, this park offers a central location near attractions in the area, a heated pool and a Jacuzzi. Dogs of all sizes are allowed for an additional $1 per night per pet for a nightly fee, and an additional $5 per night per pet for a weekly fee. Dogs may not be left unattended, and they must be leashed, and cleaned up after. This is an RV only park. There are some breed restrictions. There is a dog walk area at the campground. Multiple dogs may be allowed.

Arcata

Mad River Rapids RV Park
3501 Janes Road
Arcata, CA
707-822-7275
This modern park is located along the coastal mountains. It offers great scenery and a variety of land and water recreation. One dog up to 20 pounds is allowed at no additional fee. Dogs may not be left unattended outside, and they must be leashed and cleaned up after. Dogs are not allowed in the pool area or in buildings. The camping and tent areas also allow dogs. There is a dog walk area at the campground.

Arrowbear

Green Valley Campground
Green Valley Lake Road
Arrowbear, CA
909-337-2444
This 36 site campground is located in the San Bernardino National Forest. RVs up to 22 feet are allowed. The lake offers fishing, swimming and boating. Trails are located nearby. Dogs of all sizes are allowed for no additional fee. Dogs may not be left unattended outside, and they must be on no more than a 6 foot leash at all times, and cleaned up after. Dogs are allowed on the trails. This campground is closed during the off-season. The camping and tent areas also allow dogs. There is a dog walk area at the campground. There are no water hookups at the campgrounds. Multiple dogs may be allowed.

Arrowbear Lake

Crab Flats Campground
Forest Road 3N16
Arrowbear Lake, CA
909-337-2444

This San Bernardino National Forest campground is located at an elevation of 6,200 feet in tall pine, oak and cedar trees. It is a popular campsite and off-highway vehicle staging area. Off-road and hiking trails are located near this campground. Tent and small RV sites are available, with a maximum RV length of 15 feet. Sites are available on a first-come, first-served basis. Pets on leash are allowed and please clean up after them. Dogs are allowed on the trails. From Green Valley Road exit turn left and go about 4 miles to the Crab Flats Campground sign at Forestry (dirt road). Turn left and go about 4.5 miles. The camping and tent areas also allow dogs. There is a dog walk area at the campground. There are no electric or water hookups at the campgrounds. Multiple dogs may be allowed.

Arroyo Grande

Lake Lopez Recreation Area Campground
6820 Lopez Drive
Arroyo Grande, CA
805-788-2381
This campground has 354 campsites which overlook the lake or are nestled among oak trees. This lake is popular for fishing, camping, boating, sailing, water skiing, canoeing, bird-watching and miles of hiking trails ranging from easy to strenuous. The marina allows dogs on their boat rentals for an extra $20 fee. Other amenities at the marina include a guest laundry, grocery store and tackle shop. Dogs must be leashed at all times and people need to clean up after their pets. There is an additional fee of $2 per night per pet. Dogs are not allowed in the water, but they are allowed on the trails. Reservations for the campsites are accepted. The camping and tent areas also allow dogs. There is a dog walk area at the campground. Multiple dogs may be allowed.

Auburn - Gold Country North

Auburn Gold Country RV (formally KOA)
3550 KOA Way
Auburn, CA
530-885-0990
Dogs of all sizes are allowed for no additional fee at this recreational park. Dogs may not be left unattended, and they must be leashed and cleaned up after. They are not allowed in the pool or playground areas, or in park buildings. There are some breed restrictions. The camping and tent areas also allow dogs. There is a dog walk area at the campground. Multiple dogs may be allowed.

Rocky Rest Campground
H 49
Downieville, CA
530-288-3231
This 10 site campground is located at the Yuba River District in the Tahoe National Forest at a 2,200 foot elevation. Amenities include piped water and vault toilets. The North Yuba trailhead is located at this campground. Pets must be leashed in the campsite and please clean up after your pets. Dogs are not allowed to be left unattended outside. This campground is closed during the off-season. The camping and tent areas also allow dogs. There is a dog walk area at the campground. There are no electric or water hookups at the campgrounds. Multiple dogs may be allowed.

French Meadows Reservoir Campground
Mosquito Ridge Road
Foresthill, CA
530-367-2224
Located in the Tahoe National Forest, this 75 site campground is at an elevation of 5,300 feet. The campground is next to the French Meadows Reservoir. Camp amenities include piped water and flush/vault toilets. Pets are allowed but must be leashed in the campground. The campsite is located 36 miles east of Foresthill on Mosquito Ridge Road. Call to make a reservation. Dogs are allowed on the trails. This campground is closed during the off-season. The camping and tent areas also allow dogs. There is a dog walk area at the campground. There are no electric or water hookups at the campgrounds. Multiple dogs may be allowed.

Robinson Flat Campground
Foresthill Divide Road
Foresthill, CA
530-367-2224
This campground is located at an elevation of 6,800 feet in the Tahoe National Forest, near the Little Bald Mountain Trail. The campground offer 14 sites (7 family sites and 7 equestrian sites) on a first-come, first-served basis. Amenities include well water and vault toilets. There is no fee. Pet must be on leash in the campground. Please clean up after your pets. To get there, go 28 miles from Foresthill on Foresthill Divide Road to Robinson Flat. This campground is closed during the off-season. The camping and tent areas also allow dogs. There is a dog walk area at the campground. There are no electric or water hookups at the campgrounds. Multiple dogs may be allowed.

Lodgepole Campground
Lake Valley Reservoir
Nevada City, CA
916-386-5164
This 35 site campground is located in the Tahoe National Forest and is managed by PG&E. The campsite is located at an elevation of 5,800 feet. Pets must be leashed in the campground must be cleaned up after. There is a $1 per night per pet additional fee. To get there from I-80, take the Yuba Gap exit for .4 miles. Go around Lake Valley Reservoir for 1.2 miles. Then take right fork 2.5 miles. This campground is closed during the off-season. The camping and tent areas also allow dogs. There is a dog walk area at the campground. There are no electric or water hookups at the campgrounds. 2 dogs may be allowed.

South Yuba Campground
North Bloomfield Road
Nevada City, CA
916-985-4474
This campground has 16 sites for tents or RVs. Camp amenities include picnic tables, fire grills, piped water, pit toilets and garbage collection. The cost per site is $5 per night with a 14 day maximum stay. Sites are available on a first-come, first-served basis. Dogs may not be left unattended outside, and they must be leashed and cleaned up after. Dogs are allowed on the trails. After traveling about 10 miles on N Bloomfield Road, and you come to the one lane bridge at Edwards Crossing, go about 1.5 miles on a dirt/gravel road to the campground and trailhead. Trailers and motorhomes should take Highway 49 and then turn right at the junction of Tyler Foote Road. At the intersection of Grizzly Hill Road turn right and proceed to North Bloomfield Road. This campground is closed during the off-season. The camping and tent areas also allow dogs. There is

a dog walk area at the campground. There are no electric or water hookups at the campgrounds. Multiple dogs may be allowed.

South Yuba Campground
North Bloomfield Road
Nevada City, CA
919-985-4474
This campground has 16 sites for tents or RVs. Camp amenities include picnic tables, fire grills, piped water, pit toilets and garbage collection. The cost per site is $5 per night with a 14 day maximum stay, and are on a first-come, first-served basis. The South Yuba River Recreation Area is located about 10 miles northeast of Nevada City. Once turned on North Bloomfield Road, drive 10 miles to the South Yuba Recreation Area. From the one lane bridge at Edwards Crossing, go about 1.5 miles on a dirt/gravel road to the campground and trailhead. Trailers and motorhomes should take Highway 49 and then turn right at the junction of Tyler Foote Road. At the intersection of Grizzly Hill Road turn right and proceed to North Bloomfield Road. Dogs of all sizes are allowed at no additional fee. Dogs may not be left unattended outside, and they must be leashed and cleaned up after. Dogs are allowed on the trails. This campground is closed during the off-season. The camping and tent areas also allow dogs. There is a dog walk area at the campground. There are no electric or water hookups at the campgrounds. Multiple dogs may be allowed.

Avenue Of The Giants

Benbow Valley RV Resort and Golf Course
7000 Benbow Drive
Garberville, CA
707-923-2777
This beautiful full service resort offers many amenities in addition to a wide variety of recreation. Dogs of all sizes are allowed for an additional $3 per night per pet. Dogs may not be left unattended outside, and left inside only if they will be quiet and well behaved. Dogs must be on no more than a 6 foot leash and be cleaned up after. They are also adjacent to a state park where there are several hiking trails. This is an RV only park. This campground is closed during the off-season. There is a dog walk area at the

campground. 2 dogs may be allowed.

Humboldt Redwoods State Park Campgrounds
17119 Avenue of the Giants (H 254)
Weott, CA
707-946-2409
There are several campgrounds located in this park including Albee Creek, Burlington and Hidden Springs Campgrounds. Tent and RV sites are available. Camp amenities include picnic tables, fire rings, showers and flush toilets. While dogs are not allowed on the trails, they are allowed in the campgrounds and on miles of fire roads and access roads. These paths are used mainly for mountain biking, but dogs are allowed too. There are both steep and gently sloping fire roads. Some of the fire roads are located next to the Albee Creek Campground. Pets must be on no more than a 6 foot leash, and cleaned up after. There is no additional pet fee, but dogs must have proof of their shots. Dogs must be quiet, well behaved, and inside at night. They are not allowed in park buildings. The park is located about 45 miles south of Eureka and 20 miles north of Garberville The camping and tent areas also allow dogs. There is a dog walk area at the campground. There are no electric or water hookups at the campgrounds. Multiple dogs may be allowed.

Baker

Hole in the Wall Campground
Black Canyon Road
Baker, CA
760-928-2562
This desert park, located in the scenic Mojave National Preserve, offers various recreational pursuits to its visitors. Dogs of all sizes are allowed. There are no additional pet fees. Dogs must be on no more than a 6 foot leash and cleaned up after. Dogs must be brought in at night, and they are allowed on the trails on lead. The camping and tent areas also allow dogs. There is a dog walk area at the campground. There are no electric or water hookups at the campgrounds. Multiple dogs may be allowed.

Mohave National Preserve Campgrounds
Black Canyon Road

Baker, CA
760-252-6101
This park offers two family campgrounds with elevations ranging from 4,400 feet to 5,600 feet. The campgrounds offer tent camping and one camp offers spaces for RVs. The campsites are usually booked during deer hunting season. Spaces are available on a first-come, first-served basis. Dogs of all sizes are allowed at no additional fee. Dogs must be leashed in camp and cleaned up after. Dogs may be off lead only if they are under voice control and will not chase. Dogs are allowed on the trails, and can even go in the visitor's center. Contact the park for campground locations and more details. The camping and tent areas also allow dogs. There is a dog walk area at the campground. There are no electric or water hookups at the campgrounds. Multiple dogs may be allowed.

Bakersfield

Bakersfield Palms RV Resort
250 Fairfax Road
Bakersfield, CA
661-366-6700
This RV only park offers various recreational pursuits, and ready access to other nearby attractions. Dogs of all sizes are allowed. There are no additional pet fees. Dogs may not be left unattended outside, and they must be leashed and cleaned up after. There is a dog walk area at the campground. Multiple dogs may be allowed.

Orange Grove RV Park
1452 S Edison Road
Bakersfield, CA
661-366-4662
This RV park is on a 40 acre orange grove about eight miles east of Highway 99. Site amenities include pull through sites with up to 50 amp service. Other amenities include a rig and car wash, a children's playground, oranges available from December through March, a swimming pool, laundry facilities, propane, TV/group meeting room and a country store. Well-behaved, leashed dogs are welcome. There are no pet fees. Please clean up after your pet. The camping and tent areas also allow dogs. There is a dog walk area at the campground. Multiple dogs may be allowed.

Bakersfield KOA

Campgrounds and RV Parks - Please always call ahead to make sure an establishment is still dog-friendly.

5101 E Lerdo H
Shafter, CA
661-399-3107
Large pull through RV spaces and grassy tent sites are available at this campground. RV site amenities include a maximum length pull through of 70 feet and 50 amp service. Other campground amenities include a seasonal swimming pool, modem dataport, and LP gas. Gas stations and 24 hour restaurants are within walking distance. Dogs of all sizes are allowed for no additional fee. Dogs must be under owner's control and visual observation at all times. Dogs must be quiet, well behaved, and leashed at all times or otherwise contained. Dogs may not be left unattended outside the owner's camping equipment. There are some breed restrictions. The camping and tent areas also allow dogs. There is a dog walk area at the campground. Multiple dogs may be allowed.

Bakersfield KOA
5101 E Lerdo H
Shafter, CA
661-399-3107
Some of this park's amenities are free morning coffee, a swimming pool, and large pull thru grass sites with shade trees. Dogs of all sizes are allowed at no additional fee. Dogs may not be left unattended for long periods, and they must be well behaved, leashed and cleaned up after. There are some breed restrictions. The camping and tent areas also allow dogs. There is a dog walk area at the campground. Multiple dogs may be allowed.

Beaumont

Country Hills RV Park
14711 Manzanita Park Road
Beaumont, CA
951-845-5919
This country like park is close to many local attractions and offers a variety of services and recreational opportunities. Dogs of all sizes are allowed for an additional $1 per night per pet. Dogs may not be left unattended outside, and left inside only if they will be well behaved and physically comfortable. Dogs must be leashed and cleaned up after. No Pit Bulls are allowed. This is an RV only park. There are some breed restrictions. There is a dog walk area at the campground. 2 dogs may be allowed.

Big Bear Lake

Holloway's RV Park
398 Edgemoor Road
Big Bear Lake, CA
909-8666-5706
This RV park offers large level sites with a nice view of Big Bear Lake. RV sites offer tables, barbecues, and TV cable. Park amenities include a small convenience store, restrooms, showers, laundry room, playground with horseshoes, basketball and boat rentals. Dogs are allowed at the campgrounds and on the boat rentals. Pets must be leashed and please clean up after them. There is a dog walk area at the campground. 2 dogs may be allowed.

Pineknot Campground
Bristlecone
Big Bear Lake, CA
909-866-3437
This 52 site campground is part of the San Bernardino National Forest. It is located at an elevation of 7,000 feet. RV spaces have a maximum length of 45 feet. Amenities include water, flush toilets and picnic areas. Pets must be on leash and cannot be left unattended. Please clean up after your pets. The campground is on Bristlecone near Summit Blvd. Call to make a reservation. The camping and tent areas also allow dogs. There is a dog walk area at the campground. There are no electric or water hookups at the campgrounds. Multiple dogs may be allowed.

Serrano Campground
4533 N Shore Drive
Big Bear Lake, CA
909-866-3437
This camp area is situated among tall pines on the North Shore of Bear Lake, and some of their new facilities include showers, toilets, and telephones. Dogs of all sizes are allowed. There are no additional pet fees. Dogs may not be left unattended, and they must be leashed and cleaned up after. The camping and tent areas also allow dogs. There is a dog walk area at the campground. Multiple dogs may be allowed.

Big Bear Shores RV Resort and Yacht Club
40751 North Shore Lane
Fawnskin, CA
909-866-4151

This gated resort offers a fully equipped private health club in addition to other recreational pursuits. Dogs of all sizes are allowed at an additional $10 per night per pet. Dogs may not be left unattended outside, and not left inside unless they will be quiet and well behaved. Dogs must be leashed and cleaned up after. Dogs are allowed on the trails. There is a dog walk area at the campground. 2 dogs may be allowed.

Hanna Flat Campground
Rim of the World Drive
Fawnskin, CA
909-382-2790
This 88 site campground, of tall pines, wildflowers and wild roses, is located in the San Bernardino National Forest at an elevation of 7,000 feet. RVs up to 40 feet are allowed. Amenities include picnic tables, fire rings, paved parking, flush toilets and trash dumpster. The Hanna Flat Trailhead is located at this camp. Pets on leash are allowed and please clean up after them. Dogs may not be left unattended. To get there take Highway 18 to Big Bear Lake Dam. Go straight, do not cross over the dam. Highway 18 becomes Highway 38. Go the Fawnskin Fire Station and turn left onto the Rim of the World Drive. Go about 2.5 miles on a dirt road to the campsite. This campground is closed during the off-season. The camping and tent areas also allow dogs. There is a dog walk area at the campground. There are no electric or water hookups at the campgrounds. Multiple dogs may be allowed.

Holcomb Valley Campground
40971 North Shore Drive
Fawnskin, CA
909-866-3437
This tent and RV campground is located in the historic Holcomb Valley about a mile from the Belleville Ghost Town. See our listing under Big Bear Lake for more information about the ghost town. There is no water at the campsite. Camp amenities include toilets. The sites are on a first-come, first-served basis. Pets are allowed but must be leashed at all times, picked up after, and they cannot be left unattended. Watch out for rattlesnakes, especially during the warm summer months. The campground is located in the San Bernardino National Forest. Dogs are allowed on the trails on lead. The camping and tent

areas also allow dogs. There is a dog walk area at the campground. There are no electric or water hookups at the campgrounds. Multiple dogs may be allowed.

Big Pine

Big Pine Creek Campground
Glacier Lodge Road
Big Pine, CA
760-873-2500
This 36 site campground is located in the Inyo National Forest at an elevation of 7,700 feet. Amenities include water and space for RVs. For hiking, the trailheads for the Big Pine Canyon Trails are located here. The fee for a campsite is $13. Pets must be leashed while in the campground and please clean up after your pets. They may be off lead in the back country if they are under voice command. Dogs may not be left unattended outside, and only left inside if they will be comfortable, quiet, and well behaved. This campground is closed during the off-season. The camping and tent areas also allow dogs. There is a dog walk area at the campground. There are no electric or water hookups at the campgrounds. Multiple dogs may be allowed.

Grandview Campground
White Mountain Road
Big Pine, CA
760-873-2500
This campground is in Bristlecone Pine Forest, at 8,600 feet, in the White Mountain area of Inyo National Forest. There are no services or water available here. Dogs of all sizes are allowed at no additional fee. Dogs may not be left unattended, and they must be leashed and cleaned up after. When out of camp, on the trails, dogs may be off lead if no one is around, and they are under voice control. This campground is closed during the off-season. The camping and tent areas also allow dogs. There is a dog walk area at the campground. There are no electric or water hookups at the campgrounds. Multiple dogs may be allowed.

Big Sur

Big Sur Campground and Cabins
47000 H 1
Big Sur, CA
831-677-2322

This tent and RV campground is set amongst redwood trees along the Big Sur River. Camp amenities include some pull through sites, a general store, playground, basketball court and more. Well-behaved leashed dogs of all sizes are allowed in the tent, RV sites, and the tent cabins, but not in the hardwood cabins or around them. There is an additional fee of $4 per night per pet for the tent or RV sites. There is an additional fee of $12 per night per pet for the tent cabins. Pets must be attended at all times. People need to clean up after their pets. They are located about 5 miles from the dog-friendly Pfieffer Beach and 2.5 miles from Big Sur Station. The camping and tent areas also allow dogs. There is a dog walk area at the campground. Dogs are allowed in the camping cabins. Multiple dogs may be allowed.

Fernwood at Big Sur
47200 H 1
Big Sur, CA
831-667-2422
Home to a famous and rare Albino Redwood tree, this park provides historic sites, river campsites, a store, tavern and planned events. One of the many trails here ends at Pfeiffer Falls, a 60-foot high waterfall. Dogs of all sizes are allowed for an additional fee of $3 per night per pet for the tent or RV sites, and an additional fee of $10 per night per pet for the tent cabins. Dogs may not be left unattended, and they must be leashed and cleaned up after. Dogs are allowed on the trails unless otherwise marked. The camping and tent areas also allow dogs. There is a dog walk area at the campground. Dogs are allowed in the camping cabins.

Ventana Big Sur Campground
28106 H 1
Big Sur, CA
831-667-2712
This 40 acre campground, located in a redwood tree lined canyon, offers 80 camp sites nestled among the trees and along the edge of the stream. RV's are limited to 22 feet. Well-behaved, quiet, leashed dogs of all sizes are allowed, maximum of two dogs per site. People need to clean up after their pets. There is a $5 per night pet fee per dog. This campground is closed during the off-season. The camping and tent

areas also allow dogs. There is a dog walk area at the campground. There are no electric or water hookups at the campgrounds. 2 dogs may be allowed.

Bishop

Four Jeffrey Campground
South Lake Road
Bishop, CA
760-873-2500
This 106 site campground is located in the Inyo National Forest at an elevation of 8,100 feet. Amenities include water, space for RVs and a dump station. For hiking, the Bristlecone Pine Forest is located nearby and offers many dog-friendly trails. The fee for a campsite is $14. Pets must be leashed while in the campground and please clean up after your pets. Dogs must be quiet and friendly. This campground is closed during the off-season. The camping and tent areas also allow dogs. There is a dog walk area at the campground. There are no electric or water hookups at the campgrounds. Multiple dogs may be allowed.

Bonita

Sweetwater Summit Regional Park
3218 Summit Meadow Road
Bonita, CA
619-472-7572
This park offers spectacular views from the summit, various habitats to explore, and offers a wide variety of recreational pursuits. Dogs of all sizes are allowed for an additional $1 per night per pet, and they must have current tags, rabies, and shot records. Dogs may not be left unattended at any time, and they must be on no more than a 6 foot leash and cleaned up after. Dogs are not allowed on the trails, but they may be walked on the payment and along side the roads on leash. The camping and tent areas also allow dogs. There is a dog walk area at the campground. Multiple dogs may be allowed.

Borrego Springs

Culp Valley Primitive Camp, Anza Borrego State Park
Off Montezuma Valley Road/HS 22
Borrego Springs, CA
760-767-5311
Located in the Anza Borrego park, this park allows dogs of all sizes at

no additional fee. Dogs may not be left unattended at any time, and they must be on no more than a 6 foot leash, and cleaned up after. Dogs are not allowed on the hiking trails; they may be walked on paved or dirt roads, or in the camp area. The camping and tent areas also allow dogs. There is a dog walk area at the campground. There are no electric or water hookups at the campgrounds. Multiple dogs may be allowed.

Bridgeport

Honeymoon Flat
P. O. Box 631/Twin Lakes Road
Bridgeport, CA
760-932-7070
This campground is in the Twin Lakes Recreation Area of the Sierra Nevada Mountain Range, and there are a variety of recreational pursuits. Dog of all sizes are allowed at no additional fee. Dogs must be leashed in the camp areas, and cleaned up after at all times. Dogs may be off lead when hiking if they are under voice control, however, they may not be off lead at any time on the Robinson Head Creek Trail. This campground is closed during the off-season. The camping and tent areas also allow dogs. There is a dog walk area at the campground. There are no electric or water hookups at the campgrounds. Multiple dogs may be allowed.

California City

Sierra Trails RV Park
21282 H 14N
California City, CA
877-994-7999
This RV only park offers shade trees, cement patios, lawns, grills and picnic tables at each site, a heated pool in summer, a rec room, restrooms with showers and a laundry. Dogs of all sizes are allowed at no additional fee. Dogs may not be left unattended outside, and they must be leashed at all times, and cleaned up after. They ask that you walk your pet along the outside of the park, and in another area close by. There are some breed restrictions. Multiple dogs may be allowed.

Campo

Lake Morena County Park
2550 Lake Morena Drive

Campo, CA
619-579-4101
This park is a combination of desert, coastal, and mountain habitats. It supports a wide variety of plant and animal life. Dogs of all sizes are allowed for an additional $1 per night per pet, and they must have current tags, rabies, and shot records. Dogs may not be left unattended at any time, and they must be on no more than a 6 foot leash and cleaned up after. Dogs are not allowed on the trails, but they may be walked on the payment and along side the roads on leash. The camping and tent areas also allow dogs. There is a dog walk area at the campground. Multiple dogs may be allowed.

Carmel

Carmel by the River RV Park
27680 Schulte Road
Carmel, CA
831-624-9329
This RV park is located right next to the river. Amenities include hookups, a basketball court, recreation room and dog walk area. Per Monterey County's Ordinance, the maximum length per stay from April through September is 14 days and from October through March is 8 weeks. Well-behaved quiet dogs of all sizes are allowed, up to a maximum of three pets. Pets must be kept on a short leash and never left unattended in the campsite or in your RV. People need to clean up after their pets. There is a $2 per night per dog pet fee. The owners have dogs that usually stay at the office. There is a dog walk area at the campground. Multiple dogs may be allowed.

Castaic

Valencia Travel Resort
27946 Henry Mayo Drive (H 126)
Castaic, CA
661-257-3333
This full service park offers a pool, store, laundry room, meeting room, planned activities, and a variety of recreation. Dogs of all sizes are allowed. There are no additional pet fees. Dogs may not be left unattended outside unless they will be quiet and well behaved. They must be leashed, and cleaned up after. There is also an off-lead dog run area at this RV only park. There are some breed restrictions. There

is a dog walk area at the campground. Multiple dogs may be allowed.

Chico

Almond Grove RV Park
567 E Lassen
Chico, CA
530-342-6056
This 55 and over park offers many amenities, programs, and a variety of recreation. Dogs up to 30 pounds are allowed. There are no additional pet fees. Dogs must be quiet, well behaved, leashed and cleaned up after. This is an RV only park, and there is no limits to length of stay. There is a dog walk area at the campground. 2 dogs may be allowed.

Chowchilla

The Lakes RV and Golf Resort
1024 Robetson Blvd
Chowchilla, CA
866-665-6980
This luxury resort offers many amenities in addition to a wide variety of recreational opportunities. Dogs of all sizes are allowed at no additional fee. Dogs may not be left unattended outside, and they must be quiet, well behaved, on no more than a 6 foot leash, and cleaned up after. Dogs are not allowed in the green belt or pool/spa areas. This campground is closed during the off-season. There is a dog walk area at the campground. Multiple dogs may be allowed.

Clear Lake

Clear Lake State Park
5300 Soda Bay Road
Kelseyville, CA
707-279-4293
This park offers 149 campsites for RV or tent camping, and is located along the shores of California's largest freshwater lake. Amenities include picnic tables, restrooms, showers and grills. While dogs are not allowed on the trails or the swimming beaches at this park, they are allowed in the campgrounds and in the water at non-designated swim areas. One of the non-designated swim beaches is located between campgrounds 57 and 58. Pets must be on leash at all times, and please clean up after them. The park is located is 3.5 miles northeast of

Kelseyville. The camping and tent areas also allow dogs. There is a dog walk area at the campground. There are no electric or water hookups at the campgrounds. Multiple dogs may be allowed.

Sunset Campground
County Road 301/Forest Road M1
Upper Lake, CA
916-386-5164
This campground is located in the Mendocino National Forest and is managed by Pacific Gas and Electric. Camp amenities include 54 tables, 54 stoves, 12 toilets, water, trailer spaces and 27 grills. The Sunset Nature Trail Loop begins at this campground. There is a $12 fee per campsite and an extra $1 per night per pet fee. Dogs on leash are allowed and please clean up after them. This campground is closed during the off-season. The camping and tent areas also allow dogs. There is a dog walk area at the campground. There are no electric or water hookups at the campgrounds. 2 dogs may be allowed.

Coleville

Sonora Bridge Campground
Sonora Bridge Road
Coleville, CA
760-932-7070
Dogs of all sizes are allowed. There are no additional pet fees. Dogs may not be left unattended, and they must be leashed and cleaned up after. Dogs may be off lead on the trails only if they will respond to voice command and will not chase wildlife. Dogs are not allowed on the trails that go into Yosemite. This campground is closed during the off-season. The camping and tent areas also allow dogs. There is a dog walk area at the campground. There are no electric or water hookups at the campgrounds. Multiple dogs may be allowed.

Corning

Woodson Bridge State Rec Area
25340 South Avenue
Corning, CA
530-839-2112
This beautiful oak woodland park along the Sacramento River is home to a dense native riparian forest that is also a winter home to the Bald Eagle. The park also offers various recreational opportunities. Dogs of all sizes are allowed. There are no

additional pet fees. Dogs must be on no more than a 6 foot leash, and cleaned up after. Dogs are not allowed on the beach or on the trails, and they must be inside at night. The camping and tent areas also allow dogs. There is a dog walk area at the campground. There are no electric or water hookups at the campgrounds. Multiple dogs may be allowed.

Crescent City

Crescent City KOA
4241 H 101N
Crescent City, CA
707-464-5744
This 17 acre campground has 10 acres of camping in the redwood forest. It offers ice cream socials, pancake breakfasts, movie nights, hayrides, snack bar, bike rentals and a maximum pull through length of 60 feet with 50 amp service. Dogs of all sizes are allowed for no additional fee. Dogs must be under owner's control and visual observation at all times. Dogs must be quiet, well behaved, and be on no more than a 6 foot leash at all times, or otherwise contained. Dogs may not be left unattended outside the owner's camping equipment. There are some breed restrictions. The camping and tent areas also allow dogs. There is a dog walk area at the campground. Dogs are allowed in the camping cabins. Multiple dogs may be allowed.

De Norte Coast Redwoods State Park
7 miles S of Crescent City off H 101
Crescent City, CA
707-464-6101, ext. 5064
This predominately old growth coastal forest park is known for its steep topography and lush natural setting, and they offer guided tours, exhibits, and a variety of recreational pursuits. Dogs of all sizes are allowed. There are no additional pet fees. Dogs must be leashed and cleaned up after. Dogs are not allowed on the nature trails, but they are allowed on the beach on lead. No swimming, due to high danger, is allowed. This campground is closed during the off-season. The camping and tent areas also allow dogs. There is a dog walk area at the campground. There are no electric or water hookups at the campgrounds. Multiple dogs may be allowed.

Jedediah Smith Campground
1440 H 199
Crescent City, CA
707-464-6101
This campground is located in the Jedediah Smith Redwoods State Park and offers 106 RV or tent sites in an old growth redwood forest. RVs must be 36 feet or less. Camp amenities include restrooms, showers, fire pits, dump station and bear-proof lockers. While dogs are not allowed on any park trails, they are allowed in the campground and at the beach. They are also allowed to walk on or along Walker Road which is just west of the campground. Pets must be on no more than a 6 foot leash and attended at all times. Please clean up after your pets. There are no additional pet fees. The camping and tent areas also allow dogs. There is a dog walk area at the campground. There are no electric or water hookups at the campgrounds. Multiple dogs may be allowed.

Jedediah Smith Redwoods State Park
9 miles east of Crescent City on Highway 199.
Crescent City, CA
707-464-6101, ext. 5112
This predominately old growth coastal forest of redwoods is home to the last major free flowing river in California. The park is abundant with animal and plant life and offers a variety of interpretive programs, guided tours, and recreational pursuits. Dogs of all sizes are allowed. There are no additional pet fees. Dogs must be leashed and cleaned up after. Dogs are not allowed on the trails, but they are allowed on the beach on lead. The camping and tent areas also allow dogs. There is a dog walk area at the campground. There are no electric or water hookups at the campgrounds.

Mill Creek Campground
1375 Elk Valley Road
Crescent City, CA
707-464-9533
This park is located in a second growth Redwood forest, and offers guided walks, campfire programs, and a variety of recreational pursuits. Dogs of all sizes are allowed. There are no additional pet fees. Dogs must be on no more than a 6 foot leash and cleaned up after. Dogs are not allowed on the beach. They are

allowed on the trails unless otherwise marked. This campground is closed during the off-season. The camping and tent areas also allow dogs. There is a dog walk area at the campground. There are no electric or water hookups at the campgrounds. Multiple dogs may be allowed.

Panther Flat Campground
mile post 16.75 on Highway 199
Gasquet, CA
707-457-3131
This park, located next to the Middle Fork of Smith River, is the largest Smith River NRA campground, and offers botanical areas, various trails, and a variety of recreational pursuits. Dogs of all sizes are allowed. There are no additional pet fees. Dogs must be leashed and cleaned up after. Dogs are allowed on the trails unless otherwise marked. They are not allowed to go on the National or State Park trails that connect in areas to this park. The camping and tent areas also allow dogs. There is a dog walk area at the campground. There are no electric or water hookups at the campgrounds. Multiple dogs may be allowed.

Panther Flat Campground
Mile Post 16.75 H 199
Gasquet, CA
707-442-1721
This campground is located in the Smith River National Recreation Area and is part of the Six Rivers National Forest. The campground offers 39 tent and RV sites. RVs up to 40 feet are allowed. Amenities include flush restrooms, pay shower, potable water, picnic tables, grills, fishing, and sites with river and scenic views. Pets on leash are allowed at no additional fee, and please clean up after them. Dogs are allowed on the trails in the National Forest on lead but not on State Park trails. The camping and tent areas also allow dogs. There is a dog walk area at the campground. There are no electric or water hookups at the campgrounds. Multiple dogs may be allowed.

Crowley Lake

Crowley Lake Campground
Crowley Lake Drive
Crowley Lake, CA
760 873-2503
This campground is located in open high desert country at 7,000 feet and has 47 tent and RV sites available.

Please note that there are no trees and the winds can be strong. The area overlooks Crowley Lake which is a popular site for fishing. The campground is usually open from late April until the end of October. Camp amenities include 4 pit toilets and pull through trailer spaces. All sites are first-come, first-served. This campsite is managed by the BLM (Bureau of Land Management), and there is a $5 per night camping fee. Dogs are allowed at no additional fee, but please keep them under control, and leashed in camp. The closest convenience stores are located in Mammoth Lakes, about 10 miles north of the campground or at a very small store in the Crowley Lake area. After exiting H 395, go west through the Crowley Lake community for about 2 miles. At Crowley Lake Drive turn north and go about 2 miles. This campground is closed during the off-season. The camping and tent areas also allow dogs. There is a dog walk area at the campground. There are no electric or water hookups at the campgrounds.

Crowley Lake RV Campland
4109 Crowley Lake Drive
Crowley Lake, CA
760-935-4260
This small RV only park is about an 1/8 of a mile from H 395, and 2 dogs up to about 50 pounds are allowed, or 3 dogs if they are very small. Dogs must be quiet, well behaved, leashed at all times, and cleaned up after. There is a BLM campground about a mile and a half further that also allows dogs of all sizes for tent and RV camping. There are some breed restrictions. This campground is closed during the off-season. There is a dog walk area at the campground.

Death Valley

Death Valley National Park Campgrounds
H 190
Death Valley, CA
760-786-3200
There are 10 campgrounds to choose from at this park, ranging from 196 feet below sea level to 8,200 feet above sea level. The Emigrant campground, located at 2,100 feet, offers tent camping only. This free campground offers 10 sites with water, tables and flush toilets. The Furnace Creek

campground, located at 196 feet below sea level has 136 sites with water, tables, fireplaces, flush toilets and a dump station. Winter rates are $18 per night and less for the summertime. There are no hookups and some campgrounds do not allow generators. The Stovepipe Wells RV Campground is managed by the Stovepipe Wells Resort and offers 14 sites with full hookups but no tables or fireplaces. See our listing in Death Valley for more information about this RV park. About half of the campgrounds are open all year. Pets must be leashed and attended at all times. Please clean up after your pets. Dogs are not allowed on any trails in Death Valley National Park, but they can walk along roads. Pets are allowed up to a few hundred yards from the paved and dirt roads. The camping and tent areas also allow dogs. There is a dog walk area at the campground. Multiple dogs may be allowed.

Stovepipe Wells Village Campgrounds and RV Park
H 190
Death Valley, CA
760-786-2387
In addition to the motel, this establishment also offers a campground and RV park with full hookups. The main building has a restaurant, saloon, gift shops and swimming pool. They are located in the Death Valley National Park. Well-behaved leashed dogs are allowed for no additional fee in the camp area and there is no set number of dogs. There is a $20 refundable deposit for the motel, and only 2 dogs are allowed. Dogs are allowed in public areas only, and they are not allowed on the trails or in the canyon areas. The camping and tent areas also allow dogs. There is a dog walk area at the campground.

Dinkey Creek

Dinkey Creek Campground
Dinkey Creek Road
Dinkey Creek, CA
559-297-0706
This campground is next to Dinkey Creek in the Sierra National Forest. The campground is on a large sandy flat above the river and shaded by cedar and pine trees at an elevation of 5,400 feet. There are 128 tent and RV sites. RVs up to 35 feet are allowed. Amenities include piped water, flush toilets, picnic tables and grills. There are several trails that

start at this campground. Dogs are allowed at the campgrounds, on trails, and in the water, but only at non-designated swimming beaches. Pets must be leashed and please clean up after them. Dogs must be quiet and well behaved. This campground is closed during the off-season. The camping and tent areas also allow dogs. There is a dog walk area at the campground. There are no electric or water hookups at the campgrounds. Multiple dogs may be allowed.

Eureka

Eureka KOA
4050 N H 101
Eureka, CA
707-822-4243
Located along Humboldt Bay in the heart of the giant redwood country, this well-kept park offers a maximum length pull-through of 70 feet with 50 amp service. Some amenities include cable TV, two playgrounds, a swimming pool, family hot tub, adults-only hot tub, horseshoe pits, rental bikes, a camp store, and ice cream socials during the summer months. Dogs of all sizes are allowed for an additional fee of $3 per night per pet. Dogs must be under owner's control and visual observation at all times. Dogs must be quiet, well behaved, and be on no more than a 6 foot leash at all times, or otherwise contained. Dogs may not be left unattended outside the owner's camping equipment. There are some breed restrictions. The camping and tent areas also allow dogs. There is a dog walk area at the campground. Dogs are allowed in the camping cabins. Multiple dogs may be allowed.

Friant

Millerton Lake State Recreation Area
47597 Road 145 (campground) 5290 Millerton Road (day use)
Friant, CA
559-822-2332
This popular park offers lush rolling hills and over 40 miles of shoreline allowing for ample recreational opportunities. Dogs of all sizes are allowed. There are no additional pet fees. Dogs must be on no more than a 6 foot leash and cleaned up after. Dogs are not allowed in park buildings, on trails, or on most beaches. Dogs may be walked in the

campgrounds, along the shoreline, or on the side of the roads on lead. The camping and tent areas also allow dogs. There is a dog walk area at the campground. Multiple dogs may be allowed.

Garberville

Dean Creek Resort
4112 Redwood Drive
Redway, CA
707-923-2555
Located on the Eel River, this campground is located just 3 miles from the Avenue of the Giants attraction. Riverfront sites are available for both RVs and tent camping. Many of the RV sites have full hookups with 50 amp service available. All sites have picnic tables and barbecue grills. Other amenities include a pool, spa, sauna, coin laundry, mini-mart, meeting room, game room, playground, and restrooms. Pets are allowed but must be leashed at all times. There is an additional $1.50 per night per pet fee for the tent or RV sites. There is a $6 per night per pet additional fee for the motel rooms. Dogs may not be left unattended at any time. There are some breed restrictions. The camping and tent areas also allow dogs. There is a dog walk area at the campground. 2 dogs may be allowed.

Gorda

Kirk Creek Campground
H 1
Gorda, CA
831-385-5434
Located in the Los Padres National Forest, this campground is situated on an open bluff 100 feet above sea level and offers great views of the ocean and coastline. The beach is reached by hiking down from the campgrounds. The Kirk Creek trailhead is also located at the campground and leads to the Vicente Flat Trail which offers miles of hiking trails. Dogs are allowed in the campgrounds, on the hiking trails, and on the beach, but they must be leashed. Dogs must be cleaned up after. Be aware that there are large amounts of poison oak on the trails. RVs up to 30 feet are permitted. The campground is located about 25 miles south of Big Sur. There is no additional fee for pets, but dogs must have proof of

rabies vaccinations and current shot records. Dogs may not be left unattended outside, and left inside an RV only if they will be quiet and comfortable. The camping and tent areas also allow dogs. There is a dog walk area at the campground. There are no electric or water hookups at the campgrounds. 2 dogs may be allowed.

Plaskett Creek Campground
H 1
Gorda, CA
831-385-5434
Located in the Los Padres National Forest, this tent and RV campground is nestled among large Monterey Pine trees. The campsites are within walking distance of the dog-friendly Sand Dollar Beach. Dogs of all sizes are allowed at no additional fee. Dogs may not be left unattended outside, and left inside only if they will be quiet and comfortable. Dogs must be leashed in the campgrounds, on trails, on the beach, and have proof of current shots. The campground is about 5 miles south of the Kirk Creek and about 30 miles south of Big Sur. The camping and tent areas also allow dogs. There is a dog walk area at the campground. There are no electric or water hookups at the campgrounds. 2 dogs may be allowed.

Graeagle

Lakes Basin Campground
County Road 519
Graeagle, CA
530-836-2575
Glaciers formed the special geological features of this park that is located in the Plumas National Forest, and it is known for it's spectacular scenery and numerous clear lakes. Amenities include water, vault toilets and trailer space. Located at this campground is the trailhead for the Grassy Lake Trail. In the campground dogs must be on leash. On the trails, dogs on leash or off-leash, but under direct voice control, are allowed. Owners must clean up after their pets. This campground is closed during the off-season. The camping and tent areas also allow dogs. There is a dog walk area at the campground. There are no electric or water hookups at the campgrounds. Multiple dogs may be allowed.

Gualala

Gualala Point Regional Park Campgrounds
42401 Coast H 1
Gualala, CA
707-785-2377
This dog-friendly park offers sandy beaches, hiking trails and 20 campsites. RVs are permitted and there is a dump station. Dogs are allowed but must be on a 6 foot or less leash at all times, be cleaned up after, and have proof of rabies vaccination. There is an additional fee of $1 per night per pet. Reservations are taken by telephone at 707-565-CAMP(2267). The camping and tent areas also allow dogs. There is a dog walk area at the campground. There are no electric or water hookups at the campgrounds. Multiple dogs may be allowed.

Guatay

Laguna Campground
Sunrise H
Pine Valley, CA
619-445-6235
This 104 site campground is located in the Cleveland National Forest. It is located at an elevation of 5,600 feet and offers both tent and RV sites. RVs up to 40 feet are allowed. Flush toilets are available at this campground. Pets must be on no more than a 6 foot leash at all times, cleaned up after, and contained at night. There are no additional pet fees. The camping and tent areas also allow dogs. There is a dog walk area at the campground. There are no electric or water hookups at the campgrounds. Multiple dogs may be allowed.

Hollister

Casa de Fruta, RV Orchard Resort
10031 Pacheco Pass H
Hollister, CA
408-842-9316
This RV park is located at a popular roadside orchard resort which features a fruit stand, store, 24 hour restaurant, zoo, rock shop, gold panning, children's train ride, children's playground and picnic areas. Amenities at the RV park include full hookups, pull through sites, shady areas, TV hookups, and seasonal tent sites. Well-behaved leashed dogs are allowed. Dogs may not be left unattended. There is a $3 per night pet fee per pet. Please clean up after your pets. The resort

is located on Highway 152/Pacheco Pass, two miles east of the Highway 156 junction. The camping and tent areas also allow dogs. There is a dog walk area at the campground. Multiple dogs may be allowed.

Independence

Goodale Creek Campground
Aberdeen Cutoff Road
Independence, CA
760-872-5000
This campground is located at a 4,000 foot elevation on a volcanic flow, next to Goodale Creek. It offers great views of the Sierra Nevada Mountains. There are 62 tent and RV sites available, 5 pit toilets, picnic tables and campfire rings/stands. The campground is usually open from late April to the end of October. There are no fees, no hookups and no drinking water. All sites are on a first-come, first-served basis. Be aware of rattlesnakes in the area, especially during the summer months. The closest convenience stores are located in the towns of Independence and Big Pine. Dogs are allowed at the campground, but please keep them under control, and they must be leashed and cleaned up after. Dogs are allowed on the trails on lead. The camping and tent areas also allow dogs. There is a dog walk area at the campground. There are no electric or water hookups at the campgrounds. Multiple dogs may be allowed.

Jackson - Gold Country Central

49er Village RV Resort
18265 H 49
Plymouth, CA
800-339-6981
Nestled in the Sierra foothills, this park offers spacious, shady sites on tree-lined streets, 2 swimming pools-one year round-heated, an indoor whirlpool spa, and an on-site Deli-Espresso Cafe and Gift Shop, which is open daily at 7 a.m. Up to 3 dogs of any size are allowed for the RV section, and there is no additional fee or deposit. There are 2 pet friendly cabins; 1 dog is allowed in the studio, and up to 2 dogs are allowed in the one bedroom. There is a $100 per pet refundable deposit. Dogs may not be left unattended in the cottages or outside. Dogs must be leashed and

cleaned up after. This is an RV only park. There is a dog walk area at the campground. Dogs are allowed in the camping cabins.

Johnsondale

Redwood Meadow Campground
Off Mountain Road 50 on Western Divide H/M 107
Johnsondale, CA
559-539-2607
This campground is located in the Sequoia National Forest at an elevation of 6,100 feet. It is across the road from the Trail of a Hundred Giants. The campground offers 15 tent and small RV sites. RVs up to 16 feet are allowed. Vault toilets are located at the camp. Ideal camping is from May to October. Pets must be on no more than a 6 foot leash and attended to at all times. Please clean up after your pet. The campsite is located about 45 miles northwest of Kernville. This campground is closed during the off-season. The camping and tent areas also allow dogs. There is a dog walk area at the campground. There are no electric or water hookups at the campgrounds. Multiple dogs may be allowed.

Joshua Tree National Park

29 Palms RV Resort
4949 Desert Knoll
Twentynine Palms, CA
760-367-3320
This RV resort is located less than 10 minutes from the Joshua Tree National Park visitor center. RV sites include shade trees, and they can accommodate large motorhomes and trailers. Park amenities include a recreation hall, fitness room, tennis courts, shuffle board, heated indoor pool, laundry, showers, and restrooms. You can stay for a day, a week, or all winter. Pets on leash are welcome. There is no pet fee, just clean up after your dog. They also provide a fenced-in dog run area. Dogs may not be left unattended outside. The camping and tent areas also allow dogs. There is a dog walk area at the campground. There are special amenities given to dogs at this campground. Multiple dogs may be allowed.

Joshua Tree National Park Campgrounds
74485 National Park Drive
Twentynine Palms, CA
760-367-5500

There are nine campgrounds at this park which range from 3,000 foot to 4,500 foot elevations. Many have no fees and offer pit toilets. Only a few of the campgrounds offer water and flush toilets. Generators are not allowed between the hours of 10pm and 6am, and they are only allowed for 3 two hour periods each day. Dogs of all sizes are allowed at no additional fee. Dogs may not be left unattended, and they must be leashed and cleaned up after. Dogs are not allowed on the trails, but they are allowed on all paved roads, and the paved trail by the Visitor's Center. The camping and tent areas also allow dogs. There is a dog walk area at the campground. There are no electric or water hookups at the campgrounds. Multiple dogs may be allowed.

Julian

Cuyamaca Ranch State Park Campgrounds
12551 H 79
Descanso, CA
760-765 -0755
This scenic park has two family campgrounds, and some of the amenities include a picnic table, fire ring, barbecue, restrooms with pay showers, and water located near each site. Campsites are $20 per night May 15 through September 15, and $15 the rest of the season. There is an eight person maximum per site. You may bring your own padlock if you wish to lock the cabin during your stay. Dogs are allowed at no additional fee, but restricted to the campgrounds, picnic areas, paved roads, and the Cuyamaca Peak Fire Road. Dogs must be leashed and cleaned up after. They may not be left unattended at any time. This park is located about 15 miles south of the town of Julian. The camping and tent areas also allow dogs. Dogs are allowed in the camping cabins. There are no electric or water hookups at the campgrounds. Multiple dogs may be allowed.

Lake Cuamaca
15027 H 79
Julian, CA
760-765-0515
This campground has 40 RV sites, 14 tent sites, and 2 cabins located next to a popular fishing lake. There is a 3.5 mile trail surrounding the lake. Dogs on leash are welcome both in the campground and on the trail, but they are not allowed in the water and

must stay at least 50 feet from the shore. Dogs are, however, allowed to go on the rental boats. People must clean up after their pets. The camping and tent areas also allow dogs. There is a dog walk area at the campground. Dogs are allowed in the camping cabins. Multiple dogs may be allowed.

Pinezanita Trailer Ranch and Campground
4446 H 79
Julian, CA
760-765-0429
They have a fishing pond which is stocked with blue gill and catfish. You can find fishing tackle and bait in the Campground Registration Office. Dogs are not allowed in the cabins, but they are welcome to stay with you at your RV, trailer, or campsite. There is a $2 per day per pet charge. Pets must be on a 6 foot or shorter leash at all times. Noisy pets are cause for eviction. Carry plastic bags or a pooper scooper and pick up after your pet. The camping and tent areas also allow dogs. There is a dog walk area at the campground. Multiple dogs may be allowed.

Stagecoach Trails RV Equestrian and Wildlife Resort
7878 Great Southern Overland Stage Route of 1849
Julian, CA
760-765-2197
This scenic desert resort park has an historical, natural, cultural history to share in addition to many amenities and recreational pursuits. Dogs of all sizes are allowed at no additional fee. Dogs may not be left unattended, and they must be quiet, well behaved, leashed, and cleaned up after. Dogs are allowed on the trails unless otherwise indicated. This is an RV only park. There is a dog walk area at the campground. Multiple dogs may be allowed.

William Heise County Park
4945 Heise Park Road
Julian, CA
760-765-0650
Dogs of all sizes are allowed for an additional $1 per night per pet, and they must have current tags, rabies, and shot records. Dogs may not be left unattended at any time, and they must be on no more than a 6 foot leash and cleaned up after. Dogs are not allowed on the trails, but they may be walked on the payment and along side the roads

on leash. The camping and tent areas also allow dogs. There is a dog walk area at the campground. There are no water hookups at the campgrounds. Multiple dogs may be allowed.

June Lake

Silver Lake Resort
6957 H 158
June Lake, CA
760-648-7572
This resort, located on the shore of Silver Lake, offers great views and amenities that include a general store, cafe, showers, laundry room and picnic area. Well-behaved dogs of all sizes are allowed at no additional fee. Dogs must be leashed, and walked outside of the park, and please clean up after your pet in the Sierra National Forest. The resort is open from the end of April to mid-October. This is an RV only park. This campground is closed during the off-season. The camping and tent areas also allow dogs. There is a dog walk area at the campground. Multiple dogs may be allowed.

Silver Lake Resort
6957 H 158
June Lake, CA
760-648-7525
This historic resort, the oldest in the Eastern Sierra, offers spectacular views, an RV park with a paved patio slab and picnic table at each site, a general store, cafe, showers, restrooms, laundry room and picnic area. There is no tent camping. Well-behaved leashed pets are allowed in the RV park. They need to be walked outside of the park and please clean up after your pet in the Sierra National Forest. The resort is located on the shores of Silver Lake. This campground is closed during the off-season. There is a dog walk area at the campground. 2 dogs may be allowed.

Kernville

Rivernook Campground
14001 Sierra Way
Kernville, CA
760-376-2705
This park is nestled in 60 wooded acres along the scenic Kern River and offers a variety of land and water recreation. Dogs of all sizes are allowed. There are no additional pet

26

fees. Dogs may not be left unattended outside, and left inside only if they will be quiet, well behaved, and physically comfortable. Dogs must be leashed and cleaned up after. The camping and tent areas also allow dogs. There is a dog walk area at the campground. Multiple dogs may be allowed.

Isabella Lake KOA
15627 H 178
Weldon, CA
760-378-2001
Located near the dog-friendly Isabella Lake, this campground offers both tent sites and RV spaces. Well-behaved leashed dogs of all sizes are allowed. People need to clean up after their pets. There is no pet fee. Site amenities include a maximum length pull through of 40 feet and 30 amp service available. Other amenities include LP gas, an entrance gate, free modem dataport, snack bar and a seasonal swimming pool, playground, and adult pub. There are some breed restrictions. The camping and tent areas also allow dogs. There is a dog walk area at the campground. Multiple dogs may be allowed.

King City

San Lorenzo Campground and RV Park
1160 Broadway
King City, CA
831-385-5964
This campground is located in the dog-friendly San Lorenzo Park where leashed dogs are allowed on the hiking trails. Camp amenities include grassy tent sites, shaded RV spaces, an information center and museum, a walking trail along the river, laundry facilities, a putting green, playground, internet access kiosk, restrooms, and showers. Well-behaved leashed dogs of all sizes are allowed in the campground. Pets must be attended at all times. People need to clean up after their pets. There is a $2 per night per pet fee. Dogs are allowed on the trails, on roads, and at a place on the other side of the levy. The camping and tent areas also allow dogs. There is a dog walk area at the campground. 2 dogs may be allowed.

Klamath National Forest

East Fork Campground

Salmon River Road
Forks of Salmon, CA
530-468-5351
This Klamath National Forest campground has 9 camp sites with no water but there are vault toilets. There is no charge for a camp site. Hiking from the East Fork Campground provides access to the lakes in the Caribou Basin, Rush Creek, and Little South Fork drainages. The campground is located 27 miles southwest of Callahan next to the East and the South Forks of the Salmon River. It sits at a 2,600 foot elevation. Dogs of all sizes are allowed at no additional fee. Dogs may not be left unattended outside, except for short periods, and only if they will be quiet and well behaved. Dogs must be leashed in camp and cleaned up after. Dogs are allowed on the trails, and they may be off lead on the trails if they will respond to voice command. This campground is closed during the off-season. The camping and tent areas also allow dogs. There is a dog walk area at the campground. There are no electric or water hookups at the campgrounds. Multiple dogs may be allowed.

Bridge Flat Campground
Scott River Road
Fort Jones, CA
530-468-5351
This Klamath National Forest campground offers 4 camp sites with no water but there are vault toilets. There are no fees. Popular activities include hiking and fishing. The campground is open from May to October. The Kelsey Trail begins at this camp site. The campground is located on the Scott River approximately 17 miles from Fort Jones towards the town of Scott Bar, at a 2,000 foot elevation. Dogs must be on lead at all times in developed sites. They may be off lead on the trails if they are under voice control. Dogs may not be left unattended outside, except for short periods. This campground is closed during the off-season. The camping and tent areas also allow dogs. There is a dog walk area at the campground. There are no electric or water hookups at the campgrounds. Multiple dogs may be allowed.

Norcross Campground
Elk Creek Road
Happy Camp, CA
530-493-1777

This 6 site campground is located in the Klamath National Forest at an elevation of 2,400 feet. Amenities include vault toilets. The campground is open from May to October. This campground serves as a staging area for various trails that provide access into the Marble Mountain Wilderness. The trails are used by hikers and horseback riders. Dogs must be leashed in the campground. On trails, pets must be either leashed or off-leash but under direct voice control. Please clean up after your pets. Dogs may not be left unattended outside your unit, except for short periods. The campsite is located 16 miles south of Happy Camp on Elk Creek Road. This campground is closed during the off-season. The camping and tent areas also allow dogs. There is a dog walk area at the campground. There are no electric or water hookups at the campgrounds. Multiple dogs may be allowed.

Lagunitas

Samuel P. Taylor State Park
8889 Sir Francis Drake Blvd
Lagunitas, CA
415-488-9897
This park is home to a unique contrast of coastal redwood groves, open grassland and flowers. Amenities include water, tables, grills, flush toilets and showers. Dogs of all sizes are allowed at no additional fee. While dogs are not allowed on the hiking trails, they are allowed on the bike trail that runs about six miles through the park. The path is nearly level and follows the Northwest Pacific Railroad right-of-way. The trail is both paved and dirt and it starts near the park entrance. Dogs are also allowed in the developed areas like the campgrounds. Pets must be leashed, and please clean up after your pet. Dogs may not be left unattended. The camping and tent areas also allow dogs. There is a dog walk area at the campground. There are no electric or water hookups at the campgrounds. Multiple dogs may be allowed.

Lake Arrowhead

North Shore Campground
Torrey Road
Lake Arrowhead, CA
909-337-2444
This 27 site campground is located in

the San Bernardino National Forest at 5,300 feet. RVs up to 22 feet are allowed and there are no hookups. The trailhead for the North Shore National Recreation Trail is located at this campground. Pets on leash are allowed at no additional fee, and please clean up after them. Dogs are allowed on the trails. The camp is located near the north shore of Lake Arrowhead, about two miles northeast of the village. To get there from the Lake Arrowhead Marina, go east on Torrey Road. At the first left, take the dirt road to Forest Road 2N25 to the trailhead. This campground is closed during the off-season. The camping and tent areas also allow dogs. There is a dog walk area at the campground. There are no electric or water hookups at the campgrounds. Multiple dogs may be allowed.

Dogwood Campground
H 18
Rimforest, CA
909-337-2444
This 93 site campground is located in the San Bernardino National Forest at 5,600 feet. RVs up to 22 feet are allowed. Amenities include water, showers, and a dump station. The camp is located less than a mile from Rimforest and 3 miles from Lake Arrowhead. Pets on leash are allowed at no additional fee, and please clean up after them. Dogs are allowed on the trails. This campground is closed during the off-season. The camping and tent areas also allow dogs. There is a dog walk area at the campground. There are no electric or water hookups at the campgrounds. Multiple dogs may be allowed.

Lake Elsinore

Lake Elsinore West Marina and RV Resort
32700 Riverside Drive
Lake Elsinore, CA
951-678-1300
Located on the largest freshwater lake in Southern California, this popular resort park offers many amenities and recreational opportunities. Dogs up to 20 pounds are allowed for an additional fee of $1 per night per pet. Dogs may not be left unattended, and they must be leashed and cleaned up after. This is an RV only park. The camping and tent areas also allow dogs. There is a dog walk area at the campground. 2 dogs may be allowed.

Lake Shasta

Antler's RV Park and Campground
20682 Antlers Road
Lakehead, CA
530-238-2322
located on beautiful Shasta Lake, this park offers a multitude of amenities and recreational opportunities. Dogs of all sizes are allowed for an additional $3 per night per pet or $15 per week per pet. Dogs may not be left unattended, and they must be leashed and cleaned up after. Pets must have vaccination papers for Parvo, Rabies and Distemper in order to stay at park. These are required at check-in. The camping and tent areas also allow dogs. There is a dog walk area at the campground. 2 dogs may be allowed.

Lakeshore Inn and RV
20483 Lakeshore Drive
Lakehead, CA
530-238-2003
This campground has tall pine and oak trees and overlooks Shasta Lake. Septic and cable TV are available at some of the sites. Other amenities include a large swimming pool, mini store, gift shop, playground, picnic area, video game room, showers, guest laundry, dump station and handicap bathrooms. Well-behaved dogs are welcome. Pets should be quiet and please clean up after them. There is a $1 per day per pet fee. Dogs may not be left unattended, and they must be leashed at all times. Dogs are allowed on the trails. The camping and tent areas also allow dogs. There is a dog walk area at the campground. Multiple dogs may be allowed.

Shasta Lake RV Resort and Campground
20433 Lakeshore Drive
Lakehead, CA
530-238-2370
This RV resort and campground is located on Lake Shasta. The campground is on Shasta-Trinity National Forest land. RVs up to 60 feet are allowed. Amenities include hot showers, swimming pool, private boat dock, playground, grocery store, and more. Well-behaved leashed dogs are allowed for an additional $1 per night per pet. Please clean up after your pets. There are some breed restrictions.

The camping and tent areas also allow dogs. There is a dog walk area at the campground. 2 dogs may be allowed.

Hirz Bay Campground
Gilman Road
Shasta Lake, CA
530-275-1587
This campground is located in the Shasta-Trinity National Forest at an elevation of 1,100 feet. The campground offers 37 tent and RV campsites. RVs up to 30 feet are allowed. Amenities include drinking water, accessible restrooms, flush toilets and boat ramp. Fishing, swimming and boating are popular activities at the campground. The camp is open year round. Dogs are allowed in the lake, but not at the designated swimming beaches. Pets must be leashed and please clean up after them. The camping and tent areas also allow dogs. There is a dog walk area at the campground. There are no electric or water hookups at the campgrounds. Multiple dogs may be allowed.

Lake Tahoe

D. L. Bliss State Park
H 89
South Lake Tahoe, CA
530-525-9529
This park, at 6,200 feet, offers an impressive panoramic view of Lake Tahoe and the Tahoe Valley and a variety of recreational opportunities. Dogs are allowed in the parks at no additional fee. However, they must be kept on a leash during the day and in an enclosed vehicle or tent at night. Due to the possible danger to wildlife and other park visitors, dogs are not permitted on the trails, beaches or in the Vikingsholm area. The camping and tent areas also allow dogs. There is a dog walk area at the campground. There are no electric or water hookups at the campgrounds. Multiple dogs may be allowed.

Encore Tahoe Valley RV Resort
1175 Melba Drive
South Lake Tahoe, CA
877-717-8737
Located in South Lake Tahoe, this campground sits among towering pines and mountain vistas, and some of their amenities include volleyball and tennis courts, seasonal heated outdoor pool, pool table, playground, video game center, general store,

laundry facilities, modem hookups and even a dog run. Well-behaved leashed (at all times) dogs are welcome. Please clean up after your pet. There is no pet fee. Dogs may not be left unattended. The camping and tent areas also allow dogs. There is a dog walk area at the campground. Multiple dogs may be allowed.

Fallen Leaf Campground
Fallen Leaf Lake Road
South Lake Tahoe, CA
530-543-2600
This campground is at a 6,377 foot elevation and is located in the Lake Tahoe Management Basin Unit of the National Forest. The camp offers 250 sites and 17 are available on a first-come, first-served basis. The maximum RV length allowed is 40 feet. Amenities include water, flush toilets, fire rings, picnic tables and barbecues. There are miles of trails which begin at or near this campground. Pets on leash are allowed at no additional fee, but not at the beach; they are allowed to swim in the lake. Please clean up after your pets. Dogs are allowed on the trails. Access to the campgrounds is on a rough paved road. A regular passenger car will make it, but go slow. This campground is closed during the off-season. The camping and tent areas also allow dogs. There is a dog walk area at the campground. There are no electric or water hookups at the campgrounds. Multiple dogs may be allowed.

Lake Tahoe-South Shore KOA
760 North Highway 50
South Lake Tahoe, CA
530-577-3693
Surrounded by tall pines with a creek running through, this campground offers a variety of land and water recreation with amenities that include cable TV, 60 foot pull through sites with 30 amp, LP gas, WiFi, swimming pool, and tours. Dogs of all sizes are allowed for an additional fee of $4 per night per pet. Dogs must be under owner's control and visual observation at all times. Dogs must be quiet, well behaved, and be on no more than a 6 foot leash at all times, or otherwise contained. Dogs may not be left unattended outside the owner's camping equipment. There are some breed restrictions. This campground is closed during the off-season. The camping and tent areas also allow dogs. There is

a dog walk area at the campground. Multiple dogs may be allowed.

Meeks Bay Campground
H 89
Tahoe City, CA
530-543-2600
This campground is at 6,225 feet elevation and is located in the Lake Tahoe Management Basin Unit of the National Forest. The camp offers 40 tent and RV sites. The maximum RV length allowed is 20 feet. Amenities include water, flush toilets, fire rings, picnic tables and barbecues. Pets on leash are allowed but not at the beach. Please clean up after your pets. Dogs are allowed on the trails. The camp is about 10 miles south of Tahoe City, located near D.L. Bliss State Park. This campground is closed during the off-season. The camping and tent areas also allow dogs. There is a dog walk area at the campground. There are no electric or water hookups at the campgrounds. Multiple dogs may be allowed.

General Creek Campground
West Shore Lake Tahoe
Tahoma, CA
530-525-7982
This park is located in the Sugar Pine Point State Park, offering various habitats to explore, miles of trails, and a variety of land and water recreation. Dogs of all sizes are allowed at no additional fee. Dogs must be kept on a leash no longer than six feet and under control at all times. They are not permitted in buildings or beaches. Dogs are allowed on all paved trails. Dogs must be confined to a vehicle or tent from 10:00 p.m. to 6:00 a.m. This campground is closed during the off-season. The camping and tent areas also allow dogs. There is a dog walk area at the campground. Multiple dogs may be allowed.

Lakeside Campground
Off H 89
Truckee, CA
530-587-3558
This 30 site campground is located in the Tahoe National Forest at an elevation of 5,741 feet. Camp amenities include vault toilets. There is no water. Sites are $13 per night. The campground is located next to the reservoir and activities include fishing and swimming. Pets are allowed at no additional fee,

and they must be leashed in the campground. Dogs must be cleaned up after. They may be off lead on the trails only if they are under voice control. This campground is closed during the off-season. The camping and tent areas also allow dogs. There is a dog walk area at the campground. There are no electric or water hookups at the campgrounds. 2 dogs may be allowed.

Logger Campground, Truckee District
9646 Donner Pass Road
Truckee, CA
530-587-3558
Located high in the northern Sierra Nevada mountain range, this park offers great scenery, interpretive exhibits, miles of trails, and a variety of recreation. Dogs of all sizes are allowed. There are no additional pet fees. Dogs must be leashed in the camp areas, and cleaned up after. Dogs may be off lead on the trails if they are under voice control. This campground is closed during the off-season. The camping and tent areas also allow dogs. There is a dog walk area at the campground. There are no electric or water hookups at the campgrounds. Multiple dogs may be allowed.

Camp at the Cove
760 H 50
Zephyr Cove, NV
775-589-4907
Located in spectacular scenery, this award winning resort campground offers a wide variety of amenities and recreational opportunities. Dogs of all sizes are allowed at no additional fee for tent or RV sites. There is a $15 per night per pet additional fee for the cabins. Dogs may not be left unattended outside, or in an RV. They may be left in an RV if they will be quiet and well behaved. Dogs are not allowed on the beach or in the buildings. The camping and tent areas also allow dogs. There is a dog walk area at the campground. Dogs are allowed in the camping cabins. Multiple dogs may be allowed.

Zephyr Cove RV Park and Campground
760 H 50
Zephyr Cove, NV
775-589-4922
This campground is located within minutes of South Lake Tahoe and Stateline. RV site amenities include telephone lines, cable TV, picnic

tables, fire rings, bear proof lockers, s, and spectacular scenery. There is also a restaurant, coffee bar, general store and gift shop, and a full service marina. RVs up to 40 feet can be accommodated. Tent sites are either drive-in or walk-in sites, some of which offer lake views. Well-behaved dogs on leash are allowed for no additional fee for the tent or RV sites. There is an additional fee of $15 per night per pet for the cabins. Dogs may not be left unattended in the cabins. Dogs must be leashed and cleaned up after, and they are not allowed on the beach. The camping and tent areas also allow dogs. There is a dog walk area at the campground. Dogs are allowed in the camping cabins. Multiple dogs may be allowed.

Lakeport

Konocti Vistat Casino Resort and Marina
2755 Mission Rancheria Road
Lakeport, CA
707-262-1900
Located on beautiful, historic Clear Lake, this RV park sits along a casino that has its own 90 slip marina, and there are several recreational activities to explore. Dogs of all sizes are allowed at no additional fee. Dogs may not be left unattended, and they must be leashed and cleaned up after. Dogs are not allowed in the hotel or casino. This is an RV only park. There is a dog walk area at the campground. Multiple dogs may be allowed.

Lakeside

Lake Jennings County Park
10108 Bass Road
Lakeside, CA
619-443-2004
This popular park offers great scenery, an amphitheater, various programs and exhibits, and a wide variety of recreational pursuits. Dogs of all sizes are allowed for an additional $1 per night per pet, and they must have current tags, rabies, and shot records. Dogs may not be left unattended at any time, and they must be on no more than a 6 foot leash and cleaned up after. Dogs are not allowed on the trails, but they may be walked on the payment and along side the roads on leash. The camping and tent areas also allow dogs. There is a dog walk area at the

campground. Multiple dogs may be allowed.

Lassen Volcanic Area

Hat Creek Campground
H 89
Hat Creek, CA
530-336-5521
This campground is located in the Lassen National Forest at an elevation of 4,300 feet. The camp offers 75 campsites. Camp amenities include water, fire rings, picnic tables and restrooms. Most sites are available on a first-come, first-served basis. Some sites can be reserved. Dogs on leash are allowed at the campground and on trails. Please clean up after your dog. Dogs must be quiet, well behaved, and have current shot records. This campground is closed during the off-season. The camping and tent areas also allow dogs. There is a dog walk area at the campground. There are no electric or water hookups at the campgrounds. Multiple dogs may be allowed.

Butte Lake, Lassen Volcanic National Park
PO Box 100,
Mineral, CA
530-595-4444
This park, at 6,100 feet, sits amid a variety of landscapes and recreational pursuits. Dogs of all sizes are allowed. There are no additional pet fees. Dogs may not be left unattended outside, and they must be leashed and cleaned up after. Dogs are allowed only on paved roads, and in the developed areas of the campground. Dogs are not allowed on the trails. The campsite is located 17 miles from Old Station on Highway 44 East, then 6 miles south on a dirt road. This campground is closed during the off-season. The camping and tent areas also allow dogs. There is a dog walk area at the campground. There are no electric or water hookups at the campgrounds. Multiple dogs may be allowed.

Lassen Volcanic National Park Campgrounds
36050 H 36
Mineral, CA
530-595-4444
This park offers many campgrounds, with the largest campground having 179 sites.

Trailers up to 35 feet are permitted, and all sites are on a first-come, first-served basis. Pets must be leashed and attended at all times. Please clean up after your pet. Dogs must be well behaved, and have current shot records. Dogs are permitted on established roadways, in campgrounds, picnic areas, and in other developed areas. Dogs are not allowed on any trails or hikes in this park, but see our Lassen National Forest listing for nearby dog-friendly hiking, sightseeing and additional camping. This campground is closed during the off-season. The camping and tent areas also allow dogs. There is a dog walk area at the campground. There are no electric or water hookups at the campgrounds. Multiple dogs may be allowed.

Cave Campground
H 89
Old Station, CA
530-336-5521
This campground is located in the Lassen National Forest near the Subway Cave where you and your pooch can explore an underground lava tube. The camp is at an elevation of 4,300 feet and offers 46 campsites. Camp amenities include water, fire rings, picnic tables and restrooms. Most sites are available on a first-come, first-served basis. Some sites can be reserved. Dogs on leash are allowed at the campground and on trails. Please clean up after your dog. Dogs must be quiet, well behaved, and have current shot records. This campground is closed during the off-season. The camping and tent areas also allow dogs. There is a dog walk area at the campground. There are no electric or water hookups at the campgrounds. Multiple dogs may be allowed.

Mt Lassen/Shingletown KOA
7749 KOA Road
Shingletown, CA
530-474-3133
Located at an elevation of 3,900 feet, this twelve acre campground offers both tent and RV sites in the pines. The maximum length for pull through sites is 60 feet. Sites have 30 amp service available. Other amenities include LP gas, free modem dataport, snack bar, swimming pool during the summer, and a deli. Dogs of all sizes are allowed for no additional fee. Dogs must be under owner's control and visual observation at all times. Dogs must

be quiet, well behaved, and be on no more than a 6 foot leash at all times, or otherwise contained. Dogs may not be left unattended outside the owner's camping equipment. There is a large field where dogs may be off lead if they are well trained, and under voice command. There are some breed restrictions. This campground is closed during the off-season. The camping and tent areas also allow dogs. There is a dog walk area at the campground. Multiple dogs may be allowed.

Goumas Campground, Eagle Lake
477-050 Eagle Lake Road
Susanville, CA
530-257-4188
This primitive campground, at 5,600 feet and near Eagle Lake, offers great scenery and a host of recreational pursuits. Dogs of all sizes are allowed. There are no additional pet fees. Dogs must be on no more than a 6 foot leash at all times in the camp areas, but they may be off lead on the trails if they are under voice command and well behaved. Please clean up after your pet. This campground is closed during the off-season. The camping and tent areas also allow dogs. There is a dog walk area at the campground. There are no electric or water hookups at the campgrounds. Multiple dogs may be allowed.

Merrill Campground, Eagle Lake
477050 Eagle Lake Road
Susanville, CA
530-257-4188
Located at the south end of Eagle Lake at 5,100 feet, this park offers great scenery and a variety of land and water recreation. Dogs of all sizes are allowed. There are no additional pet fees. Dogs may not be left unattended, and they must be leashed and cleaned up after. Dogs are allowed on the trails. This campground is closed during the off-season. The camping and tent areas also allow dogs. There is a dog walk area at the campground. There are no water hookups at the campgrounds. Multiple dogs may be allowed.

Lava Beds Area

Eagles Nest RV Park
634 County Road 97A
Tionesta, CA
530-664-2081
This RV park is located 24 miles south of the town of Tulelake and 2

miles off Highway 139. Amenities include 20 full hookup pull through sites, showers, restrooms, a guest laundry, clubhouse with pool table, satellite TV, and a book exchange. Grassy tent sites are also available. Well-behaved leashed dogs are welcome for no additional fee. Please clean up after your pets. This campground is closed during the off-season. The camping and tent areas also allow dogs. There is a dog walk area at the campground. Multiple dogs may be allowed.

Indian Well Campground
1 Indian Well
Tulelake, CA
530-667-8100
This campground, located in the Lava Beds National Monument, offers 40 campsites for tents and small to medium sized RVs. Amenities include water and flush toilets. Campsites are available on a first-come, first-served basis. Pets must be on no more than a 6 foot leash and attended at all times. Please clean up after your pet. Dogs may not be left unattended. Dogs are not allowed on any trails or hikes in this park, but see our Modoc National Forest listings in this region for nearby dog-friendly hiking, sightseeing and additional camping. The camping and tent areas also allow dogs. There is a dog walk area at the campground. There are no electric or water hookups at the campgrounds. Multiple dogs may be allowed.

Medicine Lake Campground
Forest Service Road 44N38
Tulelake, CA
530-233-5811
This campground is located on the shores of Medicine Lake at a 6,700 foot elevation in the Modoc National Forest. There are 22 RV and tent sites. RVs up to 22 feet are allowed, and amenities include picnic tables, fire pits, vault toilets and potable water. Dogs on leash are allowed at the campgrounds and in the water. Please clean up after your pets. There is a $7 per vehicle fee. This campground is closed during the off-season. The camping and tent areas also allow dogs. There is a dog walk area at the campground. There are no electric or water hookups at the campgrounds. Multiple dogs may be allowed.

Lodi

Stockton/Lodi (formally KOA)
2851 East Eight Mile Road
Lodi, CA
209-334-0309
This campground offers a store, a host of amenities, planned activities, and various land and water recreation. Dogs of all sizes are allowed at no additional fee. Dogs may not be left unattended, and they must be on no more than a 6 foot leash. Dogs must be taken to the dog walk area to do their "business", and be cleaned up after at all times. There are some breed restrictions. The camping and tent areas also allow dogs. There is a dog walk area at the campground. Multiple dogs may be allowed.

Lone Pine

Lone Pine Campground
Whitney Portal Road
Lone Pine, CA
760-876-6200
This 43 site campground is located in the Inyo National Forest at an elevation of 6,000 feet. Water is available at the site. There is a $12 fee per campsite. Pets must be leashed while in the campground. Please clean up after your pets. Dogs may not be left unattended. Dogs may be off lead on the trails if they are under good voice control. The camping and tent areas also allow dogs. There is a dog walk area at the campground. There are no electric or water hookups at the campgrounds. Multiple dogs may be allowed.

Tuttle Creek Campground
Horseshoe Meadows Road
Lone Pine, CA
760-876-6200
This campground is located at 5,120 feet and is shadowed by some of the most impressive peaks in the Sierra Nevada Mountain Range. The camp is located in an open desert setting with a view of Alabama Hills and Mt. Whitney. There are 85 tent and RV sites, but no potable water. Amenities include 9 pit toilets, stream water, barbecues, fire rings and picnic tables. All sites are based on a first-come, first-served basis. This campground is managed by the BLM (Bureau of Land Management). Pets on leash are allowed and please clean up after them. Dogs may not be left unattended. They may be off lead on the trials if they are under good voice control. To get there go 3.5 miles west of Lone Pine on

31

Whitney Portal Road. Then go 1.5 miles south on Horseshoe Meadows Road and follow the sign to the campsite. This campground is closed during the off-season. The camping and tent areas also allow dogs. There is a dog walk area at the campground. There are no electric or water hookups at the campgrounds. Multiple dogs may be allowed.

Whitney Portal Campground, Inyo National Forest
Whitney Portal Road
Lone Pine, CA
760-876-6200
This camp area at 8,000 feet, is located in a national forest, and offers a wide variety of both land and water recreational opportunities. Dogs of all sizes are allowed at no additional fee. Dogs may not be left unattended, and they must be on no more than a 6 foot leash, and cleaned up after. Dogs are allowed on the trails up to the trail camp. This campground is closed during the off-season. The camping and tent areas also allow dogs. There is a dog walk area at the campground. There are no electric or water hookups at the campgrounds. Multiple dogs may be allowed.

Wildrose Campground
On Corner of H 395 and H 136
Lone Pine, CA
760-786-3200
Wildrose is a free campground at 4,100 feet in the Panamint Mountains and is not accessible to vehicles over 25 feet in length. Dogs of all sizes are allowed. There are no additional pet fees. Dogs may not be left unattended outside, and they must be leashed and cleaned up after. Dogs are not allowed off the main road or along side the main road if being walked. Dogs must remain by the vehicle otherwise, and they are not allowed on the trails. The camping and tent areas also allow dogs. There is a dog walk area at the campground. There are no electric or water hookups at the campgrounds. Multiple dogs may be allowed.

Lost Hills

Lost Hills RV Park (formally KOA)
14831 Warren Street
Lost Hills, CA
661-797-2719
Dogs of all sizes are allowed for no additional fee at this RV only park.

Dogs must be leashed and cleaned up after. There are some breed restrictions. There is a dog walk area at the campground. Multiple dogs may be allowed.

Malibu

Leo Carrillo State Park Campground
35000 Pacific Coast H (H 1)
Malibu, CA
818-880-0350
This campground offers tent and RV camping near the dog-friendly (leashes only and certain sections only) beach, tide pools, marine viewing, interpretive programs, and a variety of recreational activities. The campsites are located on the inland side of Highway 1. You can walk to the beach along a road that goes underneath the highway. Dogs on leash are allowed in the campgrounds and on a certain section of the beach. Please clean up after you pets. Dogs are not allowed in the rocky tide pool area, or on the back country trails. The camping and tent areas also allow dogs. There is a dog walk area at the campground. There are no electric or water hookups at the campgrounds. Multiple dogs may be allowed.

Malibu Beach RV Park
25801 Pacific Coast H
Malibu, CA
310-456-6052
This ocean park provide many amenities, some of which are a rec room, video game room, an outdoor game room, marine life viewing, hiking trails, and various other land and water recreational activities. Dogs of all sizes are allowed for an additional fee of $3 per night per pet. Dogs may not be left unattended, and they must be leashed at all times, and cleaned up after. This is an RV only park. There are some breed restrictions. There is a dog walk area at the campground. 2 dogs may be allowed.

Mammoth Lakes

Lake George Campground
Lake George Road
Mammoth Lakes, CA
760-924-5500
This 16 site campground is located in the Inyo National Forest at an

elevation of 9,000 feet. It is located near several trails. The fee for a campsite is $14. The sites are available on a first-come, first-served basis. Pets must be leashed while in the campground and please clean up after them. Dogs may be off lead on the trails only if they are under voice control. To get there from the intersection of Main Street and Hwy 203, take Lake Mary Road to the left. Go past Twin Lakes. You'll see a road that goes off to the left (Lake Mary Loop Rd). Go past this road, you'll want the other end of the loop. When you come to another road that also says Lake Mary Loop Rd, turn left. Then turn right onto Lake George Road and follow it to the campground. This campground is closed during the off-season. The camping and tent areas also allow dogs. There is a dog walk area at the campground. There are no electric or water hookups at the campgrounds. Multiple dogs may be allowed.

Lake Mary Campground
Lake Mary Loop Road
Mammoth Lakes, CA
760-924-5500
This 48 site campground is located in the Inyo National Forest at an elevation of 8,900 feet. It is located near several trails. The fee for a campsite is $14. The sites are available on a first-come, first-served basis. Pets must be leashed while in the campground and please clean up after them. Dogs may be off lead on the trails if they will respond to voice command. From Hwy 203, take Lake Mary Road to the left. Pass Twin Lakes and then you'll come to Lake Mary. Turn left onto Lake Mary Loop Road. This campground is closed during the off-season. The camping and tent areas also allow dogs. There is a dog walk area at the campground. There are no electric or water hookups at the campgrounds. Multiple dogs may be allowed.

Mammoth Mountain RV Park
P.O. Box 288/H 203
Mammoth Lakes, CA
760-934-3822
This RV park offers over 160 tent sites and RV sites with full hookups. Amenities include dump stations, restrooms with hot showers, laundry rooms, picnic tables, indoor heated swimming pool and spa, children's play area and RV supplies. Site rates range from $21 to $34 per night. Rates are subject to change. Pets are welcome but need to be leashed

at all times and cannot be left unattended outside, and left inside only if they will be physically comfortable and quiet. There is a $3 per night per pet fee. They are located within walking distance of shops and restaurants. The RV park is open year round. There are some breed restrictions. The camping and tent areas also allow dogs. There is a dog walk area at the campground. Multiple dogs may be allowed.

New Shady Rest Campground
Sawmill Cutoff Road
Mammoth Lakes, CA
760-924-5500
This 94 site campground is located in the Inyo National Forest at an elevation of 7,800 feet. It is located near several trails. Amenities include water, flush toilets, fire ring, showers, interpretive programs, and a visitors' center. The fee for a campsite is $13. The sites are available on a first-come, first-served basis. Pets must be leashed while in the campground and please clean up after them. This campground is closed during the off-season. The camping and tent areas also allow dogs. There is a dog walk area at the campground. There are no electric or water hookups at the campgrounds. Multiple dogs may be allowed.

Red Meadows Campground
Off H 203
Mammoth Lakes, CA
760-924-5500
This 56 site campground is located in the Inyo National Forest at an elevation of 7,600 feet. It is near the dog-friendly Devil's Postpile National Monument and hiking trails including the John Muir Trail. Amenities include water. The fee for a campsite is $15, and sites are available on a first-come, first-served basis. Pets must be leashed while in the campground and please clean up after them. From Highway 395, drive 10 miles west on Highway 203 to Minaret Summit. Then drive about 7 miles on a paved, narrow mountain road. This campground is closed during the off-season. The camping and tent areas also allow dogs. There is a dog walk area at the campground. There are no electric or water hookups at the campgrounds. Multiple dogs may be allowed.

Twin Lakes Campground, Inyo National Forest
Lake Mary Road

Mammoth Lakes, CA
760-924-5500
This forest campground located at 8,600 feet offers great scenery amid a variety of recreational activities and pursuits. Dogs of all sizes are allowed. There are no additional pet fees. Dogs may not be left unattended, and they must be leashed and cleaned up after. Dogs are allowed on the trails unless otherwise marked. This campground is closed during the off-season. The camping and tent areas also allow dogs. There is a dog walk area at the campground. There are no electric or water hookups at the campgrounds. Multiple dogs may be allowed.

Manchester

Manchester Beach/Mendocino Coast KOA
44300 Kinney Road
Manchester, CA
707-882-2375
There is a variety of land and water recreation at this park located on a spectacular five-mile stretch of sand beach on the Mendocino Coast. Dogs of all sizes are allowed for no additional fee. Dogs must be under owner's control and visual observation at all times. Dogs must be quiet, well behaved, and be on no more than a 6 foot leash at all times, or otherwise contained. Dogs may not be left unattended outside the owner's camping equipment. There are some breed restrictions. The camping and tent areas also allow dogs. There is a dog walk area at the campground. Dogs are allowed in the camping cabins. 2 dogs may be allowed.

Marin - North Bay

Bodega Dunes Campground
3095 H 1
Bodega Bay, CA
707-875-3483
This campground is located in one of the largest beach parks in the state, and offers miles of hiking trails, whale-watching sites, various nature habitats, and a variety of land and water recreation. Dogs of all sizes are allowed. There are no additional pet fees. Dogs must be on no more than a 6 foot leash at all times and cleaned up after. Dogs must be inside at night, and they are not allowed on beach adjacent to the campground or on trails. The

camping and tent areas also allow dogs. There is a dog walk area at the campground. There are no electric or water hookups at the campgrounds. Multiple dogs may be allowed.

Doran Regional Park Campgrounds
201 Doran Beach Road
Bodega Bay, CA
707-875-3540
Walk to the beach from your campsite! There are over 100 campsites in this park which features 2 miles of sandy beach. There is a dump station for RVs. Dogs are allowed for an additional fee of $1 per night per pet. Dogs must be on no more than a 6 foot leash at all times, and proof of a rabies vaccination is required. They may not be left unattended unless they will be quiet and well behaved. The number for reservations is 707-565-CAMP (2267). The camping and tent areas also allow dogs. There is a dog walk area at the campground. There are no electric or water hookups at the campgrounds. Multiple dogs may be allowed.

Westside Regional Park Campground
2400 Westshore Road
Bodega Bay, CA
707-875-3540
This park offers 38 campsites. Fishing is the popular activity at this park. Dogs are allowed but must be on a 6 foot or less leash at all times, and proof of a rabies vaccination is required. There is an additional $1 per night per pet. Dogs may not be left unattended outside unless they will be quiet and well behaved. The camping and tent areas also allow dogs. There is a dog walk area at the campground. There are no electric or water hookups at the campgrounds. Multiple dogs may be allowed.

Novato RV Park
1530 Armstrong Avenue
Novato, CA
415-897-1271
Nestled in a quiet country setting just minutes from all the attractions of the bay cities, this park offers modern amenities, and various recreation. Dogs of all sizes are allowed. There are no additional pet fees. Dogs may not be left unattended outside, and they must be quiet, well behaved, leashed, and cleaned up after. This is an RV only park. There is a dog walk area at the campground. Multiple dogs may be allowed.

Olema Ranch Campground

10155 H 1
Olema, CA
415-663-8001

This full service park features both natural forest and open meadow camp sites, a laundry, rec hall, store, Post Office, and a wide variety of activities and recreation. Dogs of all sizes are allowed for an additional $1 per night per pet. Dogs must be on no more than an 8 foot leash at all times and cleaned up after. The camping and tent areas also allow dogs. There is a dog walk area at the campground. Multiple dogs may be allowed.

San Francisco North/Petaluma KOA

20 Rainsville Road
Petaluma, CA
707-763-1492

Just north of the Golden Gate, this scenic country-style campground offers tours of the city, a petting farm, a full recreational program, swimming pool, hot tub, cable TV, and a snack bar. Friendly dogs of all sizes are allowed for no additional fee. Dogs must be under owner's control and visual observation at all times. Dogs must be quiet, well behaved, and be on no more than a 6 foot leash at all times, or otherwise contained. Dogs may not be left unattended outside the owner's camping equipment, and must be brought inside at night. There are some breed restrictions. The camping and tent areas also allow dogs. There is a dog walk area at the campground. Multiple dogs may be allowed.

Markleeville

Grover Hot Springs State Park

3415 Hot Springs Road
Markleeville, CA
530-694-2248

You will find a variety of weather and recreation at this park that is known for its mineral hot springs. Dogs of all sizes are allowed. There are no additional pet fees. Dogs may not be left unattended, and they must be leashed at all times, and cleaned up after. Dogs are not allowed in the pool area, and guests or their dogs are not allowed in the meadows. The camping and tent areas also allow dogs. There is a dog walk area at the campground. There are no electric or water hookups at the campgrounds.

Multiple dogs may be allowed.

Indian Creek Campground

Indian Creek Road
Markleeville, CA
775-885-6000

Surrounded by pine trees at 5,600 feet, this park covers 160 acres used for recreational pursuits. Dogs of all sizes are allowed. There are no additional pet fees. Dogs may not be left unattended, and they must be leashed at all times, and cleaned up after. Dogs are allowed on the trails. This campground is closed during the off-season. The camping and tent areas also allow dogs. There is a dog walk area at the campground. There are no electric or water hookups at the campgrounds.

McGee Creek

McGee Creek Campground

McGee Creek Road
McGee Creek, CA
760-873-2500

This 28 site campground is located in the Inyo National Forest at an elevation of 7,600 feet. The campsite is in an open area and adjacent to McGee Creek. Amenities include water, flush toilets and space for RVs. For hiking, the McGee Creek Trail is located within a few miles of the campground. The fee for a campsite is $15. Pets must be leashed while in the campground and please clean up after your pets. This campground is closed during the off-season. The camping and tent areas also allow dogs. There is a dog walk area at the campground. There are no electric or water hookups at the campgrounds. Multiple dogs may be allowed.

Mendocino

Pomo RV Park and Campground

17999 Tregoning Lane
Fort Bragg, CA
707-964-3373

This small scenic park offers a good variety of recreational opportunities. They have a "major holiday dog policy", wherein dogs must remain on the owners campsite only. No walking of dogs in the park is allowed on major holidays and dogs may not be left alone on campsites for any reason. Dogs of all sizes are allowed for an additional $1 per night per dog. Dogs must be

leashed and cleaned up after. There are some breed restrictions. The camping and tent areas also allow dogs. There is a dog walk area at the campground. Multiple dogs may be allowed.

Casper Beach RV Park and Campground

14441 Point Cabrilla
Mendocino, CA
707-964-3306

This RV park is located in one of the most picturesque coastal regions anywhere in the US, with such amenities as an arcade, an onsite grocery & novelty store, and host to a variety of land and water recreation. Dogs of all sizes are allowed for an additional fee of $2 per night per per pet. Dogs must be very friendly, quiet, well behaved, leashed, and cleaned up after. The camping and tent areas also allow dogs. There is a dog walk area at the campground. 2 dogs may be allowed.

Mono Lake

Glass Creek Campground

H 395
Lee Vining, CA
760-873-2408

This 50 site campground is located in the Inyo National Forest at an elevation of 7,600 feet. It is located near several trails. The fee for a campsite is $14. The sites are available on a first-come, first-served basis. Pets must be leashed while in the campground and please clean up after them. The campground is located between Lee Vining and Mammoth Lakes on Highway 395. It is at the intersection of the highway and the Crestview CalTrains Maintenance Station, about one mile north of the Crestview Rest Area. This campground is closed during the off-season. The camping and tent areas also allow dogs. There is a dog walk area at the campground. There are no electric or water hookups at the campgrounds. Multiple dogs may be allowed.

Lundy Canyon County Park Campground

Lundy Lake Road, Mono Lake
Lee Vining, CA
760-932-5440

This park, in the Mono Lake area, offers hikers a variety of trails and recreational pursuits. There are also trails to enter the Ansel Adams and

Hoover Wildernesses. Dogs of all sizes are allowed. There are no additional pet fees. Dogs must be leashed at all times and cleaned up after. Dogs are allowed on the trails on lead. This campground is closed during the off-season. The camping and tent areas also allow dogs. There is a dog walk area at the campground. There are no electric or water hookups at the campgrounds. Multiple dogs may be allowed.

Morgan Hill

Parkway Lakes RV Park
100 Ogier Avenue
Morgan Hill, CA
408-779-0244
This 110 RV space park offers a pool, mini mart, WiFi, club house, laundry, showers, and more. Dogs of all sizes are allowed for an additional fee of $1 per night per pet. Dogs must be leashed and cleaned up after. There is an area just outside the park for walking your pet. There are some breed restrictions. The camping and tent areas also allow dogs. 2 dogs may be allowed.

Mount Shasta

Mount Shasta KOA
900 N Mt Shasta Blvd
Shasta City, CA
530-926-4029
There is a variety of land, water, and air recreation at this scenic alpine park. The campground also offers 80 foot pull through sites with 50 amp, cable, LP gas, snack bar, and swimming pool. Dogs of all sizes are allowed for no additional fee. Dogs must be under owner's control and visual observation at all times. Dogs must be quiet, well behaved, and be on no more than a 6 foot leash at all times, or otherwise contained. Dogs may not be left unattended outside the owner's camping equipment. There are some breed restrictions. The camping and tent areas also allow dogs. There is a dog walk area at the campground. Dogs are allowed in the camping cabins. Multiple dogs may be allowed.

Mountain Mesa

Lake Isabella RV Resort
11936 H 178
Mountain Mesa, CA
800-787-9920
This picturesque, RV only park, is

located along Lake Isabella, and amenities include more than 40 miles of open shoreline, a full service marina, and a pool. Dogs of all sizes are allowed for an additional $1 per night per pet. Dogs may not be left unattended outside, and they must be brought in at night, leashed, and cleaned up after. There are some breed restrictions. There is a dog walk area at the campground. 2 dogs may be allowed.

Napa Valley

Napa County Fairgrounds Campground
1435 Oak Street
Calistoga, CA
707-942-5111
Located at the fairgrounds, this campground offers 46 RV/tent sites. RV sites are parallel in the parking lot and tent sites are located on an adjacent lawn. RV sites have full hookups (some have sewer). Other amenities include restrooms, showers, potable water and disabled accessible. Dogs are allowed but must be on a 10 foot or less leash. Dogs must be well behaved, and please clean up after your pet. For reservations call 707-942-5221. The camping and tent areas also allow dogs. There is a dog walk area at the campground. Multiple dogs may be allowed.

Putah Creek Resort
7600 Knoxville Road
Napa, CA
707-966-0794
This park of many mini-peninsulas along Lake Berryessa allows for lots of accessible shoreline along with land and water recreation. Dogs of all sizes are allowed for an additional $2 per night per pet. Dogs may only be left unattended on your site if they have secure water and food, will be quiet, and well behaved. Dogs must be leashed at all times and cleaned up after. There are some breed restrictions. The camping and tent areas also allow dogs. There is a dog walk area at the campground. Multiple dogs may be allowed.

Needles

Moabi Regional Park Campgrounds
Park Moabi Road

Needles, CA
760-326-3831
This park has a campground with 35 RV sites with full hookups, 120 sites with partial hookups, and unlimited tent sites. The sites are situated in the main section of the park and along 2.5 miles of shoreline. The park is located on the banks of the Colorado River and is popular for camping, fishing, boating, swimming and water skiing. Dogs can go into the water but they strongly advise against it because there are so many fast boats in the water. Dogs must be leashed and please clean up after them. There is an additional fee of $1 per night per pet. The camping and tent areas also allow dogs. There is a dog walk area at the campground. Multiple dogs may be allowed.

Needles KOA
5400 National Old Trails H
Needles, CA
760-326-4207
This desert oasis park offers 90 foot pull through sites with 50 amp service, LP gas, snack bar, swimming pool, and guided tours. Dogs of all sizes are allowed for no additional fee. Dogs must be under owner's control and visual observation at all times. Dogs must be quiet, well behaved, and be on no more than a 6 foot leash at all times, or otherwise contained. Dogs may not be left unattended outside the owner's camping equipment, and must be brought inside at night. Dogs are not allowed in the pool area or buildings. There are some breed restrictions. The camping and tent areas also allow dogs. There is a dog walk area at the campground. Dogs are allowed in the camping cabins. Multiple dogs may be allowed.

New Cuyama

Selby Campgrounds
Soda Lake Road
New Cuyama, CA
661-391-6000
Primitive camping is available at this campground which is located at the base of the Caliente Mountains and near the dog-friendly Caliente Mountain Access Trail. There are 5 picnic tables and 4 fire pits, but no shade trees. There is no garbage pickup service, electricity or drinking water. Leave vehicles along the edge of the road, do not drive to your chosen campsite. Be aware of rattlesnakes in the area. Dogs on

leash are allowed. Dogs may not be left unattended, and please clean up after your dog. The campground is about 14 miles west of New Cuyama off Hwy 166, on Soda Lake Road. There will be signs. Dogs are not allowed at Painted Rock at any time. This campground is closed during the off-season. The camping and tent areas also allow dogs. There is a dog walk area at the campground. There are no electric or water hookups at the campgrounds. Multiple dogs may be allowed.

Oakland - East Bay

Del Valle Regional Park
7000 Del Valle Road
Livermore, CA
510-562-2267
This park of almost 4,000 acres sits along a lake surrounded by rolling hills. It is a popular area for nature study, a variety of land and water recreation, and for hiking. It also serves as an entrance to the Ohlone Wilderness Trail. Dogs of all sizes are allowed for an additional $2 per night per pet, and they must have current tags, rabies, and shot records. Dogs may not be left unattended at any time, and they must be on no more than a 6 foot leash and cleaned up after. Dogs are not allowed on the beach. The gates at this park close each night at 10 pm. There are some breed restrictions. This campground is closed during the off-season. The camping and tent areas also allow dogs. There is a dog walk area at the campground. There are no electric hookups at the campgrounds. Multiple dogs may be allowed.

Anthony Chabot Regional Park
9999 Redwood Road
Oakland, CA
510-562-2267
With almost 5,000 acres this beautiful park features an amphitheater, naturalist-led campfire programs, a marksmanship range, and a full range of activities and recreation. Dogs of all sizes are allowed for an additional $2 per night per pet. Dogs may not be left unattended, and they must be leashed, and cleaned up after at all times. Dogs are not allowed on the beach. The gates at this park close at 10 pm. The camping and tent areas also allow dogs. There is a dog walk area at the campground. Multiple dogs may be allowed.

Old Creek

Big Basin Redwoods State Park
21600 Big Basin Way
Old Creek, CA
831-338-8860
This park is California's oldest park and is home to the largest continuous stand of ancient coast redwoods south of the bay area. It offers a wide variety of recreation and other activities. Dogs of all sizes are allowed. There are no additional pet fees. Dogs may not be left unattended at any time, and they must be leashed and cleaned up after. Dogs are allowed in the picnic area, the campground area, on paved roads, and the North escape road only. Dogs are not allowed anywhere at Rancho del Oso or on any other trails or interior roads. They must be kept in the RV or tent at night. Check at Park Headquarters for scheduled guided "dog walks", which are informative group hikes that give dog owners a chance to take their dogs along while learning about redwood ecology and park history. The camping and tent areas also allow dogs. There is a dog walk area at the campground. There are no electric or water hookups at the campgrounds. Multiple dogs may be allowed.

Onyx

Walker Pass Campground
H 178
Onyx, CA
661-391-6000
This BLM (Bureau of Land Management) campground has 11 walk-in sites for Pacific Crest Trail hikers and two sites are available for vehicles. Drinking water is available from spring through fall. Hitching racks and corrals are available for horses. There are no reservations or fees but donations are accepted. Dogs are allowed but need to be on leash while in the campground. They are allowed on the trails. The camping and tent areas also allow dogs. There is a dog walk area at the campground. There are no electric or water hookups at the campgrounds. Multiple dogs may be allowed.

Orange County Beaches

Bolsa Chica State Beach

Campground
Pacific Coast H
Huntington Beach, CA
714-377-5691
Most RVs can be accommodated at this campground, just let them know when making a reservation if your RV is over 25 feet. Tent camping is not allowed. Pets on leash are allowed and please clean up after them. While dogs are not allowed on this state beach, they are allowed on several miles of paved trails that follow the coast. Dogs are also allowed at the adjacent Huntington Dog Beach. The campground is located on the Pacific Coast Highway between Golden West to Warner Avenue. There is a dog walk area at the campground.

Huntington By the Sea
21871 Newland
Huntington Beach, CA
714-536-8316
If you love the beach and everything about it, then you will love this RV park, which also provides a host of amenities. Dogs of all sizes are allowed. There are no additional pet fees. Dogs may not be left unattended outside, and they must be leashed and cleaned up after. This is an RV only park. There are some breed restrictions. There is a dog walk area at the campground. Multiple dogs may be allowed.

Newport Dunes RV Park
1131 Back Bay Drive
Newport Beach, CA
949-729-3863
This waterfront resort features lush grounds, many amenities, and a variety of land and water recreation. Dogs of all sizes are allowed for an additional $2 per night per pet for the nightly fee, and an additional $5 per night per pet for the weekly fee. Dogs may not be left unattended, and they must be leashed and cleaned up after. Dogs are not allowed on the beach and anywhere on the sand. There are some breed restrictions. The camping and tent areas also allow dogs. There is a dog walk area at the campground. 2 dogs may be allowed.

Orange County South

Doheny State Beach Park
25300 Dana Point Harbor Drive
Dana Point, CA
949-496-6172
This park, nestled among the trees

on the ocean, offers exhibits, various other programs, and a variety of land and water recreation. Dogs of all sizes are allowed. There are no additional pet fees. Dogs must be leashed and cleaned up after. Dogs are not allowed on the beach. The camping and tent areas also allow dogs. There is a dog walk area at the campground. There are no electric or water hookups at the campgrounds. Multiple dogs may be allowed.

San Clemente State Beach
3030 El Avenida Del Presidente
San Clemente, CA
949-492-3156
Set among the sandstone cliffs on the ocean, this park is home to many species of land and marine life. The park offers interpretive exhibits and programs and a variety of recreational activities. Dogs of all sizes are allowed. There are no additional pet fees. Dogs may not be left unattended, and they must be well behaved, on no more than a 6 foot leash, and cleaned up after. Dogs must be brought inside at night. Dogs are not allowed on the trails or on the beach. The camping and tent areas also allow dogs. There is a dog walk area at the campground. Multiple dogs may be allowed.

Orland

Buckhorn Recreation Area
19225 Newville Road
Orland, CA
530-865-4781
This picturesque park, snuggled in the foothills of north-central California along Black Butte Lake, offers a variety of recreational pursuits and an interpretive trail. Next door is a 75-acre all-terrain park. Dogs of all sizes are allowed at no additional fee. Dogs must be on no more than a 6 foot leash at all times in the camp and trail areas. Dogs may be off lead at the backside of the lake only if they are under voice command. The camping and tent areas also allow dogs. There is a dog walk area at the campground. There are no electric or water hookups at the campgrounds. Multiple dogs may be allowed.

Palm Springs

Palm Springs Oasis RV Resort
36-100 Date Palm Drive
Cathedral City, CA

800-680-0144
Amidst spectacular views, this parks' amenities include a clubhouse, 2 swimming pools, a spa, an 18 hole executive golf course, and tennis courts to name just a few. Dogs of all sizes are allowed. There are no additional pet fees. Dogs may not be left unattended, and they must be leashed and cleaned up after. The camping and tent areas also allow dogs. There is a dog walk area at the campground. Multiple dogs may be allowed.

Indian Wells RV Resort
47-340 Jefferson Street
Indio, CA
800-789-0895
This RV only resort offers many amenities such as three swimming pools, two spas, shuffleboard courts, basketball courts, pavilion with gas grills, billiards, horseshoes, fitness area, library, modem hookup, putting green, laundry facility, computer center and even a dog run. Site amenities include full hook-ups with 50 amp service, electric, water, sewer, paved pad and patio, and phone service for stays of 30 days or longer. Well-behaved leashed dogs are welcome. Please clean up after your pet. There is no pet fee. Dogs may not be left unattended outside. There is a dog walk area at the campground. Multiple dogs may be allowed.

Palo Alto - Peninsula

San Francisco RV Resort
7000 Palmetto Avenue
Pacifica, CA
650-355-7093
Offering the only ocean view RV sites in the area with only a short walk to the beach, this modern park is also ideally situated for exploring other attractions in the area. Dogs up to 40 pounds are allowed at no additional fee. Dogs may not be left unattended, and they must be quiet, well behaved, leashed, and cleaned up after. There are two dog walks, including one on the beach. This is an RV only park. There are some breed restrictions. There is a dog walk area at the campground. 2 dogs may be allowed.

Butano State Park Campground
Off H 1 4.5 miles SE of Pescadero
Pescadero, CA
650-879-2040

The campground can accept RVs up to 27 feet, and camp amenities include picnic tables, water and vault toilets. While dogs are not allowed on the park trails, they are allowed in the campground, picnic area, all paved roads, and on miles of fire roads. Mountain biking is also allowed on the fire roads. Pets must be on a 6 foot or less leash at all times. Please clean up after them. The camping and tent areas also allow dogs. There is a dog walk area at the campground. There are no electric or water hookups at the campgrounds. Multiple dogs may be allowed.

Pearblossom

South Fork Campground
Big Rock Creek Road/Forest Road 4N11A
Pearblossom, CA
661-296-9710
This 21 site campground is located in the Angeles National Forest at an elevation of 4,500 feet. There are both tent and small RV sites up to 16 feet. Amenities include vault toilets. There are many hiking trails nearby including one which leads to the dog-friendly Devil's Punchbowl County Park. Well behaved dogs on leash are allowed and please clean up after them. Dogs may not be left unattended outside, and only left inside if they will be quiet and comfortable. The camping and tent areas also allow dogs. There is a dog walk area at the campground. There are no electric or water hookups at the campgrounds. Multiple dogs may be allowed.

Perris

Sunland Golden Village Palms
3600 W Florida Ave (H 74)
Hemet, CA
800-323-9610
This luxury RV resort offers flowered landscaping, lawns, many amenities, planned activities, and a wide variety of recreation. Dogs up to 50 pounds are allowed at no additional fee. Dogs may not be left unattended outside at any time, and only left inside if they will be quiet, well behaved, and physically comfortable. Dogs are allowed in the pet section of the park only. There are some breed restrictions. The camping and tent areas also allow dogs. There is a dog walk area at the campground. 2 dogs may be allowed.

Lake Perris Campgrounds
17801 Lake Perris Drive
Perris, CA
951-657-0676
This campground offers 434 campsites including two RV areas with full hookups. While dogs are not allowed in the lake or within 100 feet of the water, they are allowed on miles of trails including the bike trail that loops around the lake. Pets must be on no more than a 6 foot leash, and please clean up after them. Dogs may not be left unattended. The camping and tent areas also allow dogs. There is a dog walk area at the campground. Multiple dogs may be allowed.

Luiseno Campground, Lake Perris State Rec Area
17801 Lake Perris Drive
Perris, CA
951-940-5603
This campground sits among the white sands and blue waters of Lake Perris and offers a wide variety of land and water recreation. Animals must be leashed (6? or less), caged, or in a tent, motor home, or vehicle at all times, and can not be left unattended. Visitors are responsible for clean-up after their pets. No body contact with the water is allowed, and dogs may not be on the trails or the beach. The camping and tent areas also allow dogs. There is a dog walk area at the campground. Multiple dogs may be allowed.

Piedra

Pine Flat Lake Rec Area
28100 Pine Flat Road
Piedra, CA
559-488-3004
This park of 120 acres is located on the Kings River below Pine Flat Dam, has 5 day use areas in addition to the camp area, and offers a variety of recreational pursuits. Dogs of all sizes are allowed at no additional fee. Dogs may not be left unattended, and they must be on no more than a 6 foot leash at all times, and cleaned up after. Dogs are allowed on the trails. The camping and tent areas also allow dogs. There is a dog walk area at the campground. There are no electric or water hookups at the campgrounds. Multiple dogs may be allowed.

Pinecrest

Boulder Flat,
21 miles east of Pinecrest on Highway 108
Pinecrest, CA
209-965-3434
This camp area is located in the Brightman Recreation Area in a forested area along the Stanislaus River. Dogs of all sizes are allowed. There are no additional pet fees. Dogs must be well behaved, leashed in camp, and cleaned up after. Dogs may be off lead on the trails if they are under voice command and will not chase wildlife. Please refrain from taking pets to beach areas to prevent contamination. This campground is closed during the off-season. The camping and tent areas also allow dogs. There is a dog walk area at the campground. There are no electric or water hookups at the campgrounds. Multiple dogs may be allowed.

Pinecrest Lake
Pinecrest Lake Road
Pinecrest, CA
209-965-3434
Located in a timbered setting at an elevation of 5,600 feet, this scenic park offers interpretive programs and a variety of land and water recreation. Dogs of all sizes are allowed. There are no additional pet fees. Dogs must be quiet, well behaved, leashed, and cleaned up after. No dogs allowed in Day Use Area (between Pinecrest Lake Road/Pinecrest Avenue and the boat launch and the fishing pier) from May 15 to September 15. This campground is closed during the off-season. The camping and tent areas also allow dogs. There is a dog walk area at the campground. There are no electric or water hookups at the campgrounds. Multiple dogs may be allowed.

Piru

Olive Grove Campground
4780 Piru Canyon Road
Piru, CA
805-521-1500
Located at Lake Piru, this campground allows well-behaved leashed dogs in the developed campgrounds, but not in the water. However, dogs are allowed on a boat on the water. The Marina rents pontoon boats and dogs are allowed on the rentals. Campsite amenities including laundry facilities, showers, water, picnic

areas and dumping stations. Five of the RV sites have hookups. There is a $2 per day pet fee, and dogs must have current shot records. Please clean up after your pets. Dogs may not be left unattended outside. The camping and tent areas also allow dogs. There is a dog walk area at the campground. Multiple dogs may be allowed.

Placerville - Highway 50 Corridor

Ice House Campground
Forest Road 32
Pollock Pines, CA
530-644-2349
This 83 site campground is located in the El Dorado National Forest at an elevation of 5,500 feet. It is located near the Ice House Bike Trail. Camp amenities include restrooms, water, picnic tables, swimming, bicycling, hiking and more. Pets on leash are allowed in the campground, on the trails and in the water. Please clean up after your pets. Dogs are not allowed on trails into Desolation Valley. This campground is closed during the off-season. The camping and tent areas also allow dogs. There is a dog walk area at the campground. There are no electric or water hookups at the campgrounds.

Ice House Resort
Forest Road 3
Pollock Pines, CA
530-644-2348
Located in the El Dorado National Forest at 5,500 feet, this scenic park offers a variety of recreational opportunities. Dogs of all sizes are allowed. There are no additional pet fees. Dogs may not be left unattended outside, and they must be leashed and cleaned up after. This campground is closed during the off-season. The camping and tent areas also allow dogs. There is a dog walk area at the campground. There are no electric or water hookups at the campgrounds. 2 dogs may be allowed.

Sly Park Campground
4771 Sly Park Road
Pollock Pines, CA
530-644-2792
The wooded Sly Park Recreation Area offers 159 campsites at an elevation of 3,500 feet. Site amenities include a table, barbecue and fire ring. Camp amenities include water, vault toilets, and a dump

station at the park entrance. Pets on leash are allowed in the campground and on trails including the 8 to 9 mile trail which surround the lake. Dogs are not allowed in the lake. There is an additional fee of $2 per night per pet. Although open year round, call first in winter as snow causes road closures. The camping and tent areas also allow dogs. There is a dog walk area at the campground. There are no electric or water hookups at the campgrounds. Multiple dogs may be allowed.

Wench Creek Campground
Ice House Road/Forest Road 3
Pollock Pines, CA
530-644-2349
This campground is located in the El Dorado National Forest next to Union Valley Reservoir and offers 100 tent and RV campsites. Camp amenities include restrooms, water, swimming, bicycling, and hiking. Dogs are allowed in the campground, on the trails, and in the water. Pets should be leashed and please clean up after them. Dogs are not allowed to go into Desolation Valley. This campground is closed during the off-season. The camping and tent areas also allow dogs. There is a dog walk area at the campground. There are no electric or water hookups at the campgrounds. Multiple dogs may be allowed.

Placerville KOA
4655 Rock Barn Road
Shingle Springs, CA
530-676-2267
Located close to other attractions, this park offers 110 foot pull-through sites with 50 amp service, a store, petting zoo, playground, pond, swimming pool, sauna/spa, cable, WiFi, and more. Dogs of all sizes are allowed for no additional fee. Dogs must be under owner's control and visual observation at all times. Dogs must be quiet, well behaved, and be on no more than a 6 foot leash at all times, or otherwise contained. Dogs may not be left unattended outside the owner's camping equipment, and must be brought inside at night. There is a fenced in dog run area where your pet may be off lead. There are some breed restrictions. The camping and tent areas also allow dogs. There is a dog walk area at the campground. There are special amenities given to dogs at this campground. Multiple dogs may be allowed.

Plumas National Forest - Quincy

Upper Jamison Creek Campground
310 Johnsville Road
Blairsden, CA
530-836-2380
This campground is located in the scenic Sierra Plumas Eureka State Park at the foot of Eureka Mountain. Dogs of all sizes are allowed at no additional fee. Dogs may not be left unattended, and they must be quiet, leashed, and cleaned up after. Dogs are not allowed on the trails; they are allowed on Jamison Trail Road or in the back country on lead. This campground is closed during the off-season. The camping and tent areas also allow dogs. There is a dog walk area at the campground. There are no electric or water hookups at the campgrounds. Multiple dogs may be allowed.

Silver Lake Campground
Forest Road 24N29X/Silver Lake
Bucks Lake, CA
530-283-0555
This tent only campground is located in the Plumas National Forest and offers 8 campsites and vault toilets. There is no water available. Campsites are on a first-come, first-served basis. The trailhead for the Gold Lake Trail is located at this campground. In the campground dogs must be on leash. On the trails, dogs on leash or off-leash but under direct voice control are allowed. Dogs may not be left unattended. From the turn-off, travel 6.4 miles on Road 24N29X, a gravel road. This campground is closed during the off-season. The camping and tent areas also allow dogs. There is a dog walk area at the campground. There are no electric or water hookups at the campgrounds. Multiple dogs may be allowed.

Little Beaver Campground, Feather River District
off Forest Road 120/La Porte Road
La Porte, CA
530-534-6500
This campground is located at the Little Grass Valley Reservoir Recreation Area in the Plumas National Forest. There are 120 campsites, some of which offer prime lakeside sites. Amenities include water, flush toilets, trailer space, and an RV dump station.

Dogs are allowed in the campgrounds, on trails and in the water. In the campground dogs must be on leash. On the trails, dogs on leash or off-leash but under direct voice control are allowed. Dogs may not be left unattended outside. Please clean up after your pet. This campground is closed during the off-season. The camping and tent areas also allow dogs. There is a dog walk area at the campground. There are no electric or water hookups at the campgrounds. Multiple dogs may be allowed.

Pioneer RV Park
1326 Pioneer Road
Quincy, CA
530-283-0796
This pet-friendly RV park is located in the Sierra Nevada Mountains between Lassen National Park and Lake Tahoe. They have over 60 sites on 6.5 acres. RV sites have long wide pull through sites, picnic tables, 30 or 50 amp service, and satellite TV. Tent campers are also welcome. Other amenities include a laundry room, LP gas, rec room with modem hookup, big screen TV, books exchange and a ping-pong table. They are located about 1.5 miles from downtown Quincy and right next to a county park which has an Olympic size swimming pool and a playground. Well-behaved leashed dogs of all sizes are allowed. People need to clean up after their pets. There is no pet fee. There is a large area outside the park for walking your pet. The camping and tent areas also allow dogs. Multiple dogs may be allowed.

Pomona - Ontario

Los Angeles/Pomona/Fairplex KOA
2200 N White Avenue
Pomona, CA
909-593-8915
This lushly landscaped campground, is set among pine trees with the San Gabriel mountains as a backdrop. Some of the amenities provided are a club room, guided tours, a pool open year-round, a fully stocked mini market, a catering service, and it is close to many world class attractions. Dogs up to 50 pounds are allowed for no additional fee. Dogs must be under owner's control and visual observation at all times. Dogs must be quiet, well behaved, and be on no more than a 6 foot leash at all times, or otherwise

contained. Dogs may not be left unattended outside the owner's camping equipment. There are some breed restrictions. There is a dog walk area at the campground. 2 dogs may be allowed.

East Shore RV Park
1440 Camper View Road
San Dimas, CA
909-599-8355
This family RV park offers over 500 full hookup paved sites including some pull through sites. Site amenities include a grassy area, view sites, and full hookups with 20, 30 or 50 amp service. Park amenities include picnic areas, children's playground, laundry room, swimming pool, general store and market, video rentals, basketballs and volleyballs, email station, restrooms and 24 hour check-in. Well-behaved dogs are allowed in the RV park, but not in the tenting area. Pets must be leashed and please clean up after them. There is a $2 per day pet fee. Dogs may not be left unattended. This RV park is open year-round. There is a dog walk area at the campground. Multiple dogs may be allowed.

Grasshopper Flat Campground
Grizzley Flat Road (Road 112)
Portola, CA
530-836-2575
This park on Lake Davis in the Sequoia National Forest offers varied habitats, ecosystems, and a wide variety of land and water recreation. Dogs may not be left unattended, and they must be leashed at all times and cleaned up after. Dogs are allowed on the trails unless otherwise marked, and in developed areas. Dogs are not allowed in any park buildings. This campground is closed during the off-season. The camping and tent areas also allow dogs. There is a dog walk area at the campground. Multiple dogs may be allowed.

Potrero County Park
24800 Potrero Park Drive
Potrero, CA
619-478-5212
Dotted with hundred-year-old coastal oak trees and rich in natural and cultural history, this park at 2,600 feet, offers a wide variety of habitats and recreational activities. Dogs of

all sizes are allowed for an additional $1 per night per pet, and they must have current tags, rabies, and shot records. Dogs may not be left unattended at any time, and they must be on no more than a 6 foot leash and cleaned up after. Dogs are not allowed on the trails, but they may be walked on the payment and along side the roads on leash. The camping and tent areas also allow dogs. There is a dog walk area at the campground. Multiple dogs may be allowed.

Dos Picos County Park
17953 Dos Picos Park Road
Ramona, CA
760-789-2220
This park, located in a small valley sheltered by nearby mountains, is full of plant and animal life, and offers various trails and recreational pursuits. Dogs of all sizes are allowed for an additional $1 per night per pet, and they must have current tags, rabies, and shot records. Dogs may not be left unattended at any time, and they must be on no more than a 6 foot leash and cleaned up after. Dogs are not allowed on the trails, but they may be walked on the payment and along side the roads on leash. The camping and tent areas also allow dogs. There is a dog walk area at the campground. Multiple dogs may be allowed.

Mountain Gate RV Park
14161 Holiday Road
Redding, CA
530-283-0769
This RV park's amenities include full RV hookups, lighted grounds, large pull through sites, a convenience store, video rentals, cable TV, pool, rec room with pool table, email station, laundry, showers, restrooms, dump station, easy I-5 access, and an off lead, fenced pet area. Well-behaved leashed dogs are allowed. Please clean up after your pets. There is an additional fee of $1 per night per pet. The park is located 7 miles north of Redding. There are some breed restrictions. There is a dog walk area at the campground. There are special amenities given to dogs at this campground. Multiple dogs may be allowed.

Sacramento River RV Resort
6596 Riverland Drive
Redding, CA
530-365-6402
This is an RV only park located along the Sacramento River. No number or size restrictions are set on dogs for a one or two night stay, and there is no additional fee. For stays of one week or longer, there can be no more than 2 dogs and they can not be over 25 pounds, also for no additional fee. Dogs must be leashed and cleaned up after. There are some breed restrictions. There is a dog walk area at the campground.

Elk Prairie Campground
127011 Newton B. Drury Scenic Parkway
Orick, CA
707-464-6101
This campground is located in Prairie Creek Redwoods State Park. While dogs are not allowed on any park trails or the beach, they are allowed at this campground. There are 75 RV or tent sites which are next to a prairie and old growth redwood forest. RVs must be less than 27 feet. Camp amenities include restrooms, showers, fire pits, dump station and bear-proof lockers. Located just north of the campground is Cal Barrel Road. Dogs can walk on or along this 3 mile gravel road. There are not too many cars that travel along this road. Pets must be on no more than a 6 foot leash and attended to at all times. Please clean up after your pet. The camping and tent areas also allow dogs. There is a dog walk area at the campground. There are no electric or water hookups at the campgrounds. 2 dogs may be allowed.

Gold Bluffs Beach Campground
Davidson Road
Orick, CA
707-464-6101
This campground is located in Prairie Creek Redwoods State Park. While dogs are not allowed on any park trails, they are allowed at this campground and the adjoining beach. There are 29 tent sites and 25 RV sites at the beach. RVs must be less than 24 feet long and 8 feet wide. All sites are on a first-come, first-served basis. Camp amenities include restrooms, solar showers

and fire pits. Pets must be leashed and attended at all times. Please clean up after your pets. Dogs are not allowed on any established trails. They are allowed in parking lots, the campground, picnic areas, paved roads, and must stay within 100 feet of the roads. Although the campground is open year round, call ahead, as sometimes the roads are closed for repairs. The camping and tent areas also allow dogs. There is a dog walk area at the campground. There are no electric or water hookups at the campgrounds. Multiple dogs may be allowed.

Ridgecrest

Fossil Falls Campground
Cinder Road
Ridgecrest, CA
760-384-5400
This park, rich in prehistoric and modern history, features a rugged and primitive landscape as a result of ancient volcanic activity. Dogs of all sizes are allowed. There are no additional pet fees. Dogs must be leashed at all times and cleaned up after. Dogs are allowed on the trails; take caution around the cliff areas. The camping and tent areas also allow dogs. There is a dog walk area at the campground. There are no electric or water hookups at the campgrounds. Multiple dogs may be allowed.

Sacramento

Beals Point Campground
7806 Folsom-Auburn Road
Folsom, CA
916-988-0205
This park, located on shores of Folsom Lake, offers miles of hiking trails, and a wide variety of recreational opportunities. Dogs of all sizes are allowed. There are no additional pet fees. Dogs must be on no more than a 6 foot leash and cleaned up after. Dogs are not allowed at the main swimming beaches. Dogs are allowed on the trails. The camping and tent areas also allow dogs. There is a dog walk area at the campground. There are no electric or water hookups at the campgrounds. Multiple dogs may be allowed.

Cal Expo RV Park
1600 Exposition Blvd
Sacramento, CA
916-263-3000

Centrally located amid an abundance of attractions and recreational opportunities, this park also provides a laundry room, private restroom and showers, and 24 hour security. Dogs of all sizes are allowed. There are no additional pet fees. Dogs may not be left unattended outside, and only inside if they will be physically comfortable, quiet, and well behaved. Dogs must be leashed at all times, and cleaned up after. This is an RV only park. There is a dog walk area at the campground. 2 dogs may be allowed.

Sacramento Metropolitan KOA
3951 Lake Road
West Sacramento, CA
916-371-6771
This camping area, located close to many other attractions and the state capitol, offer such amenities as 65 foot pull-through sites with 50 amp service, cable, phone, swimming pool, bike rentals, and planned activities. Up to 3 dogs of all sizes are allowed for no additional fee at the tent or RV sites. There is an additional fee of $10 per night per pet for the cabins, and only 2 dogs are allowed. Guests who own any of the known aggressive breeds must sign a waiver. Dogs must be under owner's control and visual observation at all times. Dogs must be quiet, well behaved, and be on no more than a 6 foot leash at all times, or otherwise contained. Dogs may not be left unattended outside the owner's camping equipment, and must be brought inside at night. The camping and tent areas also allow dogs. There is a dog walk area at the campground. Dogs are allowed in the camping cabins.

Salinas

Laguna Seca Campground
1025 Monterey H 68
Salinas, CA
831-755-4895
The popular Laguna Seca raceway is the highlight of this park. The park also offers a rifle range and an OHV and Off-Highway Motocross Track. Dogs are not permitted on any of the tracks including the OHV area. Dogs on leash are allowed at the RV and tent campgrounds, and on hiking trails. There is an additional fee of $2 per night per pet. RV sites are paved and offer up to 30 amp service. Tent sites are dirt pads with showers, telephones

and a playground within walking distance. Camping fees are subject to change depending on events that are being held at the raceway. Call ahead for rates and reservations. The camping and tent areas also allow dogs. There is a dog walk area at the campground. 2 dogs may be allowed.

San Diego

San Diego Metro
111 N 2nd Avenue
Chula Vista, CA
619-427-3601
Only minutes from world class attractions, this resort campground also offers landscaped grounds, 65 feet pull through sites with 50 amp, cable TV, swimming pool, hot tub, sauna, and a variety of planned activities and recreation. Dogs of all sizes are allowed for no additional fee. There is a $50 refundable pet deposit for the cabins. Dogs must be under owner's control and visual observation at all times. Dogs must be quiet, well behaved, and be on no more than a 6 foot leash at all times, or otherwise contained. Dogs may not be left unattended outside the owner's camping equipment, and must be brought inside at night. There are some breed restrictions. The camping and tent areas also allow dogs. There is a dog walk area at the campground. Multiple dogs may be allowed.

Sunland RV Resort - San Diego
7407 Alvarado Road
La Mesa, CA
619-469-4697
In addition to an abundance of land and water recreation, this beautiful RV park offers all the amenities of a luxury resort. Dogs of all sizes are allowed for an additional fee of $3 per night per pet. Dogs may not be left unattended outside, and they must be leashed and cleaned up after. Dogs are not allowed in the buildings. This is an RV only park. There are some breed restrictions. There is a dog walk area at the campground. 2 dogs may be allowed.

Campland on the Bay
2211 Pacific Beach Drive
San Diego, CA

This RV park is located on Mission Bay, across the water from Sea World. They offer beach front, bay view or primitive sites. Amenities include boat slips, a boat launch, store with a market, game room and a laundry room. Dogs of all sizes are allowed for an additional fee of $3 per night per pet. They must be leashed and please clean up after them. Dogs may not be left unattended outside, and they are not allowed on the beach. The camping and tent areas also allow dogs. There is a dog walk area at the campground. 2 dogs may be allowed.

Santee Lakes Recreation Preserve
9310 Fanita Parkway
San Diego, CA
619-596-3141
This large park, also a prime bird habitat, offers 2 swimming pools, a spa, 7 scenic lakes-stocked, a laundry with shower facilities, a clubhouse, watercraft rentals, 5 playgrounds including the Kiwanis Playground for children with disabilities, and miles of paved trails. Dogs of all sizes are allowed for an additional fee of $1 per night per pet. Dogs may not be left unattended outside, and they must be leashed and cleaned up after. Dogs are allowed ONLY on the pet walks around lakes 6 and 7 and in the campground. Dogs are not allowed in any of the day use areas. The camping and tent areas also allow dogs. There is a dog walk area at the campground. 2 dogs may be allowed.

San Diego County North

San Elijo State Beach Campground
2050 Coast H
Cardiff, CA
760-753-5091
This campground offers RV sites with limited hookups. RVs up to 26 feet can use the hookup sites and RVs up to 35 feet are allowed. They offer both inland and ocean view spaces. While dogs are not allowed at this beach, you can walk to the dog-friendly Cardiff State Beach. The beach is about 1 mile south of Cardiff. Dogs may not be left unattended, and they must be leashed and cleaned up after. There are some breed restrictions. The camping and tent areas also allow dogs. There is a dog walk area at the campground. 2 dogs may be allowed.

Guajome County Park

3000 Guajome Lake Road
Oceanside, CA
760-724-4489
Rich in natural and cultural history, this park is home to a variety of diverse habitats for plant and animal life. Dogs of all sizes are allowed for an additional $1 per night per pet, and they must have current tags, rabies, and shot records. Dogs may not be left unattended at any time, and they must be on no more than a 6 foot leash and cleaned up after. Dogs are not allowed on the trails, but they may be walked on the payment and along side the roads on leash. There are some breed restrictions. The camping and tent areas also allow dogs. There is a dog walk area at the campground. Multiple dogs may be allowed.

Paradise by the Sea RV Resort
1537 S Coast H
Oceanside, CA
760-439-1376
Set between the beautiful Pacific Ocean and historic Highway 101, this park features beach and pool swimming, a rec room, hot showers, restroom and laundry facilities, and a convenience store. Dogs of all sizes are allowed for an additional fee of $1 per night per pet. Dogs may not be left unattended, and they must be leashed and cleaned up after. Dogs are not allowed on the beach. This is an RV only park. There are some breed restrictions. There is a dog walk area at the campground. Multiple dogs may be allowed.

San Diego I-15 Corridor

Sunland RV Resorts
1740 Seven Oaks Road
Escondido, CA
760-740-5000
This lushly landscaped resort park is a favorite family and pet-friendly retreat, and they have a pet walking and play area, many amenities, and a variety of recreational opportunities. Dogs of all sizes are allowed for an additional $3 per night per pet. Dogs must be leashed at all times, and cleaned up after. Dogs are not allowed in buildings or the pool area. There are some breed restrictions. There is a dog walk area at the campground. There are special amenities given to dogs at this campground. 2 dogs may be allowed.

San Fernando Valley

Birmingham RV Park
7740 Balboa Blvd
Van Nuys, CA
818-785-0949
This park offers a location central to many attractions, concrete patios with grass yards, 2 large laundry rooms, and various recreational opportunities. One dog up to 30 pounds is allowed at no additional fee. Dogs may not be left unattended, and they must be leashed and cleaned up after. This is an RV only park, and the RV must be 10 years or newer. There are some breed restrictions. There is a dog walk area at the campground.

San Francisco

Candlestick RV Park
650 Gilman Avenue
San Francisco, CA
415-822-2299
This modern park is next to it's namesake stadium and near local Bay-Area attractions. It has shuttles to downtown San Francisco, a game room, and laundry. Dogs of all sizes are allowed. There are no additional pet fees. Dogs may not be left unattended outside, and may only be left inside if they will be quiet and comfortable. Dogs must be leashed and cleaned up after. Dogs are not allowed in buildings. The RV park sits along side a state park with miles of trails, and dogs are allowed on the trails except where indicated. The camping and tent areas also allow dogs. There is a dog walk area at the campground. Multiple dogs may be allowed.

San Jose

Trailer Tel RV Park
1212 Oakland Road
San Jose, CA
408-453-3535
This full service, landscaped park offers a swimming pool, fitness room, laundry, car wash, and location to many other attractions in the area. Dogs up to 20 pounds are allowed at no additional fee. Dogs may not be left unattended outside, and they must be leashed and cleaned up after. This is an RV only park. There is a dog walk area at the campground. 2 dogs may be allowed.

San Juan Bautista

Betabel RV Park
9664 Betabel Road
San Juan Bautista, CA
831-623-2202
Located about 5 miles south of Gilroy, this RV park is set in the quiet countryside. Amenities include 30 or 50 amp service, a mini mart, seasonally heated pool, propane, club/meeting rooms, satellite TV, restrooms, showers and handicapped access. Well-behaved leashed dogs of all sizes are allowed at no additional fee. People need to clean up after their pets. There is no pet fee. Dogs may not be left unattended outside, and they may only be left inside your unit for a short time if they will be quiet and comfortable. There is a large park across from the office where dogs can run off lead if they are well behaved and under voice control. The camping and tent areas also allow dogs. There is a dog walk area at the campground. 2 dogs may be allowed.

Mission Farms RV Park & Campground
400 San Juan Hollister Road
San Juan Bautista, CA
831-623-4456
Thanks to one of our readers for recommending this campground. Close to the highway, but quiet with lots of shade trees, this RV only park offers pull thru sites, big rig access, cable TV, and laundry. The camp sites are $28 per night. There is a $2 per night per pet fee for each small dog, and there is a $4 per night per pet fee for medium to large dogs. Dogs may not be left unattended, and they must be leashed and cleaned up after. There is a dog walk area at the campground. Multiple dogs may be allowed.

San Luis Obispo

Lake San Antonio Campground
2610 San Antonio Road
Bradley, CA
805-472-2311
Lake San Antonio is a premier freshwater recreation area, located just 20 miles inland from California?s beautiful Central Coast. Lake San Antonio offers year-round activities including picnicking, camping, fishing, hiking, swimming, boating and water-skiing. Dogs of all sizes are allowed at no additional fee.

Dogs must be on no more than a 7 foot leash and be cleaned up after. Dogs are allowed on the trails. The camping and tent areas also allow dogs. There is a dog walk area at the campground. 2 dogs may be allowed.

North Beach Campground, Pismo State Beach Park
555 Pier Avenue
Oceano, CA
805-489-1869
Close to the ocean, sitting inland behind the dunes, is a beautiful campground offering a variety of land and water recreation. Dogs of all sizes are allowed. There are no additional pet fees. Dogs may not be left unattended, and they must be leashed and cleaned up after. Dogs are allowed on the trails on lead. The camping and tent areas also allow dogs. There is a dog walk area at the campground. There are no electric or water hookups at the campgrounds. Multiple dogs may be allowed.

Pacific Dunes RV Resort
1025 Silver Spur Place
Oceano, CA
760-328-4813
Walk to the dog-friendly sand dunes and beach from this campground. Well-behaved leashed dogs are welcome in the tent sites and RV spaces. Please clean up after your pet. There is no pet fee, and dogs are allowed on the trails. The RV sites are pull through or back-in with 50 amp service, water, electric, sewer hookups, cable TV and a picnic table. Other campground amenities include a volleyball court, pool table, basketball courts, horseback riding, barbecue facilities, bicycle and walking paths, general store, laundry facilities, lighted streets, restrooms/showers, modem hookup and a clubhouse. The camping and tent areas also allow dogs. There is a dog walk area at the campground. Multiple dogs may be allowed.

Lake Nacimiento Resort RV and Campgrounds
10625 Nacimiento Lake Drive
Paso Robles, CA
805-238-3256
This campground offers a variety of amenities and land and water recreation. Dogs are allowed around and in the lake at this campground, but be careful about letting your dog get too far into the

water, as there are many boats on the lake. They are also allowed on trails. Pets must be on no more than a 6 foot leash, cleaned up after, and attended at all times. There is a $10 per day charge for dogs. Proof of your dogs' rabies vaccination is required. The camping and tent areas also allow dogs. There is a dog walk area at the campground. Multiple dogs may be allowed.

Pismo Coast Village RV Park
165 S Dolliver Street
Pismo Beach, CA
805-773-1811
This 26 acre RV park is located right on the dog-friendly Pismo State Beach. There are 400 full hookup sites each with satellite TV. RVs up to 40 feet can be accommodated. Nestled right on the beach and beautifully landscaped, park amenities include a general store, arcade, guest laundry, guest modem access in lobby, heated pool, bicycle rentals and miniature golf course. The maximum stay is 29 consecutive nights. Well-behaved leashed dogs of all sizes are allowed, up to a maximum of three pets. People need to clean up after their pets. There is no pet fee. Dogs may not be left unattended outside. This RV only campground is open all year. There are some breed restrictions. There is a dog walk area at the campground. Multiple dogs may be allowed.

El Chorro Regional Park Campground
H 1
San Luis Obispo, CA
805-781-5930
This campground offers 62 campsites for tent or RV camping. Some of the RV spaces are pull through sites and can accommodate RVs up to 40 feet. All sites are available on a first-come, first-served basis. Use the self-registration envelopes upon arrival. There are several hiking trails to choose from at this park, from hiking on meadows to walking along a creek. There is an additional fee of $2 per night per pet. Dogs must be leashed at all times on the trails and in the campground. Please clean up after your pets. This park is home to the Dairy Creek Golf Course and features a day use area, barbecue facilities, volleyball courts, an off leash dog park (with two separate areas - one for smaller pets and one for larger pets), horseshoe pits, a botanical garden, softball fields and various hiking trails. The camping and tent areas also allow

dogs. There is a dog walk area at the campground. Multiple dogs may be allowed.

Santa Margarita KOA
4765 Santa Margarita Lake Road
Santa Margarita, CA
805-438-5618
Set in a rural setting with panoramic vistas, other amenities offered are 40 foot pull through sites with 30 amp, LP gas, swimming pool, and planned activities. Dogs of all sizes are allowed for no additional fee. Dogs must be under owner's control and visual observation at all times. Dogs must be quiet, well behaved, and be on no more than a 6 foot leash at all times, or otherwise contained. Dogs may not be left unattended outside the owner's camping equipment, and must be brought inside at night. In the cabins, dogs must remain in their carriers at all times. There are some breed restrictions. The camping and tent areas also allow dogs. There is a dog walk area at the campground. Dogs are allowed in the camping cabins. 2 dogs may be allowed.

Santa Margarita Lake Regional Park Camping
4695 Santa Margarita Lake Road
Santa Margarita, CA
805-781-5930
Primitive boat-in sites are available at this park. This lake is popular for fishing, boating and hiking. Swimming is not allowed at the lake because it is a reservoir which is used for city drinking water. There is a seasonal swimming pool at the park. Hiking can be enjoyed at this park which offers miles of trails, ranging from easy to strenuous. Dogs must be leashed at all times and people need to clean up after their pets. There is an additional fee of $2 per night per pet. Dogs are allowed on the trails. The camping and tent areas also allow dogs. There is a dog walk area at the campground. There are no electric or water hookups at the campgrounds. Multiple dogs may be allowed.

Santa Barbara

El Capitan State Beach
10 Refugio Beach Road
Goleta, CA
805-968-1033
Set among sycamores and oaks along El Capitán Creek, this park offers rocky tide pools, a sandy beach, and a variety of land and

water recreation. Dogs of all sizes are allowed at no additional fee. Dogs may not be left unattended at any time, and they must be leashed and cleaned up after. Dogs are not allowed on the beach. The camping and tent areas also allow dogs. There is a dog walk area at the campground. There are no electric or water hookups at the campgrounds. 2 dogs may be allowed.

Cachuma Lake Rec Area
H 154
Santa Barbara, CA
805-686-5054
This modern Santa Barbara park is well known for its natural beauty and a variety of recreational opportunities. Dogs of all sizes are allowed for an additional fee of $3 per night per dog. Dogs may not be left unattended, and they must have current rabies and shot records. Dogs must be quiet, well behaved, leashed at all times, and cleaned up after. Dogs may not be closer than 50 feet to the shore. The camping and tent areas also allow dogs. There is a dog walk area at the campground. Multiple dogs may be allowed.

Santa Cruz

New Brighton State Beach
1500 Park Avenue
Capitola, CA
831-464-6330
Rich in natural and cultural history, this park also has various marine and land habitats to explore and a variety of recreational opportunities. Dogs of all sizes are allowed. There are no additional pet fees. Dogs may not be left unattended outside, and they must be on no more than a 6 foot leash at all times, and cleaned up after. Dogs are allowed to walk on the beach. The camping and tent areas also allow dogs. There is a dog walk area at the campground. 2 dogs may be allowed.

Santa Ysabel

Lake Henshaw Resort
26439 H 76
Santa Ysabel, CA
760-782-3487
Lake Henshaw Resort, located at a lake which rests at the foot of the Palomar Mountains, is a great place for fishermen of all levels. Some of

the amenities include a sparkling pool and spa, children's playground, grocery store with all your fishing needs, clubhouse, laundry facilities, and restaurant. Dogs of all sizes are allowed at an additional $2 per night per pet. Dogs are not allowed on the furniture in the cabins and they may not be left unattended. Dogs are allowed to walk along the lakeshore and to go in the water. The camping and tent areas also allow dogs. There is a dog walk area at the campground. Dogs are allowed in the camping cabins. Multiple dogs may be allowed.

Sequoia National Park

Azalea Campground, Kings Canyon National Park
Grant Tree Road
Three Rivers, CA
559-565-3708
This scenic park, located at 6,500 feet in the Kings Canyon National Park, offers a variety of recreational pursuits. Dogs of all sizes are allowed. There are no additional pet fees. Dogs must be leashed at all times and cleaned up after. Dogs are not allowed on the hiking trails, and must stay in the camp area or on the roads. The camping and tent areas also allow dogs. There is a dog walk area at the campground. There are no electric or water hookups at the campgrounds. Multiple dogs may be allowed.

Potwisha Campground, Sequoia and Kings Canyon Nat'l Park
47050 Generals H (H 198)
Three Rivers, CA
559-565-3341
Located in a National Forest, this park offers spectacular scenery, varied habitats and elevations, and a wide variety of land and water recreation. Dogs of all sizes are allowed at no additional fee. Dogs may not be left unattended at any time. Keep in mind that dogs are not permitted on park trails and it may be too hot to leave them in the car. It is highly suggested that dogs are not brought to the park in summer as temperatures reach over 110 degrees, and there is poison oak, snakes, and ticks. Dogs are not allowed in the water or on any of the trails. Dogs may be walked in the campground, on walkways or roadways only. Dogs must be leashed at all times and cleaned up after. The camping and tent areas

also allow dogs. There is a dog walk area at the campground. There are no electric or water hookups at the campgrounds. 2 dogs may be allowed.

Sequoia and Kings Canyon National Park Campgrounds
47050 General H
Three Rivers, CA
559-565-3341
This park offers many campgrounds which range in elevation from 2,100 feet to 7,500 feet. The Lodgepole, Dorst, Grant Grove and Atwell Mill campgrounds are located near giant sequoia groves. The Lodgepole campground, located at 6,700 foot elevation, is one of the largest camps and offers 250 sites. Tent and RV camping is available, with a maximum RV length of 35 feet. Amenities at this campground include a guest laundry, deli, market, gift shop, pay showers, flush toilets and more. Some of the campgrounds are open all year. Pets must be leashed and attended at all times. Please clean up after your pet. Keep in mind that dogs are not permitted on park trails and it may be too hot to leave them in the car. Please see our listings in the towns of Johnsondale and Hume for details about nearby dog-friendly hiking, sightseeing and additional camping. A couple of the camp areas are not accessible to RV's, so research ahead. The camping and tent areas also allow dogs. There is a dog walk area at the campground. There are no electric or water hookups at the campgrounds. Multiple dogs may be allowed.

Shasta - Trinity National Forest

Lakeview Terrace Resort
Trinity Dam Blvd
Lewiston, CA
530-778-3803
This resort overlooks Lewiston Lake and features an RV park and cabin rentals. RV spaces feature pull through sites, tables and barbecues. Most of the pull through sites offer a lake view. Other amenities include a laundry facility, restrooms and showers. Well-behaved quiet leashed dogs are welcome, up to two pets per cabin or RV. Pets are not allowed in the swimming pool area and cannot not be left alone at any time, either in your RV or at the cabins. Please clean up after your pet. There is no pet fee if you stay in an RV space, but there is a $10 per

day fee for pets in the cabins. Dogs may not be left unattended in the cabins, or outside your RV. There are some breed restrictions. There is a dog walk area at the campground. 2 dogs may be allowed.

Clark Springs Campground
Off H 3
Trinity Center, CA
530-623-2121
This campground is located in the Shasta-Trinity National Forest at an elevation of 2,400 feet. The campground offers 21 tent and RV campsites. RVs up to 25 feet are allowed, and amenities include a swimming beach, boat ramp, drinking water, picnic sites, wheelchair access and flush toilets. Fishing, swimming, boating and hiking are popular activities at the campground. The Trinity Lakeshore trailhead is located here. Dogs are allowed on the trails and in the lake water but only on non-designated swimming areas. Pets must be leashed at all times in camp, and please clean up after them. Dogs may be off lead on the trails only if they are under strict voice control, and they will not chase. This campground is closed during the off-season. The camping and tent areas also allow dogs. There is a dog walk area at the campground. There are no electric or water hookups at the campgrounds. Multiple dogs may be allowed.

Hayward Flat Campground
H 3
Trinity Center, CA
530-623-2121
This campground is located on the west side of the East Fork arm of Trinity Lake in the Shasta-Trinity National Forest. The campground is at an elevation of 2,400 feet and offers 94 tent and RV campsites. RVs up to 40 feet are allowed, and amenities include drinking water and flush toilets. Fishing, swimming and boating are popular activities at the campground. Dogs may not be left unattended outside. Pets must be leashed at all times in the camp areas, and please clean up after them. Dogs may be off lead on the trails if they are under strict voice command and will not chase. This campground is closed during the off-season. The camping and tent areas also allow dogs. There is a dog walk area at the campground. There are no electric or water hookups at the campgrounds.

Multiple dogs may be allowed.

Wyntoon Resort
60260 H 3
Trinity Center, CA
530-266-3337
This 90 acre wooded resort is located at the north end of Lake Trinity and offers both RV and tent sites. The RV sites are tree shaded with 30 or 50 amp service, and will accommodate RVs up to 60 feet. Tent sites are located under pine and cedar trees and have picnic tables and barbecues. Other camp amenities include a swimming pool, clubhouse, snack bar, ping pong, showers and laundry facilities. Well-behaved leashed pets are always welcome. Please clean up after your pet. There is a $1 per day pet fee. Dogs may not be left unattended. The camping and tent areas also allow dogs. There is a dog walk area at the campground. Multiple dogs may be allowed.

Brandy Creek RV Campground
P. O. Box 188
Whiskeytown, CA
530-246-1225
This campground is part of the Whiskeytown National Recreation Area which allows dogs on trails, in the lake and on non-swimming beaches only. The camp offers paved parking spots for RVs along an access road. There are no hookups, and generators are allowed, but not during the quiet time which is usually from 10pm to 6am. All sites are on a first-come, first-served basis. Dogs must be leashed, or crated, and attended at all times. Please clean up after your pet. The campground is open all year. The camping and tent areas also allow dogs. There is a dog walk area at the campground. There are no electric or water hookups at the campgrounds. Multiple dogs may be allowed.

Oak Bottom Campgrounds
Oak Bottom Road
Whiskeytown, CA
530-359-2269
This campground offers tent sites next to Whiskeytown Lake. The campground is part of the Whiskeytown National Recreation Area which allows dogs on trails, in the lake and on non-swimming beaches only. The camp also offers RV sites. Generators are allowed but not during the quiet time which is usually from 10pm to 6am. During the summer reservations are

required and during the winter sites are on a first-come, first-served basis. Dogs must be leashed at all times while in the camp areas. Dogs may be off lead on trails only if they will respond to voice command and will not chase. Please clean up after your pet. Dogs may not be left unattended. The camping and tent areas also allow dogs. There is a dog walk area at the campground. There are no electric or water hookups at the campgrounds. Multiple dogs may be allowed.

Shaver Lake

Camp Edison at Shaver Lake
42696 Tollhouse Road
Shaver Lake, CA
559-841-3134
This campground is located at Shaver Lake in the Sierra National Forest and is managed by Southern California Edison. There are 252 campsites with electricity and free cable TV. Amenities include picnic tables, restroom with heated showers, a guest laundry, marina and a general store. Dogs are allowed at the campgrounds, on trails and in the water but only at non-designated swimming beaches. Pets must be leashed and please clean up after them. There is a $5 per night per pet fee. Dogs may not be left unattended, and they must be brought inside at night. The camping and tent areas also allow dogs. There is a dog walk area at the campground. Multiple dogs may be allowed.

Dorabelle Campground
Dorabella Street
Shaver Lake, CA
559-297-0706
This campground is next to Shaver Lake in the Sierra National Forest. Some of the sites have lake views and all of the sites have shade from dense pines trees. The camp is at an elevation of 5,500 feet. There are 68 tent and RV sites, and RVs up to 40 feet are allowed. Amenities include water, vault toilets, picnic tables and grills. Be sure to bring some mosquito repellant. There are several trails here that provide access around the lake. Dogs are allowed at the campgrounds, on trails and in the water but only at non-designated swimming beaches. Pets must be leashed and please clean up after them. Dogs may not be left unattended. This campground is closed during the off-season. The

camping and tent areas also allow dogs. There is a dog walk area at the campground. There are no electric or water hookups at the campgrounds. Multiple dogs may be allowed.

Solvang

Flying Flags RV Park and Campground
180 Avenue of the Flags
Buellton, CA
805-688-3716
This award winning campground offers beautiful landscaped grounds, grassy pull through sites with up to 50 amp service, WiFi, a guest laundry, convenience store, snack bar, pool, spa, and playground. Up to 2 dogs are allowed at no additional fee. If there are more than 2 dogs, then there is a $2 per night per pet fee. Dogs must be leashed at all times and cleaned up after. Dogs may not be left unattended outside, and they are not allowed in the pool area, playground, or in buildings. There are some breed restrictions. The camping and tent areas also allow dogs. There is a dog walk area at the campground.

Sonoma

Cloverdale KOA
1166 Asti Ridge Road
Cloverdale, CA
707-894-3337
This park is nestled among 100-year-old oak, eucalyptus and evergreen trees, and some of the amenities include a hillside pool and spa, nature trail, pond, gymnastics playground, and various land and water recreation. Dogs of all sizes are allowed for no additional fee. Dogs must be under owner's control and visual observation at all times. Dogs must be quiet, well behaved, and be on no more than a 6 foot leash at all times, or otherwise contained. Dogs may not be left unattended outside the owner's camping equipment. There are some breed restrictions. The camping and tent areas also allow dogs. There is a dog walk area at the campground. Dogs are allowed in the camping cabins. Multiple dogs may be allowed.

Casini Ranch Family Campground
22855 Moscow Road

Duncan Mills, CA
707-865-2255
This beautiful family campground lies along the Russian River, offers great scenery, fishing, trails, and a variety of recreation. Dogs of all sizes are allowed for an additional $1 per night per pet. Dogs may not be left unattended, and they must be quiet, leashed at all times, and cleaned up after. Dogs must be inside at night, and they are not allowed in the livestock areas. Dogs are allowed on the trails on lead. The camping and tent areas also allow dogs. There is a dog walk area at the campground. Multiple dogs may be allowed.

Fifes Guest Ranch
16467 H 116
Guerneville, CA
707-869-0656
Located on 15 acres and among redwood trees, this guest ranch offers individual cabins, cottages and tent camping. Amenities include a pool, volleyball court, gym and onsite massages. Well-behaved dogs of all sizes are allowed in the campsites, cabins, and cottages for an additional fee of $50 per stay. Dogs are allowed on the trails nearby and on the beach. This campground is closed during the off-season. There is a dog walk area at the campground. 2 dogs may be allowed.

Spring Lake Regional Park Campgrounds
5585 Newanga Avenue
Santa Rosa, CA
707-785-2377
This 320 acre regional park with a 72 acre lake, offers 27 campsites and miles of easy walking trails. RVs are permitted and there is a dump station. Dogs are allowed at an additional $1 per night per pet. They must be on a 6 foot or less leash and proof of a rabies vaccination is required. Dogs are not allowed around the swimming lagoon area. For reservations call 707-565-CAMP (2267). To get to the campground, take Hoen Avenue east, cross Summerfield Road, left at the stop sign (Newanga Avenue) into park. This campground is closed during the off-season. The camping and tent areas also allow dogs. There is a dog walk area at the campground. There are no electric or water hookups at the campgrounds. Multiple dogs may be allowed.

Sonoma Coast

46

Stillwater Cove Regional Park Campgrounds
22455 H 1
Jenner, CA
707-847-3245
This 210 acre park offers 17 campsites. RVs are permitted and there is a dump station. The park also features a small beach, great views of the Pacific Ocean, picnic tables and restrooms. Dogs are allowed but must be on a 6 foot or less leash and proof of a rabies vaccination is required. There is an additional fee of $1 per night per pet. Please clean up after your pet. The camping and tent areas also allow dogs. There is a dog walk area at the campground. There are no electric or water hookups at the campgrounds. Multiple dogs may be allowed.

Sonora - Gold Country South

49er RV Ranch
23223 Italian Bar Road
Columbia, CA
209-532-4978
This RV only park is located within a short distance to the dog-friendly Columbia State Historic Park. Park amenities offers full hookups, cable TV, a store, laundry, propane and a modem hookup in the store. Dogs of all sizes are allowed for no additional fee. They ask you take your pet to the pet walk area to do their business, and that you clean up after your pet at all times. Dogs may not be left unattended, and they must be well behaved, and leashed. There is a dog walk area at the campground. Multiple dogs may be allowed.

Stonyford

Letts Lake Campground
Forest Road M10
Stonyford, CA
530-934-3316
This campground is located in the Mendocino National Forest and is next to a 35 acre lake. Water-based activities include non-motorized boating, trout fishing and swimming. There are 44 campsites and camp amenities include toilets, fire rings, water and trailer space. The access road and camps are suitable for 16 to 20 foot camping trailers. The campground is at an elevation of 4,500 feet. There is a $10 per day campsite fee. Prices are subject to change. Dogs on leash are allowed at the campground, on trails and in

the water at non-designated swimming areas only. The camp is located 19 miles west of Stonyford. This campground is closed during the off-season. The camping and tent areas also allow dogs. There is a dog walk area at the campground. There are no electric or water hookups at the campgrounds. Multiple dogs may be allowed.

Temecula

Pechanga RV Resort
45000 Pechanga Parkway
Temecula, CA
951-587-0484
This RV only resort is located at the Pechanga Casino. They offer 168 sites with 20, 30 and 50 amp service, cable TV, 25 pull through sites, 3 internet access stations, a heated pool, two spas, and an attractive patio area with a full adjoining the recreation room. Well behaved, friendly dogs are allowed for no additional fee. Dogs may not be left unattended, and they must be leashed and cleaned up after. If dogs are not cleaned up after, they will ask visitors to leave. There are some breed restrictions. There is a dog walk area at the campground. 2 dogs may be allowed.

Vail Lake Wine Country RV Resort
38000 H 79 S
Temecula, CA
951-303-0173
This RV resort is located in the country, about 15 minutes from Interstate 15. There are several hiking trails throughout the RV park where you can walk with your dog. There is no additional pet fee. Dogs may not be left unattended, and they must be leashed and cleaned up after. There is a dog walk area at the campground. 2 dogs may be allowed.

Tom's Place

East Fork Campground
Rock Creek Canyon Road
Tom's Place, CA
760-873-2500
This 133 site campground is located in the Inyo National Forest at an elevation of 9,000 feet. Amenities include water, flush toilet, picnic tables and space for RVs. For hiking, there are several trailheads nearby including the Hilton Lakes and Little Lakes Valley trails. The

fee for a campsite is $15. Pets must be leashed while in the campground and please clean up after them. Dogs may not be left unattended outside. This campground is closed during the off-season. The camping and tent areas also allow dogs. There is a dog walk area at the campground. There are no electric or water hookups at the campgrounds. Multiple dogs may be allowed.

Trinidad

Patricts Point State Park
4150 Patricks Point Drive
Trinidad, CA
707-677-3570
This park offers marine viewing, rocky tide pools, a recreated Yurok village, a native American plant garden, and various recreation. Dogs of all sizes are allowed at no additional fees. Dogs may not be left unattended, and they must have current rabies and shot records. Dogs must be leashed at all times and cleaned up after. Dogs may be on paved roads or the parking area; they are not allowed on the trails or on the beach. The camping and tent areas also allow dogs. There is a dog walk area at the campground. There are no electric or water hookups at the campgrounds. Multiple dogs may be allowed.

Vacaville

Midway RV Park
4933 Midway Road
Vacaville, CA
707-446-7679
Located in a beautiful rural setting, this park offers a pool, WiFi, laundry, pull through sites, sewer hook-ups, and is centrally located to several attractions. Dogs of all sizes are allowed for an additional $1 per night per pet. Dogs may not be left unattended outside, and they must be leashed and cleaned up after. This is an RV only park. There are some breed restrictions. There is a dog walk area at the campground. Multiple dogs may be allowed.

Vineyard RV Park
4985 Midway Road
Vacaville, CA
707-693-8797
This nicely landscaped park offers a large enclosed dog walk area, a rec room, WiFi, laundry room, pool, and a variety of activities and recreation. Dogs of all sizes are allowed for an

additional $1 per night per pet by the day, or for an additional $5 per night per pet by the week. Dogs may not be left unattended outside, and they must be leashed and cleaned up after. This is an RV only park. There are some breed restrictions. There is a dog walk area at the campground. There are special amenities given to dogs at this campground. 2 dogs may be allowed.

Vallecito

Vallecito Regional Park
37349 County Route S-2
Vallecito, CA
760-765-1188
Rich in natural and cultural history, this park has been called a beautiful oasis in the desert. It offers a wide variety of recreational pursuits. Dogs of all sizes are allowed for an additional $1 per night per pet, and they must have current tags, rabies, and shot records. Dogs may not be left unattended at any time, and they must be on no more than a 6 foot leash and cleaned up after. Dogs are not allowed on the trails, but they may be walked on the payment and along side the roads on leash. This campground is closed during the off-season. The camping and tent areas also allow dogs. There is a dog walk area at the campground. There are no electric or water hookups at the campgrounds. Multiple dogs may be allowed.

Valley Springs

Acorn Campground
2713 Hogan Dam Road
Valley Springs, CA
209-772-1343
This campground, along New Hogan Lake on the Calaveras River, features an amphitheater, an interpretive trail, hiking trails, and various recreation opportunities. Dogs of all sizes are allowed. There are no additional pet fees. Dogs must be on no more than a 6 foot leash and cleaned up after. Dogs are allowed on the trails, but they are not allowed at Wrinkle Cove. The camping and tent areas also allow dogs. There is a dog walk area at the campground. There are no electric or water hookups at the campgrounds. 2 dogs may be allowed.

Victorville

Victorville/Inland Empire KOA
16530 Stoddard Wells Road
Victorville, CA
760-245-6867
A shady get-away in the high desert, this park offers a maximum pull through of 75 feet with 30 amp, LP gas, seasonal swimming pool, several planned activities, and bike rentals. Dogs of all sizes are allowed for no additional fee. Dogs must be under owner's control and visual observation at all times. Dogs must be quiet, well behaved, and be on no more than a 6 foot leash at all times, or otherwise contained. Dogs may not be left unattended outside the owner's camping equipment, and must be brought inside at night. Only dogs that are house trained are allowed in the cabins, and they must not be left inside unattended. There are some breed restrictions. The camping and tent areas also allow dogs. There is a dog walk area at the campground. Dogs are allowed in the camping cabins.

Visalia

Horse Creek Campgrounds
Horse Creek(Lake Kaweah), H 198
Visalia, CA
559-597-2301
Located on the Kaweah River in the foothills of the central Sierra Nevada Mountains, this park offers interpretive and hiking trails and a variety of land and water recreation. Dogs of all sizes are allowed. There are no additional pet fees. Dogs must be leashed and cleaned up after. Dogs are allowed on the trails. The camping and tent areas also allow dogs. There is a dog walk area at the campground. There are no electric or water hookups at the campgrounds. Multiple dogs may be allowed.

Visalia/Fresno South KOA
7480 Avenue 308
Visalia, CA
559-651-0544
Amenities include old time charm, a good location, 65 foot pull-through sites with 50 amp service, cable, LP gas, snack bar, and swimming pool. Dogs of all sizes are allowed for no additional fee. Dogs must be under owner's control and visual observation at all times. Dogs must be quiet, well behaved, and be on no more than a 6 foot leash at all times, or otherwise contained. Dogs may not be left unattended outside the owner's camping equipment,

and must be brought inside at night. There is a fenced-in dog area where your pets may be off lead. There are some breed restrictions. The camping and tent areas also allow dogs. There is a dog walk area at the campground. There are special amenities given to dogs at this campground. Multiple dogs may be allowed.

Watsonville

Mount Madonna County Park
7850 Pole Line Road
Watsonville, CA
408-355-2201
From the towering redwoods to the Monterey Bay, this 3,688 acre park offers great scenery, interpretive exhibits and programs, an amphitheater, access to an extensive 14 mile trail system, a self-guided nature trail, and a variety of recreation. Dogs of all sizes are allowed at no additional fee. Dogs must be on no more than a 6 foot leash, and cleaned up after. Dogs must be in confined areas at night. The camping and tent areas also allow dogs. There is a dog walk area at the campground. 2 dogs may be allowed.

Santa Cruz/Monterey Bay KOA
1186 San Andreas Road
Watsonville, CA
831-722-0551
This scenic family resort along the coast of Monterey Bay offers a long list of amenities, planned activities, and land and water recreation. Dogs of all sizes are allowed for no additional fee. Dogs must be under owner's control and visual observation at all times. Dogs must be quiet, well behaved, and be on no more than a 6 foot leash at all times, or otherwise contained. Dogs may not be left unattended outside the owner's camping equipment, and must be brought inside at night. Dogs are not allowed in the lodge or the play areas. There are some breed restrictions. The camping and tent areas also allow dogs. There is a dog walk area at the campground. Dogs are allowed in the camping cabins. Multiple dogs may be allowed.

Sunset State Beach
201 Sunset Beach Road
Watsonville, CA
831-763-7062
Dogs of all sizes are allowed. There

are no additional pet fees. Dogs may not be left unattended at any time, and they must be leashed and cleaned up after. Dogs are not allowed on the beach. This campground is closed during the off-season. The camping and tent areas also allow dogs. There is a dog walk area at the campground. There are no electric or water hookups at the campgrounds. 2 dogs may be allowed.

Whitehorn

Nadelos Campground
Chemise Mountain Road
Whitehorn, CA
707-825-2300
This campground offers 8 walk-in tent sites ranging from 50 to 300 feet from the parking lot. The sites are shaded by Douglas fir trees and are set along a small mountain stream. Campground amenities include picnic tables, vault toilets, drinking water and fire rings. Day use parking for the dog-friendly Chemise Mountain Trail is located at this campground. Sites are $8 per day with a maximum of 14 days per stay. Pets are allowed but must be leashed in the campground. If off leash on the trails, they must respond to voice command and not chase wildlife. Dogs may not be left unattended. To get there, take Highway 101 to Redway. Go west on Briceland/Shelter Cove Road for 22 miles and then head south on Chemise Mountain Road for 1.5 miles. Travel time from Highway 101 is about 55 minutes. The camping and tent areas also allow dogs. There is a dog walk area at the campground. There are no electric or water hookups at the campgrounds. Multiple dogs may be allowed.

Wailaki Campground
Chemise Mountain Road
Whitehorn, CA
707-825-2300
This campground offers 13 tent and trailer sites along a small mountain stream amidst large Douglas fir trees. Large RVs are not recommended on the roads to this campground. Day use parking for the dog-friendly Chemise Mountain Trail is located at this campground. Camp amenities include picnic tables, grills, water and restrooms. Sites are $8 per day with a maximum of 14 days per stay. Pets are allowed but must be leashed in the campground. If off leash on the trails, they must

respond to voice command and not chase wildlife. Dogs may not be left unattended. To get there, take Highway 101 to Redway, go west on Briceland/Shelter Cove Road for 22 miles, and then head south on Chemise Mountain Road for 2 miles. Travel time from Highway 101 is about 55 minutes. This campground is closed during the off-season. The camping and tent areas also allow dogs. There is a dog walk area at the campground. There are no electric or water hookups at the campgrounds. Multiple dogs may be allowed.

Winchester

Lake Skinner Campground
37101 Warren Road
Winchester, CA
951-926-1541
The campground is located in a 6,040 acre park which features a lake, hiking/interpretive trails, equestrian trails, seasonal swimming pool, launch ramps, boat rentals, and a camp store. Dogs are allowed on the trails and in the campgrounds, but not in the lake or within 50 feet of the lake. Dogs must be on a 6 foot or less leash and please clean up after them. There is an additional fee of $2 per night per pet. The camping and tent areas also allow dogs. There is a dog walk area at the campground. Multiple dogs may be allowed.

Yermo

Barstow/Calico KOA
35250 Outer H 15
Yermo, CA
760-254-2311
This campground is located in a desert setting about 3.5 miles from the dog-friendly Calico Ghost Town. RV site amenities include a maximum pull through length of 70 feet and 50 amp service. Other camp amenities include a seasonal swimming pool, free modem dataport, LP gas, snack bar, pavilion/meeting room, and dog walking area. Dogs of all sizes are allowed for no additional fee. Dogs must be under owner's control and visual observation at all times. Dogs must be quiet, well behaved, and be on no more than a 6 foot leash at all times or otherwise contained. Dogs may not be left unattended outside the owner's camping equipment. Dogs are not allowed in the pool or

playground areas, and may not be tied to trees. There are some breed restrictions. The camping and tent areas also allow dogs. There is a dog walk area at the campground. Multiple dogs may be allowed.

Barstow/Calico KOA
35250 Outer H 15
Yermo, CA
760-254-2311
In a convenient location midway between Los Angeles and Las Vegas, this KOA provides easy access to dozens of desert attractions and activities. Amenities include 70 foot pull through sites with 50 amp, LP Gas, modem dataport, snack bar, and a swimming pool. Dogs of all sizes are allowed for no additional fee. Dogs must be under owner's control and visual observation at all times. Dogs must be quiet, well behaved, and be on no more than a 6 foot leash at all times, or otherwise contained. Dogs may not be left unattended outside the owner's camping equipment, and must be brought inside at night. Dogs are not allowed in the pool area, buildings, or playgrounds, and they may not be tied to trees. There are some breed restrictions. The camping and tent areas also allow dogs. There is a dog walk area at the campground. Multiple dogs may be allowed.

Yosemite

Lupine/Cedar Bluff Campground
County Road 222 on South side of Bass Lake
Bass Lake, CA
559-877-2218
This campground is next to Bass Lake in the Sierra National Forest. It is at an elevation of 3,400 feet and offers shade from dense pine, oak and cedar frees. There are 113 campsites for tent and RV camping. RVs up to 40 feet are allowed, and amenities include piped water, flush toilets, picnic tables and grills. The campground is open all year. A .5 mile trail called The Way of the Mono Trail, is located near this campground. Dogs are allowed at the campgrounds, on trails and in the water but only at non-designated swimming beaches. Pets must be leashed and please clean up after them. Dogs may not be left unattended outside, and they are not allowed on the beach. Check in at the Bass Lake Campground office before heading to your campsite.

The office is located at the west end of the lake near Recreation Point. The camping and tent areas also allow dogs. There is a dog walk area at the campground. There are no electric or water hookups at the campgrounds. Multiple dogs may be allowed.

Yosemite/Mariposa KOA
6323 H 140
Midpines, CA
209-966-2201
Nestled in the pines, close to Yosemite, this campground offers such amenities as 43 foot pull through sites with 50 amp service, cable TV, swimming pool, mini golf, planned activities, and guided tours. Dogs of all sizes are allowed for an additional pet fee of $2 per night per pet. Dogs must be under owner's control and visual observation at all times. Dogs must be quiet, well behaved, and be on no more than a 6 foot leash at all times, or otherwise contained. Dogs may not be left unattended outside the owner's camping equipment, and must be brought inside at night. There are some breed restrictions. The camping and tent areas also allow dogs. There is a dog walk area at the campground. Multiple dogs may be allowed.

Yosemite National Park Campgrounds
P. O. Box 577
Yosemite National Park, CA
209-372-0200
There are 10 dog-friendly campgrounds to choose from at this visually striking national park. Pets are allowed in all campgrounds except Camp 4, Tamarack Flat, Porcupine Flat, all walk-in sites and all group campsites. Generators can be used sparingly only between 7am and 7pm. Some of the campgrounds are open all year but all are open during the summer. Reservations should be made well in advance, especially during the summer season. Dogs of all sizes are allowed at no additional fee. While this national park does not allow dogs on most of the trails, there are still about 6-7 miles of both paved and unpaved trails that allow dogs. See our Yosemite National Park listing for more details. Dogs must be on a 6 foot or less leash and attended at all times. People must also clean up after their pets. The camping and tent areas also allow dogs. There is a dog walk area at the campground. Multiple dogs may be allowed.

Yreka

Tree of Heaven Campground, Klamath National Forest
1312 Fairlane Road
Yreka, CA
530-468-5351
This park features great river access, a Birding Nature Trail and various recreation. Dogs of all sizes are allowed. There are no additional pet fees. Dogs must be leashed and cleaned up after. Dogs are allowed on the trails. The camping and tent areas also allow dogs. There is a dog walk area at the campground. There are no electric or water hookups at the campgrounds. Multiple dogs may be allowed.

Yucaipa

Yacaipa Regional Park
33900 Oak Glen Road
Yucaipa, CA
909-790-3127
Sitting on 885 acres in the foothills of the San Bernardino Mountains, this park offers a wide variety of land and water recreation. Dogs of all sizes are allowed for an additional $1 per night per pet. Dogs must be leashed and cleaned up after. The camping and tent areas also allow dogs. There is a dog walk area at the campground. Multiple dogs may be allowed.

Colorado Listings

Alamosa

Alamosa KOA
6900 Juniper Avenue
Alamosa, CO
719-589-9757
Dogs of all sizes are allowed, however there can only be up to 3 dogs at tent and RV sites, and up to 2 dogs at the cabins. There are no additional pet fees. Dogs may not be left unattended at the cabins or outside, and they must be leashed and cleaned up after. There are some breed restrictions. The camping and tent areas also allow dogs. There is a dog walk area at the campground. Dogs are allowed in the camping cabins.

Arboles

Navajo State Park
1526 County Road 982 (Box 1697)
Arboles, CO
970-883-2208
This scenic park touts a reservoir with over 15,000 acres, and offers a variety of land and water recreation in addition to the geological and historical points of interest. Dogs of all sizes are allowed at no additional fee. Dogs may not be left unattended, and they must be on no more than a 6 foot leash, and be cleaned up after. The camping and tent areas also allow dogs. There is a dog walk area at the campground. Dogs are allowed in the camping cabins. Multiple dogs may be allowed.

Basalt

Aspen Basalt Campground
20640 H 82
Basalt, CO
800-567-2773
Dogs of all sizes are allowed. There are no additional pet fees. Dogs may not be left unattended outside, and must be leashed and cleaned up after. There is a dog walk area at the campground. 2 dogs may be allowed.

Bayfield

Blue Spruce Cabins and RV Park
1875 County Road 500
Bayfield, CO
970-884-2641
Dogs of all sizes are allowed. There are no additional pet fees. Dogs may not be left out at night, or outside unattended. Dogs must be leashed and cleaned up after. There are some breed restrictions. This RV park is closed during the off-season. The camping and tent areas also allow dogs. There is a dog walk area at the campground. 2 dogs may be allowed.

Vallecito Resort
13030 County Road 501
Bayfield, CO
970-884-9458
Dogs of all sizes are allowed. There are no additional pet fees. Dogs must be leashed and cleaned up after. There are some breed restrictions. This RV park is closed during the off-season. The camping and tent areas also allow dogs.

There is a dog walk area at the campground. Dogs are allowed in the camping cabins. 2 dogs may be allowed.

Breckenridge

Tiger Run RV Resort
85 Tiger Run Road
Breckenridge, CO
800-895-9594
Dogs of all sizes are allowed. There are no additional pet fees. Dogs must be leashed and cleaned up after. There is a dog walk area at the campground. Multiple dogs may be allowed.

Buena Vista

Arrowhead Point Camping Resort
33975 H 24N
Buena Vista, CO
719-395-2323
Dogs of all sizes are allowed. There are no additional pet fees. Dogs must be leashed and cleaned up after. There are some breed restrictions. This RV park is closed during the off-season. The camping and tent areas also allow dogs. There is a dog walk area at the campground. Multiple dogs may be allowed.

Buena Vista KOA
27700 H 303
Buena Vista, CO
719-395-8318
Dogs of all sizes are allowed, and there are no additional pet fees for tent or RV sites. There is a $5 per night per pet additional fee for cabins. There can be up to 3 dogs at tent or RV sites, but only up to 2 dogs at the cabins. Dogs may not be left unattended, and they must be leashed and cleaned up after. There are some breed restrictions. This RV park is closed during the off-season. The camping and tent areas also allow dogs. There is a dog walk area at the campground. Dogs are allowed in the camping cabins.

Burlington

Bonny Lake State Park
32300 Yuma County Road 2
Burlington, CO
970-354-7306
Dogs of all sizes are allowed. There are no additional pet fees. Dogs must be on no more than a 6 foot leash, and be cleaned up after. Dogs

are allowed on the trails and at the beach, but not at the swim areas. The camping and tent areas also allow dogs. There is a dog walk area at the campground. There are no water hookups at the campground. Multiple dogs may be allowed.

Canon City

Fort Gorge RV Park
45044 H 50W
Canon City, CO
719-275-5111
Dogs of all sizes are allowed. There are no additional pet fees. Dogs may not be left unattended, and must be leashed and cleaned up after. The camping and tent areas also allow dogs. There is a dog walk area at the campground. Dogs are allowed in the camping cabins. Multiple dogs may be allowed.

Royal Gorge/Canon City KOA
559 County Road 3A
Canon City, CO
719-275-6116
Dogs of all sizes are allowed. There are no additional pet fees. Dogs may not be left unattended at the cabins, and they must be leashed and cleaned up after. This RV park is closed during the off-season. The camping and tent areas also allow dogs. There is a dog walk area at the campground. Dogs are allowed in the camping cabins. Multiple dogs may be allowed.

Yogi Bear Jellystone Park
43595 H 50
Canon City, CO
719-275-2128
Dogs of all sizes are allowed. There are no additional pet fees. Dogs may not be left unattended except for short periods. Dogs must be well behaved, quiet, leashed, and cleaned up after. There are some breed restrictions. This RV park is closed during the off-season. The camping and tent areas also allow dogs. There is a dog walk area at the campground. Multiple dogs may be allowed.

Castle Rock

Castle Rock Campground
6527 S I 25
Castle Rock, CO
303-681-3169
Dogs of all sizes are allowed. There

are no additional pet fees. Dogs must be well behaved, leashed, and cleaned up after. They also have lodges (deluxe cabins) where your dog is allowed at no extra fee. The camping and tent areas also allow dogs. There is a dog walk area at the campground. Dogs are allowed in the camping cabins. Multiple dogs may be allowed.

Central City

Gambler's Edge RV Park
605 Lake Gultch Road
Central City, CO
303-582-9345
Dogs of all sizes are allowed. There are no additional pet fees. Dogs must be leashed and cleaned up after. There are some breed restrictions. There is a dog walk area at the campground. 2 dogs may be allowed.

Clark

Steamboat Lake State Park
61105 H 129
Clark, CO
970-879-3922
This park is one of Colorado's most popular parks with year round recreational pursuits. Although the camp areas are closed in winter, there are 18 sites for RVs at the marina. Dogs of all sizes are allowed at no additional fee. Dogs may not be left unattended, and they must have current rabies and shot records. Dogs must be on no more than a 6 foot leash, and be cleaned up after. Dogs are not allowed in public swim areas or in buildings. Dogs are allowed on the trails. The camping and tent areas also allow dogs. There is a dog walk area at the campground. There are no water hookups at the campground. Multiple dogs may be allowed.

Clifton

RV Ranch at Grand Junction
3238 E I 70 Business Loop
Clifton, CO
970-434-6644
One dog of any size is allowed. There are no additional pet fees. Dogs must be leashed and cleaned up after. There are some breed restrictions. The camping and tent areas also allow dogs. There is a dog walk area at the campground.

Colorado Springs

Fountain Creek RV Park
3023 W Colorado Avenue
Colorado Springs, CO
719-633-2192
Dogs of all sizes are allowed. There are no additional pet fees. Dogs may not be left unattended, and must be leashed and cleaned up after. The camping and tent areas also allow dogs. There is a dog walk area at the campground. Multiple dogs may be allowed.

Garden of the Gods Campground
3704 W Colorado Avenue
Colorado Springs, CO
719-475-9450
Dogs of all sizes are allowed. There are no additional pet fees. Dogs must be quiet, leashed, and cleaned up after. The camping and tent areas also allow dogs. There is a dog walk area at the campground. Multiple dogs may be allowed.

Cortez

Cortez Mesa Verde KOA
27432 E H 160
Cortez, CO
970-565-9301
Dogs of all sizes are allowed. There are no additional pet fees. Dogs may not be left unattended at the cabins or outside, and they must be leashed and cleaned up after. There are some breed restrictions. This RV park is closed during the off-season. The camping and tent areas also allow dogs. There is a dog walk area at the campground. Dogs are allowed in the camping cabins. Multiple dogs may be allowed.

Echo Basin Ranch
43747 Co. Rd M
Mancos, CO
970-533-7000
Dogs of all sizes are allowed. There are no additional pet fees. Dogs must be leashed or crated at all times, and be cleaned up after. This RV park is closed during the off-season. The camping and tent areas also allow dogs. There is a dog walk area at the campground. 2 dogs may be allowed.

Mesa Verde RV Resort
35303 H 160
Mancos, CO
970-533-7421
Dogs of all sizes are allowed. There are no additional pet fees. Dogs

must be leashed and cleaned up after. There is a pet sitter on site available for $5 per pet per day. The camping and tent areas also allow dogs. There is a dog walk area at the campground. There are special amenities given to dogs at this campground. Multiple dogs may be allowed.

Mesa Verde RV Resort
35303 H 160
Mancos, CO
970-533-7421
Dogs of all sizes are allowed. There are no additional pet fees. Dogs must be leashed and cleaned up after. Dogs are not allowed in buildings or the pool area. The camping and tent areas also allow dogs. There is a dog walk area at the campground. Multiple dogs may be allowed.

Morefield Campground
34879 H 160
Mancos, CO
800-449-2288
Dogs of all sizes are allowed, and there are no additional pet fees for tent or RV sites. There is a $25 per night per pet additional fee for the lodge. Dogs may not be left unattended at the lodge at any time. Dogs must be leashed and cleaned up after. Dogs may not be left outside unattended, and they are not allowed in the buildings or on the trails. This RV park is closed during the off-season. The camping and tent areas also allow dogs. There is a dog walk area at the campground. Multiple dogs may be allowed.

Cotopaxi

Cotopaxi Arkansas River KOA
21435 H 50
Cotopaxi, CO
719-275-9308
Dogs of all sizes are allowed, and there are no additional pet fees for tent or RV sites. There is a $5 per night per pet additional fee for the cabins or motel. Dogs must be quiet, well behaved, be on no more than a 6 foot leash, and cleaned up after. Dogs may not be left unattended at any time. There are some breed restrictions. This RV park is closed during the off-season. The camping and tent areas also allow dogs. There is a dog walk area at the campground. Dogs are allowed in the camping

cabins. Multiple dogs may be allowed.

Craig

Craig KOA
2800 E H 40
Craig, CO
970-824-5105
Dogs of all sizes are allowed. There are no additional pet fees. Dogs must be leashed and cleaned up after. The camping and tent areas also allow dogs. There is a dog walk area at the campground. Dogs are allowed in the camping cabins. Multiple dogs may be allowed.

Crawford

Crawford State Park
40468 H 92 N
Crawford, CO
970-921-5721
Water recreation, fishing, and hiking are the main attractions at this scenic park. Dogs of all sizes are allowed at no additional fee. Dogs may not be left unattended, and they must be on no more than a 6 foot leash, and cleaned up after. Dogs are not allowed in buildings, or on the swim or ski beaches. The camping and tent areas also allow dogs. There is a dog walk area at the campground. Multiple dogs may be allowed.

Cripple Creek

Cripple Creek/Colorado Springs W KOA
2576 County Road 81
Cripple Creek, CO
719-689-3376
Dogs of all sizes are allowed. There are no additional pet fees. Dogs may not be left unattended at the cabins or outside. Dogs must be quiet, be on no more than a 6 foot leash, and cleaned up after. This RV park is closed during the off-season. The camping and tent areas also allow dogs. There is a dog walk area at the campground. Dogs are allowed in the camping cabins. Multiple dogs may be allowed.

Del Norte

Rio Grande National Forest
13308 W H 160
Del Norte, CO
719-852-5941
With 4 ranger districts and over a

million acres, this forest provides a variety of camping areas and trails. The diverse ecosystems support a large variety of plant, fish, mammal, and bird species. Dogs are allowed at no additional fee. Dogs may not be left unattended, and they must be leashed and cleaned up after in the camp areas. Dogs are allowed on the trails. The camping and tent areas also allow dogs. There is a dog walk area at the campground. Multiple dogs may be allowed.

Delta

Grand Mesa, Uncompahgre and Gunnison National Forests
2250 H 50
Delta, CO
970-874-6600
With more than 3 million acres of public land, there is a variety of recreational pursuits. Dogs of all sizes are allowed. There are no additional pet fees. Dogs must be leashed and cleaned up after. Dogs are allowed on the trails. This campground is closed during the off-season. The camping and tent areas also allow dogs. There is a dog walk area at the campground. There are no electric or water hookups at the campground. Multiple dogs may be allowed.

Denver

Denver Meadows RV Park
2075 Potomac Street
Aurora, CO
303-364-9483
Dogs of all sizes are allowed. There are no additional pet fees. Dogs may not be left unattended outside, and they must be leashed and cleaned up after. This is an RV only park. There are some breed restrictions. There is a dog walk area at the campground. Multiple dogs may be allowed.

Dakota Ridge RV Park
17800 W Colfax
Golden, CO
800-398-1625
Dogs of all sizes are allowed. There is a $1 per night per additional fee. Dogs must be quiet, leashed, and cleaned up after. Dogs may not be put in outside pens, or be left unattended outside. There are some breed restrictions. There is a dog walk area at the campground. Multiple dogs may be allowed.

Chatfield State Park
11500 N Roxborough Park Road
Littleton, CO
303-791-7275
In addition to a wide variety of recreational pursuits, miles of trails, and a marina, the diverse ecosystems of this park also allow for some unique educational opportunities. Dogs of all sizes are allowed at no additional fee. Dogs may not be left unattended, and they must be leashed and cleaned up after. Dogs are not allowed in public swim areas or in buildings. Dogs are allowed on the trails, and there is an area behind the dam where dogs may be off lead if they are under voice control. The camping and tent areas also allow dogs. There is a dog walk area at the campground. Multiple dogs may be allowed.

Prospect RV Park
11600 W 44th Avenue
Wheat Ridge, CO
303-424-4414
Dogs of all sizes are allowed. There are no additional pet fees. Dogs must be leashed and cleaned up after. There are some breed restrictions. There is a dog walk area at the campground. Multiple dogs may be allowed.

Divide

Mueller State Park
21045 H 67S
Divide, CO
719-687-2366
This park has over 5,000 acres of some of the most beautiful land in the state. The park offers a variety of year round recreation. Dogs are allowed at no additional fee. Dogs may not be left unattended, and they must be on no more than a 6 foot leash, and be cleaned up after. Dogs are not allowed off the pavement, and they may not go on the trails. The camping and tent areas also allow dogs. There is a dog walk area at the campground. There are no water hookups at the campground. Multiple dogs may be allowed.

Dolores

Dolores River RV Park
18680 H 145
Dolores, CO
970-882-7761
Dogs of all sizes are allowed, and

there are no additional pet fees for tent or RV sites. There may be a small one time fee for pets in cabins. This RV park is closed during the off-season. The camping and tent areas also allow dogs. There is a dog walk area at the campground. Dogs are allowed in the camping cabins. Multiple dogs may be allowed.

Durango

Alpen Rose RV Park
27847 H 550N
Durango, CO
970-247-5540
Dogs of all sizes are allowed. There are no additional pet fees. Dogs may not be left unattended outside, and must be quiet, leashed, and cleaned up after. There are a couple of dog sitters on site that will take care of your dog with walks, food and water, and play time for $10 per day per dog. This RV park is closed during the off-season. There is a dog walk area at the campground. There are special amenities given to dogs at this campground. Multiple dogs may be allowed.

Durango East KOA
30090 H 160
Durango, CO
970-247-0783
Dogs of all sizes are allowed. There are no additional pet fees. Dogs may not be left unattended, and they must be quiet, well behaved, leashed and cleaned up after. There are some breed restrictions. This RV park is closed during the off-season. The camping and tent areas also allow dogs. There is a dog walk area at the campground. Dogs are allowed in the camping cabins. Multiple dogs may be allowed.

Durango North KOA
13391 County Road 250
Durango, CO
970-247-4499
Dogs of all sizes are allowed. There are no additional pet fees. Dogs may not be left unattended, and they must be leashed and cleaned up after. This RV park is closed during the off-season. The camping and tent areas also allow dogs. There is a dog walk area at the campground. Dogs are allowed in the camping cabins. 2 dogs may be allowed.

San Juan National Forest
15 Burnett Court

Durango, CO
970-247-4874
With over 2 and a half million acres, and home to the Anasazi Heritage Center, there are historical and geological interests as well as a variety of recreational pursuits. Dogs are allowed at no additional fee. Dogs may not be left unattended, and they must be leashed and cleaned up after. Dogs are allowed on the trails, and they may be off lead in the forest if they are under voice control. This campground is closed during the off-season. The camping and tent areas also allow dogs. There is a dog walk area at the campground. There are no water hookups at the campground. Multiple dogs may be allowed.

United Campground of Durango
1322 Animas View Road
Durango, CO
970-247-3853
Dogs of all sizes are allowed. There are no additional pet fees. Dogs may not be in the buildings, or at the pool, nor left unattended. Dogs must be leashed at all times, and must be cleaned up after. This RV park is closed during the off-season. The camping and tent areas also allow dogs. There is a dog walk area at the campground. Multiple dogs may be allowed.

Estes Park

Elk Meadow Lodge and RV Resort
1665 H 66
Estes Park, CO
970-586-5342
Dogs of all sizes are allowed. There are no additional pet fees. Dogs may not be left unattended, and they must be quiet, leashed, and cleaned up after. There are some breed restrictions. This RV park is closed during the off-season. The camping and tent areas also allow dogs. There is a dog walk area at the campground. Multiple dogs may be allowed.

Estes Park KOA
2051 Big Thompson Avenue
Estes Park, CO
970-586-2888
Dogs of all sizes are allowed. There are no additional pet fees. Dogs may not be left unattended, and they must be leashed and cleaned up after. There may only be up to 2 dogs in the cabins. There are some breed restrictions. This RV park is closed

during the off-season. The camping and tent areas also allow dogs. There is a dog walk area at the campground. Dogs are allowed in the camping cabins. Multiple dogs may be allowed.

Manor RV Park
815 Riverside Drive
Estes Park, CO
970-586-3251
Dogs of all sizes are allowed. There are no additional pet fees. Dogs must be quiet, leashed, and cleaned up after. This RV park is closed during the off-season. There is a dog walk area at the campground. Multiple dogs may be allowed.

Mary's Lake Campground
2120 Mary's Lake Road
Estes Park, CO
970-586-4411
Dogs of all sizes are allowed. There are no additional pet fees. Dogs must be leashed and cleaned up after. This RV park is closed during the off-season. The camping and tent areas also allow dogs. There is a dog walk area at the campground. Multiple dogs may be allowed.

Yogi Bear Jellystone Park
5495 H 36
Estes Park, CO
970-586-4230
Dogs of all sizes are allowed. There are no additional pet fees. Dogs must be well behaved, quiet, leashed, and cleaned up after. This RV park is closed during the off-season. The camping and tent areas also allow dogs. There is a dog walk area at the campground. Multiple dogs may be allowed.

Fort Collins

Arapaho Roosevelt National Forest
2150 Center Avenue, Building E
Fort Collins, CO
970-498-2770
This park covers 22 million acres of forest and grassland in 5 states. There are about 50 campgrounds, but only 2 are open all year, and only 3 have electric hook-ups. Dogs of all sizes are allowed. There are no additional pet fees. Dogs are not allowed in any buildings, and on some of the trails as marked. Dogs must be leashed and cleaned up

after. The Arapaho Roosevelt National Forest surrounds the Rocky Mountain National Park, and the National Park doesn't allow dogs in most areas. The camping and tent areas also allow dogs. There is a dog walk area at the campground. There are no water hookups at the campground. Multiple dogs may be allowed.

Heron Lake RV Park
1910 N Taft Hill
Fort Collins, CO
877-254-4063
Dogs of all sizes are allowed. There is a $1 per day per dog, or $5 per week per dog, additional pet fee. Dogs must be leashed and cleaned up after. There are some breed restrictions. This RV park is closed during the off-season. The camping and tent areas also allow dogs. There is a dog walk area at the campground. Multiple dogs may be allowed.

Fountain

Colorado Springs South KOA
8100 Bandley Drive
Fountain, CO
719-382-7575
Dogs of all sizes are allowed, and there are no additional pet fees for tent or RV sites. There is a $3 per night per pet additional fee for cabins. Dogs may not be left unattended in the cabins or outside, and they must be leashed and cleaned up after. There are some breed restrictions. The camping and tent areas also allow dogs. There is a dog walk area at the campground. Dogs are allowed in the camping cabins. Multiple dogs may be allowed.

Fruita

Mountain RV Resort
607 H 340
Fruita, CO
970-858-3155
Dogs of all sizes are allowed, but there can only be up to 3 small dogs or 2 large dogs per site. There are no additional pet fees. Dogs must be leashed and cleaned up after. There are some breed restrictions. There is a dog walk area at the campground.

Glenwood Springs

Rock Gardens RV Resort and

Campground
1308 County Road 129
Glenwood Springs, CO
800-958-6737
Dogs of all sizes are allowed. There are no additional pet fees. Dogs must be leashed and cleaned up after. This RV park is closed during the off-season. The camping and tent areas also allow dogs. There is a dog walk area at the campground. Multiple dogs may be allowed.

White River Naional Forest
900 Grand Avenue
Glenwood Springs, CO
970-945-2521
With over 2 million acres and 8 wilderness areas, this forest provides a variety of camping areas and trails. The diverse ecosystems support a large variety of plants, fish, mammals, bird species, and recreation. Dogs are allowed at no additional fee. Dogs may not be left unattended, and they must be leashed and cleaned up after in the camp areas. Dogs are not allowed in some of the wilderness areas. This campground is closed during the off-season. The camping and tent areas also allow dogs. There is a dog walk area at the campground. Multiple dogs may be allowed.

Goodrich

Jackson Lake State Park
26363 County Road 3
Goodrich, CO
970-645-2551
This park has been referred to as an "oasis in the plains", and there are a variety of recreational pursuits offered all year. Quiet and well behaved dogs of all sizes are allowed at no additional fee. Dogs may not be left unattended, and they must be on no more than a 6 foot leash, and be cleaned up after. Dogs are not allowed on the swim or ski beaches, or in buildings. Dogs are allowed on the trails. There is an off-leash area and a pond where dogs can swim at the North end of the park. The camping and tent areas also allow dogs. There is a dog walk area at the campground. Multiple dogs may be allowed.

Gunnison

Gunnison KOA
105 County Road 50
Gunnison, CO
970-641-1358

Dogs of all sizes are allowed, but there can only be 1 large or 2 small dogs per site. There are no additional pet fees. Dogs may not be left unattended, and they must be leashed at all times, and cleaned up after. This RV park is closed during the off-season. The camping and tent areas also allow dogs. There is a dog walk area at the campground. Dogs are allowed in the camping cabins.

Gunnison Lakeside Resort
28357 H 50
Gunnison, CO
970-641-0477
Dogs of all sizes are allowed. There are no additional pet fees. Dogs may not be left unattended outside, and they must be well behaved, leashed at all times, and cleaned up after. This RV park is closed during the off-season. The camping and tent areas also allow dogs. There is a dog walk area at the campground. 2 dogs may be allowed.

Mesa RV Resort
36128 W H 50
Gunnison, CO
970-641-3186
Dogs of all sizes are allowed. There are no additional pet fees. Dogs must be quiet, leashed, and cleaned up after. This RV park is closed during the off-season. The camping and tent areas also allow dogs. There is a dog walk area at the campground. Multiple dogs may be allowed.

La Junta

La Junta KOA
26680 H 50
La Junta, CO
719-384-9580
Dogs of all sizes are allowed. There are no additional pet fees. Dogs must be quiet, be on no more than a 6 foot leash, and cleaned up after. There are some breed restrictions. The camping and tent areas also allow dogs. There is a dog walk area at the campground. Dogs are allowed in the camping cabins. Multiple dogs may be allowed.

LaPorte

Fort Collins KOA
6670 N H 287
LaPorte, CO
970-493-9758
Dogs of all sizes are allowed. There

are no additional pet fees. Dogs must be leashed and cleaned up after. Dogs are not allowed at the playground, the camp kitchen, or the bathrooms. This RV park is closed during the off-season. The camping and tent areas also allow dogs. There is a dog walk area at the campground. Dogs are allowed in the camping cabins. Multiple dogs may be allowed.

Lake George

Eleven Mile State Park
4229 County Road 92
Lake George, CO
719-748-3401
Great fishing, hiking, waterfront camping, and various water and land recreation make this a popular park. Dogs of all sizes are allowed at no additional fee. Dogs may not be left unattended, and they must be on no more than a 6 foot leash, and be cleaned up after. Dogs are not allowed in the water anywhere. Dogs are allowed on the trails. The camping and tent areas also allow dogs. There is a dog walk area at the campground. There are no water hookups at the campground. Multiple dogs may be allowed.

Limon

Limon KOA
575 Colorado Avenue
Limon, CO
719-775-2151
Dogs of all sizes are allowed. There are no additional pet fees. Dogs must be leashed and cleaned up after. There are some breed restrictions. This RV park is closed during the off-season. The camping and tent areas also allow dogs. There is a dog walk area at the campground. Dogs are allowed in the camping cabins. Multiple dogs may be allowed.

Longmont

St. Vrain State Park
3525 H 119
Longmont, CO
303-678-9402
Dogs of all sizes are allowed. There are no additional pet fees. Dogs must be leashed and cleaned up after. The camping and tent areas also allow dogs. There is a dog walk area at the campground. Multiple dogs may be allowed.

Loveland

Johnson's Corner RV Retreat
3618 SE Frontage Road
Loveland, CO
970-669-8400
Dogs of all sizes are allowed. There is a $1 per night per pet additional fee. Dogs must be leashed and cleaned up after. There is a dog walk area at the campground. Multiple dogs may be allowed.

New Castle

Elk Creek Campgrounds
0581 County Road 241
New Castle, CO
970-984-2240
Dogs of all sizes are allowed, and there are no additional pet fees for tent or RV sites. There is a $5 per night per pet additional fee for cabins. Dogs may not be left unattended, and they must be leashed and cleaned up after. There is a small fenced in area for off lead. This RV park is closed during the off-season. The camping and tent areas also allow dogs. There is a dog walk area at the campground. 2 dogs may be allowed.

Ouray

Ouray KOA
225 County Road 23
Ouray, CO
970-325-4736
Dogs of all sizes are allowed. There are no additional pet fees. Dogs may not be left unattended at the cabins or outside, and they are not allowed in the buildings. Dogs must be quiet, well behaved, be on no more than a 6 foot leash, and cleaned up after. There are some breed restrictions. This RV park is closed during the off-season. The camping and tent areas also allow dogs. There is a dog walk area at the campground. Dogs are allowed in the camping cabins. Multiple dogs may be allowed.

Pagosa Springs

Elk Meadows River Resort
5360 E H 160
Pagosa Springs, CO
970-264-5482
Dogs of all sizes are allowed. There are no additional pet fees. Dogs may not be left unattended outside unless they will be quiet and well behaved, and they must be leashed and

cleaned up after. This is an RV and rental cabins park. This RV park is closed during the off-season. There is a dog walk area at the campground. Dogs are allowed in the camping cabins. Multiple dogs may be allowed.

Pueblo

Lake Pueblo
640 Reservoir Road
Pueblo, CO
719-561-9320
There are over 9,000 acres at this scenic park, 2 full service marinas, a swim beach/waterpark, miles of hiking trails, and a variety of land and water recreation. Dogs of all sizes are allowed at no additional fee. Dogs may not be left unattended, and they must be on no more than a 6 foot leash, and be cleaned up after. Dogs are not allowed on the swim beach. The camping and tent areas also allow dogs. There is a dog walk area at the campground. There are no water hookups at the campground. Multiple dogs may be allowed.

Pike and San Isabel National Forests
2840 Kachina Drive
Pueblo, CO
719-545-8737
This forest, with it's nearly 3 million acres, unique ecosystem, flora and fauna, is one of the most diverse forest in the U.S. Campgrounds are seasonal, however the park is open year round. Dogs of all sizes are allowed. There are no additional pet fees. Dogs are allowed on the trails. Dogs must be leashed and cleaned up after. This campground is closed during the off-season. The camping and tent areas also allow dogs. There is a dog walk area at the campground. There are no water hookups at the campground. Multiple dogs may be allowed.

Pueblo KOA
4131 I 25N
Pueblo, CO
719-542-2273
Dogs of all sizes are allowed. There are no additional pet fees. Dogs may not be left unattended, and they must be leashed and cleaned up after. The camping and tent areas also allow dogs. There is a dog walk area at the campground. Dogs are allowed in the camping cabins. Multiple dogs may be

allowed.

Pueblo South/Colorado City KOA
9040 I 25S
Pueblo, CO
719-676-3376
There can be up to 2 dogs of any size, or 3 small, at the tent and RV sites at no additional fee. There is only 1 dog up to 20 pounds allowed in the cabins for an additional fee of $7 per day. There is a pet waiver to sign at check in if the dog is one of the listed aggressive breeds. Dogs may not be left unattended, and they must be quiet, well behaved, leashed, and cleaned up after. Dogs may not be tied to trees, picnic tables, or other camp property. The camping and tent areas also allow dogs. There is a dog walk area at the campground. Dogs are allowed in the camping cabins.

Ridgeway

Ridgeway State Park
28555 H 550
Ridgeway, CO
970-626-5822
This park offers a sandy swim beach, a full service marina, and is known as a very accessible recreation area for people with disabilities. Dogs of all sizes are allowed at no additional fee for tent or RV sites. There is a $10 daily additional pet fee for the yurts. Dogs may not be left unattended outside, and they must be on no more than a 6 foot leash, and be cleaned up after. Dogs are not allowed in public swim areas, but they are allowed on the trails. The camping and tent areas also allow dogs. There is a dog walk area at the campground. Dogs are allowed in the camping cabins. 2 dogs may be allowed.

Rifle

Rifle Falls State Park
575 H 325
Rifle, CO
970-625-1607
Visitors will enjoy the unusual scenery and tropical feel of this park as a result of the waterfalls and the mist they create for vegetation. Dogs of all sizes are allowed at no additional fee. Dogs may not be left unattended, and they must be on no more than a 6 foot leash, and be cleaned up after. Dogs are not allowed on the swim beach or at Harvey Gap, but they are allowed on

the trails. The camping and tent areas also allow dogs. There is a dog walk area at the campground. Multiple dogs may be allowed.

Silverton

Silver Summit RV Park
640 Mineral Street
Silverton, CO
970-387-0240
Dogs of all sizes are allowed. There are no additional pet fees. Dogs may not be left unattended, and they must be quiet, leashed, and cleaned up after. This RV park is closed during the off-season. There is a dog walk area at the campground. Multiple dogs may be allowed.

Somerset

Paonai State Park
On H 133
Somerset, CO
970-921-5721
This small primitive park offers wildflowers in abundance and a small lake for recreation. There is no drinking water available here, so bring your own. Dogs of all sizes are allowed at no additional fee. Dogs may not be left unattended, and they must be leased and cleaned up after. Dogs are not allowed in public swim areas. Dogs are allowed on the trails. The camping and tent areas also allow dogs. There is a dog walk area at the campground. There are no electric or water hookups at the campground. Multiple dogs may be allowed.

Sterling

Jellystone Park
22018 H 6
Sterling, CO
970-522-2233
Dogs of all sizes are allowed. There are no additional pet fees. Dogs must be well behaved, quiet, leashed, and cleaned up after. For those on the road in the off season, they have electric only hook-ups. This RV park is closed during the off-season. The camping and tent areas also allow dogs. There is a dog walk area at the campground. 2 dogs may be allowed.

Strasburg

Denver East/Strasburg KOA

1312 Monroe
Strasburg, CO
303-622-9274
Dogs of all sizes are allowed, and there are no additional pet fees for tent or RV sites. There is a $4 per night per pet additional fee for the cabins. Dogs are greeted at check in with a dog biscuit. Dogs may not be left unattended at the cabins or outside, and they must be leashed and cleaned up after. The camping and tent areas also allow dogs. There is a dog walk area at the campground. Dogs are allowed in the camping cabins. There are special amenities given to dogs at this campground. Multiple dogs may be allowed.

Walden

North Park/Gould/Walden KOA
53337 H 14
Walden, CO
970-723-4310
Dogs of all sizes are allowed. There are no additional pet fees. Dogs may not be left unattended, and they must be leashed and cleaned up after. This RV park is closed during the off-season. The camping and tent areas also allow dogs. There is a dog walk area at the campground. Dogs are allowed in the camping cabins. Multiple dogs may be allowed.

Wellington

Fort Collins North/Wellington KOA
4821 E County Road 70/Owl Canyon Road
Wellington, CO
970-568-7486
Dogs of all sizes are allowed. There are no additional pet fees. Dogs must be leashed and cleaned up after. The camping and tent areas also allow dogs. There is a dog walk area at the campground. Dogs are allowed in the camping cabins. Multiple dogs may be allowed.

Westcliffe

Grape Creek RV Park
56491 H 69
Westcliffe, CO
719-783-2588
Dogs of all sizes are allowed. There are no additional pet fees. Dogs must be leashed and cleaned up after. There is only one dog friendly

cabin. This RV park is closed during the off-season. The camping and tent areas also allow dogs. There is a dog walk area at the campground. Dogs are allowed in the camping cabins. Multiple dogs may be allowed.

Connecticut Listings

Ashford

Brialee RV and Tent Park
174 Laurel Lane
Ashford, CT
860-429-8359
Dogs of all sizes are allowed. There are no additional pet fees. Dogs must be leashed and under your control at all times and must be cleaned up after. The camping and tent areas also allow dogs. There is a dog walk area at the campground. 2 dogs may be allowed.

Bozrah

Acron Acres Campground
135 Lake Road
Bozrah, CT
860-859-1020
Dogs of all sizes are allowed. There are no additional pet fees. Dogs must be quiet, well behaved, leashed and cleaned up after. There are some breed restrictions. The camping and tent areas also allow dogs. There is a dog walk area at the campground. 2 dogs may be allowed.

Odetah Campground
38 Bozrah Street Extension
Bozrah, CT
860-889-4144
Dogs of all sizes are allowed to stay in the campground but are not allowed to leave your camp site. There are no additional pet fees. Dogs must be well behaved, quiet, and kept leashed. There is a dog walk area at the campground. Multiple dogs may be allowed.

E Canaan

Lone Oak Campsites
360 Norfolk
E Canaan, CT

860-824-7051
Dogs of all sizes are allowed. There are no additional pet fees. Dogs must be leashed, cleaned up after, and have proof of rabies shots. There is a dog walk area at the campground. Multiple dogs may be allowed.

East Lyme

Aces High RV Park
301 Chesterfield Road
East Lyme, CT
860-739-8858
Well behaved dogs of all sizes are allowed. There are no additional pet fees. Dogs are not allowed in other people's sites and they also have a separate swim area for them. Dogs must be quiet, leashed and cleaned up after. There is a dog walk area at the campground. Multiple dogs may be allowed.

Killingly

Stateline Camp Resort
1639 Hartford Pike
Killingly, CT
860-774-3016
Dogs of all sizes are allowed, however some breeds are not. There is a $3 per night per pet additional fee. Dogs must be well behaved, quiet, leashed, and cleaned up after. Dogs are not to be left unattended. The camping and tent areas also allow dogs. There is a dog walk area at the campground. Multiple dogs may be allowed.

Lebanon

Water's Edge Family Campground
271 Leonard Bridge Road
Lebanon, CT
860-642-7470
Dogs of all sizes are allowed. There are no additional pet fees. Dogs must be leashed and cleaned up after. Dogs are allowed in the camping cabins. 2 dogs may be allowed.

Lisbon

Ross Hill Park
170 Ross Hill Road
Lisbon, CT
860-376-9606
Pets of all sizes are allowed. There are no additional pet fees. Dogs allowed on leash only, and fecal

matter MUST BE CLEANED UP IMMEDIATELY. Failure to pick up after your pet will result in eviction. Pets are not allowed in the swimming area. This RV park is closed during the off-season. The camping and tent areas also allow dogs. There is a dog walk area at the campground. 2 dogs may be allowed.

Litchfield

Hemlock Hill Camp Resort
118 Hemlock Hill Road
Litchfield, CT
860-567-2267
One dog of any size per site is the usual allowance, however two dogs are allowed if they are both under 25 pounds. Pit Bulls, Rottweilers, and some other breeds are not allowed. Dogs must have proof of rabies shots. The camping and tent areas also allow dogs. There is a dog walk area at the campground.

North Stonington

Highland Orchards Resort Park
118 Pendelton Hill Road
North Stonington, CT
860-599-5101
Small Dogs Only. Dogs of all sizes are allowed. There is no additional fee for one dog, however each dog thereafter is a $4 per night per pet additional fee. Dogs must have proof of rabies shots, be kept leashed, and cleaned up after. The camping and tent areas also allow dogs. There is a dog walk area at the campground. Multiple dogs may be allowed.

Old Mystic

Seaport Campgrounds
P.O. Box 104
Old Mystic, CT
860-536-4044
Dogs of all sizes are allowed. There is a $2 per night per pet additional fee, and there must be proof of current rabies and immunization shots. Dogs must be kept under your control. The camping and tent areas also allow dogs. There is a dog walk area at the campground. 2 dogs may be allowed.

Preston

Strawberry Park Resort

Campground
42 Pierce Road
Preston, CT
860-886-1944
Dogs of all sizes are allowed, but some breeds are not. There are no additional pet fees. Dogs must remain on your site and are not to be walked or carried around the campground. The camping and tent areas also allow dogs. Multiple dogs may be allowed.

Salem

Salem Farms Campground
39 Alexander Road
Salem, CT
860-859-2320
Dogs of all sizes are allowed. There are no additional pet fees. Dogs must be leashed, are not allowed to be on the grass areas, and must be cleaned up after. The camping and tent areas also allow dogs. There is a dog walk area at the campground. 2 dogs may be allowed.

Witch Meadow Lake Campground
139 Witch Meadow Road
Salem, CT
860-859-1542
Dogs of all sizes are allowed. There are no additional pet fees. Dogs may not be left unattended, and they must be leashed and cleaned up after. Dogs must be kept on the campsite or walked on the dog walk trail at the back of the campground. There are some breed restrictions. This RV park is closed during the off-season. The camping and tent areas also allow dogs. There is a dog walk area at the campground. Multiple dogs may be allowed.

Tolland

Del-Aire Campground
704 Shenipsit Road
Tolland, CT
860-875-8325
Dogs of all sizes are allowed. There are no additional pet fees. Dogs must be well behaved, quiet, leashed, and cleaned up after. Dogs may not be left on site unattended. The camping and tent areas also allow dogs. There is a dog walk area at the campground. Multiple dogs may be allowed.

Woodstock

Beaver Pines Campground
1728 H 198
Woodstock, CT
860-974-0110
Dogs of all sizes are allowed at no additional fee. Dogs may not be left unattended, and they must have current rabies and shot records. Dogs must be leashed and cleaned up after. There are some breed restrictions. This RV park is closed during the off-season. The camping and tent areas also allow dogs. There is a dog walk area at the campground. Multiple dogs may be allowed.

Delaware Listings

Bear

Lums Pond State Park
1068 Howell School Road
Bear, DE
302-368-6989
This park of over 1,700 acres with a 200 surface acre lake, offers sports facilities, and a variety of land and water recreation. Dogs of all sizes are allowed at no additional fee. Dogs may not be left unattended, and they must be quiet, be on no more than a 6 foot leash, and be cleaned up after. Dogs are not allowed in buildings, in picnic areas, or on the trails. However, just past this park on Buck's Jersey Road, there is an off leash training area for dogs. This campground is closed during the off-season. The camping and tent areas also allow dogs. There is a dog walk area at the campground. There are no water hookups at the campground. Multiple dogs may be allowed.

Felton

Killens Pond State Park
5025 Killens Pond Road
Felton, DE
302-284-3412
This resort type park features an all new water park, a variety of hiking trails, nature study, and land and water recreation. Dogs of all sizes are allowed at no additional fee. Dogs may not be left unattended, and they must be on no more than a 6 foot leash, and be cleaned up after. Dogs are not allowed in the buildings, but they are allowed on the

trails. The camping and tent areas also allow dogs. There is a dog walk area at the campground. Multiple dogs may be allowed.

Laurel

Trap Pond State Park
33587 Bald Cypress Lane
Laurel, DE
302-875-2392
Trap Pond State Park offers an opportunity to explore a wetland forest and its inhabitants on both land and water and a variety of recreational activities and pursuits. Dogs of all sizes are allowed at no additional fee. Dogs may not be left unattended, and they must be leashed and cleaned up after. Dogs are not allowed in buildings. This campground is closed during the off-season. The camping and tent areas also allow dogs. There is a dog walk area at the campground. Multiple dogs may be allowed.

Lewes

G and R Campground
4075 Gun and Rod Club Road
Houston, DE
302-398-8108
Dogs of all sizes are allowed, and there are no additional pet fees for the tent or RV sites. There is a $15 per night per pet additional fee for the cabin rentals, and there are only 2 pets per cabin allowed. Dogs must be quiet and well behaved. Dogs may not be left unattended, must be leashed, and cleaned up after. There are some breed restrictions. The camping and tent areas also allow dogs. There is a dog walk area at the campground. Dogs are allowed in the camping cabins.

Cape Henlopen State Park
42 Cape Henlopen Drive
Lewes, DE
302-645-2103
This scenic park offers hiking trails with historical and environmental interests, and an observation tower, as well as a number of year round recreational activities and pursuits. Dogs of all sizes are allowed at no additional fee. Dogs may not be left unattended, and they must be leashed and cleaned up after. Dogs are not allowed in public swim areas or in buildings. Dogs are allowed on the trails. This campground is closed during the

off-season. The camping and tent areas also allow dogs. There is a dog walk area at the campground. Multiple dogs may be allowed.

Tall Pines Camping Resort
29551 Persimmon Road
Lewes, DE
302-684-0300
Dogs of all sizes are allowed. There are no additional pet fees. Dogs must be quiet, well behaved, and are not to be left unattended. They must be leashed and cleaned up after. The camping and tent areas also allow dogs. There is a dog walk area at the campground. Multiple dogs may be allowed.

Millsboro

Holly Lake Campsites
32087 Hollly Lake Road
Millsboro, DE
302-945-3410
Dogs of all sizes are allowed. There are no additional pet fees. Dogs may not be left unattended outside and they must be quiet, well behaved, leashed and cleaned up after. Dogs are allowed on the trails. This RV park is closed during the off-season. The camping and tent areas also allow dogs. There is a dog walk area at the campground. Multiple dogs may be allowed.

Rehoboth Beach

Big Oaks Family Campground
35567 Big Oaks Lane
Rehoboth Beach, DE
302-645-6838
Dogs of all sizes are allowed in the campground area but not in the rentals. There are no additional pet fees. Dogs must be on a 6 foot or shorter leash and cleaned up after. The camping and tent areas also allow dogs. There is a dog walk area at the campground. Multiple dogs may be allowed.

Delaware Seashore State Park
130 Coastal H
Rehoboth Beach, DE
302-539-7202
This park, being on the coast, offers a wide variety of water related activities. Dogs of all sizes are allowed at no additional fee. Dogs may not be left unattended, and they must be on no more than a 6 foot leash, and be cleaned up after. Dogs are not allowed in public swim areas or buildings. Dogs are allowed on the

beach at the North end, at T-Box Road, Conquest Road, and the 3 Rs. The camping and tent areas also allow dogs. There is a dog walk area at the campground. Multiple dogs may be allowed.

Wilmington Area

Delaware Motel and RV Park
235 S. Dupont Highway
New Castle, DE
302-328-3114
Dogs of all sizes are allowed. There are no additional pet fees. Dogs must be well behaved and not left unattended at any time. There is a dog walk area at the campground. Multiple dogs may be allowed.

Florida Listings

Arcadia

Toby's Resort
3550 NE H 70
Arcadia, FL
800-307-0768
Dogs up to 35 pounds are allowed. There are no additional pet fees. Dogs must be leashed and cleaned up after. The camping and tent areas also allow dogs. There is a dog walk area at the campground. 2 dogs may be allowed.

Chattahoochee

Chattahoochee/Tallahassee W KOA
2309 Flat Circle Road
Chattahoochee, FL
850-442-6657
Dogs of all sizes are allowed. There are no additional pet fees. Dogs may not be left unattended outside, and they must be well behaved, leashed, and cleaned up after. There are some breed restrictions. The camping and tent areas also allow dogs. There is a dog walk area at the campground. Dogs are allowed in the camping cabins. Multiple dogs may be allowed.

Chipley

Falling Waters State Rec Area
1130 State Park Road

Chipley, FL
850-638-6130
Features of this park are the Sink Hole Trail that takes you along a boardwalk to Florida's highest waterfall, the butterfly garden, and interpretive programs held in their amphitheater. Well behaved dogs of all sizes are allowed at no additional fee. Dogs must have current rabies and shot records, be on no more than a 6 foot leash, and be cleaned up after. Dogs are not allowed in buildings, in the lake, or on the boardwalk to the waterfall. The camping and tent areas also allow dogs. There is a dog walk area at the campground. Multiple dogs may be allowed.

Clermont

Lake Louisa State Park
7305 H 27
Clermont, FL
352-394-3969
Lake Louisa has 6 lakes, is a part of a chain of 13 lakes connected by the Palatlakaha River, has over 20 miles of hiking trails, and a variety of land and water activities. Dogs of all sizes are allowed at no additional fee. Dogs must have current rabies and shot records, be on no more than a 6 foot leash, and be cleaned up after. Dogs are not allowed in or around buildings, but they are allowed on the trails. The camping and tent areas also allow dogs. There is a dog walk area at the campground. Multiple dogs may be allowed.

Crystal River

Rock Crusher Canyon Park
275 S Rock Crusher Road
Crystal River, FL
352-795-1313
Dogs of all sizes are allowed. There are no additional pet fees. Dogs must be leashed and cleaned up after. The camping and tent areas also allow dogs. There is a dog walk area at the campground. Multiple dogs may be allowed.

Cypress Gardens

Greenfield Village RV Park
1015 H 542W
Dundee, FL
863-439-7409
Dogs of all sizes are allowed. There are no additional pet fees. Dogs

may not be left unattended outside, and they must be leashed and cleaned up after. This is a 55 years or older park. There are some breed restrictions. There is a dog walk area at the campground. 2 dogs may be allowed.

Daytona Beach

Bulow Plantation RV Resort
3345 Old Kings Road S
Flagler Beach, FL
800-782-8569
Dogs of all sizes are allowed. There are no additional pet fees. Dogs must be quiet, well behaved, leashed, and cleaned up after. There are some breed restrictions. The camping and tent areas also allow dogs. There is a dog walk area at the campground. Multiple dogs may be allowed.

Daytona North RV Resort
1701 H 1
Ormond Beach, FL
877-277-8737
Dogs of all sizes are allowed. There are no additional pet fees. Dogs must be leashed and cleaned up after. The camping and tent areas also allow dogs. There is a dog walk area at the campground. Multiple dogs may be allowed.

Tomoka State Park
2099 N Beach Street
Ormond Beach, FL
386-676-4050
This park protects a variety of wildlife habitats and endangered species and over 160 bird species. It boasts a nature trail, a museum, and a variety of land and water recreation. Dogs of all sizes are allowed at no additional fee. Dogs may not be left unattended, and they must have current rabies and shot records. Dogs must be on no more than a 6 foot leash, and be cleaned up after. Dogs are not allowed in buildings or on the beach. Dogs are allowed on the trails. The camping and tent areas also allow dogs. There is a dog walk area at the campground. Multiple dogs may be allowed.

Destin

Camping on the Gulf
1005 Emerald Coast Parkway
Destin, FL
877-226-7485
Dogs of all sizes are allowed. There

are no additional pet fees. Dogs may not be left unattended outside, and they must be leashed and cleaned up after. There is a large fine levied for dogs on the beach. The camping and tent areas also allow dogs. There is a dog walk area at the campground. 2 dogs may be allowed.

Destin RV Beach Resort
362 Miramar Beach Drive
Destin, FL
877-737-3529
Dogs of all sizes are allowed. There are no additional pet fees. Dogs must be leashed and cleaned up after. The dogs may be walked on the grass just outside of the park. 2 dogs may be allowed.

Henderson Beach State Park
17000 Emerald Coast Parkway
Destin, FL
850-837-7550
Land and water recreation is offered here with about 6000 feet of white sandy beaches, a boardwalk, and nature trails. Quiet and well behaved dogs of all sizes are allowed at no additional fee. Dogs may not be left unattended at any time, and they must have current rabies and shot records. Dogs must be on no more than a 6 foot leash, and be cleaned up after. Dogs are not allowed in buildings, on the beach, or on the Boardwalk. Dogs are allowed on all the trails. The camping and tent areas also allow dogs. There is a dog walk area at the campground. Multiple dogs may be allowed.

Estero

Koreshan State Historic Site
Corner of H 41 and Corkscrew Road
Estero, FL
239-992-0311
Guided or self-guided tours are offered here as well as a variety of recreational pursuits. Dogs of all sizes are allowed at no additional fee. Dogs may not be left unattended for more than 15 minutes if outside, and they must have current rabies and shot records. Dogs must be on no more than a 6 foot leash, and be cleaned up after. Dogs are not allowed in buildings, but they are allowed on the trails. The camping and tent areas also allow dogs. There is a dog walk area at the campground. Multiple dogs may be allowed.

Fernandina Beach

Fort Clinch State Park
2601 Atlantic Avenue
Fernandina Beach, FL
904-277-7274
This park is home to one of the most well preserved 19th century forts in America, and offers deep woods, white sandy beaches, a living history program, and a variety of recreation and trails. Dogs of all sizes are allowed at no additional fee. Dogs may not be left unattended, and they must have current rabies and shot records. Dogs must be on no more than a 6 foot leash, and be cleaned up after. Dogs are not allowed in buildings or on the beaches, but they are allowed on the trails. The camping and tent areas also allow dogs. There is a dog walk area at the campground. Multiple dogs may be allowed.

Flagler Beach

Beverly Beach Campground
2816 N Ocean Shore Blvd
Flagler Beach, FL
800-255-2706
Dogs of all sizes are allowed. There are no additional pet fees. Dogs must be quiet, leashed, and cleaned up after. Dogs may not be left unattended outside. They ask that dogs be walked just outside of the park, and they are allowed at the beach. The camping and tent areas also allow dogs. Multiple dogs may be allowed.

Gamble Rogers Memorial State Recreation Area
3100 S A1A (Ocean Shore Blvd)
Flagler Beach, FL
386-517-2086
This park is tucked between the Intracoastal Waterway and the Atlantic Ocean with the beach being the popular draw, and there is a nature trail and boat ramp also. Dogs of all sizes are allowed at no additional fee. Dogs may not be left unattended, and they must have current rabies and shot records. Dogs must be on no more than a 6 foot leash, and be cleaned up after. Dogs are not allowed in buildings or on the beach, but they are allowed on the trails. The camping and tent areas also allow dogs. There is a dog walk area at the campground. Multiple dogs may be allowed.

Fort Myers

Shady Acres RV Travel Park
19370 S Tamiami
Fort Myers, FL
888-634-4080
Dogs up to 35 pounds are allowed. There are no additional pet fees. Dogs may not be left unattended outside, and they must be leashed and cleaned up after. There are some breed restrictions. The camping and tent areas also allow dogs. There is a dog walk area at the campground. 2 dogs may be allowed.

Indian Creek RV Resort
17340 San Carlos Blvd
Fort Myers Beach, FL
800-828-6992
Dogs of all sizes are allowed. There are no additional pet fees. Dogs may not be left unattended outside, and they must be leashed and cleaned up after. There are some breed restrictions. There is a dog walk area at the campground. 2 dogs may be allowed.

Hobe Sound

Jonathan Dickinson State Park
16450 SE Federal H (H 1)
Hobe Sound, FL
772-546-2771
This park is Florida's first federally designated Wild and Scenic River, and is home to abundant wildlife in 13 natural communities. Dogs of all sizes are allowed at no additional fee. Dogs may not be left unattended, and they must have current rabies and shot records. Dogs must be on no more than a 6 foot leash, and be cleaned up after. Dogs are not allowed in buildings or any public swimming areas. The camping and tent areas also allow dogs. There is a dog walk area at the campground. Multiple dogs may be allowed.

Holt

Blackwater River State Park
7720 Deaton Bridge Road
Holt, FL
850-983-5363
This park was certified as a Registered State Natural Feature for their preserving and representation of the natural history of Florida. Dogs of all sizes are allowed at no additional fee. Dogs may not be left

unattended, and they must have current rabies and shot records. Dogs must be on no more than a 6 foot leash, and be cleaned up after. Dogs are not allowed in buildings or at the beaches. Dogs are allowed on the trails, including the Chain O'Lakes Trail. The camping and tent areas also allow dogs. There is a dog walk area at the campground. Multiple dogs may be allowed.

Jacksonville

Little Talbot Island State Park
12157 Heckscher Drive
Jacksonville, FL
904-251-2320
This park has scenic, historical, biological, and geological sites to explore. They have introduced a new interpretive program of a self-guided auto tour of the area. Dogs of all sizes are allowed at no additional fee. Dogs may not be left unattended, and they must have current rabies and shot records. Dogs must be on no more than a 6 foot leash, and be cleaned up after. Dogs are not allowed in buildings, on beaches, or in the waterways. Dogs are allowed on the trails. The camping and tent areas also allow dogs. There is a dog walk area at the campground. Multiple dogs may be allowed.

Flamingo Lake RV Resort
3640 Newcomb Road
N Jacksonville, FL
904-766-0672
Dogs of all sizes are allowed. There are no additional pet fees. Dogs may not be left unattended outside, and they must be leashed and cleaned up after. There are some breed restrictions. There is a dog walk area at the campground. Multiple dogs may be allowed.

Key West

Boyd's Key West Campground
6401 Maloney Avenue
Key West, FL
305-294-1465
Dogs of all sizes are allowed. There are no additional pet fees. Dogs may not be left unattended outside, and they must be leashed and cleaned up after. There are some breed restrictions. The camping and tent areas also allow dogs. There is a dog walk area at the campground. Multiple dogs may be allowed.

Keys

Sunshine Key RV Resort
38801 Overseas H
Big Pine Key, FL
305-872-2217
Dogs of all sizes are allowed. There are no additional pet fees. Dogs must be leashed and cleaned up after. The camping and tent areas also allow dogs. There is a dog walk area at the campground. Multiple dogs may be allowed.

John Pennekamp Coral Reef State Park
H 1, MM 102.5
Key Largo, FL
305-451-1202
This campground is located at Americas 1st undersea park where they offer boat tours, rentals, guided nature walks, and 47 full service tent and RV sites with restrooms and hot showers. Dogs are not allowed in buildings or on the boat tours. Dogs of all sizes are allowed at no additional fee. Dogs may not be left unattended outside the camping unit, and they must be quiet, well behaved, leashed and cleaned up after. Dogs are not allowed at this park for day use because they may not be left in vehicles in the parking lot. The camping and tent areas also allow dogs. There is a dog walk area at the campground. Multiple dogs may be allowed.

Sugarloaf Key/Key West KOA
251 H 939
Sugarloaf Key, FL
305-745-3549
Dogs of all sizes are allowed. There are no additional pet fees. Dogs may not be left unattended outside, and they must be leashed and cleaned up after. The camping and tent areas also allow dogs. There is a dog walk area at the campground. Dogs are allowed in the camping cabins. Multiple dogs may be allowed.

Lakeland

Sanlan Ranch Campground
3929 H 98S
Lakeland, FL
863-665-1726
Dogs of all sizes are allowed. There is $.50 per night per pet additional fee. Dogs may not be left unattended outside, and they must be leashed and cleaned up after.

Dogs must stay out of the water because of alligators. The camping and tent areas also allow dogs. There is a dog walk area at the campground. 2 dogs may be allowed.

Live Oak

Suwannee River State Park
20185 County Road 132
Live Oak, FL
386-362-2746
Rich in scenery, history, and recreation, this park offers 5 different trails and panoramic views of the great river. Dogs of all sizes are allowed at no additional fee. Dogs may not be left unattended, and they must have current rabies and shot records. Dogs must be on no more than a 6 foot leash, and be cleaned up after. Dogs are not allowed in buildings or public swim areas, but they are allowed on the trails. The camping and tent areas also allow dogs. There is a dog walk area at the campground. Multiple dogs may be allowed.

Madison

Jellystone Park
1051 SW Old St. Augustine Road
Madison, FL
800-347-0174
Dogs of all sizes are allowed. There are no additional pet fees. Dogs must be leashed and cleaned up after. Dogs are not allowed in public areas or the beach. The camping and tent areas also allow dogs. There is a dog walk area at the campground. Multiple dogs may be allowed.

Marianna

Florida Caverns State Park
3345 Caverns Road (H 166)
Marianna, FL
850-482-9598
As well as having a variety of year round recreational activities, this park offers the only guided cave tours in Florida. Dogs of all sizes are allowed at no additional fee. Dogs may not be left unattended, and they must have current rabies and shot records. Dogs must be on no more than a 6 foot leash, and be cleaned up after. Dogs are not allowed in buildings, any public swimming areas, or on the cave tours. The camping and tent areas also allow

dogs. There is a dog walk area at the campground. Multiple dogs may be allowed.

Melbourne Beach

Sebastian Inlet State Park
9700 S A1A
Melbourne Beach, FL
321-984-4852
This park offers premier saltwater fishing, 3 miles of beaches, a boat dock, and a variety of land and water recreation. Dogs of all sizes are allowed at no additional fee. Dogs may not be left unattended, and they must have current rabies and shot records. Dogs must be on no more than a 6 foot leash, and be cleaned up after. Dogs are not allowed in buildings, on the beaches, on the jetty, or catwalks. Dogs are allowed on the trails, and there is a small area at the cove where they may go in the water as long as they are still on lead. The camping and tent areas also allow dogs. There is a dog walk area at the campground. Multiple dogs may be allowed.

Naples

Collier-Seminole State Park
20200 E Tamiami Trail
Naples, FL
239-394-3397
This park displays wildlife and vegetation typical of the Everglades, a forest of tropical trees, and is a National Historic Mechanical Engineering Landmark site. Dogs of all sizes are allowed at no additional fee. Dogs may not be left unattended outside, and they must have current rabies and shot records. Dogs must be on no more than a 6 foot leash, and be cleaned up after. Dogs are not allowed in buildings, on canoe rentals, or on any of the trails. Dogs may be walked around the camp area. The camping and tent areas also allow dogs. There is a dog walk area at the campground. Multiple dogs may be allowed.

Hitching Post RV Resort
100 Barefoot Williams Road
Naples, FL
239-774-1259
Dogs of all sizes are allowed. There are no additional pet fees. Dogs must be quiet, leashed, and cleaned up after. This RV park is closed during the off-season. The camping and tent areas also allow dogs. There is a dog walk area at the

campground. Multiple dogs may be allowed.

Lake San Marino RV Resort
1000 Wiggins Pass
Naples, FL
239-597-4202
Dogs of all sizes are allowed. There are no additional pet fees. Dogs may not be tied up or left unattended outside, and they must be leashed and cleaned up after. They do have an off lead dog park on site. This a 55 years or older park. There are some breed restrictions. There is a dog walk area at the campground. There are special amenities given to dogs at this campground. 2 dogs may be allowed.

North Fort Myers

North Fort Myers RV Resort (Pioneer Village)
7974 Samville Road
North Fort Myers, FL
239-543-3303
Dogs of all sizes are allowed. There are no additional pet fees. Dogs must be leashed and cleaned up after. The camping and tent areas also allow dogs. There is a dog walk area at the campground. Multiple dogs may be allowed.

Ocala

Silver River State Park
1425 NE 58th Avenue
Ocala, FL
352-236-7148
This park has dozens of springs, 15 miles of trails, 14 distinct natural communities, a pioneer cracker village, the Silver River Museum and an Environmental Education Center. Dogs of all sizes are allowed at no additional fee. Dogs may not be left unattended, and they must have current rabies and shot records. Dogs must be on no more than a 6 foot leash, and be cleaned up after. Dogs are not allowed in or around any buildings, and dogs should not be down by the river because of alligators. The camping and tent areas also allow dogs. There is a dog walk area at the campground. Multiple dogs may be allowed.

Ochopee

Big Cypress National Preserve
521005 Tamiami Trail E/ H 41
(Vistor's Center)
Ochopee, FL
239-695-2000
This park is known for it's biological diversity and provides a wide variety of scenic, biological, and geological sites to explore in addition to the recreational pursuits. Dogs are allowed at no additional fee. Dogs may not be left unattended, and they must be leashed and cleaned up after. Dogs are not allowed in the back country or on the boardwalks. The camping and tent areas also allow dogs. There is a dog walk area at the campground. There are no water hookups at the campground. Multiple dogs may be allowed.

Big Cypress National Preserve
33100 Tamiami Trail East
Ochopee, FL
239-695-1201
This recreational paradise offers day use, camping, canoeing, kayaking, hiking, bird-watching opportunities, interpretive programs, and self guided nature walks. Dogs of all sizes are allowed for no additional fee. Dogs must be leashed at all times and cleaned up after. Dogs are allowed anywhere in the front country and the campgrounds, but they are not allowed on trails or on any of the boardwalks. The camping and tent areas also allow dogs. There is a dog walk area at the campground. There are no water hookups at the campgrounds. 2 dogs may be allowed.

Orange City

Blue Spring State Park
2100 W French Avenue
Orange City, FL
386-775-3663
Blue Spring, a scenic recreation area, is also a designated manatee refuge because the warm waters in winter create a perfect habitat for the growing population of West Indian Manatees. Dogs of all sizes are allowed at no additional fee. Dogs may not be left unattended for more than 30 minutes at a time, and they must have current rabies and shot records. Dogs must be on no more than a 6 foot leash, and be cleaned up after. Dogs are not allowed in buildings or on the beaches. Dogs are allowed on the trails. The camping and tent areas also allow dogs. There is a dog walk area at the campground. Multiple dogs may be

allowed.

Deland/Orange City KOA
1440 E Minnesota Avenue
Orange City, FL
386-775-3996
Dogs of all sizes are allowed. There are no additional pet fees. Dogs may not be left unattended, and they must be leashed and cleaned up after. There are some breed restrictions. The camping and tent areas also allow dogs. There is a dog walk area at the campground. Multiple dogs may be allowed.

Orange Lake

Grand Lake RV & Golf Resort
4555 W H 318
Orange Lake, FL
352-591-3474
Dogs of all sizes are allowed. There are no additional pet fees. Dogs must be leashed when walking around the resort and cleaned up after, but may be off lead on own site if well behaved and under voice command. The camping and tent areas also allow dogs. There is a dog walk area at the campground. Multiple dogs may be allowed.

Orlando

Wekiwa Springs State Park
1800 Wekiwa Circle
Apopka, FL
407-884-2008
There are many water and land activities year round at this park, and they have interpretive programs at their amphitheater, a nature center, and 13 miles of multi-use trails. Dogs of all sizes are allowed at no additional fee. Dogs may not be left unattended, and they must have current rabies and shot records. Dogs must be on no more than a 6 foot leash, and be cleaned up after. Dogs are not allowed in buildings, at the beach, the springs, the top of the slope, or on the boardwalk trails. Dogs are allowed on the other trails. The camping and tent areas also allow dogs. There is a dog walk area at the campground. Multiple dogs may be allowed.

Florida Camp Inn
48504 H 27
Davenport, FL
863-424-2494
Dogs of all sizes are allowed. There are no additional pet fees. Dogs may not be left unattended, and they must

be leashed and cleaned up after. The camping and tent areas also allow dogs. There is a dog walk area at the campground. Multiple dogs may be allowed.

Orlando SW/Fort Summit KOA
2525 Frontage Road
Davenport, FL
863-424-1880
Small Dogs Only. Dogs of all sizes are allowed. There are no additional pet fees. Dogs may not be left unattended outside, and they must be well behaved, leashed, and cleaned up after. There are some breed restrictions. The camping and tent areas also allow dogs. There is a dog walk area at the campground. Multiple dogs may be allowed.

Encore Tropical Palms
2650 Holiday Trail
Kissimmee, FL
800-647-2567
Dogs of all sizes are allowed. There are no additional pet fees. Dogs must be quiet, well behaved, leashed, and cleaned up after. There is a dog walk area at the campground. Multiple dogs may be allowed.

Kissimmee KOA
2643 Happy Camper Place
Kissimmee, FL
407-396-2400
Dogs of all sizes are allowed. There are no additional pet fees. Dogs may not be left unattended outside, and they must be quiet, leashed, and cleaned up after. The camping and tent areas also allow dogs. There is a dog walk area at the campground. Multiple dogs may be allowed.

Orlando SE/Lake Whippoorwill KOA
12345 Narcoossee Road
Orlando, FL
407-277-5075
Dogs of all sizes are allowed. There are no additional pet fees. Dogs may not be left unattended, and they must be leashed and cleaned up after. The camping and tent areas also allow dogs. There is a dog walk area at the campground.

Panama City Beach

Emerald Coast RV Beach Resort
1957 Allison Avenue
Panama City Beach, FL

800-232-2478
Dogs of all sizes are allowed. There are no additional pet fees. Dogs may not be left unattended outside, and they must be leashed and cleaned up after. Dogs are not allowed in any of the buildings. There are some breed restrictions. There is a dog walk area at the campground. 2 dogs may be allowed.

Raccoon River Campground
12209 Hutchison Blvd
Panama City Beach, FL
877-234-0181
Dogs of all sizes are allowed. There are no additional pet fees. Dogs must be leashed and cleaned up after. There are some breed restrictions. There is a dog walk area at the campground. Multiple dogs may be allowed.

Port Orange

Daytona Beach Campground
4601 Clyde Morris Blvd
Port Orange, FL
386-761-2663
Dogs of all sizes are allowed. There are no additional pet fees. Dogs may not be left unattended outside or in tents, and they must be quiet, leashed, and cleaned up after. There is a dog walk area just outside of the park. There are some breed restrictions. The camping and tent areas also allow dogs. Multiple dogs may be allowed.

Riddick

Encore RV Resort
16905 NW H 225
Riddick, FL
352-591-1723
Dogs of all sizes are allowed. There are no additional pet fees. Dogs may not be left unattended outside, and they must be leashed and cleaned up after. The camping and tent areas also allow dogs. There is a dog walk area at the campground. Multiple dogs may be allowed.

Sebring

Buttonwood Bay RV Resort
10001 H 27S
Sebring, FL
863-655-1122
Dogs of all sizes are allowed. There are no additional pet fees. Dogs must be leashed and cleaned up after. There are some breed

restrictions. There is a dog walk area at the campground. 2 dogs may be allowed.

Highlands Hammock State Park
5931 Hammock Road
Sebring, FL
863-386-6094
This park offers a variety of recreational pursuits, nine trails, special events, and an elevated boardwalk that traverses an old-growth cypress swamp. Dogs of all sizes are allowed at no additional fee. Dogs may not be left unattended, and they must have current rabies and shot records. Dogs must be on no more than a 6 foot leash, and be cleaned up after. Dogs are not allowed in buildings or on any of the elevated boardwalk trails. Dogs are allowed on the other trails. The camping and tent areas also allow dogs. There is a dog walk area at the campground. Multiple dogs may be allowed.

Silver Springs

Ocala National Forest
17147 E H 40
Silver Springs, FL
352-625-2520
This National forest offers interesting geological and historical sites to explore, a wide abundance of land and water recreation, and a variety of trails, including a portion of the Florida National Scenic Trail. Dogs of all sizes are allowed at no additional fee. Dogs may not be left unattended, they must have current rabies and shot records, be on no more than a 6 foot leash, and be cleaned up after. Dogs are not allowed in public swim areas, buildings, or any day use areas. Dogs are allowed on all the trails except for the short interpretive trails. The camping and tent areas also allow dogs. There is a dog walk area at the campground. Multiple dogs may be allowed.

Sopchoppy

Ochlockonee River State Park
429 State Park Road
Sopchoppy, FL
850-962-2771
This park is where the Ochlockonee and Dead rivers intersect and flow into the Gulf of Mexico. This allows a variety of year round recreation including both freshwater and saltwater fishing. Dogs of all sizes

are allowed at no additional fee. Dogs may not be left unattended outside at any time, and can only be left in your camping unit for no more than 30 minutes. Dogs must have current rabies and shot records, be on no more than a 6 foot leash, and be cleaned up after. Dogs are not allowed in buildings, in swim areas, or in the water. Dogs are allowed on the trails. The camping and tent areas also allow dogs. There is a dog walk area at the campground. Multiple dogs may be allowed.

South Florida

Juno RV Park
900 Juno Ocean Walk
Juno Beach, FL
561-622-7500
Dogs of all sizes are allowed. There is a $3 per night per pet additional fee. Dogs must be friendly, well behaved, leashed, and cleaned up after. There is a dog walk area at the campground. Multiple dogs may be allowed.

Paradise Island RV Resort
2121 NW 29th Court
Oakland Park, FL
954-485-1150
Dogs of all sizes are allowed. There are no additional pet fees. Dogs may not be left unattended outside at any time, and they must be well behaved, leashed, and cleaned up after. There is also a Bark Park about 20 minutes from the resort. There are some breed restrictions. There is a dog walk area at the campground. Multiple dogs may be allowed.

Highland Woods
850/900 NE 48th Street
Pompano Beach, FL
866-340-0649
Dogs of all sizes are allowed. There are no additional pet fees. Dogs may not be left unattended, and they must be leashed and cleaned up after. There is a dog walk area at the campground. Multiple dogs may be allowed.

Space Coast

Space Coast RV Resort
820 Barns Blvd
Rockledge, FL
321-636-2873
Dogs up to 35 pounds are allowed. There are no additional pet fees. Dogs must be walked in designated

areas only. Dogs may not be left unattended outside, and must be leashed and cleaned up after. The camping and tent areas also allow dogs. There is a dog walk area at the campground. 2 dogs may be allowed.

St Augustine

Anastasia State Park
1340-A A1A South
St Augustine, FL
904-461-2033
This park houses natural and cultural treasures with the beauty and serenity of the beaches, trails, and an archaeological site to dig in. Dogs of all sizes are allowed at no additional fee. Dogs may not be left unattended for more than 30 minutes, and they must have current rabies and shot records. Dogs must be on no more than a 6 foot leash, and be cleaned up after. Dogs are not allowed in buildings or on the beaches. Dogs are allowed on the trails. The camping and tent areas also allow dogs. There is a dog walk area at the campground. Multiple dogs may be allowed.

Anastasia State Park Campgrounds
Anastasia Park Drive
St Augustine, FL
904-461-2033
This campsite offers electric and water hookups at each camp site. RVs under 40 feet can be accommodated. Pets are allowed at the campground, in day use areas and on the 1/2 mile nature trail and the old quarry walk. Pets are not allowed on the beach, in playgrounds, bathing areas, cabins, park buildings, or concession facilities. Pets cannot be tied to trees, tables, bushes, or shelter facilities. Dogs tied at a campsite cannot be left unattended for more than 30 minutes. Dogs must be on a 6 foot or less leash and people are required to clean up after their pets. During the park's quiet hours, usually from 11pm to 8am, your pets must be inside your camping unit. To get there from I-95, take exit 311 (old exit 94). Go east on State Road 207. Turn right on State Road 312. Turn left on A1A. Go about 1.5 miles north to the main park entrance, which is on the right after your pass The Surf Station.

St. Augustine Beach KOA

525 West Pope Road
St Augustine, FL
904-471-3113
This campground is located on Anastasia Island. Both RV and tent sites are available. Campground amenities include a year round swimming pool, fishing, bicycle rentals, maximum length pull through of 70 feet, Cable TV, modem dataport, and 50 amp service available. Pets are welcome at the campground but not in the cabins. There is no extra pet fee. This KOA has a dog walk area. The campground is open year round.

Stagecoach RV Park
2711 County Road 208
St Augustine, FL
904-824-2319
Dogs of all sizes are allowed. There are no additional pet fees. Dogs must be leashed and cleaned up after. It is suggested to book 8 to 12 months in advance for the winter months. There are some breed restrictions. There is a dog walk area at the campground. Multiple dogs may be allowed.

St James City

Fort Myers/Pine Island KOA
5120 Stringfellow Road
St James City, FL
239-283-2415
Dogs of all sizes are allowed. There is a $5 per night per pet additional fee. Dogs may not be left unattended outside, and only inside if they will be quiet and well behaved. Dogs must be leashed and cleaned up after. The camping and tent areas also allow dogs. There is a dog walk area at the campground. Dogs are allowed in the camping cabins. Multiple dogs may be allowed.

Tallahassee

Apalachicola National Forest
11152 NW State Road 20
Tallahassee, FL
850-643-2282
This National Forest offers a wide variety of year round land and water recreation, interpretive exhibits, and 85 miles of various types of trails. Dogs of all sizes are allowed at no additional fee. Dogs may not be left unattended, and they must have current rabies and shot records. Dogs must be on no more than a 6 foot leash, and be cleaned up after in

the camp area. Dogs are allowed on the trails. The camping and tent areas also allow dogs. There is a dog walk area at the campground. There are no water hookups at the campground. Multiple dogs may be allowed.

Big Oak RV Park
4024 N Monroe Street
Tallahassee, FL
850-562-4660
Dogs of all sizes are allowed. There are no additional pet fees. Dogs must be quiet, well behaved, leashed, and cleaned up after. There is a dog walk area at the campground. Multiple dogs may be allowed.

Tampa Bay

Horseshoe Cove RV Resort
5100 60th Street & Caruso Road
Bradenton, FL
941-758-5335
Dogs up to about 75 pounds are allowed. There are no additional fees. Dogs must be leashed and cleaned up after. There are some breed restrictions. There is a dog walk area at the campground. 2 dogs may be allowed.

Lake Manatee State Park
20007 H 64E
Bradenton, FL
941-741-3028
This park, set along 3 miles of lake shoreline, offers both land and water recreation. Well behaved dogs of all sizes are allowed at no additional fee. Dogs may not be left unattended for more than 30 minutes at a time, and they must have current rabies and shot records. Dogs must be on no more than a 6 foot leash, and be cleaned up after. Dogs are not allowed in buildings, public swimming areas, or by the boat ramps. Dogs are allowed on the trails. The camping and tent areas also allow dogs. There is a dog walk area at the campground. Multiple dogs may be allowed.

Sarasota North Resort
800 K Road
Bradenton, FL
800-678-2131
Dogs of all sizes are allowed. There are no additional pet fees. Dogs must be leashed and cleaned up after. The camping and tent areas also allow dogs. There is a dog

walk area at the campground. Multiple dogs may be allowed.

Oscar Scherer State Park
1843 S Tamiami Trail
Osprey, FL
941-483-5956
Special events, campfire programs, guided tours, and 15 miles of trails add to the year round recreation offered here. Dogs of all sizes are allowed at designated pet sites for no additional fee. Dogs may not be left unattended, and they must have current rabies and shot records. Dogs must be leashed, and cleaned up after. Dogs are not allowed by the creek, but they are allowed on the trails. The camping and tent areas also allow dogs. There is a dog walk area at the campground. Multiple dogs may be allowed.

Clearwater/Tarpon Springs KOA
37061 H 19N
Palm Harbor, FL
727-937-8412
Dogs of all sizes are allowed. There are no additional pet fees. Dogs may not be left unattended outside, and they must be well behaved, leashed, and cleaned up after. There are some breed restrictions. There is a dog walk area at the campground. Dogs are allowed in the camping cabins. 2 dogs may be allowed.

Thonotosassa

Hillsborough River State Park
15402 H 301 N
Thonotosassa, FL
813-987-6771
Take a tour of a replica of an 1837 fort from the Second Seminole War, walk The Wetlands Restoration Trail, or enjoy the variety of land and water recreation at this park. Dogs of all sizes are allowed at no additional fee. Dogs may not be left unattended, and they must have current rabies and shot records. Dogs are not allowed in buildings, at the pool, or on canoe rentals. Dogs are allowed on the trails but they must be in designated dog areas at all times. The camping and tent areas also allow dogs. There is a dog walk area at the campground. Multiple dogs may be allowed.

White Springs

Stephen Foster Folk Culture Center State Park

P. O. Drawer G/ US 41 N
White Springs, FL
386-397-2733
This beautiful recreational nature park offers a museum, a Craft Square, miles of trails, and special events throughout the year. Dogs of all sizes are allowed at no additional fee. Dogs may not be left unattended, and they must have current rabies and shot records. Dogs must be on no more than a 6 foot leash, and be cleaned up after. Dogs are not allowed in buildings, but they are allowed on the trails. The camping and tent areas also allow dogs. There is a dog walk area at the campground. Multiple dogs may be allowed.

Suwannee Valley Campground
786 N W Street
White Springs, FL
866-397-1667
Dogs of all sizes are allowed, and there are no additional pet fees for tent or RV sites. There is a $50 one time pet fee for cabins. Dogs must have up to date shot records, and be leashed and cleaned up after. The camping and tent areas also allow dogs. There is a dog walk area at the campground. Dogs are allowed in the camping cabins. 2 dogs may be allowed.

Winterhaven

East Haven RV Park
4320 Dundee Road
Winterhaven, FL
863-324-2624
One dog of any size is allowed. There are no additional pet fees. Dogs may not be left unattended, and they must be leashed and cleaned up after. There are some breed restrictions. The camping and tent areas also allow dogs. There is a dog walk area at the campground.

Georgia Listings

Acworth

Holiday Harbor
5989 Groover's Landing
Acworth, GA
770-974-2575
Dogs of all sizes are allowed. There are no additional pet fees. Dogs

must be leashed and cleaned up after. This is an RV only park with cabin rentals, but there is only one pet friendly cabin. The camping and tent areas also allow dogs. There is a dog walk area at the campground. Dogs are allowed in the camping cabins. Multiple dogs may be allowed.

Adairsville

Harvest Moon RV Park
1001 Poplar Springs Road
Adairsville, GA
770-773-7320
Dogs of all sizes are allowed. There are no additional pet fees. Dogs may not be left unattended outside, and they must be leashed and cleaned up after. There are some breed restrictions. There is a dog walk area at the campground. 2 dogs may be allowed.

Appling

Mistletoe State Park
3723 Mistletoe Road
Appling, GA
706-541-0321
This 1,920 acre peninsula park on a 7,200 acre lake, offers a wide variety of land and water activities and recreation. Dogs of all sizes are allowed at no additional fee. Dogs may not be left unattended, and they must be leashed and cleaned up after. Dogs are not allowed around the cabin areas, however, they are allowed on the trails. The camping and tent areas also allow dogs. There is a dog walk area at the campground. Multiple dogs may be allowed.

Atlanta

Stone Mountain Park
H 78E
Stone Mountain, GA
800-385-9807
Dogs of all sizes are allowed. There are no additional pet fees. Dogs are not allowed on the laser lawn, walk up trails, posted areas, nor at any of the attractions or special events. Dogs may not be left unattended, and they must be leashed and cleaned up after. The camping and tent areas also allow dogs. There is a dog walk area at the campground. Multiple dogs may be allowed.

Atlanta Area

Brookwood RV Park
1031 Wylie Road SE
Marietta, GA
877-727-5787
Dogs of all sizes are allowed. There are no additional pet fees. Dogs must be leashed and cleaned up after. There is a dog walk area at the campground. Multiple dogs may be allowed.

Atlanta South RV Resort
281 Mount Olive Road
McDonough, GA
770-957-2610
Dogs of all sizes are allowed. There are no additional pet fees. Dogs must be leashed and cleaned up after. The camping and tent areas also allow dogs. There is a dog walk area at the campground. Multiple dogs may be allowed.

Augusta

Flynn's Inn Camping Village
3746 Peach Orchard Road
Augusta, GA
706-798-6912
Dogs up to 25 pounds are allowed. There are no additional pet fees. Dogs may not be left unattended outside, and they must be leashed and cleaned up after. There is a dog walk area at the campground. 2 dogs may be allowed.

Blairsville

Trackrock Campground and Cabins
4887 Trackrock Camp Road
Blairsville, GA
706-745-2420
Dogs of all sizes are allowed. There are no additional pet fees. Dogs must be quiet, leashed, and cleaned up after. The camping and tent areas also allow dogs. There is a dog walk area at the campground. Multiple dogs may be allowed.

Vogel State Park
7485 Vogel State Park Road
Blairsville, GA
706-745-2628
This 233 acre park with a 20 acre lake is one of the oldest and most popular parks in the state. It offers a museum, 17 miles of hiking trails with access to the Appalachian Trail nearby, and a variety of land and water recreation. Dogs of all sizes

are allowed at no additional fee. Dogs may not be left unattended, and they must be leashed and cleaned up after. Dogs are not allowed in public swim areas or in buildings. Dogs are allowed on the trails. The camping and tent areas also allow dogs. There is a dog walk area at the campground. Multiple dogs may be allowed.

Brunswick

Blythe Island Regional Park
6616 Blythe Island H (H 303)
Brunswick, GA
912-279-2812
This is a marina park that is close to other hydro attractions and offers a variety of land and water recreation. Dogs of all sizes are allowed at no additional fee. Dogs may not be left unattended, and they must be leashed and cleaned up after. Dogs are not allowed on the beaches or in buildings. Dogs are allowed on the trails. The camping and tent areas also allow dogs. There is a dog walk area at the campground. Multiple dogs may be allowed.

Calhoun

Calhoun KOA
2523 Redbud Road NE
Calhoun, GA
706-629-7511
Dogs of all sizes are allowed. There are no additional pet fees. Dogs may not be left unattended outside or in the cabins, and they must be quiet, leashed, and cleaned up after. The camping and tent areas also allow dogs. There is a dog walk area at the campground. Dogs are allowed in the camping cabins. Multiple dogs may be allowed.

Cartersville

Allatoona Landing Marine Resort
24 Allatoona Landing Road
Cartersville, GA
770-974-6089
Dogs of all sizes are allowed. There are no additional pet fees. Dogs may not be left unattended outside, and they must be leashed and cleaned up after. There are some breed restrictions. The camping and tent areas also allow dogs. There is a dog walk area at the campground. Multiple dogs may be allowed.

Red Top Mountain State Park

50 Lodge Road
Cartersville, GA
770-975-4226
This popular park of 1,562 acres along the 12,000-acre Lake Allatoona, offers over 15 miles of hiking trails, an interpretive center, and a wide variety of land and water recreation. Dogs of all sizes are allowed at no additional fee. Dogs may not be left unattended, and they must be leashed and cleaned up after. Dogs are not allowed in public swim areas or in buildings. Dogs are allowed on the trails. The camping and tent areas also allow dogs. There is a dog walk area at the campground. Multiple dogs may be allowed.

Catersville

Carterville/Cassville-White KOA
800 Cass-White Road NW
Catersville, GA
770-382-7330
Dogs of most all sizes are allowed; ex-large dogs are not. There are no additional pet fees. Dogs must be leashed and cleaned up after. There are some breed restrictions. The camping and tent areas also allow dogs. There is a dog walk area at the campground. Multiple dogs may be allowed.

Clarkesville

Moccasin Creek State Park
3655 H 197
Clarkesville, GA
706-947-3194
This scenic 32 acre park along the 2,800-acre Lake Burton, offers a wildlife observation tower, trails with access to the Appalachian Trail, and a variety of land and water activities and recreation. Dogs of all sizes are allowed at no additional fee. Dogs may not be left unattended, and they must be on no more than a 6 foot leash, and cleaned up after. Dogs are not allowed in public swim areas or in buildings. Dogs are allowed on the trails. The camping and tent areas also allow dogs. There is a dog walk area at the campground. Multiple dogs may be allowed.

Cleveland

Leisure Acres Campground
3840 W Moreland Road
Cleveland, GA

888-748-6344
Dogs of all sizes are allowed. There are no additional pet fees. Dogs must be leashed and cleaned up after. The camping and tent areas also allow dogs. There is a dog walk area at the campground. Multiple dogs may be allowed.

Cordele

Cordele KOA
373 Rockhouse Road E
Cordele, GA
229-273-5454
Dogs of all sizes are allowed, and there are no additional pet fees for tent or RV sites. There is a limit of 1 dog under 15 pounds for the cabins. Dogs must be leashed, cleaned up after, and in at night. The camping and tent areas also allow dogs. There is a dog walk area at the campground. Dogs are allowed in the camping cabins.

Veterans Memorial State Park
2459A H 280W
Cordele, GA
229-276-2371
This park of more than 1,300 acres on Lake Blackshear was established as a memorial to U.S. veterans, featuring a museum with artifacts from the Revolutionary War through the Gulf War. The park offers a variety of activities and recreation. Dogs of all sizes are allowed at no additional fee. Dogs may not be left unattended, and they must be on no more than a 6 foot leash, and be cleaned up after. Dogs are allowed on the trails. The camping and tent areas also allow dogs. There is a dog walk area at the campground. Multiple dogs may be allowed.

Dillard

River Vista Mountain Village
960 H 246
Dillard, GA
888-850-PARK (7275)
Up to 3 dogs of all sizes are allowed. There are no additional pet fees for tent or RV sites. There is a $10 per night per pet additional fee for the cabins, and only 2 dogs are allowed. Dogs may not be left unattended outside or in the cabins. Dogs must be on no more than a 6 foot leash and cleaned up after. The camping and tent areas also allow dogs. There is a dog walk area at the campground. Dogs are allowed in the camping cabins.

Elberton

Bobby Brown State Park
2509 Bobby Brown State Park Road
Elberton, GA
706-213-2046
Rich in natural and cultural history, this 655 acre park, on the shores of the 70,000-acre Clarks Hill Lake, offers a variety of land and water recreation. Dogs of all sizes are allowed at no additional fee. Dogs may not be left unattended except for short periods, they must be on no more than a 6 foot leash, and be cleaned up after. Dogs are allowed on the trails. The camping and tent areas also allow dogs. There is a dog walk area at the campground. Multiple dogs may be allowed.

Elko

Twin Oaks RV Park
305 H 26E
Elko, GA
478-987-9361
Dogs of all sizes are allowed. There are no additional pet fees. Dogs must be leashed and cleaned up after. The camping and tent areas also allow dogs. There is a dog walk area at the campground. 2 dogs may be allowed.

Fargo

Stephen Foster State Park
17515 H 177
Fargo, GA
912-637-5274
The breathtaking scenery of moss-laced cypress trees reflecting off the black swamp waters make this one of the most intriguing areas in Georgia. The park offers an interpretive center and a variety of land and water recreation. Dogs of all sizes are allowed at no additional fee. Dogs may not be left unattended outside except for short periods, and they must be leashed and cleaned up after. Dogs are not allowed on the waterways or in park buildings, however, they are allowed on the trails. The camping and tent areas also allow dogs. There is a dog walk area at the campground. Multiple dogs may be allowed.

Flovilla

Indian Springs State Park
678 Lake Clark Road
Flovilla, GA

770-504-2277
Thought to be the oldest state park in the nation, and home to a "healing" spring, this park offers a variety of land and water recreation. Dogs of all sizes are allowed at no additional fee. Dogs must be on no more than a 6 foot leash, and be cleaned up after. Dogs are not allowed in buildings or in the cabin area, however, they are allowed on the trails. The camping and tent areas also allow dogs. There is a dog walk area at the campground. Multiple dogs may be allowed.

Forsyth

Forsyth KOA
414 S Frontage Road
Forsyth, GA
478-994-2019
Dogs of all sizes are allowed. There are no additional pet fees. Dogs may not be left unattended outside, and they must be leashed, cleaned up after, and inside at night. The camping and tent areas also allow dogs. There is a dog walk area at the campground. Dogs are allowed in the camping cabins. Multiple dogs may be allowed.

Gainesville

Chattahoochee-Oconee National Forest
1755 Cleveland H
Gainesville, GA
770-297-3000
This forest has 7 district offices, 2 visitor centers, almost 900,000 acres, and diverse ecosystems that support a large variety of plants, fish, mammals, bird species, and year round recreation. Dogs of all sizes are allowed at no additional fee. Dogs may not be left unattended, and they must be leashed at all times, and be cleaned up after. The camping and tent areas also allow dogs. There is a dog walk area at the campground. Multiple dogs may be allowed.

Hartwell

Hart State Park
330 Hart State Park Road
Hartwell, GA
706-376-8756
This scenic park of 147 acres on Lake Hartwell offers a variety of land and water activities and recreation. Dogs of all sizes are

allowed at no additional fee. Dogs must be on no more than a 6 foot leash, and be cleaned up after. Dogs are allowed on the trails. The camping and tent areas also allow dogs. There is a dog walk area at the campground. Multiple dogs may be allowed.

Helen

Unicoi State Park
1788 H 356
Helen, GA
706-878-3982
This park offers programs that focus on its historical, natural, cultural, and recreational resources. Dogs of all sizes are allowed at no additional fee. Only 2 dogs are allowed in the cabins. Dogs may not be left unattended outside, and they must be on no more than a 6 foot leash, and be cleaned up after. Dogs are allowed on the trails, but not in the lodge. The camping and tent areas also allow dogs. There is a dog walk area at the campground. Dogs are allowed in the camping cabins.

Hiawassee

Georgia Mountain
1311 Music Hall Road
Hiawassee, GA
706-896-4191
Dogs of all sizes are allowed. There are no additional pet fees. Dogs are not allowed in the fair area, and they must be leashed and cleaned up after. The RV sites are open all year, but the tent sites are seasonal. The camping and tent areas also allow dogs. There is a dog walk area at the campground. Multiple dogs may be allowed.

Jackson

High Falls State Park
76 High Falls Park Drive
Jackson, GA
478-993-3053
Steeped in American history, this 1,050 acre park with 650 lake acres offers waterfalls, scenic trails, and a variety of land and water recreation. Dogs of all sizes are allowed at no additional fee. Dogs must be on no more than a 6 foot leash, and be cleaned up after. The camping and tent areas also allow dogs. There is a dog walk area at the campground. Multiple dogs may be allowed.

Jekyll Island

Jekyll Island Campground
1197 Riverview Drive
Jekyll Island, GA
866-658-3021
Dogs of all sizes are allowed. There are no additional pet fees. Dogs must be leashed and cleaned up after. The camping and tent areas also allow dogs. There is a dog walk area at the campground. Multiple dogs may be allowed.

Kingsland

Jacksonville N/Kingsland KOA
2970 Scrubby Buff Road
Kingsland, GA
912-729-3232
Dogs of all sizes are allowed. There are no additional pet fees. Dogs may not be left unattended outside, and they must be leashed and cleaned up after. The camping and tent areas also allow dogs. There is a dog walk area at the campground. Dogs are allowed in the camping cabins. Multiple dogs may be allowed.

Lake Park

Eagle's Roost RV Resort
5465 Mill Store Road
Lake Park, GA
229-559-5192
Dogs of all sizes are allowed. There are no additional pet fees. Dogs must be leashed and cleaned up after. The camping and tent areas also allow dogs. There is a dog walk area at the campground. Multiple dogs may be allowed.

Valdosta/Lake Park KOA
5300 Jewel Futch Road
Lake Park, GA
229-559-9738
Dogs of all sizes are allowed, and there are no additional pet fees for tent or RV sites. There is a $25 one time additional pet fee for the cabin and park models. Dogs may not be left unattended outside or in rentals, and they must be leashed and cleaned up after. The camping and tent areas also allow dogs. There is a dog walk area at the campground. Dogs are allowed in the camping cabins. Multiple dogs may be allowed.

Lincolnton

Elijah Clark State Park
2959 McCormick H
Lincolnton, GA
706-359-3458
Rich in American history, this 447 acre park with a 70,000 acre lake offers a variety of land and water recreation. Dogs of all sizes are allowed at no additional fee. Dogs may not be left unattended unless quiet and well behaved; they must be on no more than a 6 foot leash, and cleaned up after. Dogs are not allowed in buildings or on the beaches. Dogs are allowed on the trails. This campground is closed during the off-season. The camping and tent areas also allow dogs. There is a dog walk area at the campground. Multiple dogs may be allowed.

Millington

Meeman-Shelby State Park
910 Riddick Road
Millington, GA
901-876-5215
Dogs of all sizes are allowed, and there are no additional pet fees for tent or RV sites. There is a $10 per night per pet additional fee for the 1 pet friendly cabin. Dogs may not be left unattended outside or in the cabin, and they must be leashed and cleaned up after. The camping and tent areas also allow dogs. There is a dog walk area at the campground. Dogs are allowed in the camping cabins. 2 dogs may be allowed.

Nicholls

General Coffee State Park
46 John Coffee Road
Nicholls, GA
912-384-7082
Rich in agricultural history, and host to a cypress swamp of rare and endangered plants, this park offers an amphitheater, history and nature programs, and a variety of land and water recreation. Dogs of all sizes are allowed at no additional fee. Dogs may not be left unattended, and they must be on no more than a 6 foot leash, and be cleaned up after in camp areas. Dogs are not allowed in the buildings, however, they are allowed on the trails. The camping and tent areas also allow dogs. There is a dog walk area at the campground. Multiple dogs may be allowed.

Ochlocknee

Sugar Mill Plantation RV Park
4857 McMillan Road
Ochlocknee, GA
229-227-1451
Dogs of all sizes are allowed. There are no additional pet fees. Dogs may not be left unattended outside, and they must be leashed and cleaned up after. There are some breed restrictions. The camping and tent areas also allow dogs. There is a dog walk area at the campground. Multiple dogs may be allowed.

Pine Mountain

Pine Mountain Campground
8804 Hamilton Road
Pine Mountain, GA
706-663-4329
Dogs of all sizes are allowed. There are no additional pet fees. Dogs may not be left unattended, and they must be leashed and cleaned up after. There are some breed restrictions. The camping and tent areas also allow dogs. There is a dog walk area at the campground. Multiple dogs may be allowed.

Roosevelt State Park
2970 H 190E
Pine Mountain, GA
706-663-4858
This historical park of 9,049 acres offers spectacular views, 37 miles of hiking trails, an amphitheater and a wide variety of recreational pursuits. Dogs of all sizes are allowed at no additional fee. Dogs may not be left unattended, and they must be on no more than a 6 foot leash, and cleaned up after. Dogs are not allowed in the cottage area, at the group camp, or at the pool. Dogs are allowed on the trails. The camping and tent areas also allow dogs. There is a dog walk area at the campground. Multiple dogs may be allowed.

Rising Farm

Cloudland Canyon State Park
122 Cloudland Canyon Park Road
Rising Farm, GA
706-657-4050
Rugged geology and beautiful vistas make this one of the most scenic parks in the state, and a variety of trails and recreation are available for your use. Dogs of all sizes are allowed at no additional fee. Dogs

may not be left unattended, and they must be quiet, well behaved, leashed and cleaned up after. Dogs are not allowed in buildings. Dogs are allowed on the trails. The camping and tent areas also allow dogs. There is a dog walk area at the campground. Multiple dogs may be allowed.

Rossville

Holiday Trav-L-Park
1653 Mack Smith Road
Rossville, GA
706-891-9766
Dogs of all sizes are allowed. There are no additional pet fees. Dogs may not be left unattended outside, must be on no more than a 6 foot leashed, and be cleaned up after. The camping and tent areas also allow dogs. There is a dog walk area at the campground. 2 dogs may be allowed.

Rutledge

Hard Labor Creek State Park
Knox Chaple Road
Rutledge, GA
706-557-3001
Although best known for its golf course, there are a wide variety of land and water activities and recreation offered at this state park. Dogs of all sizes are allowed at no additional fee. Dogs must be leashed, and cleaned up after in camp areas. Dogs are not allowed in or around cottage areas or on the beach. Dogs are allowed on the trails. The camping and tent areas also allow dogs. There is a dog walk area at the campground. Multiple dogs may be allowed.

Savannah

Brookwood RV Park
Rt 5, Box 3107; on Pulaski Excelsior
Metter, GA
888-636-4616
Dogs of all sizes are allowed. There are no additional pet fees. Dogs must be leashed and cleaned up after. There is a dog walk area at the campground. Multiple dogs may be allowed.

Fort McAllister State Historic Park
3894 Fort McAllister Road
Richmond Hill, GA
912-727-2339
This park, rich in American history

and along the Colonial Coast Birding Trail, offers a Civil War museum, an Earthwork Fort, and a variety of recreational pursuits. Dogs of all sizes are allowed at no additional fee. Dogs may not be left unattended, and they must be on no more than a 6 foot leash, and be cleaned up after. Dogs are not allowed in any of the buildings, however, they are allowed on the trails. The camping and tent areas also allow dogs. There is a dog walk area at the campground. Multiple dogs may be allowed.

Savannah South KOA
4915 H 17
Richmond Hill, GA
912-765-3396
Dogs of all sizes are allowed. There are no additional pet fees. Dogs must be leashed and cleaned up after. The camping and tent areas also allow dogs. There is a dog walk area at the campground. Dogs are allowed in the camping cabins. Multiple dogs may be allowed.

Waterway RV Park
70 H 17
Richmond Hill, GA
912-756-2296
Dogs up to 75 pounds are allowed. There are no additional pet fees. Dogs may not be left unattended, and they must be leashed and cleaned up after. Dogs are not allowed to swim in the river because of alligators. There are some breed restrictions. There is a dog walk area at the campground. 2 dogs may be allowed.

Skidaway Island State Park
52 Diamond Causeway
Savannah, GA
912-598-2300
This 588 acre barrier island park along the Colonial Coast Birding Trail, offers observation towers, an interpretive center, and a variety of recreational pursuits. Dogs of all sizes are allowed at no additional fee. Dogs may not be left unattended, and they must be leashed and cleaned up after. Dogs are not allowed in buildings or in the pool area. The camping and tent areas also allow dogs. There is a dog walk area at the campground. Multiple dogs may be allowed.

Springfield

Dynasty Canine Training Facility

and RV Park
3554 H 21N
Springfield, GA
912-754-4834
Dogs of all sizes are allowed. There are no additional pet fees. Dogs may not be left unattended outside, and they must be in at dusk. Dogs must be quiet, well behaved, leashed, and cleaned up after. The Park provides wading pools for your pets in the summer, and there are 2 fenced in areas where dogs can be off lead. The camping and tent areas also allow dogs. There is a dog walk area at the campground. There are special amenities given to dogs at this campground. Multiple dogs may be allowed.

Tifton

Agirama RV Park
1392 Windmill Road
Tifton, GA
229-386-3344
Dogs of all sizes are allowed. There are no additional pet fees. Dogs may not be left unattended outside, and they must be leashed and cleaned up after. This park is along side an 1870's working village. Dogs are not allowed in any of the Museum of Agriculture or village buildings. There is a dog walk area at the campground. 2 dogs may be allowed.

Amy's South Georgia RV Park
4632 Union Road
Tifton, GA
229-386-8441
Dogs of all sizes are allowed. There are no additional pet fees. Dogs may not be left unattended outside, and they must be in at night, leashed, and cleaned up after. The camping and tent areas also allow dogs. There is a dog walk area at the campground. Multiple dogs may be allowed.

Trenton

Lookout Mountain/Chattanooga West KOA
930 Mountain Shadows Drive
Trenton, GA
706-657-6815
Dogs of all sizes are allowed. There are no additional pet fees. Dogs must be leashed and cleaned up after. There are some breed restrictions. The camping and tent areas also allow dogs. There is a dog walk area at the campground.

Dogs are allowed in the camping cabins. Multiple dogs may be allowed.

Tybee Island

River's End Campground
915 Polk Street
Tybee Island, GA
912-786-5518
Dogs of all sizes are allowed. There are no additional pet fees. Dogs may not be left unattended, or at the beach at any time, and they must be leashed and cleaned up after. The camping and tent areas also allow dogs. There is a dog walk area at the campground. Multiple dogs may be allowed.

Idaho Listings

Ahsahka

Dent Acres Rec Area
P. O. Box 48/ Well Bench Road
Ahsahka, ID
208-476-1261
This 677 acre park located on the Dworshak Reservoir offers a variety of land and water recreation. Dogs of all sizes are allowed at no additional fee. Dogs may not be left unattended outside, and they must be leashed and cleaned up after. Dogs are not allowed on the swim beach or in buildings. Dogs are allowed on the trails. This campground is closed during the off-season. The camping and tent areas also allow dogs. There is a dog walk area at the campground. Multiple dogs may be allowed.

Almo

City of Rocks National Reserve
3035 S Elba Almo Road
Almo, ID
208-824-5519
This scenic park holds geologic and historic significance in that it is home to some of the oldest rocks in America (some over 60 stories high), so rock climbing is popular here. Dogs of all sizes are allowed at no additional fee. Dogs may not be left unattended, and they must be on no more than a 6 foot leash, and be cleaned up after. Dogs must not be

allowed to dig, especially at the staging/climbing areas. Dogs are allowed on the trails. The camping and tent areas also allow dogs. There is a dog walk area at the campground. There are no electric or water hookups at the campground. Multiple dogs may be allowed.

Athol

Farragut State Park
13550 E H 54
Athol, ID
208-683-2425
With over 4,000 acres and home to the largest lake in the state, this biologically diverse park offers a variety of nature study, and land and water recreation. This park also has exhibits about their part as a Navel Training Center in WWII. Dogs of all sizes are allowed at no additional fee. Dogs may not be left unattended, and they must be quiet, well behaved, leashed and cleaned up after. Dogs are not allowed on the beach or in buildings. Dogs are allowed on the trails. The camping and tent areas also allow dogs. There is a dog walk area at the campground. Dogs are allowed in the camping cabins. Multiple dogs may be allowed.

Boise

On the River RV Park
6000 Glenwood
Boise, ID
208-375-7432
Dogs of all sizes are allowed. There are no additional pet fees. Dogs must be leashed and cleaned up after. The camping and tent areas also allow dogs. There is a dog walk area at the campground. Multiple dogs may be allowed.

Caldwell

Ambassador RV Resort
615 S Mead Parkway
Caldwell, ID
888-877-8307
Dogs of all sizes are allowed. There are no additional pet fees. Dogs must be quiet, leashed, and cleaned up after. Dogs may not be left unattended outside. There are some breed restrictions. There is a dog walk area at the campground. Multiple dogs may be allowed.

Coeur D'Alene

Coeur D'Alene KOA
10588 E Wolf Lodge Bay Road
Coeur D'Alene, ID
208-664-4471
Dogs of all sizes are allowed. There are no additional pet fees. Dogs must be quiet, leashed, and cleaned up after. This RV park is closed during the off-season. The camping and tent areas also allow dogs. There is a dog walk area at the campground. Dogs are allowed in the camping cabins. Multiple dogs may be allowed.

Blackwell Island RV Resort
800 S Marina Way
Coeur d'Alene, ID
208-665-1300
Dogs of all sizes are allowed. There are no additional pet fees. Dogs must be leashed and cleaned up after. This RV park is closed during the off-season. There is a dog walk area at the campground. Multiple dogs may be allowed.

Idaho Panhandle National Forest
3815 Schreiber Street
Coeur d'Alene, ID
208-765-7223
This forest of 2.5 million acres has more than 3,300 miles of hiking trails, and the various ecosystems support a large variety of plants, fish, mammals, bird species, and recreation. Dogs of all sizes are allowed at no additional fee. Dogs may not be left unattended, and they must be leashed and cleaned up after. Dogs are allowed on the trails. The camping and tent areas also allow dogs. There is a dog walk area at the campground. Dogs are allowed in the camping cabins. Multiple dogs may be allowed.

Coolin

Priest Lake State Park
3140 Indian Creek Park Road
Coolin, ID
208-443-6710
Steeped in history, this scenic park offers a variety of habitats, trails, and land and water recreation. Dogs of all sizes are allowed at no additional fee. Dogs may not be left unattended, and they must be quiet, be on no more than a 6 foot leash, and cleaned up after. Dogs are not allowed in the public swim area, but they are allowed at their own designated swim area and on the

trails. The camping and tent areas also allow dogs. There is a dog walk area at the campground. Dogs are allowed in the camping cabins. There are no water hookups at the campground. Multiple dogs may be allowed.

Glenns Ferry

Three Island Crossing State Park
1083 S Three Island Park Drive
Glenns Ferry, ID
208-366-2394
This park is home to The Oregon Trail History and Education Center, and offers a host of educational and historic programs and events. Dogs of all sizes are allowed at no additional fee. Dogs may not be left unattended unless they will be quiet and well behaved, and they must be leashed and cleaned up after. Dogs are not allowed in buildings or on the beach, however, they are allowed on the trails. The camping and tent areas also allow dogs. There is a dog walk area at the campground. Multiple dogs may be allowed.

Grangeville

Christmas Ranch RV Park
16967 H 95S
Grangeville, ID
208-983-2383
Dogs of all sizes are allowed. There are no additional pet fees. When out walking with your pet, they must be on a leash. Dogs may be off leash on site if they are under voice command and will not chase. Dogs must be cleaned up after at all times. There is a dog walk area at the campground. Multiple dogs may be allowed.

Nez Perce National Forest
1005 H 13
Grangeville, ID
208-983-1950
This diverse forest of 2.2 million acres provides spectacular scenery, a rich cultural history, and diverse ecosystems that support a large variety of plants animals, and recreation. Dogs of all sizes are allowed at no additional fee. Dogs may not be left unattended, and they must be leashed and cleaned up after in camp areas. Dogs are allowed on the trails except in winter when they are not allowed on the ski trails. The camping and tent areas also allow dogs. There is a dog walk area at the campground. There are no electric or water hookups at the

campground. Multiple dogs may be allowed.

Hagerman

Hagerman RV Village
18049 H 30
Hagerman, ID
208-837-4906
Dogs of all sizes are allowed. There are no additional pet fees. Dogs must be quiet, well behaved, leashed, and cleaned up after. They are allowed in the cabins, but they may not be left unattended there, and they are not allowed on the furniture. The camping and tent areas also allow dogs. There is a dog walk area at the campground. Multiple dogs may be allowed.

High Adventure River Tours RV Park
1211 E 2350 S
Hagerman, ID
208-837-9005
Scenic tours, river rafting, Dutch oven cooking, and even fresh produce in season are offered here. Well behaved dogs of all sizes are allowed at no additional fee. Dogs must be well behaved, leashed, and cleaned up after. Dogs are not allowed in the buildings, but they are allowed on the trails. The camping and tent areas also allow dogs. There is a dog walk area at the campground. There are no electric or water hookups at the campground. Multiple dogs may be allowed.

Idaho City

Boise National Forest
3833 H 21
Idaho City, ID
208-373-4100
This forest has 6 ranger districts, over 2 million acres, and diverse ecosystems that support a large variety of plants, fish, mammals, bird species, and year round recreation. Dogs of all sizes are allowed at no additional fee. Dogs may not be left unattended, and they must be leashed and cleaned up after. Dogs are not allowed on the furniture in the cabins, or in any other park buildings. Dogs are allowed on the trails. This campground is closed during the off-season. The camping and tent areas also allow dogs. There is a dog walk area at the campground. Dogs are allowed in the camping

cabins. There are no electric or water hookups at the campground. Multiple dogs may be allowed.

Idaho Falls

Caribou-Targhee National Forest
3659 East Ririe Highway
Idaho Falls, ID
208-524-7500
These 2 forests were joined in the year 2000, creating 6 ranger districts, over 3 million acres, and diverse ecosystems that support a large variety of plants, animals and year round recreation. Dogs of all sizes are allowed at no additional fee. Dogs may not be left unattended, and they must be leashed and cleaned up after. Dogs are not allowed on the West Mink Trail, but they are allowed on the other trails. This campground is closed during the off-season. The camping and tent areas also allow dogs. There is a dog walk area at the campground. There are no electric or water hookups at the campground. Multiple dogs may be allowed.

Targhee-Caribou National Forest
1405 Hollipark Drive
Idaho Falls, ID
208-524-7500
These 2 forests were joined in the year 2000, creating 7 ranger districts, over 3 million acres, and diverse ecosystems that support a large variety of plants, fish, mammals, bird species, and year round recreation. Dogs of all sizes are allowed at no additional fee. Dogs may not be left unattended, and they must be leashed and cleaned up after. Dogs are not allowed on the West Mink Trail, but they are allowed on the other trails. This campground is closed during the off-season. The camping and tent areas also allow dogs. There is a dog walk area at the campground. There are no electric or water hookups at the campground. Multiple dogs may be allowed.

Island Park

Henry's Lake State Park
3917 E 5100 N
Island Park, ID
208-558-7532
This high mountain lake park offers beautiful scenery and a variety of land and water recreational pursuits. Dogs of all sizes are allowed at no additional fee. Dogs may not be left unattended, and they must be on no

more than a 6 foot leash, and be cleaned up after. Dogs are not allowed in buildings, but they are allowed on the trails. This campground is closed during the off-season. The camping and tent areas also allow dogs. There is a dog walk area at the campground. Multiple dogs may be allowed.

Jerome

Twin Falls/Jerome KOA
5431 H 93
Jerome, ID
208-324-4169
Dogs of all sizes are allowed. There are no additional pet fees, but they request that if you rented a cabin with a dog that you sweep the cabin out before you leave. Dogs may not be left unattended, must be leashed, and cleaned up after. There are some breed restrictions. This RV park is closed during the off-season. The camping and tent areas also allow dogs. There is a dog walk area at the campground. Dogs are allowed in the camping cabins. Multiple dogs may be allowed.

Ketchum

Sawtooth National Rec Area
5 N Fort Canyon Road
Ketchum, ID
208-837-9005
Located in the Sawtooth National Forest, this recreational area provides a wide variety of year round land and water activities. Dogs of all sizes are allowed at no additional fee. Dogs may not be left unattended, and they must be leashed and cleaned up after. Dogs are allowed on the trails. The camping and tent areas also allow dogs. There is a dog walk area at the campground. There are no electric or water hookups at the campground. Multiple dogs may be allowed.

Smiley Creek Lodge
HC 64, Box 9102/ 37 miles N of Ketchum on H 75
Ketchum, ID
208-774-3547
Dogs of all sizes are allowed. There are no additional pet fees. Dogs may not be left unattended outside, and they must be leashed and cleaned up after. The camping and tent areas also allow dogs. There is a dog walk area at the campground. Multiple dogs may be allowed.

Wood River Campground / Sawtooth National Forest
12 Miles N of Ketchum on H 75
Ketchum, ID
208-726-7672
Dogs of all sizes are allowed. There are no additional pet fees. Dogs must be leashed and cleaned up after. This RV park is closed during the off-season. The camping and tent areas also allow dogs. Multiple dogs may be allowed.

Lewiston

Hells Gate State Park
4832 Hells Gate State Park
Lewiston, ID
208-799-5015
This park offers shady campsites on the Snake River along the deepest river gorge in North America, an interpretive plaza, a discovery center, tours, and various recreation. Dogs of all sizes are allowed at no additional fee. Dogs may not be left unattended, and they must be leashed at all times, and cleaned up after. Dogs are not allowed on the beach or in buildings, but they are allowed on the trails. The camping and tent areas also allow dogs. There is a dog walk area at the campground. Dogs are allowed in the camping cabins. Multiple dogs may be allowed.

Lucile

Riverfront Gardens RV Park
MM 210.5 H 95
Lucile, ID
208-628-3777
This is an RV only park. Dogs of all sizes are allowed at no additional fee. Dogs must be leashed and cleaned up after. There is a dog walk area at the campground. Multiple dogs may be allowed.

McCall

Payette National Forest
102 W Lake Street
McCall, ID
208-634-0700
From the deepest river gorge in North America to elevations of almost 9,500 feet, this diverse forest of 2.3 million acres supports a large variety of plants, fish, mammals, bird species, and recreation. Dogs of all sizes are allowed at no additional fee. Dogs

may not be left unattended, and they must be leashed and cleaned up after in camp areas. Dogs are not allowed in any buildings, but however they are allowed on the trails. This campground is closed during the off-season. The camping and tent areas also allow dogs. There is a dog walk area at the campground. There are no electric or water hookups at the campground. Multiple dogs may be allowed.

Ponderosa State Park
Miles Standish Road
McCall, ID
208-634-2164
The diverse topography of his peninsula park offers a variety of naturescapes, and the park provides educational programs, guided tours, and various year round recreation. Dogs of all sizes are allowed at no additional fee. Dogs may not be left unattended, and they must be on no more than a 6 foot leash and be cleaned up after. Dogs are not allowed on ski trails in winter, on the beach, or in park buildings; they are allowed on the trails. This campground is closed during the off-season. The camping and tent areas also allow dogs. Multiple dogs may be allowed.

Meridian

Boise Meridian RV Resort
184 Pennwood
Meridian, ID
877-894-1357
Dogs of all sizes are allowed. There are no additional pet fees. Dogs may not be left unattended, or tied to the trees or other campsite furnishings. Dogs must be leashed and cleaned up after. There are some breed restrictions. There is a dog walk area at the campground. 2 dogs may be allowed.

The Playground RV Park
1680 Overland Road
Meridian, ID
208-887-1022
Dogs of all sizes are allowed. There are no additional pet fees. Dogs must be leashed and cleaned up after. There is a dog walk area at the campground. Multiple dogs may be allowed.

Montpelier

Montpelier Creek KOA
28501 H 89N

Montpelier, ID
208-847-0863
Dogs of all sizes are allowed. There are no additional pet fees. Dogs must be leashed and cleaned up after. This RV park is closed during the off-season. The camping and tent areas also allow dogs. There is a dog walk area at the campground. Dogs are allowed in the camping cabins. 2 dogs may be allowed.

Moravia

Ro VelDo Cabins and Campgrounds
20925 H J5T
Moravia, ID
641-437-4084
Dogs of all sizes are allowed. There are no additional pet fees for tent or RV sites. There is a $50 one time additional pet fee for the cabins, which are open all year. Dogs must be quiet, well behaved, leashed, and cleaned up after. This RV park is closed during the off-season. The camping and tent areas also allow dogs. There is a dog walk area at the campground. Multiple dogs may be allowed.

Mountain Home

Bruneau Dunes State Park
27608 Sand Dunes Road
Mountain Home, ID
208-366-7919
Home to the Bruneau Dunes Observatory, and the tallest single-structured sand dune in North America at 470 feet, this high desert park offers a wide variety of nature/sky study, and land and water recreation. Dogs of all sizes are allowed at no additional fee. Dogs may not be left unattended, and they must be on no more than a 6 foot leash, and be cleaned up after in the camp areas. Dogs may be off lead out of the camp area only if they are well trained and will respond to voice command. Dogs are allowed on the trails. This campground is closed during the off-season. The camping and tent areas also allow dogs. There is a dog walk area at the campground. Multiple dogs may be allowed.

Mountain Home KOA
220 E 10th N
Mountain Home, ID
208-587-5111
Dogs of all sizes are allowed. There are no additional pet fees. Dogs

must be leashed and cleaned up after. This RV park is closed during the off-season. The camping and tent areas also allow dogs. There is a dog walk area at the campground. Dogs are allowed in the camping cabins. Multiple dogs may be allowed.

Mountain Home RV Park
2295 American Legion Blvd
Mountain Home, ID
208-890-4100
Dogs of all sizes are allowed. There are no additional pet fees. Dogs must be quiet, well behaved, and cleaned up after. Dogs may be off lead if they are under voice control. There is a dog walk area at the campground. Multiple dogs may be allowed.

Orofino

Clearwater National Forest
83544 H 12
Orofino, ID
208-476-4541
This forest has 4 ranger districts, 1.8 million acres, and has diverse ecosystems that support a large variety of plants, fish, mammals, bird species as well as year round recreation. Dogs of all sizes are allowed at no additional fee. Dogs may not be left unattended, and they must be leashed, and cleaned up after in camp areas, and especially on the beaches. Dogs are not allowed in swim areas or in buildings. Dogs are allowed on the trails. This campground is closed during the off-season. The camping and tent areas also allow dogs. There is a dog walk area at the campground. Dogs are allowed in the camping cabins. There are no electric or water hookups at the campground. Multiple dogs may be allowed.

Dworshak State Park
P. O. Box 2028/Freeman Creek Road
Orofino, ID
208-476-5994
This 850, acre park located on shores of Dworshak Reservoir, offers a variety of activities and land and water recreation. Dogs of all sizes are allowed at no additional fee. Dogs may not be left unattended, and they must be leashed at all times, and cleaned up after. Dogs are not allowed in the buildings or on the beaches. Dogs

are allowed on the trails. The camping and tent areas also allow dogs. There is a dog walk area at the campground. Dogs are allowed in the camping cabins. Multiple dogs may be allowed.

Pinehurst

Kellogg/Silver Valley KOA
801 N Division Street
Pinehurst, ID
208-682-3612
Dogs of all sizes are allowed. There are no additional pet fees. There is a $50 refundable deposit (or have credit card on file) for the cabin rentals. Dogs must be well behaved, may not be left unattended, must be leashed at all times, and cleaned up after. There is a fenced in dog run on site. This RV park is closed during the off-season. The camping and tent areas also allow dogs. There is a dog walk area at the campground. Dogs are allowed in the camping cabins. 2 dogs may be allowed.

Plummer

Heyburn State Park
1291 Chatcolet Road
Plummer, ID
208-686-1308
This park of about 5,500 acres with 2,300 acres of lake is rich in natural and cultural history. The park offers an interpretive center along with a wide variety of land and water activities and recreation. Dogs of all sizes are allowed at no additional fee. Dogs may not be left unattended except for short periods, and then only if they will be quiet and well behaved. Dogs must be on no more than a 6 foot leash, and be cleaned up after. Dogs are allowed on the trails. This campground is closed during the off-season. The camping and tent areas also allow dogs. There is a dog walk area at the campground. Dogs are allowed in the camping cabins. Multiple dogs may be allowed.

Pocatello

Pocatello KOA
9815 W Pocatello Creek Road
Pocatello, ID
208-233-6851
Dogs of all sizes are allowed. There are no additional pet fees. Dogs may not be left unattended, must be leashed, and cleaned up after. The

camping and tent areas also allow dogs. There is a dog walk area at the campground. Multiple dogs may be allowed.

Pollock

Canyon Pines Resort
10 Barn Road
Pollock, ID
208-628-4006
Dogs of all sizes are allowed. There are no additional pet fees. Dogs may not be left unattended, and must be leashed and cleaned up after. The camping and tent areas also allow dogs. There is a dog walk area at the campground. Multiple dogs may be allowed.

Post Falls

Suntree RV Park
350 N Idahline Road
Post Falls, ID
208-773-9982
Dogs of all sizes are allowed. There is a $1 per night per pet additional fee. Dogs may not be left unattended, and they must be quiet, well behaved, leashed, and cleaned up after. There is a dog walk area at the campground. 2 dogs may be allowed.

Salmon

Salmon-Chalis National Forest
50 H 93 S
Salmon, ID
208-756-5100
This forest has 7 ranger districts, is home to the largest wilderness area in the US with over 4.3 million acres, and has diverse ecosystems and year round recreation. Dogs of all sizes are allowed at no additional fee. Dogs may not be left unattended outside, and they must be leashed and cleaned up after. Dogs are not allowed in buildings, but they are allowed on the trails. This campground is closed during the off-season. The camping and tent areas also allow dogs. There is a dog walk area at the campground. There are no electric or water hookups at the campground. Multiple dogs may be allowed.

Salmon River RV Park
111 Whitetail Drive
Salmon, ID
208-894-4549
Dogs of all sizes are allowed. There

are no additional pet fees. Dogs may not be left unattended outside, and they must be quiet, well behaved, leashed, and cleaned up after. This is an RV only park. There is a dog walk area at the campground. Multiple dogs may be allowed.

Salmon-Challis National Forest
1669 H 93
Salmon, ID
208-879-4100
This forest has 7 ranger districts, is home to the largest wilderness area in the US with over 4.3 million acres, and has diverse ecosystems that support a large variety of plants, animals, and year round recreation. Dogs of all sizes are allowed at no additional fee. Dogs may not be left unattended outside, and they must be leashed and cleaned up after. Dogs are not allowed in buildings, but they are allowed on the trails. This campground is closed during the off-season. The camping and tent areas also allow dogs. There is a dog walk area at the campground. There are no electric or water hookups at the campground. Multiple dogs may be allowed.

St Charles

Bear Lake North RV Park
220 N Main
St Charles, ID
208-945-2941
Dogs of all sizes and numbers are allowed at RV sites, however only 1 dog up to 20 pounds is allowed at the cabins. There is a $1.50 per night per pet additional fee. Dogs may not be left unattended at the cabins, and they are not allowed on the beds or in the loft. The camping and tent areas also allow dogs. There is a dog walk area at the campground. Dogs are allowed in the camping cabins.

Stanley

Carmela Winery Golf Course and RV Park
1294 W Madison
Stanley, ID
208-366-2773
Dogs of all sizes are allowed at no additional fee. Dogs may only be left inside your RV for short periods, and only if they will be quiet and well behaved. Dogs must be leashed and cleaned up after. The

park has an adjoining 65 acres nearby where your dog may run off lead if they are trained and will obey voice command. The camping and tent areas also allow dogs. There is a dog walk area at the campground. Multiple dogs may be allowed.

Twin Falls

Anderson Camp
S Tipperary
Eden, ID
888-480-9400
Dogs of all sizes are allowed. There are no additional pet fees. Dogs may not be left unattended, and must be quiet, leashed, and cleaned up after. The camping and tent areas also allow dogs. There is a dog walk area at the campground. Dogs are allowed in the camping cabins. Multiple dogs may be allowed.

Sawtooth National Forest
2647 Kimberly Road E.
Twin Falls, ID
208-737-3200
In addition to archaeological and historical sites and interests, this forest of more than a million acres has diverse ecosystems support a large variety of plants, animals, and recreation. Dogs of all sizes are allowed at no additional fee. Dogs may not be left unattended, and they must be leashed and cleaned up after. Dogs are allowed on the trails. This campground is closed during the off-season. The camping and tent areas also allow dogs. There is a dog walk area at the campground. There are no electric or water hookups at the campground. Multiple dogs may be allowed.

White Bird

Hells Canyon Jet Boat Trips and Lodging
1 mile S of White Bird on Old H 95
White Bird, ID
800-469-8757
Dogs of all sizes are allowed. There are no additional pet fees. Dogs must be leashed and cleaned up after. Dogs may be left on site on leash, but please inform the office as to how long you will be gone and if you will be on the 6 hour jet boat tour. There is a motel on site that has one pet friendly room, also at no additional fee, but please, however, only 1 dog is allowed in the motel room at a time. The camping and tent areas also allow dogs. There is

a dog walk area at the campground.

Winchester

Winchester Lake State Park
Forest Road
Winchester, ID
208-924-7563
This 418 acre park, with 103 lake acres, is popular for nature study, fishing, and hiking, and offers a variety of land and water activities and recreation. Dogs of all sizes are allowed at no additional fee. Dogs may not be left unattended, and they must be well behaved, leashed and cleaned up after. Dogs are not allowed in the buildings, but they are allowed on the trails. The park has one pet-friendly yurt available. The camping and tent areas also allow dogs. There is a dog walk area at the campground. 2 dogs may be allowed.

Illinois Listings

Amboy

O'Connells' Yogi Bear Jellystone Park Camp Resort
970 Greenwing Road
Amboy, IL
815-857-3860
Dogs of all sizes are allowed. There are no additional pet fees. Dogs must be leashed and cleaned up after. This RV park is closed during the off-season. The camping and tent areas also allow dogs. There is a dog walk area at the campground. Multiple dogs may be allowed.

Benton

Benton KOA
1500 N DuQuoin Street
Benton, IL
618-439-4860
Dogs of all sizes are allowed, and there are no additional pet fees for tent or RV sites. There is a $5 one time additional pet fee for the cabins. Dogs may not be left unattended, and they must be leashed and cleaned up after. This RV park is closed during the off-season. The camping and tent areas also allow dogs. There is a dog walk area at the campground. Dogs are allowed in the

camping cabins. 2 dogs may be allowed.

Casey

Casey KOA
1248 E 1250th Road
Casey, IL
217-932-5319
Dogs of all sizes are allowed. There are no additional pet fees. Dogs may not be left unattended or placed in outside pens. Dogs must be leashed and cleaned up after. There are some breed restrictions. This RV park is closed during the off-season. The camping and tent areas also allow dogs. There is a dog walk area at the campground. Multiple dogs may be allowed.

Chandlerville

Jim Edgar Panther Creek State Park
10149 H 11
Chandlerville, IL
217-452-7741
There is a wide variety of trails in this park. Dogs of all sizes are allowed. There are no additional pet fees. Dogs must be on no more than a 10 foot leash and be cleaned up after. The camping and tent areas also allow dogs. There is a dog walk area at the campground. Multiple dogs may be allowed.

Charleston

Fox Ridge State Park
18175 State Park Road
Charleston, IL
217-345-6416
This park only closes for one month in December. Dogs of all sizes are allowed. There are no additional pet fees. Dogs must be leashed and cleaned up after. Dogs are allowed on the trails. This campground is closed during the off-season. The camping and tent areas also allow dogs. There is a dog walk area at the campground. There are no water hookups at the campground. Multiple dogs may be allowed.

Chatham

Double J Campground
9683 Palm Road
Chatham, IL
217-483-9998
Dogs of all sizes are allowed. There

are no additional pet fees. Dogs may not be left unattended or tied up outside alone. Dogs must be quiet, leashed, and cleaned up after. This RV park is closed during the off-season. The camping and tent areas also allow dogs. There is a dog walk area at the campground. Multiple dogs may be allowed.

Chebanse

Kankakee South KOA
425 E 6000 Road
Chebanse, IL
815-939-4603
Dogs of all sizes are allowed. There are no additional pet fees. Dogs may not be left unattended, and must be leashed and cleaned up after. There are some breed restrictions. This RV park is closed during the off-season. The camping and tent areas also allow dogs. There is a dog walk area at the campground. Dogs are allowed in the camping cabins. Multiple dogs may be allowed.

Chicago Area

Windy City Campground
18701 S 80th Avenue
Tinley Park, IL
708-720-0030
Dogs of all sizes are allowed. There are no additional pet fees. Dogs may not be left outside unattended, and may only be left inside if they will be comfortable and quiet. Dogs must be leashed and cleaned up after. This RV park is closed during the off-season. There is a dog walk area at the campground. 2 dogs may be allowed.

Hide-A-Way Lakes
8045 Van Emmons Road
Yorkville, IL
630-553-6323
Dogs of all sizes are allowed. There are no additional pet fees. Dogs must be quiet, well behaved, leashed, and cleaned up after. The camping and tent areas also allow dogs. There is a dog walk area at the campground. Multiple dogs may be allowed.

Clinton

Weldon Springs State Park
1159 500 North RR 2
Clinton, IL
217-935-2644
Dogs of all sizes are allowed. There

are no additional pet fees. Dogs may not be left unattended, they must be on no more than a 10 foot leash, and be cleaned up after. Dogs are allowed on the trails, but they are not allowed in the pet free zones. The camping and tent areas also allow dogs. There is a dog walk area at the campground. There are no water hookups at the campground. Multiple dogs may be allowed.

Colchester

Arglye Lake State Park
640 Argyle Park Road
Colchester, IL
309-776-3422
Dogs of all sizes are allowed. There are no additional pet fees. Dogs may not be left unattended, they must be on no more than a 10 foot leash, and be cleaned up after. Dogs are allowed on the trails. The camping and tent areas also allow dogs. There is a dog walk area at the campground. There are no water hookups at the campground. Multiple dogs may be allowed.

DeWitt

Clinton Lake State Park
H 14
DeWitt, IL
217-935-8722
Dogs of all sizes are allowed. There are no additional pet fees. Dogs may not be left unattended, they must be on no more than a 10 foot leash, and be cleaned up after. Dogs are allowed on the trails. The camping and tent areas also allow dogs. There is a dog walk area at the campground. Multiple dogs may be allowed.

Effingham

Camp Lakewood
1217 W Rickelman
Effingham, IL
217-342-6233
Dogs of all sizes are allowed. There are no additional pet fees. Dogs must be quiet, leashed, and cleaned up after. This RV park is closed during the off-season. There is a dog walk area at the campground. Multiple dogs may be allowed.

Findlay

Eagle Creek State Park

off Bruce Findley Road
Findlay, IL
217-756-8260
Dogs of all sizes are allowed. There are no additional pet fees. Dogs may not be left unattended and they must be leashed and cleaned up after. The camping and tent areas also allow dogs. There is a dog walk area at the campground. There are no water hookups at the campground. Multiple dogs may be allowed.

Galena

Palace Campground
11357 H 20W
Galena, IL
815-777-2466
Dogs of all sizes are allowed. There are no additional pet fees. Dogs may not be left unattended, must be leashed, and cleaned up after. This RV park is closed during the off-season. The camping and tent areas also allow dogs. There is a dog walk area at the campground. Dogs are allowed in the camping cabins. Multiple dogs may be allowed.

Garden Prairie

Holiday Acres Camping Resort
7050 Epworth
Garden Prairie, IL
815-547-7846
Dogs of all sizes are allowed, but there can only be one dog in the cabins. There are no additional pet fees. Dogs must be well behaved, leashed, and cleaned up after. The camping and tent areas also allow dogs. There is a dog walk area at the campground. Dogs are allowed in the camping cabins.

Goodfield

Yogi Bear Campground
RR 1 Timerberline Road
Goodfield, IL
309-965-2224
Dogs of all sizes are allowed. There are no additional pet fees. Dogs must be quiet, leashed, and cleaned up after. The camping and tent areas also allow dogs. There is a dog walk area at the campground. 2 dogs may be allowed.

Goreville

Ferne Clyffe State Park
On H 37 one mile S of Goreville
Goreville, IL
618-995-2411
Dogs of all sizes are allowed. There are no additional pet fees. Dogs may not be left unattended, and they must be quiet, well behaved, be on no more than a 10 foot leash, and be cleaned up after. Dogs are allowed on the trails, but not in any buildings. The camping and tent areas also allow dogs. There is a dog walk area at the campground. There are no water hookups at the campground. Multiple dogs may be allowed.

Harrisburg

Shawnee National Forest
Ridge Road
Harrisburg, IL
800-699-6637
This national forest has 14 campgrounds, and one of them has electric hookups. The pet policy applies to all the campgrounds. Dogs of all sizes are allowed. There are no additional pet fees. Dogs may not be left unattended, they must have a current rabies certificate and shot records, be leashed at all times, and be cleaned up after. Dogs are allowed on the trails. The camping and tent areas also allow dogs. There is a dog walk area at the campground. There are no water hookups at the campground. Multiple dogs may be allowed.

Havana

Evening Star Camping Resort
23049 H 136
Havana, IL
309-562-7590
Dogs of all sizes are allowed. There are no additional pet fees. Dogs must be quiet, leashed, and cleaned up after. The camping and tent areas also allow dogs. There is a dog walk area at the campground. 2 dogs may be allowed.

Lena

Lake Ke-aqua-na State Park
8542 Lake Road
Lena, IL
815-369-4282
This park has many year round recreational activities in and around the 715 acre park and 40 acre lake. Dogs of all sizes are allowed. There are no additional pet fees. Dogs may

not be left unattended, and they must be quiet, leashed, and cleaned up after. Dogs are allowed on the trails, but not at the beach. The camping and tent areas also allow dogs. There is a dog walk area at the campground. There are no water hookups at the campground. Multiple dogs may be allowed.

Lena KOA
10982 W H 20
Lena, IL
815-369-2612
Dogs of all sizes are allowed, and there are no additional pet fees for tent or RV sites. There is a $2 per night per pet additional fee for the cabins, and only 2 dogs are allowed. Dogs must be leashed and cleaned up after. There are some breed restrictions. This RV park is closed during the off-season. The camping and tent areas also allow dogs. There is a dog walk area at the campground. Dogs are allowed in the camping cabins.

Loves Park

Rock Cut State Park
7318 Harlem Road
Loves Park, IL
815-885-3311
This park offers about 40 miles of hiking, 23 miles of mountain biking, and about 14 miles of equestrian trails. Dogs of all sizes are allowed. There are no additional pet fees. Dogs may not be left unattended, and they must be leashed and cleaned up after. Dogs are allowed on marked trails. The camping and tent areas also allow dogs. There is a dog walk area at the campground. There are no water hookups at the campground. Multiple dogs may be allowed.

Marengo

Lehman's Lakeside RV Resort
19609 Harmony Road
Marengo, IL
815-923-4533
Dogs of all sizes are allowed. There are no additional pet fees. Dogs must be leashed and cleaned up after. This RV park is closed during the off-season. There is a dog walk area at the campground. Multiple dogs may be allowed.

Marshall

Lincoln Trail State Park
1685 1350th Road
Marshall, IL
217-826-2222
This 1,023-acre park is home to a variety of flora and is rich in wildlife. There are many scenic and historic sites, and activities year round. Dogs of all sizes are allowed. There are no additional pet fees. Dogs may not be left unattended except for very short periods, and may only be left in unit if it poses no danger to the animal. Dogs must be leashed and cleaned up after. Dogs are allowed on the trails. The camping and tent areas also allow dogs. There is a dog walk area at the campground. There are no water hookups at the campground. Multiple dogs may be allowed.

Millbrook

Jellystone Park
8574 Millbrook Road
Millbrook, IL
800-438-9644
Dogs of all sizes are allowed. There is a $3 per night per pet additional fee for tent and RV spaces, and $5 per night per pet for cabin rentals. Dogs are not allowed in trailer or park models. Dogs may not be left unattended, must be leashed, and cleaned up after. The camping and tent areas also allow dogs. There is a dog walk area at the campground. Dogs are allowed in the camping cabins. Multiple dogs may be allowed.

Miller City

Horseshoe Lake-Alexander State Park
21204 Promise Land Road
Miller City, IL
618-776-5689
Dogs of all sizes are allowed. There are no additional pet fees. Dogs may not be left unattended, and they must be leashed and cleaned up after. Dogs on lead are allowed on the trails. The camping and tent areas also allow dogs. There is a dog walk area at the campground. Multiple dogs may be allowed.

Oakwood

Kickapoo State Park
10906 Kickapoo Park Road
Oakwood, IL
217-442-4915

This recreational park allows dogs of all sizes. There are no additional pet fees. Dogs must be on no more than a 10 foot leash, be cleaned up after, and inside and quiet at night. The camping and tent areas also allow dogs. There is a dog walk area at the campground. There are no water hookups at the campground. Multiple dogs may be allowed.

Pittsfield

Pine Lakes Resort
RR3 Box 3077
Pittsfield, IL
877-808-7436
Dogs of all sizes are allowed, and there are no additional pet fees for tent or RV sites. There is a $5 per night per pet additional fee for cottages. Dogs may not be left unattended except for short periods, and they must be leashed and cleaned up after. The camping and tent areas also allow dogs. There is a dog walk area at the campground. Dogs are allowed in the camping cabins. Multiple dogs may be allowed.

Plainview

Beaver Dam State Park
14548 Beaver Dam Road
Plainview, IL
217-854-8020
Dogs of all sizes are allowed. There are no additional pet fees. Dogs must be leashed and cleaned up after. This campground is closed during the off-season. The camping and tent areas also allow dogs. There is a dog walk area at the campground. Multiple dogs may be allowed.

Rock Island

Rock Island KOA
2311 78th Avenue W
Rock Island, IL
309-787-0665
Dogs of all sizes are allowed. There are no additional pet fees. Dogs must be leashed and cleaned up after. The camping and tent areas also allow dogs. There is a dog walk area at the campground. Dogs are allowed in the camping cabins. Multiple dogs may be allowed.

Rockford

River's Edge Campground
12626 N Meridian
Rockton, IL
815-629-2526
Dogs of all sizes are allowed. There are no additional pet fees. Dogs may not be left unattended, must be leashed, and cleaned up after. This RV park is closed during the off-season. The camping and tent areas also allow dogs. There is a dog walk area at the campground. Multiple dogs may be allowed.

Savanna

Mississippi Palisades State Park
16327A H 84
Savanna, IL
815-273-2731
As well as all the recreational activities this 2,500 acre park has to offer, it has some interesting geological sites to explore ear round. This park is also rich in Native American history. Dogs of all sizes are allowed. There are no additional pet fees. Dogs may not be left unattended, and they must be leashed and cleaned up after. Stay on designated trails. The camping and tent areas also allow dogs. There is a dog walk area at the campground. There are no water hookups at the campground. Multiple dogs may be allowed.

Springfield

Springfield KOA
4320 KOA Road
Rochester, IL
217-498-7002
Dogs of all sizes are allowed. There are no additional pet fees. Dogs must be quiet, leashed, and cleaned up after. This RV park is closed during the off-season. The camping and tent areas also allow dogs. There is a dog walk area at the campground. Dogs are allowed in the camping cabins.

St Louis Area

MGM Lakeside Campground
3133 W Chain of Rocks
Granite City, IL
618-797-2820
Dogs of all sizes are allowed. There are no additional pet fees. Dogs must be leashed and cleaned up after. The camping and tent areas also allow dogs. There is a dog walk area at the campground. Multiple

dogs may be allowed.

Union

Chicago Northwest KOA
8404 S Union Road
Union, IL
815-923-4206
Dogs of all sizes are allowed. There are no additional pet fees. Dogs may not be left unattended, they must be on no more than a 6 food leash, and cleaned up after. There are some breed restrictions. This RV park is closed during the off-season. The camping and tent areas also allow dogs. There is a dog walk area at the campground. Multiple dogs may be allowed.

Utica

Hickory Hollow Campground
757 N 3029 Road
Utica, IL
815-667-4996
Dogs of all sizes are allowed. There are no additional pet fees. Dogs may not be tied to trees or other campground property, and they must be leashed and cleaned up after. This RV park is closed during the off-season. The camping and tent areas also allow dogs. There is a dog walk area at the campground. 2 dogs may be allowed.

LaSalle/Peru KOA
756 N 3150th Road
Utica, IL
815-667-4988
Dogs of all sizes are allowed. There are no additional pet fees. Dogs may not be left unattended at the cabins, and they must be leashed and cleaned up after. This RV park is closed during the off-season. The camping and tent areas also allow dogs. There is a dog walk area at the campground. Dogs are allowed in the camping cabins. Multiple dogs may be allowed.

Wilmington

Fossil Rock Recreation Area
24615 W Strip Mine Road
Wilmington, IL
815-476-6784
Dogs of all sizes are allowed. There are no additional pet fees. Dogs must be leashed and cleaned up after. There are some breed restrictions. The camping and tent

areas also allow dogs. There is a dog walk area at the campground. 2 dogs may be allowed.

Indiana Listings

Albion

Chain O' Lakes State Park
2355 E 75S
Albion, IN
260-636-2654
This park has a nature center with regular programs, many hiking trails, and 8 connecting lakes you can paddle through. Dogs of all sizes are allowed. There are no additional pet fees. Dogs must be on no more than a 6 foot leash and be cleaned up after. Dogs are allowed on all the trails. The camping and tent areas also allow dogs. There is a dog walk area at the campground. There are no water hookups at the campground. Multiple dogs may be allowed.

Angola

Oakhill Family Campground
4450 N 50W
Angola, IN
260-668-7041
Dogs of all sizes are allowed. There are no additional pet fees. Dogs must be leashed and cleaned up after. The camping and tent areas also allow dogs. There is a dog walk area at the campground. 2 dogs may be allowed.

Pokagon State Park
450 Lane 100 Lake James
Angola, IN
260-833-2012
This park has several natural lakes, a nature center, and a seasonal toboggan run. Dogs are allowed at no additional fee. Dogs may not be left unattended at any time, and they must be leashed and cleaned up after. Dogs are not allowed at the group camping area or in any of the buildings. Dogs are not allowed on the beach from Memorial Day through Labor Day. The camping and tent areas also allow dogs. There is a dog walk area at the campground. There are no water hookups at the campground. Multiple dogs may be allowed.

Auburn

Auburn/Fort Wayne North KOA
5612 County Road 11A
Auburn, IN
260-925-6747
Dogs of all sizes are allowed. There are no additional pet fees. Dogs must be quiet, well behaved, leashed, and cleaned up after. The camping and tent areas also allow dogs. There is a dog walk area at the campground. Multiple dogs may be allowed.

Battle Ground

Prophetstown State Park
4112 E State Road 4
Battle Ground, IN
765-567-4919
This park's historical and geological setting allow visitors to step back in time with a recreated Native American village and a 1920's era living history farm. Dogs of all sizes are allowed at no additional fee. Dogs may not be left unattended, and they must be on no more than a 6 foot leash, and be cleaned up after. Dogs are allowed on the trails. The camping and tent areas also allow dogs. There is a dog walk area at the campground. Multiple dogs may be allowed.

Bedford

Hoosier National Forest
811 Constitution (District office)
Bedford, IN
812-275-5987
This park has over 200,000 acres with 6 main campgrounds, several trails, and geological, scenic, and historical areas to explore. Dogs of all sizes are allowed. There are no additional pet fees. Dogs must be leashed and cleaned up after. Dogs are allowed on all of the trails. The camping and tent areas also allow dogs. There is a dog walk area at the campground.

Bloomington

Lake Monroe Village
8107 S Fairfax
Bloomington, IN
812-824-2267
Dogs of all sizes are allowed. There are no additional pet fees. Dogs must be leashed and cleaned up after. The camping and tent areas also allow dogs. There is a dog walk

area at the campground. Dogs are allowed in the camping cabins. Multiple dogs may be allowed.

Bluffton

Ouabache State Park
4930 E State Road 201
Bluffton, IN
260-824-0926
This recreational park provides plenty of hiking trails, fishing, and off season fun. Dogs are allowed at no additional fee, and they are allowed on the trails. Dogs must be on a 6 foot leash unless you are off the trails and have voice control. Dogs must be cleaned up after, and they are not allowed at the pool. The camping and tent areas also allow dogs. There is a dog walk area at the campground. There are no water hookups at the campground. Multiple dogs may be allowed.

Charleston

Charlestown State Park
3000 State Park Drive
Charleston, IN
812-256-5600
Dogs of all sizes are allowed. There are no additional pet fees. Dogs may not be left unattended, and they must be leashed and cleaned up after. Dogs are allowed on the trails. The camping and tent areas also allow dogs. There is a dog walk area at the campground. Multiple dogs may be allowed.

Cherokee

Happy Holiday RV Park
1553 Wolftown Road
Cherokee, IN
828-497-7250
Dogs of all sizes are allowed. There are no additional pet fees. Dogs may not be left unattended outside, and they must be leashed and cleaned up after. This RV park is closed during the off-season. The camping and tent areas also allow dogs. There is a dog walk area at the campground. Dogs are allowed in the camping cabins. Multiple dogs may be allowed.

Chesterton

Indiana Dunes State Park
1600 North 25 E

Chesterton, IN
219-926-1952
The dunes, the nature center, trails, and special programs throughout the year make this an interesting park. Dogs of all sizes are allowed. There are no additional pet fees. Dogs must be on no more than a 6 foot leash and be cleaned up after. Dogs are allowed on the trails, but from Memorial Day to Labor Day dogs are not allowed on the beach. The camping and tent areas also allow dogs. There is a dog walk area at the campground. Multiple dogs may be allowed.

Columbus

Woods N Waters Kampground
8855 S 300 W
Columbus, IN
812-342-1619
Dogs of all sizes are allowed. There are no additional pet fees. Dogs may not be left unattended, must be leashed, and cleaned up after. The camping and tent areas also allow dogs. There is a dog walk area at the campground. Multiple dogs may be allowed.

Corydon

O'Bannon Woods State Park
7240 Old Forest Road
Corydon, IN
812-738-8232
This 26,000 acre park is called one of the 7 hidden jewels of the Indiana parks because of it's beauty and seclusion. Dogs are allowed at no additional fee. Dogs must be on no more than a 6 foot leash and be cleaned up after. Dogs are not allowed in the buildings. This campground is closed during the off-season. The camping and tent areas also allow dogs. There is a dog walk area at the campground. There are no water hookups at the campground. Multiple dogs may be allowed.

Crawfordsville

Crawfordsville KOA
1600 Lafayette Road
Crawfordsville, IN
765-362-4190
Dogs of all sizes are allowed. There are no additional pet fees. Dogs may not be left unattended in the cabins or outside alone. Dogs must be leashed and cleaned up after. This

RV park is closed during the off-season. The camping and tent areas also allow dogs. There is a dog walk area at the campground. Dogs are allowed in the camping cabins. Multiple dogs may be allowed.

Elkhart

Elkhart Campground
25608 County Road 4
Elkhart, IN
574-264-2914
Dogs of all sizes are allowed. There are no additional pet fees. Dogs must be quiet, leashed, and cleaned up after. If you have dogs in one of the cabins they request you sweep out the cabin before you leave. Dogs must be leashed and cleaned up after. This RV park is closed during the off-season. The camping and tent areas also allow dogs. There is a dog walk area at the campground. Dogs are allowed in the camping cabins. 2 dogs may be allowed.

Freemont

Jellystone Park
140 Lane, 201 Barton Lake
Freemont, IN
260-833-1114
Dogs of all sizes are allowed. There are no additional pet fees. Dogs may not be left unattended, must be leashed, and cleaned up after. This RV park is closed during the off-season. The camping and tent areas also allow dogs. There is a dog walk area at the campground. 2 dogs may be allowed.

Gary

Oak Lake Campground
5310 E 900N
Fair Oaks, IN
219-345-3153
Dogs of all sizes are allowed, however there can only be one large dog, or two small dogs per site. There are no additional pet fees. Dogs must be quiet, leashed, and cleaned up after. This RV park is closed during the off-season. There is a dog walk area at the campground.

Geneva

Amishville RV Park
844 E 900 S
Geneva, IN

260-589-3536
Dogs of all sizes are allowed. There are no additional pet fees. Dogs must be quiet, well behaved, leashed, and cleaned up after. This RV park is closed during the off-season. The camping and tent areas also allow dogs. There is a dog walk area at the campground. Multiple dogs may be allowed.

Granger

South Bend East KOA
50707 Princess Way
Granger, IN
574-277-1335
Dogs of all sizes are allowed, and there are no additional pet fees for tent or RV sites. There is a $50 cash only refundable deposit for the cabins. Dogs must be leashed and cleaned up after. This RV park is closed during the off-season. The camping and tent areas also allow dogs. There is a dog walk area at the campground. Dogs are allowed in the camping cabins. Multiple dogs may be allowed.

Howe

Twin Mills Camping Resort
1675 W H 120
Howe, IN
260-562-3212
Dogs of all sizes and numbers are allowed, and there are no additional pet fees for tent or RV sites. There is a $25 per stay additional fee for cabins or rentals, and only 2 dogs 10 pounds or under are allowed. There must be proof of insurance for known aggressive breeds. Dogs must be leashed and cleaned up after. This RV park is closed during the off-season. The camping and tent areas also allow dogs. There is a dog walk area at the campground. Dogs are allowed in the camping cabins.

Indianapolis

Broadview Lake Campground
4850 Broadview Road
Colfax, IN
765-324-2622
Dogs of all sizes are allowed. There are no additional pet fees. Dogs must be quiet, leashed, and cleaned up after. This RV park is closed during the off-season. There is a dog walk area at the campground. Multiple dogs may be

allowed.

Heartland Resort
1613 W 300N
Greenfield, IN
317-326-3181
Dogs of all sizes are allowed. There are no additional pet fees. Dogs must be quiet, well behaved, may not be left unattended, and must be leashed and cleaned up after. Dogs are not allowed in the buildings or at the beach. The camping and tent areas also allow dogs. There is a dog walk area at the campground. 2 dogs may be allowed.

Indianapolis KOA
5896 W 200 N
Greenfield, IN
317-894-1397
Dogs of all sizes are allowed. There are no additional pet fees. Dogs may not be left unattended in the cabins, and they must be leashed and cleaned up after. This RV park is closed during the off-season. The camping and tent areas also allow dogs. There is a dog walk area at the campground. Dogs are allowed in the camping cabins. Multiple dogs may be allowed.

S & H Campground
2573 W 100N
Greenfield, IN
317-326-3208
Dogs of all sizes are allowed. There are no additional pet fees. Dogs must be leashed and cleaned up after. The camping and tent areas also allow dogs. There is a dog walk area at the campground. Multiple dogs may be allowed.

Jasonville

Shakamak State Park
6265 W State Road 48
Jasonville, IN
812-665-2158
This park offers a nature center, 3 man-made lakes, and a variety of habitats, trails, and land and water recreation. Dogs of all sizes are allowed at no additional fee. Dogs may not be left unattended, and they must be on no more than a 6 foot leash, and be cleaned up after. Dogs are allowed on the trails. The camping and tent areas also allow dogs. There is a dog walk area at the campground. There are no water hookups at the campground. Multiple dogs may be allowed.

Knightstown

Yogi Bear Campground
5964 S H 109
Knightstown, IN
765-737-6585
Dogs of all sizes are allowed. There are no additional pet fees. Dogs must be friendly, well behaved, leashed, and cleaned up after. The camping and tent areas also allow dogs. There is a dog walk area at the campground. Dogs are allowed in the camping cabins. Multiple dogs may be allowed.

Liberty

Whitewater Memorial Park
1418 S State Road 101
Liberty, IN
765-458-5565
This historical and scenic park offers a 200 acre lake and a variety of land and water recreation. Dogs of all sizes are allowed at the tent and RV sites at no additional fee. There may only be one dog in the cabins, and there are only 2 pet friendly cabins. Dogs may not be left unattended, and they must be on no more than a 6 foot leash, and be cleaned up after. Dogs are allowed on the trails. The camping and tent areas also allow dogs. There is a dog walk area at the campground. Dogs are allowed in the camping cabins. There are no water hookups at the campground.

Lincoln City

Lincoln State Park
On H 162 3 miles W of Santa Claus
Lincoln City, IN
812-937-4710
This park is a natural living history park. Dogs of all sizes are allowed. There are no additional pet fees. Dogs may not be left unattended, and they must be on no more than a 6 foot leash, and be cleaned up after. Dogs are allowed on the trails, but not on the beach. The camping and tent areas also allow dogs. There is a dog walk area at the campground. Multiple dogs may be allowed.

Madison

Clifty Falls State Park
2221 Clifty Drive
Madison, IN
812-273-8885
Great scenic hiking and a beautiful water fall offer year round beauty at this park. Dogs of all sizes are allowed. There are no additional pet fees. Dogs may not be left unattended, and they must be leashed and cleaned up after. Dogs are not allowed at the pool or in the buildings. The camping and tent areas also allow dogs. There is a dog walk area at the campground. There are no water hookups at the campground.

Marshall

Turkey Run State Park
8121 E Park Road
Marshall, IN
765-597-2635
The natural geologic wonders, a Nature Center and Planetarium, great trails, and variety of land and water recreation brings visitors to this park. Dogs of all sizes are allowed at no additional fee. Dogs may not be left unattended, and they must be on no more than a 6 foot leash, and be cleaned up after. Dogs are not allowed in the nature center or in the lake, but they are allowed on the trails. The camping and tent areas also allow dogs. There is a dog walk area at the campground. There are no water hookups at the campground. Multiple dogs may be allowed.

Michigan City

Michigan City Campground
601 N H 421
Michigan City, IN
800-813-2267
Dogs of all sizes are allowed. There are no additional pet fees. Dogs may not be left unattended, must be leashed, and cleaned up after. The camping and tent areas also allow dogs. There is a dog walk area at the campground. 2 dogs may be allowed.

Middlebury

Elkhart Co/Middlebury Exit KOA
52867 H 13
Middlebury, IN
574-825-5932
Dogs of all sizes are allowed. There are no additional pet fees. Dogs may not be left unattended at the cabins, and they must be leashed and cleaned up after. This RV park is closed during the off-season. The camping and tent areas also allow dogs. There is a dog walk area at the campground. Dogs are allowed in the camping cabins. Multiple dogs may be allowed.

Mitchell

Spring Mill State Park
3333 H 60 E
Mitchell, IN
812-849-4129
Home to the Grissom Memorial, this park also has an early 1800s pioneer village, and tours of cave sites, in addition to a variety of land and water recreation. Dogs of all sizes are allowed at no additional fee. Dogs may not be left unattended, and they must be on no more than a 6 foot leash, and be cleaned up after. Dogs are not allowed in the village or in park buildings, but they are allowed on the trails. This campground is closed during the off-season. The camping and tent areas also allow dogs. There is a dog walk area at the campground. Multiple dogs may be allowed.

Monticello

Jellystone Park
2882 N West Shafer Drive
Monticello, IN
574-583-8646
Dogs of all sizes are allowed. There are no additional pet fees. Dogs may not be left unattended, must be leashed, and cleaned up after. Pit Bulls are not allowed. This RV park is closed during the off-season. The camping and tent areas also allow dogs. There is a dog walk area at the campground. 2 dogs may be allowed.

Nashville

Westward Ho Campground
4557 E H 46
Nashville, IN
812-988-0008
Dogs of all sizes are allowed. There are no additional pet fees. Dogs may not be tied up alone outside, they must be leashed at all times, and cleaned up after. This RV park is closed during the off-season. There is a dog walk area at the campground. Multiple dogs may be allowed.

New Castle

Summit Lake State Park

5993 N Messick Road
New Castle, IN
765-766-5873
With over 2,500 acres and a large lake, this park offers a variety of nature study and land and water recreation. Dogs of all sizes are allowed at no additional fee. Dogs may not be left unattended, and they must be on no more than a 6 foot leash, and be cleaned up after. Dogs are not allowed on the beaches or in buildings, but they are allowed on the trails. The camping and tent areas also allow dogs. There is a dog walk area at the campground. Multiple dogs may be allowed.

Walnut Ridge Campground
408 County Road 300W
New Castle, IN
877-619-2559
Dogs of all sizes are allowed. There are no additional pet fees. Dogs must be leashed and cleaned up after. This RV park is closed during the off-season. The camping and tent areas also allow dogs. There is a dog walk area at the campground. Multiple dogs may be allowed.

New Harmony

Harmonie State Park
3451 Harmonie State Park Road
New Harmony, IN
812-682-4821
This park has a natural resources education center, and many trails for hiking, walking, and biking. Dogs of all sizes are allowed. There are no additional pet fees. Dogs must be on no more than a 6 foot leash and cleaned up after. Dogs are not allowed at the pool or in the buildings, but they are allowed on the trails. The camping and tent areas also allow dogs. There is a dog walk area at the campground. There are no water hookups at the campground. Multiple dogs may be allowed.

New Paris

Natural Springs Resort
500 S Washington Street
New Paris, IN
888-330-5771
Dogs of all sizes are allowed. There is a $3 per night per pet additional fee. Dogs must be leashed and cleaned up after. This RV park is closed during the off-season. There is a dog walk area at the campground. Multiple dogs may be

allowed.

North Liberty

Potatoe Creek State Park
25601 State Road 4
North Liberty, IN
574-656-8186
This park offers a nature center, a 327 acre lake, and a variety of habitats, trails, ecosystems, and land and water recreation. Dogs of all sizes are allowed at no additional fee. Dogs may not be left unattended, and they must be on no more than a 6 foot leash, and be cleaned up after. Dogs are not allowed on beaches or in buildings. Dogs are allowed on the trails. The camping and tent areas also allow dogs. There is a dog walk area at the campground. There are no water hookups at the campground. Multiple dogs may be allowed.

Pierceton

Camp Yogi Jellystone Park
1916 N 850 E
Pierceton, IN
574-594-2124
Dogs of all sizes are allowed, however there can only be 2 large or up to 3 small pets per site. There are no additional pet fees. Dogs may not be left unattended, must be leashed, and cleaned up after. There are some breed restrictions. This RV park is closed during the off-season. The camping and tent areas also allow dogs. There is a dog walk area at the campground.

Plymouth

Jellystone Park
7719 Redwood Road
Plymouth, IN
574-936-7851
Dogs of all sizes are allowed. There are no additional pet fees. Dogs may not be left unattended, must be leashed at all times, and cleaned up after. This RV park is closed during the off-season. The camping and tent areas also allow dogs. There is a dog walk area at the campground. Dogs are allowed in the camping cabins. Multiple dogs may be allowed.

Portage

Yogi Bear Campground

5300 Old Porter Road
Portage, IN
219-762-7757
Dogs of all sizes are allowed. There are no additional pet fees. Dogs are not allowed in the rentals, must be leashed, and cleaned up after. This RV park is closed during the off-season. The camping and tent areas also allow dogs. There is a dog walk area at the campground. Multiple dogs may be allowed.

Porter

Indiana Dunes National Lakeshore
1100 North Mineral Springs Road
Porter, IN
219-926-7561
The dunes, the nature center, trails, and special programs throughout the year make this an interesting place to visit. Dogs of all sizes are allowed. There are no additional pet fees. Dogs must be on no more than a 6 foot leash and be cleaned up after. From October 1st to April 30th dogs are allowed at West Beach, Camel, Dunbar, and Lakeview. They are allowed at all through the year at Central Beach and Mount Baldie. The camping and tent areas also allow dogs. There is a dog walk area at the campground. There are no water hookups at the campground. Multiple dogs may be allowed.

Remington

Caboose Lake Campground
3657 H 24
Remington, IN
877-600-CAMP (2267)
Dogs of all sizes are allowed. There are no additional pet fees. Dogs must be quiet, well behaved, not left unattended at any time, leashed, and cleaned up after. There are some breed restrictions. The camping and tent areas also allow dogs. There is a dog walk area at the campground. Multiple dogs may be allowed.

Richmond

Richmond KOA
3101 Cart Road
Richmond, IN
756-962-1219
Dogs of all sizes are allowed, and there are no additional pet fees for tent or RV sites. Two dogs up to 50 pounds are allowed at the cabins also at no additional fee. Dogs may not be left unattended, and they must

be leashed and cleaned up after. This RV park is closed during the off-season. The camping and tent areas also allow dogs. There is a dog walk area at the campground. Dogs are allowed in the camping cabins.

Santa Claus

Lake Rudolph Campground
78 N Holiday Blvd
Santa Claus, IN
877-478-3657
Dogs of all sizes are allowed. There are no additional pet fees. Dogs must be leashed and cleaned up after. This RV park is closed during the off-season. The camping and tent areas also allow dogs. There is a dog walk area at the campground. Multiple dogs may be allowed.

Scottsburg

Jellystone Park
4577 W H 56
Scottsburg, IN
812-752-4062
Dogs of all sizes are allowed. There are no additional pet fees. Dogs may not be left unattended, must be leashed, and cleaned up after. The camping and tent areas also allow dogs. There is a dog walk area at the campground. Multiple dogs may be allowed.

South Bend

Mini Mountain Campground
32351 H 2
New Carlisle, IN
574-654-3307
Dogs of all sizes are allowed. There are no additional pet fees. Dogs must have shot records, may not be left unattended, and must be leashed and cleaned up after. Although this is mostly a seasonal campground, they have a few RV sites open in the winter for those traveling through. This RV park is closed during the off-season. The camping and tent areas also allow dogs. There is a dog walk area at the campground. Multiple dogs may be allowed.

Spencer

McCormick's Creek State Park
250 McCormicks Creek Park Road
Spencer, IN
812-829-2235
In addition to the recreational

activities, this park touts beautiful waterfalls and some unique limestone formations. Dogs of all sizes are allowed. There are no additional pet fees. Dogs may not be left unattended, and they must be on no more than a 6 foot leash, and be cleaned up after. Dogs are not allowed at the pool, the group camping area, or the hotel. The camping and tent areas also allow dogs. There is a dog walk area at the campground. There are no water hookups at the campground. Multiple dogs may be allowed.

Terre Haute

Terre Haute KOA
5995 E Sony Drive
Terre Haute, IN
812-232-2457
Dogs of all sizes are allowed. There is a $5 one time fee for pets. Dogs must be leashed and cleaned up after. The camping and tent areas also allow dogs. There is a dog walk area at the campground. Dogs are allowed in the camping cabins. Multiple dogs may be allowed.

Thorntown

Old Mill Run Park
8544 W 690N
Thorntown, IN
765-436-7190
Dogs of all sizes are allowed. There are no additional pet fees. Dogs may not be left unattended or tied up alone outside. Dogs must be leashed and cleaned up after. This RV park is closed during the off-season. The camping and tent areas also allow dogs. There is a dog walk area at the campground. Dogs are allowed in the camping cabins.

Versailles

Versailles State Park
1387 E H 50
Versailles, IN
812-689-6424
A 230 acre lake and a variety of land and water recreation are offered at this park. Dogs of all sizes are allowed at no additional fee. Dogs may not be left unattended, and they must be on no more than a 6 foot leash, and be cleaned up after. Dogs are not allowed in the lake or at the group camps, but they are allowed on the

trails. The camping and tent areas also allow dogs. There is a dog walk area at the campground. There are no water hookups at the campground. Multiple dogs may be allowed.

Waveland

Shades State Park
7751 S 890 W
Waveland, IN
765-435-2810
A variety of habitats create a nature lover's paradise here, and it has become a favorite among hikers and canoeists. Dogs of all sizes are allowed at no additional fee. Dogs may not be left unattended, and they must be on no more than a 6 foot leash, and be cleaned up after. Dogs are not allowed in buildings, but they are allowed on the trails. This campground is closed during the off-season. The camping and tent areas also allow dogs. There is a dog walk area at the campground. There are no electric or water hookups at the campground. Multiple dogs may be allowed.

Winamac

Tippecanoe River State Park
4200 N H 35
Winamac, IN
574-946-3213
This park along the Tippecanoe River offers a variety of land and water recreation. Dogs of all sizes are allowed at no additional fee. Dogs may not be left unattended, and they must be leashed and cleaned up after. Dogs are not allowed in public swim areas or in buildings. Dogs are allowed on the trails. The camping and tent areas also allow dogs. There is a dog walk area at the campground. Dogs are allowed in the camping cabins. There are no water hookups at the campground. Multiple dogs may be allowed.

Iowa Listings

Adel

Des Moines West KOA
3418 L Avenue

Adel, IA
515-834-2729
Dogs of all sizes are allowed. There are no additional pet fees. Dogs must be leashed and cleaned up after. There are some breed restrictions. The camping and tent areas also allow dogs. There is a dog walk area at the campground. Multiple dogs may be allowed.

Albia

Indian Hills RV Park
100 H 34E
Albia, IA
800-728-4286
Dogs of all sizes are allowed, and there are no additional pet fees for tent or RV sites. There is a $6 per night per pet additional fee for rooms at the inn, and they are in the smoking rooms. Dogs may not be left unattended, must be well behaved, leashed and cleaned up after. There is a dog walk area at the campground. 2 dogs may be allowed.

Amana Colonies

Amana Colony RV Park
#39 38th Avenue
Amana, IA
319-622-7616
Dogs of all sizes are allowed. There are no additional pet fees. Dogs must be leashed and cleaned up after. This RV park is closed during the off-season. The camping and tent areas also allow dogs. There is a dog walk area at the campground. Multiple dogs may be allowed.

Brighton

Lake Darling State Park
111 Lake Darling Road
Brighton, IA
319-694-2323
This beautiful park of 1,417 acres with a 302-acre lake, offers various recreational pursuits. Along the parks many trails you will see a variety of plant, animal and bird species. Dogs of all sizes are allowed at no additional fee. Dogs may not be left unattended, and they must be leashed and cleaned up after. Dogs are not allowed in public swim areas or in buildings. Dogs are allowed on the trails. The camping and tent areas also allow dogs. There is a dog walk area at the campground. Dogs are allowed in the camping

cabins. There are no water hookups at the campground. Multiple dogs may be allowed.

Cedar Falls

Black Hawk Park
2410 W Lonetree Road
Cedar Falls, IA
319-266-6813
This large park offers a variety of activities and recreation. Dogs of all sizes are allowed at no additional fee. Dogs may not be left unattended at any time, and they must be quiet, be on no more than a 6 foot leash, and cleaned up after. Dogs are allowed on the trails, but not on the playground. The camping and tent areas also allow dogs. There is a dog walk area at the campground. Dogs are allowed in the camping cabins. Multiple dogs may be allowed.

Clear Lake

Clear Lake State Park
6490 S Shore Drive
Clear Lake, IA
641-357-4212
This 55 acre park sits along the southeast shore of the beautiful 3,643-acre Clear Lake. It offers a variety of land and water recreational pursuits. Dogs of all sizes are allowed at no additional fee. Dogs may not be left unattended, and they must be quiet, leashed, and cleaned up after. Dogs are not allowed on the beach. Dogs are allowed on the trails. The camping and tent areas also allow dogs. There is a dog walk area at the campground. There are no water hookups at the campground. Multiple dogs may be allowed.

Oakwood RV Park
5419 240th Street
Clear Lake, IA
641-357-4019
Dogs of all sizes are allowed. There are no additional pet fees. Dogs must be quiet, well behaved, leashed, and cleaned up after. There are some breed restrictions. This RV park is closed during the off-season. There is a dog walk area at the campground. Multiple dogs may be allowed.

Clermont

Skip A Way RV Park

3825 Harding Road
Clermont, IA
563-423-7338
Dogs of all sizes are allowed. There are no additional pet fees. Dogs may not be left unattended outside your unit, must be leashed, and cleaned up after. Dogs can be walked down by the lake and also go for a swim. The camping and tent areas also allow dogs. There is a dog walk area at the campground. Multiple dogs may be allowed.

Des Moines

Adventureland Campground
2600 Adventureland Drive
Altoona, IA
512-265-7384
Dogs of all sizes are allowed. There are no additional pet fees. Dogs may not be left unattended, must be quiet, well behaved, and cleaned up after. The camping and tent areas also allow dogs. There is a dog walk area at the campground. 2 dogs may be allowed.

Kellogg RV Park
1570 H 224
Kellogg, IA
641-526-8535
Dogs of all sizes are allowed. There are no additional pet fees. Dogs must be quiet, well behaved, leashed, and cleaned up after. This RV park is closed during the off-season. The camping and tent areas also allow dogs. There is a dog walk area at the campground. Multiple dogs may be allowed.

Rolling Acres RV Park
1601 E 36th Street
Newton, IA
641-792-2428
Dogs of all sizes are allowed. There are no additional pet fees. Dogs must be well behaved, leashed and cleaned up after. This RV park is closed during the off-season. The camping and tent areas also allow dogs. There is a dog walk area at the campground. Multiple dogs may be allowed.

Farmington

Riverview Canoes and Camping
26070 Hawk Drive
Farmington, IA
319-878-3715
Dogs of all sizes are allowed. There are no additional pet fees. Dogs may not be left unattended unless they

will be quiet and well behaved. Dogs must be leashed and cleaned up after. This RV park is closed during the off-season. The camping and tent areas also allow dogs. There is a dog walk area at the campground. Dogs are allowed in the camping cabins. Multiple dogs may be allowed.

Guthrie Center

Springbrook State park
2437 160th Road
Guthrie Center, IA
641-747-3591
This beautiful park is located along a lake shore and offers 12 miles of hiking/nature trails and a variety of land and water recreation. Dogs of all sizes are allowed at no additional fee. Dogs may not be left unattended, and they must be leashed at all times, and cleaned up after. Dogs are not allowed on beaches or in buildings. Dogs are allowed on the trails. The camping and tent areas also allow dogs. There is a dog walk area at the campground. There are no water hookups at the campground. Multiple dogs may be allowed.

Hampton

Beed's Lake State Park
1422 165th Street
Hampton, IA
641-456-2047
This popular park provides a beautiful backdrop for a wide range of land and water activities, recreation and scenic trails. Dogs of all sizes are allowed at no additional fee. Dogs may not be left unattended, and they must be leashed and cleaned up after. Dogs are not allowed on the beach or in buildings. Dogs are allowed on the trails. This campground is closed during the off-season. The camping and tent areas also allow dogs. There is a dog walk area at the campground. Multiple dogs may be allowed.

Kellogg

Rock Creek State Park
5628 Rock Creek E
Kellogg, IA
641-236-3722
This park provides a haven for many different species of birds and wildlife. In addition it is a popular recreational area with a variety of activities. Dogs of all sizes are allowed at no additional fee. Dogs may not be left unattended, and they must be leashed and cleaned up after. Dogs are not allowed in public swim areas or buildings. Dogs are allowed on the trails. The camping and tent areas also allow dogs. There is a dog walk area at the campground. There are no water hookups at the campground. Multiple dogs may be allowed.

Lehigh

Brushy Creek Rec Area
3175 290th Street
Lehigh, IA
515-543-8298
This park, with over 6,000 acres located along a creek and the Des Moines River, offers about 50 miles of multi-use trails and a variety of land and water recreation. Dogs of all sizes are allowed at no additional fee. Dogs may not be left unattended, and they must be leashed and cleaned up after in camp area. Dogs may be off lead on the trails only if they are under strict voice command and will not chase. Dogs are not allowed on the beach. The camping and tent areas also allow dogs. There is a dog walk area at the campground. Multiple dogs may be allowed.

Marshalltown

Shady Oaks RV and Campground
2370 Shady Oaks Road
Marshalltown, IA
641-752-2946
Dogs of all sizes are allowed. There are no additional pet fees. Dogs may not be left unattended, and they must be leashed and cleaned up after. This RV park is closed during the off-season. The camping and tent areas also allow dogs. There is a dog walk area at the campground. Multiple dogs may be allowed.

Milford

Emerson Bay and Lighthouse
Emerson Street
Milford, IA
712-337-3211
This park provides a variety of habitats, trails, and land and water recreation. Dogs of all sizes are allowed at no additional fee. Dogs may not be left unattended unless they will be quiet, well behaved, and comfortable. Dogs must be leashed and cleaned up after. Dogs are not allowed in public swim areas or buildings. Dogs are allowed on the trails. The camping and tent areas also allow dogs. There is a dog walk area at the campground. There are no water hookups at the campground. Multiple dogs may be allowed.

Missouri Valley

Wilson Island Rec Area
32801 Campground Lane
Missouri Valley, IA
712-642-2069
This secluded park offers a variety of land and water recreation and is home to an abundance of bird and wildlife. Dogs of all sizes are allowed at no additional fee. Dogs may not be left unattended, and they must be leashed and cleaned up after. Dogs are not allowed in the Wildlife Refuge, in public swim areas, or buildings. Dogs are allowed on the trails. The camping and tent areas also allow dogs. There is a dog walk area at the campground. There are no water hookups at the campground. Multiple dogs may be allowed.

Mount Pleasant

Old Threshers Campground
405 E Threshers Road
Mount Pleasant, IA
319-38 5-8937
Dogs of all sizes are allowed. There are no additional pet fees. Dogs may not be left unattended, and they must be leashed and cleaned up after. This RV park is closed during the off-season. The camping and tent areas also allow dogs. There is a dog walk area at the campground. Multiple dogs may be allowed.

N Liberty

Colony Country Campground
1275 Forever Green Road
N Liberty, IA
319-626-2221
Dogs of all sizes are allowed. There are no additional pet fees. Dogs must be leashed and cleaned up after. This RV park is closed during the off-season. The camping and tent areas also allow dogs. There is a dog walk area at the campground.

Multiple dogs may be allowed.

Onawa

Lewis and Clark State Park
21914 Park Loop
Onawa, IA
712-423-2829
This historic park is home to a full-sized reproduction of Lewis and Clark's keelboat, "Discovery" and, in addition to commemorative events with period reenactments, it hosts a variety of land and water recreation. Dogs of all sizes are allowed at no additional fee. Dogs may not be left unattended, and they must be leashed and cleaned up after. Dogs are not allowed on beaches or in buildings. Dogs are allowed on the trails. The camping and tent areas also allow dogs. There is a dog walk area at the campground. There are no water hookups at the campground. Multiple dogs may be allowed.

On-Ur-Wa RV Park
1111 28th Street
Onawa, IA
712-423-1387
Dogs of all sizes are allowed. There are no additional pet fees, and your pets are met with a biscuit at check in. Dogs must be leashed and cleaned up after. This RV park is closed during the off-season. There is a dog walk area at the campground. There are special amenities given to dogs at this campground. Multiple dogs may be allowed.

Onawa/Blue Lake KOA
21788 Dogwood Avenue
Onawa, IA
712-423-1633
Dogs of all sizes are allowed. There are no additional pet fees. Dogs must be quiet, well behaved, leashed, and cleaned up after. Dogs may not be left unattended. This RV park is closed during the off-season. The camping and tent areas also allow dogs. There is a dog walk area at the campground. Dogs are allowed in the camping cabins. Multiple dogs may be allowed.

Osceola

Terribles Lakeside Casino
777 Casino Drive
Osceola, IA
541-342-9511

Dogs of all sizes are allowed. There are no additional fees for the tent, RV sites, or the hotel. Dogs may not be left unattended unless they will be quiet and well behaved. Dogs must be crated if left in the motel room unattended. The camping and tent areas also allow dogs. There is a dog walk area at the campground. 2 dogs may be allowed.

Quad Cities

Interstate RV Park
8448 Fairmont
Davenport, IA
563-386-7292
Dogs of all sizes are allowed. There are no additional pet fees. Dogs may not be left unattended, must be leashed, and cleaned up after. Dogs are not allowed at the playground or pool areas. There are some breed restrictions. There is a dog walk area at the campground. Multiple dogs may be allowed.

Tipton

Hunt's Cedar River Campground
1231 306th Street
Tipton, IA
563-946-2431
Dogs of all sizes are allowed. There are no additional pet fees. Dogs must be quiet, in your unit at night, leashed, and cleaned up after. This RV park is closed during the off-season. The camping and tent areas also allow dogs. There is a dog walk area at the campground. Multiple dogs may be allowed.

W Liberty

West Liberty KOA
1961 Garfield Avenue
W Liberty, IA
319-627-2676
Dogs of all sizes are allowed. There are no additional pet fees. Dogs may not be left unattended, and must be leashed and cleaned up after. The camping and tent areas also allow dogs. There is a dog walk area at the campground. Dogs are allowed in the camping cabins. Multiple dogs may be allowed.

Waterloo

George Wyth State Park
3659 Wyth Road
Waterloo, IA

319-232-5505
This beautiful park is unique in having several water areas for a variety of activities. It also offers several miles of various trails with connecting links to other larger trails. Dogs of all sizes are allowed at no additional fee. Dogs may not be left unattended, and they must be leashed and cleaned up after. Dogs are not allowed on beaches or in buildings. Dogs are allowed on the trails. The camping and tent areas also allow dogs. There is a dog walk area at the campground. There are no water hookups at the campground. Multiple dogs may be allowed.

Kansas Listings

Abilene

Covered Wagon RV Resort
803 Buckeye
Abilene, KS
785-263-2343
Dogs of all sizes are allowed. There are no additional pet fees. Dogs must be leashed and cleaned up after. The camping and tent areas also allow dogs. There is a dog walk area at the campground. Multiple dogs may be allowed.

Colby

Bourquin's RV Park
155 E Willow
Colby, KS
785-462-3300
Dogs of all sizes are allowed. There are no additional pet fees. Dogs may not be left unattended outside, and they must be leashed and cleaned up after. The camping and tent areas also allow dogs. There is a dog walk area at the campground. Multiple dogs may be allowed.

Dodge City

Gunsmoke Trav-L-Park
11070 108 Road
Dodge City, KS
620-227-8247
Dogs of all sizes are allowed. There are no additional pet fees. Dogs may not be tied up or left unattended outside at any time. Dogs must be

well behaved, leashed, and cleaned up after. Dogs may not be walked in the tent or pool areas, and they are not allowed in the buildings. This RV park is closed during the off-season. There is a dog walk area at the campground. Multiple dogs may be allowed.

Watersports Campground
500 E Cherry
Dodge City, KS
620-225-8044
Dogs of all sizes are allowed. There are no additional pet fees. Dogs may not be left unattended except for very short periods, and they must be cleaned up after. Dogs may be off lead if they are friendly, well behaved, and they will stay by the side of owner. The camping and tent areas also allow dogs. There is a dog walk area at the campground. Multiple dogs may be allowed.

El Dorado

Deer Grove RV Park
2873 SE H 54
El Dorado, KS
316-321-6272
Dogs of all sizes are allowed. There are no additional pet fees. Dogs may not be left unattended outside, and they must be leashed and cleaned up after. The camping and tent areas also allow dogs. There is a dog walk area at the campground. Multiple dogs may be allowed.

El Dorado State Park
618 NE Bluestem Road
El Dorado, KS
316-321-7180
The largest park in the state spreads along the shores of the El Dorado Reservoir and offer a full range of recreational pursuits. I addition it boasts an amphitheater and 7 different trails. Dogs of all sizes are allowed at no additional fee. Pets must be restrained by a camper, cage, hand-held leash, or tethered chain no longer than 10 feet at all times. Dogs may not be left unattended unless quiet and very well behaved. For cabin visitors, dogs may be tied up outside, and at night they must be crated. They are not allowed on swimming beaches, or in swimming areas that are delineated by buoys/markers, or in public buildings or structures. Dogs are allowed on the trails. The camping and tent areas also allow dogs. There is a dog walk area at the campground. Multiple dogs may be

allowed.

Emporia

Emporia RV Park
1601 W H 50
Emporia, KS
620-343-3422
Dogs of all sizes are allowed. There are no additional pet fees. Dogs must be leashed and cleaned up after. There is a dog walk area at the campground. Multiple dogs may be allowed.

Farlington

Crawford State Park
I Lake Road
Farlington, KS
620-362-3671
Rich in history and spectacular scenery, this 500-acre park, with a 150 acre lake and 2 archaeological sites, offers an array of recreational pursuits. Pets must be restrained by a camper, cage, hand-held leash, or tethered chain no longer than 10 feet at all times. Dogs may not be left unattended outside. They are not allowed on swimming beaches, or in swimming areas that are delineated by buoys or other markers, or in public buildings or structures. Dogs are allowed on the trails. This campground is closed during the off-season. The camping and tent areas also allow dogs. There is a dog walk area at the campground. There are no water hookups at the campground. Multiple dogs may be allowed.

Goddard

All Seasons RV Campground
15520 W Maple Street
Goddard, KS
316-722-1154
Dogs of all sizes are allowed. There are no additional pet fees. Dogs may not be left unattended, and they must be leashed and cleaned up after. The camping and tent areas also allow dogs. There is a dog walk area at the campground. 2 dogs may be allowed.

Goodland

Goodland KOA
1114 E H 24
Goodland, KS
785-890-5701

Dogs of all sizes are allowed. There are no additional pet fees. Dogs must be well behaved, leashed, and cleaned up after. There are some breed restrictions. This RV park is closed during the off-season. The camping and tent areas also allow dogs. There is a dog walk area at the campground. Dogs are allowed in the camping cabins. Multiple dogs may be allowed.

Grantville

Topeka KOA
3366 KOA Road
Grantville, KS
785-246-3419
Dogs of all sizes are allowed. There are no additional pet fees. There is a pet waiver to sign if the dog(s) are any of the known aggressive breeds. Dogs must be quiet, leashed and cleaned up after. This RV park is closed during the off-season. The camping and tent areas also allow dogs. Dogs are allowed in the camping cabins. Multiple dogs may be allowed.

Halstead

Spring Lake Resort
1308 S Spring Lake Road
Halstead, KS
316-835-3443
Dogs of all sizes are allowed. There are no additional pet fees. Dogs must be quiet, leashed, and cleaned up after. There are some breed restrictions. The camping and tent areas also allow dogs. There is a dog walk area at the campground. Multiple dogs may be allowed.

Hesston

Cottonwood Grove RV Campground
101 E Lincoln Blvd
Hesston, KS
620-327-4173
Dogs of all sizes are allowed. There are no additional pet fees. Dogs must be quiet, well behaved, leashed, and cleaned up after. The camping and tent areas also allow dogs. There is a dog walk area at the campground. Multiple dogs may be allowed.

Hutchinson

Melody Acres Campground

2201 S Bonebreak
Hutchinson, KS
620-665-5048
Dogs up to 20 pounds are allowed.
There are no additional pet fees.
Dogs may not be left unattended,
and they must be leashed and
cleaned up after. There are some
breed restrictions. There is a dog
walk area at the campground. 2 dogs
may be allowed.

Independence

Elk City State Park
4825 Squaw Peak Road
Independence, KS
620-331-6295
Dense woodlands, blue streams, and
a variety of scenic trails make this a
popular recreational destination. Pets
must be restrained by a camper,
cage, hand-held leash, or tethered
chain no longer than 10 feet at all
times. Dogs may not be left
unattended outside, and they must
be well taken care of. They are not
allowed on swimming beaches, or in
swimming areas that are delineated
by buoys or other markers, or in
public buildings or structures. Dogs
are allowed on the trails. The
camping and tent areas also allow
dogs. There is a dog walk area at the
campground. Multiple dogs may be
allowed.

Junction City

Owl's Nest RV Campground
1912 Old H 40
Junction City, KS
785-238-0778
Dogs of all sizes are allowed. There
are no additional pet fees. Dogs
must be leashed and cleaned up
after. There is a dog walk area at the
campground. Multiple dogs may be
allowed.

Kansas City

Rutlader Outpost and RV Park
33565 Metcalf
Louisburg, KS
866-888-6779
Dogs of all sizes are allowed. There
are no additional pet fees. Dogs
must be leashed and cleaned up
after. There is a dog walk area at the
campground. Multiple dogs may be
allowed.

Lawrence

Lawrence/Kansas City KOA
1473 H 40
Lawrence, KS
785-842-3877
Dogs of all sizes are allowed. There
are no additional pet fees. Dogs
may not be left unattended outside
or in the cabins, and they must be
quiet, be on no more than a 6 foot
leash, and cleaned up after. There
are some breed restrictions. The
camping and tent areas also allow
dogs. There is a dog walk area at
the campground. Dogs are allowed
in the camping cabins. Multiple
dogs may be allowed.

Manhattan

Tuttle Creek State Park
5800A River Pond Road
Manhattan, KS
785-539-7941
Numerous trails, an 18 hole disc
golf course, excellent fishing, and a
variety of other land and water
recreation greet visitors at this park.
Pets must be restrained by a
camper, cage, hand-held leash, or
tethered chain no longer than 10
feet at all times. Dogs may not be
left unattended outside. They are
not allowed on swimming beaches,
or in swimming areas that are
delineated by buoys or other
markers, or in public buildings or
structures. Dogs are allowed on the
trails. The camping and tent areas
also allow dogs. There is a dog
walk area at the campground.
Multiple dogs may be allowed.

Milford

Milford State Park
8811 State Park Road
Milford, KS
785-238-3014
This resort like park sits along the
shores of the largest lake in the
state, and offer a multi- purpose trail
system, a full service marina and
yacht club, and various water and
land recreation. Dogs of all sizes
are allowed at no additional fee.
Pets must be restrained by a
camper, cage, hand-held leash, or
tethered chain no longer than 10
feet at all times. Dogs may not be
left unattended outside. They are
not allowed on swimming beaches,
or in swimming areas that are
delineated by buoys/markers, or in
public buildings or structures. Dogs
are allowed on the trails. The

camping and tent areas also allow
dogs. There is a dog walk area at the
campground. Multiple dogs may be
allowed.

Norton

Praire Dogs State Park
P.O. Box 431
Norton, KS
785-877-2953
This park offers a variety of
recreation, historical interpretation
programs, a 1.4 mile nature trail, and
is home to a thriving prairie dog
colony. Pets must be restrained by a
camper, cage, hand-held leash, or
tethered chain no longer than 10 feet
at all times. Dogs must be well
behaved, and may not be left
unattended outside. They are not
allowed on swimming beaches, or in
swimming areas that are delineated
by buoys or other markers, or in
public buildings or structures. Dogs
are allowed on the trails, and they
may be off lead in the wildlife area if
they will not chase and are under
voice command. The camping and
tent areas also allow dogs. There is
a dog walk area at the campground.
Multiple dogs may be allowed.

Oakley

High Plains Camping
462 H 83
Oakley, KS
785-672-3538
Dogs of all sizes are allowed. There
are no additional pet fees. Dogs may
not be left unattended outside, and
they must be leashed and cleaned
up after. The camping and tent areas
also allow dogs. There is a dog walk
area at the campground. Multiple
dogs may be allowed.

Salina

Salina KOA
1109 W Diamond Drive
Salina, KS
785-827-3182
Dogs of all sizes and numbers are
allowed at the tent or RV sites. Two
dogs of any size are allowed at the
cabins. There are no additional pet
fees. Dogs may not be left
unattended, and they must be
leashed and cleaned up after. This
RV park is closed during the off-
season. The camping and tent areas
also allow dogs. There is a dog walk
area at the campground. Dogs are

allowed in the camping cabins.

St John

Pine Haven Retreat
217 E H 50
St John, KS
620-549-3444
Dogs of all sizes are allowed. There are no additional pet fees. Dogs may not be left unattended, and they must be leashed and cleaned up after. There are some breed restrictions. The camping and tent areas also allow dogs. There is a dog walk area at the campground. 2 dogs may be allowed.

Stockton

Webster State Park
1210 Nine Road
Stockton, KS
785-425-6775
This park covers 880 acres along the shores of Webster Reservoir, and a wide variety of land and water recreation is available. Dogs of all sizes are allowed at no additional fee. Pets must be restrained by a camper, cage, hand-held leash, or tethered chain no longer than 10 feet at all times. Dogs may not be left unattended outside. They are not allowed on swimming beaches, or in swimming areas that are delineated by buoys/markers, or in public buildings or structures. Dogs are allowed on the trails. The camping and tent areas also allow dogs. There is a dog walk area at the campground. Multiple dogs may be allowed.

Topeka

Capital City RV Park
1949 SW 49th Street
Topeka, KS
785-862-5267
Dogs of all sizes are allowed. There are no additional pet fees. Dogs may not be left unattended, and they must be leashed and cleaned up after. The camping and tent areas also allow dogs. There is a dog walk area at the campground. Multiple dogs may be allowed.

Toronto

Cross Timbers State Park
144 H 105
Toronto, KS

620-637-2213
This park, with over 1000 acres and with access to a 2,800 acre reservoir, offers a variety of trails, recreational pursuits, and some of the most diverse flora and fauna in the state. Dogs of all sizes are allowed at no additional fee. Pets must be restrained by a camper, cage, hand-held leash, or tethered chain no longer than 10 feet at all times. Dogs may not be left unattended unless they will be quiet and very well behaved. They are not allowed on swimming beaches, or in swimming areas that are delineated by buoys/markers, or in public buildings or structures. Dogs are allowed on the trails. The camping and tent areas also allow dogs. There is a dog walk area at the campground. Multiple dogs may be allowed.

WaKeeney

WaKeeney KOA
I 70 S. Frontage Road, Box 170
WaKeeney, KS
785-743-5612
Dogs of all sizes are allowed, and there are no additional pet fees for tent or RV sites. There is a $25 refundable deposit for the cabins, and dogs may not be left unattended there. Dogs must be well behaved, leashed, and cleaned up after. There are some breed restrictions. This RV park is closed during the off-season. The camping and tent areas also allow dogs. There is a dog walk area at the campground. Dogs are allowed in the camping cabins. There are special amenities given to dogs at this campground. Multiple dogs may be allowed.

Wichita

USI RV Park
2920 E 33rd
Wichita, KS
316-838-8699
Dogs of all sizes are allowed. There is a pet waiver to sign at check in and there are no additional pet fees. Dogs are not allowed in any of the buildings, and they may not be left unattended. Dogs must be quiet, leashed, and cleaned up after. There is a dog walk area at the campground. Multiple dogs may be allowed.

Yoder

Hitchin Post RV Park
3415 E Switzer Road
Yoder, KS
620-727-2356
Small Dogs Only. Dogs of all sizes are allowed. There are no additional pet fees. Dogs must be quiet, well behaved, leashed, and cleaned up after. Dogs may not be left unattended outside. This is an RV only park. There is a dog walk area at the campground. Multiple dogs may be allowed.

Kentucky Listings

Bardstown

Holts Campground
2351 Templin Ave (H 1430)
Bardstown, KY
502-348-6717
Dogs of all sizes are allowed. There are no additional pet fees. Dogs must be leashed and cleaned up after. The camping and tent areas also allow dogs. There is a dog walk area at the campground. Multiple dogs may be allowed.

My Old Kentucky Home State Park
501 E Stephen Foster Avenue
Bardstown, KY
502-348-3502
Rich in culture and history this park offers living history tours, an amphitheater, and a variety of activities and recreational pursuits. Dogs of all sizes are allowed at no additional fee. Dogs may not be left unattended, and they must be leashed and cleaned up after. Dogs are not allowed in the buildings. The camping and tent areas also allow dogs. There is a dog walk area at the campground. Multiple dogs may be allowed.

Beattyville

Lago Linda Hideaway Campground
850 Black Ridge Road
Beattyville, KY
606-464-2876
Dogs of all sizes are allowed. There are no additional pet fees. Dogs may not be left unattended outside or in

the cabins, and they must be leashed and cleaned up after. There are 2 pet-friendly cabins. Dogs do stay off the furniture in the cabins, and they are not allowed in other park buildings or on other people's camp sites. The camping and tent areas also allow dogs. There is a dog walk area at the campground. Dogs are allowed in the camping cabins. 2 dogs may be allowed.

Berea

Old Kentucky RV Park
1142 Paint Lick Road
Berea, KY
859-986-1150
Dogs of all sizes are allowed. There are no additional pet fees. Dogs must be quiet, well behaved, leashed, and cleaned up after. The camping and tent areas also allow dogs. There is a dog walk area at the campground. Multiple dogs may be allowed.

Bowling Green

Beech Bend Park & Splash Lagoon Family Campground
798 Beech Bend Road
Bowling Green, KY
270-781-7634
Dogs of all sizes are allowed. There are no additional pet fees. Dogs must be quiet, well behaved, leashed, and cleaned up after. The camping and tent areas also allow dogs. There is a dog walk area at the campground. Multiple dogs may be allowed.

Bowling Green KOA
1960 Three Springs Road
Bowling Green, KY
270-843-1919
Dogs of all sizes are allowed, and there are no additional pet fees for tent or RV sites. There is a $5 per night per pet additional fee for the cabins. Dogs may not be left unattended outside or in the cabins, and they must be leashed and cleaned up after. The camping and tent areas also allow dogs. There is a dog walk area at the campground. Dogs are allowed in the camping cabins. Multiple dogs may be allowed.

Burnside

General Burnside State Park
8801 S H 27

Burnside, KY
606-561-4104
Scenic views, an 18 hole golf course, and a variety of activities and recreational pursuits are offered in the park. Dogs of all sizes are allowed at no additional fee. Dogs may not be left unattended, and they must be leashed and cleaned up after. Dogs are not allowed on the golf course. This campground is closed during the off-season. The camping and tent areas also allow dogs. There is a dog walk area at the campground. Multiple dogs may be allowed.

Cadiz

Kamptown RV Resort
4124 Rockcastle Road
Cadiz, KY
270-522-7976
Dogs of all sizes are allowed. There are no additional pet fees. Dogs must be cleaned up after. Dogs may be off lead if they are under control of owner and they are well behaved. This RV park is closed during the off-season. The camping and tent areas also allow dogs. There is a dog walk area at the campground. Multiple dogs may be allowed.

Prizer Point Marina and Resort
1777 Prizer Point Road
Cadiz, KY
270-522-3762
Dogs of all sizes are allowed, and there are no additional pet fees for tent or RV sites. There is a $25 one time fee for 1 dog and $5 for each dog thereafter for the lodge. The campsites are seasonal, but the lodge is open year around. Dogs may not be left unattended at any time, or tied up outside alone. Dogs must be leashed and cleaned up after. This RV park is closed during the off-season. The camping and tent areas also allow dogs. There is a dog walk area at the campground. Multiple dogs may be allowed.

Calvert City

Paducah/I 24/Kentucky Lake KOA
4793 H 62
Calvert City, KY
270-395-5841
Dogs of all sizes are allowed at the tent or RV sites, and there can be up to 3. There can only be 2 dogs up to 25 pounds each in the cabins. There are no additional pet fees.

Dogs may not be left unattended, and they must be leashed and cleaned up after. This RV park is closed during the off-season. The camping and tent areas also allow dogs. There is a dog walk area at the campground. Dogs are allowed in the camping cabins.

Carrollton

General Butler State Resort Park
1608 H 227
Carrollton, KY
502-723-4384
This historic resort park offers summer concerts, tours, miniature golf, trails, planned activities, and a scenic overlook, and a variety of recreational pursuits. Dogs of all sizes are allowed at no additional fee. Dogs may not be left unattended, and they must have current rabies shot records. Dogs must be leashed at all times and cleaned up after, and they may not be tied to trees or shrubs. Dogs are allowed on the trails. The camping and tent areas also allow dogs. There is a dog walk area at the campground. Multiple dogs may be allowed.

Cave City

Crystal Onyx Cave and Campground Resort
363 Prewitts Knob Road
Cave City, KY
270-773-2359
Dogs of all sizes are allowed. There are no additional pet fees. Dogs may not be left unattended outside, and they must be well behaved, and cleaned up after. Dogs may be off lead only if they are under voice command and will not chase. This RV park is closed during the off-season. The camping and tent areas also allow dogs. There is a dog walk area at the campground. 2 dogs may be allowed.

Jellystone Park
1002 Mammoth Cave Road
Cave City, KY
270-773-3840
Dogs of all sizes are allowed. There are no additional pet fees. Dogs must be leashed and cleaned up after. There are some breed restrictions. The camping and tent areas also allow dogs. There is a dog walk area at the campground. Dogs are not allowed in the camping cabins. Multiple dogs may be

allowed.

Corbin

Corbin KOA
171 E City Dam Road
Corbin, KY
806-528-1534
Up to 3 dogs are allowed at the RV sites, 2 dogs at the tent sites, and 1 dog in the cabins. There are no additional pet fees. Dogs may not be left unattended, and must be leashed and cleaned up after. The camping and tent areas also allow dogs. There is a dog walk area at the campground. Dogs are allowed in the camping cabins.

Cumberland Falls State Resort Park
7351 H 90
Corbin, KY
606-528-4121
This park, known as the "Niagara of the South", has an impressive waterfall, but only on the night of a full moon over the waterfall can you see the Moonbow, a phenomenon not found anywhere else in the Western Hemisphere. There is also a variety of trails and recreation available. Dogs of all sizes are allowed at no additional fee. Dogs may not be left unattended outside, and they must be leashed and cleaned up after. Dogs are not allowed in buildings, but they can be on the trails. The camping and tent areas also allow dogs. There is a dog walk area at the campground. Multiple dogs may be allowed.

Corinth

Three Springs Campground
595 Campground Road
Corinth, KY
859-806-3030
Dogs of all sizes are allowed. There are no additional pet fees. Dogs must be leashed and cleaned up after. Dogs may be unleashed on your site if they are under voice command, will stay on the site, and will not chase. The camping and tent areas also allow dogs. There is a dog walk area at the campground. Dogs are allowed in the camping cabins. Multiple dogs may be allowed.

Crittenden

Cincinnati South KOA

3315 Dixie H
Crittenden, KY
859-428-2000
Dogs of all sizes are allowed. There are no additional pet fees. Dogs must be leashed and cleaned up after. There are some breed restrictions. This RV park is closed during the off-season. The camping and tent areas also allow dogs. There is a dog walk area at the campground. Multiple dogs may be allowed.

Dawson Springs

Pennyrile Forest State Park
20781 Pennyrile Lodge Road
Dawson Springs, KY
270-797-3421
This park is a back-to-nature hideaway, offering interpretive programs, an 18-hole par-72 golf course, 7 easy to difficult hiking trails, and a variety of recreational pursuits. Dogs of all sizes are allowed at no additional fee. Dogs may not be left unattended unless they will be quiet and well behaved. Dogs must be leashed and cleaned up after. Dogs are allowed on the trails, but not in any park buildings. The camping and tent areas also allow dogs. There is a dog walk area at the campground. Multiple dogs may be allowed.

Eddyville

Eddy Creek Marina Resort
7612 H 93S
Eddyville, KY
270-388-2271
Dogs of all sizes are allowed. There are no additional pet fees for the camping area. There is a $100 refundable pet deposit for the lodge. Dogs must be leashed and cleaned up after. Dogs are allowed on the trails. This RV park is closed during the off-season. The camping and tent areas also allow dogs. There is a dog walk area at the campground. Multiple dogs may be allowed.

Falls of Rough

Rough River State Resort Park
450 Lodge Road
Falls of Rough, KY
270-257-2311
This park, overlooking a 5,000 acre lake, offers a wide range of activities and land and water recreation. Dogs of all sizes are

allowed at no additional fee. Dogs may not be left unattended, and they must be leashed and cleaned up after. Dogs are allowed on the trails. The camping and tent areas also allow dogs. There is a dog walk area at the campground. Multiple dogs may be allowed.

North Fork Park
14500 Falls of Rough Road
Falls of Rough Road, KY
270-257-8139
This park along Rough River Lake offers a variety of land and water recreation. Dogs of all sizes are allowed at no additional fee. Dogs may not be left unattended, and they must be on no more than a 6 foot leash, and cleaned up after. Dogs are not allowed on the beaches. This campground is closed during the off-season. The camping and tent areas also allow dogs. There is a dog walk area at the campground. Multiple dogs may be allowed.

Falmouth

Kincaid Lake State Park
565 Kincaid Park Road
Falmouth, KY
859-654-3531
This scenic park, located along a 183-acre lake, offers mini golf, hiking trails, a 9 hole golf course, and a variety of land and water recreation. Dogs of all sizes are allowed at no additional fee. Dogs may not be left unattended, and they must be leashed and cleaned up after. Dogs are not allowed in public swim areas or in buildings. Dogs are allowed on the trails. The camping and tent areas also allow dogs. There is a dog walk area at the campground. Multiple dogs may be allowed.

Franklin

Franklin KOA
2889 Scottsville Road
Franklin, KY
270-586-5622
Dogs of all sizes are allowed. There are no additional pet fees. Dogs must be leashed and cleaned up after. The camping and tent areas also allow dogs. There is a dog walk area at the campground. Dogs are allowed in the camping cabins. Multiple dogs may be allowed.

Greenup

Greenbow Lake State Park
965 Lodge Road
Greenup, KY
606-473-7324
Rich in natural and cultural history, this park offers 25 miles of nature trails and a host of land and water recreation year round. Dogs of all sizes are allowed at no additional fee. Dogs may not be left unattended, and they must be leashed and cleaned up after. Dogs are not allowed in buildings, however, they are allowed on the trails. This campground is closed during the off-season. The camping and tent areas also allow dogs. There is a dog walk area at the campground. Multiple dogs may be allowed.

Hardin

Kenlake State Resort Park
542 Kenlake Road
Hardin, KY
270-474-2211
For quiet relaxation, active recreation, or as a business retreat, this park offers nature trails, and a wide array of land and water activities year round. Dogs of all sizes are allowed at no additional fee. Dogs may not be left unattended, and they must be leashed and cleaned up after. Dogs are not allowed in buildings. Dogs are allowed on the trails. This campground is closed during the off-season. The camping and tent areas also allow dogs. There is a dog walk area at the campground. Multiple dogs may be allowed.

Hartford

Ohio County Park and Campground
2300 H 69N
Hartford, KY
270-298-4466
Dogs of all sizes are allowed. There are no additional pet fees. Dogs may not be left unattended, must be well behaved, leashed, and cleaned up after. The camping and tent areas also allow dogs. There is a dog walk area at the campground. 2 dogs may be allowed.

Horse Cave

Horse Cave KOA
109 Knob Hill Road

Horse Cave, KY
270-786-2819
Dogs of all sizes are allowed. There are no additional pet fees. Dogs must be leashed and cleaned up after. The camping and tent areas also allow dogs. There is a dog walk area at the campground. Dogs are allowed in the camping cabins. Multiple dogs may be allowed.

Jamestown

Lake Cumberland State Park
5465 State Park Road
Jamestown, KY
270-343-3111
This park offers panoramic views of the 60,000 acre lake that is considered one of best in the Eastern US for boating and fishing. It also provides interpretive programs, scenic trails and a variety of land and water recreation. Dogs of all sizes are allowed at no additional fee. Dogs may not be left unattended, and they must be leashed and cleaned up after. Dogs are not allowed in buildings. Dogs are allowed on the trails. This campground is closed during the off-season. The camping and tent areas also allow dogs. There is a dog walk area at the campground. Multiple dogs may be allowed.

Lexington

Elkhorn Campground
165 N Scruggs Lane
Frankfort, KY
502-695-9154
Dogs of all sizes are allowed, but dogs over 60 pounds must wear a harness lead. There are no additional pet fees. Dogs may not be left unattended, must be quiet, well behaved, leashed, and cleaned up after. Although they mostly close down in winter, they do have a few RV sites available for those traveling through. There are some breed restrictions. This RV park is closed during the off-season. The camping and tent areas also allow dogs. There is a dog walk area at the campground. Multiple dogs may be allowed.

Kentucky Horse Park Campground
4089 Iron Works Parkway
Lexington, KY
859-259-4257
There are many amenities at this beautiful park and a variety of

activities and recreational pursuits. Dogs of all sizes are allowed at no additional fee. Dogs may not be left unattended, and they must be on no more than a 6 foot leash, and cleaned up after. The camping and tent areas also allow dogs. There is a dog walk area at the campground. Multiple dogs may be allowed.

Louisville

Louisville Metro KOA
900 Marriott Drive
Clarksville, IN
812-282-4474
Dogs of all sizes are allowed. There are no additional pet fees. Dogs may not be left unattended outside, and they must be leashed and cleaned up after. The camping and tent areas also allow dogs. There is a dog walk area at the campground. Dogs are allowed in the camping cabins. Multiple dogs may be allowed.

Grand Trails RV Park
205 S Mulberry
Corydon, IN
812-738-9077
Dogs of all sizes are allowed, and there are no additional pet fees for tent or RV sites. There is a $25 refundable pet deposit for the cabins. Dogs may not be tied to anything belonging to the campground, and they may not be tied up alone outside. Dogs must be leashed at all times, and cleaned up after. The camping and tent areas also allow dogs. There is a dog walk area at the campground. Dogs are allowed in the camping cabins. Multiple dogs may be allowed.

Lucas

Barren River Lake State Resort
1149 State Park Road
Lucas, KY
270-646-2151
This beautiful park curves around the 10,000-acre lake, providing spectacular views and sunsets. It also offers nature trails, a regulation 18 hole golf course and a wide variety of land and water recreation. Dogs of all sizes are allowed at no additional fee. Dogs may not be left unattended, and they must be quiet, well behaved, leashed and cleaned up after. Dogs are not allowed in buildings. Dogs are allowed on the trails. This campground is closed during the off-season. The camping and tent areas also allow dogs.

There is a dog walk area at the campground. Multiple dogs may be allowed.

Mammoth Cave

Mammoth Cave National Park
P. O. Box 7
Mammoth Cave, KY
270-758-2180
This park has the longest recorded cave system in the world with over 350 miles mapped, and it provides a variety of camping areas, trails, recreation, and diverse ecosystems that support a large variety of plants, fish, mammals, and bird species. Dogs are allowed at no additional fee. Dogs may not be left unattended, and they must be leashed and cleaned up after in the camp areas. Dogs are not allowed in the caves. The park is open with tent camping year round, however, RV camping is seasonal. This campground is closed during the off-season. The camping and tent areas also allow dogs. There is a dog walk area at the campground. There are no electric or water hookups at the campground. Multiple dogs may be allowed.

Manchester

Clay County Campground
83 Crawfish Road
Manchester, KY
606-598-3449
Dogs of all sizes are allowed. There are no additional pet fees. Dogs must be well behaved, leashed, and cleaned up after. Only one dog at a time can be in the cabins. This RV park is closed during the off-season. The camping and tent areas also allow dogs. There is a dog walk area at the campground. Dogs are allowed in the camping cabins.

Middleboro

Cumberland Gap National Historical Park
H 25E South
Middleboro, KY
606-248-2817
Rich in natural and cultural history, this park is commemorated as the "doorway to the West", as it marks a major break in the formidable Appalachian Mountains. Within the park you will find a number of recreational pursuits and over 70 miles of trails. Dogs of all sizes are allowed at no additional fee. Dogs may not be left unattended unless they will be quiet and well behaved. Dogs must be leashed and cleaned up after. Dogs are allowed on the trails. The camping and tent areas also allow dogs. There is a dog walk area at the campground. There are no water hookups at the campground. Multiple dogs may be allowed.

Morehead - Cave Run Lake

Poppy Mountain Campground
8030 H 60E
Morehead, KY
606-780-4192
Dogs of all sizes are allowed. There are no additional pet fees. Dogs may not be in the stage area, and they must be leashed and cleaned up after. This RV park is closed during the off-season. The camping and tent areas also allow dogs. There is a dog walk area at the campground. Multiple dogs may be allowed.

Twin Knobs Rec Area
2375 Kentucky H
Morehead, KY
606-784-6428
This recreation area, located on a 700-acre wooded peninsula, offers interpretive programs and land and water recreation. Dogs must be leashed and cleaned up after. Dogs are allowed on the trails, but not in the public swimming areas. This campground is closed during the off-season. The camping and tent areas also allow dogs. There is a dog walk area at the campground. There are no water hookups at the campground. Multiple dogs may be allowed.

Paducah

Duck Creek RV Park & Campground
2540 John Puryear Drive
Paducah, KY
270-415-0404
Dogs of all sizes are allowed. There are no additional pet fees. Dogs must be leashed and cleaned up after. The camping and tent areas also allow dogs. There is a dog walk area at the campground. Multiple dogs may be allowed.

Parker's Lake

Eagle Falls Resort
11251 H 90
Parker's Lake, KY
888-318-2658
Dogs of all sizes are allowed, and there are no additional pet fees for tent or RV sites. There is a $10 per night per pet additional fee for the resort. Dogs must be leashed and cleaned up after. The camping and tent areas also allow dogs. There is a dog walk area at the campground. Multiple dogs may be allowed.

Renfro Valley

Renfro Valley KOA
Red Foley Road, H 25
Renfro Valley, KY
606-256-2474
Dogs of all sizes are allowed. There are no additional pet fees. Dogs may not be left unattended outside except for very short periods, and they must be leashed and cleaned up after. There are some breed restrictions. The camping and tent areas also allow dogs. There is a dog walk area at the campground. Dogs are allowed in the camping cabins.

Renfro Valley RV Park
Renfro Valley Entertainment Center
Renfro Valley, KY
606-256-2638
Dogs of all sizes are allowed. There are no additional pet fees. Dogs must be well behaved, leashed, and cleaned up after. There is a dog walk area at the campground. Multiple dogs may be allowed.

Russell Springs

Russell Springs KOA
1440 H 1383
Russell Springs, KY
270-866-5616
Dogs of all sizes are allowed. There are no additional pet fees. Dogs must be quiet, leashed, and cleaned up after. This RV park is closed during the off-season. The camping and tent areas also allow dogs. There is a dog walk area at the campground. Multiple dogs may be allowed.

Sassafras

Carr Creek State Park
2086 Smithboro Road
Sassafras, KY
606-642-4050
Featuring the longest lakefront sand

beach in the Kentucky State Park system, this park offers a full service marina, and a variety of land and water recreation. Dogs of all sizes are allowed at no additional fee. Dogs must have current tags and shot records, be leashed at all times, and cleaned up after. Dogs are not allowed on the beach or in park buildings. This campground is closed during the off-season. The camping and tent areas also allow dogs. There is a dog walk area at the campground. Multiple dogs may be allowed.

Shepherdsville

Louisville South KOA
2433 H 44E
Shepherdsville, KY
502-543-2041
Dogs of all sizes are allowed. There are no additional pet fees. Dogs may not be left unattended, and they must be leashed and cleaned up after. The camping and tent areas also allow dogs. There is a dog walk area at the campground. Dogs are allowed in the camping cabins. Multiple dogs may be allowed.

Slade

Natural Bride State Resort Park
2135 Natural Bridge Road
Slade, KY
606-663-2214
It took nature millions of years to form the natural sandstone arch for which this park is named, and it offers a nature center and a variety of recreational pursuits. Dogs of all sizes are allowed at no additional fee. Dogs may not be left unattended, and they must be leashed and cleaned up after. Dogs are not allowed in buildings or on the nature trails. This campground is closed during the off-season. The camping and tent areas also allow dogs. There is a dog walk area at the campground. Multiple dogs may be allowed.

Union

Big Bone Lick State Park
3380 Beaver Road
Union, KY
859-384-3522
Popular, historical, educational, recreational, and pre-historic, all describe this scenic park. The park is home to the Outdoor Museum, their

own buffalo herd, salty marshes with fossilized remains of prehistoric animals, and still active salt springs. Dogs of all sizes are allowed at no additional fee. Dogs may not be left unattended, and they must be leashed at all times, and cleaned up after. Dogs are allowed on the trails. The camping and tent areas also allow dogs. There is a dog walk area at the campground. Multiple dogs may be allowed.

Winchester

Daniel Boone National Forest
1700 Bypass Road
Winchester, KY
859-745-3100
This forest of over 700,000 acres is home to the Natural Arch Scenic Area, the Red River Gorge Geological Area and over 3,400 miles of sandstone cliffs. In addition, the park offers a rich cultural history, spectacular scenery, and diverse ecosystems that support a large variety of plants, animals, and recreation. Dogs of all sizes are allowed at no additional fee. Dogs may not be left unattended, and they must be leashed and cleaned up after. Dogs are allowed on the trails. The camping and tent areas also allow dogs. There is a dog walk area at the campground. Multiple dogs may be allowed.

Louisiana Listings

Amite

Natalbany Creek Campground
30218 H 16
Amite, LA
985-747-9909
Dogs of all sizes are allowed. There are no additional pet fees. Dogs may not be left unattended outside, and they must be leashed and cleaned up after. The camping and tent areas also allow dogs. There is a dog walk area at the campground. Multiple dogs may be allowed.

Carencro

Bayou Wilderness RV Resort
201 St Claire Road

Carencro, LA
337-896-0598
Dogs of all sizes are allowed. There are no additional pet fees. Dogs must be leashed and cleaned up after. There is a dog walk area at the campground. Multiple dogs may be allowed.

Chatham

Jimmy Davis State Park (AKA-Caney Creek Lake State Park
1209 State Park Road
Chatham, LA
888-677-2263
This peninsula park offers an interesting history, fishing, trails, and a host of land and water recreation. Dogs of all sizes are allowed at no additional fee. Dogs may not be left unattended, and they must be leashed at all times, and cleaned up after. Dogs are not allowed on the beach or in park buildings. Dogs are allowed on the trails. The camping and tent areas also allow dogs. There is a dog walk area at the campground. Multiple dogs may be allowed.

Coushatta

Grand Bayou Resort
Rt 5, Box 11250
Coushatta, LA
877-932-3821
Dogs of all sizes are allowed. There are no additional pet fees. Dogs must be leashed and cleaned up after. The camping and tent areas also allow dogs. There is a dog walk area at the campground. Multiple dogs may be allowed.

Denham Springs

Baton Rouge KOA
7628 Vincent Road
Denham Springs, LA
225-664-7281
Dogs of all sizes are allowed. There are no additional pet fees. Dogs may not be left unattended outside, and they must be leashed and cleaned up after. There are some breed restrictions. The camping and tent areas also allow dogs. There is a dog walk area at the campground. Multiple dogs may be allowed.

Farmerville

Lake D'arbonne State Park

3628 Evergreen Road
Farmerville, LA
888-677-5200
This serene 665 acre park with a lake of more than 15,000 acres puts its focus on natural beauty and offers a wide variety of land and water recreation. Dogs of all sizes are allowed at no additional fee. Dogs may not be left unattended, and they must be leashed and cleaned up after. Dogs are not allowed in buildings or in the screened in areas. Dogs are allowed on the trails. The camping and tent areas also allow dogs. There is a dog walk area at the campground. Multiple dogs may be allowed.

Gardner

Kincaid Lake Rec Area
Valentine Lake Road
Gardner, LA
318-793-9427
A variety of colorful trees add to the beauty of this park that offers miles of various scenic trails and a host of land and water recreation. The park is located in the Kisatchie National Forest in the Calcasieu district. Dogs of all sizes are allowed at no additional fee. Dogs may not be left unattended, and they must be leashed and cleaned up after. Dogs are allowed on the trails. The camping and tent areas also allow dogs. There is a dog walk area at the campground. Multiple dogs may be allowed.

Grand Isle

Grand Isle State Park
108 Admiral Craig Drive
Grand Isle, LA
888-787-2559
A fisherman's and bird watcher's paradise, this park offers a rich history. In addition it is home to an observation tower, a 400 foot fishing pier, and a variety of land and water recreation. Dogs of all sizes are allowed at no additional fee. Dogs may not be left unattended, and they must be leashed and cleaned up after. Dogs are not allowed in buildings, but they are allowed on the trails. The camping and tent areas also allow dogs. There is a dog walk area at the campground. Multiple dogs may be allowed.

Homer

Lake Claiborne State Park
225 State Park Road
Homer, LA
888-677-2524
This park with a pristine lake of over 6,000 acres, offers scenic trails, long sandy beaches, and a variety of land and water activities and recreation. Dogs of all sizes are allowed at no additional fee. Dogs must be well behaved, be on no more than a 5 foot leash and cleaned up after. Dogs are not allowed in buildings; they are allowed on the trails. The camping and tent areas also allow dogs. There is a dog walk area at the campground. Multiple dogs may be allowed.

Lake Charles

Jellystone Park
4200 Luke Powers Road
Lake Charles, LA
337-433-1114
Dogs of all sizes are allowed. There are no additional pet fees. Dogs must be leashed and cleaned up after. The camping and tent areas also allow dogs. There is a dog walk area at the campground. Multiple dogs may be allowed.

Minden

Caney Lakes Rec Area
194 Caney Lake Road
Minden, LA
318-927-2061
This park offers a variety of landscapes, from the National Sugar Cane Recreation Trail to two completely different types of lakes for recreation. Dogs of all sizes are allowed at no additional fee. Dogs may not be left unattended, and they must be leashed and cleaned up after. Dogs are allowed on the trails. The camping and tent areas also allow dogs. There is a dog walk area at the campground. Multiple dogs may be allowed.

Monroe

Bayou Boeuf RV Park
11791 H 165 N
Sterlington, LA
318-665-2405
Dogs of all sizes are allowed. There are no additional pet fees. Dogs must be quiet, well behaved, leashed, and cleaned up after. The camping and tent areas also allow

dogs. There is a dog walk area at the campground. Multiple dogs may be allowed.

New Orleans

New Orleans/Hammond KOA
14154 Club Deluxe Road
Hammond, LA
985-542-8094
Dogs of all sizes are allowed. There are no additional pet fees. Dogs may not be left unattended outside, and they must be leashed and cleaned up after. There is a fenced in dog park for dogs to be off-leash. The camping and tent areas also allow dogs. There is a dog walk area at the campground. There are special amenities given to dogs at this campground. Multiple dogs may be allowed.

Pineville

Kisatchie National Forest
2500 Shreveport H
Pineville, LA
318-473-7160
This park of over 600,000 acres can be described as popular, historical, educational, recreational, and a sportsman's paradise. Dogs of all sizes are allowed at no additional fee. Dogs must be leashed, and cleaned up after in the camp areas. Dogs are allowed on the trails. The camping and tent areas also allow dogs. There is a dog walk area at the campground. Multiple dogs may be allowed.

Port Allen

Cajun Country Campground
4667 Relle Lane
Port Allen, LA
800-264-8554
Dogs of all sizes are allowed. There are no additional pet fees. Dogs must be leashed and cleaned up after. There is a dog walk area at the campground. Multiple dogs may be allowed.

Robert

Jellystone Park
46049 H 445 N
Robert, LA
985-542-1507
Dogs up to 20 pounds are allowed. There are no additional pet fees. Dogs must be leashed and cleaned

up after. There are some breed restrictions. The camping and tent areas also allow dogs. There is a dog walk area at the campground. Multiple dogs may be allowed.

Scott

Lafayette KOA
537 Apollo Road
Scott, LA
337-235-2739
Dogs of all sizes are allowed. There are no additional pet fees. Dogs may not be left unattended outside, and they must be leashed and cleaned up after. The camping and tent areas also allow dogs. There is a dog walk area at the campground. Multiple dogs may be allowed.

Shreveport

Cash Point Landing
215 Cash Point Landing
Bossier City, LA
318-742-4999
Dogs of all sizes are allowed. There are no additional pet fees. Dogs must be quiet, well behaved, leashed, and cleaned up after. Dogs may be off lead on your site if they are under voice control and will not chase. This is an RV only park. There is a dog walk area at the campground. Multiple dogs may be allowed.

Shreveport/Bossier KOA
6510 W 70th Street
Shreveport, LA
318-687-1010
Dogs of all sizes are allowed. There are no additional pet fees. Dogs may not be left unattended outside, and they must be leashed and cleaned up after. There are some breed restrictions. The camping and tent areas also allow dogs. There is a dog walk area at the campground. Dogs are allowed in the camping cabins. Multiple dogs may be allowed.

Sulphur

Hidden Ponds RV Park
1207 Ravia Road
Sulphur, LA
337-583-4709
Dogs of all sizes are allowed. There are no additional pet fees. Dogs may not be left unattended outside, and they must be leashed and cleaned up after. There is a dog walk area at

the campground. Multiple dogs may be allowed.

Vidalia

River View RV Park and Resort
100 River View Parkway
Vidalia, LA
318-336-1400
Dogs of all sizes are allowed. There are no additional pet fees. Dogs must be leashed and cleaned up after. The camping and tent areas also allow dogs. There is a dog walk area at the campground. Multiple dogs may be allowed.

Maine Listings

Abbott

Balsam Woods
112 Pond Road
Abbott, ME
207-876-2731
Dogs of all sizes are allowed. There are no additional pet fees. Dogs must be leashed and cleaned up after. This RV park is closed during the off-season. The camping and tent areas also allow dogs. There is a dog walk area at the campground. Dogs are allowed in the camping cabins. Multiple dogs may be allowed.

Alfred

Walnut Grove Campground
599 Gore Road
Alfred, ME
207-324-1207
Dogs of all sizes are allowed. There are no additional pet fees. Dogs must be leashed and cleaned up after. Visitor pets are not allowed. Dogs must have current rabies records. This RV park is closed during the off-season. Only one dog is allowed per campsite. The camping and tent areas also allow dogs. There is a dog walk area at the campground.

Arundel

Hemlock Grove Campground
1299 Portland Road
Arundel, ME

207-985-0398
Dogs of all sizes are allowed. There are no additional pet fees. Dogs can be left unattended only if they are quiet, well behaved, and comfortable with owner's absence. They must be left in the tent or RV. Dogs must be leashed at all times and cleaned up after. This RV park is closed during the off-season. The camping and tent areas also allow dogs. There is a dog walk area at the campground. 2 dogs may be allowed.

Augusta

Augusta West Lakeside Resort
183 Holmes Brook Lane
Winthrop, ME
207-377-9993
Dogs of all sizes are allowed. There is a $4 per pet per stay additional fee. Dogs may not be left unattended, must be leashed, and cleaned up after. Dogs are also not allowed at the beach or the pool. This RV park is closed during the off-season. The camping and tent areas also allow dogs. There is a dog walk area at the campground. 2 dogs may be allowed.

Bangor

Paul Bunyan Campground
1862 Union Street
Bangor, ME
207-941-1177
Dogs of all sizes are allowed. There are no additional pet fees. Dogs must be leashed and cleaned up after. This RV park is closed during the off-season. The camping and tent areas also allow dogs. There is a dog walk area at the campground.

Pleasant Hill RV Park
45 Mansell Road
Hermon, ME
207-848-5127
Dogs up to 35 pounds are allowed. There is no fee for pets for the lots, but in the rentals there is a $10 per night per pet additional fee. Dogs must be leashed and cleaned up after. This RV park is closed during the off-season. The camping and tent areas also allow dogs. There is a dog walk area at the campground. Dogs are allowed in the camping cabins. 2 dogs may be allowed.

Bar Harbor

Spruce Valley Campground

136 County Road
Bar Harbor, ME
207-288-5139
Dogs of all sizes are allowed. There are no additional pet fees. Dogs may not be left unattended, must be leashed, and cleaned up after. This RV park is closed during the off-season. The camping and tent areas also allow dogs. There is a dog walk area at the campground. Multiple dogs may be allowed.

Boothbay

Beaver Dam Campground
551 H 9
Boothbay, ME
207-698-2267
Dogs of all sizes are allowed. There are no additional pet fees. Dogs may not be left unattended, must be leashed at all times, and cleaned up after. Dogs are not allowed at the playground or the beach. This RV park is closed during the off-season. The camping and tent areas also allow dogs. There is a dog walk area at the campground. Multiple dogs may be allowed.

Little Ponderosa Campground
159 Wiscasset Road
Boothbay, ME
207-633-2700
Dogs of all sizes are allowed. There are no additional pet fees. Dogs may not be left unattended unless they are well behaved and will be quiet, and then only inside your unit for short periods. Dogs must be leashed and cleaned up after. This RV park is closed during the off-season. The camping and tent areas also allow dogs. There is a dog walk area at the campground. Multiple dogs may be allowed.

Shore Hills Campground
553 Wiscaffet Road
Boothbay, ME
207-633-4782
Dogs of all sizes are allowed. There are no additional pet fees. Dogs may not be left unattended, must be leashed, and cleaned up after. This RV park is closed during the off-season. The camping and tent areas also allow dogs. There is a dog walk area at the campground. Multiple dogs may be allowed.

Brunswick

Thomas Point Beach
29 Meadow Road
Brunswick, ME
207-725-6009
Dogs up to 25 pounds are allowed. There are no additional pet fees, and pets are not allowed in the rentals. Dogs must stay on the campsite and can not be walked around the park. Dogs must be leashed at all times and cleaned up after. This RV park is closed during the off-season. The camping and tent areas also allow dogs. Multiple dogs may be allowed.

Camden

Camden Hills State Park
128 Belfast Road
Camden, ME
207-236-3109
Dogs of all sizes are allowed. There are no additional pet fees. Dogs may not be left unattended, and they must be leashed and cleaned up after. Dogs are allowed throughout the park. This campground is closed during the off-season. The camping and tent areas also allow dogs. There is a dog walk area at the campground. There are no electric or water hookups at the campground. Multiple dogs may be allowed.

Canaan

Skowhegan/Canaan
18 Cabin Row
Canaan, ME
207-474-2858
Dogs of all sizes are allowed and they are allowed in the cabins with a credit card on file. There are no additional pet fees. Dogs must be quiet and well behaved. Dogs may not be left unattended, must be leashed, and cleaned up after. Dogs are not allowed in the buildings, the pavillion, the pool or playground. This RV park is closed during the off-season. The camping and tent areas also allow dogs. There is a dog walk area at the campground. Dogs are allowed in the camping cabins.

Damariscotta

Lake Pemaquid Camping
100 Twin Cove Lane
Damariscotta, ME
207-563-5202
Dogs of all sizes are allowed. There

are no additional pet fees. Dogs must be quiet, leashed, and cleaned up after. This RV park is closed during the off-season. The camping and tent areas also allow dogs. There is a dog walk area at the campground. Dogs are allowed in the camping cabins. Multiple dogs may be allowed.

Dover-Foxcroft

Peaks-Kenny State Park
401 State Park Road
Dover-Foxcroft, ME
207-564-2003
Dogs of all sizes are allowed. There are no additional pet fees. Dogs may not be left unattended, and they must be leashed and cleaned up after at all times. Dogs are not allowed on the beach, the gravel, in the water, or the picnic areas. Dogs can be on the grass at the beach area and on all the trails. This campground is closed during the off-season. The camping and tent areas also allow dogs. There is a dog walk area at the campground. There are no electric or water hookups at the campground. Multiple dogs may be allowed.

Durham

Freeport/Durham KOA
82 Big Skye Lane
Durham, ME
207-688-4288
Dogs of all sizes are allowed, and there are no additional pet fees for tent or RV sites. There is a $10 one time additional pet fee for cabin rentals. Dogs must be quiet, leashed, and cleaned up after. There are some breed restrictions. This RV park is closed during the off-season. The camping and tent areas also allow dogs. There is a dog walk area at the campground. Dogs are allowed in the camping cabins. Multiple dogs may be allowed.

Ellsworth

Lamoine State Park
23 State Park Road
Ellsworth, ME
207-667-4778
Dogs of all sizes are allowed. There are no additional pet fees. Dogs may not be left unattended at any time, and they must be quiet, be on no more than a 4 foot leash, and be cleaned up after. Dogs may be off lead on your own site if they will stay

on site, and they are well behaved and under voice command. There are no dump stations at this park. This campground is closed during the off-season. The camping and tent areas also allow dogs. There is a dog walk area at the campground. There are no electric or water hookups at the campground. Multiple dogs may be allowed.

Freeport

Cedar Haven Campground
39 Baker Road
Freeport, ME
207-865-6254
Well behaved dogs of all sizes are allowed. There are no additional pet fees. Dogs may not be left unattended, must be leashed, and cleaned up after. There is a pond for dogs to swim in at which time they can be off lead if they are under voice control. No excessive barking is allowed. This RV park is closed during the off-season. The camping and tent areas also allow dogs. There is a dog walk area at the campground. Dogs are allowed in the camping cabins.

Greenville

Lily Bay State Park
Lily Bay Road
Greenville, ME
207-695-2700
Dogs of all sizes are allowed. There are no additional pet fees. Dogs may not be left unattended, and they must be leashed and cleaned up after. Dogs are allowed on all of the trails. This park has 2 campgrounds, and one usually closes up for the season earlier than the other. This campground is closed during the off-season. The camping and tent areas also allow dogs. There is a dog walk area at the campground. There are no electric or water hookups at the campground. Multiple dogs may be allowed.

Herman

Paul Bunyan's Wheeler Stream Campground
2202 H 2
Herman, ME
207-848-7877
Dogs of all sizes are allowed. There are no additional pet fees. Dogs may not be left unattended, must be leashed, and cleaned up after. This

RV park is closed during the off-season. The camping and tent areas also allow dogs. There is a dog walk area at the campground. Multiple dogs may be allowed.

Hermon

Pumpkin Patch
149 Billings Road
Hermon, ME
207-848-2231
Dogs of all sizes are allowed, and they are greeted here with a bone or other doggy treat when they come. There are no additional pet fees. Dogs must be leashed and cleaned up after. There are some breed restrictions. This RV park is closed during the off-season. The camping and tent areas also allow dogs. There is a dog walk area at the campground. There are special amenities given to dogs at this campground. Multiple dogs may be allowed.

Holden

Red Barn Campground
602 Main Road
Holden, ME
207-843-6011
Dogs of all sizes are allowed. There are no additional pet fees. Dogs may not be left unattended, be leashed, and cleaned up after. Dogs may not be in any of the buildings. This RV park is closed during the off-season. The camping and tent areas also allow dogs. There is a dog walk area at the campground. Multiple dogs may be allowed.

Houlton

My Brother's Place Campground
659 North Street
Houlton, ME
207-532-6739
Dogs of all sizes are allowed, however the cabins will only accept 1 dog up to 50 pounds. There are no additional pet fees. Dogs may not be left unattended, must be leashed, and cleaned up after. This RV park is closed during the off-season. The camping and tent areas also allow dogs. There is a dog walk area at the campground. Dogs are allowed in the camping cabins.

Kennebunkport

Red Apple Campground
111 Sinnott Road
Kennebunkport, ME
207-967-4927
Dogs of all sizes are allowed. There are no additional pet fees. Dogs may not be left unattended, must be leashed, and cleaned up after. This RV park is closed during the off-season. The camping and tent areas also allow dogs. There is a dog walk area at the campground. Multiple dogs may be allowed.

Medway

Katahdin Shadows Campground and Cabins
H 157
Medway, ME
207-746-9349
Dogs of all sizes are allowed. There are no additional pet fees. Dogs may not be left unattended, must be leashed, and cleaned up after. This campground is open through the winter and closes for only one month in April. This RV park is closed during the off-season. The camping and tent areas also allow dogs. There is a dog walk area at the campground. Dogs are allowed in the camping cabins. Multiple dogs may be allowed.

N Bridgton

Lakeside Pines Campground
54 Lakeside Pines Road
N Bridgton, ME
207-647-3935
Dogs of all sizes are allowed. There are no additional pet fees. Dogs must be up to date on their shots. Some breeds are not allowed. Dogs are not allowed in the rentals or on the beach. Dogs must be leashed and cleaned up after. This RV park is closed during the off-season. The camping and tent areas also allow dogs. There is a dog walk area at the campground. Multiple dogs may be allowed.

N Monmouth

Beaver Brook Campground
RFD 1 Box 1835 Wilson Pond Roa
N Monmouth, ME
207-933-2108
Dogs of all sizes are allowed. There are no additional pet fees. Dogs must be leashed and cleaned up

after. Dogs can be off leash to go swimming at the lake as long as they are under owner's control. This RV park is closed during the off-season. The camping and tent areas also allow dogs. There is a dog walk area at the campground. 2 dogs may be allowed.

Naples

Naples Campground
295 Sebago Road
Naples, ME
207-693-5267
Dogs of all sizes are allowed. There are no additional pet fees. Dogs must be friendly, not left unattended, be leashed, and cleaned up after. Dogs are not allowed in the rentals. This RV park is closed during the off-season. The camping and tent areas also allow dogs. There is a dog walk area at the campground. 2 dogs may be allowed.

Old Orchard Beach

Hid'n Pines Family Campground
8 Cascade Road
Old Orchard Beach, ME
207-934-2352
One dog of any size is allowed. There is a pet policy to sign at check in and there are no additional pet fees. Dogs may not be left unattended at any time and must be leashed and cleaned up after. Dogs are not allowed in the pool or bathroom areas. There are some breed restrictions. This RV park is closed during the off-season. The camping and tent areas also allow dogs. There is a dog walk area at the campground.

Powder Horn Family Camping Resort
48 Cascade Road
Old Orchard Beach, ME
207-934-4733
Dogs of all sizes are allowed. There is a pet policy to sign at check in and there are no additional pet fees. Dogs may not be left unattended at any time, and they are not allowed at the tents, buildings, or common areas. This RV park is closed during the off-season. There is a dog walk area at the campground. Multiple dogs may be allowed.

Wild Acres Family Camping Resort
179 Saco Avenue
Old Orchard Beach, ME

207-934-2535
Dogs of all sizes are allowed. There are no additional pet fees. There is a pet policy to sign at check in and there are no additional fees. Dogs may not be left unattended, must be leashed, and cleaned up after. This RV park is closed during the off-season. The camping and tent areas also allow dogs. There is a dog walk area at the campground. Multiple dogs may be allowed.

Phippsburg

Meadowbrook Camping
33 Meadowbrook Road
Phippsburg, ME
207-443-4967
Dogs of all sizes are allowed. There are no additional pet fees. Dogs may not be left unattended, must be leashed, and cleaned up after. Dogs are not allowed in the rentals. The camping and tent areas also allow dogs. There is a dog walk area at the campground. Multiple dogs may be allowed.

Portland

Bayley's Camping Resort
275 Pine Point Road
Scarborough, ME
207-883-6043
Dogs of all sizes are allowed. There is a pet policy to sign at check in and there are no additional pet fees. Dogs may not be left unattended, must be leashed, and cleaned up after. Children are not allowed to walk the dogs. This RV park is closed during the off-season. The camping and tent areas also allow dogs. There is a dog walk area at the campground. Multiple dogs may be allowed.

Wassamki Springs
56 Soco Street
Scarborough, ME
207-839-4276
Well behaved dogs of all sizes are allowed. There are no additional pet fees. Dogs may not be left unattended, must be leashed, and cleaned up after. There are some breed restrictions. This RV park is closed during the off-season. There is a dog walk area at the campground. 2 dogs may be allowed.

Pownal

Blueberry Pond Camping
218 Poland Range Road
Pownal, ME
207-688-4421
Dogs of all sizes are allowed. There are no additional pet fees. Dogs must be well behaved, leashed, and cleaned up after. This RV park is closed during the off-season. The camping and tent areas also allow dogs. There is a dog walk area at the campground. Dogs are allowed in the camping cabins. Multiple dogs may be allowed.

Rangeley

Rangeley Lake State Park
South Shore Drive
Rangeley, ME
207-864-3858
Dogs of all sizes are allowed. There are no additional pet fees. Dogs may not be left unattended, and they must be well behaved, leashed at all times, and be cleaned up after. Dogs are allowed on all the trails in the park. This campground is closed during the off-season. The camping and tent areas also allow dogs. There is a dog walk area at the campground. There are no electric or water hookups at the campground. Multiple dogs may be allowed.

Richmond

Augusta/Gardiner KOA
30 Mallard Drive
Richmond, ME
207-582-5086
Dogs of all sizes are allowed. There are no additional pet fees. There is only one pet friendly cabin available, so early booking would be advised. Dogs must be leashed and cleaned up after. There are some breed restrictions. This RV park is closed during the off-season. The camping and tent areas also allow dogs. There is a dog walk area at the campground. Dogs are allowed in the camping cabins. Multiple dogs may be allowed.

Rockport

Camden Hills RV Resort
30 Applewood Road
Rockport, ME
207-236-2498
Dogs of all sizes are allowed. There are no additional pet fees. Dogs may not be left unattended, must be leashed, and cleaned up after. This

RV park is closed during the off-season. There is a dog walk area at the campground. 2 dogs may be allowed.

Megunticook Campground
On H 1
Rockport, ME
207-594-2428
Dogs of all sizes are allowed. There are no additional pet fees. Dogs must be quiet and well behaved. Dogs may not be left unattended, must be leashed, and cleaned up after. There are some breed restrictions. This RV park is closed during the off-season. The camping and tent areas also allow dogs. There is a dog walk area at the campground. Dogs are allowed in the camping cabins. Multiple dogs may be allowed.

Saco

KOA Saco/Portland South
814 Portland Road
Saco, ME
207-282-0502
Dogs of all sizes are allowed, and there are no additional pet fees for tent or RV sites. There is a $15 one time fee plus a $100 refundable pet deposit for cabin rentals. Dogs may not be left unattended, must be leashed, and cleaned up after. This RV park is closed during the off-season. The camping and tent areas also allow dogs. There is a dog walk area at the campground. Dogs are allowed in the camping cabins. Multiple dogs may be allowed.

Trenton

Timberland Acres Campground
57 Bar Harbor
Trenton, ME
207-667-3600
Dogs of all sizes are allowed. There are no additional pet fees. Dogs may not be left unattended, must be leashed, and cleaned up after. This RV park is closed during the off-season. The camping and tent areas also allow dogs. There is a dog walk area at the campground. 2 dogs may be allowed.

Weld

Mt Blue State Park
299 Center Hill Road
Weld, ME
207-585-2347

Dogs of all sizes are allowed. There are no additional pet fees. Dogs may not be left unattended at any time, and they must be leashed and cleaned up after. Dogs are not allowed on Webb Beach, or anywhere on the sand, but they may go up to the tree line at the beach. Dogs are allowed on leash throughout the park, and at the boat launch area for swimming. The camping and tent areas also allow dogs. There is a dog walk area at the campground. There are no electric or water hookups at the campground. 2 dogs may be allowed.

Wells

Sea-Vu Campground
1733 Post Road
Wells, ME
207-646-7732
Dogs of all sizes are allowed. There are no additional pet fees. Dogs must be leashed and cleaned up after. This RV park is closed during the off-season. The camping and tent areas also allow dogs. There is a dog walk area at the campground. Multiple dogs may be allowed.

Well Beach Resort
1000 Post Road
Wells, ME
207-646-7570
Dogs of all sizes are allowed. There are no additional pet fees for 2 pets per site. There is a $7 per night per pet additional fee if over 2 dogs. Dogs must be leashed and cleaned up after. This RV park is closed during the off-season. There is a dog walk area at the campground. Multiple dogs may be allowed.

York Harbor

Libby's Oceanside Camp
725 York Street
York Harbor, ME
207-363-4171
Dogs of all sizes are allowed. There are no additional pet fees. Dogs must be leashed and cleaned up after. Dogs are allowed to go to the beach before 8AM and after 6PM. This RV park is closed during the off-season. The camping and tent areas also allow dogs. There is a dog walk area at the campground. 2 dogs may be allowed.

Maryland Listings

Baltimore

Bar Harbor
4228 Birch Avenue
Abingdon, MD
410-679-0880
Dogs up to 35 pounds are allowed. There are no additional pet fees. Dogs are not allowed in any of the rentals. There are some breed restrictions. There is a dog walk area at the campground. 2 dogs may be allowed.

Berlin

Frontier Town
8428 Stephen Decatur H
Berlin, MD
410-641-0880
Friendly dogs of all sizes are allowed. There are no additional pet fees. Dogs may not be left unattended, must be leashed, and cleaned up after. Dogs are not allowed in the rentals. There are some breed restrictions. This RV park is closed during the off-season. The camping and tent areas also allow dogs. There is a dog walk area at the campground. 2 dogs may be allowed.

Carlisle

Western Village RV Park
200 Greenview Drive
Carlisle, MD
717-243-1179
Dogs of all sizes are allowed. There are no additional pet fees. Dogs may not be left unattended, must be leashed, and cleaned up after. Dogs are not allowed on other guests' sites. There is a dog walk area at the campground. Multiple dogs may be allowed.

Clarksburg

Little Bennet Regional Park
23701 Frederick Road
Clarksburg, MD
301-972-9222
This scenic park of 3,600 acres and 20 miles of trails offers a variety of activities and recreational pursuits. Dogs of all sizes are allowed at no

additional fee. Dogs may not be left unattended, and they must be on no more than a 6 foot leash, and be cleaned up after. This campground is closed during the off-season. The camping and tent areas also allow dogs. There is a dog walk area at the campground. There are no water hookups at the campground. Multiple dogs may be allowed.

Ellicott City

Patapsco Valley State Park
8020 Baltimore National Pike
Ellicott City, MD
410-461-5005
This scenic park of 14,000 acres runs along 32 miles of shoreline, and features the world's longest multiple-arched stone railroad bridge, a 300 foot suspension bridge, a variety of trails, and various land and water recreation. Dogs of all sizes are allowed at no additional fee. Dogs may not be left unattended outside, and they must be leashed and cleaned up after. Dogs are not allowed to use the trails at the main entrance of the park or to be in developed areas. They are allowed only on marked trails, on the road, or just outside the park. This campground is closed during the off-season. The camping and tent areas also allow dogs. There is a dog walk area at the campground. Multiple dogs may be allowed.

Flintstone

Greenridge State Forest
28700 Headquarters Drive NE
Flintstone, MD
301-478-3124
The second largest forest in the state, this 44,000-acre oak-hickory forest offers a variety of trails, various land and water recreation, and some spectacular lookout points. Dogs of all sizes are allowed at no additional fee. Dogs may not be left unattended, they must be leashed, and cleaned up after in camp areas. Dogs are allowed on the trails. This campground is closed during the off-season. The camping and tent areas also allow dogs. There is a dog walk area at the campground. There are no electric or water hookups at the campground. Multiple dogs may be allowed.

Rocky Gap State Park
12500 Pleasant Valley Road
Flintstone, MD

301-777-2139
This resort like scenic park has over 3,000 land acres, 243 lake acres, a variety of trails, and various year round activities for land and water recreation. Dogs of all sizes are allowed at no additional fee. Dogs may not be left unattended, and they must be leashed and cleaned up after. Dogs are not allowed on beaches, in buildings, or picnic areas. Dogs are allowed on the trails. This campground is closed during the off-season. The camping and tent areas also allow dogs. There is a dog walk area at the campground. Dogs are allowed in the camping cabins. There are no water hookups at the campground. Multiple dogs may be allowed.

Freeland

Morris Meadows
1523 Freeland Road
Freeland, MD
410-329-6636
Dogs of all sizes are allowed. There are no additional pet fees. Dogs must have current shot records, may not be left unattend, and must be on no more than a 6 foot leash and cleaned up after. There are some breed restrictions. The camping and tent areas also allow dogs. There is a dog walk area at the campground. 2 dogs may be allowed.

Gardners

Mountain Creek Campground
349 Pine Grove Road
Gardners, MD
717-486-7681
Dogs of all sizes are allowed. There are no additional pet fees. Dogs must be quiet, well behaved, leashed, and cleaned up after. This RV park is closed during the off-season. The camping and tent areas also allow dogs. There is a dog walk area at the campground. Multiple dogs may be allowed.

Grantsville

Big Run State Park
349 Headquarters Lane
Grantsville, MD
301-895-5453
This park of about 300 acres offers land and water recreation, but by being surrounded by the Savage River State Forest, visitors are

offered an even wider variety of options. Dogs of all sizes are allowed at no additional fee. Dogs may not be left unattended, and they must be leashed and cleaned up after. Dogs are allowed on the trails. The camping and tent areas also allow dogs. There is a dog walk area at the campground. There are no electric or water hookups at the campground. Multiple dogs may be allowed.

Savage River State Forest
349 Headquarters Lane
Grantsville, MD
301-895-5759
With 54,000 land acres, of which 12,000 is designate wildlands, this hardwood forest has a wide variety of nature study and land and water recreation. Dogs of all sizes are allowed at no additional fee. Dogs may not be left unattended outside, and they must be leashed and cleaned up after. Dogs are allowed on the trails. The camping and tent areas also allow dogs. There is a dog walk area at the campground. There are no electric or water hookups at the campground. Multiple dogs may be allowed.

Jarrettsville

Susquehanna State Park
3318 Rocks Chrome Hill Road
Jarrettsville, MD
410-557-7994
A variety of land and water recreation, and a wide range of trails varying in length and difficulty greet visitors at this park. Dogs of all sizes are allowed at no additional fee. Dogs may not be left unattended, and they must be on no more than a 10 foot leash, and be cleaned up after. Dogs are not allowed in picnic areas or buildings. Dogs are allowed on the trails. This campground is closed during the off-season. The camping and tent areas also allow dogs. There is a dog walk area at the campground. There are no water hookups at the campground. Multiple dogs may be allowed.

Millersville

Washington DE, NE KOA
768 Cecil Avenue N
Millersville, MD
410-923-2771
Dogs of all sizes are allowed. There are no additional pet fees. Dogs may not be left unattended, must be leashed, and cleaned up after. Dogs

are not allowed at the lodge. This RV park is closed during the off-season. The camping and tent areas also allow dogs. There is a dog walk area at the campground. Dogs are allowed in the camping cabins. Multiple dogs may be allowed.

Nanticoke

Roaring Point
2360 Nanticoke Wharf Road
Nanticoke, MD
410-873-2553
Dogs of all sizes are allowed. There are no additional pet fees. Dogs must be well behaved, not left unattended, be leashed, and cleaned up after. This RV park is closed during the off-season. The camping and tent areas also allow dogs. There is a dog walk area at the campground.

North East

Elk Neck State Park
4395 Turkey Point Road
North East, MD
410-287-5333
This peninsula park is home to the Turkey Point Lighthouse, and offers a diversified topography for a variety of activities and recreation. Dogs of all sizes are allowed at no additional fee. Dogs may not be left unattended outside, and they must be leashed and cleaned up after. Dogs are not allowed on the beach, in buildings, or in day use areas. Dogs are allowed in the NE loop, at the "Y" pet area, and on the trails. The camping and tent areas also allow dogs. There is a dog walk area at the campground. Multiple dogs may be allowed.

Oakland

Garrett State Forest
222 Herrington Lane
Oakland, MD
301-334-2038
This forest displays a wide variety of trees, abundant wildlife, glimpses of beaver ponds and cranberry bogs and provides various land and water recreation. Dogs of all sizes are allowed at no additional fee. Dogs may not be left unattended, and they may be off lead if they are well behaved and under voice control. Dogs are allowed on the trails. The camping and tent areas also allow dogs. There is a dog walk area at the campground. There are no electric or

water hookups at the campground. Multiple dogs may be allowed.

Potomac State Forest
1431 Camp Road
Oakland, MD
301-334-2038
Mountain forests, valleys, rushing streams, scenic trails, and a variety of land and water recreation are offered at this state forest. Dogs are allowed at no additional fee. Dogs may be off lead if they are under voice control and will not chase or bother other animals or visitors. Dogs may not be left unattended outside. Dogs are allowed on the trails. This campground is closed during the off-season. The camping and tent areas also allow dogs. There is a dog walk area at the campground. There are no electric or water hookups at the campground. Multiple dogs may be allowed.

Swallow Falls State Park
222 Harrington Lane
Oakland, MD
301-387-6938
Hike through old growth forest at this mountain park that is home to Maryland's highest waterfall, and some of the states most breathtaking scenery. Dogs are not allowed in the day use area or on the trails between the Saturday before Memorial Day and Labor Day. Dogs may not be left unattended outside, and they must be leashed and cleaned up after. This campground is closed during the off-season. The camping and tent areas also allow dogs. There is a dog walk area at the campground. Multiple dogs may be allowed.

Ocean City

Ocean City Campground
105 70th Street
Ocean City, MD
410-524-7601
Dogs of all sizes are allowed. There are no additional pet fees. Pets must be on a leash and exercised outside of the campground property. Dogs must be leashed and cleaned up after. Pets cannot be left unattended inside or outside of camper at any time. No pets in tents or RV's without air conditioning. The camping and tent areas also allow dogs. Multiple dogs may be allowed.

Queen Anne

Tuckahoe State Park
13070 Crouse Mill Road
Queen Anne, MD
410-820-1668
This park offers a 60 acre lake, 20 miles of scenic multi-use trails, and an arboretum that encompasses 500 acres of park land with almost three miles of surfaced walkways featuring tagged native species of trees and shrubs. Dogs of all sizes are allowed at no additional fee. Dogs must be on leash, and when in camp, cleaned up after. Dogs are allowed on the trails, but not in the lake area. This campground is closed during the off-season. The camping and tent areas also allow dogs. There is a dog walk area at the campground. There are no water hookups at the campground. Multiple dogs may be allowed.

Schellsburg

Shawnee Sleepy Hollow Campground
147 Sleepy Hollow Road
Schellsburg, MD
814-733-4380
Dogs up to about 65 pounds are allowed. There is a $1 per night per pet additional fee. Dogs must be quiet, well behaved, leashed and cleaned up after. There are some breed restrictions. This RV park is closed during the off-season. The camping and tent areas also allow dogs. There is a dog walk area at the campground. Multiple dogs may be allowed.

Scotland

Point Lookout State Park
11175 Point Lookout Road
Scotland, MD
301-872-5688
There are over 1000 recreational acres at this historic, peninsula park which is home to the Civil War Museum/Marshland Nature Center. Dogs of all sizes are allowed at no additional fee. Dogs may not be left unattended, and they must be on no more than a 6 foot leash, and be cleaned up after. Pets are allowed in all areas of Malone Circle, Tulip Loop, Green's Point Loop, Hoffman's Loop, on the paved portion of the causeway, and on the beach north of the causeway to the entrance of Tanner's Creek. They are NOT permitted in any other day use area

or trail, including the beach or picnic area. There is one camping loop left open in the winter for self contained RVs. The camping and tent areas also allow dogs. There is a dog walk area at the campground. Multiple dogs may be allowed.

Snow Hill

Pocomoke River State Park
3461 Worchester H
Snow Hill, MD
410-632-2566
This wooded park features the Great Cypress Swamp which runs through the park. It offers a variety of nature study, activities, and recreation. Dogs of all sizes are allowed at no additional fee. Dogs may not be left unattended, and they must be leashed and cleaned up after. Dogs are not allowed in non-pet loop areas, but they are allowed on the trails. Dogs are allowed at the Milburn Landing area but not at Shad Landing. This campground is closed during the off-season. The camping and tent areas also allow dogs. There is a dog walk area at the campground. There are no water hookups at the campground. Multiple dogs may be allowed.

Swanton

Deep Creek Lake State Park
898 State Park Road
Swanton, MD
301-387-5563
This year round park offers an educational/interpretive center with hands on exhibits, trails varying from moderate to difficult, and a variety of land and water recreation. Dogs of all sizes are allowed at no additional fee. Dogs may not be left unattended, and they must be leashed and cleaned up after. Dogs are not allowed in picnic, swim areas, or in buildings. Dogs are allowed on the trails. This campground is closed during the off-season. The camping and tent areas also allow dogs. There is a dog walk area at the campground. There are no water hookups at the campground. Multiple dogs may be allowed.

Taylor's Island

Taylor's Island Family Campground
4362 Bay Shore Road

Taylor's Island, MD
410-397-3275
Dogs of all sizes are allowed. There are no additional pet fees. Dogs may not be left unattended except for short periods, and they must be quiet, well behaved, leashed, and cleaned up after. The camping and tent areas also allow dogs. There is a dog walk area at the campground. Multiple dogs may be allowed.

Thurmont

Catoctin Mountain Park
6602 Foxville Road
Thurmont, MD
301-663-9388
This 5,810-acre hardwood forest park comes complete with rushing streams, scenic vistas, and a variety of recreational pursuits. Dogs of all sizes are allowed at no additional fee. Dogs may not be left unattended, and they must be quiet, be on no more than a 6 foot leash, and be cleaned up after. Dogs are allowed at Owens Creek Campground and on the trails. They are not allowed in camps 1, 2 and 4, the youth camp, or in the Adirondack backcountry shelters. Dogs are also not allowed at the waterfall in the adjoining state park, or left in the car at that location. This campground is closed during the off-season. The camping and tent areas also allow dogs. There is a dog walk area at the campground. There are no electric or water hookups at the campground. Multiple dogs may be allowed.

Grambrill State Park
14039 Catoctin Hollow Road
Thurmont, MD
301-271-7574
Some points of interests at this park of over 1,100 acres include 3 native stone scenic overlooks, a good variety of trails, interpretive programs, and a nature center. Dogs of all sizes are allowed at no additional fee. Dogs may not be left unattended, and they must be leashed and cleaned up after. Dogs are allowed on the trails and throughout the park, unless otherwise posted. This campground is closed during the off-season. The camping and tent areas also allow dogs. There is a dog walk area at the campground. There are no water hookups at the campground. Multiple dogs may be allowed.

Washington Suburbs

Cherry Hill Park
9800 Cherry Hill Road
College Park, MD
800-801-6449
Dogs of all sizes are allowed. There are no additional pet fees. Dogs must be well behaved, not be left unattended, be leashed, and cleaned up after. The camping and tent areas also allow dogs. There is a dog walk area at the campground. Multiple dogs may be allowed.

Duncan's Family Campground
5381 Sands Beach Road
Lothian, MD
410-741-9558
Dogs of all sizes are allowed. There are no additional pet fees. Dogs must be quiet, leashed, and cleaned up after. Dogs may not be left tied up at the site. The camping and tent areas also allow dogs. There is a dog walk area at the campground. Multiple dogs may be allowed.

Whaleyville

Fort Whaley
11224 Dale Road
Whaleyville, MD
410-641-9785
Dogs of all sizes are allowed. There are no additional pet fees. Dogs must be well behaved, leashed, and cleaned up after. Dogs may only be left inside of your unit if there is air conditioning and if they will be quiet. The camping and tent areas also allow dogs. There is a dog walk area at the campground. Multiple dogs may be allowed.

Williamsport

KOA Hagerstown/Snug Harbor
11759 Snug Harbor Lane
Williamsport, MD
301-223-7571
Dogs of all sizes are allowed. There are no additional pet fees. Dogs must be quiet, be on no more than a 6 foot leash, and be cleaned up after. This RV park is closed during the off-season. The camping and tent areas also allow dogs. There is a dog walk area at the campground. Dogs are allowed in the camping cabins. Multiple dogs may be allowed.

Yogi Bear Jellystone Park
16519 Lappans Road
Williamsport, MD

800-421-7116
Dogs of all sizes are allowed. There are no additional pet fees. Dogs must be leashed and cleaned up after. Dogs are not allowed at the cabins. The camping and tent areas also allow dogs. There is a dog walk area at the campground. 2 dogs may be allowed.

Woodbine

Ramblin Pines Campground
801 Hoods Mill Road
Woodbine, MD
410-795-5161
Dogs of all sizes are allowed. There are no additional pet fees. Dogs may not be left unattended, and they must be leashed and cleaned up after. There is a fenced in dog run area where pets may be off lead. There are some breed restrictions. The camping and tent areas also allow dogs. There is a dog walk area at the campground. Multiple dogs may be allowed.

Massachusetts Listings

Baldwinville

Otter River State Forest
86 Winchendon Road
Baldwinville, MA
978-939-8962
Dogs of all sizes are allowed. There are no additional pet fees. Dogs may not be left unattended, and they must be leashed and cleaned up after. Dogs are allowed on all of the trails, but they are not allowed in the water. This campground is closed during the off-season. The camping and tent areas also allow dogs. There is a dog walk area at the campground. There are no electric or water hookups at the campground. Multiple dogs may be allowed.

Barre

Coldbrook Resort and Campground
864 Old Coldbrook Road
Barre, MA
978-355-2090
Dogs of all sizes are allowed. There is a $5 per night per pet additional

fee. Dogs may not be left unattended, and they must be leashed and cleaned up after. This RV park is closed during the off-season. The camping and tent areas also allow dogs. There is a dog walk area at the campground. 2 dogs may be allowed.

Bellingham

Circle Farm
131 Main Street
Bellingham, MA
508-966-1136
Well behaved dogs of all sizes are allowed. There are no additional pet fees. Dogs must be quiet, leashed, and cleaned up after. Multiple dogs may be allowed.

Boston Area

Normandy Farms
72 West Street
Foxboro, MA
508-543-7600
Well behaved dogs of all sizes are allowed. There are no additional pet fees. Dogs must be quiet, leashed, cleaned up after, and not left unattended at any time. Multiple dogs may be allowed.

Boston Minuteman Campground
264 Ayer Road
Littleton, MA
877-677-0042
Well behaved dogs of all sizes are allowed. There are no additional pet fees. Dogs must be quiet, leashed, and cleaned up after. There is a dog walk area at the campground. Multiple dogs may be allowed.

KOA
438 Plymouth Street
Middleboro, MA
508-947-6435
Dogs of all sizes are allowed. There are no additional pet fees. Dogs may not be left unattended, must be quiet at night, be leashed, and cleaned up after. This RV park is closed during the off-season. The camping and tent areas also allow dogs. There is a dog walk area at the campground. Multiple dogs may be allowed.

Winter Island Park
50 Winter Island Road
Salem, MA
978-745-9430
This is a marine recreational park, and dogs of all sizes are allowed.

There are no additional pet fees. Dogs may not be left unattended outside, and may only be left inside your unit if it will not cause a danger to the animal. They must have a current rabies certificate and shot records. Dogs must be quiet during quiet hours, leashed, and cleaned up after. Dogs are allowed on the trails, but not on the beach or in the buildings. Although the campground is seasonal, the park is open year round from 7 am to 10 pm. This campground is closed during the off-season. The camping and tent areas also allow dogs. There is a dog walk area at the campground. There are no electric or water hookups at the campground. 2 dogs may be allowed.

Rusnik Campground
115 Lafayette Road
Salisbury, MA
978-462-9551
Well behaved dogs of all sizes are allowed. There are no additional pet fees. Dogs must be quiet, leashed, and cleaned up after. Multiple dogs may be allowed.

Bourne

Bay View Campgrounds
260 McArthur Blvd
Bourne, MA
508-759-7610
Dogs of all sizes are allowed. There are no additional pet fees. Dogs must be quiet, leashed, cleaned up after, and not left unattended at any time. There is a dog walk area at the campground. Multiple dogs may be allowed.

Bourne Scenic Park Campground
370 Scenic Highway
Bourne, MA
508-759-7873
Dogs of all sizes are allowed. There are no additional pet fees. Dogs must be quiet, leashed, and cleaned up after. Multiple dogs may be allowed.

Cape Cod

Nickerson State Park
3488 Main Street
Brewster, MA
508-896-3491
Dogs of all sizes are allowed. There are no additional pet fees. Dogs may not be left unattended, they must have current rabies certificate and

shot records, be leashed, and cleaned up after. Dogs are allowed on all the trails. Dogs are not allowed at the Yurt cabins. The campground is seasonal but the park is open year round from 8am to 8pm, and in winter from dawn to dusk. This campground is closed during the off-season. The camping and tent areas also allow dogs. There is a dog walk area at the campground. There are no electric or water hookups at the campground. Multiple dogs may be allowed.

Nickerson State Park Campgrounds
Route 6A
Brewster, MA
508-896-3491
This state park has 1900 acres of land and offers over 400 campsites. Your dog is welcome at the campgrounds, but they ask that your dog never be left unattended. Dogs are also allowed on the hiking trails, and paved trails. Dogs are not allowed in the pond or on public beaches. However, you can take your dog to an uncrowded beach, where there are not many other people. Dogs must be leashed and you must have proof of your dog's rabies vaccination.

Camper's Haven
184 Old Wharf Road
Dennisport, MA
508-398-2811
One dog of any size is allowed during their off season, which begins after Labor Day. There are no additional pet fees. Dogs must be quiet, leashed, cleaned up after, and not left unattended.

Peter's Pond Park
185 Cotuit Road
Sandwich, MA
508-477-1775
Dogs of all sizes are allowed in the RV section only. There is one street where they park all the RVs. There are no additional pet fees. Dogs must be leashed and cleaned up after. There is a dog walk area at the campground. Multiple dogs may be allowed.

Shawme-Crowell State Forest
42 Main Street
Sandwich, MA
508-888-0351
Dogs of all sizes are allowed. There are no additional pet fees. Dogs may not be left unattended, they must have current rabies certificate and

shot records, be leashed, and cleaned up after. Dogs are allowed on all of the trails. The forest is open from 8am to 8pm daily. The camping and tent areas also allow dogs. There is a dog walk area at the campground. There are no electric or water hookups at the campground. Multiple dogs may be allowed.

Charlemont

Mohawk Trail State Forest
On H 2
Charlemont, MA
413-339-5504
Dogs of all sizes are allowed. There are no additional pet fees. Dogs may not be left unattended, they must have current rabies certificate and shot records, be leashed, and cleaned up after. Dogs are allowed on all the trails. This campground is closed during the off-season. The camping and tent areas also allow dogs. There is a dog walk area at the campground. Dogs are allowed in the camping cabins. There are no electric or water hookups at the campground. Multiple dogs may be allowed.

Chester

Walker Island Family Camping Resort
27 Route 20
Chester, MA
413-354-2295
Dogs of all sizes are allowed. There are no additional pet fees. Dogs may not be left unattended, and they must be quiet, friendly, leashed, and cleaned up after. Dogs must have proof of current shots. Dogs are not allowed in the pool area, or in buildings. This RV park is closed during the off-season. The camping and tent areas also allow dogs. There is a dog walk area at the campground. Multiple dogs may be allowed.

Clarksburg

Clarksburg State Park
1199 Middle Road
Clarksburg, MA
413-664-8345
Dogs of all sizes are allowed. There are no additional pet fees. Dogs may not be left unattended, and they must have a current rabies certificate and shot records. Dogs

must be quiet during quiet hours, leashed, and cleaned up after. Dogs are allowed on the trails, but not on the beach or in the swim area. Although the campground is seasonal, the park is open year round. This campground is closed during the off-season. The camping and tent areas also allow dogs. There is a dog walk area at the campground. There are no electric or water hookups at the campground. Multiple dogs may be allowed.

E Falmouth

Cape Cod Camp Resort
176 Thomas Landers Road
E Falmouth, MA
508-548-1458
Dogs of all sizes are allowed, however Rottweilers, Pit Bulls and other fighting breeds are not. There is a $4 per night per pet additional fee and there must be proof of shots; either tags or paperwork. Dogs must be cleaned up after, leashed, and not left unattended at any time. Multiple dogs may be allowed.

E Taunton

Massasoit State Park
1361 Middleboro
E Taunton, MA
508-822-7405
Dogs of all sizes are allowed. There are no additional pet fees. Dogs may not be left unattended, they must have current rabies certificate and shot records, be quiet, well behaved, leashed, and cleaned up after. Dogs are allowed on the trails. This campground is closed during the off-season. The camping and tent areas also allow dogs. There is a dog walk area at the campground. There are no water hookups at the campground. Multiple dogs may be allowed.

Erving

Erving State Forest
Laurel Lake Road
Erving, MA
978-544-3939
Dogs of all sizes are allowed. There are no additional pet fees. Dogs may not be left unattended, they must have current rabies certificate and shot records, be leashed, and cleaned up after. Dogs are allowed on all of the trails, but not on the beach. This campground is closed

during the off-season. The camping and tent areas also allow dogs. There is a dog walk area at the campground. There are no electric or water hookups at the campground. Multiple dogs may be allowed.

Granville

Prospect Mountain Campground
1349 Main Road (H 57)
Granville, MA
888-550-4PMC (762)
Dogs of all sizes are allowed. There are no additional pet fees. Dogs may not be left unattended outside, and left inside only for short periods. There is a day kennel close by for your pet when you will be gone longer. Dogs must be leashed and cleaned up after. This RV park is closed during the off-season. The camping and tent areas also allow dogs. There is a dog walk area at the campground. Multiple dogs may be allowed.

Hingham

Wompatuck State Park
Union Street
Hingham, MA
781-749-7160
Dogs of all sizes are allowed. There are no additional pet fees. Dogs may not be left unattended, they must have current rabies certificate and shot records, be leashed, and cleaned up after. Dogs are allowed on all the trails. This campground is closed during the off-season. The camping and tent areas also allow dogs. There is a dog walk area at the campground. There are no water hookups at the campground. Multiple dogs may be allowed.

Lanesborough

Hidden Valley Campground
15 Scott Road (Box700)
Lanesborough, MA
413-447-9419
Only one dog is allowed for the local residents, however, out of town travelers with 2 dogs are allowed if they are both small. They are allowed in the RV area only, not the campsites. Dogs must be quiet, be on a 6 foot max leash, cleaned up after, and not left unattended at any time. There are some breed restrictions.

Lee

October Mountain State Forest
317 Woodland Road
Lee, MA
413-243-1778
Dogs of all sizes are allowed. There are no additional pet fees. Dogs may not be left unattended, they must have current rabies certificate and shot records, be on no more than a 10 foot leash, and be cleaned up after. Dogs are allowed on all the trails, but they are not allowed in any buildings. This campground is closed during the off-season. The camping and tent areas also allow dogs. There is a dog walk area at the campground. There are no electric or water hookups at the campground. Multiple dogs may be allowed.

Monson

Sunset View Farms
57 Town Farm Road
Monson, MA
413-267-9269
Dogs of all sizes are allowed. There are no additional pet fees. Dogs must have current rabies shots, be leashed, and cleaned up after. Dogs may not be left unattended. 2 dogs may be allowed.

North Andover

H arold Parker State Forest
305 Middleton Road
North Andover, MA
978-686-3391
Dogs of all sizes are allowed. There are no additional pet fees. Dogs may not be left unattended, they must have current rabies certificate and shot records, be quiet, leashed, and cleaned up after. Dogs are allowed on all the trails. This campground is closed during the off-season. The camping and tent areas also allow dogs. There is a dog walk area at the campground. There are no electric or water hookups at the campground. Multiple dogs may be allowed.

Oakham

Pine Acres Family Camping Resort
203 Bechan Road
Oakham, MA
508-882-9509
Dogs of all sizes are allowed. There

is a $2 per night per pet additional fee. Dogs must be leashed and cleaned up after. The camping and tent areas also allow dogs. There is a dog walk area at the campground. 2 dogs may be allowed.

Pittsfield

Pittsfield State Forest
1041 Cascade Street
Pittsfield, MA
413-442-8992
Dogs of all sizes are allowed. There are no additional pet fees. Dogs may not be left unattended, they must have a current rabies certificate and shot records, be on no more than a 10 foot leash, and be cleaned up after. Dogs are allowed on all of the trails, but not at the swimming area. This campground is closed during the off-season. The camping and tent areas also allow dogs. There is a dog walk area at the campground. There are no electric or water hookups at the campground. Multiple dogs may be allowed.

Plainfield

Peppermint Park Camping Resort
169 Grant Street
Plainfield, MA
413-634-5385
Dogs of all sizes are allowed. There is a $10 per night per pet additional fee and dogs must have proof of up to date shots. Dogs must be leashed, cleaned up after, and can not be left unattended. The camping and tent areas also allow dogs. There is a dog walk area at the campground. Multiple dogs may be allowed.

Plymouth

Ellis Haven Family Campground
531 Furnace Road
Plymouth, MA
508-746-0803
Dogs of all sizes are allowed. There is a $2 per night additional fee for a dog. Dogs may not be left unattended outside, and they must be leashed and cleaned up after. This RV park is closed during the off-season. Only one dog is allowed per campsite. The camping and tent areas also allow dogs. There is a dog walk area at the campground.

Salisbury

Black Bear Campgrounds
54 Main Street
Salisbury, MA
978-462-3183
Dogs up to 35 pounds are allowed. There are no additional pet fees, but pets must have proof of rabies shots. Dogs must be well behaved and cleaned up after. 2 dogs may be allowed.

Savoy

Savoy Mountain State Forest
Central Shaft Road
Savoy, MA
413-663-8469
Dogs of all sizes are allowed. There are no additional pet fees. Dogs may not be left unattended, and they must have a current rabies certificate and shot records. Dogs must be quiet during quiet hours, be leashed, and cleaned up after. This campground is closed during the off-season. The camping and tent areas also allow dogs. There is a dog walk area at the campground. There are no electric or water hookups at the campground. Multiple dogs may be allowed.

Shelburne Falls

Country Aire Campground
1753 Mohaw Trail
Shelburne Falls, MA
413-625-2996
Well behaved dogs of all sizes are allowed. There are no additional pet fees. Dogs must be quiet, leashed, cleaned up after, and not left unattended. Multiple dogs may be allowed.

South Carver

Myles Standish State Forest
1941 Cranberry Road
South Carver, MA
508-866-2526
Dogs of all sizes are allowed. There are no additional pet fees. Dogs may not be left unattended, and they must have a current rabies certificate and shot records. Dogs must be quiet during quiet hours, be leashed, and cleaned up after. Dogs are allowed on the trails, but not on the beach or swim areas, and not in the buildings. This campground is closed during the off-season. The camping and tent areas also allow dogs. There is a dog walk area at the campground. There are no electric or water hookups at the campground. Multiple

dogs may be allowed.

Sturbridge

Jellystone Park
30 River Road
Sturbridge, MA
508-347-9570
Dogs of all sizes are allowed. There are no additional pet fees. The camping and tent areas also allow dogs. There is a dog walk area at the campground. Multiple dogs may be allowed.

Wells State Park
159 Walker Pond Road
Sturbridge, MA
508-347-9257
Dogs of all sizes are allowed. There are no additional pet fees. Dogs may not be left unattended, they must have a current rabies certificate and shot records, be leashed at all times, and cleaned up after. Dogs are allowed on all the trails, but not on the beach. This campground is closed during the off-season. The camping and tent areas also allow dogs. There is a dog walk area at the campground. There are no electric or water hookups at the campground. Multiple dogs may be allowed.

Wales

Oak Haven Family Campground
22 Main Street
Wales, MA
413-245-7148
Dogs of all sizes are allowed. There are no additional pet fees. Dogs must have current rabies records, be leashed, and cleaned up after. 2 dogs may be allowed.

Washington

Summit Hill Campground
34 Old Middlefield
Washington, MA
413-623-5761
Dogs of all sizes are allowed. There are no additional pet fees, and rabies shots and licenses must be up to date. There is a dog walk area at the campground. 2 dogs may be allowed.

Webster

KOA-Webster/Sturbridge
106 Douglas Road

Webster, MA
508-943-1895
Dogs of all sizes are allowed. There are no additional pet fees. Dogs must be leashed and cleaned up after. There are some breed restrictions. This RV park is closed during the off-season. The camping and tent areas also allow dogs. There is a dog walk area at the campground. Multiple dogs may be allowed.

West Brookfield

The Old Sawmill Campground
Box 377 Longhill Road
West Brookfield, MA
508-867-2427
Dogs of all sizes are allowed. There are no additional pet fees. Dogs must be leashed and cleaned up after. 2 dogs may be allowed.

Westford

Wyman's Beach Family Camping
48 Wyman's Beach Road
Westford, MA
978-692-6287
Well behaved dogs of all sizes are allowed. There are no additional pet fees. Dogs must remain in one's own site and be leashed at all times. There is a dog walk area close by that you can drive to. Dogs are allowed in the camping cabins. Multiple dogs may be allowed.

Westport Point

Horseneck Beach State Reservations
On H 88
Westport Point, MA
508-636-8817
This park is popular because of it's almost 2 miles of beaches and it's salt marsh. Dogs of all sizes are allowed. There are no additional pet fees. Dogs may not be left unattended, and they must have a current rabies certificate and shot records. Dogs must be quiet during quiet hours, be leashed, and cleaned up after. Dogs are allowed on the trails, but not on the beach, in the buildings, or at the sand dunes. This campground is closed during the off-season. The camping and tent areas also allow dogs. There is a dog walk area at the campground. There are no water hookups at the campground. Multiple dogs may be allowed.

Campgrounds and RV Parks - Please always call ahead to make sure an establishment is still dog-friendly.

Whately

White Birch Campground
214 North Street
Whately, MA
800-244-4941
Dogs of all sizes are allowed. There are no additional pet fees. Dogs must be quiet, leashed, and cleaned up after. Multiple dogs may be allowed.

Michigan Listings

Adrian

Sequoia Campgrounds
2675 Gady Road
Adrian, MI
517-264-5531
Dogs of all sizes are allowed. There are no additional pet fees. Dogs must be leashed and cleaned up after. The camping and tent areas also allow dogs. There is a dog walk area at the campground. 2 dogs may be allowed.

Allegan

Hungry Horse Campground
2016 142nd Avenue
Allegan, MI
616-681-9843
Dogs of all sizes are allowed. There are no additional pet fees. Dogs must be leashed and cleaned up after. This RV park is closed during the off-season. There is a dog walk area at the campground. Multiple dogs may be allowed.

Augres

City of Augres Riverfront Park
522 Park Street
Augres, MI
989-876-8310
Dogs of all sizes are allowed. There are no additional pet fees. Dogs must be leashed and cleaned up after. This RV park is closed during the off-season. The camping and tent areas also allow dogs. There is a dog walk area at the campground. Multiple dogs may be allowed.

Bellaire

Chain-O-Lakes Campground
7231 S H 88
Bellaire, MI
231-533-8432
Dogs of all sizes are allowed. There are no additional pet fees. Dogs must be friendly, be on leash, and cleaned up after. Dogs may not be left unattended at any time. The camping and tent areas also allow dogs. There is a dog walk area at the campground. Dogs are allowed in the camping cabins. Multiple dogs may be allowed.

Benton Harbor

House of David Travel Trailer Park
1019 E Empire
Benton Harbor, MI
269-927-3302
Dogs of all sizes are allowed. There are no additional pet fees. Dogs must be leashed and cleaned up after. There are some breed restrictions. The camping and tent areas also allow dogs. There is a dog walk area at the campground. Dogs are allowed in the camping cabins. 2 dogs may be allowed.

Benzonia

Vacation Trailer Park
2080 Benzie H
Benzonia, MI
231-882-5101
Dogs of all sizes are allowed. There are no additional pet fees. Dogs must be quiet, well behaved, and leashed and cleaned up after. The camping and tent areas also allow dogs. There is a dog walk area at the campground. Multiple dogs may be allowed.

Big Bend

Big Bend Family Campground
513 Conrad Road
Big Bend, MI
989-653-2267
Dogs of all sizes are allowed. There are no additional pet fees. Dogs can go in the river and the lake, otherwise they must be leashed at all times and cleaned up after. This RV park is closed during the off-season. The camping and tent areas also allow dogs. There is a dog walk area at the campground. Dogs are allowed in the camping cabins. Multiple dogs may be allowed.

Brimley

Brimley State Park
9200 W 6 Mile Road
Brimley, MI
906-248-3422
This park is located along the shore of Whitefish Bay. Its activities include land and water recreation and an explorer program. Dogs of all sizes are allowed at no additional fee. Dogs may not be left unattended, they must be on no more than a 6 foot leash, and be cleaned up after. Dogs are not allowed on the beach, on any sand, or in buildings. This campground is closed during the off-season. The camping and tent areas also allow dogs. There is a dog walk area at the campground. There are no water hookups at the campground. Multiple dogs may be allowed.

Buchanan

Fuller's Resort and Campground
1622 E Clearlake Road
Buchanan, MI
269-695-3785
Dogs of all sizes are allowed. There are no additional pet fees. Dogs must be leashed, cleaned up after, and are not allowed on the beach. There are some breed restrictions. The camping and tent areas also allow dogs. There is a dog walk area at the campground. Multiple dogs may be allowed.

Buckley

Traverse City KOA
9700 H 37
Buckley, MI
231-269-4562
Dogs of all sizes are allowed. There are no additional pet fees. Dogs must be leashed and cleaned up after. Dogs are not allowed at the lodge or rentals. There are some breed restrictions. This RV park is closed during the off-season. The camping and tent areas also allow dogs. There is a dog walk area at the campground. Multiple dogs may be allowed.

Cadillac

Camp Cadillac
10621 E 34th Road (Boon Road)
Cadillac, MI
231-775-9724

110

One dog of any size or 2 small dogs are allowed. There are no additional pet fees. Dogs must be leashed and cleaned up after. The camping and tent areas also allow dogs. There is a dog walk area at the campground.

Nuron-Manistee National Forest
1755 S Mitchell Street
Cadillac, MI
616-775-2421
These 2 forests combined have over a million acres and there is ample outdoor recreation year round. Dogs are allowed at no additional fee. Dogs may not be left unattended, they must be leashed, and they are not allowed on the beaches. This campground is closed during the off-season. The camping and tent areas also allow dogs. There is a dog walk area at the campground. Multiple dogs may be allowed.

Cass City

Evergreen Park, Sanilac County
4731 Van Dyke
Cass City, MI
989-872-6600
Dogs of all sizes are allowed. There are no additional pet fees. Dogs must be leashed and cleaned up after. The camping and tent areas also allow dogs. There is a dog walk area at the campground. 2 dogs may be allowed.

Cedar Springs

Lakeside Camp Park
13677 White Creek Avenue
Cedar Springs, MI
616-696-1735
Dogs of all sizes are allowed. There are no additional pet fees. Dogs must be leashed and cleaned up after. There are some breed restrictions. The camping and tent areas also allow dogs. There is a dog walk area at the campground. 2 dogs may be allowed.

Cedarville

Cedarville RV
634 Grove Street
Cedarville, MI
906-484-3351
Dogs of all sizes are allowed. There are no additional pet fees. Three dogs can be accepted if they are all small. Dogs may not be left unattended, must be leashed, and cleaned up after. The camping and

tent areas also allow dogs. There is a dog walk area at the campground.

Cement City

Irish Hills Campground
16230 US H 12
Cement City, MI
517-592-6751
Dogs of all sizes are allowed. There are no additional pet fees. Dogs must be leashed and cleaned up after. The camping and tent areas also allow dogs. There is a dog walk area at the campground. Multiple dogs may be allowed.

Cheboygan

Cheboygan State Park
4490 Beach Road
Cheboygan, MI
231-798-3711
A variety of year round recreational activities, beautiful beaches and trails greet visitors at this park. Well behaved dogs are allowed at no additional fee. Dogs may not be left unattended, and they must be leashed and cleaned up after. Dogs are not allowed in public swim areas or in buildings. Dogs are allowed on the trails. This campground is closed during the off-season. The camping and tent areas also allow dogs. There is a dog walk area at the campground. There are no water hookups at the campground. Multiple dogs may be allowed.

Chelsea

Waterloo Recreation Area
16345 McClure Road
Chelsea, MI
734-475-8307
This recreation area provides over 20,000 acres with 47 miles of hiking trails, 11 lakes, glacial topography, and an abundance of flora and fauna. No alcohol is allowed here from April 15 through Labor Day. The Sugarloag camp area is seasonal, but the Portage area is open all year. Dogs of all sizes are allowed at no additional fee. Dogs may not be left unattended at any time, including in automobiles, and they must have a current rabies certificate and shot records. Dogs must be quiet, well behaved, be on no more than a 6 foot leash, and be cleaned up after. Dogs are allowed on the trails, and at the picnic

areas. Dogs are not allowed in buildings, day use areas, at the beaches or in the water. The camping and tent areas also allow dogs. There is a dog walk area at the campground. There are no water hookups at the campground. Multiple dogs may be allowed.

Coldwater

Waffle Farm Camp
790 N Union City Road
Coldwater, MI
517-278-4315
Dogs of all sizes are allowed. There are no additional pet fees. Dogs must be quiet, well behaved, and in your unit by 11PM. Dogs must be kept leashed and cleaned up after. This RV park is closed during the off-season. The camping and tent areas also allow dogs. There is a dog walk area at the campground. Multiple dogs may be allowed.

Copper Harbor

Fort Wilkins Historic State Park
One mile E. of Copper Harbor on US 41 (B0x 71)
Copper Harbor, MI
906-289-4215
This historical park is a restored and reconstructed 1844 Army Outpost. Costumed interpreters show and explain how life was at this time. There is also a lighthouse museum on site. Dogs of all sizes are allowed. There are no additional pet fees. Dogs may not be left unattended at any time, including in automobiles, and they must have a current rabies certificate and shot records. Dogs must be quiet, well behaved, be on no more than a 6 foot leash, and be cleaned up after. Dogs are allowed on the trails, and at the picnic areas. Dogs are not allowed in buildings, day use areas, at the beaches or in the water. This campground is closed during the off-season. The camping and tent areas also allow dogs. There is a dog walk area at the campground. There are no water hookups at the campground. Multiple dogs may be allowed.

Crystal Falls

Bewabic State Park
1933 US Highway 2 W (720 Idlewild Rd.)
Crystal Falls, MI
906-875-3324

This recreational park has among it's amenities access to Fortune Lake for boating, swimming and fishing. Dogs of all sizes are allowed. There are no additional pet fees. Dogs may not be left unattended at any time, including in automobiles, and they must have a current rabies certificate and shot records. Dogs must be quiet, well behaved, be on no more than a 6 foot leash, and be cleaned up after. Dogs are allowed on the trails, and at the picnic areas. Dogs are not allowed in buildings, day use areas, at the beaches or in the water. This campground is closed during the off-season. The camping and tent areas also allow dogs. There is a dog walk area at the campground. There are no water hookups at the campground. Multiple dogs may be allowed.

Decatur

Oak Shores Campground
86882 County Road 215
Decatur, MI
269-423-7370
Dogs of all sizes are allowed. There are no additional pet fees. Dogs may not be left unattended, must be leashed, and cleaned up after. The camping and tent areas also allow dogs. There is a dog walk area at the campground. Multiple dogs may be allowed.

Detroit

Wayne County Fairgrounds and RV Park
10871 Quirk Road
Belleville, MI
734-697-7002
Dogs of all sizes are allowed. There are no additional pet fees. Dogs must be leashed and cleaned up after. This RV park is closed during the off-season. There is a dog walk area at the campground. Multiple dogs may be allowed.

Harbortown RV Resort
14931 La Plaisance
Monroe, MI
734-384-4700
Dogs of all sizes are allowed. There are no additional pet fees. Dogs may not be left unattended, must be leashed, and cleaned up after. The camping and tent areas also allow dogs. There is a dog walk area at the campground. Multiple dogs may be allowed.

Durand

Walnut Hills
7685 Lehring
Durand, MI
989-634-9782
Dogs of all sizes are allowed. There are no additional pet fees. Dogs must be quiet and may not be left unattended. They must be on no more than a 6 foot leash and cleaned up after. Dogs can not be in the campground building, the beach, or the lake. This RV park is closed during the off-season. The camping and tent areas also allow dogs. There is a dog walk area at the campground. Multiple dogs may be allowed.

Emmett

Emmett KOA
3864 Breen Road
Emmett, MI
810-395-7042
Dogs of all sizes are allowed. There are no additional pet fees. Dogs must be quiet, well behaved, not left unattended, and leashed and cleaned up after. Dogs are not allowed in the lake. This RV park is closed during the off-season. The camping and tent areas also allow dogs. There is a dog walk area at the campground. Multiple dogs may be allowed.

Fenwick

Snow Lake Campground
644 E Snows Lake Road
Fenwick, MI
989-248-3224
Dogs of all sizes are allowed. There are no additional pet fees. Dogs may not be left unattended, must be leashed, and cleaned up after. There are some breed restrictions. The camping and tent areas also allow dogs. There is a dog walk area at the campground. Multiple dogs may be allowed.

Frankenmuth

Frankenmuth Jellystone Park
1339 Weiss Street
Frankenmuth, MI
989-652-6668
Dogs of all sizes are allowed. There are no additional pet fees. Dogs may not be left unattended, must be leashed, and cleaned up after. The camping and tent areas also allow

dogs. There is a dog walk area at the campground. Multiple dogs may be allowed.

Gaylord

Gaylord KOA
5101 Campfires Parkway
Gaylord, MI
989-939-8723
Dogs of all sizes are allowed. There are no additional pet fees. Dogs may not be left unattended, must be leashed, and cleaned up after. This RV park is closed during the off-season. The camping and tent areas also allow dogs. There is a dog walk area at the campground. Dogs are allowed in the camping cabins. Multiple dogs may be allowed.

Grand Haven

Grand Haven State Park
1001 Harbor Avenue
Grand Haven, MI
616-847-1309
This park, along Lake Michigan and Grand River, offers summer recreation, scenic views, sandy beaches, and the Grand River Pier and Lighthouse. Foot day traffic is allowed in winter. Dogs of all sizes are allowed at no additional fee. Dogs may not be left unattended, they must be on no more than a 6 foot leash, and be cleaned up after. Dogs are not allowed at public swim beaches or in buildings. This campground is closed during the off-season. The camping and tent areas also allow dogs. There is a dog walk area at the campground. There are no water hookups at the campground. Multiple dogs may be allowed.

Yogi Bear's Jellystone Park Camp-Resort
10990 H 31N
Grand Haven, MI
616-842-9395
This resort like park offers a wide variety of activities and recreational pursuits. Dogs of all sizes are allowed at no additional fee. Dogs may not be left unattended, and they must be quiet, well behaved, leashed and cleaned up after. Dogs are not allowed on the playground. This campground is closed during the off-season. The camping and tent areas also allow dogs. There is a dog walk area at the campground. 2 dogs may be allowed.

Campgrounds and RV Parks - Please always call ahead to make sure an establishment is still dog-friendly.

Grand Junction

Warner Camp on Lester Lake
60 55th Street
Grand Junction, MI
269-434-6844
Dogs of all sizes are allowed. There are no additional pet fees. Dogs must be leashed and cleaned up after, and are not allowed on the beach. This RV park is closed during the off-season. The camping and tent areas also allow dogs. There is a dog walk area at the campground. Dogs are allowed in the camping cabins. Multiple dogs may be allowed.

Grand Rapids

Woodchip Campground
7501 Burlingame SW
Byron Center, MI
616-878-9050
Dogs of all sizes are allowed. There are no additional pet fees. Dogs must be leashed and cleaned up after. There are some breed restrictions. The camping and tent areas also allow dogs. There is a dog walk area at the campground. Multiple dogs may be allowed.

Grass Lake

Apple Creek Campground
11185 Orban Road
Grass Lake, MI
517-522-3467
Dogs of all sizes are allowed. There are no additional pet fees. Dogs may not be left unattended, must be leashed, and cleaned up after. This RV park is closed during the off-season. The camping and tent areas also allow dogs. There is a dog walk area at the campground. Multiple dogs may be allowed.

Grayling

Jellystone Park
370 W 4 Mile Road
Grayling, MI
989-348-2157
Dogs of all sizes are allowed. There are no additional pet fees. Dogs must be well behaved, be leashed, and cleaned up after. This RV park is closed during the off-season. The camping and tent areas also allow dogs. There is a dog walk area at the campground. Multiple dogs may be allowed.

Harrison

Wilson State Park
910 N 1st Street
Harrison, MI
989-539-3021
Dogs of all sizes are allowed. There are no additional pet fees. Dogs may not be left unattended at any time, including in automobiles, and they must have a current rabies certificate and shot records. Dogs must be quiet, well behaved, be on no more than a 6 foot leash, and be cleaned up after. Dogs are allowed on the trails, and at the picnic areas. Dogs are not allowed in buildings, day use areas, at the beaches or in the water. This campground is closed during the off-season. The camping and tent areas also allow dogs. There is a dog walk area at the campground. There are no water hookups at the campground. Multiple dogs may be allowed.

Holland

Oak Grove Resort
2011 Ottawa Beach Road
Holland, MI
616-399-9230
Dogs of all sizes are allowed. There is a $3 per night per dog additional fee. Dogs must be leashed and cleaned up after. The camping and tent areas also allow dogs. There is a dog walk area at the campground. Multiple dogs may be allowed.

Interlochen

Interlochen State Park
15 miles SW of Traverse City on H 137.
Interlochen, MI
231-276-9511
Dogs of all sizes are allowed. There are no additional pet fees. Dogs may not be left unattended at any time, including in automobiles, and they must have a current rabies certificate and shot records. Dogs must be quiet, well behaved, be on no more than a 6 foot leash, and be cleaned up after. Dogs are allowed on the trails and at the picnic areas. Dogs are not allowed in buildings, day use areas, at the beaches or in the water. This campground is closed during the off-season. The camping and tent areas also allow dogs. There is a dog walk area at the campground. There are no water hookups at the campground.

Multiple dogs may be allowed.

Jackson

Greenwood Campgrounds
2401 Hilton Road
Jackson, MI
517-522-8600
Dogs of all sizes are allowed. There are no additional pet fees. Dogs must be leashed and cleaned up after. This RV park is closed during the off-season. The camping and tent areas also allow dogs. There is a dog walk area at the campground. Multiple dogs may be allowed.

Lakeport

Lakeport State Park
7605 Lakeshore Road
Lakeport, MI
810-327-6765
Dogs of all sizes are allowed. There are no additional pet fees. Dogs may not be left unattended at any time, including in automobiles, and they must have a current rabies certificate and shot records. Dogs must be quiet, well behaved, be on no more than a 6 foot leash, and be cleaned up after. Dogs are allowed on the trails, and at the picnic areas. Dogs are not allowed in buildings, day use areas, at the beaches or in the water. This campground is closed during the off-season. The camping and tent areas also allow dogs. There is a dog walk area at the campground. There are no water hookups at the campground. Multiple dogs may be allowed.

Lansing

Lansing Campground
5339 S Aurelius Road
Lansing, MI
517-393-3200
Dogs of all sizes are allowed. There are no additional pet fees. Dogs must be well behaved, leashed, and cleaned up after. This RV park is closed during the off-season. There is a dog walk area at the campground. Multiple dogs may be allowed.

Linwood

Hoyles Marina and Campground
135 S Linwood Beach Road
Linwood, MI
989-697-3153

Dogs of all sizes are allowed. There are no additional pet fees. Dogs may be off leash in some areas as long as there is control by owner and your dog will not run after people or pets, otherwise they must be leashed and cleaned up after. Dogs must be quiet, especially at night, and be well behaved. Dogs may not be left unattended. The camping and tent areas also allow dogs. There is a dog walk area at the campground. Multiple dogs may be allowed.

Lower Peninsula

Campers Cove RV Park
505 Long Rapids Road
Alpena, MI
989-356-3708
Dogs of all sizes are allowed. There are no additional pet fees. Dogs must be quiet, well behaved, leashed and cleaned up after. There are some breed restrictions. The camping and tent areas also allow dogs. There is a dog walk area at the campground. Multiple dogs may be allowed.

Ludington

Ludington State Park
Lakeshore Drive
Ludington, MI
231-843-2423
This parks sits between 2 lakes with miles of shoreline on both with much to offer. There is a lighthouse, 18 miles of trails, an interactive and interpretive visitor's center, and a one of a kind canoe trail. Dogs of all sizes are allowed at no additional fee. Dogs may not be left unattended, they must be on no more than a 6 foot leash, and be cleaned up after. Dogs are not allowed in swim areas or in buildings, but they are allowed on the trails. This campground is closed during the off-season. The camping and tent areas also allow dogs. There is a dog walk area at the campground. There are no water hookups at the campground. Multiple dogs may be allowed.

Mackinaw City

Mackinaw City/Mackinac Island KOA
566 Trailsend Road
Mackinaw City, MI
231-436-5643
Dogs of all sizes are allowed. There

are no additional pet fees, but there can only be one pet per adult per site. Dogs may not be left unattended, must be leashed, and cleaned up after. Dogs are not allowed in the cabins, tents, or pop ups. There are some breed restrictions. This RV park is closed during the off-season. There is a dog walk area at the campground.

Mackinaw Mill Creek Camping
9730 H 23
Mackinaw City, MI
231-436-5584
Dogs of all sizes are allowed. There are no additional pet fees. Dogs must be leashed and cleaned up after, and they are not allowed on the beach. The camping and tent areas also allow dogs. There is a dog walk area at the campground. Multiple dogs may be allowed.

St. Ignace/Mackinac Island KOA
1242 H 2 W
St Ignace, MI
906-643-9303
Dogs of all sizes are allowed. There are no additional pet fees. Dogs may not be left unattended, must be leashed, and cleaned up after. This RV park is closed during the off-season. The camping and tent areas also allow dogs. There is a dog walk area at the campground. Dogs are allowed in the camping cabins. Multiple dogs may be allowed.

Marenisco

Lake Gogebic State Park
N 9995 H 64
Marenisco, MI
906-842-3341
This recreational park has about a mile of lake frontage on the largest inland lake in the Upper Peninsula. Dogs of all sizes are allowed. There are no additional pet fees. Dogs may not be left unattended at any time, including in automobiles, and they must have a current rabies certificate and shot records. Dogs must be quiet, well behaved, be on no more than a 6 foot leash, and be cleaned up after. Dogs are allowed on the trails, and at the picnic areas. Dogs are not allowed in buildings, day use areas, at the beaches or in the water. This campground is closed during the off-season. The camping and tent areas also allow dogs. There is a dog walk area at the campground. There are no water hookups at the

campground. Multiple dogs may be allowed.

Mears

Jellystone Park
8239 W Hazel
Mears, MI
231-873-4502
Dogs of all sizes are allowed. There are no additional pet fees. Dogs may not be left unattended, must be leashed, and cleaned up after. This RV park is closed during the off-season. The camping and tent areas also allow dogs. There is a dog walk area at the campground. Multiple dogs may be allowed.

Moscow

Moscow Maples RV Park
8291 E Chicago
Moscow, MI
517-688-9853
Dogs of all sizes are allowed. There are no additional pet fees. Dogs may not be left unattended, must be leashed, and cleaned up after. This RV park is closed during the off-season. The camping and tent areas also allow dogs. There is a dog walk area at the campground. Multiple dogs may be allowed.

Munising

Pictured Rocks National Lakshore Park
N8391 Sand Point Road
Munising, MI
906-387-3700
Michigan state highways 28 and 94 lead to Munising, and H-77 leads to Grand Marais. H-58 and other spur roads provide access throughout the lakeshore. Dogs of all sizes are allowed. There are no additional pet fees. Dogs may not be left unattended, they must have a current rabies certificate and shot records, be leashed, and cleaned up after. Dogs are allowed at Miner's Castle, Miner's Beach, 12 Mile Beach, and Hurricane River. Dogs are not allowed on any of the back country trails. The camping and tent areas also allow dogs. There is a dog walk area at the campground. There are no electric or water hookups at the campground. Multiple dogs may be allowed.

Wandering Wheels Campground
E10102 H 28E

Munising, MI
906-387-3315
Dogs of all sizes are allowed. There are no additional pet fees. Dogs must be leashed and cleaned up after. This RV park is closed during the off-season. The camping and tent areas also allow dogs. There is a dog walk area at the campground. Dogs are allowed in the camping cabins. Multiple dogs may be allowed.

Muskegon

Muskegon
3500 N Strand
Muskegon, MI
231-766-3900
Dogs of all sizes are allowed. There are no additional pet fees. Dogs may not be left unattended, must be leashed, and cleaned up after. Dogs are allowed at the backside of the lake. There are some breed restrictions. This RV park is closed during the off-season. The camping and tent areas also allow dogs. There is a dog walk area at the campground. Multiple dogs may be allowed.

P.J. Hoffmaster State Park
6585 Lake Harbor Road
Muskegon, MI
231-798-3711
This park offers forest-covered dunes with nearly three miles of Lake Michigan shore, a designated wildlife site, a year round interpretive program, and the Sand Dune Visitor's Center is considered a top attraction. Dogs are allowed at no additional fee. Dogs may not be left unattended, and they must be leashed and cleaned up after. Dogs are not allowed on the beach, but they are allowed on the trails. This campground is closed during the off-season. The camping and tent areas also allow dogs. There is a dog walk area at the campground. There are no water hookups at the campground. Multiple dogs may be allowed.

Back Forty Ranch
5900 S Water Road
Rothbury, MI
231-894-4444
Dogs of all sizes are allowed. There are no additional pet fees for RV spaces, however there is a $25 per night per pet additional fee for the Back 40 Cabins plus a $100 refundable deposit. Dogs may not be

left unattended except for short periods and if they will be well behaved in owner's absence. Dogs must be leashed and cleaned up after. The camping and tent areas also allow dogs. There is a dog walk area at the campground. Dogs are allowed in the camping cabins. Multiple dogs may be allowed.

Newberry

Newberry KOA
13724 H 28
Newberry, MI
906-293-5762
Dogs of all sizes are allowed. There are no additional pet fees. Dogs may not be left unattended, must be leashed, and cleaned up after. This RV park is closed during the off-season. The camping and tent areas also allow dogs. There is a dog walk area at the campground. Dogs are allowed in the camping cabins. Multiple dogs may be allowed.

Ontonagon

Porcupine Mountains Wilderness State Park
33303 Headquarters Road
Ontonagon, MI
906-885-5275
This park is home to one of the few remaining large wilderness areas in the region. Dogs of all sizes are allowed. There are no additional pet fees. Dogs may not be left unattended at any time, including in automobiles, and they must have a current rabies certificate and shot records. Dogs must be quiet, well behaved, be on no more than a 6 foot leash, and be cleaned up after. Dogs are allowed on the trails, and at the picnic areas. Dogs are not allowed in buildings, day use areas, at the beaches or in the water. This campground is closed during the off-season. The camping and tent areas also allow dogs. There is a dog walk area at the campground. There are no water hookups at the campground. Multiple dogs may be allowed.

Oscoda

Oscoda KOA
3591 Forest Road
Oscoda, MI
989-739-5115
Dogs of all sizes are allowed. There

are no additional pet fees. Dogs must be leashed and cleaned up after. This RV park is closed during the off-season. The camping and tent areas also allow dogs. There is a dog walk area at the campground. Multiple dogs may be allowed.

Paradise

Tahquamenon Falls State Park
41382 W H 123
Paradise, MI
906-492-3415
This park has modern, semi-modern, and rustic camping areas to offer in addition to several recreation activities. This park is mostly known for having one of the largest waterfalls east of the Mississippi, as well as several other waterfalls. Dogs of all sizes are allowed. There are no additional pet fees. Dogs may not be left unattended at any time, including in automobiles, and they must have a current rabies certificate and shot records. Dogs must be quiet, well behaved, be on no more than a 6 foot leash, and be cleaned up after. Dogs are allowed on the trails, and at the picnic areas. Dogs are not allowed in buildings, day use areas, at the beaches or in the water. This campground is closed during the off-season. The camping and tent areas also allow dogs. There is a dog walk area at the campground. There are no water hookups at the campground. Multiple dogs may be allowed.

Petersburg

Monroe Co/Toledo North KOA
US 23 at Summerfield Road
Petersburg, MI
734-856-4972
Dogs of all sizes are allowed. There is a $5 per night per pet additional fee. Dogs are not allowed in the rentals. Dogs may not be left unattended, must be leashed, and cleaned up after. There are some breed restrictions. This RV park is closed during the off-season. The camping and tent areas also allow dogs. There is a dog walk area at the campground. Multiple dogs may be allowed.

Petoskey

Petoskey KOA
1800 N H 31
Petoskey, MI

231-347-0005
Dogs of all sizes are allowed. There are no additional pet fees. Dogs may not be left unattended, must be leashed, and cleaned up after. Dogs are allowed in the cabins but not the park models. This RV park is closed during the off-season. The camping and tent areas also allow dogs. There is a dog walk area at the campground. Dogs are allowed in the camping cabins. Multiple dogs may be allowed.

Port Austin

Duggans Family Campground
2941 Port Austin Road
Port Austin, MI
989-738-5160
Dogs of all sizes are allowed. There are no additional pet fees. Dogs must be quiet and well behaved. Dogs may not be left unattended, must be leashed, and cleaned up after. This RV park is closed during the off-season. The camping and tent areas also allow dogs. There is a dog walk area at the campground. Multiple dogs may be allowed.

Rapid River

Whitefish Hill RV Park
8455 H 2
Rapid River, MI
800-476-6515
Dogs of all sizes are allowed. There are no additional pet fees for the RV or camp sites, however there is a $50 refundable pet deposit for any of their rentals. Dogs must be leashed and cleaned up after. The camping and tent areas also allow dogs. There is a dog walk area at the campground. Multiple dogs may be allowed.

Riverside

Coloma/St Joseph KOA
3527 Coloma Road
Riverside, MI
269-849-3333
Dogs of all sizes are allowed. There are no additional pet fees. Dogs may not be left unattended, must be leashed, and cleaned up after. There are some breed restrictions. This RV park is closed during the off-season. The camping and tent areas also allow dogs. There is a dog walk area at the campground. Dogs are allowed in the camping cabins. 2 dogs may be allowed.

Roscommon

Higgins Hills RV Park
3800 Federal H
Roscommon, MI
989-275-8151
Dogs of all sizes are allowed. There are no additional pet fees. Dogs must be quiet and not left unattended. They must be leashed and cleaned up after. There are some breed restrictions. There is a dog walk area at the campground. 2 dogs may be allowed.

North Higgins Lake State Park
11747 N Higgins Lake Drive
Roscommon, MI
989-821-6125
This park was once the world's largest seedling nursery which led in part to a large population of animals, birds, trees and plants. Dogs of all sizes are allowed at no additional fee. Dogs may not be left unattended, they must be on no more than a 6 foot leash, and be cleaned up after. Dogs are allowed on the trails, but they are not allowed on the beach, in buildings, or on ski trails in winter. This campground is closed during the off-season. The camping and tent areas also allow dogs. There is a dog walk area at the campground. There are no water hookups at the campground. Multiple dogs may be allowed.

Saginaw Area

Valley Plaza Resort
5215 Bay City Road
Midland, MI
989-496-2159
One dog of any size is allowed. There are no additional pet fees. Dogs must be well behaved, leashed, and cleaned up after. This RV park is closed during the off-season. The camping and tent areas also allow dogs. There is a dog walk area at the campground.

Stanwood

River Ridge Resort
22265 8 mile Road
Stanwood, MI
877-287-4837
Dogs of all sizes are allowed. There is a $3 per night per dog additional fee. Dogs must be leashed and cleaned up after. There is a dog walk area at the campground.

Multiple dogs may be allowed.

Sumner

Leisure Lake Campground
505 S Warner Road
Sumner, MI
989-875-4689
Dogs of all sizes are allowed. There are no additional pet fees. Dogs must be quiet, not left unattended, leashed and cleaned up after. Dogs are not allowed at the beach area of the lake, but they are allowed at the east end. This RV park is closed during the off-season. The camping and tent areas also allow dogs. There is a dog walk area at the campground. Multiple dogs may be allowed.

Traverse City

Holiday Park Campground
4860 H 31S
Traverse City, MI
231-938-4410
Dogs of all sizes are allowed. There are no additional pet fees. Dogs must be leashed and cleaned up after. This RV park is closed during the off-season. The camping and tent areas also allow dogs. There is a dog walk area at the campground. Multiple dogs may be allowed.

Tustin

Cadillac Woods Campground
23163 H 115
Tustin, MI
231-825-2012
Dogs of all sizes are allowed. There are no additional pet fees. Dogs may not be left unattended, must be leashed and cleaned up after. Dogs are allowed off leash at your site if the dog will not chase people or pets, and will stay on the site. The camping and tent areas also allow dogs. There is a dog walk area at the campground. Dogs are allowed in the camping cabins. Multiple dogs may be allowed.

Upper Peninsula

Ottawa National Forest
E6248 US 2 (Supervisor's Office)
Ironwood, MI
906-932-1330
This park covers nearly a million acres in the states of Michigan and Wisconsin. Dogs of all sizes are

allowed. There are no additional pet fees. Dogs may not be left unattended, they must have a current rabies certificate and shot records, be leashed, and cleaned up after. Dogs are allowed on all the trails. The camping and tent areas also allow dogs. There is a dog walk area at the campground. Multiple dogs may be allowed.

White Lake

Highland Recreation Area
5200 E Highland Road
White Lake, MI
248-889-3750
There are a variety of trails at this park of about 5,900 acres, with 4 lakes, a doggy trail, and activities for all seasons. Dogs of all sizes are allowed at no additional fee. Dogs may not be left unattended, they must be on no more than a 6 foot leash, and be cleaned up after. Dogs are allowed on marked trails, but they are not allowed in public swim areas or in buildings. This campground is closed during the off-season. The camping and tent areas also allow dogs. There is a dog walk area at the campground. There are no electric or water hookups at the campground. Multiple dogs may be allowed.

Williamsburg

Traverse Bay RV Resort
5555 H 72E
Williamsburg, MI
231-938-5800
Dogs of all sizes are allowed. There are no additional pet fees. Dogs must be leashed and cleaned up after. This RV park is closed during the off-season. There is a dog walk area at the campground. 2 dogs may be allowed.

Ypsilanti

Detroit/Greenfield KOA
6680 Bunton Road
Ypsilanti, MI
734-482-7222
Dogs of all sizes are allowed. There are no additional pet fees. Dogs must be leashed and cleaned up after, and may not go in the lake. This RV park is closed during the off-season. The camping and tent areas also allow dogs. There is a dog walk area at the campground. Multiple dogs may be allowed.

Zeeland

Dutch Treat Camping
10300 Gordon Street
Zeeland, MI
616-772-4303
Dogs of all sizes are allowed. There are no additional pet fees. Dogs may not be left unattended, must be well behaved, leashed, and cleaned up after. The camping and tent areas also allow dogs. There is a dog walk area at the campground. Multiple dogs may be allowed.

Minnesota Listings

Altura

Whitewater State Park
19041 H 74
Altura, MN
507-932-3007
This popular park offers easy-to-challenging hiking trails. Dogs of all sizes are allowed at no additional fee. Dogs may not be left unattended, and they must be leashed and cleaned up after. Dogs are not allowed in public swim areas or buildings. Dogs are allowed on the trails. The camping and tent areas also allow dogs. There is a dog walk area at the campground. There are no water hookups at the campground. Multiple dogs may be allowed.

Austin

Beaver Trails Campground and RV Park
21943 630th Avenue
Austin, MN
507-584-6611
Dogs of all sizes are allowed. There are no additional pet fees. Dogs must be leashed and cleaned up after. There are some breed restrictions. This RV park is closed during the off-season. The camping and tent areas also allow dogs. There is a dog walk area at the campground. Dogs are allowed in the camping cabins. Multiple dogs may be allowed.

Bemidji

Bemidji KOA

510 Brightstar Road NW
Bemidji, MN
218-444-7562
Dogs of all sizes are allowed, and there are no additional pet fees for tent or RV sites. There is a $5 per pet per stay additional fee for the lodge and cabins. Dogs must be on no more than a 6 foot leash, and be cleaned up after. This RV park is closed during the off-season. The camping and tent areas also allow dogs. There is a dog walk area at the campground. Dogs are allowed in the camping cabins. Multiple dogs may be allowed.

Brainard

Crow Wing State Park
3124 State Park Road
Brainard, MN
218-825-3075
This scenic park offers an interpretive exhibit, 18 miles of hiking trails, and a variety of recreation. Dogs of all sizes are allowed at no additional fee. Dogs may not be left unattended except for very short periods, and they must be on no more than a 6 foot leash, and cleaned up after. Dogs are allowed on the trails, except for the ski trails in winter. The camping and tent areas also allow dogs. There is a dog walk area at the campground. There are no water hookups at the campground. Multiple dogs may be allowed.

Cannon Falls

Lake Byllesby Regional Park
7650 Echo Point Road
Cannon Falls, MN
507-263-4447
This beautiful park, located along Lake Byllesby Reservoir, offers a variety of year round land and water recreation. Dogs of all sizes are allowed at no additional fee. Dogs may not be left unattended, and they must be on no more than a 6 foot leash, and cleaned up after. Dogs may not be tied to trees, plants, buildings, or park equipment. Dogs are allowed on the trails. This campground is closed during the off-season. The camping and tent areas also allow dogs. There is a dog walk area at the campground. Multiple dogs may be allowed.

Cass Lake

Chippewa National Forest

Norway Beach Road
Cass Lake, MN
218-335-8600
Steeped in a rich history and culture, this 1.6 million acre forest with 1300 lakes provides a variety of camping areas, miles of trails, recreation pursuits, and diverse ecosystems that support a large variety of plants and animals. Dogs are allowed at no additional fee. Dogs may not be left unattended, and they must be leashed and cleaned up after in the camp areas. This campground is closed during the off-season. The camping and tent areas also allow dogs. There is a dog walk area at the campground. There are no water hookups at the campground. Multiple dogs may be allowed.

Stonypoint Resort

5510 H 2 NW
Cass Lake, MN
507-584-6611
Dogs of all sizes are allowed. There is a $2 per night per pet additional fee. Dogs must be well behaved, house trained, leashed, and cleaned up after. This RV park is closed during the off-season. The camping and tent areas also allow dogs. There is a dog walk area at the campground. Dogs are allowed in the camping cabins. Multiple dogs may be allowed.

Cloquet

Cloquet/Duluth KOA

1381 Carlton Road
Cloquet, MN
218-879-5726
Dogs of all sizes are allowed. There are no additional pet fees. Dogs must be leashed and cleaned up after. This RV park is closed during the off-season. The camping and tent areas also allow dogs. There is a dog walk area at the campground. Dogs are allowed in the camping cabins. 2 dogs may be allowed.

Currie

Lake Shetek State Park

163 State Park Road
Currie, MN
507-763-3256
This 1,100 acre park, born of glacial activity, is rich in natural and cultural history and offer 14 miles of hiking trails. It also houses an interpretive trail over a causeway to Loon Island (a bird sanctuary) and a variety of land and water recreation. Dogs of all sizes are allowed at no additional fee. Dogs may not be left unattended, and they must be on no more than a 6 foot leash at all times, and cleaned up after. Dogs are not allowed on beaches or in buildings. Dogs are allowed on trails. There is a shoreline access for dogs to go swimming. The camping and tent areas also allow dogs. There is a dog walk area at the campground. There are no water hookups at the campground. Multiple dogs may be allowed.

Deer River

Lake Winnibigoshish Rec Area and Dam

County Road 9
Deer River, MN
218-326-6128
This park is on a premier fishing lake with a dam built by the Corp of Engineers (on National Register of Historical Places), and offers spectacular views, abundant plant and wildlife, and various recreational pursuits. Dogs of all sizes are allowed at no additional fee. Dogs may not be left unattended unless they will be quiet and well behaved, and then only for a short time. Dog must be on no more than a 6 foot leash, and cleaned up after. Dogs are allowed on the trails. This campground is closed during the off-season. The camping and tent areas also allow dogs. There is a dog walk area at the campground. There are no water hookups at the campground. Multiple dogs may be allowed.

Detroit Lakes

Long Lake Campsite

17421 W Long Lake Road
Detroit Lakes, MN
218-847-8920
Dogs of all sizes are allowed. There are no additional pet fees. Dogs must be quiet, well behaved, leashed, and cleaned up after. Dogs may not be on the beach. This RV park is closed during the off-season. There is a dog walk area at the campground. Multiple dogs may be allowed.

Duluth

Indian Point Campground

7500 Pulaski
Duluth, MN
218-628-4977
Dogs of all sizes are allowed. There are no additional pet fees. Dogs must be quiet and well behaved, especially if they are left alone on site. This RV park is closed during the off-season. The camping and tent areas also allow dogs. There is a dog walk area at the campground. 2 dogs may be allowed.

Superior National Forest

8901 Grand Avenue Place
Duluth, MN
218-626-4300
This forest of over 3 million acres provides a variety of camping areas, trails, recreation, and diverse ecosystems. Dogs are allowed at no additional fee. Dogs may not be left unattended, and they must be leashed and cleaned up after in the camp areas. Dogs are not allowed on the beach or in buildings. This campground is closed during the off-season. The camping and tent areas also allow dogs. There is a dog walk area at the campground. There are no water hookups at the campground. Multiple dogs may be allowed.

Fairmont

Flying Goose Campground

2521 115th Street
Fairmont, MN
507-235-3458
Dogs of all sizes are allowed. There are no additional pet fees. Dogs may not be left unattended, and must be leashed and cleaned up after. This RV park is closed during the off-season. The camping and tent areas also allow dogs. There is a dog walk area at the campground. Multiple dogs may be allowed.

Grand Rapids

Pokegama Lake and Dam

34385 H 2
Grand Rapids, MN
218-326-6128
This scenic park lies along the Mississippi River and offers a variety of activities and recreation. Dogs of all sizes are allowed at no additional fee. Dogs may not be left unattended unless they will be quiet and well behaved, and only then for short periods. Dogs must be on no more than a 6 foot leash, and cleaned up after. This campground is closed during the off-season. The camping

and tent areas also allow dogs. There is a dog walk area at the campground. There are no water hookups at the campground. Multiple dogs may be allowed.

Gilbert

Sherwood Forest Campground
PO box 548
Gilbert, MN
218-748-2221
This popular park provides a variety of land and water recreational pursuits. Dogs of all sizes are allowed at no additional fee. Dogs may not be left unattended at any time; they must be quiet, well behaved, be leashed, and cleaned up after. Dogs are allowed on the trails. Dogs are not allowed on beaches or in buildings. This campground is closed during the off-season. The camping and tent areas also allow dogs. There is a dog walk area at the campground. Multiple dogs may be allowed.

Hayward

Albert Lea/Austin KOA
84259 County Road 46
Hayward, MN
507-373-5170
Dogs of all sizes are allowed. There are no additional pet fees. Dogs must be well behaved, leashed, and cleaned up after. This RV park is closed during the off-season. The camping and tent areas also allow dogs. There is a dog walk area at the campground. Dogs are allowed in the camping cabins. Multiple dogs may be allowed.

Hinckley

St Croix State Park
30065 St Croix Park Road
Hinckley, MN
320-384-6591
With over 34,000 acres along 2 great rivers, this scenic park offers a fire tower, miles of multi-use trails, and a variety of land and water recreation. Dogs may not be left unattended, and they must be on no more than a 6 foot leash and be cleaned up after. Dogs are not allowed on ski trails in the winter or in buildings. Dogs are allowed on the trails. The camping and tent areas also allow dogs. There is a dog walk area at the campground. There are no water hookups at the campground. Multiple

dogs may be allowed.

Isle

Father Hennepin State Park
41294 Father Hennepin Park Road
Isle, MN
320-676-8763
A large sandy beach, panoramic views, a hardwood forest, and a rocky shoreline all greet the hiker at this 316 acre recreational park. Dogs of all sizes are allowed at no additional fee. Dogs may not be left unattended; they must be quiet, well behaved, be on no more than a 6 foot leash, and cleaned up after. Dogs are allowed on the trails. Dogs are not allowed in swim areas or in buildings. The camping and tent areas also allow dogs. There is a dog walk area at the campground. There are no water hookups at the campground. Multiple dogs may be allowed.

Jackson

Jackson KOA
2035 H 71N
Jackson, MN
507-847-3825
Dogs of all sizes are allowed, and there are no additional pet fees for the tent or RV sites. There is a $5 one time additional pet fee for cabin rentals. Dogs must be leashed and cleaned up after. This RV park is closed during the off-season. The camping and tent areas also allow dogs. There is a dog walk area at the campground. Dogs are allowed in the camping cabins. Multiple dogs may be allowed.

Jasper

Split Rock Creek State Park
336 50th Avenue
Jasper, MN
507-348-7908
This 1,303 acre park provides a variety of habitats for birds and wildlife, interpretive exhibits, self guided trails, and various land and water recreational pursuits. The off-season phone number is 507-283-1307. Dogs of all sizes are allowed at no additional fee. Dogs may not be left unattended, and they must be on no more than a 6 foot leash, and cleaned up after. Dogs are allowed on the trails. This campground is closed during the off-season. The camping and tent

areas also allow dogs. There is a dog walk area at the campground. There are no water hookups at the campground. Multiple dogs may be allowed.

Jordan

Minneapolis Southwest KOA
3315 W 166th Street
Jordan, MN
952-492-6440
Dogs of all sizes are allowed. There is a $1 per night per pet additional fee. There is an additional refundable pet deposit of $50 for the cabin rentals. Dogs must be leashed and cleaned up after. This RV park is closed during the off-season. The camping and tent areas also allow dogs. There is a dog walk area at the campground. Dogs are allowed in the camping cabins. 2 dogs may be allowed.

Little Falls

Charles Lindbergh State Park
1516 Lindberg Drive S
Little Falls, MN
320-616-2525
Born from ancient glaciers and rich in natural and cultural history, this park, located on the Mississippi River, offers a wide variety of land and water recreation. Dogs of all sizes are allowed at no additional fee. Dogs may not be left unattended, and they must be quiet, well behaved, be on no more than a 6 foot leash at all times, and cleaned up after. Dogs are not allowed in buildings or on beaches. Dogs are allowed on the trails, except not on the ski trails in winter. The camping and tent areas also allow dogs. There is a dog walk area at the campground. There are no water hookups at the campground. Multiple dogs may be allowed.

Luverne

Blue Mounds State Park
1410 161st Street
Luverne, MN
507-283-1307
This recreational park is full of natural surprises like the 100 foot straight-up Sioux quartzite cliff, a bison herd, and an historic site with a mystery. They also offer an interpretive center and 13 miles of hiking trails. Dogs of all sizes are allowed at no additional fee. Dogs

may not be left unattended, and they must be on no more than a 6 foot leash, and cleaned up after. Dogs are not allowed on beaches or in buildings. Dogs are allowed on trails. The camping and tent areas also allow dogs. There is a dog walk area at the campground. There is no water hookups at the campground. Multiple dogs may be allowed.

Minneapolis - St Paul

Greenwood Campground
13797 190th Street E
Hastings, MN
651-437-5269
Dogs of all sizes are allowed. There are no additional pet fees. Dogs must be quiet, leashed, and cleaned up after. This RV park is closed during the off-season. There is a dog walk area at the campground. 2 dogs may be allowed.

Minneapolis Northwest KOA
10410 Brockton
Maple Grove, MN
763-420-2255
Dogs of all sizes are allowed. There are no additional pet fees. Dogs may not be tied up outside alone, must be leashed, and cleaned up after. There are some breed restrictions. This RV park is closed during the off-season. The camping and tent areas also allow dogs. There is a dog walk area at the campground. 2 dogs may be allowed.

Dakotah Meadows RV Park
2341 Park Place
Prior Lake, MN
952-445-8800
Dogs of all sizes are allowed. There are no additional pet fees. Dogs must be leashed and cleaned up after. There is a dog walk area at the campground. Multiple dogs may be allowed.

St Paul East KOA
568 Cottage Grove
Woodbury, MN
651-436-6436
Dogs of all sizes are allowed. There are no additional pet fees. Dogs must be quiet, well behaved, leashed, and cleaned up after. There are some breed restrictions. This RV park is closed during the off-season. The camping and tent areas also allow dogs. There is a dog walk area at the campground. Dogs are allowed in the camping cabins. Multiple dogs may be allowed.

Monticello

River Terrace Park
1335 River Street W
Monticello, MN
763-295-2264
Dogs of all sizes are allowed. There are no additional pet fees unless staying monthly. Dogs must be quiet, well behaved, leashed, and cleaned up after. This RV park is closed during the off-season. The camping and tent areas also allow dogs. There is a dog walk area at the campground. Multiple dogs may be allowed.

Moorhead

Moorhead/Fargo KOA
4396 28th Avenue S
Moorhead, MN
218-233-0671
Dogs of all sizes are allowed. There are no additional pet fees. Dogs must be well behaved, may not be left unattended, must be leashed, and cleaned up after. This RV park is closed during the off-season. The camping and tent areas also allow dogs. There is a dog walk area at the campground. Dogs are allowed in the camping cabins. Multiple dogs may be allowed.

New Ulm

Flandrau State Park
1300 Summit Avenue
New Ulm, MN
507-233-9800
This popular park lies along the Big Cottonwood River and offers a scenic diverse terrain, 8 miles of trails, an interpretive exhibit, and a variety of land and water recreation. Dogs of all sizes are allowed at no additional fee. Dogs may not be left unattended, and they must be on no more than a 6 foot leash, and cleaned up after. Dogs are allowed on the trails, except the ski trails in winter. Dogs are not allowed by the pool or in buildings. The camping and tent areas also allow dogs. There is a dog walk area at the campground. There are no water hookups at the campground. Multiple dogs may be allowed.

Flandrau State Park
1300 Summit Avenue
New Ulm, MN
507-233-9800
This popular park lies along the Big

Cottonwood River and offers a scenic diverse terrain, 8 miles of trails, an interpretive exhibit, and a variety of land and water recreation. Dogs of all sizes are allowed at no additional fee. Dogs may not be left unattended, and they must be on no more than a 6 foot leash, and cleaned up after. Dogs are allowed on the trails, except the ski trails in winter. Dogs are not allowed by the pool or in buildings. The camping and tent areas also allow dogs. There is a dog walk area at the campground. There are no water hookups at the campground. Multiple dogs may be allowed.

Ortonville

Big Stone Lake State Park
35889 Meadowbrook State Park Road
Ortonville, MN
320-839-3663
This 986 acre park offers an Environmental Education Center and various land and water recreation. Dogs of all sizes are allowed at no additional fee. Dogs may not be left unattended; they must be quiet, well behaved, be on no more than a 6 foot leash, and cleaned up after. Dogs are allowed on the trails. Dogs are not allowed on beaches or in buildings. The off-season phone number is 320-734-4450. This campground is closed during the off-season. The camping and tent areas also allow dogs. There is a dog walk area at the campground. There are no water hookups at the campground. Multiple dogs may be allowed.

Owatonna

Hope Oak Knoll Campground
9545 County Road 3
Owatonna, MN
507-451-2998
Dogs of all sizes are allowed. There are no additional pet fees. Dogs may not be left unattended, and must be leashed and cleaned up after. This RV park is closed during the off-season. The camping and tent areas also allow dogs. There is a dog walk area at the campground. Multiple dogs may be allowed.

Park Rapids

Big Pines
501 S Central

Park Rapids, MN
218-732-4483
Dogs of all sizes are allowed. There are no additional pet fees. Dogs must be leashed and cleaned up after. This RV park is closed during the off-season. The camping and tent areas also allow dogs. There is a dog walk area at the campground. Multiple dogs may be allowed.

Itasca State Park
36750 Main Park Drive
Park Rapids, MN
218-266-2100
As Minnesota's oldest state park, there is a rich blend of natural and cultural history here. The park is National Register Historic District and offers a variety of trails, interpretive exhibits and programs, tours, and plenty of recreational pursuits. Dogs of all sizes are allowed at no additional fee. Dogs may not be left unattended at any time; they must be quiet, well behaved, be on no more than a 6 foot leash or crated at all times, and cleaned up after. Dogs are allowed on the trails, except the ski trails in winter. Dogs are not allowed on beaches or in buildings. This campground is closed during the off-season. The camping and tent areas also allow dogs. There is a dog walk area at the campground. There are no water hookups at the campground. Multiple dogs may be allowed.

Preston

Forestville/Mystery Cave State Park
Route 2, Box 128/H 118
Preston, MN
507-352-5111
You will see natural wonders below and above ground at this historic park including a restored 1800's village, an interpretive exhibit, tours, nature programs, and a variety of recreational pursuits. Dogs of all sizes are allowed at no additional fee. Dogs may not be left unattended at any time; they must be quiet, well behaved, be on no more than a 6 foot leash or crated at all times, and cleaned up after. Dogs are allowed on the trails, except the ski trails in winter. Dogs are not allowed on beaches or in buildings. The camping and tent areas also allow dogs. There is a dog walk area at the campground. There are no water hookups at the campground. Multiple dogs may be allowed.

Old Barn Resort
Rt 3 Box 57
Preston, MN
507-467-2512 ext 1
This popular recreation area has some unique features, like a three season indoor pool, access to the 60 mile Root River State Trail, caves, a museum, beautiful scenery and abundant wildlife. Pets are welcome, at no additional fee, if they are kept on a leash, cleaned up after and are quiet so as not to disturb other campers. They are not allowed in the pool or in any part of the buildings on the grounds including the barn itself. Pets may not be left at campsites unattended. This campground is closed during the off-season. The camping and tent areas also allow dogs. There is a dog walk area at the campground. Multiple dogs may be allowed.

Rochester

Rochester/Marion KOA
5232 65th Avenue SE
Rochester, MN
507-288-0785
Dogs of all sizes are allowed. There are no additional pet fees. Dogs must be leashed and cleaned up after. There are some breed restrictions. This RV park is closed during the off-season. The camping and tent areas also allow dogs. There is a dog walk area at the campground. Multiple dogs may be allowed.

St Cloud

St Cloud Campground
2491 2nd Street SE
St Cloud, MN
320-251-4463
Dogs of all sizes are allowed. There are no additional pet fees. Dogs must be leashed and cleaned up after. Dogs are not allowed in the buildings or at the pool area. This RV park is closed during the off-season. The camping and tent areas also allow dogs. There is a dog walk area at the campground.

St Croix

William O'Brien State Park
16821 O'Brien Trail N
St Croix, MN
651-433-0500
Set along the banks of the St Croix River, this picturesque park offers several miles of multi-use trails (12 miles hiking), interpretive exhibits, naturalist programs, and a variety of land and water recreation. Dogs of all sizes are allowed at no additional fee. Dogs may not be left unattended, and they must be on no more than a 6 foot leash, and cleaned up after. Dogs are allowed on the trails, except the ski trails in winter. Dogs are not allowed in swim areas or in buildings. The camping and tent areas also allow dogs. There is a dog walk area at the campground. There are no water hookups at the campground. Multiple dogs may be allowed.

Starbuck

Glacial Lakes State Park
25022 County Road 41
Starbuck, MN
320-239-2860
Born from glacial activity, this park is home to a wide variety of plants, birds, and wildlife, and provides a variety of trails, an interpretive exhibit and various recreational pursuits. Dogs of all sizes are allowed at no additional fee. Dogs may not be left unattended; they must be quiet, well behaved, be on no more than a 6 foot leash or crated at all times, and cleaned up after. Dogs are allowed on the trails, except the ski trails in winter. Dogs are not allowed in swim areas or in buildings. Dogs may not be tied to the trees or other park equipment. The camping and tent areas also allow dogs. There is a dog walk area at the campground. There are no water hookups at the campground. Multiple dogs may be allowed.

Taylors Falls

Interstate State Park
P. O. Box 254/H 8
Taylors Falls, MN
651-465-5711
Unique geology intrigues visitors at this state park. At least 10 different lava flows are exposed in the park along with two distinct glacial deposits. The park also offers an interpretive exhibit and various trails and recreation. Dogs of all sizes are allowed at no additional fee. Dogs may not be left unattended at any time; they must be quiet, well behaved, be on no more than a 6 foot leash or crated at all times, and cleaned up after. Dogs are allowed

on the trails, except the ski trails in winter. Dogs are not allowed on beaches or in buildings. The camping and tent areas also allow dogs. There is a dog walk area at the campground. There are no water hookups at the campground. Multiple dogs may be allowed.

Waseca

Kiesler's Campground
14360 H 14E
Waseca, MN
800-533-4642
Dogs of all sizes are allowed. There are no additional pet fees. Dogs may not be left unattended. Dogs must be quiet, well behaved, leashed, and cleaned up after. This RV park is closed during the off-season. The camping and tent areas also allow dogs. There is a dog walk area at the campground. Multiple dogs may be allowed.

Watson

Lac Qui Parle State Park
14047 20th Street NW
Watson, MN
320-734-4450
The Dakota Indians called this the "lake that speaks" because it is a stop over for thousands of migratory Canada geese and other waterfowl. The park offers a variety of land and water recreation. Dogs of all sizes are allowed at no additional fee. Dogs may not be left unattended, and they must be quiet, well behaved, on no more than a 6 foot leash, and cleaned up after. Dogs are allowed on the trails. The camping and tent areas also allow dogs. There is a dog walk area at the campground. Multiple dogs may be allowed.

Mississippi Listings

Ackerman

Tombigbee National Forest
H 15S
Ackerman, MS
662-285-3264
This 66,600 acre forest provides a variety of camping areas, trails, recreation, and diverse ecosystems

that support a large variety of plants, fish, mammals, and bird species. Dogs are allowed at no additional fee. Dogs may not be left unattended, and they must be leashed and cleaned up after in the camp areas. Dogs are allowed on the trails. This campground is closed during the off-season. The camping and tent areas also allow dogs. There is a dog walk area at the campground. There are no electric or water hookups at the campground. Multiple dogs may be allowed.

Bryam

Swinging Bridge RV Park
100 Holiday Rambler Lane
Bryam, MS
800-297-9127
Dogs of all sizes are allowed. There are no additional pet fees. Dogs may not be left unattended outside, and they must be leashed and cleaned up after. There are some breed restrictions. There is a dog walk area at the campground. Multiple dogs may be allowed.

Canton

Movietown RV Park
109 Movietown Drive
Canton, MS
601-859-7990
Dogs of all sizes are allowed. There are no additional pet fees. Dogs may not be left unattended outside, and they must be quiet, well behaved, leashed and cleaned up after. The camping and tent areas also allow dogs. There is a dog walk area at the campground. Multiple dogs may be allowed.

Collinsville

Twitley Branch Camping Area
9200 Hamrick Road
Collinsville, MS
601-626-8068
Dogs are allowed at no additional fee. Dogs may not be left unattended unless they will be quiet and very well behaved, and they may not be left outside unattended at any time. Dogs must be leashed and cleaned up after. Dogs are not allowed on the beach or in buildings. The camping and tent areas also allow dogs. There is a dog walk area at the campground. Multiple dogs may be allowed.

Columbia

Mimosa Landing Campground
501 Rustique Brick Drive
Columbia, MS
866-736-9700
Dogs of all sizes are allowed. There are no additional pet fees. Dogs must be leashed and cleaned up after. There is a dog walk area at the campground. 2 dogs may be allowed.

Columbus

Lake Lowndes State Park
3319 Lake Lowndes Road
Columbus, MS
662-328-2110
This scenic park sits along a 150 acre lake, and offers a wide array of land and water activities and recreation. It also hosts an amphitheater and a nature trail. Dogs are allowed at no additional fee. Dogs may not be left unattended outside, and they must be leashed and cleaned up after. Dogs are allowed on the trails. The camping and tent areas also allow dogs. There is a dog walk area at the campground. Multiple dogs may be allowed.

Forest

Bienville National Forest
3473 H 35S
Forest, MS
601-469-3811
This working forest of 178,000 acres provides a variety of camping areas, trails, recreation, and diverse ecosystems that support a large variety of plants, fish, mammals, and bird species. Dogs are allowed at no additional fee. Dogs may not be left unattended, and they must be leashed and cleaned up after in the camp areas. This campground is closed during the off-season. The camping and tent areas also allow dogs. There is a dog walk area at the campground. Multiple dogs may be allowed.

Glen

Little Creek Ranch
181 County Road 345
Glen, MS
662-287-0362
Dogs of all sizes are allowed. There are no additional pet fees. Dogs must be quiet, well behaved,

leashed, and cleaned up after. The camping and tent areas also allow dogs. There is a dog walk area at the campground. Multiple dogs may be allowed.

Hattiesburg

Paul Johnson State Park
319 Geiger Lake Road
Hattiesburg, MS
601-582-7721
Surrounded by deep forest, this scenic park offers a variety of habitats, the "Trail of the Southern Pines" that features two lookout towers, and a variety of land and water recreation. Dogs of all sizes are allowed at no additional fee. Dogs may not be left unattended, and they must be leashed and cleaned up after. Dogs are not allowed in or around the cabins or on the beach. Dogs are allowed on the trails. The camping and tent areas also allow dogs. There is a dog walk area at the campground. Multiple dogs may be allowed.

Holly Springs

Wall Doxey
3946 H 7 S
Holly Springs, MS
662-252-4231
Rich in natural beauty and located along the shores of a 60 acre spring fed lake, this park offers a variety of land and water activities, recreation, and trails. Dogs of all sizes are allowed at no additional fee. Dogs may not be left unattended unless they will be quiet, well behaved, and then only for short periods. Dogs must be leashed and cleaned up after, and they are allowed on the trails. The camping and tent areas also allow dogs. There is a dog walk area at the campground. Multiple dogs may be allowed.

Wall Doxey State Park
3946 H 7S
Holly Springs, MS
662-252-4231
This park sits along a 60-acre spring-fed lake, and offers an abundance of outdoor recreation and activities. Dogs of all sizes are allowed at no additional fee. Dogs may not be left unattended except for short periods and only if they will be quiet and well behaved. Dogs must be leashed and cleaned up after. Dogs are allowed on the trails. The camping and tent areas also allow dogs. There is a

dog walk area at the campground. Multiple dogs may be allowed.

Jackson

LeFleur's Bluff State Park
2140 Riverside Drive
Jackson, MS
601-987-3923
Rich in cultural heritage, this 305 acre park features a nine-hole golf course with a driving range, a variety of trails, and various land and water activities and recreation. Dogs of all sizes are allowed at no additional fee. Dogs may not be left unattended, and they must be leashed and cleaned up after. Dogs are not allowed in the playground area. Dogs are allowed on the trails. The camping and tent areas also allow dogs. There is a dog walk area at the campground. Multiple dogs may be allowed.

Meridian

Nanabe Creek Campground
1933 Russell Mount Gilliad Road
Meridian, MS
601-485-4711
Dogs of all sizes are allowed. There are no additional pet fees. Dogs must be leashed, cleaned up after, and walked in designated pet areas. The camping and tent areas also allow dogs. There is a dog walk area at the campground. Multiple dogs may be allowed.

Morton

Roosevelt State Park
2149 H 13 S
Morton, MS
601-732-6316
This park features panoramic views and hosts a variety of land and water activities and recreation. Dogs of all sizes are allowed at no additional fee. Dogs may not be left unattended, and they must be quiet, well behaved, leashed and cleaned up after in camp areas. Dogs are not allowed in any of the buildings, however, they are allowed on the trail. The camping and tent areas also allow dogs. There is a dog walk area at the campground. Multiple dogs may be allowed.

Roosevelt State Park
2149 H 13 S
Morton, MS
601-732-6316

This picturesque park provides a panoramic view of the Bienville National Forest. It also provides a wide variety of recreational pursuits and numerous trails. Dogs of all sizes are allowed at no additional fee. Dogs may not be left unattended, and they must be quiet, well behaved, leashed and cleaned up after. Dogs are not allowed in buildings, but they are allowed on the trails. The camping and tent areas also allow dogs. There is a dog walk area at the campground. Multiple dogs may be allowed.

Oxford

Holly Springs National Forest
1000 Front Street
Oxford, MS
662-236-6550
This forest provides a variety of camping areas, trails, recreation, and diverse ecosystems that support a large variety of plants, fish, mammals, and bird species. Dogs are allowed at no additional fee. Dogs may not be left unattended, and they must be leashed and cleaned up after in the camp areas. Dogs are not allowed on the beach, however, they are allowed on the trails. The camping and tent areas also allow dogs. There is a dog walk area at the campground. Multiple dogs may be allowed.

Philadelphia

Frog Level RV Park
1532 H 16W
Philadelphia, MS
601-650-0044
Dogs of all sizes are allowed. There are no additional pet fees. Dogs must be leashed and cleaned up after, and they can be walk just outside of the park. There are some breed restrictions. Multiple dogs may be allowed.

Robinsonville

Grand Casino RV Resort
13615 Old H 61N
Robinsonville, MS
800-946-4946
Dogs of all sizes are allowed in selected areas. There are no additional pet fees. Dogs may not be left unattended outside, and they must be leashed and cleaned up after. This is an RV only park. There is a dog walk area at the

campground. Multiple dogs may be allowed.

Sam's Town RV Park and Casino
1477 Casino Strip Resort Blvd
Robinsonville, MS
800-946-0711
Dogs up to 25 pounds are allowed. There are no additional pet fees. Dogs may not be left unattended outside, and they must be inside at night. Dogs must be leashed and cleaned up after. This is an RV only park. There is a dog walk area at the campground. Multiple dogs may be allowed.

Rolling Fork

Delta National Forest
20380 H 61
Rolling Fork, MS
662-873-6256
This 60,000 acre forest is the only bottomland hardwood ecosystem in the National Forest System. Delta National Forest supports various important natural habitats and offers a variety of trails and recreation. Dogs of all sizes are allowed at no additional fee. Dogs may not be left unattended, and they must be leashed and cleaned up after. Dogs are allowed on the trails. The camping and tent areas also allow dogs. There is a dog walk area at the campground. There are no electric or water hookups at the campground. Multiple dogs may be allowed.

Sardis

John W Kyle State Park
4235 State Park Road
Sardis, MS
662-487-1345
This scenic park sits along the picturesque Sardis Reservoir, and offers a wide variety of land and water activities and recreation. Dogs of all sizes are allowed at no additional fee. Dogs may not be left unattended except for short periods, and they must be quiet, well behaved, leashed, and cleaned up after. Dogs are allowed on the trails. The camping and tent areas also allow dogs. There is a dog walk area at the campground. Multiple dogs may be allowed.

John W Kyle State Park
4235 State Park Road
Sardis, MS
662-487-1345
This park, located on the picturesque

Sardis Reservoir, offers a variety of land and water activities, recreation, and trails. Dogs of all sizes are allowed at no additional fee. Dogs may not be left unattended unless they will be quiet, well behaved, and only for short periods. Dogs must be leashed and cleaned up after, and they are allowed on the trails. The camping and tent areas also allow dogs. There is a dog walk area at the campground. Multiple dogs may be allowed.

Toomsuba

Meridian East/Toomsuba KOA
3953 KOA Campground Road
Toomsuba, MS
601-632-1684
Dogs up to 50 pounds are allowed. There are no additional pet fees. Dogs must be quiet, be on no more than a 6 foot leash, and be cleaned up after. There are some breed restrictions. The camping and tent areas also allow dogs. There is a dog walk area at the campground. 2 dogs may be allowed.

Vicksburg

Rivertown Campground
5900 H 61S
Vicksburg, MS
601-630-9995
Dogs of all sizes are allowed. There are no additional pet fees. Dogs may not be left unattended, and they must be quiet, well behaved, leashed, and cleaned up after. There is a dog walk area at the campground. Multiple dogs may be allowed.

Vicksburg Battlefield
4407 N Frontage Road
Vicksburg, MS
601-636-2025
Dogs of all sizes are allowed. There are no additional pet fees. Dogs must be leashed and cleaned up after. The camping and tent areas also allow dogs. There is a dog walk area at the campground. Multiple dogs may be allowed.

Wesson

Lake Lincoln State Park
2573 Sunset Road
Wesson, MS
601-643-9044
This serene park, nestled among

towering hardwood trees along the shores of Lake Lincoln, offers a nature trail and a variety of land and water activities and recreation. Dogs of all sizes are allowed at no additional fee. Dogs may not be left unattended, and they must be leashed and cleaned up after. Dogs are not allowed on the beach or in buildings. The camping and tent areas also allow dogs. There is a dog walk area at the campground. Multiple dogs may be allowed.

Lake Lincoln State Park
2573 Sunset Road
Wesson, MS
601-643-9044
This scenic park is shaded by towering hardwood trees. The park offers easy access to several nearby attractions and a variety of land and water recreation and trails. Dogs of all sizes are allowed at no additional fee. Dogs may not be left unattended, and they must be leashed and cleaned up after. Dogs are not allowed on beaches or in buildings. Dogs are allowed on the trails. The camping and tent areas also allow dogs. There is a dog walk area at the campground. Multiple dogs may be allowed.

Missouri Listings

Arrow Rock

Arrow Rock State Historical Park
P.O. Box 1
Arrow Rock, MO
660-837-3330
Steeped in American history, this park offers "living history" reenactments, guided walking tours and land and water recreation. Dogs of all sizes are allowed at no additional fee. Dogs may not be left unattended, and they must be on no more than a 10 foot leash, and be cleaned up after. Dogs are not allowed in buildings, but they are allowed on the trail. The camping and tent areas also allow dogs. There is a dog walk area at the campground. There are no water hookups at the campground. Multiple dogs may be allowed.

Branson

Branson KOA
1025 Headwaters Road
Branson, MO
417-334-7450
Dogs of all sizes are allowed. There are no additional pet fees. Dogs may not be left unattended outside, and they must be quiet, leashed, and cleaned up after. There are some breed restrictions. This RV park is closed during the off-season. The camping and tent areas also allow dogs. There is a dog walk area at the campground. Dogs are allowed in the camping cabins. Multiple dogs may be allowed.

Branson Shenanigan RV Park
3675 Keeter Street
Branson, MO
417-334-1920
Dogs of all sizes are allowed. There are no additional pet fees. Dogs may not be left outside unattended. Dogs must be quiet, well behaved, leashed, and cleaned up after. This RV park is closed during the off-season. The camping and tent areas also allow dogs. There is a dog walk area at the campground. Multiple dogs may be allowed.

Branson Stagecoach RV Park
5751 H 165
Branson, MO
417-335-8185
Dogs of all sizes are allowed, and there are no additional pet fees for tent or RV sites. There is a $25 refundable deposit for the cabins, and only 2 dogs up to 20 pounds are allowed. Dogs must be leashed and cleaned up after. There are some breed restrictions. The camping and tent areas also allow dogs. There is a dog walk area at the campground. Dogs are allowed in the camping cabins.

Cooper Creek Campground
471 Cooper Creek Road
Branson, MO
417-334-5250
Dogs of all sizes are allowed, and there are no additional pet fees for tent or RV sites. There is a $7 per night per pet additional fee for the cabins. Dogs must be leashed and cleaned up after. The camping and tent areas also allow dogs. There is a dog walk area at the campground. Dogs are allowed in the camping cabins. Multiple dogs may be allowed.

Cassville

Roaring River State Park
Rt 4 Box 4100
Cassville, MO
417-847-2539
This park's geology adds breathtaking beauty, diverse plant life, and unusual rock formations to a wide array of land and water activities and recreation. Dogs of all sizes are allowed at no additional fee. Dogs may not be left unattended, and they must be on no more than a 10 foot leash, and be cleaned up after. Dogs are not allowed in buildings, but they are allowed on the trails. The camping and tent areas also allow dogs. There is a dog walk area at the campground. There are no water hookups at the campground. Multiple dogs may be allowed.

Columbia

Cottonwoods RV Park
5170 Oakland Gravel Road
Columbia, MO
573-474-2747
Dogs of all sizes are allowed. There are no additional pet fees. Dogs may not be left unattended, and must be leashed and cleaned up after. There is a dog walk area at the campground. There are special amenities given to dogs at this campground. Multiple dogs may be allowed.

Finger Lakes State Park
1505 E Peabody Road
Columbia, MO
573-443-5315
This 1,131-acre park was once a coal mining operation, and now visitors enjoy wildflowers, rolling hills and running streams, in addition to a variety of recreational pursuits. Dogs of all sizes are allowed at no additional fee. Dogs may not be left unattended, and they must be on no more than a 10 foot leash, and be cleaned up after. Dogs are not allowed on the beach or in buildings. It is suggested that dogs be walked on the trails in the Rocky Fork Conservation area next to the park because Finger Lakes is an off-road ATV park for which the trails are used. The camping and tent areas also allow dogs. There is a dog walk area at the campground. There are no water hookups at the campground. Multiple dogs may be allowed.

Eagleville

Eagle Ridge RV Park
22708 W 182nd Street
Eagleville, MO
660-867-5518
Dogs of all sizes are allowed. There are no additional pet fees. Dogs must be leashed and cleaned up after. The camping and tent areas also allow dogs. There is a dog walk area at the campground. Multiple dogs may be allowed.

Granite City

Northeast/I 270/Granite City KOA
3157 Chain of Rocks Road
Granite City, MO
618-931-5160
Dogs of all sizes are allowed, and there are no additional pet fees for tent or RV sites. There is a $2.50 per night per pet additional fee for the cabins. Dogs must be quiet, well behaved, leashed, and cleaned up after. There are some breed restrictions. This RV park is closed during the off-season. The camping and tent areas also allow dogs. There is a dog walk area at the campground. Dogs are allowed in the camping cabins. Multiple dogs may be allowed.

Hannibal

Mark Twain Cave and Campgrounds
300 Cave Hollow Road
Hannibal, MO
573-221-1656
Dogs of all sizes are allowed. There are no additional pet fees. Dogs must be leashed and cleaned up after. There are some breed restrictions. The camping and tent areas also allow dogs. There is a dog walk area at the campground. Multiple dogs may be allowed.

Higginsville

Interstate RV Park
On Old H 40
Higginsville, MO
800-690-2267
Dogs of all sizes are allowed. There are no additional pet fees. Dogs must be leashed and cleaned up after. The camping and tent areas also allow dogs. There is a dog walk area at the campground. Multiple dogs may be allowed.

Jackson

Trail of Tear State Park
429 Moccasin Springs
Jackson, MO
573-334-1711
This park, of almost 3,500 acres along the Mississippi River, is a memorial to the forced relocation of several Cherokee tribes and has interpretive exhibits about their journeys. The park now provides a wide variety of land and water activities and recreation. Dogs of all sizes are allowed at no additional fee. Dogs must be leashed and cleaned up after, and they are not allowed in buildings. Dog are allowed on the trails. The camping and tent areas also allow dogs. There is a dog walk area at the campground. Multiple dogs may be allowed.

Joplin

Joplin KOA
4359 H 43
Joplin, MO
417-623-2246
Dogs of all sizes are allowed. There are no additional pet fees. Dogs must be leashed and cleaned up after. The camping and tent areas also allow dogs. There is a dog walk area at the campground. Dogs are allowed in the camping cabins. Multiple dogs may be allowed.

Kaiser

Lake of the Ozarks
403 H 134
Kaiser, MO
573-348-2694
This park of more than 1,700 acres, stretches along the shores of one of Michigan's largest lakes, and offers guided tours of the Ozark Caverns, 12 scenic multi-use trails, and a variety of land and water recreation. Dogs of all sizes are allowed at no additional fee. Dogs may not be left unattended, and they must be on no more than a 10 foot leash, and be cleaned up after. Dogs are not allowed on the beach, in the water, or in buildings. For cabin visitors, dogs may be tied up outside, and at night they must be crated (inside or out). The camping and tent areas also allow dogs. There is a dog walk area at the campground. There are no water hookups at the campground. Multiple dogs may be allowed.

Kansas City

Trailside RV Park
1000 R.D. Mize Road
Grain Valley, MO
816-229-2267
Dogs of all sizes are allowed. There are no additional pet fees. Dogs must be well behaved, leashed, and cleaned up after. The camping and tent areas also allow dogs. There is a dog walk area at the campground. Multiple dogs may be allowed.

Basswood Country RV Resort
15880 Inter Urban Road
Platte City, MO
816-858-5556
Dogs of all sizes are allowed. There are no additional pet fees. Dogs may not be left unattended, must be quiet, leashed, and cleaned up after. There is a dog walk area at the campground. Multiple dogs may be allowed.

Kimberling City

Water's Edge
72 Marina Way
Kimberling City, MO
417-739-5377
Dogs of all sizes are allowed, and there are no additional pet fees for tent or RV sites. There is a $50 refundable deposit for the cabins, and only 1 small dog is allowed. Dogs may not be left unattended, must be leashed, and cleaned up after. Dogs may swim at the lake, but not in the public swim area. The camping and tent areas also allow dogs. There is a dog walk area at the campground. Dogs are allowed in the camping cabins.

Kirksville

Thousand Hills State Park
2431 H 157
Kirksville, MO
660-665-6995
This 3,215-acre park with a 573 acre lake features an interpretive shelter that displays the park's petroglyphs and offers an array of activities and recreation. Dogs of all sizes are allowed at no additional fee. Dogs must be leashed and cleaned up after. Dogs must be quiet, well behaved, and may not be left unattended outside or inside for long periods. Dogs are allowed on the trails. The camping and tent areas also allow dogs. There is a

dog walk area at the campground. There are no water hookups at the campground. Multiple dogs may be allowed.

Lake Ozark

Osage Beach RV Park
3949 Campground Drive
Lake Ozark, MO
573-348-3445
Dogs of all sizes are allowed. There are no additional pet fees. Dogs may not be left unattended, must be leashed, and cleaned up after. This RV park is closed during the off-season. The camping and tent areas also allow dogs. There is a dog walk area at the campground. 2 dogs may be allowed.

Riverview RV Park
398 Woodriver Road
Lake Ozark, MO
573-365-1122
Dogs of all sizes are allowed. There are no additional pet fees. Dogs must be quiet, well behaved, leashed, and cleaned up after. There are some breed restrictions. This RV park is closed during the off-season. The camping and tent areas also allow dogs. There is a dog walk area at the campground. Multiple dogs may be allowed.

Lebanon

Bennett Spring State Park
26250 H 64A
Lebanon, MO
417-532-4338
Home of the 4th largest natural spring in the state, this scenic park has a history of mills of one form or another, and now it provides naturalist programs and ample recreational opportunities. Dogs of all sizes are allowed at no additional fee. Dogs may not be left unattended, and they must be quiet, well behaved, be on no more than a 10 foot leash, and cleaned up after. Dogs are not allowed in buildings, but they are allowed on the trails. There are some breed restrictions. The camping and tent areas also allow dogs. There is a dog walk area at the campground. Multiple dogs may be allowed.

Macon

Long Branch Lake State Park
28615 Visitors Center Road

Macon, MO
660-773-5229
A great destination for water enthusiasts as well as nature lovers, this park of over 1,800 acres offers a variety of recreational pursuits. Dogs of all sizes are allowed at no additional fee. Dogs may not be left unattended outside, and they must be on no more than a 10 foot leash, and be cleaned up after. Dogs are not allowed on the beach, but they are allowed on the trails. The camping and tent areas also allow dogs. There is a dog walk area at the campground. There are no water hookups at the campground. 2 dogs may be allowed.

Montgomery City

Lazy Day Campground
214 H J
Montgomery City, MO
573-564-2949
Dogs of all sizes are allowed. There are no additional pet fees. Dogs must be leashed and cleaned up after. The camping and tent areas also allow dogs. There is a dog walk area at the campground.

Oak Grove

Kansas City East/Oak Grove KOA
303 NE 3rd
Oak Grove, MO
816-690-6660
Dogs of all sizes are allowed. There are no additional pet fees. Dogs must be quiet, leashed, and cleaned up after. There are some breed restrictions. The camping and tent areas also allow dogs. There is a dog walk area at the campground. Multiple dogs may be allowed.

Ozark

Ozark RV Park
320 N 20th Street
Ozark, MO
417-581-3203
Dogs of all sizes are allowed. There are no additional pet fees. Dogs must be leashed and cleaned up after. There is a dog walk area at the campground. Multiple dogs may be allowed.

Pacific

Jellystone Park
5300 Foxcreek Road

Pacific, MO
636-938-5925
Dogs of all sizes are allowed. There are no additional pet fees. Dogs may not be left unattended, must be leashed, and cleaned up after. This RV park is closed during the off-season. The camping and tent areas also allow dogs. There is a dog walk area at the campground. Multiple dogs may be allowed.

Perryville

Perryville/Cape Girardeau KOA
89 KOA Lane
Perryville, MO
573-547-8303
Dogs of all sizes are allowed, and there are no additional pet fees for tent or RV sites. There is a $5 one time fee per pet for the cabins. Dogs may not be left unattended outside, and they must leashed and cleaned up after. This RV park is closed during the off-season. The camping and tent areas also allow dogs. There is a dog walk area at the campground. Dogs are allowed in the camping cabins. 2 dogs may be allowed.

Phillipsburg

Lebanon KOA
18376 Campground Road
Phillipsburg, MO
417-532-3422
Dogs of all sizes are allowed. There are no additional pet fees. Dogs must be leashed and cleaned up after. There are some breed restrictions. This RV park is closed during the off-season. The camping and tent areas also allow dogs. There is a dog walk area at the campground. Multiple dogs may be allowed.

Pittsburg

Pomme de Terre State Park
HC 77, Box 890
Pittsburg, MO
417-852-4291
This park sits on both sides of Pomme de Terre Lake, and offer a full service marina, large beaches, trails, and various recreation. Dogs of all sizes are allowed at no additional fee. Dogs may not be left unattended, and they must be on no more than a 10 foot leash, and be cleaned up after. Dogs may not be in the buildings or on the beaches,

but the are allowed on the trails. The camping and tent areas also allow dogs. There is a dog walk area at the campground. There are no water hookups at the campground. Multiple dogs may be allowed.

Portageville

Hayti/Portageville KOA
2824 MO State E Outer Road
Portageville, MO
573-359-1580
Dogs of all sizes are allowed. There are no additional pet fees. Dogs must be leashed and cleaned up after. There are some breed restrictions. This RV park is closed during the off-season. The camping and tent areas also allow dogs. There is a dog walk area at the campground. Multiple dogs may be allowed.

Red Lodge

Red Lodge KOA
7464 H 212
Red Lodge, MO
406-446-2364
Dogs of all sizes and numbers are allowed, and they must be quiet and well behaved. There are no additional pet fees for tent or RV sites. Only one dog is allowed in the cabins with no additional fee. Dogs may not be tied up outside alone, and can only be left in your RV if it is cool. Dogs may not be left unattended, must be leashed, and cleaned up after. This RV park is closed during the off-season. The camping and tent areas also allow dogs. There is a dog walk area at the campground. Dogs are allowed in the camping cabins.

Revere

Battle of Athens State Historical Park
RR1, Box 26, H CC
Revere, MO
660-877-3871
This park offers exhibits and tours interpreting the battle of the northernmost Civil War battle which took place here. In addition, the park offers a variety of trails and recreational pursuits. Dogs of all sizes are allowed at no additional fee. Dogs may not be left unattended, and they must be on no more than a 10 foot leash, and be cleaned up after. Dogs are not

allowed in the buildings, but they are allowed on the trails. The camping and tent areas also allow dogs. There is a dog walk area at the campground. There are no water hookups at the campground. Multiple dogs may be allowed.

Rock Port

Rock Port KOA
1409 H 136W
Rock Port, MO
660-744-5485
Dogs of all sizes are allowed. There are no additional pet fees. Dogs in the cabins must be housebroken. Dogs must be well behaved, leashed, and cleaned up after. This RV park is closed during the off-season. The camping and tent areas also allow dogs. There is a dog walk area at the campground. Dogs are allowed in the camping cabins. Multiple dogs may be allowed.

Rolla

Mark Twain National Forest
401 Fairgrounds Road
Rolla, MO
573-364-4621
This scenic park supports a variety of habitats, trails, and year round land and water activities. Dogs of all sizes are allowed at no cost. Dogs must be leashed at all times in the camp area, and cleaned up after. Dogs may only be left unattended for short periods, and only if the dog will be quiet and well behaved. Dogs are allowed on the trails. This campground is closed during the off-season. The camping and tent areas also allow dogs. There is a dog walk area at the campground. There are no water hookups at the campground. Multiple dogs may be allowed.

Rushville

Lewis and Clark State Park
801 Lake Crest Blvd
Rushville, MO
816-579-5564
This 200 acre park along the shores of Lewis and Clark Lake, offer an interesting history as well as a variety of land and water recreation. Dogs of all sizes are allowed at no additional fee. Dogs may not be left unattended or in vehicles, and they must be on no more than a 10 foot leash, and be cleaned up after. Dogs are not

allowed in swim areas or on public beaches. Dogs may not be left outside at night, and they must have ID tags. Dogs are allowed on the trails unless otherwise marked. The camping and tent areas also allow dogs. There is a dog walk area at the campground. There are no water hookups at the campground. Multiple dogs may be allowed.

Shelby

Lewis and Clark RV Park
Box 369, Front Street
Shelby, MO
406-434-2710
Dogs of all sizes are allowed. There are no additional pet fees. Dogs must be quiet, leashed, and cleaned up after. Dogs may not be left unattended. The camping and tent areas also allow dogs. There is a dog walk area at the campground. 2 dogs may be allowed.

Springfield

Springfield KOA
5775 W Farm Road 140
Springfield, MO
417-831-3645
Dogs of all sizes are allowed. There are no additional pet fees. Dogs may not be tied up or left unattended outside, and they must be leashed and cleaned up after. The camping and tent areas also allow dogs. There is a dog walk area at the campground. Dogs are allowed in the camping cabins. Multiple dogs may be allowed.

Traveler's Park Campground
425 S Trailview Road
Springfield, MO
417-866-4226
Dogs of all sizes are allowed. There are no additional pet fees. Dogs must be quiet, leashed, and cleaned up after. This RV park is closed during the off-season. There is a dog walk area at the campground. 2 dogs may be allowed.

St Louis

St Louis South KOA
8000 Metropolitan Blvd
Barnhart, MO
636-479-4449
Dogs of all sizes are allowed. There

are no additional pet fees. Dogs may not be left unattended outside, and they must be leashed and cleaned up after. The camping and tent areas also allow dogs. There is a dog walk area at the campground. Dogs are allowed in the camping cabins. Multiple dogs may be allowed.

St Louis West KOA
18475 Old H 66
Eureka, MO
636-257-3018
Dogs of all sizes are allowed. There are no additional pet fees. Dogs may not be left unattended outside, and they must be leashed and cleaned up after. Dogs must be crated at all times when they are in a cabin. This RV park is closed during the off-season. The camping and tent areas also allow dogs. There is a dog walk area at the campground. Dogs are allowed in the camping cabins. Multiple dogs may be allowed.

Sundermeier RV Park
111 Transit Street
St Charles, MO
636-940-0111
Dogs of all sizes are allowed. There are no additional pet fees. Dogs must be leashed and cleaned up after. There are some breed restrictions. There is a dog walk area at the campground. Multiple dogs may be allowed.

Beacon RV Park
822 S Belt H
St Joseph, MO
816-279-5417
Dogs of all sizes are allowed. There are no additional pet fees. Dogs may not be left unattended at any time, must be well behaved, leashed, and cleaned up after. There is a dog walk area at the campground. Multiple dogs may be allowed.

Pin Oak Creek RV Park
1302 H 8AT
Villa Ridge, MO
636-451-5656
Dogs of all sizes are allowed. There is a pet policy to sign at check in, and there are no additional pet fees. Dogs may not be left unattended or tied up outside alone. Dogs must be leashed and cleaned up after. The camping and tent areas also allow dogs. There is a dog walk area at the campground. Multiple dogs may be allowed.

Stanton

Stanton/Meramec KOA
74 H 'W'
Stanton, MO
573-927-5215
Dogs of all sizes are allowed. There are no additional pet fees. Dogs may not be left unattended, and they must be leashed and cleaned up after. This RV park is closed during the off-season. The camping and tent areas also allow dogs. There is a dog walk area at the campground. Dogs are allowed in the camping cabins. Multiple dogs may be allowed.

Stoutsville

Mark Twain State Park
20057 State Park Office Road
Stoutsville, MO
573-565-3440
This historical park, located on Mark Twain Lake, offers a variety of habitats, trails, and land and water recreation. Dogs of all sizes are allowed at no additional fee. Dogs may not be left unattended, and they must be on no more than a 6 foot leash, and be cleaned up after. Dogs are not allowed on the beach or in buildings. Dogs are allowed on the trails. The camping and tent areas also allow dogs. There is a dog walk area at the campground. There are no water hookups at the campground. Multiple dogs may be allowed.

Three Forks

Three Forks KOA
15 KOA Road
Three Forks, MO
406-285-3611
Dogs of all sizes are allowed. There are no additional pet fees. Dogs may not be left outside unattended, and they must be quiet and well behaved. Dogs must be leashed and cleaned up after. This RV park is closed during the off-season. The camping and tent areas also allow dogs. There is a dog walk area at the campground. Multiple dogs may be allowed.

Williamsville

Lake Wappapello State Park
HC 2, Box 102
Williamsville, MO
573-297-3232
This park of over 1,800 acres, nestled by a lake and surrounded by Ozark forests, provides a variety of

habitats, trails, and land and water recreation. Dogs of all sizes are allowed at no additional fee. Dogs may not be left unattended, and they must be leashed and cleaned up after in camp areas. Dogs are not allowed on the beach, in buildings, or tied to park trees. Dogs are allowed on the trails. For cabin visitors, dogs may be tied up outside, and at night they must be crated. Cabins are seasonal. The camping and tent areas also allow dogs. There is a dog walk area at the campground. There are no water hookups at the campground. Multiple dogs may be allowed.

Lake Wappapello State Park
Rt 2, Box 102; the end of H 172
Williamsville, MO
573-297-3232
Stroll the miles of trails, relax, or enjoy the various land and water recreation offered at this scenic park. Dogs of all sizes are allowed at no additional fee. Dogs may not be left unattended or in vehicles, and they must be on no more than a 10 foot leash, and be cleaned up after. Dogs are not allowed in swim areas or on public beaches. Dogs may not be left outside at night, and they must have ID tags. Dogs are allowed on the trails unless otherwise marked. The camping and tent areas also allow dogs. There is a dog walk area at the campground. There are no water hookups at the campground. Multiple dogs may be allowed.

Montana Listings

Alberton

Rivers Edge Resort
22 S Frontage Road E
Alberton, MT
406-722-3338
Dogs of all sizes are allowed. There are no additional pet fees. Dogs may not be left unattended outside, and they must be leashed and cleaned up after. There is also a motel on site that will allow up to 2 dogs per room with a $25 refundable deposit. The camping and tent areas also allow dogs. There is a dog walk area at the campground. Multiple dogs may be allowed.

Alder

Alder/Virginia City KOA
2280 H 287
Alder, MT
406-842-5677
Dogs of all sizes are allowed. There are no additional pet fees. Dogs must be quiet, leashed, and cleaned up after. There are some breed restrictions. The camping and tent areas also allow dogs. There is a dog walk area at the campground. Multiple dogs may be allowed.

Belt

Fort Ponderosa Campground
568 Arminton Road
Belt, MT
406-277-3232
Dogs of all sizes are allowed. There are no additional pet fees. Dogs must be leashed and cleaned up after. This RV park is closed during the off-season. The camping and tent areas also allow dogs. There is a dog walk area at the campground. Multiple dogs may be allowed.

Big Arm

Big Arm State Park
425 Big Arm Road
Big Arm, MT
406-849-5255
The phone numbers at the parks are subject to change each year, but 406-752-5501 is the year round contact number. All the Montana state parks are along a shoreline and this park of over 500 acres offers a variety of land and water recreation. Dogs of all sizes are allowed. There are no additional pet fees. Dogs may not be left unattended, they must be on no more than a 10 foot leash, and be cleaned up after. Dogs are allowed on the trails. This campground is closed during the off-season. The camping and tent areas also allow dogs. There is a dog walk area at the campground. There are no electric or water hookups at the campground. Multiple dogs may be allowed.

Big Fork

Wayfarers State Park
8600 H 35
Big Fork, MT
406-837-4196
Some parks discontinue phone

service and get new numbers the following season, but 406-752-5501 is a non-changing number for park information. This scenic park located on Flathead Lake offers a variety of land and water recreation. Dogs of all sizes are allowed at no additional fee. Dogs may not be left unattended, and they must be quiet, well behaved, be on no more than a 10 foot leash, and be cleaned up after. Dogs are not allowed in public swim areas, but they are allowed on the trails. This campground is closed during the off-season. The camping and tent areas also allow dogs. There is a dog walk area at the campground. There are no water hookups at the campground. Multiple dogs may be allowed.

Yellow Bay State Park
17215 Eastshore
Big Fork, MT
406-752-5501
This scenic park, sitting in the heart of sweet cherry orchards with a wide sandy beach area, creates a rather beautiful setting for visitors and a variety of land and water recreation. Dogs of all sizes are allowed at no additional fee. Dogs may not be left unattended, and they must be quiet, well behaved, be on no more than a 10 foot leash, and be cleaned up after. Dogs are not allowed in public swim areas, but they are allowed on the trails. This campground is closed during the off-season. The camping and tent areas also allow dogs. There is a dog walk area at the campground. There are no electric or water hookups at the campground. Multiple dogs may be allowed.

Billings

Billings KOA
547 Garden Avenue
Billings, MT
406-252-3104
Dogs of all sizes are allowed. There are no additional pet fees. Dogs must be well behaved, leashed, and cleaned up after. This RV park is closed during the off-season. The camping and tent areas also allow dogs. There is a dog walk area at the campground. Multiple dogs may be allowed.

Custer National Forest
1310 Main Street
Billings, MT
406-657-6200
This forest of nearly 1.3 million acres, of which almost half is

designated wilderness, provides spectacular scenery, a rich cultural history, and diverse ecosystems that support a large variety of plants, fish, mammals, bird species, and year round recreation. Dogs of all sizes are allowed at no additional fee. Dogs may not be left unattended, and they must be leashed and cleaned up after. Dogs are not allowed in public swim areas, but they are allowed on the trails. This campground is closed during the off-season. The camping and tent areas also allow dogs. There is a dog walk area at the campground. There are no electric or water hookups at the campground. Multiple dogs may be allowed.

Trailer Village RV Park
325 S Billings Blvd
Billings, MT
406-248-8685
Dogs of all sizes are allowed. There are no additional pet fees. Dogs must be leashed and cleaned up after. There is a dog walk area at the campground. 2 dogs may be allowed.

Yellowstone River Campground
309 Garden Avenue
Billings, MT
406-259-0878
Dogs of all sizes are allowed. There are no additional pet fees. Dogs must be leashed and cleaned up after. This RV park is closed during the off-season. The camping and tent areas also allow dogs. There is a dog walk area at the campground. Multiple dogs may be allowed.

Bozeman

Bozeman KOA
81123 Gallatin Road
Bozeman, MT
406-587-3030
Dogs of all sizes are allowed. There are no additional pet fees. Dogs must be leashed and cleaned up after. The camping and tent areas also allow dogs. There is a dog walk area at the campground. Dogs are allowed in the camping cabins. Multiple dogs may be allowed.

Sunrise Campground
31842 Frontage Road
Bozeman, MT
877-437-2095
Dogs of all sizes are allowed. There

are no additional pet fees. Dogs may not be tied up outside alone, and they may not be left unattended unless they will be quiet, well behaved, and comfortable. Dogs must be leashed, cleaned up after, and brought in at night. This RV park is closed during the off-season. The camping and tent areas also allow dogs. There is a dog walk area at the campground. Multiple dogs may be allowed.

Butte

Butte KOA
1601 Kaw Avenue
Butte, MT
406-782-8080
Dogs of all sizes are allowed. There are no additional pet fees. Dogs must be quiet, leashed, and cleaned up after. This RV park is closed during the off-season. The camping and tent areas also allow dogs. There is a dog walk area at the campground. Dogs are allowed in the camping cabins. Multiple dogs may be allowed.

Choteau

Choteau KOA
85 H 221
Choteau, MT
406-466-2615
Dogs of all sizes are allowed. There are no additional pet fees. Dogs must be leashed and cleaned up after. This RV park is closed during the off-season. The camping and tent areas also allow dogs. There is a dog walk area at the campground. Dogs are allowed in the camping cabins. Multiple dogs may be allowed.

Deer Lodge

Deer Lodge KOA
330 Park Street
Deer Lodge, MT
406-846-1629
Dogs of all sizes are allowed. There are no additional pet fees. Dogs may not be left unattended at any time, must be leashed, and cleaned up after. This RV park is closed during the off-season. The camping and tent areas also allow dogs. There is a dog walk area at the campground. Dogs are allowed in the camping cabins. Multiple dogs may be allowed.

Dillon

Bannack State Park
4200 Bannack Road
Dillon, MT
406-834-3413
Some parks discontinue phone service and get new numbers the following season, but 406-752-5501 is a non-changing number for park information. This park, located on Grasshopper Creek, is a registered historic landmark, and offers a variety of land and water recreation. Dogs of all sizes are allowed at no additional fee. Dogs may not be left unattended, and they must be quiet, well behaved, be on no more than a 10 foot leash, and be cleaned up after. Dogs are not allowed in public swim areas, but they are allowed on the trails. This campground is closed during the off-season. The camping and tent areas also allow dogs. There is a dog walk area at the campground. There are no electric or water hookups at the campground. Multiple dogs may be allowed.

Deerlodge (Beaverhead) National Forest
420 Barrett Street
Dillon, MT
406-683-3900
This is a year round diverse recreational and working forest covering over 3 million acres in eight counties. Dogs are allowed at no additional fee. Dogs may not be left unattended, and they must be leashed and cleaned up after. Dogs are allowed on the trails, and they may be off lead in the forest as long as there is voice control. This campground is closed during the off-season. The camping and tent areas also allow dogs. There is a dog walk area at the campground. Dogs are allowed in the camping cabins. There are no electric or water hookups at the campground. Multiple dogs may be allowed.

Dillon KOA
735 Park Street
Dillon, MT
406-683-2749
Dogs of all sizes are allowed. There are no additional pet fees. Dogs must be leashed and cleaned up after. Dogs are not allowed on the beds in the cabins. There are some breed restrictions. The camping and tent areas also allow dogs. There is a dog walk area at the campground. Dogs are allowed in the camping cabins. Multiple dogs may be allowed.

East Big Timber

Big Timber KOA
693 H 10
East Big Timber, MT
406-932-6569
Dogs of all sizes are allowed, and there are no additional pet fees for tent or RV sites. Up to three medium to small dogs or up to 2 large dogs are allowed at tent or RV sites. Only one dog is allowed in the cabins and there is an additional $5 fee per night. Dogs may not be left unattended, must be quiet, leashed, and cleaned up after. There are some breed restrictions. This RV park is closed during the off-season. The camping and tent areas also allow dogs. There is a dog walk area at the campground. Dogs are allowed in the camping cabins.

Ennis

Ennis Village RV
5034 H 287
Ennis, MT
866-682-5272
Dogs of all sizes are allowed. There are no additional pet fees. Dogs must be leashed and cleaned up after. This RV park is closed during the off-season. The camping and tent areas also allow dogs. There is a dog walk area at the campground. Multiple dogs may be allowed.

Fairmont

Fairmont RV Park
1700 Fairmont Road
Fairmont, MT
406-797-3505
Dogs of all sizes are allowed. There are no additional pet fees. Dogs may not be left unattended outside, and they must be leashed and cleaned up after. Dogs are also allowed at the teepee sites at no additional fee. This RV park is closed during the off-season. The camping and tent areas also allow dogs. There is a dog walk area at the campground. Multiple dogs may be allowed.

Finley Point

Finley Point State Park
3000 S Finley Point
Finley Point, MT
406-887-2715
Some parks discontinue phone service and get new numbers each season, but 406-752-5501 is a non-changing number for park information. This small, 16 site park, sits in a secluded pine forest on Flathead Lake, and offers a variety of water and land recreation. Dogs of all sizes are allowed at no additional fee. Dogs may not be left unattended, and they must be quiet, well behaved, be on no more than a 10 foot leash, and be cleaned up after. Dogs are not allowed in public swim areas, but they are allowed on the trails. This campground is closed during the off-season. The camping and tent areas also allow dogs. There is a dog walk area at the campground. There are no electric or water hookups at the campground. Multiple dogs may be allowed.

Fort Smith

Bighorn Canyon National Rec Area
5 Avenue B from H 313
Fort Smith, MT
406-666-2412
There are over 189,000 acres of wilderness in this forest, with 1,500 miles of trails, and there are several ways to enter. An additional ranger station is at 2013 Eastside 2nd Street, Sheridan, WY 82801, 307-674-2600. Dogs are allowed at no additional fee, and they are allowed on all the trails. Dogs may not be left unattended, and they must be leashed and cleaned up after. The camping and tent areas also allow dogs. There is a dog walk area at the campground. There are no electric or water hookups at the campground. Multiple dogs may be allowed.

Gardiner

Rocky Mountain Campground
14 Gardine
Gardiner, MT
877-534-6931
Dogs of all sizes are allowed. There are no additional pet fees. Dogs must be leashed and cleaned up after. This RV park is closed during the off-season. The camping and tent areas also allow dogs. There is a dog walk area at the campground.

Garryowen

7th Ranch RV Camp

7th Ranch & Reno Creek Road
Garryowen, MT
800-371-7963
Dogs of all sizes are allowed. There are no additional pet fees. Dogs must be quiet, well behaved, leashed, and cleaned up after. This RV park is closed during the off-season. The camping and tent areas also allow dogs. There is a dog walk area at the campground. Multiple dogs may be allowed.

Glacier National Park

Flathead National Forest
1935 3rd Ave. E
Kalispell, MT
406-758-5200
This year round forest provides natural resources in addition to a wide variety of recreational pursuits. Dogs are allowed at no additional fee. Dogs may not be left unattended outside, and may be left inside only if it presents no danger to the animal. Dogs must be quiet, well behaved, leashed and cleaned up after. Dogs are not allowed on the public beach, the picnic areas, or on cross-country ski trails. Dogs may be off lead in the forest as long as they are under voice control. Dogs must be on lead in Jewel Basin, and they are allowed on the hiking trails. There is one dog friendly cabin available in Star Meadows. This campground is closed during the off-season. The camping and tent areas also allow dogs. There is a dog walk area at the campground. There are no electric or water hookups at the campground. Multiple dogs may be allowed.

Lake Mary Ronan State Park
490 N Meridian
Kalispell, MT
406-849-5082
Camping, fishing, swimming, and walking the trails are the popular pastimes at this park. Dogs are allowed at no additional fee. Dogs may not be left unattended, and they must be leashed and cleaned up after. Dogs are not allowed in buildings or in public swim areas, but they are allowed on the trails. This campground is closed during the off-season. The camping and tent areas also allow dogs. There is a dog walk area at the campground. There are no electric or water hookups at the campground. Multiple dogs may be allowed.

Whitefish/Kalispell N KOA

5121 H 93D
Whitefish, MT
406-862-4242
Dogs of all sizes are allowed. There are no additional pet fees. Dogs must leashed and cleaned up after. Dogs may be left unattended if they will be quiet. The camping and tent areas also allow dogs. There is a dog walk area at the campground. Dogs are allowed in the camping cabins. Multiple dogs may be allowed.

Glasgow

Cottonwood Inn
45 First Avenue NE
Glasgow, MT
800-321-8213
Dogs of all sizes are allowed. There are no additional pet fees. Dogs may not be left unattended, and must be well behaved, leashed, and cleaned up after. This RV park is closed during the off-season. There is a dog walk area at the campground. Multiple dogs may be allowed.

Great Falls

Ackley Lake State Park
4600 Giant Srings Road
Great Falls, MT
406-454-5840
This park of 160 acres offers a variety of land and water recreation. Dogs of all sizes are allowed. There are no additional pet fees. Dogs may not be left unattended, they must be on no more than a 10 foot leash, and be cleaned up after. Dogs are allowed on the trails. The camping and tent areas also allow dogs. There is a dog walk area at the campground. There are no electric or water hookups at the campground. Multiple dogs may be allowed.

Dick's RV Park
1403 11th Street SW
Great Falls, MT
406-452-0333
Dogs of all sizes are allowed. There are no additional pet fees. Dogs must be leashed and cleaned up after. The camping and tent areas also allow dogs. There is a dog walk area at the campground. Multiple dogs may be allowed.

Great Falls KOA
1500 51st Street S

Great Falls, MT
406-727-3191
Dogs of all sizes are allowed. There are no additional pet fees. Dogs may not be left unattended, must be leashed, and cleaned up after. The camping and tent areas also allow dogs. There is a dog walk area at the campground. Dogs are allowed in the camping cabins. Multiple dogs may be allowed.

Lewis and Clark National Forest
1101 15th Street N.
Great Falls, MT
406-791-7700
This forest covers almost 2 million acres, reaches over 9000 feet, has a designated Natural Research area of over 10,000 acres, the National Historic Trail Interpretive Center, and a variety of trails. Dogs are allowed at no additional fee. Dogs may not be left unattended, and they must be leashed and cleaned up after. Dogs are not allowed in public swim areas or buildings. Dogs are allowed on the trails. The camping and tent areas also allow dogs. There is a dog walk area at the campground. Multiple dogs may be allowed.

Hamilton

Bitterroot National Forest
1801 N 1st Street
Hamilton, MT
406-363-7100
This forest of 1.6 million acres has 4 ranger districts, more than 1,600 miles of multi-use trails, and very diverse ecosystems that support a large variety of plants, fish, mammals, bird species, as well as recreational pursuits. Dogs are allowed at no additional fee. Dogs may not be left unattended, and they must be well behaved, leashed and cleaned up after in the camp areas. Dogs may be off lead in the forest if they are under voice command and will not chase the wildlife. This campground is closed during the off-season. The camping and tent areas also allow dogs. There is a dog walk area at the campground. Dogs are allowed in the camping cabins. There are no water hookups at the campground. Multiple dogs may be allowed.

Hardin

Hardin KOA
RR 1
Hardin, MT

406-665-1635
Dogs of all sizes are allowed. There are no additional pet fees. Dogs must be leashed and cleaned up after. There are some breed restrictions. This RV park is closed during the off-season. The camping and tent areas also allow dogs. There is a dog walk area at the campground. Multiple dogs may be allowed.

Helena

Helena Campground
5820 N Montana Avenue
Helena, MT
406-458-4714
Dogs of all sizes are allowed. There are no additional pet fees. Dogs may not be left unattended outside, and they must be quiet, be on no more than a 6 foot leash, and be cleaned up after. This RV park is closed during the off-season. The camping and tent areas also allow dogs. There is a dog walk area at the campground. 2 dogs may be allowed.

Helena National Forest
2880 Skyway Drive
Helena, MT
406-449-5201
This recreational and working forest covers almost a million acres and straddles the Continental Divide creating very diverse geology and topography regions. Dogs are allowed at no additional fee. Dogs must be leashed when in the camp area and when on the trails if there are other visitors present. They may be off leash only if they are well behaved, will not chase, and are under voice control. The camping and tent areas also allow dogs. There is a dog walk area at the campground. There are no electric or water hookups at the campground. Multiple dogs may be allowed.

Hungry Horse

Timber Wolf Resort
9105 H 2E
Hungry Horse, MT
406-387-9653
Dogs of all sizes are allowed. There is a $3 per night per pet additional fee for the tent or RV sites. There is a $10 per night per pet additional fee for the cabins. Dogs may not be left unattended, and they must be leashed at all times, and cleaned up after. Dogs are allowed on the trails.

The camping and tent areas also allow dogs. There is a dog walk area at the campground. Dogs are allowed in the camping cabins. Multiple dogs may be allowed.

Joliet

Cooney State Park
Boyd County Road
Joliet, MT
406-445-2326
This park is one of the most popular parks in south central Montana, and it provides a variety of land and water recreation. Dogs of all sizes are allowed at no additional fee. Dogs may not be left unattended, and they must be leashed and cleaned up after. Dogs are not allowed at the Marshall Cove campground, on swim beaches, or in buildings. Dogs are allowed on the trails. This campground is closed during the off-season. The camping and tent areas also allow dogs. There is a dog walk area at the campground. There are no water hookups at the campground. Multiple dogs may be allowed.

Jordon

Hell Creek State Park
H 59/25 miles north of Jordon
Jordon, MT
406-234-0900
This park is located on Fort Peck Lake, and provides a variety of water and land recreation. Dogs are allowed at no additional fee. Dogs may not be left unattended, and they must be leashed and cleaned up after. This campground is closed during the off-season. The camping and tent areas also allow dogs. There is a dog walk area at the campground. There are no electric or water hookups at the campground. Multiple dogs may be allowed.

Kallispell

Flathead Lake State Park
490 N Meridian
Kallispell, MT
406-844-3066
All the Montana state parks are along a shoreline and this park of almost 130 acres, and considered the most private, offers a variety of land and water recreation. Dogs of all sizes are allowed at no additional fee. Dogs may not be left

unattended, they must be quiet, well behaved, on no more than a 10 foot leash, and be cleaned up after. Dogs are not allowed at public swim areas, but they are allowed on the trails. This campground is closed during the off-season. The camping and tent areas also allow dogs. There is a dog walk area at the campground. There are no electric or water hookups at the campground. Multiple dogs may be allowed.

Lakeside

West Shore State Park
9264 H 93S
Lakeside, MT
406-844-3066
Some parks discontinue phone service and get new numbers the following season, but 406-752-5501 is a non-changing number for park information. This secluded park sits along Flathead Lake and provides a variety of land and water recreation. Dogs of all sizes are allowed at no additional fee. Dogs may not be left unattended, and they must be quiet, well behaved, be on no more than a 10 foot leash, and be cleaned up after. Dogs are not allowed in public swim areas, but they are allowed on the trails. The camping and tent areas also allow dogs. There is a dog walk area at the campground. There are no water hookups at the campground. Multiple dogs may be allowed.

Laurel

Pelican RV Park
11360 S Frontage
Laurel, MT
406-628-4324
Dogs of all sizes are allowed, and there are no additional pet fees for tent or RV sites. There is a $10 one time fee for up to 2 dogs, and a $20 one time fee for 3 dogs at the motel. Dogs must be leashed and cleaned up after. The camping and tent areas also allow dogs. There is a dog walk area at the campground. Multiple dogs may be allowed.

Libby

Kootenai National Forest
1101 Hwy. 2 West
Libby, MT
406-293-6211
This forest is open year round, and it provides a wealth of natural

resources and an abundance of recreational activities. There are lookouts that can be rented, and dogs are allowed there. Dogs are allowed at no additional fee. Dogs may not be left unattended, and they must be leashed and cleaned up after. Dogs are not allowed on the beaches or in buildings, but they are allowed on the trails. Canoe Gultch campground is located at 12557 H 37. This campground is closed during the off-season. The camping and tent areas also allow dogs. There is a dog walk area at the campground. There are no water hookups at the campground.

Livingston

Livingston/Paradise Valley KOA
163 Pine Creek Road
Livingston, MT
406-222-0992
Dogs of all sizes are allowed. There are no additional pet fees. Dogs may not be left unattended, must be leashed, and cleaned up after. This RV park is closed during the off-season. The camping and tent areas also allow dogs. There is a dog walk area at the campground. Dogs are allowed in the camping cabins. Multiple dogs may be allowed.

Miles City

Miles City KOA
1 Palmer Street
Miles City, MT
406-232-3991
Dogs of all sizes are allowed. There are no additional pet fees. Dogs may not be tied up outside unless an adult is present, and they can only be left in your RV if they will be quiet and comfortable. Dogs must be well behaved, leashed, and cleaned up after. There are some breed restrictions. This RV park is closed during the off-season. The camping and tent areas also allow dogs. There is a dog walk area at the campground. Multiple dogs may be allowed.

Missoula

Beavertail Hill State Park
3201 Spurgin Road
Missoula, MT
406-542-5500
Some parks discontinue phone service and get new numbers the following season, but 406-752-5501

is a non-changing number for park information. This park, along Flathead Lake, offers a variety of land and water recreation, and a one hour walking nature trail. Dogs of all sizes are allowed at no additional fee. Dogs may not be left unattended, and they must be quiet, well behaved, be on no more than a 10 foot leash, and be cleaned up after. Dogs are not allowed in public swim areas or buildings, but they are allowed on the trails. This campground is closed during the off-season. The camping and tent areas also allow dogs. There is a dog walk area at the campground. There are no water hookups at the campground. Multiple dogs may be allowed.

Jellystone Park
9900 Jellystone Drive
Missoula, MT
406-543-9400
Dogs of all sizes are allowed. There are no additional pet fees. Dogs must be leashed and cleaned up after. This RV park is closed during the off-season. The camping and tent areas also allow dogs. There is a dog walk area at the campground. 2 dogs may be allowed.

Lolo National Forest
Building 24, Fort Missoula
Missoula, MT
406-329-3750
With 5 ranger districts, and over 2 million acres, this forest provides a variety of camping areas and trails. The diverse ecosystems support innumerable plant, fish, mammal, and bird species. Dogs are allowed at no additional fee. Dogs must be leashed and cleaned up after in the camp areas. The camping and tent areas also allow dogs. There is a dog walk area at the campground. Multiple dogs may be allowed.

Missoula KOA
3450 Tina Avenue
Missoula, MT
406-549-0881
Dogs of all sizes are allowed. There are no additional pet fees. Dogs may not be left unattended, must be leashed, and cleaned up after. The camping and tent areas also allow dogs. There is a dog walk area at the campground. Dogs are allowed in the camping cabins. Multiple dogs may be allowed.

Polson

Polson/Flathead KOA
200 Irvine Flats Road
Polson, MT
406-883-2151
Dogs of all sizes are allowed. There are no additional pet fees. Dogs may not be left unattended, must be leashed, and cleaned up after. This RV park is closed during the off-season. The camping and tent areas also allow dogs. There is a dog walk area at the campground. 2 dogs may be allowed.

St Mary

St Mary/East Glacier
106 W Shore Road
St Mary, MT
406-732-4122
Dogs of all sizes are allowed. There are no additional pet fees. Dogs may be left for short periods, and someone in the office needs to know the dog is unattended. Dogs must be leashed and cleaned up after. There are some breed restrictions. This RV park is closed during the off-season. The camping and tent areas also allow dogs. There is a dog walk area at the campground. Dogs are allowed in the camping cabins. Multiple dogs may be allowed.

St Regis

Campground St Regis
44 Frontage Road
St Regis, MT
406-649-2470
Dogs of all sizes are allowed. There are no additional pet fees. Dogs must be leashed and cleaned up after. This RV park is closed during the off-season. The camping and tent areas also allow dogs. There is a dog walk area at the campground. Multiple dogs may be allowed.

Nugget Campground
E of Stop Sign on Main Street
St Regis, MT
888-800-0125
Dogs of all sizes are allowed. There are no additional pet fees. Dogs must be leashed and cleaned up after. The camping and tent areas also allow dogs. There is a dog walk area at the campground. Dogs are allowed in the camping cabins. Multiple dogs may be allowed.

West Glacier

Glacier Campground
MM 152 H 2, 1 mile W of W Glacier
West Glacier, MT
406-387-5689
Dogs of all sizes are allowed. There are no additional pet fees. Dogs must be quiet, well behaved, leashed, and cleaned up after. Dogs may not be left unattended at any time. This RV park is closed during the off-season. The camping and tent areas also allow dogs. There is a dog walk area at the campground. Dogs are allowed in the camping cabins. Multiple dogs may be allowed.

Glacier National Park
On H 2 (Going to the Sun Road)
West Glacier, MT
406-888-7800
This forest covers more than a million acres and provides recreation for all seasons. Dogs are allowed at no additional fee. Dogs may not be left unattended, and they must be leashed and cleaned up after. Dogs are allowed in developed areas only and on the main road through the park. Dogs are not allowed in the back country or on any of the trails. The camping and tent areas also allow dogs. There is a dog walk area at the campground. There are no electric or water hookups at the campground. Multiple dogs may be allowed.

West Glacier KOA
355 Half Moon Flats Road
West Glacier, MT
406-387-5341
Dogs of all sizes are allowed. There are no additional pet fees. Dogs must be well behaved, quiet, leashed, and cleaned up after. Dogs may not be left unattended. There is a local dog sitter available. This RV park is closed during the off-season. The camping and tent areas also allow dogs. There is a dog walk area at the campground. Dogs are allowed in the camping cabins. Multiple dogs may be allowed.

Whitehall

Lewis and Clark Caverns State Park
1455 H 2E
Whitehall, MT
406-287-3541
Montana's first state park is home to one of the most highly decorated

limestone caverns in the Northwest, and the park offers a variety of hiking trails, a visitor center and an amphitheater. Dogs of all sizes are allowed at no additional fee. Dogs may not be left unattended, and they must be leashed and cleaned up after. Dogs are not allowed in food service areas, in the caverns, or on guided tours. Dogs may be in the Visitor's Center if they are not busy. As of 2006 they will be offering 2 kennels free of charge for visitors who would like to take the caverns tour. Dogs are allowed on the other trails. This campground is closed during the off-season. The camping and tent areas also allow dogs. There is a dog walk area at the campground. Dogs are allowed in the camping cabins. There are no electric or water hookups at the campground. Multiple dogs may be allowed.

Pipestone RV Park
41 Bluebird Lane
Whitehall, MT
406-287-5224
Dogs of all sizes are allowed. There are no additional pet fees. Dogs must be quiet, well behaved, leashed, and cleaned up after. Dogs may not be left unattended. The camping and tent areas also allow dogs. There is a dog walk area at the campground. Multiple dogs may be allowed.

Wolf Creek

Holter Lake Recreation Area
Recreation Road
Wolf Creek, MT
406-494-5059
All the Montana state parks are along a shoreline and this park of offers a variety of land and water recreation. Dogs of all sizes are allowed. There are no additional pet fees. Dogs may not be left unattended, they must be on no more than a 10 foot leash, and be cleaned up after. Dogs are not allowed on the beach but they are allowed on the trails. The camping and tent areas also allow dogs. There is a dog walk area at the campground. There are no electric or water hookups at the campground. Multiple dogs may be allowed.

Yellowstone - Grand Teton

Lionshead RV Resort

1545 Targhee Pass H
W Yellowstone, MT
406-646-7662
Dogs of all sizes are allowed. There are no additional pet fees. Dogs must be leased and cleaned up after. This RV park is closed during the off-season. The camping and tent areas also allow dogs. There is a dog walk area at the campground. Multiple dogs may be allowed.

Madison Arm Resort
5475 Madison Arm Road
West Yellowstone, MT
406-646-9328
Dogs of all sizes are allowed. There are no additional pet fees. Dogs may not be left unattended, and they must be leashed at all times, and cleaned up after. This RV park is closed during the off-season. The camping and tent areas also allow dogs. There is a dog walk area at the campground. 2 dogs may be allowed.

Yellowstone Grizzly RV Park
210 S Electric Street
West Yellowstone, MT
406-646-4466
Dogs of all sizes are allowed. There are no additional pet fees. Dogs must be quiet, well behaved, leashed, and cleaned up after. Dogs may not be left unattended. There is a forest nearby where they can run if they are under voice command. This RV park is closed during the off-season. The camping and tent areas also allow dogs. There is a dog walk area at the campground. Dogs are allowed in the camping cabins. Multiple dogs may be allowed.

Nebraska Listings

Ashland

Eugene T. Mahoney State Park
28500 W Park H
Ashland, NE
402-944-2523
This modern resort park offers many amenities including a family aquatic center, a 70-foot observation tower, and a wide variety of land and water activities and recreation. Dogs of all sizes are allowed at no additional fee. Dogs may not be left unattended outside, or in the cabin unless crated. Dogs must be leashed and

cleaned up after. Dogs are not allowed in park buildings, but they are allowed on the trails. The state reservation phone number is 402-471-1414. The camping and tent areas also allow dogs. There is a dog walk area at the campground. Dogs are allowed in the camping cabins. Multiple dogs may be allowed.

Bayard

Chimney Rock Pioneer Crossing
On County Road 75 @ H 92
Bayard, NE
305-586-1988
Dogs of all sizes are allowed. There are no additional pet fees. The camping and tent areas also allow dogs. There is a dog walk area at the campground. Multiple dogs may be allowed.

Flying Bee Ranch
6755 County Road 42
Bayard, NE
888-534-2341
Dogs of all sizes are allowed. There are no additional pet fees for the tent or RV sites. There is an $8 per night per pet additional fee for the cabins. Dogs may not be left unattended unless they will be quiet and well behaved. Dogs must be leashed and cleaned up after. The camping and tent areas also allow dogs. There is a dog walk area at the campground. Dogs are allowed in the camping cabins. Multiple dogs may be allowed.

Brule

Eagle Canyon Hideaway
1086 Lakeview W Road
Brule, NE
866-866-5253
Dogs of all sizes are allowed. There are no additional pet fees. Dogs must be quiet, leashed, and cleaned up after. The camping and tent areas also allow dogs. There is a dog walk area at the campground. Dogs are allowed in the camping cabins. Multiple dogs may be allowed.

Chadron

Chadron State Park
15951 H 385
Chadron, NE
308-432-6167
This scenic 972 acre park at an elevation of 5000 feet sits inside the Nebraska National Forest and offers a variety of land and water activities and recreation. Dogs of all sizes are allowed at no additional fee. Dogs may not be left unattended at any time, and they must be on no more than a 6 foot leash, and be cleaned up after. Dogs are allowed on the trails. The state reservation phone number is 402-471-1414. The camping and tent areas also allow dogs. There is a dog walk area at the campground. Dogs are allowed in the camping cabins. There are no water hookups at the campground. Multiple dogs may be allowed.

Nebraska National Forest
125 N Main Street
Chadron, NE
308-432-0300
Comprised of 3 national grasslands, 2 national forests, and home to the oldest national tree nursery, this forest provides diverse ecosystems that support a large variety of plants, fish, mammals, bird species, and year round recreation. Dogs of all sizes are allowed at no additional fee. Dogs may not be left unattended, and they must be leashed and cleaned up after. Dogs are allowed on the trails. The camping and tent areas also allow dogs. There is a dog walk area at the campground. There are no water hookups at the campground. Multiple dogs may be allowed.

Crawford

Fort Robinson State Park
3200 H 20
Crawford, NE
308-665-2900
This historically rich park of over 22,000 acres is home to their own herds of buffalo and longhorn. The park offers an interpretive museum as well as a variety of land and water activities and recreation. Dogs of all sizes are allowed at no additional fee. Dogs may not be left unattended at any time, and they must be on no more than a 6 foot leash, and be cleaned up after. Dogs are not allowed in buildings, but they are allowed on the trails. The state reservation phone number is 402-471-1414. The camping and tent areas also allow dogs. There is a dog walk area at the campground. Dogs are allowed in the camping cabins. There are no water hookups at the campground.

Multiple dogs may be allowed.

Crofton

Lewis and Clark State Rec Area
54731 897 Road (H 121)
Crofton, NE
402-388-4169
With over 9,000 acres along the states' 2nd largest lake, this park offers a wide variety of land and water activities and recreation. Dogs of all sizes are allowed at no additional fee. Dogs may not be left unattended at any time, and they must be on no more than a 6 foot leash, and be cleaned up after. Dogs are not allowed on the furniture in the cabins, on the beaches, or other park buildings. Dogs are allowed on the trails. The state reservation phone number is 402-471-1414. The camping and tent areas also allow dogs. There is a dog walk area at the campground. Dogs are allowed in the camping cabins. There are no water hookups at the campground. Multiple dogs may be allowed.

Doniphan

Grand Island KOA
904 South B Road
Doniphan, NE
402-886-2249
Dogs of all sizes are allowed, and there are no additional pet fees for tent or RV sites. There is a $5 per night per pet additional fee for the cabins. Dogs may not be left unattended, and they must be quiet, leashed, and cleaned up after. Dogs are not allowed in the buildings or the playground, and they must be in at night. This RV park is closed during the off-season. The camping and tent areas also allow dogs. There is a dog walk area at the campground. Dogs are allowed in the camping cabins. Multiple dogs may be allowed.

Mormon Island State Rec Area
7425 S H 281
Doniphan, NE
308-385-6211
This park is home to a spectacular gathering each spring of hundreds of thousands of sandhill cranes (the world's largest concentration)and serves as a link in the "Chain of Lakes". Dogs of all sizes are allowed at no additional fee. Dogs may not be left unattended, and they must be on no more than a 6 foot leash, and be cleaned up after. The camping

and tent areas also allow dogs. There is a dog walk area at the campground. There are no water hookups at the campground. Multiple dogs may be allowed.

Elwood

Johnson Lake State Rec Area
1 E. Park Drive 25A
Elwood, NE
308-785-2685
This fairly small park borders a 2,000 plus acre lake and provides a variety of land and water recreation. Dogs of all sizes are allowed at no additional fee. Dogs may not be left unattended unless they are crated and comfortable, and they must be on no more than a 6 foot leash, and be cleaned up after. Dogs are not allowed in park buildings. The state reservation phone number is 402-471-1414. The camping and tent areas also allow dogs. There is a dog walk area at the campground. There are no water hookups at the campground. Multiple dogs may be allowed.

Fairbury

Rock Creek Station State Historic Park
57426 710th Road
Fairbury, NE
402-729-5777
This park is rich in it's history and provides an excellent interpretive center in addition to a variety of hiking trails, activities and recreational pursuits. Well behaved dogs of all sizes are allowed at no additional fee. Dogs must be on no more than a 6 foot leash, and be cleaned up after. Dogs are not allowed in buildings, but they are allowed on the trails. The state reservation phone number is 402-471-1414. The camping and tent areas also allow dogs. There is a dog walk area at the campground. There are no water hookups at the campground. Multiple dogs may be allowed.

Gothenburg

Gothenburhg KOA
1102 S Lake Avenue
Gothenburg, NE
308-537-7387
Dogs of all sizes are allowed. There are no additional pet fees. Dogs may not be left unattended, and must be

leashed and cleaned up after. There are some breed restrictions. This RV park is closed during the off-season. The camping and tent areas also allow dogs. There is a dog walk area at the campground. Dogs are allowed in the camping cabins. Multiple dogs may be allowed.

Greenwood

Pine Grove RV Park
23403 Mynard Road
Greenwood, NE
402-994-3550
Dogs of all sizes are allowed. There are no additional pet fees. With the exception of an off lead area, dogs must be leashed. Dogs must be quiet and cleaned up after. The camping and tent areas also allow dogs. There is a dog walk area at the campground. Multiple dogs may be allowed.

Gretna

Linoma Beach Resort
17106 S 255th Street
Gretna, NE
402-332-4500
Dogs of all sizes are allowed. There are no additional pet fees. Dogs may not be left unattended outside, and they must be leashed and cleaned up after. Dogs must stay within the campers area, and they are not allowed on the beaches at any time. Barking dogs are not allowed. This is an RV only park. This RV park is closed during the off-season. There are no water hookups at the campgrounds. 2 dogs may be allowed.

West Omaha KOA
14601 H 6
Gretna, NE
402-332-3010
Dogs of all sizes are allowed. There are no additional pet fees. Dogs must be leashed and cleaned up after. There are some breed restrictions. This RV park is closed during the off-season. The camping and tent areas also allow dogs. There is a dog walk area at the campground. Dogs are allowed in the camping cabins. Multiple dogs may be allowed.

Kimball

Kimball KOA
4334 Link 53E
Kimball, NE
308-235-4404
Dogs of all sizes are allowed. There are no additional pet fees. Dogs may not be left unattended, and they must be leashed and cleaned up after. This RV park is closed during the off-season. The camping and tent areas also allow dogs. There is a dog walk area at the campground. Dogs are allowed in the camping cabins. Multiple dogs may be allowed.

Twin Pines RV Camp
1508 S H 71
Kimball, NE
308-235-3231
Dogs of all sizes are allowed. There are no additional pet fees. Dogs may not be left unattended, and they must be leashed and cleaned up after. The camping and tent areas also allow dogs. There is a dog walk area at the campground. Multiple dogs may be allowed.

Lincoln

Camp A Way
200 Camper's Circle
Lincoln, NE
866-719-2267
Dogs of all sizes are allowed. There are no additional pet fees. Dogs may not be left unattended, and they must be leashed and cleaned up after. The camping and tent areas also allow dogs. There is a dog walk area at the campground. Multiple dogs may be allowed.

Maxwell

Fort McPherson Campground
12567 Valley View Road
Maxwell, NE
308-582-4320
Dogs of all sizes are allowed. There are no additional pet fees. Dogs may be off lead when there is no one else around and if they are under voice control. Otherwise dogs must be leashed and cleaned up after. Dogs may not be left unattended. There is 1 cabin and a ranch house that sleeps 6, that is also pet friendly. This RV park is closed during the off-season. The camping and tent areas also allow dogs. There is a dog walk area at the campground. Dogs are allowed in the camping cabins. Multiple dogs may be allowed.

Niobrara

Niobrara State Park
89261 522nd Avenue
Niobrara, NE
402-85 7-3373
This park of over 1,600 acres offers opportunities for nature study in addition to providing an interpretive center, more than 14 miles of trails, and a wide range of land and water recreation. Dogs of all sizes are allowed at no additional fee. Dogs may not be left unattended outside, and they must be on no more than a 6 foot leash, and be cleaned up after. Dogs are not allowed on the furniture or bed in the cabins, and they must be placed in a crate if left inside. Dogs are not allowed in the pool area, but they are allowed on the trails. The state reservation phone number is 402-471-1414. The camping and tent areas also allow dogs. There is a dog walk area at the campground. Dogs are allowed in the camping cabins. There are no water hookups at the campground. Multiple dogs may be allowed.

North Platte

Holiday Trav-L-Park
601 Halligan Drive
North Platte, NE
308-534-2265
Dogs of all sizes are allowed. There are no additional pet fees. Dogs may not be left unattended at any time, and they must be leashed and cleaned up after. The camping and tent areas also allow dogs. There is a dog walk area at the campground. Multiple dogs may be allowed.

Lake Maloney State Rec Area
301 E State Farm Road
North Platte, NE
308-535-8025
This recreational park sits along a 1000 acre lake. Dogs of all sizes are allowed at no additional fee. Dogs must be leashed and cleaned up after. The camping and tent areas also allow dogs. There is a dog walk area at the campground. There are no water hookups at the campground. Multiple dogs may be allowed.

Ogallala

Lake Ogallala State Rec Area
1475 H 61N
Ogallala, NE

308-284-8800
This modern park is located in a shady spot below the Kingsley Dam Hydroelectric Plant, and offers both land and water recreation. Dogs of all sizes are allowed at no additional fee. Dogs may not be left unattended, and they must be leashed and cleaned up after. Dogs are allowed on the trails. The camping and tent areas also allow dogs. There is a dog walk area at the campground. There are no water hookups at the campground. Multiple dogs may be allowed.

Ponca

Ponca State Park
88090 Spur 26E
Ponca, NE
402-755-2284
This picturesque park, rich in history, is home to one of the state's most comprehensive outdoor/environmental education programs, and provides a variety of outdoor recreation. Dogs of all sizes are allowed at no additional fee. Dogs may not be left unattended in the cabins, and they must be leashed at all times, and cleaned up after. Dogs are not allowed in the pool area or buildings, and they may be left tied outside only if they will be quiet and well behaved. Dogs are allowed on the trails. The state reservation phone number is 402-471-1414. The camping and tent areas also allow dogs. There is a dog walk area at the campground. Dogs are allowed in the camping cabins. There are no water hookups at the campground. Multiple dogs may be allowed.

Potter

Buffalo Point RV Park and Motel
8175 H 30
Potter, NE
308-879-4400
Dogs of all sizes are allowed. There are no additional pet fees. Dogs must be quiet, leashed, and cleaned up after. There is also a motel on site that allowes dogs. The camping and tent areas also allow dogs. There is a dog walk area at the campground. Dogs are allowed in the camping cabins. Multiple dogs may be allowed.

Scottsbluff

Scottsbluff/Chimney Rock KOA
180037 KOA Drive
Scottsbluff, NE
308-635-3760
Dogs of all sizes are allowed. There are no additional pet fees. Dogs may not be left unattended, and they must be quiet, leashed, and cleaned up after. Dogs may not be tied to the trees or tables. This RV park is closed during the off-season. The camping and tent areas also allow dogs. There is a dog walk area at the campground. Dogs are allowed in the camping cabins. Multiple dogs may be allowed.

Valentine

Fishberry Campground
5 miles N of Valentine on H 83
Valentine, NE
866-376-1662
Dogs of all sizes are allowed. There are no additional pet fees. Dogs must be quiet, well behaved, leashed, and cleaned up after. Sites are available by reservation only after November 1st. The camping and tent areas also allow dogs. There is a dog walk area at the campground. Multiple dogs may be allowed.

Waco

Double Nickel Campground
905 Road S
Waco, NE
402-728-5558
Dogs of all sizes are allowed. There are no additional pet fees. Dogs may not be left unattended outside, and they must be leashed and cleaned up after. This RV park is closed during the off-season. The camping and tent areas also allow dogs. There is a dog walk area at the campground.

Wood River

Wood River Motel and RV Park
11774 S H 11
Wood River, NE
308-583-2256
Dogs of all sizes are allowed, and there are no additional pet fees for tent or RV sites. There is a motel on site, and there is a $5 per night per pet additional fee. Dogs may not be left unattended in the motel room or outside, and they must be leashed and cleaned up after. The camping and tent areas also allow dogs.

There is a dog walk area at the campground. Multiple dogs may be allowed.

Nevada Listings

Austin

Berlin-Ichthyosaur State Park
HC 61 Box 61200/H 844
Austin, NV
775-964-2440
Nestled at 7,000 feet on the Shoshone mountain range, this park preserves a true Nevada ghost town. It also features archeological sites, extensive self guided hiking trails, a nature trail to the Fossil Shelter, tours and various recreational pursuits. It is first come, first serve camping. Dogs of all sizes are allowed at no additional fee. Dogs may not be left unattended outside, and only inside if they will be quiet and comfortable. Dogs must be leashed and cleaned up after. Dogs are allowed on the trails. The camping and tent areas also allow dogs. There is a dog walk area at the campground. There are no electric hookups at the campgrounds. Multiple dogs may be allowed.

Beatty

Baileys Hot Springs RV Park
6 miles N of Beatty on H 95
Beatty, NV
775-553-2395
Visitors come from all over to enjoy the hot springs here. Dogs of all sizes are allowed at no additional fee. Dogs must be leashed and cleaned up after. There are some breed restrictions. The camping and tent areas also allow dogs. There is a dog walk area at the campground. Multiple dogs may be allowed.

Boulder City

Lake Mead RV Village
268 Lakeshore Road
Boulder City, NV
702-293-2540
Offering beautiful views, this RV park, conveniently located to a variety of attractions, also offers a convenience store, laundry facility, 2 boat launches, and a variety of land and water recreation. Dogs of all

sizes are allowed at no additional fee. Dogs may not be left unattended at any time, and they must be quiet, well behaved, leashed at all times, and cleaned up after. This is an RV only park. There is a dog walk area at the campground. 2 dogs may be allowed.

Caliente

Beaver Dam State Park
P. O. Box 985
Caliente, NV
775-726-3564
This remote, primitive 2,393-acre park features deep canyons, pine forests, a flowing stream, numerous beaver dams, hiking, and interpretive trails. Due to flood damage and dangerous conditions, it is strongly advised to check conditions before going to the dam site and the exposed mud flats behind the dam. Dogs of all sizes are allowed at no additional fee. Dogs must be leashed and cleaned up after. Dogs are allowed on the trails. The camping and tent areas also allow dogs. There is a dog walk area at the campground. There are no electric hookups at the campgrounds. 2 dogs may be allowed.

Carson City

Washoe Lake State Park
4855 East Lake Blvd
Carson City, NV
775-687-4319
This scenic park features a wetlands area with a viewing tower, an interpretive display, nature study and bird watching, hiking, horseback riding, water sports, boat launches, 2 comfort stations with showers, and access to trails and trailheads. Dogs of all sizes are allowed. There are no additional pet fees. Dogs may not be left unattended outside, and they must be leashed and cleaned up after. Dogs may be off lead when other people are not around and they are under voice control. Dogs are allowed on the beach and trails. The camping and tent areas also allow dogs. There is a dog walk area at the campground. There are no electric or water hookups at the campgrounds. Multiple dogs may be allowed.

Dayton

Dayton State Park
P. O. Box 1478
Dayton, NV
775-687-5678
The Carson River flows through this park giving visitors fishing opportunities and water activities. The park also offers hiking trails, an interpretive trail, a historic site and various recreation. Dogs of all sizes are allowed at no additional fee. Please keep dogs on a leash in populated areas and clean up after them. Dogs may not be left unattended outside, and they are not allowed in the pavilion area or on the lawns. The camping and tent areas also allow dogs. There is a dog walk area at the campground. There are no electric or water hookups at the campgrounds. Multiple dogs may be allowed.

Elko

Double Dice RV Park
3730 Idaho Street
Elko, NV
775-738-5642
This RV park offers 140 sites with amenities that include 30 or 50 amp electric, instant phone, 43 channel TV, 75 pull through sites for rigs up to 65 feet, a game room, laundry room, free email/web center, and showers. Tent sites are also available. Well-behaved leashed dogs are welcome. Please clean up after your pets. There is a $1 per night per pet additional fee. Dogs must be leashed, and taken to the dog run to relieve themselves. They are not allowed on the grass. Dogs may not be left outside, and they may be left inside only if they will be quiet and comfortable. The camping and tent areas also allow dogs. There is a dog walk area at the campground. Multiple dogs may be allowed.

Wild Horse State Recreation Area
HC 31, Box 26/H 225
Elko, NV
775-758-6493
Located on the northeast shore of Wild Horse Reservoir, this park is popular for camping, picnicking, hunting, fishing, boating, and hiking. The park also offers a boat launch, showers and a dump station. Dogs of all sizes are allowed. There are no additional pet fees. Dogs must be well behaved, on no more than a 6

foot leash, and cleaned up after. The camping and tent areas also allow dogs. There is a dog walk area at the campground. There are no electric or water hookups at the campgrounds. Multiple dogs may be allowed.

Ely

Cave Lake State Park
P. O. Box 151761
Ely, NV
775-728-4467
This park, along a 32 acre reservoir at 7,300 feet, offers outstanding views, opportunities for nature study and photography, a boat launch, interpretive presentations, winter programs, hiking trails, and more. Dogs of all sizes are allowed at no additional fee. Dogs must be leashed and cleaned up after. Dogs are not allowed in buildings. They are allowed on the trails. The camping and tent areas also allow dogs. There is a dog walk area at the campground. There are no electric or water hookups at the campgrounds. Multiple dogs may be allowed.

Ely Koa
H 93
Ely, NV
775-289-3413
Well landscaped grounds and location make this a popular park, with amenities that include 85 foot pull-through sites with 50 amp service, cable TV, LP gas, and WiFi. Dogs of all sizes are allowed for no additional fee, and there is a pet waiver to sign. There is a $25 refundable pet deposit for the cabins. Dogs must be under owner's control and visual observation at all times. Dogs must be quiet, well behaved, and be on no more than a 6 foot leash at all times, or otherwise contained. Dogs may not be left unattended outside the owner's camping equipment, and must be brought inside at night. Dogs are not allowed on the grass except by the dog walk. There are some breed restrictions. The camping and tent areas also allow dogs. There is a dog walk area at the campground. Dogs are allowed in the camping cabins. Multiple dogs may be allowed.

Ward Charcoal Ovens State Historic Park
P. O. Box 151761
Ely, NV
775-728-4460

Although mostly known for its historic six beehive-shaped charcoal ovens, this park also offers outstanding geologic sites, trails consisting of several miles of different views and ecotypes, and various other recreation. Dogs of all sizes are allowed at no additional fee. Dogs may not be left unattended outside, and left inside only if they will be quiet and comfortable. Dogs must be on no more than a 6 foot leash and be cleaned up after. Dogs are allowed on the trails. The camping and tent areas also allow dogs. There is a dog walk area at the campground. There are no electric or water hookups at the campgrounds. Multiple dogs may be allowed.

Las Vegas

Las Vegas KOA at Circus Circus
500 Circus Circus Drive
Las Vegas, NV
702-733-9707
Located on the Las Vegas Strip, this RV mostly park offers 80 foot pull-through sites with 50 amp service, LP Gas, WiFi, snack bar, swimming pool, hot tub, sauna, and guided tours. Dogs of all sizes are allowed for no additional fee. Dogs must be under owner's control and visual observation at all times. Dogs must be quiet, well behaved, and be on no more than a 6 foot leash at all times, or otherwise contained. Dogs may not be left unattended outside the owner's camping equipment, and must be brought inside at night. There are some breed restrictions. There is a dog walk area at the campground. Multiple dogs may be allowed.

Oasis Las Vegas RV Resort
2711 W Windmill Lane
Las Vegas, NV
800-566-4707
This premier RV park offers beautifully landscaped sites, beachfront family pool and waterfalls, adult pool and spa, 18-hole putting course, fitness center, store, restaurant, and a variety of recreational pursuits. Dogs of all sizes are allowed at no additional fee. Dogs may not be left unattended at any time, and they must be leashed and cleaned up after at all times. There is a $50 fine if the dogs are not picked up after. Dogs are not allowed in the non-pet section of the park. There is a fenced in dog run area where they

may be off lead, but still must be cleaned up after. This is an RV only park. There are some breed restrictions. There is a dog walk area at the campground. There are special amenities given to dogs at this campground. 2 dogs may be allowed.

Laughlin

Fiesta RV Resort
3190 H 95
Bullhead City, AZ
800-982-1750
Dogs of all sizes are allowed. There are no additional pet fees. Dogs must be walked out of the park and be leashed and cleaned up after. Dogs must be quiet and well behaved. There is a dog walk area at the campground. Multiple dogs may be allowed.

Silver View RV Resort
1501 Gold Rush Road
Bullhead City, AZ
928-763-5500
With spectacular views from the bluffs overlooking the Colorado River, this 5 star resort offers a mini mart and deli, clubhouse, swimming pool/Jacuzzi, and laundry. Two dogs under 40 pounds or one dog over 40 pounds is allowed at no additional fee. Dogs may not be left unattended outside, and they must be leashed and cleaned up after. Dogs are not allowed on the grass areas. There is a dog run on site where pets may be off lead. There are some breed restrictions. The camping and tent areas also allow dogs. There is a dog walk area at the campground.

Big Bend of the Colorado
P. O. Box 32850
Laughlin, NV
702-298-1859
Located on the shores of the Colorado River, this desert park offers a variety of land and water recreation. Dogs of all sizes are allowed at no additional fee. Dogs must be on no more than a 6 foot leash and be cleaned up after. The camping and tent areas also allow dogs. There is a dog walk area at the campground. There are no electric or water hookups at the campgrounds. 2 dogs may be allowed.

Don Laughlin's Riverside RV Resort

1650 S Casino Drive
Laughlin, NV
702-298-2535
This RV only park, located across the street from the Riverside Resort Hotel, offers 740 full hookup RV sites. Amenities include laundry facilities, showers, and 24 hour security. Well-behaved leashed dogs are allowed. Please clean up after your pets. There is no pet fee. Dogs may not be left unattended outside, and left inside only if they will be quiet and comfortable. There is a dog walk area at the campground. Multiple dogs may be allowed.

Lovelock

Rye Patch State Recreation Area
2505 Rye Patch Reservoir Road
Lovelock, NV
775-538-7321
Rich in natural and cultural history, this park along a 22-mile long reservoir, offers archaeological sites, and a variety of land and water recreation. Dogs of all sizes are allowed at no additional fee. Dogs may not be left unattended outside, and they must be on no more than a 6 foot leash, and cleaned up after. The camping and tent areas also allow dogs. There is a dog walk area at the campground. There are no electric or water hookups at the campgrounds. Multiple dogs may be allowed.

Minden

Silver City RV Resort
3165 H 395N
Minden, NV
775-267-3359
This RV campground offers a covered pool and spa, fish pond, fitness club, store, laundry facilities, gaming, and various other recreational pursuits. Dogs of all sizes are allowed for an additional $1 per night per pet. Dogs may not be left unattended outside, and they must be leashed and cleaned up after. This is an RV only park. There are some breed restrictions. There is a dog walk area at the campground. 2 dogs may be allowed.

Overton

Valley of Fire State Park
P. O. Box 515/ Valley of Fire Road
Overton, NV
702-397-2088

Unusual red sandstone formations mark this park with a facinating array of shapes, and they offer interpretive exhibits, numerous trails, historic sites, various recreation, and a visitor's center. Dogs of all sizes are allowed at no additional fee. Dogs may not be left unattended outside, and they must be leashed and cleaned up after. Dogs are allowed on the trails. The camping and tent areas also allow dogs. There is a dog walk area at the campground. There are no electric or water hookups at the campgrounds. Multiple dogs may be allowed.

Pahrump

Lakeside Casino RV Park
5870 S Homestead Road
Pahrump, NV
775-751-7770
This lushly landscaped RV resort offers historic old west charm among its many amenities which include watercraft rentals, laundry facilities, swimming lagoon, swimming pool and Jacuzzi. Dogs of all sizes are allowed. There are no additional pet fees. Dogs may not be left unattended outside, and left inside if they will be quiet and comfortable. They must be leashed and cleaned up after. Dogs are not allowed in the lake, on the beach, or in the pool area. This is an RV only park. There are some breed restrictions. There is a dog walk area at the campground. 2 dogs may be allowed.

Panaca

Cathedral Gorge State Park
333 Cathedral Gorge Road
Panaca, NV
775-728-4460
This park features dramatic scenic canyons, a rich history, interpretive displays, opportunities for nature study and photography, ranger programs, several trails and a variety of recreation. Dogs of all sizes are allowed for no additional fee. Dogs may not be left unattended for long periods, and only for a short time if they will be comfortable, quiet, and well behaved. Dogs are allowed on the trails. The camping and tent areas also allow dogs. There is a dog walk area at the campground. There are no electric or water hookups at the campgrounds. 2

dogs may be allowed.

Pioche

Echo Canyon State Park
HC 74, Box 295
Pioche, NV
775-962-5103
This 1080-acre park, with a 65 acre reservoir, supports a good variety of plant and animal life. It offers a rich archeological and agricultural history to explore in addition to various recreational pursuits. Dogs of all sizes are allowed at no additional fee. Dogs must be leashed in the camp area, and cleaned up after. Dogs are allowed on the trails. The camping and tent areas also allow dogs. There is a dog walk area at the campground. There are no electric or water hookups at the campgrounds. Multiple dogs may be allowed.

Spring Valley State Park
HC74, Box 201
Pioche, NV
775-962-5102
This high desert park, along a 65 acre reservoir, offers a rich cultural history in addition to a variety of amenities and recreational pursuits. Dogs of all sizes are allowed for no additional fee. Dogs may not be left unattended, except for short periods, and then only if they will be quiet and well behaved. Dogs must be on no more than a 6 foot leash and cleaned up after. When there are not a lot of people around, dogs may be off lead if they are under voice control and will not chase. The camping and tent areas also allow dogs. There is a dog walk area at the campground. There are no electric or water hookups at the campgrounds. Multiple dogs may be allowed.

Reno

Bonanza Terrace RV Park
4800 Stoltz Road
Reno, NV
775-329-9624
This RV park is located two miles north of downtown Reno off Highway 395. The Bonanza Casino is across the street from the RV park. RV sites include a gravel parking pad, up to 50 amp electric, water, sewer and phone line. RVs up to 40 feet are welcome. Well-behaved, leashed, and quiet pets accompanied by their owner are welcome. There is a $1 per night pet fee. Please clean up

after your pet. Dogs may not be left unattended outside. There are some breed restrictions. There is a dog walk area at the campground. Multiple dogs may be allowed.

Reno KOA
2500 E 2nd Street
Reno, NV
775-789-2147
Located at the Reno Hilton, there is an abundance of activities and recreation available, and amenities include 24 hour security, 65 foot pull through sites with 50 amp service, LP gas, snack bar, seasonal swimming pool, hot tub/sauna, mini golf, and guided tours. Dogs of all sizes are allowed for no additional fee. Dogs must be under owner's control and visual observation at all times. Dogs must be quiet, well behaved, and be on no more than a 6 foot leash at all times, or otherwise contained, and cleaned up after. Management will ask guests to leave if they do not clean up after their dogs. Dogs may not be left unattended outside the owner's camping equipment, and must be brought inside at night. There are some breed restrictions. The camping and tent areas also allow dogs. There is a dog walk area at the campground. Multiple dogs may be allowed.

Reno RV Park
735 Mill Street
Reno, NV
775-323-3381
This RV park is located about 4 blocks from the casinos. They offer restrooms, showers, 24 hour security, electric gates, propane available, recreation area, picnic area and more. Well-behaved leashed dogs are welcome. Please clean up after your pets. There is no pet fee. Dogs may not be left unattended. The camping and tent areas also allow dogs. There is a dog walk area at the campground. Multiple dogs may be allowed.

Rivers Edge RV Park
1405 S Rock Blvd
Sparks, NV
775-358-8533
Dogs of all sizes are allowed. There are no additional pet fees. Dogs may not be left unattended outside, and they must be leashed and cleaned up after. Dogs are allowed on the trails. This is an RV only park. There is a dog walk area at the campground. Multiple dogs may be

allowed.

Sparks Marina RV Park
1200 E Lincoln Way
Sparks, NV
775-851-8888
This modern, well landscaped park offers a small store, large clubhouse, pool, spa, free cable, laundry facilities, large pull through sites, and 3 fenced dog run areas. Dogs up to about 50 pounds are allowed at no additional fee. Dogs must be leashed and cleaned up after. This is an RV only park, and RVs must be 10 years old or newer. There are some breed restrictions. There is a dog walk area at the campground. There are special amenities given to dogs at this campground. 2 dogs may be allowed.

Silver Springs

Fort Churchill State Historic Park
1000 H 95A
Silver Springs, NV
775-577-2345
Rich in American history, this park offers a visitor's center with exhibits and artifacts, hiking, historic and environmental education, and access to the Carson River for canoeing. Dogs of all sizes are allowed at no additional fee. Dogs may not be left unattended for long periods, and only then if they will be quiet and well behaved. Dogs must be on no more than a 6 foot leash, or crated, and cleaned up after. Dogs are allowed on the trails unless otherwise marked. The camping and tent areas also allow dogs. There is a dog walk area at the campground. There are no electric or water hookups at the campgrounds. Multiple dogs may be allowed.

Silver Springs Beach
1971 Fir Street
Silver Springs, NV
775-577-2226
This park, located in the high desert of the Lahontan State Rec Area along a 17 mile reservoir, offers a variety of amenities and recreational opportunities. Dogs of all sizes are allowed at no additional fee. Dogs must be on no more than a 6 foot leash and cleaned up after. Dogs are allowed to go to the beach and on the trails. The camping and tent areas also allow dogs. There is a dog walk area at the campground. There are no electric or water

hookups at the campgrounds. 2 dogs may be allowed.

Spring Creek

South Fork State Recreation Area
353 Lower South Fork Unit 8
Spring Creek, NV
775-744-4346
Surrounded by 2,200 acres of wildlife-filled meadow lands and rolling hills, this park, with a 1,650 acre reservoir, is popular for hunting, boating, hiking, winter sports, and wildlife viewing. Friendly dogs of all sizes are allowed for no additional fee. Dogs must be on no more than a 6 foot leash and be cleaned up after. The camping and tent areas also allow dogs. There is a dog walk area at the campground. There are no electric or water hookups at the campgrounds. Multiple dogs may be allowed.

Verdi

Gold Ranch Casino and RV Resort
320 Gold Ranch Road
Verdi, NV
877-792-6789
A few miles from Reno, nestled among the trees of the Sierra Nevada mountain range, this modern, luxury resort offers a 24 hour convenience store, an Arco gas station, clean showers, laundry facilities, clubhouse, heated pool/spa, and wide pull through sites. Dogs of all sizes are allowed. There are no additional pet fees. Dogs may not be left unattended outside, and they must be leashed and cleaned up after. This is an RV only park. There is a dog walk area at the campground.

Virginia City

Virginia City RV Park
355 N 'F' Street
Virginia City, NV
775-847-0999
Located just two blocks from downtown Virginia City, this park offers 50 RV sites, and amenities include phone equipped spaces, showers, swimming pool, tennis courts park access, onsite market and deli, video rentals, laundry facility, slot machines and tent camping. Well-behaved leashed dogs are allowed. Please clean up after your pets, and do not leave them unattended. Reservations are

accepted for busy periods. The park is open all year. The camping and tent areas also allow dogs. There is a dog walk area at the campground. 2 dogs may be allowed.

West Wendover

Wendover KOA
651 N Camper Drive
West Wendover, NV
775-664-3221
Located just 10 miles from the world-famous Bonneville Salt Flats and next to 2 casinos, this oasis park offers large pull through sites, seasonal heated outdoor pool, mini golf, a grocery and souvenir shop, laundry and much more. Dogs of all sizes are allowed for no additional fee. Dogs must be under owner's control and visual observation at all times. Dogs must be quiet, well behaved, and be on no more than a 6 foot leash at all times, or otherwise contained, and cleaned up after. Dogs may not be left unattended outside the owner's camping equipment or alone in the cabins, and they must be brought inside at night. There are some breed restrictions. The camping and tent areas also allow dogs. There is a dog walk area at the campground. Dogs are allowed in the camping cabins. Multiple dogs may be allowed.

Winnemucca

Model T RV Park
1130 W Winnemucca Blvd
Winnemucca, NV
775-623-2588
This RV only park is located in town within walking distance of many services. Amenities include laundry facilities, a seasonal pool, restrooms and showers. Well-behaved leashed pets are allowed. There is no pet fee, just please clean up after your pet. The RV park is part of the Model T Casino and Winnemucca Quality Inn. There is a dog walk area at the campground. Multiple dogs may be allowed.

New Hampshire Listings

Ascutney

Wilgus State Park
On H 5
Ascutney, NH
802-674-5422
Dogs of all sizes are allowed. There are no additional pet fees. Dogs may not be left unattended, and they must be leashed and cleaned up after. Dogs are not allowed on the beach, the picnic areas, the day use area, and they must have proof of rabies shots. This campground is closed during the off-season. The camping and tent areas also allow dogs. There is a dog walk area at the campground. Multiple dogs may be allowed.

Ashland

Jellystone Park
35 Jellystone Park
Ashland, NH
603-968-9000
Dogs of all sizes are allowed. There are no additional pet fees. Dogs must have a valid rabies certificate, can not be left unattended, and must be leashed and cleaned up after. This RV park is closed during the off-season. The camping and tent areas also allow dogs. There is a dog walk area at the campground. Multiple dogs may be allowed.

Bristol

Davidson's Countryside Campgrounds
100 Schofield Road
Bristol, NH
603-744-2403
Dogs of all sizes are allowed. There are no additional pet fees. Dogs must be well behaved, leashed, and cleaned up after. This RV park is closed during the off-season. The camping and tent areas also allow dogs. There is a dog walk area at the campground. Multiple dogs may be allowed.

Center Ossipee

Terrace Pines Campground
110 Terrace Pine
Center Ossipee, NH
603-539-6210
Dogs of all sizes are allowed. There are no additional pet fees. Dogs may not be left unattended, must be leashed, and cleaned up after. This RV park is closed during the off-

season. The camping and tent areas also allow dogs. There is a dog walk area at the campground. Dogs are allowed in the camping cabins. Multiple dogs may be allowed.

Conroy

Chocorua Camping Village
893 White Mountain H
Chocorua, NH
603-323-8536
Small Dogs Only. One dog about 50 pounds or two dogs that total 35 pounds are allowed. There are no additional pet fees. Dogs must be leashed and cleaned up after. There is a swim area for dogs where they can be off leash. There are some breed restrictions. This RV park is closed during the off-season. The camping and tent areas also allow dogs. There is a dog walk area at the campground. Dogs are allowed in the camping cabins.

Epsom

Circle 9 Ranch
39 Windymere Drive
Epsom, NH
603-736-9656
Dogs of all sizes are allowed. There are no additional pet fees. Dogs must be leashed at all times and be cleaned up after. There is a dog walk area at the campground. Multiple dogs may be allowed.

Franconia

Fransted Family Campground
974 Profile Road
Franconia, NH
603-823-5675
Dogs of all sizes are allowed. There are no additional pet fees. Dogs may not be left unattended, must be leashed, and cleaned up after. There are some breed restrictions. This RV park is closed during the off-season. Only one dog is allowed per campsite. The camping and tent areas also allow dogs. There is a dog walk area at the campground.

Freedom

Danforth Bay Camping Resort
196 Shawtown Road
Freedom, NH
603-539-2069
Dogs of all sizes are allowed. There are no additional pet fees. Dogs

must have current shot records, and be leashed and cleaned up after. Dogs are not allowed at the pool or beach. There are some breed restrictions. This RV park is closed during the off-season. The camping and tent areas also allow dogs. There is a dog walk area at the campground. 2 dogs may be allowed.

Hampton Falls

Wakeda Campground
294 Exeter Road
Hampton Falls, NH
603-772-5274
Dogs of all sizes are allowed. There are no additional pet fees. Dogs may not be left unattended, must be leashed, and cleaned up after. This RV park is closed during the off-season. The camping and tent areas also allow dogs. There is a dog walk area at the campground. Dogs are allowed in the camping cabins. Multiple dogs may be allowed.

Henniker

Mile-Away Campground
41 Old West Hockington Road
Henniker, NH
603-428-7616
Dogs of all sizes are allowed. There are no additional pet fees. Dogs must be leashed and cleaned up after. This RV park is closed during the off-season. The camping and tent areas also allow dogs. There is a dog walk area at the campground. Multiple dogs may be allowed.

Jefferson

Lantern Resort Motel and Campground
571 Presidential H
Jefferson, NH
603-586-7151
Dogs of all sizes are allowed. There are no additional pet fees. Dogs must be leashed and cleaned up after. Dogs may be left inside your unit for short periods if they will be quiet and well behaved. Dogs are not allowed at the motel. This RV park is closed during the off-season. The camping and tent areas also allow dogs. There is a dog walk area at the campground. Multiple dogs may be allowed.

Lancaster

Mountain Lake Campground
485 Prospect Street
Lancaster, NH
603-788-4509
Dogs of all sizes are allowed. There is a $2 per night per pet additional fee, and dogs must have current rabies and shot records. Dogs must be leashed and cleaned up after. There are some breed restrictions. This RV park is closed during the off-season. The camping and tent areas also allow dogs. There is a dog walk area at the campground. 2 dogs may be allowed.

Roger's Campground
10 Roger's Campground Road
Lancaster, NH
603-788-4885
Dogs of all sizes are allowed. There are no additional pet fees. Dogs must be leashed and cleaned up after. Dogs are not allowed at the motel or other rentals. This RV park is closed during the off-season. The camping and tent areas also allow dogs. There is a dog walk area at the campground. Multiple dogs may be allowed.

Laconia

White Mountain National Forest
719 Main Street
Laconia, NH
603-528-8721
Dogs of all sizes are allowed. There are no additional pet fees. Dogs may not be left unattended, and they must be quiet, leashed, and cleaned up after. Dogs are allowed on most trails in the forest. There is a trail map that can be ordered ahead or at seen at the entrances of the park. Since there is private and state owned land, dogs are not allowed, in the park, they request adherence to the map. There are 22 campgrounds in this national forest. The camping and tent areas also allow dogs. There is a dog walk area at the campground. There are no electric or water hookups at the campground. Multiple dogs may be allowed.

Lisbon

KOA Littleton/Lisbon
2154 Route 302
Lisbon, NH
603-838-5525
Dogs of all sizes are allowed. There are no additional pet fees. Dogs

may not be left unattended, must be well behaved, leashed, and cleaned up after. There are some breed restrictions. This RV park is closed during the off-season. The camping and tent areas also allow dogs. There is a dog walk area at the campground. Multiple dogs may be allowed.

Littleton

Crazy Horse Campground
788 Hiltop Road
Littleton, NH
603-444-2204
Dogs of all sizes are allowed. There are no additional pet fees. Dogs must have current rabies records, be leashed, and cleaned up after. The camping and tent areas also allow dogs. There is a dog walk area at the campground. 2 dogs may be allowed.

Milton

Mi-te-jo Campground
111 Mi-te-jo Road
Milton, NH
603-652-9022
Dogs of all sizes are allowed. There are no additional pet fees. Dogs may not be left unattended, must be leashed, and cleaned up after. Dogs are not allowed on the ball field, the playground, or the beach. This RV park is closed during the off-season. The camping and tent areas also allow dogs. There is a dog walk area at the campground. 2 dogs may be allowed.

Moultonborough

Pine Woods Campground
65 Barrett Place
Moultonborough, NH
603-253-6251
Dogs of all sizes are allowed. There are no additional pet fees. Dogs may not be left unattended, must be leashed, and cleaned up after. Dogs are allowed to go to the lake about a 15 minute walk away. This RV park is closed during the off-season. The camping and tent areas also allow dogs. There is a dog walk area at the campground. Multiple dogs may be allowed.

N Conway

Beach Camping Area

776 White Mountain H
N Conway, NH
603-447-2723
Dogs of all sizes are allowed. There is a $2 per night per pet additional fee. Dogs may not be left unattended, must be leashed, and cleaned up after. Dogs are not allowed at the river. This RV park is closed during the off-season. The camping and tent areas also allow dogs. There is a dog walk area at the campground. Multiple dogs may be allowed.

Saco River Camping
1550 White Mountain H
N Conway, NH
603-356-3360
Dogs of all sizes are allowed. There is a $2 per night per pet additional fee. Dogs may not be left unattended, and must be leashed and cleaned up after. Dogs are not allowed at the beach or pool, the playground, or the office. There are some breed restrictions. This RV park is closed during the off-season. The camping and tent areas also allow dogs. There is a dog walk area at the campground. 2 dogs may be allowed.

New Boston

Friendly Beaver Campground
Old Coach Road
New Boston, NH
603-487-5570
Dogs of all sizes are allowed. There are no additional pet fees. Dogs must be leashed, cleaned up after, and brought in after dark. The camping and tent areas also allow dogs. There is a dog walk area at the campground. Multiple dogs may be allowed.

New Hampton

Twin Tamarack Family Camping
431 Twin Tamarack Road
New Hampton, NH
603-279-4387
Dogs of all sizes are allowed. There are no additional pet fees. Dogs may not be left unattended, must be leashed, and cleaned up after. There are some breed restrictions. This RV park is closed during the off-season. The camping and tent areas also allow dogs. There is a dog walk area at the campground. Multiple dogs may be allowed.

Orford

Jacob's Brook
46 Highbridge Road
Orford, NH
603-353-9210
Dogs of all sizes are allowed. There are no additional pet fees. Normally only 2 dogs are allowed per site, but more may be accepted if you let them know in advance. Dogs must be well behaved, leashed, and cleaned up after. This RV park is closed during the off-season. The camping and tent areas also allow dogs. There is a dog walk area at the campground.

Raymond

Pine Acres Family Campground
74 Freetown Road
Raymond, NH
603-895-2519
Dogs of all sizes are allowed. There are no additional pet fees. Dogs may not be left unattended, must be leashed and cleaned up after. Dogs are not allowed at the beach or the pavillion This RV park is closed during the off-season. The camping and tent areas also allow dogs. There is a dog walk area at the campground. Multiple dogs may be allowed.

Richmond

Shir-roy Camping
100 Athol Road
Richmond, NH
603-239-4768
Dogs of all sizes are allowed. There are no additional pet fees. Dogs may not be left unattended, must be leashed, and cleaned up after. This RV park is closed during the off-season. The camping and tent areas also allow dogs. There is a dog walk area at the campground. Multiple dogs may be allowed.

Rindge

Woodmore Family Campground
21 Woodmore Drive
Rindge, NH
603-899-3362
Dogs of all sizes are allowed. There are no additional pet fees. Dogs must be quiet, well behaved, leashed, and cleaned up after. Dogs may not be left unattended. This RV park is closed during the off-season. The camping and tent

areas also allow dogs. There is a dog walk area at the campground. Dogs are allowed in the camping cabins. Multiple dogs may be allowed.

Shelburne

Timberland Camping Area
809 H 2
Shelburne, NH
603-466-3872
Dogs of all sizes are allowed. There are no additional pet fees. Dogs must be leashed and cleaned up after. There are some breed restrictions. The camping and tent areas also allow dogs. There is a dog walk area at the campground. 2 dogs may be allowed.

Tamworth

Tamworth Camping
194 Depot Road
Tamworth, NH
603-323-8031
Dogs of all sizes are allowed. There are no additional pet fees. Dogs must have current rabies and shot records, and be leashed and cleaned up after. There is a river nearby where you can take your pet. This RV park is closed during the off-season. The camping and tent areas also allow dogs. There is a dog walk area at the campground. Multiple dogs may be allowed.

Twin Mountain

KOA Twin Mountain
372 H 115
Twin Mountain, NH
603-846-5559
Dogs of all sizes are allowed. There are no additional pet fees. Dogs must be leashed and cleaned up after. This RV park is closed during the off-season. The camping and tent areas also allow dogs. There is a dog walk area at the campground. 2 dogs may be allowed.

Weare

Cold Springs RV and Camp Resort
62 Barnard Hill Road
Weare, NH
603-529-2528
Dogs of all sizes are allowed. There is a $2 per night per pet additional fee. Dogs must be quiet, well behaved, leashed, and cleaned up

after. Dogs are not allowed at the beach or pool. Visitor dogs are not allowed. This RV park is closed during the off-season. The camping and tent areas also allow dogs. There is a dog walk area at the campground. Multiple dogs may be allowed.

Winchester

Forest Lake Campground
331 Keene Road
Winchester, NH
603-239-4267
Dogs of all sizes are allowed. There are no additional pet fees. Dogs must be leashed and cleaned up after. There are some breed restrictions. This RV park is closed during the off-season. The camping and tent areas also allow dogs. There is a dog walk area at the campground. Multiple dogs may be allowed.

Woodstock

KOA Woodstock
1001 Eastside Road
Woodstock, NH
603-745-8008
Dogs of all sizes are allowed. There are no additional pet fees. Dogs must be leashed and cleaned up after. This RV park is closed during the off-season. The camping and tent areas also allow dogs. There is a dog walk area at the campground. Dogs are allowed in the camping cabins. Multiple dogs may be allowed.

New Jersey Listings

Atlantic City

Shady Pines Camping Resort
443 S 6th Avenue
Absecon Highlands, NJ
609-652-1516
One dog of any size is allowed. There are no additional pet fees. Dogs must be leashed and cleaned up after. The camping and tent areas also allow dogs. There is a dog walk area at the campground.

Buens

Buena Vista Camping Park
775 Harding Highway
Buens, NJ
856-697-5555
Dogs of all sizes are allowed, however some breeds are not. There are no additional pet fees. Dogs must be well behaved, quiet, leashed, and cleaned up after. The camping and tent areas also allow dogs. There is a dog walk area at the campground. Multiple dogs may be allowed.

Cape May

Pomona Campground
Oak Drive
Cape May, NJ
609-965-2123
Dogs of all sizes are allowed. There are no additional pet fees. Dogs must be well behaved, quiet, leashed, and cleaned up after. The camping and tent areas also allow dogs. There is a dog walk area at the campground. Multiple dogs may be allowed.

Seashore Campsites
720 Seashore Road
Cape May, NJ
609-884-4010
Dogs of all sizes are allowed. There are no additional pet fees. Dogs must be leashed, cleaned up after, and not left unattended. The camping and tent areas also allow dogs. There is a dog walk area at the campground. Multiple dogs may be allowed.

Cape May Courthouse

Big Timber Lake Camping Resort
116 Swainton-Goshen Road
Cape May Courthouse, NJ
609-465-4456
Dogs of all sizes are allowed. There are no additional pet fees. Dogs may not be left unattended, and they must be leashed and cleaned up after. This RV park is closed during the off-season. The camping and tent areas also allow dogs. There is a dog walk area at the campground. Multiple dogs may be allowed.

Clarksboro

Timberlane Campground
117 Timberlane Road
Clarksboro, NJ
856-423-6677

Dogs of all sizes are allowed. There are no additional pet fees. Dogs may not be left unattended, and they must be quiet, leashed, and cleaned up after. The camping and tent areas also allow dogs. There is a dog walk area at the campground. Multiple dogs may be allowed.

Egg Harbor

Holly Acres RV Park
218 S Frankfurt Avenue
Egg Harbor, NJ
609-965-3387
Dogs of all sizes are allowed. There are no additional pet fees. Dogs may not be left unattended outside, and they must be quiet, well behaved, leashed and cleaned up after. There are some breed restrictions. This RV park is closed during the off-season. There is a dog walk area at the campground. Multiple dogs may be allowed.

Elmer

Yogi Bear Tall Pines
49 Beal Road
Elmer, NJ
800-252-2890
Dogs of all sizes are allowed, some breeds are not. There are no additional pet fees. Dogs must be leashed, cleaned up after, and not left unattended. This RV park is closed during the off-season. The camping and tent areas also allow dogs. There is a dog walk area at the campground. Dogs are allowed in the camping cabins.

Freehold

Turkey Pond Swamp Campground
200 Georgia Road
Freehold, NJ
732-842-4000
Dogs of all sizes are allowed. There are no additional pet fees. Dogs may not be left unattended except for short periods, and they must be quiet, leashed, and cleaned up after. The camping and tent areas also allow dogs. There is a dog walk area at the campground. Multiple dogs may be allowed.

Hamburg

Beaver Hill Campground
120 Big Springs Road
Hamburg, NJ

973-827-0670
Dogs of all sizes are allowed. There is a $1 per night per pet additional fee. Dogs must be leashed, cleaned up after, and not left unattended. The camping and tent areas also allow dogs. There is a dog walk area at the campground. Multiple dogs may be allowed.

Jackson

Butterfly Camping Resort
360 Butterfly Road
Jackson, NJ
732-928-2107
Dogs of all sizes are allowed, some breeds are not. There are no additional pet fees. Dogs must be leashed and cleaned up after. The camping and tent areas also allow dogs. There is a dog walk area at the campground. 2 dogs may be allowed.

Tip Tam Camping Resort
301 Brewer's Bridge Road
Jackson, NJ
877-TIP-TAM1
Dogs of all sizes are allowed, however some breeds are not. There are no additional pet fees. Dogs must remain on your own site, be leashed, and cleaned up after. The camping and tent areas also allow dogs. 2 dogs may be allowed.

Marmora

Whipporwill Campground
810 S Shore Road
Marmora, NJ
609-390-3458
Dogs of all sizes are allowed. There are no additional pet fees. Dogs must be quiet and well behaved. They are allowed to be off lead on your site if they will stay regardless of what goes by. Dogs must otherwise be leashed and cleaned up after. The camping and tent areas also allow dogs. There is a dog walk area at the campground. Multiple dogs may be allowed.

May's Landing

Winding River Campground
6752 Weymouth Road
May's Landing, NJ
609-625-3191
Dogs of all sizes are allowed. There are no additional pet fees. Dogs must be quiet, leashed, cleaned up after, and have current shot records.

The camping and tent areas also allow dogs. There is a dog walk area at the campground. 2 dogs may be allowed.

Mays Landing

Yogi Bear's Jellystone Park
1079 12th Avenue
Mays Landing, NJ
609-476-2811
Dogs of all sizes are allowed. There are no additional pet fees. Dogs must have a valid rabies certificate, be well behaved, leashed, and cleaned up after. The camping and tent areas also allow dogs. There is a dog walk area at the campground. 2 dogs may be allowed.

Montague

Cedar Ridge Campground
205 River Road
Montague, NJ
973-293-3512
One dog of any size is allowed. There are no additional pet fees. Dogs may not be left unattended at any time, and they must be leashed and cleaned up after. Dogs must be licensed and have up to date shot records. There are some breed restrictions. This RV park is closed during the off-season. The camping and tent areas also allow dogs. There is a dog walk area at the campground.

New Gretna

Timberline Lake
345 H 679
New Gretna, NJ
609-296-7900
Well behaved dogs of all sizes are allowed. There are no additional pet fees. Dogs must be friendly, leashed, and cleaned up after. All dogs must have recent shot records. The camping and tent areas also allow dogs. There is a dog walk area at the campground. 2 dogs may be allowed.

North Shore

Pine Cone Resort
340 Georgia Road
Pine Cone, NJ
732-462-2230
Dogs up to about 75 pounds are allowed; some breeds are not. There are no additional pet fees.

Dogs must be leashed, cleaned up after, and not left unattended. Only one dog is allowed per campsite. The camping and tent areas also allow dogs. There is a dog walk area at the campground.

Northern New Jersey

Liberty Harbor RV Park
11 Marin Blvd
Jersey City, NJ
201-387-7500
Dogs of all sizes are allowed. There are no additional pet fees. Dogs must be leashed, cleaned up after, and not be left unattended. There is a dog walk area at the campground. Multiple dogs may be allowed.

Ocean View

Ocean View Resort
2555 H 9
Ocean View, NJ
609-624-1675
Dogs of all sizes are allowed. There are no additional pet fees. Dogs must be leashed and cleaned up after. There is a dog walk area at the campground. 2 dogs may be allowed.

Pine Haven Camping Resort
2339 H 9
Ocean View, NJ
609-624-3437
Dogs of all sizes are allowed. There are no additional pet fees. Dogs must be leashed and cleaned up after. The camping and tent areas also allow dogs. Multiple dogs may be allowed.

Pilesgrove

Four Seasons Family Campground
158 Woodstown Road
Pilesgrove, NJ
856-769-3635
Dogs of all sizes are allowed. There are no additional pet fees. Dogs may not be left unattended outside, and they must be leashed and cleaned up after. Dogs are not allowed on the beach or at the playground, and they are not allowed in or around the cabin areas. Dogs must be licensed and have current shot records. The camping and tent areas also allow dogs. There is a dog walk area at the campground. Multiple dogs may be allowed.

Tuckerton

Atlantic City North Family Campground
Stage Road
Tuckerton, NJ
609-296-9163
Dogs of all sizes are allowed. There are no additional pet fees. Dogs may not be left unattended outside or in the cabins, and they must be leashed and cleaned up after. This RV park is closed during the off-season. The camping and tent areas also allow dogs. There is a dog walk area at the campground. Dogs are allowed in the camping cabins. Multiple dogs may be allowed.

West Creek

Sea Pirate Campground
Bay side of H 9, Box 271
West Creek, NJ
609-296-7400
Up to two dogs of any size are allowed at the tent and RV sites at no additional fee. Basic Cabins and 2 Room Basic Cabins allow one pet at $5 per night with a $200 security deposit. Dogs may not be left unattended, and they must be leashed and cleaned up after. This RV park is closed during the off-season. The camping and tent areas also allow dogs. There is a dog walk area at the campground. Dogs are allowed in the camping cabins.

New Mexico Listings

Alamogordo

Alamogordo Roadrunner Campground
412 24th Street
Alamogordo, NM
877-437-3003
Dogs of all sizes are allowed. There are no additional pet fees. Dogs may not be left unattended outside, and they must be leashed and cleaned up after. The camping and tent areas also allow dogs. There is a dog walk area at the campground. Multiple dogs may be allowed.

Lincoln National Forest
1101 New York Avenue
Alamogordo, NM
505-434-7200
Home of Smokey Bear, this forest of over a million acres has diverse ecosystems that support a large variety of plants, fish, mammals, bird species, and recreation. Dogs of all sizes are allowed at no additional fee. Dogs may not be left unattended, and they must be leashed and cleaned up after in camp areas. Dogs may be off lead in the forest if they are well trained and under voice control. Dogs are allowed on the trails. The camping and tent areas also allow dogs. There is a dog walk area at the campground. There are no electric or water hookups at the campground. Multiple dogs may be allowed.

Oliver Lee Memorial State Park
409 Dog Canyon Road
Alamogordo, NM
505-437-8284
This oasis in the desert features historical exhibits and guided tours of a fully restored 19th century ranch house. Dogs of all sizes are allowed at no additional fee. Dogs may not be left unattended outside, and they must be, quiet, well behaved, leashed and cleaned up after. Dogs are allowed on the trails. The camping and tent areas also allow dogs. There is a dog walk area at the campground. Multiple dogs may be allowed.

Albuquerque

Albuquerque Central KOA
12400 Skyline Road NE
Albuquerque, NM
505-296-2729
Dogs of all sizes are allowed. There are no additional pet fees. Dogs may not be left unattended outside, and they must be well behaved, leashed, and cleaned up after. There are some breed restrictions. The camping and tent areas also allow dogs. There is a dog walk area at the campground. Dogs are allowed in the camping cabins. Multiple dogs may be allowed.

Enchanted Trails
14305 Central
Albuquerque, NM
505-831-6317
Dogs of all sizes are allowed. There are no additional pet fees. Dogs may not be left unattended outside, and they must be leashed and

cleaned up after. There is a dog walk area at the campground. Multiple dogs may be allowed.

High Desert RV Park
13000 W Frontage Road SW
Albuquerque, NM
866-839-9035
Dogs of all sizes are allowed. There are no additional pet fees. Dogs may not be penned or left unattended outside, and they must be leashed and cleaned up after. There is a dog walk area at the campground. Multiple dogs may be allowed.

Aztec

Ruins Road RV Park
312 Ruins Road
Aztec, NM
505-334-3160
Dogs of all sizes are allowed. There are no additional pet fees. Dogs may not be left unattended outside, and they must be leashed and cleaned up after. The camping and tent areas also allow dogs. There is a dog walk area at the campground. Multiple dogs may be allowed.

Bernalillo

Albuquerque N/Bernalillo KOA
555 S Hill Road
Bernalillo, NM
505-867-5227
Dogs of all sizes are allowed. There are no additional pet fees. Dogs may not be left unattended, and they must be quiet, leashed, and cleaned up after. Dogs may not be on the grass, in the store, the bathrooms, or the cafe. There is a fenced area for off lead. The camping and tent areas also allow dogs. There is a dog walk area at the campground. Dogs are allowed in the camping cabins. Multiple dogs may be allowed.

Caballo

Caballo Lake State Park
Box 32; On H 187
Caballo, NM
505-743-3942
Main attractions here are the migration of Bald and Golden Eagles and 2 cactus gardens, in addition to a variety of land and water recreation. Dogs of all sizes are allowed at no additional fee. Dogs must be leashed and cleaned up after, and they are allowed on the

trails. The camping and tent areas also allow dogs. There is a dog walk area at the campground. Multiple dogs may be allowed.

Percha Dam State Park
Box 32; on H 187
Caballo, NM
505-743-3942
This 80 acre park along the Rio Grande offers fishing and hiking, nature study, and a variety of land and water recreation. Dogs of all sizes are allowed at no additional fee. Dogs may not be left unattended, and they must be leashed and cleaned up after. Dogs are allowed on the trails. The camping and tent areas also allow dogs. There is a dog walk area at the campground. Multiple dogs may be allowed.

Carlsbad

Brantley Lake State Park
Capitan Reef Road
Carlsbad, NM
505-457-2384
With 3000 land acres and 4000 lake acres, this park offers a variety of recreational pursuits and planned activities throughout the year. Dogs of all sizes are allowed at no additional fee. Dogs must be leashed and cleaned up after in the camp areas. Dogs may be off lead in the primitive areas if they are under voice control. The camping and tent areas also allow dogs. There is a dog walk area at the campground. Multiple dogs may be allowed.

Windmill RV Park
3624 National Parks H (H 62/180N)
Carlsbad, NM
505-887-1387
Dogs of all sizes are allowed. There are no additional pet fees. Dogs may not be left unattended outside, and they must be leashed and cleaned up after. This is an RV only park. There is a dog walk area at the campground. Multiple dogs may be allowed.

Cedar Crest

Turquoise Trail Campground
22 Calvary Road
Cedar Crest, NM
505-281-2005
Dogs of all sizes are allowed. There are no additional pet fees. Dogs must be leashed and cleaned up after. There is also an archeological

museum on site. The camping and tent areas also allow dogs. There is a dog walk area at the campground. Multiple dogs may be allowed.

Chama

Little Creek Resort
2631 S H 84/64
Chama, NM
505-756-2382
Dogs of all sizes are allowed. There are no additional pet fees. Dogs may not be left unattended outside, and they must be leashed and cleaned up after. The camping and tent areas also allow dogs. There is a dog walk area at the campground. Dogs are allowed in the camping cabins.

Rio Chama RV Park
182 N H 17
Chama, NM
505-756-2303
Dogs of all sizes are allowed. There are no additional pet fees. Dogs must be leashed and cleaned up after. This RV park is closed during the off-season. There is a dog walk area at the campground. 2 dogs may be allowed.

Clayton

Clayton Lake State Park
141 Clayton Lake Road
Clayton, NM
505-374-8808
This parks' main attraction is more than 500 dinosaur footprints that have been preserved and identified. There is also a variety of land and water recreation at this high mountain desert park. Dogs of all sizes are allowed at no additional fee. Dogs may not be left unattended, and they must be quiet, well behaved, be on no more than a 10 foot leash, and be cleaned up after. Dogs are allowed on the trails. The camping and tent areas also allow dogs. There is a dog walk area at the campground. Multiple dogs may be allowed.

Columbus

Pancho Villa State Park
400 W H 9
Columbus, NM
505-532-2711
This historical park features an extensive exhibit depicting an armed invasion by Pancho Villa and

interpretive trails that wind through extensive botanical gardens. Dogs of all sizes are allowed at no additional fee. Dogs may not be left unattended, and they must be on no more than a 10 foot leash, and be cleaned up after. Dogs are not allowed in the buildings, but they are allowed on the trails. The camping and tent areas also allow dogs. There is a dog walk area at the campground. Multiple dogs may be allowed.

Conchas Dam

Conchas Lake State Park
Box 967; On H 104
Conchas Dam, NM
505-868-2270
This park offers ancient sites, one of the largest lakes in New Mexico, and a variety of land and water recreation. Dogs of all sizes are allowed at no additional fee. Dogs may not be left unattended, they must be quiet, be on no more than a 10 foot leash and be cleaned up after. The camping and tent areas also allow dogs. There is a dog walk area at the campground. Multiple dogs may be allowed.

Deming

Little Vineyard
2901 E Pine
Deming, NM
505-546-3560
Dogs of all sizes are allowed. There are no additional pet fees. Dogs must be leashed and cleaned up after. There is a dog walk area at the campground. Multiple dogs may be allowed.

Roadrunner RV Park
2849 E Pine Street
Deming, NM
505-546-6960
Dogs of all sizes are allowed. There are no additional pet fees. Dogs must be quiet, leashed, and cleaned up after. There is a dog walk area at the campground. Multiple dogs may be allowed.

Rockhound State Park
P. O. Box 1064
Deming, NM
505-546-6182
This park is a favorite for rockhounds, and it also has trails varying in difficulty and elevations that offer breathtaking scenery. Dogs

of all sizes are allowed at no additional fee. Dogs may not be left unattended, and they must be on no more than a 10 foot leash, and be cleaned up after. Dogs are allowed on the trails. The camping and tent areas also allow dogs. There is a dog walk area at the campground. Multiple dogs may be allowed.

Eagle Nest

Cimmarron Canyon State Park
2959 H 64
Eagle Nest, NM
505-377-6271
This high mountain park of over 33,000 acres is also part of the Colin Neblett Wildlife Area, and offers a variety of nature study and recreation. Dogs of all sizes are allowed at no additional fee. Dogs may not be left unattended, and they must be on no more than a 10 foot leash and be cleaned up after. Dogs are allowed on the trails. The camping and tent areas also allow dogs. There is a dog walk area at the campground. Multiple dogs may be allowed.

Elephant Butte

Elephant Butte Lake
Box 13; H 195/171
Elephant Butte, NM
505-744-5421
Scenic Elephant Butte Lake can be described as educational, recreational and pre-historic. Dogs of all sizes are allowed at no additional fee. Dogs may not be left unattended, and they must be leashed and cleaned up after. Dogs are allowed on the trails. The camping and tent areas also allow dogs. There is a dog walk area at the campground. Multiple dogs may be allowed.

Farmington

Downs RV Park
5701 H 64
Farmington, NM
505-325-7094
Dogs of all sizes are allowed. There are no additional pet fees. Dogs may not be left unattended outside, and they must be leashed and cleaned up after. The camping and tent areas also allow dogs. There is a dog walk area at the campground. Multiple dogs may be allowed.

Faywood

City of Rocks State Park
Box 50; On H 61
Faywood, NM
505-536-2800
This park is home to some of the most unusual rock formations in the world, and since it is so dark the park has also implemented a Stars-N-Parks program with a Star Observatory. Cactus gardens and scenic hiking trails are also an attraction. Dogs of all sizes are allowed at no additional fee. Dogs may not be left unattended, and they must be leashed and cleaned up after. Dogs are allowed on the trails. The camping and tent areas also allow dogs. There is a dog walk area at the campground. Multiple dogs may be allowed.

Fort Sumner

Sumner Lake State Park
HC 64, Box 125
Fort Sumner, NM
505-355-2541
This historical park is popular for water activities and nature study. Dogs of all sizes are allowed at no additional fee. Dogs may not be left unattended, and they must be leashed and cleaned up after. The camping and tent areas also allow dogs. There is a dog walk area at the campground. Multiple dogs may be allowed.

Gallup

USA RV Park
2925 W H 66
Gallup, NM
505-863-5021
Dogs of all sizes are allowed. There is a pet policy to sign at check in and there are no additional pet fees. County ordinance requires that, by law, dogs be walked to the dog walk area to defecate and/or urinate. Dogs may not be left unattended outside, and they must be quiet, well behaved, be on no more than a 6 foot leash, and be cleaned up after. Dogs must be walked on asphalt only-no other surfaces, and dogs are not allowed to approach other campers or their pets. Dogs are not allowed by the office, cook areas, telephones, playground, restrooms, picnic tables, or the laundries. Adults only may walk the dogs, and dog cages or pens are not allowed. There are some breed

restrictions. There is a dog walk area at the campground. Multiple dogs may be allowed.

Guadalupita

Coyote Creek State Park
Box 477, MM 17 H 434
Guadalupita, NM
505-387-2328
This scenic park is surround by forests of spruce, pine, and fields of wildflowers, and the creek is considered to be the best stocked in the state. Dogs of all sizes are allowed at no additional fee. Dogs may not be left unattended, and they must be quiet, be on no more than a 10 foot leash, and be cleaned up after. Dogs are allowed on the trails. The camping and tent areas also allow dogs. There is a dog walk area at the campground. Multiple dogs may be allowed.

Morphy Lake State Park
Box 477; Morphy Lake Road
Guadalupita, NM
505-387-2328
This secluded, pack-in/out park with a well stocked lake, is reached by foot or a high clearance vehicle. There is no drinking water available, and it is suggested to check road conditions before going. Dogs of all sizes are allowed at no additional fee. Dogs may not be left unattended, and they must be on no more than a 10 foot leash at all times, and be cleaned up after. Dogs are allowed on the trails. This campground is closed during the off-season. The camping and tent areas also allow dogs. There is a dog walk area at the campground. There are no electric or water hookups at the campground. Multiple dogs may be allowed.

Jemez Springs

Fenton Lake State Park
455 Fenton Lake Road
Jemez Springs, NM
505-829-3630
This park, surrounded by pine forest with a 35 acre lake, sits at an elevation of 7900 feet, and offers a variety of recreation for all seasons. Dogs of all sizes are allowed at no additional fee. Dogs may not be left unattended, and they must be leashed and cleaned up after. Dogs are allowed on the trails. The camping and tent areas also allow dogs. There is a dog walk area at the

campground. There are no water hookups at the campground. Multiple dogs may be allowed.

Las Cruces

Hacienda RV and Rally Resort
740 Stern Drive
Las Cruces, NM
888-686-9090
Dogs of all sizes are allowed. There are no additional pet fees. Dogs must be leashed and cleaned up after. There is a fenced in area where dogs may be off lead. There is a dog walk area at the campground. Multiple dogs may be allowed.

The Coachlight Inn and RV Park
301 S Motel Blvd
Las Cruces, NM
505-526-3301
Dogs of all sizes are allowed. There are no additional pet fees for the RV sites. There is an additional $5 per night per pet fee for small dogs at the inn, and an additional $10 per night per pet fee for medium to large dogs. There are only 2 dogs allowed per room, and no more than 3 for the RV area. This is an RV only park. There is a dog walk area at the campground.

Las Vegas

Storrie Lake State Park
HC 33, Box 109 #2
Las Vegas, NM
505-425-7278
This park with 1,100 acres of lake surface, offers a wide variety of water recreation, an interesting history, and plenty of trails. Dogs of all sizes are allowed at no additional fee. Dogs may not be left unattended, and they must be on no more than a 10 foot leash, and be cleaned up after. Dogs are allowed on the trails. This campground is closed during the off-season. The camping and tent areas also allow dogs. There is a dog walk area at the campground. Multiple dogs may be allowed.

Logan

Ute Lake State Park
1800 540 Loop
Logan, NM
505-487-2284
Nature study, round-the-clock fishing, scenic trails, and a variety of land and water recreation make this a popular park. Dogs of all sizes are

allowed at no additional fee. Dogs may not be left unattended, and they must be leashed and cleaned up after. Dogs are allowed on the trails unless otherwise marked. The camping and tent areas also allow dogs. There is a dog walk area at the campground. Multiple dogs may be allowed.

Los Ojos

Heron Lake State Park
Box 159; MM 6 H 95
Los Ojos, NM
505-588-7470
Ideal for both winter and summer sports at 7200 feet, this scenic park also has a trail that leads to a suspension bridge that crosses the river. Dogs of all sizes are allowed at no additional fee. Dogs may not be left unattended, and they must be leashed and cleaned up after. Dogs are allowed on the trails. The camping and tent areas also allow dogs. There is a dog walk area at the campground. Multiple dogs may be allowed.

Mountainair

Manzano Mountains State Park
HC66, Box 202
Mountainair, NM
505-847-2820
This park of 160 acres at 7600 foot altitude has a wide variety of trees and is an important bird fly zone. The park will also provide a field check list for the birds. Dogs of all sizes are allowed at no additional fee. Dogs may not be left unattended, and they must quiet, well behaved, be on no more than a 10 foot leash, and be cleaned up after. Dogs are allowed on the trails. This campground is closed during the off-season. The camping and tent areas also allow dogs. There is a dog walk area at the campground. There are no water hookups at the campground. Multiple dogs may be allowed.

Nageezi

Chaco Culture National Historical Park
P. O. Box 220
Nageezi, NM
505-786-7014
This park has a rich cultural history; it is part of the Chaco Night Sky Program, and a variety of trails here

will lead you by petroglyphs and historic writings. There are no services here, so you must bring your own food and water. Dogs of all sizes are allowed at no additional fee. Dogs may not be left unattended, and they must be quiet, well behaved, leashed, and cleaned up after. Dogs are allowed on the trails unless otherwise marked. The camping and tent areas also allow dogs. There is a dog walk area at the campground. There are no electric or water hookups at the campground. Multiple dogs may be allowed.

Navajo Dam

Navajo Lake State Park
1448 H 511 #1
Navajo Dam, NM
505-632-2278
With over 21,000 land acres and an almost 16,000 acre lake, this park offers interpretive exhibits, 2 full service marinas, and a wide variety of land and water recreation. Dogs of all sizes are allowed at no additional fee. Dogs may not be left unattended, and they must be on no more than a 10 foot leash, and be cleaned up after. Dogs are allowed on the trails. The camping and tent areas also allow dogs. There is a dog walk area at the campground. Multiple dogs may be allowed.

Portales

Oasis State Park
1891 Oasis Road
Portales, NM
505-356-5331
This park of 193 acres, set among the cottonwood trees and shifting sand dunes, offers a small fishing lake and more than 80 species of birds. Dogs of all sizes are allowed at no additional fee. Dogs may not be left unattended outside or for long periods inside, and they must be on no more than a 10 foot leash, and be cleaned up after. Dogs are not allowed in the water, but they are allowed on the trails. The camping and tent areas also allow dogs. There is a dog walk area at the campground. Multiple dogs may be allowed.

Prewitt

Bluewater Lake State Park
Box 3419/ at end of H 412
Prewitt, NM

505-876-2391
This year round recreational park offers great fishing, a wide variety of birds, a visitor's center, and plenty of hiking trails. Dogs are allowed at no additional fee. Dogs must be leashed and cleaned up after. Dogs are allowed on the trails. The camping and tent areas also allow dogs. There is a dog walk area at the campground. There are no water hookups at the campground. Multiple dogs may be allowed.

Radium Springs

Leasburg Dam State Park
P.O. Box 6
Radium Springs, NM
505-524-4068
This park along the Rio Grande offers a variety of land and water recreation. Dogs of all sizes are allowed at no additional fee. Dogs may not be left unattended, and they must be leashed and cleaned up after. Dogs are allowed on the trails. The camping and tent areas also allow dogs. There is a dog walk area at the campground. There are no water hookups at the campground. Multiple dogs may be allowed.

Raton

Sugarite Canyon State Park
HCR 63, Box 386
Raton, NM
505-445-5607
With 3,600 land acres at an altitude of 7,800 feet and a lake with 120 acres, this scenic park provides a variety of year round recreation. Dogs of all sizes are allowed at no additional fee. Dogs may not be left unattended outside or left in the unit for long periods, and they must be leashed and cleaned up after. Dogs are not allowed in public swim areas or in buildings. Dogs are allowed on the trails. The camping and tent areas also allow dogs. There is a dog walk area at the campground. Multiple dogs may be allowed.

Red River

River Ranch
1501 W Main (H 38)
Red River, NM
505-754-2293
Dogs of all sizes are allowed. There are no additional pet fees. Dogs may not be left unattended outside, and they must be quiet, well behaved,

leashed and cleaned up after. This RV park is closed during the off-season. The camping and tent areas also allow dogs. There is a dog walk area at the campground. Multiple dogs may be allowed.

Rodeo

Rustys RV Ranch
22 Estrella Parkway
Rodeo, NM
505-557-2526
Dogs of all sizes are allowed. There are no additional pet fees. Dogs may not be left unattended outside, and they must be leashed in camp, and cleaned up after. Dogs may be off lead on the trails if they are under voice command and will not chase wildlife. They have 1 pet friendly rental trailer. The camping and tent areas also allow dogs. There is a dog walk area at the campground. Multiple dogs may be allowed.

Roswell

Bottomless Lakes State Park
HC 12, Box 1200; On H 409
Roswell, NM
505-624-6058
This park has 1400 acres and 7 small lakes and offers a variety of recreational pursuits. Dogs of all sizes are allowed at no additional fee. Dogs may not be left unattended, and they must be leashed and cleaned up after. The camping and tent areas also allow dogs. There is a dog walk area at the campground. Multiple dogs may be allowed.

Red Barn RV Park
2806 E 2nd Street
Roswell, NM
505-623-4897
Dogs of all sizes are allowed. There are no additional pet fees. Dogs must be leashed and cleaned up after. There is a dog walk area at the campground. Multiple dogs may be allowed.

Town and Country RV Park
331 W Brasher Road
Roswell, NM
505-624-1833
Dogs of all sizes are allowed. There are no additional pet fees. Dogs may not be tied up or left unattended outside, and they must be leashed and cleaned up after.

The camping and tent areas also allow dogs. There is a dog walk area at the campground. Multiple dogs may be allowed.

Santa Fe

Hyde Memorial State Park
740 Hyde Park Road
Santa Fe, NM
505-983-7175
Located in the Sangre de Cristo Mountains at 8500 feet, this park offers beautiful scenery, quiet settings, and year round recreation. Dogs of all sizes are allowed at no additional fee. Dogs may not be left unattended, and they must be leashed and cleaned up after. Dogs are allowed on the trails. This campground is closed during the off-season. The camping and tent areas also allow dogs. There is a dog walk area at the campground. Multiple dogs may be allowed.

Rancheros de Santa Fe
736 Old Las Vegas H
Santa Fe, NM
800-426-9259
Dogs of all sizes are allowed. There are no additional pet fees. Dogs may not be left unattended, and they must be quiet, leashed, and cleaned up after. There is a fenced in Doggy Corral for off lead. The camping and tent areas also allow dogs. There is a dog walk area at the campground. Dogs are allowed in the camping cabins. Multiple dogs may be allowed.

Santa Fe National Forest
1474 Rodeo Road
Santa Fe, NM
505-438-7840
This forest of 1.6 million acres at an altitude of over 13,000 feet. It offers diverse ecosystems that support a large variety of plants, fish, mammals, bird species, and recreation. Dogs of all sizes are allowed at no additional fee. Dogs may not be left unattended, and they must be leashed and cleaned up after. Dogs are allowed on the trails. The camping and tent areas also allow dogs. There is a dog walk area at the campground. There are no electric or water hookups at the campground. Multiple dogs may be allowed.

Santa Fe Skies RV Park
14 Browncastle Ranch

Santa Fe, NM
505-473-5946
Dogs of all sizes are allowed. There are no additional pet fees. Dogs must be cleaned up after. Dogs may be off leash if they are friendly and under owner's control. Dogs must be quiet and well behaved. There is a dog walk area at the campground. Multiple dogs may be allowed.

Trailer Ranch RV Resort
3471 Cerrillos
Santa Fe, NM
505-471-9970
Dogs of all sizes are allowed. There are no additional pet fees. Dogs must be quiet, well behaved, leashed, and cleaned up after. This is a 55 plus resort so at least one of the campers must be 55 or older. There are some breed restrictions. There is a dog walk area at the campground. Multiple dogs may be allowed.

Santa Rosa

Santa Rosa Campground
2136 Historic H 66
Santa Rosa, NM
505-472-3126
Dogs of all sizes are allowed. There are no additional pet fees. Dogs may be walked anywhere in the park, but they must be taken to the dog walk to relieve themselves. Dogs must be leashed and cleaned up after. The camping and tent areas also allow dogs. There is a dog walk area at the campground. Dogs are allowed in the camping cabins. Multiple dogs may be allowed.

Santa Rosa Lake State Park
P.O. Box 384
Santa Rosa, NM
505-472-3110
With 500 land acres and 3,800 lake acres, this park offers a variety of land and water recreation and nature study. Dogs of all sizes are allowed at no additional fee. Dogs may not be left unattended, and they must be on no more than a 10 foot leash, and be cleaned up after. Dogs are allowed on the trails. The camping and tent areas also allow dogs. There is a dog walk area at the campground. Multiple dogs may be allowed.

Silver City

Gila National Forest

3005 Camino Del Bosque
Silver City, NM
505-388-8201
This forest has 6 ranger districts, covers 3.3 million acres, and has diverse ecosystems that support a large variety of plants, fish, mammals, bird species, and recreation. Dogs of all sizes are allowed at no additional fee. Dogs may not be left unattended, and they must be leashed and cleaned up after. Dogs are not allowed at the cliff dwellings or on the trail to the dwellings, however, they are allowed on the other trails unless marked. The camping and tent areas also allow dogs. There is a dog walk area at the campground. There are no electric or water hookups at the campground. Multiple dogs may be allowed.

Sumner

Valley View RV Park
401 E Sumner Avenue
Sumner, NM
505-355-2380
Dogs of all sizes are allowed. There are no additional pet fees. Dogs may not be left unattended outside, and they must be leashed and cleaned up after. This park only closes for the first 2 weeks in January each year. There is a dog walk area at the campground. Multiple dogs may be allowed.

Taos

Carson National Forest
208 Cruz Alta
Taos, NM
505-758-6200
This forest has 6 ranger districts, covers 1.5 million acres, is home to the states highest mountain at 13,161 feet, and it's diverse ecosystems support a large variety of plants, animals, and recreation. Dogs of all sizes are allowed at no additional fee. Dogs may not be left unattended, and they must be leashed and cleaned up after. Dogs are allowed on trails. The camping and tent areas also allow dogs. There is a dog walk area at the campground. There are no electric or water hookups at the campground. Multiple dogs may be allowed.

Enchanted Moon RV Park and Campground
HC 71 Box 59

Taos, NM
505-758-3338
Dogs of all sizes are allowed. There are no additional pet fees. Dogs must be leashed and cleaned up after. This RV park is closed during the off-season. The camping and tent areas also allow dogs. There is a dog walk area at the campground.

Tierra Amarilla

El Vado Lake State Park
Box 367; El Vado State Park Road
Tierra Amarilla, NM
505-588-7247
With over 1700 land acres and a lake with 3200 acres, this park has a variety of nature study and land and water recreation. Dogs of all sizes are allowed at no additional fee. Dogs may not be left unattended, and they must be on no more than a 10 foot leash, and be cleaned up after. Dogs are allowed on the trails. The camping and tent areas also allow dogs. There is a dog walk area at the campground. There are no water hookups at the campground. Multiple dogs may be allowed.

Tijeras

Cibola National Forest
11776 H 337
Tijeras, NM
505-346-3900
This forest has 6 ranger districts, almost 2 million acres with 5 wilderness areas, and diverse ecosystems that support a large variety of plants, animals, and recreation. Dogs of all sizes are allowed at no additional fee. Dogs may not be left unattended, and they must be leashed and cleaned up after. Dogs are not allowed in buildings, but they are allowed on the trails. The camping and tent areas also allow dogs. There is a dog walk area at the campground. There are no electric or water hookups at the campground. Multiple dogs may be allowed.

Truth or Consequences

Cielo Vista RV Resort
501 S Broadway
Truth or Consequences, NM
505-894-3738
Dogs of all sizes are allowed. There are no additional pet fees. Dogs may not be left unattended, and they must be quiet, well behaved, be on no

more than a 6 foot leash, and cleaned up after. There is a dog walk area at the campground. Multiple dogs may be allowed.

Tucumcari

Mountain Road RV Park
1700 Mountain Road
Tucumcari, NM
505-461-9628
Dogs of all sizes are allowed. There are no additional pet fees. Dogs may be walked anywhere in the park, but they must be taken to one of the dog walks to relieve themselves. Dogs may not be left unattended outside, and they must be leashed and cleaned up after. The camping and tent areas also allow dogs. There is a dog walk area at the campground. Multiple dogs may be allowed.

Villanueva

Villanueva State Park
P. O. Box 40
Villanueva, NM
505-421-2957
A scenic, riverside canyon park, there are a variety of land and water recreational pursuits and places to explore. Dogs of all sizes are allowed at no additional fee. Dogs may not be left unattended, and they must be on no more than a 10 foot leash, and be cleaned up after. Dogs are not allowed in buildings, but they are allowed on the trails. This campground is closed during the off-season. The camping and tent areas also allow dogs. Dogs are allowed in the camping cabins. Multiple dogs may be allowed.

White's City

White City Resort
17 Carlsbad Caverns Highway
White's City, NM
800-228-3767
Dogs of all sizes are allowed. There are no additional pet fees for the tent or RV sites. There is a $10 per night per pet additional fee for the Walnut Inn. Dogs must be quiet, well behaved, leashed, and cleaned up after. The camping and tent areas also allow dogs. There is a dog walk area at the campground. Multiple dogs may be allowed.

New York Listings

Adirondacks

Schroon River Resort
969 E Schroon River Road
Diamond Point, NY
518-623-3954
Dogs of all sizes are allowed. There are no additional pet fees. Current shot records and proof of insurance is required for some breeds. Dogs must be leashed and cleaned up after. The camping and tent areas also allow dogs. There is a dog walk area at the campground. Multiple dogs may be allowed.

Lake George RV Park
74 State H 149
Lake George, NY
518-792-3775
Dogs of all sizes are allowed. There are no additional pet fees. Dogs must be leashed, cleaned up after, and not left unattended. The camping and tent areas also allow dogs. There is a dog walk area at the campground. 2 dogs may be allowed.

KOA Lake George/Saratoga
564 Lake Avenue
Lake Luzerne, NY
518-696-2615
Dogs of all sizes are allowed. There are no additional pet fees. Dogs must be leashed and cleaned up after. There are some breed restrictions. This RV park is closed during the off-season. The camping and tent areas also allow dogs. There is a dog walk area at the campground. Multiple dogs may be allowed.

Plattsburgh RV Park
7182 H 9N
Plattsburgh, NY
518-563-3915
Dogs of all sizes are allowed. There are no additional pet fees. Dogs must be well behaved and under control of owner. Dogs must be leashed and cleaned up after. The camping and tent areas also allow dogs. There is a dog walk area at the campground. Dogs are allowed in the camping cabins. Multiple dogs may be allowed.

KOA Lake Placid/Whiteface Mountain
77 Foxfarm Road

Wilmington, NY
518-946-7878
Dogs of all sizes are allowed in the camp and RV sites, but only one dog up to 40 pounds is allowed in the cabin. There are no additional pet fees. Dogs may not be left unattended and must have a valid rabies certificate. They must be leashed and cleaned up after. There are some breed restrictions. This RV park is closed during the off-season. The camping and tent areas also allow dogs. There is a dog walk area at the campground. Dogs are allowed in the camping cabins.

Alexandria

Keywaydin State Park
45165 H 12
Alexandria, NY
315-482-3331
Dogs of all sizes are allowed. There are no additional pet fees. Dogs may not be left unattended, they must have a current rabies certificate and shot records, be well behaved, on no more than a 6 foot leash, and be cleaned up after. Dogs are allowed on the trails, but not in the picnic or bathroom areas. This campground is closed during the off-season. The camping and tent areas also allow dogs. There is a dog walk area at the campground. There are no water hookups at the campground. Multiple dogs may be allowed.

Austerlitz

Woodland Hills Campground
386 Foghill Road
Austerlitz, NY
518-392-3557
Dogs of all sizes are allowed. There are no additional pet fees. Dogs must be quiet, leashed, and cleaned up after. The camping and tent areas also allow dogs. There is a dog walk area at the campground. Multiple dogs may be allowed.

Averill Park

Alps Family Campground
1928 State H 43
Averill Park, NY
518-674-5565
Dogs of all sizes are allowed. There are no additional pet fees. Dogs must have proof of rabies shots, be leashed, cleaned up after, and not left unattended. The camping and tent areas also allow dogs. There is

a dog walk area at the campground. Multiple dogs may be allowed.

Binghampton

Kellystone Park
51 Hawkins Road
Nineveh, NY
607-639-1090
Dogs of all sizes are allowed, however some breeds are not. There are no additional pet fees. Dogs must be quiet, well behaved, leashed, and cleaned up after. The camping and tent areas also allow dogs. There is a dog walk area at the campground. Multiple dogs may be allowed.

Brocton

Lake Erie State Park
5905 H 5
Brocton, NY
716-792-9214
Dogs of all sizes are allowed. There are no additional pet fees. Dogs may not be left unattended, they must have a current rabies certificate and shot records, be leashed, and cleaned up after. Dogs are allowed on the trails and down by the lake, but they are not allowed to be tied to the trees. This campground is closed during the off-season. The camping and tent areas also allow dogs. There is a dog walk area at the campground. Dogs are allowed in the camping cabins. There are no water hookups at the campground. Multiple dogs may be allowed.

Cambridge

Lake Lauderdale Campground
744 Country Route 61
Cambridge, NY
518-677-8855
Dogs of all sizes are allowed. There are no additional pet fees. Dogs must be well behaved, leashed, and cleaned up after. Dogs are not to be left unattended. The camping and tent areas also allow dogs. There is a dog walk area at the campground. Multiple dogs may be allowed.

Castile

Letchworth State Park
#1 Letchworth
Castile, NY
585-493-3600
Dogs of all sizes are allowed. There

are no additional pet fees. Dogs may not be left unattended, they must have a current rabies certificate and shot records, be quiet, on no more than a 6 foot leash, and be cleaned up after. Dogs are allowed on the outside trails, but they must stay in the pet area of the park, and they are not allowed in any of the buildings. This campground is closed during the off-season. The camping and tent areas also allow dogs. There is a dog walk area at the campground. There are no water hookups at the campground. Multiple dogs may be allowed.

Catskills

Nickerson Park Campground
378 Stryker Road
Gilboa, NY
607-588-7327
Dogs of all sizes are allowed. There are no additional pet fees. Dogs must be quiet, well behaved, leashed, and cleaned up after. This establishment also shares the New York trail system. The camping and tent areas also allow dogs. There is a dog walk area at the campground. Multiple dogs may be allowed.

Whip-O-Will Family Campsite
644 H 31
Roundtop, NY
518-622-3277
Dogs of all sizes are allowed. There are no additional pet fees. Dogs must be kept under control, on a leash, and cleaned up after. The camping and tent areas also allow dogs. There is a dog walk area at the campground. Multiple dogs may be allowed.

Chateauga

High Falls Park Campground
34 Cemetary Road
Chateauga, NY
518-497-3156
Dogs of all sizes are allowed. There are no additional pet fees. Dogs must be kept leashed and cleaned up after. The camping and tent areas also allow dogs. There is a dog walk area at the campground. Multiple dogs may be allowed.

Chenango Forks

Chenango Valley State Park
153 State Park Road

Chenango Forks, NY
607-648-5251
Dogs of all sizes are allowed. There are no additional pet fees. Dogs may not be left unattended, they must have a current rabies certificate and shot records. Dogs must be quiet, leashed, and cleaned up after. Dogs are allowed on the trails, but not on the beach or in the water. Although the campground is seasonal, the park is open year round. This campground is closed during the off-season. The camping and tent areas also allow dogs. There is a dog walk area at the campground. Dogs are allowed in the camping cabins. Multiple dogs may be allowed.

Clayton

Grass Point State Park
36661 Cedar Point State Park Drive
Clayton, NY
315-686-4472
Dogs of all sizes are allowed. There are no additional pet fees. Dogs may not be left unattended, they must have a current rabies certificate and shot records, be well behaved, on no more than a 6 foot leash, and be cleaned up after. Dogs are allowed on the trails, but not in the picnic or bathroom areas. This campground is closed during the off-season. The camping and tent areas also allow dogs. There is a dog walk area at the campground. There are no water hookups at the campground. Multiple dogs may be allowed.

Merry Knoll 1000 Islands Campground
38115 H 12E
Clayton, NY
315-686-3055
Dogs of all sizes are allowed. There are no additional pet fees. Dogs must be quiet, leashed, and cleaned up after. The camping and tent areas also allow dogs. There is a dog walk area at the campground. Multiple dogs may be allowed.

Cooperstown

KOA Cooperstown
565 Ostrander Road
Cooperstown, NY
315-858-0236
Dogs of all sizes are allowed. There are no additional pet fees. Dogs are allowed at the cabins but must be kept off the beds. There is a large field where dogs can run off leash if

they will come to your command. Otherwise dogs must be leashed and cleaned up after. Dogs may not be left unattended except for short periods, and only if the dog is well behaved and comfortable with a short absence. This RV park is closed during the off-season. The camping and tent areas also allow dogs. There is a dog walk area at the campground. Dogs are allowed in the camping cabins. Multiple dogs may be allowed.

Shadowbrook Campground
2149 County H 31
Cooperstown, NY
607-264-8431
Dogs of all sizes are allowed, however some breeds are not. There are no additional pet fees. Dogs must be leashed and cleaned up after. The camping and tent areas also allow dogs. There is a dog walk area at the campground. 2 dogs may be allowed.

Corinth

Alpine Lake RV Resort
78 Heath Road
Corinth, NY
518-654-6260
Dogs of all sizes are allowed, however some breeds are not. There are no additional pet fees. Dogs must have proof of rabies shots, be leashed, and cleaned up after. The camping and tent areas also allow dogs. There is a dog walk area at the campground. 2 dogs may be allowed.

Dansville

Sugar Creek Glen Campground
11288 Poagf Hole Road
Dansville, NY
585-335-6294
Dogs of all sizes are allowed. There is a pet policy to sign at check in and there are no additional pet fees. Dogs must not be left unattended for very long periods, and only if they are quiet and well behaved. Dogs must be leashed and cleaned up after. The camping and tent areas also allow dogs. There is a dog walk area at the campground. Dogs are allowed in the camping cabins. Multiple dogs may be allowed.

Dexter

Black River Bay Campground

16129 Foster Park Road (Box541)
Dexter, NY
315-639-3735
Dogs of all sizes are allowed, however only 2 dogs are allowed per site or 3 dogs are ok if they are all small. There are no additional pet fees. Dogs must be leashed and cleaned up after. The camping and tent areas also allow dogs. There is a dog walk area at the campground.

Fair Haven

Fair Haven Beach State Park
14985 Park Road
Fair Haven, NY
315-947-5205
Dogs of all sizes are allowed. There are no additional pet fees. Dogs may not be left unattended, they must have a current rabies certificate and shot records, be on no more than a 6 foot leash, and be cleaned up after. Dogs are allowed on the trails, but they are not allowed on any sandy areas, at the beach, or in the water. Although the campground is seasonal, some cabins remain open all year. This campground is closed during the off-season. The camping and tent areas also allow dogs. There is a dog walk area at the campground. Dogs are allowed in the camping cabins. There are no water hookups at the campground. Multiple dogs may be allowed.

Farmington

KOA Canandaigua/Rochester
5374 FarmingtonTownline Road
Farmington, NY
585-398-3582
Dogs of all sizes are allowed. There is no additional pet fee for RV or tent sites, however there is a $25 refundable pet deposit when renting the cabins. Dogs may not be left unattended; they must be quiet, well behaved, leashed, and cleaned up after. There are some breed restrictions. This RV park is closed during the off-season. The camping and tent areas also allow dogs. There is a dog walk area at the campground. Dogs are allowed in the camping cabins. Multiple dogs may be allowed.

Finger Lakes

Hickory Hill Family Camping Resort

7531 Country Route 13
Bath, NY
607-776-4345
Dogs of all sizes are allowed. There are no additional fees for pets staying at the campsites, however there is a $20 one time fee per unit for the rentals. Dogs are not to be left unattended at the site, must be leashed at all times, and cleaned up after. The camping and tent areas also allow dogs. There is a dog walk area at the campground. Dogs are allowed in the camping cabins. 2 dogs may be allowed.

Ferenbaugh Campsites
4248 State H 414
Corning, NY
607-962-6193
Dogs up to 25 pounds are allowed. There are no additional pet fees. Dogs must be leashed, cleaned up after, and may not be left unattended. The camping and tent areas also allow dogs. There is a dog walk area at the campground. Dogs are allowed in the camping cabins. 2 dogs may be allowed.

Spruce Row Campsite & RV Park
2271 Kraft Road
Ithaca, NY
607-387-9225
Dogs of all sizes are allowed. There are no additional pet fees. Dogs must be under control of owners. The camping and tent areas also allow dogs. There is a dog walk area at the campground. Multiple dogs may be allowed.

Florida

Black Bear Campground
197 Wheeler Road
Florida, NY
845-651-7717
Dogs of all sizes are allowed, however some breeds are not. There are no additional pet fees. Dogs must be well behaved, leashed, and cleaned up after. The camping and tent areas also allow dogs. There is a dog walk area at the campground. Dogs are allowed in the camping cabins. 2 dogs may be allowed.

Franklin

KOA Unadilla/Oneonta
242 Union Church Road
Franklin, NY
607-369-9030
Dogs of all sizes are allowed. There are no additional pet fees. Dogs may

not be left unattended, and must be leashed and cleaned up after. This RV park is closed during the off-season. The camping and tent areas also allow dogs. There is a dog walk area at the campground. 2 dogs may be allowed.

Gansevoort

Lake George Resort
427 Fortsville Road
Gansevoort, NY
518-792-3519
Dogs of all sizes are allowed. There are no additional pet fees. Proof of up to date shots and insurance papers for some breeds is required. Dogs must be leashed and cleaned up after. The camping and tent areas also allow dogs. There is a dog walk area at the campground. Multiple dogs may be allowed.

Gardiner

Jellystone Park
50 Bevier Road
Gardiner, NY
845-255-5193
Dogs of all sizes are allowed. There are no additional pet fees. Dogs must be quiet at night, be leashed, and cleaned up after. This RV park is closed during the off-season. There is a dog walk area at the campground. 2 dogs may be allowed.

Garrattsville

Yogi Bear Jellystone Park at Crystal Lake
111 East Turtle Lake Road
Garrattsville, NY
607-965-8265
Dogs of all sizes are allowed, except in the rentals. There is no fee if there are only 2 dogs; if there are more, it is $1.50 per night per pet additional fee. Dogs must have a current rabies certificate, be leashed, and cleaned up after. Dogs are not allowed at the pool, pavilion, playground, the rentals, or in the buildings. This RV park is closed during the off-season. The camping and tent areas also allow dogs. There is a dog walk area at the campground. Multiple dogs may be allowed.

Greenfield Center

Sarasota Springs Resort

265 Brigham Road
Greenfield Center, NY
518-893-0537
Dogs of all sizes are allowed. There are no additional pet fees. Dogs must have proof of shots, be leashed, and cleaned up after. The camping and tent areas also allow dogs. There is a dog walk area at the campground. Multiple dogs may be allowed.

Greenfield Park

Skyway Camping Resort
99 Mountain Dale Road
Greenfield Park, NY
845-647-5747
Dogs of all sizes are allowed, however some breeds are not. There are no additional pet fees. Dogs must be leashed and cleaned up after. The camping and tent areas also allow dogs. There is a dog walk area at the campground. 2 dogs may be allowed.

Greenport

Eastern Long Island Kampgrounds
On Queen Street
Greenport, NY
631-477-0022
Dogs of all sizes are allowed, however some breeds are not. There are no additional pet fees. Dogs must have proof of rabies shots. Dogs must be leashed, cleaned up after, and not left unattended. The camping and tent areas also allow dogs. There is a dog walk area at the campground. 2 dogs may be allowed.

Henderson Harbor

Association Island RV Resort & Marina
Snowshoe Road
Henderson Harbor, NY
315-938-5655
Dogs of all sizes are allowed, however some breeds are not. There are no additional pet fees. Dogs must be leashed, cleaned up after, and have proof of rabies shots. The camping and tent areas also allow dogs. There is a dog walk area at the campground. Multiple dogs may be allowed.

Herkimer

KOA Herkimer
800 Mohawk Street
Herkimer, NY
315-891-7355
Dogs of all sizes are allowed. There are no additional pet fees. Dog must be leashed and cleaned up after. This RV park is closed during the off-season. The camping and tent areas also allow dogs. There is a dog walk area at the campground. Multiple dogs may be allowed.

Mexico

Jellystone Park
601 County Road 16
Mexico, NY
315-963-7096
One dog of any size is allowed, some breeds are not. There are no additional pet fees. Dogs must be walked in the pet walk area only, not around the park. Dogs may not be left unattended and must be leashed and cleaned up after. This RV park is closed during the off-season. The camping and tent areas also allow dogs. There is a dog walk area at the campground.

Mount Vision

Meadow-Vale Campsites
505 Gilbert Lake Road
Mount Vision, NY
607-293-8802
Dogs of all sizes are allowed, however some breeds are not. There are no additional pet fees. Dogs must be leashed and cleaned up after. The camping and tent areas also allow dogs. There is a dog walk area at the campground.

Natural Bridge

KOA Natural Bridge/Watertown
6081 State H 3
Natural Bridge, NY
315-644-4880
Dogs of all sizes are allowed. There are no additional pet fees. Dogs must be leashed and cleaned up after. This RV park is closed during the off-season. The camping and tent areas also allow dogs. There is a dog walk area at the campground. Multiple dogs may be allowed.

New York

Liberty Harbor RV Park
11 Marin Blvd

Jersey City, NJ
201-387-7500
Dogs of all sizes are allowed. There are no additional pet fees. Dogs must be leashed, cleaned up after, and not be left unattended. There is a dog walk area at the campground. Multiple dogs may be allowed.

North Java

Jellystone Park
5204 Youngers Road
North Java, NY
585-457-9644
Dogs of all sizes are allowed. There are no additional pet fees unless staying in the pet friendly Boo Boo Chalets. Then there would be an additional $25 per unit. Dogs must be quiet, well behaved, leashed and cleaned up after. Dogs may not be left unattended. This RV park is closed during the off-season. The camping and tent areas also allow dogs. There is a dog walk area at the campground. Dogs are allowed in the camping cabins. 2 dogs may be allowed.

Oxford

Bowman Lake State Park
745 Bilven Sherman Road
Oxford, NY
607-334-2718
Dogs of all sizes are allowed. There are no additional pet fees. Dogs may not be left unattended and they must have a current rabies certificate and shot record. Dogs must be quiet, well behaved, on no more than a 6 foot leash, and be cleaned up after. Dogs are allowed on the trails, but not on the beach or in any of the buildings. The camping and tent areas also allow dogs. There is a dog walk area at the campground. There are no electric or water hookups at the campground. Multiple dogs may be allowed.

Plattekill

KOA Newburgh/NYC North
119 Freetown Highway
Plattekill, NY
845-564-2836
Dogs of all sizes are allowed. There are no additional pet fees. Dogs must be leashed and cleaned up after. This RV park is closed during the off-season. The camping and tent areas also allow dogs. There is a dog walk area at the campground.

Dogs are allowed in the camping cabins. Multiple dogs may be allowed.

Pulaski

Brennan Beach RV Resort
80 Brennan's Beach Road
Pulaski, NY
315-298-2242
Dogs of all sizes are allowed. There are no additional pet fees. Dogs must be leased and cleaned up after. The camping and tent areas also allow dogs. There is a dog walk area at the campground. 2 dogs may be allowed.

Selkirk Sores State Park
7101 H 3
Pulaski, NY
315-298-5737
Dogs of all sizes are allowed. There are no additional pet fees. Dogs may not be left unattended, and they must have a current rabies certificate and shot record, be on no more than a 6 foot leash, and be cleaned up after. Dogs are allowed on the trails and at the beach. This campground is closed during the off-season. The camping and tent areas also allow dogs. There is a dog walk area at the campground. Dogs are allowed in the camping cabins. There are no water hookups at the campground. Multiple dogs may be allowed.

Randolph

Pope Haven Campgrounds
11948 Pope Road
Randolph, NY
716-358-4900
Dogs of all sizes are allowed. There are no additional pet fees. Dogs must have proof of rabies shots, and be leashed and cleaned up after. They must also be quiet and well behaved. The camping and tent areas also allow dogs. There is a dog walk area at the campground. Multiple dogs may be allowed.

Rochester

Genesee Country Campgrounds
40 Flinthill Road
Caledonia, NY
585-538-4200
Dogs of all sizes are allowed. There are no additional pet fees. Dogs must be leashed and cleaned up after. The camping and tent areas

also allow dogs. There is a dog walk area at the campground. Dogs are allowed in the camping cabins. 2 dogs may be allowed.

Saugerties

KOA Saugerties/Woodstock
882 H212
Saugerties, NY
845-246-4089
Dogs of all sizes are allowed. There are no additional fees for site rentals, however there is a $4 per night per pet additional fee for the cabins. Dogs must be leashed and cleaned up after. There are some breed restrictions. This RV park is closed during the off-season. The camping and tent areas also allow dogs. There is a dog walk area at the campground. Dogs are allowed in the camping cabins. Multiple dogs may be allowed.

Sodus Point

South Shore RV Park
7867 Lake Road
Sodus Point, NY
315-483-8679
Dogs of all sizes are allowed. There are no additional pet fees. Dogs must be quiet, leashed, and cleaned up after. Dogs must not be left unattended at any time, especially in the cabins. The camping and tent areas also allow dogs. There is a dog walk area at the campground. Dogs are allowed in the camping cabins. Multiple dogs may be allowed.

Stow

Camp Chautauqua Camping Resort
3900 Westlake Road
Stow, NY
716-789-3435
Dogs of all sizes are allowed. There are no additional pet fees. Shot records must be up to date, and dogs must be kept under owner's control and be quiet during the night. The camping and tent areas also allow dogs. There is a dog walk area at the campground. 2 dogs may be allowed.

Swan Lake

Swan Lake Camplands
106 Fulton Road

Swan Lake, NY
845-292-4781
Dogs of all sizes are allowed. There are no additional pet fees. Dogs must be leased and cleaned up after. The camping and tent areas also allow dogs. There is a dog walk area at the campground. Dogs are allowed in the camping cabins. Multiple dogs may be allowed.

Verona

Turning Stone RV Park
5065 State H 365
Verona, NY
315-361-7275
Dogs of all sizes are allowed. There are no additional pet fees. Dogs must be leased and cleaned up after. If your dog will remain next to you and not chase other dogs or people, it can be off leash on your own site. There is a dog walk area at the campground. Multiple dogs may be allowed.

Wasrrensburg

Schroon River Campsites
74 State H 149
Wasrrensburg, NY
518-623-2171
Dogs of all sizes are allowed. There are no additional pet fees. Dogs must be well behaved, cleaned up after, and not left unattended. The camping and tent areas also allow dogs. There is a dog walk area at the campground. Multiple dogs may be allowed.

Waterport

Lakeside Beach State Park
Lakeside, H 18
Waterport, NY
585-682-4888
Dogs of all sizes are allowed. There are no additional pet fees. Dogs may not be left unattended, they must have a current rabies certificate and shot records, be on no more than a 6 foot leash, and be cleaned up after. Dogs are allowed on the trails, but when in the campground they must stay in the camping loops that are designated for pets. This campground is closed during the off-season. The camping and tent areas also allow dogs. There are no water hookups at the campground. Multiple dogs may be allowed.

Watkins Glen

KOA Watkins Glen/Corning
1710 H 414
Watkins Glen, NY
607-535-7404
Dogs of all sizes are allowed. There are no additional pet fees. Dogs may not be left unattended, and must be leashed and cleaned up after. This RV park is closed during the off-season. The camping and tent areas also allow dogs. There is a dog walk area at the campground. 2 dogs may be allowed.

Watkins Glen State Park

3530 H 419
Watkins Glen, NY
607-535-4511
Dogs of all sizes are allowed. There are no additional pet fees. Dogs may not be left unattended, they must have a current rabies certificate and shot records, be on no more than a 6 foot leash, and cleaned up after. Dogs are not allowed at the pool or in the buildings. Dogs are allowed on all the trails except the Main Gorge Trail. The Rim Trails are open all year. This campground is closed during the off-season. The camping and tent areas also allow dogs. There is a dog walk area at the campground. There are no water hookups at the campground. 2 dogs may be allowed.

Westfield

KOA Westfield/Lake Erie
8001 H 5
Westfield, NY
716-326-3573
Dogs of all sizes are allowed. There are no additional pet fees. Dogs may not be left unattended, and must be leashed and cleaned up after. This RV park is closed during the off-season. The camping and tent areas also allow dogs. There is a dog walk area at the campground. Dogs are allowed in the camping cabins. Multiple dogs may be allowed.

Woodridge

Jellystone Park at Birchwood Acres
85 Martinfeld Road, Box 482
Woodridge, NY
845-434-4743
One dog of any size is allowed, except in the rentals or lodge. Dogs may not be left unattended, must be leashed, and cleaned up after. There are some breed restrictions. This RV park is closed during the off-season. The camping and tent areas also allow dogs. There is a dog walk area at the campground.

North Carolina Listings

Albemarle

Morrow Mountain State Park
49104 Morrow Mountain Road
Albemarle, NC
704-982-4402
Rich in natural and cultural history, this park offers an exhibit hall and a historic site, an amphitheater, 15 miles of blazed hiking trails, and a wide variety of land and water activities and recreation. Dogs of all sizes are allowed at no additional fee. Dogs may not be left unattended, and they must be on no more than a 6 foot leash, and be cleaned up after. Dogs are not allowed in buildings, however they are allowed on the trails. The camping and tent areas also allow dogs. There is a dog walk area at the campground. There are no electric or water hookups at the campground. Multiple dogs may be allowed.

Apex

Jordan Lake State Park
280 State Park Road
Apex, NC
919-362-0586
Rich in natural and cultural history, this scenic park can be described as popular, historical, educational, recreational, and even pre-historic. Dogs of all sizes are allowed at no additional fee. Dogs may not be left unattended unless they will be quiet and well behaved. Dogs must be on no more than a 6 foot leash, and cleaned up after. Dogs are not allowed in buildings or on the beaches, however, they are allowed on the trails. The camping and tent areas also allow dogs. There is a dog walk area at the campground. Multiple dogs may be allowed.

Jordan Lake State Park

280 State Park Road
Apex, NC
919-362-0586
Rich in ancient American history and home to one of the largest summertime homes of the bald eagle, this park offers educational and interpretive programs, a variety of trails, and various recreation. Dogs of all sizes are allowed at no additional fee. Dogs may not be left unattended, and they must be on no more than a 6 foot leash, and cleaned up after. The camping and tent areas also allow dogs. There is a dog walk area at the campground. Multiple dogs may be allowed.

Asheville

Bear Creek RV Park
81 S Bear Creek Road
Asheville, NC
828-253-0798
Dogs of all sizes are allowed. There are no additional pet fees for the first two dogs. For more than 2 dogs, there is a $5 per night per pet additional fee. Dogs must be leashed and cleaned up after. The camping and tent areas also allow dogs. There is a dog walk area at the campground. Multiple dogs may be allowed.

Pisgah National Forest
1001 Pisgah H (H276)
Asheville, NC
828-877-3350
This forest's diverse ecosystems support a large variety of trails, plants, fish, mammals, bird species, recreation, and is also home to the Looking Glass Falls. Dogs of all sizes are allowed at no additional fee. Dogs may not be left unattended, and they must be leashed and cleaned up after. Dogs are not allowed in buildings, however, they are allowed on the trails. Dogs are not allowed on the trails in the Great Smoky Mountains National Forest that adjoins the park. The camping and tent areas also allow dogs. There is a dog walk area at the campground. There are no electric or water hookups at the campground. Multiple dogs may be allowed.

Balsam

Moonshine Creek Campground
27 Moonshine Creek Trail
Balsam, NC
828-586-6666

Dogs of all sizes are allowed. There are no additional pet fees. Dogs must be leashed and cleaned up after. This RV park is closed during the off-season. The camping and tent areas also allow dogs. There is a dog walk area at the campground. Multiple dogs may be allowed.

Bat Cave

Creekside Mountain Camping
24 Chimney View Road
Bat Cave, NC
800-248-8118
Dogs of all sizes are allowed. There are no additional pet fees. Dogs may not be left unattended, and they must be quiet, leashed, and cleaned up after. The camping and tent areas also allow dogs. There is a dog walk area at the campground. 2 dogs may be allowed.

Boone

Boone KOA
123 Harmony Mountain Lane
Boone, NC
828-264-7250
Dogs of all sizes are allowed. There are no additional pet fees. Dogs may not be left unattended, and they must be leashed and cleaned up after. This RV park is closed during the off-season. The camping and tent areas also allow dogs. There is a dog walk area at the campground. Dogs are allowed in the camping cabins. Multiple dogs may be allowed.

Bottineau

Lake Metigoshe State Park
#2 Lake Metigoshe State Park
Bottineau, NC
701-263-4651
This park of 1,551 acres, located along the shores of Lake Metigoshe, is a popular destination that offer various trails, educational and interpretive programs, and a variety of recreational pursuits. Dogs of all sizes are allowed at no additional fee. Dogs may not be left unattended-including inside vehicles, and they must have current tags and rabies shot records. Dogs must be quiet, well behaved, on no more than a 6 foot leash or crated, and be cleaned up after. Dogs may not be tied to any native vegetation or camp property, and digging is not allowed. Dogs

are not allowed in public swim areas, the playground, or any buildings. Dogs are allowed on the trails, except the ski trails in winter. There are some breed restrictions. This campground is closed during the off-season. The camping and tent areas also allow dogs. There is a dog walk area at the campground. There are no water hookups at the campground. Multiple dogs may be allowed.

Candler

Asheville West KOA
309 Wiggins Road
Candler, NC
828-665-7015
Dogs of all sizes are allowed. There are no additional pet fees. Dogs must be leashed and cleaned up after. There are some breed restrictions. The camping and tent areas also allow dogs. There is a dog walk area at the campground. Dogs are allowed in the camping cabins. Multiple dogs may be allowed.

Carolina Beach

Carolina Beach State Park
1010 State Park Road
Carolina Beach, NC
910-458-8206
Steeped in both history and natural diversity, this park offers an interpretive center, a variety of distinct habitats, miles of hiking trails-including the Venus Flytrap Trail, and a variety of activities and recreation. Dogs of all sizes are allowed at no additional fee. Dogs may not be left unattended, and they must be on no more than a 6 foot leash, and be cleaned up after. Dogs are not allowed on the beaches or in buildings, however they are allowed on the trails. The camping and tent areas also allow dogs. There is a dog walk area at the campground. There are no electric or water hookups at the campground. Multiple dogs may be allowed.

Cedar Mountain

Black Forest Family Camping Resort
100 Summer Road
Cedar Mountain, NC
828-884-2267
Dogs of all sizes are allowed. There are no additional pet fees. Dogs

must be leashed and cleaned up after. This RV park is closed during the off-season. The camping and tent areas also allow dogs. There is a dog walk area at the campground. Multiple dogs may be allowed.

Charlotte

Charlotte/Fort Mill KOA
940 Gold Hill Road
Fort Mill, NC
803-548-1148
Dogs of all sizes are allowed. There are no additional pet fees. Dogs may not be left unattended, and they must be leashed and cleaned up after. The camping and tent areas also allow dogs. There is a dog walk area at the campground. Multiple dogs may be allowed.

Cherokee

Cherokee/Great Smokies KOA
92 KOA Campground Road
Cherokee, NC
828-497-9711
Dogs of all sizes are allowed. There are no additional pet fees. Dogs may not be left unattended, and they must be leashed and cleaned up after. The camping and tent areas also allow dogs. There is a dog walk area at the campground. Dogs are allowed in the camping cabins. Multiple dogs may be allowed.

Yogi in the Smokies
317 Galamore Bridge Road
Cherokee, NC
828-497-9151
Dogs of all sizes are allowed. There are no additional pet fees. Dogs may not be left unattended, must be quiet, leashed, and cleaned up after. This RV park is closed during the off-season. The camping and tent areas also allow dogs. There is a dog walk area at the campground. Multiple dogs may be allowed.

Concord

Fleetwood RV Racing Camping Resort
6600 Speedway Blvd
Concord, NC
704-455-4445
Dogs of all sizes are allowed. There are no additional pet fees. Dogs may not be left unattended outside, and they must be leashed and cleaned up after. There is a dog walk area at the campground. Multiple dogs may

be allowed.

Creswell

Pettigrew State Park
2252 Lakeshore Road
Creswell, NC
252-797-4475
A blend of natural and cultural history, this park offers a variety of educational and interpretive programs, trails with a 350-foot boardwalk that cuts through a cypress swamp, and a variety of land and water recreation. Dogs of all sizes are allowed at no additional fee. Dogs may not be left unattended, and they must be on no more than a 6 foot leash, and cleaned up after. Dogs are not allowed in the buildings, however, they are allowed on the trails. The camping and tent areas also allow dogs. There is a dog walk area at the campground. There are no electric or water hookups at the campground. Multiple dogs may be allowed.

Pettigrew State Park
2252 Lakeshore Road
Creswell, NC
252-797-44751
A blend of ancient mystery, history, culture, nature, and recreation are offered at this more than 1,200 acre park with a 16,600 acre lake. Dogs of all sizes are allowed at no additional fee. Dogs may not be left unattended, and they must be on no more than a 6 foot leash, and cleaned up after. Dogs are not allowed in buildings, but they are allowed on the trails. The camping and tent areas also allow dogs. There is a dog walk area at the campground. There are no electric or water hookups at the campground. Multiple dogs may be allowed.

Danbury

Hanging Rock State Park
State Road 2015
Danbury, NC
336-593-8480
Picturesque cascades and waterfalls, high rock cliffs, 18 miles of trails, and spectacular views are all located here. In addition, the park hosts an interactive interpretive center and a variety of land and water activities and recreation. Dogs of all sizes are allowed at no additional fee. Dogs

may not be left unattended, and they must be on no more than a 6 foot leash, and be cleaned up after. Dogs are not allowed in swim areas or in buildings. Dogs are allowed on the trails. The camping and tent areas also allow dogs. There is a dog walk area at the campground. There are no electric or water hookups at the campground. Multiple dogs may be allowed.

Elizabethtown

Jones Lake State Park
4117 H 242N
Elizabethtown, NC
910-588-4550
This 2,208-acre park is a nature lover's delight, and offers educational and interpretive programs as well as a variety of trails and recreational pursuits. Dogs of all sizes are allowed at no additional fee. Dogs may not be left unattended, and they must be on no more than a 6 foot leash, and cleaned up after. Dogs are not allowed in swim areas, however they are allowed on the trails. There is only one site that has an electric hook-ups. The camping and tent areas also allow dogs. There is a dog walk area at the campground. There are no electric or water hookups at the campground. Multiple dogs may be allowed.

Emerald Isle

Holiday Trav-L-Park Resort
9102 Coast Guard Road
Emerald Isle, NC
252-354-2250
Dogs of all sizes are allowed. There is a $5 per night per pet additional fee. Dogs must be leashed and cleaned up after. This RV park is closed during the off-season. There is a dog walk area at the campground. Multiple dogs may be allowed.

Enfield

Enfield/Rocky Mount KOA
101 Bell Acres
Enfield, NC
252-445-5925
Dogs of all sizes are allowed, and there are no additional pet fees for tent or RV sites. There is a $2 per night per pet additional fee for the cabins. Dogs may not be left unattended in the cabins or outside, and they must be leashed and

cleaned up after. There are some breed restrictions. The camping and tent areas also allow dogs. There is a dog walk area at the campground. Dogs are allowed in the camping cabins. Multiple dogs may be allowed.

Flat Rock

Lakewood RV Resort
915 Ballenger Road
Flat Rock, NC
888-819-4200
Dogs of all sizes are allowed. There are no additional pet fees. Dogs are not allowed at any of the rentals, the clubhouse, or in any of the buildings. Dogs may not be left unattended, and they must be leashed and cleaned up after. There is a dog walk area at the campground. 2 dogs may be allowed.

Fletcher

Rutledge Lake RV Park
170 Rutledge Road
Fletcher, NC
828-654-7873
Dogs up to about 70 pounds are allowed. There are no additional pet fees. Dogs may not be left unattended outside, and they must be inside at night. Dogs must be well behaved, leashed and cleaned up after. There are some breed restrictions. The camping and tent areas also allow dogs. There is a dog walk area at the campground. Multiple dogs may be allowed.

Frisco

Frisco Woods Campground
53124 H 12
Frisco, NC
800-948-3942
Dogs of all sizes are allowed. There is an additional $5 one time fee per pet. Dogs may not be left unattended, and they must be leashed and cleaned up after. This RV park is closed during the off-season. The camping and tent areas also allow dogs. There is a dog walk area at the campground. Dogs are allowed in the camping cabins. Multiple dogs may be allowed.

Gatesville

Merchants Millpond State Park
71 H 158E

Gatesville, NC
252-357-1191
Called an "Enchanted Forest" as a result of the mingling of coastal pond and southern swamp forest, this is one of the rarest ecological communities in the state. The park offers a wide variety of recreational and educational pursuits. Dogs of all sizes are allowed at no additional fee. Dogs may not be left unattended unless they will be quiet and well behaved. Dogs must be on no more than a 6 foot leash, and cleaned up after. Dogs are allowed on the trails. The camping and tent areas also allow dogs. There is a dog walk area at the campground. There are no electric or water hookups at the campground. Multiple dogs may be allowed.

Harkers Island

Cape Lookout National Seashore
131 Charles Street
Harkers Island, NC
252-728-2250
Although isolated, the natural and historic features provide an incentive to visit Cape Lookout. It offers interpretive programs, a lighthouse complex, and a variety of land and water activities and recreation. This park is either reached by private boat or by ferry. One of three ferries runs all year, the Local Yocal Ferry. Dogs may ride the ferry for an additional $6 fee per pet and dogs must be leashed at all times. Dogs of all sizes are allowed at no additional fee. Dogs may not be left unattended, and they must be on no more than a 6 foot leash, and cleaned up after. The camping and tent areas also allow dogs. There is a dog walk area at the campground. There are no electric or water hookups at the campground. 2 dogs may be allowed.

Hatteras Village

Hatteras Sands
57316 Eagle Pass Road
Hatteras Village, NC
252-986-2422
Dogs of all sizes are allowed. There is a $2 per night per pet additional fee. Dogs may not be left unattended, and they must be leashed and cleaned up after. This RV park is closed during the off-season. The camping and tent areas also allow dogs. There is a

dog walk area at the campground. Dogs are allowed in the camping cabins. Multiple dogs may be allowed.

Henderson

Kerr Lake State Rec Area
6254 Satterwhite Point Road
Henderson, NC
252-438-7791
This park offers abundant wildlife, educational and interpretive programs, an accessible nature trail with an overlook, an amphitheater, and a variety of land and water activities and recreation. Dogs of all sizes are allowed at no additional fee. Dogs may not be left unattended, and they must be on no more than a 6 foot leash, and cleaned up after. Dogs are not allowed in buildings, however, they are allowed on trails. The camping and tent areas also allow dogs. There is a dog walk area at the campground. Multiple dogs may be allowed.

Kerr Lake State Rec Area
6254 Satterwhite Point Road
Henderson, NC
252-438-7791
This park touts a 50,000-acre man-made lake with many miles of wooded shoreline and provides a variety of land and water recreation areas, woodlands, trails, and wildlife habitats. Dogs of all sizes are allowed at no additional fee. Dogs may not be left unattended, and they must be on no more than a 6 foot leash at all times, and cleaned up after. Dogs are not allowed in buildings, but they are allowed on the trails. The camping and tent areas also allow dogs. There is a dog walk area at the campground. Multiple dogs may be allowed.

Highlands

Nantahala National Forest
2010 Flat Mountain Road
Highlands, NC
828-526-3765
This forest, the largest in the state with over half a million acres, provides over 600 miles of hiking trails, diverse ecosystems that support a large variety of plants, fish, mammals, bird species, and various recreational pursuits. Dogs of all sizes are allowed at no additional fee. Dogs may not be left unattended, and they must be

leashed and cleaned up after. Dogs are not allowed in buildings, however, they are allowed on the trails. Dogs are not allowed on the trails in the Great Smokey Mountains National Forest that adjoin the park. The camping and tent areas also allow dogs. There is a dog walk area at the campground. There are no electric or water hookups at the campground. Multiple dogs may be allowed.

Hollister

Medoc Mountain State Park
1541 Medoc State Park Road/ H 1322
Hollister, NC
252-586-6588
This park is home to a large variety of plant and animal life and offers educational and interpretive programs, 7 different trails, and various recreational pursuits. Dogs of all sizes are allowed at no additional fee. Dogs may not be left unattended except for short periods, and they must be on no more than a 6 foot leash, and cleaned up after. Dogs are not allowed in buildings, but they are allowed on the trails. The camping and tent areas also allow dogs. There is a dog walk area at the campground. Multiple dogs may be allowed.

Manteo

Cape Hatteras National Seashore
1401 National Park Drive
Manteo, NC
252-473-2111
This park offers a captivating combination of natural and cultural resources. The park is rich in maritime history, is stretched over 70 miles of barrier islands and offers a variety of recreational pursuits. Dogs of all sizes are allowed at no additional fee. Dogs may not be left unattended, and they must be on no more than a 6 foot leash or crated, and cleaned up after. Dogs are not allowed in public swim areas, however, they are allowed on the trails. The camping and tent areas also allow dogs. There is a dog walk area at the campground. There are no electric or water hookups at the campground. 2 dogs may be allowed.

Marion

Buck Creek Campground
2576 Toms Creek Road
Marion, NC
828-724-4888
Dogs up to 100 pounds are allowed. There are no additional pet fees. Dogs may not be left unattended outside, and they must be leashed and cleaned up after. There are some breed restrictions. This RV park is closed during the off-season. There is a dog walk area at the campground. Multiple dogs may be allowed.

Jellystone Park at Hidden Valley Campground
1210 Deacon Drive
Marion, NC
828-652-7208
Dogs of all sizes are allowed. There are no additional pet fees. Dogs must be leashed and cleaned up after. This RV park is closed during the off-season. The camping and tent areas also allow dogs. There is a dog walk area at the campground. Multiple dogs may be allowed.

New Bern

Croatan National Forest
141 E Fisher Street
New Bern, NC
252-393-7352
This park, called the "Land of Many Ecosystems", has various habitats providing for some unusual plant life and a wide range of birds and wildlife. The park also provides interpretive trails, hiking trails and recreational pursuits. Dogs may not be left unattended, and they must be leashed and cleaned up after. Dogs are allowed on the trails. The camping and tent areas also allow dogs. There is a dog walk area at the campground. Multiple dogs may be allowed.

New Bern
1565 B Street
New Bern, NC
252-638-2556
Dogs of all sizes are allowed. There are no additional pet fees. Dogs must be leashed and cleaned up after. There are 2 fenced in areas for off lead. There are some breed restrictions. The camping and tent areas also allow dogs. There is a dog walk area at the campground. Dogs are allowed in the camping cabins. Multiple dogs may be allowed.

Oak Island

Long Beach Campground
5011 E Oak Island Drive
Oak Island, NC
910-278-5737
Dogs of all sizes are allowed. There are no additional pet fees. Dogs must be leashed and cleaned up after. Dogs are allowed at the beach. The camping and tent areas also allow dogs. There is a dog walk area at the campground. Multiple dogs may be allowed.

Piney Creek

Rivercamp USA
2221 Kings Creek Road
Piney Creek, NC
336-359-2267
Dogs of all sizes are allowed. There are no additional pet fees. Dogs may not be left unattended outside, and they must be quiet, leashed, and cleaned up after. This RV park is closed during the off-season. The camping and tent areas also allow dogs. There is a dog walk area at the campground. Multiple dogs may be allowed.

Pinnacle

Pilot Mountain State Park
1792 Pilot Knob Park Road
Pinnacle, NC
336-352-2355
Dedicated as a National Natural Landmark, this park offers a wide variety of land and water recreational activities. In addition, it has educational and interpretive programs and many miles of scenic hiking trails. Dogs of all sizes are allowed at no additional fee. Dogs may not be left unattended, and they must be on no more than a 6 foot leash, and cleaned up after. Dogs are allowed on the trails. This campground is closed during the off-season. The camping and tent areas also allow dogs. There is a dog walk area at the campground. There are no electric or water hookups at the campground. Multiple dogs may be allowed.

Raleigh

William Umstead State Park
8801 Glenwood Avenue
Raleigh, NC
919-571-4170
Rich in natural and cultural history,

this scenic park offers educational and interpretive programs, an interactive exhibit hall, 20 miles of hiking trails and a variety of land and water recreation. Dogs of all sizes are allowed at no additional fee. Dogs may not be left unattended, and they must be on no more than a 6 foot leash, and cleaned up after. Dogs are not allowed in public swim areas or in buildings. Dogs are allowed on the trails. The camping and tent areas also allow dogs. There is a dog walk area at the campground. There are no electric or water hookups at the campground.

Roaring Gap

Stone Mountain State Park
3042 Frank Parkway
Roaring Gap, NC
336-957-8185
Designated as a National Natural Landmark in 1975, this park is home to a magnificent 600-foot granite dome, 16 miles of scenic trails, and a variety of recreational pursuits. Dogs of all sizes are allowed at no additional fee. Dogs may not be left unattended, and they must be on no more than a 6 foot leash at all times, and cleaned up after. Dogs are not allowed in buildings, however, they are allowed on the trails. The camping and tent areas also allow dogs. There is a dog walk area at the campground. Multiple dogs may be allowed.

Rodanthe

Camp Hatteras Campground
24798 H 12
Rodanthe, NC
252-987-2777
Dogs of all sizes are allowed. There is a $2 per night additional pet fee for up to 3 dogs. Dogs are not allowed in the clubhouse, and they may not be tied to cars, porches, or tables. Dogs may not be left unattended outside, and they must be leashed and cleaned up after. The camping and tent areas also allow dogs. There is a dog walk area at the campground. Multiple dogs may be allowed.

Cape Hatteras KOA
25099 H 12
Rodanthe, NC
252-987-2307
Dogs of all sizes are allowed, and there are no additional pet fees for tent or RV sites. There is a $5 one time pet fee for the cabins. Dogs

may not be left unattended, and must be leashed and cleaned up after. This RV park is closed during the off-season. The camping and tent areas also allow dogs. There is a dog walk area at the campground. Dogs are allowed in the camping cabins. Multiple dogs may be allowed.

Rutherfordton

Four Paws Kingdom
335 Lazy Creek Drive
Rutherfordton, NC
828-287-7324
Dogs of all sizes are allowed, however some breeds are not. There are no additional pet fees, and dogs must be cleaned up after. There are 2 park areas where your dog can run off leash; one for the large dogs and one for the smaller dogs. There is a pond dedicated for dogs and a bath house with a dog grooming area. The camping and tent areas also allow dogs. There is a dog walk area at the campground. Dogs are allowed in the camping cabins. 2 dogs may be allowed.

Selma

Selma/Smithfield KOA
428 Campground Road
Selma, NC
919-965-5923
Dogs of all sizes are allowed. There are no additional pet fees. Dogs may not be left unattended outside, and they must be in at night. Dogs must be quiet, leashed, and cleaned up after. The camping and tent areas also allow dogs. There is a dog walk area at the campground. Multiple dogs may be allowed.

Seven Springs

Cliffs of the Neuse State Park
345A Park Entrance Road
Seven Springs, NC
919-778-6234
Rich in geological and biological history, this park offers a museum, educational and interpretive programs, and a variety of recreational pursuits. Dogs of all sizes are allowed at no additional fee. Dogs may not be left unattended, and they must be on no more than a 6 foot leash, and cleaned up after. Dogs are not allowed in the swim areas or in buildings, however, they are

allowed on the trails. The camping and tent areas also allow dogs. There is a dog walk area at the campground. There are no electric or water hookups at the campground. Multiple dogs may be allowed.

Sherrills Ford

Wildlife Woods Campground
4582 Beaver Blvd
Sherrills Ford, NC
704-483-5611
Dogs of all sizes are allowed. There are no additional pet fees. Dogs may not be left unattended, and they must be leashed and cleaned up after. There are some breed restrictions. The camping and tent areas also allow dogs. There is a dog walk area at the campground. Multiple dogs may be allowed.

Statesville

Statesville KOA
162 KOA Lane
Statesville, NC
704-873-5560
Dogs of all sizes are allowed. There are no additional pet fees. Dogs may not be left unattended, and they must be quiet, leashed, and cleaned up after. There are some breed restrictions. The camping and tent areas also allow dogs. There is a dog walk area at the campground. Multiple dogs may be allowed.

Sunset Beach

Shallotte/Brunswick Beaches KOA
7200 KOA Drive
Sunset Beach, NC
910-579-7562
Dogs of all sizes are allowed. There are no additional pet fees. Dogs may not be left unattended, and they must be up to date on shots, leashed, and cleaned up after. The camping and tent areas also allow dogs. There is a dog walk area at the campground. Multiple dogs may be allowed.

Swannanoa

Asheville East KOA
2708 H 70 E
Swannanoa, NC
828-686-3121
Dogs of all sizes are allowed. There are no additional pet fees. Dogs may not be left unattended, and they must be quiet, leashed, and cleaned up

after. The camping and tent areas also allow dogs. There is a dog walk area at the campground. Dogs are allowed in the camping cabins. Multiple dogs may be allowed.

Mama Gerties Hideaway Campground
15 Uphill Road
Swannanoa, NC
828-686-4258
Dogs of all sizes are allowed, and there are no additional pet fees for tent or RV sites. There is a $5 per night per pet additional fee for the cabins. Dogs may not be left unattended, and they must be quiet, well behaved, leashed, and cleaned up after. There are some breed restrictions. The camping and tent areas also allow dogs. There is a dog walk area at the campground. Dogs are allowed in the camping cabins. 2 dogs may be allowed.

Yogi Bear's Jellystone Park Resort @ Daddy Joe's
626 Richard Wright Road
Tabor City, NC
910-653-2155
Dogs of all sizes are allowed. There are no additional pet fees. Dogs must be leashed and cleaned up after. The camping and tent areas also allow dogs. There is a dog walk area at the campground. Multiple dogs may be allowed.

Lake Norman State Park
159 Inland Sea Lane
Troutman, NC
704-528-6350
This park offers 13 miles of shoreline along the largest lake in the state and there is an abundant variety of plant and animal life. The park also offers educational and interpretive programs and a variety of trails and recreation. Dogs of all sizes are allowed at no additional fee. Dogs may not be left unattended, and they must be on no more than a 6 foot leash, and cleaned up after. Dogs are not allowed in swim areas or buildings, and they must be inside at night. Dogs are allowed on the trails. This campground is closed during the off-season. The camping and tent areas also allow dogs. There is a dog walk area at the campground. There are no electric or water hookups at the campground. Multiple

dogs may be allowed.

Lake Norman State Park
159 Inland Sea Lane
Troutman, NC
704-528-6350
Located along the state's largest manmade lake, this park supports a wide variety of plant and animal life, provides educational and interpretive programs, and various land and water activities. Dogs of all sizes are allowed at no additional fee. Dogs may not be left unattended, and they must be on no more than a 6 foot leash, and cleaned up after. Dogs are not allowed in public swim areas or buildings, and they must be in your unit at night. Dogs are allowed on the trails. This campground is closed during the off-season. The camping and tent areas also allow dogs. There is a dog walk area at the campground. There are no electric or water hookups at the campground. Multiple dogs may be allowed.

Uwharrie National Forest
789 H 24/27E
Troy, NC
910-576-6391
This forest's diverse ecosystems support a large variety of plants, fish, mammals, bird species, trails, and recreation. Dogs of all sizes are allowed at no additional fee. Dogs may not be left unattended, and they must be leashed and cleaned up after. Dogs are not allowed in buildings. Dogs are allowed on the trails. The camping and tent areas also allow dogs. There is a dog walk area at the campground. There are no water hookups at the campground. Multiple dogs may be allowed.

Fayetteville/Wade KOA
6250 Wade Stedman Road
Wade, NC
910-484-5500
Dogs of all sizes are allowed, and there are no additional pet fees for tent or RV sites. There is a $6 one time pet fee for the cabins. Dogs may not be left unattended, and must be quiet, leashed, and cleaned up after. The camping and tent areas also allow dogs. There is a dog walk area at the campground.

Dogs are allowed in the camping cabins. Multiple dogs may be allowed.

Falls Lake State Park
13304 Creedmoor Road (H 50)
Wake Forest, NC
919-676-1027
This park of 26,000 acres of woodlands with a 12,000-acre lake, offers educational and interpretive programs, trails with access to the Mountains-to-Sea Trail, and a variety of land and water activities and recreation. Dogs of all sizes are allowed at no additional fee. Dogs may not be left unattended, and they must be on no more than a 6 foot leash, and cleaned up after. Dogs are not allowed in swim areas or in buildings, however, they are allowed on the trails. The camping and tent areas also allow dogs. There is a dog walk area at the campground. Multiple dogs may be allowed.

Falls Lake State Park
13304 Creedmoor Road
Wake Forest, NC
919-676-1027
This 26,000 acre park of woodlands with a 12,000-acre lake provides a variety of habitats, and offers a portion of the Mountains-to-Sea Trail, educational and interpretive programs, and various recreational pursuits. Dogs of all sizes are allowed at no additional fee. Dogs may not be left unattended, and they must be on no more than a 6 foot leash, and cleaned up after. Dogs are not allowed in the swim areas or in buildings, but they are allowed on the trails. The camping and tent areas also allow dogs. There is a dog walk area at the campground. Multiple dogs may be allowed.

Wilmington KOA
7415 Market Street
Wilmington, NC
800-454-7705
Three dogs up to 20 pounds are allowed, and there are no additional pet fees for tent or RV sites. There is a $50 refundable pet deposit for the cabins, and there may only be up to two 20 pound dogs. Dogs may not be left unattended outside at any time, and they must be leashed and cleaned up after. There are some breed restrictions. There is a dog

walk area at the campground. Dogs are allowed in the camping cabins.

Winston - Salem

Lake Meyers RV Resort
2862 H 64W
Mocksville, NC
336-492-7736
Dogs of all sizes are allowed. There are no additional pet fees. Dogs may not be left unattended outside, and they must be quiet, leashed, and cleaned up after. The camping and tent areas also allow dogs. There is a dog walk area at the campground. Multiple dogs may be allowed.

North Dakota Listings

Arvilla

Turtle River State Park
3084 Park Avenue
Arvilla, ND
701-594-4445
Because of its environmental diversity, this entire 784 acre park is a nature sanctuary, and offers a variety of trails and land and water recreation. Dogs of all sizes are allowed at no additional fee. Dogs may not be left unattended anywhere, including vehicles, and they must have current tags and rabies shot records. Dogs must be quiet, well behaved, on no more than a 6 foot leash or crated, and be cleaned up after. Dogs may not be tied to any native vegetation or camp property, and digging is not allowed. Dogs are not allowed in public swim areas, the playground, or any buildings. Dogs are allowed on the trails, except the ski trails in winter. There are some breed restrictions. The camping and tent areas also allow dogs. There is a dog walk area at the campground. There are no water hookups at the campground. Multiple dogs may be allowed.

Bismarck

Bismarck KOA
3720 Centennial Road
Bismarck, ND
701-222-2662
Dogs of all sizes are allowed. There

are no additional pet fees. Dogs must be leashed and cleaned up after. This RV park is closed during the off-season. The camping and tent areas also allow dogs. There is a dog walk area at the campground. Dogs are allowed in the camping cabins. Multiple dogs may be allowed.

Casselton

Governor's RV Park and Campground
2050 Governor's Drive
Casselton, ND
701-347-4524
Dogs of all sizes are allowed. There are no additional pet fees for the tent or RV sites. There is a $9 per night per pet additional fee for the hotel, which is open year around. Dogs may not be left unattended outside, and they must be leashed and cleaned up after. Dogs may be kenneled when out of the hotel room if they will be quiet. This RV park is closed during the off-season. The camping and tent areas also allow dogs. There is a dog walk area at the campground. 2 dogs may be allowed.

Cavalier

Icelandic State Park
13571 H 5
Cavalier, ND
701-265-4561
Rich in natural beauty and cultural heritage, this park is home to the Gunlogson Homestead and Nature Preserve and the Pioneer Heritage Center. It also offers a wide variety of recreational pursuits. Dogs of all sizes are allowed at no additional fee. Dogs may not be left unattended anywhere, including vehicles, and they must have current tags and rabies shot records. Dogs must be quiet, well behaved, on no more than a 6 foot leash or crated, and be cleaned up after. Dogs may not be tied to any native vegetation or camp property, and digging is not allowed. Dogs are not allowed in public swim areas, the playground, or any buildings. Dogs are allowed on the trails, except the ski trails in winter. There are some breed restrictions. The camping and tent areas also allow dogs. There is a dog walk area at the campground. There are no water hookups at the campground. Multiple dogs may be

allowed.

Devil's Lake

Woodland Resort
1012 Woodland Drive
Devil's Lake, ND
701-662-5996
Dogs of all sizes are allowed. There are no additional pet fees for tent or RV sites. There is a $10 per night per pet, or $50 per week per pet, additional fee for the lodge, motel, or cabins. Dogs may not be left unattended, and they must be leashed and cleaned up after. The camping and tent areas also allow dogs. There is a dog walk area at the campground. Dogs are allowed in the camping cabins. Multiple dogs may be allowed.

Devils Island

Devils Lake State Park, Grahams Island
152 S. Duncan Road
Devils Island, ND
701-766-4015
This scenic park of over 1,100 acres on the shores of Devil's Lake offers an activity center, miles of trails, and a variety of land and water recreation. Dogs of all sizes are allowed at no additional fee. Dogs may not be left unattended anywhere, including vehicles, and they must have current tags and rabies shot records. Dogs must be quiet, well behaved, on no more than a 6 foot leash or crated, and be cleaned up after. Dogs may not be tied to any native vegetation or camp property, and digging is not allowed. Dogs are not allowed in public swim areas, the playground, or any buildings. Dogs are allowed on the trails, except the ski trails in winter. There are some breed restrictions. The camping and tent areas also allow dogs. There is a dog walk area at the campground. There are no water hookups at the campground. Multiple dogs may be allowed.

Epping

Lewis and Clark State Park
4904 119th Road NW
Epping, ND
701-859-3071
This 490 acre park on the shores of Lake Sakakawea offers an extensive trail system and a variety of land and water recreation. Dogs of all sizes

are allowed at no additional fee. Dogs may not be left unattended anywhere, including vehicles, and they must have current tags and rabies shot records. Dogs must be quiet, well behaved, on no more than a 6 foot leash or crated, and be cleaned up after. Dogs may not be tied to any native vegetation or camp property, and digging is not allowed. Dogs are not allowed in public swim areas, the playground, or any buildings. Dogs are allowed on the trails, except the ski trails in winter. The camping and tent areas also allow dogs. There is a dog walk area at the campground. There are no water hookups at the campground. Multiple dogs may be allowed.

Garrison

Fort Stevenson State Park
1252 A 41st Avenue NW
Garrison, ND
701-337-5576
This 438 acre park on Lake Sakakawea offers an arboretum, prairie dog town, interpretive trails, planned activities, and various land and water recreation. Dogs of all sizes are allowed at no additional fee. Dogs may not be left unattended anywhere, including vehicles, and they must have current tags and rabies shot records. Dogs must be quiet, well behaved, on no more than a 6 foot leash or crated, and be cleaned up after. Dogs may not be tied to any native vegetation or camp property, and digging is not allowed. Dogs are not allowed in public swim areas, the playground, or any buildings. Dogs are allowed on the trails, except the ski trails in winter. This campground is closed during the off-season. The camping and tent areas also allow dogs. There is a dog walk area at the campground. There are no water hookups at the campground. Multiple dogs may be allowed.

Indian Hills Resort
7302 14th Street NW
Garrison, ND
701-743-4122
Dogs of all sizes are allowed. There are no additional pet fees. Dogs may not be left unattended, and they must be quiet, well behaved, leashed and cleaned up after. Dogs may be off lead when no other people are around and you have them under voice control. This RV park is closed during the off-season. The camping and tent areas also allow dogs.

There is a dog walk area at the campground. Multiple dogs may be allowed.

Grand Forks

Grand Forks Campground
4796 S 42nd Street
Grand Forks, ND
701-772-6108
Dogs of all sizes are allowed. There are no additional pet fees. Dogs must be leashed and cleaned up after. There are some breed restrictions. This RV park is closed during the off-season. The camping and tent areas also allow dogs. There is a dog walk area at the campground. Multiple dogs may be allowed.

Jamestown

Frontier Fort Campground
1838 3rd Avenue SE
Jamestown, ND
701-252-7492
Dogs of all sizes are allowed. There are no additional pet fees. Dogs must be quiet, well behaved, leashed, and cleaned up after. The camping and tent areas also allow dogs. There is a dog walk area at the campground. Multiple dogs may be allowed.

Jamestown Campground
3605 80th Avenue
Jamestown, ND
701-252-6262
Dogs of all sizes are allowed. There are no additional pet fees. Dogs must be quiet, well behaved, leashed and cleaned up after. This RV park is closed during the off-season. The camping and tent areas also allow dogs. There is a dog walk area at the campground. Multiple dogs may be allowed.

Mandan

Fort Abraham Lincoln State Park
4480 Fort Lincoln Road
Mandan, ND
701-667-6340
Rich in military and early Native American history, this park is home to the Custer House and a reconstructed Indian village. The park provides a variety of recreational pursuits. Dogs of all sizes are allowed at no additional fee. Dogs may not be left unattended anywhere, including

vehicles, and they must have current tags and rabies shot records. Dogs must be quiet, well behaved, on no more than a 6 foot leash or crated, and be cleaned up after. Dogs may not be tied to any native vegetation or camp property, and digging is not allowed. Dogs are not allowed in public swim areas, the playground, or any buildings. Dogs are allowed on the trails, except the ski trails in winter. The camping and tent areas also allow dogs. There is a dog walk area at the campground. There are no water hookups at the campground. Multiple dogs may be allowed.

Minot

KOA - Minot
5261 H 52E
Minot, ND
701-839-7400
Dogs of all sizes are allowed. There are no additional pet fees. Dogs must be leashed and cleaned up after. This RV park is closed during the off-season. The camping and tent areas also allow dogs. There is a dog walk area at the campground. Multiple dogs may be allowed.

Roughrider Campground
500 54th Street NW
Minot, ND
701-852-8442
Dogs of all sizes are allowed. There are no additional pet fees. Dogs may not be left unattended, and must be leashed and cleaned up after. This RV park is closed during the off-season. There is a dog walk area at the campground. Multiple dogs may be allowed.

St Michael

Spirit Lake Casino and Resort
7889 H 57
St Michael, ND
701-766-4747
Dogs of all sizes are allowed, and there are no additional pet fees for tent or RV sites. There is a $25 per stay per pet additional fee for the lodge. Dogs must be leashed and cleaned up after. The camping and tent areas also allow dogs. There is a dog walk area at the campground. Multiple dogs may be allowed.

Williston

Prairie Acres RV Park
13853 H 2W
Williston, ND
701-572-4860
Dogs of all sizes are allowed. There are no additional pet fees. Dogs may not be left unattended, and must be leashed and cleaned up after. This RV park is closed during the off-season. There is a dog walk area at the campground. Multiple dogs may be allowed.

Ohio Listings

Stonelick State Park
3294 Elk Lake Road
Afton, OH
513-734-4323
Dogs of all sizes are allowed. There are no additional pet fees. Dogs may not be left unattended at any time, they must be on no more than a 6 foot leash, and be cleaned up after. Dogs must be walked in the designated pet section of the park, and they are not allowed on the beaches, or in any of the park buildings. Dogs must be quiet and well behaved. The camping and tent areas also allow dogs. There is a dog walk area at the campground. 2 dogs may be allowed.

Portage Lakes State Park Campground
5031 Manchester Road
Akron, OH
330-644-2220
The campground at this state park offers 74 sites with no electric hookups. Campground amenities include vault latrines, a dump station and nearby hiking trails. Up to two dogs per pet campsite are allowed and they must be leashed and cleaned up after.

Camp Toodik
7700 Twp Road 462
Loudonville, OH
800-322-2663
This family campground is located in the foothills of the Appalachian

Mountains in Holmes County. They offer both tent and RV sites with full hookups and pull through sites. Amenities include canoe and kayak rentals, heated swimming pool, fishing in the river or pond, walking trails, miniature golf, shuffleboard, sand volleyball, horseshoes, playground, game room, recreation hall, picnic shelter and laundry room. Pets are welcome but need to be leashed, cleaned up after and are not allowed in the cabins or cottages. There are no pet fees. Dogs are also allowed in the canoe rentals. The campground is located off I-71. Take exit #173.

Mohican Campground
3058 State Route 3 South
Loudonville, OH
419-994-2267
This campground offers full hookup sites and primitive camping sites with picnic tables and fire rings. Pets are allowed at the campground but must be leashed and cleaned up after. Pets are not allowed in the pavilion, patio, or any public buildings. Pets are strictly not allowed in or near the cabins (guide or service dogs are exempted from this regulation). There is a $2 per night per pet fee.

Mohican State Park Campground
3116 State Route 3
Loudonville, OH

The campground at this state park offers 120 sites with electricity, fire rings and picnic tables. Full hookups are available at 33 sites. Campground amenities include showers, flush toilets, a dump station and nearby hiking trails. Up to two dogs per pet campsite are allowed and they must be leashed and cleaned up after.

Malabar Farm State Park Campground
4050 Bromfield Road
Lucas, OH
419-892-2784
The campground at this state park offers 15 primitive camp sites with no electric hookups. Campground amenities include restrooms, a dump station and nearby hiking trails. Up to two dogs per pet campsite are allowed and they must be leashed and cleaned up after.

Scenic Hills RV Park
4483 TR 367
Millersburg, OH

330-893-3607
Located in the heart of Amish country, this RV park offers over 80 full hookups, 40 pull thru sites, modem hookup, dump station available, fire rings, picnic tables and open sites on a grassy hilltop. Pets are welcome but need to be leashed, cleaned up after and not left unattended. The park is located one mile east of Berlin, 500 feet south on TR 367/Hiland Road.

Pymatuning State Park Campground
6260 Pymatuning Lake Road
Andover, OH
440-293-6030
The campground at this state park offers tent and trailer camping with 349 sites with electrical hookups and 21 sites with no electricity. Campground amenities include heated shower houses, flush toilets, laundry facilities, playgrounds, basketball and volleyball courts, and nearby hiking trails. Up to two dogs per pet campsite are allowed and they must be leashed and cleaned up after.

Paint Creek State Park Campground
14265 US Route 50
Bainbridge, OH
937-365-1401
The campground at this state park offers 195 sites with electric hookups. Campground amenities include hot showers, flush toilets, laundry facilities, a dump station and nearby hiking trails and swimming. Up to two dogs per pet campsite are allowed and they must be leashed and cleaned up after.

Clearwater Lake Campgrounds
2845 State Route 50
Batavia, OH
513-625-9893
This campground offers over 65 sites with full hookups and tent sites along the lake. Amenities include a bath and laundry house, playground, shelter and fishing lake. Pets are welcome but need to be leashed and cleaned up after. The campground is open from the beginning of April through the end of October.

East Fork State Park
2837 Old State Park
Batavia, OH
513-724-6521
Dogs of all sizes are allowed. There are no additional pet fees. Dogs may not be left unattended, and they must have a current rabies certificate and shot records. Dogs must be quiet during quiet hours, be well behaved, on no more than a 6 foot leash, and be cleaned up after. Dogs are allowed on the trails, but not on the beach or in the water. Dogs must stay in the pet designated areas. This campground is closed during the off-season. The camping and tent areas also allow dogs. There is a dog walk area at the campground. 2 dogs may be allowed.

Baylor

Baylor Beach Park Family Camping
8725 Manchester Avenue SW
Baylor, OH
888-922-9567
Dogs up to about 60 pounds are allowed. There are no additional pet fees. Dogs must be leashed and cleaned up after. Dogs are not allowed at the waterpark or the beach. There are some breed restrictions. This RV park is closed during the off-season. The camping and tent areas also allow dogs. There is a dog walk area at the campground. 2 dogs may be allowed.

Bellville

Jellystone Park
6500 Black Road
Bellville, OH
419-886-CAMP (2267)
Dogs of all sizes are allowed. There are no additional pet fees. Dogs must be leashed and cleaned up after. There are some breed restrictions. This RV park is closed during the off-season. The camping and tent areas also allow dogs. There is a dog walk area at the campground. Dogs are allowed in the camping cabins. 2 dogs may be allowed.

Belmont

Barkcamp State Park Campground
65330 Barkamp Road
Belmont, OH

740-484-4064
The campground at this state park offers 125 shaded and sunny sites with electrical hookups. Campground amenities include hot showers, tables, fire rings, two wheelchair accessible sites, a dump station and nearby hiking trails and lake. Up to two dogs per pet campsite are allowed and they must be leashed and cleaned up after.

Bloomingdale

Top O' The Caves Campground
26780 Chapel Ridge Road
Bloomingdale, OH
800-967-2434
Dogs of all sizes are allowed, and there are no additional pet fees for tent or RV sites which are open only for the season. There is a $25 one time fee per pet additional fee for the cabins, which are open all year. Dogs must be leashed and cleaned up after. This RV park is closed during the off-season. The camping and tent areas also allow dogs. There is a dog walk area at the campground. Dogs are allowed in the camping cabins. 2 dogs may be allowed.

Blue Rock

Muskingum River State Park
7924 Cutler Lake Road
Blue Rock, OH
740-674-4794
The campground at this state park offers 20 sites and pets are allowed in the camping area at Ellis. Campground amenities water, toilets, fire rings, and picnic tables. Up to two dogs per pet campsite are allowed and they must be leashed and cleaned up after.

Brookville

Dayton KOA
7796 Wellbaum Road
Brookville, OH
937-833-3888
Dogs of all sizes are allowed. There are no additional pet fees. Dogs must be quiet, well behaved, leashed, and cleaned up after. There are some breed restrictions. This RV park is closed during the off-season. The camping and tent areas also allow dogs. There is a dog walk area at the campground. Dogs are allowed in the camping cabins. Multiple dogs may be

allowed.

Buckeye Lake

Buckeye Lake/Columbus East KOA
4460 Walnut Road
Buckeye Lake, OH
740-928-0706
Dogs of all sizes are allowed. There are no additional pet fees. Dogs may not be left unattended, be on no more than a 6 foot leash, and cleaned up after. There is a large fenced in area where dogs can run off lead. There are some breed restrictions. This RV park is closed during the off-season. The camping and tent areas also allow dogs. There is a dog walk area at the campground. 2 dogs may be allowed.

Butler

Butler/Mohican KOA
6918 Bunker Hills Road S
Butler, OH
419-883-3314
Dogs of all sizes are allowed. There is a $5 per pet per stay additional fee. Dogs must be well behaved, leashed, and cleaned up after. There are some breed restrictions. This RV park is closed during the off-season. The camping and tent areas also allow dogs. There is a dog walk area at the campground. Dogs are allowed in the camping cabins. Multiple dogs may be allowed.

Caldwell

Wolf Run State Park Campground
16170 Wolf Run Road
Caldwell, OH
740-732-5035
The campground at this state park offers 71 sites with electrical hookups and 67 without electric. Campground amenities include showers, toilets, laundry facilities and nearby hiking trails. Up to two dogs per pet campsite are allowed and they must be leashed and cleaned up after.

Cambridge

Hillview Acres Campground
66271 Wolfs Den Road
Cambridge, OH
740-439-3348
Amenities include water and

electrical hookups, dump station, free showers, playgrounds, nearby hiking and a camping cabin. The campground is open from mid-April to the end of October. Pets are welcome but must be leashed and cleaned up after. There are no pet fees.

Spring Valley Campground
8000 Dozer Road
Cambridge, OH
740-439-9291
Dogs of all sizes are allowed. There are no additional pet fees. Dogs must be leashed and cleaned up after. The camping and tent areas also allow dogs. There is a dog walk area at the campground. Multiple dogs may be allowed.

Canton

Canton/East Sparta KOA
3232 Downing Street SW
East Sparta, OH
330-484-3901
Pull through sites up to 50 feet are available as well as 50 amp service. Amenities include a seasonal swimming pool, modem dataport (fee), LP gas (fee) and mini golf (fee). The RV park is open all year. Pets are welcome but are not allowed in the cottages. There are no pet fees.

Cincinnati

Miami Whitewater Forest Campground
various entrances
Crosby, OH
513-521-PARK
Open from the beginning of March to late October, this campground offers 46 electric sites which cost about $18 per night per site. Campground amenities include parking pads, fire rings, picnic tables, shower building, dump facility and nearby hiking trails. Pets are allowed but must be on a 6 foot or less leash, under control, and picked up after. Pooper scooper dispensers are located at each trailhead and are available from the Park District Rangers. To get to the park, take I-74 to Dry Fork Road exit, turn right on Dry Fork Road, turn right on West Road to the park entrance. The park is also accessible from Route 128 to Mt. Hope Road.

Indian Springs Campground
3306 Stateline Road
N Bend, OH

513-353-9244
Dogs of all sizes are allowed. There are no additional pet fees. Dogs must be leashed, and cleaned up after. There are some breed restrictions. The camping and tent areas also allow dogs. There is a dog walk area at the campground. 2 dogs may be allowed.

Winton Woods Campground
Winton Road
Springfield Township, OH
513-521-PARK
Open from late February to early November, this campground offers 100 sites with full and electric hookups. Prices range from $18 to $26 per night. Campground amenities include picnic tables, fire rings, access to a heated shower building, dump station, laundry room, playground, camp store and nearby hiking trails. A 3 night stay is required on holidays. Pets are allowed but must be on a 6 foot or less leash, under control, and picked up after. Pooper scooper dispensers are located at each trailhead and are available from the Park District Rangers. To get to the park, take I-275 to the Winton Road-Forest Park exit, and head south on Winton Road to the park entrances on left and right. The park is also accessible via the Ronald Reagan-Cross County Highway. Take the Winton Road exit, and head north on Winton Road to the park entrances on the left and right.

Circleville

A.W. Marion State Park Campground
7317 Warner-Huffer Road
Circleville, OH
740-869-3124
The campground at this state park offers 58 wooded sites for tents and trailers. Twenty-nine of the sites have electrical hookups. Campground amenities include toilets, water and nearby hiking trails. Up to two dogs per pet campsite are allowed and they must be leashed and cleaned up after.

Cleveland

Kool Lakes Family RV park
12990 H 282
Parkman, OH
440-548-8436
Dogs of all sizes are allowed. There

are no additional pet fees. Dogs must be leashed and cleaned up after. Dogs are not allowed at the beach or in the water. This RV park is closed during the off-season. There is a dog walk area at the campground. Multiple dogs may be allowed.

Country Acres Campground
9850 Minyoung Road
Ravenna, OH
866-813-4321
Dogs of all sizes are allowed. There are no additional pet fees. Dogs must be quiet, may not be left unattended, must be leashed, and cleaned up after. This RV park is closed during the off-season. The camping and tent areas also allow dogs. There is a dog walk area at the campground. Multiple dogs may be allowed.

College Corner

Hueston Woods State Park Campground
6301 Park Office Road
College Corner, OH
513-523-6347
The campground at this state park offers 252 sites with electrical hookups and 236 sites with no electric. Campground amenities include showers, flush toilets, laundry, a trailer waste station and nearby hiking trails. Up to two dogs per pet campsite are allowed and they must be leashed and cleaned up after.

Columbus

Crosscreek Camping Resort
3190 S Old State
Delaware, OH
740-549-2267
Dogs of all sizes are allowed. There are no additional pet fees. Dogs may not be left unattended at any time, must be leashed, and cleaned up after. Proof of liability insurance is required if the dog is on the list for aggressive breeds. They are open all year, but with limited services after Thanksgiving. The camping and tent areas also allow dogs. There is a dog walk area at the campground. Multiple dogs may be allowed.

Conneaut

Evergreen Lake Park Campground
703 Center Road

Conneaut, OH
440-599-8802
This 70 acre campground offers over 250 campsites with water and electric hookups, many with full hookups. Amenities include flush toilets, sinks, hot showers, tables, fire rings, public phones, RV parts and service department, snack bar, pizza shop, pool tables, video games, playgrounds, Sunday Church services, shuffleboard, tetherball, horseshoe pits, sand volleyball court and mini golf. Pets are allowed but need to be leashed and cleaned up after. There is no pet fee. The campground is open from the beginning of May to mid-October.

Cortland

Mosquito Lake State Park Campground
1439 State Route 305
Cortland, OH
330-637-2856
The campground at this state park offers 234 sites of which 218 sites have electric hookups. The majority of camp sites are located in a mature forest and the rest of the sites offer lakeshore access and vistas. Campground amenities include a shower building, flush toilets and nearby hiking trails and swimming. Up to two dogs per pet campsite are allowed and they must be leashed and cleaned up after.

Delaware

Alum Creek State Park
3615 S. Old State Road
Delaware, OH
740-548-4039
Dogs of all sizes are allowed. There are no additional pet fees. Dogs may not be left unattended, and they must be leashed and cleaned up after. Dogs are allowed on the trails in the North Camp only. The camping and tent areas also allow dogs. There is a dog walk area at the campground. There are no water hookups at the campground. Multiple dogs may be allowed.

Alum Creek State Park Campgrounds
3615 S. Old State Road
Delaware, OH
740-548-4631
The campground at this state park offers 289 woody and sunny sites with electric hookups. Many of the sites also offer water and sewer

hookups. Campground amenities include heated showers, toilets and nearby hiking trails. Up to two dogs per pet campsite are allowed and they must be leashed and cleaned up after.

Delaware State Park Campground
5202 US 23 North
Delaware, OH
740-369-2761
The campground at this state park offers 211 tent and trailer sites with electric hookups. Campground amenities include flush toilets, showers, laundry facilities, dump station, and nearby hiking trails and swimming areas. Up to two dogs per pet campsite are allowed and they must be leashed and cleaned up after. To get there from Columbus, go north on US 23. Go 5 miles north of the city of Delaware and the park entrance is on the east side of the road at the traffic light.

Deneva

Indian Creek Camping Resort
4710 Lake Road E
Deneva, OH
440-466-8191
Dogs of all sizes are allowed. There are no additional pet fees. Dogs must be well behaved, leashed, and cleaned up after. Dogs may be left for short periods if they will be quiet. They are open in winter without water. The camping and tent areas also allow dogs. There is a dog walk area at the campground. Multiple dogs may be allowed.

E Sparta

Canton/East Sparta KOA
3232 Downing SW
E Sparta, OH
330-484-3901
Dogs of all sizes are allowed. There are no additional pet fees. Dogs must be quiet, leashed, and cleaned up after. There are some breed restrictions. The camping and tent areas also allow dogs. There is a dog walk area at the campground. Multiple dogs may be allowed.

East Liverpool

Beaver Creek State Park Campground
12021 Echo Dell Road
East Liverpool, OH

330-385-3091
The campground at this state park offers 53 sites with no electric hookups. Campground amenities include tables, fire rings, pit latrines, a dump station and nearby hiking trails. Up to two dogs per pet campsite are allowed and they must be leashed and cleaned up after.

Fayette

Harrison Lake State Park Campground
26246 Harrison Lake Road
Fayette, OH
419-237-2593
The campground at this state park offers 199 campsites of which 144 have electric hookups. Amenities include showers, flush toilets, a dump station and nearby hiking trails. They have designated sites for campers with pets and offer self-serve "mutt mitts" for cleaning up after your pooch. Up to two dogs per campsite are allowed and they must be leashed and cleaned up after. To get there from Toledo, take U.S. 20 West through Fayette to County Road 27. Turn left and drive 2 miles to the park.

Findlay

Pleasant View
12611 Township Road 218
Van Buren, OH
419-299-3897
Dogs of all sizes are allowed. There are no additional pet fees. Dogs must be well behaved, leashed, and cleaned up after. This RV park is closed during the off-season. The camping and tent areas also allow dogs. There is a dog walk area at the campground. Multiple dogs may be allowed.

Van Buren State Park Campgrounds
12259 Township Rd. 218
Van Buren, OH
419-832-7662
This park offers a campground with 40 non-electric sites and a multi-use campground for general and horse camping with 38 non-electric sites. Camp amenities include tables, pit toilets, and hiking trails. There are certain designated sites for campers with pets. Up to two dogs per campsite are allowed and they must be leashed and cleaned up after.

Geneva-on-the-Lake

Geneva State Park Campground
4499 Padanarum Road
Geneva, OH
440-466-8400
The campground at this state park offers 88 shaded or sunny sites with electric hookups. Campground amenities include showers, flush toilets and nearby hiking trails. Up to two dogs per pet campsite are allowed and they must be leashed and cleaned up after. To get there from Cleveland, take Interstate 90 east to Route 534 north. The park entrance is six miles north on Route 534, on the left.

Indian Creek Camping Resort
4710 Lake Road East
Geneva-on-the-Lake, OH
440-466-8191
This 110 acre campground offers tent sites and RV sites with full hookups. Big rigs are welcome. Campground amenities include restrooms, heated adult pool for people 21 years and older, heated family pool, coin guest laundry, playground, game room, 18 hole miniature golf, church services, lounge and more. Pets are allowed but need to be kept on a leash, cleaned up after and not left attended. There are no pet fees.

Hillsboro

Rocky Fork State Park
9800 North Shore Drive
Hillsboro, OH
937-393-4284
Dogs of all sizes are allowed. There are no additional pet fees. Dogs may not be left unattended, and they must be leashed and cleaned up after. Dogs are allowed on the trails, but not at the beach swim area. The camping and tent areas also allow dogs. There is a dog walk area at the campground. There are no water hookups at the campground. 2 dogs may be allowed.

Rocky Fork State Park Campground
9800 North Shore Drive
Hillsboro, OH
937-393-4284
The campground at this state park offers 230 tent and trailer sites, of which 130 have electricity, 80 are non-electric and 20 have full hookups. Campground amenities include showers, flush toilets,

laundry facilities, dump station, camp store, volleyball and playground equipment, miniature golf course, tether ball, basketball court, horseshoe pits and nearby hiking trails. Games and sporting equipment can be loaned to registered campers. Up to two dogs per pet campsite are allowed and they must be leashed and cleaned up after.

Hocking Hills

Strouds Run State Park Campground
11661 State Park Road
Athens, OH
740-592-2302
The campground at this state park offers 75 non-electric camp sites for tents or trailers. Campground amenities include toilets, waste drains, picnic tables, fire rings and nearby hiking trails and lake. Up to two dogs per pet campsite are allowed and they must be leashed and cleaned up after.

Forest Haven Campground
2342 Walnut Creek Road
Chillicothe, OH
740-774-1203
This campground is open year round and offers spacious shaded sites. Both full hookup and primitive sites are available. Campground amenities include flush toilets, hot showers, TV/VCR/Video rentals, laundry facility, two playgrounds, bike rentals, swim area, camp store, paddle boats, small fishing lake, horseshoe pit, game room, dump station, book exchange, Halloween campout, basketball court, Internet access and tent rentals. Pets are allowed but need to be leashed and cleaned up after. There is no pet fee.

Great Seal State Park Campground
635 Rocky Road
Chillicothe, OH

The campground at this state park offers 15 campsites with pressurized water, vault latrines, a playground and a shelterhouse. The campground is located adjacent to Sugarloaf Mountain. Amenities include nearby hiking trails. Up to two dogs per campsite are allowed and they must be leashed and cleaned up after. To get there from Columbus, take U.S. 23 South

through Circleville 17 miles to the Delano Exit. Follow the signs to the park. The park is located 3 miles east off of U.S. 23.

Burr Oak State Park Campground
10220 Burr Oak Lodge Road
Glouster, OH
740-767-3570
The campground at this state park offers 100 non-electric sites for campers. Campground amenities include showers, flush toilets, a dump station and nearby hiking trails and lake. Up to two dogs per pet campsite are allowed and they must be leashed and cleaned up after.

Smoke Rise Ranch Resort Camping
6751 Hunterdon Road
Glouster, OH
740-767-2624
This working cattle ranch offers a campground with both tent and RV sites. Sites with no hookups are about $16 per night. Sites with electricity and water hookups are about $20 per night. Rates include two adults and two children. There is a $8 fee per additional person. Dogs are welcome in the campground but need to be leashed and cleaned up after. Pets are not allowed in the cabins.

Lancaster RV Campground
2151 W Fair Avenue
Lancaster, OH
740-653-2261
Dogs of all sizes are allowed. There are no additional pet fees. Dogs must be leashed and cleaned up after. This RV park is closed during the off-season. The camping and tent areas also allow dogs. There is a dog walk area at the campground. Multiple dogs may be allowed.

Palmerosa Campground
19217 Keifel Road
Laurelville, OH
740-385-3799
This horseman's campground is located next to Hocking Hills State Forest and offers both RV sites with electric hookups and primitive camp sites. You are welcome with or without horses. Camp amenities include hot showers, outhouses, picnic tables, dump facilities, and a small tack and gift shop. Pets are welcome but need to be leashed and under control, and cleaned up after. There is a $5 one time per stay pet fee per pet.

Salt Creek Retreats
17549 Crawford Road
Laurelville, OH
614-397-3422
These vacation rentals are located near the Hocking Hills area. They offer one cabin rental and one yurt rental (rustic with no electricity or plumbing). Both rentals are furnished. The cabin has air conditioning and a gas furnace. Depending on the season and day of the week, rates for the cabin range from about $90 to $125 per night for up to four people. Yurt rates range from $50 to $65 per night for up to six people. Extra people can be accommodated if they bring their own tent. There is a $10 charge per night per extra person. Pets and children are welcome. There is a $15 one time per stay pet fee. Rental rates are subject to change. Call for details about payment.

Caveman Retreats Campgrounds and Cabin Rentals
18693 State Route 664S
Logan, OH
740-385-9485
This campground is on 20 wooded acres and situated on a working Christmas tree farm. They have primitive tent sites, electric hookup sites and furnished rustic cabins. Camp amenities include restrooms, picnic tables and fire rings. Pets are allowed and there is a $10 per night pet fee if you stay in one of the rustic cabins. Pets need to be leashed and cleaned up after. Camping sites start at about $18 per night and rustic cabins start at about $90 per night.

Hocking Hills State Park
20160 H 664
Logan, OH
740-385-6841
Dogs of all sizes are allowed. There are no additional pet fees. Dogs may not be left unattended, must be on no more than a 6 foot leash, and be cleaned up after. This RV park is closed during the off-season. The camping and tent areas also allow dogs. There is a dog walk area at the campground. Multiple dogs may be allowed.

Hocking Hills State Park Campground
19852 State Route 664 South
Logan, OH
740-385-6842
The campground at this state park offers 159 electric sites with 20 to 50 amp electric hookups and 13 non-electric sites. All sites have a paved pad for up to a 50 foot unit. Campground amenities include heated showers, flush toilets, laundry facility, camp store, swimming pool, playgrounds, a volleyball court and nearby hiking trails. Up to two dogs per campsite are allowed and they must be leashed and cleaned up after. To get there from Columbus, take U.S. 33 East through Lancaster to Logan and exit onto State Route 664 South.

Scenic View Family Campground
29150 Pattor Road
Logan, OH
740-385-4295
Dogs of all sizes are allowed. There are no additional pet fees. Dogs must be leashed and cleaned up after. There are some breed restrictions. This RV park is closed during the off-season. There is a dog walk area at the campground. 2 dogs may be allowed.

Lake Hope State Park Campground
27331 State Route 278
McArthur, OH
740-596-5253

Top O' The Caves Camping
26780 Chapel Ridge Road
South Bloomingville, OH
800-967-2434
This 60 acre resort offers the largest campground in the Hocking Hills. They are surrounded by dog-friendly state parks (dogs on leash) which you can walk to from your site. They have both tent camping and full RV hookups. Each site includes a picnic table and fire ring. Resort amenities include two modern shower houses with hot water, a large swimming pool, kids playground, mini golf, large game arcade, gift shop, laundry facilities and Sunday worship services. Pets are welcome and there are no pet fees. Please keep your dog leashed and clean up after them. The resort also offers cabins rentals that allow dogs. The resort is located on Chapel Ridge Road, near Highway 374.

Jackson

Lazy Dog Camp Resort & Noah's Ark Animal Farm
1527 McGiffins Road
Jackson, OH
800-282-2167
Dogs of all sizes are allowed at the tent and RV sites. Small dogs only, under 15 pounds are allowed at the cabins. There are no additional pet fees. Dogs must be leashed and cleaned up after. Dogs are not allowed at the lake, nor at the Noah's Ark Animal Farm. The camping and tent areas also allow dogs. There is a dog walk area at the campground. Dogs are allowed in the camping cabins.

Lake Erie Island Region

Kelleys Island State Park Campground
Division Street
Kelleys Island, OH
419-746-2546
The family campground at this state park offers 82 electric sites and 45 non-electric sites. Campground amenities include showers, flush toilets, a dump station, volleyball court, playground, beaches and six miles of hiking trails. Pets are welcome in the designated pet camp sites. Up to two dogs per campsite are allowed and they must be leashed and cleaned up after. There is a $1 per pet fee. To get there you will need to take a ferry to the island. Kelleys Island Ferry Boat Line operates year round, weather permitting, and offers passenger and limited vehicle service from Marblehead, Ohio to the island. Leashed pets are welcome on the ferry. Once on Kelleys Island, go west on E. Lakeshore Drive and turn right on Division Street. The park is at the end of Division Street on the right.

Cedarlane RV Park
2926 NE Catawba Road
Port Clinton, OH
419-797-9907
Dogs of all sizes are allowed. There are no additional pet fees. Dogs may not be left unattended, must be leashed, and cleaned up after. This RV park is closed during the off-season. The camping and tent areas also allow dogs. There is a dog walk area at the campground. 2 dogs may be allowed.

East Harbor State Park Campground
Route 269
Port Clinton, OH
419-734-4424

The campground at this state park is the largest in the Ohio State Park system. It offers 365 sites with electric hookups and 205 with no electric. Campground amenities include showers, flush toilets, dump station, camp store and nearby hiking trails. Up to two dogs per pet campsite are allowed and they must be leashed and cleaned up after. To get there from Cleveland, take State Route 2 West to State Route 269 North. The park is located on State Route 269. To get there from Port Clinton, go east on Route 163 to Route 269 north.

Shade Acres RV Campground
1810 W. Catawba Road
Port Clinton, OH
419-797-4681
RV sites include water and electric service, picnic tables, fire rings, shade and a concrete patio. Amenities include a small playground. Pets are allowed in the RV sites but not in the tent camping sites. There is no pet fee.

Sleepy Hollows Family Camping
2817 E. Harbor Road
Port Clinton, OH
419-734-3556
This campground offers tent sites and RV sites, some of which have electric hookups. Amenities include wooded sites, picnic tables, fire rings, dump station, firewood sales and a boat storage area. Pets are allowed but you will need to register your pet at the office. Pets must be leashed and cleaned up after. The RV park is open from mid-May to mid-October. They are located four miles east of Port Clinton on State Route 163.

Camper Village RV Park
One Cedar Point Drive
Sandusky, OH
419-627-2106
This RV park is located at Cedar Point Amusement Park. The campground offers over 200 camp sites. There are 111 electric only sites and 97 full hookup sites. Tent camping or ground fires are not permitted. Amenities include restrooms, shower facilities, guest laundry, picnic tables and camping supply store. Pets are allowed but must be on leash and not left unattended. Pets can be boarded at Cedar Point's Pet Check during park operating hours for $10 per day during the day only.

South Bass Island State Park Campground
Catawba Avenue
South Bass Island, OH
419-285-2112
The campground at this state park offers 125 non-electric camp sites and 10 full service sites with electric, water and sewer hookups. Amenities include showers, flush toilets and a dump station. This 32 acre state park does not allow dogs on the beach and does not really have any hiking trails. Up to two dogs per campsite are allowed and they must be leashed and cleaned up after. There is a $1 per pet fee. To get there you will need to take a ferry to South Bass Island. Miller Boat Line departs from Catawba and Jet Express departs from Port Clinton. Both ferries go to the island and both allow leashed dogs. Jet Express requires that dogs stay on the outside deck. While both ferries offer passenger transportation, Miller Boat Line also offers limited vehicle service. Once on the island, you can either drive your own car or rent a dog-friendly golf cart. From the village, take Catawba Avenue until you reach the park.

Lakeside-Marblehead

East Harbor State Park
1169 N Buck Road
Lakeside-Marblehead, OH
866-644-6727
There are many recreational activities to enjoy at this park as it is located along the shores of Lake Erie and it has the largest campground in the Ohio Park System. Dogs of all sizes are allowed. There are no additional pet fees. Dogs may not be left unattended at any time, they must be on no more than a 6 foot leash, and be cleaned up after. Dogs must be walked in the pet designated areas of the park. Dogs must be quiet, well behaved, and have current rabies and shot records. The camping and tent areas also allow dogs. There is a dog walk area at the campground. There are no water hookups at the campground. 2 dogs may be allowed.

Lakeview

Indian Lake State Park Campground

12774 State Route 235 N
Lakeview, OH
937-843-2717
The campground at this state park offers 441 tent and trailer sites, most of which have electrical hookups. Campground amenities include heated shower houses, flush toilets, laundry facility and nearby hiking trails and swimming area. Up to two dogs per pet campsite are allowed and they must be leashed and cleaned up after. To get there from Columbus, take U.S. 33 towards Marysville. The park is about an hour and 15 minutes northwest on U.S. 33.

Lisbon

Lock 30 RV Campground Resort
45529 Middle Beaver Road
Lisbon, OH
330-424-9197
This campground offers RV sites with full hookups with extra space around your site. Amenities include picnic tables, fire rings, hiking and biking trails, vending machines, game room, book exchange, playground, toddler playground, basketball, volleyball, horseshoes, bathrooms with showers, private fishing lake, river access, private dog swim area and hiking paths to the actual un-restored Lock 30 of the historic Sandy & Beaver Canal. Pets are welcome but need to be leashed and cleaned up after. There is no extra pet fee.

Lore City

Salt Fork State Park Campgrounds
14755 Cadiz Road
Lore City, OH
740-439-3521
The campground at this state park offers 212 sites all with electrical hookups. Campground amenities include heated shower houses, flush toilets, a dump station and nearby hiking trails. Up to two dogs per pet campsite are allowed and they must be leashed and cleaned up after.

Louisville

Cutty's Sunset Camping Resort
8050 Edison Street NE
Louisville, OH
330-935-2431
Dogs of all sizes are allowed. There are no additional pet fees. Dogs must be leashed and cleaned up

after. This RV park is closed during the off-season. The camping and tent areas also allow dogs. There is a dog walk area at the campground. 2 dogs may be allowed.

Mantua

Jellystone Park
3392 H 82
Mantua, OH
330-562-9100
Dogs of all sizes are allowed. There are no additional pet fees. Dogs must be leashed and cleaned up after. Dogs are not allowed in the rentals or at the beach. This RV park is closed during the off-season. The camping and tent areas also allow dogs. There is a dog walk area at the campground. Multiple dogs may be allowed.

McClure

Mary Jane Thurston State Park Campground
1-466 State Route 65
McClure, OH
419-832-7662
The campground at this state park offers 35 sites with no electric hookups. Fifteen of the sites are for walk-in tent camping only. Campground amenities include restrooms, a nearby dump station and nearby hiking trails. Up to two dogs per campsite are allowed and they must be leashed and cleaned up after.

Mount Gilead

Mount Gilead State Park Campground
4119 State Route 95
Mount Gilead, OH
419-946-1961
The campground at this state park is set in a scenic pine forest and offers 59 sites with electrical hookups. Campground amenities include a camp store, fire rings, picnic tables, waste water drains, toilets and hiking trails. Up to two dogs per campsite are allowed and they must be leashed and cleaned up after.

Mount Sterling

Deer Creek State Park
20635 Waterloo Road
Mount Sterling, OH
740-869-3508

Dogs of all sizes are allowed. There are no additional pet fees. Dogs may not be left unattended, and they must be on no more than a 6 foot leash, and be cleaned up after. Dogs are not allowed on the swim beach, in any of the buildings, or on the trails. The camping and tent areas also allow dogs. There is a dog walk area at the campground. There are no water hookups at the campground. 2 dogs may be allowed.

Deer Creek State Park Campground
20635 Waterloo Road
Mount Sterling, OH
740-869-3124

N Lawrence

Clay's Park Resort
13190 Patterson Road
N Lawrence, OH
800-860-4FUN (386)
Dogs of all sizes are allowed. There are no additional pet fees. Dogs must be leashed and cleaned up after. Dogs may not be tied up outside unattended. There are some breed restrictions. This RV park is closed during the off-season. The camping and tent areas also allow dogs. There is a dog walk area at the campground. 2 dogs may be allowed.

Nashport

Dillon State Park Campground
5265 Dillon Hills Drive
Nashport, OH
740-453-4377
The campground at this state park offers 195 sites and 183 of them have electrical hookups. There are also walk-in sites which offer primitive camping. Campground amenities include showers, flush toilets, a dump station, guest laundry, store with groceries, nearby hiking trails. Up to two dogs per pet campsite are allowed and they must be leashed and cleaned up after.

Newbury

Punderson State Park Campground
11755 Kinsman Road
Newbury, OH
440-564-2279

The campground at this state park, once a former Indian village, offers 196 sites with electrical hookups. Five of the sites have full hookups with electricity, water and sewer service. Campground amenities include showers, flush toilets and nearby hiking and swimming. Up to two dogs per pet campsite are allowed and they must be leashed and cleaned up after.

Pleasant Plain

Stonelick State Park Campground
2895 Lake Drive
Pleasant Plain, OH
513-625-7544
The campground at this state park offers 115 sites with electrical hookups. Campground amenities include showers, flush toilets, camp store, laundry facilities, a dump station and nearby hiking trails. Up to two dogs per pet campsite are allowed and they must be leashed and cleaned up after.

Portsmouth

Shawnee State Park
4404 H 125
Portsmouth, OH
740-858-4561
Dogs of all sizes are allowed. There are no additional pet fees. Dogs may not be left unattended, they must be quiet, well behaved, be on no more than a 6 foot leash, and be cleaned up after. The camping and tent areas also allow dogs. There is a dog walk area at the campground. There are no water hookups at the campground. 2 dogs may be allowed.

Shawnee State Park Campground
4404 State Route 125
Portsmouth, OH
740-858-6652
The campground at this state park offers 103 tent and trailer sites with electrical hookups. Campground amenities include heater shower houses, flush toilets, laundry facilities, a dump station and nearby hiking trails and swimming. Up to two dogs per pet campsite are allowed and they must be leashed and cleaned up after.

Put-in-Bay

Fox's Den Campground
140 Conlan Road

Put-in-Bay, OH
419-285-5001
This campground offers over 60 sites with water and electric hookups. Amenities include a laundry facility, camp store, showers, fire rings and dump station. Pets are allowed but need to be leashed and cleaned up after.

Quincy

OakDale Camp
4611 State Route 235 South
Quincy, OH
937-585-6232
This campground offers over 100 campsites with water and electric at each site. Amenities include a shower house with flush toilets, dump stations, trees and wildlife. Pets are welcome, but must be quiet and kept on a leash. There are no pet fees. They are open from April 1 to October 1.

Ravenna

West Branch State Park Campground
5708 Esworthy Road
Ravenna, OH
330-296-3239
The campground at this state park offers 103 sites, 50 of which have 50 amp electric hookups. Campground amenities include heated showers, flush toilets, laundry facilities, a trailer dump station and nearby hiking trails. Up to two dogs per pet campsite are allowed and they must be leashed and cleaned up after.

Reedsville

Forked Run State Park Campground
63300 State Route 124
Reedsville, OH
740-378-6206
The campground at this state park offers 80 electric sites and 100 non-electric sites. Campground amenities include showers, a dump station and nearby hiking trails and lake. Up to two dogs per pet campsite are allowed and they must be leashed and cleaned up after.

Ronmey

Middle Ridge Campground
HC 65, Box 4965 (on Middle Ridge Road)

Ronmey, OH
304-822-8020
Dogs of all sizes are allowed. There are no additional pet fees. Dogs may not be left unattended, must be quiet, well behaved, leashed, and cleaned up after. This RV park is closed during the off-season. The camping and tent areas also allow dogs. There is a dog walk area at the campground. Multiple dogs may be allowed.

Shelby

Shelby/Mansfield KOA
6787 Baker 47
Shelby, OH
419-347-1392
Dogs of all sizes are allowed. There are no additional pet fees. Dogs may not be left unattended at any time, must be on no more than a 6 foot leash, and be cleaned up after. There are some breed restrictions. This RV park is closed during the off-season. The camping and tent areas also allow dogs. There is a dog walk area at the campground. Multiple dogs may be allowed.

Springfield

Buck Creek State Park
1901 Buck Creek Lane
Springfield, OH
937-322-5284
Dogs of all sizes are allowed. There are no additional pet fees. Dogs may not be left unattended, and they must be leashed and cleaned up after. Dogs are not allowed in the water at the swimming area, or any of the sandy areas on the beach, the picnic areas, or in any of the buildings. Dogs must stay in the designated pet areas. The camping and tent areas also allow dogs. There is a dog walk area at the campground. There are no water hookups at the campground. 2 dogs may be allowed.

Buck Creek State Park Campground
1901 Buck Creek Lane
Springfield, OH
937-322-5284
The campground at this state park offers 111 camp sites of which 89 have electricity. Campground amenities include showers, flush toilets, dump station and nearby hiking trails and swim beach. Up to two dogs per pet campsite are allowed and they must be leashed

and cleaned up after. The park is about 48 miles from Columbus. To get there from Columbus, take Interstate 70 west to exit #62 to Route 40 west. Go 3 miles to the first traffic light and turn right on North Bird Road to Buck Creek Lane.

Enon Beach Campground
2401 Enon Road
Springfield, OH
937-882-6431
Dogs of all sizes are allowed. There are no additional pet fees. Dogs may not be left unattended, must be leashed, and cleaned up after. Dogs may go to the lake, but not be on the beach area. The camping and tent areas also allow dogs. There is a dog walk area at the campground. Multiple dogs may be allowed.

St Marys

Grand Lake Saint Marys State Park Campground
834 Edgewater Drive
St Marys, OH
419-394-3611
The campground at this state park offers 210 sites of which 142 have electricity. Campground amenities include flush toilets, laundry, showers, a dump station, and the lake for recreation. Up to two dogs per pet campsite are allowed and they must be leashed and cleaned up after. To get there from Columbus, head west on Route 33 to St. Marys (33 becomes 29 at St. Marys). Stay on the four lane road to Route 364, then go south to 703. Take 730/364 East to the park entrance.

Lake Loramie State Park Campground
834 Edgewater Drive
St Marys, OH
419-394-3611
The campground at this state park offers 161 sites with electric hookups. Campground amenities include shaded waterfront sites, showers, flush toilets, a dump station, nearby hiking trails and swimming areas. Up to two dogs per pet campsite are allowed and they must be leashed, and are not allowed inside any buildings.

Streetsboro

Mar-Lynn Lake Park
187 State Route 303

Streetsboro, OH
330-650-2552
This campground offers full hookup sites, water and electric only sites, pull thru sites and rustic tent sites. Pets are welcome but not in the cabins. Dogs must be leashed, cleaned up after and cannot be left unattended.

Toledo

Maumee Bay State Park Campground
1400 State Park Road
Oregon, OH
419-836-7758
The campground at this state park offers 252 sites with electric hookups. Campground amenities include showers, flush toilets, playground equipment and nearby hiking trails. Up to two dogs per pet campsite are allowed and they must be leashed and cleaned up after.

Toledo East/Stony Ridge KOA
24787 Luckey Road
Perrysburg, OH
419-837-6848
Dogs of all sizes are allowed. There are no additional pet fees. Dogs must be leashed and cleaned up after. This RV park is closed during the off-season. The camping and tent areas also allow dogs. There is a dog walk area at the campground. There are special amenities given to dogs at this campground. Multiple dogs may be allowed.

Wapakoneta

Wapakoneta/Lima S KOA
14719 Cemetary Road
Wapakoneta, OH
419-738-6016
Dogs of all sizes are allowed. There are no additional pet fees. Dogs must be leashed and cleaned up after. There are some breed restrictions. This RV park is closed during the off-season. The camping and tent areas also allow dogs. There is a dog walk area at the campground. Multiple dogs may be allowed.

Waynesville

Caesar Creek State Park
8750 E H 74
Waynesville, OH
513-897-3055

Dogs of all sizes are allowed. There are no additional pet fees. Dogs may not be left unattended, they must be on no more than a 6 foot leash, and be cleaned up after. Dogs must stay in the pet section of the campground. The camping and tent areas also allow dogs. There is a dog walk area at the campground. There are no water hookups at the campground. Multiple dogs may be allowed.

Caesar Creek State Park Campground
8570 East S.R. 73
Waynesville, OH
513-897-3055
The campground at this state park offers 285 shady and sunny sites with electrical hookups. Campground amenities include showers, flush toilets and nearby hiking trails. Up to two dogs per pet campsite are allowed and they must be leashed and cleaned up after. To get there from Cincinnati, take Interstate 71 north to Route 73. Turn right onto Route 73. Then turn left onto Route 380 and left on Center Road.

Wellington

Findley State Park Campground
25381 State Route 58
Wellington, OH
440-647-4490
The campground at this state park offers 272 both sunny and shaded sites with no electric hookups. Campground amenities include showers, flush toilets, laundry facilities, dump station, game room, fully stocked camp store, recreation area with sand volleyball, a basketball court, two horseshoe pits and nearby hiking trails. Up to two dogs per pet campsite are allowed and they must be leashed and cleaned up after. To get there from Cleveland, take Interstate 480 west to Route 10 west and continue to Route 20 west. Then go to Route 58 south and go ten miles. The park is 2.5 miles south of Wellington on the east side of the road.

Whistler

Riverside Whistler Camping and Cabins
8018 Mons Road
Whistler, OH
604-905-5533
Dogs of all sizes are allowed. There

is a $2.50 per night per pet additional fee for the tent and RV sites, and for the one pet friendly cabin. Dogs may not be left unattended at any time, especially inside the RVs in the summer. Dogs must be leashed and cleaned up after. The camping and tent areas also allow dogs. There is a dog walk area at the campground. Dogs are allowed in the camping cabins. Multiple dogs may be allowed.

Wilmington

Beechwood Acres Camping Resort
855 Yankee Road
Wilmington, OH
937-289-2202
This campground is located near Cowan State Park which allows dogs on the hiking trails. Camp amenities include tent and RV sites with hookups, heated swimming pool, game room, bike rentals, onsite convenience store, showers, laundry facilities, playground and golf cart train rides for children. Pets are welcome but need to be leashed and cleaned up after. Pets are not allowed in the cabins. There is a $1 per day pet fee.

Cowan Lake State Park
1750 Osborn Road
Wilmington, OH
937-382-1096
Dogs of all sizes are allowed. There are no additional pet fees. Dogs may not be left unattended, they must be quiet, well behaved, be on no more than a 6 foot leash, and be cleaned up after. Dogs must be walked in designated pet areas only. The camping and tent areas also allow dogs. There is a dog walk area at the campground. There are no water hookups at the campground. 2 dogs may be allowed.

Cowan Lake State Park Campground
1750 Osborn Road
Wilmington, OH
937-382-1096
The campground at this state park offers 254 tent or trailer sites, of which 237 sites have electricity and 17 non-electric sites. Four sites are wheelchair accessible. Campground amenities include a shower house, flush toilets, laundry facilities, a dump station and nearby hiking trails. Up to two dogs per pet campsite are allowed and they must

be leashed and cleaned up after.

Yellow Springs

John Bryan State Park Campground
3790 State Route 370
Yellow Springs, OH
937-767-1274
The campground at this state park offers 10 sites with electrical hookups and 89 sites without electric. Campground amenities include some shaded sites, picnic tables, fire rings, toilets, drinking water, a dump station and nearby hiking trails. Up to two dogs per pet campsite are allowed and they must be leashed and cleaned up after.

Oklahoma Listings

Ardmore

Lake Murray State Park
204 Scenic State H 77
Ardmore, OK
580-223-4044
This is Oklahoma's oldest and largest state park, offering an ATV area, an 18 hole golf course, a nature center, and a wide variety of additional land and water activities and recreation. Dogs of all sizes are allowed at no additional fee. Dogs may not be left unattended, and they must be on no more than a 10 foot leash, and be cleaned up after. Dogs are not allowed on the beach, but they are allowed on the trails. The camping and tent areas also allow dogs. There is a dog walk area at the campground. Dogs are allowed in the camping cabins. Multiple dogs may be allowed.

Bartlesville

Riverside RV Resort
11211 SE Adams Blvd
Bartlesville, OK
888-572-1241
Dogs of all sizes are allowed. There are no additional pet fees. Dogs may not be left unattended outside, and they must be leashed and cleaned up after. There is an 11 mile city maintained walking/biking trail that passes by this resort. There is a dog walk area at the campground.

Multiple dogs may be allowed.

Beaver

Beaver Dunes State Park
H 270
Beaver, OK
580-625-3373
This 520 acre park has 300 acres of sand dunes, perfect for off-roading, hiking and biking. Dogs of all sizes are allowed at no additional fee. Dogs may not be left unattended, and they must be on no more than a 10 foot leash, and be cleaned up after. Dogs are allowed on the trails. This campground is closed during the off-season. The camping and tent areas also allow dogs. There is a dog walk area at the campground. Dogs are allowed in the camping cabins. Multiple dogs may be allowed.

Broken Bow

Broken Bend Resort Park
H 259A
Broken Bow, OK
580-494-6300
This resort park offers an 18 hole golf course, an amphitheater, a nature center, and a wide variety of land and water activities and recreation. Dogs of all sizes are allowed at no additional fee. Dogs may not be left unattended outside, and they must be leashed and cleaned up after in the park. Dogs may be uncrated in the cabins when left inside, only if they are very well behaved and not for long periods. Dogs are allowed on the trails. The camping and tent areas also allow dogs. There is a dog walk area at the campground. Dogs are allowed in the camping cabins. Multiple dogs may be allowed.

Calumet

El Reno West KOA
301 S Walbaum Road
Calumet, OK
405-884-2595
Dogs of all sizes are allowed. There are no additional pet fees. Dogs must be leashed and cleaned up after. This RV park is closed during the off-season. The camping and tent areas also allow dogs. There is a dog walk area at the campground. Dogs are allowed in the camping cabins. Multiple dogs may be allowed.

Canute

Elk City/Clinton KOA
Clinton Lake Road
Canute, OK
580-592-4409
Dogs of all sizes are allowed, and there are no additional pet fees for tent or RV sites. There is a $5 per night per pet additional fee for the cabins. Dogs may not be tied to the trees or left unattended,and they must be quiet, well behaved, leashed, and cleaned up after. There are some breed restrictions. The camping and tent areas also allow dogs. There is a dog walk area at the campground. Dogs are allowed in the camping cabins. Multiple dogs may be allowed.

Catoosa

Tulsa Northeast KOA
19605 E Skelly Drive
Catoosa, OK
918-266-4227
Dogs of all sizes are allowed. There are no additional pet fees. Dogs must be leashed and cleaned up after. There are some breed restrictions. The camping and tent areas also allow dogs. There is a dog walk area at the campground. Dogs are allowed in the camping cabins. Multiple dogs may be allowed.

Chandler

Bell Cow Lake Equestrian Campground and Trails
Lake Road
Chandler, OK
405-258-1460
Dogs of all sizes are allowed. There are no additional pet fees. Dogs may not be left unattended, and they must be leashed and cleaned up after. Dogs are not allowed in the swim area. This RV park is closed during the off-season. The camping and tent areas also allow dogs. There is a dog walk area at the campground. Multiple dogs may be allowed.

Oak Glen RV Park
3 1/2 miles East of Chandler on H 66
Chandler, OK
800-521-6681
Dogs of all sizes are allowed. There are no additional pet fees. Dogs must be leashed and cleaned up after. The camping and tent areas also allow dogs. There is a dog walk

area at the campground. Multiple dogs may be allowed.

Checotah

Checotah/Henryetta KOA
On I 40 @Pierce Road (HC 68, Box750)
Checotah, OK
918-473-6511
Dogs of all sizes are allowed, and there are no additional pet fees for tent or RV sites. There is a $5 one time additional pet fee for cabins. Dogs must be leashed and cleaned up after. There are some breed restrictions. The camping and tent areas also allow dogs. There is a dog walk area at the campground. Dogs are allowed in the camping cabins. Multiple dogs may be allowed.

Clayton

Clayton Lake State Park
HC 60 Box 33-10/ H 271
Clayton, OK
918-569-7981
This park of over 500 acres has a 95 acre lake and offers a variety of land and water recreation. Dogs of all sizes are allowed at no additional fee. Dogs may not be left unattended, and they must be leashed and cleaned up after. However, if there are no other people around and your dog will respond to voice command, they may be off lead when out of the camp area. Dogs are allowed on the trails. The camping and tent areas also allow dogs. There is a dog walk area at the campground. Dogs are allowed in the camping cabins.

Colbert

Colbert KOA
411 Sherrard Street
Colbert, OK
580-296-2485
Dogs of all sizes are allowed. There are no additional pet fees. Dogs may not be left unattended at the cabins or outside, and they must be leashed and cleaned up after. There are some breed restrictions. The camping and tent areas also allow dogs. There is a dog walk area at the campground. Dogs are allowed in the camping cabins. Multiple dogs may be allowed.

Davis

Dreamweaver RV Resort
110 Kay Star Trail
Davis, OK
580-369-3399
Dogs of all sizes are allowed. There are no additional pet fees. Large dogs must be leashed; smaller dogs may be off lead if they are well behaved and under voice control. Dogs may not be left unattended, and they must be friendly and cleaned up after. There is a creek nearby where dogs are also allowed. There is a dog walk area at the campground. Multiple dogs may be allowed.

Elk City

Elk Creek RV Park
317 E 20th
Elk City, OK
580-225-7865
Dogs of all sizes are allowed. There are no additional pet fees. Dogs may not be left unattended outside, and they must leashed and cleaned up after. Dogs must be quiet, and in at night. The camping and tent areas also allow dogs. There is a dog walk area at the campground. Multiple dogs may be allowed.

Fairland

Twin Bridges State Park
14801 S H 137
Fairland, OK
918-540-2545
This small park is known for its fishing and offers a variety of recreational pursuits. Well behaved dogs of all sizes are allowed at no additional fee. Dogs may not be left unattended, and they must be leashed at all times, and be cleaned up after. Dogs are allowed on the trails. The camping and tent areas also allow dogs. There is a dog walk area at the campground. There are no water hookups at the campground. Multiple dogs may be allowed.

Gore

Marval Resort
Marval Lane
Gore, OK
800-340-4280
Dogs of all sizes are allowed, and there are no additional pet fees for tent or RV sites. There is a $20 one

time additional pet fee for the cabins. Dogs may not be left unattended, and they must be on no more than a 10 foot leash, and cleaned up after. The camping and tent areas also allow dogs. There is a dog walk area at the campground. Dogs are allowed in the camping cabins. Multiple dogs may be allowed.

Grand Lake Towne

Water's Edge RV and Cabin Resort
446714 E 355th
Grand Lake Towne, OK
918-782-1444
Dogs of all sizes are allowed. There are no additional pet fees. Dogs may be off leash only if they are good under voice command. Dogs must be quiet, well behaved, and cleaned up after. This is an RV only park. The camping and tent areas also allow dogs. There is a dog walk area at the campground. Multiple dogs may be allowed.

Grove

Bear's Den Resort
25301 H 59
Grove, OK
918-786-6196
Dogs of all sizes are allowed. There are no additional pet fees. Dogs may not be left unattended, and they must be quiet, well behaved, leashed, and cleaned up after. The camping and tent areas also allow dogs. There is a dog walk area at the campground. 2 dogs may be allowed.

Cedar Oaks RV Resort
1550 83rd Street NW
Grove, OK
800-880-8884
Dogs of all sizes are allowed. There are no additional pet fees. Dogs may not be left unattended, and they must be leashed and cleaned up after. There is a fenced in area for off lead. There is a dog walk area at the campground. Multiple dogs may be allowed.

Hinton

Red Rock Canyon State Park
H 281 S
Hinton, OK
405-542-6344
This canyon park adds rock climbing to their other recreational activities, and it is a great place for hiking and exploring. Well behaved dogs of all

sizes are allowed at no additional fee. Dogs may not be left unattended, and they must have current rabies and shot records. Dogs must be on no more than a 10 foot leash at all times. Dogs are allowed on the trails. The camping and tent areas also allow dogs. There is a dog walk area at the campground. Multiple dogs may be allowed.

Hodgen

Big Cedar Adventure Park
21823 H 63
Hodgen, OK
918-651-3271
Dogs of all sizes are allowed. There are no additional pet fees for tent or RV sites. There is an additional one time pet fee of $20 for each 1 to 3 days stay for the 1 pet friendly cabin. Dogs may not be left unattended, and they must be leashed and cleaned up after. The camping and tent areas also allow dogs. There is a dog walk area at the campground. Dogs are allowed in the camping cabins. Multiple dogs may be allowed.

Marietta

Ardmore/Marietta KOA
Oswalt Road (Rt 1, Box 640)
Marietta, OK
580-276-2800
Dogs of all sizes are allowed. There are no additional pet fees. Dogs must be quiet, leashed, and cleaned up after. The camping and tent areas also allow dogs. There is a dog walk area at the campground. Dogs are allowed in the camping cabins. Multiple dogs may be allowed.

Oklahoma City

Oklahoma City East KOA
6200 S Choctaw Road
Choctaw, OK
405-391-5000
Dogs of all sizes are allowed. There are no additional pet fees. Dogs may not be left unattended outside, and they must be leashed and cleaned up after. There are some breed restrictions. The camping and tent areas also allow dogs. There is a dog walk area at the campground. Multiple dogs may be allowed.

Abe's RV Park
12115 N I 35 Service Road

Oklahoma City, OK
405-478-0278
Dogs of all sizes are allowed. There are no additional pet fees. Dogs must be leashed and cleaned up after. There are some breed restrictions. There is a dog walk area at the campground. Multiple dogs may be allowed.

Roadrunner RV Park
4800 S I-35
Oklahoma City, OK
405-677-2373
Small Dogs Only. Dogs of all sizes are allowed. There are no additional pet fees. Dogs may not be left unattended, and they must be leashed and cleaned up after. Only one dog is allowed if the stay is a long one. There is a dog walk area at the campground. 2 dogs may be allowed.

Rockwell RV Park
720 S Rockwell
Oklahoma City, OK
405-787-5992
Dogs of all sizes are allowed. There are no additional pet fees. Dogs must be leashed and cleaned up after. The camping and tent areas also allow dogs. There is a dog walk area at the campground. Multiple dogs may be allowed.

Porter

Crossroads RV Park
6476 35th Street W
Porter, OK
918-686-9104
Dogs up to 50 pounds are allowed. There is a $1 per night per pet additional fee. Dogs must be leashed and cleaned up after. There is a dog walk area at the campground. 2 dogs may be allowed.

Sallisaw

Sallisaw KOA
1908 Power Drive
Sallisaw, OK
918-775-2792
Dogs of all sizes are allowed. There are no additional pet fees. Dogs may not be penned or left unattended outside, and they must be leashed and cleaned up after. The camping and tent areas also allow dogs. There is a dog walk area at the campground. Dogs are allowed in the camping cabins. Multiple dogs may be allowed.

Smithville

Ato Z Guest Ranch
64599 Ashby Road
Smithville, OK
580-244-3729
Dogs of all sizes are allowed. There are no additional pet fees. Dogs may not be left unattended, and they must be leashed and cleaned up after. They request guests do not walk dogs on the trails with the horses. The camping and tent areas also allow dogs. There is a dog walk area at the campground. Multiple dogs may be allowed.

Sulphur

Arbuckle RV Resort
700 Charles Cooper Memorial Road
Sulphur, OK
580-622-6338
Dogs of all sizes are allowed. There are no additional pet fees. Dogs may not be left unattended outside, and they must be quiet, well behaved, leashed, and cleaned up after. This is an RV mostly park, but they do have a few places for tents. There are some breed restrictions. The camping and tent areas also allow dogs. There is a dog walk area at the campground. Multiple dogs may be allowed.

Chickasaw National Rec Area
1 Perimeter Road
Sulphur, OK
580-622-3165
This park has significant geological and hydrological importance, and features various ecosystems along with a variety of activities and land and water recreation. Dogs of all sizes are allowed at no additional fee. Dogs may not be left unattended, and they must be leashed and cleaned up after. Dogs are not allowed on trails behind the Nature Center, but they are allowed on the other trails. The camping and tent areas also allow dogs. There is a dog walk area at the campground. There are no water hookups at the campground. Multiple dogs may be allowed.

Tulsa

Mingo RV Park
801 N Mingo
Tulsa, OK
800-932-8824
Dogs of all sizes are allowed. There

are no additional pet fees. Dogs must be leashed and cleaned up after. There is a dog walk area at the campground. 2 dogs may be allowed.

Tulsa Warrior Campground
5131 S Union
Tulsa, OK
800-426-3199
Dogs of all sizes are allowed. There are no additional pet fees. Dogs may not be left unattended at any time, and they must be leashed and cleaned up after. There is a dog walk area at the campground. Multiple dogs may be allowed.

Vinita

Water's Edge RV Resort
446714 E 355th
Vinita, OK
918-782-1444
Dogs of all sizes are allowed. There are no additional pet fees. Dogs must be leashed and cleaned up after. This RV park is closed during the off-season. The camping and tent areas also allow dogs. There is a dog walk area at the campground. Multiple dogs may be allowed.

Watonga

Roman Nose State Resort Park
H 8 A
Watonga, OK
580-623-4215
Dogs of all sizes are allowed. There are no additional pet fees. Dogs may not be left unattended, and they must be well behaved, be on no more than a 10 foot leash, and cleaned up after. The camping and tent areas also allow dogs. There is a dog walk area at the campground. Dogs are allowed in the camping cabins. Multiple dogs may be allowed.

Oregon Listings

Albany

Albany/Corvallis KOA
33775 Oakville Road S
Albany, OR
541-967-8521
Dogs of all sizes are allowed. There are no additional pet fees. Dogs

must be quiet, well behaved, be on no more than a 6 foot leash, and be cleaned up after. There are some breed restrictions. The camping and tent areas also allow dogs. There is a dog walk area at the campground.

Baker City

Mountain View Holiday T rav-L-Park
2845 Hughes Lane
Baker City, OR
541-523-4824
Dogs up to 30 pounds are allowed. There are no additional pet fees. Dogs may not be left unattended, and must be quiet, leashed and cleaned up after. There are some breed restrictions. The camping and tent areas also allow dogs. There is a dog walk area at the campground. 2 dogs may be allowed.

Oregon Trails West RV Park
42534 N Cedar Road
Baker City, OR
888-523-3236
Dogs of all sizes are allowed. There are no additional pet fees. Dogs must be quiet, leashed and cleaned up after. Dogs may not be left unattended. The camping and tent areas also allow dogs. There is a dog walk area at the campground. Multiple dogs may be allowed.

Wallowa-Whitman National Forest
1550 Dewey Avenue
Baker City, OR
541-523-6391
These forests were combined creating 2.3 million acres of spectacular scenery, hundreds of miles of trails, and diverse ecosystems that support a large variety of plants, animals, and recreation. Dogs of all sizes are allowed at no additional fee. Dogs may not be left unattended, and they must be leashed and cleaned up after in camp areas. Dogs are allowed on the trails. This campground is closed during the off-season. The camping and tent areas also allow dogs. There is a dog walk area at the campground. Multiple dogs may be allowed.

Bandon

Bandon by the Sea RV Park
49612 H 101

Bandon, OR
541-347-5155
Dogs of all sizes are allowed. There are no additional pet fees. Dogs must be well behaved, leashed, and cleaned up after. Dogs may be left in your RV only if they will be comfortable and quiet, and they are not allowed at the club house. There is a dog walk area at the campground. Multiple dogs may be allowed.

Bullards Beach State Park
52470 H 101
Bandon, OR
541-347-2209
This is a large, family-oriented park nestled among the pines along the Coquille River, and offers an historic lighthouse with tours (seasonal) as well as various recreational pursuits. When visiting the park you can bring your binoculars for viewing the wildlife refuge just across the river. Dogs of all sizes are allowed at no additional fee. Dogs may not be left unattended except for short periods, and only if they will be quiet and well behaved. Dogs must be on no more than a 6 foot leash, and cleaned up after. Dogs are allowed on the trails. The camping and tent areas also allow dogs. There is a dog walk area at the campground. Multiple dogs may be allowed.

Bend

Deschutes National Forest
1001 SW Emkay Drive
Bend, OR
541-383-5300
Rich in natural and cultural history, this forest is home to the Newberry National Volcanic Monument, 8 wilderness areas and hundreds of miles of trails. The park also offers many diverse scenic and recreational opportunities. Dogs of all sizes are allowed at no additional fee. Dogs must be leashed and cleaned up after. This campground is closed during the off-season. The camping and tent areas also allow dogs. There is a dog walk area at the campground. Multiple dogs may be allowed.

Sisters/Bend KOA
67667 H 20W
Bend, OR
541-549-3021
Dogs of all sizes are allowed. There are no additional pet fees. Dogs must be leashed and cleaned up after. This RV park is closed during

the off-season. The camping and tent areas also allow dogs. There is a dog walk area at the campground. Multiple dogs may be allowed.

Boardman

Driftwood RV Resort
800 W Kunze Lane
Boardman, OR
541-481-2262
Dogs up to 30 pounds are allowed. There is a $1 per night per pet additional pet fee. Dogs may not be left unattended, and must be leashed and cleaned up after. The camping and tent areas also allow dogs. There is a dog walk area at the campground. 2 dogs may be allowed.

Brookings

At Rivers Edge RV Park
98203 S Bank Chetco River Road
Brookings, OR
541-469-3356
Dogs of all sizes are allowed. There are no additional pet fees. Dogs may not be left unattended unless they will be quiet and well behaved. Dogs must be leashed and cleaned up after. Dogs may be off lead on your site only if they are under voice command and will not chase. The camping and tent areas also allow dogs. There is a dog walk area at the campground. 2 dogs may be allowed.

Harris Beach State Park
1655 H 101N
Brookings, OR
541-469-2021
This park sits along the coastline making marine mammal watching a favorite here. The park also offers interpretive events, nature programs, trails, and a variety of land and water recreation. Dogs of all sizes are allowed at no additional fee. Dogs may not be left unattended; they must be on no more than a 6 foot leash or crated, and cleaned up after. Dogs are allowed on the trails. Dogs are not allowed in buildings. The camping and tent areas also allow dogs. There is a dog walk area at the campground. Multiple dogs may be allowed.

Cannon Beach

Cannon Beach RV Resort

340 Elk Creek Road
Cannon Beach, OR
800-847-2231
Dogs of all sizes are allowed. There are no additional pet fees. Dogs may not be left unattended, and they must be well behaved, leashed, and cleaned up after. There is a dog walk area at the campground. Multiple dogs may be allowed.

Sea Ranch RV Park and Stables
415 1st Street
Cannon Beach, OR
503-436-2815
Dogs of all sizes are allowed. There is a $2 per night per pet additional fee. Dogs may not be left unattended, and they must be leashed and cleaned up after. Dogs must be friendly to other animals because there are a variety of animals on site, including a free range bunny population. The camping and tent areas also allow dogs. There is a dog walk area at the campground. Multiple dogs may be allowed.

Cascade Locks

Cascade Locks/Portland East KOA
841 NW Forest Lane
Cascade Locks, OR
541-374-8668
Dogs of all sizes are allowed. There are no additional pet fees. Dogs may not be left unattended at any time, must be leashed, and cleaned up after. There are some breed restrictions. This RV park is closed during the off-season. The camping and tent areas also allow dogs. There is a dog walk area at the campground. Dogs are allowed in the camping cabins. Multiple dogs may be allowed.

Central Point

Medford/Gold Hill KOA
12297 Blackwell Road
Central Point, OR
541-855-7710
Dogs of all sizes are allowed. There are no additional pet fees. Dogs must be quiet, well behaved, leashed, and cleaned up after. Dogs may not be left unattended, and may be left outside alone only if they are in an enclosed pen. There are some breed restrictions. The camping and tent areas also allow dogs. There is a dog walk area at

the campground. Dogs are allowed in the camping cabins. Multiple dogs may be allowed.

Charleston

Charleston Marina RV Park
63402 King Fisher Road
Charleston, OR
541-888-2548
Dogs of all sizes are allowed. There are no additional pet fees. Dogs may not be left unattended, and they must be leashed and cleaned up after. This RV park is closed during the off-season. The camping and tent areas also allow dogs. There is a dog walk area at the campground. Multiple dogs may be allowed.

Coos Bay

Lucky Loggers RV Park
250 E Johnson
Coos Bay, OR
541-267-6003
Dogs of all sizes are allowed. There are no additional pet fees. Dogs must be leashed and cleaned up after. There is a dog walk area at the campground. Multiple dogs may be allowed.

Midway RV Park
92478 Cape Arago H
Coos Bay, OR
541-888-9300
Dogs up to 50 pounds are allowed. There are no additional pet fees. Dogs must be leashed and cleaned up after. There is a dog walk area at the campground. 2 dogs may be allowed.

Sunset Bay State Park
89814 Cape Arago
Coos Bay, OR
541-888-4902
This picturesque park, along the Oregon coast, features sandy beaches sheltered by towering sea cliffs, interpretive and nature programs, a network of hiking trails, and a variety of land and water recreation. Dogs of all sizes are allowed at no additional fee, and they must have current tags, rabies, and shot records. Dogs may not be left unattended; they must be on no more than a 6 foot leash, and cleaned up after. Dogs are allowed on the trails except where marked. Dogs are not allowed in Shore Acres. The camping and tent areas also allow dogs. There is a dog walk area

at the campground. Multiple dogs may be allowed.

Corvallis

Siuslaw National Forest
4077 SW Research Way
Corvallis, OR
541-750-7000
This very diverse and productive forest of over 630,000 acres has unique and varying ecosystems to explore and offers a wide variety of land and water recreation. Dogs of all sizes are allowed at no additional fee. Dogs may not be left unattended, and they must be leashed and cleaned up after. Dogs are not allowed in public swim areas or buildings. Dogs are allowed on the trails. The camping and tent areas also allow dogs. There is a dog walk area at the campground. There are no water hookups at the campground. Multiple dogs may be allowed.

Crater Lake

Crater Lake National Park
P.O. Box 7/S Entrance Road
Crater Lake, OR
541-594-2211
This beautiful and historical lake park is a very diverse area. It is almost 90% wilderness and supports a large variety of plants, fish, mammals, bird species, and recreation. Dogs of all sizes are allowed at no additional fee. Dogs may not be left unattended, and they must be leashed and cleaned up after. Dogs are not allowed in buildings or in the Rim Village area in the winter. Dogs are allowed on the trails. This campground is closed during the off-season. The camping and tent areas also allow dogs. There is a dog walk area at the campground. Multiple dogs may be allowed.

Culver

Madras/Culver KOA
2435 SW Jericho Lane
Culver, OR
541-546-3046
Dogs of all sizes are allowed, and there are no additional pet fees for up to 2 dogs. If there are more than 2 dogs, the fee is $2 per night per pet. Dogs must be leashed and cleaned up after. There are some breed restrictions. This RV park is closed during the off-season. The camping

and tent areas also allow dogs. There is a dog walk area at the campground. Multiple dogs may be allowed.

The Cove Palisades State Park
7300 SW Jordan Road
Culver, OR
541-546-3412
This high desert park features a myriad of water and land recreational opportunities, 10 miles of hiking trails, a designated off-leash area for your dog, historic sites, and special events and programs throughout the year. Dogs of all sizes are allowed at no additional fee. Dogs may not be left unattended, and they must be on no more than a 6 foot leash and cleaned up after. Dogs are not allowed in any of the swim areas, in buildings, or where posted as such. Dogs are allowed on the trails. The camping and tent areas also allow dogs. There is a dog walk area at the campground. There are special amenities given to dogs at this campground. Multiple dogs may be allowed.

Detroit

Detroit Lake State Recreation Area
44000 N Santiam H SE
Detroit, OR
503-854-3346
This scenic park sits along a beautiful 400-foot-deep lake located in the Cascade Mountains. It features nature programs, interpretive tours and exhibits, various special events, and a variety of land and water recreation. Dogs of all sizes are allowed at no additional fee. Dogs may not be left unattended, and they must be on no more than a 6 foot leash, and cleaned up after. Dogs are allowed on the trails. This campground is closed during the off-season. The camping and tent areas also allow dogs. There is a dog walk area at the campground. Multiple dogs may be allowed.

Diamond Lake

Diamond Lake RV Park
3500 Diamond Lake Loop
Diamond Lake, OR
541-793-3318
Dogs of all sizes are allowed, but only 2 large or 3 small dogs are allowed per site. There are no

additional pet fees. Dogs must be leashed and cleaned up after. This RV park is closed during the off-season. There is a dog walk area at the campground.

Eugene

Premier RV Resorts
33022 Van Duyn Road
Eugene, OR
541-686-3152
Dogs of all sizes are allowed. There are no additional pet fees. Dogs must be leashed and cleaned up after. There is a small fenced in area for off lead. There is a dog walk area at the campground. Multiple dogs may be allowed.

Shamrock RV Village
4531 Franklin Blvd
Eugene, OR
541-747-7473
Dogs of all sizes are allowed. There are no additional pet fees. Dogs must be leashed and cleaned up after. There are some breed restrictions. There is a dog walk area at the campground. Multiple dogs may be allowed.

Florence

Jessie M Honeyman Memorial State Park
84505 H 101S
Florence, OR
541-997-3641
This park has the second largest overnight camping area in the state and features two miles of sand dunes, two natural freshwater lakes, an ATV area, interpretive and nature programs, and a variety of land and water recreation. Dogs of all sizes are allowed at no additional fee. Dogs may not be left unattended, and they must be on no more than a 6 foot leash, and cleaned up after. Dogs are allowed on the trails, but they are not allowed in buildings or yurts. The camping and tent areas also allow dogs. There is a dog walk area at the campground. Multiple dogs may be allowed.

Mercer Lake Resort
88875 Bay Berry Lane
Florence, OR
800-355-3633
Dogs of all sizes are allowed. There is a $5 per night per pet additional fee. Dogs may not be left unattended, and they must be

leashed and cleaned up after. This is an RV only park. There is a dog walk area at the campground. 2 dogs may be allowed.

Woahink Lake RV Resort
83570 H 101 S
Florence, OR
541-997-6454
Dogs up to about 50 pounds are allowed, and there can only be 2 small or one medium sized dog per site. Dogs must be leashed and cleaned up after. There are some breed restrictions. This RV park is closed during the off-season. There is a dog walk area at the campground.

Gold Beach

Four Seasons RV Resort
96526 N Bank Road
Gold Beach, OR
800-248-4503
Dogs of all sizes are allowed. There are no additional pet fees. Dogs must be leashed and cleaned up after. There is a dog walk area at the campground. 2 dogs may be allowed.

Indian Creek Resort
94680 Jerry's Flat Road
Gold Beach, OR
541-247-7704
Dogs of all sizes are allowed, and there are no additional fees for tent or RV sites. There is a $20 one time additional pet fee for cabins. Dogs may not be left unattended outside, and they must be leashed and cleaned up after. Dogs must be quiet and well behaved. The camping and tent areas also allow dogs. There is a dog walk area at the campground. Dogs are allowed in the camping cabins. 2 dogs may be allowed.

Turtle Rock RV Resort
28788 Hunter Creek Loop
Gold Beach, OR
541-247-9203
Dogs of all sizes are allowed. There are no additional pet fees for one pet, either at the tent and RV sites or the cabins. For more than one dog there is a $4 per night per pet additional fee for the tent and RV sites, and a $15 per night per pet additional pet fee for the cabins. Dogs must be leashed and cleaned up after. The camping and tent areas also allow dogs. There is a dog walk

area at the campground. Dogs are allowed in the camping cabins. Multiple dogs may be allowed.

Gold Hill

Valley of the Rouge State Park
I 5 AT Exit 45B
Gold Hill, OR
541-582-1118
This scenic park sits along the river made famous by novelist and avid fisherman Zane Grey. It offers a self-guided interpretive walking trail, nature programs, and a variety of land and water recreation. Dogs of all sizes are allowed at no additional fee. Dogs may not be left unattended, be on no more than a 6 foot, and cleaned up after in camp areas. Dogs are allowed on the trails, and they may be off lead there if they will not chase and they are under voice command. The camping and tent areas also allow dogs. There is a dog walk area at the campground. Multiple dogs may be allowed.

Grants Pass

Jack's Landing RV Resort
247 NE Morgan Lane
Grants Pass, OR
541-472-1144
Dogs of all sizes are allowed. There are no additional pet fees. Dogs may not be placed in outdoor pens or be left unattended. They may be left in the RV if comfortable and quiet. Dogs must be leashed and cleaned up after. There is a dog walk area at the campground. Multiple dogs may be allowed.

Siskiyou National Forest
2164 NE Spalding Avenue
Grants Pass, OR
541-471-6500
Rogue River and Siskiyou National Forests were combined creating 1.8 million acres of spectacular scenery, hundreds of miles of trails, and diverse ecosystems that support a large variety of plants, animals, and recreation. Dogs of all sizes are allowed at no additional fee. Dogs may not be left unattended, and they must be leashed and cleaned up after in camp areas. Dogs are allowed off lead in the forest if they will not chase and if they are under strict voice control. This campground is closed during the off-season. The camping and tent areas also allow

dogs. There is a dog walk area at the campground. Multiple dogs may be allowed.

Hammond

Astoria/Seaside KOA
1100 Northwest Ridge Road
Hammond, OR
503-861-2606
Dogs of all sizes are allowed. There is a $2 per night per pet additional fee. Dogs may not be left unattended, must be leashed, and cleaned up after. There are some breed restrictions. The camping and tent areas also allow dogs. There is a dog walk area at the campground. Dogs are allowed in the camping cabins. 2 dogs may be allowed.

Fort Stevens State Park
100 Peter Ierdale
Hammond, OR
503-861-1671
Born out of the need for military defense this historic park offers programs and exhibits on its history, a nature/visitor center, several trails, various habitats, and a variety of land and water recreation. Dogs of all sizes are allowed at no additional fee. Dogs may not be left unattended, and they must be on no more than a 6 foot leash, and cleaned up after. Dogs are allowed off lead on South Beach, and they are allowed on the trails. The camping and tent areas also allow dogs. There is a dog walk area at the campground. Multiple dogs may be allowed.

Hornbrook

Blue Heron RV Park
6930 Copco Road
Hornbrook, OR
530-475-3270
Dogs of all sizes are allowed. There is a $1 per night per pet additional fee. Dogs must be leashed and cleaned up after. There is a dog walk area at the campground. Multiple dogs may be allowed.

John Day

Malheur National Forest
431 Patterson Bridge Road
John Day, OR
541-575-3000
This 1.7 million acre forest offers spectacular scenery, hundreds of miles of trails, and diverse

ecosystems that support a large variety of plants, animals, and recreation. Dogs of all sizes are allowed at no additional fee. Dogs may not be left unattended, and they must be leashed and cleaned up after. This campground is closed during the off-season. The camping and tent areas also allow dogs. There is a dog walk area at the campground. There are no electric or water hookups at the campground. Multiple dogs may be allowed.

Joseph

Park at the River
59879 Wallowa Lake H
Joseph, OR
541-432-8800
Dogs of all sizes are allowed. There are no additional pet fees. Dogs may not be left unattended, and must be well behaved, leashed, and cleaned up after. Dogs are not allowed at any of the rentals. There is a dog walk area at the campground. Multiple dogs may be allowed.

Klamath Falls

Fremont- WINEMA National Forest
2819 Dahlia Street
Klamath Falls, OR
541-883-6714
The Fremont-Winema National Forests were combined creating 2.3 million acres of spectacular scenery, hundreds of miles of trails, and diverse ecosystems that support a large variety of plants, animals, and recreation. Dogs of all sizes are allowed at no additional fee. Dogs may not be left unattended, and they must be leashed and cleaned up after in camp areas. Dogs may be off lead in the forest if they will not chase and they are under voice control. Dogs are not allowed in buildings. This campground is closed during the off-season. The camping and tent areas also allow dogs. There is a dog walk area at the campground. There are no electric or water hookups at the campground. Multiple dogs may be allowed.

Klamath Falls KOA
3435 Shasta Way
Klamath Falls, OR
541-884-4644
Dogs of all sizes are allowed. There are no additional pet fees. Dogs may not be left unattended, and they must be leashed and cleaned up after. There is a large fenced in area

where dogs may run off lead. The camping and tent areas also allow dogs. There is a dog walk area at the campground. Multiple dogs may be allowed.

LaPine

LaPine State Park
15800 State Recreation Road
LaPine, OR
541-536-2071
This park, home to the oldest tree in Oregon aged about 500 years, offers access to 2 rivers, 10 miles of trails, a museum, and a variety of land and water recreation. Dogs of all sizes are allowed at no additional fee. Dogs may not be left unattended, and they must be on no more than a 6 foot leash, and cleaned up after. Dogs are allowed on trails unless otherwise marked. The camping and tent areas also allow dogs. There is a dog walk area at the campground. Multiple dogs may be allowed.

Lakeview

FREEMONT-Winema National Forest
1301 S G Street
Lakeview, OR
541-947-2151
The Fremont-Winema National Forests were combined creating 2.3 million acres of spectacular scenery, hundreds of miles of trails, and diverse ecosystems that support a large variety of plants, animals, and recreation. Dogs of all sizes are allowed at no additional fee. Dogs may not be left unattended, and they must be leashed and cleaned up after. This campground is closed during the off-season. The camping and tent areas also allow dogs. There is a dog walk area at the campground. There are no electric or water hookups at the campground. Multiple dogs may be allowed.

Langlois

Bandon/Port Orford KOA
46612 H 101
Langlois, OR
541-348-2358
Dogs of all sizes are allowed. There are no additional pet fees. Dogs must be leashed and cleaned up after. There are some breed restrictions. The camping and tent

areas also allow dogs. There is a dog walk area at the campground. 2 dogs may be allowed.

Lebanon

Premier RV Resort
31958 Bellinger Scale Road
Lebanon, OR
541-259-0070
Dogs of all sizes are allowed. There are no additional pet fees. Dogs may not be left unattended, and must be leashed and cleaned up after. There is a fenced dog run area for off lead. There is a dog walk area at the campground. Multiple dogs may be allowed.

McKenzie Bridge

Willamette National Forest
57600 McKenzie H
McKenzie Bridge, OR
541-822-3381
This forest has over a million and a half acres of high mountains, cascading streams, narrow canyons, and diverse ecosystems that support a large variety of plants, animals, and recreation. Dogs of all sizes are allowed at no additional fee. Dogs may not be left unattended, and they must be leashed and cleaned up after in camp. Dogs may be off lead on the trails only if they will not chase, and if they are under strict voice command. The camping and tent areas also allow dogs. There is a dog walk area at the campground. There are no electric or water hookups at the campground. Multiple dogs may be allowed.

Medford

Rogue River National Forest
333 W 8th Street
Medford, OR
541-858-2200
Rogue River and Siskiyou National Forests were combined creating 1.8 million acres of spectacular scenery, hundreds of miles of trails, and diverse ecosystems that support a large variety of plants, animals, and recreation. Dogs of all sizes are allowed at no additional fee. Dogs may not be left unattended, and they must be leashed and cleaned up after in camp areas. Dogs are allowed off lead in the forest if they will not chase and if they are under strict voice control. This campground is closed during the off-season. The

camping and tent areas also allow dogs. There is a dog walk area at the campground. There are no water hookups at the campground. Multiple dogs may be allowed.

Mosier

Memaloose State Park
Box 472
Mosier, OR
541-478-3008
This oasis like park offers interpretive exhibits and events, nature programs, various day and night programs and a variety of land and water recreation. Dogs of all sizes are allowed at no additional fee. Dogs may not be left unattended unless they will be quiet and well behaved, and they must be on no more than a 6 foot leash, and cleaned up after. Dogs are allowed on the trails unless otherwise marked, and they may be off lead on trails if they are under strict voice command. This campground is closed during the off-season. The camping and tent areas also allow dogs. There is a dog walk area at the campground. Multiple dogs may be allowed.

Myrtle Creek

On the River Golf & RV Resort
111 Whitson Lane
Myrtle Creek, OR
541-679-3505
Dogs of all sizes are allowed. There are no additional pet fees. Dogs may not be left unattended outside, and they must be leashed and cleaned up after. There are some breed restrictions. The camping and tent areas also allow dogs. There is a dog walk area at the campground. Multiple dogs may be allowed.

Netarts

Netarts Bay RV Park and Marina
2260 Bilyeu Avenue
Netarts, OR
503-842-7774
Dogs of all sizes are allowed. There are no additional pet fees. Dogs must be leashed and cleaned up after. There are some breed restrictions. There is a dog walk area at the campground. 2 dogs may be allowed.

Newport

Beverly Beach State Park
198 NE 123rd Street
Newport, OR
541-265-9278
This forest-sheltered campground sits along the Oregon coast providing a long sandy seashore to explore. It provides nature programs, trails, interpretive programs, and a variety of recreational pursuits. Dogs of all sizes are allowed at no additional fee. Dogs may not be left unattended, and they must be on no more than a 6 foot leash, and cleaned up after. Dogs are allowed on trails unless otherwise marked. The camping and tent areas also allow dogs. There is a dog walk area at the campground. Multiple dogs may be allowed.

North Bend

Oregon Dunes KOA
68632 H 101
North Bend, OR
541-756-4851
Dogs of all sizes are allowed. There are no additional pet fees. Dogs must be leashed and cleaned up after, and walked by an adult. Dogs are not allowed to be left unattended outside, but they may be left in your auto or RV if they will be comfortable and quiet. The camping and tent areas also allow dogs. There is a dog walk area at the campground. Multiple dogs may be allowed.

Otis

Lincoln City KOA
5298 NE Park Lane
Otis, OR
541-994-2961
Dogs of all sizes are allowed. There is a pet policy to sign at check in and there are no additional pet fees. Dogs must be leashed and cleaned up after. There are some breed restrictions. The camping and tent areas also allow dogs. There is a dog walk area at the campground. Multiple dogs may be allowed.

Pacific City

Cape Kiwanda RV Resort
33305 Cape Kiwanda Drive
Pacific City, OR
503-965-6230
Dogs of all sizes are allowed. There

are no additional pet fees. Dogs must be leashed and cleaned up after. There is a dog walk area at the campground. Multiple dogs may be allowed.

Pendleton

Umatilla National Forest
2517 SW Hailey Avenue
Pendleton, OR
541-278-3716
This forest of nearly 1.4 million acres provides spectacular scenery, a rich cultural history, and diverse ecosystems that support a large variety of plants, animals, and recreation. Dogs of all sizes are allowed at no additional fee. Dogs may not be left unattended; they must be quiet, well behaved, be on no more than a 6 foot leash, and cleaned up after in camp areas. Dogs are allowed on the trails. This campground is closed during the off-season. The camping and tent areas also allow dogs. There is a dog walk area at the campground. Dogs are allowed in the camping cabins. There are no electric or water hookups at the campground. Multiple dogs may be allowed.

Phoenix

Holiday RV Park
201 Fern Valley Road
Phoenix, OR
800-452-7970
Dogs up to 25 pounds are allowed. There are no additional pet fees. Dogs may not be left unattended outside, and they must be leashed and cleaned up after. There is a dog walk area at the campground. 2 dogs may be allowed.

Portland

Jantzen Beach RV Park
1503 N Hayden Island Drive
Portland, OR
503-289-7626
One dog of any size is allowed. There are no additional pet fees. Dogs may not be left unattended outside, and they must be leashed and cleaned up after. This is an RV only park. There are some breed restrictions. There is a dog walk area at the campground.

Riverside RV Park
24310 S H 99E
Portland, OR

503-263-3000
Dogs up to 40 pounds are allowed. There are no additional pet fees. Dogs may not be left unattended outside, and they must be quiet, leashed, and cleaned up after. There is a dog walk area at the campground. Multiple dogs may be allowed.

Portland Area

Portland Fairview RV Park
21401 NE Sandy Blvd
Fairview, OR
503-661-1047
Dogs of all sizes are allowed. There are no additional pet fees. Dogs must be quiet, friendly, well behaved, leashed, and cleaned up after. Dogs may not be left unattended outside. There are some breed restrictions. There is a dog walk area at the campground. Multiple dogs may be allowed.

Rolling Hills RV Park
20145 NE Sandy Blvd
Fairview, OR
503-666-7282
Dogs of all sizes are allowed. There are no additional pet fees. Dogs may not be left unattended or chained outside alone. Dogs must be leashed and cleaned up after. There are some breed restrictions. There is a dog walk area at the campground. Multiple dogs may be allowed.

RV Park of Portland
6645 SW Nyberg Road
Tualatin, OR
503-692-0225
Dogs of all sizes are allowed, but only 1 dog may be over 40 pounds, and St. Bernards are not allowed. There are no additional pet fees. Dogs may not be left unattended outside, and they must be leashed and cleaned up after. There are some breed restrictions. There is a dog walk area at the campground.

Prineville

Ochoco National Forest
3160 SE 3rd Street
Prineville, OR
541-416-6500
The Ochoco and Deschutes Forests were combined creating 2.5 million acres of spectacular scenery, hundreds of miles of trails, diverse ecosystems and recreation. Dogs of

all sizes are allowed at no additional fee. Dogs may not be left unattended, and they must be leashed and cleaned up after in camp areas. Dogs may be off lead in the forest on the trails if they will not chase wildlife and if they are under strict voice control. Dogs are not allowed in buildings. This campground is closed during the off-season. The camping and tent areas also allow dogs. There is a dog walk area at the campground. There are no electric or water hookups at the campground. Multiple dogs may be allowed.

Prineville Reservoir State Park
19020 SE Parkland Drive
Prineville, OR
541-447-4363
This park and reservoir offer a wide variety of land and water recreation, nature programs, trails, and interpretive events and tours. Dogs of all sizes are allowed at no additional fee. Dogs may not be left unattended, and they must be on no more than a 6 foot leash, and cleaned up after. Dogs are not allowed in cabins or in the cabin area. Dogs are allowed on the trails. The camping and tent areas also allow dogs. There is a dog walk area at the campground. Multiple dogs may be allowed.

Roseburg

Rising River RV Park
5579 Grange Road
Roseburg, OR
541-679-7256
Dogs of all sizes are allowed. There are no additional pet fees. Dogs may not be left unattended outside, and they must be leashed and cleaned up after. There are some breed restrictions. There is a dog walk area at the campground. 2 dogs may be allowed.

Umpqua National Forest
2900 Stewart Parkway
Roseburg, OR
541-750-7000
This forest of almost a million acres is home to one of the largest developed recreational facilities within the Forest Service. It offers a diverse topography that provides for a wide variety of habitats, naturescapes and recreational activities. Dogs of all sizes are allowed at no additional fee. Dogs may not be left unattended; they must be quiet, well behaved, be on

no more than a 6 foot leash, and cleaned up after in camp areas. Dogs are allowed on the trails, but they say to use caution on the horse and ATV trails. The camping and tent areas also allow dogs. There is a dog walk area at the campground. There are no electric or water hookups at the campground. Multiple dogs may be allowed.

Salem

Premier RV Resorts
4700 H 22
Salem, OR
503-364-7714
Dogs of all sizes are allowed. There are no additional pet fees. Dogs must be quiet, well behaved, leashed, and cleaned up after. Dogs may not be left unattended outside. There is a dog walk area at the campground. Multiple dogs may be allowed.

Salem Campground
3700 Hager's Grove Road
Salem, OR
503-581-6736
Dogs of all sizes are allowed. There are no additional pet fees. Dogs must be leashed and cleaned up after. There are some breed restrictions. There is a dog walk area at the campground. 2 dogs may be allowed.

Sandy

Mount Hood National Forest
16400 Champion Way
Sandy, OR
503-668-1700
This beautiful forest of more than a million acres offers hundreds of miles of trails, interpretive programs, and diverse ecosystems that support a large variety of plants, animals, and recreation. Dogs of all sizes are allowed at no additional fee. Dogs may not be left unattended, and they must be leashed and cleaned up after. Dogs are allowed on the trails. This campground is closed during the off-season. The camping and tent areas also allow dogs. There is a dog walk area at the campground. There are no electric or water hookups at the campground.

St Paul

Champoeg State Heritage Area
Champoeg Road

St Paul, OR
503-678-1251, ext 221
Located on the banks of the Willamette River, this scenic park has a rich historic past, and offers historic tours, living history demonstrations, nature and history programs, and a wide variety of land and water activities. Dogs of all sizes are allowed at no additional fee. Dogs may not be left unattended, and they must be on no more than a 6 foot leash, and cleaned up after. Dogs are not allowed in buildings. There is a large off-leash area located at the west end of the park for your pet to run. The camping and tent areas also allow dogs. There is a dog walk area at the campground. There are special amenities given to dogs at this campground. Multiple dogs may be allowed.

Tillamook

Cape Lookout State Park
13000 Whiskey Creek Road W
Tillamook, OR
503-842-4981
This lush coastal forest park offers spectacular views, marine watching, hiking trails, interpretive tours, historic programs, and a variety of recreational pursuits. Dogs of all sizes are allowed at no additional fee. Dogs may not be left unattended, and they must be on no more than a 6 foot leash, and cleaned up after. Dogs are allowed on trails unless otherwise marked. The camping and tent areas also allow dogs. There is a dog walk area at the campground. Multiple dogs may be allowed.

Waldport

Waldport/Newport KOA
1330 NW Pacific Coast H
Waldport, OR
541-563-2250
Dogs of all sizes are allowed. There are no additional pet fees. Dogs must be on no more than a 6 foot leash(retractable leashes are not allowed), and cleaned up after. There are some breed restrictions. The camping and tent areas also allow dogs. There is a dog walk area at the campground. There are special amenities given to dogs at this campground. Multiple dogs may be allowed.

Welches

Mt Hood Village
65000 E H 26
Welches, OR
800-255-3069
One dog of any size is allowed, and there are no additional pet fees for tent or RV sites. There is a $10 one time additional pet fee for the cabin. Dogs must be quiet, well behaved, leashed, and cleaned up after. There are some breed restrictions. The camping and tent areas also allow dogs. There is a dog walk area at the campground. Dogs are allowed in the camping cabins.

Wilderville

Grants Pass/Redwood Hwy KOA
13370 Redwood H
Wilderville, OR
541-476-6508
Dogs of all sizes are allowed. There are no additional pet fees. Dogs may not be tied to the picnic tables, and they must be leashed and cleaned up after. Dogs must be taken to the specified dog walk area to do their business. There are some breed restrictions. The camping and tent areas also allow dogs. There is a dog walk area at the campground. Multiple dogs may be allowed.

Winchester Bay

The Marina RV Resort
End of Marina Way
Winchester Bay, OR
541-271-0287
Dogs of all sizes are allowed. There are no additional pet fees. Dogs may not be left unattended, and they must be well behaved, leashed and cleaned up after. There is a dog walk area at the campground. Multiple dogs may be allowed.

Pennsylvania Listings

Barnsville

Locust Lake State Park
220 Locust Lake Road
Barnsville, PA
570-467-2404
This park offers over 1000 acres of land and water recreation, with a number of trails varying in difficulty. Day use visitors can only bring pets to the park when the campground is closed. Dogs of all sizes are allowed with campers. There is a $2 per night per pet additional fee. Dogs are to be walked in designated walking areas of the campground. Dogs must have current shot records and rabies certificate, be quiet, and well behaved. Dogs are allowed on the trails and day use areas, but they are not allowed on the beach, in any swim areas, or in buildings. Dogs may not be left unattended except for very short periods; then they must be left inside your unit, weather permitting. The camping and tent areas also allow dogs. There is a dog walk area at the campground. There are no water hookups at the campground. 2 dogs may be allowed.

Bellefonte

Bellefonte/State College KOA
2481 Jacksonville Road
Bellefonte, PA
814-355-7912
Dogs of all sizes are allowed. There are no additional pet fees. Dogs must be leashed and cleaned up after. This RV park is closed during the off-season. The camping and tent areas also allow dogs. There is a dog walk area at the campground. Dogs are allowed in the camping cabins. Multiple dogs may be allowed.

Bowmansville

Sun Valley Campground
451 Maple Grove Road
Bowmansville, PA
717-445-6262
Dogs of all sizes are allowed. There are no additional pet fees. Dogs must be leashed and cleaned up after. This RV park is closed during the off-season. The camping and tent areas also allow dogs. There is a dog walk area at the campground. Multiple dogs may be allowed.

Bradford

Kinzua East KOA
Klondike Road, Kinzua Heights
Bradford, PA
814-368-3662
One dog of any size is allowed. There are no additional pet fees.

Dogs may not be left unattended, must be leashed, and cleaned up after. There are some breed restrictions. This RV park is closed during the off-season. The camping and tent areas also allow dogs. There is a dog walk area at the campground.

Chambersburg

Twin Bridge Meadow Campground
1345 Twin Bridges Road
Chambersburg, PA
717-369-2216
Dogs of all sizes are allowed. There are no additional pet fees. Dogs may not be left unattended, must be leashed, and cleaned up after. There are some breed restrictions. This RV park is closed during the off-season. The camping and tent areas also allow dogs. There is a dog walk area at the campground. 2 dogs may be allowed.

Clearville

Hidden Springs Campground
815 Beans Cove Road
Clearville, PA
814-767-9676
Dogs of all sizes are allowed. There are no additional pet fees. Dogs must be quiet, leashed, and cleaned up after. This RV park is closed during the off-season. The camping and tent areas also allow dogs. There is a dog walk area at the campground. Multiple dogs may be allowed.

Cooksburg

Cook Forest State Park
(Box 120) On River Road
Cooksburg, PA
814-744-8407
Dogs of all sizes are allowed. There is a $2 per night per pet additional fee. Dogs may not be left unattended, they must have a current rabies certificate and shot records, be leashed, and cleaned up after. Dogs are allowed on the trails. There is a separate section for campers with pets, and pets must be kept in that area when not on the trails. They are not allowed beyond the contact station that leads to the non-pet area. The camping and tent areas also allow dogs. There is a dog walk area at the campground. There are no water hookups at the campground. 2 dogs may be

allowed.

Dairy

Keystone State Park
1150 Keystone Park Road
Dairy, PA
724-668-2939
Dogs of all sizes are allowed. There is a $2 per night per pet additional fee. Pets are to be walked in designated walking areas of the campground and on designated pet walkways when accessing other areas of the park from the campground. Dogs must be leashed, under physical control at all times, and cleaned up after. Pet food must remain inside the camping unit, and dogs must have current shot records and a rabies certificate, be quiet, and well behaved. Dogs are allowed on the trails and day use areas, but they are not allowed on the beach, in any swim areas, or in any of the buildings. Dogs may not be left unattended except for very short periods; then they must be left inside your unit, weather permitting. Dogs are allowed on the trails. This campground is closed during the off-season. The camping and tent areas also allow dogs. There is a dog walk area at the campground. There are no water hookups at the campground. 2 dogs may be allowed.

Denver

Hickory Run Camping Resort
285 Greenville Road
Denver, PA
717-336-5564
Dogs of all sizes are allowed. There are no additional pet fees. Dogs must be leashed and cleaned up after. They can be left in your unit if they are well behaved, and there is sufficient cooling. This RV park is closed during the off-season. The camping and tent areas also allow dogs. There is a dog walk area at the campground. Multiple dogs may be allowed.

Dutch Country

Spring Gulch
475 Lynch Road
New Holland, PA
866-864-8524
Dogs of all sizes are allowed. There are no additional pet fees. Dogs

must be well behaved, leashed, and cleaned up after. Dogs are not allowed in the rentals This RV park is closed during the off-season. The camping and tent areas also allow dogs. There is a dog walk area at the campground. 2 dogs may be allowed.

Elizabethtown

Hershey Conewago Campground
1590 Hershey Road
Elizabethtown, PA
717-367-1179
Dogs of all sizes are allowed. There are no additional pet fees. Dogs may not be left unattended at any time, must be leashed, and cleaned up after. This RV park is closed during the off-season. The camping and tent areas also allow dogs. There is a dog walk area at the campground. Multiple dogs may be allowed.

Elverson

French Creek State Park
843 Park Road
Elverson, PA
610-582-9680
Dogs of all sizes are allowed. There is a $2 per night per pet additional fee. Pets are to be walked in designated walking areas of the campground and on designated pet walkways when accessing other areas of the park from the campground. Dogs must be leashed and under physical control at all times, and pet waste must be disposed of quickly and properly. Pet food must remain inside the camping unit, and dogs must have current rabies certificate and shot records, be quiet and well behaved. Dogs are allowed on the trails and in day use areas, but they are not allowed in the swim areas or in any of the buildings. Dogs may not be left unattended except for very short periods; then they must be left inside your unit, weather permitting. There are some breed restrictions. The camping and tent areas also allow dogs. There is a dog walk area at the campground. There are no water hookups at the campground. 2 dogs may be allowed.

Galeton

Lyman Run State Park
454 Lyman Run Road
Galeton, PA

814-435-5010

Dogs of all sizes are allowed. There is a $2 per night per pet additional fee. Pets are to be walked in designated walking areas of the campground and on designated pet walkways when accessing other areas of the park from the campground. Dogs must be leashed, under physical control at all times, and cleaned up after. Pet food must remain inside the camping unit, and dogs must have current shot records and a rabies certificate, be quiet, and well behaved. Dogs are allowed on the trails and day use areas, but they are not allowed on the beach, in any swim areas, or in any of the buildings. Dogs may not be left unattended except for very short periods; then they must be left inside your unit, weather permitting. Dogs are allowed on the trails. This campground is closed during the off-season. The camping and tent areas also allow dogs. There is a dog walk area at the campground. There are no water hookups at the campground. 2 dogs may be allowed.

Gettysburg

Drummer Boy Camping Resort
1300 Hanover Road
Gettysburg, PA
800-293-2808
Dogs of all sizes are allowed. There are no additional pet fees. Dogs may not be left unattended, must be leashed, and cleaned up after. They are also not allowed to be tied up outside alone or be in any of the buildings. This RV park is closed during the off-season. The camping and tent areas also allow dogs. There is a dog walk area at the campground. 2 dogs may be allowed.

Gettysburg/Battlefield KOA
20 Knox Road
Gettysburg, PA
717-642-5713
Dogs of all sizes are allowed, and there are no additional pet fees for tent or RV sites. There is a $10 one time pet fee for cabin rentals. Dogs may not be left unattended at any time, must be leashed, and cleaned up after. This RV park is closed during the off-season. The camping and tent areas also allow dogs. There is a dog walk area at the campground. Dogs are allowed in the camping cabins. Multiple dogs may be allowed.

Round Top Campground
180 Night Road
Gettysburg, PA
717-334-9565
Dogs of all sizes are allowed. There are no additional pet fees. Dogs may not be left unattended, must be leashed, and cleaned up after. Dogs are not allowed in the rentals. The camping and tent areas also allow dogs. There is a dog walk area at the campground. Multiple dogs may be allowed.

Hanover

Codorus State Park
1066 Blooming Grove Rd
Hanover, PA
717-637-2418
Dogs of all sizes are allowed. There is a $2 per night per pet additional fee. Dogs are to be leashed and under physical control at all times. Pet food must remain inside the camping unit, and pet waste must be disposed of quickly and properly. Pets are to be walked in designated walking areas of the campground and on designated pet walkways when accessing other areas of the park from the campground. Dogs are not permitted in swimming areas or inside buildings, they must have current rabies certificate and shot records, be quiet, and well behaved. Dogs may not be left unattended except for very short periods, and then they must be inside, weather permitting. Dogs on lead are allowed on the trails. There are some breed restrictions. This campground is closed during the off-season. The camping and tent areas also allow dogs. There is a dog walk area at the campground. There are no water hookups at the campground. 2 dogs may be allowed.

Hookstown

Raccoon Creek State Park
3000 State Route 18
Hookstown, PA
724-899-2200
Dogs of all sizes are allowed. There is a $2 per night per pet additional fee. Pets are to be walked in designated walking areas of the campground and on designated pet walkways when accessing other areas of the park from the campground. Dogs must be leashed, under physical control at

all times, and cleaned up after. Pet food must remain inside the camping unit, and dogs must have current shot records and a rabies certificate, be quiet, and well behaved. Dogs are allowed on the trails and day use areas, but they are not allowed on the beach, in any swim areas, or in any of the buildings. Dogs may not be left unattended except for very short periods; then they must be left inside your unit, weather permitting. Dogs are allowed on all the trails. This campground is closed during the off-season. The camping and tent areas also allow dogs. There is a dog walk area at the campground. There are no water hookups at the campground. 2 dogs may be allowed.

Hummelstown

Hershey Highmeadow Campground
1200 Matlock Road
Hummelstown, PA
717-534-8999
Dogs of all sizes are allowed. There are no additional pet fees. Dogs must be leashed and cleaned up after. There is a dog walk area at the campground. Multiple dogs may be allowed.

Huntington

Penn Roosevelt
Stone Creek Road
Huntington, PA
814-667-1800
Dogs of all sizes are allowed. There is a $2 per night per pet additional fee. Pets are to be walked in designated walking areas of the campground and on designated pet walkways when accessing other areas of the park from the campground. Dogs must be leashed, under physical control at all times, and cleaned up after. Pet food must remain inside the camping unit, and dogs must have current shot records and a rabies certificate, be quiet, and well behaved. Dogs are allowed on the trails and day use areas, but they are not allowed on the beach, in any swim areas, or in any of the buildings. Dogs may not be left unattended except for very short periods; then they must be left inside your unit, weather permitting. Dogs are allowed on the trails. The camping and tent areas also allow dogs. There is a dog walk area at the campground. There are no electric or

water hookups at the campground. 2 dogs may be allowed.

Jamestown

Pymatuning State Park
2660 Williamsfield Road
Jamestown, PA
724-932-3141
Dogs of all sizes are allowed. There is a $2 per night per pet additional fee. Pets are to be walked in designated walking areas of the campground and on designated pet walkways when accessing other areas of the park from the campground. Dogs must be leashed, under physical control at all times, and cleaned up after. Pet food must remain inside the camping unit, and dogs must have current shot records and a rabies certificate, be quiet, and well behaved. Dogs are allowed on the trails and day use areas, but they are not allowed on the beach, in any swim areas, or in any of the buildings. Dogs may not be left unattended at any time. The campground in this park that allows pets is the Tuttle Campground, and it is accessed off H 285. Although the campground is seasonal, the park is open year round. This campground is closed during the off-season. The camping and tent areas also allow dogs. There is a dog walk area at the campground. There are no water hookups at the campground. 2 dogs may be allowed.

Jonestown

Jonestown/I-81,78 KOA
145 Old Route 22
Jonestown, PA
717-865-2526
Dogs of all sizes are allowed, but there can only be 1 large dog or 2 small dogs per site. There are no additional pet fees. Dogs may not be left unattended, and they must be leashed and cleaned up after. There are some breed restrictions. This RV park is closed during the off-season. The camping and tent areas also allow dogs. There is a dog walk area at the campground.

Knox

Wolf's Camping Resort
308 Timberwolf Run
Knox, PA
814-797-1103
Dogs of all sizes are allowed. There

are no additional pet fees. Dogs must be quiet, well behaved, not left unattended, and leashed and cleaned up after. There is limited winter camping. The camping and tent areas also allow dogs. There is a dog walk area at the campground. Multiple dogs may be allowed.

Lenhartsville

Blue Rocks Family Campground
341 Sousley Road
Lenhartsville, PA
610-756-6366
Dogs of all sizes are allowed. There are no additional pet fees. Dogs must have current shot records and be quiet and well behaved. Dogs must be leashed and cleaned up after. This RV park is closed during the off-season. The camping and tent areas also allow dogs. There is a dog walk area at the campground. Multiple dogs may be allowed.

Robin Hill Camping Resort
149 Robin Hill Road
Lenhartsville, PA
610-756-6117
Dogs of all sizes are allowed. There are no additional pet fees. Dogs must be well behaved, not left unattended, and be leashed and cleaned up after. This RV park is closed during the off-season. The camping and tent areas also allow dogs. There is a dog walk area at the campground. Multiple dogs may be allowed.

Manheim

Pinch Pond Family Campground
2649 Camp Road
Manheim, PA
717-665-7120
Dogs of all sizes are allowed. There are no additional pet fees. Dogs must be leashed and cleaned up after. This RV park is closed during the off-season. The camping and tent areas also allow dogs. There is a dog walk area at the campground. Multiple dogs may be allowed.

McKean

Erie KOA
6645 West Road
McKean, PA
814-476-7706
Dogs of all sizes are allowed. There are no additional pet fees. Dogs may not be left unattended, must be

leashed, and cleaned up after. This RV park is closed during the off-season. The camping and tent areas also allow dogs. There is a dog walk area at the campground. Dogs are allowed in the camping cabins. Multiple dogs may be allowed.

Meadville

Brookdale Family Campground
25164 H 27
Meadville, PA
814-789-3251
Dogs of all sizes are allowed. There are no additional pet fees. Dogs must be quiet, be leashed at all times, and be cleaned up after. Dogs may not be tied up outside alone. They can be left in the camper or RV if they are well behaved and have cool air. This RV park is closed during the off-season. The camping and tent areas also allow dogs. There is a dog walk area at the campground. Multiple dogs may be allowed.

Mercer

Mercer/Grove City KOA
1337 Butler Pike
Mercer, PA
724-748-3160
Dogs of all sizes are allowed. There are no additional pet fees. Dogs must be well behaved, leashed, and cleaned up after. This RV park is closed during the off-season. The camping and tent areas also allow dogs. There is a dog walk area at the campground. Dogs are allowed in the camping cabins. Multiple dogs may be allowed.

Mifflinburg

Hidden Valley Campgrounds
162 Hidden Valley Lane
Mifflinburg, PA
570-966-1330
Dogs of all sizes are allowed. There are no additional pet fees. Dogs must be quiet, well behaved, leashed, and cleaned up after. This RV park is closed during the off-season. The camping and tent areas also allow dogs. There is a dog walk area at the campground. Multiple dogs may be allowed.

Mill Run

Jelllystone Park

839 Mill Run Road
Mill Run, PA
724-455-2929
Dogs of all sizes are allowed. There is a $2 per night per pet additional fee. Dogs must be leashed and cleaned up after. Dogs are not allowed in the rentals. The camping and tent areas also allow dogs. There is a dog walk area at the campground. Multiple dogs may be allowed.

New Columbia

Nittany Mountain Campground
2751 Miller's Bottom Road
New Columbia, PA
570-568-5541
One dog of any size is allowed in the rentals. Dogs of all sizes are allowed in the camping and RV area. There is a $1 per night per pet additional fee. Dogs must be leashed and cleaned up after. This RV park is closed during the off-season. The camping and tent areas also allow dogs. There is a dog walk area at the campground. Dogs are allowed in the camping cabins.

New Tripoli

Allentown KOA
6750 KOA Drive
New Tripoli, PA
610-298-2160
Dogs of all sizes are allowed. There are no additional pet fees. Dogs must be leashed and cleaned up after. There are some breed restrictions. This RV park is closed during the off-season. The camping and tent areas also allow dogs. There is a dog walk area at the campground. Multiple dogs may be allowed.

Northumberland

Yogi-on-the-River
213 Yogi Blvd
Northumberland, PA
570-473-8021
Dogs of all sizes are allowed. There are no additional pet fees. Dogs may not be left unattended, must be leashed, and cleaned up after. Dogs are allowed to go to the river, but you may not access the river across other sites. This RV park is closed during the off-season. The camping and tent areas also allow dogs. There is a dog walk area at the campground. 2 dogs may be

allowed.

Oil City

Oil Creek State Park
305 State Park Road
Oil City, PA
814-676-5915
This park is home to the world's first commercial oil well, and there are trails that wind throughout. There is no tent or RV camping, and there are no cabins. They have trail shelters available. Dogs of all sizes are allowed. There is a $2 per night per pet additional fee. Dogs must be leashed and cleaned up after. Dogs are allowed on the trails and at the day use areas. There is a dog walk area at the campground. There are no electric or water hookups at the campground. 2 dogs may be allowed.

Patton

Prince Gallitzin State Park
966 Marina Road
Patton, PA
814-674-1000
Dogs of all sizes are allowed. There is a $2 per night per pet additional fee. Pets are to be walked in designated walking areas of the campground and on designated pet walkways when accessing other areas of the park from the campground. Dogs must be leashed, under physical control at all times, and pet waste must be disposed of quickly and properly. Pet food must remain inside the camping unit, and dogs must have a current rabies certificate and shot records, be quiet and well behaved. Dogs are allowed on the trails and day use areas, but they are not allowed in the swim areas or in any of the buildings. Dogs can be at the boat launch area and on the trails. Dogs may not be left unattended except for very short periods; then they must be left inside your unit, weather permitting. This campground is closed during the off-season. The camping and tent areas also allow dogs. There is a dog walk area at the campground. There are no water hookups at the campground. 2 dogs may be allowed.

Philadelphia

Timberland Campground

117 Timber Lane
Clarksboro, NJ
856-423-6677
Dogs of all sizes are allowed. There are no additional pet fees. Dogs must be quiet and well behaved. Dogs may not be left unattended, must be leashed, and cleaned up after. The camping and tent areas also allow dogs. There is a dog walk area at the campground. Multiple dogs may be allowed.

Philadelphia/West Chester KOA
1659 Embreeville Road
Coatsville, PA
610-486-0447
Well behaved and friendly dogs of all sizes are allowed. There are no additional pet fees. Dogs may not be left unattended, must be leashed, and cleaned up after. This RV park is closed during the off-season. The camping and tent areas also allow dogs. There is a dog walk area at the campground. Multiple dogs may be allowed.

Pine Grove

Pine Grove KOA
1445 Suedburg Road
Pine Grove, PA
717-865-4602
Dogs of all sizes are allowed. There are no additional pet fees. Dogs must be quiet, leashed, and cleaned up after. There are some breed restrictions. The camping and tent areas also allow dogs. There is a dog walk area at the campground. Dogs are allowed in the camping cabins. Multiple dogs may be allowed.

Pittsburgh

Bear Run Campground
184 Badger Hill Road
Portersville, PA
888-737-2605
Dogs of all sizes are allowed. There are no additional pet fees. Dogs must be leashed and cleaned up after. Dogs are not allowed in the buildings or rentals. There are some breed restrictions. This RV park is closed during the off-season. The camping and tent areas also allow dogs. There is a dog walk area at the campground. 2 dogs may be allowed.

Madison/Pittsburgh SE KOA
119 Tanglewood Lane
Ruffs Dale, PA

724-722-4444
Dogs of all sizes are allowed. There are no additional pet fees. Dogs must be leashed and cleaned up after. There are some breed restrictions. This RV park is closed during the off-season. The camping and tent areas also allow dogs. There is a dog walk area at the campground. Dogs are allowed in the camping cabins. Multiple dogs may be allowed.

Keen Lake Camping and Cottage Resort
155 Keen Lake Road
Waymart, PA
570-488-5522
Dogs of all sizes are allowed, and there are no additional pet fees for RV or tent sites. There is a $50 one time additional pet fee for a cottage rental plus a $250 refundable pet deposit. Dogs must be quiet, may not be left unattended, and must be leashed and cleaned up after. This RV park is closed during the off-season. The camping and tent areas also allow dogs. There is a dog walk area at the campground. Dogs are allowed in the camping cabins. 2 dogs may be allowed.

Poconos

Delaware Water Gap KOA
233 Hollow Road
E Stroudsburg, PA
570-223-8000
Dogs of all sizes are allowed. There are no additional pet fees. Dogs must be leased and cleaned up after. There are some breed restrictions. This RV park is closed during the off-season. The camping and tent areas also allow dogs. There is a dog walk area at the campground. Multiple dogs may be allowed.

Mountain Vista Campground
50 Taylor Drive
E Stroudsburg, PA
570-223-0111
Dogs of all sizes are allowed. There are no additional pet fees. Dogs must be well behaved, leashed, and cleaned up after. This RV park is closed during the off-season. The camping and tent areas also allow dogs. There is a dog walk area at the campground. Multiple dogs may be allowed.

Otter Lake Camp Resort
4805 Marshall's Creek Road
E Stroudsburg, PA

570-223-0123
Dogs of all sizes are allowed. There are no additional pet fees. Dogs may not be left unattended, must be leashed, and cleaned up after. The camping and tent areas also allow dogs. There is a dog walk area at the campground. Multiple dogs may be allowed.

Tri-State RV Park
200 Shay Lane
Matamoras, PA
800-562-2663
Dogs of all sizes are allowed. There are no additional pet fees. Dogs must have current shot records, be leashed, and cleaned up after. There is a dog walk area at the campground.

Hickory Run State Park
On H 534
White Haven, PA
570-443-0400
Dogs of all sizes are allowed. There is a $2 per night per pet additional fee. Pets are to be walked in designated walking areas of the campground and on designated pet walkways when accessing other areas of the park from the campground. Dogs must be leashed and under physical control at all times, and pet waste must be disposed of quickly and properly. Pet food must remain inside the camping unit, and dogs must have current rabies certificate and shot records, be quiet and well behaved. Dogs are allowed on the trails and day use areas, but they are not allowed in the swim areas or in any of the buildings. Dogs may not be left unattended except for very short periods; then they must be left inside your unit, weather permitting. There are some breed restrictions. This campground is closed during the off-season. The camping and tent areas also allow dogs. There is a dog walk area at the campground. There are no water hookups at the campground. 2 dogs may be allowed.

Quarryville

Jellystone Park
340 Blackburn Road
Quarryville, PA
717-786-3458
Dogs of all sizes are allowed. There are no additional pet fees. Dogs must be quiet and well behaved. Dogs may not be left unattended, must be leashed, and cleaned up

after. This RV park is closed during the off-season. The camping and tent areas also allow dogs. There is a dog walk area at the campground. 2 dogs may be allowed.

Schellsburg

Shawnee State Park
132 State Park Road
Schellsburg, PA
814-733-4218
Dogs of all sizes are allowed. There is a $2 per night per pet additional fee. Pets are to be walked in designated walking areas of the campground and on designated pet walkways when accessing other areas of the park from the campground. Dogs must be leashed and under physical control at all times, and pet waste must be disposed of quickly and properly. Pet food must remain inside the camping unit, and dogs must have current rabies certificate and shot records, be quiet and well behaved. Dogs are allowed on the trails and day use areas, but they are not allowed on any sand areas, at the beach shoreline, or in any of the buildings. Dogs may not be left unattended except for very short periods; then they must be left inside your unit, weather permitting. There are some breed restrictions. This campground is closed during the off-season. The camping and tent areas also allow dogs. There is a dog walk area at the campground. There are no water hookups at the campground. 2 dogs may be allowed.

Shartlesville

Appalachian Campsites
60 Motel Drive
Shartlesville, PA
610-488-6319
Dogs of all sizes are allowed. There are no additional pet fees. Dogs must be leashed and cleaned up after. The camping and tent areas also allow dogs. There is a dog walk area at the campground. 2 dogs may be allowed.

Slippery Rock

Cooper's Lake Campground
205 Currie Road
Slippery Rock, PA
724-368-8710
Friendly dogs of all sizes are allowed. There are no additional pet

fees. Dogs must be quiet, not left unattended, leashed and cleaned up after. The camp closes for the month of August every year. This RV park is closed during the off-season. The camping and tent areas also allow dogs. There is a dog walk area at the campground. Multiple dogs may be allowed.

Somerset

Kooser State Park
934 Glades Pike
Somerset, PA
814-445-7725
Dogs of all sizes are allowed. There is a $2 per night per pet additional fee. Pets are to be walked in designated walking areas of the campground and on designated pet walkways when accessing other areas of the park from the campground. Dogs must be leashed, under physical control at all times, and cleaned up after. Pet food must remain inside the camping unit, and dogs must have current shot records and a rabies certificate, be quiet, and well behaved. Dogs are allowed on the trails and day use areas, but they are not allowed on the beach, in any swim areas, or in any of the buildings. Dogs may not be left unattended except for very short periods; then they must be left inside your unit, weather permitting. Dogs are allowed on the trails. The camping and tent areas also allow dogs. There is a dog walk area at the campground. There are no water hookups at the campground. 2 dogs may be allowed.

Tobyhanna

Tobyhanna State Park
On H 423
Tobyhanna, PA
570-894-8336
Dogs of all sizes are allowed. There is a $2 per night per pet additional fee. Pets are to be walked in designated walking areas of the campground and on designated pet walkways when accessing other areas of the park from the campground. Dogs must be leashed, under physical control at all times, and cleaned up after. Pet food must remain inside the camping unit, and dogs must have current shot records and a rabies certificate, be quiet, and well behaved. Dogs are allowed on the trails and day use areas, but they are not allowed on the beach, in any

swim areas, or in any of the buildings. Dogs may not be left unattended except for very short periods; then they must be left inside your unit, weather permitting. Dogs are allowed on the trails. This campground is closed during the off-season. The camping and tent areas also allow dogs. There is a dog walk area at the campground. There are no electric or water hookups at the campground. 2 dogs may be allowed.

Upper Black Eddy

Colonial Woods Family Camping Resort
545 Lonely Cottage Drive
Upper Black Eddy, PA
610-847-5808
Dogs of all sizes are allowed. There are no additional pet fees. Dogs must be quiet, well behaved, leashed, and cleaned up after. This RV park is closed during the off-season. The camping and tent areas also allow dogs. There is a dog walk area at the campground. Multiple dogs may be allowed.

Warren

Allegheny National Forest
222 Liberty Street
Warren, PA
814-723-5150
This park is located in northwestern Pennsylvania and covers over 24,000 acres. Dogs of all sizes are allowed. There are no additional pet fees. Dogs may not be left unattended, and they must have a current rabies certificate and shot records. Dogs must be quiet during quiet hours, be leashed, and cleaned up after. Dogs are allowed on the trails, but not on the beach or in the buildings. This campground is closed during the off-season. The camping and tent areas also allow dogs. There is a dog walk area at the campground. There are no water hookups at the campground. Multiple dogs may be allowed.

Washington

Washington KOA
7 KOA Road
Washington, PA
724-225-7590
Dogs of all sizes are allowed. There are no additional pet fees. In the

cabins there can only be one large dog or two small dogs. There are a couple of more dogs allowed on tent and RV sites. Dogs must be leashed and cleaned up after. The camping and tent areas also allow dogs. There is a dog walk area at the campground. Dogs are allowed in the camping cabins.

Wyoming

Frances Slocum State Park
565 Mount Olivet Road
Wyoming, PA
570-696-3525
Dogs of all sizes are allowed. There is a $2 per night per pet additional fee. Pets are to be walked in designated walking areas of the campground and on designated pet walkways when accessing other areas of the park from the campground. Dogs must be leashed, under physical control at all times, and cleaned up after. Pet food must remain inside the camping unit, and dogs must have current shot records and a rabies certificate, be quiet, and well behaved. Dogs are allowed on the trails and day use areas, but they are not allowed on the beach, in any swim areas, or in any of the buildings. Dogs may not be left unattended except for very short periods; then they must be left inside your unit, weather permitting. Dogs are allowed on the trails. The camping and tent areas also allow dogs. There is a dog walk area at the campground. There are no water hookups at the campground. 2 dogs may be allowed.

Rhode Island Listings

Chepachet

George Washington Management Area
2185 Putnam Park
Chepachet, RI
401-568-2248
Dogs of all sizes are allowed. There are no additional pet fees. Dogs may not be left unattended, they must have current rabies certificate and shot records, be leashed, and cleaned up after. Dogs are allowed on the trails, but not on the beach.

This campground is closed during the off-season. The camping and tent areas also allow dogs. There is a dog walk area at the campground. There are no electric or water hookups at the campground. Multiple dogs may be allowed.

Foster

Ginny-B Campground
7 Harrington Road
Foster, RI
401-397-9477
Dogs of all sizes are allowed. There are no additional pet fees. Dogs must be well behaved, leashed, and cleaned up after. The camping and tent areas also allow dogs. Multiple dogs may be allowed.

Hope Valley

Whispering Pines
41 Sawmill Road
Hope Valley, RI
401-539-7011
Well behaved dogs of all sizes are allowed. There are no additional pet fees. No aggressive dogs are allowed, and they must be kept leashed and cleaned up after. There are some breed restrictions. Multiple dogs may be allowed.

N Scituate

Holiday Acres Camping Resort
591 Snakehill Road
N Scituate, RI
401-934-0780
Dogs of all sizes are allowed, however some breeds are not. There are no additional pet fees. Dogs must be well behaved and they are not allowed on other sites or the beach. They must be leashed and cleaned up after. The camping and tent areas also allow dogs. There is a dog walk area at the campground. 2 dogs may be allowed.

Newport

Goose Creek Resort
350 Red Barn Road
Newport, RI
866-839-2628
Dogs of all sizes are allowed. There are no additional pet fees. Dogs must be leashed and cleaned up after. There are some breed restrictions. There is a dog walk area at the campground. Multiple dogs

may be allowed.

Providence

Bowdish Lake
40 Safari Road
Glocester, RI
401-568-8890
Dogs of all sizes are allowed, but some breeds are not. There is a $10 per night per pet additional fee. Dogs must be well behaved, leashed, and cleaned up after. The camping and tent areas also allow dogs. There is a dog walk area at the campground. Multiple dogs may be allowed.

Wakefield

Wordon Pond Family Campground
416 A Worden Pond Road
Wakefield, RI
401-789-9113
Dogs of all sizes are allowed. There are no additional pet fees. Dogs must be leashed and cleaned up after. This RV park is closed during the off-season. The camping and tent areas also allow dogs. There is a dog walk area at the campground. 2 dogs may be allowed.

West Kingston

Wawaloam Campground
510 Gardner Road
West Kingston, RI
401-294-3039
Dogs of all sizes are allowed. There is a $3 per night per pet additional fee. Dogs must be leashed and cleaned up after. The camping and tent areas also allow dogs. There is a dog walk area at the campground. 2 dogs may be allowed.

South Carolina Listings

Anderson

Anderson/Lake Hartwell KOA
200 Wham Road
Anderson, SC
864-287-3161
Dogs of all sizes are allowed. There are no additional pet fees. Dogs

may not be left unattended, and they must be quiet, well behaved, leashed, and cleaned up after. The camping and tent areas also allow dogs. There is a dog walk area at the campground. Dogs are allowed in the camping cabins. Multiple dogs may be allowed.

Blacksburg

Kings Mountain State Park
1277 Park Road
Blacksburg, SC
803-222-3209
Rich in American history, this picturesque park offers self guided tours of a living history farm in addition to various land and water recreation. Dogs of all sizes are allowed at no additional fee. Dogs may not be left unattended unless they will be quiet and well behaved, and they must be on no more than a 6 foot leash, and cleaned up after. Dogs are allowed on the trails. The camping and tent areas also allow dogs. There is a dog walk area at the campground. Multiple dogs may be allowed.

Calhoun Falls

Calhoun Falls State Park
46 Maintenance Shop Road
Calhoun Falls, SC
864-447-8269
This park, located on one of the states most popular fishing lakes, also provides a scenic trail, nature study opportunities, and a variety of recreation. Dogs of all sizes are allowed at no additional fee. Dogs may not be left unattended, and they must be on no more than a 6 foot leash, and be cleaned up after in camp areas. Dogs are not allowed in buildings or on the beach. Dogs are allowed on the trails. The camping and tent areas also allow dogs. There is a dog walk area at the campground. Multiple dogs may be allowed.

Charleston

James Island County Park Campground
871 Riverland Drive
Charleston, SC
843-795-7275
Dogs of all sizes are allowed. There are no additional pet fees. Dogs may not be left unattended outside, and may only be left inside an RV if there

is temperature control. Dogs must be quiet during quiet hours, leashed, and cleaned up after. There is an a fenced in Dog Park where dogs may run off lead. The camping and tent areas also allow dogs. There is a dog walk area at the campground. Multiple dogs may be allowed.

Oak Plantation Campground
3540 Savannah H
Charleston, SC
843-766-5936
Dogs of all sizes are allowed. There are no additional pet fees. Dogs may not be left unattended outside, they must be leashed at all times, and cleaned up after. There is a large fenced in dog run where dogs may run off lead. There is a dog walk area at the campground. 2 dogs may be allowed.

Mt Pleasant/Charleston KOA
3157 H 17
Mount Pleasant, SC
843-849-5177
Dogs of all sizes are allowed. There are no additional pet fees. Dogs may not be left unattended outside, and they must be leashed and cleaned up after. The camping and tent areas also allow dogs. There is a dog walk area at the campground. Dogs are allowed in the camping cabins. Multiple dogs may be allowed.

Columbia

Sesquicentennial State Park
9564 Two Notch Road
Columbia, SC
803-788-2706
This park of over 1,400 acres with a 30 acre lake, offers scenic trails, interpretive programs, and a variety of land and water recreation. Dogs of all sizes are allowed at no additional fee. Dogs may not be left unattended, and they must be on no more than a 6 foot leash, and be cleaned up after. Dogs are not allowed in buildings, but they are allowed on the trails. The camping and tent areas also allow dogs. There is a dog walk area at the campground. Multiple dogs may be allowed.

Barnyard RV Park
201 Oak Drive
Lexington, SC
803-957-1238
Dogs of all sizes are allowed. There are no additional pet fees. Dogs must be leashed and cleaned up

after. There is a dog walk area at the campground. Multiple dogs may be allowed.

Conway

Big Cypress Lake RV Park
6531 Browns Way Shortcut Road
Conway, SC
843-397-1800
Dogs of all sizes are allowed. There are no additional pet fees. Dogs must be quiet, well behaved, leashed, and cleaned up after. The camping and tent areas also allow dogs. There is a dog walk area at the campground. Multiple dogs may be allowed.

Edisto Beach

Edisto Beach State Park
8377 State Cabin Road
Edisto Beach, SC
843-869-2156
This 1,255 acre park is home to a dense maritime forest, expansive salt marshes, an interactive interpretive center, and a variety of land and water recreation. Dogs of all sizes are allowed at no additional fee. Dogs may not be left unattended outside unless they will be quiet and very well behaved. Dogs must be on no more than a 6 foot leash, and be cleaned up after. Dogs are allowed on the trails. The camping and tent areas also allow dogs. There is a dog walk area at the campground. Multiple dogs may be allowed.

Fair Play

Lake Hartwell State Rec Area
19138 A H 11S
Fair Play, SC
864-972-3352
Sports enthusiasts, campers, and nature lovers all like the easy access to this park with 14 miles of Lake Hartwell shoreline. Dogs of all sizes are allowed at no additional fee. Dogs may not be left unattended outside, and may only be left inside if they will be quiet, well behaved, and comfortable. Dogs must be on no more than a 6 foot leash, and be cleaned up after. Dogs are allowed on the trails. The camping and tent areas also allow dogs. There is a dog walk area at the campground. Multiple dogs may be allowed.

Florence

Florence KOA
1115 E Campground Road
Florence, SC
843-665-7007
Dogs of all sizes are allowed. There are no additional pet fees. Dogs may not be left unattended, even at the dog pen area. Dogs must be leashed and cleaned up after. The camping and tent areas also allow dogs. There is a dog walk area at the campground. Dogs are allowed in the camping cabins. Multiple dogs may be allowed.

Hamer

South of the Border Campground
3346 H 301N
Hamer, SC
843-774-2411
Dogs of all sizes are allowed. There are no additional pet fees. Dogs may not be left unattended, and they must be leashed and cleaned up after. There is also the South of the Border Motel on site that allows dogs at no extra fee. The camping and tent areas also allow dogs. There is a dog walk area at the campground. Multiple dogs may be allowed.

Hilton Head Island

Hilton Head Island Motor Coach Resort
133 L Street
Hilton Head Island, SC
800-722-2365
Dogs of all sizes are allowed. There are no additional pet fees. Dogs must be leashed at all times and cleaned up after. This is an RV only, Class A resort. There is a dog walk area at the campground. Multiple dogs may be allowed.

Hollywood

Lake Aire RV Park Campground
4375 H 162
Hollywood, SC
843-571-1271
Dogs of all sizes are allowed. There are no additional pet fees. Dogs may not be left unattended, and may only be left in the RV if there is temperature control. Dogs must be well behaved, friendly, leashed, and cleaned up after. There is a dog walk area at the campground. Multiple dogs may be allowed.

Campgrounds and RV Parks - Please always call ahead to make sure an establishment is still dog-friendly.

Huntington Island

Hunting Island State Park
2555 Sea Island Parkway
Huntington Island, SC
843-838-2011
This semi-tropical park acts as a preserve for its abundant wildlife, offers an historic 19th-century lighthouse for spectacular views, and a variety of recreation. Dogs of all sizes are allowed at no additional fee. Dogs may not be left unattended, and they must be leashed at all times, and cleaned up after. Dogs are not allowed in or around the cabins or in other park buildings, but they are allowed on the trails. The camping and tent areas also allow dogs. There is a dog walk area at the campground. Multiple dogs may be allowed.

Ladson

Charleston KOA
9494 H 78
Ladson, SC
843-797-1045
Dogs of all sizes are allowed. There are no additional pet fees. Dogs may not be left unattended, and they must be leashed and cleaned up after. The camping and tent areas also allow dogs. There is a dog walk area at the campground. Dogs are allowed in the camping cabins.

McClellanville

Francis Marion National Forest
1015 Pinckney
McClellanville, SC
843-887-3257
This forest's diverse ecosystems support a large variety of plants, fish, mammals, bird species, and recreation. Dogs of all sizes are allowed at no additional fee. Dogs may not be left unattended, and they must be leashed and cleaned up after. On the trails, dogs must be under verbal or physical restraint at all times; keep in mind they are multi-use trails and use a leash when populated. The camping and tent areas also allow dogs. There is a dog walk area at the campground. There are no water hookups at the campground. Multiple dogs may be allowed.

McCormick

Baker Creek State Park

863 State Park Road
McCormick, SC
864-443-2457
This park provides a variety of quality recreation amid undisturbed natural resources, a 10 mile mountain biking/hiking trail, and opportunities for nature study. Dogs of all sizes are allowed at no additional fee. Dogs may not be left unattended outside, and they may only be left inside if they will be quiet, well behaved, and comfortable. Dogs must be on no more than a 6 foot leash, and be cleaned up after. Dogs are not allowed in park buildings, but they are allowed on the trails. The camping and tent areas also allow dogs. There is a dog walk area at the campground. Multiple dogs may be allowed.

Mountain Rest

Oconee State Park
624 State Park Road
Mountain Rest, SC
864-638-5353
This more than 1,100 acre park offers 2 small lakes, 8 hiking trails, a variety of wildlife, and is the trailhead for the 85-mile Foothills Trail. Dogs of all sizes are allowed at no additional fee. Dogs may not be left unattended, and they must be quiet, leashed and cleaned up after. Dogs are not allowed in public swim areas or in buildings. Dogs are allowed on the trails. The camping and tent areas also allow dogs. There is a dog walk area at the campground. Multiple dogs may be allowed.

Murrells Inlet

Huntington Beach State Park
16148 Ocean H (H 17)
Murrells Inlet, SC
843-237-4440
The natural coastal environment at this park provides a variety of trails and boardwalks, various land and water recreation, and it is a prime habitat for birds. Dogs of all sizes are allowed at no additional fee. Dogs may not be left unattended, and they must be leashed and cleaned up after. Dogs are not allowed in buildings, but they are allowed on the trails. The camping and tent areas also allow dogs. There is a dog walk area at the campground. Multiple dogs may be allowed.

Myrtle Beach

Willow Tree Resort
520 Southern Sights Drive
Longs, SC
866-207-2267
Dogs of all sizes are allowed. There are no additional pet fees. Dogs may not be left unattended outside, and they must be leashed and cleaned up after. The camping and tent areas also allow dogs. There is a dog walk area at the campground. Multiple dogs may be allowed.

Apache Family Campground
9700 Kings Road
Myrtle Beach, SC
843-449-7323
Dogs of all sizes are allowed. There are no additional pet fees. Dogs must be leashed and cleaned up after. There are some breed restrictions. The camping and tent areas also allow dogs. There is a dog walk area at the campground. Multiple dogs may be allowed.

Myrtle Beach KOA
613 5th Avenue S
Myrtle Beach, SC
843-448-3421
Dogs of all sizes are allowed. There are no additional pet fees. Dogs must be quiet, well behaved, leashed, and cleaned up after. There are some breed restrictions. The camping and tent areas also allow dogs. There is a dog walk area at the campground. Multiple dogs may be allowed.

Myrtle Beach State Park
4401 S Kings H
Myrtle Beach, SC
843-238-5325
This popular 312 acre oceanfront park offers educational programs at their nature center, a fishing pier, miles of trails, and various land and water recreation. Dogs may be left on site if they will be quiet, well behaved, and comfortable. Dogs must be leashed at all times, and cleaned up after. Dogs are not allowed in buildings, but they are allowed on the trails. The camping and tent areas also allow dogs. There is a dog walk area at the campground. Multiple dogs may be allowed.

Myrtle Beach Travel Park
10108 Kings Road
Myrtle Beach, SC
843-449-3714

Dogs of all sizes are allowed. There are no additional pet fees. Dogs must be quiet, well behaved, leashed, and cleaned up after. The camping and tent areas also allow dogs. There is a dog walk area at the campground. Multiple dogs may be allowed.

Pirateland Family Campground
5401 S Kings Road
Myrtle Beach, SC
843-238-5155
Dogs of all sizes are allowed. There are no additional pet fees. Dogs may not be left unattended at any time, and they must be on no more than a 6 foot leash, and be cleaned up after. There are some breed restrictions. The camping and tent areas also allow dogs. There is a dog walk area at the campground. Multiple dogs may be allowed.

Ninety-Six

Lake Greenwood State Rec Area
302 State Park Road
Ninety-Six, SC
864-543-3535
This 914-acre park covers five peninsulas on beautiful Lake Greenwood offering ample fishing, hiking, lake shore camping, and an interactive educational center. Dogs of all sizes are allowed at no additional fee. Dogs may not be left unattended unless for a shore time, and only if they will be quiet and well behaved. Dogs must be leashed at all times, and cleaned up after. Dogs are not allowed in any of the buildings, but they are allowed on the trails. The camping and tent areas also allow dogs. There is a dog walk area at the campground. Multiple dogs may be allowed.

Pickens

Table Rock State Park
158 Ellison Lane
Pickens, SC
864-878-9813
This park is listed on the National Register of Historic Places, and offers two lakes, challenging hiking trails, and a variety of land and water recreation. Dogs of all sizes are allowed at no additional fee. Dogs must be leashed at all times, and cleaned up after. Dogs may be left on site for shore periods if they will be comfortable, quiet and well behaved. Dogs are allowed on the trails. The camping and tent areas

also allow dogs. There is a dog walk area at the campground. Multiple dogs may be allowed.

Plum Branch

Hamilton Branch State Rec Area
111 Campground Road
Plum Branch, SC
864-333-2223
This 731 acre park takes up almost an entire peninsula, allowing for ample fishing, hiking, and lakeside camping. Dogs of all sizes are allowed at no additional fee. Dogs must be on no more than a 6 foot leash and be cleaned up after. Dogs are allowed on the trails. The camping and tent areas also allow dogs. There is a dog walk area at the campground. Multiple dogs may be allowed.

Prosperity

Dreher Island State Park
3677 State Park Road
Prosperity, SC
803-364-4152
This park, located on Lake Murray, offers various land and water recreation. The park is unique in that it consists of three islands linked together, and to the mainland, by bridge and causeway. Dogs of all sizes are allowed at no additional fee. Dogs may not be left unattended, and they must be on no more than a 6 foot leash, and be cleaned up after. Dogs are not allowed in the villa, the lodge area, or in park buildings, but they are allowed on the trails. The camping and tent areas also allow dogs. There is a dog walk area at the campground. Multiple dogs may be allowed.

Simpsonville

Scuffletown USA
603 Scuffletown Road
Simpsonville, SC
864-967-2276
Dogs of all sizes are allowed. There are no additional pet fees. Dogs must be leashed and cleaned up after. The camping and tent areas also allow dogs. There is a dog walk area at the campground. Multiple dogs may be allowed.

Swansea

River Bottom Farms
357 Cedar Creek Road
Swansea, SC
803-568-4182
Dogs of all sizes are allowed. There are no additional pet fees. Dogs must be well behaved, leashed, and cleaned up after. There are some breed restrictions. The camping and tent areas also allow dogs. There is a dog walk area at the campground. Dogs are allowed in the camping cabins. Multiple dogs may be allowed.

Townville

Lake Hartwell Camping and Cabins
400 Ponderosa Point
Townville, SC
888-427-8935
Dogs of all sizes are allowed, and there are no additional pet fees for tent or RV sites. There is a $25 one time pet fee for the cabins. Dogs must be leashed and cleaned up after. There are some breed restrictions. The camping and tent areas also allow dogs. There is a dog walk area at the campground. Multiple dogs may be allowed.

W Union

Crooked Creek RV Park
777 Arvee lane
W Union, SC
864-882-5040
Dogs of all sizes are allowed. There are no additional pet fees. Dogs are not allowed in the buildings or the pool area, and they must be leashed and cleaned up after. The camping and tent areas also allow dogs. There is a dog walk area at the campground. Multiple dogs may be allowed.

Whitmeyer

Sumter National Forest
H 66
Whitmeyer, SC
803-276-4810
This forest' diverse ecosystems support a large variety of plants, fish, mammals, bird species, and recreation. Dogs of all sizes are allowed at no additional fee. Dogs may not be left unattended, and they must be leashed and cleaned up after. On the trails, dogs must be under verbal or physical restraint at all times; keep in mind they are multi-

use trails and use a leash when populated. The camping and tent areas also allow dogs. There is a dog walk area at the campground. There are no electric or water hookups at the campground. Multiple dogs may be allowed.

Winnsboro

Lake Wateree State Rec Area
881 State Park Road
Winnsboro, SC
803-482-6401
This 238 acre park along a more than a 13,000 acre lake provides premier fishing, lake shore camping, hiking, and a variety of recreational pursuits. Dogs of all sizes are allowed at no additional fee. Dogs may not be left unattended at any time, and they must be on no more than a 6 foot leash, and be cleaned up after. Dogs are not allowed in the swim areas or in buildings. Dogs are allowed on the trails. The camping and tent areas also allow dogs. There is a dog walk area at the campground. Multiple dogs may be allowed.

Yemassee

Point South KOA
14 Campground Road
Yemassee, SC
843-726-5733
Dogs of all sizes are allowed. There are no additional pet fees. Dogs may not be left unattended, and they must be leashed and cleaned up after. There are some breed restrictions. The camping and tent areas also allow dogs. There is a dog walk area at the campground. Dogs are allowed in the camping cabins. Multiple dogs may be allowed.

South Dakota Listings

Brandon

Yogi Bear Jellystone Park
26014 478th Avenue
Brandon, SD
605-332-2233
Dogs of all sizes are allowed. There are no additional pet fees. Dogs must be leashed and cleaned up

after. Pets allowed in cabins with a security deposit or a credit card on file. This RV park is closed during the off-season. The camping and tent areas also allow dogs. There is a dog walk area at the campground. Dogs are allowed in the camping cabins. Multiple dogs may be allowed.

Brookings

Oakwood Lakes State Park
46109 202nd Street
Brookings, SD
605-627-5441
Born from ancient glaciers, this park is rich in natural and cultural history and offers historical sites, an archeology display, an almost 3,000 acre lake, and a variety of land and water recreation. Dogs of all sizes are allowed at no additional fee. Dogs may not be left unattended unless they will be quiet and well behaved. Dogs must be leashed and cleaned up after. Dogs are not allowed on beaches or in buildings. Dogs are allowed on the trails. The camping and tent areas also allow dogs. There is a dog walk area at the campground. Multiple dogs may be allowed.

Canton

Newton Hills State Park
28771 482nd Avenue
Canton, SD
605-987-2263
Born from ancient glaciers and rich in folklore, natural, and cultural history, this park features ancient burial mounds, folk music concerts, hiking trails, and a variety of recreational pursuits. Dogs of all sizes are allowed at no additional fee. Dogs may not be left unattended unless they will be quiet and very well behaved. Dogs must be leashed and cleaned up after. Dogs are not allowed in buildings. Dogs are allowed on the trails. The camping and tent areas also allow dogs. There is a dog walk area at the campground. There are no water hookups at the campground. Multiple dogs may be allowed.

Deadwood

Deadwood KOA
1 mile W of Deadwood on H 14A
Deadwood, SD
605-578-3830

Dogs of all sizes are allowed. There are no additional pet fees. Dogs may not be left unattended in the cabins or outside. Dogs must be leashed and cleaned up after. This RV park is closed during the off-season. The camping and tent areas also allow dogs. There is a dog walk area at the campground. Dogs are allowed in the camping cabins. Multiple dogs may be allowed.

Fort Pierre

Griffen Park
222 E Dakota Street
Fort Pierre, SD
605-773-7407
This park offers a variety of recreational pursuits, trails, and year round activities. Dogs of all sizes are allowed at no additional fee. Dogs must be quiet, leashed and cleaned up after. Dogs are not allowed on the beach. Dogs are allowed on the trials. The camping and tent areas also allow dogs. There is a dog walk area at the campground. Multiple dogs may be allowed.

Oahe Downstream Rec Area
20439 Marina Loop Road
Fort Pierre, SD
605-223-7722
This park is located on the south side of the dam that was built by the Corp, creating one of the largest constructed reservoirs in the US, and offers a wide range of activities and recreation. Dogs of all sizes are allowed at no additional fee. Dogs may not be left unattended, and they must be on no more than a 10 foot leash, and cleaned up after in camp areas. Dogs may be off lead in the off season if they are well behaved and under strict voice command. Dogs are not allowed on the swim beach or in buildings. Dogs are allowed on the trails. This campground is closed during the off-season. The camping and tent areas also allow dogs. There is a dog walk area at the campground. There are no water hookups at the campground. Multiple dogs may be allowed.

Garretson

Palisades State Park
25495 485th Avenue
Garretson, SD
605-594-3824
Born from ancient glaciers and rich in natural and cultural history, this park

offers a variety of hiking and climbing trails and various other recreational pursuits. Dogs of all sizes are allowed at no additional fee. Dogs may not be left unattended, and they must be leashed and cleaned up after. Dogs are not allowed in buildings. Dogs are allowed on the trails. This campground is closed during the off-season. The camping and tent areas also allow dogs. There is a dog walk area at the campground. There are no water hookups at the campground. Multiple dogs may be allowed.

Hot Springs

Angostura Rec Area
HC 52 Box 131-A
Hot Springs, SD
605-745-6996
Located along one of the largest reservoirs in western SD, this park provides a variety of land and water activities and recreation. Dogs of all sizes are allowed at no additional fee. Dogs may not be left unattended at any time; they must be on no more than a 10 foot leash, and be cleaned up after. The camping and tent areas also allow dogs. There is a dog walk area at the campground. There are no water hookups at the campground. Multiple dogs may be allowed.

Hot Springs KOA
HCR 52, Box 112-C
Hot Springs, SD
605-745-6449
Dogs of all sizes are allowed, and there are no additional pet fees for tent or RV sites. There is a $3 per night additional fee for pets in the cabins. Dogs must be quiet, well behaved, leashed and cleaned up after. This RV park is closed during the off-season. The camping and tent areas also allow dogs. There is a dog walk area at the campground. Dogs are allowed in the camping cabins. Multiple dogs may be allowed.

Interior

Badland National Park
25216 Ben Reifel Place
Interior, SD
605-433-5361
This park of 244,000 acres of sharply eroded buttes, pinnacles, spires, and home to the largest protected mixed grass prairie in the US, offers

interpretive programs, an active paleontological dig site, and a variety of recreational pursuits. Dogs of all sizes are allowed at no additional fee. Dogs may not be left unattended at any time-including in automobiles, and they must be leashed and cleaned up after. Dogs are not allowed on the trails or grass, and are to remain on asphalt areas. The camping and tent areas also allow dogs. There is a dog walk area at the campground. There are no electric or water hookups at the campground. Multiple dogs may be allowed.

Badlands/White River KOA
20720 H 44
Interior, SD
605-433-5337
Dogs of all sizes are allowed. There are no additional pet fees. Dogs may not be left unattended unless they will be quiet. Dogs must be leashed and cleaned up after. They have a Pet Park where your dog can be off leash. This RV park is closed during the off-season. The camping and tent areas also allow dogs. There is a dog walk area at the campground. There are special amenities given to dogs at this campground. Multiple dogs may be allowed.

Kennebec

Kennebec KOA
311 S H 273
Kennebec, SD
605-869-2300
Dogs of all sizes are allowed. There are no additional pet fees. Dogs must be leashed and cleaned up after. A pet waiver must be signed if the dog(s) are any of the known aggressive breeds. This RV park is closed during the off-season. The camping and tent areas also allow dogs. There is a dog walk area at the campground. Dogs are allowed in the camping cabins. Multiple dogs may be allowed.

Midland

Belvidere East KOA
24201 H 63
Midland, SD
605-344-2247
Dogs of all sizes are allowed. There are no additional pet fees. Dogs must be leashed and cleaned up after. There is a fenced in pet playground where dogs may be off

leash. This RV park is closed during the off-season. The camping and tent areas also allow dogs. There is a dog walk area at the campground. Multiple dogs may be allowed.

Mitchell

Dakota Campground
1800 Spruce
Mitchell, SD
605-996-9432
Dogs of all sizes are allowed. There are no additional pet fees. Dogs may not be left unattended, they must be quiet, leashed, and cleaned up after. This RV park is closed during the off-season. The camping and tent areas also allow dogs. There is a dog walk area at the campground. Multiple dogs may be allowed.

Mitchell KOA
41244 H 38
Mitchell, SD
605-996-1131
Dogs of all sizes are allowed. There are no additional pet fees. Dogs must be quiet, well behaved, leashed, and cleaned up after. This RV park is closed during the off-season. The camping and tent areas also allow dogs. There is a dog walk area at the campground. Dogs are allowed in the camping cabins. Multiple dogs may be allowed.

Rondees Campground
911 East K
Mitchell, SD
605-996-0769
Dogs of all sizes are allowed. There are no additional pet fees. Dogs may not be left unattended outside, and they must be quiet, well behaved, leashed, and cleaned up after. This RV park is closed during the off-season. The camping and tent areas also allow dogs. There is a dog walk area at the campground. Multiple dogs may be allowed.

Mobridge

Indian Creek Rec Area
12905 288th Avenue
Mobridge, SD
605-845-7112
Beautiful river views from the rolling hills of this park make this a popular destination. In addition to its historical interest, the park offers a marina, a hiking trail, and a variety of recreational pursuits. Dogs of all sizes are allowed at no additional

fee. Dogs may not be left unattended, and they must be on no more than a 6 foot leash, and cleaned up after. The camping and tent areas also allow dogs. There is a dog walk area at the campground. There are no water hookups at the campground. Multiple dogs may be allowed.

Mount Rushmore - Black Hills

Black Hills National Forest
25041 N H 16
Custer, SD
605-673-9200
This 1.2 million acre forest, at altitudes up to 7,242 feet, offers 1,300 miles of streams, over 13,000 acres of wilderness, 2 scenic byways and over 450 miles of trails. Dogs of all sizes are allowed at no additional fee. Dogs may not be left unattended, and they must be leashed in the camp areas, and cleaned up after. Dogs may be off lead in the forest only if they are under strict voice command and will not chase wildlife. The camping and tent areas also allow dogs. There is a dog walk area at the campground. There are no electric or water hookups at the campground. Multiple dogs may be allowed.

Custer State Park
13329 H 16A
Custer, SD
605-255-4515
Steeped in natural and cultural history, this park of 71,000 acres of spectacular terrain offers living history demonstrations, guided nature walks, gold-panning excursions, one of the largest bison herds in the world and a variety of recreational pursuits. Dogs of all sizes are allowed at no additional fee. Dogs may not be left unattended, and they must be leashed and cleaned up after in camp areas. Dogs are allowed on the trails, and they may be off lead then only if they are under strict voice command. Dogs are not allowed on beaches or in buildings. The camping and tent areas also allow dogs. There is a dog walk area at the campground. There are no electric or water hookups at the campground. Multiple dogs may be allowed.

KOA Campground
U.S. Highway 16
Custer, SD

605-673-4304
This KOA campground is located in the Black Hills. They have tent sites, RV campsites and pet-friendly Kamping Kabins. Amenities include a heated pool, croquet, a playground, snack bar, modem dataport, maximum pull through length of 60 feet and 50 amp service available. Well-behaved leashed dogs are allowed and there is a dog walk area on the premises. Please remember to clean up after your pet. The campground is open from April 15 to October 1. They are located 3 miles west of the town of Custer on Highway 1 towards Jewel Cave and New Castle, Wyoming. Mt. Rushmore is about a 30 minute drive from the campground, possibly more if there is traffic.

The Flintstones Bedrock City Campground
US Highways 16 and 385
Custer, SD
605-673-4079
Enjoy a camping or RV stay at this Flintstone's themed campground. The camp sites are located in an open meadow hilltop location. This full service campground offers tent camping and RV camping. Amenities include full hookups, showers, laundry facility, store, heating swimming pool and arcade. Also on site is the Flintstone's theme park which offers a miniature train ride around the park, several playgrounds, a Flintmobile car ride, gift shop, and a drive-in restaurant which has Brontoburgers, Chickasaurus and more. They are open from mid May until the beginning of September. Well-behaved leashed dogs are welcome, but are not allowed inside any buildings, including the camping cabins. Pets are allowed in the theme park including on the miniature train ride and at the outdoor dining seats at the drive-in restaurant. Please remember to clean up after your pet.

The Roost Resort
12462 H 16 A
Custer, SD
605-673-2326
Dogs of all sizes are allowed at no additional fee for tent or RV sites. For the cabins, there is a $5 per night per pet additional fee for a small dog, and a $10 per night per pet additional fee for medium to large dogs. Dogs may not be left unattended, and they must be quiet,

well behaved, leashed, and cleaned up after. The camping and tent areas also allow dogs. There is a dog walk area at the campground. Dogs are allowed in the camping cabins. Multiple dogs may be allowed.

Crooked Creek Resort
24184 S H 385/16
Hill City, SD
800-252-8486
Dogs of all sizes are allowed. There are no additional pet fees. Dogs may not be left unattended, and they must be leashed and cleaned up after. This RV park is closed during the off-season. The camping and tent areas also allow dogs. There is a dog walk area at the campground. Dogs are allowed in the camping cabins. 2 dogs may be allowed.

Horse Thief Campground
24391 H 87
Hill City, SD
605-574-2668
Dogs of all sizes are allowed. There are no additional pet fees. Dogs may not be left unattended, and they must be leashed and cleaned up after. This RV park is closed during the off-season. The camping and tent areas also allow dogs. There is a dog walk area at the campground. Multiple dogs may be allowed.

KOA Campground and Resort
12620 Highway 244
Hill City, SD
605-574-2525
This KOA Campground is located at an elevation of 5,400 feet and is just 5 miles from Mt. Rushmore. The campground is adjacent to the Peter Norbeck Wildlife Preserve and the Black Elk Wilderness Area and minutes to Custer State Park. They have almost 500 tent sites and RV campsites, and 55 Kamping Kabins with one or two bedroom options. Amenities include 2 outdoor pools, 3 hot tubs, sauna, waterslide, mini-golf, volleyball court, basketball court, fishing pond, hayrides, evening movies, paddle boats, bike rentals, restaurant, laundry facilities, comfort stations and dump stations. Well-behaved leashed dogs are allowed in the campground, and in the cabins, some of which have bathrooms. Please remember to clean up after your pet.

Rafter J Bar Ranch
12325 Rafter J Road
Hill City, SD

605-574-2527
Dogs of all sizes are allowed. There are no additional pet fees. Dogs may not be left unattended, they must be quiet, leashed, and cleaned up after. This RV park is closed during the off-season. The camping and tent areas also allow dogs. There is a dog walk area at the campground. Multiple dogs may be allowed.

Berry Patch Campground
1860 E North Street
Rapid City, SD
800-658-4566
Dogs of all sizes are allowed. There are no additional pet fees. Dogs may not be left unattended outside, and must be leashed and cleaned up after. The camping and tent areas also allow dogs. There is a dog walk area at the campground. Multiple dogs may be allowed.

Happy Holiday Resort
8990 H 16S
Rapid City, SD
605-342-7365
Dogs of all sizes are allowed. There is a $1 one time additional fee per pet. Dogs may not be left unattended outside, and they must be leashed and cleaned up after. The camping and tent areas also allow dogs. There is a dog walk area at the campground. Multiple dogs may be allowed.

Jellystone Park
7001 S H 16
Rapid City, SD
605-341-8554
Dogs of all sizes are allowed. There are no additional pet fees. Dogs may not be left unattended, must be leashed, and cleaned up after. There is a dog run area where dogs can run off leash if they are well behaved and are under voice control. Dogs are not allowed in the front sites, by the pool, in the cabins, or in the buildings. This RV park is closed during the off-season. The camping and tent areas also allow dogs. There is a dog walk area at the campground. Multiple dogs may be allowed.

KOA Campground
P.O. Box 2592
Rapid City, SD
605-348-2111
This KOA campground is off of I-90 in Rapid City and is located about an hour from the area's popular attractions. They have tent sites, RV campsites and pet-friendly Kamping Kabins. Well-behaved leashed dogs are allowed in the campground and in the cabins. Please remember to clean up after your pet. Amenities include a swimming pool, hot tub/sauna, snack bar, modem dataport, cable TV, maximum pull through length of 60 feet and 50 amp service available. The campground is open from April 15 to October 15. Upon arrival, they usually have a grab bag with treats for pets. There are some breed restrictions.

Rushmore Shadows
23645 Clubhouse Drive
Rapid City, SD
800-231-0425
Dogs of all sizes are allowed. There are no additional pet fees. Dogs may not be left unattended, and must be leashed and cleaned up after. This RV park is closed during the off-season. The camping and tent areas also allow dogs. There is a dog walk area at the campground. Multiple dogs may be allowed.

N Sioux City

Sioux City KOA
601 Streeter Drive
N Sioux City, SD
605-232-4519
Dogs of all sizes are allowed. There are no additional pet fees. Dogs must be well behaved, leashed, and cleaned up after. This RV park is closed during the off-season. The camping and tent areas also allow dogs. There is a dog walk area at the campground. Dogs are allowed in the camping cabins. Multiple dogs may be allowed.

Salem

Camp America
25495 H 81
Salem, SD
605-425-9085
Dogs of all sizes are allowed. There are no additional pet fees. Dogs must be leashed at all times, and cleaned up after. This RV park is closed during the off-season. The camping and tent areas also allow dogs. There is a dog walk area at the campground. Multiple dogs may be allowed.

Sioux Falls

Sioux Falls KOA
1401 E Robur Drive
Sioux Falls, SD
605-332-9987
Dogs of all sizes are allowed. There are no additional pet fees. Dogs must be well behaved, leashed, and cleaned up after. This RV park is closed during the off-season. The camping and tent areas also allow dogs. There is a dog walk area at the campground. Dogs are allowed in the camping cabins. Multiple dogs may be allowed.

Spearfish

Spearfish KOA
41 H 14
Spearfish, SD
605-642-4633
Dogs of all sizes are allowed. There are no additional pet fees. Dogs may not be left unattended at any time, and they must be leashed and cleaned up after. There are some breed restrictions. This RV park is closed during the off-season. The camping and tent areas also allow dogs. There is a dog walk area at the campground. Multiple dogs may be allowed.

Sturgis

Bear Butte State Park
PO Box 688; E Hwy 79
Sturgis, SD
605-347-5240
Rich in geology, history, and culture, this park features interpretive programs, an education center, a variety of trails, and various recreational pursuits. Dogs of all sizes are allowed at no additional fee. Dogs may not be left unattended at any time; they must be on no more than a 10 foot leash, and be cleaned up after. Dogs are allowed on all the trails except the Summit Trail. Dogs are not allowed in park buildings. The camping and tent areas also allow dogs. There is a dog walk area at the campground. There are no electric or water hookups at the campground. Multiple dogs may be allowed.

Elkview Campground
13014 Pleasant Valley Road
Sturgis, SD
877-478-5162
Dogs of all sizes are allowed. There are no additional pet fees. Dogs may not be left unattended unless they will be quiet and well behaved. Dogs

must be leashed and cleaned up after. This RV park is closed during the off-season. The camping and tent areas also allow dogs. There is a dog walk area at the campground. Multiple dogs may be allowed.

Tea

Red Barn RV Park
47003 272nd Street
Tea, SD
605-368-2268
Dogs of all sizes are allowed. There are no additional pet fees. Dogs may not be left unattended, and must be leashed and cleaned up after. This RV park is closed during the off-season. There is a dog walk area at the campground. Multiple dogs may be allowed.

Wall

Arrow Campground
PO Box 366
Wall, SD
605-279-2112
Dogs of all sizes are allowed. There are no additional pet fees. Dogs may not be left unattended outside, and they must be leashed and cleaned up after. Dogs are not allowed at the playground. The camping and tent areas also allow dogs. There is a dog walk area at the campground. Multiple dogs may be allowed.

Sleepy Hollow Campground
116 4th Avenue W
Wall, SD
605-279-2100
Dogs of all sizes are allowed. There are no additional pet fees. Dogs must be leashed and cleaned up after. Dogs are not allowed in buildings or on the lawn by the office. This RV park is closed during the off-season. The camping and tent areas also allow dogs. There is a dog walk area at the campground. Multiple dogs may be allowed.

Yankton

Chief White Crane Rec Area
43349 Hwy 52
Yankton, SD
605-668-2985
This park is rich in history, but their main feature is being a winter home for the American Eagle, and motor vehicles are not allowed in the park from November 1st through March

31 due to nesting. Dogs of all sizes are allowed at no additional fee. Dogs may not be left unattended, and they must be leashed and cleaned up after. Dogs are not allowed in public swim areas or in buildings. Dogs are allowed on the trails. This campground is closed during the off-season. The camping and tent areas also allow dogs. There is a dog walk area at the campground. Multiple dogs may be allowed.

Tennessee Listings

Benton

Cherokee National Forest
3171 H 64
Benton, TN
423-476-9700
This scenic park of over 640,000 acres is in one of the world's most diverse areas and supports a large variety of plants, fish, mammals, bird species, and recreation. Dogs of all sizes are allowed at no additional fee. Dogs may not be left unattended except for short periods, and they ask that you inform the office of your absence. Dogs must be leashed at all times and cleaned up after in camp areas. Dogs are allowed on the trails. The camping and tent areas also allow dogs. There is a dog walk area at the campground. There are no electric or water hookups at the campground.

Blountville

Bristol/Kingsport KOA
425 Rocky Branch Road
Blountville, TN
423-323-7790
Dogs of all sizes are allowed. There are no additional pet fees. Dogs may not be tied up or left unattended outside, and they must be leashed and cleaned up after. There is a fenced in dog run area, and a Kennel Day Care on site for $10 per day per pet. The camping and tent areas also allow dogs. There is a dog walk area at the campground. There are special amenities given to dogs at this campground. Multiple dogs may be allowed.

Buchanan

Paris Landing State Park
16055 H 79 N
Buchanan, TN
731-641-4465
This 841 acre park along the shores of the Tennessee River offers a variety of land and water recreation. Dogs of all sizes are allowed at no additional fee for camping. There is an additional fee of $10 per night per pet for the lodge and for the 1 pet friendly cabin. Dogs may not be left unattended, and they must be leashed and cleaned up after. Dogs are allowed on the trails. The camping and tent areas also allow dogs. There is a dog walk area at the campground. Dogs are allowed in the camping cabins. Multiple dogs may be allowed.

Burns

Montgomery Bell State Park
1020 Jackson Hill Road
Burns, TN
615-797-9052
This park of over 3,700 acres offers a variety of naturalist interpretive programs in addition to various land and water recreation. Dogs of all sizes are allowed at no additional fee for the camping area. There is a $10 per night per pet additional fee for the 1 pet friendly cabin and the lodge. Dogs must be leashed at all times and cleaned up after. Dogs are not allowed in the lake or in park buildings; they are allowed on the trails. The camping and tent areas also allow dogs. There is a dog walk area at the campground. Dogs are allowed in the camping cabins. Multiple dogs may be allowed.

Caryville

Cove Lake State Park
110 Cove Lake Lane
Caryville, TN
423-566-9701
This mountain valley park on 673 acres offers a variety of land and water activities and recreational pursuits. Dogs of all sizes are allowed at no additional fee. Dogs may not be left unattended, and they must be leashed and cleaned up after. Dogs are not allowed in buildings. Dogs are allowed on the trails. The camping and tent areas also allow dogs. There is a dog walk area at the campground. Multiple

dogs may be allowed.

Royal Blue RV Resort
305 Luther Seiber Road
Caryville, TN
423-566-4847
Dogs of all sizes are allowed. There are no additional pet fees. Dogs must be quiet, leashed, and cleaned up after. The camping and tent areas also allow dogs. There is a dog walk area at the campground. Multiple dogs may be allowed.

Clarksville

Clarksville RV Park and Campground
1270 Tyler Road
Clarksville, TN
931-648-8638
Dogs of all sizes are allowed. There are no additional pet fees. Dogs may not be left unattended outside, must be leashed, and cleaned up after. The camping and tent areas also allow dogs. There is a dog walk area at the campground. Multiple dogs may be allowed.

Cornersville

Texas T Campground
2499 Lynnville H
Cornersville, TN
931-293-2500
Dogs of all sizes are allowed. There are no additional pet fees. Dogs must be leashed and cleaned up after. The camping and tent areas also allow dogs. There is a dog walk area at the campground. Multiple dogs may be allowed.

Crossville

Ballyhoo Campground
256 Werthwyle Drive
Crossville, TN
931-484-0860
Dogs of all sizes are allowed, up to three, and there are no additional pet fees for tent or RV sites. There is a $5 one time additional pet fee for the cabins, and only one dog is allowed. Dogs must be well behaved, leashed, and cleaned up after. There are some breed restrictions. The camping and tent areas also allow dogs. There is a dog walk area at the campground. Dogs are allowed in the camping cabins.

Cumberland Mountain State Park
24 Office Dirve

Crossville, TN
931-484-6138
This 1,720-acre park is said to be the largest timbered plateau in America, and offers interpretive programs, scenic trails, and a variety of land and water recreation. Dogs are allowed at no additional fee for tent or RV sites. There is an additional $5 per night per pet fee for the cabins. Dogs must be leashed and cleaned up after. Dogs are allowed on the trails. The camping and tent areas also allow dogs. There is a dog walk area at the campground. Dogs are allowed in the camping cabins. Multiple dogs may be allowed.

Roam and Roost RV Campground
255 Fairview Drive
Crossville, TN
931-707-1414
Dogs of all sizes are allowed. There are no additional pet fees. Dogs must be well behaved, leashed, and cleaned up after. There are some breed restrictions. This RV park is closed during the off-season. There is a dog walk area at the campground. 2 dogs may be allowed.

Harrison

Harrison Bay State Park
8411 Harrison Bay Road
Harrison, TN
423-344-2272
This scenic wooded park of 1,200 acres with 40 miles of shoreline holds historical interest and provides a variety of land and water activities. Dogs of all sizes are allowed at no additional fee. Dogs may not be left unattended for long periods, and they must be leashed and cleaned up after. Dogs are not allowed in public swim areas or in buildings. Dogs are allowed on the trails. The camping and tent areas also allow dogs. There is a dog walk area at the campground. Multiple dogs may be allowed.

Henderson

Chickasaw State Rustic Park
20 Cabin Lane
Henderson, TN
731-989-5141
This scenic park has over 1,280 acres for recreation, and a variety of trails as well as land and water

activities. Dogs of all sizes are allowed at no additional fee for the tent and RV sites. There is a $10 per night per pet additional fee for the cabins. Dogs may not be left unattended for very long or left out at night. Dogs must be leashed and be cleaned up after. Dogs are allowed on the trails. The camping and tent areas also allow dogs. There is a dog walk area at the campground. Dogs are allowed in the camping cabins. Multiple dogs may be allowed.

Hilham

Standing Stone State Park
1674 Standing Stone Park H (H 52)
Hilham, TN
931-823-6347
This scenic 1100 acre park hosts a variety of activities and recreational pursuits. Dogs of all sizes are allowed at no additional fee for the camping area. There is a $10 additional pet fee for the 1st night, and $5 per night per pet thereafter, for the 1 pet friendly cabin. Dogs may not be left unattended, and they must be leashed at all times, and cleaned up after. Dogs are allowed on the trails. The camping and tent areas also allow dogs. There is a dog walk area at the campground. Dogs are allowed in the camping cabins.

Hurricane Mills

Buffalo/I-40/Exit 143 KOA
473 Barren Hollow Road
Hurricane Mills, TN
931-296-1306
Dogs of all sizes are allowed, but there can only be up to 2 large or three small dogs per site. There are no additional pet fees. Dogs may not be left unattended, and they must be quiet, well behaved, leashed, and cleaned up after. There are some breed restrictions. The camping and tent areas also allow dogs. There is a dog walk area at the campground. Dogs are allowed in the camping cabins.

Loretta Lynn's Ranch
44 Hurricane Mills
Hurricane Mills, TN
931-296-7700
Dogs of all sizes are allowed. There are no additional pet fees. Dogs are not allowed on tours or in the buildings. Dogs must be in at night, leashed, and cleaned up after. The

camping and tent areas also allow dogs. There is a dog walk area at the campground. Multiple dogs may be allowed.

Jellico

Indian Mountain State Park
143 State Park Circle
Jellico, TN
423-784-7958
This beautiful 200 acre park provides nature study in addition to a variety of land and water recreation. Dogs of all sizes are allowed at no additional fee. Dogs may not be left unattended, and they must be leashed and cleaned up after. Dogs are allowed on the trails. The camping and tent areas also allow dogs. There is a dog walk area at the campground. Multiple dogs may be allowed.

Kingsport

Warriors Path State Park
490 Hemlock Road
Kingsport, TN
423-239-8531
This park got it's name from being an ancient war and trading path of the Cherokees, and now this scenic area provides a variety of land and water activities and recreation. Dogs of all sizes are allowed at no additional fee. Dogs may not be left unattended for very long and then only if they will be quiet and very well behaved. Dogs must be leashed and cleaned up after. Dogs are not allowed on the beach or in the buildings. Dogs are allowed on the trails. The camping and tent areas also allow dogs. There is a dog walk area at the campground. Multiple dogs may be allowed.

Knoxville

Southlake RV Park
3730 Maryville Pike
Knoxville, TN
865-573-1837
Dogs of all sizes are allowed. There are no additional pet fees. Dogs may not be left unattended outside, must be leashed, and cleaned up after. The camping and tent areas also allow dogs. There is a dog walk area at the campground. Multiple dogs may be allowed.

Kodak

Knoxville East KOA
241 KOA Way
Kodak, TN
865-933-6393
Dogs of all sizes are allowed. There are no additional pet fees. Dogs must be quiet, well behaved, leashed, and cleaned up after. This RV park is closed during the off-season. The camping and tent areas also allow dogs. There is a dog walk area at the campground. Multiple dogs may be allowed.

Lawrenceburg

David Crockett State Park
1400 W Gaines Street
Lawrenceburg, TN
931-762-9408
This historically rich park offers a museum, interpretive programs, and a variety of land and water activities and recreation. Dogs of all sizes are allowed at no additional fee. Dogs may not be left unattended, and they must have current rabies and shot records. Dogs must be leashed at all times and cleaned up after. Dogs are not allowed in buildings, but they are allowed on the trails. The camping and tent areas also allow dogs. There is a dog walk area at the campground. Multiple dogs may be allowed.

Lebanon

Cedars of Lebanon State Park
328 Cedar Forest Road
Lebanon, TN
615-443-2769
Because of the unique ecosystems of this park, 19 rare and endangered species of plants grow profusely only at this spot on Earth. In addition to nature study and programs, there are a variety of land and water recreational activities. Dogs of all sizes are allowed at no additional fee for the camp area, but there is a $5 per night per pet additional fee for the 1 pet friendly cabin. Dogs may not be left unattended for very long, and they must be quiet, well behaved, leashed, and cleaned up after. Dogs are not allowed in buildings, but they are allowed on the trails. The camping and tent areas also allow dogs. There is a dog walk area at the campground. Dogs are allowed in the camping cabins. Multiple dogs may be allowed.

Countryside RV Resort
2100 Safari Camp Road
Lebanon, TN
615-449-5527
Dogs of all sizes are allowed. There are no additional pet fees. Dogs must be leashed and cleaned up after. The camping and tent areas also allow dogs. There is a dog walk area at the campground. Multiple dogs may be allowed.

Timberline Campground
1204 Murfreesboro Road
Lebanon, TN
615-449-2831
Dogs up to 50 pounds are allowed. There are no additional pet fees. Dogs may not be left unattended outside, must be leashed, and cleaned up after. The camping and tent areas also allow dogs. There is a dog walk area at the campground. 2 dogs may be allowed.

Lenoir City

Soaring Eagle Campground
3152 Buttermilk Road W
Lenoir City, TN
865-376-9017
Dogs up to 50 pounds are allowed. There are no additional pet fees. Dogs are not allowed at the picnic or playground area. Dogs must be leashed and cleaned up after. There are some breed restrictions. The camping and tent areas also allow dogs. There is a dog walk area at the campground. 2 dogs may be allowed.

Manchester

Manchester KOA
586 Campground Road
Manchester, TN
931-728-9777
Dogs of all sizes are allowed. There are no additional pet fees. There is a pet waiver to sign for cabin rentals. Dogs may not be left unattended outside, and they must be quiet, leashed, and cleaned up after. There is a field nearby where dogs may run off lead if they are well behaved, and under voice control. The camping and tent areas also allow dogs. There is a dog walk area at the campground. Dogs are allowed in the camping cabins. Multiple dogs may be allowed.

Old Stone Fort State

Archaeological Historic Park
732 Stone Fort Drive
Manchester, TN
931-723-5073
In addition to recreational pursuits, this historic park offers educational and entertaining programs regarding the preservation, protection, and study of the area and Native American cultures. Dogs of all sizes are allowed at no additional fee. Dogs may not be left unattended for very long, and they must be leashed and cleaned up after. Dogs are not allowed on the mounds or in the buildings, but they are allowed on the trails. The camping and tent areas also allow dogs. There is a dog walk area at the campground. Multiple dogs may be allowed.

McDonald

Chattanooga North/Cleveland KOA
648 Pleasant Grove Road
McDonald, TN
423-472-8928
Two dogs of any size are allowed at the tent or RV sites. There can only be one dog up to 20 pounds in the cabins. There is a pet policy to sign at check in and there are no additional pet fees. Dogs may not be left unattended outside, and they must be leashed and cleaned up after. The camping and tent areas also allow dogs. There is a dog walk area at the campground. Dogs are allowed in the camping cabins.

Memphis

Memphis Graceland RV Park and Campground
3691 Elvis Presley Blvd
Memphis, TN
901-396-7125
Dogs of all sizes are allowed. There are no additional pet fees. Dogs must be leashed and cleaned up after. The camping and tent areas also allow dogs. There is a dog walk area at the campground. Multiple dogs may be allowed.

T. O. Fuller State Park
1500 W Mitchell Road
Memphis, TN
901-543-7581
This park of over 1100 acres is within the city limits of Memphis, is mostly forested, and offers an Olympic sized swimming pool, an 18 hole golf course, and acres of grassy fields. Dogs of all sizes are allowed at no additional fee. Dogs may not be left

unattended, and they must be leashed and cleaned up after. Dogs are not allowed on the golf course, but they are allowed on the trails. The camping and tent areas also allow dogs. There is a dog walk area at the campground. Multiple dogs may be allowed.

Tom Sawyer's Mississippi River RV Park
1286 S 8th Street
West Memphis, AR
870-735-9770
Dogs of all sizes are allowed. There are no additional pet fees. Dogs must be quiet, well behaved, leashed, and cleaned up after. Dogs are also welcome to swim at the river. The camping and tent areas also allow dogs. There is a dog walk area at the campground. Multiple dogs may be allowed.

Millington

Meeman-Shelby Forest State Park
910 Riddick Road
Millington, TN
901-876-5215
A museum and interactive nature center are offered here in addition to providing a variety of recreation areas, woodlands, trails, and wildlife habitats. Dogs of all sizes are allowed at no additional fee for the camping areas. There is a $10 per night per pet fee for the 1st night, and $5 per night per pet for each night thereafter for the 1 pet friendly cabin. Dogs must be leashed at all times. Dogs are allowed on the trails. The camping and tent areas also allow dogs. There is a dog walk area at the campground. Dogs are allowed in the camping cabins. Multiple dogs may be allowed.

Morristown

Panther Creek State Park
2010 Panther Creek Road
Morristown, TN
423-587-7046
This park, of over 1,400 acres located on the shores of the Cherokee Reservoir, provides 13 scenic hiking and biking trails (of which 5 are hiking only), and a variety of land and water recreation. Dogs of all sizes are allowed at no additional fee. Dogs may not be left unattended, and they must be leashed. They request dogs do their

business off trails, or they must be cleaned up after. The camping and tent areas also allow dogs. There is a dog walk area at the campground. Multiple dogs may be allowed.

Nashville

Brown County State Park
1450 State Road 46 W
Nashville, TN
812-988-6406
Dogs of all sizes are allowed. There are no additional pet fees. Dogs may not be left unattended, and they must be leashed and cleaned up after. The camping and tent areas also allow dogs. There is a dog walk area at the campground. There are no water hookups at the campground. Multiple dogs may be allowed.

Jellystone Park
2572 Music Valley Drive
Nashville, TN
615-889-4225
Dogs of all sizes are allowed. There are no additional pet fees. Dogs may not be left unattended, must be leashed, and cleaned up after. They are also not allowed to be tied up outside unless an adult is present. There are some breed restrictions. The camping and tent areas also allow dogs. There is a dog walk area at the campground. Multiple dogs may be allowed.

Two Rivers Campground
2616 Music Valley Drive
Nashville, TN
615-883-8559
Dogs of all sizes are allowed. There are no additional pet fees. Dogs may not be left unattended, must be well behaved, leashed, and cleaned up after. The camping and tent areas also allow dogs. There is a dog walk area at the campground. Multiple dogs may be allowed.

Pikeville

Fall Creek Falls State Park
2009 Village Camp Road
Pikeville, TN
423-881-5298
Sparkling streams, gorges, cascading waterfalls, a variety of scenic trails, ecosystems, and abundant recreation make this park a popular destination. Dogs of all sizes are allowed at no additional fee for camping areas. There is a $10 (plus tax)per night per pet additional fee

for the 1 pet friendly cabin or the lodge. Dogs must be leashed and cleaned up after. Dogs are not allowed on the Overnight Trail, but they are allowed on the other trails. The camping and tent areas also allow dogs. There is a dog walk area at the campground. Dogs are allowed in the camping cabins. Multiple dogs may be allowed.

Ringgold

Chattanooga South/Lookout Mtn KOA
199 KOA Blvd
Ringgold, TN
706-937-4166
Dogs of all sizes are allowed, and there are no additional pet fees for tent or RV sites. There is a $10 per night additional pet fee for the cabins. There can be up to 3 dogs at the tent or RV sites and up to 2 dogs at the cabins. Dogs may not be placed in outdoor pens, and may not be left unattended outside. Dogs must be leashed and cleaned up after. There are some breed restrictions. The camping and tent areas also allow dogs. There is a dog walk area at the campground. Dogs are allowed in the camping cabins.

Rock Island

Rock Island State Park
82 Beach Road
Rock Island, TN
931-686-2471
The Great Falls of the Caney Fork River add to the scenic beauty of this park that provides a variety of special programs, activities, and recreation. Dogs of all sizes are allowed at no additional fee. Dogs may not be left unattended outside, and they must be leashed and cleaned up after. Dogs are allowed on the trails. The camping and tent areas also allow dogs. There is a dog walk area at the campground. Multiple dogs may be allowed.

Sevierville

River Plantation RV Park
1004 Parkway
Sevierville, TN
865-429-5267
Dogs of all sizes are allowed. There are no additional pet fees. Dogs must be leashed and cleaned up after. There is a dog walk area at the

campground. Multiple dogs may be allowed.

Silver Point

Edgar Evins State Park
1630 Edgar Evins Park Road
Silver Point, TN
931-858-2446
This park of over 6,000 acres is along the shores of one of the most beautiful reservoirs in Tennessee and provides miles of hiking trails, opportunities for nature study, and a variety of land and water recreation. Dogs of all sizes are allowed at no additional fee for the camping area. There is a $10 per night per pet additional fee for the cabins, and dogs must be 30 pounds or under. The cabins are closed for one month in off season. Dogs may not be left unattended, and they must be leashed and cleaned up after. Dogs are allowed on the trails. The camping and tent areas also allow dogs. There is a dog walk area at the campground. Dogs are allowed in the camping cabins.

The Smoky Mountains

Arrow Creek Campground
4721 E Parkway
Gatlinburg, TN
865-430-7433
Dogs of all sizes and numbers are allowed for tent and RV sites. Only 2 dogs are allowed in the cabins. There are no additional pet fees. Dogs may not be left unattended, must be quiet, leashed, and cleaned up after. This RV park is closed during the off-season. The camping and tent areas also allow dogs. There is a dog walk area at the campground. Dogs are allowed in the camping cabins.

Great Smoky Jellystone
4946 Hooper H
Gatlinburg, TN
423-487-5534
Dogs up to 75 pounds are allowed. There are no additional pet fees. Dogs must be well behaved, not left unattended, be leashed, and cleaned up after. There are some breed restrictions. This RV park is closed during the off-season There is a dog walk area at the campground. 2 dogs may be allowed.

Great Smoky Mountains National

Park
107 Park Headquarters Road
Gatlinburg, TN
865-436-1200
Rich in history, this popular park is well known for its beauty, diversity of plant and animal life, and its educational and recreational pursuits. Dogs of all sizes are allowed at no additional fee. Dogs may not be left unattended at any time, and they must be on no more than a 6 foot leash, and be cleaned up after. Dogs can be wherever an automobile can be. They are not allowed on the hiking trails. The camping and tent areas also allow dogs. There is a dog walk area at the campground. There are no electric or water hookups at the campground. Multiple dogs may be allowed.

Smoky Bear Campground
4857 E Parkway
Gatlinburg, TN
865-436-8372
Dogs of all sizes are allowed at the tent and RV sites. Small dogs only are allowed in the rentals or cabins. There are no additional pet fees. Dogs may not be left unattended except for very short periods. Dogs must be leashed and cleaned up after. This RV park is closed during the off-season. The camping and tent areas also allow dogs. There is a dog walk area at the campground. Dogs are allowed in the camping cabins. Multiple dogs may be allowed.

Twin Creek RV Resort
E Parkway
Gatlinburg, TN
865-436-7081
Dogs of all sizes are allowed. There are no additional pet fees. Canvas or Pop-up trailers are not allowed with pets. Dogs may not be left unattended, and dog pens are not allowed. Dogs must be leashed and cleaned up after. There are some breed restrictions. There is a dog walk area at the campground. 2 dogs may be allowed.

Riveredge RV Park
4220 Huskey Street
Pigeon Forge, TN
865-453-5813
Dogs of all sizes are allowed. There are no additional pet fees. Dogs must in your RV and not left outside alone when gone. Dogs must be leashed and cleaned up after. There is a dog walk area at the

campground. Multiple dogs may be allowed.

Townsend

Little River Village Campground
8533 H 73
Townsend, TN
865-448-2241
Dogs of all sizes are allowed. There are no additional pet fees. Dogs may not be left unattended, must be quiet, leashed, and cleaned up after. The camping and tent areas also allow dogs. There is a dog walk area at the campground. Multiple dogs may be allowed.

Tremont Hills Campground
118 Stables Drive
Townsend, TN
865-448-6363
Dogs of all sizes are allowed. There are no additional pet fees. Dogs may not be left unattended, and must be leashed and cleaned up after. The camping and tent areas also allow dogs. There is a dog walk area at the campground. Multiple dogs may be allowed.

Winchester

Tims Ford State Park
570 Tims Ford Drive
Winchester, TN
931-962-1183
Known as one of the best bass fishing areas in the south, this park also holds archaeological interest, and is host to a variety of recreation. Dogs of all sizes are allowed at no additional fee for the camping area. There is a $10 per night per pet additional fee for the cabins. Dogs may not be left unattended, and they must be leashed and cleaned up after. Dogs are not allowed in buildings. The camping and tent areas also allow dogs. There is a dog walk area at the campground. Dogs are allowed in the camping cabins. Multiple dogs may be allowed.

Texas Listings

Abilene

Abilene KOA

4851 W Stamford Street
Abilene, TX
915-672-3681
Dogs of all sizes are allowed. There are no additional pet fees. Dogs must be leashed and cleaned up after. Dogs may be left unattended for short periods, and only if they will be quiet and well behaved. There is a fenced dog run for off lead. There are some breed restrictions. The camping and tent areas also allow dogs. There is a dog walk area at the campground. Dogs are allowed in the camping cabins. Multiple dogs may be allowed.

Alpine

Lost Alaskan RV Park
2401 N H 118
Alpine, TX
800-837-3604
Dogs of all sizes are allowed. There are no additional pet fees. Dogs must be leashed and cleaned up after. There is a fenced "Paw Paw Park" on site for off lead. There is a dog walk area at the campground. There are special amenities given to dogs at this campground. Multiple dogs may be allowed.

Stillwell Trailer Park
HC 65, Box 430 (H 2627)
Alpine, TX
432-376-2244
Dogs of all sizes are allowed at no additional fee. Dogs may not be left unattended, and they must be leased and cleaned up after. The camping and tent areas also allow dogs. There is a dog walk area at the campground. Multiple dogs may be allowed.

Amarillo

Amarillo KOA
1100 Folsom Road
Amarillo, TX
806-335-1762
Dogs of all sizes are allowed, and there are no additional pet fees for tent or RV sites. There is a $5 per night per pet additional fee for the cabins. Dogs must be leashed and cleaned up after. There are some breed restrictions. The camping and tent areas also allow dogs. There is a dog walk area at the campground. Dogs are allowed in the camping cabins. Multiple dogs may be allowed.

Amarillo Ranch
1414 Sunrise
Amarillo, TX
806-373-4962
Dogs of all sizes are allowed. There are no additional pet fees. Dogs may not be left unattended outside, and they may only be left inside if there is climate control. Dogs must be leashed and cleaned up after. There is a dog walk area at the campground. Multiple dogs may be allowed.

Fort Amarillo RV Resort
10101 Amarillo Blvd
Amarillo, TX
806-331-1700
Dogs of all sizes are allowed. There are no additional pet fees. Dogs must be leashed and cleaned up after. There is a dog run for off lead. Dogs are not allowed in the courtyard or at the putting green. There is a dog walk area at the campground. Multiple dogs may be allowed.

Atlanta

Atlanta State Park
927 Park Road 42
Atlanta, TX
903-796-6476
With 1,475 acres and 170 miles of shoreline, this park has plenty of hiking and nature trails, and is home to a variety of plants, birds, and wildlife. Dogs of all sizes are allowed at no additional fee. Dogs may not be left unattended, they must have current rabies and shot records, be on no more than a 6 foot leash, and be cleaned up after. Dogs are not allowed in public swim areas. The camping and tent areas also allow dogs. There is a dog walk area at the campground. Multiple dogs may be allowed.

Austin

Austin Lone Star RV Resort
7009 S IH 35
Austin, TX
512-444-6322
Dogs of all sizes are allowed. There are no additional pet fees. Dogs may not be left unattended outside, and they must be leashed and cleaned up after. There are some breed restrictions. The camping and tent areas also allow dogs. There is a dog walk area at the campground. Multiple dogs may be allowed.

Oak Forest RV Park
8207 Canoga Avenue
Austin, TX
800-478-7275
Dogs of all sizes are allowed. There are no additional pet fees. Dogs may not be left unattended, and they must be leashed and cleaned up after. There is a fenced dog run for off lead. There are some breed restrictions. There is a dog walk area at the campground. Multiple dogs may be allowed.

Bandera

Pioneer Rivers Resort
1203 Maple
Bandera, TX
830-796-3751
Dogs of all sizes are allowed. There are no additional pet fees. Dogs must be leashed and cleaned up after. There are some breed restrictions. The camping and tent areas also allow dogs. There is a dog walk area at the campground. Multiple dogs may be allowed.

Bastrop

Bastrop State Park
130 H 21E
Bastrop, TX
512-321-2101
This recreational park boasts several trails and an 18-hole golf course against it's scenic land and water background. Dogs of all sizes are allowed at no additional fee. Dogs may not be left unattended, they must have current rabies and shot records, be on no more than a 6 foot leash, and be cleaned up after. Dogs are not allowed in public swim areas or buildings. Dogs are allowed on the trails. The camping and tent areas also allow dogs. There is a dog walk area at the campground. Multiple dogs may be allowed.

Baytown

Houston East/Baytown KOA
11810 I-10E
Baytown, TX
281-383-3618
Dogs of all sizes are allowed. There are no additional pet fees. Dogs must be leashed and cleaned up after. The camping and tent areas also allow dogs. There is a dog walk area at the campground. Multiple dogs may be allowed.

Bellmead

Waco North KOA
24132 N I 35
Waco, TX
254-826-3869
Dogs of all sizes are allowed. There are no additional pet fees. Dogs may not be left unattended outside, and they must be leashed and cleaned up after. The camping and tent areas also allow dogs. There is a dog walk area at the campground. Multiple dogs may be allowed.

i 35 RV Park
1513 N I 35
Waco, TX
254-829-0698
Dogs of all sizes are allowed. There are no additional pet fees. Dogs must be leashed and cleaned up after. There are some breed restrictions. There is a dog walk area at the campground. 2 dogs may be allowed.

Belton

Belton/Temple/Killeen KOA
2901 S I 35
Belton, TX
254-939-1961
Dogs of all sizes are allowed. There are no additional pet fees. Dogs may not be left unattended outside, and they must be on no more than a 6 foot leash, and cleaned up after. The camping and tent areas also allow dogs. There is a dog walk area at the campground. Dogs are allowed in the camping cabins. Multiple dogs may be allowed.

Blanco

Blanco State Park
101 Park Road 23
Blanco, TX
830-833-4333
This park offers land and water recreation year round. Dogs of all sizes are allowed at no additional fee. Dogs may not be left unattended, they must have current rabies and shot records, be on no more than a 6 foot leash, and be cleaned up after. Dogs are not allowed in buildings or at the river. Dogs are allowed on the trails. The camping and tent areas also allow dogs. There is a dog walk area at the campground. Multiple dogs may be allowed.

Brookshire

Houston West/Brookshire KOA
35303 Cooper Road
Brookshire, TX
281-375-5678
Dogs of all sizes are allowed. There are no additional pet fees. Dogs may not be left unattended, and they must be leashed and cleaned up after. The camping and tent areas also allow dogs. There is a dog walk area at the campground. Multiple dogs may be allowed.

Brownsville

Breeze Lake RV Campground
1710 N Vermillion
Brownsville, TX
956-831-4427
Dogs of all sizes are allowed. There are no additional pet fees. Dogs may not be left unattended outside, and they must be on no more than a 6 foot leash, and be cleaned up after. There is a dog walk area at the campground. Multiple dogs may be allowed.

Paul's RV Park
1129 N Minnesota Avenue
Brownsville, TX
800-352-5010
Dogs of all sizes are allowed. There are no additional pet fees. Dogs may not be left unattended outside, and they must be leashed and cleaned up after. The owner is known to carry dog biscuits around so he can have treats all his four legged guests. There are some breed restrictions. The camping and tent areas also allow dogs. There is a dog walk area at the campground. Multiple dogs may be allowed.

Rio RV Park
8801 Boca Chica
Brownsville, TX
956-831-4653
This park offers a free shuttle to the Mexican border, where you can walk across for shopping. A dog is allowed on the shuttle to Mexico. Dogs up to 30 pounds are allowed. There are no additional pet fees. Dogs may not be left unattended, or be in any of the buildings, and they must have a current rabies certificate and shot records. Dogs must be quiet, well behaved, leashed and cleaned up after. If a cabin will be needed with a pet, they suggest calling ahead. There are some breed restrictions. The camping and tent

areas also allow dogs. There is a dog walk area at the campground. Dogs are allowed in the camping cabins. 2 dogs may be allowed.

Brownwood

Lake Brownwood State Park
200 State H Park Road 15
Brownwood, TX
325-784-5223
Lake Brownwood State Park offers over 500 acres, a reservoir, 2 1/2 miles of trails, a half mile nature trail and a variety of year round recreation. Dogs of all sizes are allowed at no additional fee. Dogs may not be left unattended, they must have current rabies and shot records, be on no more than a 6 foot leash, and be cleaned up after. Dogs are not allowed in the buildings or shelters. Dogs are allowed on the trails. The camping and tent areas also allow dogs. There is a dog walk area at the campground. Multiple dogs may be allowed.

Bryan

Primrose Lane
2929 Stevens Drive
Bryan, TX
979-778-0119
Dogs of all sizes are allowed. There are no additional pet fees. Dogs must be leashed and cleaned up after. The camping and tent areas also allow dogs. There is a dog walk area at the campground. Multiple dogs may be allowed.

Burnet

Inks Lake State Park
3630 Park Road 4W
Burnet, TX
512-793-2223
Inks Lake, surrounded by granite hills, is one of the lakes located in the Highland Lakes chain of 7 lake. Inks Lake State Park offers a variety of land and water recreation. Dogs of all sizes are allowed at no additional fee. Dogs may not be left unattended, they must have current rabies and shot records, be leashed at all times, and be cleaned up after. Dogs are not allowed in public swim areas or buildings. Dogs are allowed on the trails, and there is a designated dog swim area. The camping and tent areas also allow dogs. There is a dog walk area at the campground. Multiple dogs may be

allowed.

Caddo

Possum Kingdom State Park
3901 Park Road 35
Caddo, TX
940-549-1803
This park of over 1500 acres is adjacent to Possum Kingdom Lake that has over 20,000 acres of water. There are a variety of land and water recreational activities. The park is open for day use during the winter season. Dogs of all sizes are allowed at no additional fee. Dogs may not be left unattended, they must have current rabies and shot records, be on no more than a 6 foot leash, and be cleaned up after. Dogs are not allowed in public swim areas or any buildings. Dogs are allowed on the trails. This campground is closed during the off-season. The camping and tent areas also allow dogs. There is a dog walk area at the campground. Multiple dogs may be allowed.

Calliham

Choke Canyon State Park
Park Road 8
Calliham, TX
361-786-3868
The habitats at this park provide some of the best areas for birds and bird watchers, and there is a wildlife educational center, a mile long bird trail, and 2 miles of hiking trails. Dogs of all sizes are allowed at no additional fee. Dogs may not be left unattended, they must have current rabies and shot records, be leashed, and cleaned up after. Dogs are not allowed in public swim areas or buildings. Dogs are allowed on the trails. The camping and tent areas also allow dogs. There is a dog walk area at the campground. Multiple dogs may be allowed.

Canyon

Palo Duro Canyon State Park
11450 Park Road 5
Canyon, TX
806-488-2227
This scenic, historical, and geologically rich park is known as the Grand Canyon of Texas. It's diverse habitats allow for an abundant variety of flora and fauna, and recreational pursuits. The park

closes the gates at 5 pm in winter and 10 pm in summer, so you must call ahead if you are coming to the campground for the first time and are going to arrive after the gates close. Dogs of all sizes are allowed at no additional fee. Dogs may not be left unattended, they must have current rabies and shot records, be on no more than a 6 foot leash, and be cleaned up after. Dogs are not allowed in buildings, but they may be on the trails. The camping and tent areas also allow dogs. There is a dog walk area at the campground. Multiple dogs may be allowed.

Cedar Hill

Cedar Hill State Park
1570 W FM 1382
Cedar Hill, TX
972-291-3900
Cedar Hill State Park is an urban nature preserve of over 1,800 acres located on a 7500 acre reservoir. It is home to the Penn Farm Agricultural History Center. Well behaved dogs of all sizes are allowed at no additional fee. Dogs may not be left unattended, they must have current rabies and shot records, be on no more than a 6 foot leash, and be cleaned up after. Dogs are not allowed in buildings or in public swim areas, but they are allowed on trails. The camping and tent areas also allow dogs. There is a dog walk area at the campground. Multiple dogs may be allowed.

Comstock

Seminole Canyon State Park & Historic Site
Box 820/ H 90 W
Comstock, TX
432-292-4464
This park is over 2000 acres and provides a historical study of ancient peoples and pictograph sites. There are nature and interpretive attractions, and land and water recreation. No hiking is allowed in the canyon area without a guide. Dogs of all sizes are allowed at no additional fee. Dogs may not be left unattended, they must have current rabies and shot records, be on no more than a 6 foot leash at all times, and be cleaned up after. Dogs are not allowed in buildings or on guided tours. Dogs are allowed on hiking trails. The camping and tent areas also allow dogs. There is a dog walk area at the campground. Multiple

dogs may be allowed.

Concan

Garner State Park
234 RR 1050
Concan, TX
830-232-6132
High mesas, deep canyons, an abundance of plant and animal life, and a variety of recreation greet visitors to this park. Dogs of all sizes are allowed at no additional fee. Dogs may not be left unattended, they must have current rabies and shot records, be on no more than a 6 foot leash, and be cleaned up after. Dogs are not allowed in public swim areas or buildings. Dogs are allowed on the trails. The camping and tent areas also allow dogs. There is a dog walk area at the campground. Multiple dogs may be allowed.

Cooper

Cooper Lake State Park/South Suphur Unit
1664 Farm Road 1529
Cooper, TX
903-395-3100
The South Sulphur Unit of Cooper Lake is over 2,000 acres of land and water recreation, with sandy beaches, an outdoor amphitheater, and miles of trails. Due to budget cuts this park is only open for day use and/or camping on Friday, Saturday, and Sunday. Dogs of all sizes are allowed at no additional fee. Dogs may not be left unattended, they must have current rabies and shot records, be on no more than a 6 foot leash, and be cleaned up after. Dogs are not allowed in public swim areas or buildings. Dogs are allowed on the trails. The camping and tent areas also allow dogs. There is a dog walk area at the campground. Multiple dogs may be allowed.

Corpus Christi

Hatch RV Park
3101 Up River Road
Corpus Christi, TX
361-883-9781
Dogs up to 40 pounds are allowed, and they can be no taller than 20 inches from the shoulder to the ground. There are no additional pet fees. Dogs must be leashed and cleaned up after. There is a dog walk area at the campground. 2 dogs may

be allowed.

Sea Breeze RV Park
1026 Sea Breeze Lane
Portland, TX
361-643-0744
Dogs of all sizes are allowed. There are no additional pet fees. Dogs may not be left unattended outside, nor inside unless weather permits. Dogs must be leashed and cleaned up after. There are some breed restrictions. There is a dog walk area at the campground. 2 dogs may be allowed.

Pioneer Beach Resort
120 Gulfwinds Drive
Port Aransas, TX
888-480-3246
Dogs of all sizes are allowed. There are no additional pet fees. Dogs must be leashed and cleaned up after. There are some breed restrictions. There is a dog walk area at the campground. 2 dogs may be allowed.

Daingerfield

Daingerfield State Park
455 Park Road 17
Daingerfield, TX
903-645-2921
With over 550 land acres and an 80 acre lake, there are plenty of recreational pursuits at this park. Dogs of all sizes are allowed at no additional fee. Dogs may not be left unattended, they must have current rabies and shot records, be on no more than a 6 foot leash, and be cleaned up after. Dogs are not allowed in public swim areas or buildings. Dogs are allowed on the trails. The camping and tent areas also allow dogs. There is a dog walk area at the campground. Multiple dogs may be allowed.

Dallas - Fort Worth Area

Treetops RV Village
1901 W Arbrook
Arlington, TX
817-467-7943
Dogs of all sizes are allowed, but there can only be 2 large dogs or 3 if they are very small. There are no additional pet fees. Dogs may not be left unattended outside, and may not be left inside RV unless the conditions are safe and comfortable. Dogs must be leashed

and cleaned up after. There are some breed restrictions. There is a dog walk area at the campground.

RV Ranch
2301 S I 35W
Burleson, TX
888-855-9091
Dogs of all sizes are allowed. There are no additional pet fees. Dogs may not be left unattended outside, and they must be quiet, leashed, and cleaned up after. There are some breed restrictions. There is a dog walk area at the campground. Multiple dogs may be allowed.

Sandy Lake RV Park
1915 Sandy Lake Road
Carrollton, TX
972-242-6808
Dogs up to 40 pounds are allowed. There are no additional pet fees. Dogs may not be left unattended outside or put in outside pens, and they must be quiet, leashed, and cleaned up after. There is a dog walk area at the campground. 2 dogs may be allowed.

Decatur

Caddo-LBJ National Grasslands
1400 H 81/287
Decatur, TX
940-627-5475
With Caddo at almost 18,000 acres with 3 lakes, and the LBJ Grasslands at over 20,000 acres, this forest provides a wide variety of habitats, trails, nature study, and land and water recreation. Dogs of all sizes are allowed at no additional fee. Dogs may not be left unattended, and they must be on no more than a 6 foot leash, unless being used for hunting during a designated hunting season where the uses of dogs are legal. Dogs are allowed everywhere unless otherwise posted. The camping and tent areas also allow dogs. There is a dog walk area at the campground. There are no electric or water hookups at the campground. Multiple dogs may be allowed.

Denison

Eisenhower State Park
50 Park Road 20
Denison, TX
903-465-1956
A variety of nature sites, land and water recreation, interpretive programs, and trails greet visitor's here. Dogs of all sizes are allowed at

no additional fee. Dogs may not be left unattended, they must have current rabies and shot records, be on no more than a 6 foot leash, and be cleaned up after. Dogs are not allowed in public swim areas or buildings. Dogs are allowed on the trails. The camping and tent areas also allow dogs. There is a dog walk area at the campground. Multiple dogs may be allowed.

Dickinson

Green Caye RV Park
2401 Owens Drive
Dickinson, TX
280-337-0289
Dogs of all sizes are allowed. There are no additional pet fees. Dogs must be leashed and cleaned up after. There is a dog walk area at the campground. Multiple dogs may be allowed.

El Paso

El Paso Roadrunner RV Park
1212 LaFayette
El Paso, TX
915-598-4469
Dogs of all sizes are allowed. There are no additional pet fees. Dogs must be quiet, leashed, and cleaned up after. There is a dog walk area at the campground. Multiple dogs may be allowed.

Sampson RV Park
11300 Gateway Blvd
El Paso, TX
915-859-8383
Dogs of all sizes are allowed. There are no additional pet fees. Dogs may not be left unattended outside, and they must be leashed and cleaned up after. There is a dog walk area at the campground. Multiple dogs may be allowed.

Fentress

Leisure Camp & RV Park
1 River Lane
Fentress, TX
512-488-2563
Dogs of all sizes are allowed. There are no additional pet fees. Dogs must be leashed and cleaned up after. There is a fenced pet park area. Dogs are not allowed in public swim areas. The camping and tent areas also allow dogs. There is a dog walk area at the campground. Multiple dogs may be allowed.

Fort Davis

Fort Davis Motor Inn & Campground
I Mile N of Fort Davis on H 17N
Fort Davis, TX
800-803-2847
Dogs of all sizes are allowed. There are no additional pet fees. Dogs may not be left unattended, and they must be leashed and cleaned up after. There is also an inn on site that allows dogs for a $10 per night per pet additional fee in a smoking room only. There is a dog walk area at the campground. 2 dogs may be allowed.

Fredericksburg

Fredericksburg
5681 H 290E
Fredericksburg, TX
830-997-4796
Dogs of all sizes are allowed, but there can only be 2 dogs per site unless they are under 10 pounds, then there can be up to 3. There are no additional pet fees. Dogs must be leashed, cleaned up after, and inside at night. There are some breed restrictions. The camping and tent areas also allow dogs. There is a dog walk area at the campground.

Oakwood RV Resort
#78 FM 2093
Fredericksburg, TX
830-997-9817
Dogs of all sizes are allowed. There are no additional pet fees. Dogs may not be left unattended, and they must be quiet, leashed, and cleaned up after. The camping and tent areas also allow dogs. There is a dog walk area at the campground.

Galveston

Dellanera RV Park
10901 San Louis Pass Road
Galveston, TX
409-797-5102
Dogs of all sizes are allowed. There are no additional pet fees. Dogs may not be left unattended outside, they must be in at night, and leashed and cleaned up after. There is a dog walk area at the campground. Multiple dogs may be allowed.

Galveston Island State Park
14901 FM 3005
Galveston, TX

409-737-1222
This recreational island park offers a variety of land and water activities. Dogs of all sizes are allowed at no additional fee. Dogs may not be left unattended, they must have current rabies and shot records, be on no more than a 6 foot leash at all times, and be cleaned up after. Dogs are not allowed in public swim areas or buildings. Dogs are allowed on the trails. The camping and tent areas also allow dogs. There is a dog walk area at the campground. Multiple dogs may be allowed.

Marina Bay RV Resort
925 FM 2094
Kemeh, TX
281-334-9944
Dogs of all sizes are allowed. There are no additional pet fees. Dogs must be leashed, cleaned up after, and walked in designated areas. There is a dog walk area at the campground. 2 dogs may be allowed.

Space Center RV Resort
301 Gulf Freeway S
League City, TX
888-846-3478
Dogs of all sizes are allowed. There are no additional pet fees. Dogs may not be left unattended outside, and they must be leashed and cleaned up after. There is a dog walk area at the campground. 2 dogs may be allowed.

Goodlett

Ole Towne Cotton Gin RV Park
230 Market Street
Goodlett, TX
940-674-2477
Dogs of all sizes are allowed, and there are no additional pet fees for tent or RV sites. There is a $35 one time pet fee for the cabins. Dogs may not be left unattended, and they must be leashed and cleaned up after. The camping and tent areas also allow dogs. There is a dog walk area at the campground. Dogs are allowed in the camping cabins. Multiple dogs may be allowed.

Grand Prairie

Trader's Village
2602 Mayfield Road
Grand Prairie, TX
972-647-8205
Dogs of all sizes are allowed. There

are no additional pet fees. Dogs may not be left unattended outside, and they must be leashed and cleaned up after. The camping and tent areas also allow dogs. There is a dog walk area at the campground. 2 dogs may be allowed.

Trader's Village RV Park
2602 Mayfield Road
Grand Prairie, TX
972-647-8205
Dogs up to 40 pounds are allowed at no additional fee. Dogs must be leashed, cleaned up after, and walked in designated areas. The camping and tent areas also allow dogs. There is a dog walk area at the campground. 2 dogs may be allowed.

Hemphill

Sabine National Forest
201 S Palm
Hemphill, TX
409-787-2791
This ecologically diverse forest provides archeological, historic, and prehistoric sites to explore in addition to offering a variety of trails, and land and water recreation. Dogs of all sizes are allowed at no additional fee. Dogs may not be left unattended; they must be cleaned up after in camp areas, and be on no more than a 6 foot leash unless being used for hunting during a designated hunting season where the uses of dogs are legal. Dogs are allowed everywhere in the park unless posted. The camping and tent areas also allow dogs. There is a dog walk area at the campground. There are no water hookups at the campground. Multiple dogs may be allowed.

Houston

All Star RV Resort
10650 SW Plaza Court
Houston, TX
713-981-6814
Dogs of all sizes are allowed. There are no additional pet fees. Dogs must be leashed and cleaned up after. There is a dog walk area at the campground. Multiple dogs may be allowed.

Houston Central KOA
1620 Peachleaf
Houston, TX
281-442-3700
Dogs of all sizes are allowed. There

are no additional pet fees. Dogs may not be left unattended outside, and they must be leashed and cleaned up after. There is only 1 pet friendly cabin. There are some breed restrictions. The camping and tent areas also allow dogs. There is a dog walk area at the campground. Dogs are allowed in the camping cabins. Multiple dogs may be allowed.

Houston Leisure RV Resort
1601 S Main Street
Houston, TX
281-426-3576
Dogs of all sizes are allowed. There are no additional pet fees. Dogs may not be left unattended outside, and they must be leashed and cleaned up after. The camping and tent areas also allow dogs. There is a dog walk area at the campground. Multiple dogs may be allowed.

Trader's Village
7979 N Eldridge Road
Houston, TX
281-890-5500
Dogs of all sizes are allowed. There are no additional pet fees. Dogs may not be left unattended, and they must be leashed and cleaned up after. There is a dog walk area at the campground. Multiple dogs may be allowed.

Huntsville

Huntsville State Park
Park Road 40
Huntsville, TX
936-295-5644
This park of over 2000 acres, with a 210 acre lake, offers a variety of naturescapes and land and water recreation. Dogs of all sizes are allowed at no additional fee. Dogs may not be left unattended, they must have current rabies and shot records, be on no more than a 6 foot leash, and be cleaned up after. Dogs are not allowed in buildings, in public swim or sandy beach areas. Dogs are not allowed in the water anywhere. Dogs are allowed on the trails. The camping and tent areas also allow dogs. There is a dog walk area at the campground. Multiple dogs may be allowed.

Johnson City

Pedernales Falls State Park
2585 Park Road 6026

Johnson City, TX
830-868-7304
Pedernales Falls draws visitors from all over to it's scenic overlook. The park also offers more than 150 species of birds, abundant plant and animal life and a variety of recreation. They close only for a couple of weeks each January. Dogs of all sizes are allowed at no additional fee. Dogs may not be left unattended, they must have current rabies and shot records, be on no more than a 6 foot leash, and be cleaned up after. Dogs are not allowed in public swim areas or buildings. Dogs are not allowed in the river anywhere. Dogs are allowed on the trails. The camping and tent areas also allow dogs. There is a dog walk area at the campground. Multiple dogs may be allowed.

Junction

Junction KOA
2145 Main Street
Junction, TX
325-446-3138
Dogs of all sizes are allowed. There are no additional pet fees. Dogs may not be left unattended, and they must be on no more than a 6 foot leash, and be cleaned up after. Dogs are not allowed on the playground, at the pool, or at the bathrooms. There are some breed restrictions. The camping and tent areas also allow dogs. There is a dog walk area at the campground. Multiple dogs may be allowed.

Karnack

Caddo Lake State Park
245 Park Road 2
Karnack, TX
903-679-3351
This lush park offers a nature study of the bayous and offers a variety of land and water pursuits. Dogs of all sizes are allowed at no additional fee. Dogs may not be left unattended, they must have current rabies and shot records, be on no more than a 6 foot leash, and be cleaned up after. Dogs are not allowed in buildings or anywhere in the water. Dogs are allowed on the trails. The camping and tent areas also allow dogs. There is a dog walk area at the campground. Multiple dogs may be allowed.

Kennard

Davy Crockett National Forest
Rt 1, Box 55 FS
Kennard, TX
936-655-2299
This forest has more than 160,000 acres of streams, recreation areas, woodlands, and a variety of trails and wildlife habitats. Dogs of all sizes are allowed at no additional fee. Dogs may not be left unattended, and they must be on no more than a 6 foot leash unless being used for hunting during a designated hunting season where the uses of dogs are legal. Dogs are allowed everywhere unless otherwise posted. The camping and tent areas also allow dogs. There is a dog walk area at the campground. There are no electric or water hookups at the campground. Multiple dogs may be allowed.

Kerrville

Kerrville KOA
2950 Goat Creek Road
Kerrville, TX
830-895-1665
Dogs of all sizes are allowed. There are no additional pet fees. Dogs may not be left unattended outside, and they must be leashed and cleaned up after. The camping and tent areas also allow dogs. There is a dog walk area at the campground. Dogs are allowed in the camping cabins. Multiple dogs may be allowed.

La Feria

Kenwood RV Resort
1201 N Main #1
La Feria, TX
856-797-1851
Dogs of all sizes are allowed, but there can only be 1 large dog or 2 small dogs per site. There are no additional pet fees. Dogs may not be left unattended outside, and no outdoor kennels are allowed. Dogs must be leashed and cleaned up after. This is a 55 years or older park. There is a dog walk area at the campground.

Lubbock

Lubbock KOA
5502 County Road 6300
Lubbock, TX
806-762-8653
Dogs of all sizes are allowed. There are no additional pet fees. Dogs may not be left unattended outside, and

they must be leashed and cleaned up after. The camping and tent areas also allow dogs. There is a dog walk area at the campground. Dogs are allowed in the camping cabins. Multiple dogs may be allowed.

Lubbock RV Park
4811 N I 27
Lubbock, TX
806-747-2366
Dogs of all sizes are allowed. There are no additional pet fees. Dogs must be leashed and cleaned up after. There is a dog walk area at the campground. Multiple dogs may be allowed.

Lufkin

Angelina National Forest
111 Walnut Ridge Road
Zavalla, TX
936-897-1068
With more than 150,000 acres and a 114,550 acre lake, this forests diverse ecosystems support a large variety of plants, fish, mammals, bird species, and recreation. Dogs of all sizes are allowed at no additional fee. Dogs may not be left unattended, and they must be on no more than a 6 foot leash, unless being used for hunting during a designated hunting season where the uses of dogs are legal. Dogs are allowed everywhere in the forest unless otherwise posted. The camping and tent areas also allow dogs. There is a dog walk area at the campground. There are no electric or water hookups at the campground. Multiple dogs may be allowed.

Mathis

Lake Corpus Christi State Park
Park Road 25
Mathis, TX
361-547-2635
This park of over 14,000 acres, with a 21,000 acre lake, gives way to a variety of naturescapes and land and water recreation. Dogs of all sizes are allowed at no additional fee. Dogs may not be left unattended, they must have current rabies and shot records, be on no more than a 6 foot leash, and be cleaned up after. Dogs are not allowed in public swim areas or buildings. Dogs are allowed on the trails, and in the water if they are still on lead. The camping and tent

areas also allow dogs. There is a dog walk area at the campground. Multiple dogs may be allowed.

Lake Corpus Christi/Mathis KOA
101 C ounty Road 371
Mathis, TX
361-547-5201
Dogs of all sizes are allowed. There are no additional pet fees. Dogs must be well behaved, leashed, and cleaned up after. The camping and tent areas also allow dogs. There is a dog walk area at the campground. Dogs are allowed in the camping cabins.

Meridian

Meridian State Park
173 Park Road 7
Meridian, TX
254-435-2536
A hiking trail circles this park's 72-acre lake, creating a haven for fishing enthusiasts and nature lovers alike. Dogs of all sizes are allowed at no additional fee. Dogs may not be left unattended, they must have current rabies and shot records, be on no more than a 6 foot leash, and be cleaned up after. Dogs are not allowed in public swim areas or buildings. Dogs are allowed on the trails. The camping and tent areas also allow dogs. There is a dog walk area at the campground. Multiple dogs may be allowed.

Mexia

Fort Parker State Park
194 Park Road 28
Mexia, TX
254-562-5751
This park of over 1,400 acres, with a 700 acre lake, offers a variety of naturescapes and land and water recreation. Dogs of all sizes are allowed at no additional fee. Dogs may not be left unattended, they must have current rabies and shot records, be on no more than a 6 foot leash, and be cleaned up after. Dogs are not allowed in public swim areas or buildings. Dogs are allowed on the trails. The camping and tent areas also allow dogs. There is a dog walk area at the campground. Multiple dogs may be allowed.

Millsap

Hillbilly Haven Campground
10885 I-20W

Millsap, TX
817-341-4009
Dogs of all sizes are allowed. There are no additional pet fees. Dogs may not be left unattended, and they must be quiet, leashed, and cleaned up after. The camping and tent areas also allow dogs. There is a dog walk area at the campground. Multiple dogs may be allowed.

Mineral Wells

Lake Mineral Wells State Park and Trailway
100 Park Road 71
Mineral Wells, TX
940-328-1171
This park of over 2000 acres, with a 210 acre lake, offers a variety of naturescapes, land and water recreation, and has a 20 mile trailway that connects to other trails. Dogs of all sizes are allowed at no additional fee. Dogs may not be left unattended, they must have current rabies and shot records, be on no more than a 6 foot leash, and be cleaned up after. Dogs are not allowed on the beaches or in buildings. Dogs are allowed on the trails. The camping and tent areas also allow dogs. There is a dog walk area at the campground. Multiple dogs may be allowed.

Mission

Bentsen Palm Village RV Park
2500 S Benson Pond Drive
Mission, TX
956-585-5568
Dogs of all sizes are allowed. There are no additional pet fees. Dogs may not be left unattended outside, and they must be quiet, leashed, and cleaned up after. Pets must be walked in assigned areas. This is a 50 years old or older resort. There is a dog walk area at the campground. Multiple dogs may be allowed.

Bentson-Rio Grande Valley State Park
2800 Bentson Palm Drive
Mission, TX
956-585-1107
This parks is known for the variety of birds that live here. Vehicles are not allowed inside this park, and they do have a tram to transport visitors inside or they can walk in. Dogs are allowed at no additional fee, but they are not allowed on the trams. Dogs may not be left unattended, they must have current rabies and shot

records, be on no more than a 6 foot leash, and be cleaned up after. Dogs are not allowed in buildings. Dogs are allowed on the trails. The camping and tent areas also allow dogs. There is a dog walk area at the campground. There are no electric or water hookups at the campground. Multiple dogs may be allowed.

Monahans

Monahans Sandhills State Park
Park Road 41
Monahans, TX
432-943-2092
There are over 3,800 acres of sand dunes to explore at this park, as well as an interpretive program, hands on exhibits, and a working oil well. Due to budget cuts, the park may only be open from Thursday through Sundays. Dogs of all sizes are allowed at no additional fee. Dogs may not be left unattended, they must have current rabies and shot records, be on no more than a 6 foot leash, and be cleaned up after. Dogs are allowed on the trails. The camping and tent areas also allow dogs. There is a dog walk area at the campground. Multiple dogs may be allowed.

Mount Pleasant

Mt Pleasant KOA
2322 Greenhill Road
Mount Pleasant, TX
903-572-5005
Dogs of all sizes are allowed. There are no additional pet fees. Dogs must be leashed and cleaned up after. Dogs may not be left unattended, but they may be outside alone in the RV. There are some breed restrictions. The camping and tent areas also allow dogs. There is a dog walk area at the campground. Dogs are allowed in the camping cabins. Multiple dogs may be allowed.

Needville

Brazos Bend State Park
21901 FM 762/Crab River Road
Needville, TX
979-553-5101
This lush park is home to the George Observatory, more than 270 species of birds, and a variety of land and water recreation. Dogs of

all sizes are allowed at no additional fee. Dogs may not be left unattended, they must have current rabies and shot records, be on no more than a 6 foot leash, and be cleaned up after. Dogs are not allowed in public swim areas or buildings. Dogs are not allowed to drink out of or be by the water anywhere. Dogs are allowed on the trails. The camping and tent areas also allow dogs. There is a dog walk area at the campground. Multiple dogs may be allowed.

New Waverly

Sam Houston National Forest
394 FM 1375 W
New Waverly, TX
936-344-6205
This forest of more than 160,000 acres has a variety of recreation areas, woodlands, wildlife habitats, and the 128-mile Lone Star Hiking Trail also winds through it. Dogs are allowed at no additional fee. Dogs may not be left unattended; they must be cleaned up after in camp, and be on no more than a 6 foot leash unless being used for hunting during a designated hunting season where the uses of dogs are legal. Dogs are allowed everywhere unless otherwise posted. The camping and tent areas also allow dogs. There is a dog walk area at the campground. There are no water hookups at the campground. Multiple dogs may be allowed.

Newton

Artesian Springs Resort
Rt 1 Box 670-12 H 26/26
Newton, TX
409-379-8826
Dogs of all sizes are allowed, and there are no additional pet fees for tent or RV sites. There is a $25 pet fee for the cabins, $15 of which, is refundable, and only 2 dogs up to 25 pounds each is allowed. Dogs may not be left unattended, and they must be leashed and cleaned up after. There are some breed restrictions. This RV park is closed during the off-season. The camping and tent areas also allow dogs. There is a dog walk area at the campground. Dogs are allowed in the camping cabins.

Odessa

Midessa Oil Patch RV Park

4220 S County Road 1290
Odessa, TX
432-563-2368
Dogs of all sizes are allowed. There are no additional pet fees. Dogs may not be left unattended outside, and they must be leashed and cleaned up after. There is a fenced pet run for off lead. The camping and tent areas also allow dogs. There is a dog walk area at the campground. Multiple dogs may be allowed.

Palacios

Serendipity Bay Resort
1001 Main Street
Palacios, TX
361-972-5454
Dogs of all sizes are allowed. There are no additional pet fees. Dogs may not be left unattended, and they must be leashed and cleaned up after. There are 2 fishing piers in the park. There are some breed restrictions. There is a dog walk area at the campground. Multiple dogs may be allowed.

Port Aransas

Island RV Resort
Avenue G & 6th Street
Port Aransas, TX
361-749-5600
Dogs of all sizes are allowed. There are no additional pet fees. Dogs may not be left outside unattended, and they must be leashed and cleaned up after at all times. There is a walking path of a couple of miles across the street from the RV park, and dogs are also allowed to walk along the beach. There are some breed restrictions. The camping and tent areas also allow dogs. There is a dog walk area at the campground. 2 dogs may be allowed.

Mustang Island State Park
17047 H 364
Port Aransas, TX
361-749-5246
This park offers a variety of recreational pursuits within its almost 4000 acres and 5 miles of beaches. Dogs of all sizes are allowed at no additional fee. Dogs may not be left unattended, they must have current rabies and shot records, be on no more than a 6 foot leash, and be cleaned up after. Dogs are not allowed in public swim areas or buildings. Dogs are allowed on the trails. The camping and tent areas also allow dogs. There is a dog walk

area at the campground. Multiple dogs may be allowed.

Presidio

Big Bend Ranch State Park
The River Road (H 170)
Presidio, TX
432-424-3327
Almost 300,000 acres of Chihuahuan Desert wilderness with a vast variety of plant and animal life await visitors here. This park is mostly for primitive camping. Dogs are allowed at no additional fee. Dogs may not be left unattended, and they must be leased and cleaned up after. Dogs are not allowed in public swim areas or in buildings. Dogs are allowed on the trails, but they are not allowed on the guided river trips. The camping and tent areas also allow dogs. There is a dog walk area at the campground. There are no electric or water hookups at the campground. Multiple dogs may be allowed.

Quanah

Copper Breaks State Park
777 Park Road 62
Quanah, TX
940-839-4331
This year round park offers 2 lakes, 10 miles of trails, summer educational and interpretive programs, a wide variety of plant and wildlife, and a natural history museum (open Friday through Sunday). Dogs of all sizes are allowed at no additional fee. Dogs may not be left unattended, they must have current rabies and shot records, be on no more than a 6 foot leash, and be cleaned up after. Well behaved dogs are allowed in the museum when they are not real busy. Dogs are allowed on the trails. They will allow only fully self-contained RVs to stay in off season. This campground is closed during the off-season. The camping and tent areas also allow dogs. There is a dog walk area at the campground. Multiple dogs may be allowed.

Quitaque

Caprock Canyons State Park
P.O. Box 204 (on FM 1065)
Quitaque, TX
806-455-1492
There are over 15,000 acres and

almost 90 miles of multi-use trails at this scenic park, creating a variety of habitats, ecosystems and land and water recreation. Dogs of all sizes are allowed at no additional fee. Dogs may not be left unattended, and they must have current rabies and shot records. Dogs must be on no more than a 6 foot leash, and be cleaned up after. Dogs are allowed on the trails. This campground is closed during the off-season. The camping and tent areas also allow dogs. There is a dog walk area at the campground. There are no water hookups at the campground. Multiple dogs may be allowed.

San Angelo

San Angelo KOA
6699 Knickerbocker Road
San Angelo, TX
325-949-3242
Dogs of all sizes are allowed. There are no additional pet fees. Dogs may not be left unattended outside, and they must be leashed and cleaned up after. Dogs may not be at the pool or in the buildings. There is a fenced pen area where dogs may be left for short periods. There are some breed restrictions. The camping and tent areas also allow dogs. There is a dog walk area at the campground. Dogs are allowed in the camping cabins. Multiple dogs may be allowed.

San Angelo State Park
3900-2 Mercedes
San Angelo, TX
325-949-4757
Activities are year round at this park that covers four ecological zones, and it offers a variety of tours, trails, plants, animals, birds, and recreation. Dogs of all sizes are allowed at no additional fee. Dogs may not be left unattended, they must have current rabies and shot records, be on no more than a 6 foot leash, and be cleaned up after. Dogs are not allowed in public swim areas or buildings. Dogs are allowed on the trails. The camping and tent areas also allow dogs. There is a dog walk area at the campground. Multiple dogs may be allowed.

San Antonio

Admiralty RV Resort
1485 N Ellison Drive
San Antonio, TX

800-999-7872
Dogs of all sizes are allowed. There are no additional pet fees. Dogs must be leashed and cleaned up after. There is a dog walk area at the campground. Multiple dogs may be allowed.

Blazing Star RV Resort
1120 W H 1604N
San Antonio, TX
210-680-7827
Dogs of all sizes are allowed. There are no additional pet fees. Dogs may not be left unattended outside, and they may be left inside only if they are quiet and comfortable. Dogs must be leashed and cleaned up after. There are some breed restrictions. The camping and tent areas also allow dogs. There is a dog walk area at the campground. 2 dogs may be allowed.

San Antonio KOA
602 Gembler Road
San Antonio, TX
210-224-9296
Dogs of all sizes are allowed. There are no additional pet fees. Dogs may not be left unattended outside, and they must be quiet, leashed, and cleaned up after. There are some breed restrictions. The camping and tent areas also allow dogs. There is a dog walk area at the campground. Dogs are allowed in the camping cabins. 2 dogs may be allowed.

Traveler's World RV Resort
2617 Roosevelt Avenue
San Antonio, TX
210-532-8310
Dogs of all sizes are allowed. There are no additional pet fees. Dogs may not be left unattended outside, and they must be leashed and cleaned up after. There is a dog walk area at the campground. Multiple dogs may be allowed.

San Marcos

Canyon Trail RV Resort
6050 IH 35S
San Marcos, TX
888-616-3540
One dog up to 10 pounds is allowed. There are no additional pet fees. Dogs must be leashed and cleaned up after. There are some breed restrictions. There is a dog walk area at the campground.

Schertz

Stone Creek RV Park
18905 IH 35N
Schertz, TX
830-609-7759
Dogs of all sizes are allowed. There are no additional pet fees. Dogs may not be left unattended outside, and they must be leashed and cleaned up after. There are some breed restrictions. The camping and tent areas also allow dogs. There is a dog walk area at the campground. Multiple dogs may be allowed.

Shannon

Natchez Trace RV Park
189 County Road 506
Shannon, TX
662-767-8609
Dogs of all sizes are allowed. There are no additional pet fees. Dogs must be quiet, well behaved, leashed, and cleaned up after. There is a dog walk area at the campground. Multiple dogs may be allowed.

Smithville

Buescher State Park
100 Park Road 1E
Smithville, TX
512-237-2241
There are over a 1,000 acres with a small lake at this park that provides a variety of recreational and nature pursuits. Well behaved dogs of all sizes are allowed at no additional fee. Dogs may not be left unattended, they must have current rabies and shot records, be on no more than a 6 foot leash, and be cleaned up after. Dogs are not allowed in public swim areas or buildings. Dogs are allowed on the trail. The camping and tent areas also allow dogs. There is a dog walk area at the campground. Multiple dogs may be allowed.

Snyder

Wagon Wheel Guest Ranch
5996 County Road 2128
Snyder, TX
325-573-2348
This guest ranch offers a country music venue and a variety of recreational pursuits. Dogs of all sizes are allowed at no additional fee. Dogs may not be left unattended, they must have current rabies and shot records, be on no

more than a 6 foot leash, and be cleaned up after. Dogs are not allowed in buildings. Dogs are allowed on the trails. The camping and tent areas also allow dogs. There is a dog walk area at the campground. Multiple dogs may be allowed.

Somerville

Lake Somerville State Park and Trailway (AKA-Birch Creek SP)
14222 Park Road 57
Somerville, TX
979-535-7763
A multitude of land and water recreational opportunities await visitors at this park. Dogs of all sizes are allowed at no additional fee. Dogs may not be left unattended, they must have current rabies and shot records, be on no more than a 6 foot leash, and be cleaned up after. Dogs are not allowed in public swim areas or buildings. Dogs are allowed on the trails. The camping and tent areas also allow dogs. There is a dog walk area at the campground. Multiple dogs may be allowed.

Spring Branch

Guadalupe River State Park
3350 Park Road 31
Spring Branch, TX
830-438-2656
This park of almost 2000 acres with 5 miles of riverfront offers a variety of naturescapes, land and water recreation, and a guided interpretive tour. Dogs of all sizes are allowed at no additional fee. Dogs may not be left unattended, they must have current rabies and shot records, be on no more than a 6 foot leash at all times, and be cleaned up after. Dogs are not allowed in public swim areas or buildings. Dogs are allowed on the trails but not on the guided tours. The camping and tent areas also allow dogs. There is a dog walk area at the campground. Multiple dogs may be allowed.

Study Butte

Study Butte RV Park
On H 118
Study Butte, TX
432-371-2468
Well behaved dogs of all sizes are allowed at no additional fee. Dogs may not be left unattended, and they must be leashed and cleaned up

after. The camping and tent areas also allow dogs. There is a dog walk area at the campground. Multiple dogs may be allowed.

Terlingua Oasis RV Park
At H 118 & H 170
Study Butte, TX
432-371-2218
Dogs of all sizes are allowed at no additional fee for tent or RV sites. Dogs may not be left unattended, and they must be leashed and cleaned up after. There is a motel on site that also allows dogs in smoking rooms only at $5 per night per pet. Dogs are allowed on the trails inside the campground. The camping and tent areas also allow dogs. There is a dog walk area at the campground. Multiple dogs may be allowed.

Terlingua

Big Bend Motor Inn & RV Campground
100 Main Street
Terlingua, TX
800-848-2363
Dogs of all sizes are allowed, but there can only be one large dog or two small dogs per site. There are no additional pet fees. Dogs may not be left unattended, and they must be leashed and cleaned up after. There is a motel on site that also allows dogs at $5 per night per pet additional fee in a smoking room only. There is a dog walk area at the campground.

Big Bend RV Park
Terlingua Creek Bridge
Terlingua, TX
432-371-2250
Dogs are allowed at no additional fee. Dogs may not be left unattended, and they must be leashed and cleaned up after. Dogs are not allowed in public swim areas or in buildings. Dogs are allowed on the trails. This park also has a restaurant where your pet may join you on the patio. The camping and tent areas also allow dogs. There is a dog walk area at the campground. Multiple dogs may be allowed.

Texarkana

Texarkana KOA
500 W 53rd Street
Texarkana, TX
903-792-5521
Dogs of all sizes are allowed, and there are no additional pet fees for

tent or RV sites. There is a $10 one time additional pet fee for the cabins. Dogs must be leashed and cleaned up after. The camping and tent areas also allow dogs. There is a dog walk area at the campground. Dogs are allowed in the camping cabins. Multiple dogs may be allowed.

Toledo

Cowtown RV Park
7000 I-20
Toledo, TX
817-441-7878
Dogs of all sizes are allowed. There are no additional pet fees. Dogs may not be left unattended outside, and they must be leashed and cleaned up after. They also have 2 fenced in dog run areas. There are some breed restrictions. The camping and tent areas also allow dogs. There is a dog walk area at the campground. Multiple dogs may be allowed.

Valley View

Ray Roberts Lake State Park
100 PW 4153/Johnson Branck
Valley View, TX
940-637-2294
This state park consists of 2 units: The second unit is Isle du Bois, located at 100 PW 4137, Pilot Point, TX, 76258,(940-686-2148). There is a variety of land and water recreation offered in both areas, and they also have an interpretive and educational program. Dogs of all sizes are allowed at no additional fee. Dogs may not be left unattended, they must have current rabies and shot records, be on no more than a 6 foot leash, and be cleaned up after. Dogs are not allowed on the beaches or in buildings. Dogs are allowed on the trails. The camping and tent areas also allow dogs. There is a dog walk area at the campground. Multiple dogs may be allowed.

Van Horn

Van Horn KOA
10 Kamper's Lane
Van Horn, TX
432-283-2728
Dogs of all sizes are allowed. There are no additional pet fees. Dogs may not be left unattended outside, and they must be leashed and

cleaned up after. The camping and tent areas also allow dogs. There is a dog walk area at the campground. Dogs are allowed in the camping cabins. Multiple dogs may be allowed.

Vanderpool

Lost Maples State Natural Area
37221 H 187
Vanderpool, TX
830-966-3413
With over 2,000 acres on the Sabinal River, this park offers a variety of nature and archaeological study, in addition to land and water recreation. Dogs of all sizes are allowed at no additional fee. Dogs may not be left unattended, and they must be on no more than a 6 foot leash, and be cleaned up after. Dogs are not allowed in public swim areas or buildings. Dogs are allowed on the trails. The campgrounds are closed for a couple of weeks each year in January for hunting. The camping and tent areas also allow dogs. There is a dog walk area at the campground. Multiple dogs may be allowed.

Waller

Jellystone Park
34843 Betka Road
Waller, TX
979-826-4111
Dogs of all sizes are allowed. There are no additional pet fees. Dogs must be quiet, well behaved, may not be left unattended, and must be leashed and cleaned up after. Dogs must be quiet and may not be tied up outside alone. The camping and tent areas also allow dogs. There is a dog walk area at the campground. 2 dogs may be allowed.

Whitney

Lake Whitney State Park
Box 1175; (on FM-1244)
Whitney, TX
254-694-3793
This park of more than 1200 acres runs along the east shore of Lake Whitney and offers a variety of nature study and land and water recreation. Dogs of all sizes are allowed at no additional fee. Dogs may not be left unattended, and they must be on no more than a 6 foot leash, and be cleaned up after. Dogs are not allowed in the swim or day

use areas, but they are allowed on the trails. The camping and tent areas also allow dogs. There is a dog walk area at the campground. Multiple dogs may be allowed.

Wichita Falls

Wichita Falls RV Park
2944 Seymour H
Wichita Falls, TX
940-723-1532
Dogs of all sizes are allowed. There are no additional pet fees. Dogs may not be left unattended outside, and they must be leashed and cleaned up after. There is a dog walk area at the campground. Multiple dogs may be allowed.

Utah Listings

Beaver

Beaver KOA
1428 Manderfield Road
Beaver, UT
435-438-2924
Dogs of all sizes are allowed. There are no additional pet fees. Dogs must be leashed and cleaned up after. This RV park is closed during the off-season. The camping and tent areas also allow dogs. There is a dog walk area at the campground. Dogs are allowed in the camping cabins. Multiple dogs may be allowed.

Blanding

Goosenecks State Park
660 West 400 North/End of H 316
Blanding, UT
435-678-2238
This park shares 300 million years of geologic history with its visitors from an observation shelter located at 1000 feet over the San Juan River. From here you can see the path of the river's erosion. Dogs are allowed at no additional fee. Dogs may be off lead if there is voice control. The camping and tent areas also allow dogs. There is a dog walk area at the campground. There are no electric or water hookups at the campground. Multiple dogs may be allowed.

Bluff

Cadillac Ranch
640 E Main
Bluff, UT
800-538-6195
Dogs of all sizes are allowed. There are no additional pet fees. Dogs must be leashed and cleaned up after. The camping and tent areas also allow dogs. There is a dog walk area at the campground. Multiple dogs may be allowed.

Bryce Canyon

Ruby's Inn, RV Park, and Campground
1280 H 63S
Bryce, UT
435-834-5301
Dogs of all sizes are allowed. There are no additional pet fees. Dogs must be leashed and cleaned up after. This RV park is closed during the off-season. The camping and tent areas also allow dogs. There is a dog walk area at the campground. Multiple dogs may be allowed.

Panguitch KOA
555 Main Street
Panguitch, UT
435-676-2225
Dogs of all sizes are allowed. There are no additional pet fees. Dogs must be leashed and cleaned up after. This RV park is closed during the off-season. The camping and tent areas also allow dogs. There is a dog walk area at the campground. Multiple dogs may be allowed.

Paradise RV Park
2153 N H 89
Panguitch, UT
435-676-8348
Dogs of all sizes are allowed at the tent and RV sites. Only small, lightly furred dogs are allowed at the cabins. There are no additional pet fees. Dogs may not be left unattended, and they must be leashed and cleaned up after. This RV park is closed during the off-season. The camping and tent areas also allow dogs. There is a dog walk area at the campground. Dogs are allowed in the camping cabins.

Red Canyon RV Park
3279 H 12
Panguitch, UT
435-676-2690
Dogs of all sizes are allowed. There are no additional pet fees. Dogs

must be leashed and cleaned up after. This RV park is closed during the off-season. The camping and tent areas also allow dogs. There is a dog walk area at the campground. 2 dogs may be allowed.

Cannonville

Cannonville/Bryce Valley KOA
H 12 at Red Rocks Road
Cannonville, UT
435-679-8988
Dogs of all sizes are allowed. There are no additional pet fees. Dogs must be well behaved, leashed, and cleaned up after. This RV park is closed during the off-season. The camping and tent areas also allow dogs. There is a dog walk area at the campground. Dogs are allowed in the camping cabins. Multiple dogs may be allowed.

Canonville

Kodachrome Basin State Park
P.O. Box 180069/ Cottonwood Road
Canonville, UT
435-679-8562
This park offers a unique desert beauty as a result of geological activity that created the many trails and massive, colorful sandstone chimneys. Dogs are allowed at no additional fee. Dogs may not be left unattended, and they must be on no more than a 6 foot leash, and be cleaned up after. Dogs are allowed on the trails. The camping and tent areas also allow dogs. There is a dog walk area at the campground. There are no electric or water hookups at the campground. Multiple dogs may be allowed.

Cedar City

Cedar City KOA
1121 N Main
Cedar City, UT
435-586-9872
There can be up to 3 dogs of any size for the tent or RV sites, and there are no additional pet fees. There is a $5 per night per pet additional fee for the cabins, and only up to 2 dogs are allowed. Dogs may not be left unattended, and they must be leashed and cleaned up after. There are some breed restrictions. The camping and tent areas also allow dogs. There is a dog walk area at the campground. Dogs are allowed in the camping

cabins.

Dixie National Forest
1789 N Wedgewood Lane
Cedar City, UT
435-865-3700
This is the largest National Forest in Utah and dogs of all sizes are allowed. There are no additional pet fees. Dogs may not be left unattended, and they must be leashed and cleaned up after. Dogs are allowed on all the trails, but they are not allowed on the beaches or in the water. This campground is closed during the off-season. The camping and tent areas also allow dogs. There is a dog walk area at the campground. Multiple dogs may be allowed.

Cortez

Hovenweep Campground/Hovenweep National Monument
On H 10 (McElmo Route)
Cortez, UT
970-562-4282
This park is the safeguard for six prehistoric, Puebloan-era villages, and offers a variety of historical, geological, and scenic sites. Dogs are allowed at no additional fee. Dogs may not be left unattended outside, and they must be leashed and cleaned up after. Dogs are allowed on the trails, and they must stay on the trails. The camping and tent areas also allow dogs. There is a dog walk area at the campground. There are no electric or water hookups at the campground. Multiple dogs may be allowed.

Dinosaur National Monument

Ashley National Forest
355 N Vernal Avenue
Vernal, UT
435-789-1181
Dogs of all sizes are allowed. There are no additional pet fees. Dogs may not be left unattended, and they must be leashed and cleaned up after. This campground is closed during the off-season. The camping and tent areas also allow dogs. There is a dog walk area at the campground. Multiple dogs may be allowed.

Vernal/Dinosaurland KOA
930 N Vernal Avenue
Vernal, UT
435-789-2148

Dogs of all sizes are allowed. There are no additional pet fees. Dogs may not be left unattended at any time, and they must be quiet, leashed, and cleaned up after. Only 2 dogs at a time are allowed in the cabins, and up to 3 dogs at the tent or RV sites. There are some breed restrictions. This RV park is closed during the off-season. The camping and tent areas also allow dogs. There is a dog walk area at the campground. Dogs are allowed in the camping cabins.

Escalante

Escalante State Park
710 N Reservoir Road
Escalante, UT
435-826-4466
This park, along the Wide Hollow Reservoir, has a couple of popular trails; The Petrified Forest Trail which winds through lava flows and petrified wood, and for more of a challenge there is the Sleeping Rainbows trail. Dogs are allowed at no additional fee. Dogs may not be left unattended, and they must be leashed and cleaned up after. Dogs are allowed on the trails. The camping and tent areas also allow dogs. There is a dog walk area at the campground. There are no electric or water hookups at the campground. Multiple dogs may be allowed.

Fillmore

Fillmore KOA
900 S 410 W
Fillmore, UT
435-743-4420
Dogs of all sizes are allowed, and there can be up to 3 dogs at the tent and RV sites. Two small dogs only are allowed at the cabins, and they must stay off the beds. There are no additional pet fees. Dogs are not allowed at the playground or the pool, and they must be leashed and cleaned up after. There are some breed restrictions. This RV park is closed during the off-season. The camping and tent areas also allow dogs. There is a dog walk area at the campground. Dogs are allowed in the camping cabins.

Garden City

Bear Lake State Park
Box 184/ Off H 30

Garden City, UT
435-946-3343
This beautiful lake park is located high in the Rocky Mountains and is open year round. Dogs are allowed at no additional fee. Dogs may not be left unattended, and they must be leashed and cleaned up after. Dogs may be off lead when out of the camp areas if there is voice control. Dogs are allowed on the trails unless otherwise marked. This campground is closed during the off-season. The camping and tent areas also allow dogs. There is a dog walk area at the campground. Multiple dogs may be allowed.

Bear Lake/Garden City KOA
485 N Bear Lake Blvd
Garden City, UT
435-946-3454
Dogs of all sizes are allowed. There are no additional pet fees. Dogs may not be left unattended, and they must be leashed and cleaned up after. There is an off leash dog run area. The tent and RV sites are seasonal, and the cabins stay open all year. There are some breed restrictions. The camping and tent areas allow dogs. There is a dog walk area at the campground. Dogs are allowed in the camping cabins. Multiple dogs may be allowed.

Glendale

Glendale KOA
11 Koa Street
Glendale, UT
435-648-2490
Dogs of all sizes are allowed. There are no additional pet fees. Dogs must be leashed and cleaned up after. There is a fenced in dog run for off lead. This RV park is closed during the off-season. The camping and tent areas also allow dogs. There is a dog walk area at the campground. Multiple dogs may be allowed.

Green River

Green River State Park
125 Fairway Avenue
Green River, UT
435-564-3633
This park has it's own recreational activities and a golf course, but is is also a central point to access other recreational areas and trails. Dogs are allowed at no additional fee. Dogs may not be left unattended, and they must be leashed and

cleaned up after. Dogs are allowed on the trails. This campground is closed during the off-season. The camping and tent areas also allow dogs. There is a dog walk area at the campground. There are no electric or water hookups at the campground. Multiple dogs may be allowed.

United Campground of Green River
910 E Main Street
Green River, UT
435-564-8195
Dogs of all sizes are allowed. There are no additional pet fees. Dogs must be leashed and cleaned up after. The camping and tent areas also allow dogs. There is a dog walk area at the campground. Multiple dogs may be allowed.

Hanksville

Goblin Valley State Park
P.O. Box 637/Hanksville Road
Hanksville, UT
435-564-3633
Goblin Valley is so named as a result of the unusual rock formations and the scenery of the park. Dogs are allowed at no additional fee. Dogs may not be left unattended, and they must be leashed and cleaned up after. Dogs are allowed on the trails. The camping and tent areas also allow dogs. There is a dog walk area at the campground. There are no electric or water hookups at the campground. Multiple dogs may be allowed.

Huntington

Huntington State Park
P.O. Box 1343/ On H 10
Huntington, UT
435-687-2491
The beautiful reservoir here is surrounded by sandstone cliffs, and a variety of recreation is available. Dogs are allowed at no additional fee. Dogs may not be left unattended, and they must be leashed and cleaned up after. Dogs are allowed on the trails. The camping and tent areas also allow dogs. There is a dog walk area at the campground. There are no electric or water hookups at the campground. Multiple dogs may be allowed.

Hurricane

Brentwood RV Resort

15N 3700W
Hurricane, UT
800-447-2239
One dog of any size is allowed. There are no additional pet fees. Dogs must be leashed and cleaned up after. There is a dog walk area at the campground.

Kanab

Coral Pink Sand Dunes State Park
P.O. Box 95/Coral Springs Road
Kanab, UT
435-648-2800
This park offer a unique geologic feature since it is the only major sand dune field on the Colorado Plateau. There is plenty of hiking and ATV trails. Dogs are allowed at no additional fee. Dogs may not be left unattended, and they must be leashed and cleaned up after. Dogs are allowed on the trails with the exception of the ATV trails. The camping and tent areas also allow dogs. There is a dog walk area at the campground. There are no electric or water hookups at the campground. Multiple dogs may be allowed.

Kanab RV Corral
483 S 100 E
Kanab, UT
435-644-5330
Dogs of all sizes are allowed. There are no additional pet fees. Dogs may not be left unattended, and they must be leashed and cleaned up after. There is a dog walk area at the campground. Multiple dogs may be allowed.

Kaysville

Cherry Hill RV Resort
1325 S Main
Kaysville, UT
801-451-5379
Dogs of all sizes are allowed. There are no additional pet fees. Dogs must be well behaved, leashed, and cleaned up after. Dogs may only be left alone if they will be quiet and comfortable. The camping and tent areas also allow dogs. There is a dog walk area at the campground. Multiple dogs may be allowed.

Lake Powell

Bullfrog Resort and Marina

Campground
On H 276
Lake Powell, UT
435-684-7000
Every Summer this park has interpretive programs about the ancestral Puebloans who lived here, and about the geology and wildlife of the area, but there are also activities year round. There is a car ferry that travels across the lake and dogs are allowed on the 30 minute ride. For ferry crossing times call (435)684-3000. Dogs are also allowed in the rentals, on the trails (unless otherwise marked), and on rented boats. Dogs must be leashed and cleaned up after. Dogs are not allowed at the ruins. The camping and tent areas also allow dogs. There is a dog walk area at the campground. Multiple dogs may be allowed.

Village Center at Halls Crossing Marina
End of H 276
Lake Powell, UT
435-684-7000
Every Summer this park has interpretive programs about the ancestral Puebloans who lived here, and about the geology and wildlife of the area, but there are activities year round. There is a car ferry that travels across the lake and dogs are allowed on the 30 minute ride. For ferry crossing times call (435)684-3000. Dogs are also allowed in the rentals, on the trails (unless otherwise marked), and on the rented houseboats. Dogs must be leashed and cleaned up after. Dogs are not allowed at the ruins. The camping and tent areas also allow dogs. There is a dog walk area at the campground. Multiple dogs may be allowed.

Manila

Flaming Gorge/Manila KOA
H 43 & 3rd W
Manila, UT
435-784-3184
Dogs of all sizes are allowed. There is a $10 cash only refundable pet deposit. Dogs must be leashed and cleaned up after. This RV park is closed during the off-season. The camping and tent areas also allow dogs. There is a dog walk area at the campground. Dogs are allowed in the camping cabins. Multiple dogs may be allowed.

Midway

Wasatch Mountain State Park
1281 Warm Springs Road
Midway, UT
435-654-1791
This recreational park is open year round, has a 36 hole golf course, and is Utah's most developed state park. Dogs are allowed at no additional fee. Dogs must be leashed and cleaned up after. Dogs are allowed on the trails, but they are not allowed on the golf course. This campground is closed during the off-season. The camping and tent areas also allow dogs. There is a dog walk area at the campground. There are no electric or water hookups at the campground. Multiple dogs may be allowed.

Moab

Arch View Resort
10 miles N of Moab on H 191
Moab, UT
435-259-7854
Dogs of all sizes are allowed. There are no additional pet fees. Dogs must be quiet, well behaved, leashed, and cleaned up after. This RV park is closed during the off-season. The camping and tent areas also allow dogs. There is a dog walk area at the campground. Dogs are allowed in the camping cabins. Multiple dogs may be allowed.

Canyonlands Campground
555 S Main Street
Moab, UT
800-522-6848
Dogs of all sizes are allowed. There are no additional pet fees. Dogs may not be left unattended, and they must be quiet, leashed, and cleaned up after. The camping and tent areas also allow dogs. There is a dog walk area at the campground. Multiple dogs may be allowed.

Dead Horse Point State Park
P.O. Box 609/At End of H 313
Moab, UT
435-259-2614
This park, Utah's Grand Canyon, is known for having the most spectacular views in all of the Utah parks. Dead Horse Point towers over 2000 feet over the Colorado River. Dogs must be leashed in the campground and cleaned up after. Dogs are allowed on the trails. The camping and tent areas also allow dogs. There is a dog walk area at the campground. There are no water

hookups at the campground. Multiple dogs may be allowed.

Moab KOA
3225 S H 191
Moab, UT
435-259-6682
Dogs of all sizes and numbers are allowed, and there is a $5 one time fee for tent or RV sites. Dogs may not be left unattended outside, or inside an RV unless there is air conditioning. There is a $5 one time fee for the cabins also, only 2 dogs are allowed, and they must be crated if left. Dogs must be quiet, leashed, and cleaned up after. There are some breed restrictions. This RV park is closed during the off-season. The camping and tent areas also allow dogs. There is a dog walk area at the campground. Dogs are allowed in the camping cabins.

Squaw Flat Campground/Canyonlands National Park
End of H 211
Moab, UT
435-259-4711 (Needles)
This park provides a colorful landscape of sedimentary sandstone created by the erosion of the Colorado River and it's tributaries. Dogs are allowed on the main roads and in the campground. Dogs are not allowed on the trails, in the back country, or on the 4-wheel drive trails. Dogs must be leashed and cleaned up after. The closest services and gas are about 50 miles away in Monticello. The camping and tent areas also allow dogs. There is a dog walk area at the campground. There are no electric or water hookups at the campground. Multiple dogs may be allowed.

Monument Valley

Gouldings RV Park
1000 Main Street
Monument Valley, UT
435-727-3235
Both tent sites and full hookup RV sites are offered at this campground. Rates are from $16 to $26 per site per night. The rates are for two people. There is a $3 per night extra fee per additional person. Well-behaved leashed pets are welcome. Campground amenities includes a view of Monument Valley, heated indoor

pool, guest laundry, hot showers, grocery store, playground and cable TV. The campground is located north of the Arizona and Utah border, adjacent to the Navajo Tribal Park in Monument Valley. They are open year round with limited service from November 1 to March 14. There is a dog walk area at the campground. Multiple dogs may be allowed.

Perry

Brigham City/Perry South KOA
1040 W 3600 S
Perry, UT
435-723-5503
Dogs of all sizes are allowed. There are no additional pet fees. Dogs must be leashed and cleaned up after. There are some breed restrictions. This RV park is closed during the off-season. The camping and tent areas also allow dogs. There is a dog walk area at the campground. Multiple dogs may be allowed.

Price

Manti-La Sal National Forest
599 W. Price River Dr.
Price, UT
435-636-3500
This forest of more than 1.4 million acres, with elevations from 5,000 feet to over 12,000 feet, provides a variety of landscapes and year round recreational opportunities. Dogs are allowed at no additional fee. Dogs may not be left unattended, and they must be leashed and cleaned up after when in camp areas. Dogs may be off lead in the forest if there is voice control. Dogs are allowed on the trails. This campground is closed during the off-season. The camping and tent areas also allow dogs. There are no electric or water hookups at the campground. Multiple dogs may be allowed.

Provo

Lakeside RV Campground
4000 W Center Street
Provo, UT
801-373-5267
Dogs of all sizes are allowed. There are no additional pet fees. Dogs may not be left unattended at any time, and they must be quiet, leashed, and cleaned up after. Dogs are not allowed in the store, at the pool, or at the playground. The camping and

tent areas also allow dogs. There is a dog walk area at the campground. Multiple dogs may be allowed.

Provo KOA
320N 2050 W
Provo, UT
801-375-2994
Dogs of all sizes are allowed. There are no additional pet fees. Dogs may not be left unattended at the cabins, and they must be leashed and cleaned up after. The camping and tent areas also allow dogs. There is a dog walk area at the campground. Dogs are allowed in the camping cabins. Multiple dogs may be allowed.

Uinta National Forest
88 W 100 N
Provo, UT
801-377-5780
Dogs of all sizes are allowed. There are no additional pet fees. Dogs may not be left unattended, and they must be quiet, well behaved, leashed, and cleaned up after. This campground is closed during the off-season. The camping and tent areas also allow dogs. There is a dog walk area at the campground. There are no water hookups at the campground. Multiple dogs may be allowed.

Richfield

Fishlake National Forest
115 East 900 North
Richfield, UT
435-896-9233
Dogs of all sizes are allowed. There are no additional pet fees. Dogs may not be left unattended, and they must be leashed and cleaned up after. Dogs are allowed on the trails. This campground is closed during the off-season. The camping and tent areas also allow dogs. There is a dog walk area at the campground. Multiple dogs may be allowed.

Richfield KOA
600 W 600 S
Richfield, UT
435-896-6674
Dogs up to about 75 pounds are allowed. There are no additional pet fees. Dogs may not be left unattended, and they must be quiet, leashed, and cleaned up after. There are some breed restrictions. This RV park is closed during the off-season. The camping and tent areas also allow dogs. There is a dog walk area at the campground. 2 dogs may be

allowed.

Salt Lake City

Sunset Campground
Farmington Canyon
Farmington City, UT
877-444-6777
This campground is located at an elevation of 6,400 feet in the Wasatch-Cache National Forest, east of Farmington City and north of Salt Lake City. There are 16 camp sites with tables, fire circles and grills. Campground amenities include toilets and drinking water but no trash cans or RV hookups. The maximum vehicle length allowed is 28 feet. Sites are paved with pull-thru capabilities. Some of the sites are shaded and wheelchair accessible. Dogs must be leashed at the campgrounds and on the 1/2 mile Sunset Trail. Please clean up after your pets. All camp sites are first come, first serve and no reservations are accepted. The campground is open from June through October. To get there from Salt Lake City, head north on Interstate 15 and take the Farmington Exit. At the stop sign, turn right. Go to 100 East Street and turn left (heading north). Take this road 5.3 miles up the canyon (Farmington Canyon) to the campground.

Salt Lake City KOA
1400 W North Temple
Salt Lake City, UT
801-355-1214
Dogs of all sizes are allowed. There are no additional pet fees. Dogs may not be left unattended, and they must be quiet, well behaved, leashed, and cleaned up after. The camping and tent areas also allow dogs. There is a dog walk area at the campground. Multiple dogs may be allowed.

Wasatch -Cache National Forest
3285 East 3800 S
Salt Lake City, UT
801-466-6411
There are ample recreational opportunities in this forest of over a million acres comprised of high desert and alpine landscapes with 6 ranger districts. Dogs are allowed at no additional fee. Dogs may not be left unattended, and they must be leashed and cleaned up after. Dogs are allowed on the trails, but they are not allowed in any watershed areas. The camping and tent areas

also allow dogs. There is a dog walk area at the campground. There are no water hookups at the campground. Multiple dogs may be allowed.

Quail Run RV Park
9230 S State Street
Sandy, UT
801-255-9300
Dogs of all sizes are allowed. There are no additional pet fees. Dogs must be quiet, well behaved, leashed, and cleaned up after. Dogs may not be left unattended, or chained to the lamp posts or trees. Multiple dogs may be allowed.

Springville

East Bay RV Park
1750 W 1600N
Springville, UT
801-491-0700
Small Dogs Only. Dogs of all sizes are allowed. There are no additional pet fees. Dogs may not be left unattended, and they must be quiet, be on no more than a 6 foot leash, and cleaned up after. Dogs may not be on the lawns or at the golf course. Dogs may not be tied to fire hydrants or other park property, and outside dog fences or kennels are not allowed. There are some breed restrictions. There is a dog walk area at the campground. 2 dogs may be allowed.

St George

Snow Canyon State Park
1002 Snow Canyon Drive (H 18)
St George, UT
435-628-2255
Sand dunes, quiet beauty, and many trails bring visitors to this park. Dogs are allowed at no additional fee. Dogs may not be left unattended, and they must be leashed and cleaned up after. Dogs are allowed on the Whiptail Trail and the West Canyon Trail only. The camping and tent areas also allow dogs. There is a dog walk area at the campground. Multiple dogs may be allowed.

Templeview RV Resort
975 S Main
St George, UT
800-381-0321
Dogs of all sizes are allowed. There are no additional pet fees unless the stay is monthly; then there is a $5 additional pet fee. Dogs must be

leashed and cleaned up after. The camping and tent areas also allow dogs. There is a dog walk area at the campground. 2 dogs may be allowed.

Sterling

Palisade State Park
2200 Palisade Road
Sterling, UT
435-835-7275
The Palisade Reservoir of 70 acres provides many water sports. There is a golf course, driving range, several trails, and Six-Mile Canyon for the off-roaders. Dogs are allowed at no additional fee. Dogs may not be left unattended, and they must be leashed and cleaned up after. Dogs are allowed on the trails. The camping and tent areas also allow dogs. There is a dog walk area at the campground. Multiple dogs may be allowed.

Syracuse

Antelope Island State Park
4528 West 1700 South
Syracuse, UT
801-773-2941
This park is Utah's largest island with over 28,000 acres, and is reached via a 2 lane causeway. This park has a unique history, with biological, geological, and plenty of recreational opportunities to pursue. Dogs are allowed at no additional fee. Dogs may not be left unattended, and they must be leashed and cleaned up after. Dogs are allowed on all but 2 of the trails and the beach. The camping and tent areas also allow dogs. There is a dog walk area at the campground. There are no electric or water hookups at the campground. Multiple dogs may be allowed.

Virgin

Zion River Resort
730 E H 9
Virgin, UT
800-838-8594
Dogs of all sizes are allowed. There are no additional pet fees. Dogs must be leashed and cleaned up after. There is a fenced in area where dogs may run off lead. There is a dog walk area at the campground. 2 dogs may be allowed.

Willard

Willard Bay State Park
900 West 650 North #A/ On H 315
Willard, UT
435-734-9494
Willard Bay has 2 marinas open to the public, and is a freshwater reservoir providing fresh water for farming as well as recreation. Dogs are allowed at no additional fee. Dogs may not be left unattended, and they must be leashed and cleaned up after. Dogs are allowed on the trails. The camping and tent areas also allow dogs. There is a dog walk area at the campground. Multiple dogs may be allowed.

Zion National Park

Quail Creek State Park
H 318 M.P. #2
Hurricane, UT
435-879-2378
This park provides a variety of year round recreation, and the man-made reservoir here is known for the warmth of its water in the summer. Dogs are allowed at no additional fee. Dogs must be on no more than a 6 foot leash and be cleaned up after. Dogs are not allowed on the beach between the grass areas. The camping and tent areas also allow dogs. There is a dog walk area at the campground. There are no electric or water hookups at the campground. Multiple dogs may be allowed.

Red Cliffs Recreation Area
4.5 miles from Leeds on I-15
Leeds, UT
435-688-3246
This recreational site has 10 campsites among the bright colored canyon walls of the area. Dogs are allowed at no additional fee, and they must be leashed and cleaned up after. Information and maps can be gotten from the BLM office at 345 E. Riverside Drive, St. George, Utah. The camping and tent areas also allow dogs. There is a dog walk area at the campground. There are no electric or water hookups at the campground. Multiple dogs may be allowed.

Zion Canyon Campground & Resort
479 Zion Park Blvd
Springdale, UT
435-772-3237
Dogs of all sizes are allowed. There

are no additional pet fees. Dogs may not be left inside a tent or outside on any site unattended, and they may be left in an RV only if there is air conditioning. Dogs must be quiet, well behaved, leashed, and cleaned up after. There are some breed restrictions. The camping and tent areas also allow dogs. There is a dog walk area at the campground. 2 dogs may be allowed.

Vermont Listings

Alburg

Alburg RV Resort
1 Blue Rock Road
Alburg, VT
802-796-3733
Dogs of all sizes are allowed. There are no additional pet fees. Dogs are not allowed at the pool or lake, must be leashed at all times, and cleaned up after. This RV park is closed during the off-season. There is a dog walk area at the campground. Multiple dogs may be allowed.

Arlington

Camping on the Battenkill
Route 7A-Camping on the Battenkill
Arlington, VT
802-375-6663
Dogs of all sizes are allowed. There are no additional pet fees. Dogs must have a current rabies certificate, be on leash and cleaned up after. This RV park is closed during the off-season. There is a dog walk area at the campground. Multiple dogs may be allowed.

Bennington

Greenwood Lodge and Campsites
311 Greenwood Drive
Bennington, VT
802-442-2547
Dogs of all sizes are allowed. There are no additional pet fees. Dogs must have their shot records and they may not be left unattended. Dogs must be quiet, leashed and cleaned up after. They are allowed to swim at the lake and be off lead at that time if the owner has voice control, but they may not swim in any of the ponds. This RV park is closed during the off-season. The camping

and tent areas also allow dogs. There is a dog walk area at the campground. 2 dogs may be allowed.

Brandon

Smoke Rise Campground
2111 Grove Street
Brandon, VT
802-247-6984
Dogs of all sizes are allowed. There are no additional pet fees. Dogs may not be left unattended, must be leashed, and cleaned up after. This RV park is closed during the off-season. The camping and tent areas also allow dogs. There is a dog walk area at the campground. Multiple dogs may be allowed.

Burlington

Lone Pine Campsites
52 Sunset View Road
Colchester, VT
802-878-5447
One dog of any size is allowed. There are no additional pet fees. Dogs may not be left unattended, must be leashed, and cleaned up after. There are some breed restrictions. This RV park is closed during the off-season. The camping and tent areas also allow dogs. There is a dog walk area at the campground.

Cavendish

Canton Place Campground
2419 East Road
Cavendish, VT
802-226-7767
Dogs of all sizes are allowed. There are no additional pet fees. Dogs must be leashed and cleaned up after. This RV park is closed during the off-season. The camping and tent areas also allow dogs. There is a dog walk area at the campground. Multiple dogs may be allowed.

Champlain

Grand Isle State Park
36 E Shore Road S
Champlain, VT
802-372-4300
Dogs of all sizes are allowed. There are no additional pet fees. Dogs may not be left unattended, and they must be leashed and cleaned up after. Dogs are not allowed on the beach.

Dogs must have up to date shot records. Dogs on lead are allowed on all the trails and throughout the park. This campground is closed during the off-season. The camping and tent areas also allow dogs. There is a dog walk area at the campground. There are no electric or water hookups at the campground. Multiple dogs may be allowed.

Danville

Sugar Ridge RV Village
24 Old Stage Coach Road
Danville, VT
802-684-2550
Dogs of all sizes are allowed. There are no additional pet fees. Dogs must current rabies certificate, and be leashed and cleaned up after. Dogs are not allowed in the rentals. This RV park is closed during the off-season. There is a dog walk area at the campground. Multiple dogs may be allowed.

Dorset

Dorset RV Park
1567 H 30
Dorset, VT
802-867-5754
Dogs of all sizes are allowed. There are no additional pet fees. Dogs may not be left unattended, must be leashed, and cleaned up after. This RV park is closed during the off-season. The camping and tent areas also allow dogs. There is a dog walk area at the campground. Multiple dogs may be allowed.

E. Thetford

Rest N Nest Campground
300 Latham
E. Thetford, VT
802-785-2997
Dogs of all sizes are allowed. There are no additional pet fees. Dogs may not be left unattended, must be leashed, and cleaned up after. This RV park is closed during the off-season. The camping and tent areas also allow dogs. There is a dog walk area at the campground. Multiple dogs may be allowed.

East Dorset

Emerald Lakes State Park
75 Emerald Lake Lane

East Dorset, VT
802-254-2610
Dogs of all sizes are allowed. There are no additional pet fees. Dogs may not be left unattended at any time, they must be on no more than a 10 foot leash, and be cleaned up after. Dogs are not allowed in any day use areas, including parking lots, picnic areas, playgrounds, beaches, or buildings. Dogs must be at least 6 months old and have a current rabies certificate and shot records. Dogs on leash are allowed on the trails. The camping and tent areas also allow dogs. There is a dog walk area at the campground. There are no electric or water hookups at the campground. Multiple dogs may be allowed.

East Dummerston

KOA Brattleboro N
1238 US Route 5
East Dummerston, VT
802-254-5908
Dogs of all sizes are allowed. There are no additional pet fees. Dogs must be leashed and cleaned up after. This RV park is closed during the off-season. The camping and tent areas also allow dogs. There is a dog walk area at the campground. 2 dogs may be allowed.

Enosburg Falls

Lake Carmi State Park
460 Marsh Farm Rd
Enosburg Falls, VT
802-933-8383
Dogs of all sizes are allowed. There are no additional pet fees. Dogs may not be left unattended at any time, they must be on no more than a 10 foot leash, and be cleaned up after. Dogs are not allowed in any day use areas, including parking lots, picnic areas, beach and swim areas, playgrounds, or buildings. Dogs must be at least 6 months old and have a current rabies certificate and shot records. Dogs on lead are allowed on the trails. The camping and tent areas also allow dogs. There is a dog walk area at the campground. Dogs are allowed in the camping cabins. There are no electric or water hookups at the campground. Multiple dogs may be allowed.

Fair Haven

Bomoseen State Park
22 Cedar Mountain Rd,

Fair Haven, VT
802-265-4242
Dogs of all sizes are allowed. There are no additional pet fees. Dogs may not be left unattended at any time, they must be on no more than a 10 foot leash, and be cleaned up after. Dogs are not allowed in any day use areas, including parking lots, picnic areas, beach and swim areas, playgrounds, or buildings. Dogs must be at least 6 months old and have a current rabies certificate and shot records. Dogs on leash are allowed on the trails. The camping and tent areas also allow dogs. There is a dog walk area at the campground. There are no electric or water hookups at the campground. Multiple dogs may be allowed.

Groton

Big Deer State Park
303 Boulder Beach Road
Groton, VT
802-372-4300
Dogs of all sizes are allowed. There are no additional pet fees. Dogs may not be left unattended, and they must be on no more than a 10 foot leash, and be cleaned up after. Dogs are not allowed at the swim beach, however dogs are allowed to swim at the beach by the boat docks. Dogs must have current rabies shot records. There are a series of trails nearby, and dogs on lead are allowed. This campground is closed during the off-season. The camping and tent areas also allow dogs. There is a dog walk area at the campground. There are no electric or water hookups at the campground. Multiple dogs may be allowed.

Stillwatere State Park
44 Stillwater Road
Groton, VT
802-584-3822
Dogs of all sizes are allowed. There are no additional pet fees. Dogs may not be left unattended, they must be on no more than a 10 foot leash, and be cleaned up after. Dogs are not allowed at the swim beach, however dogs are allowed to swim at the beach by the boat docks. Dogs must have current rabies shot records. There are a series of trails nearby, and dogs on lead are allowed. This campground is closed during the off-season. The camping and tent areas also allow dogs. There is a dog walk area at the campground. There are no electric or water hookups at the campground. Multiple dogs may be

allowed.

Guilford

Fort Dummer State Park
517 Old Guilford
Guilford, VT
802-254-2610
Dogs of all sizes are allowed. There are no additional pet fees. Dogs may not be left unattended at any time, they must be on no more than a 10 foot leash, and be cleaned up after. Dogs are not allowed in any day use areas, including parking lots, picnic areas, playgrounds, or buildings. Dogs must be at least 6 months old and have a current rabies certificate and shot records. The camping and tent areas also allow dogs. There is a dog walk area at the campground. There are no electric or water hookups at the campground. Multiple dogs may be allowed.

Hubbarton

Lake Bomoseen Campground
18 Campground Drive
Hubbarton, VT
802-273-2061
Dogs of all sizes are allowed. There is a $1 per night per pet additional fee. Dogs may not be left unattended, must be leashed, and cleaned up after. Dogs must have shot records. There are some breed restrictions. This RV park is closed during the off-season. The camping and tent areas also allow dogs. There is a dog walk area at the campground. Multiple dogs may be allowed.

Irasburg

Tree Corners
3540 H 58
Irasburg, VT
802-754-6042
One small dog up to about 15 pounds is allowed. There are no additional pet fees. This RV park is closed during the off-season. Only one dog is allowed per campsite. The camping and tent areas also allow dogs. There is a dog walk area at the campground. Dogs are allowed in the camping cabins.

Island Pond

Brighton State Park

102 State Park Road
Island Pond, VT
802-723-4360
Dogs of all sizes are allowed. There are no additional pet fees. Dogs may not be left unattended at any time, and they must be quiet, well behaved, leashed and cleaned up after. Dogs are not allowed on the beach, the trails, the day use areas, or the buildings. Dogs must have up to date rabies shot records and a current license. This campground is closed during the off-season. The camping and tent areas also allow dogs. There is a dog walk area at the campground. There are no electric or water hookups at the campground. Multiple dogs may be allowed.

Jamaica

Jamaica State Park
285 Salmon Hole Lane
Jamaica, VT
802-874-4600
Dogs of all sizes are allowed. There are no additional pet fees. Dogs may not be left unattended at any time, they must be on no more than a 10 foot leash, and be cleaned up after. Dogs are not allowed in any day use areas, including parking lots, picnic areas, beach and swim areas, playgrounds, or buildings. Dogs must be at least 6 months old and have a current rabies certificate and shot records. Dogs on leash are allowed on all the trails, except the children's nature trail. The camping and tent areas also allow dogs. There is a dog walk area at the campground. There are no electric or water hookups at the campground. Multiple dogs may be allowed.

Lake Elmore

Elmore State Park
856 H 12
Lake Elmore, VT
802-888-2982
Dogs of all sizes are allowed. There are no additional pet fees. Dogs may not be left unattended, and they must be leashed and cleaned up after. Dogs are not allowed on the beach, the picnic areas, or in day use areas. Dogs on lead are allowed on the trails. Dogs must have current rabies shot records. This campground is closed during the off-season. The camping and tent areas also allow dogs. There is a dog walk area at the campground. There are no electric or water hookups at the campground.

Multiple dogs may be allowed.

Marshfield

New Discovery State Park
4239 H 232
Marshfield, VT
802-426-3042
Dogs of all sizes are allowed. There are no additional pet fees. Dogs may not be left unattended at any time, they must be on no more than a 10 foot leash, and be cleaned up after. Dogs are not allowed in any day use areas, including parking lots, picnic areas, playgrounds, or buildings. Dogs must be at least 6 months old and have a current rabies certificate and shot records. Dogs on leash are allowed on the trails. The camping and tent areas also allow dogs. There is a dog walk area at the campground. There are no electric or water hookups at the campground. Multiple dogs may be allowed.

Milton

Homestead Campgrounds
864 Ethan Allen H
Milton, VT
802-524-2356
Dogs of all sizes are allowed. There are no additional pet fees. Dogs must be well behaved, be on a leash, and cleaned up after. This RV park is closed during the off-season. The camping and tent areas also allow dogs. There is a dog walk area at the campground. Multiple dogs may be allowed.

Montpelier

Green Valley Campground
1368 H 2
Montpelier, VT
802-223-6217
Dogs of all sizes are allowed. There are no additional pet fees. Dogs may not be left unattended, must be leashed, and cleaned up after. This RV park is closed during the off-season. The camping and tent areas also allow dogs. There is a dog walk area at the campground. Multiple dogs may be allowed.

North Hero

North Hero State Park
3803 Lakeview Drive
North Hero, VT
802-372-8727

Dogs of all sizes are allowed. There are no additional pet fees. Dogs may not be left unattended at any time, they must be on no more than a 10 foot leash, and be cleaned up after. Dogs are not allowed in any day use areas, including parking lots, picnic areas, pools, beaches, playgrounds, or buildings. Dogs must be at least 6 months old and have a current rabies certificate and shot records. Dogs on leash are allowed on the trails. The camping and tent areas also allow dogs. There is a dog walk area at the campground. There are no electric or water hookups at the campground. Multiple dogs may be allowed.

Perkinsville

Crown Point Camping
131 Bishop Camp Road
Perkinsville, VT
802-263-5555
Dogs of all sizes are allowed. There are no additional pet fees. Dogs must be well behaved and leashed and cleaned up after. The camping and tent areas also allow dogs. There is a dog walk area at the campground. Multiple dogs may be allowed.

Plymouth

Coolidge State Park
855 Coolidge State Park Road
Plymouth, VT
802-672-3612
Dogs of all sizes are allowed. There are no additional pet fees. Dogs may not be left unattended, and they must be leashed and cleaned up after. Dogs must have current rabies shot records. Dog on lead are allowed on the trails. This campground is closed during the off-season. The camping and tent areas also allow dogs. There is a dog walk area at the campground. There are no electric or water hookups at the campground. Multiple dogs may be allowed.

Poultney

Lake St Catherine State Park
3034 H 30S
Poultney, VT
802-287-9158
Dogs of all sizes are allowed. There are no additional pet fees. Dogs may not be left unattended at any

time, they must be on no more than a 10 foot leash, and be cleaned up after. Dogs are not allowed in any day use areas, including parking lots, picnic areas, pools, beaches, playgrounds, or buildings. Dogs must be quiet during quiet hours. Dogs must be at least 6 months old and have a current rabies certificate and shot records. Dogs on leash are allowed on the trails. The camping and tent areas also allow dogs. There is a dog walk area at the campground. There are no electric or water hookups at the campground. Multiple dogs may be allowed.

Randolph Center

Lake Champagne Campground
53 Lake Champagne Drive
Randolph Center, VT
802-728-5293
Dogs of all sizes are allowed. There are no additional pet fees. Dogs must be leashed and cleaned up after; they are not allowed on the beach or the picnic areas. This RV park is closed during the off-season. The camping and tent areas also allow dogs. There is a dog walk area at the campground. Multiple dogs may be allowed.

Rutlant

Green Mountain National Forest
On H 7N
Rutlant, VT
802-747-6700
Dogs of all sizes are allowed. There are no additional pet fees. Dogs may not be left unattended, and they must be well behaved, leashed, and cleaned up after. Dogs are not allowed in the picnic or pond areas. Dogs on lead are allowed on all the trails. There are 7 campgrounds in this national forest, 2 remain open all year. The camping and tent areas also allow dogs. There is a dog walk area at the campground. There are no electric or water hookups at the campground. Multiple dogs may be allowed.

Salisbury

Lake Dunmore
1457 Lake Dunmore Road
Salisbury, VT
802-352-4501
Dogs of all sizes are allowed. There are no additional pet fees. Dogs must have current shot records, be

well behaved, and be leashed and cleaned up after. This RV park is closed during the off-season. The camping and tent areas also allow dogs. There is a dog walk area at the campground. 2 dogs may be allowed.

Shelburne

Shelburne Camping Area
4385 Shelburne Road
Shelburne, VT
802-985-2540
Dogs of all sizes are allowed. There are no additional pet fees. Dogs may not be left unattended, must be leashed at all times, and cleaned up after. The camping and tent areas also allow dogs. There is a dog walk area at the campground. Multiple dogs may be allowed.

South Hero

Apple Island Resort
Box 183 H 2
South Hero, VT
802-372-5398
Dogs of all sizes are allowed. There are no additional pet fees. Dogs may not be left unattended, must be leashed, and cleaned up after. This RV park is closed during the off-season. The camping and tent areas also allow dogs. There is a dog walk area at the campground. There are allowed in the camping cabins. Multiple dogs may be allowed.

St Johnsbury

Moose River Campground
2870 Portland Street
St Johnsbury, VT
802-748-4334
Dogs of all sizes are allowed. There are no additional pet fees. Dogs must be quiet and may not be left unattended. Dogs must be leashed and cleaned up after. Pets are not allowed in any of the rentals. This RV park is closed during the off-season. The camping and tent areas also allow dogs. There is a dog walk area at the campground. Multiple dogs may be allowed.

Stowe

Smuggler's Notch State Park
6443 Mountain Road
Stowe, VT
802-253-4014

Dogs of all sizes are allowed. There are no additional pet fees. Dogs may not be left unattended, and they must be leashed and cleaned up after. Dogs must have current rabies shot records. Dogs on lead are allowed on all the trails. Dogs are not allowed at Camp Plymouth. This campground is closed during the off-season. The camping and tent areas also allow dogs. There is a dog walk area at the campground. There are no electric or water hookups at the campground. Multiple dogs may be allowed.

Thetford Center

Thetford Hill State Park
622 Academy Road
Thetford Center, VT
802-785-2266
Dogs of all sizes are allowed. There are no additional pet fees. Dogs may not be left unattended at any time, they must be on no more than a 10 foot leash, and be cleaned up after. Dogs are not allowed in any day use areas, including parking lots, picnic areas, beach and swim areas, playgrounds, or buildings. Dogs must be at least 6 months old and have a current rabies certificate and shot records. Dogs on leash are allowed on the trails. The camping and tent areas also allow dogs. There is a dog walk area at the campground. There are no electric or water hookups at the campground. Multiple dogs may be allowed.

Townshend

Bald Mountain Campground
1760 State Forest Road
Townshend, VT
802-365-7510
Dogs of all sizes are allowed. There are no additional pet fees. Dogs may not be left unattended, and must be leashed and cleaned up after. This RV park is closed during the off-season. The camping and tent areas also allow dogs. There is a dog walk area at the campground. Multiple dogs may be allowed.

Vergennes

Button Bay State Park
5 Button Bay State Park Road
Vergennes, VT
802-475-2377
Dogs of all sizes are allowed. There

are no additional pet fees. Dogs may not be left unattended at any time, they must be on no more than a 10 foot leash, and be cleaned up after. Dogs are not allowed in any day use areas, including parking lots, picnic areas, beach and swim areas, playgrounds, or buildings. Dogs must be at least 6 months old and have a current rabies certificate and shot records. Dogs on leash are allowed on the trails in the pet section only. The camping and tent areas also allow dogs. There is a dog walk area at the campground. There are no electric or water hookups at the campground. Multiple dogs may be allowed.

White River Junction

Pine Valley RV Resort
3700 Woodstock Road
White River Junction, VT
802-296-6711
Dogs of all sizes are allowed. There are no additional pet fees. Dogs must be well behaved, not left unattended, and must be leashed and cleaned up after. There are some breed restrictions. This RV park is closed during the off-season. There is a dog walk area at the campground. Multiple dogs may be allowed.

Quechee Gorge State Park
764 Dewey Mills Road
White River Junction, VT
802-295-2990
Dogs of all sizes are allowed. There are no additional pet fees. Dogs may not be left unattended at any time, they must be on no more than a 10 foot leash, and be cleaned up after. Dogs are not allowed in any day use areas, including parking lots, picnic areas, beach and swim areas, playgrounds, or buildings. Dogs must be at least 6 months old and have a current rabies certificate and shot records. Dogs on leash are allowed on the trails. The camping and tent areas also allow dogs. There is a dog walk area at the campground. There are no electric or water hookups at the campground. Multiple dogs may be allowed.

Williamstown

Limehurst Lake Campground
4104 H 14
Williamstown, VT
802-433-6662
Dogs of all sizes are allowed. There

are no additional pet fees. Dogs must be quiet, well behaved, and leashed and cleaned up after. There are some breed restrictions. This RV park is closed during the off-season. The camping and tent areas also allow dogs. There is a dog walk area at the campground. Dogs are allowed in the camping cabins. Multiple dogs may be allowed.

Windsor

Ascutney State Park
1826 Back Mountain Road
Windsor, VT
802-674-2060
Dogs of all sizes are allowed. There are no additional pet fees. Dogs may not be left unattended at any time, they must be on no more than a 10 foot leash, and be cleaned up after. Dogs are not allowed in any day use areas, including parking lots, picnic areas, beach and swim areas, playgrounds, or buildings. Dogs must be at least 6 months old and have a current rabies certificate and shot records. Dogs on leash are allowed on the trails. The camping and tent areas also allow dogs. There is a dog walk area at the campground. There are no electric or water hookups at the campground. Multiple dogs may be allowed.

Woodford

Woodford State Park
142 State Park Road
Woodford, VT
802-447-7169
Dogs of all sizes are allowed. There are no additional pet fees. Dogs must be quiet, not be left unattended at any time, be on no more than a 10 foot leash, and be cleaned up after. Dogs are not allowed in any day use areas, including parking lots, picnic areas, beach and swim areas, playgrounds, or buildings. Dogs must be at least 6 months old and have a current rabies certificate and shot records. Dogs on leash are allowed on the trails. The camping and tent areas also allow dogs. There is a dog walk area at the campground. There are no electric or water hookups at the campground. Multiple dogs may be allowed.

Virginia Listings

Appomattox

Holiday Lake State Park
Rt 2, Box 622; State Park Road 692
Appomattox, VA
434-248-6308
A paradise for the outdoor enthusiast, this park offers a variety of land and water activities, and recreational pursuits. Dogs of all sizes are allowed for $3 per night per dog. Dogs must be leashed and cleaned up after. Dogs may be left tethered on site if they will be quiet, well behaved, are shaded, and have food and water. Dogs are allowed on the trails, but they are not allowed in the lake. The camping and tent areas also allow dogs. There is a dog walk area at the campground. Multiple dogs may be allowed.

Breaks

Breaks Interstate Park
769 H 80
Breaks, VA
276-865-4413
This year round 4,600 acre park has often been called the "Little Grand Canyon", and in addition to panoramic views, there is a wide variety of land and water activities. Dogs are allowed at no additional fee for camping; there is a $7 per night per pet additional fee for the lodge. Dogs may not be left unattended in rooms, but they may be tethered in the camp area if they will be well behaved, quiet, and checked in on. Dogs are allowed on the trails. This campground is closed during the off-season. The camping and tent areas also allow dogs. There is a dog walk area at the campground. Dogs are allowed in the camping cabins. Multiple dogs may be allowed.

Charlottesville

Charlottesville KOA
3825 Red Hill Lane
Charlottesville, VA
434-296-9881
Dogs of all sizes are allowed. There are no additional pet fees. Dogs must be leashed and cleaned up after. This RV park is closed during the off-season. The camping and tent areas also allow dogs. There is a dog walk area at the campground.

Multiple dogs may be allowed.

Chesterfield

Pocohontas State Park
10301 State Park Road
Chesterfield, VA
804-796-4255
Popular, educational, multi-functional, and recreational, all describe this year round park. Dogs of all sizes are allowed for an additional $3 per night per pet. Dogs may not be left unattended outside or in a tent, and they must be leashed and cleaned up after. Dogs are not allowed in food areas or at the pool. Dogs are allowed on the trails. This campground is closed during the off-season. The camping and tent areas also allow dogs. There is a dog walk area at the campground. Multiple dogs may be allowed.

Clarksville

Occoneechee State Park
1192 Occoneechee Park Road
Clarksville, VA
434-374-2210
This historical park is located on Virginia's largest lake and offers a variety of land and water recreation, however, swimming is not allowed. Dogs of all sizes are allowed at $3 per dog per day for the camp area. Dogs may not be left unattended unless very well behaved, and they must have current rabies and shot records. Dogs must be on no more than a 6 foot leash, and be cleaned up after. This campground is closed during the off-season. The camping and tent areas also allow dogs. There is a dog walk area at the campground. Multiple dogs may be allowed.

Clifton Forge

Douthat State Park
Rt 1, Box 212
Clifton Forge, VA
540-862-8100
This park, a Nationally Registered Historic District, offers interpretive programs, more than 40 miles of hiking trails, and a variety of land and water events and recreation. Dogs of all sizes are allowed for $3 per night per pet for the camp area, and at $5 per night per pet for the cabins. Dogs may not be left unattended, and they must be leashed and cleaned up after. Dogs are not allowed at the

lodge or on the beach, but they are allowed on the trails. This campground is closed during the off-season. The camping and tent areas also allow dogs. There is a dog walk area at the campground. Dogs are allowed in the camping cabins. Multiple dogs may be allowed.

Cumberland

Bear Creek State Park
929 Oak Hill Road
Cumberland, VA
804-492-4410
This park of 326 acres has a lake of 40 acres, and offers fishing, hiking, nature study, and a variety of land and water recreation. Dogs of all sizes are allowed for an additional fee of $3 per night per pet. Dogs may not be left unattended, and they must be on no more than a 6 foot leash, and be cleaned up after. Dogs are not allowed on the beach or in the water. Dogs are allowed on the trails. This campground is closed during the off-season. The camping and tent areas also allow dogs. There is a dog walk area at the campground. Multiple dogs may be allowed.

Duffield

Natural Tunnel State Park
Rt 3, Box 250
Duffield, VA
276-940-2674
This park offers a visitor center, an amphitheater, interpretive programs, a wide variety of recreational pursuits, and more, but its amazing natural tunnel is the real attraction. Dogs of all sizes are allowed for an additional fee of $3 per night per pet. Dogs may not be left unattended, they must be leashed at all times, and cleaned up after. Dogs are allowed on the trails. This campground is closed during the off-season. The camping and tent areas also allow dogs. There is a dog walk area at the campground. Multiple dogs may be allowed.

Emporia

Jellystone Park
2940 Sussex Drive
Emporia, VA
434-634-3115
Dogs of all sizes are allowed. There are no additional pet fees. Dogs must be well behaved, may not be left unattended, and be leashed and

cleaned up after. Dogs are not allowed in the buildings or at the playground. The camping and tent areas also allow dogs. There is a dog walk area at the campground. Multiple dogs may be allowed.

Fredericksburg

Fredericksburg/Washington DC S KOA
7400 Brookside Lane
Fredericksburg, VA
540-898-7252
Dogs of all sizes are allowed. There are no additional pet fees, for tent or RV sites. There is a $5 per night per pet additional fee for cabins. Dogs must be quiet, well behaved, leashed, and cleaned up after. The camping and tent areas also allow dogs. There is a dog walk area at the campground. Dogs are allowed in the camping cabins. 2 dogs may be allowed.

Gladstone

James River State Park
Rt 1, Box 787
Gladstone, VA
434-933-4355
A fairly new park offers 20 miles of multiple use trails, three fishing ponds, and various activities and recreation. Dogs of all sizes are allowed for an additional $3 per night per pet for camping, and for $5 per night per pet for cabins. Cabins are available year round. Dogs may not be left unattended, and they must be leashed in camp areas, and cleaned up after. Dogs are allowed on the trails. The camping and tent areas also allow dogs. There is a dog walk area at the campground. Dogs are allowed in the camping cabins. There are no electric or water hookups at the campground. Multiple dogs may be allowed.

Green Bay

Twin Lakes State Park
788 Twin Lakes Road
Green Bay, VA
434-392-3435
This secluded park also provides a conference center in addition to a variety of lakefront activities, recreation, and interpretive programs. Dogs of all sizes are allowed for an additional $3 per night per pet for camping, and for

$5 per night per pet for cabins. Cabins are available year round. Dogs may not be left unattended, and they must be leashed and cleaned up after. Dogs are not allowed on the beach or in the lake, but they are allowed on the trails. This campground is closed during the off-season. The camping and tent areas also allow dogs. There is a dog walk area at the campground. Dogs are allowed in the camping cabins. Multiple dogs may be allowed.

Harrisonburg

Harrisonburg/New Market
12480 Mountain Valley Road
Broadway, VA
540-896-8929
Up to 2 dogs are allowed per RV or tent site, at no additional fee. There is a $20 per stay fee for one dog only in the cabins. Dogs may not be left unattended, must be leashed, and cleaned up after. The camping and tent areas also allow dogs. There is a dog walk area at the campground. Dogs are allowed in the camping cabins.

Huddleston

Smith Mountain State Park
1235 State Park Road
Huddleston, VA
540-297-6066
Hardwood and pine forests, secluded coves and picturesque vistas are the backdrop for a variety of trails, land,water activities, and recreation at this year round park. Dogs of all sizes are allowed for an additional $3 per night per pet for camping, and for $5 per night per pet for cabins. Cabins are available year round. Dogs may not be tied to trees, and they must be leashed and cleaned up after. Dogs may only be left unattended if they will be quiet and well behaved in owners' absence. Dogs are allowed on the trails. This campground is closed during the off-season. The camping and tent areas also allow dogs. There is a dog walk area at the campground. Dogs are allowed in the camping cabins. Multiple dogs may be allowed.

Lorton

Pohick Bay Regional Park
6501 Pohick Bay Drive
Lorton, VA

703-339-6104
In addition to the natural beauty of this park a variety of land and water activities and recreation are offered. Dogs of all sizes are allowed at no additional fee. Dogs may not be left unattended, and they must be leashed and cleaned up after. Dogs are allowed on the trails. The camping and tent areas also allow dogs. There is a dog walk area at the campground. There are no water hookups at the campground. Multiple dogs may be allowed.

Luray

Jellystone Park
2250 H 211E
Luray, VA
540-743-4002
Dogs of all sizes are allowed. There are no additional pet fees. Dogs must be well behaved, leashed, and cleaned up after. Dogs are not allowed to be left staked outside your unit. They may be left inside your RV if they will be quiet. This RV park is closed during the off-season. The camping and tent areas also allow dogs. There is a dog walk area at the campground. Dogs are not allowed in the camping cabins. Multiple dogs may be allowed.

Marion

Hungry Mother State Park
2854 Park Blvd
Marion, VA
276-781-7400
This park is rich in folklore and history, and offers interpretive programs, a variety of land and water activities, and recreation. Dogs of all sizes are allowed for an additional $3 per night per pet for camping, and for $5 per night per pet for cabins. Cabins are available year round. Dogs may not be left unattended, and they must be leashed and cleaned up after. Dogs are not allowed on the beaches or in buildings, but they are allowed on the trails. This campground is closed during the off-season. The camping and tent areas also allow dogs. There is a dog walk area at the campground. Dogs are allowed in the camping cabins. Multiple dogs may be allowed.

Mouth of Wilson

Grayson Highlands State Park

829 Grayson Highland Lane
Mouth of Wilson, VA
276-579-7092
Fishing, 9 hiking trails and land and water recreation are offered at this scenic park. Dogs of all sizes are allowed for an additional $3 per night per pet. Dogs may not be left unattended, and they must be leashed in camp and cleaned up after. Dogs are not allowed in buildings or in the wilderness area. Dogs are allowed on the trails. This campground is closed during the off-season. The camping and tent areas also allow dogs. There is a dog walk area at the campground. 2 dogs may be allowed.

Natural Bridge

Natural Bridge/Lexington KOA
214 Killdeer Lane
Natural Bridge, VA
540-291-2770
Dogs of all sizes are allowed, and there can be more than two dogs. There are no additional pet fees for tent or RV sites. There is a $5 per stay per pet additional fee for cabins, and there can be 2 dogs. Dogs must be well behaved, leashed, and cleaned up after. The camping and tent areas also allow dogs. There is a dog walk area at the campground. Dogs are allowed in the camping cabins.

Natural Bridge Station

Yogi Bear at Natural Bridge
16 Recreation Lane
Natural Bridge Station, VA
540-291-2727
This scenic park, located along the James River, offers a variety of land and water activities and recreational pursuits. Dogs of all sizes are allowed at no additional fee. Dogs may not be left unattended, and they must be leashed and cleaned up after. Dogs are not allowed on the beach, the game area, food areas, or in buildings. Dogs are allowed on the trails. This campground is closed during the off-season. The camping and tent areas also allow dogs. There is a dog walk area at the campground. Dogs are allowed in the camping cabins. 2 dogs may be allowed.

Northern Virginia

Bull Run Regional Park

7700 Bull Run Drive
Centreville, VA
703-631-0550
This scenic park offers year round recreation, and is close to Washington DC, and other area attractions. Dogs of all sizes are allowed at no additional fee. Dogs may not be left unattended, and they must be leashed and cleaned up after. Dogs are not allowed in the pool area, but they are allowed on the trails. The camping and tent areas also allow dogs. There is a dog walk area at the campground. There are no water hookups at the campground. Multiple dogs may be allowed.

Lake Fairfax Park
1400 Lake Fairfax Drive
Reston, VA
703-471-5415
This park of 476 acres, with an 18 acre lake, offers fishing, hiking, nature study, and a variety of land and water recreation. Dogs of all sizes are allowed at no additional fee. Dogs may not be left unattended outside, and they must be leashed and cleaned up after. Dogs are not allowed on the athletic fields, but they are allowed on the trails. The camping and tent areas also allow dogs. There is a dog walk area at the campground. There are no water hookups at the campground. Multiple dogs may be allowed.

Petersburg

Petersburg KOA
2809 Cortland Road
Petersburg, VA
804-732-8345
Dogs of all sizes are allowed. There are no additional pet fees. Dogs must be quiet, leashed, and cleaned up after. The camping and tent areas also allow dogs. There is a dog walk area at the campground. Dogs are allowed in the camping cabins. Multiple dogs may be allowed.

Reedville

Chesapeake Bay/Smith Island KOA
382 Campground Road
Reedville, VA
804-453-3430
Dogs of all sizes are allowed. There are no additional pet fees. Dogs must be well behaved, leashed, and cleaned up after. Dogs may not be at the pool or in the buildings. There

231

are some breed restrictions. This RV park is closed during the off-season. The camping and tent areas also allow dogs. There is a dog walk area at the campground. Multiple dogs may be allowed.

Scottsburg

Staunton River State Park
1170 Staunton Trail
Scottsburg, VA
434-572-4623
This year round park covers almost 1,600 acres, is home to the largest lake in Virginia, offers interpretive programs, and a variety of land and water recreation. Dogs of all sizes are allowed for an additional $3 per night per pet for camping, and for $5 per night per pet for cabins. Cabins are available year round. Dogs may not be left unattended outside or in a tent, and they must be leashed and cleaned up after. Dogs are not allowed in the pool area, but they are allowed on the trails. This campground is closed during the off-season. The camping and tent areas also allow dogs. There is a dog walk area at the campground. Dogs are allowed in the camping cabins. Multiple dogs may be allowed.

Stuart

Fairy Stone State Park
967 Fairystone Lake Drive
Stuart, VA
276-930-2424
Rich in folklore, this park of 4,868 acres with a 168 acre lake provides a variety of land and water recreation, but the Fairy Stones (naturally formed crosses in small rocks) are the real attraction in this park. Dogs of all sizes are allowed for an additional $3 per night per pet for camping, and for $5 per night per pet for cabins. Cabins are available year round. Dogs must be leashed and cleaned up after in camp areas. Dogs are not allowed on the beach, in the water, or at the conference center. Dogs are allowed on the trails. This campground is closed during the off-season. The camping and tent areas also allow dogs. There is a dog walk area at the campground. Dogs are allowed in the camping cabins. Multiple dogs may be allowed.

Surry

Chippokes Plantation
695 Chippokes Park Road
Surry, VA
757-294-3625
As one of the oldest working farms in the US, Chippokes is a living historical exhibit, and among the cultivated gardens and woodlands, all the traditional recreation is offered. Dogs of all sizes are allowed for an additional $3 per night per pet. Dogs may not be left unattended, and they must be on no more than a 6 foot leash, and be cleaned up after. Dogs are not allowed in the buildings, but they are allowed on the trails unless otherwise marked. This campground is closed during the off-season. The camping and tent areas also allow dogs. There is a dog walk area at the campground. Multiple dogs may be allowed.

Triangle

Prince William Forest Park
18100 Park Headquarters Road
Triangle, VA
703-221-7181
With over 19,000 acres, this park offers a variety of nature study, and land and water recreation. Dogs of all sizes are allowed at no additional fee. Dogs may not be left unattended, and they must be on no more than a 6 foot leash, and be cleaned up after. Dogs are not allowed in the Chopawamsic backcountry, Turkey Run Ridge Group Campground, or in the buildings. Dogs are allowed on the trails. The camping and tent areas also allow dogs. There is a dog walk area at the campground. There are no electric or water hookups at the campground. Multiple dogs may be allowed.

Verona

Staunton/Verona KOA
296 Riner Lane
Verona, VA
540-248-2746
Dogs of all sizes are allowed, and there are no additional pet fees for tent or RV sites. There is a $10 per night per pet additional fee for cabins. Dogs must be leashed and cleaned up after. This RV park is closed during the off-season. The camping and tent areas also allow dogs. There is a dog walk area at the campground. Dogs are allowed in the camping cabins. Multiple

dogs may be allowed.

Virginia Beach Area

First Landing State Park
2500 Shore Drive
Virginia Beach, VA
757-412-2300
This park offers exhibits, 3 indoor aquariums, interpretive programs, and almost 20 miles of hiking trails. Dogs of all sizes are allowed for an additional $3 per night per pet for camping, and for $5 per night per pet for cabins. Cabins are available year round. Dogs may not be left unattended, and they must have current rabies and shot records. Dogs are allowed on the trails. This campground is closed during the off-season. The camping and tent areas also allow dogs. There is a dog walk area at the campground. Dogs are allowed in the camping cabins. Multiple dogs may be allowed.

Virginia Beach KOA
1240 General Booth Blvd
Virginia Beach, VA
757-428-1444
Dogs of all sizes are allowed. There are no additional pet fees. Dogs must be leashed and cleaned up after. Dogs are not allowed to be in an outside pen unattended. There is a dog walk area at the campground. Multiple dogs may be allowed.

Williamsburg

Williamsburg KOA
5210 Newman Road
Williamsburg, VA
757-565-2907
Dogs of all sizes are allowed. There are no additional pet fees. Dogs must be leashed and cleaned up after. This RV park is closed during the off-season. The camping and tent areas also allow dogs. There is a dog walk area at the campground. Multiple dogs may be allowed.

Williamsburg/Colonial KOA
4000 Newman Road
Williamsburg, VA
757-565-2734
Dogs of all sizes are allowed. There are no additional pet fees. Dogs must be leashed and cleaned up after. This RV park is closed during the off-season. The camping and tent areas also allow dogs. There is a dog walk area at the campground. Multiple dogs may be allowed.

Wytheville

Whtheville KOA
231 KOA Road
Wytheville, VA
276-228-2601
Dogs of all sizes are allowed. There are no additional pet fees. Dogs must be leashed and cleaned up after. There are some breed restrictions. The camping and tent areas also allow dogs. There is a dog walk area at the campground. Dogs are allowed in the camping cabins. Multiple dogs may be allowed.

Washington Listings

Anacortes

Fidalgo Bay Resort
4701 Fidalgo Bay Road
Anacortes, WA
360-293-5353
Dogs of all sizes are allowed. There are no additional pet fees. Dogs may not be left unattended, and they must be quiet, well behaved, leashed at all times, and cleaned up after. Dogs may not be kenneled outside. This is an RV only park. There is a dog walk area at the campground. 2 dogs may be allowed.

Pioneer Trails RV Resort
7337 Miller Road
Anacortes, WA
360-293-5355
Dogs of all sizes are allowed. There is a $2 per night per pet additional fee. Dogs must be leashed and cleaned up after. Dogs are not allowed in the covered wagons. There are some breed restrictions. There is a dog walk area at the campground. 2 dogs may be allowed.

Anatone

Fields Spring State Park
992 Park Road
Anatone, WA
509-256-3332
This state park has a variety of year round land and water recreational activities. Dogs of all sizes are allowed at no additional fee. Dogs

may not be left unattended, and they must be leashed and cleaned up after. Dogs are allowed on the trails, but they are not allowed at any public swim areas. The camping and tent areas also allow dogs. There is a dog walk area at the campground. There are no electric or water hookups at the campground. Multiple dogs may be allowed.

Ashford

Mount Rainier National Park
Tahoma Woods Star Route (H706)
Ashford, WA
360-569-2211
This park is home to Mount Rainier, an active volcano encrusted by ice, and at 14,411 feet it towers 8,000 feet above the surrounding Cascades peaks and creates it own weather. There is a variety of land and water recreation. Dogs are allowed at no additional fee. Dogs must be leashed and cleaned up after. Dogs are not allowed in any of the buildings, or on any of the trails except for the Pacific Coast Trail. Dogs must otherwise stay on the roads and parking lots of the camp areas. This campground is closed during the off-season. The camping and tent areas also allow dogs. There is a dog walk area at the campground. There are no electric or water hookups at the campground. Multiple dogs may be allowed.

Bagley

Jellystone Park
11354 County H X
Bagley, WA
608-996-2201
Dogs of all sizes are allowed. There are no additional pet fees. Dogs must be leashed and cleaned up after. This RV park is closed during the off-season. The camping and tent areas also allow dogs. There is a dog walk area at the campground. Multiple dogs may be allowed.

Wyalusing State Park
13081 State Park lane
Bagley, WA
608-996-2261
This park holds historical significance as one of Wisconsin's oldest parks. It has over 24 miles of trails, including a canoe trail, water and land recreation, an interpretive center, and more. Dogs are allowed

at no additional fee. Dogs may not be left unattended, and they must be leashed and cleaned up after. Dogs are not allowed in the picnic areas, in buildings, on cross-country ski trails once there is snow, or on the Sugar Maple Nature trail. Dogs are allowed on the hiking trails, and they may be off lead when out of the camp area if there is voice control. The camping and tent areas also allow dogs. There is a dog walk area at the campground. There are no water hookups at the campground. Multiple dogs may be allowed.

Bainbridge Island

Fay Bainbridge State Park
15446 Sunrise Drive NE
Bainbridge Island, WA
206-842-3931
This 17 acre marine camping park, with 1,420 feet of saltwater shoreline, offers excellent scenery and a host of water and land recreation. Dogs of all sizes are allowed at no additional fee. Dogs may not be left unattended, and they must be leashed and cleaned up after. Dogs are not allowed in park buildings, however they are allowed on the trails. The camping and tent areas also allow dogs. There is a dog walk area at the campground. Multiple dogs may be allowed.

Bay Center

Bay Center/Willapa Bay KOA
457 Bay Center Road
Bay Center, WA
360-875-6344
Dogs of all sizes are allowed. There are no additional pet fees. Dogs may not be left unattended outside, must be quiet, leashed, and cleaned up after. Dogs are met at the door with doggy treats. Dogs are not allowed on the playground, at the cabins, or in the buildings. There are some breed restrictions. This RV park is closed during the off-season. The camping and tent areas also allow dogs. There is a dog walk area at the campground. There are special amenities given to dogs at this campground. Multiple dogs may be allowed.

Bellingham

Bellingham RV Park
3939 Bennett Drive
Bellingham, WA

360-752-1224
Dogs of all sizes are allowed. There are no additional pet fees. Dogs must be leashed and cleaned up after. There are some breed restrictions. The camping and tent areas also allow dogs. There is a dog walk area at the campground. Multiple dogs may be allowed.

Larrabee State Park
245 Chuckanut Drive
Bellingham, WA
360-676-2093
This year round recreational park features 8,100 feet of saltwater shoreline, 2 freshwater lakes, and many miles of trails to explore. The I-5 route is suggested for larger RVs. Dogs of all sizes are allowed at no additional fee. Dogs may not be left unattended, and they must be leashed and cleaned up after. Dogs are allowed on the trails, but not in any buildings. The camping and tent areas also allow dogs. There is a dog walk area at the campground. Multiple dogs may be allowed.

Blaine

Birch Bay State Park
5105 Helwig
Blaine, WA
360-371-2800
Year around recreation is offered at this park. There are 194 acres with over 8,200 feet of saltwater shoreline, a rich archeological history, miles of trails, and a variety of land and water activities. Dogs of all sizes are allowed at no additional fee. Dogs may not be left unattended at any time, they must be on no more than a 6 foot leash, and be cleaned up after. Dogs are allowed on the trails, but they are not allowed on the beach. The camping and tent areas also allow dogs. There is a dog walk area at the campground. Multiple dogs may be allowed.

Bothell

Lake Pleasant RV Park
24025 Bothell Everett H SE
Bothell, WA
425-487-1785
Dogs of all sizes are allowed. There are no additional pet fees. Dogs must be leashed and cleaned up after. There are some breed restrictions. There is a dog walk area at the campground. 2 dogs may be allowed.

Bremerton

Illahee State Park
3540 Bahia Vista
Bremerton, WA
360-478-6460
This park is a marine camping park with almost 1800 feet of saltwater frontage. There is only 1 site that has hook-ups. Dogs of all sizes are allowed. There are no additional pet fees. Dogs may not be left unattended, and they must be leashed and cleaned up after. Dogs are allowed on the trails, but not in any buildings. The camping and tent areas also allow dogs. There is a dog walk area at the campground. There are no electric or water hookups at the campground. Multiple dogs may be allowed.

Burlington

Burlington/Anacortes KOA
6397 N Green Road
Burlington, WA
360-724-5511
Dogs of all sizes are allowed. There are no additional pet fees. Dogs must be well behaved, quiet, be on no more than a 6 foot leash, and be cleaned up after. Dogs may not be left unattended at any time and can not be on the beds in the cabins. The camping and tent areas also allow dogs. There is a dog walk area at the campground. Dogs are allowed in the camping cabins. Multiple dogs may be allowed.

Castle Rock

Seaquest State Park
Spirit Lake H
Castle Rock, WA
206-274-8633
There are 475 acres at this year round recreational park with 8 miles of hiking trails, over a mile of lake shoreline, and a variety of activities. Dogs of all sizes are allowed at no additional fee. Dogs may not be left unattended at any time, they must be on no more than a 6 foot leash, and be cleaned up after. Dogs are allowed on the trails. The camping and tent areas also allow dogs. There is a dog walk area at the campground.

Chehalis

Chehalis/H 12 KOA
118 h 12

Chehalis, WA
360-262-9220
Dogs of all sizes are allowed. There are no additional pet fees. Dogs may not be left unattended, must be leashed, and cleaned up after. The camping and tent areas also allow dogs. There is a dog walk area at the campground. Dogs are allowed in the camping cabins. 2 dogs may be allowed.

Cheney

Klinks Williams Lake Resort
18617 Williams Lake Road
Cheney, WA
509-235-2391
Dogs of all sizes are allowed. There are no additional pet fees. Dogs must be friendly, well behaved, leashed, and cleaned up after. Dogs are not allowed at the beach. There are some breed restrictions. This RV park is closed during the off-season. The camping and tent areas also allow dogs. There is a dog walk area at the campground. 2 dogs may be allowed.

Clarkston

Granite Lake RV Resort
306 Granite Lake Drive
Clarkston, WA
509-751-1635
Dogs of all sizes are allowed. There is no fee for one dog. If you have a 2nd dog there is an additional fee of $1 per day. Dogs may not be left unattended, and if needed, there is a dog sitter on site. Dogs may walk along the river, and they must be leashed and cleaned up after. There are some breed restrictions. There is a dog walk area at the campground. 2 dogs may be allowed.

Colville

Colville National Forest
765 Main (Forest Supervisor's Office)
Colville, WA
509-684-7000
Dogs of all sizes are allowed. There are no additional pet fees. Dogs may not be left unattended, and they must be leashed and cleaned up after. There are some beaches that dogs are allowed on, but they are not allowed at any of the public swim areas. Dogs are allowed on the trails unless otherwise marked. This campground is closed during the off-season. The camping and tent areas

also allow dogs. There is a dog walk area at the campground. There are no electric or water hookups at the campground. Multiple dogs may be allowed.

Concrete

Concrete/Grandy Creek KOA
7370 Russell Road
Concrete, WA
360-826-3554
Dogs of all sizes are allowed. There are no additional pet fees. Dogs may not be left unattended at any time, must be leashed, and cleaned up after. There are some breed restrictions. This RV park is closed during the off-season. The camping and tent areas also allow dogs. There is a dog walk area at the campground. Dogs are allowed in the camping cabins. Multiple dogs may be allowed.

Cougar

Lone Fir Motel and RV Resort
16806 Lewis River Road
Cougar, WA
360-238-5210
Dogs of all sizes and numbers are allowed, and there are no additional pet fees for the tent and RV sites. There is a $10 per night per pet additional fee for the motel and only 2 dogs are allowed per room. Dogs must be quiet, well behaved, leashed, and cleaned up after. The camping and tent areas also allow dogs. There is a dog walk area at the campground. Dogs are allowed in the camping cabins. Multiple dogs may be allowed.

Coulee City

Sun Lakes Park Resort
34228 Park Lake Road NE
Coulee City, WA
509-632-5291
Dogs of all sizes are allowed. There is a $7 per night per pet additional fee for the cabins, tent or RV sites. Dogs may not be left unattended, are not allowed at the swim beach, and must be leashed and cleaned up after. There is an area where the dogs are also allowed to go swim. This RV park is closed during the off-season. The camping and tent areas also allow dogs. There is a dog walk area at the campground. Dogs are allowed in the camping cabins. Multiple dogs may be allowed.

Sun Lakes State Park
H 17, 2 miles W of Coulee City
Coulee City, WA
509-632-5583
This park is home to one of the great geological wonders of North America; a stark cliff is the only remnant of a once grand waterfall 10 times the size of Niagara Falls. There is also more than 4,000 acres with over 73,000 feet of shoreline to explore. Dogs of all sizes are allowed at no additional fee. Dogs may not be left unattended at any time, they must be on no more than a 6 foot leash, and be cleaned up after. Dogs are allowed on the trails, but not at any public swim areas or buildings. This campground is closed during the off-season. The camping and tent areas also allow dogs. There is a dog walk area at the campground. There are no water hookups at the campground. Multiple dogs may be allowed.

Coulee Dam

Lake Roosevelt National Recreation area
Spring Canyon Road
Coulee Dam, WA
509-633-9441
This year round recreational area has 28 campgrounds around the lake, miles of trails, and a variety of fun activities. Dogs of all sizes are allowed at no additional fee. Dogs may not be left unattended, and they must be leashed and cleaned up after. Dogs are allowed on the trails, but not in any day use or public swim areas. The camping and tent areas also allow dogs. There is a dog walk area at the campground. There are no electric or water hookups at the campground. Multiple dogs may be allowed.

Coupeville

Fort Ebey State Park
400 Hill Valley Drive
Coupeville, WA
360-678-4636
Popular, historical, educational, recreational, and pre-historic, all describe this scenic park that offer interpretive programs and several miles of trails. Dogs of all sizes are allowed at no additional fee. Dogs may not be left unattended, and they must be leashed and cleaned up after. Dogs are allowed on the

trails. The camping and tent areas also allow dogs. There is a dog walk area at the campground. Multiple dogs may be allowed.

Electric City

Coulee Playland Resort
401 Coulee Blvd E (H 155)
Electric City, WA
509-633-2671
Dogs of all sizes are allowed. There are no additional pet fees. Dogs may not be left unattended outside, and they must be leashed and cleaned up after. This RV park is closed during the off-season. The camping and tent areas also allow dogs. There is a dog walk area at the campground. Multiple dogs may be allowed.

Steamboat Rock State Park
Banks Lake
Electric City, WA
509-633-1304
This park with more than 3,500 acres along Banks Lake is an oasis in desert surroundings, and a variety of activities and recreation are offered. Dogs of all sizes are allowed at no additional fee. Dogs may not be left unattended, and they must be leashed and cleaned up after. Dogs are not allowed in public swim areas or in buildings. Dogs are allowed on the trails. The camping and tent areas also allow dogs. There is a dog walk area at the campground. Multiple dogs may be allowed.

Ellensburg

Ellensburg KOA
32 Thorp H S
Ellensburg, WA
509-925-9319
Dogs of all sizes are allowed. There are no additional pet fees. Dogs may not be left unattended, must be leashed, and cleaned up after. Dogs are allowed at the river, but the river is very swift. The camping and tent areas also allow dogs. There is a dog walk area at the campground. Multiple dogs may be allowed.

Ephrata

Oasis RV Park and Golf
2541 Basin Street SW
Ephrata, WA
509-754-5102
Dogs of all sizes are allowed. There are no additional pet fees. Dogs may

not be left unattended, must be well behaved, leashed, and cleaned up after. This RV park is closed during the off-season. There is a dog walk area at the campground. Multiple dogs may be allowed.

Everett

Lakeside Park
12321 H 99S
Everett, WA
425-347-2970
Dogs of all sizes are allowed. There are no additional pet fees. Dogs may not be left unattended at any time, must be leashed, and cleaned up after. The camping and tent areas also allow dogs. There is a dog walk area at the campground. 2 dogs may be allowed.

Maple Grove RV Resort
12417 H 99
Everett, WA
425-423-9608
Dogs of all sizes are allowed. There are no additional pet fees. Dogs may not be tied up outside alone, and they must be leashed and cleaned up after. There is a dog walk area at the campground. 2 dogs may be allowed.

Federal Way

Dash Point State Park
5700 SW Dash Point Road
Federal Way, WA
253-661-4955
This park has 11 miles of trails and 3,301 feet of saltwater shoreline on Puget Sound. Dogs of all sizes are allowed. There are no additional pet fees. Dogs may not be left unattended, they must be on no more than an 8 foot leash, and be cleaned up after. Dogs are allowed on the trails and beach but not in buildings. This campground is closed during the off-season. The camping and tent areas also allow dogs. There is a dog walk area at the campground. Multiple dogs may be allowed.

Dash Point State Park
5700 SW Dash Point Road
Federal Way, WA
253-661-4955
This 398-acre park, with 3,301 feet of saltwater shoreline on the Puget Sound, offers an amphitheater, interpretive programs, nature study, and a variety of land and water

recreation. Dogs of all sizes are allowed at no additional fee. Dogs may not be left unattended, and they must be on no more than an 8 foot leash, and be cleaned up after. Dogs are not allowed in buildings, but they are allowed on the trails unless otherwise marked. The camping and tent areas also allow dogs. There is a dog walk area at the campground. Multiple dogs may be allowed.

Ferndale

The Cedars RV Resort
6335 Portal Way
Ferndale, WA
360-384-2622
Dogs of all sizes are allowed. There is a $2 per night per pet additional fee. Dogs must be leashed and cleaned up after, and they are not allowed at the playground or in the buildings. The camping and tent areas also allow dogs. There is a dog walk area at the campground. Multiple dogs may be allowed.

Gig Harbor

Gig Harbor RV Resort
9515 Burnham Drive NW
Gig Harbor, WA
253-858-8138
Dogs of all sizes are allowed. There are no additional pet fees. Dogs may not be left outside alone, must be leashed at all times, and cleaned up after. The camping and tent areas also allow dogs. There is a dog walk area at the campground. Multiple dogs may be allowed.

Ilwaco

Ilwaco/Long Beach KOA
1509 H 101
Ilwaco, WA
360-642-3292
Dogs of all sizes are allowed. There are no additional pet fees. Dogs must be leashed and cleaned up after. There is an off leash fenced in area for dogs also. There are some breed restrictions. This RV park is closed during the off-season. The camping and tent areas also allow dogs. There is a dog walk area at the campground. 2 dogs may be allowed.

Kent

Seattle/Tacoma KOA
5801 S 212th Street
Kent, WA
253-872-8652
Dogs of all sizes are allowed. There are no additional pet fees. Dogs must have current shot records, be leashed, and cleaned up after. Dogs may be left in your RV if they will be quiet and comfortable. There are some breed restrictions. The camping and tent areas also allow dogs. There is a dog walk area at the campground. Multiple dogs may be allowed.

LaPush

Lonesome Creek RV Park
490 Ocean Drive
LaPush, WA
360-374-4338
Dogs of all sizes are allowed. There are no additional pet fees. Dogs must be leashed and cleaned up after. The camping and tent areas also allow dogs. There is a dog walk area at the campground.

Leavenworth

Lake Wenatchee State Park
21588A H 207
Leavenworth, WA
509-662-0420
This 489 acre park along a glacier fed lake offers an amphitheater, interpretive programs, nature study, a variety of trails, and various land and water activities and recreation. Dogs of all sizes are allowed at no additional fee. Dogs may not be left unattended, and they must be leashed and cleaned up after. Dogs are not allowed in buildings, but they are allowed on the trails. The camping and tent areas also allow dogs. There is a dog walk area at the campground. Multiple dogs may be allowed.

Leavenworth/Wenatchee KOA
11401 Riverbend Drive
Leavenworth, WA
509-548-7709
Dogs of all sizes are allowed. There are no additional pet fees. Dogs must be leashed and cleaned up after. Dogs may be left unattended if they are quiet and well behaved. There are some breed restrictions. This RV park is closed during the off-season. The camping and tent areas also allow dogs. There is a dog walk area at the campground. Multiple dogs may be allowed.

Long Beach

Andersen's RV Park on the Ocean
1400 138th Street (H 103)
Long Beach, WA
800-645-6795
Dogs of all sizes are allowed. There are no additional pet fees. Dogs may not be left unattended unless they will be very quiet and well behaved. Dogs must be leashed and cleaned up after. Dogs may be off lead along the beach only if they will respond to voice command. This is an RV only park. There is a dog walk area at the campground. Multiple dogs may be allowed.

Lopez Island

Spencer Spit State Park
521A Baker View Road
Lopez Island, WA
360-468-2251
There is a 45 minute ferry ride from Anacordes to this park, and dogs must remain on the car deck during the crossing. This is a marine and camping park along the Strait of Juan de Fuca, and beachcoming and nature study are favorites here. Pets must be on a leash and under physical control at all times. Dogs are not permitted on designated swimming beaches. Dogs are allowed on the trails. The camping and tent areas also allow dogs. There is a dog walk area at the campground. There are no electric or water hookups at the campground. 2 dogs may be allowed.

Lynden

Lynden/Bellingham KOA
8717 Line Road
Lynden, WA
360-354-4772
Dogs of all sizes are allowed. There are no additional pet fees. Dogs must be well behaved, leashed, and cleaned up after. The camping and tent areas also allow dogs. There is a dog walk area at the campground. Multiple dogs may be allowed.

Lynnwood

Twin Cedars RV Park
17826 H 99N
Lynnwood, WA
425-742-5540
Dogs of all sizes are allowed. There are no additional pet fees. Dogs may not be left unattended, must be

leashed, and cleaned up after. Dogs may be off leash at the dog run if they are well behaved. There is a dog walk area at the campground. Multiple dogs may be allowed.

Mead

Mount Spokane State Park
26107 Mount Spokane Park Drive
Mead, WA
509-238-4258
This almost 14,000 acre park offers over one hundred miles of hiking trails, interpretive activities and a variety of year round recreation. Dogs of all sizes are allowed at no additional fee. Dogs may not be left unattended, they must be on no more than an 8 foot leash, and be cleaned up after. Dogs are not allowed in building, however, they are allowed on the trails. This campground is closed during the off-season. The camping and tent areas also allow dogs. There is a dog walk area at the campground. There are no electric or water hookups at the campground. Multiple dogs may be allowed.

Montesano

Lake Sylvia State Park
1812 Lake Sylvia Road
Montesano, WA
360-249-3621
This 233-acre camping park with 15,000 feet of freshwater shoreline is rich with logging lore and history. It offers 5 miles of hiking trails, and a variety of land and water recreation. Dogs of all sizes are allowed at no additional fee. Dogs may not be left unattended, and they must be quiet, well behaved, be on no more than an 8 foot leash, and be cleaned up after. Dogs are not allowed in public swim areas, buildings, or in the Environmental Learning Center area. This campground is closed during the off-season. The camping and tent areas also allow dogs. There is a dog walk area at the campground. There are no electric or water hookups at the campground. Multiple dogs may be allowed.

Mount Vernon

Riverbend RV Park
305 W Stewart Road
Mount Vernon, WA

360-428-4044
Dogs up to 25 pounds are allowed. There are no additional pet fees. Dogs must be leashed and cleaned up after. There are some breed restrictions. The camping and tent areas also allow dogs. There is a dog walk area at the campground. 2 dogs may be allowed.

Mountlake Terrace

Mt. Baker-Snoqualmie National Forest
21905 64th Avenue W
Mountlake Terrace, WA
425-775-9702
Snoqualmie National Forest extends more than 140 miles along the west side of the Cascade Mountains and offers a wide variety of recreational activities year round. Dogs of all sizes are allowed at no additional fee. Dogs may not be left unattended, and they must be leashed and cleaned up after. Dogs are allowed on the trails, but not in public swim areas. This campground is closed during the off-season. The camping and tent areas also allow dogs. There is a dog walk area at the campground. There are no electric or water hookups at the campground. Multiple dogs may be allowed.

Nine Mile Falls

Riverside State Park
Charles Road
Nine Mile Falls, WA
509-465-5064
This 10,000-acre park along the Spokane Rivers offers interpretive centers, 55 miles of scenic hiking trails, opportunities for nature study, and a variety of land and water recreation. Dogs of all sizes are allowed at no additional fee. Dogs may not be left unattended, and they must be leashed at all times, and cleaned up after. Dogs are not allowed in the natural heritage area or in the Spokane River. Dogs are allowed on the trails. The camping and tent areas also allow dogs. There is a dog walk area at the campground. Multiple dogs may be allowed.

Nordland

Fort Flager State Park
10541 Flagler Road
Nordland, WA
360-385-1259

This historic, 784-acre marine park, sits atop a high bluff overlooking the Puget Sound, and offers a museum, interpretive programs, several miles of trails, and land and water activities. Dogs are allowed at no additional fee. Dogs may not be left unattended, and they must be leashed and cleaned up after. Dogs are not allowed in any of the buildings, but they are allowed on the trails. The camping and tent areas also allow dogs. There is a dog walk area at the campground. Multiple dogs may be allowed.

Oak Harbor

North Whidbey RV Park
565 W Coronet Bay Road
Oak Harbor, WA
360-675-9597
Dogs of all sizes are allowed. There are no additional pet fees. Dogs may not be left unattended, or tied up outside alone. Dogs must be leashed and cleaned up after. There is a dog walk area at the campground. Multiple dogs may be allowed.

Ocean Park

Ocean Park Resort
25904 R Street
Ocean Park, WA
360-665-4585
Dogs of all sizes and numbers are allowed, and there are no additional pet fees. There is a $7 per night per pet additional fee for the motel, and only 2 dogs are allowed per room. Dogs must be leashed and cleaned up after. There are some breed restrictions. The camping and tent areas also allow dogs. There is a dog walk area at the campground. Multiple dogs may be allowed.

Okanogan

Okanogan National Forest
1240 South Second Avenue
Okanogan, WA
509-826-3275
This forest of a million and a half acres has a variety of water and land recreation year round. Dogs are allowed at no additional fee. Dogs may not be left unattended, and they must be leashed and cleaned up after. Dogs are not allowed in the back country, and on many of the trails. Dogs must remain on paved areas or on marked trails. This campground is closed during the off-

season. The camping and tent areas also allow dogs. There is a dog walk area at the campground. There are no electric or water hookups at the campground. Multiple dogs may be allowed.

Olympia

Olympic National Forest
1835 Black Lk Blvd SW
Olympia, WA
360-956-23300
This park is a unique geographic province in that it contains 5 different major landscapes, and is home to an astounding diversity of plants, animals, and recreational pursuits. The campground at Round Creek is the only camp area that stays open year round. Dogs of all sizes are allowed at no additional fee. Dogs may not be left unattended, and they must be leashed and cleaned up after. Dogs are allowed on the trails. The camping and tent areas also allow dogs. There is a dog walk area at the campground. Dogs are allowed in the camping cabins. There are no electric or water hookups at the campground. Multiple dogs may be allowed.

Otis Orchards

Spokane KOA
N 3025 Barker Road
Otis Orchards, WA
509-924-4722
Dogs of all sizes are allowed. There are no additional pet fees. Dogs may not be left unattended, can be on no more than a 6 foot leash, and must be cleaned up after. There are some breed restrictions. The camping and tent areas also allow dogs. There is a dog walk area at the campground. Dogs are allowed in the camping cabins. Multiple dogs may be allowed.

Pacific Beach

Pacific Beach State Park
On H 109
Pacific Beach, WA
360-276-4297
This 10 acre camping park, with 2,300 feet of ocean shoreline, offers a variety of land and water recreation. Dogs of all sizes are allowed at no additional fee. Dogs may not be left unattended, and they must be quiet, well behaved,

be on no more than an 8 foot leash, and be cleaned up after. Dogs are not allowed in public swim areas or buildings. Dogs are allowed on the trails. This campground is closed during the off-season. The camping and tent areas also allow dogs. There is a dog walk area at the campground. Multiple dogs may be allowed.

Pasco

Sandy Heights RV Park
8801 St Thomas Drive
Pasco, WA
877-894-1357
Dogs of all sizes are allowed. There are no additional pet fees. Dogs must be leashed and cleaned up after. There are some breed restrictions. There is a dog walk area at the campground. 2 dogs may be allowed.

Pendleton

Mountain View RV Park
1375 SE 3rd Street
Pendleton, WA
866-302-3311
Dogs of all sizes are allowed. There are no additional pet fees. Dogs must be leashed and cleaned up after. There are some breed restrictions. The camping and tent areas also allow dogs. There is a dog walk area at the campground. 2 dogs may be allowed.

Port Angeles

Log Cabin Resort
3183E Beach Road
Port Angeles, WA
360-928-3325
This resort style park offers spectacular scenery, a variety of accommodations as well as recreational pursuits. Dogs of all sizes are allowed at no additional fee for RV sites, however there is a $10 (plus tax)per night per pet additional fee for the rustic cabins. Dogs may not be left unattended, and they must be leashed and cleaned up after. Dogs are not allowed on the trails in the Olympic National Forest area. There is a dog walk area at the campground. Dogs are allowed in the camping cabins. Multiple dogs may be allowed.

Olympia National Park
600 East Park Avenue

Port Angeles, WA
360-452-4501
From rainforest to glacier capped mountains, this forest's diverse and impressive eco-system is home to 8 plants and 15 animals that are not found anywhere else on earth. It also provides an abundant variety of year round recreational pursuits. Dogs of all sizes are allowed at no additional fee. Dogs may not be left unattended, and they must be leashed and cleaned up after. Dogs are allowed in the camp areas and the parking lot at Hurricane Ridge; dogs are not allowed on the trails. The camping and tent areas also allow dogs. There is a dog walk area at the campground. There are no electric or water hookups at the campground. Multiple dogs may be allowed.

Port Angeles/Swquim KOA
80 O'Brien Road
Port Angeles, WA
360-457-5916
Dogs of all sizes are allowed. There are no additional pet fees. Dogs may not be left unattended, must be on no more than a 6 foot leash, and cleaned up after. There are some breed restrictions. This RV park is closed during the off-season. The camping and tent areas also allow dogs. There is a dog walk area at the campground. 2 dogs may be allowed.

Port Townsend

Point Hudson Resort Marina and RV Park
103 Hudson
Port Townsend, WA
360-385-2828
Dogs of all sizes are allowed. There are no additional pet fees. Dogs must be leashed and cleaned up after. Dogs are allowed to go to the beach, and if you bring them in the office they usually have doggy treats on hand. There is a dog walk area at the campground. There are special amenities given to dogs at this campground. Multiple dogs may be allowed.

Prosser

Wine Country RV Park
330 Merlot Drive
Prosser, WA
800-726-4969
Dogs of all sizes are allowed. There are no additional pet fees. Dogs

must be quiet, well behaved, leashed, and cleaned up after. No stakes are allowed put in the ground to tie your pet to. Dogs are allowed to run in the field across the street unleashed as long as there is control by the owner. The camping and tent areas also allow dogs. There is a dog walk area at the campground. Multiple dogs may be allowed.

Richland

Horn Rapids RV Resort
2640 Kings Gate Way
Richland, WA
509-375-9913
Dogs of all sizes are allowed. There are no additional pet fees. Dogs must be leashed and cleaned up after. There is a dog run and a dog bathing area on site. There is a dog walk area at the campground. Multiple dogs may be allowed.

Rochester

Outback RV Park
19100 Huntington
Rochester, WA
360-273-0585
Dogs of all sizes are allowed. There are no additional pet fees. Dogs may not be left unattended at any time, or tied up outside alone. Dogs must be leashed and cleaned up after. There is a dog walk area at the campground. 2 dogs may be allowed.

San Juan Island

Lakedale Resort
4313 Roche Harbor Road
Friday Harbor, WA
360-378-2350
Dogs of all sizes are allowed. There is a $2 per night per pet additional fee for tent or RV sites. There is a $20 per night per pet additional fee for the lodge, however, depending on size and number, the fee for the lodge is flexible. Dogs may not be left unattended, and they must be quiet, well behaved, leashed, and cleaned up after. A ferry from Anacortes off I 5, or other ferries in the area will transport your pet on the car deck only. The camping and tent areas also allow dogs. There is a dog walk area at the campground. Dogs are allowed in the camping cabins. Multiple dogs may be allowed.

Seattle

Blue Sky RV Park
9002 302nd Avenue SE
Seattle, WA
425-222-7910
Dogs of all sizes are allowed. There are no additional pet fees. Dogs may not be left tied up outside alone, and must be leashed and cleaned up after. There is a dog walk area at the campground. Multiple dogs may be allowed.

Seattle Area

Trailer Inns RV Park
15531SE 37th
Bellevue, WA
425-747-9181
Dogs up to 25 pounds are allowed. There are no additional pet fees. Dogs must be leashed and cleaned up after. There is a dog walk area at the campground. 2 dogs may be allowed.

Issaquah Highlands
10610 Renton Issaquah Road
Issaquah, WA
425-392-2351
Dogs of all sizes are allowed. There are no additional pet fees. Dogs must be leashed and cleaned up after. The camping and tent areas also allow dogs. There is a dog walk area at the campground. 2 dogs may be allowed.

Eagle Tree RV Park
16280 H 305
Poulsbo, WA
360-598-5988
Dogs of all sizes are allowed. There are no additional pet fees. Dogs may not be tied up outside alone, must be leashed, and cleaned up after. There are some breed restrictions. There is a dog walk area at the campground. Multiple dogs may be allowed.

Sedro-Wooley

North Cascades National Park
810 State Route 20
Sedro-Wooley, WA
360-856-5700
Know as the North American Alps, the North Cascades National Park is home to an astounding diversity of plants and animals, and provides a variety of recreational pursuits. Dogs of all sizes are allowed at no additional fee. Dogs may not be left unattended, and they must be

leashed and cleaned up after. Dogs are allowed at the Ross Lake National Recreation area, and on close-in trails. Dogs are not allowed in the back country. This campground is closed during the off-season. The camping and tent areas also allow dogs. There is a dog walk area at the campground. There are no electric or water hookups at the campground. Multiple dogs may be allowed.

Sequim

Rainbows End RV Park
261831 H 101
Sequim, WA
360-683-3863
Dogs of all sizes are allowed. There are no additional pet fees. Dogs may not be left unattended, must be leashed, and cleaned up after. There is, however, a large fenced in doggy play yard where they can run off leash. The camping and tent areas also allow dogs. There is a dog walk area at the campground. 2 dogs may be allowed.

Skamania

Beacon Rock State Park
34841 h 14
Skamania, WA
360-427-8265
Beacon Rock, the core of an ancient volcano, provides technical rock climbing, and the more than 20 miles of trails offers some outstanding panoramic views at this park. Dogs of all sizes are allowed at no additional fee. Dogs may not be left unattended, and they must be leashed and cleaned up after. Dogs are not allowed in any park buildings, but they are allowed on the trails. This campground is closed during the off-season. The camping and tent areas also allow dogs. There is a dog walk area at the campground. There are no electric or water hookups at the campground. Multiple dogs may be allowed.

Spokane

Alderwood RV Resort
14007 N Newport H
Spokane, WA
509-467-5320
Dogs of all sizes are allowed. There are no additional pet fees. Dogs may not be left outside alone, and outside pens for pets are not allowed. Dogs

must be leashed and cleaned up after. The camping and tent areas also allow dogs. There is a dog walk area at the campground. Multiple dogs may be allowed.

Spokane Valley

Trailer Inns RV Park
6021 E 4th
Spokane Valley, WA
509-535-1811
Dogs of all sizes are allowed. There are no additional pet fees for up to 2 dogs, and there is no deposit unless you stay by the month. If there are more than 2 dogs, the fee is $3 per night per pet. Dogs may not be left unattended, must be leashed, and cleaned up after. There is a dog walk area at the campground. Multiple dogs may be allowed.

Stanwood

Wenberg State Park
15430 E Lake Goodwin Road
Stanwood, WA
360-652-7417
This 46 acre camping park, with 1,140 feet of freshwater shoreline, offers great fishing and a variety of land and water recreation. Dogs of all sizes are allowed at no additional fee. Dogs may not be left unattended, and they must be leashed at all times, and cleaned up after. Dogs are not allowed in public swim areas or in buildings. The camping and tent areas also allow dogs. There is a dog walk area at the campground. Multiple dogs may be allowed.

Toppenish

Yakama Nation RV Resort
280 Buster Road
Toppenish, WA
509-865-2000
Dogs of all sizes are allowed. There are no additional pet fees. Dogs must be leashed and cleaned up after. In addition to tent and RV sites, they have teepee sites, and dogs are allowed there also. There are some breed restrictions. The camping and tent areas also allow dogs. There is a dog walk area at the campground. Multiple dogs may be allowed.

Vancouver

Gifford Pinchot National Forest
10600 N.E. 51st Circle
Vancouver, WA
360-891-5000
There are 67 campgrounds in this forest, and it is also home to the Mount St. Helens National Volcanic Monument. Dogs are not allowed out of the car at the monument. Dogs of all sizes are allowed, and there are no additional pet fees. Dogs may not be left unattended, and they must be quiet, leashed, and cleaned up after. Dogs must be walked in designated areas. This campground is closed during the off-season. The camping and tent areas also allow dogs. There is a dog walk area at the campground. There are no electric or water hookups at the campground. Multiple dogs may be allowed.

Vancouver RV Park
7603 NE 13th Avenue
Vancouver, WA
360-695-1158
Dogs of all sizes are allowed. There are no additional pet fees. Dogs may not be left unattended or tied up alone outside. Dogs must be quiet, well behaved, leashed, and cleaned up after. There are some breed restrictions. The camping and tent areas also allow dogs. There is a dog walk area at the campground. 2 dogs may be allowed.

Walla Walla

Fairway RV Resort
50 W George Street (entrance Burns St)
Walla Walla, WA
509-525-8282
Dogs of all sizes are allowed. There are no additional pet fees for 2 dogs. If there are more than 2 dogs, then the fee is $1 per night per pet additional. Dogs may not be left unattended or staked outside alone, they must be leashed, and cleaned up after. The camping and tent areas also allow dogs. There is a dog walk area at the campground. Multiple dogs may be allowed.

Wenatchee

Wenatchee National Forest
215 Melody Lane (forest HQ)
Wenatchee, WA
509-664-9200
This forest is divided into 6 ranger districts and covers 2.2 million acres with a variety of trails totaling about 2,500 miles. Dogs of all sizes are

allowed at no additional fee. Dogs may not be left unattended, and they must be leashed and cleaned up after in camp areas. Dogs are allowed on the trails, but they are not allowed in public swim areas or any buildings. The camping and tent areas also allow dogs. There is a dog walk area at the campground. There are no electric or water hookups at the campground. Multiple dogs may be allowed.

Westport

Totem RV Park
2421 N Nyhus
Westport, WA
360-268-0025
Dogs of all sizes are allowed. There are no additional pet fees. Dogs may not be left unattended, and they must be quiet, well behaved, leashed, and cleaned up after. If you would like to view this area from their tower, the site is westportcam.com. The camping and tent areas also allow dogs. There is a dog walk area at the campground. Multiple dogs may be allowed.

White Salmon

Bridge RV Park & Campground
65271 H 14
White Salmon, WA
509-493-1111
Dogs of all sizes are allowed. There is a $1 per night per pet additional fee. Dogs may not be left unattended, and they must be quiet, well behaved, leashed, and cleaned up after. The camping and tent areas also allow dogs. There is a dog walk area at the campground. Multiple dogs may be allowed.

Winthrop

Winthrop/N Cascades National Park KOA
1114 H 20
Winthrop, WA
509-996-2258
Dogs of all sizes are allowed. There are no additional pet fees. Dogs must be leashed and cleaned up after. Dogs may be left unattended if they are quiet and well behaved, and you can also tie your pet by the office. This RV park is closed during the off-season. The camping and tent areas also allow dogs. There is a dog walk area at the campground. Dogs are allowed in the camping

cabins. Multiple dogs may be allowed.

Woodland

Columbia Riverfront RV Park
1881 Pike Road
Woodland, WA
360-225-8051
Dogs of all sizes are allowed. There are no additional pet fees for up to 2 pets. If there are more than 3 dogs, then the fee is an additional $1 per night per pet. Dogs must be leashed and cleaned up after, and they are allowed at the beach. There are some breed restrictions. There is a dog walk area at the campground. 2 dogs may be allowed.

Yakima

Trailer Inns RV Park
1610 N 1st Street
Yakima, WA
509-452-9561
Dogs of all sizes are allowed. There are no additional pet fees. Dogs may not be left unattended, or tied up outside alone. Dogs must be leashed and cleaned up after. The camping and tent areas also allow dogs. There is a dog walk area at the campground. Multiple dogs may be allowed.

Yakima KOA
1500 Keys Road
Yakima, WA
509-248-5882
Dogs of all sizes are allowed. There are no additional pet fees. Dogs must be well behaved, leashed, and cleaned up after. There are some breed restrictions. The camping and tent areas also allow dogs. There is a dog walk area at the campground. Dogs are allowed in the camping cabins. 2 dogs may be allowed.

West Virginia Listings

Barboursville

Beech Fork State Park
5601 Longbranch Road
Barboursville, WV

304-528-5794
This park provides more than 3000 acres of recreational fun and nature study. Dogs of all sizes are allowed at no additional fee. Dogs may not be left unattended, and they must be well behaved, be on no more than a 10 foot leash, and cleaned up after. Dogs are not allowed in the pool area, but they are allowed on the trails. The camping and tent areas also allow dogs. There is a dog walk area at the campground. Multiple dogs may be allowed.

Bruceton Mills

Big Bear Lake Campground
Hazelton Big Bear Lake Road
Bruceton Mills, WV
304-379-4382
Dogs of all sizes are allowed. There are no additional pet fees. Dogs may not be left unattended, and they must be leashed and cleaned up after. This RV park is closed during the off-season. The camping and tent areas also allow dogs. There is a dog walk area at the campground. Dogs are allowed in the camping cabins. There are no water hookups at the campgrounds. Multiple dogs may be allowed.

Buckhannon

Audra State Park
Rt. 4, Box 564/County Road 11
Buckhannon, WV
304-457-1162
Audra State Park has a heavily wooded riverside campground that offers a variety of land and water recreation. Dogs of all sizes are allowed at no additional fee. Dogs may not be left unattended, and they must be on no more than a 6 foot leash, and be cleaned up after. Dogs are allowed on the trails unless otherwise marked. This campground is closed during the off-season. The camping and tent areas also allow dogs. There is a dog walk area at the campground. There are no electric or water hookups at the campground. Multiple dogs may be allowed.

Caldwell

Greenbrier State Forest
HC 30, Box 154; Harts Run Road
Caldwell, WV
304-536-1944
This heavily forested, mountainous park of 5,100 acres offers

magnificent views, a seasonal nature program, and a variety of land and water recreation. Dogs of all sizes are allowed at no additional fee. Dogs may not be left unattended, and they must be on no more than a 10 foot leash, and be cleaned up after in camp areas. Dogs are not allowed in the pool area, but they are allowed on the trails. This campground is closed during the off-season. The camping and tent areas also allow dogs. There is a dog walk area at the campground. There are no water hookups at the campground. Multiple dogs may be allowed.

Camp Creek

Camp Creek State Park
2390 Camp Creek Road
Camp Creek, WV
304-425-9481
This scenic mountain park offers a variety of trails, land and water recreation, and it is also adjacent to the Camp Creek State Forest. Dogs of all sizes are allowed at no additional fee. Dogs may not be left unattended, and they must be leashed and cleaned up after. Dogs are allowed on the trails. This campground is closed during the off-season. The camping and tent areas also allow dogs. There is a dog walk area at the campground. There are no water hookups at the campground. Multiple dogs may be allowed.

Charleston

Kanawha State Forest
Rt 2 Box 285
Charleston, WV
304-558-3500
This 9,300-acre forest is known for its diverse wildflower and bird populations in addition to being a popular picnic, biking and hiking destination. Dogs of all sizes are allowed at no additional fee. Dogs must be on lead in high use areas, and only off lead if they are well behaved, and under voice command. Dogs are allowed on the trails. This campground is closed during the off-season. The camping and tent areas also allow dogs. There is a dog walk area at the campground. Multiple dogs may be allowed.

Clifftop

Babcock State Park
HC 35, Box 150
Clifftop, WV
304-438-3004
This park offers over 4,000 acres of rugged beauty and a variety of recreational pursuits. Of special interest is the Glade Creek Grist Mill that actually provides cornmeal and buckwheat flours for purchase. Dogs of all sizes are allowed at no additional fee. Dogs may not be left unattended, and they must be leashed and cleaned up after. Dogs are not allowed in buildings, but they are allowed on the trails. This campground is closed during the off-season. The camping and tent areas also allow dogs. There is a dog walk area at the campground. There are no water hookups at the campground. Multiple dogs may be allowed.

Davis

Canaan Valley Resort Campground
32 Canaan Valley
Davis, WV
304-866-4121
Located in the Canaan Valley State Park, this campground allows pets. They offer full hookups and can accommodate RVs up to 50 feet. Camp sites are under $20 per day during the winter and $25 per day during the summer. They have discounts for seniors and AAA members. For an extra fee, the resort offers tennis courts, an exercise room and a sauna. This park also has 18 miles of hiking and mountain biking trails. Many of the trails are linked to other trails in the 1 million acre Monongahela National Forest. Pets must be on a 10 foot or less leash at all times including in the campground and on the state park trails.

Elkins

Jellystone Park
Route 33 E Faulkner Road
Elkins, WV
304-637-8898
Dogs of all sizes are allowed. There are no additional pet fees. Dogs must be quiet, leashed, and cleaned up after. This RV park is closed during the off-season. The camping and tent areas also allow dogs. There is a dog walk area at the campground. Dogs are allowed in the camping cabins. 2 dogs may

be allowed.

Monongahela National Forest
200 Sycamore Street
Elkins, WV
304-636-1800
This forest has 6 ranger districts, almost a million acres, and diverse ecosystems that support a large variety of plants, animals, and recreation. Dogs of all sizes are allowed at no additional fee. Dogs may not be left unattended, and they must be leashed and cleaned up after in the camp areas. Dogs are allowed on the trails. The camping and tent areas also allow dogs. There is a dog walk area at the campground. There are no water hookups at the campground. Multiple dogs may be allowed.

Revelle's River Resort
9 Faulkner Road
Elkins, WV
877-988-2267
Dogs of all sizes are allowed, and there are no additional pet fees for tent or RV sites. There is a $5 per night per pet additional fee plus a cash security deposit of $50 for the regular cabins, and the same daily fee plus a $100 deposit for the upscale cabins. Dogs must be leashed and cleaned up after. The camping and tent areas also allow dogs. There is a dog walk area at the campground. Dogs are allowed in the camping cabins. 2 dogs may be allowed.

Gap Mills

Moncove Lake State Park
HC 83, Box 73A
Gap Mills, WV
304-772-3450
This park of 250 acres has an adjoining 500 acre wildlife management area and a 144 acre lake in addition to a variety of land and water recreational pursuits. Dogs of all sizes are allowed at no additional fee. Dogs may not be left unattended, and they must be quiet, well behaved, leashed and cleaned up after. This campground is closed during the off-season. The camping and tent areas also allow dogs. There is a dog walk area at the campground. There are no water hookups at the campground. Multiple dogs may be allowed.

Glen Jean

Gauley River National Rec Area
Box 246, 104 Main Street
Glen Jean, WV
304-465-0508
This park has a wide variety of natural and cultural features, and offer various land and water recreation. There are also two free flowing rivers that pass through scenic gorges and valleys offering class V+ rapids. Dogs of all sizes are allowed at no additional fee. Dogs must be leashed at all times, and cleaned up after. Dogs may be left on site if they are well behaved, quiet, and left comfortable. The camping and tent areas also allow dogs. There is a dog walk area at the campground. There are no electric or water hookups at the campground. Multiple dogs may be allowed.

Glenville

Cedar Creek State Park
2947 Cedar Creek Road
Glenville, WV
304-462-7158
This park offers 2,483 lush acres of rolling hills, wide valleys, and a variety of recreational pursuits. Dogs of all sizes are allowed at no additional fee. Dogs may not be left unattended, and they must be quiet, well behaved, leashed and cleaned up after. Dogs are not allowed in buildings or at the pool, but they are allowed on the trails. This campground is closed during the off-season. The camping and tent areas also allow dogs. There is a dog walk area at the campground. Multiple dogs may be allowed.

Grafton

Tygart Lake State Park
Rt 1, Box 260
Grafton, WV
304-265-6144
Nestled in the foothills of the Allegheny Mountains, this 1,740-acre lake park offers programs on the park's natural and cultural history in addition to a variety of land and water recreation. Dogs of all sizes are allowed at no additional fee. Dogs may not be left unattended, and they must be leashed and cleaned up after. Dogs are allowed on the trails. This campground is closed during the off-season. The camping and tent areas also allow dogs. There is a dog walk area at the campground. Multiple dogs may be allowed.

Hacker Valley

Holly River State Park
P.O. Box 70
Hacker Valley, WV
304-493-6353
The heavily forested mountains surrounding this park of 8,000 acres give a feeling of solitude and privacy. There are quite a variety of recreational pursuits and more than 40 miles of hiking trails within the park. Dogs of all sizes are allowed at no additional fee. Dogs may not be left unattended, and they must be leashed and cleaned up after. Dogs are allowed on the trails unless otherwise marked. This campground is closed during the off-season. The camping and tent areas also allow dogs. There is a dog walk area at the campground. There are no water hookups at the campground. Multiple dogs may be allowed.

Harpers Ferry

Harpers Ferry/Washington DC NW KOA
343 Campground Road
Harpers Ferry, WV
304-535-6895
Dogs of all sizes are allowed. There is a $3 per pet per stay additional fee. Dogs must be leashed and cleaned up after. There are some breed restrictions. The camping and tent areas also allow dogs. There is a dog walk area at the campground. Dogs are allowed in the camping cabins. Multiple dogs may be allowed.

Hinton

Bluestone State Park
HC 78, Box 3; Bluestone State Park Road
Hinton, WV
304-466-2805
Bluestone State Park holds historical value, covers over 2,100 acres, is adjacent to the states' third largest lake, and hosts a variety of land and water recreation. Dogs of all sizes are allowed at no additional fee. Dogs may not be left unattended outside, and they must be quiet, well behaved, leashed and cleaned up after. Dogs are not allowed in the pool area, but they are allowed on the trails. This campground is closed during the off-season. The camping and tent areas also allow dogs. There is a dog walk area at the campground. There are no water hookups at the campground. Multiple dogs may be allowed.

Logan

Chief Logan State Park
General Delivery
Logan, WV
304-792-7125
This 4,000 acre park offers a modern restaurant, an outdoor amphitheater, a wildlife center, miles of trails, and a variety of recreational pursuits. Dogs of all sizes are allowed at no additional fee. Dogs must be well behaved, leashed, and cleaned up after. Dogs are not allowed at the wildlife exhibit or at the pool, but they are allowed on the trails. This campground is closed during the off-season. The camping and tent areas also allow dogs. There is a dog walk area at the campground. Multiple dogs may be allowed.

Milton

Fox Fire Resort
Route 2, Box 655
Milton, WV
304-743-5622
Dogs of all sizes are allowed. There are no additional pet fees. Dogs must be leashed and cleaned up after. This RV park is closed during the off-season. There are some breed restrictions. 2 dogs may be allowed.

Mullens

Twin Falls Resort State Park
Bear Hole Road
Mullens, WV
304-294-4000
Nestled in rugged mountains, Twin Falls Resort State Park is great for nature lovers and sports enthusiasts, offering 9 scenic trails, a championship golf course, and various recreation. Dogs of all sizes are allowed at no additional fee. Dogs may not be left unattended, and they must be leashed and cleaned up after. Dogs are not allowed in public swim areas or in buildings. Dogs are allowed on the trails. The camping and tent areas also allow dogs. There is a dog walk area at the campground. There are no water hookups at the campground. Multiple dogs may be allowed.

Pipestem

Pipestem Resort State Park
P. O. Box 150
Pipestem, WV
304-466-1800
Located in the mountains of West Virginia, this scenic resort park is home to an aerial tram, an 18 hole golf course, and a variety of recreational pursuits. Dogs of all sizes are allowed at no additional fee, and they must be quiet and well behaved. Dogs may not be left unattended for long periods, and they must be leashed and cleaned up after. Dogs are not allowed in public swim areas or in buildings. Dogs are allowed on the trails. The camping and tent areas also allow dogs. There is a dog walk area at the campground. Multiple dogs may be allowed.

Seneca Rocks

Yokum's Vacationland
HC 59, Box 3
Seneca Rocks, WV
800-772-8343
Dogs of all sizes are allowed, and there are no additional pet fees for tent or RV sites. There is a $10 per night per pet additional fee for the motel. Dogs must be leashed and cleaned up after. The camping and tent areas also allow dogs. There is a dog walk area at the campground. Dogs are allowed in the camping cabins. Multiple dogs may be allowed.

Springfield

Milleson's Walnut Grove Campground
28/5 Milleson's Road
Springfield, WV
304-822-5284
Dogs of all sizes are allowed at no additional fee. Dogs may not be left unattended outside, and they must have current rabies and shot records. Dogs must be leashed and cleaned up after. There are some breed restrictions. This RV park is closed during the off-season. The camping and tent areas also allow dogs. There is a dog walk area at the campground. Multiple dogs may be allowed.

Triadelphia

Wheelings Dallas Pike Campground
Road 1, Box 231
Triadelphia, WV
304-547-0940
Dogs of all sizes are allowed. There are no additional pet fees. Dogs must be leashed and cleaned up after. There are some breed restrictions. The camping and tent areas also allow dogs. There is a dog walk area at the campground. Multiple dogs may be allowed.

Wisconsin Listings

Alma Center

Hixton/Alma Center KOA
N9657 H 95
Alma Center, WI
715-964-2508
Dogs of all sizes are allowed, however, if they are large dogs, there are only 2 dogs allowed per site. There are no additional pet fees. Dogs must be quiet and well behaved. Dogs may not be left unattended, must be leashed, and cleaned up after. There is a large fenced-in area for dogs to run off leash. This RV park is closed during the off-season. The camping and tent areas also allow dogs. There is a dog walk area at the campground. There are special amenities given to dogs at this campground.

Ashland

Apostle Islands National Lakeshore
415 Washington Avenue
Bayfield, WI
715-779-3379
This national lakeshore consists of a series of 21 islands and is home to some of the nations finest historic lighthouses. The park is accessible only by watercraft, but the ferry and the excursion boats don't allow dogs, so private boats or charters should be used with pets. Once on the islands, dogs may not be left unattended, and they must be on no more than a 6 foot leash, and be cleaned up after. This campground is closed during the off-season. The camping and tent areas also allow dogs. There is a dog walk area at the campground. There are no electric or water hookups at the campground. Multiple dogs may be allowed.

Baraboo

Baraboo Hill Campground
E 10545 Terrytown Road
Baraboo, WI
800-226-7242
Dogs of all sizes are allowed. There are no additional pet fees. Dogs may not be left unattended, must be leashed, and cleaned up after. This RV park is closed during the off-season. The camping and tent areas also allow dogs. There is a dog walk area at the campground. Multiple dogs may be allowed.

Devil's Lake State Park
5975 Park Road
Baraboo, WI
608-356-8301
Dogs of all sizes are allowed. There are no additional pet fees. Dogs may not be left unattended, and they must be on no more than an 8 foot leash, and be cleaned up after. Dogs are not allowed on the beach, the picnic areas, the playground, or in any of the buildings. They are allowed on all the trails except the ParFrey Glen Trail. There are 4 camps in this park; 3 family camps, and 1 group camp. The pet policy is the same at all camps. The camping and tent areas also allow dogs. There is a dog walk area at the campground. Dogs are allowed in the camping cabins. There are no water hookups at the campground. Multiple dogs may be allowed.

Mirror Lake State Park
E10320 Fern Dell Road
Baraboo, WI
608-254-2333
This park and lake offers a variety of recreational pursuits year round. Dogs of all sizes are allowed. There are no additional pet fees. Dogs may not be left unattended at any time, they must be on no more than an 8 foot leash at all times, be cleaned up after, and be in your unit at night. Dogs must have a current rabies certificate and shot records. Dogs are not allowed at the picnic area, in buildings, at the beach, and not on the nature trail. Dogs are allowed on the hiking trails. The camping and tent areas also allow dogs. There is a dog walk area at the campground. There are no electric or water hookups at the campground. Multiple dogs may be allowed.

Natural Bridge State Park
S5975 Park Road
Baraboo, WI
608-356-8301
A natural arch of sandstone with a rock shelter used by people over 11,000 years ago is a point of interest at this park. Dogs of all sizes are allowed at no additional fee. Dogs may not be left unattended at any time, they must be on no more than an 8 foot leash, be cleaned up after, and be in your unit at night. Dogs must have a current rabies certificate and shot records. Dogs are not allowed at the picnic area, in buildings, at the beach, playgrounds, and not on the nature trails. Dogs are not allowed at the Natural Bridge or on the main trail to it. Dogs are allowed on the hiking trails. The camping and tent areas also allow dogs. There is a dog walk area at the campground. There are no water hookups at the campground. Multiple dogs may be allowed.

Rocky Arbor State Park
E10320 Fern Dell Road
Baraboo, WI
608-339-6881
This park is only open from Memorial to Labor Day, and their off season phone number is 608-254-2333. Dogs of all sizes are allowed at no additional fee. Dogs may not be left unattended, they must be on no more than an 8 foot leash, be cleaned up after, and be in your unit at night. Dogs must have a current rabies certificate and shot records. Dogs are not allowed at the picnic area, in buildings, and not on the nature trails. Dogs are allowed on the hiking trails. This campground is closed during the off-season. The camping and tent areas also allow dogs. There is a dog walk area at the campground. There are no water hookups at the campground. Multiple dogs may be allowed.

Yogi Bear's Waterpark Camp Resort
S 1915 Ishnala Road
Baraboo, WI
608-254-2568
Dogs of all sizes are allowed. There are no additional pet fees. Dogs must be quiet, well behaved, leashed, and cleaned up after. This RV park is closed during the off-season. The camping and tent areas also allow dogs. There is a dog walk area at the campground. Multiple dogs may be allowed.

Big Flats

Pineland Camping Park
916 H 13
Big Flats, WI
608-564-7818
Dogs of all sizes are allowed. There are no additional pet fees. Dogs must be leashed and cleaned up after. There are some breed restrictions. This RV park is closed during the off-season. The camping and tent areas also allow dogs. There is a dog walk area at the campground. Multiple dogs may be allowed.

Black River Falls

Black River State Forest
10325 H 12 E
Black River Falls, WI
715-284-4103
This recreational park has a variety of activities year round. There are many scenic and geological sites along its many trails and glacial remnants. Dogs of all sizes are allowed. There are no additional pet fees. Dogs may not be left unattended at any time, they must be on no more than an 8 foot leash, be cleaned up after, and they must be in your unit at night. Dogs must have a current rabies certificate and shot records. Dogs are not allowed at the picnic area, in buildings, at the beach, and not on the nature trails. Dogs are allowed on the hiking trails, and they are allowed to go in the water as long as it is not near a swim area. The camping and tent areas also allow dogs. There is a dog walk area at the campground. There are no water hookups at the campground. Multiple dogs may be allowed.

Blue Mounds

Blue Mound State Park
4350 Mound Park Road
Blue Mounds, WI
608-437-5711
Dogs of all sizes are allowed. There are no additional pet fees. Dogs may not be left unattended, and they must be on no more than a 6 foot leash, and be cleaned up after. Dogs are not allowed on the nature trails, at the picnic areas, or at the pool. The camping and tent areas also allow dogs. There is a dog walk area at the campground. Multiple dogs may be allowed.

Boulder Junction

Northern-Highland American Legion State Forest
4125 County H M
Boulder Junction, WI
715-385-2727
This forest has many recreational activities with more than 225,000 acres of lakes and forest. Dogs of all sizes are allowed at no additional fee. Dogs may not be left unattended, they must be on no more than an 8 foot leash, be cleaned up after, and be in your unit at night. Dogs are not allowed on the nature trails, but they are allowed on the hiking trails. The camping and tent areas also allow dogs. There is a dog walk area at the campground. There are no electric or water hookups at the campground. Multiple dogs may be allowed.

Caledonia

Jellystone Park
8425 H 38
Caledonia, WI
262-835-2526
Dogs of all sizes are allowed. There are no additional pet fees. Dogs must be quiet, well behaved, leashed, and cleaned up after. This RV park is closed during the off-season. The camping and tent areas also allow dogs. There is a dog walk area at the campground. Multiple dogs may be allowed.

Camp Douglas

Mill Bluff State Park
15819 Funnel Rd.
Camp Douglas, WI
608-427-6692
The unusual, tall bluffs rising abruptly from the flat plains create a variety of picturesque rock formations at this park which is one of nine units of the Ice Age National Scientific Reserve. Dogs are allowed off lead in the forest if they are under voice control and will not chase other animals. Dogs must be on lead and cleaned up after in the camping areas. Dogs are allowed on the trails, but not in the swim areas. The camping and tent areas also allow dogs. There is

a dog walk area at the campground. There are no electric or water hookups at the campground. Multiple dogs may be allowed.

Cascade

Hoeft's Resort
W9070 Crooked Lake Drive
Cascade, WI
262-626-2221
One dog of any size is allowed. There are no additional pet fees. Dogs are not allowed at the cabins or at the beach. Dogs must be leashed and cleaned up after. This RV park is closed during the off-season. The camping and tent areas also allow dogs. There is a dog walk area at the campground.

Cassville

Nelson Dewey State Park
12190 County Road V V
Cassville, WI
608-725-5374
This park is along the Mississippi River and was the home to Wisconsin's first governor. There is also a reconstructed 1890 village on site. Dogs may not be left unattended, and they must be leashed and cleaned up after. Dogs are not allowed in the picnic areas, the buildings, or the nature trail. Dogs are allowed on the hiking trails. The camping and tent areas also allow dogs. There is a dog walk area at the campground. There are no water hookups at the campground. Multiple dogs may be allowed.

Chippewa Falls

Lake Wissota State Park
18127 County H O
Chippewa Falls, WI
715-382-4574
This park has a permanent fishing pier to accommodate those with disabilities, and 17.4 miles of hiking trails, with a favorite being the 1-mile self-guided Beaver Meadow Nature Trail. Dogs are allowed at no additional fee. Dogs may not be left unattended, and they must be on no more than an 8 foot leash, and be cleaned up after. Dogs are not allowed at the groomed picnic areas, the Nature Trail, and certain marked areas. The camping and tent areas also allow dogs. There is a dog walk area at the campground. There are no water hookups at the

campground. Multiple dogs may be allowed.

Cornell

Brunet Island State Park
23125 255th Street
Cornell, WI
715-239-6888
Dogs of all sizes are allowed. There are no additional pet fees. Dogs may not be left unattended, and they must be leashed and cleaned up after. Dogs are not allowed on the beach, in the picnic areas, any of the buildings, or on the one 3/4 mile guided Jean Burnet Trail. There are many other trails where dogs are allowed. There is also a pet run area where they have set up a mini picnic area with tables. The camping and tent areas also allow dogs. There is a dog walk area at the campground. There are no water hookups at the campground. Multiple dogs may be allowed.

DeForest

Madison KOA
4859 CTH-V
DeForest, WI
608-846-4528
Dogs of all sizes are allowed. There are no additional pet fees. Dogs may not be left unattended, must be leashed, and cleaned up after. Dogs are not allowed at the playground or in the rentals. This RV park is closed during the off-season. The camping and tent areas also allow dogs. There is a dog walk area at the campground. Multiple dogs may be allowed.

Delafield

Lapham Peak Unit, Kettle Moraine State Forest
W 329 N 846 County Road C
Delafield, WI
262-646-3025
Along the Ice Age Trail in this park there is a campsite that must be backpacked into. The southern unit of this park has tent and RV camping. Lapham Peak has over 21 miles of hiking trails, more than 17 miles of cross country ski trails, and a lookout tower at the highest point in Waukesha County. Dogs are allowed at no additional fee. Dogs may not be left unattended, and they must be leashed and cleaned up after. Dogs are allowed on the

trails, but they are not allowed in the picnic areas, or on ski trails after snow. The camping and tent areas also allow dogs. There is a dog walk area at the campground. There are no electric or water hookups at the campground. Multiple dogs may be allowed.

Dells

Arrowhead Resort Campground
W1530 Arrowhead Road
Dells, WI
608-254-7244
Dogs of all sizes are allowed. There are no additional pet fees. Dogs are not allowed in the rentals, they may not be left unattended, and must be leashed and cleaned up after. This RV park is closed during the off-season. The camping and tent areas also allow dogs. There is a dog walk area at the campground. 2 dogs may be allowed.

Depere

Apple Creek Family Campground
3831 County Road U
Depere, WI
920-532-0132
Dogs of all sizes are allowed. There are no additional pet fees. Dogs must be well behaved, leashed, and cleaned up after. Dogs may be left for short times in your unit if they will be quiet. There are some breed restrictions. This RV park is closed during the off-season. The camping and tent areas also allow dogs. There is a dog walk area at the campground. 2 dogs may be allowed.

Dodgeville

Governor Dodge State Park
4175 H 23
Dodgeville, WI
608-935-2315
Dogs of all sizes are allowed. There are no additional pet fees. Dogs may not be left unattended, they must be on no more than an 8 foot leash, and be cleaned up after. Dogs are not allowed on the beach, and at certain picnic areas. There is a separate picnic area where dogs are allowed. Dogs are allowed on lead throughout the park. The camping and tent areas also allow dogs. There is a dog walk area at the campground. There are no water hookups at the campground. Multiple dogs may be

allowed.

Door Peninsula

Newport State Park
475 County Highway NP
Ellison Bay, WI
920-854-2500
This park offers an interpretive center and a naturalist program. There is a variety of year round activities and there is almost 40 miles of trails. Dogs of all sizes are allowed at no additional fee. Dogs may not be left unattended at any time, they must be leashed, cleaned up after, and be in your unit at night. Dogs must have a current rabies certificate and shot records. Dogs are not allowed at the picnic area, in buildings, or at the swim beach. Dogs do not have to be on lead in the woods as long as there is voice control. Dogs are allowed on the trails. The camping and tent areas also allow dogs. There is a dog walk area at the campground. There are no electric or water hookups at the campground. Multiple dogs may be allowed.

Peninsula State Park
9462 Shore Road
Fish Creek, WI
920-868-3258
There is a wide variety of activities at this park of over 3,700 acres, with an observation tower, a summer theater, a 125 year old lighthouse, and many trails. Dogs of all sizes are allowed at no additional fee. Dogs may not be left unattended at any time, they must be leashed, cleaned up after, and be in your unit at night. Dogs must have a current rabies certificate and shot records. Dogs are not allowed at the picnic areas, in buildings, at the beach, the groomed ski trails, or on the nature trails. Dogs are allowed on the hiking trails. The camping and tent areas also allow dogs. There is a dog walk area at the campground. There are no water hookups at the campground. Multiple dogs may be allowed.

Jellystone Park
3677 May Road
Sturgeon Bay, WI
920-743-9001
Dogs of all sizes are allowed. There are no additional pet fees. Dogs must be leashed and cleaned up after. This RV park is closed during the off-season. The camping and tent areas also allow dogs. There is a dog walk area at the campground.

Multiple dogs may be allowed.

Potawatomi State Park
3740 Park Drive
Sturgeon Bay, WI
920-746-2890
This park offers land and water recreation, a variety of trails, and a 75-foot observation tower that rises above the forest canopy. Dogs are allowed at no additional fee. Dogs may not be left unattended, and they must be leashed and cleaned up after. Dogs are not allowed at picnic areas or in buildings. Dogs can be off lead by the water as long as they are under voice control, and they are allowed on the trails. The camping and tent areas also allow dogs. There is a dog walk area at the campground. There are no water hookups at the campground. Multiple dogs may be allowed.

Dundee

Kettle Moraine State Forest-Northern Unit
N1765 H G
Dundee, WI
262-626-2116
Dogs of all sizes are allowed. There are no additional pet fees. Dogs may not be left unattended, and they must be well behaved, leashed, and cleaned up after. Dogs are not allowed on certain smaller nature trails, but there are several trails they can be on. This information is available at the Forest Headquarters in the park. This forest has 2 campgrounds. The camping and tent areas also allow dogs. There is a dog walk area at the campground. There are no water hookups at the campground. Multiple dogs may be allowed.

Eagle

Kettle Moraine State Forest-Southern Unit
S91 W39091 Highway 59
Eagle, WI
262-594-6200
Dogs of all sizes are allowed. There are no additional pet fees. Dogs may not be left unattended at any time, they must be on no more than an 8 foot leash at all times, be cleaned up after, and be in your unit at night. Dogs must have a current rabies certificate and shot records. Dogs are not allowed at the picnic area, in buildings, at the beach, and not on the nature trails. Dogs are

allowed on the hiking trails. The camping and tent areas also allow dogs. There is a dog walk area at the campground. There are no water hookups at the campground. Multiple dogs may be allowed.

Fond Du Lac

Fond Du Luc KOA
5099 H B
Fond Du Lac, WI
920-477-2300
Dogs of all sizes are allowed, and there are no additional pet fees for tent or RV sites. There is a $5 one time additional pet fee for cabin rentals. Dogs must be well behaved, leashed, and cleaned up after. This RV park is closed during the off-season. The camping and tent areas also allow dogs. There is a dog walk area at the campground. Dogs are allowed in the camping cabins. Multiple dogs may be allowed.

Fort Atkinson

Jellystone Park
N 551 Wishing Well Drive
Fort Atkinson, WI
920-568-4100
Dogs of all sizes are allowed. There are no additional pet fees. Dogs may not be left unattended, must be quiet, leashed, and cleaned up after. There are some breed restrictions. This RV park is closed during the off-season. The camping and tent areas also allow dogs. There is a dog walk area at the campground. Multiple dogs may be allowed.

Fountain City

Merrick State Park
S2965 H 35
Fountain City, WI
608-687-4936
You can dock your boat at your campsite at this park. Dogs are allowed at no additional fee. Dogs may not be left unattended, they must be on no more than an 8 foot leash, be cleaned up after, and be in your unit at night. Dogs must have a current rabies certificate and shot records. With the exception of one marked picnic area, dogs are not allowed in picnic areas, in buildings, at the beach, or on the nature trails. Dogs are allowed on the hiking trails. The camping and tent areas also allow dogs. There is a dog walk area at the campground. There are no

water hookups at the campground. Multiple dogs may be allowed.

Fremont

Yogi Bear's Jellystone Park
E6506 H 110
Fremont, WI
920-446-3420
Dogs of all sizes are allowed. There are no additional pet fees. Dogs must be quiet, well behaved, leashed, and cleaned up after. This RV park is closed during the off-season. The camping and tent areas also allow dogs. There is a dog walk area at the campground. Multiple dogs may be allowed.

Friendship

Roche-A-Cri State Park
1767 H 13
Friendship, WI
608-339-6881
A 303 step wooden stairway takes you to the top of the 300-foot high rock outcropping called the Roche-A-Cri Mound offering panoramic views of the park. Dogs are allowed in camping areas, on roads, and in other areas of the park not developed for public use. Dogs are not allowed on the stairway. Dogs may not be left unattended, they must be quiet, on no more than an 8 foot leash, and be cleaned up after. Dogs are not allowed on the beach, the picnic areas, playgrounds, on cross-country ski trails or nature trails. Dogs are allowed on the hiking trails. The off season phone number is 608-565-2789. The camping and tent areas also allow dogs. There is a dog walk area at the campground. There are no water hookups at the campground. Multiple dogs may be allowed.

Glenbeulah

Westward Ho Camp Resort
N5456 Division Road
Glenbeulah, WI
920-526-3407
Dogs of all sizes are allowed. There are no additional pet fees. Dogs may not be left unattended, must be leashed, and cleaned up after. This RV park is closed during the off-season. The camping and tent areas also allow dogs. There is a dog walk area at the campground. Multiple dogs may be allowed.

Grantsburg

Governor Knowles State Forest
(Box 367) H 70 @ St Croix River & entrances in WI & MN
Grantsburg, WI
715-463-2898
Dogs of all sizes are allowed. There are no additional pet fees. Dogs may not be left unattended at any time, they must be on no more than an 8 foot leash and be cleaned up after. Dogs are allowed on all the trails, except the ski trail in the winter. Dogs on lead are allowed throughout the forest, at the picnic area, and at the Wayside just before entering the park. This campground is closed during the off-season. The camping and tent areas also allow dogs. There is a dog walk area at the campground. There are no electric or water hookups at the campground. Multiple dogs may be allowed.

Hartford

Pike Lake Unit - Kettle Moraine State Forest
3544 Kettle Moraine Road
Hartford, WI
262-670-3400
This park is located in the middle of the Kettle Moraine. The year round park is known for it's glacial landscapes. There are many trails here. Dogs are allowed at no additional fee. Dogs may not be left unattended, and they must be leashed and cleaned up after. Dogs are not allowed on the beach, the picnic areas, the self-guided nature trails, or the groomed ski trails. Dogs are allowed on the hiking trails. This campground is closed during the off-season. The camping and tent areas also allow dogs. There is a dog walk area at the campground. There are no water hookups at the campground. Multiple dogs may be allowed.

Hayward

Hayward KOA
11544 N H 63
Hayward, WI
715-634-2331
Dogs of all sizes are allowed. There are no additional pet fees. Dogs must be leashed and cleaned up after. Dogs may be left alone if they will be quiet and well behaved. Dogs must be crated when left unattended in the cabins. There are

some breed restrictions. This RV park is closed during the off-season. The camping and tent areas also allow dogs. There is a dog walk area at the campground. Dogs are allowed in the camping cabins. Multiple dogs may be allowed.

Hudson

Willow River State Park
1034 County H A
Hudson, WI
715-386-5931
There is year round recreation at this park of almost 3,000 acres. There are trails of varying difficulty, a nature center, and scenic overlooks. Dogs of all sizes are allowed at no additional fee. Dogs may not be left unattended, they must be on no more than a 6 foot leash, and be cleaned up after. Dogs are not allowed in the picnic areas, in buildings, at the beach, on ski trails, or on the nature trails. Dogs are allowed on the hiking trails. The camping and tent areas also allow dogs. There is a dog walk area at the campground. There are no water hookups at the campground. Multiple dogs may be allowed.

Kansasville

Richard Bong State Recreation Area
26313 Burlington Road
Kansasville, WI
262-878-5600
This recreational park has numerous activities year round. Dogs are allowed at no additional fee. Dogs may not be left unattended, and they must be leashed and cleaned up after. Dogs are not allowed on the beach, the picnic shelters, in buildings, or the self-guided nature trails. Dogs are allowed on the hiking trails. The camping and tent areas also allow dogs. There is a dog walk area at the campground. There are no water hookups at the campground. Multiple dogs may be allowed.

Knowlton

Lake Dubay Shores Campground
1713 Dubay Drive
Knowlton, WI
715-457-2484
Dogs of all sizes are allowed. There is a $1 per night per pet additional fee. Dogs must be leashed and

cleaned up after. They may be left in your RV if they will be quiet. This RV park is closed during the off-season. The camping and tent areas also allow dogs. There is a dog walk area at the campground. Multiple dogs may be allowed.

La Crosse

Neshonoc Lakeside Camp Resort
N4668 H 16
West Salem, WI
608-786-1792
Dogs of all sizes are allowed. There are no additional pet fees. Dogs must be leashed and cleaned up after. There are some breed restrictions. This RV park is closed during the off-season. The camping and tent areas also allow dogs. There is a dog walk area at the campground. 2 dogs may be allowed.

Lake Geneva

Big Foot Beach State Park
1550 S. Lake Shore Drive
Lake Geneva, WI
262-248-2528
This park offers hiking and nature trails. Dogs of all sizes are allowed. There are no additional pet fees. Dogs may not be left unattended, and they must be leashed and cleaned up after. Dogs are not allowed on the beach or at the picnic areas. The camping and tent areas also allow dogs. There is a dog walk area at the campground. There are no water hookups at the campground. Multiple dogs may be allowed.

Madison

Crystal Lake Campground
N550 Gannon Road
Lodi, WI
608-592-5607
Dogs of all sizes are allowed. If there is only one dog there is no fee. If there are more than one the fee is $5 per night per dog. Dogs may not be left unattended, must be leashed, and cleaned up after. Dogs may swim from the pier, but they may not be in the swim zone or on the beach. This RV park is closed during the off-season. The camping and tent areas also allow dogs. There is a dog walk area at the campground. Multiple dogs may be allowed.

Mellen

Copper Falls State Park
Copper Falls Road
Mellen, WI
715-274-5125
Dogs of all sizes are allowed. There are no additional pet fees. Dogs may not be left unattended, and they must be quiet, well behaved, leashed and cleaned up after. Dogs are not allowed on the beach, in the picnic areas, the main hiking trail, or in any of the buildings. There is a specified walking trail for dogs. There are two campgrounds in the park, and the pet rules apply at both. The camping and tent areas also allow dogs. There is a dog walk area at the campground. There are no water hookups at the campground. Multiple dogs may be allowed.

Mercer

Turtle Flambeau Scenic Water Area
3291 State House Circle
Mercer, WI
715-332-5271
This park has 60 campsites and is accessible by boat only from seven public boat landings and from private resorts. It provides for a variety of plants, fish, mammals, bird species, and recreational opportunities. Dogs are allowed at no additional fee. Dogs may not be left unattended, and they must be leashed at all times and cleaned up after. Dogs are allowed on the trails. This campground is closed during the off-season. The camping and tent areas also allow dogs. There is a dog walk area at the campground. There are no water hookups at the campground. Multiple dogs may be allowed.

Merrill

Council Grounds State Park
N 1895 Council Grounds Drive
Merrill, WI
715-536-8773
Dogs of all sizes are allowed. There are no additional pet fees. Dogs may not be left unattended, they must be on no more than an 8 foot leash, and be cleaned up after. Dogs are not allowed on the beach or picnic areas. Dogs are allowed on the trails. This campground is closed during the off-season. The camping and tent areas also allow

dogs. There is a dog walk area at the campground. There are no water hookups at the campground. Multiple dogs may be allowed.

Milton

Hidden Valley RV Resort
872 E State Road 59
Milton, WI
608-868-4141
Dogs of all sizes are allowed. There are no additional pet fees. Dogs may be left in RV if the inside is cool but they may not be left unattended for long periods. Dogs are not allowed in the play areas, and must be leashed and cleaned up after. This RV park is closed during the off-season. The camping and tent areas also allow dogs. There is a dog walk area at the campground. Multiple dogs may be allowed.

Milwaukee

Wisconsin State Fair RV Park
601 S 76th Street
Milwaukee, WI
414-266-7035
Dogs of all sizes are allowed. There are no additional pet fees. Dogs must be well behaved, quiet, leashed, and cleaned up after. Dogs may be left in your RV if they will be quiet and it is cool. There is a dog walk area at the campground. Multiple dogs may be allowed.

Montello

Wilderness Campground
N1499 H 22
Montello, WI
608-297-2002
One dog of any size is allowed. There are no additional pet fees. Dogs may not be left unattended, must be leashed, and cleaned up after. This RV park is closed during the off-season. The camping and tent areas also allow dogs. There is a dog walk area at the campground.

Necedah

Buckhorn State Park
W8450 Buckhorn Avenue
Necedah, WI
608-565-2789
Dogs of all sizes are allowed. There are no additional pet fees. Dogs may not be left unattended, and they must be leashed at all times, and be

cleaned up after. Dogs are not allowed in the picnic areas, at the shelters, or in any of the buildings. Dogs are also not allowed on the 303 step stairway that is next to the park. There is electric provided at the handicap site only. The camping and tent areas also allow dogs. There is a dog walk area at the campground. There are no electric or water hookups at the campground. Multiple dogs may be allowed.

New Glarus

New Glarus Woods State Park
W5446 County Trunk H NN
New Glarus, WI
608-527-2335
Restoration programs, interpretive programs, an active Amphitheater, hiking, recreation, and more makes this a pretty busy park. Dogs are allowed at no additional fee. Dogs may not be left unattended, they must be on no more than an 8 foot leash, be cleaned up after, and be in at night. Dogs must have a current rabies certificate and shot records. Dogs are not allowed in the picnic area, at the playground, in buildings, at the beach, or on nature trails. Dogs are allowed on the hiking trails. The camping and tent areas also allow dogs. There is a dog walk area at the campground. There are no water hookups at the campground. Multiple dogs may be allowed.

Oakdale

Oakdale KOA
200 J Street
Oakdale, WI
608-372-5622
Dogs of all sizes are allowed. There are no additional pet fees. Dogs must be leashed and cleaned up after. There are some breed restrictions. This RV park is closed during the off-season. The camping and tent areas also allow dogs. There is a dog walk area at the campground. Multiple dogs may be allowed.

Ontario

Wildcat Mountain State Park
E13660 State Highway 33, PO Box 99
Ontario, WI
608-337-4775
This park of more than 3,600 acres offers more than 25 miles of hiking trails, an interpretive nature trail, a variety of other trails, and a nature center. Dogs are allowed at no additional fee. Dogs may not be left unattended, and they must be leashed and cleaned up after except when in the woods. Dogs are allowed on the trails. The camping and tent areas also allow dogs. There is a dog walk area at the campground. There are no electric or water hookups at the campground. Multiple dogs may be allowed.

Park Falls

Chequamegon National Forest
1170 4th Avenue S
Park Falls, WI
715-762-2461
This forest provides a wide variety of camping areas and trails, and the diverse ecosystems support a large variety of plants, fish, mammals, and bird species. Dogs are allowed at no additional fee. Dogs may not be left unattended, and they must be leashed and cleaned up after in the camp areas. Dogs are not allowed on the beaches or in buildings, but they are allowed on the trails. The camping and tent areas also allow dogs. There is a dog walk area at the campground. There are no water hookups at the campground.

Rhinelander

Chequamegon/Nicolet National Forest
68 S Stevens Street -Nicolet Division
Rhinelander, WI
715-362-2461
This forest provides a variety of camping areas and trails, and the diverse ecosystems here support a large variety of plants, fish, mammals, and bird species. Dogs are allowed at no additional fee. Dogs may not be left unattended, and they must be leashed and cleaned up after in the camp areas. Dogs are allowed on the trails unless otherwise marked. The camping and tent areas also allow dogs. There is a dog walk area at the campground. There are no electric or water hookups at the campground. Multiple dogs may be allowed.

Rice Lake

Rice Lake/Spooner KOA
1876 29 3/4 Avenue
Rice Lake, WI
715-234-2360
Dogs of all sizes are allowed, and there are no additional pet fees for tent or RV sites. There is a $5 per night per pet additional pet fee for cabin rentals. Dogs may not be left alone except in your own RV, and only if they will be quiet and well behaved. Dogs must be leashed and cleaned up after. This RV park is closed during the off-season. The camping and tent areas also allow dogs. There is a dog walk area at the campground. Dogs are allowed in the camping cabins. Multiple dogs may be allowed.

Saxon

Frontier Campground & RV Park
11296 W H 2
Saxon, WI
715-893-2461
Dogs of all sizes are allowed. There are no additional pet fees. Dogs must be well behaved, quiet, leashed, and cleaned up after. The camping and tent areas also allow dogs. There is a dog walk area at the campground. Multiple dogs may be allowed.

Sheboygan

Kohler-Andrae State Park
1020 Beach Park Lane
Sheboygan, WI
920-451-4080
Dogs of all sizes are allowed. There are no additional pet fees. Dogs may not be left unattended, they must be leashed at all times, and be cleaned up after. There is a separate picnic area for those with dogs, and dogs are not allowed in the buildings. There is a pet area map in the office that shows what trails and areas that are pet friendly. The camping and tent areas also allow dogs. There is a dog walk area at the campground. There are no water hookups at the campground. Multiple dogs may be allowed.

Sherwood

High Cliff State Park
N7630 State Park Road
Sherwood, WI
920-989-1106
Dogs of all sizes are allowed. There

are no additional pet fees. Dogs may not be left unattended, and they must be leashed and cleaned up after. Dogs are not allowed on the beach, the picnic areas, or on the grass. Dogs on lead are allowed on the trails. The camping and tent areas also allow dogs. There is a dog walk area at the campground. There are no water hookups at the campground. Multiple dogs may be allowed.

Spring Green

Lower Wisconsin State Riverway/Tower Hill State Park
5808 County Road C
Spring Green, WI
608-588-2116
This park has a vast variety of archaeological, scenic, and historical sites to explore. Dogs are allowed at no additional fee. Dogs may not be left unattended, and they must be leashed and cleaned up after. Dogs are allowed on the trails. This campground is closed during the off-season. The camping and tent areas also allow dogs. There is a dog walk area at the campground. There are no electric or water hookups at the campground. Multiple dogs may be allowed.

St Croix Falls

Interstate State Park
851 H 35S
St Croix Falls, WI
715-483-3747
Dogs of all sizes are allowed. There are no additional pet fees. Dogs may not be left unattended, they must be well behaved, on no more than an 8 foot leash, and be cleaned up after. Dogs are not allowed on the 2 nature trails or at the picnic area. This park has 2 campgrounds. The north campground closes for the winter. The camping and tent areas also allow dogs. There is a dog walk area at the campground. There are no electric or water hookups at the campground. Multiple dogs may be allowed.

Stoughton

Lake Kegonsa State Park
2405 Door Creek Road
Stoughton, WI
608-873-9695
Kegonsa means "lake of many fishes", and it is as well known for it's

great fishing and its nature trails and woodlands, the effigy mounds, and other natural sites. Dogs are allowed at no additional fee. Dogs are not allowed at swim or sheltered picnic areas, the ski trails once there is snow, or any other posted "no pets" area. Dogs may not be left unattended, and they must be leashed and cleaned up after. This campground is closed during the off-season. The camping and tent areas also allow dogs. There is a dog walk area at the campground. There are no electric or water hookups at the campground. Multiple dogs may be allowed.

Superior

Pattison State Park
6294 S State Road 35
Superior, WI
715-399-3111
This park features the highest waterfalls in Wisconsin, and there are naturalist-guided hikes here as well as many other recreational pursuits. Dogs of all sizes are allowed at no additional fee. Dogs may not be left unattended at any time, they must be well behaved, leashed, cleaned up after, and be in your unit at night. Dogs must have a current rabies certificate and shot records. Dogs are not allowed at the picnic area, in buildings, at the beach, and not on the nature trails. Dogs are allowed on the hiking trails and at the river. There is also a 4 table picnic area where dogs are allowed. The camping and tent areas also allow dogs. There is a dog walk area at the campground. There are no water hookups at the campground. Multiple dogs may be allowed.

Trempealeau

Perrot State Park
W26247 Sullivan Road
Trempealeau, WI
608-534-6409
This park has access to the Great River State Trail and year round recreation. Dogs of all sizes are allowed at no additional fee. Dogs may not be left unattended, they must be on no more than an 8 foot leash, be cleaned up after, and be in your unit at night. Dogs must have a current rabies certificate and shot records. Dogs are not allowed at the picnic area, in buildings, and not on the nature trails. Dogs are

allowed on the hiking trails. The camping and tent areas also allow dogs. There is a dog walk area at the campground. There are no water hookups at the campground. Multiple dogs may be allowed.

Two Rivers

Point Beach State Forest
9400 County H O
Two Rivers, WI
920-794-7480
There are high sand dunes, woods, and more than five miles of undeveloped Lake Michigan shoreline to explore within walking distance of each site. Dogs are allowed at no additional fee. Dogs may not be left unattended, and they must be quiet, leashed and cleaned up after. Dogs are not allowed on the beach, in buildings, north of the lighthouse, on the Swales Nature Trail, or the groomed ski trails. Dogs may be off lead if hunting or swimming, and they are allowed on hiking trails, and south of the lighthouse on the beach. The camping and tent areas also allow dogs. There is a dog walk area at the campground. There are no water hookups at the campground. Multiple dogs may be allowed.

Warrens

Jellystone Park
1500 Jellystone Park Drive
Warrens, WI
608-378-4303
Dogs of all sizes are allowed. There are no additional pet fees. Dogs may not be left unattended, must be well behaved, be leashed, and cleaned up after. Dogs are not allowed in the buildings, the water park, the fishing lake, or the beach and pool areas. The camping and tent areas also allow dogs. There is a dog walk area at the campground. 2 dogs may be allowed.

Waupaca

Hartman Creek State Park
N2480 Hartman Creek Road
Waupaca, WI
715-258-2372
This park offers a variety of trails, a sandy beach swimming area, and 7 lakes (no gas motors) for recreation. Dogs of all sizes are allowed. There are no additional pet fees. Dogs may not be left unattended at any time,

they must be on no more than an 8 foot leash, be cleaned up after, and be in your unit at night. Dogs must have a current rabies certificate and shot records. Dogs are not allowed at the picnic area, in the buildings, or at the beach. Dogs are allowed on the hiking trails, but not on the equestrian trails. Generator use is prohibited. The camping and tent areas also allow dogs. There is a dog walk area at the campground. There are no water hookups at the campground. Multiple dogs may be allowed.

Wausau

Rib Mountain State Park
4200 Park Road
Wausau, WI
715-842-2522
A spectacular view over one of the oldest geological formations on earth is offered from the 60 observation towers at this park. The park is open all year. Dogs of all sizes are allowed at no additional fee. Dogs may not be left unattended, they must be on no more than an 8 foot leash, be cleaned up after, and be in your unit at night. Dogs must have a current rabies certificate and shot records. Dogs are not allowed at the picnic area, in the buildings, or on the nature trails. Dogs are allowed on the hiking trails. This campground is closed during the off-season. The camping and tent areas also allow dogs. There is a dog walk area at the campground. There are no water hookups at the campground. Multiple dogs may be allowed.

Wausaukee

Menominee River Natural Resources Area
Verhayen Lane
Wausaukee, WI
715-856-9160
Campers at this park will need to hike in or canoe to camp sites, as it is mostly limited to foot traffic. Dogs may be off lead if they are under voice control and will not chase other animals. Dogs are restricted to a lead during nesting times, which is usually from mid-April through June. Dogs may not be left unattended at any time. This campground is closed during the off-season. The camping and tent areas also allow dogs. There is a dog walk area at the campground. There are no electric or water hookups at the campground.

Multiple dogs may be allowed.

Winter

Flambeau River State Forest
W1613 CR W
Winter, WI
715-332-5271
Dogs of all sizes are allowed. There are no additional pet fees. Dogs may not be left unattended, they must be quiet, be on no more than an 8 foot leash, and be cleaned up after. Dogs are allowed on the trails, but not in public use or picnic areas. The camping and tent areas also allow dogs. There is a dog walk area at the campground. There are no electric or water hookups at the campground. Multiple dogs may be allowed.

Wisconsin Dells

Wisconsin Dells KOA
S 235 Stand Rock Road
Wisconsin Dells, WI
608-254-4177
Dogs of all sizes are allowed. There are no additional pet fees. Dogs may not be left unattended at any time. They must be leashed, and cleaned up after. There are some breed restrictions. This RV park is closed during the off-season. The camping and tent areas also allow dogs. There is a dog walk area at the campground. Multiple dogs may be allowed.

Woodruff

Willow Flowage Scenic Waters Area
Cedar Falls Road
Woodruff, WI
715-356-5211
This wilderness area has more than 106 islands and covers more than 17,000 acres. Dogs are allowed at no additional fee. Dogs may not be left unattended, and they must be leashed and cleaned up after. Dogs are not allowed on the public beach swimming areas, the picnic areas, or nature trails. Dogs are allowed on the hiking trails, and they may be off lead when out of the camp areas if there is voice control. This campground is closed during the off-season. The camping and tent areas also allow dogs. There is a dog walk area at the campground. There are no electric or water hookups at the campground.

Multiple dogs may be allowed.

Wyoming Listings

Buffalo

Buffalo KOA
87 H 16E
Buffalo, WY
307-684-5423
Dogs of all sizes are allowed, and there are no additional pet fees for tent or RV sites. There is a $5 per night per pet additional fee for the cabins. Dogs must be leashed and cleaned up after. Dogs may not be left unattended outside or in the cabins. This RV park is closed during the off-season. The camping and tent areas also allow dogs. There is a dog walk area at the campground. Dogs are allowed in the camping cabins. Multiple dogs may be allowed.

Deer Park RV Park
Box 568, On H 16E
Buffalo, WY
307-684-5722
Dogs of all sizes are allowed. There are no additional pet fees. Dogs must be quiet, well behaved, leashed, and cleaned up after. Dogs may not be left unattended. This RV park is closed during the off-season. There is a dog walk area at the campground. Multiple dogs may be allowed.

Indian Campground
660 E Hart Street
Buffalo, WY
307-684-9601
Dogs of all sizes are allowed, however there can only be up to 3 dogs at tent and RV sites, and up to 2 dogs at the cabins. There are no additional pet fees. Dogs may not be left unattended, and they must be leashed and cleaned up after. This RV park is closed during the off-season. The camping and tent areas also allow dogs. There is a dog walk area at the campground. Dogs are allowed in the camping cabins.

Casper

Casper KOA
1101 Prairie Lane

Casper, WY
307-577-1664
Dogs of all sizes are allowed. There are no additional pet fees. Dogs must be leashed and cleaned up after. This RV park is closed during the off-season. The camping and tent areas also allow dogs. There is a dog walk area at the campground. Dogs are allowed in the camping cabins. Multiple dogs may be allowed.

Fort Casper Campground
4205 Fort Caspar Road
Casper, WY
888-243-7709
Dogs of all sizes are allowed. There are no additional pet fees. Dogs may not be left unattended for very long at a time, nor placed in outdoor kennels, or tied up outside alone. Dogs must be well behaved, leashed, and cleaned up after. There are some breed restrictions. This RV park is closed during the off-season. The camping and tent areas also allow dogs. There is a dog walk area at the campground. 2 dogs may be allowed.

Cheyenne

Cheyenne KOA
8800 Archer Frontage Road
Cheyenne, WY
307-638-8840
Dogs of all sizes are allowed. There are no additional pet fees. Dogs must be quiet, well behaved, leashed, and cleaned up after. The camping and tent areas also allow dogs. There is a dog walk area at the campground. Dogs are allowed in the camping cabins. Multiple dogs may be allowed.

Curt Gowdy State Park
1319 Hynds Lodge Road
Cheyenne, WY
307-632-7946
This park has two lakes, an amphitheater, and many hiking trails. Well behaved dogs of all sizes are allowed. There are no additional pet fees. Dogs may not be left unattended, they must be on no more than a 10 foot leash, and be cleaned up after. Dogs are not allowed on public beaches or in buildings. The camping and tent areas also allow dogs. There is a dog walk area at the campground. There are no electric or water hookups at the campground. Multiple dogs may be allowed.

Terry Bison Ranch
51 I 25 Service Road E
Cheyenne, WY
307-634-4171
Dogs of all sizes are allowed. There are no additional pet fees. Dogs must be leashed and cleaned up after. The camping and tent areas also allow dogs. There is a dog walk area at the campground. Multiple dogs may be allowed.

Cody

Buffalo Bill State Park
47 Lakeside Road
Cody, WY
307-587-9227
Dogs of all sizes are allowed. There are no additional pet fees. Dogs may not be left unattended, they must be on no more than a 10 foot leash, and be cleaned up after. Dogs are not allowed in public eating places, buildings, or designated beach areas. This campground is closed during the off-season. The camping and tent areas also allow dogs. There is a dog walk area at the campground. There are no water hookups at the campground. Multiple dogs may be allowed.

Cody KOA
5561 Greybull H
Cody, WY
307-587-2369
Dogs of all sizes are allowed. There are no additional pet fees. Dogs must be leashed and cleaned up after. There are some breed restrictions. This RV park is closed during the off-season. The camping and tent areas also allow dogs. There is a dog walk area at the campground. Dogs are allowed in the camping cabins. Multiple dogs may be allowed.

Ponderosa Campground
1815 8th Street
Cody, WY
307-587-9203
Dogs of all sizes are allowed. There are no additional pet fees. Dogs must be leashed and cleaned up after. Dogs may not be left unattended at the cabins or outside. This RV park is closed during the off-season. The camping and tent areas also allow dogs. There is a dog walk area at the campground. Dogs are allowed in the camping

cabins. Multiple dogs may be allowed.

Shoshone National Forest
203 A Yellowstone Avenue
Cody, WY
307-527-6241
This park has 2.4 million acres of recreational land, and it is also the first National Forest in the United States. Dogs of all sizes are allowed. There are no additional pet fees. Dogs must be leashed and cleaned up after, and they are allowed on the trails. Dogs may be off lead in the forest if they are under voice control. The camping and tent areas also allow dogs. There is a dog walk area at the campground. There are no water hookups at the campground. Multiple dogs may be allowed.

Custer

Big Pine Campground
12084 Big Pine Road
Custer, WY
800-235-3981
Dogs of all sizes are allowed. There are no additional pet fees. Dogs must be leashed and cleaned up after. There are some breed restrictions. The camping and tent areas also allow dogs. There is a dog walk area at the campground. Multiple dogs may be allowed.

Crazy Horse Kampground
1116 N 5th Street
Custer, WY
605-673-2565
Dogs of all sizes are allowed. There are no additional pet fees. Dogs may not be left unattended, they must be well behaved, leashed, and cleaned up after. This RV park is closed during the off-season. The camping and tent areas also allow dogs. There is a dog walk area at the campground. Dogs are allowed in the camping cabins. Multiple dogs may be allowed.

Devils Tower

Devils Tower KOA
60 H 110
Devils Tower, WY
307-467-5395
Dogs of all sizes are allowed. There are no additional pet fees. Dogs must be leashed and cleaned up after. This RV park is closed during the off-season. The camping and tent areas also allow dogs. There is

a dog walk area at the campground. Dogs are allowed in the camping cabins. Multiple dogs may be allowed.

Douglas

Douglas KOA
168 H 91
Douglas, WY
307-358-2164
Dogs of all sizes are allowed. There are no additional pet fees. Dogs must be leashed and cleaned up after. There is a fenced in dog run where dogs are allowed to run off lead. This RV park is closed during the off-season. The camping and tent areas also allow dogs. There is a dog walk area at the campground. Multiple dogs may be allowed.

Gilette

High Plains Campground
1500 S Garner Lake Road
Gilette, WY
307-687-7339
Dogs of all sizes are allowed. There are no additional pet fees. Dogs may not be left unattended outside, and they must be leashed at all times and cleaned up after. Dogs must be friendly and well behaved. The camping and tent areas also allow dogs. There is a dog walk area at the campground. Multiple dogs may be allowed.

Glendo

Glendo State Park
397 Glendo Park Road
Glendo, WY
307-735-4433
There are scenic, historical, and geological sites to explore at this recreational park. Dogs of all sizes are allowed. There are no additional pet fees. Dogs must be leashed at all times with the exception of the pheasant hunting event. Dogs must be cleaned up after. The camping and tent areas also allow dogs. There is a dog walk area at the campground. There are no electric or water hookups at the campground. Multiple dogs may be allowed.

Grand Teton

Grand Teton Park RV Resort
Box 92, 6 miles E of Moran
Grand Teton, WY

307-733-1980
Dogs of all sizes are allowed. There are no additional pet fees. Dogs must be leashed at all times and cleaned up after. The camping and tent areas also allow dogs. There is a dog walk area at the campground. Multiple dogs may be allowed.

Greybull

Greybull KOA
333 N 2nd Street
Greybull, WY
307-765-2555
Dogs of all sizes are allowed. There are no additional pet fees. Dogs must be leashed and cleaned up after. There are some breed restrictions. This RV park is closed during the off-season. The camping and tent areas also allow dogs. There is a dog walk area at the campground. Dogs are allowed in the camping cabins. Multiple dogs may be allowed.

Guernsey

Guernsey State Park
On H 317
Guernsey, WY
307-836-2334
This is a recreational park and lake, however there are 2 times a year when they drain the lake. So check ahead if you want water sports. Dogs of all sizes are allowed. There are no additional pet fees. Dogs may not be left unattended, and they must be leashed and cleaned up after. Dogs are allowed on the trails, but some of the beaches are restricted. This campground is closed during the off-season. The camping and tent areas also allow dogs. There is a dog walk area at the campground. Multiple dogs may be allowed.

Hawk Springs Recreation Area
3 miles south of Hawk Springs off H 85
Guernsey, WY
307-836-2334
Dogs of all sizes are allowed. There are no additional pet fees. Dogs must be leashed and cleaned up after. The camping and tent areas also allow dogs. There is a dog walk area at the campground. There are no electric or water hookups at the campground. Multiple dogs may be allowed.

Lander

Sinks Canyon State Park
3079 Sinks Canyon Road
Lander, WY
307-332-6333
Throughout the summer experts on the Sinks Canyon area present weekly programs on it's botany, history, geology, and wildlife. Dogs are allowed everywhere in the park and on the trails. Dogs may not be left unattended, and they must be leashed and cleaned up after. There are no additional pet fees. This campground is closed during the off-season. The camping and tent areas also allow dogs. There is a dog walk area at the campground. There are no electric or water hookups at the campground. Multiple dogs may be allowed.

Sleeping Bear Ranch and RV Resort
715 E Main Street (H 287)
Lander, WY
307-332-5159
Dogs of all sizes are allowed. There are no additional pet fees. Dogs must be well behaved, leashed, and cleaned up after. The camping and tent areas also allow dogs. There is a dog walk area at the campground. Multiple dogs may be allowed.

Laramie

Laramie KOA
1271 W Baker Street
Laramie, WY
307-742-6553
Dogs of all sizes and numbers are allowed. There are no additional pet fees. There are only 2 dogs allowed at the cabins. Dogs must be leashed and cleaned up after. There are some breed restrictions. The camping and tent areas also allow dogs. There is a dog walk area at the campground. Dogs are allowed in the camping cabins.

Medicine Bow - Routt National Forests
2468 Jackson Street
Laramie, WY
307-745-2300
This forest of nearly 3 million acres has 13 designated wilderness areas and its diverse ecosystems support a large variety of plants, fish, mammals, bird species, and recreation. Dogs of all sizes are allowed at no additional fee. Dogs may not be left unattended, and they

must be leased and cleaned up after. Dogs are allowed on the trails. This campground is closed during the off-season. The camping and tent areas also allow dogs. There is a dog walk area at the campground. Dogs are allowed in the camping cabins. There are no electric or water hookups at the campground. Multiple dogs may be allowed.

Lyman

Lyman KOA
1531N H 413
Lyman, WY
307-786-2188
Dogs of all sizes are allowed. There are no additional pet fees. Dogs must be leashed at all times and must be cleaned up after. This RV park is closed during the off-season. The camping and tent areas also allow dogs. There is a dog walk area at the campground. Multiple dogs may be allowed.

Moorcroft

Keyhole State Park
353 McKean Road
Moorcroft, WY
307-756-3596
This recreational park has 9 campgrounds, all overlooking the lake, and touts more than 200 species of birds. Dogs of all sizes are allowed. There are no additional pet fees. Dogs are allowed on the trails, but they are not allowed in the stores, public eating areas, the swim beach, or any buildings. The camping and tent areas also allow dogs. There is a dog walk area at the campground. There are no electric or water hookups at the campground. Multiple dogs may be allowed.

Moran

Flagg Ranch Resort
Box 187, 2 miles S of Yellowstonw
Moran, WY
800-443-2311
Dogs of all sizes are allowed, and there are no additional pet fees for tent or RV sites. There is a $10 per night per pet additional fee for the cabins. Dogs must be leashed and cleaned up after. This RV park is closed during the off-season. The camping and tent areas also allow dogs. There is a dog walk area at the campground. Dogs are allowed in the camping cabins. Multiple dogs may

be allowed.

Oacoma

Oasis Campground
1003 H 16
Oacoma, WY
605-734-6959
Dogs of all sizes are allowed. There are no additional pet fees. Dogs may be off lead if they are friendly and well behaved, but they must be cleaned up after at all times. This RV park is closed during the off-season. The camping and tent areas also allow dogs. There is a dog walk area at the campground. Multiple dogs may be allowed.

Piedmont

Elk Creek Resort and RV Park
8220 Elk Creek Road
Piedmont, WY
800-846-2267
Dogs of all sizes are allowed. There are no additional pet fees. Dogs must be leashed and cleaned up after. Dogs must be placed in a crate or taken with owner for cabin rentals. The camping and tent areas also allow dogs. There is a dog walk area at the campground. Dogs are allowed in the camping cabins. Multiple dogs may be allowed.

Pine Bluffs

Pine Bluffs RV Park
10 Paint Brush Road
Pine Bluffs, WY
800-294-4968
Dogs of all sizes are allowed. There are no additional pet fees. Dogs must be leashed and cleaned up after. The camping and tent areas also allow dogs. There is a dog walk area at the campground. Multiple dogs may be allowed.

Rawlins

Rawlins KOA
205 E H 71
Rawlins, WY
307-328-2021
Dogs of all sizes are allowed. There are no additional pet fees. Dogs may not be left unattended, and must be leashed, and cleaned up after. There are some breed restrictions. This RV park is closed during the off-season. The camping and tent areas also allow dogs.

There is a dog walk area at the campground. Dogs are allowed in the camping cabins. Multiple dogs may be allowed.

Western Hills Campground
2500 Wagon Circle Road
Rawlins, WY
888-568-3040
Dogs of all sizes are allowed. There are no additional pet fees. Dogs are not allowed to be tied to bumpers, poles, picnic tables, or any campground equipment. Dogs must be leashed and cleaned up after. There is a fenced in play area where dogs may be off lead. Dogs must be well behaved and not left unattended at any time. The camping and tent areas also allow dogs. There is a dog walk area at the campground. Multiple dogs may be allowed.

Riverton

Wind River RV Park
1618 E Park Avenue
Riverton, WY
800-528-3913
Dogs of all sizes are allowed. There are no additional pet fees. Dogs must be quiet, well behaved, leashed, and cleaned up after. This is an RV mostly park. They can make exception and place a tent on the lawn, but they water the lawns automatically everyday. There is a dog walk area at the campground. Multiple dogs may be allowed.

Rock Springs

Rock Springs KOA
86 Foothill Blvd
Rock Springs, WY
307-362-3063
Dogs of all sizes are allowed. There are no additional pet fees. Dogs may not be tied up outside unattended. Dogs must be leashed and cleaned up after. There are some breed restrictions. This RV park is closed during the off-season. The camping and tent areas also allow dogs. There is a dog walk area at the campground. Dogs are allowed in the camping cabins. Multiple dogs may be allowed.

Sheridan

Bighorn National Forest
2013 Eastside 2nd Street
Sheridan, WY
307-674-2600

The forest is open year round, but the campgrounds are mostly seasonal. Dogs of all sizes are allowed. There are no additional pet fees. Dogs are allowed on all the trails except for the ski trails in winter. This campground is closed during the off-season. The camping and tent areas also allow dogs. There is a dog walk area at the campground. There are no water hookups at the campground. Multiple dogs may be allowed.

Sheridan/Big Horn Mountains KOA
63 Decker Road
Sheridan, WY
307-674-8766
Dogs of all sizes are allowed. There are no additional pet fees. Well trained dogs may be off lead. Dogs must be cleaned up after. This RV park is closed during the off-season. The camping and tent areas also allow dogs. There is a dog walk area at the campground. Dogs are allowed in the camping cabins. Multiple dogs may be allowed.

Shoshoni

Boysen State Park
15 Ash, Boysen Route
Shoshoni, WY
307-876-2796
Dogs of all sizes are allowed. There are no additional pet fees. Dogs may not be left unattended, and they must be leashed and cleaned up after. Dogs are allowed on the trails, but not at the swim beaches. The camping and tent areas also allow dogs. There is a dog walk area at the campground. There are no electric or water hookups at the campground. Multiple dogs may be allowed.

Thermopolis

Eagle RV Park
204 H 20S
Thermopolis, WY
888-865-5707
Dogs of all sizes are allowed. There are no additional pet fees. Dogs must be quiet, leashed, and cleaned up after. This RV park is closed during the off-season. The camping and tent areas also allow dogs. There is a dog walk area at the campground. Dogs are allowed in the camping cabins. Multiple dogs may be allowed.

Fountain of Youth
250 H 20N

Thermopolis, WY
307-864-3265
Dogs of all sizes are allowed. There are no additional pet fees. Dogs are not allowed by the pool, and they must be leashed and cleaned up after. This RV park is closed during the off-season. The camping and tent areas also allow dogs. There is a dog walk area at the campground. Multiple dogs may be allowed.

Yellowstone - Grand Teton

Campgrounds in Grand Teton
Various
Grand Teton National Park, WY
800-628-9988
Dogs on leash are allowed in campgrounds thoughout Grand Teton National Park. Pets may not be left unattended and must be cleaned up after.

Colter Bay Campground
Colter Bay
Grand Teton National Park, WY
800-628-9988
This RV Park is located in Grand Teton National Park. It is the only RV Park in the park with electric hookups and the only one that will handle campers over 30 feet in length. Dogs on leash are allowed in the RV park.

Lizard Creek Campground
North End of Park
Grand Teton National Park, WY
800-672-6012
This RV Park and campground is located at the north end of Grand Teton National Park. This RV park has no electric hookups but does have water and dumping. RVs less than 30 feet in length are allowed. The campground is open seasonally from about June to September. Dogs on leash are allowed in the campground. No reservations are accepted, it is first come first serve.

Signal Mountain
16 Miles north of Jenny Lake
Grand Teton National Park, WY
800-672-6012
This RV Park and campground is located at the north end of Grand Teton National Park. This RV park has no electric hookups but does have water and dumping. RVs less than 30 feet in length are allowed. The campground is open seasonally from about May to

October. Dogs on leash are allowed in the campground. No reservations are accepted, it is first come first serve.

Bridger-Teton National Forest
340 Cash Street
Jackson, WY
307-739-5500
This park covers 3.4 million acres, and it is first come first serve for camping. Dogs of all sizes are allowed. There are no additional pet fees. Although it is not advised, dogs may be off lead in the forest if you have voice control. Dogs must be cleaned up after and they must be on leash in the camp areas. The camping and tent areas also allow dogs. There is a dog walk area at the campground. There are no electric or water hookups at the campground. 2 dogs may be allowed.

Jackson South/Hoback Junction KOA
9705 S H 89
Jackson, WY
307-733-7078
Dogs of all sizes are allowed. There are no additional pet fees. Dogs may not be left unattended, and must be quiet, leashed, and cleaned up after. There are some breed restrictions. This RV park is closed during the off-season. The camping and tent areas also allow dogs. There is a dog walk area at the campground. Dogs are allowed in the camping cabins. Multiple dogs may be allowed.

Virginian RV Resort
750 W Broadway
Jackson, WY
307-733-7189
Dogs of all sizes are allowed. There are no additional pet fees. Dogs must be leashed and cleaned up after. This RV park is closed during the off-season. There is a dog walk area at the campground. Multiple dogs may be allowed.

Teton Village/Jackson West KOA
2780 Moose Wilson Road
Teton Village, WY
307-733-5354
Dogs of all sizes are allowed. There are no additional pet fees. Dogs may not be left unattended, and they must be leashed and cleaned up after. There are some breed restrictions. This RV park is closed during the off-season. The camping and tent areas also allow dogs. There is a dog walk

area at the campground. Dogs are allowed in the camping cabins. Multiple dogs may be allowed.

Yellowstone Park/West Entrance KOA
3305 Targhee Pass H
W Yellowstone, WY
406-646-7606
Dogs of all sizes are allowed. There are no additional pet fees. Dogs may not be left unattended in the cabins, and they must be leashed and cleaned up after. There are some breed restrictions. This RV park is closed during the off-season. The camping and tent areas also allow dogs. There is a dog walk area at the campground. Dogs are allowed in the camping cabins. Multiple dogs may be allowed.

Campsites in Yellowstone National Park
Throughout
Yellowstone National Park, WY
307-344-7311
All Yellowstone campgrounds allow pets. Pets must be leashed at all times. Pets may not be left unattended, may not bark continuously, and must be cleaned up after. Pets are not allowed on park trails and must not be more than 100 feet from a roadway or parking area outside of the campground.

Fishing Bridge RV Park
Lake Yellowstone
Yellowstone National Park, WY
307-344-7311
This RV Park is located in the middle of Yellowstone National Park on the north side of Lake Yellowstone. It is open seasonally from May through October. Dogs are required to be on leash at all times.

Canada Listings

Alberta Listings

Anahim Lake

Tweedsmuir South Provincial Park
40 kilometers west of Anahim Lake
Anahim Lake, AB
250-397-2523
Of special note, they suggest caution and to call ahead to check road conditions on Highway 20 as it has up to an 18% grade in places. This park provides spectacular scenery, a rich cultural history, and diverse ecosystems that support a large variety of plants, animals, and recreation. Dogs of all sizes are allowed at no additional fee. Dogs may not be left unattended, and they must be leashed and cleaned up after. Dogs are allowed on the trails on leash. This campground is closed during the off-season. The camping and tent areas also allow dogs. There is a dog walk area at the campground. There are no electric or water hookups at the campground. Multiple dogs may be allowed.

Balzac

Whispering Spruce Campground
Range Road 10, 262195
Balzac, AB
403-226-0097
Dogs of all sizes are allowed. There is a pet policy to sign at check in and there are no additional pet fees. Dogs must be quiet, well behaved, may not be left unattended, and must be leashed and cleaned up after. Dogs are not allowed in the picnic or playground areas. This RV park is closed during the off-season. There is a dog walk area at the campground. Multiple dogs may be allowed.

Banff

Banff National Park of Canada
224 Banff Avenue
Banff, AB
403-762-1550
Nestled in the Canadian Rocky Mountains, this park is home to a national historic site, and offers interpretive programs/events, opportunities for nature study, and a wide range of land, water, and ice recreation. Dogs of all sizes are allowed at no additional fee. Dogs may not be left unattended at any time, and they must be inside your unit at night. Dogs must be leashed and cleaned up after. The camping and tent areas also allow dogs. There is a dog walk area at the campground.

Brooks

Dinosaur Provincial Park
Prairie Road 30
Brooks, AB
403-378-3700
Dogs of all sizes are allowed. There are no additional pet fees. Dogs must be leashed and cleaned up after. The camping and tent areas also allow dogs. There is a dog walk area at the campground. Multiple dogs may be allowed.

Calgary

Hinton/Jasper KOA
4720 Vegas Road NW
Calgary, AB
403-288-8351
Dogs of all sizes are allowed, and there are no additional pet fees for the tent or RV sites. There is a $10 per night per pet additional fee for the cabins. Dogs must be leashed and cleaned up after. There are some breed restrictions. This RV park is closed during the off-season. The camping and tent areas also allow dogs. There is a dog walk area at the campground. Dogs are allowed in the camping cabins. 2 dogs may be allowed.

Pine Creek RV Campground
On McCloud Trail
Calgary, AB
403-256-3002
Dogs of all sizes are allowed. There are no additional pet fees. Dogs must be well behaved, leashed, and cleaned up after. There is an off-lead fenced in area for the dogs to run. This RV park is closed during the off-season. There is a dog walk area at the campground. 2 dogs may be allowed.

Symon's Valley RV Park
260011 Symon's Valley Road NW
Calgary, AB
403-274-4574
Dogs of all sizes are allowed. There are no additional pet fees. Dogs must be leashed and cleaned up after. There is a dog walk area at the campground. 2 dogs may be allowed.

Campbell River, Vancouver Island

Elk Falls Provincial Park; Quinsam Campground
H 28
Campbell River, Vancouver Island, AB
250-248-9460
This park has been called "The Salmon Capitol of the World", but also offers an extensive network of forest trails, a waterfall, and a variety of land and water recreation. Dogs of all sizes are allowed at no additional fee. Dogs may not be left unattended, and they must be quiet, well behaved, leashed and cleaned up after. Dogs are allowed on the trails on leash. The camping and tent areas also allow dogs. There is a dog walk area at the campground. There are no electric or water hookups at the campground. Multiple dogs may be allowed.

Canmore

Spring Creek Mountain Village
502 3rd Avenue
Canmore, AB
403-678-5111
Dogs of all sizes are allowed. There is a $2 per night per dog additional fee. Dogs must be leashed and cleaned up after. There is a dog walk area at the campground. Multiple dogs may be allowed.

Edmonton

Glowing Embers RV Park
26309 Acheson
Edmonton, AB
877-785-7275
Dogs of all sizes are allowed. There are no additional pet fees. Dogs must be leashed and cleaned up after. The camping and tent areas also allow dogs. There is a dog walk area at the campground. Multiple dogs may be allowed.

Whitemud Creek Gold and RV Park
3428 156th Street SW
Edmonton, AB
780-988-6800
Dogs of all sizes are allowed. There are no additional pet fees. Dogs

must be leashed and cleaned up after. There is a dog walk area at the campground. 2 dogs may be allowed.

Edson

East of Eden Campground and RV Park
162 Range Road
Edson, AB
780-723-2287
Dogs of all sizes are allowed. There are no additional pet fees. Dogs must be quiet, well behaved, leashed, and cleaned up after. Dogs may not be left unattended outside, and may not be tied to any of the trees. There may be a minimal pet fee per night. This RV park is closed during the off-season. There is a dog walk area at the campground. 2 dogs may be allowed.

Fort Saskatchewan

Elk Island National Park of Canada
Site 4, RR #1
Fort Saskatchewan, AB
780-922-5790
This striking park is home to some of the most endangered habitats in Canada, to herds of free roaming bison, moose, elk, and deer. With 250 species of birds it is also a bird watcher's paradise. The park offers a variety of year round recreational pursuits. Dogs of all sizes are allowed at no additional fee. Dogs may not be left unattended, and they must be leashed and cleaned up after. Pets and pet food must be brought in at night. Dogs are allowed on the trails on lead. This campground is closed during the off-season. The camping and tent areas also allow dogs. There is a dog walk area at the campground. Multiple dogs may be allowed.

Hinton

Best Canadian Motor Inn and RV Park
386 Smith Street
Hinton, AB
780-865-5099
Dogs of all sizes and numbers are allowed, and there are no additional pet fees for RV sites. There is a $25 per night per pet additional fee for up to 2 dog at the motel, and pets are allowed in the smoking rooms only. Dogs must be quiet, well behaved, leashed, and cleaned up after. Dogs

may not be left unattended at any time. There is a dog walk area at the campground.

Jasper

Jasper National Park of Canada
500 Connaught Drive
Jasper, AB
780-852-6176
Born from glaciers and rich in natural history, this park is home to delicate and carefully protected ecosystems and more than 660 miles of trails. The park is home to highest mountain in Alberta and there are a variety of recreational pursuits available. Dogs of all sizes are allowed at no additional fee. Dogs may not be left unattended, and they must be leashed at all times, and cleaned up after. Pets and pet food must be brought inside at night. Dogs are allowed on trails on lead, unless otherwise marked. The camping and tent areas also allow dogs. There is a dog walk area at the campground. Multiple dogs may be allowed.

Lac Lac La Biche

Sir Winston Churchill Provincial Park
End of H 36N
Lac Lac La Biche, AB
780-623-4144
Located on an island accessible by a 2.5 km causeway, this park is host to more than 200 bird species. It offers various trails including a boardwalk trail that goes through a 300-year-old boreal forest and a variety of land and water recreation. Dogs of all sizes are allowed at no additional fee. Dogs may not be left unattended, and they must be quiet, well behaved, leashed and cleaned up after. Dogs are not allowed on the beach or in buildings, however, they are allowed on the trails on leash. This campground is closed during the off-season. The camping and tent areas also allow dogs. There is a dog walk area at the campground. Multiple dogs may be allowed.

Medicine Hat

Wild Rose Trailer Park
28B Camp Drive SW
Medicine Hat, AB
403-526-2248
Dogs of all sizes are allowed. There

are no additional pet fees. Dogs may not be left unattended, must be leashed, and cleaned up after. There is a dog walk area at the campground. Multiple dogs may be allowed.

Okanagan Lake

Fintry Provincial Park and Protected Area
Fintry Delta Road
Okanagan Lake, AB
250-260-3590
With two dramatically different topographical areas, this park has a variety of habitats, trails, historical features, a spectacular triple waterfall, and various land and water recreation to offer. Dogs of all sizes are allowed at no additional fee. Dogs may not be left unattended, and they must be quiet, well behaved, leashed at all times, and cleaned up after. Dogs are not allowed on the swim beach, but they are allowed on the trails on leash. This campground is closed during the off-season. The camping and tent areas also allow dogs. There is a dog walk area at the campground. There are no electric or water hookups at the campground. Multiple dogs may be allowed.

Pine Lake

Green Acres
Box 66
Pine Lake, AB
403-886-4833
Dogs of all sizes are allowed. There are no additional pet fees. Dogs must be leashed and cleaned up after. This RV park is closed during the off-season. There is a dog walk area at the campground. Multiple dogs may be allowed.

Terrace

Nisga'a Memorial Lava Bed Provincial Park
Kalum Lake Drive N
Terrace, AB
250-638-8490
These parks were combined to protect and interpret the natural features and native culture of the area. It also affords visitors the unique opportunity to explore a volcanic landscape. They offer guided tours, special events, and various trails and recreation. Dogs of all sizes are allowed at no additional

fee. Dogs may not be left unattended, and they must be leashed and cleaned up after. Dogs are not allowed on the quided tour trail to the volcano, however, they are allowed on the other trails on leash. This campground is closed during the off-season. The camping and tent areas also allow dogs. There is a dog walk area at the campground. There are no electric or water hookups at the campground. Multiple dogs may be allowed.

Vermilion

Vermilion Campground
5301 48th Street
Vermilion, AB
780-853-4372
Dogs of all sizes are allowed. There are no additional pet fees. Dogs must be leashed and cleaned up after. This RV park is closed during the off-season. The camping and tent areas also allow dogs. There is a dog walk area at the campground. Multiple dogs may be allowed.

British Columbia Listings

Burnaby

Burnaby Cariboo RV Park
8765 Cariboo Place
Burnaby, BC
604-420-1722
One dog of any size is allowed. There are no additional pet fees. Dogs may not be left unattended nor left tied up outside alone. Dogs must be leashed and cleaned up after. This RV park is closed during the off-season. The camping and tent areas also allow dogs. There is a dog walk area at the campground.

Burns Lake

Beaver Point Resort
16272 H 35
Burns Lake, BC
250-695-6519
Dogs of all sizes are allowed. There are no additional pet fees. Dogs must be leashed at all times and cleaned up after. Well behaved and quiet dogs may be left unattended at

your site. This RV park is closed during the off-season. The camping and tent areas also allow dogs. There is a dog walk area at the campground. Multiple dogs may be allowed.

Burns Lake KOA
4 miles E of Burns Lake on H 16
Burns Lake, BC
250-692-3105
Dogs of all sizes are allowed. There are no additional pet fees. Dogs may not be left unattended, must be leashed, and cleaned up after. This RV park is closed during the off-season. The camping and tent areas also allow dogs. There is a dog walk area at the campground. Dogs are allowed in the camping cabins. Multiple dogs may be allowed.

Cache Creek

Brookside Campsite
1621 E Trans Canada H
Cache Creek, BC
250-457-6633
Dogs of all sizes are allowed. There are no additional pet fees. Dogs may not be left unattended, must be leashed, and cleaned up after. This RV park is closed during the off-season. The camping and tent areas also allow dogs. There is a dog walk area at the campground. Multiple dogs may be allowed.

Campbell River

Ripple Rock RV Park
15011 Browns Bay Road
Campbell River, BC
250-287-7108
Dogs of all sizes are allowed. There are no additional pet fees. Dogs must be leashed and cleaned up after. This RV park is closed during the off-season. The camping and tent areas also allow dogs. There is a dog walk area at the campground. Multiple dogs may be allowed.

Salmon Point
2176 Salmon Point Road
Campbell River, BC
250-923-6605
Dogs of all sizes are allowed. There is a $1 per night per pet additional fee for small dogs, and a $2 per night per pet additional fee for medium to large dogs. Dogs must be leashed and cleaned up after. The camping and tent areas also allow dogs. There is a dog walk

area at the campground. Dogs are allowed in the camping cabins. Multiple dogs may be allowed.

Chilliwack

Cottonwood Meadows RV Country Club
44280 Luckakuck
Chilliwack, BC
604-824-7275
Small Dogs Only. One dog of any size is allowed. There are no additional pet fees. Dogs are not allowed to be tied up outside alone, and they must be leashed and cleaned up after. The camping and tent areas also allow dogs. There is a dog walk area at the campground.

Christina Lake

Cascade Cove RV Park
1120 River Road
Christina Lake, BC
250-447-9510
One dog of any size is allowed. There are no additional pet fees. Dogs may not be left unattended, must be leashed, and cleaned up after. There are some breed restrictions. This RV park is closed during the off-season. The camping and tent areas also allow dogs. There is a dog walk area at the campground.

Clearwater

Clearwater/Well Gray KOA
373 Clearwater Valley Road
Clearwater, BC
250-674-3909
Dogs of all sizes are allowed, and there are no additional pet fees for tent or RV sites. There is a $5 per night per pet additional fee for the motel. Dogs must be leashed and cleaned up after. This RV park is closed during the off-season. The camping and tent areas also allow dogs. There is a dog walk area at the campground. 2 dogs may be allowed.

Crofton

Osborne Bay Resort
1450 Charlette Street
Crofton, BC
250-246-4787
Friendly dogs of all sizes are allowed, and there are no additional pet fees for tent or RV sites. Up to

two very well behaved dogs are allowed in the cottages, and there is no extra fee unless it is an extra large, or heavy shedding dog. Dogs may not be left unattended in cottages, and they must be leashed and cleaned up after. The camping and tent areas also allow dogs. There is a dog walk area at the campground. Dogs are allowed in the camping cabins.

Dawson Creek

Mile Zero Park and Campground
1901 Alaska Avenue
Dawson Creek, BC
250-782-2590
Dogs of all sizes are allowed. There are no additional pet fees. Dogs may not be left unattended, must be leashed, and cleaned up after. This RV park is closed during the off-season. The camping and tent areas also allow dogs. There is a dog walk area at the campground. Multiple dogs may be allowed.

Dease Lake

Dease Lake RV Park
M.P. 488 H 37
Dease Lake, BC
250-771-4666
Dogs of all sizes are allowed. There are no additional pet fees. Dogs must be leashed and cleaned up after. This RV park is closed during the off-season. There is a dog walk area at the campground. Multiple dogs may be allowed.

Fairmont

Fairmont Hot Springs Resort
5225 Fairmont Hot Springs
Fairmont, BC
800-663-4979/ask for RV
Dogs of all sizes are allowed. There are no additional pet fees. Dogs must be quiet, leashed, and cleaned up after. This RV park is closed during the off-season. The camping and tent areas also allow dogs. There is a dog walk area at the campground. Multiple dogs may be allowed.

Field

Yoho National Park of Canada
P. O. Box 99/H 1
Field, BC
250-343-6783

This visually impressive park is home to a wide variety of habitats, spectacular waterfalls, towering rock walls, and a unique ecology. It offers more than 400 km of trails, interpretive signs and exhibits and various recreation. Dogs of all sizes are allowed at no additional fee. Dogs may not be left unattended, and they must be leashed and cleaned up after. Dogs are allowed on the trails on leash. This campground is closed during the off-season. The camping and tent areas also allow dogs. There is a dog walk area at the campground. There are no electric or water hookups at the campground. Multiple dogs may be allowed.

Fort Nelson

Fort Nelson
M.P. 293 Alaska H
Fort Nelson, BC
250-774-7270
Dogs of all sizes are allowed. There are no additional pet fees. Dogs must be leashed and cleaned up after when in the campgrounds. This RV park is closed during the off-season. The camping and tent areas also allow dogs. There is a dog walk area at the campground. Multiple dogs may be allowed.

Westend Campground
M.P. 304 Alaska H
Fort Nelson, BC
250-774-2340
Dogs of all sizes are allowed. There are no additional pet fees. Dogs must be leashed and cleaned up after. This RV park is closed during the off-season. The camping and tent areas also allow dogs. There is a dog walk area at the campground. Multiple dogs may be allowed.

Fort St John

Ross H. Maclean Rotary RV Park
13016 Lakeshore Drive
Fort St John, BC
250-785-1700
Dogs of all sizes are allowed. There are no additional pet fees. Dogs must be friendly, well behaved, leashed, and cleaned up after. Dogs can be walked by the lake. There are some breed restrictions. This RV park is closed during the off-season. The camping and tent areas also allow dogs. There is a dog walk area at the campground. Multiple dogs may be allowed.

Harrison

Harrison Springs Camping and RV Park
740 Hot Springs Road
Harrison, BC
604-796-8900
Dogs of all sizes are allowed, but only small dogs, 10 pounds or under, are allowed in the cabins. There are no additional pet fees. Dogs must be quiet, friendly, may not be left alone, must be leashed at all times, and cleaned up after. This RV park is closed during the off-season. The camping and tent areas also allow dogs. There is a dog walk area at the campground. Dogs are allowed in the camping cabins. Multiple dogs may be allowed.

Hope

Hope Valley Campground
62280 Flood Hope Road
Hope, BC
604-869-9857
Dogs of all sizes are allowed. There are no additional pet fees. Dogs may not be left unattended, must be leashed, and cleaned up after. This RV park is closed during the off-season. The camping and tent areas also allow dogs. There is a dog walk area at the campground. Multiple dogs may be allowed.

Iskut

Tatogga Lake Resort
At about M.P. 390 on H 37 (Box 5995)
Iskut, BC
250-234-3526
Dogs of all sizes are allowed at the tent and RV site, but only one dog is allowed in the cabins. There are no additional pet fees. Dogs may be off leash if well behaved. This RV park is closed during the off-season. The camping and tent areas also allow dogs. There is a dog walk area at the campground. Dogs are allowed in the camping cabins.

Jade City

Jade City RV Park
At about Mile Post 603/604 on H 37
Jade City, BC
250-239-3022
Dogs of all sizes are allowed. There are no additional pet fees. Dogs must be leashed and cleaned up after while in the campground, but

there is a big field close by where they can run off leash. This RV park is closed during the off-season. There is a dog walk area at the campground. Multiple dogs may be allowed.

Kitwanga

Cassiar RV Park
1535 Barcalow Road
Kitwanga, BC
250-849-5799
Dogs of all sizes are allowed. There are no additional pet fees. Dogs must be leashed and cleaned up after. This RV park is closed during the off-season. There is a dog walk area at the campground. Multiple dogs may be allowed.

Mill Bay

Bamberton Provincial Park
Mill Bay Road
Mill Bay, BC
250-474-1336
This park features a warm water bay, a long sandy beach, and a variety of recreational areas, woodlands, trails, and wildlife habitats. Dogs of all sizes are allowed at no additional fee. Dogs may not be left unattended except for short periods and then only if they will be quiet and well behaved. Dogs must be leashed and cleaned up after. Dogs are not allowed on the beach, however, they can be on the trails on lead. The camping and tent areas also allow dogs. There is a dog walk area at the campground. There are no electric or water hookups at the campground. Multiple dogs may be allowed.

Muncho Lake

J and H Wilderness Resort and RV Park
M.P. 463 Alaska H
Muncho Lake, BC
250-776-3453
Dogs of all sizes are allowed. There are no additional pet fees. Dogs may not be left unattended, must be leashed, and cleaned up after. This RV park is closed during the off-season. The camping and tent areas also allow dogs. There is a dog walk area at the campground. Multiple dogs may be allowed.

Northern Rockies Lodge
M.P. 462 Alaska H
Muncho Lake, BC

250-776-3481
Dogs of all sizes are allowed, and there are no additional pet fees for tent or RV sites. There is a $10 per night per pet additional fee for the lodge. Dogs may not be left unattended, must be leashed, and cleaned up after. The camping and tent areas also allow dogs. There is a dog walk area at the campground. 2 dogs may be allowed.

Oliver

Oliver/Gallagher Lake KOA
RR2 Site 41, Comp 8
Oliver, BC
250-498-3358
Dogs of all sizes are allowed. There are no additional pet fees. Dogs must be quiet, well behaved, leashed, and cleaned up after. Dogs are not allowed on the beach sites. This RV park is closed during the off-season. The camping and tent areas also allow dogs. There is a dog walk area at the campground. Multiple dogs may be allowed.

Osoyoos

Nk'Mip Resort
8000 45th Street
Osoyoos, BC
250-495-7279
Dogs of all sizes are allowed. There is a $4 per night per pet additional fee. Dogs may not be left unattended in the Yurts and may only be left in RVs if weather permits, or if the units have air conditioning. Dogs must be leashed and cleaned up after. There is a dog walk area at the campground. 2 dogs may be allowed.

Parksville

Parks Sands Beach Resort
105 E Island H
Parksville, BC
250-248-3171
Dogs of all sizes are allowed. There are no additional pet fees. Dogs may not be left unattended, and they must be leashed at all times, and cleaned up after. Dogs are not allowed on the beach at any time between March 1st and April 30th. This park is located on Vancouver Island and is accessible by ferry. Most of the ferry companies will allow dogs on the auto deck only. The camping and tent areas also allow dogs. There is a dog walk

area at the campground. Multiple dogs may be allowed.

Surfside RV Resort
200 N Corfield Street
Parksville, BC
866-642-2001
Dogs of all sizes are allowed. There are no additional pet fees. Dogs must be well behaved, may not be left unattended, must be leashed, and cleaned up after. There is a dog walk area at the campground. 2 dogs may be allowed.

Pink Mountain

Pink Mountain Campsite
M.P. 143 Alaska H
Pink Mountain, BC
250-772-5133
Dogs of all sizes are allowed. There are no additional pet fees. Dogs must be leashed and cleaned up after. Dogs may not be in the store or in the store parking lot. The camping and tent areas also allow dogs. There is a dog walk area at the campground. Dogs are allowed in the camping cabins. Multiple dogs may be allowed.

Prince George

Blue Spruce RV Park
4433 Kimbal Road
Prince George, BC
877-964-7272
Dogs of all sizes are allowed. There are no additional pet fees. Dogs may not be left unattended, must be leashed, and cleaned up after. Dogs are not allowed in the buildings. This RV park is closed during the off-season. The camping and tent areas also allow dogs. There is a dog walk area at the campground. Multiple dogs may be allowed.

Hartway RV Park
7729 S Kelly Road
Prince George, BC
250-962-8848
Dogs of all sizes are allowed. There are no additional pet fees. Dogs may not be left unattended at any time, must be leashed, and cleaned up after. This RV park is closed during the off-season. The camping and tent areas also allow dogs. There is a dog walk area at the campground. Multiple dogs may be allowed.

Sintich Trailer Park
7817 H 97

Prince George, BC
250-963-9862
Dogs of all sizes are allowed. There are no additional pet fees. Dogs must be leashed and cleaned up after. This RV park is closed during the off-season. The camping and tent areas also allow dogs. There is a dog walk area at the campground. Multiple dogs may be allowed.

Queen Charlotte

Gwaii Haanas National Park Reserve & Haida Heritage Site
P. O. Box 37
Queen Charlotte, BC
250-559-8818
Comprised of some 138 islands that stretch 90 kilometers from north to south, the rugged beauty and rich ecology of this park will allow visitors to have a complete wilderness experience. On islands where you may camp, you may only camp on the beaches. It is recommended that visitors not bring their pets with them into Gwaii Haanas, but if you do, when onshore, your pet must be kept on a leash at all times with an adult. They encourage you not to bring your pet ashore at any of the Watchmen sites. Hotspring Island is closed to pets. You must also register for an orientation prior to being allowed to this park. Only one dog is allowed per campsite. There is a dog walk area at the campground. There are no electric or water hookups at the campground.

Quesnel

Lake Daze Lakeside Resort
714 Ritchie Road
Quesnel, BC
250-992-6700
Dogs of all sizes are allowed. There are no additional pet fees. Dogs must be well behaved, may not be left unattended, must be leashed, and cleaned up after. This RV park is closed during the off-season. The camping and tent areas also allow dogs. There is a dog walk area at the campground. Multiple dogs may be allowed.

Radium Hot Springs

Kootenay National Park of Canada
P. O. Box 220/ Kootenay Parkway
Radium Hot Springs, BC
250-347-9615
This park offers a diversity of

naturescapes, elevations, climates, ecology, and recreation to its visitors. Dogs of all sizes are allowed at no additional fee. Dogs may not be left unattended, and they must be leashed and cleaned up after. Pets and pet food must be brought inside at night. Dogs are allowed on the trails on lead. This campground is closed during the off-season. The camping and tent areas also allow dogs. There is a dog walk area at the campground. Multiple dogs may be allowed.

Revelstoke

Canyon Hot Springs Resort
35 KM E of Revelstoke on H 1
Revelstoke, BC
250-837-2420
One dog of any size is allowed. There are no additional pet fees. Dogs may not be left unattended, must be leashed, and cleaned up after. This RV park is closed during the off-season. The camping and tent areas also allow dogs. There is a dog walk area at the campground.

Glacier National Park of Canada
P.O. Box 350
Revelstoke, BC
250-837-7500
Born from ancient glaciers and rich in natural history, this park protects unique old growth forests and critical habitats for threatened and endangered wildlife. Home to the Rogers Pass National Historic Site, the park offers interpretive programs as well as a variety of recreational pursuits. Dogs of all sizes are allowed at no additional fee. Dogs may not be left unattended, and they must be leashed and cleaned up after. Pets and pet food must be brought inside at night. Dogs are not allowed at Balu Pass, but they are allowed on the trails on lead. This campground is closed during the off-season. The camping and tent areas also allow dogs. There is a dog walk area at the campground. There are no electric or water hookups at the campground. Multiple dogs may be allowed.

Lamplighter Campground
1760 Nixon
Revelstoke, BC
250-837-3385

Dogs of all sizes are allowed. There are no additional pet fees. Dogs may not be left unattended, must be leashed, and cleaned up after. This RV park is closed during the off-season. The camping and tent areas also allow dogs. There is a dog walk area at the campground. Multiple dogs may be allowed.

Revelstoke KOA
2411 KOA Road
Revelstoke, BC
250-837-2085
Dogs of all sizes are allowed. There are no additional pet fees. Dogs must be leashed and cleaned up after. This RV park is closed during the off-season. The camping and tent areas also allow dogs. There is a dog walk area at the campground. 2 dogs may be allowed.

Williamson's Lake Campground
1816 Williamson Lake Road
Revelstoke, BC
250-837-5512
Dogs of all sizes are allowed. There are no additional pet fees. Dogs may not be left unattended, must be leashed, quiet, and cleaned up after. Dogs are not allowed on the beach nor at the cabins. They do have one teepee on site where dogs are welcome. This RV park is closed during the off-season. The camping and tent areas also allow dogs. There is a dog walk area at the campground. Multiple dogs may be allowed.

Scotch Creek

Shuswap Lake Provincial Park
Squilax Road
Scotch Creek, BC
250-955-0861
This very popular park offers a variety of habitats, scenic views, numerous trails, and various recreational pursuits. Dogs of all sizes are allowed at no additional fee. Dogs may not be left unattended, and they must be leashed and cleaned up after. Dogs may be off lead when in your camp only if they are under voice control, and will not leave the perimeter of your site. Dogs are not allowed in beach areas, beach trails, park buildings, or day-use areas, however, a stretch of beach is available adjacent to the boat launch where visitors may swim with their dogs. Dogs are allowed on the trails on leash. This campground is closed

during the off-season. The camping and tent areas also allow dogs. There is a dog walk area at the campground. There are no electric or water hookups at the campground. Multiple dogs may be allowed.

Sicamous

Sicamous KOA
3250 Oxboro Road
Sicamous, BC
250-836-2507
Dogs of all sizes are allowed, and there are no additional pet fees for tent or RV sites. There is a $5 per night per pet additional fee for cabins. Dogs may not be left unattended, must be leashed, and cleaned up after. This RV park is closed during the off-season. The camping and tent areas also allow dogs. There is a dog walk area at the campground. Dogs are allowed in the camping cabins. Multiple dogs may be allowed.

St John

Sourdough Pete's RV Park
MM 45 Alaska H
St John, BC
250-785-9255
Dogs up to about 50 pounds are allowed. There are no additional pet fees. Dogs must be friendly, well behaved, leashed, and cleaned up after. The camping and tent areas also allow dogs. There is a dog walk area at the campground. 2 dogs may be allowed.

Stewart

Bear River RV Park
2200 Davis Street
Stewart, BC
250-636-9205
Dogs of all sizes are allowed. There are no additional pet fees. Dogs must be quiet, may not be left unattended, must be leashed, and cleaned up after. This RV park is closed during the off-season. There is a dog walk area at the campground. Multiple dogs may be allowed.

Summerland

Okanagan Lake Provincial Park
On H 97, 11 km N of Summerland
Summerland, BC
250-494-6500

This park offers panoramic views, interpretive programs, sandy beaches, self-guided trails, and a variety of land and water recreation. Dogs of all sizes are allowed at no additional fee. Dogs may not be left unattended, and they must be leashed and cleaned up after. Dogs are not allowed in buildings, on beaches, or in the back country. This campground is closed during the off-season. The camping and tent areas also allow dogs. There is a dog walk area at the campground. There are no electric or water hookups at the campground.

Surrey

Dogwood Campground and RV Park
15151 112th Avenue
Surrey, BC
604-583-5585
Dogs of all sizes are allowed. There are no additional pet fees. Dogs must be leashed and cleaned up after. There are some breed restrictions. The camping and tent areas also allow dogs. There is a dog walk area at the campground. 2 dogs may be allowed.

Hazelmere RV Park
18843 8th Avenue
Surrey, BC
877-501-5007
Dogs of all sizes and numbers are allowed, however there can only be two dogs at a time in the cabins. There are no additional pet fees. Dogs must be quiet, well behaved, leashed and cleaned up after. Dogs are not to be left unattended in the cabins at any time. The camping and tent areas also allow dogs. There is a dog walk area at the campground. Dogs are allowed in the camping cabins.

Terrace

Lakelse Lake Provincial Park
P. O. Box 1124
Terrace, BC
250-638-8490
Surrounded by mountains, this scenic park offers a variety of habitats, trails, ecosystems, and land and water recreation. Dogs of all sizes are allowed at no additional fee. Dogs may not be left unattended, and they must be leashed and cleaned up after. Dogs are not allowed on the beach or in buildings; they are allowed on the

trails on leash. This campground is closed during the off-season. The camping and tent areas also allow dogs. There is a dog walk area at the campground. There are no electric or water hookups at the campground. Multiple dogs may be allowed.

Toad River

Toad River Lodge and RV
M.P. 422 Alaska H
Toad River, BC
250-232-5401
Dogs of all sizes and numbers are allowed, and there are no additional pet fees for tent or RV sites. There is a $5 per night per pet additional fee for the lodge, and only 2 dogs are allowed. Dogs must be leashed and cleaned up after. They may be left alone in your camper if they will be quiet. The camping and tent areas also allow dogs. There is a dog walk area at the campground.

Tofino

Mussel Beach Campground
Gravel Road, Section 54 off Port Albion Road
Tofino, BC
250-537-2081
Dogs of all sizes are allowed. There are no additional pet fees. Dogs may not be left unattended outside, and they must be leashed and cleaned up after. Dogs may be off lead only if they respond to voice control. This park is on Vancouver Island, is accessible by ferry, and dogs are allowed on most of them on the auto deck only. The camping and tent areas also allow dogs. There is a dog walk area at the campground. There are no electric or water hookups at the campgrounds. Multiple dogs may be allowed.

Ucluelet

Pacific Rim National Park Reserve of Canada
2185 Ocean Terrace Road
Ucluelet, BC
250-726-7721
This park has an abundance of natural and cultural treasures, is home to the rare ecosystem of a lush coastal temperate rainforest, and offers a wide variety of trails, long beaches and various recreational pursuits. Dogs of all sizes are allowed at no additional fee. Dogs may not be left unattended, and they

must be leashed and cleaned up after. Dogs are not allowed in buildings. Dogs are allowed on the trails on lead. This campground is closed during the off-season. The camping and tent areas also allow dogs. There is a dog walk area at the campground. There are no electric or water hookups at the campground. Multiple dogs may be allowed.

Victoria

Gulf Islands
2220 Harbour Road
Sidney, BC
250-654-4000
Spread 35 km over 15 islands, this first national park reserve of the 21st century, was initiated to protect the ecological integrity of the area, and to provide an educational experience of the culture and of the coastal island landscape. The islands are reached by ferry and other watercraft. BC Ferry will transport pets, but they must remain on vehicle decks for the duration of the voyage. This campground is closed during the off-season. The camping and tent areas also allow dogs. There is a dog walk area at the campground. There are no electric or water hookups at the campground. Multiple dogs may be allowed.

Fort Victoria RV Park
340 Island H
Victoria, BC
250-479-8112
Dogs of all sizes are allowed. There are no additional pet fees. Dogs may not be left unattended, must be leashed, and cleaned up after. There is a dog walk area at the campground. 2 dogs may be allowed.

Victoria West KOA
230 Trans-Canada H 1
Victoria, BC
250-478-3332
Dogs of all sizes are allowed. There are no additional pet fees. Dogs must be friendly, leashed, and cleaned up after. Dogs may be off leash on the dog walk if they are under voice control. This RV park is closed during the off-season. The camping and tent areas also allow dogs. There is a dog walk area at the campground. Dogs are allowed in the camping cabins. Multiple dogs may be allowed.

Weir's Beach RV Resort

5191 William Head Road
Victoria, BC
250-478-3323
Dogs of all sizes are allowed. There are no additional pet fees. Dogs must be leashed when in the park and cleaned up after. Dogs can be off leash at the river. There is a dog walk area at the campground. Multiple dogs may be allowed.

Westbay Oceanfront RV Park
453 Head Street
Victoria, BC
250-385-1831
Dogs of all sizes are allowed. There are no additional pet fees. Dogs must be leashed and cleaned up after. There are some breed restrictions. The camping and tent areas also allow dogs. There is a dog walk area at the campground. 2 dogs may be allowed.

Manitoba Listings

Brandon

Curran Park Campground
Box 6, 305 RR 3
Brandon, MB
204-571-0750
Dogs of all sizes are allowed. There are no additional pet fees. Dogs must be leashed and cleaned up after. This RV park is closed during the off-season. The camping and tent areas also allow dogs. There is a dog walk area at the campground. Multiple dogs may be allowed.

Meadowlark Campground
1629 Middleton
Brandon, MB
204-728-7205
Dogs of all sizes are allowed. There are no additional pet fees. Dogs must be quiet, leashed, and cleaned up after. This RV park is closed during the off-season. The camping and tent areas also allow dogs. There is a dog walk area at the campground. Multiple dogs may be allowed.

Dauphin

Rainbow Beach Campground
17 km E of Dauphin on H 20
Dauphin, MB

204-638-9493
Dogs of all sizes are allowed. There are no additional pet fees. Dogs must be leashed and cleaned up after, and they may not be on the beach. This RV park is closed during the off-season. The camping and tent areas also allow dogs. There is a dog walk area at the campground. Multiple dogs may be allowed.

Hadashville

Whitemouth River RV Park and Campground
On Government Jet Road
Hadashville, MB
204-426-5367
One dog of any size is allowed. There are no additional pet fees. Dogs must be leashed and cleaned up after. This RV park is closed during the off-season. The camping and tent areas also allow dogs. There is a dog walk area at the campground.

Portage la Prairie

Miller's Camping Resort
6 miles E of Portage on H 1
Portage la Prairie, MB
204-857-4255
Dogs of all sizes are allowed. There are no additional pet fees. Dogs must be quiet, leashed, and cleaned up after. This RV park is closed during the off-season. The camping and tent areas also allow dogs. There is a dog walk area at the campground. Multiple dogs may be allowed.

Portage Campground
8 miles E of Portage on H 1
Portage la Prairie, MB
204-267-2191
Dogs of all sizes are allowed. There are no additional pet fees. Dogs must be quiet, leashed, and cleaned up after. This RV park is closed during the off-season. The camping and tent areas also allow dogs. There is a dog walk area at the campground. 2 dogs may be allowed.

Shediac

Wikiwak Campground
55 S Cove
Shediac, MB
506-532-6713
Dogs of all sizes are allowed. There are no additional pet fees. Dogs

must be quiet, well behaved, leashed and cleaned up after. Dogs may not be left unattended. This RV park is closed during the off-season. The camping and tent areas also allow dogs. There is a dog walk area at the campground. Multiple dogs may be allowed.

St Malo

Debonair Campground
P. O. Box 68
St Malo, MB
204-347-5543
Dogs of all sizes are allowed. There are no additional pet fees. Dogs may not be left unattended outside, and may be left inside only if they will be quiet and well behaved. Dogs must be leashed and cleaned up after. This RV park is closed during the off-season. The camping and tent areas also allow dogs. There is a dog walk area at the campground. Multiple dogs may be allowed.

Swan River

Duck Mountain Provincial Park
P. O. Box 640
Swan River, MB
204-734-3429
This park of forested hills and river valleys offers a variety of trails and abundant year round recreation. Dogs of all sizes are allowed at no additional fee. Dogs may not be left unattended, and they must be leashed and cleaned up after. Dogs are allowed on the trails on leash. This campground is closed during the off-season. The camping and tent areas also allow dogs. There is a dog walk area at the campground. There are no water hookups at the campground. Multiple dogs may be allowed.

Virden

Virden's Lion's Campground
Corner &th and H 257
Virden, MB
204-748-6393
Dogs of all sizes are allowed. There are no additional pet fees. Dogs must be leashed and cleaned up after. This RV park is closed during the off-season. The camping and tent areas also allow dogs. There is a dog walk area at the campground. Multiple dogs may be allowed.

Wasagaming

Riding Mountain National Park of Canada
On H 10
Wasagaming, MB
204-848-7275
This park is an island mountain reserve that is home to a wide range of plant and animal life. It also offers panoramic views, numerous hiking trails, a lookout tower, and various recreational pursuits. Dogs of all sizes are allowed at no additional fee. Dogs may not be left unattended, and they must be leashed at all times, and cleaned up after. Dogs are not allowed on the beach. Dogs are allowed on the trails on lead. This campground is closed during the off-season. The camping and tent areas also allow dogs. There is a dog walk area at the campground. Multiple dogs may be allowed.

West Hawk Lake

Whitelshell Provincial Park
P. O. Box 119
West Hawk Lake, MB
204-349-2245
You will find rock alignments (petroforms) throughout this park that was created by natives over 8000 years ago. The park also offers interpretive programs, guided trails and is home to some of the province's nicest hiking trails. Dogs of all sizes are allowed at no additional fee. Dogs may not be left unattended, and they must be leashed and cleaned up after. Dogs are not allowed on the beach, however, they are allowed on trails on leash. This campground is closed during the off-season. The camping and tent areas also allow dogs. There is a dog walk area at the campground. Multiple dogs may be allowed.

Winnipeg

Bird's Hill Provincial Park
On Lagimodiere/H 59
Winnipeg, MB
888-482-2267
Dogs of all sizes are allowed. There are no additional pet fees. Dogs must be leashed and cleaned up for, and they are not allowed on the beach. This RV park is closed during the off-season. The camping and tent areas also allow dogs.

There is a dog walk area at the campground. Multiple dogs may be allowed.

Northgate Trailer Park
2695 Main
Winnipeg, MB
204-339-6631
Dogs of all sizes are allowed. There are no additional pet fees. Dogs must be leashed and cleaned up after. This RV park is closed during the off-season. The camping and tent areas also allow dogs. There is a dog walk area at the campground. Multiple dogs may be allowed.

Traveller's RV Resort
56001 Murdock Road
Winnipeg, MB
204-256-2186
Dogs of all sizes are allowed. There are no additional pet fees. Dogs must be leashed and cleaned up after. This RV park is closed during the off-season. The camping and tent areas also allow dogs. There is a dog walk area at the campground. Multiple dogs may be allowed.

New Brunswick Listings

Alma

Fundy National Park of Canada
P.O.Box 1001
Alma, NB
506-887-6000
This forest protects some of the last remaining wilderness in the area, and an interesting feature here are the tidal fluctuations in the Bay of Fundy, which are the highest in the world. They offer year round recreation and interpretive programs during the summer. Dogs of all sizes are allowed at no additional fee. Dogs may not be left unattended, and they must be leashed and cleaned up after. Pets and pet food must be brought in at night. Dogs are allowed on the trails on lead. This campground is closed during the off-season. The camping and tent areas also allow dogs. There is a dog walk area at the campground. Multiple dogs may be allowed.

Cap Pele

Sandy Beach Tent and Trailer Park
380 Bas-cap-pele
Cap Pele, NB
506-577-2218
Dogs of all sizes are allowed. There are no additional pet fees. Dogs may not be left unattended, must be leashed, and cleaned up after. This RV park is closed during the off-season. The camping and tent areas also allow dogs. There is a dog walk area at the campground. Multiple dogs may be allowed.

Edmundston

Camping St Basile
14411 Road 144
Edmundston, NB
506-263-1183
Dogs of all sizes are allowed. There are no additional pet fees. Dogs must be leashed and cleaned up after. This RV park is closed during the off-season. The camping and tent areas also allow dogs. There is a dog walk area at the campground. Multiple dogs may be allowed.

Fredericton

Hartt Island RV Resort
2475 Woodstock Road
Fredericton, NB
866-462-9400
Dogs of all sizes are allowed. There are no additional pet fees. Dogs must be leashed and cleaned up after. This RV park is closed during the off-season. The camping and tent areas also allow dogs. There is a dog walk area at the campground. Multiple dogs may be allowed.

Grand Barachois

Camping Plage Gagnon Beach
30 Plage Ganon Beach Road
Grand Barachois, NB
800-658-2828
Dogs of all sizes are allowed. There are no additional pet fees. Dogs must be quiet, well behaved, leashed, and cleaned up after. This RV park is closed during the off-season. The camping and tent areas also allow dogs. There is a dog walk area at the campground. Multiple dogs may be allowed.

Hopewell Cape

Ponderosa Pines Camping

4325 H 114
Hopewell Cape, NB
800-822-8800
Dogs of all sizes are allowed. There are no additional pet fees. Dogs must be leashed and cleaned up after. This RV park is closed during the off-season. The camping and tent areas also allow dogs. There is a dog walk area at the campground. Multiple dogs may be allowed.

Kouchibouguac National Park

Kouchibouguac National Park of Canada
186, Route 117
Kouchibouguac National Park, NB
506-876-2443
This wilderness park offers spectacular scenery and diverse ecosystems that support a large variety of plants, fish, mammals, bird species. It also offers 60 km of trails and year round recreation. Dogs of all sizes are allowed at no additional fee. Dogs may not be left unattended, and they must be quiet, well behaved, leashed and cleaned up after. Dogs are not allowed on the beach. Dogs are allowed on the trails on lead. The camping and tent areas also allow dogs. There is a dog walk area at the campground. There are no water hookups at the campground. Multiple dogs may be allowed.

Moncton

Camper's City RV Park
138 Queens Way Drive
Moncton, NB
877-512-7868
Dogs of all sizes are allowed. There are no additional pet fees. Dogs must be leashed and cleaned up after. This RV park is closed during the off-season. The camping and tent areas also allow dogs. There is a dog walk area at the campground. Dogs are allowed in the camping cabins. Multiple dogs may be allowed.

Stonehurst Trailer Park
47915 Homestead Road
Moncton, NB
506-852-4162
Dogs of all sizes are allowed. There are no additional pet fees. Dogs must be leashed and cleaned up after. This RV park is closed during the off-season. The camping and tent areas also allow dogs. There is a dog walk area at the campground.

Multiple dogs may be allowed.

Saint Jacques

Camping Panoramic
14 Road Albert
Saint Jacques, NB
506-739-6544
Dogs of all sizes are allowed. There are no additional pet fees. Dogs must be leashed and cleaned up after. This RV park is closed during the off-season. The camping and tent areas also allow dogs. There is a dog walk area at the campground. Multiple dogs may be allowed.

Saint John

Rockwood Park
142 Lakeside Drive S
Saint John, NB
506-652-4050
Dogs of all sizes are allowed. There are no additional pet fees. Dogs must be leashed and cleaned up after. This RV park is closed during the off-season. The camping and tent areas also allow dogs. There is a dog walk area at the campground. Multiple dogs may be allowed.

Saint Louis-de-Kent

National Daigles Park
10787 H 134
Saint Louis-de-Kent, NB
877-324-4531
Dogs of all sizes are allowed. There are no additional pet fees. Dogs may not be left unattended, must be leashed, and cleaned up after. This RV park is closed during the off-season. The camping and tent areas also allow dogs. There is a dog walk area at the campground. 2 dogs may be allowed.

St Martins

Century Farm Family Campground
670 Ocean Wave Drive
St Martins, NB
866-394-4400
Dogs of all sizes and numbers are allowed, but only 2 dogs are allowed per cabin, and they are not to be on the furniture. There are no additional pet fees. Dogs may not be left unattended, must be well behaved, leashed, and cleaned up after. This RV park is closed during the off-season. The camping and tent areas also allow dogs. There is a dog walk

area at the campground. Dogs are allowed in the camping cabins. Multiple dogs may be allowed.

Woodstock

Jellystone Park at Kozy Acres
174 Hemlock Street
Woodstock, NB
506-328-6287
Dogs of all sizes are allowed. There are no additional pet fees. Dogs must be leashed and cleaned up after. This RV park is closed during the off-season. The camping and tent areas also allow dogs. There is a dog walk area at the campground. Multiple dogs may be allowed.

Newfoundland Listings

Arnold's Cove

Arnold's Cove RV Park
5 km E of Arnold's Cove on H 1
Arnold's Cove, NF
709-685-6767
Dogs of all sizes are allowed. There are no additional pet fees. Dogs must be leashed and cleaned up after. This RV park is closed during the off-season. The camping and tent areas also allow dogs. There is a dog walk area at the campground.

Doyles

Grand Codroy RV Camping Park
On Doyle Station Road
Doyles, NF
877-955-2520
Dogs of all sizes are allowed. There are no additional pet fees. Dogs must be leashed and cleaned up after. This RV park is closed during the off-season. The camping and tent areas also allow dogs. There is a dog walk area at the campground. Multiple dogs may be allowed.

Eastport

Eastport Peninsula Sunshine Park
On the Road to the Beaches-H 310
Eastport, NF
709-677-2438
Dogs of all sizes are allowed. There are no additional pet fees. Dogs

must be leashed and cleaned up after. This RV park is closed during the off-season. The camping and tent areas also allow dogs. There is a dog walk area at the campground. Dogs are allowed in the camping cabins. Multiple dogs may be allowed.

Glovertown

Terra Nova National Park of Canada
Trans Canada #1
Glovertown, NF
709-533-2801
Trails wind from bogs, ponds, and rolling forested hills to the rugged cliffs and inlets of the coastal region, offering a variety of habitats and recreational opportunities. Dogs of all sizes are allowed at no additional fee. Dogs may not be left unattended, and they must be leashed and cleaned up after. Dogs are not allowed on the beach. Dogs are allowed on the trails on lead. The camping and tent areas also allow dogs. There is a dog walk area at the campground. Multiple dogs may be allowed.

Green's Harbour

Golden Arm Trailer Park
12 miles from H 1 on H 80
Green's Harbour, NF
709-582-3600
One dog of any size is allowed. There are no additional pet fees. Dogs must be leashed and cleaned up after. Long hair/shedding type dogs are not allowed in the cabins, and they must stay off the furniture. This RV park is closed during the off-season. The camping and tent areas also allow dogs. There is a dog walk area at the campground. Dogs are allowed in the camping cabins.

Lomand River

Lomand River Lodge
10 km from H 430 on H 431
Lomand River, NF
877-456-6663
Dogs of all sizes are allowed. There are no additional pet fees. Dogs may not be left unattended, especially at the cabins. Dogs must be leashed and cleaned up after. This RV park is closed during the off-season. The camping and tent areas also allow dogs. There is a

dog walk area at the campground. Dogs are allowed in the camping cabins. Multiple dogs may be allowed.

Rocky Harbour

Gros Morne National Park of Canada
P.O. Box 130
Rocky Harbour, NF
709-458-2417
Designated as a UNESCO World Heritage Site, this park, rich in natural beauty, offers unique geological features, an in depth Discovery Center, a wide variety of plant, marine, and animal life, and a multitude of recreational activities. Dogs of all sizes are allowed at no additional fee. Dogs may not be left unattended, and they must be leashed and cleaned up after. Pets and pet food must be brought inside at night. Dogs are allowed on the trails on lead unless otherwise marked. This campground is closed during the off-season. The camping and tent areas also allow dogs. There is a dog walk area at the campground. There are no electric or water hookups at the campground. Multiple dogs may be allowed.

South Brook

Kona Beach Trailer Park
On H 1 80 80 km W of Grand Falls
South Brook, NF
709-657-2400
Dogs of all sizes are allowed. There are no additional pet fees. Dogs must be leashed and cleaned up after. This RV park is closed during the off-season. The camping and tent areas also allow dogs. There is a dog walk area at the campground. Multiple dogs may be allowed.

St Johns

Pippy RV Park
34 Nagles Place
St Johns, NF
709-737-3669
Dogs of all sizes are allowed. There are no additional pet fees. Dogs must be quiet, well behaved, leashed, and cleaned up after. This RV park is closed during the off-season. The camping and tent areas also allow dogs. There is a dog walk area at the campground. Multiple dogs may be allowed.

Northwest Territories Listings

Fort Simpson

Nahanni National Park Reserve of Canada
P. O. Box 348
Fort Simpson, NT
867-695-3151
The raw nature and breathtaking scenery of this park will give the adventurous visitor a true wilderness experience. The park is accessible only by aircraft. It provides tent camping only and there are no concessions at this park. Dogs are allowed at no additional fee. Dogs may not be left unattended at any time, and they must be leashed at all times. Dogs are not allowed on river trips or tours. There are no developed trails or roads in or to the park. Only one dog is allowed per campsite. The camping and tent areas also allow dogs. There is a dog walk area at the campground. There are no electric or water hookups at the campground.

Fort Smith

Wood Buffalo National Park of Canada
149 McDoogle Road
Fort Smith, NT
867-872-7900
This park is a UNESCO World Heritage Site, it is Canada's largest national park and has been recognized as a critical habitat for migratory birds. The park offers a variety of interesting trails and various recreational pursuits. Dogs of all sizes are allowed at no additional fee. Dogs may not be left unattended, and they must be leashed and cleaned up after. Dogs are allowed on the trails on leash. The camping and tent areas also allow dogs. There is a dog walk area at the campground. There are no electric or water hookups at the campground. Multiple dogs may be allowed.

Pangnirtung

Auyuittuq National Park of Canada
P. O. Box 353

Pangnirtung, NT
867-473-2500
This park lies at the Arctic Circle and is still vibrant with ongoing glacial activity. It is accessible by air only; being a 5 hour trip from the closest departure area. You will find everything from steep-walled ocean fjords, to jagged mountain peaks, and deep valleys. The are no services available at all. Dogs must be leashed and with you at all times. This campground is closed during the off-season. There are no electric or water hookups at the campground.

Sachs Harbour

Aulavik National Park of Canada
Box 29
Sachs Harbour, NT
867-690-3904
Rich in pre-historic history, this arctic park is an isolated wilderness area with a variety of landscapes from seacoasts, river valleys and polar deserts to the buttes and badlands. It is only accessible by air. There are no services at all or developed trails. Dogs are allowed if they can make the flight, and must be kept with owners at all times. This campground is closed during the off-season. There are no electric or water hookups at the campground.

Nova Scotia Listings

Baddeck

Baddeck Cabot Trail Campground
9584 Trans Canada H 105
Baddeck, NS
902-295-2288
Dogs of all sizes are allowed. There are no additional pet fees. Dogs must be leashed and cleaned up after. This RV park is closed during the off-season. The camping and tent areas also allow dogs. There is a dog walk area at the campground. Dogs are allowed in the camping cabins. Multiple dogs may be allowed.

Barwick

Plantation Campground and RV Park
210 W Steadmon Road
Barwick, NS
888-363-8882
Dogs of all sizes are allowed at the tent and RV sites, but there can only be up to 2 small dogs (under 15 pounds) in the cabins. There are no additional pet fees. Dogs must be leashed and cleaned up after. This RV park is closed during the off-season. The camping and tent areas also allow dogs. There is a dog walk area at the campground. Dogs are allowed in the camping cabins.

Cheticamp

Cape Breton Highlands National Park of Canada
16648 Cabot Trail
Cheticamp, NS
902-224-2306
Rich in natural and cultural heritage with a human heritage dating back to the ice age, this park provides spectacular scenery, abundant wildlife, and a variety of recreational pursuits. Dogs of all sizes are allowed at no additional fee. Dogs may not be left unattended unless they will be quiet and well behaved. Dogs must be leashed and cleaned up after. Dogs are allowed on the trails, unless otherwise marked, and they are not allowed on the Skyline Trial. The camping and tent areas also allow dogs. There is a dog walk area at the campground. Multiple dogs may be allowed.

Five Islands

Sand Point Beach Campground
412 Wharf Road
Five Islands, NS
902-254-2755
Dogs of all sizes are allowed. There are no additional pet fees. Dogs must be leashed and cleaned up after. This RV park is closed during the off-season. The camping and tent areas also allow dogs. There is a dog walk area at the campground. Multiple dogs may be allowed.

Halifax

Woodhaven RV Park
1757 Hammonds Pines Road
Halifax, NS
902-835-2271
Dogs of all sizes are allowed. There

are no additional pet fees. Dogs may not be left unattended, must be leashed, and cleaned up after. This RV park is closed during the off-season. The camping and tent areas also allow dogs. There is a dog walk area at the campground. Multiple dogs may be allowed.

Hubbards

Hubbards Beach Campground
226 Shore Club Road
Hubbards, NS
902-857-9460
Dogs of all sizes are allowed. There are no additional pet fees. Dogs must be well behaved, leashed and cleaned up after, and may not be on the beach. This RV park is closed during the off-season. The camping and tent areas also allow dogs. There is a dog walk area at the campground. Multiple dogs may be allowed.

Kingston

Jellystone Park
43 Boo Boo Blvd
Kingston, NS
888-225-7773
Dogs of all sizes are allowed. There are no additional pet fees. Dogs must be leashed and cleaned up after. This RV park is closed during the off-season. The camping and tent areas also allow dogs. There is a dog walk area at the campground. Multiple dogs may be allowed.

New Harris

Seal Island/North Sydney KOA
3779 New Harris Road
New Harris, NS
902-674-2145
Dogs of all sizes are allowed. There are no additional pet fees. Dogs may not be left outside unattended, must be leashed, and cleaned up after. This RV park is closed during the off-season. The camping and tent areas also allow dogs. There is a dog walk area at the campground. Dogs are allowed in the camping cabins. Multiple dogs may be allowed.

Pictou

Harbour Light Campground
2881 Tree Brooks
Pictou, NS
902-485-5733

Dogs of all sizes are allowed. There are no additional pet fees. Dogs must be leashed and cleaned up after, and they are not allowed on the beach. This RV park is closed during the off-season. The camping and tent areas also allow dogs. There is a dog walk area at the campground. Multiple dogs may be allowed.

S Harbour

Hide-Away Campground
401 Shore Road
S Harbour, NS
902-383-2116
Dogs of all sizes are allowed. There are no additional pet fees. Dogs must be leashed and cleaned up after. Dogs are allowed at the beach, and only 1 dog is allowed in the cabins. This RV park is closed during the off-season. The camping and tent areas also allow dogs. There is a dog walk area at the campground. Multiple dogs may be allowed.

Seafoam

Seafoam Campground
3493 River John
Seafoam, NS
902-351-3122
Dogs of all sizes are allowed. There are no additional pet fees. Dogs must be leashed and cleaned up after, and they are allowed to go to the beach area. This RV park is closed during the off-season. The camping and tent areas also allow dogs. There is a dog walk area at the campground. Multiple dogs may be allowed.

Sydeny

River Ryan Campground
5779 Union H
New Waterford, NS
902-862-8367
Dogs of all sizes are allowed. There are no additional pet fees. Dogs may not be left unattended, must be leashed, and cleaned up after. This RV park is closed during the off-season. The camping and tent areas also allow dogs. There is a dog walk area at the campground. Multiple dogs may be allowed.

Sydney

Arm of Gold Campground
Corner of Church Street and H 105
Little Bras d'or, NS
866-736-6516
Dogs of all sizes are allowed. There are no additional pet fees. Dogs must be leashed and cleaned up after. This RV park is closed during the off-season. The camping and tent areas also allow dogs. There is a dog walk area at the campground. Multiple dogs may be allowed.

Truro

Scotia Pine Campground
On Route 2
Truro, NS
877-893-3666
Dogs of all sizes are allowed. There are no additional pet fees. Dogs may not be left unattended, must be leashed, and cleaned up after. This RV park is closed during the off-season. The camping and tent areas also allow dogs. There is a dog walk area at the campground. Dogs are allowed in the camping cabins. Multiple dogs may be allowed.

Upper Sackville

Halifax West KOA
3070 H 1
Upper Sackville, NS
902-865-4342
Dogs of all sizes are allowed. There are no additional pet fees. Dogs must be quiet, well behaved, leashed, and cleaned up after. Dogs may not be left unattended. This RV park is closed during the off-season. The camping and tent areas also allow dogs. There is a dog walk area at the campground. Dogs are allowed in the camping cabins. Multiple dogs may be allowed.

Ontario Listings

Important – Ontario has banned Pit Bulls and similar dogs from the province. Please see dogfriendly.com/bsl for more information.

Amherstburg

Jellystone Park
4610 County Road 18
Amherstburg, ON
519-736-3201
Dogs of all sizes are allowed. There are no additional pet fees. Dogs must be leashed and cleaned up

after. This RV park is closed during the off-season. The camping and tent areas also allow dogs. Multiple dogs may be allowed.

Barrie

Barrie KOA
3138 Penetanguishene Road
Barrie, ON
705-726-6128
Dogs of all sizes are allowed. There are no additional pet fees. Dogs may not be left unattended, must be on no more than a 6 foot leash, and cleaned up after. There are some breed restrictions. This RV park is closed during the off-season. The camping and tent areas also allow dogs. There is a dog walk area at the campground. Dogs are allowed in the camping cabins. Multiple dogs may be allowed.

Barry's Bay

Chippawa Easy Living Camping and RV Park
RR 1, 835 Chippawa Road
Barry's Bay, ON
613-267-8507
Dogs of all sizes are allowed. There are no additional pet fees. Dogs must be leashed and cleaned up after. There are some breed restrictions. This RV park is closed during the off-season. The camping and tent areas also allow dogs. There is a dog walk area at the campground. 2 dogs may be allowed.

Bradford

Yogi Bear's Jellystone Park
3666 Simcoe Road 88
Bradford, ON
905-775-1377
Dogs of all sizes are allowed. There are no additional pet fees. Dogs must be well behaved, leashed and cleaned up after. Pit bull breeds are not allowed. This RV park is closed during the off-season. The camping and tent areas also allow dogs. There is a dog walk area at the campground. Multiple dogs may be allowed.

Brighton

Brighton/401 KOA
15043 Telephone Road
Brighton, ON

613-475-2186
Dogs of all sizes are allowed. There are no additional pet fees. Dogs must be leashed and cleaned up after. There are some breed restrictions. This RV park is closed during the off-season. The camping and tent areas also allow dogs. There is a dog walk area at the campground. Dogs are allowed in the camping cabins. Multiple dogs may be allowed.

Cambridge

Valens Conservation Area
1691 Regional Park Road 97
Cambridge, ON
905-525-2183
Dogs of all sizes are allowed. There are no additional pet fees. Dogs must be leashed and cleaned up after. Dogs are not allowed at the sand beach, but they are allowed at the doggy beach. There are some breed restrictions. The camping and tent areas also allow dogs. There is a dog walk area at the campground. Multiple dogs may be allowed.

Campbellville

Toronto West KOA
9301 Second Line Nassagaweya,
RR 1
Campbellville, ON
905-845-2495
Dogs of all sizes are allowed. There are no additional pet fees. Dogs must be well behaved, may not be left unattended, and must be leashed and cleaned up after. No visitor pets are allowed. They offer a complimentary dog sitting service for up to 2 dogs and they also greet your dog with pet treats at the door. There are some breed restrictions. This RV park is closed during the off-season. The camping and tent areas also allow dogs. There is a dog walk area at the campground. There are special amenities given to dogs at this campground. Multiple dogs may be allowed.

Cardinal

Cardinal KOA
609 Pittston Road
Cardinal, ON
613-657-4536
Dogs of all sizes are allowed. There are no additional pet fees. Dogs may not be left unattended, must be leashed, and cleaned up after.

There are some breed restrictions. This RV park is closed during the off-season. The camping and tent areas also allow dogs. There is a dog walk area at the campground. Dogs are allowed in the camping cabins. Multiple dogs may be allowed.

Cherry Valley

Quinte's Isle Campark
237 Salmon Point Road
Cherry Valley, ON
613-476-6310
Dogs of all sizes are allowed. There are no additional pet fees. Dogs must be leashed and cleaned up after. The camping and tent areas also allow dogs. There is a dog walk area at the campground. Multiple dogs may be allowed.

Cookstown

Toronto North/Cookstown KOA
139 Reive Blvd
Cookstown, ON
705-458-2267
Dogs of all sizes are allowed. There are no additional pet fees. Dogs must be well behaved, may not be left unattended, and must be leashed and cleaned up after. There are some breed restrictions. This RV park is closed during the off-season. The camping and tent areas also allow dogs. There is a dog walk area at the campground. Multiple dogs may be allowed.

Forest

Carolinian Forest Campground
9589 Ipperwash Road
Forest, ON
519-243-2258
One dog of any size is allowed. There are no additional pet fees. Dogs may not be left unattended, must be quiet and well behaved, and leashed and cleaned up after. Dogs are allowed at the beach. There are some breed restrictions. This RV park is closed during the off-season. The camping and tent areas also allow dogs. There is a dog walk area at the campground.

Gravenhurst

Gravenhurst/Muskoka KOA
1083 Reay Road E
Gravenhurst, ON
705-687-2333

Dogs of all sizes are allowed. There are no additional pet fees. Dogs may not be left unattended, must be leashed, and cleaned up after. There are some breed restrictions. This RV park is closed during the off-season. The camping and tent areas also allow dogs. There is a dog walk area at the campground. Multiple dogs may be allowed.

Heron Bay

Pukaskwa National Park of Canada
P. O. Box 212/h 627
Heron Bay, ON
807-229-0801
Rich in ancient and modern history, this beautiful park is the only wilderness national park in Ontario, and offers a variety of habitats, wildlife, trails, and recreation. Dogs of all sizes are allowed at no additional fee. Dogs may not be left unattended, and they must be quiet, leashed, and cleaned up after. Dogs are not allowed in the back country, but they are allowed on the day trails on lead. The camping and tent areas also allow dogs. There is a dog walk area at the campground. There are no water hookups at the campground. Multiple dogs may be allowed.

Ipperwash Beach

Our Ponderosa Family Campground
9338 W Ipperwash Road
Ipperwash Beach, ON
888-786-2267
Dogs of all sizes are allowed. There are no additional pet fees. Dogs must be leashed at all times and cleaned up after. This RV park is closed during the off-season. The camping and tent areas also allow dogs. There is a dog walk area at the campground. Multiple dogs may be allowed.

Johnstown

Grenville Park
2323 County Road 2 RR3
Johnstown, ON
613-925-2000
Dogs of all sizes are allowed. There are no additional pet fees. Dogs must be leashed and cleaned up after. Dogs may not be on the furniture or beds in the cabin. This RV park is closed during the off-

season. The camping and tent areas also allow dogs. There is a dog walk area at the campground. Dogs are allowed in the camping cabins. Multiple dogs may be allowed.

Kapuskasing

Rene Brunelle Provincial Park
Provincinial Park Road
Kapuskasing, ON
705-367-2692
Dogs of all sizes are allowed. There are no additional pet fees. Dogs must be leashed and cleaned up after, and they are not allowed on the beach. This RV park is closed during the off-season. The camping and tent areas also allow dogs. There is a dog walk area at the campground. Multiple dogs may be allowed.

Kincardine

Aintree Trailer Park
2435 Huron Consession 12 Road
Kincardine, ON
519-396-8533
Dogs of all sizes are allowed. There are no additional pet fees. Dogs may not be left unattended, must be quiet, leashed, and cleaned up after. Dogs are allowed at the beach. This RV park is closed during the off-season. The camping and tent areas also allow dogs. There is a dog walk area at the campground. Multiple dogs may be allowed.

Kingston

1000 Islands/Kingston KOA
2039 Cordukes Road
Kingston, ON
613-546-6140
Friendly dogs of all sizes are allowed. There are no additional pet fees. Dogs may not be left unattended, must be leashed, and cleaned up after. There are some breed restrictions. This RV park is closed during the off-season. The camping and tent areas also allow dogs. There is a dog walk area at the campground. Dogs are allowed in the camping cabins. Multiple dogs may be allowed.

Lake Ontario Park
1000 King Street W
Kingston, ON
613-542-6574

Dogs of all sizes are allowed. There are no additional pet fees. Dogs must be leashed and cleaned up after. This RV park is closed during the off-season. The camping and tent areas also allow dogs. There is a dog walk area at the campground. Multiple dogs may be allowed.

Rideau Acres
1014 Cunningham Road
Kingston, ON
613-546-2711
Dogs of all sizes are allowed. There are no additional pet fees. Dogs must be leashed and cleaned up after, and may not be on the beach. This RV park is closed during the off-season. The camping and tent areas also allow dogs. There is a dog walk area at the campground. Multiple dogs may be allowed.

Kitchener

Bingeman's Campground
425 Bingeman's Drive
Kitchener, ON
519-744-1002
Dogs of all sizes are allowed. There are no additional pet fees. Dogs may not be left unattended, must be quiet, well behaved, leashed at all times and cleaned up after. There are some breed restrictions. This RV park is closed during the off-season. The camping and tent areas also allow dogs. There is a dog walk area at the campground. Multiple dogs may be allowed.

Lans Downe

1000 Islands Camping Resort
382 1000 Islands Parkway
Lans Downe, ON
613-659-3058
Dogs of all sizes are allowed. There are no additional pet fees. Dogs must be leashed and cleaned up after. There are some breed restrictions. This RV park is closed during the off-season. The camping and tent areas also allow dogs. There is a dog walk area at the campground.

Lansdowne

1000 Islands/Ivy Lea KOA
514 1000 Islands Parkway
Lansdowne, ON
613-659-2817
Dogs of all sizes are allowed. There are no additional pet fees. Dogs

must be quiet, well behaved, leashed, and cleaned up after. There are some breed restrictions. This RV park is closed during the off-season. The camping and tent areas also allow dogs. There is a dog walk area at the campground. Dogs are allowed in the camping cabins. Multiple dogs may be allowed.

London

London/401 KOA
136 Cromarty Drive
London, ON
519-644-0222
Dogs of all sizes are allowed. There are no additional pet fees. Dogs must be leashed and cleaned up after. There are some breed restrictions. This RV park is closed during the off-season. The camping and tent areas also allow dogs. There is a dog walk area at the campground. 2 dogs may be allowed.

Madawaska

All Star Resort
1 Major Lake Road
Madawaska, ON
613-637-5592
Dogs of all sizes are allowed, and there are no additional pet fees for tent or RV sites, which are seasonal. There is a $10 per night per pet additional fee for the cabins, and the cabins are available year around. Dogs must be leashed and cleaned up after. This RV park is closed during the off-season. The camping and tent areas also allow dogs. There is a dog walk area at the campground. Dogs are allowed in camping cabins. 2 dogs may be allowed.

Mallorytown

1000 Islands/Mallorytown KOA
1477 County Road 2
Mallorytown, ON
613-923-5339
Dogs of all sizes are allowed. There are no additional pet fees. Dogs may not be left unattended, must be leashed, and cleaned up after. Dogs must be crated in the cabins when left, and at night. There are some breed restrictions. This RV park is closed during the off-season. The camping and tent areas also allow dogs. There is a dog walk area at the campground. Dogs are allowed in the

camping cabins. Multiple dogs may be allowed.

St. Lawrence Islands National Park of Canada
2 County Road 5, RR3
Mallorytown, ON
613-923-5261
A very lush and complex park of more than 20 islands and about 90 islets, it is accessible only by watercraft. There is a 100 acre compound at the mainland headquarters which offers a nature trial and exhibits. Dogs of all sizes are allowed at no additional fee. Dogs must be leashed at all times and be cleaned up after. The park does not make any arrangements for water transport. This campground is closed during the off-season. Only one dog is allowed per campsite. The camping and tent areas also allow dogs. There is a dog walk area at the campground. There are no electric or water hookups at the campground.

Marmora

Marmora KOA
178 KOA Campground Road
Marmora, ON
613-472-2233
Dogs of all sizes are allowed. There are no additional pet fees. Dogs may not be left unattended, must be leashed, and cleaned up after. There are some breed restrictions. This RV park is closed during the off-season. The camping and tent areas also allow dogs. There is a dog walk area at the campground. Dogs are allowed in the camping cabins. Multiple dogs may be allowed.

McGregor

Wildwood Golf and RV Resort
11112 11 Consession
McGregor, ON
519-726-6176
Dogs of all sizes are allowed. There are no additional pet fees. Dogs must be leashed and cleaned up after. There are some breed restrictions. This RV park is closed during the off-season. There is a dog walk area at the campground. Multiple dogs may be allowed.

Midland

Georgian Bay Island National

Park of Canada
P. O. Box 9
Midland, ON
705-526-9804, ext. 235
This park, accessible by boat and only for tent camping, offers spectacular landscapes, diverse habitats, the rugged beauty of the Canadian Shield, an incredible variety of plants and animals, and a variety of year round recreation. Dogs of all sizes are allowed at no additional fee. Dogs may not be left unattended, and they must be leashed and cleaned up after. Pets and pet food must be brought in at night. Dogs are allowed on the trails on lead. This campground is closed during the off-season. The camping and tent areas also allow dogs. There is a dog walk area at the campground. There are no electric or water hookups at the campground. Multiple dogs may be allowed.

Smith's Camp
736 King Street
Midland, ON
705-526-4339
Dogs of all sizes are allowed. There are no additional pet fees. Dogs must be quiet, have up to date shot records, be leashed at all times, and cleaned up after. Dogs are not allowed on the beach. There are some breed restrictions. This RV park is closed during the off-season. The camping and tent areas also allow dogs. There is a dog walk area at the campground. 2 dogs may be allowed.

Niagara Falls

KOA Niagara Falls
2570 Grand Island Blvd
Grand Island, NY
716-773-7583
Dogs of all sizes are allowed. There are no additional pet fees. Dogs must be friendly, well behaved, leashed, and cleaned up after. This RV park is closed during the off-season. The camping and tent areas also allow dogs. There is a dog walk area at the campground. Multiple dogs may be allowed.

Campark Resort
9387 Lundy's Lane
Niagara Falls, ON
877-226-7275
Dogs of all sizes are allowed. There are no additional pet fees. Dogs may not be left outside unattended or be at the pool area. Dogs must be

leashed and cleaned up after. This RV park is closed during the off-season. The camping and tent areas also allow dogs. There is a dog walk area at the campground. Due to Ontario law Pit Bulls and similar dogs are not allowed. Multiple dogs may be allowed.

Jellystone Park
8676 Oakwood Drive
Niagara Falls, ON
905-354-1432
One dog of any size is allowed. There are no additional pet fees. Dogs are not allowed in rentals or tents. Dogs may not be left unattended, must be leashed, and cleaned up after. Due to Ontario law Pit Bulls and similar dogs are not allowed. This RV park is closed during the off-season. There is a dog walk area at the campground.

King Waldorf's Tent and Trailer Park
9015 Stanley S Avenue
Niagara Falls, ON
905-295-8191
Dogs of all sizes are allowed. There are no additional pet fees. Dogs may not be left unattended, must be leashed, and cleaned up after. This RV park is closed during the off-season. The camping and tent areas also allow dogs. There is a dog walk area at the campground. Due to Ontario law Pit Bulls and similar dogs are not allowed. Multiple dogs may be allowed.

Niagara Falls KOA
8625 Lundy's Lane
Niagara Falls, ON
905-356-2267
Dogs of all sizes are allowed. There are no additional pet fees. Dogs must be well behaved, may not be left unattended, and must be leashed and cleaned up after. Dogs are not allowed in the rentals or the buildings. There are some breed restrictions. This RV park is closed during the off-season. The camping and tent areas also allow dogs. There is a dog walk area at the campground. 2 dogs may be allowed.

KOA Niagara Falls N/Lewiston
1250 Pletcher Road
Youngstown, NY
716-754-8013
Dogs of all sizes are allowed. There are no additional pet fees. Dogs may not be left unattended, and must be

leashed and cleaned up after. There are some breed restrictions. This RV park is closed during the off-season. The camping and tent areas also allow dogs. There is a dog walk area at the campground. Dogs are allowed in the camping cabins. Multiple dogs may be allowed.

North Bay

Champlain Tent and Trailer Park
1202 Premier Road
North Bay, ON
705-474-4669
Dogs of all sizes are allowed. There are no additional pet fees. Dogs must be quiet, well behaved, leashed, and cleaned up after. This RV park is closed during the off-season. The camping and tent areas also allow dogs. There is a dog walk area at the campground. Multiple dogs may be allowed.

Ottawa

Poplar Grove Tourist Camp
6154 Bank Street
Ottawa, ON
613-821-2973
Dogs of all sizes are allowed. There are no additional pet fees. Dogs must be quiet, leashed, and cleaned up after. There are some breed restrictions. This RV park is closed during the off-season. The camping and tent areas also allow dogs. There is a dog walk area at the campground. 2 dogs may be allowed.

Rec-Land
1566 Canaan Road
Ottawa, ON
613-833-2974
Dogs of all sizes are allowed. There are no additional pet fees. Dogs must be leashed and cleaned up after. There are some breed restrictions. This RV park is closed during the off-season. The camping and tent areas also allow dogs. Multiple dogs may be allowed.

Owen Sound

Owen Sound KOA
RR6 28th Avenue E
Owen Sound, ON
519-371-1331
One dog of any size is allowed. There are no additional pet fees. Dogs must be quiet and well

behaved. Dogs may not be left unattended, must be leashed, and cleaned up after. There are some breed restrictions. This RV park is closed during the off-season. The camping and tent areas also allow dogs. There is a dog walk area at the campground.

Palgrave

Leisure Time Park
8431 H 9
Palgrave, ON
905-880-4921
Dogs of all sizes are allowed. There are no additional pet fees. Dogs may not be left unattended, must be quiet, well behaved, leashed and cleaned up after. There are some breed restrictions. This RV park is closed during the off-season. The camping and tent areas also allow dogs. There is a dog walk area at the campground. Multiple dogs may be allowed.

Parry Sound

Parry Sound KOA
276 Rankin Lake Road
Parry Sound, ON
705-378-2721
Dogs of all sizes are allowed. There are no additional pet fees. Dogs must be quiet, may not be left unattended, and must be leashed and cleaned up after. There are some breed restrictions. This RV park is closed during the off-season. The camping and tent areas also allow dogs. There is a dog walk area at the campground. Dogs are allowed in the camping cabins. Multiple dogs may be allowed.

Phedford

The Dunes Campground
9910 Northville Cresent
Phedford, ON
519-243-2500
Dogs of all sizes are allowed. There are no additional pet fees. Dogs must be leashed at all times and cleaned up after. There are some breed restrictions. This RV park is closed during the off-season. The camping and tent areas also allow dogs. There is a dog walk area at the campground. 2 dogs may be allowed.

Renfrew

Renfrew KOA
2826 Johnston Road
Renfrew, ON
613-432-6280
Dogs of all sizes are allowed. There are no additional pet fees. Dogs must be leashed and cleaned up after. There are some breed restrictions. This RV park is closed during the off-season. The camping and tent areas also allow dogs. There is a dog walk area at the campground. Multiple dogs may be allowed.

Restoule

Cedar Grove Camp
6845 H 534
Restoule, ON
705-729-2030
Dogs of all sizes are allowed, and there may be up to 3 dogs in the tent or RV areas, but only 2 dogs are allowed per cabin. There are no additional pet fees. Dogs may not be left unattended unless they will be quiet and well behaved, and they must be leashed and cleaned up after. This RV park is closed during the off-season. The camping and tent areas also allow dogs. There is a dog walk area at the campground. Dogs are allowed in the camping cabins. There are no water hookups at the campgrounds.

Ruthven

Leisure Lake Campgroud
510 County Road 31
Ruthven, ON
519-326-1255
Dogs of all sizes are allowed. There are no additional pet fees. Dogs must be quiet, well behaved, leashed, and cleaned up after. This RV park is closed during the off-season. The camping and tent areas also allow dogs. There is a dog walk area at the campground. Multiple dogs may be allowed.

Sauble Beach

Sauble Beach Resort Camp
877 County Road 8
Sauble Beach, ON
519-422-1101
Dogs of all sizes are allowed. There are no additional pet fees. Dogs may not be left unattended, must be leashed, and cleaned up after. There are some breed restrictions. This RV park is closed during the off-season. The camping and tent areas also allow dogs. There is a dog walk area at the campground. Multiple dogs may be allowed.

Woodland Park Family Campground

47 Sauble Falls Parkway
Sauble Beach, ON
519-422-1161
Dogs of all sizes are allowed. There is no fee for one dog. If there are two dogs, then the fee is $2 per night per dog. Dogs are not allowed on the beach, and must be leashed and cleaned up after. There are some breed restrictions. This RV park is closed during the off-season. The camping and tent areas also allow dogs. There is a dog walk area at the campground. 2 dogs may be allowed.

Sault Ste. Marie

Sault Ste Marie KOA
501 5th Line
Sault Ste. Marie, ON
705-759-2344
Dogs of all sizes are allowed. There are no additional pet fees. Dogs must be leashed and cleaned up after. They may be left for only short periods and only if they will be quiet and well behaved. There are some breed restrictions. This RV park is closed during the off-season. The camping and tent areas also allow dogs. There is a dog walk area at the campground. Dogs are allowed in the camping cabins. Multiple dogs may be allowed.

Sheguiandah

Batman's Trailer Park
11408 H 6
Sheguiandah, ON
705-368-2180
Dogs of all sizes are allowed. There are no additional pet fees. Dogs may not be left unattended, must be quiet, leashed at all times, and cleaned up after. This RV park is closed during the off-season. The camping and tent areas also allow dogs. There is a dog walk area at the campground. Multiple dogs may be allowed.

Spragge

Spragge KOA
4696 H 17
Spragge, ON
705-849-2210
Dogs of all sizes are allowed, but they want to know ahead of time if you have large dogs so they can provide a space to accommodate. There are no additional pet fees. Dogs must be quiet and well behaved. Dogs may not be left unattended, must be leashed, and cleaned up after. Your dog can run off leash at the river if there is voice control and no one is around. There are some breed restrictions. This RV park is closed during the off-season. The camping and tent areas also allow dogs. There is a dog walk area at the campground. Dogs are allowed in the camping cabins. Multiple dogs may be allowed.

Sudbury

Carol's Campsite
2388 Richard Lake Drive
Sudbury, ON
705-522-5570
Dogs up to 15 pounds are allowed. There are no additional pet fees. Dogs may not be left unattended, must be leashed, and cleaned up after. This RV park is closed during the off-season. The camping and tent areas also allow dogs. There is a dog walk area at the campground. 2 dogs may be allowed.

Thorndale

River View Campground
22164 Valley View Road
Thorndale, ON
866-447-7197
Dogs of all sizes are allowed. There are no additional pet fees. Dogs must be leashed and cleaned up after. This RV park is closed during the off-season. The camping and tent areas also allow dogs. There is a dog walk area at the campground. Multiple dogs may be allowed.

Thunder Bay

Thunder Bay KOA
162 Spruce River Road
Thunder Bay, ON
807-683-6221
Dogs of all sizes are allowed. There are no additional pet fees. Dogs must be leashed and cleaned up after. Some breeds are not allowed. This RV park is closed during the off-season. The camping and tent areas also allow dogs. There is a dog walk

area at the campground. Dogs are allowed in the camping cabins. Multiple dogs may be allowed.

Tobermory

Bruce Peninsula National Park of Canada
P.O. Box 189
Tobermory, ON
519-596-2263
This park, sitting in the heart of a World Biosphere Reserve, is home to the largest remaining chunk of natural habitat in Southern Ontario. The park offers thousand year old cedar trees and an array of habitats from clear lakes to dense forests and rare alvars. Dogs of all sizes are allowed at no additional fee. Dogs may not be left unattended, and they must be leashed at all times and cleaned up after. Dogs are allowed on the trails on lead. This campground is closed during the off-season. The camping and tent areas also allow dogs. There is a dog walk area at the campground. There are no water hookups at the campground. Multiple dogs may be allowed.

Toronto

Glen Rouge Campground
7450 Kingston Road
Toronto, ON
416-338-2267
Dogs of all sizes are allowed. There are no additional pet fees. Dogs may not be left unattended, must be leashed, and cleaned up after. This RV park is closed during the off-season. The camping and tent areas also allow dogs. There is a dog walk area at the campground. There are some breed restrictions. Multiple dogs may be allowed.

Toronto Area

Indian Line Campground
7625 Finch Avenue W
Brampton, ON
905-678-1233
Dogs of all sizes are allowed. There are no additional pet fees. Dogs may not be left unattended, must be leashed, and cleaned up after. This RV park is closed during the off-season. The camping and tent areas also allow dogs. There is a dog walk area at the campground. There are some breed restrictions. Multiple dogs may be allowed.

Milton Heights Campground
8690 Tremaine Road
Milton, ON
905-878-6781
Dogs of all sizes are allowed. There are no additional pet fees. Dogs may not be left unattended, must be leashed, and cleaned up after. There are some breed restrictions. The camping and tent areas also allow dogs. There is a dog walk area at the campground. Multiple dogs may be allowed.

Wiarton

Roth Park Family Campground
Burford Lake Road
Wiarton, ON
519-534-0145
Dogs of all sizes are allowed. There are no additional pet fees. Dogs may not be left unattended unless they will be quiet and well behaved, and they must be leashed and cleaned up after. This RV park is closed during the off-season. The camping and tent areas also allow dogs. There is a dog walk area at the campground. Dogs are allowed in the camping cabins. Multiple dogs may be allowed.

Prince Edward Island Listings

Cavendish

Cavendish KOA
198 Forest Hill Lane
Cavendish, PE
902-963-2079
Dogs of all sizes are allowed. There are no additional pet fees. Dogs may not be left unattended, must be leashed, and cleaned up after. Dogs must be well behaved and friendly. A dog sitter is sometimes available. There are some breed restrictions. This RV park is closed during the off-season. The camping and tent areas also allow dogs. There is a dog walk area at the campground. Dogs are allowed in the camping cabins. Multiple dogs may be allowed.

Charlottetown

Prince Edward Island National Park of Canada
2 Palmers Lane
Charlottetown, PE
902-672-6350
Dogs of all sizes are allowed at no additional fee. Dogs may not be left unattended, and they must be leashed and cleaned up after. Dogs are not allowed on the beaches from mid-April to the end of October. Dogs are allowed on the trails on lead. This campground is closed during the off-season. The camping and tent areas also allow dogs. There is a dog walk area at the campground. Multiple dogs may be allowed.

Quebec Listings

Bromont

Camping Carrousel
1699 Shephard Street
Bromont, PQ
450-534-2404
Dogs of all sizes are allowed. There are no additional pet fees. Dogs are not allowed at the pool or the beach, and they must be leashed and cleaned up after. This RV park is closed during the off-season. The camping and tent areas also allow dogs. There is a dog walk area at the campground. Multiple dogs may be allowed.

Camping Parc Bromont
24 La Fontanie
Bromont, PQ
450-534-2712
Dogs of all sizes are allowed. There are no additional pet fees. Dogs must be quiet, well behaved, leashed, and cleaned up after. This RV park is closed during the off-season. The camping and tent areas also allow dogs. There is a dog walk area at the campground. 2 dogs may be allowed.

Cabano

Camping Cabano
71 Road 185
Cabano, PQ
418-854-9133
Dogs of all sizes are allowed. There are no additional pet fees. Dogs must be leashed and cleaned up

after. The camping and tent areas also allow dogs. There is a dog walk area at the campground. 2 dogs may be allowed.

Drummondville

Camping La Detente
1580 Fontaine Bleau
Drummondville, PQ
819-478-0651
Dogs of all sizes are allowed. There are no additional pet fees. Dogs must be leashed and cleaned up after. This RV park is closed during the off-season. The camping and tent areas also allow dogs. There is a dog walk area at the campground. Multiple dogs may be allowed.

Gaspe

Forillon National Park of Canada
122 Gaspe Boulevard
Gaspe, PQ
418-368-5505
Home to the Grande-Grave National Heritage Site and located on the Gaspé Peninsula, this park features spectacular scenery, a long rich cultural history, marine and wildlife viewing, and a variety of year round recreation. Dogs of all sizes are allowed at no additional fee. Dogs may not be left unattended outside, and they must be leashed and cleaned up after. Pets and pet food must be brought inside at night. Dogs are allowed on the trails on lead. This campground is closed during the off-season. The camping and tent areas also allow dogs. There is a dog walk area at the campground. Multiple dogs may be allowed.

Gracefield

Camping Pionnier
184 Road 105
Gracefield, PQ
819-463-4163
Dogs of all sizes are allowed. There are no additional pet fees. Dogs must be leashed and cleaned up after. This RV park is closed during the off-season. Only one dog is allowed per campsite. The camping and tent areas also allow dogs. There is a dog walk area at the campground.

La Tuque

La Tuque Campground
15 Road 155N
La Tuque, PQ
819-523-4561
Dogs of all sizes are allowed, however there can only be up to 2 dogs any size or up to 3 small dogs per site. There are no additional pet fees. Dogs must be leashed and cleaned up after. This RV park is closed during the off-season. The camping and tent areas also allow dogs. There is a dog walk area at the campground.

Montreal

Camping de Compton
24 Chemin De La Station
Compton, PQ
800-563-5277
Dogs of all sizes are allowed. There are no additional pet fees. Dogs must be leashed and cleaned up after. This RV park is closed during the off-season. The camping and tent areas also allow dogs. There is a dog walk area at the campground. Multiple dogs may be allowed.

Montreal West KOA
171 H 338
Coteau du Lac, PQ
450-763-5625
Dogs of all sizes are allowed. There are no additional pet fees. Dogs must be quiet, well behaved, leashed, and cleaned up after. This RV park is closed during the off-season. The camping and tent areas also allow dogs. There is a dog walk area at the campground. Multiple dogs may be allowed.

Camping Lac LaFontaine
110 Boul
Grand Heron, PQ
450-431-7373
Dogs of all sizes are allowed. There is a $3 per stay per pet additional fee. Dogs must be leashed and cleaned up after. This RV park is closed during the off-season. The camping and tent areas also allow dogs. There is a dog walk area at the campground. 2 dogs may be allowed.

Camping Alouette
3449 L'Industrie
Saint-Mathieu-de-beloeil, PQ
450-464-1661
Dogs of all sizes are allowed. There is a $1 per night per pet additional fee. Dogs must be leashed and cleaned up after. This RV park is

closed during the off-season. The camping and tent areas also allow dogs. There is a dog walk area at the campground. Multiple dogs may be allowed.

Norte Dame du Laus

Tarmigan Campground
907 Ch. Poisson Blanc
Norte Dame du Laus, PQ
819-767-2559
Dogs of all sizes are allowed for an additional $3.50 per night per pet for the tent or RV area, and an additional fee of $5 per night per pet for the cottages. Dogs may not be left unattended, and they must be leashed and cleaned up after. There is an area where the dog may run off lead, but only if they are well behaved, under voice control, and will not chase, as there are several other animals residing at this park. This RV park is closed during the off-season. The camping and tent areas also allow dogs. There is a dog walk area at the campground. Dogs are allowed in the camping cabins. Multiple dogs may be allowed.

Quebec City

Camping Plage Fortier
1400 Lucen Francoes
L'ange-Gardien, PQ
888-226-7387
Dogs of all sizes are allowed. There are no additional pet fees. Dogs may not be left unattended, must be leashed, and cleaned up after. This RV park is closed during the off-season. The camping and tent areas also allow dogs. There is a dog walk area at the campground. Multiple dogs may be allowed.

Camping Aeroport
2050 Aeroport
Quebec City, PQ
800-294-1574
Dogs of all sizes are allowed. There are no additional pet fees. Dogs must be quiet, well behaved, leashed, and cleaned up after. This RV park is closed during the off-season. The camping and tent areas also allow dogs. There is a dog walk area at the campground. Multiple dogs may be allowed.

Camping Parc Beaumont
432 Fleuve
Quebec City, PQ
418-837-3787
Dogs of all sizes are allowed. There

are no additional pet fees. Dogs must be leashed and cleaned up after. This RV park is closed during the off-season. The camping and tent areas also allow dogs. There is a dog walk area at the campground. 2 dogs may be allowed.

Rimouski

Motel and Camping de l'Anse
1105 St. Hermaine Blvd
Rimouski, PQ
418-721-0322
Dogs of all sizes are allowed. There are no additional pet fees. Dogs must be quiet, well behaved, leashed, and cleaned up after. This RV park is closed during the off-season. The camping and tent areas also allow dogs. There is a dog walk area at the campground. 2 dogs may be allowed.

Riviere-du-loup

Camping Du Quai
70 Ancrage
Riviere-du-loup, PQ
418-860-3111
Dogs of all sizes are allowed. There are no additional pet fees. Dogs must be leashed and cleaned up after. This RV park is closed during the off-season. The camping and tent areas also allow dogs. There is a dog walk area at the campground. 2 dogs may be allowed.

Shawinigan

La Mauricie National Park of Canada
702 5th Street, Box 160, Stn. Bureau-chef
Shawinigan, PQ
819-538-3232
This park offers spectacular scenery, diverse ecosystems, a five day hiking trail through the Laurentian forest, an interpretation center, a nature observatory, and a variety of recreation. Dogs of all sizes are allowed at no additional fee. Dogs may not be left unattended at any time, and they must be leashed and cleaned up after. Dogs are strictly forbidden in the forest, in watercraft, on beaches, on hiking trails, and in all public buildings. In camp areas, dogs and their food must be brought inside at night. The camping and tent areas also allow dogs. There is a dog walk area at the campground. There are no water hookups at the

campground. Multiple dogs may be allowed.

St Nicolas

Quebec City KOA
684 Chemin Olivier Street
St Nicolas, PQ
418-831-1813
Dogs of all sizes are allowed, but they want to know ahead of time how many pets there are so they can place accordingly. There are no additional pet fees. Dogs must be well behaved, leashed, and cleaned up after. There is one pet friendly cabin available, and they offer a complimentary dog walking service. There are some breed restrictions. This RV park is closed during the off-season. The camping and tent areas also allow dogs. There is a dog walk area at the campground. Dogs are allowed in the camping cabins. Multiple dogs may be allowed.

St Philippe de Laprairie

Montreal South KOA
130 Monette Blvd
St Philippe de Laprairie, PQ
450-659-8626
Dogs of all sizes are allowed, and there are no additional pet fees for tent or RV sites. There is only one dog allowed in the cabins and there is a $20 refundable deposit. Dogs may not be left unattended outside, they must be leashed, and cleaned up after. This RV park is closed during the off-season. The camping and tent areas also allow dogs. There is a dog walk area at the campground. Dogs are allowed in the camping cabins.

Saskatchewan Listings

Assiniboia

Assiniboia Regional Park
Off Center Street
Assiniboia, SK
306-642-5620
Dogs of all sizes are allowed. There are no additional pet fees. Dogs must be cleaned up after. They may be off leash if well behaved and

under control of owner. This RV park is closed during the off-season. The camping and tent areas also allow dogs. There is a dog walk area at the campground. Multiple dogs may be allowed.

Chaplin

Silver Dollar RV Park and Campground
Corner of H 1 and H 19
Chaplin, SK
306-395-2332
Dogs of all sizes are allowed. There are no additional pet fees. This RV park is closed during the off-season. The camping and tent areas also allow dogs. There is a dog walk area at the campground. Multiple dogs may be allowed.

Craven

Craven World Campground
Russ Hill Road
Craven, SK
306-731-3336
Dogs of all sizes are allowed. There are no additional pet fees. Dogs may not be left unattended outside, and they must be leashed and cleaned up after. This RV park is closed during the off-season. The camping and tent areas also allow dogs. There is a dog walk area at the campground. Multiple dogs may be allowed.

Indian Head

Indian Head KOA
1100 McKay Street
Indian Head, SK
306-695-3635
Dogs of all sizes are allowed. There is a $2 per night per pet additional fee. Dogs must be leashed and cleaned up after. This RV park is closed during the off-season. The camping and tent areas also allow dogs. There is a dog walk area at the campground. Dogs are allowed in the camping cabins. Multiple dogs may be allowed.

Little Bear Lake

Moose Horn Lodge and Campground
Mile 62 Hanson Lake Road
Little Bear Lake, SK
306-426-2700
Dogs of all sizes are allowed. There

are no additional pet fees. Dogs must be quiet, well behaved, leashed, and cleaned up after. This RV park is closed during the off-season. The camping and tent areas also allow dogs. There is a dog walk area at the campground. Dogs are allowed in the camping cabins. Multiple dogs may be allowed.

Lloydminster

Weaver Park Campground
On H 16 at Bar Colony Museum
Lloydminster, SK
306-825-3726
Dogs of all sizes are allowed. There are no additional pet fees. Dogs must be leashed and cleaned up after. This RV park is closed during the off-season. The camping and tent areas also allow dogs. There is a dog walk area at the campground. Multiple dogs may be allowed.

Meadow Lake

Lion's Regional Park
On H 4 at H 55
Meadow Lake, SK
306-236-4447
Dogs of all sizes are allowed. There are no additional pet fees. Dogs must be leashed and cleaned up after. Dogs may be tied up outside, only if they are very friendly. This RV park is closed during the off-season. The camping and tent areas also allow dogs. There is a dog walk area at the campground. Multiple dogs may be allowed.

Moose Jaw

Besant Trans-Canada Campground
25 miles W of Moose Jaw on H 1
Moose Jaw, SK
306-756-2700
Dogs of all sizes are allowed. There are no additional pet fees. Dogs must be leashed and cleaned up after. Dogs can be at the creek but not the beach. This RV park is closed during the off-season. The camping and tent areas also allow dogs. There is a dog walk area at the campground. Multiple dogs may be allowed.

Prairie Oasis Campground and Motel
955 Thatcher
Moose Jaw, SK
306-693-8888

Dogs of all sizes are allowed. There are no additional pet fees. Dogs must be quiet, leashed, and cleaned up after. There is also a motel on site that accepts dogs at no extra fee. This RV park is closed during the off-season. The camping and tent areas also allow dogs. There is a dog walk area at the campground. 2 dogs may be allowed.

River Park Campground
300 River Drive
Moose Jaw, SK
306-692-5474
Dogs of all sizes are allowed. There are no additional pet fees. Dogs may not be left unattended, must be leashed, and cleaned up after. This RV park is closed during the off-season. The camping and tent areas also allow dogs. There is a dog walk area at the campground. Multiple dogs may be allowed.

Moosomin

Fieldstone Campground
Box 1524
Moosomin, SK
306-435-2677
Dogs of all sizes are allowed, and up to 3 small dogs or up to 2 average size dogs are allowed per site. There are no additional pet fees. Dogs must be leashed and cleaned up after. This RV park is closed during the off-season. The camping and tent areas also allow dogs. There is a dog walk area at the campground.

North Battleford

David Laird Campground
Box 1383
North Battleford, SK
306-445-3552
Dogs of all sizes are allowed. There are no additional pet fees. Dogs must be leashed and cleaned up after. This RV park is closed during the off-season. The camping and tent areas also allow dogs. There is a dog walk area at the campground. Multiple dogs may be allowed.

Prince Albert

Country View Motel and RV Park
4 km S on H 2S
Prince Albert, SK
306-764-2374

Dogs of all sizes and numbers are allowed on tent and RV sites, and there are no additional pet fees. Only 2 dogs are allowed per room (smoking only) at the motel, which is open all year, and also for no additional fee. Dogs must be well behaved, not left unattended, and leashed and cleaned up after. This RV park is closed during the off-season. The camping and tent areas also allow dogs. There is a dog walk area at the campground.

Prince Albert Exhibition RV Park
6th and 10th Street E
Prince Albert, SK
306-764-1611
Dogs of all sizes are allowed. There are no additional pet fees. Dogs must be quiet, well behaved, leashed, and cleaned up after. This RV park is closed during the off-season. The camping and tent areas also allow dogs. There is a dog walk area at the campground. Multiple dogs may be allowed.

Regina

Buffalo Lookout Campground
2 miles E of Regina on H 1
Regina, SK
306-525-1448
Dogs of all sizes are allowed. There are no additional pet fees. Dogs must be leashed and cleaned up after. This RV park is closed during the off-season. The camping and tent areas also allow dogs. There is a dog walk area at the campground. Multiple dogs may be allowed.

Kings Acres Campground
I km E of Regina on H 1, N service road
Regina, SK
306-522-1619
Dogs of all sizes are allowed. There are no additional pet fees. Dogs may not be left unattended, must be leashed, and cleaned up after. This RV park is closed during the off-season. The camping and tent areas also allow dogs. There is a dog walk area at the campground. Multiple dogs may be allowed.

Sherwood Forest Country Club
RR 2 Box 16
Regina, SK
306-545-0330
Dogs of all sizes are allowed. There are no additional pet fees. Dogs must be leashed and cleaned up after. This RV park is closed during

the off-season. The camping and tent areas also allow dogs. There is a dog walk area at the campground. Multiple dogs may be allowed.

Saskatoon

Gordon Howe Campground
Avenue P South
Saskatoon, SK
306-975-3328
Dogs of all sizes are allowed. There are no additional pet fees. Dogs may not be left unattended, must be quiet, leashed, and cleaned up after. This RV park is closed during the off-season. The camping and tent areas also allow dogs. There is a dog walk area at the campground. Multiple dogs may be allowed.

Saskatoon 16 West RV Park
Corner of 71st Street and H 16
Saskatoon, SK
306-931-8905
Dogs of all sizes are allowed. There are no additional pet fees. Dogs must be leashed and cleaned up after. This RV park is closed during the off-season. There is a dog walk area at the campground. Multiple dogs may be allowed.

Swift Current

Ponderosa Campground
On H 1 a quarter mile E of
Swift Current, SK
306-773-5000
Dogs of all sizes are allowed. There are no additional pet fees. Dogs must be quiet, well behaved, leashed, and cleaned up after. This RV park is closed during the off-season. The camping and tent areas also allow dogs. There is a dog walk area at the campground. Multiple dogs may be allowed.

Trail Campground
701 11th Avenue NW
Swift Current, SK
306-773-8088
Dogs of all sizes are allowed. There are no additional pet fees. Dogs may not be left unattended, must be leashed, and cleaned up after. This RV park is closed during the off-season. The camping and tent areas also allow dogs. There is a dog walk area at the campground. Multiple dogs may be allowed.

Val Marie

Grasslands National Park of Canada
P. O. Box 150
Val Marie, SK
306-298-2257
This is the first national park in Canada to preserve a portion of the vast mixed prairie grasslands. It offers guided hikes, interpretive trails, bird watching, and a variety of other recreational pursuits. Dogs of all sizes are allowed at no additional fee. Dogs may not be left unattended, and they must be leashed and cleaned up after. Pets and pet food must be brought inside at night. Dogs are allowed on the trails on lead, unless otherwise marked. The camping and tent areas also allow dogs. There is a dog walk area at the campground. There are no electric or water hookups at the campground. Multiple dogs may be allowed.

Waskesiu Lake

Prince Albert National Park of Canada
P. O. Box 100
Waskesiu Lake, SK
306-663-4522
This park is full of natural and cultural wonders. It is the only fully protected white pelican nesting colony in Canada and also features a free-range herd of bison, special events, interpretive programs, and a variety of recreational pursuits. Dogs of all sizes are allowed at no additional fee. Dogs may not be left unattended at any time, and they must be leashed and cleaned up after. Dogs are allowed on the trails on lead unless otherwise marked. This campground is closed during the off-season. The camping and tent areas also allow dogs. There is a dog walk area at the campground. Multiple dogs may be allowed.

Yorkton

Yorkton City Campground
On H 16 W of Yorkton
Yorkton, SK
306-786-1757
Dogs of all sizes are allowed. There are no additional pet fees. Dogs must be leashed and cleaned up after. This RV park is closed during the off-season. The camping and tent areas also allow dogs. There is a dog walk area at the campground. Multiple dogs may be allowed.

Yukon Listings

Beaver Creek

Westmark RV Park
M.P. 1202 Alaska H
Beaver Creek, YU
867-862-7501
Dogs of all sizes are allowed, and there are no additional pet fees for tent or RV sites. There is a $15 per night per dog additional fee for the hotel, and only two dogs are allowed with two adults; 1 dog if there is a family. Dogs must be quiet, leashed, and cleaned up after. Dogs can also walk along the creek. This RV park is closed during the off-season. The camping and tent areas also allow dogs. There is a dog walk area at the campground.

Carcross

Spirit Lake Wilderness Resort
M.M. 72.1 S Klondike H
Carcross, YU
866-739-8566
Dogs of all sizes are allowed for tent or RV sites, and there are no additional pet fees. There is a $5 per night per pet additional fee for the Motel. Dogs must be well behaved, only 2 maximum are allowed, and dogs are not allowed on the beds. Dogs may not be left unattended at any time, must be leashed, and cleaned up after. This RV park is closed during the off-season. The camping and tent areas also allow dogs. There is a dog walk area at the campground.

Carmacks

Hotel Carmacks RV Park
Free Gold Road
Carmacks, YU
867-863-5221
Dogs of all sizes are allowed. There are no additional pet fees. Dogs must be leashed and cleaned up after. There is a motel on site that has one pet friendly room, also for no additional pet fee. This RV park is closed during the off-season. There is a dog walk area at the campground. 2 dogs may be allowed.

Campgrounds and RV Parks - Please always call ahead to make sure an establishment is still dog-friendly.

Dawson City

Bonanza Gold RV Park
715.2 N Klondike H
Dawson City, YU
888-993-6789
Dogs of all sizes are allowed, and there are no additional pet fees for tent or RV sites. There is a $20 one time fee per pet for the Motel. Dogs must be leashed and cleaned up after. This RV park is closed during the off-season. The camping and tent areas also allow dogs. There is a dog walk area at the campground.

Gold Rush Campground
Between 4th & 5th Streets on York Street
Dawson City, YU
867-993-5247
Dogs of all sizes are allowed. There are no additional pet fees. Dogs may not be tied up outside unattended, must be leashed, and cleaned up after. This RV park is closed during the off-season. The camping and tent areas also allow dogs. There is a dog walk area at the campground. Multiple dogs may be allowed.

Guggieville RV Park
M.M. 712 Bonanza Gold Road
Dawson City, YU
867-993-5008
Dogs of all sizes are allowed. There are no additional pet fees. Dogs must be leashed and cleaned up after. There are some breed restrictions. This RV park is closed during the off-season. There is a dog walk area at the campground. Multiple dogs may be allowed.

Destruction Bay

Destruction Bay Lodge
M.M. 1083 Alaska H
Destruction Bay, YU
867-841-5332
Dogs of all sizes are allowed. There are no additional pet fees for either the camp/RV sites or the Lodge. Dogs must be well behaved and cleaned up after. They can be off leash as long as they show no aggressive behavior, and are under voice control. This RV park is closed during the off-season. The camping and tent areas also allow dogs. There is a dog walk area at the campground. Multiple dogs may be allowed.

Eagle Plains

Eagle Plains Hotel and Campground
On the Dempster H
Eagle Plains, YU
867-993-2453
Dogs of all sizes are allowed. There are no additional pet fees. Dogs must be well behaved, quiet, and cleaned up after. They may be off lead if they are under voice control. The camping and tent areas also allow dogs. There is a dog walk area at the campground. Multiple dogs may be allowed.

Haines Junction

Fas Gas RV Park
M.M. 270 Alaska H
Haines Junction, YU
867-634-2505
Dogs of all sizes are allowed, and there are no additional pet fees for tent or RV sites. There is a $10 per night per pet additional fee for the 1 pet friendly cabin. Dogs must be leashed and cleaned up after. This RV park is closed during the off-season. The camping and tent areas also allow dogs. There is a dog walk area at the campground. Dogs are allowed in the camping cabins.

Kluane National Park and Reserve of Canada
P. O. Box 5495/ 117 Logan Street
Haines Junction, YU
867-634-7250
Home to lush valleys, immense ice fields, and high mountains, this park is a nationally significant example of Canada's North Coast Mountains natural and cultural heritage. There are a variety of land and water recreational pursuits within the park. Dogs of all sizes are allowed at no additional fee. Dogs may not be left unattended, and they must be leashed and cleaned up after. Pets and pet food must be inside at night. Dogs are allowed on the trails on lead. This campground is closed during the off-season. The camping and tent areas also allow dogs. There is a dog walk area at the campground. There are no electric or water hookups at the campground. Multiple dogs may be allowed.

Kluane RV Kampground
2 minuets N of Haines Jct (M.M. 1016) on Alaska H
Haines Junction, YU
867-634-2709
Dogs of all sizes are allowed. There are no additional pet fees. Dogs must be leashed and cleaned up after. This RV park is closed during the off-season. The camping and tent areas also allow dogs. There is a dog walk area at the campground. Multiple dogs may be allowed.

Iron Creek

Iron Creek Lodge & RV
596 Alaska H
Iron Creek, YU
867-536-2266
Dogs of all sizes and numbers are allowed, and there are no additional pet fees for tent or RV sites. There is a $5 per night per pet additional fee for the lodge, and only 2 dogs are allowed. No extra large dogs are allowed at the lodge, and there is only one pet friendly room. The camping and tent areas also allow dogs. There is a dog walk area at the campground.

Johnson's Crossing

Johnson's Crossing Campground
M.M. 1347 Alaska H
Johnson's Crossing, YU
867-390-2607
Dogs of all sizes are allowed. There are no additional pet fees. Dogs must be leashed and cleaned up after. The camping and tent areas also allow dogs. There is a dog walk area at the campground. Multiple dogs may be allowed.

Keno City

Keno City RV Park
On Main Street behind Museum
Keno City, YU
867-995-2792
Dogs of all sizes are allowed. There are no additional pet fees. Dogs must be well behaved, leashed, and cleaned up after. This RV park is closed during the off-season. The camping and tent areas also allow dogs. There is a dog walk area at the campground. Multiple dogs may be allowed.

Kluane Wilderness Village

Kluane Wilderness Village Campground
1118 Alaska H
Kluane Wilderness Village, YU

867-841-4141
Dogs of all sizes are allowed, and there are no additional pet fees for the tent or RV sites. There is a $5 per night per pet additional fee for the motel. Up to 3 dogs can be on tent or RV sites and up to 2 dogs at the motel. Dogs must be friendly, well behaved, leashed, and cleaned up after. The camping and tent areas also allow dogs. There is a dog walk area at the campground.

Mayo

Bedrock Motel and RV Park
Lot 99 Silvertrail H
Mayo, YU
867-996-2290
Dogs of all sizes are allowed. There are no additional pet fees. Dogs may not be left unattended at any time, must be leashed, and cleaned up after. The RV park is seasonal, but the motel is open year around. This RV park is closed during the off-season. The camping and tent areas also allow dogs. There is a dog walk area at the campground. 2 dogs may be allowed.

Teslin

Dawson Peaks Resort and RV Park
KM 1232 Alaska H
Teslin, YU
867-390-2244
Dogs of all sizes are allowed. There are no additional pet fees. Only 1 lightly furred dog is allowed at the lodge, and they are not allowed on the furniture. More than 2 dogs are allowed at the tent and RV sites. Dogs must be leashed at all times, and cleaned up after. This RV park is closed during the off-season. The camping and tent areas also allow dogs. There is a dog walk area at the campground.

Watson Lake

Baby Nugget RV Park
KM 1003 Alaska H (M.M. 650)
Watson Lake, YU
867-536-2307
Dogs of all sizes are allowed, and there are no additional pet fees for tent or RV sites. There is a $10 per night per pet additional fee for the lodge and cabins. Dogs must be leashed and cleaned up after at all times. This RV park is closed during the off-season. The camping and

tent areas also allow dogs. There is a dog walk area at the campground. Dogs are allowed in the camping cabins. Multiple dogs may be allowed.

Campground Services Campground
18 Adela Trail
Watson Lake, YU
867-536-7448
Dogs of all sizes are allowed. There are no additional pet fees. Dogs must be leashed and cleaned up after. This RV park is closed during the off-season. The camping and tent areas also allow dogs. There is a dog walk area at the campground. Multiple dogs may be allowed.

Racheria RV Park
M.M. 710 Alaska H (70 miles past Watson Lake)
Watson Lake, YU
867-851-6456
Dogs of all sizes are allowed, and there are no additional pet fees for the tent or RV sites. There is a $10 per night per pet additional fee for the lodge. Dogs may not be left unattended, must be leashed, and cleaned up after. This RV park is closed during the off-season. The camping and tent areas also allow dogs. There is a dog walk area at the campground. Multiple dogs may be allowed.

Whitehorse

Caribou RV Park
KM 1403 (M.M. 873) Alaska H
Whitehorse, YU
867-668-2961
Dogs of all sizes are allowed. There are no additional pet fees. Dogs may be off lead if they are under voice control, and they must be cleaned up after. This RV park is closed during the off-season. The camping and tent areas also allow dogs. There is a dog walk area at the campground. Multiple dogs may be allowed.

Hi Country RV Park
91374 Alaska H
Whitehorse, YU
877-458-3806
Dogs of all sizes are allowed. There are no additional pet fees. Dogs must be quiet, well behaved, leashed, and cleaned up after. This RV park is closed during the off-season. The camping and tent areas also allow dogs. There is a

dog walk area at the campground. Multiple dogs may be allowed.

Pioneer RV Park
91091 Alaska H
Whitehorse, YU
867-668-5944
Dogs of all sizes are allowed. There are no additional pet fees. Dogs must be leashed and cleaned up after. This RV park is closed during the off-season. The camping and tent areas also allow dogs. There is a dog walk area at the campground. Multiple dogs may be allowed.

Chapter 2
Dog-Friendly Camping Cabins

United States Listings

Alabama Listings

Birmingham

Birmingham South Campground
222 H 33
Pelham, AL
205-664-8832
Dogs of all sizes are allowed. There are no additional pet fees. Dogs must be leashed and cleaned up after. The camping and tent areas also allow dogs. There is a dog walk area at the campground. Dogs are allowed in the camping cabins. Multiple dogs may be allowed.

Delta

Cheaha Resort State Park
19644 H 281S
Delta, AL
256-488-5111
This park is at the highest peak in the state and is surrounded by national forest. It offers spectacular scenery, provides 6 hiking trails and a variety of land and water activities and recreation. Dogs of all sizes are allowed at no additional fee for the camp area. There is a $10 per night per pet additional fee for the cabin or chalets. Dogs may not be left unattended, and they must be leashed at all times, and cleaned up after. Dogs are not allowed on the beaches or in buildings. Dogs are allowed on the trails. The camping and tent areas also allow dogs. There is a dog walk area at the campground. Dogs are allowed in the camping cabins. Multiple dogs may be allowed.

Arizona Listings

Amando

Mountain View RV Ranch
2843 E Frontage Road
Amando, AZ
520-398-9401
Dogs of all sizes are allowed. There are no additional pet fees. Dogs must be quiet, well behaved, leashed, and cleaned up after. The camping and tent areas also allow dogs. There is a dog walk area at the campground. Dogs are allowed in the camping cabins. Multiple dogs may be allowed.

Apache Junction

Mesa/Apache Junction KOA
1540 S Tomahawk Road
Apache Junction, AZ
480-982-4015
Dogs of all sizes are allowed, and there are no additional pet fees for tent or RV sites. There is a $25 refundable deposit for the cabins and only 2 dogs are allowed. Dogs may not be left unattended, and they must be leashed and cleaned up after. There are some breed restrictions. The camping and tent areas also allow dogs. There is a dog walk area at the campground. Dogs are allowed in the camping cabins. Multiple dogs may be allowed.

Benson

Benson KOA
180 W Four Feathers
Benson, AZ
520-586-3977
Dogs of all sizes are allowed, and there are no additional pet fees for tent or RV sites. There is a $5 one time fee per pet for the cabins. Dogs may not be left unattended outside, and they must be leashed and cleaned up after. The camping and tent areas also allow dogs. There is a dog walk area at the campground. Dogs are allowed in the camping cabins. 2 dogs may be allowed.

Casa Grande

Val Vista Winter Village
16680 W Val Vista Blvd
Casa Grande, AZ
520-836-7800
Dogs up to 25 pounds are allowed. There are no additional pet fees. At least one person must be 55 or over. There is a pet section in the park, and dogs must be walked in that designated area. Dogs must be leashed and cleaned up after. There are some breed restrictions. There is a dog walk area at the campground. Dogs are allowed in the camping cabins. Multiple dogs may be allowed.

Cornville

Lo Lo Mai Springs
11505 Lo Lo Mai Road
Cornville, AZ
928-634-4700
Dogs of all sizes are allowed. There is a $3 per night per pet additonal fee for tent and RV sites, and there is a $5 per night per pet additional fee for cabins. Dogs may not be left unattended at any time, and they must be leashed and cleaned up after. The camping and tent areas also allow dogs. There is a dog walk area at the campground. Dogs are allowed in the camping cabins. 2 dogs may be allowed.

Lo Lo Mai Springs Outdoor Resort
11505 Lo Lo Mai Road
Cornville, AZ
928-634-4700
Abundant springs in this area provides lush foliage creating a rich oasis for recreation in the high desert. Amenities offered at this campground include hot showers, a spring fed pond, clean restrooms, a heated swimming pool, jacuzzi, convenience store, club house, children's playground, ball and game courts, and a variety of recreational pursuits. Dogs of all sizes are allowed. There is a $3 per night per pet additional fee for the campground or the cabins. Dogs are not allowed in the cottages. Dogs must be leashed and cleaned up after. Dogs are allowed throughout the park, but not at the pool or in buildings. The camping and tent areas also allow dogs. There is a dog walk area at the campground. Dogs are allowed in the camping cabins. 2 dogs may be allowed.

Flagstaff

Flagstaff KOA
5803 N H 89
Flagstaff, AZ
928-526-9926
Dogs of all sizes are allowed. There are no additional pet fees. Dogs may not be left unattended outside, and they must be leashed and cleaned up after. The camping and tent areas also allow dogs. There is a dog walk area at the campground. Dogs are allowed in the camping cabins. Multiple dogs may be allowed.

Camping Cabins - Please always call ahead to make sure an establishment is still dog-friendly.

Grand Canyon

Grand Canyon/Williams KOA
5333 H 64
Williams, AZ
928-635-2307
Dogs of all sizes are allowed. There are no additional pet fees. Dogs may not be left unattended, and they must be quiet, leashed, and cleaned up after. There are some breed restrictions. This RV park is closed during the off-season. The camping and tent areas also allow dogs. There is a dog walk area at the campground. Dogs are allowed in the camping cabins. Multiple dogs may be allowed.

Kaibab National Forest
Railroad Blvd
Williams, AZ
928-635-8200
This picturesque forest of 1.6 million acres borders both the north and south rims of the Grand Canyon. It is the largest contiguous ponderosa pine forest in US and its diverse ecosystems support a large variety of plants, fish, mammals, bird species, and recreation. Dogs of all sizes are allowed at no additional fee. Dogs may not be left unattended except for shore periods, and they must be leashed and cleaned up after in camp areas. Dogs may be off lead on the trails if no one is around, they will not chase wildlife, and are under strict voice command. The camping and tent areas also allow dogs. There is a dog walk area at the campground. Dogs are allowed in the camping cabins. There are no electric or water hookups at the campground. Multiple dogs may be allowed.

Williams/Circle Pines KOA
1000 Circle Pines Road
Williams, AZ
928-635-2626
Dogs of all sizes are allowed. There are no additional pet fees. Dogs may not be left unattended outside, and they must be leashed and cleaned up after. Dogs must be crated when left in a cabin. There are some breed restrictions. The camping and tent areas also allow dogs. There is a dog walk area at the campground. Dogs are allowed in the camping cabins. Multiple dogs may be allowed.

Kingman

Kingman KOA
3820 N Roosevelt
Kingman, AZ
928-757-4397
Dogs of all sizes are allowed. There are no additional pet fees. There is, however, a $20 refundable deposit for the cabins. Dogs must be leashed and cleaned up after. There are some breed restrictions. The camping and tent areas also allow dogs. There is a dog walk area at the campground. Dogs are allowed in the camping cabins. Multiple dogs may be allowed.

Safford

Roper Lake State Park
101 E. Roper Lake Road
Safford, AZ
928-428-6760
This park has 2 camping sections, and offers a model Indian village, land and water recreation, and a natural hot spring. Dogs are allowed at no additional fee. Dogs may not be left unattended, and they must be leashed and cleaned up after. Dogs are not allowed in park buildings or on the beach, but they are allowed on the trails. The camping and tent areas also allow dogs. There is a dog walk area at the campground. Dogs are allowed in the camping cabins. Multiple dogs may be allowed.

St Johns

Lyman Lake State Park
On H 180/191 11 miles E of St Johns
St Johns, AZ
928-337-4441
This park shares the ancient historic Pueblo Trail, and offers many sites of interest and villages of the Hopi people. Dogs of all sizes are allowed, and there are no additional pet fees for tent or RV sites. There is a $5 one time additional pet fee for the cabins. Dogs must be leashed and cleaned up after. The camping and tent areas also allow dogs. There is a dog walk area at the campground. Dogs are allowed in the camping cabins. Multiple dogs may be allowed.

Arkansas Listings

Alma

Fort Smith/Alma KOA
3539 N H 71
Alma, AR
479-632-2704
Dogs of all sizes are allowed. There are no additional pet fees. Dogs must be leashed and cleaned up after, and they may not be on the playground. There is only 1 pet friendly cabin. There are some breed restrictions. The camping and tent areas also allow dogs. There is a dog walk area at the campground. Dogs are allowed in the camping cabins.

Eureka Springs

Eureka Springs Kettle Campground
4119 E Van Buren (H 62)
Eureka Springs, AR
479-253-9100
Up to 3 dogs of all sizes are allowed, and there are no additional pet fees for the tent or RV sites. There is a $10 one time additional pet fee for the cabins, and only 2 dogs are allowed up to 50 pounds. Dogs may not be left unattended outside, and left in your RV only (not in cabins at all) if they will be quiet, well behaved, and comfortable. Dogs must be leashed and cleaned up after. Dogs are not allowed in buildings or in the pool area. The camping and tent areas also allow dogs. There is a dog walk area at the campground. Dogs are allowed in the camping cabins.

Hot Springs

Hot Springs National Park KOA
838 McClendon Road
Hot Springs, AR
501-624-5912
Dogs of all sizes are allowed. There are no additional pet fees. Dogs must be leashed and cleaned up after. The camping and tent areas also allow dogs. There is a dog walk area at the campground. Dogs are allowed in the camping cabins. Multiple dogs may be allowed.

Jasper

Dogwood Springs Jasper Resort
P.O. Box 157/On H 7 one mile N
Jasper, AR
870-446-2163
Well behaved dogs of all sizes are

allowed at no additional fee for the tent or RV sites. There is a $10 per night per pet additional fee for the cabins, plus a $50 refundable deposit that is refundable by mail 7 days after checkout. Dogs may not be left unattended at any time, and they must be quiet, leashed at all times, and cleaned up after. Your visitors may not have a dog on the property or in their vehicle on the property, for any reason, at anytime. The camping and tent areas also allow dogs. There is a dog walk area at the campground. Dogs are allowed in the camping cabins. Multiple dogs may be allowed.

Little Rock

Little Rock North/Jct I 40 KOA
7820 Crystal Hill Road
N Little Rock, AR
501-758-4598
Dogs of all sizes are allowed. There are no additional pet fees. Dogs may not be left unattended outside, and they must be leashed and cleaned up after. There is a fenced dog area. There is only 1 pet friendly cabin. The camping and tent areas also allow dogs. There is a dog walk area at the campground. Dogs are allowed in the camping cabins. Multiple dogs may be allowed.

Morrilton

Morrilton/Conway KOA
30 Kamper Lane
Morrilton, AR
501-354-8262
Dogs of all sizes are allowed. There are no additional pet fees. Dogs may not be left unattended outside, and they must be leashed and cleaned up after. This RV park is closed during the off-season. The camping and tent areas also allow dogs. There is a dog walk area at the campground. Dogs are allowed in the camping cabins. Multiple dogs may be allowed.

Mountain Home

White Buffalo Resort
418 White Buffalo Trail
Mountain Home, AR
870-425-8555
Dogs of all sizes are allowed at no additional fee for the tent or RV sites. There is a $10 per night per pet additional fee for the cabins. Dogs may not be left unattended outside or

in the cabins or tents. Dogs are not allowed on the furniture in the cabins. Dogs may only be left in an RV if they will be quiet and well behaved. The camping and tent areas also allow dogs. There is a dog walk area at the campground. Dogs are allowed in the camping cabins. 2 dogs may be allowed.

Yellville

Sherwood Forest RV Park & Campground
216 MC Road 5042
Yellville, AR
870-449-3452
Dogs of all sizes are allowed. There are no additional pet fees. Dogs may not be left unattended, and they must be leashed and cleaned up after. The camping and tent areas also allow dogs. There is a dog walk area at the campground. Dogs are allowed in the camping cabins. Multiple dogs may be allowed.

California Listings

Big Sur

Big Sur Campground and Cabins
47000 H 1
Big Sur, CA
831-677-2322
This tent and RV campground is set amongst redwood trees along the Big Sur River. Camp amenities include some pull through sites, a general store, playground, basketball court and more. Well-behaved leashed dogs of all sizes are allowed in the tent, RV sites, and the tent cabins, but not in the hardwood cabins or around them. There is an additional fee of $4 per night per pet for the tent or RV sites. There is an additional fee of $12 per night per pet for the tent cabins. Pets must be attended at all times. People need to clean up after their pets. They are located about 5 miles from the dog-friendly Pfieffer Beach and 2.5 miles from Big Sur Station. The camping and tent areas also allow dogs. There is a dog walk area at the campground. Dogs are allowed in the camping cabins. Multiple dogs may be allowed.

Fernwood at Big Sur
47200 H 1
Big Sur, CA
831-667-2422
Home to a famous and rare Albino Redwood tree, this park provides historic sites, river campsites, a store, tavern and planned events. One of the many trails here ends at Pfeiffer Falls, a 60-foot high waterfall. Dogs of all sizes are allowed for an additional fee of $3 per night per pet for the tent or RV sites, and an additional fee of $10 per night per pet for the tent cabins. Dogs may not be left unattended, and they must be leashed and cleaned up after. Dogs are allowed on the trails unless otherwise marked. The camping and tent areas also allow dogs. There is a dog walk area at the campground. Dogs are allowed in the camping cabins.

Crescent City

Crescent City KOA
4241 H 101N
Crescent City, CA
707-464-5744
This 17 acre campground has 10 acres of camping in the redwood forest. It offers ice cream socials, pancake breakfasts, movie nights, hayrides, snack bar, bike rentals and a maximum pull through length of 60 feet with 50 amp service. Dogs of all sizes are allowed for no additional fee. Dogs must be under owner's control and visual observation at all times. Dogs must be quiet, well behaved, and be on no more than a 6 foot leash at all times, or otherwise contained. Dogs may not be left unattended outside the owner's camping equipment. There are some breed restrictions. The camping and tent areas also allow dogs. There is a dog walk area at the campground. Dogs are allowed in the camping cabins. Multiple dogs may be allowed.

Eureka

Eureka KOA
4050 N H 101
Eureka, CA
707-822-4243
Located along Humboldt Bay in the heart of the giant redwood country, this well-kept park offers a maximum length pull-through of 70 feet with 50 amp service. Some amenities include cable TV, two playgrounds, a

swimming pool, family hot tub, adults-only hot tub, horseshoe pits, rental bikes, a camp store, and ice cream socials during the summer months. Dogs of all sizes are allowed for an additional fee of $3 per night per pet. Dogs must be under owner's control and visual observation at all times. Dogs must be quiet, well behaved, and be on no more than a 6 foot leash at all times, or otherwise contained. Dogs may not be left unattended outside the owner's camping equipment. There are some breed restrictions. The camping and tent areas also allow dogs. There is a dog walk area at the campground. Dogs are allowed in the camping cabins. Multiple dogs may be allowed.

Jackson - Gold Country Central

49er Village RV Resort
18265 H 49
Plymouth, CA
800-339-6981
Nestled in the Sierra foothills, this park offers spacious, shady sites on tree-lined streets, 2 swimming pools-one year round-heated, an indoor whirlpool spa, and an on-site Deli-Espresso Cafe and Gift Shop, which is open daily at 7 a.m. Up to 3 dogs of any size are allowed for the RV section, and there is no additional fee or deposit. There are 2 pet friendly cabins; 1 dog is allowed in the studio, and up to 2 dogs are allowed in the one bedroom. There is a $100 per pet refundable deposit. Dogs may not be left unattended in the cottages or outside. Dogs must be leashed and cleaned up after. This is an RV only park. There is a dog walk area at the campground. Dogs are allowed in the camping cabins.

Julian

Cuyamaca Ranch State Park Campgrounds
12551 H 79
Descanso, CA
760-765 -0755
This scenic park has two family campgrounds, and some of the amenities include a picnic table, fire ring, barbecue, restrooms with pay showers, and water located near each site. Campsites are $20 per night May 15 through September 15, and $15 the rest of the season. There is an eight person maximum per site. You may bring your own

padlock if you wish to lock the cabin during your stay. Dogs are allowed at no additional fee, but restricted to the campgrounds, picnic areas, paved roads, and the Cuyamaca Peak Fire Road. Dogs must be leashed and cleaned up after. They may not be left unattended at any time. This park is located about 15 miles south of the town of Julian. The camping and tent areas also allow dogs. Dogs are allowed in the camping cabins. There are no electric or water hookups at the campgrounds. Multiple dogs may be allowed.

Lake Cuamaca
15027 H 79
Julian, CA
760-765-0515
This campground has 40 RV sites, 14 tent sites, and 2 cabins located next a popular fishing lake. There is a 3.5 mile trail surrounding the lake. Dogs on leash are welcome both in the campground and on the trail, but they are not allowed in the water and must stay at least 50 feet from the shore. Dogs are, however, allowed to go on the rental boats. People must clean up after their pets. The camping and tent areas also allow dogs. There is a dog walk area at the campground. Dogs are allowed in the camping cabins. Multiple dogs may be allowed.

Lake Tahoe

Camp at the Cove
760 H 50
Zephyr Cove, NV
775-589-4907
Located in spectacular scenery, this award winning resort campground offers a wide variety of amenities and recreational opportunities. Dogs of all sizes are allowed at no additional fee for tent or RV sites. There is a $15 per night per pet additional fee for the cabins. Dogs may not be left unattended outside, or in a tent. They may be left in an RV if they will be quiet and well behaved. Dogs are not allowed on the beach or in the buildings. The camping and tent areas also allow dogs. There is a dog walk area at the campground. Dogs are allowed in the camping cabins. Multiple dogs may be allowed.

Zephyr Cove RV Park and Campground
760 H 50

Zephyr Cove, NV
775-589-4922
This campground is located within minutes of South Lake Tahoe and Stateline. RV site amenities include telephone lines, cable TV, picnic tables, fire rings, bear proof lockers, BBQs, and spectacular scenery. There is also a restaurant, coffee bar, general store and gift shop, and a full service marina. RVs up to 40 feet can be accommodated. Tent sites are either drive-in or walk-in sites, some of which offer lake views. Well-behaved dogs on leash are allowed for no additional fee for the tent or RV sites. There is an additional fee of $15 per night per pet for the cabins. Dogs may not be left unattended in the cabins. Dogs must be leashed and cleaned up after, and they are not allowed on the beach. The camping and tent areas also allow dogs. There is a dog walk area at the campground. Dogs are allowed in the camping cabins. Multiple dogs may be allowed.

Manchester

Manchester Beach/Mendocino Coast KOA
44300 Kinney Road
Manchester, CA
707-882-2375
There is a variety of land and water recreation at this park located on a spectacular five-mile stretch of sand beach on the Mendocino Coast. Dogs of all sizes are allowed for no additional fee. Dogs must be under owner's control and visual observation at all times. Dogs must be quiet, well behaved, and be on no more than a 6 foot leash at all times, or otherwise contained. Dogs may not be left unattended outside the owner's camping equipment. There are some breed restrictions. The camping and tent areas also allow dogs. There is a dog walk area at the campground. Dogs are allowed in the camping cabins. 2 dogs may be allowed.

Mount Shasta

Mount Shasta KOA
900 N Mt Shasta Blvd
Shasta City, CA
530-926-4029
There is a variety of land, water, and air recreation at this scenic alpine park. The campground also offers 80 foot pull through sites with 50 amp, cable, LP gas, snack bar, and

swimming pool. Dogs of all sizes are allowed for no additional fee. Dogs must be under owner's control and visual observation at all times. Dogs must be quiet, well behaved, and be on no more than a 6 foot leash at all times, or otherwise contained. Dogs may not be left unattended outside the owner's camping equipment. There are some breed restrictions. The camping and tent areas also allow dogs. There is a dog walk area at the campground. Dogs are allowed in the camping cabins. Multiple dogs may be allowed.

Needles

Needles KOA
5400 National Old Trails H
Needles, CA
760-326-4207
This desert oasis park offers 90 foot pull through sites with 50 amp service, LP gas, snack bar, swimming pool, and guided tours. Dogs of all sizes are allowed for no additional fee. Dogs must be under owner's control and visual observation at all times. Dogs must be quiet, well behaved, and be on no more than a 6 foot leash at all times, or otherwise contained. Dogs may not be left unattended outside the owner's camping equipment, and must be brought inside at night. Dogs are not allowed in the pool area or buildings. There are some breed restrictions. The camping and tent areas also allow dogs. There is a dog walk area at the campground. Dogs are allowed in the camping cabins. Multiple dogs may be allowed.

Sacramento

Sacramento Metropolitan KOA
3951 Lake Road
West Sacramento, CA
916-371-6771
This camping area, located close to many other attractions and the state capitol, offer such amenities as 65 foot pull-through sites with 50 amp service, cable, phone, swimming pool, bike rentals, and planned activities. Up to 3 dogs of all sizes are allowed for no additional fee at the tent or RV sites. There is an additional fee of $10 per night per pet for the cabins, and only 2 dogs are allowed. Guests who own any of the known aggressive breeds must sign a waiver. Dogs must be under owner's control and visual

observation at all times. Dogs must be quiet, well behaved, and be on no more than a 6 foot leash at all times, or otherwise contained. Dogs may not be left unattended outside the owner's camping equipment, and must be brought inside at night. The camping and tent areas also allow dogs. There is a dog walk area at the campground. Dogs are allowed in the camping cabins.

San Luis Obispo

Santa Margarita KOA
4765 Santa Margarita Lake Road
Santa Margarita, CA
805-438-5618
Set in a rural setting with panoramic vistas, other amenities offered are 40 foot pull through sites with 30 amp, LP gas, swimming pool, and planned activities. Dogs of all sizes are allowed for no additional fee. Dogs must be under owner's control and visual observation at all times. Dogs must be quiet, well behaved, and be on no more than a 6 foot leash at all times, or otherwise contained. Dogs may not be left unattended outside the owner's camping equipment, and must be brought inside at night. In the cabins, dogs must remain in their carriers at all times. There are some breed restrictions. The camping and tent areas also allow dogs. There is a dog walk area at the campground. Dogs are allowed in the camping cabins. 2 dogs may be allowed.

Santa Ysabel

Lake Henshaw Resort
26439 H 76
Santa Ysabel, CA
760-782-3487
Lake Henshaw Resort, located at a lake which rests at the foot of the Palomar Mountains, is a great place for fishermen of all levels. Some of the amenities include a sparkling pool and spa, children's playground, grocery store with all your fishing needs, clubhouse, laundry facilities, and restaurant. Dogs of all sizes are allowed at an additional $2 per night per pet. Dogs are not allowed on the furniture in the cabins and they may not be left unattended. Dogs are allowed to walk along the lakeshore and to go in the water. The camping and tent areas also allow dogs. There is a dog walk area at the campground. Dogs are allowed in the camping cabins.

Multiple dogs may be allowed.

Shasta - Trinity National Forest

Lakeview Terrace Resort
Trinity Dam Blvd
Lewiston, CA
530-778-3803
This resort overlooks Lewiston Lake and features an RV park and cabin rentals. RV spaces feature pull through sites, tables and barbecues. Most of the pull through sites offer a lake view. Other amenities include a laundry facility, restrooms and showers. Well-behaved quiet leashed dogs are welcome, up to two pets per cabin or RV. Pets are not allowed in the swimming pool area and cannot not be left alone at any time, either in your RV or at the cabins. Please clean up after your pet. There is no pet fee if you stay in an RV space, but there is a $10 per day fee for pets in the cabins. Dogs may not be left unattended in the cabins, or outside your RV. There are some breed restrictions. There is a dog walk area at the campground. 2 dogs may be allowed.

Sonoma

Cloverdale KOA
1166 Asti Ridge Road
Cloverdale, CA
707-894-3337
This park is nestled among 100-year-old oak, eucalyptus and evergreen trees, and some of the amenities include a hillside pool and spa, nature trail, pond, gymnastics playground, and various land and water recreation. Dogs of all sizes are allowed for no additional fee. Dogs must be under owner's control and visual observation at all times. Dogs must be quiet, well behaved, and be on no more than a 6 foot leash at all times, or otherwise contained. Dogs may not be left unattended outside the owner's camping equipment. There are some breed restrictions. The camping and tent areas also allow dogs. There is a dog walk area at the campground. Dogs are allowed in the camping cabins. Multiple dogs may be allowed.

Victorville

Victorville/Inland Empire KOA
16530 Stoddard Wells Road
Victorville, CA

760-245-6867
A shady get-away in the high desert, this park offers a maximum pull through of 75 feet with 30 amp, LP gas, seasonal swimming pool, several planned activities, and bike rentals. Dogs of all sizes are allowed for no additional fee. Dogs must be under owner's control and visual observation at all times. Dogs must be quiet, well behaved, and be on no more than a 6 foot leash at all times, or otherwise contained. Dogs may not be left unattended outside the owner's camping equipment, and must be brought inside at night. Only dogs that are house trained are allowed in the cabins, and they must not be left inside unattended. There are some breed restrictions. The camping and tent areas also allow dogs. There is a dog walk area at the campground. Dogs are allowed in the camping cabins.

Watsonville

Santa Cruz/Monterey Bay KOA
1186 San Andreas Road
Watsonville, CA
831-722-0551
This scenic family resort along the coast of Monterey Bay offers a long list of amenities, planned activities, and land and water recreation. Dogs of all sizes are allowed for no additional fee. Dogs must be under owner's control and visual observation at all times. Dogs must be quiet, well behaved, and be on no more than a 6 foot leash at all times, or otherwise contained. Dogs may not be left unattended outside the owner's camping equipment, and must be brought inside at night. Dogs are not allowed in the lodge or the play areas. There are some breed restrictions. The camping and tent areas also allow dogs. There is a dog walk area at the campground. Dogs are allowed in the camping cabins. Multiple dogs may be allowed.

Colorado Listings

Alamosa

Alamosa KOA
6900 Juniper Avenue
Alamosa, CO

719-589-9757
Dogs of all sizes are allowed, however there can only be up to 3 dogs at tent and RV sites, and up to 2 dogs at the cabins. There are no additional pet fees. Dogs may not be left unattended at the cabins or outside, and they must be leashed and cleaned up after. There are some breed restrictions. The camping and tent areas also allow dogs. There is a dog walk area at the campground. Dogs are allowed in the camping cabins.

Arboles

Navajo State Park
1526 County Road 982 (Box 1697)
Arboles, CO
970-883-2208
This scenic park touts a reservoir with over 15,000 acres, and offers a variety of land and water recreation in addition to the geological and historical points of interest. Dogs of all sizes are allowed at no additional fee. Dogs may not be left unattended, and they must be on no more than a 6 foot leash, and be cleaned up after. The camping and tent areas also allow dogs. There is a dog walk area at the campground. Dogs are allowed in the camping cabins. Multiple dogs may be allowed.

Bayfield

Vallecito Resort
13030 County Road 501
Bayfield, CO
970-884-9458
Dogs of all sizes are allowed. There are no additional pet fees. Dogs must be leashed and cleaned up after. There are some breed restrictions. This RV park is closed during the off-season. The camping and tent areas also allow dogs. There is a dog walk area at the campground. Dogs are allowed in the camping cabins. 2 dogs may be allowed.

Buena Vista

Buena Vista KOA
27700 H 303
Buena Vista, CO
719-395-8318
Dogs of all sizes are allowed, and there are no additional pet fees for tent or RV sites. There is a $5 per night per pet additional fee for

cabins. There can be up to 3 dogs at tent or RV sites, but only up to 2 dogs at the cabins. Dogs may not be left unattended, and they must be leashed and cleaned up after. There are some breed restrictions. This RV park is closed during the off-season. The camping and tent areas also allow dogs. There is a dog walk area at the campground. Dogs are allowed in the camping cabins.

Canon City

Fort Gorge RV Park
45044 H 50W
Canon City, CO
719-275-5111
Dogs of all sizes are allowed. There are no additional pet fees. Dogs may not be left unattended, and must be leashed and cleaned up after. The camping and tent areas also allow dogs. There is a dog walk area at the campground. Dogs are allowed in the camping cabins. Multiple dogs may be allowed.

Royal Gorge/Canon City KOA
559 County Road 3A
Canon City, CO
719-275-6116
Dogs of all sizes are allowed. There are no additional pet fees. Dogs may not be left unattended at the cabins, and they must be leashed and cleaned up after. This RV park is closed during the off-season. The camping and tent areas also allow dogs. There is a dog walk area at the campground. Dogs are allowed in the camping cabins. Multiple dogs may be allowed.

Castle Rock

Castle Rock Campground
6527 S I 25
Castle Rock, CO
303-681-3169
Dogs of all sizes are allowed. There are no additional pet fees. Dogs must be well behaved, leashed, and cleaned up after. They also have lodges (deluxe cabins) where your dog is allowed at no extra fee. The camping and tent areas also allow dogs. There is a dog walk area at the campground. Dogs are allowed in the camping cabins. Multiple dogs may be allowed.

Cortez

Cortez Mesa Verde KOA

27432 E H 160
Cortez, CO
970-565-9301
Dogs of all sizes are allowed. There are no additional pet fees. Dogs may not be left unattended at the cabins or outside, and they must be leashed and cleaned up after. There are some breed restrictions. This RV park is closed during the off-season. The camping and tent areas also allow dogs. There is a dog walk area at the campground. Dogs are allowed in the camping cabins. Multiple dogs may be allowed.

Cotopaxi

Cotopaxi Arkansas River KOA
21435 H 50
Cotopaxi, CO
719-275-9308
Dogs of all sizes are allowed, and there are no additional pet fees for tent or RV sites. There is a $5 per night per pet additional fee for the cabins or motel. Dogs must be quiet, well behaved, be on no more than a 6 foot leash, and cleaned up after. Dogs may not be left unattended at any time. There are some breed restrictions. This RV park is closed during the off-season. The camping and tent areas also allow dogs. There is a dog walk area at the campground. Dogs are allowed in the camping cabins. Multiple dogs may be allowed.

Craig

Craig KOA
2800 E H 40
Craig, CO
970-824-5105
Dogs of all sizes are allowed. There are no additional pet fees. Dogs must be leashed and cleaned up after. The camping and tent areas also allow dogs. There is a dog walk area at the campground. Dogs are allowed in the camping cabins. Multiple dogs may be allowed.

Cripple Creek

Cripple Creek/Colorado Springs W KOA
2576 County Road 81
Cripple Creek, CO
719-689-3376
Dogs of all sizes are allowed. There are no additional pet fees. Dogs may not be left unattended at the cabins or outside. Dogs must be quiet, be

on no more than a 6 foot leash, and cleaned up after. This RV park is closed during the off-season. The camping and tent areas also allow dogs. There is a dog walk area at the campground. Dogs are allowed in the camping cabins. Multiple dogs may be allowed.

Dolores

Dolores River RV Park
18680 H 145
Dolores, CO
970-882-7761
Dogs of all sizes are allowed, and there are no additional pet fees for tent or RV sites. There may be a small one time fee for pets in cabins. This RV park is closed during the off-season. The camping and tent areas also allow dogs. There is a dog walk area at the campground. Dogs are allowed in the camping cabins. Multiple dogs may be allowed.

Durango

Durango East KOA
30090 H 160
Durango, CO
970-247-0783
Dogs of all sizes are allowed. There are no additional pet fees. Dogs may not be left unattended, and they must be quiet, well behaved, leashed and cleaned up after. There are some breed restrictions. This RV park is closed during the off-season. The camping and tent areas also allow dogs. There is a dog walk area at the campground. Dogs are allowed in the camping cabins. Multiple dogs may be allowed.

Durango North KOA
13391 County Road 250
Durango, CO
970-247-4499
Dogs of all sizes are allowed. There are no additional pet fees. Dogs may not be left unattended, and they must be leashed and cleaned up after. This RV park is closed during the off-season. The camping and tent areas also allow dogs. There is a dog walk area at the campground. Dogs are allowed in the camping cabins. 2 dogs may be allowed.

Estes Park

Estes Park KOA
2051 Big Thompson Avenue
Estes Park, CO
970-586-2888
Dogs of all sizes are allowed. There are no additional pet fees. Dogs may not be left unattended, and they must be leashed and cleaned up after. There may only be up to 2 dogs in the cabins. There are some breed restrictions. This RV park is closed during the off-season. The camping and tent areas also allow dogs. There is a dog walk area at the campground. Dogs are allowed in the camping cabins. Multiple dogs may be allowed.

Fountain

Colorado Springs South KOA
8100 Bandley Drive
Fountain, CO
719-382-7575
Dogs of all sizes are allowed, and there are no additional pet fees for tent or RV sites. There is a $3 per night per pet additional fee for cabins. Dogs may not be left unattended in the cabins or outside, and they must be leashed and cleaned up after. There are some breed restrictions. The camping and tent areas also allow dogs. There is a dog walk area at the campground. Dogs are allowed in the camping cabins. Multiple dogs may be allowed.

Gunnison

Gunnison KOA
105 County Road 50
Gunnison, CO
970-641-1358
Dogs of all sizes are allowed, but there can only be 1 large or 2 small dogs per site. There are no additional pet fees. Dogs may not be left unattended, and they must be leashed at all times, and cleaned up after. This RV park is closed during the off-season. The camping and tent areas also allow dogs. There is a dog walk area at the campground. Dogs are allowed in the camping cabins.

La Junta

La Junta KOA
26680 H 50
La Junta, CO
719-384-9580
Dogs of all sizes are allowed. There

are no additional pet fees. Dogs must be quiet, be on no more than a 6 foot leash, and cleaned up after. There are some breed restrictions. The camping and tent areas also allow dogs. There is a dog walk area at the campground. Dogs are allowed in the camping cabins. Multiple dogs may be allowed.

LaPorte

Fort Collins KOA
6670 N H 287
LaPorte, CO
970-493-9758
Dogs of all sizes are allowed. There are no additional pet fees. Dogs must be leashed and cleaned up after. Dogs are not allowed at the playground, the camp kitchen, or the bathrooms. This RV park is closed during the off-season. The camping and tent areas also allow dogs. There is a dog walk area at the campground. Dogs are allowed in the camping cabins. Multiple dogs may be allowed.

Limon

Limon KOA
575 Colorado Avenue
Limon, CO
719-775-2151
Dogs of all sizes are allowed. There are no additional pet fees. Dogs must be leashed and cleaned up after. There are some breed restrictions. This RV park is closed during the off-season. The camping and tent areas also allow dogs. There is a dog walk area at the campground. Dogs are allowed in the camping cabins. Multiple dogs may be allowed.

Ouray

Ouray KOA
225 County Road 23
Ouray, CO
970-325-4736
Dogs of all sizes are allowed. There are no additional pet fees. Dogs may not be left unattended at the cabins or outside, and they are not allowed in the buildings. Dogs must be quiet, well behaved, be on no more than a 6 foot leash, and cleaned up after. There are some breed restrictions. This RV park is closed during the off-season. The camping and tent areas also allow dogs. There is a dog walk area at the campground. Dogs are

allowed in the camping cabins. Multiple dogs may be allowed.

Pagosa Springs

Elk Meadows River Resort
5360 E H 160
Pagosa Springs, CO
970-264-5482
Dogs of all sizes are allowed. There are no additional pet fees. Dogs may not be left unattended outside unless they will be quiet and well behaved, and they must be leashed and cleaned up after. This is an RV and rental cabins park. This RV park is closed during the off-season. There is a dog walk area at the campground. Dogs are allowed in the camping cabins. Multiple dogs may be allowed.

Pueblo

Pueblo KOA
4131 I 25N
Pueblo, CO
719-542-2273
Dogs of all sizes are allowed. There are no additional pet fees. Dogs may not be left unattended, and they must be leashed and cleaned up after. The camping and tent areas also allow dogs. There is a dog walk area at the campground. Dogs are allowed in the camping cabins. Multiple dogs may be allowed.

Pueblo South/Colorado City KOA
9040 I 25S
Pueblo, CO
719-676-3376
There can be up to 2 dogs of any size, or 3 small, at the tent and RV sites at no additional fee. There is only 1 dog up to 20 pounds allowed in the cabins for an additional fee of $7 per day. There is a pet waiver to sign at check in if the dog is one of the listed aggressive breeds. Dogs may not be left unattended, and they must be quiet, well behaved, leashed, and cleaned up after. Dogs may not be tied to trees, picnic tables, or other camp property. The camping and tent areas also allow dogs. There is a dog walk area at the campground. Dogs are allowed in the camping cabins.

Ridgeway

Ridgeway State Park

28555 H 550
Ridgeway, CO
970-626-5822
This park offers a sandy swim beach, a full service marina, and is known as a very accessible recreation area for people with disabilities. Dogs of all sizes are allowed at no additional fee for tent or RV sites. There is a $10 daily additional pet fee for the yurts. Dogs may not be left unattended outside, and they must be on no more than a 6 foot leash, and be cleaned up after. Dogs are not allowed in public swim areas, but they are allowed on the trails. The camping and tent areas also allow dogs. There is a dog walk area at the campground. Dogs are allowed in the camping cabins. 2 dogs may be allowed.

Strasburg

Denver East/Strasburg KOA
1312 Monroe
Strasburg, CO
303-622-9274
Dogs of all sizes are allowed, and there are no additional pet fees for tent or RV sites. There is a $4 per night per pet additional fee for the cabins. Dogs are greeted at check in with a dog biscuit. Dogs may not be left unattended at the cabins or outside, and they must be leashed and cleaned up after. The camping and tent areas also allow dogs. There is a dog walk area at the campground. Dogs are allowed in the camping cabins. There are special amenities given to dogs at this campground. Multiple dogs may be allowed.

Walden

North Park/Gould/Walden KOA
53337 H 14
Walden, CO
970-723-4310
Dogs of all sizes are allowed. There are no additional pet fees. Dogs may not be left unattended, and they must be leashed and cleaned up after. This RV park is closed during the off-season. The camping and tent areas also allow dogs. There is a dog walk area at the campground. Dogs are allowed in the camping cabins. Multiple dogs may be allowed.

Wellington

Fort Collins North/Wellington KOA

4821 E County Road 70/Owl Canyon Road
Wellington, CO
970-568-7486
Dogs of all sizes are allowed. There are no additional pet fees. Dogs must be leashed and cleaned up after. The camping and tent areas also allow dogs. There is a dog walk area at the campground. Dogs are allowed in the camping cabins. Multiple dogs may be allowed.

Westcliffe

Grape Creek RV Park
56491 H 69
Westcliffe, CO
719-783-2588
Dogs of all sizes are allowed. There are no additional pet fees. Dogs must be leashed and cleaned up after. There is only one dog friendly cabin. This RV park is closed during the off-season. The camping and tent areas also allow dogs. There is a dog walk area at the campground. Dogs are allowed in the camping cabins. Multiple dogs may be allowed.

Connecticut Listings

Lebanon

Water's Edge Family Campground
271 Leonard Bridge Road
Lebanon, CT
860-642-7470
Dogs of all sizes are allowed. There are no additional pet fees. Dogs must be leashed and cleaned up after. Dogs are allowed in the camping cabins. 2 dogs may be allowed.

Delaware Listings

Lewes

G and R Campground
4075 Gun and Rod Club Road
Houston, DE

302-398-8108
Dogs of all sizes are allowed, and there are no additional pet fees for the tent or RV sites. There is a $15 per night per pet additional fee for the cabin rentals, and there are only 2 pets per cabin allowed. Dogs must be quiet and well behaved. Dogs may not be left unattended, must be leashed, and cleaned up after. There are some breed restrictions. The camping and tent areas also allow dogs. There is a dog walk area at the campground. Dogs are allowed in the camping cabins.

Florida Listings

Chattahoochee

Chattahoochee/Tallahassee W KOA
2309 Flat Circle Road
Chattahoochee, FL
850-442-6657
Dogs of all sizes are allowed. There are no additional pet fees. Dogs may not be left unattended outside, and they must be well behaved, leashed, and cleaned up after. There are some breed restrictions. The camping and tent areas also allow dogs. There is a dog walk area at the campground. Dogs are allowed in the camping cabins. Multiple dogs may be allowed.

Keys

Sugarloaf Key/Key West KOA
251 H 939
Sugarloaf Key, FL
305-745-3549
Dogs of all sizes are allowed. There are no additional pet fees. Dogs may not be left unattended outside, and they must be leashed and cleaned up after. The camping and tent areas also allow dogs. There is a dog walk area at the campground. Dogs are allowed in the camping cabins. Multiple dogs may be allowed.

St James City

Fort Myers/Pine Island KOA
5120 Stringfellow Road
St James City, FL
239-283-2415

Dogs of all sizes are allowed. There is a $5 per night per pet additional fee. Dogs may not be left unattended outside, and only inside if they will be quiet and well behaved. Dogs must be leashed and cleaned up after. The camping and tent areas also allow dogs. There is a dog walk area at the campground. Dogs are allowed in the camping cabins. Multiple dogs may be allowed.

Tampa Bay

Clearwater/Tarpon Springs KOA
37061 H 19N
Palm Harbor, FL
727-937-8412
Dogs of all sizes are allowed. There are no additional pet fees. Dogs may not be left unattended outside, and they must be well behaved, leashed, and cleaned up after. There are some breed restrictions. There is a dog walk area at the campground. Dogs are allowed in the camping cabins. 2 dogs may be allowed.

White Springs

Suwannee Valley Campground
786 N W Street
White Springs, FL
866-397-1667
Dogs of all sizes are allowed, and there are no additional pet fees for tent or RV sites. There is a $50 one time pet fee for cabins. Dogs must have up to date shot records, and be leashed and cleaned up after. The camping and tent areas also allow dogs. There is a dog walk area at the campground. Dogs are allowed in the camping cabins. 2 dogs may be allowed.

Georgia Listings

Acworth

Holiday Harbor
5989 Groover's Landing
Acworth, GA
770-974-2575
Dogs of all sizes are allowed. There are no additional pet fees. Dogs must be leashed and cleaned up after. This is an RV only park with cabin rentals, but there is only one pet friendly cabin. The camping and

tent areas also allow dogs. There is a dog walk area at the campground. Dogs are allowed in the camping cabins. Multiple dogs may be allowed.

Calhoun

Calhoun KOA
2523 Redbud Road NE
Calhoun, GA
706-629-7511
Dogs of all sizes are allowed. There are no additional pet fees. Dogs may not be left unattended outside or in the cabins, and they must be quiet, leashed, and cleaned up after. The camping and tent areas also allow dogs. There is a dog walk area at the campground. Dogs are allowed in the camping cabins. Multiple dogs may be allowed.

Cordele

Cordele KOA
373 Rockhouse Road E
Cordele, GA
229-273-5454
Dogs of all sizes are allowed, and there are no additional pet fees for tent or RV sites. There is a limit of 1 dog under 15 pounds for the cabins. Dogs must be leashed, cleaned up after, and in at night. The camping and tent areas also allow dogs. There is a dog walk area at the campground. Dogs are allowed in the camping cabins.

Dillard

River Vista Mountain Village
960 H 246
Dillard, GA
888-850-PARK (7275)
Up to 3 dogs of all sizes are allowed. There are no additional pet fees for tent or RV sites. There is a $10 per night per pet additional fee for the cabins, and only 2 dogs are allowed. Dogs may not be left unattended outside or in the cabins. Dogs must be on no more than a 6 foot leash and cleaned up after. The camping and tent areas also allow dogs. There is a dog walk area at the campground. Dogs are allowed in the camping cabins.

Forsyth

Forsyth KOA
414 S Frontage Road

Forsyth, GA
478-994-2019
Dogs of all sizes are allowed. There are no additional pet fees. Dogs may not be left unattended outside, and they must be leashed, cleaned up after, and inside at night. The camping and tent areas also allow dogs. There is a dog walk area at the campground. Dogs are allowed in the camping cabins. Multiple dogs may be allowed.

Helen

Unicoi State Park
1788 H 356
Helen, GA
706-878-3982
This park offers programs that focus on its historical, natural, cultural, and recreational resources. Dogs of all sizes are allowed at no additional fee. Only 2 dogs are allowed in the cabins. Dogs may not be left unattended outside, and they must be on no more than a 6 foot leash, and be cleaned up after. Dogs are allowed on the trails, but not in the lodge. The camping and tent areas also allow dogs. There is a dog walk area at the campground. Dogs are allowed in the camping cabins.

Kingsland

Jacksonville N/Kingsland KOA
2970 Scrubby Buff Road
Kingsland, GA
912-729-3232
Dogs of all sizes are allowed. There are no additional pet fees. Dogs may not be left unattended outside, and they must be leashed and cleaned up after. The camping and tent areas also allow dogs. There is a dog walk area at the campground. Dogs are allowed in the camping cabins. Multiple dogs may be allowed.

Lake Park

Valdosta/Lake Park KOA
5300 Jewel Futch Road
Lake Park, GA
229-559-9738
Dogs of all sizes are allowed, and there are no additional pet fees for tent or RV sites. There is a $25 one time additional pet fee for the cabin and park models. Dogs may not be left unattended outside or in rentals, and they must be leashed and cleaned up after. The camping and

tent areas also allow dogs. There is a dog walk area at the campground. Dogs are allowed in the camping cabins. Multiple dogs may be allowed.

Millington

Meeman-Shelby State Park
910 Riddick Road
Millington, GA
901-876-5215
Dogs of all sizes are allowed, and there are no additional pet fees for tent or RV sites. There is a $10 per night per pet additional fee for the 1 pet friendly cabin. Dogs may not be left unattended outside or in the cabin, and they must be leashed and cleaned up after. The camping and tent areas also allow dogs. There is a dog walk area at the campground. Dogs are allowed in the camping cabins. 2 dogs may be allowed.

Savannah

Savannah South KOA
4915 H 17
Richmond Hill, GA
912-765-3396
Dogs of all sizes are allowed. There are no additional pet fees. Dogs must be leashed and cleaned up after. The camping and tent areas also allow dogs. There is a dog walk area at the campground. Dogs are allowed in the camping cabins. Multiple dogs may be allowed.

Trenton

Lookout Mountain/Chattanooga West KOA
930 Mountain Shadows Drive
Trenton, GA
706-657-6815
Dogs of all sizes are allowed. There are no additional pet fees. Dogs must be leashed and cleaned up after. There are some breed restrictions. The camping and tent areas also allow dogs. There is a dog walk area at the campground. Dogs are allowed in the camping cabins. Multiple dogs may be allowed.

Idaho Listings

Athol

Farragut State Park
13550 E H 54
Athol, ID
208-683-2425
With over 4,000 acres and home to the largest lake in the state, this biologically diverse park offers a variety of nature study, and land and water recreation. This park also has exhibits about their part as a Navel Training Center in WWII. Dogs of all sizes are allowed at no additional fee. Dogs may not be left unattended, and they must be quiet, well behaved, leashed and cleaned up after. Dogs are not allowed on the beach or in buildings. Dogs are allowed on the trails. The camping and tent areas also allow dogs. There is a dog walk area at the campground. Dogs are allowed in the camping cabins. Multiple dogs may be allowed.

Coeur D'Alene

Coeur D'Alene KOA
10588 E Wolf Lodge Bay Road
Coeur D'Alene, ID
208-664-4471
Dogs of all sizes are allowed. There are no additional pet fees. Dogs must be quiet, leashed, and cleaned up after. This RV park is closed during the off-season. The camping and tent areas also allow dogs. There is a dog walk area at the campground. Dogs are allowed in the camping cabins. Multiple dogs may be allowed.

Idaho Panhandle National Forest
3815 Schreiber Street
Coeur d'Alene, ID
208-765-7223
This forest of 2.5 million acres has more than 3,300 miles of hiking trails, and the various ecosystems support a large variety of plants, fish, mammals, bird species, and recreation. Dogs of all sizes are allowed at no additional fee. Dogs may not be left unattended, and they must be leashed and cleaned up after. Dogs are allowed on the trails. The camping and tent areas also allow dogs. There is a dog walk area at the campground. Dogs are allowed in the camping cabins. Multiple dogs may be allowed.

Coolin

Priest Lake State Park
3140 Indian Creek Park Road
Coolin, ID
208-443-6710
Steeped in history, this scenic park offers a variety of habitats, trails, and land and water recreation. Dogs of all sizes are allowed at no additional fee. Dogs may not be left unattended, and they must be quiet, be on no more than a 6 foot leash, and cleaned up after. Dogs are not allowed in the public swim area, but they are allowed at their own designated swim area and on the trails. The camping and tent areas also allow dogs. There is a dog walk area at the campground. Dogs are allowed in the camping cabins. There are no water hookups at the campground. Multiple dogs may be allowed.

Idaho City

Boise National Forest
3833 H 21
Idaho City, ID
208-373-4100
This forest has 6 ranger districts, over 2 million acres, and diverse ecosystems that support a large variety of plants, fish, mammals, bird species, and year round recreation. Dogs of all sizes are allowed at no additional fee. Dogs may not be left unattended, and they must be leashed and cleaned up after. Dogs are not allowed on the furniture in the cabins, or in any other park buildings. Dogs are allowed on the trails. This campground is closed during the off-season. The camping and tent areas also allow dogs. There is a dog walk area at the campground. Dogs are allowed in the camping cabins. There are no electric or water hookups at the campground. Multiple dogs may be allowed.

Jerome

Twin Falls/Jerome KOA
5431 H 93
Jerome, ID
208-324-4169
Dogs of all sizes are allowed. There are no additional pet fees, but they request that if you rented a cabin with a dog that you sweep the cabin out before you leave. Dogs may not be left unattended, must be leashed, and cleaned up after. There are some breed restrictions. This RV park is closed during the

off-season. The camping and tent areas also allow dogs. There is a dog walk area at the campground. Dogs are allowed in the camping cabins. Multiple dogs may be allowed.

Lewiston

Hells Gate State Park
4832 Hells Gate State Park
Lewiston, ID
208-799-5015
This park offers shady campsites on the Snake River along the deepest river gorge in North America, an interpretive plaza, a discovery center, tours, and various recreation. Dogs of all sizes are allowed at no additional fee. Dogs may not be left unattended, and they must be leashed at all times, and cleaned up after. Dogs are not allowed on the beach or in buildings, but they are allowed on the trails. The camping and tent areas also allow dogs. There is a dog walk area at the campground. Dogs are allowed in the camping cabins. Multiple dogs may be allowed.

Montpelier

Montpelier Creek KOA
28501 H 89N
Montpelier, ID
208-847-0863
Dogs of all sizes are allowed. There are no additional pet fees. Dogs must be leashed and cleaned up after. This RV park is closed during the off-season. The camping and tent areas also allow dogs. There is a dog walk area at the campground. Dogs are allowed in the camping cabins. 2 dogs may be allowed.

Mountain Home

Mountain Home KOA
220 E 10th N
Mountain Home, ID
208-587-5111
Dogs of all sizes are allowed. There are no additional pet fees. Dogs must be leashed and cleaned up after. This RV park is closed during the off-season. The camping and tent areas also allow dogs. There is a dog walk area at the campground. Dogs are allowed in the camping cabins. Multiple dogs may be allowed.

Orofino

Clearwater National Forest
83544 H 12
Orofino, ID
208-476-4541
This forest has 4 ranger districts, 1.8 million acres, and has diverse ecosystems that support a large variety of plants, fish, mammals, bird species as well as year round recreation. Dogs of all sizes are allowed at no additional fee. Dogs may not be left unattended, and they must be leashed, and cleaned up after in camp areas, and especially on the beaches. Dogs are not allowed in swim areas or in buildings. Dogs are allowed on the trails. This campground is closed during the off-season. The camping and tent areas also allow dogs. There is a dog walk area at the campground. Dogs are allowed in the camping cabins. There are no electric or water hookups at the campground. Multiple dogs may be allowed.

Dworshak State Park
P. O. Box 2028/Freeman Creek Road
Orofino, ID
208-476-5994
This 850, acre park located on shores of Dworshak Reservoir, offers a variety of activities and land and water recreation. Dogs of all sizes are allowed at no additional fee. Dogs may not be left unattended, and they must be leashed at all times, and cleaned up after. Dogs are not allowed in the buildings or on the beaches. Dogs are allowed on the trails. The camping and tent areas also allow dogs. There is a dog walk area at the campground. Dogs are allowed in the camping cabins. Multiple dogs may be allowed.

Pinehurst

Kellogg/Silver Valley KOA
801 N Division Street
Pinehurst, ID
208-682-3612
Dogs of all sizes are allowed. There are no additional pet fees. There is a $50 refundable deposit (or have credit card on file) for the cabin rentals. Dogs must be well behaved, may not be left unattended, must be leashed at all times, and cleaned up after. There is a fenced in dog run on site. This RV park is closed during the off-season. The camping and

tent areas also allow dogs. There is a dog walk area at the campground. Dogs are allowed in the camping cabins. 2 dogs may be allowed.

Plummer

Heyburn State Park
1291 Chatcolet Road
Plummer, ID
208-686-1308
This park of about 5,500 acres with 2,300 acres of lake is rich in natural and cultural history. The park offers an interpretive center along with a wide variety of land and water activities and recreation. Dogs of all sizes are allowed at no additional fee. Dogs may not be left unattended except for short periods, and then only if they will be quiet and well behaved. Dogs must be on no more than a 6 foot leash, and be cleaned up after. Dogs are allowed on the trails. This campground is closed during the off-season. The camping and tent areas also allow dogs. There is a dog walk area at the campground. Dogs are allowed in the camping cabins. Multiple dogs may be allowed.

St Charles

Bear Lake North RV Park
220 N Main
St Charles, ID
208-945-2941
Dogs of all sizes and numbers are allowed at RV sites, however only 1 dog up to 20 pounds is allowed at the cabins. There is a $1.50 per night per pet additional fee. Dogs may not be left unattended at the cabins, and they are not allowed on the beds or in the loft. The camping and tent areas also allow dogs. There is a dog walk area at the campground. Dogs are allowed in the camping cabins.

Twin Falls

Anderson Camp
S Tipperary
Eden, ID
888-480-9400
Dogs of all sizes are allowed. There are no additional pet fees. Dogs may not be left unattended, and must be quiet, leashed, and cleaned up after. The camping and tent areas also allow dogs. There is a dog walk area at the campground. Dogs are allowed in the camping

cabins. Multiple dogs may be allowed.

Illinois Listings

Benton

Benton KOA
1500 N DuQuoin Street
Benton, IL
618-439-4860
Dogs of all sizes are allowed, and there are no additional pet fees for tent or RV sites. There is a $5 one time additional pet fee for the cabins. Dogs may not be left unattended, and they must be leashed and cleaned up after. This RV park is closed during the off-season. The camping and tent areas also allow dogs. There is a dog walk area at the campground. Dogs are allowed in the camping cabins. 2 dogs may be allowed.

Chebanse

Kankakee South KOA
425 E 6000 Road
Chebanse, IL
815-939-4603
Dogs of all sizes are allowed. There are no additional pet fees. Dogs may not be left unattended, and must be leashed and cleaned up after. There are some breed restrictions. This RV park is closed during the off-season. The camping and tent areas also allow dogs. There is a dog walk area at the campground. Dogs are allowed in the camping cabins. Multiple dogs may be allowed.

Galena

Palace Campground
11357 H 20W
Galena, IL
815-777-2466
Dogs of all sizes are allowed. There are no additional pet fees. Dogs may not be left unattended, must be leashed, and cleaned up after. This RV park is closed during the off-season. The camping and tent areas also allow dogs. There is a dog walk area at the campground. Dogs are allowed in the camping cabins. Multiple dogs may be allowed.

Garden Prairie

Holiday Acres Camping Resort
7050 Epworth
Garden Prairie, IL
815-547-7846
Dogs of all sizes are allowed, but there can only be one dog in the cabins. There are no additional pet fees. Dogs must be well behaved, leashed, and cleaned up after. The camping and tent areas also allow dogs. There is a dog walk area at the campground. Dogs are allowed in the camping cabins.

Lena

Lena KOA
10982 W H 20
Lena, IL
815-369-2612
Dogs of all sizes are allowed, and there are no additional pet fees for tent or RV sites. There is a $2 per night per pet additional fee for the cabins, and only 2 dogs are allowed. Dogs must be leashed and cleaned up after. There are some breed restrictions. This RV park is closed during the off-season. The camping and tent areas also allow dogs. There is a dog walk area at the campground. Dogs are allowed in the camping cabins.

Millbrook

Jellystone Park
8574 Millbrook Road
Millbrook, IL
800-438-9644
Dogs of all sizes are allowed. There is a $3 per night per pet additional fee for tent and RV spaces, and $5 per night per pet for cabin rentals. Dogs are not allowed in trailor or park models. Dogs may not be left unattended, must be leashed, and cleaned up after. The camping and tent areas also allow dogs. There is a dog walk area at the campground. Dogs are allowed in the camping cabins. Multiple dogs may be allowed.

Pittsfield

Pine Lakes Resort
RR3 Box 3077
Pittsfield, IL
877-808-7436
Dogs of all sizes are allowed, and there are no additional pet fees for tent or RV sites. There is a $5 per

night per pet additional fee for cottages. Dogs may not be left unattended except for short periods, and they must be leashed and cleaned up after. The camping and tent areas also allow dogs. There is a dog walk area at the campground. Dogs are allowed in the camping cabins. Multiple dogs may be allowed.

Rock Island

Rock Island KOA
2311 78th Avenue W
Rock Island, IL
309-787-0665
Dogs of all sizes are allowed. There are no additional pet fees. Dogs must be leashed and cleaned up after. The camping and tent areas also allow dogs. There is a dog walk area at the campground. Dogs are allowed in the camping cabins. Multiple dogs may be allowed.

Springfield

Springfield KOA
4320 KOA Road
Rochester, IL
217-498-7002
Dogs of all sizes are allowed. There are no additional pet fees. Dogs must be quiet, leashed, and cleaned up after. This RV park is closed during the off-season. The camping and tent areas also allow dogs. There is a dog walk area at the campground. Dogs are allowed in the camping cabins.

Utica

LaSalle/Peru KOA
756 N 3150th Road
Utica, IL
815-667-4988
Dogs of all sizes are allowed. There are no additional pet fees. Dogs may not be left unattended at the cabins, and they must be leashed and cleaned up after. This RV park is closed during the off-season. The camping and tent areas also allow dogs. There is a dog walk area at the campground. Dogs are allowed in the camping cabins. Multiple dogs may be allowed.

Indiana Listings

Bloomington

Lake Monroe Village
8107 S Fairfax
Bloomington, IN
812-824-2267
Dogs of all sizes are allowed. There are no additional pet fees. Dogs must be leashed and cleaned up after. The camping and tent areas also allow dogs. There is a dog walk area at the campground. Dogs are allowed in the camping cabins. Multiple dogs may be allowed.

Cherokee

Happy Holiday RV Park
1553 Wolftown Road
Cherokee, IN
828-497-7250
Dogs of all sizes are allowed. There are no additional pet fees. Dogs may not be left unattended outside, and they must be leashed and cleaned up after. This RV park is closed during the off-season. The camping and tent areas also allow dogs. There is a dog walk area at the campground. Dogs are allowed in the camping cabins. Multiple dogs may be allowed.

Crawfordsville

Crawfordsville KOA
1600 Lafayette Road
Crawfordsville, IN
765-362-4190
Dogs of all sizes are allowed. There are no additional pet fees. Dogs may not be left unattended in the cabins or outside alone. Dogs must be leashed and cleaned up after. This RV park is closed during the off-season. The camping and tent areas also allow dogs. There is a dog walk area at the campground. Dogs are allowed in the camping cabins. Multiple dogs may be allowed.

Elkhart

Elkhart Campground
25608 County Road 4
Elkhart, IN
574-264-2914
Dogs of all sizes are allowed. There are no additional pet fees. Dogs must be quiet, leashed, and cleaned up after. If you have dogs in one of the cabins they request you sweep

out the cabin before you leave. Dogs must be leashed and cleaned up after. This RV park is closed during the off-season. The camping and tent areas also allow dogs. There is a dog walk area at the campground. Dogs are allowed in the camping cabins. 2 dogs may be allowed.

Granger

South Bend East KOA
50707 Princess Way
Granger, IN
574-277-1335
Dogs of all sizes are allowed, and there are no additional pet fees for tent or RV sites. There is a $50 cash only refundable deposit for the cabins. Dogs must be leashed and cleaned up after. This RV park is closed during the off-season. The camping and tent areas also allow dogs. There is a dog walk area at the campground. Dogs are allowed in the camping cabins. Multiple dogs may be allowed.

Howe

Twin Mills Camping Resort
1675 W H 120
Howe, IN
260-562-3212
Dogs of all sizes and numbers are allowed, and there are no additional pet fees for tent or RV sites. There is a $25 per stay additional fee for cabins or rentals, and only 2 dogs 10 pounds or under are allowed. There must be proof of insurance for known aggressive breeds. Dogs must be leashed and cleaned up after. This RV park is closed during the off-season. The camping and tent areas also allow dogs. There is a dog walk area at the campground. Dogs are allowed in the camping cabins.

Indianapolis

Indianapolis KOA
5896 W 200 N
Greenfield, IN
317-894-1397
Dogs of all sizes are allowed. There are no additional pet fees. Dogs may not be left unattended in the cabins, and they must be leashed and cleaned up after. This RV park is closed during the off-season. The camping and tent areas also allow dogs. There is a dog walk area at the campground. Dogs are allowed in the camping cabins. Multiple dogs may

be allowed.

Knightstown

Yogi Bear Campground
5964 S H 109
Knightstown, IN
765-737-6585
Dogs of all sizes are allowed. There are no additional pet fees. Dogs must be friendly, well behaved, leashed, and cleaned up after. The camping and tent areas also allow dogs. There is a dog walk area at the campground. Dogs are allowed in the camping cabins. Multiple dogs may be allowed.

Liberty

Whitewater Memorial Park
1418 S State Road 101
Liberty, IN
765-458-5565
This historical and scenic park offers a 200 acre lake and a variety of land and water recreation. Dogs of all sizes are allowed at the tent and RV sites at no additional fee. There may only be one dog in the cabins, and there are only 2 pet friendly cabins. Dogs may not be left unattended, and they must be on no more than a 6 foot leash, and be cleaned up after. Dogs are allowed on the trails. The camping and tent areas also allow dogs. There is a dog walk area at the campground. Dogs are allowed in the camping cabins. There are no water hookups at the campground.

Middlebury

Elkhart Co/Middlebury Exit KOA
52867 H 13
Middlebury, IN
574-825-5932
Dogs of all sizes are allowed. There are no additional pet fees. Dogs may not be left unattended at the cabins, and they must be leashed and cleaned up after. This RV park is closed during the off-season. The camping and tent areas also allow dogs. There is a dog walk area at the campground. Dogs are allowed in the camping cabins. Multiple dogs may be allowed.

Plymouth

Jellystone Park
7719 Redwood Road

Plymouth, IN
574-936-7851
Dogs of all sizes are allowed. There are no additional pet fees. Dogs may not be left unattended, must be leashed at all times, and cleaned up after. This RV park is closed during the off-season. The camping and tent areas also allow dogs. There is a dog walk area at the campground. Dogs are allowed in the camping cabins. Multiple dogs may be allowed.

Richmond

Richmond KOA
3101 Cart Road
Richmond, IN
756-962-1219
Dogs of all sizes are allowed, and there are no additional pet fees for tent or RV sites. Two dogs up to 50 pounds are allowed at the cabins also at no additional fee. Dogs may not be left unattended, and they must be leashed and cleaned up after. This RV park is closed during the off-season. The camping and tent areas also allow dogs. There is a dog walk area at the campground. Dogs are allowed in the camping cabins.

Terre Haute

Terre Haute KOA
5995 E Sony Drive
Terre Haute, IN
812-232-2457
Dogs of all sizes are allowed. There is a $5 one time fee for pets. Dogs must be leashed and cleaned up after. The camping and tent areas also allow dogs. There is a dog walk area at the campground. Dogs are allowed in the camping cabins. Multiple dogs may be allowed.

Thorntown

Old Mill Run Park
8544 W 690N
Thorntown, IN
765-436-7190
Dogs of all sizes are allowed. There are no additional pet fees. Dogs may not be left unattended or tied up alone outside. Dogs must be leashed and cleaned up after. This RV park is closed during the off-season. The camping and tent areas also allow dogs. There is a dog walk area at the campground. Dogs are allowed in the camping cabins.

Winamac

Tippecanoe River State Park
4200 N H 35
Winamac, IN
574-946-3213
This park along the Tippecanoe River offers a variety of land and water recreation. Dogs of all sizes are allowed at no additional fee. Dogs may not be left unattended, and they must be leased and cleaned up after. Dogs are not allowed in public swim areas or in buildings. Dogs are allowed on the trails. The camping and tent areas also allow dogs. There is a dog walk area at the campground. Dogs are allowed in the camping cabins. There are no water hookups at the campground. Multiple dogs may be allowed.

Iowa Listings

Brighton

Lake Darling State Park
111 Lake Darling Road
Brighton, IA
319-694-2323
This beautiful park of 1,417 acres with a 302-acre lake, offers various recreational pursuits. Along the parks many trails you will see a variety of plant, animal and bird species. Dogs of all sizes are allowed at no additional fee. Dogs may not be left unattended, and they must be leashed and cleaned up after. Dogs are not allowed in public swim areas or in buildings. Dogs are allowed on the trails. The camping and tent areas also allow dogs. There is a dog walk area at the campground. Dogs are allowed in the camping cabins. There are no water hookups at the campground. Multiple dogs may be allowed.

Cedar Falls

Black Hawk Park
2410 W Lonetree Road
Cedar Falls, IA
319-266-6813
This large park offers a variety of activities and recreation. Dogs of all sizes are allowed at no additional fee. Dogs may not be left unattended at any time, and they must be quiet,

be on no more than a 6 foot leash, and cleaned up after. Dogs are allowed on the trails, but not on the playground. The camping and tent areas also allow dogs. There is a dog walk area at the campground. Dogs are allowed in the camping cabins. Multiple dogs may be allowed.

Farmington

Riverview Canoes and Camping
26070 Hawk Drive
Farmington, IA
319-878-3715
Dogs of all sizes are allowed. There are no additional pet fees. Dogs may not be left unattended unless they will be quiet and well behaved. Dogs must be leashed and cleaned up after. This RV park is closed during the off-season. The camping and tent areas also allow dogs. There is a dog walk area at the campground. Dogs are allowed in the camping cabins. Multiple dogs may be allowed.

Onawa

Onawa/Blue Lake KOA
21788 Dogwood Avenue
Onawa, IA
712-423-1633
Dogs of all sizes are allowed. There are no additional pet fees. Dogs must be quiet, well behaved, leashed, and cleaned up after. Dogs may not be left unattended. This RV park is closed during the off-season. The camping and tent areas also allow dogs. There is a dog walk area at the campground. Dogs are allowed in the camping cabins. Multiple dogs may be allowed.

W Liberty

West Liberty KOA
1961 Garfield Avenue
W Liberty, IA
319-627-2676
Dogs of all sizes are allowed. There are no additional pet fees. Dogs may not be left unattended, and must be leashed and cleaned up after. The camping and tent areas also allow dogs. There is a dog walk area at the campground. Dogs are allowed in the camping cabins. Multiple dogs may be allowed.

Kansas Listings

Goodland

Goodland KOA
1114 E H 24
Goodland, KS
785-890-5701
Dogs of all sizes are allowed. There are no additional pet fees. Dogs must be well behaved, leashed, and cleaned up after. There are some breed restrictions. This RV park is closed during the off-season. The camping and tent areas also allow dogs. There is a dog walk area at the campground. Dogs are allowed in the camping cabins. Multiple dogs may be allowed.

Grantville

Topeka KOA
3366 KOA Road
Grantville, KS
785-246-3419
Dogs of all sizes are allowed. There are no additional pet fees. There is a pet waiver to sign if the dog(s) are any of the known aggressive breeds. Dogs must be quiet, leashed and cleaned up after. This RV park is closed during the off-season. The camping and tent areas also allow dogs. Dogs are allowed in the camping cabins. Multiple dogs may be allowed.

Lawrence

Lawrence/Kansas City KOA
1473 H 40
Lawrence, KS
785-842-3877
Dogs of all sizes are allowed. There are no additional pet fees. Dogs may not be left unattended outside or in the cabins, and they must be quiet, be on no more than a 6 foot leash, and cleaned up after. There are some breed restrictions. The camping and tent areas also allow dogs. There is a dog walk area at the campground. Dogs are allowed in the camping cabins. Multiple dogs may be allowed.

Salina

Salina KOA

1109 W Diamond Drive
Salina, KS
785-827-3182
Dogs of all sizes and numbers are allowed at the tent or RV sites. Two dogs of any size are allowed at the cabins. There are no additional pet fees. Dogs may not be left unattended, and they must be leashed and cleaned up after. This RV park is closed during the off-season. The camping and tent areas also allow dogs. There is a dog walk area at the campground. Dogs are allowed in the camping cabins.

WaKeeney

WaKeeney KOA
I 70 S. Frontage Road, Box 170
WaKeeney, KS
785-743-5612
Dogs of all sizes are allowed, and there are no additional pet fees for tent or RV sites. There is a $25 refundable deposit for the cabins, and dogs may not be left unattended there. Dogs must be well behaved, leashed, and cleaned up after. There are some breed restrictions. This RV park is closed during the off-season. The camping and tent areas also allow dogs. There is a dog walk area at the campground. Dogs are allowed in the camping cabins. There are special amenities given to dogs at this campground. Multiple dogs may be allowed.

Kentucky Listings

Beattyville

Lago Linda Hideaway Campground
850 Black Ridge Road
Beattyville, KY
606-464-2876
Dogs of all sizes are allowed. There are no additional pet fees. Dogs may not be left unattended outside or in the cabins, and they must be leashed and cleaned up after. There are 2 pet-friendly cabins. Dogs are to stay off the furniture in the cabins, and they are not allowed in other park buildings or on other people's camp sites. The camping and tent areas also allow dogs. There is a dog walk area at the campground. Dogs are allowed in the camping

cabins. 2 dogs may be allowed.

Bowling Green

Bowling Green KOA
1960 Three Springs Road
Bowling Green, KY
270-843-1919
Dogs of all sizes are allowed, and there are no additional pet fees for tent or RV sites. There is a $5 per night per pet additional fee for the cabins. Dogs may not be left unattended outside or in the cabins, and they must be leashed and cleaned up after. The camping and tent areas also allow dogs. There is a dog walk area at the campground. Dogs are allowed in the camping cabins. Multiple dogs may be allowed.

Calvert City

Paducah/I 24/Kentucky Lake KOA
4793 H 62
Calvert City, KY
270-395-5841
Dogs of all sizes are allowed at the tent or RV sites, and there can be up to 3. There can only be 2 dogs up to 25 pounds each in the cabins. There are no additional pet fees. Dogs may not be left unattended, and they must be leashed and cleaned up after. This RV park is closed during the off-season. The camping and tent areas also allow dogs. There is a dog walk area at the campground. Dogs are allowed in the camping cabins.

Corbin

Corbin KOA
171 E City Dam Road
Corbin, KY
806-528-1534
Up to 3 dogs are allowed at the RV sites, 2 dogs at the tent sites, and 1 dog in the cabins. There are no additional pet fees. Dogs may not be left unattended, and must be leashed and cleaned up after. The camping and tent areas also allow dogs. There is a dog walk area at the campground. Dogs are allowed in the camping cabins.

Corinth

Three Springs Campground
595 Campground Road
Corinth, KY

859-806-3030
Dogs of all sizes are allowed. There are no additional pet fees. Dogs must be leashed and cleaned up after. Dogs may be unleashed on your site if they are under voice command, will stay on the site, and will not chase. The camping and tent areas also allow dogs. There is a dog walk area at the campground. Dogs are allowed in the camping cabins. Multiple dogs may be allowed.

Franklin

Franklin KOA
2889 Scottsville Road
Franklin, KY
270-586-5622
Dogs of all sizes are allowed. There are no additional pet fees. Dogs must be leashed and cleaned up after. The camping and tent areas also allow dogs. There is a dog walk area at the campground. Dogs are allowed in the camping cabins. Multiple dogs may be allowed.

Horse Cave

Horse Cave KOA
109 Knob Hill Road
Horse Cave, KY
270-786-2819
Dogs of all sizes are allowed. There are no additional pet fees. Dogs must be leashed and cleaned up after. The camping and tent areas also allow dogs. There is a dog walk area at the campground. Dogs are allowed in the camping cabins. Multiple dogs may be allowed.

Louisville

Louisville Metro KOA
900 Marriott Drive
Clarksville, IN
812-282-4474
Dogs of all sizes are allowed. There are no additional pet fees. Dogs may not be left unattended outside, and they must be leashed and cleaned up after. The camping and tent areas also allow dogs. There is a dog walk area at the campground. Dogs are allowed in the camping cabins. Multiple dogs may be allowed.

Grand Trails RV Park
205 S Mulberry
Corydon, IN
812-738-9077
Dogs of all sizes are allowed, and

there are no additional pet fees for tent or RV sites. There is a $25 refundable pet deposit for the cabins. Dogs may not be tied to anything belonging to the campground, and they may not be tied up alone outside. Dogs must be leashed at all times, and cleaned up after. The camping and tent areas also allow dogs. There is a dog walk area at the campground. Dogs are allowed in the camping cabins. Multiple dogs may be allowed.

Manchester

Clay County Campground
83 Crawfish Road
Manchester, KY
606-598-3449
Dogs of all sizes are allowed. There are no additional pet fees. Dogs must be well behaved, leashed, and cleaned up after. Only one dog at a time can be in the cabins. This RV park is closed during the off-season. The camping and tent areas also allow dogs. There is a dog walk area at the campground. Dogs are allowed in the camping cabins.

Renfro Valley

Renfro Valley KOA
Red Foley Road, H 25
Renfro Valley, KY
606-256-2474
Dogs of all sizes are allowed. There are no additional pet fees. Dogs may not be left unattended outside except for very short periods, and they must be leashed and cleaned up after. There are some breed restrictions. The camping and tent areas also allow dogs. There is a dog walk area at the campground. Dogs are allowed in the camping cabins.

Shepherdsville

Louisville South KOA
2433 H 44E
Shepherdsville, KY
502-543-2041
Dogs of all sizes are allowed. There are no additional pet fees. Dogs may not be left unattended, and they must be leashed and cleaned up after. The camping and tent areas also allow dogs. There is a dog walk area at the campground. Dogs are allowed in the camping cabins. Multiple dogs may be allowed.

Louisiana Listings

Shreveport

Shreveport/Bossier KOA
6510 W 70th Street
Shreveport, LA
318-687-1010
Dogs of all sizes are allowed. There are no additional pet fees. Dogs may not be left unattended outside, and they must be leashed and cleaned up after. There are some breed restrictions. The camping and tent areas also allow dogs. There is a dog walk area at the campground. Dogs are allowed in the camping cabins. Multiple dogs may be allowed.

Maine Listings

Abbott

Balsam Woods
112 Pond Road
Abbott, ME
207-876-2731
Dogs of all sizes are allowed. There are no additional pet fees. Dogs must be leashed and cleaned up after. This RV park is closed during the off-season. The camping and tent areas also allow dogs. There is a dog walk area at the campground. Dogs are allowed in the camping cabins. Multiple dogs may be allowed.

Bangor

Pleasant Hill RV Park
45 Mansell Road
Hermon, ME
207-848-5127
Dogs up to 35 pounds are allowed. There is no fee for pets for the lots, but in the rentals there is a $10 per night per pet additional fee. Dogs must be leashed and cleaned up after. This RV park is closed during the off-season. The camping and tent areas also allow dogs. There is a dog walk area at the campground. Dogs are allowed in the camping cabins. 2 dogs may be allowed.

Canaan

Skowhegan/Canaan
18 Cabin Row
Canaan, ME
207-474-2858
Dogs of all sizes are allowed and they are allowed in the cabins with a credit card on file. There are no additional pet fees. Dogs must be quiet and well behaved. Dogs may not be left unattended, must be leashed, and cleaned up after. Dogs are not allowed in the buildings, the pavillion, the pool or playground. This RV park is closed during the off-season. The camping and tent areas also allow dogs. There is a dog walk area at the campground. Dogs are allowed in the camping cabins.

Damariscotta

Lake Pemaquid Camping
100 Twin Cove Lane
Damariscotta, ME
207-563-5202
Dogs of all sizes are allowed. There are no additional pet fees. Dogs must be quiet, leashed, and cleaned up after. This RV park is closed during the off-season. The camping and tent areas also allow dogs. There is a dog walk area at the campground. Dogs are allowed in the camping cabins. Multiple dogs may be allowed.

Durham

Freeport/Durham KOA
82 Big Skye Lane
Durham, ME
207-688-4288
Dogs of all sizes are allowed, and there are no additional pet fees for tent or RV sites. There is a $10 one time additional pet fee for cabin rentals. Dogs must be quiet, leashed, and cleaned up after. There are some breed restrictions. This RV park is closed during the off-season. The camping and tent areas also allow dogs. There is a dog walk area at the campground. Dogs are allowed in the camping cabins. Multiple dogs may be allowed.

Freeport

Cedar Haven Campground
39 Baker Road
Freeport, ME
207-865-6254
Well behaved dogs of all sizes are

allowed. There are no additional pet fees. Dogs may not be left unattended, must be leashed, and cleaned up after. There is a pond for dogs to swim in at which time they can be off lead if they are under voice control. No excessive barking is allowed. This RV park is closed during the off-season. The camping and tent areas also allow dogs. There is a dog walk area at the campground. Dogs are allowed in the camping cabins.

Houlton

My Brother's Place Campground
659 North Street
Houlton, ME
207-532-6739
Dogs of all sizes are allowed, however the cabins will only accept 1 dog up to 50 pounds. There are no additional pet fees. Dogs may not be left unattended, must be leashed, and cleaned up after. This RV park is closed during the off-season. The camping and tent areas also allow dogs. There is a dog walk area at the campground. Dogs are allowed in the camping cabins.

Medway

Katahdin Shadows Campground and Cabins
H 157
Medway, ME
207-746-9349
Dogs of all sizes are allowed. There are no additional pet fees. Dogs may not be left unattended, must be leashed, and cleaned up after. This campground is open through the winter and closes for only one month in April. This RV park is closed during the off-season. The camping and tent areas also allow dogs. There is a dog walk area at the campground. Dogs are allowed in the camping cabins. Multiple dogs may be allowed.

Pownal

Blueberry Pond Camping
218 Poland Range Road
Pownal, ME
207-688-4421
Dogs of all sizes are allowed. There are no additional pet fees. Dogs must be well behaved, leashed, and cleaned up after. This RV park is closed during the off-season. The camping and tent areas also allow

dogs. There is a dog walk area at the campground. Dogs are allowed in the camping cabins. Multiple dogs may be allowed.

Richmond

Augusta/Gardiner KOA
30 Mallard Drive
Richmond, ME
207-582-5086
Dogs of all sizes are allowed. There are no additional pet fees. There is only one pet friendly cabin available, so early booking would be advised. Dogs must be leashed and cleaned up after. There are some breed restrictions. This RV park is closed during the off-season. The camping and tent areas also allow dogs. There is a dog walk area at the campground. Dogs are allowed in the camping cabins. Multiple dogs may be allowed.

Rockport

Megunticook Campground
On H 1
Rockport, ME
207-594-2428
Dogs of all sizes are allowed. There are no additional pet fees. Dogs must be quiet and well behaved. Dogs may not be left unattended, must be leashed, and cleaned up after. There are some breed restrictions. This RV park is closed during the off-season. The camping and tent areas also allow dogs. There is a dog walk area at the campground. Dogs are allowed in the camping cabins. Multiple dogs may be allowed.

Saco

KOA Saco/Portland South
814 Portland Road
Saco, ME
207-282-0502
Dogs of all sizes are allowed, and there are no additional pet fees for tent or RV sites. There is a $15 one time fee plus a $100 refundable pet deposit for cabin rentals. Dogs may not be left unattended, must be leashed, and cleaned up after. This RV park is closed during the off-season. The camping and tent areas also allow dogs. There is a dog walk area at the campground. Dogs are allowed in the camping cabins. Multiple dogs may be allowed.

Maryland Listings

Flintstone

Rocky Gap State Park
12500 Pleasant Valley Road
Flintstone, MD
301-777-2139
This resort like scenic park has over 3,000 land acres, 243 lake acres, a variety of trails, and various year round activities for land and water recreation. Dogs of all sizes are allowed at no additional fee. Dogs may not be left unattended, and they must be leashed and cleaned up after. Dogs are not allowed on beaches, in buildings, or picnic areas. Dogs are allowed on the trails. This campground is closed during the off-season. The camping and tent areas also allow dogs. There is a dog walk area at the campground. Dogs are allowed in the camping cabins. There are no water hookups at the campground. Multiple dogs may be allowed.

Millersville

Washington DE, NE KOA
768 Cecil Avenue N
Millersville, MD
410-923-2771
Dogs of all sizes are allowed. There are no additional pet fees. Dogs may not be left unattended, must be leashed, and cleaned up after. Dogs are not allowed at the lodge. This RV park is closed during the off-season. The camping and tent areas also allow dogs. There is a dog walk area at the campground. Dogs are allowed in the camping cabins. Multiple dogs may be allowed.

Williamsport

KOA Hagerstown/Snug Harbor
11759 Snug Harbor Lane
Williamsport, MD
301-223-7571
Dogs of all sizes are allowed. There are no additional pet fees. Dogs must be quiet, be on no more than a 6 foot leash, and be cleaned up after. This RV park is closed during the off-season. The camping and tent areas also allow dogs. There is a dog walk

area at the campground. Dogs are allowed in the camping cabins. Multiple dogs may be allowed.

Massachusetts Listings

Charlemont

Mohawk Trail State Forest
On H 2
Charlemont, MA
413-339-5504
Dogs of all sizes are allowed. There are no additional pet fees. Dogs may not be left unattended, they must have current rabies certificate and shot records, be leashed, and cleaned up after. Dogs are allowed on all the trails. This campground is closed during the off-season. The camping and tent areas also allow dogs. There is a dog walk area at the campground. Dogs are allowed in the camping cabins. There are no electric or water hookups at the campground. Multiple dogs may be allowed.

Westford

Wyman's Beach Family Camping
48 Wyman's Beach Road
Westford, MA
978-692-6287
Well behaved dogs of all sizes are allowed. There are no additional pet fees. Dogs must remain in one's own site and be leashed at all times. There is a dog walk area close by that you can drive to. Dogs are allowed in the camping cabins. Multiple dogs may be allowed.

Michigan Listings

Bellaire

Chain-O-Lakes Campground
7231 S H 88
Bellaire, MI
231-533-8432
Dogs of all sizes are allowed. There are no additional pet fees. Dogs must be friendly, be on leash, and cleaned up after. Dogs may not be

left unattended at any time. The camping and tent areas also allow dogs. There is a dog walk area at the campground. Dogs are allowed in the camping cabins. Multiple dogs may be allowed.

Benton Harbor

House of David Travel Trailer Park
1019 E Empire
Benton Harbor, MI
269-927-3302
Dogs of all sizes are allowed. There are no additional pet fees. Dogs must be leashed and cleaned up after. There are some breed restrictions. The camping and tent areas also allow dogs. There is a dog walk area at the campground. Dogs are allowed in the camping cabins. 2 dogs may be allowed.

Big Bend

Big Bend Family Campground
513 Conrad Road
Big Bend, MI
989-653-2267
Dogs of all sizes are allowed. There are no additional pet fees. Dogs can go in the river and the lake, otherwise they must be leashed at all times and cleaned up after. This RV park is closed during the off-season. The camping and tent areas also allow dogs. There is a dog walk area at the campground. Dogs are allowed in the camping cabins. Multiple dogs may be allowed.

Gaylord

Gaylord KOA
5101 Campfires Parkway
Gaylord, MI
989-939-8723
Dogs of all sizes are allowed. There are no additional pet fees. Dogs may not be left unattended, must be leashed, and cleaned up after. This RV park is closed during the off-season. The camping and tent areas also allow dogs. There is a dog walk area at the campground. Dogs are allowed in the camping cabins. Multiple dogs may be allowed.

Grand Junction

Warner Camp on Lester Lake

60 55th Street
Grand Junction, MI
269-434-6844
Dogs of all sizes are allowed. There are no additional pet fees. Dogs must be leashed and cleaned up after, and are not allowed on the beach. This RV park is closed during the off-season. The camping and tent areas also allow dogs. There is a dog walk area at the campground. Dogs are allowed in the camping cabins. Multiple dogs may be allowed.

Mackinaw City

St. Ignace/Mackinac Island KOA
1242 H 2 W
St Ignace, MI
906-643-9303
Dogs of all sizes are allowed. There are no additional pet fees. Dogs may not be left unattended, must be leashed, and cleaned up after. This RV park is closed during the off-season. The camping and tent areas also allow dogs. There is a dog walk area at the campground. Dogs are allowed in the camping cabins. Multiple dogs may be allowed.

Munising

Wandering Wheels Campground
E10102 H 28E
Munising, MI
906-387-3315
Dogs of all sizes are allowed. There are no additional pet fees. Dogs must be leashed and cleaned up after. This RV park is closed during the off-season. The camping and tent areas also allow dogs. There is a dog walk area at the campground. Dogs are allowed in the camping cabins. Multiple dogs may be allowed.

Muskegon

Back Forty Ranch
5900 S Water Road
Rothbury, MI
231-894-4444
Dogs of all sizes are allowed. There are no additional pet fees for RV spaces, however there is a $25 per night per pet additional fee for the Back 40 Cabins plus a $100 refundable deposit. Dogs may not be left unattended except for short periods and if they will be well behaved in owner's absence. Dogs must be leashed and cleaned up

after. The camping and tent areas also allow dogs. There is a dog walk area at the campground. Dogs are allowed in the camping cabins. Multiple dogs may be allowed.

Newberry

Newberry KOA
13724 H 28
Newberry, MI
906-293-5762
Dogs of all sizes are allowed. There are no additional pet fees. Dogs may not be left unattended, must be leashed, and cleaned up after. This RV park is closed during the off-season. The camping and tent areas also allow dogs. There is a dog walk area at the campground. Dogs are allowed in the camping cabins. Multiple dogs may be allowed.

Petoskey

Petoskey KOA
1800 N H 31
Petoskey, MI
231-347-0005
Dogs of all sizes are allowed. There are no additional pet fees. Dogs may not be left unattended, must be leashed, and cleaned up after. Dogs are allowed in the cabins but not the park models. This RV park is closed during the off-season. The camping and tent areas also allow dogs. There is a dog walk area at the campground. Dogs are allowed in the camping cabins. Multiple dogs may be allowed.

Riverside

Coloma/St Joseph KOA
3527 Coloma Road
Riverside, MI
269-849-3333
Dogs of all sizes are allowed. There are no additional pet fees. Dogs may not be left unattended, must be leashed, and cleaned up after. There are some breed restrictions. This RV park is closed during the off-season. The camping and tent areas also allow dogs. There is a dog walk area at the campground. Dogs are allowed in the camping cabins. 2 dogs may be allowed.

Tustin

Cadillac Woods Campground
23163 H 115

Tustin, MI
231-825-2012
Dogs of all sizes are allowed. There are no additional pet fees. Dogs may not be left unattended, must be leashed and cleaned up after. Dogs are allowed off leash at your site if the dog will not chase people or pets, and will stay on the site. The camping and tent areas also allow dogs. There is a dog walk area at the campground. Dogs are allowed in the camping cabins. Multiple dogs may be allowed.

Minnesota Listings

Austin

Beaver Trails Campground and RV Park
21943 630th Avenue
Austin, MN
507-584-6611
Dogs of all sizes are allowed. There are no additional pet fees. Dogs must be leashed and cleaned up after. There are some breed restrictions. This RV park is closed during the off-season. The camping and tent areas also allow dogs. There is a dog walk area at the campground. Dogs are allowed in the camping cabins. Multiple dogs may be allowed.

Bemidji

Bemidji KOA
510 Brightstar Road NW
Bemidji, MN
218-444-7562
Dogs of all sizes are allowed, and there are no additional pet fees for tent or RV sites. There is a $5 per pet per stay additional fee for the lodge and cabins. Dogs must be on no more than a 6 foot leash, and be cleaned up after. This RV park is closed during the off-season. The camping and tent areas also allow dogs. There is a dog walk area at the campground. Dogs are allowed in the camping cabins. Multiple dogs may be allowed.

Cass Lake

Stonypoint Resort
5510 H 2 NW
Cass Lake, MN

507-584-6611
Dogs of all sizes are allowed. There is a $2 per night per pet additional fee. Dogs must be well behaved, house trained, leashed, and cleaned up after. This RV park is closed during the off-season. The camping and tent areas also allow dogs. There is a dog walk area at the campground. Dogs are allowed in the camping cabins. Multiple dogs may be allowed.

Cloquet

Cloquet/Duluth KOA
1381 Carlton Road
Cloquet, MN
218-879-5726
Dogs of all sizes are allowed. There are no additional pet fees. Dogs must be leashed and cleaned up after. This RV park is closed during the off-season. The camping and tent areas also allow dogs. There is a dog walk area at the campground. Dogs are allowed in the camping cabins. 2 dogs may be allowed.

Hayward

Albert Lea/Austin KOA
84259 County Road 46
Hayward, MN
507-373-5170
Dogs of all sizes are allowed. There are no additional pet fees. Dogs must be well behaved, leashed, and cleaned up after. This RV park is closed during the off-season. The camping and tent areas also allow dogs. There is a dog walk area at the campground. Dogs are allowed in the camping cabins. Multiple dogs may be allowed.

Jackson

Jackson KOA
2035 H 71N
Jackson, MN
507-847-3825
Dogs of all sizes are allowed, and there are no additional pet fees for the tent or RV sites. There is a $5 one time additional pet fee for cabin rentals. Dogs must be leashed and cleaned up after. This RV park is closed during the off-season. The camping and tent areas also allow dogs. There is a dog walk area at the campground. Dogs are allowed in the camping cabins. Multiple dogs may be allowed.

Jordan

Minneapolis Southwest KOA
3315 W 166th Street
Jordan, MN
952-492-6440
Dogs of all sizes are allowed. There is a $1 per night per pet additional fee. There is an additional refundable pet deposit of $50 for the cabin rentals. Dogs must be leashed and cleaned up after. This RV park is closed during the off-season. The camping and tent areas also allow dogs. There is a dog walk area at the campground. Dogs are allowed in the camping cabins. 2 dogs may be allowed.

Minneapolis - St Paul

St Paul East KOA
568 Cottage Grove
Woodbury, MN
651-436-6436
Dogs of all sizes are allowed. There are no additional pet fees. Dogs must be quiet, well behaved, leashed, and cleaned up after. There are some breed restrictions. This RV park is closed during the off-season. The camping and tent areas also allow dogs. There is a dog walk area at the campground. Dogs are allowed in the camping cabins. Multiple dogs may be allowed.

Moorhead

Moorhead/Fargo KOA
4396 28th Avenue S
Moorhead, MN
218-233-0671
Dogs of all sizes are allowed. There are no additional pet fees. Dogs must be well behaved, may not be left unattended, must be leashed, and cleaned up after. This RV park is closed during the off-season. The camping and tent areas also allow dogs. There is a dog walk area at the campground. Dogs are allowed in the camping cabins. Multiple dogs may be allowed.

Missouri Listings

Branson

Branson KOA

1025 Headwaters Road
Branson, MO
417-334-7450
Dogs of all sizes are allowed. There are no additional pet fees. Dogs may not be left unattended outside, and they must be quiet, leashed, and cleaned up after. There are some breed restrictions. This RV park is closed during the off-season. The camping and tent areas also allow dogs. There is a dog walk area at the campground. Dogs are allowed in the camping cabins. Multiple dogs may be allowed.

Branson Stagecoach RV Park
5751 H 165
Branson, MO
417-335-8185
Dogs of all sizes are allowed, and there are no additional pet fees for tent or RV sites. There is a $25 refundable deposit for the cabins, and only 2 dogs up to 20 pounds are allowed. Dogs must be leashed and cleaned up after. There are some breed restrictions. The camping and tent areas also allow dogs. There is a dog walk area at the campground. Dogs are allowed in the camping cabins.

Cooper Creek Campground
471 Cooper Creek Road
Branson, MO
417-334-5250
Dogs of all sizes are allowed, and there are no additional pet fees for tent or RV sites. There is a $7 per night per pet additional fee for the cabins. Dogs must be leashed and cleaned up after. The camping and tent areas also allow dogs. There is a dog walk area at the campground. Dogs are allowed in the camping cabins. Multiple dogs may be allowed.

Granite City

Northeast/I 270/Granite City KOA
3157 Chain of Rocks Road
Granite City, MO
618-931-5160
Dogs of all sizes are allowed, and there are no additional pet fees for tent or RV sites. There is a $2.50 per night per pet additional fee for the cabins. Dogs must be quiet, well behaved, leashed, and cleaned up after. There are some breed restrictions. This RV park is closed during the off-season. The camping and tent areas also allow dogs. There is a dog walk area at the

campground. Dogs are allowed in the camping cabins. Multiple dogs may be allowed.

Joplin

Joplin KOA
4359 H 43
Joplin, MO
417-623-2246
Dogs of all sizes are allowed. There are no additional pet fees. Dogs must be leashed and cleaned up after. The camping and tent areas also allow dogs. There is a dog walk area at the campground. Dogs are allowed in the camping cabins. Multiple dogs may be allowed.

Kimberling City

Water's Edge
72 Marina Way
Kimberling City, MO
417-739-5377
Dogs of all sizes are allowed, and there are no additional pet fees for tent or RV sites. There is a $50 refundable deposit for the cabins, and only 1 small dog is allowed. Dogs may not be left unattended, must be leashed, and cleaned up after. Dogs may swim at the lake, but not in the public swim area. The camping and tent areas also allow dogs. There is a dog walk area at the campground. Dogs are allowed in the camping cabins.

Perryville

Perryville/Cape Girardeau KOA
89 KOA Lane
Perryville, MO
573-547-8303
Dogs of all sizes are allowed, and there are no additional pet fees for tent or RV sites. There is a $5 one time fee per pet for the cabins. Dogs may not be left unattended outside, and they must be leashed and cleaned up after. This RV park is closed during the off-season. The camping and tent areas also allow dogs. There is a dog walk area at the campground. Dogs are allowed in the camping cabins. 2 dogs may be allowed.

Red Lodge

Red Lodge KOA
7464 H 212
Red Lodge, MO

406-446-2364
Dogs of all sizes and numbers are allowed, and they must be quiet and well behaved. There are no additional pet fees for tent or RV sites. Only one dog is allowed in the cabins with no additional fee. Dogs may not be tied up outside alone, and can only be left in your RV if it is cool. Dogs may not be left unattended, must be leashed, and cleaned up after. This RV park is closed during the off-season. The camping and tent areas also allow dogs. There is a dog walk area at the campground. Dogs are allowed in the camping cabins.

Rock Port

Rock Port KOA
1409 H 136W
Rock Port, MO
660-744-5485
Dogs of all sizes are allowed. There are no additional pet fees. Dogs in the cabins must be housebroken. Dogs must be well behaved, leashed, and cleaned up after. This RV park is closed during the off-season. The camping and tent areas also allow dogs. There is a dog walk area at the campground. Dogs are allowed in the camping cabins. Multiple dogs may be allowed.

Springfield

Springfield KOA
5775 W Farm Road 140
Springfield, MO
417-831-3645
Dogs of all sizes are allowed. There are no additional pet fees. Dogs may not be tied up or left unattended outside, and they must be leashed and cleaned up after. The camping and tent areas also allow dogs. There is a dog walk area at the campground. Dogs are allowed in the camping cabins. Multiple dogs may be allowed.

St Louis

St Louis South KOA
8000 Metropolitan Blvd
Barnhart, MO
636-479-4449
Dogs of all sizes are allowed. There are no additional pet fees. Dogs may not be left unattended outside, and they must be leashed and cleaned up after. The camping and tent areas also allow dogs. There is a dog walk

area at the campground. Dogs are allowed in the camping cabins. Multiple dogs may be allowed.

St Louis West KOA
18475 Old H 66
Eureka, MO
636-257-3018
Dogs of all sizes are allowed. There are no additional pet fees. Dogs may not be left unattended outside, and they must be leashed and cleaned up after. Dogs must be crated at all times when they are in a cabin. This RV park is closed during the off-season. The camping and tent areas also allow dogs. There is a dog walk area at the campground. Dogs are allowed in the camping cabins. Multiple dogs may be allowed.

Stanton

Stanton/Meramec KOA
74 H 'W'
Stanton, MO
573-927-5215
Dogs of all sizes are allowed. There are no additional pet fees. Dogs may not be left unattended, and they must be leashed and cleaned up after. This RV park is closed during the off-season. The camping and tent areas also allow dogs. There is a dog walk area at the campground. Dogs are allowed in the camping cabins. Multiple dogs may be allowed.

Montana Listings

Bozeman

Bozeman KOA
81123 Gallatin Road
Bozeman, MT
406-587-3030
Dogs of all sizes are allowed. There are no additional pet fees. Dogs must be leashed and cleaned up after. The camping and tent areas also allow dogs. There is a dog walk area at the campground. Dogs are allowed in the camping cabins. Multiple dogs may be allowed.

Butte

Butte KOA

1601 Kaw Avenue
Butte, MT
406-782-8080
Dogs of all sizes are allowed. There are no additional pet fees. Dogs must be quiet, leashed, and cleaned up after. This RV park is closed during the off-season. The camping and tent areas also allow dogs. There is a dog walk area at the campground. Dogs are allowed in the camping cabins. Multiple dogs may be allowed.

Choteau

Choteau KOA
85 H 221
Choteau, MT
406-466-2615
Dogs of all sizes are allowed. There are no additional pet fees. Dogs must be leashed and cleaned up after. This RV park is closed during the off-season. The camping and tent areas also allow dogs. There is a dog walk area at the campground. Dogs are allowed in the camping cabins. Multiple dogs may be allowed.

Deer Lodge

Deer Lodge KOA
330 Park Street
Deer Lodge, MT
406-846-1629
Dogs of all sizes are allowed. There are no additional pet fees. Dogs may not be left unattended at any time, must be leashed, and cleaned up after. This RV park is closed during the off-season. The camping and tent areas also allow dogs. There is a dog walk area at the campground. Dogs are allowed in the camping cabins. Multiple dogs may be allowed.

Dillon

Deerlodge (Beaverhead) National Forest
420 Barrett Street
Dillon, MT
406-683-3900
This is a year round diverse recreational and working forest covering over 3 million acres in eight counties. Dogs are allowed at no additional fee. Dogs may not be left unattended, and they must be leashed and cleaned up after. Dogs are allowed on the trails, and they may be off lead in the forest as long

as there is voice control. This campground is closed during the off-season. The camping and tent areas also allow dogs. There is a dog walk area at the campground. Dogs are allowed in the camping cabins. There are no electric or water hookups at the campground. Multiple dogs may be allowed.

Dillon KOA
735 Park Street
Dillon, MT
406-683-2749
Dogs of all sizes are allowed. There are no additional pet fees. Dogs must be leashed and cleaned up after. Dogs are not allowed on the beds in the cabins. There are some breed restrictions. The camping and tent areas also allow dogs. There is a dog walk area at the campground. Dogs are allowed in the camping cabins. Multiple dogs may be allowed.

East Big Timber

Big Timber KOA
693 H 10
East Big Timber, MT
406-932-6569
Dogs of all sizes are allowed, and there are no additional pet fees for tent or RV sites. Up to three medium to small dogs or up to 2 large dogs are allowed at tent or RV sites. Only one dog is allowed in the cabins and there is an additional $5 fee per night. Dogs may not be left unattended, must be quiet, leashed, and cleaned up after. There are some breed restrictions. This RV park is closed during the off-season. The camping and tent areas also allow dogs. There is a dog walk area at the campground. Dogs are allowed in the camping cabins.

Glacier National Park

Whitefish/Kalispell N KOA
5121 H 93D
Whitefish, MT
406-862-4242
Dogs of all sizes are allowed. There are no additional pet fees. Dogs must leashed and cleaned up after. Dogs may be left unattended if they will be quiet. The camping and tent areas also allow dogs. There is a dog walk area at the campground. Dogs are allowed in the camping cabins. Multiple dogs may be allowed.

Great Falls

Great Falls KOA
1500 51st Street S
Great Falls, MT
406-727-3191
Dogs of all sizes are allowed. There are no additional pet fees. Dogs may not be left unattended, must be leashed, and cleaned up after. The camping and tent areas also allow dogs. There is a dog walk area at the campground. Dogs are allowed in the camping cabins. Multiple dogs may be allowed.

Hamilton

Bitterroot National Forest
1801 N 1st Street
Hamilton, MT
406-363-7100
This forest of 1.6 million acres has 4 ranger districts, more than 1,600 miles of multi-use trails, and very diverse ecosystems that support a large variety of plants, fish, mammals, bird species, as well as recreational pursuits. Dogs are allowed at no additional fee. Dogs may not be left unattended, and they must be well behaved, leashed and cleaned up after in the camp areas. Dogs may be off lead in the forest if they are under voice command and will not chase the wildlife. This campground is closed during the off-season. The camping and tent areas also allow dogs. There is a dog walk area at the campground. Dogs are allowed in the camping cabins. There are no water hookups at the campground. Multiple dogs may be allowed.

Hungry Horse

Timber Wolf Resort
9105 H 2E
Hungry Horse, MT
406-387-9653
Dogs of all sizes are allowed. There is a $3 per night per pet additional fee for the tent or RV sites. There is a $10 per night per pet additional fee for the cabins. Dogs may not be left unattended, and they must be leashed at all times, and cleaned up after. Dogs are allowed on the trails. The camping and tent areas also allow dogs. There is a dog walk area at the campground. Dogs are allowed in the camping cabins. Multiple dogs may be allowed.

Livingston

Livingston/Paradise Valley KOA
163 Pine Creek Road
Livingston, MT
406-222-0992
Dogs of all sizes are allowed. There are no additional pet fees. Dogs may not be left unattended, must be leashed, and cleaned up after. This RV park is closed during the off-season. The camping and tent areas also allow dogs. There is a dog walk area at the campground. Dogs are allowed in the camping cabins. Multiple dogs may be allowed.

Missoula

Missoula KOA
3450 Tina Avenue
Missoula, MT
406-549-0881
Dogs of all sizes are allowed. There are no additional pet fees. Dogs may not be left unattended, must be leashed, and cleaned up after. The camping and tent areas also allow dogs. There is a dog walk area at the campground. Dogs are allowed in the camping cabins. Multiple dogs may be allowed.

St Mary

St Mary/East Glacier
106 W Shore Road
St Mary, MT
406-732-4122
Dogs of all sizes are allowed. There are no additional pet fees. Dogs may be left for short periods, and someone in the office needs to know the dog is unattended. Dogs must be leashed and cleaned up after. There are some breed restrictions. This RV park is closed during the off-season. The camping and tent areas also allow dogs. There is a dog walk area at the campground. Dogs are allowed in the camping cabins. Multiple dogs may be allowed.

St Regis

Nugget Campground
E of Stop Sign on Main Street
St Regis, MT
888-800-0125
Dogs of all sizes are allowed. There are no additional pet fees. Dogs must be leashed and cleaned up after. The camping and tent areas also allow dogs. There is a dog walk area at the campground. Dogs are

allowed in the camping cabins. Multiple dogs may be allowed.

West Glacier

Glacier Campground
MM 152 H 2, 1 mile W of W Glacier
West Glacier, MT
406-387-5689
Dogs of all sizes are allowed. There are no additional pet fees. Dogs must be quiet, well behaved, leashed, and cleaned up after. Dogs may not be left unattended at any time. This RV park is closed during the off-season. The camping and tent areas also allow dogs. There is a dog walk area at the campground. Dogs are allowed in the camping cabins. Multiple dogs may be allowed.

West Glacier KOA
355 Half Moon Flats Road
West Glacier, MT
406-387-5341
Dogs of all sizes are allowed. There are no additional pet fees. Dogs must be well behaved, quiet, leashed, and cleaned up after. Dogs may not be left unattended. There is a local dog sitter available. This RV park is closed during the off-season. The camping and tent areas also allow dogs. There is a dog walk area at the campground. Dogs are allowed in the camping cabins. Multiple dogs may be allowed.

Whitehall

Lewis and Clark Caverns State Park
1455 H 2E
Whitehall, MT
406-287-3541
Montana's first state park is home to one of the most highly decorated limestone caverns in the Northwest, and the park offers a variety of hiking trails, a visitor center and an amphitheater. Dogs of all sizes are allowed at no additional fee. Dogs may not be left unattended, and they must be leashed and cleaned up after. Dogs are not allowed in food service areas, in the caverns, or on guided tours. Dogs may be in the Visitor's Center if they are not busy. As of 2006 they will be offering 2 kennels free of charge for visitors who would like to take the caverns tour. Dogs are allowed on the other trails. This campground is closed during the off-season. The camping and tent areas also allow dogs.

There is a dog walk area at the campground. Dogs are allowed in the camping cabins. There are no electric or water hookups at the campground. Multiple dogs may be allowed.

Yellowstone - Grand Teton

Yellowstone Grizzly RV Park
210 S Electric Street
West Yellowstone, MT
406-646-4466
Dogs of all sizes are allowed. There are no additional pet fees. Dogs must be quiet, well behaved, leashed, and cleaned up after. Dogs may not be left unattended. There is a forest nearby where they can run if they are under voice command. This RV park is closed during the off-season. The camping and tent areas also allow dogs. There is a dog walk area at the campground. Dogs are allowed in the camping cabins. Multiple dogs may be allowed.

Nebraska Listings

Ashland

Eugene T. Mahoney State Park
28500 W Park H
Ashland, NE
402-944-2523
This modern resort park offers many amenities including a family aquatic center, a 70-foot observation tower, and a wide variety of land and water activities and recreation. Dogs of all sizes are allowed at no additional fee. Dogs may not be left unattended outside, or in the cabin unless crated. Dogs must be leashed and cleaned up after. Dogs are not allowed in park buildings, but they are allowed on the trails. The state reservation phone number is 402-471-1414. The camping and tent areas also allow dogs. There is a dog walk area at the campground. Dogs are allowed in the camping cabins. Multiple dogs may be allowed.

Bayard

Flying Bee Ranch
6755 County Road 42

Bayard, NE
888-534-2341
Dogs of all sizes are allowed. There are no additional pet fees for the tent or RV sites. There is an $8 per night per pet additional fee for the cabins. Dogs may not be left unattended unless they will be quiet and well behaved. Dogs must be leashed and cleaned up after. The camping and tent areas also allow dogs. There is a dog walk area at the campground. Dogs are allowed in the camping cabins. Multiple dogs may be allowed.

Brule

Eagle Canyon Hideaway
1086 Lakeview W Road
Brule, NE
866-866-5253
Dogs of all sizes are allowed. There are no additional pet fees. Dogs must be quiet, leashed, and cleaned up after. The camping and tent areas also allow dogs. There is a dog walk area at the campground. Dogs are allowed in the camping cabins. Multiple dogs may be allowed.

Chadron

Chadron State Park
15951 H 385
Chadron, NE
308-432-6167
This scenic 972 acre park at an elevation of 5000 feet sits inside the Nebraska National Forest and offers a variety of land and water activities and recreation. Dogs of all sizes are allowed at no additional fee. Dogs may not be left unattended at any time, and they must be on no more than a 6 foot leash, and be cleaned up after. Dogs are allowed on the trails. The state reservation phone number is 402-471-1414. The camping and tent areas also allow dogs. There is a dog walk area at the campground. Dogs are allowed in the camping cabins. There are no water hookups at the campground. Multiple dogs may be allowed.

Crawford

Fort Robinson State Park
3200 H 20
Crawford, NE
308-665-2900
This historically rich park of over 22,000 acres is home to their own herds of buffalo and longhorn. The

park offers an interpretive museum as well as a variety of land and water activities and recreation. Dogs of all sizes are allowed at no additional fee. Dogs may not be left unattended at any time, and they must be on no more than a 6 foot leash, and be cleaned up after. Dogs are not allowed in buildings, but they are allowed on the trails. The state reservation phone number is 402-471-1414. The camping and tent areas also allow dogs. There is a dog walk area at the campground. Dogs are allowed in the camping cabins. There are no water hookups at the campground. Multiple dogs may be allowed.

Crofton

Lewis and Clark State Rec Area
54731 897 Road (H 121)
Crofton, NE
402-388-4169
With over 9,000 acres along the states' 2nd largest lake, this park offers a wide variety of land and water activities and recreation. Dogs of all sizes are allowed at no additional fee. Dogs may not be left unattended at any time, and they must be on no more than a 6 foot leash, and be cleaned up after. Dogs are not allowed on the furniture in the cabins, on the beaches, or other park buildings. Dogs are allowed on the trails. The state reservation phone number is 402-471-1414. The camping and tent areas also allow dogs. There is a dog walk area at the campground. Dogs are allowed in the camping cabins. There are no water hookups at the campground. Multiple dogs may be allowed.

Doniphan

Grand Island KOA
904 South B Road
Doniphan, NE
402-886-2249
Dogs of all sizes are allowed, and there are no additional pet fees for tent or RV sites. There is a $5 per night per pet additional fee for the cabins. Dogs may not be left unattended, and they must be quiet, leashed, and cleaned up after. Dogs are not allowed in the buildings or the playground, and they must be in at night. This RV park is closed during the off-season. The camping and tent areas also allow dogs. There is a dog walk area at the campground. Dogs are allowed in the

camping cabins. Multiple dogs may be allowed.

Gothenburg

Gothenburhg KOA
1102 S Lake Avenue
Gothenburg, NE
308-537-7387
Dogs of all sizes are allowed. There are no additional pet fees. Dogs may not be left unattended, and must be leashed and cleaned up after. There are some breed restrictions. This RV park is closed during the off-season. The camping and tent areas also allow dogs. There is a dog walk area at the campground. Dogs are allowed in the camping cabins. Multiple dogs may be allowed.

Gretna

West Omaha KOA
14601 H 6
Gretna, NE
402-332-3010
Dogs of all sizes are allowed. There are no additional pet fees. Dogs must be leashed and cleaned up after. There are some breed restrictions. This RV park is closed during the off-season. The camping and tent areas also allow dogs. There is a dog walk area at the campground. Dogs are allowed in the camping cabins. Multiple dogs may be allowed.

Kimball

Kimball KOA
4334 Link 53E
Kimball, NE
308-235-4404
Dogs of all sizes are allowed. There are no additional pet fees. Dogs may not be left unattended, and they must be leashed and cleaned up after. This RV park is closed during the off-season. The camping and tent areas also allow dogs. There is a dog walk area at the campground. Dogs are allowed in the camping cabins. Multiple dogs may be allowed.

Maxwell

Fort McPherson Campground
12567 Valley View Road
Maxwell, NE
308-582-4320

Dogs of all sizes are allowed. There are no additional pet fees. Dogs may be off lead when there is no one else around and if they are under voice control. Otherwise dogs must be leashed and cleaned up after. Dogs may not be left unattended. There is 1 cabin and a ranch house that sleeps 6, that is also pet friendly. This RV park is closed during the off-season. The camping and tent areas also allow dogs. There is a dog walk area at the campground. Dogs are allowed in the camping cabins. Multiple dogs may be allowed.

Niobrara

Niobrara State Park
89261 522nd Avenue
Niobrara, NE
402-85 7-3373
This park of over 1,600 acres offers opportunities for nature study in addition to providing an interpretive center, more than 14 miles of trails, and a wide range of land and water recreation. Dogs of all sizes are allowed at no additional fee. Dogs may not be left unattended outside, and they must be on no more than a 6 foot leash, and be cleaned up after. Dogs are not allowed on the furniture or bed in the cabins, and they must be placed in a crate if left inside. Dogs are not allowed in the pool area, but they are allowed on the trails. The state reservation phone number is 402-471-1414. The camping and tent areas also allow dogs. There is a dog walk area at the campground. Dogs are allowed in the camping cabins. There are no water hookups at the campground. Multiple dogs may be allowed.

Ponca

Ponca State Park
88090 Spur 26E
Ponca, NE
402-755-2284
This picturesque park, rich in history, is home to one of the state's most comprehensive outdoor/environmental education programs, and provides a variety of outdoor recreation. Dogs of all sizes are allowed at no additional fee. Dogs may not be left unattended in the cabins, and they must be leashed at all times, and cleaned up after. Dogs are not allowed in the pool area or buildings, and they may be left tied outside only if they will be quiet and well behaved. Dogs are

allowed on the trails. The state reservation phone number is 402-471-1414. The camping and tent areas also allow dogs. There is a dog walk area at the campground. Dogs are allowed in the camping cabins. There are no water hookups at the campground. Multiple dogs may be allowed.

Potter

Buffalo Point RV Park and Motel
8175 H 30
Potter, NE
308-879-4400
Dogs of all sizes are allowed. There are no additional pet fees. Dogs must be quiet, leashed, and cleaned up after. There is also a motel on site that allowes dogs. The camping and tent areas also allow dogs. There is a dog walk area at the campground. Dogs are allowed in the camping cabins. Multiple dogs may be allowed.

Scottsbluff

Scottsbluff/Chimney Rock KOA
180037 KOA Drive
Scottsbluff, NE
308-635-3760
Dogs of all sizes are allowed. There are no additional pet fees. Dogs may not be left unattended, and they must be quiet, leashed, and cleaned up after. Dogs may not be tied to the trees or tables. This RV park is closed during the off-season. The camping and tent areas also allow dogs. There is a dog walk area at the campground. Dogs are allowed in the camping cabins. Multiple dogs may be allowed.

Nevada Listings

Ely

Ely Koa
H 93
Ely, NV
775-289-3413
Well landscaped grounds and location make this a popular park, with amenities that include 85 foot pull-through sites with 50 amp service, cable TV, LP gas, and WiFi. Dogs of all sizes are allowed for no

additional fee, and there is a pet waiver to sign. There is a $25 refundable pet deposit for the cabins. Dogs must be under owner's control and visual observation at all times. Dogs must be quiet, well behaved, and be on no more than a 6 foot leash at all times, or otherwise contained. Dogs may not be left unattended outside the owner's camping equipment, and must be brought inside at night. Dogs are not allowed on the grass except by the dog walk. There are some breed restrictions. The camping and tent areas also allow dogs. There is a dog walk area at the campground. Dogs are allowed in the camping cabins. Multiple dogs may be allowed.

West Wendover

Wendover KOA
651 N Camper Drive
West Wendover, NV
775-664-3221
Located just 10 miles from the world-famous Bonneville Salt Flats and next to 2 casinos, this oasis park offers large pull through sites, seasonal heated outdoor pool, mini golf, a grocery and souvenir shop, laundry and much more. Dogs of all sizes are allowed for no additional fee. Dogs must be under owner's control and visual observation at all times. Dogs must be quiet, well behaved, and be on no more than a 6 foot leash at all times, or otherwise contained, and cleaned up after. Dogs may not be left unattended outside the owner's camping equipment or alone in the cabins, and they must be brought inside at night. There are some breed restrictions. The camping and tent areas also allow dogs. There is a dog walk area at the campground. Dogs are allowed in the camping cabins. Multiple dogs may be allowed.

New Hampshire Listings

Center Ossipee

Terrace Pines Campground
110 Terrace Pine
Center Ossipee, NH

603-539-6210
Dogs of all sizes are allowed. There are no additional pet fees. Dogs may not be left unattended, must be leashed, and cleaned up after. This RV park is closed during the off-season. The camping and tent areas also allow dogs. There is a dog walk area at the campground. Dogs are allowed in the camping cabins. Multiple dogs may be allowed.

Conroy

Chocorua Camping Village
893 White Mountain H
Chocorua, NH
603-323-8536
Small Dogs Only. One dog about 50 pounds or two dogs that total 35 pounds are allowed. There are no additional pet fees. Dogs must be leashed and cleaned up after. There is a swim area for dogs where they can be off leash. There are some breed restrictions. This RV park is closed during the off-season. The camping and tent areas also allow dogs. There is a dog walk area at the campground. Dogs are allowed in the camping cabins.

Hampton Falls

Wakeda Campground
294 Exeter Road
Hampton Falls, NH
603-772-5274
Dogs of all sizes are allowed. There are no additional pet fees. Dogs may not be left unattended, must be leashed, and cleaned up after. This RV park is closed during the off-season. The camping and tent areas also allow dogs. There is a dog walk area at the campground. Dogs are allowed in the camping cabins. Multiple dogs may be allowed.

Rindge

Woodmore Family Campground
21 Woodmore Drive
Rindge, NH
603-899-3362
Dogs of all sizes are allowed. There are no additional pet fees. Dogs must be quiet, well behaved, leashed, and cleaned up after. Dogs may not be left unattended. This RV park is closed during the off-season. The camping and tent areas also allow dogs. There is a dog walk area at the campground. Dogs are allowed in the camping cabins.

Multiple dogs may be allowed.

Woodstock

KOA Woodstock
1001 Eastside Road
Woodstock, NH
603-745-8008
Dogs of all sizes are allowed. There are no additional pet fees. Dogs must be leashed and cleaned up after. This RV park is closed during the off-season. The camping and tent areas also allow dogs. There is a dog walk area at the campground. Dogs are allowed in the camping cabins. Multiple dogs may be allowed.

New Jersey Listings

Elmer

Yogi Bear Tall Pines
49 Beal Road
Elmer, NJ
800-252-2890
Dogs of all sizes are allowed, some breeds are not. There are no additional pet fees. Dogs must be leashed, cleaned up after, and not left unattended. This RV park is closed during the off-season. The camping and tent areas also allow dogs. There is a dog walk area at the campground. Dogs are allowed in the camping cabins.

Tuckerton

Atlantic City North Family Campground
Stage Road
Tuckerton, NJ
609-296-9163
Dogs of all sizes are allowed. There are no additional pet fees. Dogs may not be left unattended outside or in the cabins, and they must be leashed and cleaned up after. This RV park is closed during the off-season. The camping and tent areas also allow dogs. There is a dog walk area at the campground. Dogs are allowed in the camping cabins. Multiple dogs may be allowed.

West Creek

Sea Pirate Campground
Bay side of H 9, Box 271
West Creek, NJ
609-296-7400
Up to two dogs of any size are allowed at the tent and RV sites at no additional fee. Basic Cabins and 2 Room Basic Cabins allow one pet at $5 per night with a $200 security deposit. Dogs may not be left unattended, and they must be leashed and cleaned up after. This RV park is closed during the off-season. The camping and tent areas also allow dogs. There is a dog walk area at the campground. Dogs are allowed in the camping cabins.

New Mexico Listings

Albuquerque

Albuquerque Central KOA
12400 Skyline Road NE
Albuquerque, NM
505-296-2729
Dogs of all sizes are allowed. There are no additional pet fees. Dogs may not be left unattended outside, and they must be well behaved, leashed, and cleaned up after. There are some breed restrictions. The camping and tent areas also allow dogs. There is a dog walk area at the campground. Dogs are allowed in the camping cabins. Multiple dogs may be allowed.

Bernalillo

Albuquerque N/Bernalillo KOA
555 S Hill Road
Bernalillo, NM
505-867-5227
Dogs of all sizes are allowed. There are no additional pet fees. Dogs may not be left unattended, and they must be quiet, leashed, and cleaned up after. Dogs may not be on the grass, in the store, the bathrooms, or the cafe. There is a fenced area for off lead. The camping and tent areas also allow dogs. There is a dog walk area at the campground. Dogs are allowed in the camping cabins. Multiple dogs may be allowed.

Chama

Little Creek Resort
2631 S H 84/64
Chama, NM
505-756-2382
Dogs of all sizes are allowed. There are no additional pet fees. Dogs may not be left unattended outside, and they must be leashed and cleaned up after. The camping and tent areas also allow dogs. There is a dog walk area at the campground. Dogs are allowed in the camping cabins.

Santa Fe

Rancheros de Santa Fe
736 Old Las Vegas H
Santa Fe, NM
800-426-9259
Dogs of all sizes are allowed. There are no additional pet fees. Dogs may not be left unattended, and they must be quiet, leashed, and cleaned up after. There is a fenced in Doggy Corral for off lead. The camping and tent areas also allow dogs. There is a dog walk area at the campground. Dogs are allowed in the camping cabins. Multiple dogs may be allowed.

Santa Rosa

Santa Rosa Campground
2136 Historic H 66
Santa Rosa, NM
505-472-3126
Dogs of all sizes are allowed. There are no additional pet fees. Dogs may be walked anywhere in the park, but they must be taken to the dog walk to relieve themselves. Dogs must be leashed and cleaned up after. The camping and tent areas also allow dogs. There is a dog walk area at the campground. Dogs are allowed in the camping cabins. Multiple dogs may be allowed.

Villanueva

Villanueva State Park
P. O. Box 40
Villanueva, NM
505-421-2957
A scenic, riverside canyon park, there are a variety of land and water recreational pursuits and places to explore. Dogs of all sizes are allowed at no additional fee. Dogs may not be left unattended, and they must be on no more than a 10 foot leash, and

be cleaned up after. Dogs are not allowed in buildings, but they are allowed on the trails. This campground is closed during the off-season. The camping and tent areas also allow dogs. Dogs are allowed in the camping cabins. Multiple dogs may be allowed.

New York Listings

Adirondacks

Plattsburgh RV Park
7182 H 9N
Plattsburgh, NY
518-563-3915
Dogs of all sizes are allowed. There are no additional pet fees. Dogs must be well behaved and under control of owner. Dogs must be leashed and cleaned up after. The camping and tent areas also allow dogs. There is a dog walk area at the campground. Dogs are allowed in the camping cabins. Multiple dogs may be allowed.

KOA Lake Placid/Whiteface Mountain
77 Foxfarm Road
Wilmington, NY
518-946-7878
Dogs of all sizes are allowed in the camp and RV sites, but only one dog up to 40 pounds is allowed in the cabin. There are no additional pet fees. Dogs may not be left unattended and must have a valid rabies certificate. They must be leashed and cleaned up after. There are some breed restrictions. This RV park is closed during the off-season. The camping and tent areas also allow dogs. There is a dog walk area at the campground. Dogs are allowed in the camping cabins.

Brocton

Lake Erie State Park
5905 H 5
Brocton, NY
716-792-9214
Dogs of all sizes are allowed. There are no additional pet fees. Dogs may not be left unattended, they must have a current rabies certificate and shot records, be leashed, and cleaned up after. Dogs are allowed on the trails and down by the lake,

but they are not allowed to be tied to the trees. This campground is closed during the off-season. The camping and tent areas also allow dogs. There is a dog walk area at the campground. Dogs are allowed in the camping cabins. There are no water hookups at the campground. Multiple dogs may be allowed.

Chenango Forks

Chenango Valley State Park
153 State Park Road
Chenango Forks, NY
607-648-5251
Dogs of all sizes are allowed. There are no additional pet fees. Dogs may not be left unattended, they must have a current rabies certificate and shot records. Dogs must be quiet, leashed, and cleaned up after. Dogs are allowed on the trails, but not on the beach or in the water. Although the campground is seasonal, the park is open year round. This campground is closed during the off-season. The camping and tent areas also allow dogs. There is a dog walk area at the campground. Dogs are allowed in the camping cabins. Multiple dogs may be allowed.

Cooperstown

KOA Cooperstown
565 Ostrander Road
Cooperstown, NY
315-858-0236
Dogs of all sizes are allowed. There are no additional pet fees. Dogs are allowed at the cabins but must be kept off the beds. There is a large field where dogs can run off leash if they will come to your command. Otherwise dogs must be leashed and cleaned up after. Dogs may not be left unattended except for short periods, and only if the dog is well behaved and comfortable with a short absence. This RV park is closed during the off-season. The camping and tent areas also allow dogs. There is a dog walk area at the campground. Dogs are allowed in the camping cabins. Multiple dogs may be allowed.

Dansville

Sugar Creek Glen Campground
11288 Poagf Hole Road
Dansville, NY
585-335-6294

Dogs of all sizes are allowed. There is a pet policy to sign at check in and there are no additional pet fees. Dogs must not be left unattended for very long periods, and only if they are quiet and well behaved. Dogs must be leashed and cleaned up after. The camping and tent areas also allow dogs. There is a dog walk area at the campground. Dogs are allowed in the camping cabins. Multiple dogs may be allowed.

Fair Haven

Fair Haven Beach State Park
14985 Park Road
Fair Haven, NY
315-947-5205
Dogs of all sizes are allowed. There are no additional pet fees. Dogs may not be left unattended, they must have a current rabies certificate and shot records, be on no more than a 6 foot leash, and be cleaned up after. Dogs are allowed on the trails, but they are not allowed on any sandy areas, at the beach, or in the water. Although the campground is seasonal, some cabins remain open all year. This campground is closed during the off-season. The camping and tent areas also allow dogs. There is a dog walk area at the campground. Dogs are allowed in the camping cabins. There are no water hookups at the campground. Multiple dogs may be allowed.

Farmington

KOA Canandaigua/Rochester
5374 FarmingtonTownline Road
Farmington, NY
585-398-3582
Dogs of all sizes are allowed. There is no additional pet fee for RV or tent sites, however there is a $25 refundable pet deposit when renting the cabins. Dogs may not be left unattended; they must be quiet, well behaved, leashed, and cleaned up after. There are some breed restrictions. This RV park is closed during the off-season. The camping and tent areas also allow dogs. There is a dog walk area at the campground. Dogs are allowed in the camping cabins. Multiple dogs may be allowed.

Finger Lakes

Hickory Hill Family Camping Resort

7531 Country Route 13
Bath, NY
607-776-4345
Dogs of all sizes are allowed. There are no additional fees for pets staying at the campsites, however there is a $20 one time fee per unit for the rentals. Dogs are not to be left unattended at the site, must be leashed at all times, and cleaned up after. The camping and tent areas also allow dogs. There is a dog walk area at the campground. Dogs are allowed in the camping cabins. 2 dogs may be allowed.

Ferenbaugh Campsites
4248 State H 414
Corning, NY
607-962-6193
Dogs up to 25 pounds are allowed. There are no additional pet fees. Dogs must be leashed, cleaned up after, and may not be left unattended. The camping and tent areas also allow dogs. There is a dog walk area at the campground. Dogs are allowed in the camping cabins. 2 dogs may be allowed.

Florida

Black Bear Campground
197 Wheeler Road
Florida, NY
845-651-7717
Dogs of all sizes are allowed, however some breeds are not. There are no additional pet fees. Dogs must be well behaved, leashed, and cleaned up after. The camping and tent areas also allow dogs. There is a dog walk area at the campground. Dogs are allowed in the camping cabins. 2 dogs may be allowed.

North Java

Jellystone Park
5204 Youngers Road
North Java, NY
585-457-9644
Dogs of all sizes are allowed. There are no additional pet fees unless staying in the pet friendly Boo Boo Chalets. Then there would be an additional $25 per unit. Dogs must be quiet, well behaved, leashed and cleaned up after. Dogs may not be left unattended. This RV park is closed during the off-season. The camping and tent areas also allow dogs. There is a dog walk area at the campground. Dogs are allowed in the camping cabins. 2 dogs may be allowed.

Plattekill

KOA Newburgh/NYC North
119 Freetown Highway
Plattekill, NY
845-564-2836
Dogs of all sizes are allowed. There are no additional pet fees. Dogs must be leashed and cleaned up after. This RV park is closed during the off-season. The camping and tent areas also allow dogs. There is a dog walk area at the campground. Dogs are allowed in the camping cabins. Multiple dogs may be allowed.

Pulaski

Selkirk Sores State Park
7101 H 3
Pulaski, NY
315-298-5737
Dogs of all sizes are allowed. There are no additional pet fees. Dogs may not be left unattended, and they must have a current rabies certificate and shot record, be on no more than a 6 foot leash, and be cleaned up after. Dogs are allowed on the trails and at the beach. This campground is closed during the off-season. The camping and tent areas also allow dogs. There is a dog walk area at the campground. Dogs are allowed in the camping cabins. There are no water hookups at the campground. Multiple dogs may be allowed.

Rochester

Genesee Country Campgrounds
40 Flinthill Road
Caledonia, NY
585-538-4200
Dogs of all sizes are allowed. There are no additional pet fees. Dogs must be leashed and cleaned up after. The camping and tent areas also allow dogs. There is a dog walk area at the campground. Dogs are allowed in the camping cabins. 2 dogs may be allowed.

Saugerties

KOA Saugerties/Woodstock
882 H212
Saugerties, NY
845-246-4089
Dogs of all sizes are allowed. There are no additional fees for site rentals, however there is a $4 per night per pet additional fee for the cabins. Dogs must be leashed and cleaned up after. There are some breed restrictions. This RV park is closed during the off-season. The camping and tent areas also allow dogs. There is a dog walk area at the campground. Dogs are allowed in the camping cabins. Multiple dogs may be allowed.

Sodus Point

South Shore RV Park
7867 Lake Road
Sodus Point, NY
315-483-8679
Dogs of all sizes are allowed. There are no additional pet fees. Dogs must be quiet, leashed, and cleaned up after. Dogs must not be left unattended at any time, especially in the cabins. The camping and tent areas also allow dogs. There is a dog walk area at the campground. Dogs are allowed in the camping cabins. Multiple dogs may be allowed.

Swan Lake

Swan Lake Camplands
106 Fulton Road
Swan Lake, NY
845-292-4781
Dogs of all sizes are allowed. There are no additional pet fees. Dogs must be leased and cleaned up after. The camping and tent areas also allow dogs. There is a dog walk area at the campground. Dogs are allowed in the camping cabins. Multiple dogs may be allowed.

Westfield

KOA Westfield/Lake Erie
8001 H 5
Westfield, NY
716-326-3573
Dogs of all sizes are allowed. There are no additional pet fees. Dogs may not be left unattended, and must be leashed and cleaned up after. This RV park is closed during the off-season. The camping and tent areas also allow dogs. There is a dog walk area at the campground. Dogs are allowed in the camping cabins. Multiple dogs may be allowed.

North Carolina

Listings

Boone

Boone KOA
123 Harmony Mountain Lane
Boone, NC
828-264-7250
Dogs of all sizes are allowed. There are no additional pet fees. Dogs may not be left unattended, and they must be leashed and cleaned up after. This RV park is closed during the off-season. The camping and tent areas also allow dogs. There is a dog walk area at the campground. Dogs are allowed in the camping cabins. Multiple dogs may be allowed.

Candler

Asheville West KOA
309 Wiggins Road
Candler, NC
828-665-7015
Dogs of all sizes are allowed. There are no additional pet fees. Dogs must be leashed and cleaned up after. There are some breed restrictions. The camping and tent areas also allow dogs. There is a dog walk area at the campground. Dogs are allowed in the camping cabins. Multiple dogs may be allowed.

Cherokee

Cherokee/Great Smokies KOA
92 KOA Campground Road
Cherokee, NC
828-497-9711
Dogs of all sizes are allowed. There are no additional pet fees. Dogs may not be left unattended, and they must be leashed and cleaned up after. The camping and tent areas also allow dogs. There is a dog walk area at the campground. Dogs are allowed in the camping cabins. Multiple dogs may be allowed.

Enfield

Enfield/Rocky Mount KOA
101 Bell Acres
Enfield, NC
252-445-5925
Dogs of all sizes are allowed, and there are no additional pet fees for tent or RV sites. There is a $2 per night per pet additional fee for the cabins. Dogs may not be left unattended in the cabins or outside, and they must be leashed and cleaned up after. There are some breed restrictions. The camping and tent areas also allow dogs. There is a dog walk area at the campground. Dogs are allowed in the camping cabins. Multiple dogs may be allowed.

Frisco

Frisco Woods Campground
53124 H 12
Frisco, NC
800-948-3942
Dogs of all sizes are allowed. There is an additional $5 one time fee per pet. Dogs may not be left unattended, and they must be leashed and cleaned up after. This RV park is closed during the off-season. The camping and tent areas also allow dogs. There is a dog walk area at the campground. Dogs are allowed in the camping cabins. Multiple dogs may be allowed.

Hatteras Village

Hatteras Sands
57316 Eagle Pass Road
Hatteras Village, NC
252-986-2422
Dogs of all sizes are allowed. There is a $2 per night per pet additional fee. Dogs may not be left unattended, and they must be leashed and cleaned up after. This RV park is closed during the off-season. The camping and tent areas also allow dogs. There is a dog walk area at the campground. Dogs are allowed in the camping cabins. Multiple dogs may be allowed.

New Bern

New Bern
1565 B Street
New Bern, NC
252-638-2556
Dogs of all sizes are allowed. There are no additional pet fees. Dogs must be leashed and cleaned up after. There are 2 fenced in areas for off lead. There are some breed restrictions. The camping and tent areas also allow dogs. There is a dog walk area at the campground. Dogs are allowed in the camping cabins. Multiple dogs may be allowed.

Rodanthe

Cape Hatteras KOA
25099 H 12
Rodanthe, NC
252-987-2307
Dogs of all sizes are allowed, and there are no additional pet fees for tent or RV sites. There is a $5 one time pet fee for the cabins. Dogs may not be left unattended, and must be leashed and cleaned up after. This RV park is closed during the off-season. The camping and tent areas also allow dogs. There is a dog walk area at the campground. Dogs are allowed in the camping cabins. Multiple dogs may be allowed.

Rutherfordton

Four Paws Kingdom
335 Lazy Creek Drive
Rutherfordton, NC
828-287-7324
Dogs of all sizes are allowed, however some breeds are not. There are no additional pet fees, and dogs must be cleaned up after. There are 2 park areas where your dog can run off leash; one for the large dogs and one for the smaller dogs. There is a pond dedicated for dogs and a bath house with a dog grooming area. The camping and tent areas also allow dogs. There is a dog walk area at the campground. Dogs are allowed in the camping cabins. 2 dogs may be allowed.

Swannanoa

Asheville East KOA
2708 H 70 E
Swannanoa, NC
828-686-3121
Dogs of all sizes are allowed. There are no additional pet fees. Dogs may not be left unattended, and they must be quiet, leashed, and cleaned up after. The camping and tent areas also allow dogs. There is a dog walk area at the campground. Dogs are allowed in the camping cabins. Multiple dogs may be allowed.

Mama Gerties Hideaway Campground
15 Uphill Road
Swannanoa, NC
828-686-4258
Dogs of all sizes are allowed, and there are no additional pet fees for

tent or RV sites. There is a $5 per night per pet additional fee for the cabins. Dogs may not be left unattended, and they must be quiet, well behaved, leashed, and cleaned up after. There are some breed restrictions. The camping and tent areas also allow dogs. There is a dog walk area at the campground. Dogs are allowed in the camping cabins. 2 dogs may be allowed.

Wade

Fayetteville/Wade KOA
6250 Wade Stedman Road
Wade, NC
910-484-5500
Dogs of all sizes are allowed, and there are no additional pet fees for tent or RV sites. There is a $6 one time pet fee for the cabins. Dogs may not be left unattended, and must be quiet, leashed, and cleaned up after. The camping and tent areas also allow dogs. There is a dog walk area at the campground. Dogs are allowed in the camping cabins. Multiple dogs may be allowed.

Wilmington

Wilmington KOA
7415 Market Street
Wilmington, NC
800-454-7705
Three dogs up to 20 pounds are allowed, and there are no additional pet fees for tent or RV sites. There is a $50 refundable pet deposit for the cabins, and there may only be up to two 20 pound dogs. Dogs may not be left unattended outside at any time, and they must be leashed and cleaned up after. There are some breed restrictions. There is a dog walk area at the campground. Dogs are allowed in the camping cabins.

North Dakota Listings

Bismarck

Bismarck KOA
3720 Centennial Road
Bismarck, ND
701-222-2662
Dogs of all sizes are allowed. There are no additional pet fees. Dogs

must be leashed and cleaned up after. This RV park is closed during the off-season. The camping and tent areas also allow dogs. There is a dog walk area at the campground. Dogs are allowed in the camping cabins. Multiple dogs may be allowed.

Devil's Lake

Woodland Resort
1012 Woodland Drive
Devil's Lake, ND
701-662-5996
Dogs of all sizes are allowed. There are no additional pet fees for tent or RV sites. There is a $10 per night per pet, or $50 per week per pet, addtional fee for the lodge, motel, or cabins. Dogs may not be left unattended, and they must be leashed and cleaned up after. The camping and tent areas also allow dogs. There is a dog walk area at the campground. Dogs are allowed in the camping cabins. Multiple dogs may be allowed.

Ohio Listings

Bellville

Jellystone Park
6500 Black Road
Bellville, OH
419-886-CAMP (2267)
Dogs of all sizes are allowed. There are no additional pet fees. Dogs must be leashed and cleaned up after. There are some breed restrictions. This RV park is closed during the off-season. The camping and tent areas also allow dogs. There is a dog walk area at the campground. Dogs are allowed in the camping cabins. 2 dogs may be allowed.

Bloomingdale

Top O' The Caves Campground
26780 Chapel Ridge Road
Bloomingdale, OH
800-967-2434
Dogs of all sizes are allowed, and there are no additional pet fees for tent or RV sites which are open only for the season. There is a $25 one time fee per pet additional fee for

the cabins, which are open all year. Dogs must be leashed and cleaned up after. This RV park is closed during the off-season. The camping and tent areas also allow dogs. There is a dog walk area at the campground. Dogs are allowed in the camping cabins. 2 dogs may be allowed.

Brookville

Dayton KOA
7796 Wellbaum Road
Brookville, OH
937-833-3888
Dogs of all sizes are allowed. There are no additional pet fees. Dogs must be quiet, well behaved, leashed, and cleaned up after. There are some breed restrictions. This RV park is closed during the off-season. The camping and tent areas also allow dogs. There is a dog walk area at the campground. Dogs are allowed in the camping cabins. Multiple dogs may be allowed.

Butler

Butler/Mohican KOA
6918 Bunker Hills Road S
Butler, OH
419-883-3314
Dogs of all sizes are allowed. There is a $5 per pet per stay additional fee. Dogs must be well behaved, leashed, and cleaned up after. There are some breed restrictions. This RV park is closed during the off-season. The camping and tent areas also allow dogs. There is a dog walk area at the campground. Dogs are allowed in the camping cabins. Multiple dogs may be allowed.

Jackson

Lazy Dog Camp Resort & Noah's Ark Animal Farm
1527 McGiffins Road
Jackson, OH
800-282-2167
Dogs of all sizes are allowed at the tent and RV sites. Small dogs only, under 15 pounds are allowed at the cabins. There are no additional pet fees. Dogs must be leashed and cleaned up after. Dogs are not allowed at the lake, nor at the Noah's Ark Animal Farm. The camping and tent areas also allow dogs. There is a dog walk area at the campground. Dogs are allowed in the camping cabins.

Whistler

Riverside Whistler Camping and Cabins
8018 Mons Road
Whistler, OH
604-905-5533
Dogs of all sizes are allowed. There is a $2.50 per night per pet additional fee for the tent and RV sites, and for the one pet friendly cabin. Dogs may not be left unattended at any time, especially inside the RVs in the summer. Dogs must be leashed and cleaned up after. The camping and tent areas also allow dogs. There is a dog walk area at the campground. Dogs are allowed in the camping cabins. Multiple dogs may be allowed.

Oklahoma Listings

Ardmore

Lake Murray State Park
204 Scenic State H 77
Ardmore, OK
580-223-4044
This is Oklahoma's oldest and largest state park, offering an ATV area, an 18 hole golf course, a nature center, and a wide variety of additional land and water activities and recreation. Dogs of all sizes are allowed at no additional fee. Dogs may not be left unattended, and they must be on no more than a 10 foot leash, and be cleaned up after. Dogs are not allowed on the beach, but they are allowed on the trails. The camping and tent areas also allow dogs. There is a dog walk area at the campground. Dogs are allowed in the camping cabins. Multiple dogs may be allowed.

Beaver

Beaver Dunes State Park
H 270
Beaver, OK
580-625-3373
This 520 acre park has 300 acres of sand dunes, perfect for off-roading, hiking and biking. Dogs of all sizes are allowed at no additional fee. Dogs may not be left unattended, and they must be on no more than a 10 foot leash, and be cleaned up after. Dogs are allowed on the trails.

This campground is closed during the off-season. The camping and tent areas also allow dogs. There is a dog walk area at the campground. Dogs are allowed in the camping cabins. Multiple dogs may be allowed.

Broken Bow

Broken Bend Resort Park
H 259A
Broken Bow, OK
580-494-6300
This resort park offers an 18 hole golf course, an amphitheater, a nature center, and a wide variety of land and water activities and recreation. Dogs of all sizes are allowed at no additional fee. Dogs may not be left unattended outside, and they must be leashed and cleaned up after in the park. Dogs may be uncrated in the cabins when left inside, only if they are very well behaved and not for long periods. Dogs are allowed on the trails. The camping and tent areas also allow dogs. There is a dog walk area at the campground. Dogs are allowed in the camping cabins. Multiple dogs may be allowed.

Calumet

El Reno West KOA
301 S Walbaum Road
Calumet, OK
405-884-2595
Dogs of all sizes are allowed. There are no additional pet fees. Dogs must be leashed and cleaned up after. This RV park is closed during the off-season. The camping and tent areas also allow dogs. There is a dog walk area at the campground. Dogs are allowed in the camping cabins. Multiple dogs may be allowed.

Canute

Elk City/Clinton KOA
Clinton Lake Road
Canute, OK
580-592-4409
Dogs of all sizes are allowed, and there are no additional pet fees for tent or RV sites. There is a $5 per night per pet additional fee for the cabins. Dogs may not be tied to the trees or left unattended, and they must be quiet, well behaved, leashed, and cleaned up after. There are some breed restrictions.

The camping and tent areas also allow dogs. There is a dog walk area at the campground. Dogs are allowed in the camping cabins. Multiple dogs may be allowed.

Catoosa

Tulsa Northeast KOA
19605 E Skelly Drive
Catoosa, OK
918-266-4227
Dogs of all sizes are allowed. There are no additional pet fees. Dogs must be leashed and cleaned up after. There are some breed restrictions. The camping and tent areas also allow dogs. There is a dog walk area at the campground. Dogs are allowed in the camping cabins. Multiple dogs may be allowed.

Checotah

Checotah/Henryetta KOA
On I 40 @Pierce Road (HC 68, Box750)
Checotah, OK
918-473-6511
Dogs of all sizes are allowed, and there are no additional pet fees for tent or RV sites. There is a $5 one time additional pet fee for cabins. Dogs must be leashed and cleaned up after. There are some breed restrictions. The camping and tent areas also allow dogs. There is a dog walk area at the campground. Dogs are allowed in the camping cabins. Multiple dogs may be allowed.

Clayton

Clayton Lake State Park
HC 60 Box 33-10/ H 271
Clayton, OK
918-569-7981
This park of over 500 acres has a 95 acre lake and offers a variety of land and water recreation. Dogs of all sizes are allowed at no additional fee. Dogs may not be left unattended, and they must be leashed and cleaned up after. However, if there are no other people around and your dog will respond to voice command, they may be off lead when out of the camp area. Dogs are allowed on the trails. The camping and tent areas also allow dogs. There is a dog walk area at the campground. Dogs are allowed in the camping cabins.

Colbert

Colbert KOA
411 Sherrard Street
Colbert, OK
580-296-2485
Dogs of all sizes are allowed. There are no additional pet fees. Dogs may not be left unattended at the cabins or outside, and they must be leashed and cleaned up after. There are some breed restrictions. The camping and tent areas also allow dogs. There is a dog walk area at the campground. Dogs are allowed in the camping cabins. Multiple dogs may be allowed.

Gore

Marval Resort
Marval Lane
Gore, OK
800-340-4280
Dogs of all sizes are allowed, and there are no additional pet fees for tent or RV sites. There is a $20 one time additional pet fee for the cabins. Dogs may not be left unattended, and they must be on no more than a 10 foot leash, and cleaned up after. The camping and tent areas also allow dogs. There is a dog walk area at the campground. Dogs are allowed in the camping cabins. Multiple dogs may be allowed.

Hodgen

Big Cedar Adventure Park
21823 H 63
Hodgen, OK
918-651-3271
Dogs of all sizes are allowed. There are no additional pet fees for tent or RV sites. There is an additional one time pet fee of $20 for each 1 to 3 days stay for the 1 pet friendly cabin. Dogs may not be left unattended, and they must be leashed and cleaned up after. The camping and tent areas also allow dogs. There is a dog walk area at the campground. Dogs are allowed in the camping cabins. Multiple dogs may be allowed.

Marietta

Ardmore/Marietta KOA
Oswalt Road (Rt 1, Box 640)
Marietta, OK
580-276-2800
Dogs of all sizes are allowed. There are no additional pet fees. Dogs must be quiet, leashed, and cleaned up after. The camping and tent areas also allow dogs. There is a dog walk area at the campground. Dogs are allowed in the camping cabins. Multiple dogs may be allowed.

Sallisaw

Sallisaw KOA
1908 Power Drive
Sallisaw, OK
918-775-2792
Dogs of all sizes are allowed. There are no additional pet fees. Dogs may not be penned or left unattended outside, and they must be leashed and cleaned up after. The camping and tent areas also allow dogs. There is a dog walk area at the campground. Dogs are allowed in the camping cabins. Multiple dogs may be allowed.

Watonga

Roman Nose State Resort Park
H 8 A
Watonga, OK
580-623-4215
Dogs of all sizes are allowed. There are no additional pet fees. Dogs may not be left unattended, and they must be well behaved, be on no more than a 10 foot leash, and cleaned up after. The camping and tent areas also allow dogs. There is a dog walk area at the campground. Dogs are allowed in the camping cabins. Multiple dogs may be allowed.

Oregon Listings

Cascade Locks

Cascade Locks/Portland East KOA
841 NW Forest Lane
Cascade Locks, OR
541-374-8668
Dogs of all sizes are allowed. There are no additional pet fees. Dogs may not be left unattended at any time, must be leashed, and cleaned up after. There are some breed restrictions. This RV park is closed during the off-season. The camping and tent areas also allow dogs.

There is a dog walk area at the campground. Dogs are allowed in the camping cabins. Multiple dogs may be allowed.

Central Point

Medford/Gold Hill KOA
12297 Blackwell Road
Central Point, OR
541-855-7710
Dogs of all sizes are allowed. There are no additional pet fees. Dogs must be quiet, leashed, and cleaned up after. Dogs may not be left unattended, and may be left outside alone only if they are in an enclosed pen. There are some breed restrictions. The camping and tent areas also allow dogs. There is a dog walk area at the campground. Dogs are allowed in the camping cabins. Multiple dogs may be allowed.

Gold Beach

Indian Creek Resort
94680 Jerry's Flat Road
Gold Beach, OR
541-247-7704
Dogs of all sizes are allowed, and there are no additional pet fees for tent or RV sites. There is a $20 one time additional pet fee for cabins. Dogs may not be left unattended outside, and they must be leashed and cleaned up after. Dogs must be quiet and well behaved. The camping and tent areas also allow dogs. There is a dog walk area at the campground. Dogs are allowed in the camping cabins. 2 dogs may be allowed.

Turtle Rock RV Resort
28788 Hunter Creek Loop
Gold Beach, OR
541-247-9203
Dogs of all sizes are allowed. There are no additional pet fees for one pet, either at the tent and RV sites or the cabins. For more than one dog there is a $4 per night per pet additional fee for the tent and RV sites, and a $15 per night per pet additional pet fee for the cabins. Dogs must be leashed and cleaned up after. The camping and tent areas also allow dogs. There is a dog walk area at the campground. Dogs are allowed in the camping cabins. Multiple dogs may be allowed.

Hammond

Astoria/Seaside KOA
1100 Northwest Ridge Road
Hammond, OR
503-861-2606
Dogs of all sizes are allowed. There is a $2 per night per pet additional fee. Dogs may not be left unattended, must be leashed, and cleaned up after. There are some breed restrictions. The camping and tent areas also allow dogs. There is a dog walk area at the campground. Dogs are allowed in the camping cabins. 2 dogs may be allowed.

Pendleton

Umatilla National Forest
2517 SW Hailey Avenue
Pendleton, OR
541-278-3716
This forest of nearly 1.4 million acres provides spectacular scenery, a rich cultural history, and diverse ecosystems that support a large variety of plants, animals, and recreation. Dogs of all sizes are allowed at no additional fee. Dogs may not be left unattended; they must be quiet, well behaved, be on no more than a 6 foot leash, and cleaned up after in camp areas. Dogs are allowed on the trails. This campground is closed during the off-season. The camping and tent areas also allow dogs. There is a dog walk area at the campground. Dogs are allowed in the camping cabins. There are no electric or water hookups at the campground. Multiple dogs may be allowed.

Welches

Mt Hood Village
65000 E H 26
Welches, OR
800-255-3069
One dog of any size is allowed, and there are no additional pet fees for tent or RV sites. There is a $10 one time pet fee for the cabin. Dogs must be quiet, well behaved, leashed, and cleaned up after. There are some breed restrictions. The camping and tent areas also allow dogs. There is a dog walk area at the campground. Dogs are allowed in the camping cabins.

Pennsylvania

Listings

Bellefonte

Bellefonte/State College KOA
2481 Jacksonville Road
Bellefonte, PA
814-355-7912
Dogs of all sizes are allowed. There are no additional pet fees. Dogs must be leashed and cleaned up after. This RV park is closed during the off-season. The camping and tent areas also allow dogs. There is a dog walk area at the campground. Dogs are allowed in the camping cabins. Multiple dogs may be allowed.

Gettysburg

Gettysburg/Battlefield KOA
20 Knox Road
Gettysburg, PA
717-642-5713
Dogs of all sizes are allowed, and there are no additional pet fees for tent or RV sites. There is a $10 one time pet fee for cabin rentals. Dogs may not be left unattended at any time, must be leashed, and cleaned up after. This RV park is closed during the off-season. The camping and tent areas also allow dogs. There is a dog walk area at the campground. Dogs are allowed in the camping cabins. Multiple dogs may be allowed.

McKean

Erie KOA
6645 West Road
McKean, PA
814-476-7706
Dogs of all sizes are allowed. There are no additional pet fees. Dogs may not be left unattended, must be leashed, and cleaned up after. This RV park is closed during the off-season. The camping and tent areas also allow dogs. There is a dog walk area at the campground. Dogs are allowed in the camping cabins. Multiple dogs may be allowed.

Mercer

Mercer/Grove City KOA
1337 Butler Pike
Mercer, PA

724-748-3160
Dogs of all sizes are allowed. There are no additional pet fees. Dogs must be well behaved, leashed, and cleaned up after. This RV park is closed during the off-season. The camping and tent areas also allow dogs. There is a dog walk area at the campground. Dogs are allowed in the camping cabins. Multiple dogs may be allowed.

New Columbia

Nittany Mountain Campground
2751 Miller's Bottom Road
New Columbia, PA
570-568-5541
One dog of any size is allowed in the rentals. Dogs of all sizes are allowed in the camping and RV area. There is a $1 per night per pet additional fee. Dogs must be leashed and cleaned up after. This RV park is closed during the off-season. The camping and tent areas also allow dogs. There is a dog walk area at the campground. Dogs are allowed in the camping cabins.

Pine Grove

Pine Grove KOA
1445 Suedburg Road
Pine Grove, PA
717-865-4602
Dogs of all sizes are allowed. There are no additional pet fees. Dogs must be quiet, leashed, and cleaned up after. There are some breed restrictions. The camping and tent areas also allow dogs. There is a dog walk area at the campground. Dogs are allowed in the camping cabins. Multiple dogs may be allowed.

Pittsburgh

Madison/Pittsburgh SE KOA
119 Tanglewood Lane
Ruffs Dale, PA
724-722-4444
Dogs of all sizes are allowed. There are no additional pet fees. Dogs must be leashed and cleaned up after. There are some breed restrictions. This RV park is closed during the off-season. The camping and tent areas also allow dogs. There is a dog walk area at the campground. Dogs are allowed in the camping cabins. Multiple dogs may be allowed.

Keen Lake Camping and Cottage Resort
155 Keen Lake Road
Waymart, PA
570-488-5522
Dogs of all sizes are allowed, and there are no additional pet fees for RV or tent sites. There is a $50 one time additional pet fee for a cottage rental plus a $250 refundable pet deposit. Dogs must be quiet, may not be left unattended, and must be leashed and cleaned up after. This RV park is closed during the off-season. The camping and tent areas also allow dogs. There is a dog walk area at the campground. Dogs are allowed in the camping cabins. 2 dogs may be allowed.

Washington

Washington KOA
7 KOA Road
Washington, PA
724-225-7590
Dogs of all sizes are allowed. There are no additional pet fees. In the cabins there can only be one large dog or two small dogs. There are a couple of more dogs allowed on tent and rv sites. Dogs must be leashed and cleaned up after. The camping and tent areas also allow dogs. There is a dog walk area at the campground. Dogs are allowed in the camping cabins.

South Carolina Listings

Anderson

Anderson/Lake Hartwell KOA
200 Wham Road
Anderson, SC
864-287-3161
Dogs of all sizes are allowed. There are no additional pet fees. Dogs may not be left unattended, and they must be quiet, well behaved, leashed, and cleaned up after. The camping and tent areas also allow dogs. There is a dog walk area at the campground. Dogs are allowed in the camping cabins. Multiple dogs may be allowed.

Charleston

Mt Pleasant/Charleston KOA
3157 H 17
Mount Pleasant, SC
843-849-5177
Dogs of all sizes are allowed. There are no additional pet fees. Dogs may not be left unattended outside, and they must be leashed and cleaned up after. The camping and tent areas also allow dogs. There is a dog walk area at the campground. Dogs are allowed in the camping cabins. Multiple dogs may be allowed.

Florence

Florence KOA
1115 E Campground Road
Florence, SC
843-665-7007
Dogs of all sizes are allowed. There are no additional pet fees. Dogs may not be left unattended, even at the dog pen area. Dogs must be leashed and cleaned up after. The camping and tent areas also allow dogs. There is a dog walk area at the campground. Dogs are allowed in the camping cabins. Multiple dogs may be allowed.

Ladson

Charleston KOA
9494 H 78
Ladson, SC
843-797-1045
Dogs of all sizes are allowed. There are no additional pet fees. Dogs may not be left unattended, and they must be leashed and cleaned up after. The camping and tent areas also allow dogs. There is a dog walk area at the campground. Dogs are allowed in the camping cabins.

Swansea

River Bottom Farms
357 Cedar Creek Road
Swansea, SC
803-568-4182
Dogs of all sizes are allowed. There are no additional pet fees. Dogs must be well behaved, leashed, and cleaned up after. There are some breed restrictions. The camping and tent areas also allow dogs. There is a dog walk area at the campground. Dogs are allowed in the camping cabins. Multiple dogs may be allowed.

Yemassee

Point South KOA
14 Campground Road
Yemassee, SC
843-726-5733
Dogs of all sizes are allowed. There are no additional pet fees. Dogs may not be left unattended, and they must be leashed and cleaned up after. There are some breed restrictions. The camping and tent areas also allow dogs. There is a dog walk area at the campground. Dogs are allowed in the camping cabins. Multiple dogs may be allowed.

South Dakota Listings

Brandon

Yogi Bear Jellystone Park
26014 478th Avenue
Brandon, SD
605-332-2233
Dogs of all sizes are allowed. There are no additional pet fees. Dogs must be leashed and cleaned up after. Pets allowed in cabins with a security deposit or a credit card on file. This RV park is closed during the off-season. The camping and tent areas also allow dogs. There is a dog walk area at the campground. Dogs are allowed in the camping cabins. Multiple dogs may be allowed.

Deadwood

Deadwood KOA
1 mile W of Deadwood on H 14A
Deadwood, SD
605-578-3830
Dogs of all sizes are allowed. There are no additional pet fees. Dogs may not be left unattended in the cabins or outside. Dogs must be leashed and cleaned up after. This RV park is closed during the off-season. The camping and tent areas also allow dogs. There is a dog walk area at the campground. Dogs are allowed in the camping cabins. Multiple dogs may be allowed.

Hot Springs

Hot Springs KOA

HCR 52, Box 112-C
Hot Springs, SD
605-745-6449
Dogs of all sizes are allowed, and there are no additional pet fees for tent or RV sites. There is a $3 per night additional fee for pets in the cabins. Dogs must be quiet, well behaved, leashed and cleaned up after. This RV park is closed during the off-season. The camping and tent areas also allow dogs. There is a dog walk area at the campground. Dogs are allowed in the camping cabins. Multiple dogs may be allowed.

Kennebec

Kennebec KOA
311 S H 273
Kennebec, SD
605-869-2300
Dogs of all sizes are allowed. There are no additional pet fees. Dogs must be leashed and cleaned up after. A pet waiver must be signed if the dog(s) are any of the known aggressive breeds. This RV park is closed during the off-season. The camping and tent areas also allow dogs. There is a dog walk area at the campground. Dogs are allowed in the camping cabins. Multiple dogs may be allowed.

Mitchell

Mitchell KOA
41244 H 38
Mitchell, SD
605-996-1131
Dogs of all sizes are allowed. There are no additional pet fees. Dogs must be quiet, well behaved, leashed, and cleaned up after. This RV park is closed during the off-season. The camping and tent areas also allow dogs. There is a dog walk area at the campground. Dogs are allowed in the camping cabins. Multiple dogs may be allowed.

Mount Rushmore - Black Hills

KOA Campground
U.S. Highway 16
Custer, SD
605-673-4304
This KOA campground is located in the Black Hills. They have tent sites, RV campsites and pet-friendly Kamping Kabins. Amenities include a heated pool, croquet, a playground, snack bar, modem dataport,

maximum pull through length of 60 feet and 50 amp service available. Well-behaved leashed dogs are allowed and there is a dog walk area on the premises. Please remember to clean up after your pet. The campground is open from April 15 to October 1. They are located 3 miles west of the town of Custer on Highway 1 towards Jewel Cave and New Castle, Wyoming. Mt. Rushmore is about a 30 minute drive from the campground, possibly more if there is traffic.

The Roost Resort
12462 H 16 A
Custer, SD
605-673-2326
Dogs of all sizes are allowed at no additional fee for tent or RV sites. For the cabins, there is a $5 per night per pet additional fee for a small dog, and a $10 per night per pet additional fee for medium to large dogs. Dogs may not be left unattended, and they must be quiet, well behaved, leashed, and cleaned up after. The camping and tent areas also allow dogs. There is a dog walk area at the campground. Dogs are allowed in the camping cabins. Multiple dogs may be allowed.

Crooked Creek Resort
24184 S H 385/16
Hill City, SD
800-252-8486
Dogs of all sizes are allowed. There are no additional pet fees. Dogs may not be left unattended, and they must be leashed and cleaned up after. This RV park is closed during the off-season. The camping and tent areas also allow dogs. There is a dog walk area at the campground. Dogs are allowed in the camping cabins. 2 dogs may be allowed.

KOA Campground
P.O. Box 2592
Rapid City, SD
605-348-2111
This KOA campground is off of I-90 in Rapid City and is located about an hour from the area's popular attractions. They have tent sites, RV campsites and pet-friendly Kamping Kabins. Well-behaved leashed dogs are allowed in the campground and in the cabins. Please remember to clean up after your pet. Amenities include a swimming pool, hot tub/sauna, snack bar, modem dataport, cable

TV, maximum pull through length of 60 feet and 50 amp service available. The campground is open from April 15 to October 15. Upon arrival, they usually have a grab bag with treats for pets. There are some breed restrictions.

N Sioux City

Sioux City KOA
601 Streeter Drive
N Sioux City, SD
605-232-4519
Dogs of all sizes are allowed. There are no additional pet fees. Dogs must be well behaved, leashed, and cleaned up after. This RV park is closed during the off-season. The camping and tent areas also allow dogs. There is a dog walk area at the campground. Dogs are allowed in the camping cabins. Multiple dogs may be allowed.

Sioux Falls

Sioux Falls KOA
1401 E Robur Drive
Sioux Falls, SD
605-332-9987
Dogs of all sizes are allowed. There are no additional pet fees. Dogs must be well behaved, leashed, and cleaned up after. This RV park is closed during the off-season. The camping and tent areas also allow dogs. There is a dog walk area at the campground. Dogs are allowed in the camping cabins. Multiple dogs may be allowed.

Tennessee Listings

Buchanan

Paris Landing State Park
16055 H 79 N
Buchanan, TN
731-641-4465
This 841 acre park along the shores of the Tennessee River offers a variety of land and water recreation. Dogs of all sizes are allowed at no additional fee for camping. There is an additional fee of $10 per night per pet for the lodge and for the 1 pet friendly cabin. Dogs may not be left unattended, and they must be leashed and cleaned up after. Dogs

are allowed on the trails. The camping and tent areas also allow dogs. There is a dog walk area at the campground. Dogs are allowed in the camping cabins. Multiple dogs may be allowed.

Burns

Montgomery Bell State Park
1020 Jackson Hill Road
Burns, TN
615-797-9052
This park of over 3,700 acres offers a variety of naturalist interpretive programs in addition to various land and water recreation. Dogs of all sizes are allowed at no additional fee for the camping area. There is a $10 per night per pet additional fee for the 1 pet friendly cabin and the lodge. Dogs must be leashed at all times and cleaned up after. Dogs are not allowed in the lake or in park buildings; they are allowed on the trails. The camping and tent areas also allow dogs. There is a dog walk area at the campground. Dogs are allowed in the camping cabins. Multiple dogs may be allowed.

Crossville

Cumberland Mountain State Park
24 Office Dirve
Crossville, TN
931-484-6138
This 1,720-acre park is said to be the largest timbered plateau in America, and offers interpretive programs, scenic trails, and a variety of land and water recreation. Dogs are allowed at no additional fee for tent or RV sites. There is an additional $5 per night per pet fee for the cabins. Dogs must be leashed and cleaned up after. Dogs are allowed on the trails. The camping and tent areas also allow dogs. There is a dog walk area at the campground. Dogs are allowed in the camping cabins. Multiple dogs may be allowed.

Crossville

Ballyhoo Campground
256 Werthwyle Drive
Crossville, TN
931-484-0860
Dogs of all sizes are allowed, up to three, and there are no additional pet fees for tent or RV sites. There is a $5 one time additional pet fee for the cabins, and only one dog is allowed. Dogs must be well behaved,

leashed, and cleaned up after. There are some breed restrictions. The camping and tent areas also allow dogs. There is a dog walk area at the campground. Dogs are allowed in the camping cabins.

Henderson

Chickasaw State Rustic Park
20 Cabin Lane
Henderson, TN
731-989-5141
This scenic park has over 1,280 acres for recreation, and a variety of trails as well as land and water activities. Dogs of all sizes are allowed at no additional fee for the tent and RV sites. There is a $10 per night per pet additional fee for the cabins. Dogs may not be left unattended for very long or left out at night. Dogs must be leashed and be cleaned up after. Dogs are allowed on the trails. The camping and tent areas also allow dogs. There is a dog walk area at the campground. Dogs are allowed in the camping cabins. Multiple dogs may be allowed.

Hilham

Standing Stone State Park
1674 Standing Stone Park H (H 52)
Hilham, TN
931-823-6347
This scenic 1100 acre park hosts a variety of activities and recreational pursuits. Dogs of all sizes are allowed at no additional fee for the camping area. There is a $10 additional pet fee for the 1st night, and $5 per night per pet thereafter, for the 1 pet friendly cabin. Dogs may not be left unattended, and they must be leashed at all times, and cleaned up after. Dogs are allowed on the trails. The camping and tent areas also allow dogs. There is a dog walk area at the campground. Dogs are allowed in the camping cabins.

Hurricane Mills

Buffalo/I-40/Exit 143 KOA
473 Barren Hollow Road
Hurricane Mills, TN
931-296-1306
Dogs of all sizes are allowed, but there can only be up to 2 large or three small dogs per site. There are no additional pet fees. Dogs may not be left unattended, and they

must be quiet, well behaved, leashed, and cleaned up after. There are some breed restrictions. The camping and tent areas also allow dogs. There is a dog walk area at the campground. Dogs are allowed in the camping cabins.

Lebanon

Cedars of Lebanon State Park
328 Cedar Forest Road
Lebanon, TN
615-443-2769
Because of the unique ecosystems of this park, 19 rare and endangered species of plants grow profusely only at this spot on Earth. In addition to nature study and programs, there are a variety of land and water recreational activities. Dogs of all sizes are allowed at no additional fee for the camp area, but there is a $5 per night per pet additional fee for the 1 pet friendly cabin. Dogs may not be left unattended for very long, and they must be quiet, well behaved, leashed and cleaned up after. Dogs are not allowed in buildings, but they are allowed on the trails. The camping and tent areas also allow dogs. There is a dog walk area at the campground. Dogs are allowed in the camping cabins. Multiple dogs may be allowed.

Manchester

Manchester KOA
586 Campground Road
Manchester, TN
931-728-9777
Dogs of all sizes are allowed. There are no additional pet fees. There is a pet waiver to sign for cabin rentals. Dogs may not be left unattended outside, and they must be quiet, leashed, and cleaned up after. There is a field nearby where dogs may run off lead if they are well behaved, and under voice control. The camping and tent areas also allow dogs. There is a dog walk area at the campground. Dogs are allowed in the camping cabins. Multiple dogs may be allowed.

McDonald

Chattanooga North/Cleveland KOA
648 Pleasant Grove Road
McDonald, TN
423-472-8928
Two dogs of any size are allowed at the tent or RV sites. There can only

be one dog up to 20 pounds in the cabins. There is a pet policy to sign at check in and there are no additional pet fees. Dogs may not be left unattended outside, and they must be leashed and cleaned up after. The camping and tent areas also allow dogs. There is a dog walk area at the campground. Dogs are allowed in the camping cabins.

Millington

Meeman-Shelby Forest State Park
910 Riddick Road
Millington, TN
901-876-5215
A museum and interactive nature center are offered here in addition to providing a variety of recreation areas, woodlands, trails, and wildlife habitats. Dogs of all sizes are allowed at no additional fee for the camping areas. There is a $10 per night per pet fee for the 1st night, and $5 per night per pet fee for each night thereafter for the 1 pet friendly cabin. Dogs must be leashed at all times. Dogs are allowed on the trails. The camping and tent areas also allow dogs. There is a dog walk area at the campground. Dogs are allowed in the camping cabins. Multiple dogs may be allowed.

Pikeville

Fall Creek Falls State Park
2009 Village Camp Road
Pikeville, TN
423-881-5298
Sparkling streams, gorges, cascading waterfalls, a variety of scenic trails, ecosystems, and abundant recreation make this park a popular destination. Dogs of all sizes are allowed at no additional fee for camping areas. There is a $10 (plus tax)per night per pet additional fee for the 1 pet friendly cabin or the lodge. Dogs must be leashed and cleaned up after. Dogs are not allowed on the Overnight Trail, but they are allowed on the other trails. The camping and tent areas also allow dogs. There is a dog walk area at the campground. Dogs are allowed in the camping cabins. Multiple dogs may be allowed.

Ringgold

Chattanooga South/Lookout Mtn KOA
199 KOA Blvd

Ringgold, TN
706-937-4166
Dogs of all sizes are allowed, and there are no additional pet fees for tent or RV sites. There is a $10 per night additional pet fee for the cabins. There can be up to 3 dogs at the tent or RV sites and up to 2 dogs at the cabins. Dogs may not be placed in outdoor pens, and may not be left unattended outside. Dogs must be leashed and cleaned up after. There are some breed restrictions. The camping and tent areas also allow dogs. There is a dog walk area at the campground. Dogs are allowed in the camping cabins.

Silver Point

Edgar Evins State Park
1630 Edgar Evins Park Road
Silver Point, TN
931-858-2446
This park of over 6,000 acres is along the shores of one of the most beautiful reservoirs in Tennessee and provides miles of hiking trails, opportunities for nature study, and a variety of land and water recreation. Dogs of all sizes are allowed at no additional fee for the camping area. There is a $10 per night per pet additional fee for the cabins, and dogs must be 30 pounds or under. The cabins are closed for one month in off season. Dogs may not be left unattended, and they must be leashed and cleaned up after. Dogs are allowed on the trails. The camping and tent areas also allow dogs. There is a dog walk area at the campground. Dogs are allowed in the camping cabins.

The Smoky Mountains

Arrow Creek Campground
4721 E Parkway
Gatlinburg, TN
865-430-7433
Dogs of all sizes and numbers are allowed for tent and RV sites. Only 2 dogs are allowed in the cabins. There are no additional pet fees. Dogs may not be left unattended, must be quiet, leashed, and cleaned up after. This RV park is closed during the off-season. The camping and tent areas also allow dogs. There is a dog walk area at the campground. Dogs are allowed in the camping cabins.

Smoky Bear Campground

4857 E Parkway
Gatlinburg, TN
865-436-8372
Dogs of all sizes are allowed at the tent and RV sites. Small dogs only are allowed in the rentals or cabins. There are no additional pet fees. Dogs may not be left unattended except for very short periods. Dogs must be leashed and cleaned up after. This RV park is closed during the off-season. The camping and tent areas also allow dogs. There is a dog walk area at the campground. Dogs are allowed in the camping cabins. Multiple dogs may be allowed.

Winchester

Tims Ford State Park
570 Tims Ford Drive
Winchester, TN
931-962-1183
Known as one of the best bass fishing areas in the south, this park also holds archaeological interest, and is host to a variety of recreation. Dogs of all sizes are allowed at no additional fee for the camping area. There is a $10 per night per pet additional fee for the cabins. Dogs may not be left unattended, and they must be leashed and cleaned up after. Dogs are not allowed in buildings. The camping and tent areas also allow dogs. There is a dog walk area at the campground. Dogs are allowed in the camping cabins. Multiple dogs may be allowed.

Texas Listings

Abilene

Abilene KOA
4851 W Stamford Street
Abilene, TX
915-672-3681
Dogs of all sizes are allowed. There are no additional pet fees. Dogs must be leashed and cleaned up after. Dogs may be left unattended for short periods, and only if they will be quiet and well behaved. There is a fenced dog run for off lead. There are some breed restrictions. The camping and tent areas also allow dogs. There is a dog walk area at the campground. Dogs are allowed in the

camping cabins. Multiple dogs may be allowed.

Amarillo

Amarillo KOA
1100 Folsom Road
Amarillo, TX
806-335-1762
Dogs of all sizes are allowed, and there are no additional pet fees for tent or RV sites. There is a $5 per night per pet additional fee for the cabins. Dogs must be leashed and cleaned up after. There are some breed restrictions. The camping and tent areas also allow dogs. There is a dog walk area at the campground. Dogs are allowed in the camping cabins. Multiple dogs may be allowed.

Belton

Belton/Temple/Killeen KOA
2901 S I 35
Belton, TX
254-939-1961
Dogs of all sizes are allowed. There are no additional pet fees. Dogs may not be left unattended outside, and they must be on no more than a 6 foot leash, and cleaned up after. The camping and tent areas also allow dogs. There is a dog walk area at the campground. Dogs are allowed in the camping cabins. Multiple dogs may be allowed.

Brownsville

Rio RV Park
8801 Boca Chica
Brownsville, TX
956-831-4653
This park offers a free shuttle to the Mexican border, where you can walk across for shopping. A dog is allowed on the shuttle to Mexico. Dogs up to 30 pounds are allowed. There are no additional pet fees. Dogs may not be left unattended, or be in any of the buildings, and they must have a current rabies certificate and shot records. Dogs must be quiet, well behaved, leashed and cleaned up after. If a cabin will be needed with a pet, they suggest calling ahead. There are some breed restrictions. The camping and tent areas also allow dogs. There is a dog walk area at the campground. Dogs are allowed in the camping cabins. 2 dogs may be allowed.

Goodlett

Ole Towne Cotton Gin RV Park
230 Market Street
Goodlett, TX
940-674-2477
Dogs of all sizes are allowed, and there are no additional pet fees for tent or RV sites. There is a $35 one time pet fee for the cabins. Dogs may not be left unattended, and they must be leashed and cleaned up after. The camping and tent areas also allow dogs. There is a dog walk area at the campground. Dogs are allowed in the camping cabins. Multiple dogs may be allowed.

Houston

Houston Central KOA
1620 Peachleaf
Houston, TX
281-442-3700
Dogs of all sizes are allowed. There are no additional pet fees. Dogs may not be left unattended outside, and they must be leashed and cleaned up after. There is only 1 pet friendly cabin. There are some breed restrictions. The camping and tent areas also allow dogs. There is a dog walk area at the campground. Dogs are allowed in the camping cabins. Multiple dogs may be allowed.

Kerrville

Kerrville KOA
2950 Goat Creek Road
Kerrville, TX
830-895-1665
Dogs of all sizes are allowed. There are no additional pet fees. Dogs may not be left unattended outside, and they must be leashed and cleaned up after. The camping and tent areas also allow dogs. There is a dog walk area at the campground. Dogs are allowed in the camping cabins. Multiple dogs may be allowed.

Lubbock

Lubbock KOA
5502 County Road 6300
Lubbock, TX
806-762-8653
Dogs of all sizes are allowed. There are no additional pet fees. Dogs may not be left unattended outside, and they must be leashed and

cleaned up after. The camping and tent areas also allow dogs. There is a dog walk area at the campground. Dogs are allowed in the camping cabins. Multiple dogs may be allowed.

Mathis

Lake Corpus Christi/Mathis KOA
101 C ounty Road 371
Mathis, TX
361-547-5201
Dogs of all sizes are allowed. There are no additional pet fees. Dogs must be well behaved, leashed, and cleaned up after. The camping and tent areas also allow dogs. There is a dog walk area at the campground. Dogs are allowed in the camping cabins.

Mount Pleasant

Mt Pleasant KOA
2322 Greenhill Road
Mount Pleasant, TX
903-572-5005
Dogs of all sizes are allowed. There are no additional pet fees. Dogs must be leashed and cleaned up after. Dogs may not be left unattended, but they may be outside alone as long as there is an adult in the RV. There are some breed restrictions. The camping and tent areas also allow dogs. There is a dog walk area at the campground. Dogs are allowed in the camping cabins. Multiple dogs may be allowed.

Newton

Artesian Springs Resort
Rt 1 Box 670-12 H 26/26
Newton, TX
409-379-8826
Dogs of all sizes are allowed, and there are no additional pet fees for tent or RV sites. There is a $25 pet fee for the cabins, $15 of which, is refundable, and only 2 dogs up to 25 pounds each is allowed. Dogs may not be left unattended, and they must be leashed and cleaned up after. There are some breed restrictions. This RV park is closed during the off-season. The camping and tent areas also allow dogs. There is a dog walk area at the campground. Dogs are allowed in the camping cabins.

San Angelo

San Angelo KOA
6699 Knickerbocker Road
San Angelo, TX
325-949-3242
Dogs of all sizes are allowed. There are no additional pet fees. Dogs may not be left unattended outside, and they must be leashed and cleaned up after. Dogs may not be at the pool or in the buildings. There is a fenced pen area where dogs may be left for short periods. There are some breed restrictions. The camping and tent areas also allow dogs. There is a dog walk area at the campground. Dogs are allowed in the camping cabins. Multiple dogs may be allowed.

San Antonio

San Antonio KOA
602 Gembler Road
San Antonio, TX
210-224-9296
Dogs of all sizes are allowed. There are no additional pet fees. Dogs may not be left unattended outside, and they must be quiet, leashed, and cleaned up after. There are some breed restrictions. The camping and tent areas also allow dogs. There is a dog walk area at the campground. Dogs are allowed in the camping cabins. 2 dogs may be allowed.

Texarkana

Texarkana KOA
500 W 53rd Street
Texarkana, TX
903-792-5521
Dogs of all sizes are allowed, and there are no additional pet fees for tent or RV sites. There is a $10 one time additional pet fee for the cabins. Dogs must be leashed and cleaned up after. The camping and tent areas also allow dogs. There is a dog walk area at the campground. Dogs are allowed in the camping cabins. Multiple dogs may be allowed.

Van Horn

Van Horn KOA
10 Kamper's Lane
Van Horn, TX
432-283-2728
Dogs of all sizes are allowed. There are no additional pet fees. Dogs may not be left unattended outside, and they must be leashed and cleaned up after. The camping and tent areas

also allow dogs. There is a dog walk area at the campground. Dogs are allowed in the camping cabins. Multiple dogs may be allowed.

Utah Listings

Beaver

Beaver KOA
1428 Manderfield Road
Beaver, UT
435-438-2924
Dogs of all sizes are allowed. There are no additional pet fees. Dogs must be leashed and cleaned up after. This RV park is closed during the off-season. The camping and tent areas also allow dogs. There is a dog walk area at the campground. Dogs are allowed in the camping cabins. Multiple dogs may be allowed.

Bryce Canyon

Paradise RV Park
2153 N H 89
Panguitch, UT
435-676-8348
Dogs of all sizes are allowed at the tent and RV sites. Only small, lightly furred dogs are allowed at the cabins. There are no additional pet fees. Dogs may not be left unattended, and they must be leashed and cleaned up after. This RV park is closed during the off-season. The camping and tent areas also allow dogs. There is a dog walk area at the campground. Dogs are allowed in the camping cabins.

Cannonville

Cannonville/Bryce Valley KOA
H 12 at Red Rocks Road
Cannonville, UT
435-679-8988
Dogs of all sizes are allowed. There are no additional pet fees. Dogs must be well behaved, leashed, and cleaned up after. This RV park is closed during the off-season. The camping and tent areas also allow dogs. There is a dog walk area at the campground. Dogs are allowed in the camping cabins. Multiple dogs may be allowed.

Cedar City

Cedar City KOA
1121 N Main
Cedar City, UT
435-586-9872
There can be up to 3 dogs of any size for the tent or RV sites, and there are no additional pet fees. There is a $5 per night per pet additional fee for the cabins, and only up to 2 dogs are allowed. Dogs may not be left unattended, and they must be leashed and cleaned up after. There are some breed restrictions. The camping and tent areas also allow dogs. There is a dog walk area at the campground. Dogs are allowed in the camping cabins.

Dinosaur National Monument

Vernal/Dinosaurland KOA
930 N Vernal Avenue
Vernal, UT
435-789-2148
Dogs of all sizes are allowed. There are no additional pet fees. Dogs may not be left unattended at any time, and they must be quiet, leashed, and cleaned up after. Only 2 dogs at a time are allowed in the cabins, and up to 3 dogs at the tent or RV sites. There are some breed restrictions. This RV park is closed during the off-season. The camping and tent areas also allow dogs. There is a dog walk area at the campground. Dogs are allowed in the camping cabins.

Fillmore

Fillmore KOA
900 S 410 W
Fillmore, UT
435-743-4420
Dogs of all sizes are allowed, and there can be up to 3 dogs at the tent and RV sites. Two small dogs only are allowed at the cabins, and they must stay off the beds. There are no additional pet fees. Dogs are not allowed at the playground or the pool, and they must be leashed and cleaned up after. There are some breed restrictions. This RV park is closed during the off-season. The camping and tent areas also allow dogs. There is a dog walk area at the campground. Dogs are allowed in the camping cabins.

Garden City

Bear Lake/Garden City KOA
485 N Bear Lake Blvd
Garden City, UT
435-946-3454
Dogs of all sizes are allowed. There are no additional pet fees. Dogs may not be left unattended, and they must be leashed and cleaned up after. There is an off leash dog run area. The tent and RV sites are seasonal, and the cabins stay open all year. There are some breed restrictions. The camping and tent areas also allow dogs. There is a dog walk area at the campground. Dogs are allowed in the camping cabins. Multiple dogs may be allowed.

Manila

Flaming Gorge/Manila KOA
H 43 & 3rd W
Manila, UT
435-784-3184
Dogs of all sizes are allowed. There is a $10 cash only refundable pet deposit. Dogs must be leashed and cleaned up after. This RV park is closed during the off-season. The camping and tent areas also allow dogs. There is a dog walk area at the campground. Dogs are allowed in the camping cabins. Multiple dogs may be allowed.

Moab

Arch View Resort
10 miles N of Moab on H 191
Moab, UT
435-259-7854
Dogs of all sizes are allowed. There are no additional pet fees. Dogs must be quiet, well behaved, leashed, and cleaned up after. This RV park is closed during the off-season. The camping and tent areas also allow dogs. There is a dog walk area at the campground. Dogs are allowed in the camping cabins. Multiple dogs may be allowed.

Moab KOA
3225 S H 191
Moab, UT
435-259-6682
Dogs of all sizes and numbers are allowed, and there is a $5 one time fee for tent or RV sites. Dogs may not be left unattended outside, or inside an RV unless there is air conditioning. There is a $5 one time fee for the cabins also, only 2 dogs are allowed, and they must be crated if left. Dogs must be quiet, leashed, and cleaned up after. There are

some breed restrictions. This RV park is closed during the off-season. The camping and tent areas also allow dogs. There is a dog walk area at the campground. Dogs are allowed in the camping cabins.

Provo

Provo KOA
320N 2050 W
Provo, UT
801-375-2994
Dogs of all sizes are allowed. There are no additional pet fees. Dogs may not be left unattended at the cabins, and they must be leashed and cleaned up after. The camping and tent areas also allow dogs. There is a dog walk area at the campground. Dogs are allowed in the camping cabins. Multiple dogs may be allowed.

Vermont Listings

Enosburg Falls

Lake Carmi State Park
460 Marsh Farm Rd
Enosburg Falls, VT
802-933-8383
Dogs of all sizes are allowed. There are no additional pet fees. Dogs may not be left unattended at any time, they must be on no more than a 10 foot leash, and be cleaned up after. Dogs are not allowed in any day use areas, including parking lots, picnic areas, beach and swim areas, playgrounds, or buildings. Dogs must be at least 6 months old and have a current rabies certificate and shot records. Dogs on lead are allowed on the trails. The camping and tent areas also allow dogs. There is a dog walk area at the campground. Dogs are allowed in the camping cabins. There are no electric or water hookups at the campground. Multiple dogs may be allowed.

Irasburg

Tree Corners
3540 H 58
Irasburg, VT
802-754-6042

One small dog up to about 15 pounds is allowed. There are no additional pet fees. This RV park is closed during the off-season. Only one dog is allowed per campsite. The camping and tent areas also allow dogs. There is a dog walk area at the campground. Dogs are allowed in the camping cabins.

South Hero

Apple Island Resort
Box 183 H 2
South Hero, VT
802-372-5398
Dogs of all sizes are allowed. There are no additional pet fees. Dogs may not be left unattended, must be leashed, and cleaned up after. This RV park is closed during the off-season. The camping and tent areas also allow dogs. There is a dog walk area at the campground. Dogs are allowed in the camping cabins. Multiple dogs may be allowed.

Williamstown

Limehurst Lake Campground
4104 H 14
Williamstown, VT
802-433-6662
Dogs of all sizes are allowed. There are no additional pet fees. Dogs must be quiet, well behaved, and leashed and cleaned up after. There are some breed restrictions. This RV park is closed during the off-season. The camping and tent areas also allow dogs. There is a dog walk area at the campground. Dogs are allowed in the camping cabins. Multiple dogs may be allowed.

Virginia Listings

Breaks

Breaks Interstate Park
769 H 80
Breaks, VA
276-865-4413
This year round 4,600 acre park has often been called the "Little Grand Canyon", and in addition to panoramic views, there is a wide variety of land and water activities. Dogs are allowed at no additional fee for camping; there is a $7 per night

per pet additional fee for the lodge. Dogs may not be left unattended in rooms, but they may be tethered in the camp area if they will be well behaved, quiet, and checked in on. Dogs are allowed on the trails. This campground is closed during the off-season. The camping and tent areas also allow dogs. There is a dog walk area at the campground. Dogs are allowed in the camping cabins. Multiple dogs may be allowed.

Clifton Forge

Douthat State Park
Rt 1, Box 212
Clifton Forge, VA
540-862-8100
This park, a Nationally Registered Historic District, offers interpretive programs, more than 40 miles of hiking trails, and a variety of land and water events and recreation. Dogs of all sizes are allowed for $3 per night per pet for the camp area, and at $5 per night per pet for the cabins. Dogs may not be left unattended, and they must be leashed and cleaned up after. Dogs are not allowed at the lodge or on the beach, but they are allowed on the trails. This campground is closed during the off-season. The camping and tent areas also allow dogs. There is a dog walk area at the campground. Dogs are allowed in the camping cabins. Multiple dogs may be allowed.

Fredericksburg

Fredericksburg/Washington DC S KOA
7400 Brookside Lane
Fredericksburg, VA
540-898-7252
Dogs of all sizes are allowed. There are no additional pet fees, for tent or RV sites. There is a $5 per night per pet addtional fee for cabins. Dogs must be quiet, well behaved, leashed, and cleaned up after. The camping and tent areas also allow dogs. There is a dog walk area at the campground. Dogs are allowed in the camping cabins. 2 dogs may be allowed.

Gladstone

James River State Park
Rt 1, Box 787
Gladstone, VA
434-933-4355
A fairly new park offers 20 miles of

multiple use trails, three fishing ponds, and various activities and recreation. Dogs of all sizes are allowed for an additional $3 per night per pet for camping, and for $5 per night per pet for cabins. Cabins are available year round. Dogs may not be left unattended, and they must be leashed in camp areas, and cleaned up after. Dogs are allowed on the trails. The camping and tent areas also allow dogs. There is a dog walk area at the campground. Dogs are allowed in the camping cabins. There are no electric or water hookups at the campground. Multiple dogs may be allowed.

Green Bay

Twin Lakes State Park
788 Twin Lakes Road
Green Bay, VA
434-392-3435
This secluded park also provides a conference center in addition to a variety of lakefront activities, recreation, and interpretive programs. Dogs of all sizes are allowed for an additional $3 per night per pet for camping, and for $5 per night per pet for cabins. Cabins are available year round. Dogs may not be left unattended, and they must be leashed and cleaned up after. Dogs are not allowed on the beach or in the lake, but they are allowed on the trails. This campground is closed during the off-season. The camping and tent areas also allow dogs. There is a dog walk area at the campground. Dogs are allowed in the camping cabins. Multiple dogs may be allowed.

Harrisonburg

Harrisonburg/New Market
12480 Mountain Valley Road
Broadway, VA
540-896-8929
Up to 2 dogs are allowed per RV or tent site, at no additional fee. There is a $20 per stay fee for one dog only in the cabins. Dogs may not be left unattended, must be leashed, and cleaned up after. The camping and tent areas also allow dogs. There is a dog walk area at the campground. Dogs are allowed in the camping cabins.

Huddleston

Smith Mountain State Park
1235 State Park Road
Huddleston, VA
540-297-6066
Hardwood and pine forests, secluded coves and picturesque vistas are the backdrop for a variety of trails, land,water activities, and recreation at this year round park. Dogs of all sizes are allowed for an additional $3 per night per pet for camping, and for $5 per night per pet for cabins. Cabins are available year round. Dogs may not be tied to trees, and they must be leashed and cleaned up after. Dogs may only be left unattended if they will be quiet and well behaved in owners' absence. Dogs are allowed on the trails. This campground is closed during the off-season. The camping and tent areas also allow dogs. There is a dog walk area at the campground. Dogs are allowed in the camping cabins. Multiple dogs may be allowed.

Marion

Hungry Mother State Park
2854 Park Blvd
Marion, VA
276-781-7400
This park is rich in folklore and history, and offers interpretive programs, a variety of land and water activities, and recreation. Dogs of all sizes are allowed for an additional $3 per night per pet for camping, and for $5 per night per pet for cabins. Cabins are available year round. Dogs may not be left unattended, and they must be leashed and cleaned up after. Dogs are not allowed on the beaches or in buildings, but they are allowed on the trails. This campground is closed during the off-season. The camping and tent areas also allow dogs. There is a dog walk area at the campground. Dogs are allowed in the camping cabins. Multiple dogs may be allowed.

Natural Bridge

Natural Bridge/Lexington KOA
214 Killdeer Lane
Natural Bridge, VA
540-291-2770
Dogs of all sizes are allowed, and there can be more than two dogs. There are no additional pet fees for tent or RV sites. There is a $5 per stay per pet additional fee for cabins, and there can be 2 dogs. Dogs must

be well behaved, leashed, and cleaned up after. The camping and tent areas also allow dogs. There is a dog walk area at the campground. Dogs are allowed in the camping cabins.

Natural Bridge Station

Yogi Bear at Natural Bridge
16 Recreation Lane
Natural Bridge Station, VA
540-291-2727
This scenic park, located along the James River, offers a variety of land and water activities and recreational pursuits. Dogs of all sizes are allowed at no additional fee. Dogs may not be left unattended, and they must be leashed and cleaned up after. Dogs are not allowed on the beach, the game area, food areas, or in buildings. Dogs are allowed on the trails. This campground is closed during the off-season. The camping and tent areas also allow dogs. There is a dog walk area at the campground. Dogs are allowed in the camping cabins. 2 dogs may be allowed.

Petersburg

Petersburg KOA
2809 Cortland Road
Petersburg, VA
804-732-8345
Dogs of all sizes are allowed. There are no additional pet fees. Dogs must be quiet, leashed, and cleaned up after. The camping and tent areas also allow dogs. There is a dog walk area at the campground. Dogs are allowed in the camping cabins. Multiple dogs may be allowed.

Scottsburg

Staunton River State Park
1170 Staunton Trail
Scottsburg, VA
434-572-4623
This year round park covers almost 1,600 acres, is home to the largest lake in Virginia, offers interpretive programs, and a variety of land and water recreation. Dogs of all sizes are allowed for an additional $3 per night per pet for camping, and for $5 per night per pet for cabins. Cabins are available year round. Dogs may not be left unattended outside or in a tent, and they must be leashed and cleaned up after. Dogs are not allowed in the pool area, but they are

allowed on the trails. This campground is closed during the off-season. The camping and tent areas also allow dogs. There is a dog walk area at the campground. Dogs are allowed in the camping cabins. Multiple dogs may be allowed.

Stuart

Fairy Stone State Park
967 Fairystone Lake Drive
Stuart, VA
276-930-2424
Rich in folklore, this park of 4,868 acres with a 168 acre lake provides a variety of land and water recreation, but the Fairy Stones (naturally formed crosses in small rocks) are the real attraction in this park. Dogs of all sizes are allowed for an additional $3 per night per pet for camping, and for $5 per night per pet for cabins. Cabins are available year round. Dogs must be leashed and cleaned up after in camp areas. Dogs are not allowed on the beach, in the water, or at the conference center. Dogs are allowed on the trails. This campground is closed during the off-season. The camping and tent areas also allow dogs. There is a dog walk area at the campground. Dogs are allowed in the camping cabins. Multiple dogs may be allowed.

Verona

Staunton/Verona KOA
296 Riner Lane
Verona, VA
540-248-2746
Dogs of all sizes are allowed, and there are no additional pet fees for tent or RV sites. There is a $10 per night per pet additional fee for cabins. Dogs must be leashed and cleaned up after. This RV park is closed during the off-season. The camping and tent areas also allow dogs. There is a dog walk area at the campground. Dogs are allowed in the camping cabins. Multiple dogs may be allowed.

Virginia Beach Area

First Landing State Park
2500 Shore Drive
Virginia Beach, VA
757-412-2300
This park offers exhibits, 3 indoor

aquariums, interpretive programs, and almost 20 miles of hiking trails. Dogs of all sizes are allowed for an additional $3 per night per pet for camping, and for $5 per night per pet for cabins. Cabins are available year round. Dogs may not be left unattended, and they must have current rabies and shot records. Dogs are allowed on the trails. This campground is closed during the off-season. The camping and tent areas also allow dogs. There is a dog walk area at the campground. Dogs are allowed in the camping cabins. Multiple dogs may be allowed.

Wytheville

Whtheville KOA
231 KOA Road
Wytheville, VA
276-228-2601
Dogs of all sizes are allowed. There are no additional pet fees. Dogs must be leashed and cleaned up after. There are some breed restrictions. The camping and tent areas also allow dogs. There is a dog walk area at the campground. Dogs are allowed in the camping cabins. Multiple dogs may be allowed.

Washington Listings

Burlington

Burlington/Anacortes KOA
6397 N Green Road
Burlington, WA
360-724-5511
Dogs of all sizes are allowed. There are no additional pet fees. Dogs must be well behaved, quiet, be on no more than a 6 foot leash, and be cleaned up after. Dogs may not be left unattended at any time and can not be on the beds in the cabins. The camping and tent areas also allow dogs. There is a dog walk area at the campground. Dogs are allowed in the camping cabins. Multiple dogs may be allowed.

Chehalis

Chehalis/H 12 KOA
118 h 12

Chehalis, WA
360-262-9220
Dogs of all sizes are allowed. There are no additional pet fees. Dogs may not be left unattended, must be leashed, and cleaned up after. The camping and tent areas also allow dogs. There is a dog walk area at the campground. Dogs are allowed in the camping cabins. 2 dogs may be allowed.

Concrete

Concrete/Grandy Creek KOA
7370 Russell Road
Concrete, WA
360-826-3554
Dogs of all sizes are allowed. There are no additional pet fees. Dogs may not be left unattended at any time, must be leashed, and cleaned up after. There are some breed restrictions. This RV park is closed during the off-season. The camping and tent areas also allow dogs. There is a dog walk area at the campground. Dogs are allowed in the camping cabins. Multiple dogs may be allowed.

Cougar

Lone Fir Motel and RV Resort
16806 Lewis River Road
Cougar, WA
360-238-5210
Dogs of all sizes and numbers are allowed, and there are no additional pet fees for the tent and RV sites. There is a $10 per night per pet additional fee for the motel and only 2 dogs are allowed per room. Dogs must be quiet, well behaved, leashed, and cleaned up after. The camping and tent areas also allow dogs. There is a dog walk area at the campground. Dogs are allowed in the camping cabins. Multiple dogs may be allowed.

Coulee City

Sun Lakes Park Resort
34228 Park Lake Road NE
Coulee City, WA
509-632-5291
Dogs of all sizes are allowed. There is a $7 per night per pet additional fee for the cabins, tent or RV sites. Dogs may not be left unattended, are not allowed at the swim beach, and must be leashed and cleaned up after. There is an area where the dogs are also allowed to go swim.

This RV park is closed during the off-season. The camping and tent areas also allow dogs. There is a dog walk area at the campground. Dogs are allowed in the camping cabins. Multiple dogs may be allowed.

Olympia

Olympic National Forest
1835 Black Lk Blvd SW
Olympia, WA
360-956-23300
This park is a unique geographic province in that it contains 5 different major landscapes, and is home to an astounding diversity of plants, animals, and recreational pursuits. The campground at Round Creek is the only camp area that stays open year round. Dogs of all sizes are allowed at no additional fee. Dogs may not be left unattended, and they must be leashed and cleaned up after. Dogs are allowed on the trails. The camping and tent areas also allow dogs. There is a dog walk area at the campground. Dogs are allowed in the camping cabins. There are no electric or water hookups at the campground. Multiple dogs may be allowed.

Otis Orchards

Spokane KOA
N 3025 Barker Road
Otis Orchards, WA
509-924-4722
Dogs of all sizes are allowed. There are no additional pet fees. Dogs may not be left unattended, can be on no more than a 6 foot leash, and must be cleaned up after. There are some breed restrictions. The camping and tent areas also allow dogs. There is a dog walk area at the campground. Dogs are allowed in the camping cabins. Multiple dogs may be allowed.

Port Angeles

Log Cabin Resort
3183E Beach Road
Port Angeles, WA
360-928-3325
This resort style park offers spectacular scenery, a variety of accommodations as well as recreational pursuits. Dogs of all sizes are allowed at no additional fee for RV sites, however there is a

$10(plus tax)per night per pet additional fee for the rustic cabins. Dogs may not be left unattended, and they must be leashed and cleaned up after. Dogs are not allowed on the trails in the Olympic National Forest area. There is a dog walk area at the campground. Dogs are allowed in the camping cabins. Multiple dogs may be allowed.

San Juan Island

Lakedale Resort
4313 Roche Harbor Road
Friday Harbor, WA
360-378-2350
Dogs of all sizes are allowed. There is a $2 per night per pet additional fee for tent or RV sites. There is a $20 per night per pet additional fee for the lodge, however, depending on size and number, the fee for the lodge is flexible. Dogs may not be left unattended, and they must be quiet, well behaved, leashed, and cleaned up after. A ferry from Anacortes off I 5, or other ferries in the area will transport your pet on the car deck only. The camping and tent areas also allow dogs. There is a dog walk area at the campground. Dogs are allowed in the camping cabins. Multiple dogs may be allowed.

Winthrop

Winthrop/N Cascades National Park KOA
1114 H 20
Winthrop, WA
509-996-2258
Dogs of all sizes are allowed. There are no additional pet fees. Dogs must be leashed and cleaned up after. Dogs may be left unattended if they are quiet and well behaved, and you can also tie your pet by the office. This RV park is closed during the off-season. The camping and tent areas also allow dogs. There is a dog walk area at the campground. Dogs are allowed in the camping cabins. Multiple dogs may be allowed.

Yakima

Yakima KOA
1500 Keys Road
Yakima, WA
509-248-5882
Dogs of all sizes are allowed. There are no additional pet fees. Dogs

must be well behaved, leashed, and cleaned up after. There are some breed restrictions. The camping and tent areas also allow dogs. There is a dog walk area at the campground. Dogs are allowed in the camping cabins. 2 dogs may be allowed.

West Virginia Listings

Bruceton Mills

Big Bear Lake Campground
Hazelton Big Bear Lake Road
Bruceton Mills, WV
304-379-4382
Dogs of all sizes are allowed. There are no additional pet fees. Dogs may not be left unattended, and they must be leashed and cleaned up after. This RV park is closed during the off-season. The camping and tent areas also allow dogs. There is a dog walk area at the campground. Dogs are allowed in the camping cabins. There are no water hookups at the campgrounds. Multiple dogs may be allowed.

Elkins

Jellystone Park
Route 33 E Faulkner Road
Elkins, WV
304-637-8898
Dogs of all sizes are allowed. There are no additional pet fees. Dogs must be quiet, leashed, and cleaned up after. This RV park is closed during the off-season. The camping and tent areas also allow dogs. There is a dog walk area at the campground. Dogs are allowed in the camping cabins. 2 dogs may be allowed.

Revelle's River Resort
9 Faulkner Road
Elkins, WV
877-988-2267
Dogs of all sizes are allowed, and there are no additional pet fees for tent or RV sites. There is a $5 per night per pet additional fee plus a cash security deposit of $50 for the regular cabins, and the same daily fee plus a $100 deposit for the upscale cabins. Dogs must be leashed and cleaned up after. The camping and tent areas also allow

dogs. There is a dog walk area at the campground. Dogs are allowed in the camping cabins. 2 dogs may be allowed.

Harpers Ferry

Harpers Ferry/Washington DC NW KOA
343 Campground Road
Harpers Ferry, WV
304-535-6895
Dogs of all sizes are allowed. There is a $3 per pet per stay additional fee. Dogs must be leashed and cleaned up after. There are some breed restrictions. The camping and tent areas also allow dogs. There is a dog walk area at the campground. Dogs are allowed in the camping cabins. Multiple dogs may be allowed.

Seneca Rocks

Yokum's Vacationland
HC 59, Box 3
Seneca Rocks, WV
800-772-8343
Dogs of all sizes are allowed, and there are no additional pet fees for tent or RV sites. There is a $10 per night per pet additional fee for the motel. Dogs must be leashed and cleaned up after. The camping and tent areas also allow dogs. There is a dog walk area at the campground. Dogs are allowed in the camping cabins. Multiple dogs may be allowed.

Wisconsin Listings

Baraboo

Devil's Lake State Park
5975 Park Road
Baraboo, WI
608-356-8301
Dogs of all sizes are allowed. There are no additional pet fees. Dogs may not be left unattended, and they must be on no more than an 8 foot leash, and be cleaned up after. Dogs are not allowed on the beach, the picnic areas, the playground, or in any of the buildings. They are allowed on all the trails except the ParFrey Glen Trail. There are 4 camps in this park; 3 family camps,

and 1 group camp. The pet policy is the same at all camps. The camping and tent areas also allow dogs. There is a dog walk area at the campground. Dogs are allowed in the camping cabins. There are no water hookups at the campground. Multiple dogs may be allowed.

Fond Du Lac

Fond Du Luc KOA
5099 H B
Fond Du Lac, WI
920-477-2300
Dogs of all sizes are allowed, and there are no additional pet fees for tent or RV sites. There is a $5 one time additional pet fee for cabin rentals. Dogs must be well behaved, leashed, and cleaned up after. This RV park is closed during the off-season. The camping and tent areas also allow dogs. There is a dog walk area at the campground. Dogs are allowed in the camping cabins. Multiple dogs may be allowed.

Hayward

Hayward KOA
11544 N H 63
Hayward, WI
715-634-2331
Dogs of all sizes are allowed. There are no additional pet fees. Dogs must be leashed and cleaned up after. Dogs may be left alone if they will be quiet and well behaved. Dogs must be crated when left unattended in the cabins. There are some breed restrictions. This RV park is closed during the off-season. The camping and tent areas also allow dogs. There is a dog walk area at the campground. Dogs are allowed in the camping cabins. Multiple dogs may be allowed.

Rice Lake

Rice Lake/Spooner KOA
1876 29 3/4 Avenue
Rice Lake, WI
715-234-2360
Dogs of all sizes are allowed, and there are no additional pet fees for tent or RV sites. There is a $5 per night per pet additional pet fee for cabin rentals. Dogs may not be left alone except in your own RV, and only if they will be quiet and well behaved. Dogs must be leashed and cleaned up after. This RV park is closed during the off-season. The

camping and tent areas also allow dogs. There is a dog walk area at the campground. Dogs are allowed in the camping cabins. Multiple dogs may be allowed.

Wyoming Listings

Buffalo

Buffalo KOA
87 H 16E
Buffalo, WY
307-684-5423
Dogs of all sizes are allowed, and there are no additional pet fees for tent or RV sites. There is a $5 per night per pet additional fee for the cabins. Dogs must be leashed and cleaned up after. Dogs may not be left unattended outside or in the cabins. This RV park is closed during the off-season. The camping and tent areas also allow dogs. There is a dog walk area at the campground. Dogs are allowed in the camping cabins. Multiple dogs may be allowed.

Indian Campground
660 E Hart Street
Buffalo, WY
307-684-9601
Dogs of all sizes are allowed, however there can only be up to 3 dogs at tent and RV sites, and up to 2 dogs at the cabins. There are no additional pet fees. Dogs may not be left unattended, and they must be leashed and cleaned up after. This RV park is closed during the off-season. The camping and tent areas also allow dogs. There is a dog walk area at the campground. Dogs are allowed in the camping cabins.

Casper

Casper KOA
1101 Prairie Lane
Casper, WY
307-577-1664
Dogs of all sizes are allowed. There are no additional pet fees. Dogs must be leashed and cleaned up after. This RV park is closed during the off-season. The camping and tent areas also allow dogs. There is a dog walk area at the campground. Dogs are allowed in the camping cabins. Multiple dogs may be allowed.

Cheyenne

Cheyenne KOA
8800 Archer Frontage Road
Cheyenne, WY
307-638-8840
Dogs of all sizes are allowed. There are no additional pet fees. Dogs must be quiet, well behaved, leashed, and cleaned up after. The camping and tent areas also allow dogs. There is a dog walk area at the campground. Dogs are allowed in the camping cabins. Multiple dogs may be allowed.

Cody

Cody KOA
5561 Greybull H
Cody, WY
307-587-2369
Dogs of all sizes are allowed. There are no additional pet fees. Dogs must be leashed and cleaned up after. There are some breed restrictions. This RV park is closed during the off-season. The camping and tent areas also allow dogs. There is a dog walk area at the campground. Dogs are allowed in the camping cabins. Multiple dogs may be allowed.

Ponderosa Campground
1815 8th Street
Cody, WY
307-587-9203
Dogs of all sizes are allowed. There are no additional pet fees. Dogs must be leashed and cleaned up after. Dogs may not be left unattended at the cabins or outside. This RV park is closed during the off-season. The camping and tent areas also allow dogs. There is a dog walk area at the campground. Dogs are allowed in the camping cabins. Multiple dogs may be allowed.

Custer

Crazy Horse Kampground
1116 N 5th Street
Custer, WY
605-673-2565
Dogs of all sizes are allowed. There are no additional pet fees. Dogs may not be left unattended, they must be well behaved, leashed, and cleaned up after. This RV park is closed during the off-season. The

camping and tent areas also allow dogs. There is a dog walk area at the campground. Dogs are allowed in the camping cabins. Multiple dogs may be allowed.

Devils Tower

Devils Tower KOA
60 H 110
Devils Tower, WY
307-467-5395
Dogs of all sizes are allowed. There are no additional pet fees. Dogs must be leashed and cleaned up after. This RV park is closed during the off-season. The camping and tent areas also allow dogs. There is a dog walk area at the campground. Dogs are allowed in the camping cabins. Multiple dogs may be allowed.

Greybull

Greybull KOA
333 N 2nd Street
Greybull, WY
307-765-2555
Dogs of all sizes are allowed. There are no additional pet fees. Dogs must be leashed and cleaned up after. There are some breed restrictions. This RV park is closed during the off-season. The camping and tent areas also allow dogs. There is a dog walk area at the campground. Dogs are allowed in the camping cabins. Multiple dogs may be allowed.

Laramie

Laramie KOA
1271 W Baker Street
Laramie, WY
307-742-6553
Dogs of all sizes and numbers are allowed. There are no additional pet fees. There are only 2 dogs allowed at the cabins. Dogs must be leashed and cleaned up after. There are some breed restrictions. The camping and tent areas also allow dogs. There is a dog walk area at the campground. Dogs are allowed in the camping cabins.

Medicine Bow - Routt National Forests
2468 Jackson Street
Laramie, WY
307-745-2300
This forest of nearly 3 million acres has 13 designated wilderness areas

and its diverse ecosystems support a large variety of plants, fish, mammals, bird species, and recreation. Dogs of all sizes are allowed at no additional fee. Dogs may not be left unattended, and they must be leashed and cleaned up after. Dogs are allowed on the trails. This campground is closed during the off-season. The camping and tent areas also allow dogs. There is a dog walk area at the campground. Dogs are allowed in the camping cabins. There are no electric or water hookups at the campground. Multiple dogs may be allowed.

Moran

Flagg Ranch Resort
Box 187, 2 miles S of Yellowstonw
Moran, WY
800-443-2311
Dogs of all sizes are allowed, and there are no additional pet fees for tent or rv sites. There is a $10 per night per pet additional fee for the cabins. Dogs must be leashed and cleaned up after. This RV park is closed during the off-season. The camping and tent areas also allow dogs. There is a dog walk area at the campground. Dogs are allowed in the camping cabins. Multiple dogs may be allowed.

Piedmont

Elk Creek Resort and RV Park
8220 Elk Creek Road
Piedmont, WY
800-846-2267
Dogs of all sizes are allowed. There are no additional pet fees. Dogs must be leashed and cleaned up after. Dogs must be placed in a crate or taken with owner for cabin rentals. The camping and tent areas also allow dogs. There is a dog walk area at the campground. Dogs are allowed in the camping cabins. Multiple dogs may be allowed.

Rawlins

Rawlins KOA
205 E H 71
Rawlins, WY
307-328-2021
Dogs of all sizes are allowed. There are no additional pet fees. Dogs may not be left unattended, and must be leashed, and cleaned up after. There are some breed restrictions. This RV park is closed during the off-season.

The camping and tent areas also allow dogs. There is a dog walk area at the campground. Dogs are allowed in the camping cabins. Multiple dogs may be allowed.

Rock Springs

Rock Springs KOA
86 Foothill Blvd
Rock Springs, WY
307-362-3063
Dogs of all sizes are allowed. There are no additional pet fees. Dogs may not be tied up outside unattended. Dogs must be leashed and cleaned up after. There are some breed restrictions. This RV park is closed during the off-season. The camping and tent areas also allow dogs. There is a dog walk area at the campground. Dogs are allowed in the camping cabins. Multiple dogs may be allowed.

Sheridan

Sheridan/Big Horn Mountains KOA
63 Decker Road
Sheridan, WY
307-674-8766
Dogs of all sizes are allowed. There are no additional pet fees. Well trained dogs may be off lead. Dogs must be cleaned up after. This RV park is closed during the off-season. The camping and tent areas also allow dogs. There is a dog walk area at the campground. Dogs are allowed in the camping cabins. Multiple dogs may be allowed.

Thermopolis

Eagle RV Park
204 H 20S
Thermopolis, WY
888-865-5707
Dogs of all sizes are allowed. There are no additional pet fees. Dogs must be quiet, leashed, and cleaned up after. This RV park is closed during the off-season. The camping and tent areas also allow dogs. There is a dog walk area at the campground. Dogs are allowed in the camping cabins. Multiple dogs may be allowed.

Yellowstone - Grand Teton

Jackson South/Hoback Junction KOA
9705 S H 89
Jackson, WY
307-733-7078
Dogs of all sizes are allowed. There are no additional pet fees. Dogs may not be left unattended, and must be quiet, leashed, and cleaned up after. There are some breed restrictions. This RV park is closed during the off-season. The camping and tent areas also allow dogs. There is a dog walk area at the campground. Dogs are allowed in the camping cabins. Multiple dogs may be allowed.

Teton Village/Jackson West KOA
2780 Moose Wilson Road
Teton Village, WY
307-733-5354
Dogs of all sizes are allowed. There are no additional pet fees. Dogs may not be left unattended, and they must be leashed and cleaned up after. There are some breed restrictions. This RV park is closed during the off-season. The camping and tent areas also allow dogs. There is a dog walk area at the campground. Dogs are allowed in the camping cabins. Multiple dogs may be allowed.

Yellowstone Park/West Entrance KOA
3305 Targhee Pass H
W Yellowstone, WY
406-646-7606
Dogs of all sizes are allowed. There are no additional pet fees. Dogs may not be left unattended in the cabins, and they must be leashed and cleaned up after. There are some breed restrictions. This RV park is closed during the off-season. The camping and tent areas also allow dogs. There is a dog walk area at the campground. Dogs are allowed in the camping cabins. Multiple dogs may be allowed.

Canada Listings

Alberta Listings

Calgary

Hinton/Jasper KOA
4720 Vegas Road NW
Calgary, AB
403-288-8351
Dogs of all sizes are allowed, and there are no additional pet fees for the tent or RV sites. There is a $10 per night per pet additional fee for the cabins. Dogs must be leashed and cleaned up after. There are some breed restrictions. This RV park is closed during the off-season. The camping and tent areas also allow dogs. There is a dog walk area at the campground. Dogs are allowed in the camping cabins. 2 dogs may be allowed.

British Columbia Listings

Burns Lake

Burns Lake KOA
4 miles E of Burns Lake on H 16
Burns Lake, BC
250-692-3105
Dogs of all sizes are allowed. There are no additional pet fees. Dogs may not be left unattended, must be leashed, and cleaned up after. This RV park is closed during the off-season. The camping and tent areas also allow dogs. There is a dog walk area at the campground. Dogs are allowed in the camping cabins. Multiple dogs may be allowed.

Campbell River

Salmon Point
2176 Salmon Point Road
Campbell River, BC
250-923-6605
Dogs of all sizes are allowed. There is a $1 per night per pet additional fee for small dogs, and a $2 per night per pet additional fee for medium to large dogs. Dogs must be leashed and cleaned up after. The camping and tent areas also allow dogs. There is a dog walk area at the campground. Dogs are allowed in the camping cabins. Multiple dogs may be allowed.

Crofton

Osborne Bay Resort
1450 Charlette Street
Crofton, BC
250-246-4787
Friendly dogs of all sizes are allowed, and there are no additional pet fees for tent or RV sites. Up to two very well behaved dogs are allowed in the cottages, and there is no extra fee unless it is an extra large, or heavy shedding dog. Dogs may not be left unattended in cottages, and they must be leashed and cleaned up after. The camping and tent areas also allow dogs. There is a dog walk area at the campground. Dogs are allowed in the camping cabins.

Harrison

Harrison Springs Camping and RV Park
740 Hot Springs Road
Harrison, BC
604-796-8900
Dogs of all sizes are allowed, but only small dogs, 10 pounds or under, are allowed in the cabins. There are no additional pet fees. Dogs must be quiet, friendly, may not be left alone, must be leashed at all times, and cleaned up after. This RV park is closed during the off-season. The camping and tent areas also allow dogs. There is a dog walk area at the campground. Dogs are allowed in the camping cabins. Multiple dogs may be allowed.

Iskut

Tatogga Lake Resort
At about M.P. 390 on H 37 (Box 5995)
Iskut, BC
250-234-3526
Dogs of all sizes are allowed at the tent and RV site, but only one dog is allowed in the cabins. There are no additional pet fees. Dogs may be off leash if well behaved. This RV park is closed during the off-season. The camping and tent areas also allow dogs. There is a dog walk area at the campground. Dogs are allowed in the camping cabins.

Pink Mountain

Pink Mountain Campsite
M.P. 143 Alaska H
Pink Mountain, BC
250-772-5133
Dogs of all sizes are allowed. There are no additional pet fees. Dogs must be leashed and cleaned up after. Dogs may not be in the store or in the store parking lot. The camping and tent areas also allow dogs. There is a dog walk area at the campground. Dogs are allowed in the camping cabins. Multiple dogs may be allowed.

Sicamous

Sicamous KOA
3250 Oxboro Road
Sicamous, BC
250-836-2507
Dogs of all sizes are allowed, and there are no additional pet fees for tent or RV sites. There is a $5 per night per pet additional fee for cabins. Dogs may not be left unattended, must be leashed, and cleaned up after. This RV park is closed during the off-season. The camping and tent areas also allow dogs. There is a dog walk area at the campground. Dogs are allowed in the camping cabins. Multiple dogs may be allowed.

Surrey

Hazelmere RV Park
18843 8th Avenue
Surrey, BC
877-501-5007
Dogs of all sizes and numbers are allowed, however there can only be two dogs at a time in the cabins. There are no additional pet fees. Dogs must be quiet, well behaved, leashed and cleaned up after. Dogs are not to be left unattended in the cabins at any time. The camping and tent areas also allow dogs. There is a dog walk area at the campground. Dogs are allowed in the camping cabins.

Victoria

Victoria West KOA
230 Trans-Canada H 1
Victoria, BC

250-478-3332
Dogs of all sizes are allowed. There are no additional pet fees. Dogs must be friendly, leashed, and cleaned up after. Dogs may be off leash on the dog walk if they are under voice control. This RV park is closed during the off-season. The camping and tent areas also allow dogs. There is a dog walk area at the campground. Dogs are allowed in the camping cabins. Multiple dogs may be allowed.

New Brunswick Listings

Camper's City RV Park
138 Queens Way Drive
Moncton, NB
877-512-7868
Dogs of all sizes are allowed. There are no additional pet fees. Dogs must be leashed and cleaned up after. This RV park is closed during the off-season. The camping and tent areas also allow dogs. There is a dog walk area at the campground. Dogs are allowed in the camping cabins. Multiple dogs may be allowed.

Century Farm Family Campground
670 Ocean Wave Drive
St Martins, NB
866-394-4400
Dogs of all sizes and numbers are allowed, but only 2 dogs are allowed per cabin, and they are not to be on the furniture. There are no additional pet fees. Dogs may not be left unattended, must be well behaved, leashed, and cleaned up after. This RV park is closed during the off-season. The camping and tent areas also allow dogs. There is a dog walk area at the campground. Dogs are allowed in the camping cabins. Multiple dogs may be allowed.

Newfoundland Listings

Eastport Peninsula Sunshine Park
On the Road to the Beaches-H 310
Eastport, NF
709-677-2438
Dogs of all sizes are allowed. There are no additional pet fees. Dogs must be leashed and cleaned up after. This RV park is closed during the off-season. The camping and tent areas also allow dogs. There is a dog walk area at the campground. Dogs are allowed in the camping cabins. Multiple dogs may be allowed.

Golden Arm Trailer Park
12 miles from H 1 on H 80
Green's Harbour, NF
709-582-3600
One dog of any size is allowed. There are no additional pet fees. Dogs must be leashed and cleaned up after. Long hair/shedding type dogs are not allowed in the cabins, and they must stay off the furniture. This RV park is closed during the off-season. The camping and tent areas also allow dogs. There is a dog walk area at the campground. Dogs are allowed in the camping cabins.

Lomand River Lodge
10 km from H 430 on H 431
Lomand River, NF
877-456-6663
Dogs of all sizes are allowed. There are no additional pet fees. Dogs may not be left unattended, especially at the cabins. Dogs must be leashed and cleaned up after. This RV park is closed during the off-season. The camping and tent areas also allow dogs. There is a dog walk area at the campground. Dogs are allowed in the camping cabins. Multiple dogs may be allowed.

Nova Scotia Listings

Baddeck Cabot Trail Campground
9584 Trans Canada H 105
Baddeck, NS
902-295-2288
Dogs of all sizes are allowed. There are no additional pet fees. Dogs must be leashed and cleaned up after. This RV park is closed during the off-season. The camping and tent areas also allow dogs. There is a dog walk area at the campground. Dogs are allowed in the camping cabins. Multiple dogs may be allowed.

Plantation Campground and RV Park
210 W Steadmon Road
Barwick, NS
888-363-8882
Dogs of all sizes are allowed at the tent and RV sites, but there can only be up to 2 small dogs (under 15 pounds) in the cabins. There are no additional pet fees. Dogs must be leashed and cleaned up after. This RV park is closed during the off-season. The camping and tent areas also allow dogs. There is a dog walk area at the campground. Dogs are allowed in the camping cabins.

Seal Island/North Sydney KOA
3779 New Harris Road
New Harris, NS
902-674-2145
Dogs of all sizes are allowed. There are no additional pet fees. Dogs may not be left outside unattended, must be leashed, and cleaned up after. This RV park is closed during the off-season. The camping and tent areas also allow dogs. There is a dog walk area at the campground. Dogs are allowed in the camping cabins. Multiple dogs may be allowed.

Scotia Pine Campground
On Route 2
Truro, NS
877-893-3666
Dogs of all sizes are allowed. There are no additional pet fees. Dogs may not be left unattended, must be leashed, and cleaned up after. This RV park is closed during the off-season. The camping and tent areas also allow dogs. There is a dog walk

area at the campground. Dogs are allowed in the camping cabins. Multiple dogs may be allowed.

Upper Sackville

Halifax West KOA
3070 H 1
Upper Sackville, NS
902-865-4342
Dogs of all sizes are allowed. There are no additional pet fees. Dogs must be quiet, well behaved, leashed, and cleaned up after. Dogs may not be left unattended. This RV park is closed during the off-season. The camping and tent areas also allow dogs. There is a dog walk area at the campground. Dogs are allowed in the camping cabins. Multiple dogs may be allowed.

Ontario Listings

Barrie

Barrie KOA
3138 Penetanguishene Road
Barrie, ON
705-726-6128
Dogs of all sizes are allowed. There are no additional pet fees. Dogs may not be left unattended, must be on no more than a 6 foot leash, and cleaned up after. There are some breed restrictions. This RV park is closed during the off-season. The camping and tent areas also allow dogs. There is a dog walk area at the campground. Dogs are allowed in the camping cabins. Multiple dogs may be allowed.

Brighton

Brighton/401 KOA
15043 Telephone Road
Brighton, ON
613-475-2186
Dogs of all sizes are allowed. There are no additional pet fees. Dogs must be leashed and cleaned up after. There are some breed restrictions. This RV park is closed during the off-season. The camping and tent areas also allow dogs. There is a dog walk area at the campground. Dogs are allowed in the camping cabins. Multiple dogs may be allowed.

Cardinal

Cardinal KOA
609 Pittston Road
Cardinal, ON
613-657-4536
Dogs of all sizes are allowed. There are no additional pet fees. Dogs may not be left unattended, must be leashed, and cleaned up after. There are some breed restrictions. This RV park is closed during the off-season. The camping and tent areas also allow dogs. There is a dog walk area at the campground. Dogs are allowed in the camping cabins. Multiple dogs may be allowed.

Johnstown

Grenville Park
2323 County Road 2 RR3
Johnstown, ON
613-925-2000
Dogs of all sizes are allowed. There are no additional pet fees. Dogs must be leashed and cleaned up after. Dogs may not be on the furniture or beds in the cabin. This RV park is closed during the off-season. The camping and tent areas also allow dogs. There is a dog walk area at the campground. Dogs are allowed in the camping cabins. Multiple dogs may be allowed.

Kingston

1000 Islands/Kingston KOA
2039 Cordukes Road
Kingston, ON
613-546-6140
Friendly dogs of all sizes are allowed. There are no additional pet fees. Dogs may not be left unattended, must be leashed, and cleaned up after. There are some breed restrictions. This RV park is closed during the off-season. The camping and tent areas also allow dogs. There is a dog walk area at the campground. Dogs are allowed in the camping cabins. Multiple dogs may be allowed.

Lansdowne

1000 Islands/Ivy Lea KOA
514 1000 Islands Parkway
Lansdowne, ON
613-659-2817
Dogs of all sizes are allowed. There are no additional pet fees. Dogs

must be quiet, well behaved, leashed, and cleaned up after. There are some breed restrictions. This RV park is closed during the off-season. The camping and tent areas also allow dogs. There is a dog walk area at the campground. Dogs are allowed in the camping cabins. Multiple dogs may be allowed.

Madawaska

All Star Resort
1 Major Lake Road
Madawaska, ON
613-637-5592
Dogs of all sizes are allowed, and there are no additional pet fees for tent or RV sites, which are seasonal. There is a $10 per night per pet additional fee for the cabins, and the cabins are available year around. Dogs must be leashed and cleaned up after. This RV park is closed during the off-season. The camping and tent areas also allow dogs. There is a dog walk area at the campground. Dogs are allowed in the camping cabins. 2 dogs may be allowed.

Mallorytown

1000 Islands/Mallorytown KOA
1477 County Road 2
Mallorytown, ON
613-923-5339
Dogs of all sizes are allowed. There are no additional pet fees. Dogs may not be left unattended, must be leashed, and cleaned up after. Dogs must be crated in the cabins when left, and at night. There are some breed restrictions. This RV park is closed during the off-season. The camping and tent areas also allow dogs. There is a dog walk area at the campground. Dogs are allowed in the camping cabins. Multiple dogs may be allowed.

Marmora

Marmora KOA
178 KOA Campground Road
Marmora, ON
613-472-2233
Dogs of all sizes are allowed. There are no additional pet fees. Dogs may not be left unattended, must be leashed, and cleaned up after. There are some breed restrictions. This RV park is closed during the off-season. The camping and tent areas also allow dogs. There is a dog walk area

at the campground. Dogs are allowed in the camping cabins. Multiple dogs may be allowed.

Niagara Falls

KOA Niagara Falls N/Lewiston
1250 Pletcher Road
Youngstown, NY
716-754-8013
Dogs of all sizes are allowed. There are no additional pet fees. Dogs may not be left unattended, and must be leashed and cleaned up after. There are some breed restrictions. This RV park is closed during the off-season. The camping and tent areas also allow dogs. There is a dog walk area at the campground. Dogs are allowed in the camping cabins. Multiple dogs may be allowed.

Parry Sound

Parry Sound KOA
276 Rankin Lake Road
Parry Sound, ON
705-378-2721
Dogs of all sizes are allowed. There are no additional pet fees. Dogs must be quiet, may not be left unattended, and must be leashed and cleaned up after. There are some breed restrictions. This RV park is closed during the off-season. The camping and tent areas also allow dogs. There is a dog walk area at the campground. Dogs are allowed in the camping cabins. Multiple dogs may be allowed.

Restoule

Cedar Grove Camp
6845 H 534
Restoule, ON
705-729-2030
Dogs of all sizes are allowed, and there may be up to 3 dogs in the tent or RV areas, but only 2 dogs are allowed per cabin. There are no additional pet fees. Dogs may not be left unattended unless they will be quiet and well behaved, and they must be leashed and cleaned up after. This RV park is closed during the off-season. The camping and tent areas also allow dogs. There is a dog walk area at the campground. Dogs are allowed in the camping cabins. There are no water hookups at the campgrounds.

Sault Ste. Marie

Sault Ste Marie KOA
501 5th Line
Sault Ste. Marie, ON
705-759-2344
Dogs of all sizes are allowed. There are no additional pet fees. Dogs must be leashed and cleaned up after. They may be left for only short periods and only if they will be quiet and well behaved. There are some breed restrictions. This RV park is closed during the off-season. The camping and tent areas also allow dogs. There is a dog walk area at the campground. Dogs are allowed in the camping cabins. Multiple dogs may be allowed.

Spragge

Spragge KOA
4696 H 17
Spragge, ON
705-849-2210
Dogs of all sizes are allowed, but they want to know ahead of time if you have large dogs so they can provide a space to accommodate. There are no additional pet fees. Dogs must be quiet and well behaved. Dogs may not be left unattended, must be leashed, and cleaned up after. Your dog can run off leash at the river if there is voice control and no one is around. There are some breed restrictions. This RV park is closed during the off-season. The camping and tent areas also allow dogs. There is a dog walk area at the campground. Dogs are allowed in the camping cabins. Multiple dogs may be allowed.

Thunder Bay

Thunder Bay KOA
162 Spruce River Road
Thunder Bay, ON
807-683-6221
Dogs of all sizes are allowed. There are no additional pet fees. Dogs must be leashed and cleaned up after. Some breeds are not allowed. This RV park is closed during the off-season. The camping and tent areas also allow dogs. There is a dog walk area at the campground. Dogs are allowed in the camping cabins. Multiple dogs may be allowed.

Wiarton

Roth Park Family Campground
Burford Lake Road
Wiarton, ON
519-534-0145
Dogs of all sizes are allowed. There are no additional pet fees. Dogs may not be left unattended unless they will be quiet and well behaved, and they must be leashed and cleaned up after. This RV park is closed during the off-season. The camping and tent areas also allow dogs. There is a dog walk area at the campground. Dogs are allowed in the camping cabins. Multiple dogs may be allowed.

Prince Edward Island Listings

Cavendish

Cavendish KOA
198 Forest Hill Lane
Cavendish, PE
902-963-2079
Dogs of all sizes are allowed. There are no additional pet fees. Dogs may not be left unattended, must be leashed, and cleaned up after. Dogs must be well behaved and friendly. A dog sitter is sometimes availabe. There are some breed restrictions. This RV park is closed during the off-season. The camping and tent areas also allow dogs. There is a dog walk area at the campground. Dogs are allowed in the camping cabins. Multiple dogs may be allowed.

Quebec Listings

Norte Dame du Laus

Tarmigan Campground
907 Ch. Poisson Blanc
Norte Dame du Laus, PQ
819-767-2559
Dogs of all sizes are allowed for an additional $3.50 per night per pet for the tent or RV area, and an additional fee of $5 per night per pet for the cottages. Dogs may not be left unattended, and they must be leashed and cleaned up after. There is an area where the dog may run off

lead, but only if they are well behaved, under voice control, and will not chase, as there are several other animals residing at this park. This RV park is closed during the off-season. The camping and tent areas also allow dogs. There is a dog walk area at the campground. Dogs are allowed in the camping cabins. Multiple dogs may be allowed.

St Nicolas

Quebec City KOA
684 Chemin Olivier Street
St Nicolas, PQ
418-831-1813
Dogs of all sizes are allowed, but they want to know ahead of time how many pets there are so they can place accordingly. There are no additional pet fees. Dogs must be well behaved, leashed, and cleaned up after. There is one pet friendly cabin available, and they offer a complimentary dog walking service. There are some breed restrictions. This RV park is closed during the off-season. The camping and tent areas also allow dogs. There is a dog walk area at the campground. Dogs are allowed in the camping cabins. Multiple dogs may be allowed.

St Philippe de Laprairie

Montreal South KOA
130 Monette Blvd
St Philippe de Laprairie, PQ
450-659-8626
Dogs of all sizes are allowed, and there are no additional pet fees for tent or RV sites. There is only one dog allowed in the cabins and there is a $20 refundable deposit. Dogs may not be left unattended outside, they must be leashed, and cleaned up after. This RV park is closed during the off-season. The camping and tent areas also allow dogs. There is a dog walk area at the campground. Dogs are allowed in the camping cabins.

Saskatchewan Listings

Indian Head

Indian Head KOA

1100 McKay Street
Indian Head, SK
306-695-3635
Dogs of all sizes are allowed. There is a $2 per night per pet additional fee. Dogs must be leashed and cleaned up after. This RV park is closed during the off-season. The camping and tent areas also allow dogs. There is a dog walk area at the campground. Dogs are allowed in the camping cabins. Multiple dogs may be allowed.

Little Bear Lake

Moose Horn Lodge and Campground
Mile 62 Hanson Lake Road
Little Bear Lake, SK
306-426-2700
Dogs of all sizes are allowed. There are no additional pet fees. Dogs must be quiet, well behaved, leashed, and cleaned up after. This RV park is closed during the off-season. The camping and tent areas also allow dogs. There is a dog walk area at the campground. Dogs are allowed in the camping cabins. Multiple dogs may be allowed.

Yukon Listings

Haines Junction

Fas Gas RV Park
M.M. 270 Alaska H
Haines Junction, YU
867-634-2505
Dogs of all sizes are allowed, and there are no additional pet fees for tent or RV sites. There is a $10 per night per pet additional fee for the 1 pet friendly cabin. Dogs must be leashed and cleaned up after. This RV park is closed during the off-season. The camping and tent areas also allow dogs. There is a dog walk area at the campground. Dogs are allowed in the camping cabins.

Watson Lake

Baby Nugget RV Park
KM 1003 Alaska H (M.M. 650)
Watson Lake, YU
867-536-2307

Dogs of all sizes are allowed, and there are no additional pet fees for tent or RV sites. There is a $10 per night per pet addtional fee for the lodge and cabins. Dogs must be leashed and cleaned up after at all times. This RV park is closed during the off-season. The camping and tent areas also allow dogs. There is a dog walk area at the campground. Dogs are allowed in the camping cabins. Multiple dogs may be allowed.

Chapter 3

Dog-Friendly Beach Guides

Maine Beaches

Bar Harbor

Hadley Point Beach
Highway 3
Bar Harbor, ME

Dogs are allowed on the beach, but must be leashed. The beach is located about 10 minutes northwest of downtown Bar Harbor, near Eden.

Portland

East End Beach
Cutter Street
Portland, ME
207-874-8793
Dogs are only allowed on this beach from the day after Labor Day to the day before Memorial Day. Dogs are not allowed on the beach from Memorial Day through Labor Day. During the months that dogs are allowed, they can be off-leash but need to be under direct voice control. People need to make sure they pick up their dog's waste with a plastic bag and throw it away in a trash can.

Old Orchard
Cutter Street
Portland, ME
207-874-8793
Dogs are only allowed on this beach from the day after Labor Day to the day before Memorial Day. Dogs are not allowed on the beach from Memorial Day through Labor Day. During the months that dogs are allowed, they can be off-leash but need to be under direct voice control. People need to make sure they pick up their dog's waste with a plastic bag and throw it away in a trash can.

Old Orchard Beach

Old Orchard Beach City Beach

Old Orchard Beach, ME
207-934-0860
Leashed dogs are allowed on this beach at all hours from the day after Labor Day to the day before Memorial Day. Dogs are not allowed on the beach from Memorial Day through Labor Day except before 8 am and after 4 pm. People need to make sure they pick up their dog's waste with a plastic bag and throw it away in a trash can.

Kennebunk

Kennebunk Beaches
Beach Avenue
Kennebunk, ME

Dogs are allowed with certain restrictions. During the summertime, from about Memorial Day weekend through Labor Day weekend, leashed dogs are only allowed on the beach before 8am and after 6pm. During the rest of the year, dogs are allowed on the beach during park hours. There are a string of beaches, including Kennebunk, Gooch's and Mother's, that make up a nice stretch of wide sandy beaches. People need to clean up after their pets. The beaches are located on Beach Avenue, off Routes 9 and 35.

Kennebunkport

Goose Rocks Beach
Dyke Street
Kennebunkport, ME

Leashed dogs are allowed, with certain restrictions. From June 15 through September 15, dogs are only allowed on the beach before 8am and after 6pm. During the rest of the year, dogs are allowed on the beach during park hours. People need to clean up after their pets. The beach is located about 3 miles east of Cape Porpoise. From Route 9, exit onto Dyke Street.

Wells

Wells Beach
Route 1
Wells, ME
207-646-2451
Leashed dogs are allowed, with certain restrictions. During the summer, from June 16 through September 15, dogs are only allowed on the beach before 8am and after 6pm. The rest of the year, dogs are allowed on the beach during all park hours. There are seven miles of sandy beaches in Wells. People are required to clean up after their pets.

York

Long Sands Beach
Route 1A
York, ME
207-363-4422
Leashed dogs are allowed, with certain restrictions. During the summertime, from about Memorial Day weekend through Labor Day weekend, dogs are only allowed on the beach before 8am and after 6pm. During the off-season, dogs are allowed during all park hours. This beach offers a 1.5 mile sandy beach. Metered parking and private lots are available. The beach and bathhouse are also handicap accessible. People are required to clean up after their pets.

Short Sands Beach
Route 1A
York, ME
207-363-4422
Leashed dogs are allowed, with certain restrictions. During the summertime, from about Memorial Day weekend through Labor Day weekend, dogs are only allowed on the beach before 8am and after 6pm. During the off-season, dogs are allowed during all park hours. At the beach, there is a large parking area and a playground. People are required to clean up after their pets.

York Harbor Beach
Route 1A
York, ME
207-363-4422
Leashed dogs are allowed, with certain restrictions. During the summertime, from about Memorial Day weekend through Labor Day weekend, dogs are only allowed on the beach before 8am and after 6pm. During the off-season, dogs are allowed during all park hours. This park offers a sandy beach nestled against a rocky shoreline. There is limited parking. People are required to clean up after their pets.

Massachusetts Beaches

Boston

Carson Beach
I-93 and William Day Blvd

Boston, MA
617-727-5114
Dogs are only allowed on the beach during the off-season. Pets are not allowed from Memorial Day weekend through Labor Day weekend. Dogs must be leashed and people are required to clean up after their pets.

Cape Cod

Barnstable Town Beaches
off Route 6A
Barnstable, MA
508-790-6345
Dogs are allowed only during the off-season, from September 15 to May 15. Dogs must be on leash or under voice control. People need to clean up after their pets. The town of Barnstable oversees Hyannis beaches and the following beaches: Craigville, Kalmus, and Sandy Neck. Before you go, always verify the seasonal dates and times when dogs are allowed on the beach.

Chatham Town Beaches
off Route 28
Chatham, MA
508-945-5100
Dogs are allowed only during the off-season, from mid September to end the end of May. Dogs must be leashed and people need to clean up after their pets. The town of Chatham oversees the following beaches: Hardings, Light, and Ridgevale. Before you go, always verify the seasonal dates and times when dogs are allowed on the beach.

Dennis Town Beaches
Route 6A
Dennis, MA
508-394-8300
Dogs are allowed only during the off-season, from after Labor Day up to Memorial Day. There is one exception. Dogs are allowed year-round on the four wheel drive area of Chapin Beach. Dogs must be leashed on all town beaches, and people need to clean up after their pets. The town of Dennis oversees the following beaches: Chapin, Mayflower, Howes Street and Sea Street. Before you go, always verify the seasonal dates and times when dogs are allowed on the beach.

Falmouth Town Beaches
off Route 28
Falmouth, MA
508-457-2567
Dogs are allowed during the summer, only before 9am and after

5pm. During the off-season, dogs are allowed all day. Dogs must be leashed and people need to clean up after their pets. The town of Falmouth oversees the following beaches: Menauhant, Surf Drive, and Old Silver. Before you go, always verify the seasonal dates and times when dogs are allowed on the beach.

Harwich Town Beach
off Route 28
Harwich, MA
508-430-7514
Dogs are allowed only during the off-season, from October to mid-May. Dogs must be on leash or under voice control. People need to clean up after their pets. The town of Harwich oversees Red River Beach. Before you go, always verify the seasonal dates and times when dogs are allowed on the beach.

Orleans Town Beaches
off Route 28
Orleans, MA
508-240-3775
Dogs are allowed only during the off-season, from after Labor Day to the Friday before Memorial Day. Dogs are allowed off leash, but must be under voice control. People need to clean up after their pets. The town of Orleans oversees Nauset and Skaket beaches. Before you go, always verify the seasonal dates and times when dogs are allowed on the beach.

Provincetown Town Beaches
off Route 6
Provincetown, MA
508-487-7000
Dogs on leash are allowed year-round. During the summer, from 6am to 9am, dogs are allowed off-leash. The town of Provincetown oversees the following beaches: Herring Cove and Race Point. Before you go, always verify the seasonal dates and times when dogs are allowed on the beach.

Sandwich Town Beaches
off Route 6A
Sandwich, MA
508-888-4361
Dogs are allowed only during the off-season, from October through March. Dogs must be leashed and people need to clean up after their pets. The town of Sandwich oversees the following beaches: East Sandwich and Town Neck. Before you go, always verify the seasonal dates and times when

dogs are allowed on the beach.

Truro Town Beaches
off Route 6
Truro, MA
508-487-2702
Dogs are allowed during the summer, only before 9am and after 6pm. This policy is in effect from about the third weekend in June through Labor Day. During the off-season, dogs are allowed all day. Dogs must be leashed and people need to clean up after their pets. The town of Truro oversees the following beaches: Ballston, Corn Hill, Fisher, Great Hollow, Head of the Meadow, Longnook and Ryder. Before you go, always verify the seasonal dates and times when dogs are allowed on the beach.

Cape Cod National Seashore
Route 6
Wellfleet, MA
508-349-3785
The park offers a 40 mile stretch of pristine sandy beaches. Dogs on leash are allowed year-round on all of the seashore beaches, except for seasonally posted nesting or lifeguarded beaches. Leashed pets are also allowed on fire roads, and the Head of the Meadow bicycle trail in Truro. Check with the visitor center or rangers for details about fire road locations. To get there from Boston, take Route 3 south to the Sagamore Bridge. Take Route 6 east towards Eastham.

Wellfleet Town Beaches
off Route 6
Wellfleet, MA
508-349-9818
Dogs are allowed during the summer, only before 9am and after 6pm. During the off-season, from after Labor Day to the end of June, dogs are allowed all day. Dogs must be leashed and people need to clean up after their pets. The town of Wellfleet oversees the following beaches: Marconi, Cahoon Hollow, and White Crest. Before you go, always verify the seasonal dates and times when dogs are allowed on the beach.

Marthas Vineyard

Joseph Sylvia State Beach
Beach Road
Edgartown, MA
508-696-3840
Dogs are allowed during the summer, only before 9am and after

5pm. You will need to keep your dog away from any bird nesting areas, which should have signs posted. During the off-season, from mid-September to mid-April, dogs are allowed all day. This beach is about 2 miles long. Dogs must be leashed and people need to clean up after their pets. Before you go, always verify the seasonal dates and times when dogs are allowed on the beach.

Norton Point Beach
end of Katama Road
Edgartown, MA
508-696-3840
Dogs are allowed during the summer, only before 9am and after 5pm. You will need to keep your dog away from any bird nesting areas, which should have signs posted. During the off-season, from mid-September to mid-April, dogs are allowed all day. This beach is about 2.5 miles long. Dogs must be leashed and people need to clean up after their pets. Before you go, always verify the seasonal dates and times when dogs are allowed on the beach.

South Beach State Park
Katama Road
Edgartown, MA
508-693-0085
Dogs are allowed during the summer, only after 5pm. During the off-season, from mid-September to mid-April, dogs are allowed all day. This 3 mile beach is located on the South Shore. Dogs must be leashed and people need to clean up after their pets. Before you go, always verify the seasonal dates and times when dogs are allowed on the beach.

Eastville Point Beach
At bridge near Vineyard Haven
Oak Bluffs, MA
508-696-3840
Dogs are allowed during the summer, only before 9am and after 5pm. You will need to keep your dog away from any bird nesting areas, which should have signs posted. During the off-season, from mid-September to mid-April, dogs are allowed all day. Dogs must be leashed and people need to clean up after their pets. Before you go, always verify the seasonal dates and times when dogs are allowed on the beach.

Nantucket

Nantucket Island Beaches
various locations
Nantucket, MA
508-228-1700
Dogs are allowed during the summer on beaches with lifeguards only before 9am and after 5pm. On beaches that have no lifeguards, or during the winter months, dogs are allowed all day on the beach. Dogs must always be leashed. Before you go, always verify the seasonal dates and times when dogs are allowed on the beach.

Rhode Island Beaches

Newport

Salty Brine State Beach
254 Great Road
Narragansett, RI
401-789-3563
Dogs are only allowed on the beach during the off-season, from October 1 through March 31. Pets must be on leash and people are required to clean up after their pets. However, according to a representative at the Rhode Island State Parks Department, in a conversation with them July 2004, the rules may change in the future to have no dogs on the beach year round. To get there, take I-95 to Route 4 South. Then take Route 1 South to Route 108 South to Point Judith. If you are there during the summer, take the dog-friendly ferry at Pt. Judith to Block Island where leashed dogs are allowed year-round on the island beaches.

Easton's Beach
Memorial Blvd.
Newport, RI
401-847-6875
Dogs are only allowed on the beach during the off-season. They are not allowed on the beach from Memorial Day weekend through Labor Day weekend. Pets must be on leash and people need to clean up after their pets. The beach is located off Route 138A (Memorial Blvd.). There is a parking fee.

Block Island

Block Island Beaches
Corn Neck Road
Block Island, RI
401-466-2982
Dogs are allowed year-round on the island beaches, but they must be leashed and people are required to clean up after their pets. To get to the beaches, take a right out of town and follow Corn Neck Road. To get to the island, you will need to take the Block Island Ferry which allows leashed dogs. The ferry from Port Judith, RI to Block Island operates daily. If you are taking the ferry from Newport, RI or New London, CT to the island, please note these ferries only operate during the summer. If you are bringing a vehicle on the ferry, reservations are required. Call the Block Island Ferry at 401-783-4613 for auto reservations.

South Kingston

East Matunuck State Beach
950 Succotash Road
South Kingston, RI
401-789-8585
Dogs are only allowed on the beach during the off-season, from October 1 through March 31. Pets must be on leash and people are required to clean up after their pets. However, according to a representative at the Rhode Island State Parks Department, in a conversation with them July 2004, the rules may change in the future to have no dogs on the beach year round. To get there, take I-95 to Route 4 South. Then take Route 1 South to East Matunuck Exit and follow the signs to the state beach.

Charlestown

East Beach State Beach
East Beach Road
Charlestown, RI
401-322-0450
Dogs are only allowed on the beach during the off-season, from October 1 through March 31. Pets must be on leash and people are required to clean up after their pets. However, according to a representative at the Rhode Island State Parks Department, in a conversation with them July 2004, the rules may change in the future to have no dogs on the beach year round. To get there, take I-95 to Route 4 South. Then take Route 1 South to East

Beach exit in Charlestown.

Westerly

Misquamicut State Beach
257 Atlantic Avenue
Westerly, RI
401-596-9097
Dogs are only allowed on the beach during the off-season, from October 1 through March 31. Pets must be on leash and people are required to clean up after their pets. However, according to a representative at the Rhode Island State Parks Department, in a conversation to them July 2004, the rules may change in the future to have no dogs on the beach year round. To get there, take I-95 to Route 4 South. Then take Route 1 South to Westerly. Follow the signs to the state beach.

Connecticut Beaches

Fairfield

Town of Fairfield Beaches
off Highway 1
Fairfield, CT
203-256-3010
Dogs are only allowed on the town beaches during the off-season. Pets are not allowed on the beaches from April 1 through October 1. Dogs must be on leash and people need to clean up after their pets.

New York Beaches

Long Island

Camp Hero State Park
50 South Fairview Avenue
Montauk, NY
631-668-3781
The park boasts some of the best surf fishing spots in the world. Dogs on a 6 foot or less leash are allowed on the beach year-round, but not in the picnic areas. To get to the park, take Route 27 (Sunrise Highway)

east to the end. The park is about 130 miles from New York City.

Hither Hills State Park
50 South Fairview Avenue
Montauk, NY
631-668-2554
This park offers visitors a sandy ocean beach. Dogs are allowed with certain restrictions. During the off-season, dogs are allowed on the beach. During the summer, dogs are not allowed on the beach, except for the undeveloped area on the other side of the freeway. Dogs must be on a 6 foot or less leash and people need to clean up after their pets. Dogs are not allowed in buildings or on walkways and they are not allowed in the camping, bathing and picnic areas.

Montauk Point State Park
50 South Fairview Avenue
Montauk, NY
631-668-3781
This park is located on the eastern tip of Long Island. Dogs are allowed on the beach, but not near the food area. Dogs must be on a 6 foot or less leash and people need to clean up after their pets. Dogs are not allowed in buildings or on walkways and they are not allowed in the camping, bathing and picnic areas. Please note that dogs are not allowed in the adjacent Montauk Downs State Park. The park is located 132 miles from Manhattan, off Sunrise Highway (Route 27).

New York

Prospect Park Dog Beach
Prospect Park - Brooklyn
New York, NY
212-NEW-YORK
This man made, concrete beach was designed for our canine friends. It is located in Prospect Park, off 9th Street on the path leading down from the Tennis House. Dogs may only be off-leash before 9 am and after 9 pm in the summer and after 5 pm in the winter. People are not permitted to swim in the dog pool. There is a fence to keep the dogs in so you don't have to chase them across the pond.

New Jersey Beaches

North Shore

Island Beach State Park
off Route 35
Seaside Park, NJ
732-793-0506
There are certain restrictions for pets on the beach. During the summer, dogs on a 6 foot or less leash are allowed on the beach, but not on the designated swimming beaches. Ask the ranger when you arrive, as to which part of the beach allows dogs. During the off-season, dogs are allowed on all of the beaches, but must be on a 6 foot or less leash. People are required to clean up after their pets. To get to the park, take Route 37 east. Then take Route 35 south to the park entrance.

Cape May

Higbee Beach Wildlife Management Area
County Road 641
Cape May, NJ
609-628-2103
This park offers a 1 1/2 mile stretch of beach. The beach is managed specifically to provide habitat for migratory wildlife. Dogs on leash and under control are allowed at the beach. To get there, take SR 109 west to US9. Turn left onto US9 and go to the first traffic light. Turn left onto County Road 162 (Seashore Rd.). Then turn right onto Country Road 641 (New England Rd.). Take CR641 for 2 miles to the end and the beach access parking area. Parking areas near the beach may be closed during the summer. The park is open daily from dawn to dusk.

Cape May Point State Park
Lighthouse Avenue
Cape May Point, NJ
609-884-2159
Dogs are only allowed on the beach during the off-season. Pets are not allowed from April 15 through September 15. Pets must be on a 6 foot or less leash and people need to clean up after their pets. The park is located off the southern end of the Garden State Parkway. Go over the Cape May Bridge to Lafayette Street. At the intersection, go right onto Route 606 (Sunset Blvd.), then turn left onto Lighthouse Ave.

Delaware Beaches

Cape Henlopen State Park
42 Cape Henlopen Drive
Lewes, DE
302-645-8983
This park draws thousands of visitors who enjoy sunbathing and ocean swimming. Dogs on a 6 foot or less leash are allowed on the beach, with some exceptions. Dogs are not allowed on the two swimming beaches during the summer, but they are allowed on surfing and fishing beaches, bike paths and some of the trails. Pets are not allowed on the fishing pier. During the off-season, dogs are allowed on any of the beaches, but still need to be leashed. People are required to clean up after their pets. The park is located one mile east of Lewes, 1/2 mile past the Cape May-Lewes Ferry Terminal.

Delaware Seashore State Park
Inlet 850
Rehoboth Beach, DE
302-227-2800
This park offers six miles of ocean and bay shoreline. Dogs on a 6 foot or less leash are allowed on the beach, with a couple of exceptions. Dogs are not allowed at the lifeguarded swimming areas. However, there are plenty of non-guarded beaches where people with dogs can walk or sunbathe. During the off-season, dogs are allowed on any of the beaches, but still need to be leashed. People are required to clean up after their pets. The park is located south of Dewey Beach, along Route 1.

Rehoboth Beach
off Route 1
Rehoboth Beach, DE
302-227-6181
From April 1 to October 31, pets are not allowed on the beach or boardwalk at any time. However, during the off-season, dogs are allowed but need to be leashed and cleaned up after. The beach is located off Route 1, north of Dewey Beach.

Dewey Beach
Coastal Highway/Route 1
Dewey Beach, DE
302-227-1110
Dogs are allowed on the beach year-round only with a special license and with certain hour restrictions during the summer season. A special license is required for your dog to go on the beach. You do not have to be a resident of Dewey Beach to get the license. You can obtain one from the Town of Dewey Beach during regular business hours at 105 Rodney Avenue in Dewey Beach. The cost is $5 per dog and is good for the lifetime of your dog. During the summer, from May 15 to September 15, dogs are only allowed before 9:30am and after 5:30pm. During the off-season there are no hourly restrictions. Year-round, dogs can be off-leash but need to be under your control at all times and cleaned up after.

Bethany Beach
off Route 1
Bethany Beach, DE
302-539-8011
From May 15 to September 30, pets are not allowed on the beach or boardwalk at any time. But during the off-season, dogs are allowed but need to be leashed and cleaned up after.

South Bethany Beach
off Route 1
South Bethany, DE
302-539-3653
From May 15 to October 15, dogs are not allowed on the beach at any time. The rest of the year, during the off-season, dogs are allowed on the beach. Pets must be leashed and cleaned up after. The beach is located off Route 1, south of Dewey Beach.

Fenwick Island Beach
off Route 1
Fenwick Island, DE
302-539-2000
From May 1 to September 30, dogs are not allowed on the beach at any time. The rest of the year, pets are allowed on the beach but must be leashed and cleaned up after. The beach is located of Route 1, south of Dewey Beach.

Maryland Beaches

Downs Park Dog Beach
8311 John Downs Loop
Pasadena, MD
410-222-6230
This dog beach is located on Chesapeake Bay, not on the ocean. People are not permitted to go swimming, but dogs can run off-leash at this beach. The dog beach is closed every Tuesday. Dogs on leash are also allowed in Downs Park. People need to clean up after their pets. Take Route 100 until it merges with Moutain Road (Rt. 177 East). Follow Mt. Road for about 3.5 miles and the park entrance will be on your right. The dog beach is located in the northeast corner of the park.

Quiet Waters Park Dog Beach
600 Quiet Waters Park Road
Annapolis, MD
410-222-1777
This park is located on Chesapeake Bay, not on the ocean. Dogs are welcome to run off-leash at this dog beach and dog park. The dog park is closed every Tuesday. Leashed dogs are also allowed at Quiet Waters Park. The park offers over 6 miles of scenic paved trails, and a large multi-level children's playground. People need to clean up after their pets. To get there, take Route 665 until it ends and merges with Forrest Drive. Take Forrest Drive for 2 miles and then turn right onto Hillsmere Drive. The park entrance is about 100 yards on the right. The dog beach is located to the left of the South River overlook. Park in Lot N.

Elm's Beach Park
Bay Forest Road
Hermanville, MD
301-475-4572
The park is located on Chesapeake

Bay, not on the ocean. Enjoy great views of the bay or swim at the beach. Dogs on leash are allowed at the beach. People need to clean up after their pets. Take Route 235 to Bay Forest Road and then go 3 miles. The park will be on the left.

Ocean City

Ocean City Beaches
Route 528
Ocean City, MD
1-800-OC-OCEAN
Dogs are only allowed during certain times of the year on this city beach. Pets are not allowed on the beach or boardwalk at any time from May 1 through September 30. The rest of the year, dogs are allowed on the beach and boardwalk, but must be on leash and people must clean up after them.

Assateague Island

Assateague Island National Seashore
Route 611
Assateague Island, MD
410-641-1441
Dogs on leash are allowed on beaches, except for any lifeguarded swimming beaches (will be marked off with flags). There are plenty of beaches to enjoy at this park that are not lifeguarded swimming beaches. Dogs are not allowed on trails in the park. The park is located eight miles south of Ocean City, at the end of Route 611.

Virginia Beaches

Virginia Beach Area

Back Bay National Wildlife Refuge
Sandpiper Road
Virginia Beach, VA
757-721-2412
Dogs are only allowed on the beach during the off-season. Dogs are only allowed on the beach from October 1 through March 31. Pets must be leashed (on leashes up to 10 feet long) and people need to clean up after their pets. This park is located approximately 15 miles south of Virginia Beach. From I-64, exit to I-264 East (towards the oceanfront).

Then take Birdneck Road Exit (Exit 22), turn right onto Birdneck Road. Go about 3-4 miles and then turn right on General Booth Blvd. Go about 5 miles. After crossing the Nimmo Parkway, pay attention to road signs. Get into the left lane so you can turn left at the next traffic light. Turn left onto Princess Anne Rd. The road turns into Sandbridge Rd. Keep driving and then turn right onto Sandpiper Road just past the fire station. Follow Sandpiper Road for about 4 miles to the end of the road.

First Landing State Park
2500 Shore Drive
Virginia Beach, VA
757-412-2300
Dogs on a 6 foot or less leash are allowed year-round on the beach. People need to clean up after their pet. All pets must have a rabies tag on their collar or proof of a rabies vaccine. To get there, take I-64. Then take the Northampton Blvd/US 13 North (Exit 282). You will pass eight lights and then turn right at the Shore Drive/US 60 exit. Turn right onto Shore Drive and go about 4.5 miles to the park entrance.

Virginia Beach Public Beaches
off Highway 60
Virginia Beach, VA
757-437-4919
Dogs are only allowed during off-season on Virginia Beach public beaches. From the Friday before Memorial Day through Labor Day weekend, pets are not allowed on public sand beaches, the boardwalk or the grassy area west of the boardwalk, from Rudee Inlet to 42nd Street. People are required to clean up after their pets and dogs must be leashed.

North Carolina Beaches

Nags Head

Nags Head Beach
Highway 158
Nags Head, NC
252-441-8144
Dogs on leash are allowed year-round on this beach in the Outer

Banks. People need to clean up after their pets.

Manteo

Cape Hatteras National Seashore
Highway 12
Manteo, NC
252-473-2111
This park offers long stretches of pristine beach. Dogs on a 6 foot or less leash are allowed year-round, except on any designated swimming beaches. Most of the beaches are non-designated swim beaches. People are required to clean up after their pets.

Atlantic Beach

Fort Macon State Park
Highway 58
Atlantic Beach, NC
252-726-3775
This park offers beach access. Dogs on a 6 foot leash or less are allowed on the beach, but not inside the Civil War fort located in the park. People need to clean up after their pets. The park is located on the eastern end of Bogue Banks, south of Morehead City.

Kure Beach

Ft. Fisher State Recreation Area
Highway 421
Kure Beach, NC
910-458-5798
Enjoy miles of beachcombing, sunbathing or hunting for shells at this beach. Dogs on leash are allowed everywhere on the beach, except for swimming areas that have lifeguards on duty. People need to clean up after their pets. The park is located on the southern tip of Pleasure Island, near Wilmington.

South Carolina Beaches

Myrtle Beach

Myrtle Beach City Beaches
off Interstate 73
Myrtle Beach, SC
843-281-2662

There are certain restrictions for pets on the beach. Dogs are not allowed on the right of way of Ocean Blvd. (part of I-73), between 21st Avenue North and 13th Avenue South during March 1 through September 30. From Memorial Day weekend through Labor Day weekend, leashed dogs are allowed on Myrtle Beach city beaches before 9am and after 5pm. During off-season, leashed dogs are allowed on the city beaches anytime during park hours. People need to clean up after their pets.

Myrtle Beach State Park
4401 South Kings Highway
Myrtle Beach, SC
843-238-5325
This is one of the most popluar public beaches on the South Carolina coast. It is located in the heart of the Grand Strand. During the summertime, dogs are only allowed during certain hours. From June through August, dogs are only allowed on the beach after 4pm. For all other months of the year, dogs are allowed on the beach anytime during park hours. Dogs must be on leash at all times. People are required to clean up after their pets.

Murrells Inlet

Huntington Beach State Park
16148 Ocean Highway
Murrells Inlet, SC
843-234-4440
This beach is the best preserved beach on the Grand Strand. Dogs on a 6 foot or less leash are allowed on the beach. People need to clean up after their pets.

Folly Beach

Folly Beach County Park
Ashley Avenue
Folly Beach, SC
843-588-2426
Dogs are only allowed during the off-season at this beach. They are not allowed from May 1 through September 30. But the rest of the year, dogs on leash are allowed on the beach during park hours. People are required to clean up after their pets. The park is located on the west end of Folly Island. On the island, turn right at Ashley Avenue stoplight and go to the end of the road.

Kiawah

Beachwalker County Park
Beachwalker Drive
Kiawah, SC
843-768-2395
Dogs on leash are allowed year-round at this beach. People are required to clean up after their pets. The park is located on the west end of Kiawah Island. Take Bohicket Road to the island. Just before the island security gate, turn right on Beachwalker Drive. Follow the road to the park.

Edisto Island

Edisto Beach State Park
8377 State Cabin Road
Edisto Island, SC
843-869-2756
Sunbathe, beachcomb or hunt for seashells on this 1.5 mile long beach. This park also has a 4 mile nature trail that winds through a maritime forest with great vistas that overlook the salt marsh. Dogs on a 6 foot or less leash are allowed on the beach and on the trails. People need to clean up after their pets.

Hunting Island

Hunting Island State Park
2555 Sea Island Parkway
Hunting Island, SC
843-838-2011
This park offers over 4 miles of beach. Dogs on a 6 foot or less leash are allowed on the beach and on the trails at this state park. People need to clean up after their pets.

Hilton Head Island

Alder Lane Beach Access
S. Forest Beach Drive
Hilton Head Island, SC
843-341-4600
This beach has restricted seasons and hours for dogs. During the summertime, from the Friday before Memorial Day through the Tuesday after Labor Day, dogs can only be on the beach before 10am and then after 5pm (they are not allowed from 10am to 5pm). Pets must be leashed. During the off-season and winter months, from April 1 through the Thursday before Memorial Day, dogs must be on a leash between 10am and 5pm. From the Tuesday after Labor Day through September 30, dogs again must be on a leash between 10am and 5pm. At all other times, dogs may be off-leash, but must be under direct, positive voice control. People are required to clean up after their pets. There are 22 metered spaces for beach parking. The cost is a quarter for each 15 minutes.

Coligny Beach Park
Coligny Circle
Hilton Head Island, SC
843-341-4600
This beach has restricted seasons and hours for dogs. During the summertime, from the Friday before Memorial Day through the Tuesday after Labor Day, dogs can only be on the beach before 10am and then after 5pm (they are not allowed from 10am to 5pm). Pets must be leashed. During the off-season and winter months, from April 1 through the Thursday before Memorial Day, dogs must be on a leash between 10am and 5pm. From the Tuesday after Labor Day through September 30, dogs again must be on a leash between 10am and 5pm. At all other times, dogs may be off-leash, but must be under direct, positive voice control. People are required to clean up after their pets. There are 30 metered spaces for beach parking. The cost is a quarter for each 15 minutes. A flat fee of $4 is charged at the parking lot on Fridays through Sundays and holidays.

Folly Field Beach Park
Folly Field Road
Hilton Head Island, SC
843-341-4600
This beach has restricted seasons and hours for dogs. During the summertime, from the Friday before Memorial Day through the Tuesday after Labor Day, dogs can only be on the beach before 10am and then after 5pm (they are not allowed from 10am to 5pm). Pets must be leashed. During the off-season and winter months, from April 1 through the Thursday before Memorial Day, dogs must be on a leash between 10am and 5pm. From the Tuesday after Labor Day through September 30, dogs again must be on a leash between 10am and 5pm. At all other times, dogs may be off-leash, but must be under direct, positive voice control. People are required to clean up after their pets. There are 52 metered spaces for beach parking. The cost is a quarter for each 15 minutes.

Georgia Beaches

St Simons Island

Little St. Simons Island Beaches
off U.S. 17
St Simons Island, GA
912-554-7566
Dogs are allowed, but only during
certain hours in the summer. From
Memorial Day through Labor Day,
dogs are allowed on the beach
before 9:30am and after 4pm. During
the rest of the year, dogs are allowed
anytime during park hours. Dogs
must be on leash and people need to
clean up after their pets.

St. Simons Island Beaches
off U.S. 17
St Simons Island, GA
912-554-7566
Dogs are allowed, but only during
certain hours in the summer. From
Memorial Day through Labor Day,
dogs are allowed on the beach
before 9:30am and after 4pm. During
the rest of the year, dogs are allowed
anytime during park hours. Dogs
must be on leash and people need to
clean up after their pets.

Jekyll Island

Jekyll Island Beaches and Trails
off SR 520
Jekyll Island, GA
877-453-5955
Dogs on leash are welcome year
round on the beach and the paved
and dirt trails. There are about 10
miles of beaches and 20 miles of
inland paved and dirt trails. It is
recommended that your pooch stay
on the paved trails instead of the dirt
trails during the warm summer
months because there are too many
ticks along the dirt trails. On warmer
days you might choose a beach walk
rather than the inland trails anyway
because of the cooler ocean
breezes.

Florida Beaches

Amelia Island

Fernandina City Beach
14th St at the Atlantic Ocean
Fernandina Beach, FL
904-277-7305
The Fernandina City beach allows
dogs on leash. The beach is about
2 miles long. Please make sure that
you pick up after your dog.

Jacksonville

Dogwood Park Lake Bow Wow
7407 Salisbury Rd South
Jacksonville, FL
904-296-3636
This dog park and beach is great for
any size canine. It has 25 acres that
are fenced in a 42 acre park. Dogs
can be off leash in any part of the
park. The park offers picnic tables,
a pond for small dogs, a pond for
large dogs (Lake Bow Wow),
shower for dogs, warm water for
dog baths, tennis balls and toys for
play, a playground with games for
your dogs, trails to walk on, and bag
stations for cleanup. Locals can
become members for the year for
about $24.00 per month or out-of-
town visitors can pay about $11 for
a one time visit.

Huguenot Memorial Park
10980 Hecksher Drive
Jacksonville, FL
904-251-3335
Dogs are allowed in the park and on
the beach. Dogs must be leashed
and people need to clean up after
their dogs. The park is located off
A1A.

Katheryn Abby Hanna Park Beach
500 Wonderland Dr
Jacksonville, FL
904-249-4700
Dogs are allowed in this park for
camping, hiking, picnics and on the
dog friendly beach.

St Augustine

Fort Matanzas National Monument
8635 A1A South
St Augustine, FL
904-471-0116
Dogs on 6 ft leash are allowed in
this National monument. Dogs are
allowed in the park, on the beach,
and on the trails. They are not
allowed in the visitor center, boats,
or fort.

St Augustine Lighthouse and

Museum
81 Lighthouse Avenue
St Augustine, FL
904-829-0745
Dogs on leash are allowed on the
grounds of the lighthouse and beach
area. There are some tables for
picnics or bring a blanket. There is a
fee to enter the lighthouse grounds.

Flagler Beach

Flagler Beach
A1A
Flagler Beach, FL
386-517-2000
Dogs are allowed north of 10th
Street and south of 10th Street. They
are not allowed on or near the pier at
10th Street. Dogs must be on leash
and people need to clean up after
their dogs.

Daytona Beach

Smyrna Dunes Park
Highway 1
New Smyrna Beach, FL
386-424-2935
Dogs are not allowed on the ocean
beach, but are allowed almost
everywhere else, including on the
inlet beach and river. Bottle-nosed
dolphins are typically seen in the
inlet as well as the ocean. Dogs must
be leashed and people need to clean
up after their pets. The park is
located on the north end of New
Smyrna Beach.

Ponce Inlet

Lighthouse Point Park
A1A
Ponce Inlet, FL
386-239-7873
You might see some dolphins along
the shoreline at this park. The park is
also frequented by people watching a
space shuttle launch out of Cape
Canaveral. If you go during a shuttle
launch, be sure to hold on tight to
your pooch, as the shuttles can
become very, very noisy and loud.
Dogs on leash are allowed at the
park and on the beach. Please clean
up after your dog. This park is
located at the southern point of
Ponce Inlet.

Fort Pierce

Fort Pierce Inlet State Park
905 Shorewinds Drive

344

Fort Pierce, FL
772-468-3985
Dogs are not allowed on the ocean beach, but they are allowed on the cove beach. Pets must be leashed and people need to clean up after their pets. The park is located four miles east of Ft. Pierce, via North Causeway.

South Florida

Canine Beach
East End of Sunrise Blvd
Fort Lauderdale, FL
954-761-5346
There is a 100 yard stretch of beach which dogs can use. Dogs must be on leash when they are not in the water. The beach is open to dogs only on Friday, Saturday and Sundays. In winter, the hours are 3 pm - 7 pm and the summer hours are 5 pm - 9 pm. A permit is required to use the canine beach. There are annual permits available for $25 for residents of the city or $40 for non-residents or you can get a one weekend permit for $5.65. Permits can be purchased at Parks and Recreation Department, 1350 W. Broward Boulevard. Call (954) 761-5346 for permit information.

Jupiter Beach
A1A at Xanadu Road
Jupiter, FL

The beach is about 2 miles long. Please follow the dog rules on the beach so that dogs will continue to be allowed here. Dogs must be leashed on the beach. Please clean up after your dog as well.

Hobe Sound National Wildlife Refuge
North Beach Road
Jupiter Island, FL
772-546-6141
This refuge has sea turtle nesting areas and endangered species like the scrub jay and gopher tortoise. Dogs on leash are allowed at the beach. The leash law is enforced and people need to clean up after their pets. The park headquarters is located 2 miles south of SR 708 (Bridge Road) on U.S. 1. The beach is located 1.5 miles north of Bridge Road on North Beach Road.

Miami

Rickenbacker Causeway Beach
Rickenbacker Causeway
Miami, FL

This beach extends the length of the Rickenbacker Causeway from Downtown Miami to Key Biscayne. Dogs are allowed on the entire stretch. There are two types of beach, a Tree lined Dirt beach and a standard type of sandy beach further towards Key Biscayne. Dogs should be leashed on the beach.

Keys

Veteran's Memorial Park
Highway 1
Duck Key, FL
305-872-2411
Dogs on leash are allowed at this park and on the beach. People need to clean up after their pets. The park is located near mile marker 40, off Highway 1.

Anne's Beach
Highway 1
Islamorada, FL

Dog on leash are allowed at this beach. Please clean up after your dog. The beach is located around mile markers 72 to 74. There should be a sign.

Key West

Dog Beach
Vernon Ave and Waddell Ave
Key West, FL

This tiny stretch of beach is the only beach we found in Key West that a dog can go to.

Naples

Delnor-Wiggins Pass State Park
11100 Gulfshore Drive
Naples, FL
239-597-6196
Dogs are not allowed on the beaches in this park, but they can take dip in the water at the boat and canoe launch only. Dogs must be on leash. Please clean up after your dog. This park is located six miles west of Exit 17 on I-75.

Sanibel Island

Algiers Beach
Algiers Lane
Sanibel, FL
239-472-6477

This beach is located in Gulfside City Park. Dogs on leash are allowed and people need to clean up after their pets. Picnic tables and restrooms are available. There is an hourly parking fee. This beach is located about mid-way on the island. From the Sanibel causeway, turn right onto Periwinkle Way. Turn left onto Casa Ybel Rd and then left on Algiers Lane.

Bowman's Beach
Bowman Beach Road
Sanibel, FL
239-472-6477
Walk over a bridge to get to the beach. Dogs on leash are allowed and people need to clean up after their pets. Picnic tables are available. This beach is located on the west side of the island, near Captiva. From the Sanibel causeway, turn right on Periwinkle Way. Turn right on Palm Ridge Rd and then continue on Sanibel-Captiva Road. Turn left onto Bowman's Beach Rd.

Lighthouse Park Beach
Periwinkle Way
Sanibel, FL
239-472-6477
This park offers a long thin stretch of beach. Dogs on leash are allowed and people need to clean up after their pets. Picnic tables are available. This park is located on the east end of the island. From Causeway Road, turn onto Periwinkle Way.

Tarpon Bay Road Beach
Tarpon Bay Road
Sanibel, FL
239-472-6477
Take a short walk from the parking lot to the beach. Dogs on leash are allowed and people need to clean up after their pets. Picnic tables and restrooms are available. There is an hourly parking fee. This beach is located mid-way on the island. From the Sanibel causeway, turn right onto Periwinkle Way. Then turn left onto Tarpon Bay Road.

Fort Myers

Fort Myers Dog Beach
3410 Palm Beach Blvd
Fort Myers Beach, FL
239-461-7400
Dogs are allowed off leash on this section of the beach. Cleanup stations are provided. Must have a copy of health records with you at all times. The beach is run by Lees

County Parks and Recreation.

Lee County Off-Leash Dog Beach Park
Route 865
Fort Myers Beach, FL

Dogs are allowed off-leash at this beach. Please clean up after your dog and stay within the dog park boundaries. Dog Beach is located south of Ft. Myers Beach and north of Bonita Beach on Route 865. Parking is available near New Pass Bridge.

Tampa Bay

De Soto National Memorial Beach Area
PO Box 15390
Bradenton, FL
941-792-0458
Dogs must be on leash and must be cleaned up after in this park. Leashed dogs are allowed in the beach area, which is past a hut following a shell path.

Honeymoon Island State Park
1 Causeway Blvd.
Dunedin, FL
727-469-5942
Dogs on a 6 foot or less leash are allowed on part of the beach. Please ask the rangers for details when you arrive at the park. The park is located at the extreme west end of SR 586, north of Dunedin.

Gandy Bridge Causeway
Gandy Bridge east end
St Petersburg, FL

This stretch of beach allows dogs to run and go swimming. We even saw a horse here. Dogs should be leashed on the beach.

Pinellas Causeway Beach
Pinellas Bayway
St Petersburg, FL

This stretch of beach is open to humans and dogs. Dogs should be on leash on the beach.

Davis Island Dog Park
Severn Ave and Martinique Ave
Tampa, FL

This dog beach is fenced and offers a large parking area and even a doggie shower. To get there go towards Davis Island and head for the Peter Knight Airport. Loop

around until you reach the water (the airport should be on the left). Thanks to one of our readers for the updated information.

Dog Island

Dog Island Park

Dog Island, FL
850-697-2585
This island is a small remote island that is accessible only by boat, ferry or airplane. Dogs are allowed on the beach, but must be on leash. This island is south of Carrabelle.

Carrabelle

Carrabelle Beach
Carrabelle Beach Rd
Carrabelle, FL
850-697-2585
Dogs are allowed on this beach, but the following rules apply. Dogs must be on leash when near sunbathers. In areas where there are no sunbathers, dogs can be off-leash, but must be under direct voice control. Picnic areas and restrooms are available. The beach is located 1.5 miles west of town.

St George Island

Public Access Beaches
Gulf Beach Drive
St George Island, FL

St. George Island beaches have been consistently ranked as one of the top 10 beaches in America. One third of the island is Florida state park land which does not allow dogs. But the rest of the island offers Franklin County public beaches, which do allow dogs on a 6 foot leash or off-leash and under direct voice control.

Port St Joe

Cape San Blas Barrier Dunes

Port St Joe, FL

Dogs are allowed on the beaches off and on (if busy) leash. It is recommended to have health records of your pets. Pet Stations are scattered thru out for cleanup.

Mississippi Beaches

Bay St Louis

Hancock County Beaches
Beach Blvd.
Bay St Louis, MS
228-463-9222
Dogs on leash are allowed on Hancock County beaches. People need to clean up after their pets. The county beaches are located along the coast, between the cities of Waveland and Bay St. Louis.

Louisiana Beaches

Grand Isle

Grand Isle State Park
Admiral Craik Drive
Grand Isle, LA
985-797-2559
Dogs on leash are allowed at the beaches, except for some designated swimming areas. This park offers many recreational opportunities like fishing, crabbing, sunbathing, nature watching and camping. Leashed pets are also allowed at the campsites. The park is located on the east end of Grand Isle, off Highway 1 on Admiral Craik Drive. It is about 2 hours outside of New Orleans.

Texas Beaches

Galveston

Big Reef Nature Park
Boddeker Drive
Galveston, TX
409-765-5023
Take a walkway to the beach which runs parallel to Bolivar Rd. Dogs on leash are allowed on the beach. People need to clean up after their pets. There are no day use fees. This park is part of East Beach which does not allow dogs on the pavilion.

The beach is located on the east end of Galveston Isle, off Boddeker Drive.

Dellanera RV Park
FM 3005 at 7 Mile Rd.
Galveston, TX
409-740-0390
This RV park offers 1,000 feet of sandy beach. Dogs on leash are allowed on the beach and at the RV spaces. People need to clean up after their pets. There are over 60 full RV hookups, over 20 partial hookups and day parking. Picnic tables and restrooms are available at this park. There is a $5 day parking fee. RV spaces are about $25 and up.

Galveston Island State Park
14901 FM 3005
Galveston, TX
409-737-1222
Leashed dogs are allowed on the beach and at the campsites. There is a $3 per person (over 13 years old) day use fee. There is no charge for children 12 and under. The park can be reached from Interstate 45 by exiting right onto 61st Street and traveling south on 61st Street to its intersection with Seawall Boulevard and then right (west) on Seawall (FM 3005) 10 miles to the park entrance.

Stewart Beach
6th and Seawall Boulevard
Galveston, TX
409-765-5023
This is one of the best family beaches in Galveston. Many family-oriented events including a sandcastle competition are held at this beach. Restrooms, umbrella and chair rentals, and volleyball courts are available. There is a $7 per car admission fee. Dogs on leash are allowed on the beach. People need to clean up after their pets. The beach is located at 6th Street and Seawall Blvd.

Cole Park
Ocean Drive
Corpus Christi, TX
800-766-2322
Dogs on leash are allowed on the beach. People need to clean up after their pets.

Padre Island National Seashore
Highway 22
Padre Island, TX

361-949-8068
Visitors to this beach can swim, sunbathe, hunt for shells or just enjoy a walk. About 800,000 visitors per year come to this park. Dogs on leash are allowed on the beach. People need to clean up after their pets. There is a minimal day use fee. The park is located on Padre Island, southeast of Corpus Christi.

South Padre Island

Andy Bowie Park
Park Road 100
South Padre Island, TX
956-761-3704
Dogs on leash are allowed on the beach. People need to clean up after their pets. There is a minimal day use fee. This park is located on the northern end of South Padre Island.

Edwin K. Atwood Park
Park Road 100
South Padre Island, TX
956-761-3704
This beach offers 20 miles of beach driving. Dogs on leash are allowed on the beach. People need to clean up after their pets. There is a minimal day use fee. This park is located almost 1.5 miles north of Andy Bowie Park.

Isla Blanca Park
Park Road 100
South Padre Island, TX
956-761-5493
This popular beach offers about a mile of clean, white beach. Picnic tables, restrooms, and RV spaces are available at this park. Dogs on leash are allowed on the beach. People need to clean up after their pets. There is a minimal day use fee. The park is located on the southern tip of South Padre Island.

Pennsylvania Beaches

Erie

Presque Isle State Park Beach
PA Route 832
Erie, PA
814-833-7424

This state park offers beaches and almost 11 miles of hiking trails. Popular activities at the park include surfing, swimming, boating, hiking, in-line skating and bicycling. Dogs are allowed on a 6 foot or less leash at the park including on the hiking trails and only on beaches that are not guarded by lifeguard staff. Dogs can go into the water, still on leash, but people can only wade in up to their knees since there are no lifeguards in those areas. The unguarded beaches are located throughout the park, but if you want to know exact locations, please stop at the park office for details. The park is located four miles west of downtown Erie, off Route 832.

Ohio Beaches

Geneva-on-the-Lake

Geneva State Park
4499 Padanarum Road
Geneva, OH
440-466-8400
While dogs are cannot go on the swim beach, they can go in the water outside of the designated swim beach. Pets must be leashed and cleaned up after. To get there from Cleveland, take Interstate 90 east to Route 534 north. The park entrance is six miles north on Route 534, on the left.

Lake Erie Island Region

Kelleys Island State Park Beach
Division Street
Kelleys Island, OH
419-746-2546
While pets are not allowed at the small 100 foot swimming beach, they are welcome to join you at the "long beach" but you will need to keep them away from other beachgoers. Pets must be leashed and cleaned up after. To get there you will need to take a ferry to the island. Kelleys Island Ferry Boat Line operates year round, weather permitting, and offers passenger and limited vehicle service from Marblehead, Ohio to the island. Leashed pets are welcome on the ferry. Once on Kelleys Island, go west on E. Lakeshore Drive and turn right on Division Street. The park is at the end of Division Street on the

right.

Catawba Island State Park Beach
4049 East Moores Dock Rd.
Port Clinton, OH
419-797-4530
Swimming is permitted on this small beach but there are no lifeguards. Dogs are welcome at the beach but need to be leashed when not in the water. The park is off of State Route 53.

East Harbor State Park Beach
Route 269
Port Clinton, OH
419-734-4424
While dogs are not allowed on any sandy beach at this park, they can take a dip in the pond which is located off the exit road, next to the shelter road. Pets must be leashed and cleaned up after. To get there from Cleveland, take State Route 2 West to State Route 269 North. The park is located on State Route 269. To get there from Port Clinton, go east on Route 163 to Route 269 north.

Toledo

Maumee Bay State Park Beach
1400 State Park Road
Oregon, OH
419-836-7758
While dogs are not allowed at any beaches at this park, either on the Lake Erie shore or at the park's inland lake, dogs are permitted to take a dip in the water at the end of the inland lake which is on the south side of the road. Pets must be leashed even when in the water, and cleaned up after.

Michigan Beaches

Detroit

Algonac State Park Beach
off I-94
Algonac, MI
810-765-5605
Leashed dogs are allowed on the beach. If they swim in the water, they have to be under your control at all times. Pets need to be attended and cleaned up after. To get there, take I-94 to Exit 243. Drive east about 19 miles to the park.

Burt Lake

Burt Lake State Park Beach
Old 27 Highway
Burt Lake, MI
231-238-9392
This is not a Great Lakes beach, but is conveniently located off of I-75. While dogs are not allowed on the swimming beach, there is a special designated spot where dogs can go into the water. It is near campsite lot number 42, off Road 1, at the west end of the park. The road leads to the beach and dog run. Pets must be on a 6 foot or less leash and attended at all times.

Cheboygan

Aloha State Park Beach
off I-75
Cheboygan, MI
231-625-2522
This is not a Great Lakes beach, but is conveniently located off of I-75. The park has a special pet swimming area which is located by the playground. Pets need to be leashed and cleaned up after. The park is located 7 miles south of Cheboygan and 25 miles from the Mackinac Bridge.

Mackinaw City

Wilderness State Park Beach
Wilderness Park Drive
Mackinaw City, MI
231-436-5381
Dogs are not allowed at the beach but they can swim in the water on the other side of the boat launch. Pets must be a on a 6 foot or less leash and cleaned up after. The park is located 11 miles west of Mackinaw City.

Boyne City

Young State Park Beach
C56 off 131
Boyne City, MI
231-582-7523
While dogs are not allowed on the beach, they can go into the water past the boat launch. There is a sandy and rocky area that leads to the water. Pets must be leashed and attended at all times and cleaned up after.

Empire

Sleeping Bear Dunes National Lakeshore Beaches
off M-72
Empire, MI
231-326-5134
While pets are not allowed in certain areas of the park like the islands, Dune Climb, back-country campsites, or inside buildings, they are allowed on some trails, campgrounds and on the following beaches. Pets are welcome on the the south side of the beach at Esch Road (south of Empire), on the south side of Peterson Beach and on Empire Beach. Dogs must be leashed at all times and cleaned up after. To get there from Traverse City, take M-72 west to Empire.

North Muskegon

Muskegon State Park Beach
Exit M-120 off US 31
North Muskegon, MI
231-744-3480
Dogs are only allowed at the portion of beach where Memorial Drive and Scenic Drive meet. Parking is available on the lake side. Pets must be leashed and cleaned up after.

Stevensville

Grand Mere State Park Beach
Thornton Drive
Stevensville, MI
269-426-4013
Dogs on leash are allowed at the beach and on the hiking trails. The one mile beach is located along the shoreline of Lake Michigan. Remember to clean up after your pet. To get there, take I-94 south of St. Joseph and take Exit 22. Go west .25 miles to Thornton Drive and head south on Thornton for .5 miles.

Indiana Beaches

Porter

Indiana Dunes National Lakeshore
off Highway I-94
Porter, IN
219-926-7561x225
Dogs are not allowed on all of the beaches, but are allowed on two beaches which are located at the far east side of the park. One of the

348

beaches is near Mt. Baldy and the other is near Central Avenue. Check with the visitor center when you arrive for exact locations. Pets are also allowed on some of the trails, campground and picnic area but must be leashed and cleaned up after. The park is located on Lake Michigan. To get there, take Highway 94 east and take Exit 26 Chesterton/49 North and head north.

Illinois Beaches

Chicago

Belmont Harbor Dog Beach located on Belmont Ave off Lake Shore Dr
Chicago, IL

Dogs are allowed in this small fenced beach area on-leash. The city may ticket dog owners whose dogs are off-leash even though it is often used as an off-leash area by some people.

Montrose Harbor Dog Beach
Lake Shore Drive
Chicago, IL
312-742-7529
Dogs are allowed on part of the beach near Montrose. Dogs can run leash-free on the beach. Please note that people who violate the leash law by not having their dog on a leash between the parking lot and the beach are being fined with $75 tickets, so be sure to bring your dog's leash. Beginning in September, 2005 all dogs that use the dog parks are required to have an annual permit. The permits cost $35 for the first dog and $15 for additional dogs. Proof of certain vaccinations are also required.

Wisconsin Beaches

Belgium

Harrington Beach State Park
531 Highway D
Belgium, WI
262-285-3015
Pets are allowed only on part of South Beach. They must be leashed

except while swimming in the water. But once out of the water, they need to be leashed. Pets are also allowed at one of the picnic areas and on all trails except for the nature trail. Please remember to clean up after your pet.

Sheboygan

Kohler-Andrae State Park Beach
1020 Beach Park Lane
Sheboygan, WI
920-451-4080
Pets are not allowed on the swimming beaches but they are allowed only on the beach area north of the nature center. Pets must be on an 8 foot or less leash and cleaned up after. Pets can be off leash only in the water but if one paw hits the sand, he or she must be back on leash or you may get a citation from a park ranger. Dogs are also allowed at certain campsites and on the regular hiking trails but not on nature trails, in the picnic areas or the playground.

Two Rivers

Point Beach State Forest
9400 County Highway O
Two Rivers, WI
920-794-7480
Pets are allowed only on a certain part of the beach, located south of the lighthouse. Dogs must be leashed at all times including on the beach and are not allowed in the picnic areas except for the one near the beach that allows dogs. Pets are also allowed on some of the park trails. Please remember to clean up after your pet.

Door Peninsula

Potawatomi State Park Beach
3740 Park Drive
Sturgeon Bay, WI
920-746-2890
Dogs are allowed on the beach but must be leashed except when in the water. To get there from Green Bay, take Highway 57 north. Go about 37 miles to County Highway PD. Turn north onto Highway PD and go 2.4 miles to the park entrance.

Ashland

Apostle Islands National Lakeshore
Route 1

Bayfield, WI
715-779-3398
You will pretty much need your own boat to access this park and beach as the boat cruise tours do not allow pets. If you do have a boat and can reach the islands, dogs are allowed on the trails, in the back-country campgrounds and on the beaches but must be on a 6 foot or less leash at all times. People need to clean up after their pets.

California Beaches

San Diego

North Beach Dog Run
Ocean Blvd.
Coronado, CA

This dog beach is located in the city of Coronado at the end of Ocean Blvd next to the U.S. Naval Station entrance. Park on the street and walk along the Naval Station fence until you reach the ocean and then bear right. There will be signs posted for the North Beach Dog Run.

La Jolla Shores Beach
Camino Del Oro
La Jolla, CA
619-221-8900
Leashed dogs are allowed on this beach and the adjacent Kellogg Park from 6pm to 9am. The beach is about 1/2 mile long. To get there, take Hwy 5 to the La Jolla Village Drive exit heading west. Turn left onto Torrey Pines Rd. Then turn right onto La Jolla Shores Drive. Go 4-5 blocks and turn left onto Vallecitos. Go straight until you reach the beach and Kellogg Park.

Point La Jolla Beaches
Coast Blvd.
La Jolla, CA
619-221-8900
Leashed dogs are allowed on this beach and the walkway (paved and dirt trails) from 6pm to 9am. The beaches and walkway are at least a 1/2 mile long and might continue further. To get there, exit La Jolla Village Drive West from Hwy 5. Turn left onto Torrey Pines Rd. Turn right on Prospect and then park or turn right onto Coast Blvd. Parking is limited around the village area.

Dog Beach
Point Loma Blvd.
Ocean Beach, CA
619-221-8900
Dogs are allowed to run off leash at this beach anytime during the day. This is a very popular dog beach which attracts lots and lots of dogs on warm days. To get there, take Hwy 8 West until it ends and then it becomes Sunset Cliffs Blvd. Then make a right turn onto Point Loma Blvd and follow the signs to Ocean Beach's Dog Beach.

Ocean Beach
Point Loma Blvd.
Ocean Beach, CA
619-221-8900
Leashed dogs are allowed on this beach from 6pm to 9am. The beach is about 1/2 mile long. To get there, take Hwy 8 West until it ends and then it becomes Sunset Cliffs Blvd. Then make a right turn onto Point Loma Blvd and follow the signs to Ocean Beach Park. A separate beach called Dog Beach is at the north end of this beach which allows dogs to run off-leash.

Fiesta Island
Fiesta Island Road
San Diego, CA
619-221-8900
On this island, dogs are allowed to run off-leash anywhere outside the fenced areas, anytime during the day. It is mostly sand which is perfect for those beach loving hounds. You might, however, want to stay on the north end of the island. The south end was used as the city's sludge area (mud and sediment, and possibly smelly) processing facility. The island is often used to launch jet-skis and motorboats. There is a one-way road that goes around the island and there are no fences, so please make sure your dog stays away from the road. About half way around the island, there is a completely fenced area on the beach. Please note that the fully enclosed area is not a dog park. The city of San Diego informed us that is supposed to be locked and is not intended to be used as a dog park even though there may occasionally be dogs running in this off-limits area.

San Diego County North

Cardiff State Beach
Old Highway 101

Cardiff, CA
760-753-5091
This is a gently sloping sandy beach with warm water. Popular activities include swimming, surfing and beachcombing. Dogs on leash are allowed and please clean up after your pets. The beach is located on Old Highway 101, one mile south of Cardiff.

Del Mar Beach
Seventeenth Street
Del Mar, CA
858-755-1556
Dogs are allowed on the beach as follows. South of 17th Street, dogs are allowed on a 6 foot leash year-round. Between 17th Street and 29th Street, dogs are allowed on a 6 foot leash from October through May (from June through September, dogs are not allowed at all). Between 29th Street and northern city limits, dogs are allowed without a leash, but must be under voice control from October through May (from June through September, dogs must be on a 6 foot leash). Owners must clean up after their dogs.

Rivermouth Beach
Highway 101
Del Mar, CA

This beach allows voice controlled dogs to run leash free from September 15 through June 15 (no specified hours). Leashes are required during mid-summer tourist season from mid June to mid Sept. Fans of this beach are trying to convince the Del Mar City council to extend the leash-free period to year round. The beach is located on Highway 101 just south of Border Avenue at the north end of the City of Del Mar. Thanks to one of our readers for recommending this beach.

Orange County South

Main Beach
Pacific Hwy (Hwy 1)
Laguna Beach, CA
949-497-3311
Dogs are allowed on this beach between 6pm and 8am, June 1 to September 16. The rest of the year, they are allowed on the beach from dawn until dusk. Dogs must be on a leash at all times.

Orange County Beaches

Corona Del Mar State Beach
Iris Street and Ocean Blvd.
Corona Del Mar, CA
949-644-3151
This is a popular beach for swimming, surfing and diving. The sandy beach is about a half mile long. Dogs are allowed on this beach during certain hours. They are allowed before 9am and after 5pm, year round. Pets must be on a 6 foot or less leash. Tickets will be issued if your dog is off leash.

Huntington Dog Beach
Pacific Coast Hwy (Hwy 1)
Huntington Beach, CA
714-841-8644
This beautiful beach is about a mile long and allows dogs from 5 am to 10 pm. Dogs must be under control but may be off leash and owners must pick up after them. Dogs are only allowed on the beach between Golden West Street and Seapoint Ave. Please adhere to these rules as there are only a couple of dog-friendly beaches left in the entire Los Angeles area. The beach is located off the Pacific Coast Hwy (Hwy 1) at Golden West Street. Please remember to pick up after your dog... the city wanted to prohibit dogs in 1997 because of the dog waste left on the beach. But thanks to The Preservation Society of Huntington Dog Beach (http://www.dogbeach.org), it continues to be dog-friendly. City ordinances require owners to pick up after their dogs.

Newport and Balboa Beaches
Balboa Blvd.
Newport Beach, CA
949-644-3211
There are several smaller beaches which run along Balboa Blvd. Dogs are only allowed before 9am and after 5pm, year round. Pets must be on a 6 foot or less leash and are required to clean up after their pets. Tickets will be issued if your dog is off leash. The beaches are located along Balboa Blvd and ample parking is located near the Balboa and Newport Piers.

Long Beach Area

Long Beach Dog Beach Zone
between Roycroft and Argonne Avenues
Long Beach, CA
562-570-3100
This 3 acre off-leash unfenced dog

beach is the only off-leash dog beach in Los Angeles County. It is open daily from 6am until 8pm. It opened on August 1, 2003. The "zone" is 235 yards along the water and 60 yards deep. There is a fresh water fountain called the "Fountain of Woof" which is located near the restrooms at the end of Granada Avenue, near the Dog Zone. Only one dog is allowed per adult and dog owners are entirely responsible for their dog's actions. The beach is located between Roycroft and Argonne avenues in Belmont Shore, Long Beach. It is a few blocks east of the Belmont Pier and Olympic pool. From Ocean Blvd, enter at Bennett Avenue for the beachfront metered parking lot. The cost is 25 cents for each 15 minutes from 8am until 6pm daily. Parking is free after 5pm in the beachfront lot at the end of Granada Avenue. You can check with the website http://www.hautedogs.org for updates and additional rules about the Long Beach Dog Beach Zone.

Malibu

Leo Carrillo State Beach
Hwy 1
Malibu, CA
818-880-0350
This beach is one of the very few dog-friendly beaches in the Los Angeles area. In a press release dated November 27, 2002, the California State Parks clarified the rules for dogs at Leo Carrillo State Beach. We thank the State Parks for this clear announcement of the regulations. Dogs are allowed on a maximum 6 foot leash when accompanied by a person capable of controlling the dog on all beach WEST (up coast) of lifeguard tower 3 at Leo Carrillo State Park, Staircase Beach, County Line Beach, and all Beaches within Point Mugu State Park. Dogs are NOT allowed EAST of lifeguard tower 3 at Leo Carrillo State Beach at any time. And please note that dogs are not allowed in the tide pools at Leo Carrillo. There should be signs posted. A small general store is located on the mountain side of the freeway. Here you can grab some snacks and other items. The park is located on Hwy 1, approximately 30 miles northwest of Santa Monica. We ask that all dog people closely obey these regulations so that the beach continues to be dog-friendly.

Ventura - Oxnard

Hollywood Beach
various addresses
Oxnard, CA

This beach is located on the west side of the Channel Islands Harbor. The beach is 4 miles southwest of Oxnard. Dogs must be on leash and owners must clean up after their pets. Thanks to one of our readers for recommending this beach.

Oxnard Shores Beach
Harbor Blvd.
Oxnard, CA

This beach stretches for miles. If you enter at 5th Street and go north, there are no houses and very few people. Dogs must be on leash and owners must clean up after their pets. Thanks to one of our readers for recommending this beach.

Silverstrand Beach
various addresses
Oxnard, CA

This beach is located between the Channel Islands Harbor and the U.S. Naval Construction Battalion Center. The beach is 4 miles southwest of Oxnard. Dogs must be on leash and owners must clean up after their pets. Thanks to one of our readers for recommending this beach.

Santa Barbara

Goleta Beach County Park
5990 Sandspit Road
Goleta, CA
805-568-2460
Leashed dogs are allowed at this county beach. The beach and park are about 1/2 mile long. There are picnic tables and a children's playground at the park. It's located near the Santa Barbara Municipal Airport in Goleta, just north of Santa Barbara. To get there, take Hwy 101 to Hwy 217 and head west. Before you reach UC Santa Barbara, there will be an exit for Goleta Beach.

Arroyo Burro Beach County Park
2981 Cliff Drive
Santa Barbara, CA
805-967-1300
Leashed dogs are allowed at this

county beach and park. The beach is about 1/2 mile long and it is adjacent to a palm-lined grassy area with picnic tables. To get to the beach from Hwy 101, exit Las Positas Rd/Hwy 225. Head south (towards the ocean). When the street ends, turn right onto Cliff Drive. The beach will be on the left.

Arroyo Burro Off-Leash Beach
Cliff Drive
Santa Barbara, CA

While dogs are not allowed off-leash at the Arroyo Burro Beach County Park (both the beach and grass area), they are allowed to run leash free on the adjacent beach. The dog beach starts east of the slough at Arroyo Burro and stretches almost to the stairs at Mesa Lane. To get to the off-leash area, walk your leashed dog from the parking lot to the beach, turn left and cross the slough. At this point you can remove your dog's leash.

Rincon Park and Beach
Bates Road
Santa Barbara, CA

This beach is at Rincon Point which has some of the best surfing waves in the world. In the winter, it is very popular with surfers. In the summer, it is a popular swimming beach. Year-round, leashed dogs are welcome. The beach is about 1/2-1 mile long. Next to the parking lot there are picnic tables, phones and restrooms. The beach is in Santa Barbara County, about 15-20 minutes south of Santa Barbara. To get there from Santa Barbara, take Hwy 101 south and go past Carpinteria. Take the Bates Rd exit towards the ocean. When the road ends, turn right into the Rincon Park and Beach parking lot.

San Luis Obispo

Cayucos State Beach
Cayucos Drive
Cayucos, CA
805-781-5200
This state beach allows leashed dogs. The beach is located in the small town of Cayucos. To get to the beach from Hwy 1, exit Cayucos Drive and head west. There is a parking lot and parking along the street.

Oceano Dunes State Vehicular

Recreation Area
Highway 1
Oceano, CA
805-473-7220
This 3,600 acre off road area offers 5 1/2 miles of beach which is open for vehicle use. Pets on leash are allowed too. Swimming, surfing, horseback riding and bird watching are all popular activities at the beach. The park is located three miles south of Pismo Beach off Highway 1.

Lake Nacimento Resort Day Use Area
10625 Nacimiento Lake Drive
Paso Robles, CA
805-238-3256
In addition to the campgrounds and RV area, this resort also offers day use of the lake. Dogs can swim in the water, but be very careful of boats, as this is a popular lake for water-skiing. Day use fees vary by season and location, but in general rates are about $5 to $8 per person. Senior discounts are available. Dogs are an extra $5 per day. Proof of your dog's rabies vaccination is required.

Pismo State Beach
Grand Ave.
Pismo Beach, CA
805-489-2684
Leashed dogs are allowed on this state beach. This beach is popular for walking, sunbathing, swimming and the annual winter migration of millions of monarch butterflies (the park has the largest over-wintering colony of monarch butterflies in the U.S.). To get there from Hwy 101, exit 4th Street and head south. In about a mile, turn right onto Grand Ave. You can park along the road.

Coastal Access
off Hearst Drive
San Simeon, CA

There is parking just north of the Best Western Hotel, next to the "Coastal Access" sign. Dogs must be on leash.

Gorda

Kirk Creek Beach and Trailhead
Highway 1
Gorda, CA
831-385-5434
Both the Kirk Creek Beach and hiking trails allow dogs. Pets must be leashed. You can park next to the Kirk Creek Campground and either hike down to the beach or start

hiking at the Kirk Creek Trailhead which leads to the Vicente Flat Trail where you can hike for miles with your dog. The beach and trailhead is part of the Los Padres National Forest and is located about 25 miles south of Big Sur.

Sand Dollar Beach
Highway 1
Gorda, CA
805-434-1996
Walk down a path to one of the longest sandy beaches on the Big Sur Coast. This national forest managed beach is popular for surfing, fishing and walking. Dogs must be on leash and people need to clean up after their pets. There is a minimal day use fee. The dog-friendly Plaskett Creek Campground is within walking distance. This beach is part of the Los Padres National Forest and is located about 5 miles south of the Kirk Creek and about 30 miles south of Big Sur.

Willow Creek Beach
Highway 1
Gorda, CA
831-385-5434
Dogs on leash are allowed at this day use beach and picnic area. The beach is part of the Los Padres National Forest and is located about 35 miles south of Big Sur.

Big Sur

Pfieffer Beach
Sycamore Road
Big Sur, CA
805-968-6640
Dogs on leash are allowed at this day use beach which is located in the Los Padres National Forest. The beach is located in Big Sur, south of the Big Sur Ranger Station. From Big Sur, start heading south on Highway 1 and look carefully for Sycamore Road. Take Sycamore Road just over 2 miles to the beach. There is a $5 entrance fee per car.

Carmel

Carmel City Beach
Ocean Avenue
Carmel, CA
831-624-9423
This beach is within walking distance (about 7 blocks) from the quaint village of Carmel. There are a couple of hotels and several

restaurants that are within walking distance of the beach. Your pooch is allowed to run off-leash as long as he or she is under voice control. To get there, take the Ocean Avenue exit from Hwy 1 and follow Ocean Ave to the end.

Carmel River State Beach
Carmelo Street
Carmel, CA
831-624-9423
This beach is just south of Carmel. It has approximately a mile of beach and leashes are required. It's located on Carmelo Street.

Garrapata State Park
Highway 1
Carmel, CA
831-649-2836
There are two miles of beach front at this park. Dogs are allowed but must be on a 6 foot or less leash and people need to clean up after their pets. The beach is on Highway 1, about 6 1/2 miles south of Rio Road in Carmel. It is about 18 miles north of Big Sur.

Monterey

Monterey Recreation Trail
various (see comments)
Monterey, CA

Take a walk on the Monterey Recreation Trail and experience the beautiful scenery that makes Monterey so famous. This paved trail extends for miles, starting at Fisherman's Wharf and ending in the city of Pacific Grove. Dogs must be leashed. Along the path there are a few small beaches that allow dogs such as the one south of Fisherman's Wharf and another beach behind Ghiradelli Ice Cream on Cannery Row. Along the path you'll find a few more outdoor places to eat near Cannery Row and by the Monterey Bay Aquarium. Look at the Restaurants section for more info.

Monterey State Beach
various (see comments)
Monterey, CA
831-649-2836
Take your water loving and beach loving dog to this awesome beach in Monterey. There are various starting points, but it basically stretches from Hwy 1 and the Del Rey Oaks Exit down to Fisherman's Wharf. Various beaches make up this 2 mile (each way) stretch of beach, but leashed

dogs are allowed on all of them . If you want to extend your walk, you can continue on the paved Monterey Recreation Trail which goes all the way to Pacific Grove. There are a few smaller dog-friendly beaches along the paved trail.

Asilomar State Beach
Along Sunset Drive
Pacific Grove, CA
831-372-4076
Dogs are permitted on leash on the beach and the scenic walking trails. If you walk south along the beach and go across the stream that leads into the ocean, you can take your dog off-leash, but he or she must be under strict voice control and within your sight at all times.

Santa Cruz

Rio Del Mar Beach
Rio Del Mar
Aptos, CA
831-685-6500
Dogs on leash are allowed at this beach which offers a wide strip of sand. From Highway 1, take the Rio Del Mar exit.

Davenport Beach
Hwy 1
Davenport, CA
831-462-8333
This beautiful beach is surrounded by high bluffs and cliff trails. Leashes are required. To get to the beach from Santa Cruz, head north on Hwy 1 for about 10 miles.

Manresa State Beach
San Andreas Road
Manresa, CA
831-761-1795
Surfing and surf fishing are both popular activities at this beach. Dogs are allowed on the beach, but must be leashed. To get there from Aptos, head south on Highway 1. Take San Andreas Road southwest for several miles until you reach Manresa. Upon reaching the coast, you will find the first beach access point.

East Cliff Coast Access Points
East Cliff Drive
Santa Cruz, CA
831-454-7900
There are many small dog-friendly beaches and coastal access points that stretch along East Cliff Drive between 12th Avenue to 41st Avenue. This is not one long beach because the water comes up to cliffs

in certain areas and breaks it up into many smaller beaches. Dogs are allowed on leash. Parking is on city streets along East Cliff or the numbered avenues. To get there from Hwy 17 south, take the Hwy 1 exit south towards Watsonville. Take the exit towards Soquel Drive. Turn left onto Soquel Avenue. Turn right onto 17th Avenue. Continue straight until you reach East Cliff Drive. From here, you can head north or south on East Cliff Drive and park anywhere between 12th and 41st street to access the beaches.

Its Beach
West Cliff Drive
Santa Cruz, CA
831-429-3777
Your dog can go leash free from sunrise to 10am and 4pm until sunset. It is not a large beach, but enough for your water loving dog to take a dip in the water and get lots of sand between his or her paws. According to the sign, dogs are not allowed between 10am and 4pm. It is located on West Cliff Drive, just north of the Lighthouse, and south of Columbia Street. It is also across from the Lighthouse Field off-leash area. To get there, head south on Hwy 17. Take the Hwy 1 North exit, heading towards Half Moon Bay and Hwy 9. Merge onto Mission Street (Hwy 1). Turn left onto Swift Street. Then turn left on West Cliff Drive. The beach and limited parking will be on the right.

Seabright Beach
Seabright Ave
Santa Cruz, CA
831-429-2850
This beach is located south of the Santa Cruz Beach Boardwalk and north of the Santa Cruz Harbor. Dogs are allowed on leash. Fire rings are available for beach bonfires. It is open from sunrise to sunset. To get there from Hwy 17 south, exit Ocean Street on the left towards the beaches. Merge onto Ocean Street. Turn left onto East Cliff Drive and stay straight to go onto Murray Street. Then turn right onto Seabright Ave. Seabright Ave will take you to the beach (near the corner of East Cliff Drive and Seabright).

Twin Lakes State Beach
East Cliff Drive
Santa Cruz, CA
831-429-2850

This beach is one of the area's warmest beaches, due to its location at the entrance of Schwann Lagoon. Dogs are allowed on leash. The beach is located just south of the Santa Cruz Harbor where Aldo's Restaurant is located. Fire rings for beach bonfires, outdoor showers and restrooms are available. It is open from sunrise to sunset. To get there from Hwy 17 south, exit Ocean Street on the left towards beaches. Merge onto Ocean Street. Turn left onto East Cliff Drive and stay straight to go onto Murray Street. Murray Street becomes Eaton Street. Turn right onto 7th Avenue.

Palo Alto - Peninsula

Blufftop Coastal Park
Poplar Street
Half Moon Bay, CA
650-726-8297
Leashed dogs are allowed at this beach. The beach is located on the west end of Poplar Street, off Highway 1.

Montara State Beach
Highway 1
Half Moon Bay, CA
650-726-8819
Dogs on leash are allowed at this beach. Please clean up after your pets. The beach is located 8 miles north of Half Moon Bay on Highway 1. There are two beach access points. The first access point is across from Second Street, immediately south of the Outrigger Restaurant. The second access point is about a 1/2 mile north on the ocean side of Highway 1. Both access points have steep paths down to the beach.

Surfer's Beach
Highway 1
Half Moon Bay, CA
650-726-8297
Dogs on leash are allowed on the beach. It is located at Highway 1 and Coronado Street.

Esplanade Beach
Esplanade
Pacifica, CA
650-738-7381
This beach offers an off-leash area for dogs. To get to the beach, take the stairs at the end of Esplanade. Esplanade is just north of Manor Drive, off Highway 1.

Bean Hollow State Beach
Highway 1
Pescadero, CA
650-879-2170
This is a very rocky beach with not much sand. Dogs are allowed but must be on a 6 foot or less leash. Please clean up after your pets. The beach is located 3 miles south of Pescadero on Highway 1.

San Francisco

Baker Beach
Golden Gate Natl Rec Area
San Francisco, CA

This dog-friendly beach in the Golden Gate National Recreation Area has a great view of the Golden Gate Bridge. The beach is located approx. 1.5 to 2 miles south of the Golden Gate Bridge. From Lincoln Avenue, turn onto Bowley Street and head towards the ocean. There is a parking lot next to the beach.

Fort Funston/Burton Beach
Skyline Blvd./Hwy 35
San Francisco, CA

This is a very popular dog-friendly park and beach. In the past, dogs have been allowed off-leash. However, currently all dogs must be on leash. Fort Funston is part of the Golden Gate National Recreation Area. There are trails that run through the dunes & ice plant from the parking lot above with good access to the beach below. It overlooks the southern end of Ocean Beach, with a large parking area accessible from Skyline Boulevard. There is also a water faucet and trough at the parking lot for thirsty pups. It's located off Skyline Blvd. (also known Hwy 35) by John Muir Drive. It is south of Ocean Beach. Thanks to one of our readers for this info. Expect to see lots and lots of dogs having a great time. But not to worry, there is plenty of room for everyone.

Ocean Beach
Great Hwy
San Francisco, CA
415-556-8642
You'll get a chance to stretch your legs at this beach which has about 4 miles of sand. The beach runs parallel to the Great Highway (north of Fort Funston). There are several access points including Sloat Blvd., Fulton Street or Lincoln Way. This

beach has a mix of off-leash and leash required areas. Thanks to the San Francisco Dog Owners Group (SFDOG) for providing the following information: Dogs must be on leash on Ocean Beach between Sloat Blvd and Stairwell #21 (roughly at Fulton). North of Fulton to the Cliff House and South of Sloat for several miles are still okay for off-leash dogs, however parts of these areas may be impassible at high tide. The Golden Gate National Rec Area (GGNRA) strictly enforces the on-leash area between Sloat and Fulton. They usually give no warning tickets ($50 fine). As with all other leash required areas, we encourage dog owners to comply with the rules.

Marin - North Bay

Doran Regional Park
201 Doran Beach Road
Bodega Bay, CA
707-875-3540
This park offers 2 miles of sandy beach. It is a popular place to picnic, walk, surf, fish and fly kites. Dogs are allowed but must be on a 6 foot or less leash and proof of a rabies vaccination is required. There is a minimal parking fee. The park is located south of Bodega Bay.

Agate Beach
Elm Road
Bolinas, CA
415-499-6387
During low tide, this 6 acre park provides access to almost 2 miles of shoreline. Leashed dogs are allowed.

Muir Beach
Hwy 1
Muir Beach, CA

Dogs on leash are allowed on Muir Beach with you. Please clean up after your dog on the beach. To get to Muir Beach from Hwy 101 take Hwy 1 North from the north side of the Golden Gate Bridge.

Point Reyes National Seashore

Olema, CA
415-464-5100
Leashed dogs (on a 6 foot or less leash) are allowed on four beaches. The dog-friendly beaches are the Limantour Beach, Kehoe Beach, North Beach and South Beach. Dogs are not allowed on the hiking

trails. However, they are allowed on some hiking trails that are adjacent to Point Reyes. For a map of dog-friendly hiking trails, please stop by the Visitor Center. Point Reyes is located about an hour north of San Francisco. From Highway 101, exit at Sir Francis Drake Highway, and continue west on Sir Francis Drake to Olema. To find the Visitor Center, turn right in Olema onto Route 1 and then make a left onto Bear Valley Road. The Visitor Center will be on the left.

Upton Beach
Highway 1
Stinson Beach, CA
415-499-6387
Dogs not allowed on the National Park section of Stinson Beach but are allowed at Upton Beach which is under Marin County's jurisdiction. This beach is located north of the National Park. Dogs are permitted without leash but under direct and immediate control.

Gualala

Gualala Point Regional Park Beach
42401 Coast Highway 1
Gualala, CA
707-565-2041
This county park offers sandy beaches, hiking trails, campsites, picnic tables and restrooms. Dogs are allowed on the beach, on the trails, and in the campground, but they must be on a 6 foot or less leash. People also need to clean up after their pets. There is a $3 day use fee.

Mendocino

MacKerricher State Park
Highway 1
Fort Bragg, CA
707-964-9112
Dogs are allowed on the beach, but not on any park trails. Pets must be leashed and people need to clean up after their pets. Picnic areas, restrooms and campsites (including an ADA restroom and campsites), are available at this park. The park is located three miles north of Fort Bragg on Highway 1, near the town of Cleone.

Big River Beach
N. Big River Road
Mendocino, CA
707-937-5804
This small beach is located just

south of downtown Mendocino. There are two ways to get there. One way is to head south of town on Hwy 1 and turn left on N. Big River Rd. The beach will be on the right. The second way is to take Hwy 1 and exit Main Street/Jackson heading towards the coastline. In about 1/4-1/2 mile there will be a Chevron Gas Station and a historic church on the left. Park and then walk behind the church to the trailhead. Follow the trail, bearing left when appropriate, and there will be a wooden staircase that goes down to Big River Beach. Dogs must be on leash.

Van Damme State Beach
Highway 1
Mendocino, CA

This small beach is located in the town of Little River which is approximately 2 miles south of Mendocino. It is part of Van Damme State Park which is located across Highway 1. Most California State Parks, including this one, do not allow dogs on the hiking trails. Fortunately this one allows dogs on the beach. There is no parking fee at the beach and dogs must be on leash.

Westport

Westport-Union Landing State Beach
Highway 1
Westport, CA
707-937-5804
This park offers about 2 miles of sandy beach. Dogs must be on a 6 foot or less leash at all times and people need to clean up after their pets. Picnic tables, restrooms (including an ADA restroom) and campsites are available at this park. Dogs are also allowed at the campsites, but not on any park trails. The park is located off Highway 1, about 2 miles north of Westport or 19 miles north of Fort Bragg.

Eureka

Samoa Dunes Recreation Area
New Navy Base Road
Samoa, CA
707-825-2300
The Bureau of Land Management oversees this 300 acre sand dune park. It is a popular spot for off-highway vehicles which can use about 140 of the park's acres. Dogs are allowed on leash or off-leash but under voice control. Even if your dog

runs off-leash, the park service requests that you still bring a leash just in case. To get there, take Highway 255 and turn south on New Navy Base Road. Go about four miles to the parking area.

Arcata

Mad River Beach County Park
Mad River Road
Arcata, CA
707-445-7651
Enjoy walking or jogging for several miles on this beach. Dogs on leash are allowed. The park is located about 4-5 miles north of Arcata. To get there, take Highway 101 and exit Giuntoli Lane. Then go north onto Heindon Rd. Turn left onto Miller Rd. Turn right on Mad River Road and follow it to the park.

Clam Beach County Park
Highway 101
McKinleyville, CA
707-445-7651
This beach is popular for fishing, swimming, picnicking and beachcombing. Of course, there are also plenty of clams. Dogs on leash are allowed on the beach and at the campgrounds. There are no day use fees. The park is located off Highway 101, about eight miles north of Arcata.

Trinidad

Trinidad State Beach
Highway 101
Trinidad, CA
707-677-3570
Dogs are unofficially allowed at College Cove beach, as long as they are leashed and under control. The residents in this area are trying keep this beach dog-friendly, but the rules can change at any time. Please call ahead to verify.

Redwood National and State Parks

Gold Bluffs Beach
Davison Road
Orick, CA
707-464-6101
Dogs are allowed on this beach, but not on any trails within this park. Picnic tables and campgrounds are available at the beach. Pets are also allowed at road accessible picnic areas and campgrounds. Dogs must be on a 6 foot or less

leash and people need to pick up after their pets. The beach is located off Highway 101. Take Highway 101 heading north. Pass Orick and drive about 3-4 miles, then exit Davison Rd. Head towards the coast on an unpaved road (trailers are not allowed on the unpaved road).

Crescent City

Beachfront Park
Front Street
Crescent City, CA
707-464-9507
Dogs are allowed at park and the beach, but must be leashed. Please clean up after your pets. To get there, take Highway 101 to Front Street. Follow Front Street to the park.

Crescent Beach
Enderts Beach Road
Crescent City, CA
707-464-6101
While dogs are not allowed on any trails in Redwood National Park, they are allowed on a couple of beaches, including Crescent Beach. Enjoy beachcombing or bird watching at this beach. Pets are also allowed at road accessible picnic areas and campgrounds. Dogs must be on a 6 foot or less leash and people need to pick up after their pets. The beach is located off Highway 101, about 3 to 4 miles south of Crescent City. Exit Enderts Beach Road and head south.

Oregon Beaches

Brookings

Harris Beach State Park
Highway 101
Brookings, OR
541-469-2021
The park offers sandy beaches for beachcombing, whale watching, and sunset viewing. Picnic tables, restrooms (including an ADA

restroom) and shaded campsites are available at this park. There is a minimal day use fee. Leashed dogs are allowed on the beach. Dogs are also allowed at the campgrounds. They must be on a six foot or less leash at all times and people are required to clean up after their pets. On beaches located outside of Oregon State Park boundaries, dogs might be allowed off-leash and under direct voice control, please look for signs or postings. This park is located off U.S. Highway 101, just north of Brookings.

McVay Rock State Recreation Site
Highway 101
Brookings, OR
800-551-6949
This beach is a popular spot for clamming, whale watching and walking. Picnic tables and restrooms are available at this park. There are no day use fees. Dogs are allowed on the beach. They must be on a six foot or less leash at all times and people are required to clean up after their pets. On beaches located outside of Oregon State Park boundaries, dogs might be allowed off-leash and under direct voice control, please look for signs or postings. This park is located off U.S. Highway 101, just south of Brookings.

Samuel H. Boardman State Scenic Corridor
Highway 101
Brookings, OR
800-551-6949
Steep coastline at this 12 mile long corridor is interrupted by small sandy beaches. Picnic tables, restrooms (including an ADA restroom), and a hiking trail are available at this park. There are no day use fees. Leashed dogs are allowed on the beach. Dogs are also allowed on the hiking trail. They must be on a six foot or less leash at all times and people are required to clean up after their pets. On beaches located outside of Oregon State Park boundaries, dogs might be allowed off-leash and under direct voice control, please look for signs or postings. This park is located off U.S. Highway 101, 4 miles north of Brookings.

Gold Beach

Pistol River State Scenic Viewpoint
Highway 101
Gold Beach, OR
800-551-6949
This beach is popular for ocean windsurfing. There has even been windsurfing national championships held at this beach. Picnic tables and restrooms are available here. There are no day use fees. Dogs are allowed on the beach. They must be on a six foot or less leash at all times and people are required to clean up after their pets. On beaches located outside of Oregon State Park boundaries, dogs might be allowed off-leash and under direct voice control, please look for signs or postings. This park is located off U.S. Highway 101, 11 miles south of Gold Beach.

Port Orford

Cape Blanco State Park
Highway 101
Port Orford, OR
541-332-6774
Take a stroll on the beach or hike on over eight miles of trails which offer spectacular ocean vistas. Picnic tables, restrooms, hiking and campgrounds are available at this park. There is a minimal day use fee. Leashed dogs are allowed on the beach. Dogs are also allowed on hiking trails and campgrounds. They must be on a six foot or less leash at all times and people are required to clean up after their pets. On beaches located outside of Oregon State Park boundaries, dogs might be allowed off-leash and under direct voice control, please look for signs or postings. This park is located off U.S. Highway 101, 9 miles north of Port Orford.

Humbug Mountain State Park
Highway 101
Port Orford, OR
541-332-6774
This beach is frequented by windsurfers and scuba divers. A popular activity at this park is hiking to the top of Humbug Mountain (elevation 1,756 feet) . Picnic tables, restrooms, hiking and campgrounds are available at this park. There is a minimal day use fee. Leashed dogs are allowed on the beach. Dogs are also allowed on hiking trails and campgrounds. They must be on a six foot or less leash at all times and people are required to clean up after their pets. On beaches located outside of Oregon State Park boundaries, dogs might be allowed off-leash and under direct voice control, please look for signs or postings. This park

is located off U.S. Highway 101, 6 miles south of Port Orford.

Bandon

Bullards Beach State Park
Highway 101
Bandon, OR
541-347-2209
Enjoy a walk along the beach at this park. Picnic tables, restrooms, hiking and campgrounds are available at the park. There is a minimal day use fees. Leashed dogs are allowed on the beach. Dogs are also allowed on hiking trails and campgrounds. They must be on a six foot or less leash at all times and people are required to clean up after their pets. On beaches located outside of Oregon State Park boundaries, dogs might be allowed off-leash and under direct voice control, please look for signs or postings. This park is located off U.S. Highway 101, 2 miles north of Bandon.

Seven Devils State Recreation Site
Highway 101
Bandon, OR
800-551-6949
Enjoy several miles of beach at this park. Picnic tables are available at this park. There are no day use fees. Dogs are allowed on the beach. They must be on a six foot or less leash at all times and people are required to clean up after their pets. On beaches located outside of Oregon State Park boundaries, dogs might be allowed off-leash and under direct voice control, please look for signs or postings. This park is located off U.S. Highway 101, 10 miles north of Bandon.

Coos Bay

Sunset Bay State Park
Highway 101
Coos Bay, OR
541-888-4902
This park offers sandy beaches protected by towering sea cliffs. The campgrounds located at the park are within a short walk to the beach. You will also find a network of hiking trails here and in two adjacent parks. Picnic tables and restrooms (including an ADA restroom) are available at this park. There is a minimal day use fee. Leashed dogs are allowed on the beach. Dogs are also allowed on hiking trails and campgrounds. They must be on a six foot or less leash at all times and

people are required to clean up after their pets. On beaches located outside of Oregon State Park boundaries, dogs might be allowed off-leash and under direct voice control, please look for signs or postings. This park is located off U.S. Highway 101, 12 miles southwest of Coos Bay.

Florence

Carl G. Washburne Memorial State Park
Highway 101
Florence, OR
541-547-3416
This park offers five miles of sandy beach. Picnic tables, restrooms, hiking and campgrounds are available at this park. There is a day use fee. Leashed dogs are allowed on the beach. Dogs are also allowed on hiking trails and campgrounds. They must be on a six foot or less leash at all times and people are required to clean up after their pets. On beaches located outside of Oregon State Park boundaries, dogs might be allowed off-leash and under direct voice control, please look for signs or postings. This park is located off U.S. Highway 101, 14 miles north of Florence.

Heceta Head Lighthouse State Scenic Viewpoint
Highway 101
Florence, OR
800-551-6949
Go for a walk above the beach or explore the natural caves and tidepools and relax. This is a great spot for whale watching. According to the Oregon State Parks Division, the lighthouse located on the west side of 1,000-foot-high Heceta Head (205 feet above ocean) is one of the most photographed on the Oregon coast. Picnic tables, restrooms and hiking are available at this park. There is a $3 day use fee. Leashed dogs are allowed on the beach. Dogs are also allowed on hiking trails. They must be on a six foot or less leash at all times and people are required to clean up after their pets. On beaches located outside of Oregon State Park boundaries, dogs might be allowed off-leash and under direct voice control, please look for signs or postings. This park is located off U.S. Highway 101, 13 miles north of Florence.

Yachats

Neptune State Scenic Viewpoint
Highway 101
Yachats, OR
800-551-6949
During low tide at this beach you can walk south and visit a natural cave and tidepools. Or sit and relax at one of the picnic tables that overlooks the beach below. Restrooms (including an ADA restroom) are available at this park. There are no day use fees. Dogs are allowed on the beach. They must be on a six foot or less leash at all times and people are required to clean up after their pets. On beaches located outside of Oregon State Park boundaries, dogs might be allowed off-leash and under direct voice control, please look for signs or postings. This park is located off U.S. Highway 101,

Yachats State Recreation Area
Highway 101
Yachats, OR
800-551-6949
This beach is a popular spot for whale watching, salmon fishing, and exploring tidepools. Picnic tables and restrooms are available at this park. There are no day use fees. Dogs are allowed on the beach. They must be on a six foot or less leash at all times and people are required to clean up after their pets. On beaches located outside of Oregon State Park boundaries, dogs might be allowed off-leash and under direct voice control, please look for signs or postings. This park is located off U.S. Highway 101 in Yachats.

Waldport

Beachside State Recreation Site
Highway 101
Waldport, OR
541-563-3220
Enjoy miles of broad sandy beach at this park or stay at one of the campground sites that are located just seconds from the beach. Picnic tables, restrooms (including an ADA restroom), and hiking are also available at this park. There is a day use fees. Leashed dogs are allowed on the beach. Dogs are also allowed on hiking trails and campgrounds. They must be on a six foot or less leash at all times and people are required to clean up after their pets. On beaches located

outside of Oregon State Park boundaries, dogs might be allowed off-leash and under direct voice control, please look for signs or postings. This park is located off U.S. Highway 101, 4 miles south of Waldport.

Governor Patterson Memorial State Recreation Site
Highway 101
Waldport, OR
800-551-6949
This park offers miles of flat, sandy beach. It is also an excellent location for whale watching. Picnic tables and restrooms are available at this park. There are no day use fees. Dogs are allowed on the beach. They must be on a six foot or less leash at all times and people are required to clean up after their pets. On beaches located outside of Oregon State Park boundaries, dogs might be allowed off-leash and under direct voice control, please look for signs or postings. This park is located off U.S. Highway 101, 1 mile south of Waldport.

Newport

Agate Beach State Recreation Site
Highway 101
Newport, OR
800-551-6949
This beach is popular with surfers. Walk through a tunnel to get to the beach. According to the Oregon State Parks Division, many years ago Newport farmers led cattle westward through the tunnel to the ocean salt. Picnic tables and restrooms are available at this park. There is no day use fees. Dogs are allowed on the beach. They must be on a six foot or less leash at all times and people are required to clean up after their pets. On beaches located outside of Oregon State Park boundaries, dogs might be allowed off-leash and under direct voice control, please look for signs or postings. This park is located off U.S. Highway 101, 1 mile north of Newport.

Beverly Beach State Park
Highway 101
Newport, OR
541-265-9278
To get to the beach, there is a walkway underneath the highway that leads to the ocean. Picnic tables, restrooms (including an ADA restroom), a walking trail and campgrounds are available at this

park. There is a day use fee. Leashed dogs are allowed on the beach. Dogs are also allowed on the walking trail and campgrounds. They must be on a six foot or less leash at all times and people are required to clean up after their pets. On beaches located outside of Oregon State Park boundaries, dogs might be allowed off-leash and under direct voice control, please look for signs or postings. This park is located off U.S. Highway 101, 7 miles north of Newport.

Devils Punch Bowl State Natural Area
Highway 101
Newport, OR
800-551-6949
This is a popular beach for surfing. Picnic tables, restrooms and hiking are available at this park. There are no day use fees. Leashed dogs are allowed on the beach. Dogs are also allowed on hiking trails. They must be on a six foot or less leash at all times and people are required to clean up after their pets. On beaches located outside of Oregon State Park boundaries, dogs might be allowed off-leash and under direct voice control, please look for signs or postings. This park is located off U.S. Highway 101, 8 miles north of Newport.

South Beach State Park
Highway 101
Newport, OR
541-867-4715
This beach offers many recreational opportunities like beachcombing, fishing, windsurfing and crabbing. Picnic tables, restrooms (including an ADA restroom), hiking (including an ADA hiking trail), and campgrounds are available at this park. There is a day use fee. Leashed dogs are allowed on the beach. Dogs are also allowed on hiking trails and campgrounds. They must be on a six foot or less leash at all times and people are required to clean up after their pets. On beaches located outside of Oregon State Park boundaries, dogs might be allowed off-leash and under direct voice control, please look for signs or postings. This park is located off U.S. Highway 101, 2 miles south of Newport.

Depoe Bay

Fogarty Creek State Recreation Area

Highway 101
Depoe Bay, OR
800-551-6949
This beach and park offer some of the best birdwatching and tidepooling. Picnic tables and hiking are available at this park. There is a $3 day use fees. Leashed dogs are allowed on the beach. Dogs are also allowed on hiking trails. They must be on a six foot or less leash at all times and people are required to clean up after their pets. On beaches located outside of Oregon State Park boundaries, dogs might be allowed off-leash and under direct voice control, please look for signs or postings. This park is located off U.S. Highway 101, 2 miles north of Depoe Bay.

Lincoln City

D River State Recreation Site
Highway 101
Lincoln City, OR
800-551-6949
This beach, located right off the highway, is a popular and typically windy beach. According to the Oregon State Parks Division, this park is home to a pair of the world's largest kite festivals every spring and fall which gives Lincoln City the name Kite Capital of the World. Restrooms are available at the park. Dogs are allowed on the beach. They must be on a six foot or less leash at all times and people are required to clean up after their pets. On beaches located outside of Oregon State Park boundaries, dogs might be allowed off-leash and under direct voice control, please look for signs or postings. This park is located off U.S. Highway 101 in Lincoln City.

Roads End State Recreation Site
Highway 101
Lincoln City, OR
800-551-6949
There is a short trail here that leads down to the beach. Picnic tables are available at this park. There are no day use fees. Dogs are allowed on the beach. They must be on a six foot or less leash at all times and people are required to clean up after their pets. On beaches located outside of Oregon State Park boundaries, dogs might be allowed off-leash and under direct voice control, please look for signs or postings. This park is located off U.S. Highway 101, 1 mile north of Lincoln City.

Neskowin

Neskowin Beach State Recreation Site
Highway 101
Neskowin, OR
800-551-6949
Not really any facilities (picnic tables, etc.) here, but a good place to enjoy the beach. Dogs are allowed on the beach. Dogs are allowed on the beach. They must be on a six foot or less leash at all times and people are required to clean up after their pets. On beaches located outside of Oregon State Park boundaries, dogs might be allowed off-leash and under direct voice control, please look for signs or postings. This park is located off U.S. Highway 101 in Neskowin.

Pacific City

Bob Straub State Park
Highway 101
Pacific City, OR
800-551-6949
This is a nice stretch of beach to walk along. Picnic tables and restrooms (including an ADA restroom) are available at this park. There are no day use fees. Dogs are allowed on the beach. They must be on a six foot or less leash at all times and people are required to clean up after their pets. On beaches located outside of Oregon State Park boundaries, dogs might be allowed off-leash and under direct voice control, please look for signs or postings. This park is located off U.S. Highway 101 in Pacific City.

Cape Kiwanda State Natural Area
Highway 101
Pacific City, OR
800-551-6949
This beach and park is a good spot for marine mammal watching, hang gliding and kite flying. Picnic tables are available at this park. There are no day use fees. Dogs are allowed on the beach. They must be on a six foot or less leash at all times and people are required to clean up after their pets. On beaches located outside of Oregon State Park boundaries, dogs might be allowed off-leash and under direct voice control, please look for signs or postings. This park is located off U.S. Highway 101, 1 mile north of Pacific City.

Tillamook

Cape Lookout State Park
Highway 101
Tillamook, OR
503-842-4981
This is a popular beach during the summer. The beach is a short distance from the parking area. It is located about an hour and half west of Portland. Picnic tables, restrooms (including an ADA restroom), hiking trails and campgrounds are available at this park. There is a $3 day use fee. Leashed dogs are allowed on the beach. Dogs are also allowed on hiking trails and campgrounds. They must be on a six foot or less leash at all times and people are required to clean up after their pets. On beaches located outside of Oregon State Park boundaries, dogs might be allowed off-leash and under direct voice control, please look for signs or postings. This park is located off U.S. Highway 101, 12 miles southwest of Tillamook.

Cape Meares State Scenic Viewpoint
Highway 101
Tillamook, OR
800-551-6949
The beach is located south of the scenic viewpoint. The viewpoint is situated on a headland, about 200 feet above the ocean. According to the Oregon State Parks Division, bird watchers can view the largest colony of nesting common murres (this site is one of the most populous colonies of nesting sea birds on the continent. Bald eagles and a peregrine falcon have also been known to nest near here. In winter and spring, this park is an excellent location for viewing whale migrations. Picnic tables, restrooms and hiking are available at this park. There are no day use fees. Leashed dogs are allowed on the beach. Dogs are also allowed on hiking trails. They must be on a six foot or less leash at all times and people are required to clean up after their pets. On beaches located outside of Oregon State Park boundaries, dogs might be allowed off-leash and under direct voice control, please look for signs or postings. This park is located off U.S. Highway 101, 10 miles west of Tillamook.

Rockaway Beach

Manhattan Beach State Recreation Site
Highway 101
Rockaway Beach, OR

800-551-6949
The beach is a short walk from the parking area. Picnic tables are available at this park. There are no day use fees. Dogs are allowed on the beach. They must be on a six foot or less leash at all times and people are required to clean up after their pets. On beaches located outside of Oregon State Park boundaries, dogs might be allowed off-leash and under direct voice control, please look for signs or postings. This park is located off U.S. Highway 101, 2 miles north of Rockaway Beach.

Manzanita

Nehalem Bay State Park
Highway 101
Manzanita, OR
503-368-5154
The beach can be reached by a short walk over the dunes. This park is a popular place for fishing and crabbing. Picnic tables, restrooms (including an ADA restroom), hiking and camping are available at this park. There is a $3 day use fee. Leashed dogs are allowed on the beach. Dogs are also allowed on hiking trails and campgrounds. They must be on a six foot or less leash at all times and people are required to clean up after their pets. On beaches located outside of Oregon State Park boundaries, dogs might be allowed off-leash and under direct voice control, please look for signs or postings. This park is located off U.S. Highway 101, 3 miles south of Manzanita Junction.

Oswald West State Park
Highway 101
Manzanita, OR
800-551-6949
The beach is located just a quarter of a mile from the parking areas. It is a popular beach that is frequented by windsurfers and boogie boarders. Picnic tables, restrooms, hiking, and campgrounds are available at this park. There are no day use fees. Leashed dogs are allowed on the beach. Dogs are also allowed on hiking trails and campgrounds. They must be on a six foot or less leash at all times and people are required to clean up after their pets. On beaches located outside of Oregon State Park boundaries, dogs might be allowed off-leash and under direct voice control, please

look for signs or postings. This park is located off U.S. Highway 101, 10 miles south of Cannon Beach.

Cannon Beach

Arcadia Beach State Recreation Site
Highway 101
Cannon Beach, OR
800-551-6949
This sandy ocean beach is just a few feet from where you can park your car. Picnic tables and restrooms are available at this park. There are no day use fees. Dogs are allowed on the beach. They must be on a six foot or less leash at all times and people are required to clean up after their pets. On beaches located outside of Oregon State Park boundaries, dogs might be allowed off-leash and under direct voice control, please look for signs or postings. This park is located off U.S. Highway 101, 3 miles south of Cannon Beach.

Ecola State Park
Highway 101
Cannon Beach, OR
503-436-2844
According to the Oregon State Parks Division, this park is one of the most photographed locations in Oregon. To reach the beach, you will need to walk down a trail. Restrooms, hiking and primitive campgrounds are available at this park. There is a $3 day use fee. Leashed dogs are allowed on the beach. Dogs are also allowed on hiking trails and campgrounds. They must be on a six foot or less leash at all times and people are required to clean up after their pets. On beaches located outside of Oregon State Park boundaries, dogs might be allowed off-leash and under direct voice control, please look for signs or postings. This park is located off U.S. Highway 101, 2 miles north of Cannon Beach.

Hug Point State Recreation Site
Highway 101
Cannon Beach, OR
800-551-6949
According to the Oregon State Parks Division, people used to travel via stagecoach along this beach before the highway was built. Today you can walk along the original trail which was carved into the point by stagecoaches. The trail is located north of the parking area. Visitors can also explore two caves around

the point, but be aware of high tide. Some people have become stranded at high tide when exploring the point! This beach is easily accessible from the parking area. Picnic tables and restrooms are available at this park. There are no day use fees. Dogs are allowed on the beach. They must be on a six foot or less leash at all times and people are required to clean up after their pets. On beaches located outside of Oregon State Park boundaries, dogs might be allowed off-leash and under direct voice control, please look for signs or postings. This park is located off U.S. Highway 101, 5 miles south of Cannon Beach.

Tolovana Beach State Recreation Site
Highway 101
Cannon Beach, OR
800-551-6949
Indian Beach is popular with surfers. There is a short walk down to the beach. Picnic tables are available at this park. There are no day fees. Dogs are allowed on the beach. They must be on a six foot or less leash at all times and people are required to clean up after their pets. On beaches located outside of Oregon State Park boundaries, dogs might be allowed off-leash and under direct voice control, please look for signs or postings. This park is located off U.S. Highway 101, 1 mile south of Cannon Beach.

Seaside

Del Rey Beach State Recreation Site
Highway 101
Seaside, OR
800-551-6949
There is a short trail to the beach. There is no day use fee. Dogs are allowed on the beach. They must be on a six foot or less leash at all times and people are required to clean up after their pets. On beaches located outside of Oregon State Park boundaries, dogs might be allowed off-leash and under direct voice control, please look for signs or postings. This park is located off U.S. Highway 101, 2 miles north of Gearhart.

Warrenton

Fort Stevens State Park
Highway 101
Warrenton, OR

503-861-1671
There are miles of ocean beach. Picnic tables, restrooms (including an ADA restroom), hiking and campgrounds are available at this park. There is a $3 day use fee. Leashed dogs are allowed on the beach. Dogs are also allowed on hiking trails and campgrounds. They must be on a six foot or less leash at all times and people are required to clean up after their pets. On beaches located outside of Oregon State Park boundaries, dogs might be allowed off-leash and under direct voice control, please look for signs or postings. This park is located off U.S. Highway 101, 10 miles west of Astoria.

Washington Beaches

Ilwaco

Fort Canby State Park
Highway 101
Ilwaco, WA
360-902-8844
This park offers 27 miles of ocean beach and 7 miles of hiking trails. Enjoy excellent views of the ocean, Columbia River and two lighthouses. Picnic tables, restrooms (including an ADA restroom), hiking and campgrounds (includes ADA campsites) are available at this park. Leashed dogs are allowed on the beach. Dogs are also allowed on hiking trails and campgrounds. They must be on a eight foot or less leash at all times and people are required to clean up after their pets. This park is located two miles southwest of Ilwaco. From Seattle, Take I-5 south to Olympia, SR 8 west to Montesano. From there, take U.S. Hwy. 101 south to Long Beach Peninsula.

Ocean Park

Pacific Pines State Park
Highway 101
Ocean Park, WA
360-902-8844
Fishing, crabbing, clamming and beachcombing are popular activities at this beach. Picnic tables and a restroom are available at this park. Dogs are allowed on the beach.

They must be on a eight foot or less leash at all times and people are required to clean up after their pets. This park is located approximately one mile north of Ocean Park. From north or south, take Hwy. 101 until you reach Ocean Park. Continue on Vernon St. until you reach 271st St.

Grayland

Grayland Beach State Park
Highway 105
Grayland, WA
360-902-8844
This 412 acre park offers beautiful ocean frontage and full hookup campsites (including ADA campsites). Leashed dogs are allowed on the beach. Dogs are also allowed at the campgrounds. They must be on a eight foot or less leash at all times and people are required to clean up after their pets. This park is located five miles south of Westport. From Aberdeen, drive 22 miles on Highway 105 south to Grayland. Traveling through the town, watch for park signs.

Westport

Twin Harbors State Park
Highway 105
Westport, WA
360-902-8844
This beach is popular for beachcombing, bird watching, and fishing. Picnic tables, restrooms (including an ADA restroom), and campgrounds (includes ADA campgrounds) are available at this park. Leashed dogs are allowed on the beach. Dogs are also allowed at the campgrounds. They must be on a eight foot or less leash at all times and people are required to clean up after their pets. This park is located three miles south of Westport on Highway 105. From Aberdeen,

Westport Light State Park
Ocean Avenue
Westport, WA
360-902-8844
Enjoy the panoramic view at this park or take the easy access trail to the beach. Swimming in the ocean here is not advised because of variable currents or rip tides. Picnic tables, restrooms (including an ADA restroom), and a 1.3 mile paved trail (also an ADA trail) are available at this park. Leashed dogs are allowed on the beach. Dogs are also allowed on the paved trail. They must be on a

eight foot or less leash at all times and people are required to clean up after their pets. This park is located on the Pacific Ocean at Westport, 22 miles southwest of Aberdeen. To get there from Westport, drive west on Ocean Ave. about one mile to park entrance.

Ocean Shores

Damon Point State Park
Point Brown Avenue
Ocean Shores, WA
360-902-8844
Located on the southeastern tip of the Ocean Shores Peninsula, this one mile long beach offers views of the Olympic Mountains, Mount Rainer, and Grays Harbor. Picnic tables are available at this park. Dogs are allowed on the beach. They must be on a eight foot or less leash at all times and people are required to clean up after their pets. To get there from From Hoquiam, take SR 109 and SR 115 to Point Brown Ave. in the town of Ocean Shores. Proceed south on Point Brown Ave. through town, approximately 4.5 miles. Just past the marina, turn left into park entrance.

Ocean City State Park
State Route 115
Ocean Shores, WA
360-902-8844
Beachcombing, clamming, surfing, bird watching, kite flying and winter storm watching are all popular activites at this beach. Picnic tables, restrooms, and campgrounds (including ADA campgrounds) are available at this park. Leashed dogs are allowed on the beach. Dogs are also allowed at the campgrounds. They must be on a eight foot or less leash at all times and people are required to clean up after their pets. This park is located on the coast one-and-a-half miles north of Ocean Shores on Hwy. 115. From Hoquiam, drive 16 miles west on SR 109, then turn south on SR 115 and drive 1.2 miles to the park.

Copalis Beach

Griffith-Priday State Park
State Route 109
Copalis Beach, WA
360-902-8844
This beach extends from the beach through low dunes to a river and then north to the river's mouth. Picnic tables and restrooms are available at

this park. Dogs are allowed on the beach. They must be on a eight foot or less leash at all times and people are required to clean up after their pets. This park is located 21 miles northwest of Hoquiam. From Hoquiam, go north on SR 109 for 21 miles. At Copalis Beach, at the sign for Benner Rd., turn left (west).

Pacific Beach

Pacific Beach State Park
State Route 109
Pacific Beach, WA
360-902-8844
The beach is the focal point at this 10 acre state park. This sandy ocean beach is great for beachcombing, wildlife watching, windy walks and kite flying. Picnic tables, restrooms (including an ADA restroom), and campgrounds (some are ADA accessible) are available at this park. Leashed dogs are allowed on the beach. Dogs are also allowed in the campgrounds. They must be on a eight foot or less leash at all times and people are required to clean up after their pets. This park is located 15 miles north of Ocean Shores, off SR 109. From Hoquiam, follow SR 109, 30 miles northwest to the town of Pacific Beach. The park is located in town.

Port Angeles

Kalaloch Beach
Olympic National Park
Port Angeles, WA
360-962-2283
Dogs are allowed on leash, during daytime hours only, on Kalaloch Beach along the Pacific Ocean and from Rialto Beach north to Ellen Creek. These beaches are in Olympic National Park, but please note that pets are not permitted on this national park's trails, meadows, beaches (except Kalaloch and Rialto beaches) or in any undeveloped area of the park. For those folks and dogs who want to hike on a trail, try the adjacent dog-friendly Olympic National Forest. Kalaloch Beach is located off Highway 101 in Olympic National Park.

Federal Way

Dash Point State Park
Dash Point Rd.
Federal Way, WA

360-902-8844
This beach offers great views of Puget Sound. Picnic tables, restrooms, 11 miles of hiking trails and campgrounds are available at this park. Leashed dogs are allowed on the beach. Pets are not permitted on designated swimming beaches. However, there is usually a non-designated swimming beach area as well. Dogs are also allowed on hiking trails and campgrounds. They must be on a eight foot or less leash at all times and people are required to clean up after their pets. This park is located on the west side of Federal Way in the vicinity of Seattle. From Highway 5, exit at the 320th St. exit (exit #143). Take 320th St. west approximately four miles. When 320th St. ends at a T-intersection, make a right onto 47th St. When 47th St. ends at a T-intersection, turn left onto Hwy. 509/ Dash Point Rd. Drive about two miles to the park. (West side of street is the campground side, and east side is the day-use area.)

Des Moines

Saltwater State Park
Marine View Drive
Des Moines, WA
360-902-8844
This state beach is located on Puget Sound, halfway between the cities of Tacoma and Seattle (near the Sea-Tac international airport). Picnic tables, restrooms and campgrounds are available at this park. Leashed dogs are allowed on the beach. Pets are not permitted on designated swimming beaches. However, there is usually a non-designated swimming beach area as well. Dogs are also allowed at the campgrounds. They must be on a eight foot or less leash at all times and people are required to clean up after their pets. To get there from the north, take exit #149 off of I-5. Go west, then turn south on Hwy. 99 (sign missing). Follow the signs into the park. Turn right on 240th at the Midway Drive-in. Turn left on Marine View Dr. and turn right into the park.

Seattle

Sand Point Magnuson Park Dog Off-Leash Beach and Area
7400 Sand Point Way NE
Seattle, WA
206-684-4075
This leash free dog park covers

about 9 acres and is the biggest fully fenced off-leash park in Seattle. It also offers an access point to the lake where your pooch is welcome to take a dip in the fresh lake water. To find the dog park, take Sand Point Way Northeast and enter the park at Northeast 74th Street. Go straight and park near the playground and sports fields. The main gate to the off-leash area is located at the southeast corner of the main parking lot. Dogs must be leashed until you enter the off-leash area.

Bainbridge Island

Fay Bainbridge State Park
Sunset Drive NE
Bainbridge Island, WA
360-902-8844
This park is located on the northeast side of Bainbridge Island on Puget Sound. On a clear day, you can see Mt. Rainier and Mt. Baker from the beach. Picnic tables, restrooms and campgrounds are available at this park. Leashed dogs are allowed on the beach. Pets are not permitted on designated swimming beaches. However, there is usually a non-designated swimming beach area as well. Dogs are also allowed at the campgrounds. They must be on a eight foot or less leash at all times and people are required to clean up after their pets. To get there from From Poulsbo, take Hwy. 305 toward Bainbridge Island. Cross the Agate Pass Bridge. After three miles, come to stoplight and big brown sign with directions to park. Turn left at traffic light onto Day Rd. NE. Travel approximately two miles to a T-intersection. Turn left onto Sunrise Drive NE, and continue to park entrance, about two miles away.

Oak Harbor

Fort Ebey State Park
Hill Valley Drive
Oak Harbor, WA
360-902-8844
This 600+ acre park is popular for hiking and camping, but also offers a saltwater beach. Picnic tables and restrooms (including an ADA restroom) are available at this park. Leashed dogs are allowed on the saltwater beach. Dogs are also allowed on hiking trails and campgrounds. They must be on a eight foot or less leash at all times and people are required to clean up after their pets. To get to the park

from Seattle, take exit #189 off of I-5, just south of Everett. Follow signs for the Mukilteo/ Clinton ferry. Take the ferry to Clinton on Whidbey Island. Dogs are allowed on the ferry. Once on Whidbey Island, follow Hwy. 525 north, which becomes Hwy. 20. Two miles north of Coupeville, turn left on Libbey Rd. and follow it 1.5 miles to Hill Valley Dr. Turn left and enter park.

Joseph Whidbey State Park
Swantown Rd
Oak Harbor, WA
360-902-8844
This 112 acre park offers one of the best beaches on Whidbey Island. Picnic tables, restrooms, and several miles of hiking trails (including a half mile ADA hiking trail) are available at this park. Leashed dogs are allowed on the beach. Pets are not permitted on designated swimming beaches. However, there is usually a non-designated swimming beach area as well. Dogs are also allowed on hiking trails. They must be on a eight foot or less leash at all times and people are required to clean up after their pets. To get there from the south, drive north on Hwy. 20. Just before Oak Harbor, turn left on Swantown Rd. and follow it about three miles.

San Juan Island

South Beach
125 Spring Street
Friday Harbor, WA
360-378-2902
Dogs on leash are allowed at South Beach, which is located at the American Camp in the San Juan Island National Historic Park.

Lopez Island

Spencer Spit State Park
Bakerview Road
Lopez Island, WA
360-902-8844
Located in the San Juan Islands, this lagoon beach offers great crabbing, clamming and beachcombing. Picnic tables, restrooms, campgrounds and 2 miles of hiking trails are available at this park. Leashed dogs are allowed on the beach. Pets are not permitted on designated swimming beaches. However, there is usually a non-designated swimming beach area as well. Dogs are also allowed

on hiking trails and campgrounds. They must be on a eight foot or less leash at all times and people are required to clean up after their pets. This park is located on Lopez Island in the San Juan Islands. It is a 45-minute Washington State Ferry ride from Anacortes. Dogs are allowed on the ferry. Once on Lopez Island, follow Ferry Rd. Go left at Center Rd., then left at Cross Rd. Turn right at Port Stanley and left at Bakerview Rd. Follow Bakerview Rd. straight into park. For ferry rates and schedules, call 206-464-6400.

Blaine

Birch Bay State Park
Grandview
Blaine, WA
360-902-8844
This beach, located near the Canadian border, offers panoramic coastal views. Picnic tables, restrooms (including an ADA restroom), and campgrounds (including ADA campsites) are available at this park. Leashed dogs are allowed on the beach. Pets are not permitted on designated swimming beaches. However, there is usually a non-designated swimming beach area as well. Dogs are also allowed in the campgrounds. They must be on a eight foot or less leash at all times and people are required to clean up after their pets. This park is located 20 miles north of Bellingham and ten miles south of Blaine. From the south take exit #266 off of I-5. Go left on Grandview for seven miles, then right on Jackson for one mile, then turn left onto Helweg. From the north take exit #266 off of I-5, and turn right onto Grandview.

British Columbia Beaches

Vancouver

Spanish Banks West
NW Marine Drive
Vancouver, BC
604-257-8400

This beach allows dogs off-leash. Dogs are allowed from 6am to 10pm. People are required to clean up after their dogs. The beach is located off NW Marine Drive, at the entrance to Pacific Spirit Park.

Sunset Beach
off Beach Avenue
Vancouver, BC
604-257-8400
This bay beach allows dogs off-leash. Dogs are allowed from 6am to 10pm. People are required to clean up after their dogs. The beach is located near Beach Avenue, under the Burrard Bridge. It is behind the Aquatic Centre east of the ferry dock.

Vanier Park
Chestnut
Vancouver, BC
604-257-8400
This beach allows dogs off-leash. Dogs are allowed from 6am to 10am and then from 5pm to 10pm. People are required to clean up after their dogs. The beach is located on Chestnut at English Bay.

Victoria

Beacon Hill Park Off-Leash Beach
Dallas Road
Victoria, BC
250-385-5711
Dogs are allowed off-leash at the gravel beach in Beacon Hill Park. People are required to clean up after their dogs. The beach is located in downtown Victoria, along Dallas Road, between Douglas Street and Cook Street.

Chapter 4

Off-Leash Dog Parks

Arizona Dog Parks

Flagstaff

Thorpe Park Bark Park
191 N. Thorpe Road
Flagstaff, AZ
928-779-7690
This 1.5 acre dog park is double-gated and has benches, picnic tables, and a water fountain.

Lake Havasu City

Lions Dog Park
1340 McCulloch Blvd.
Lake Havasu City, AZ
928-453-8686
This dog park is located with the London Bridge Beach park. The grassy off-leash area is completely fenced and offers a water feature, hydrants, benches, and shade. Dogs are not allowed along the Bridgewater Channel, parking lots or other areas of London Bridge Beach. Dogs must be on leash when outside the off-leash area.

Phoenix

Desert Vista Off-Leash Dog Park
11800 North Desert Vista
Fountain Hills, AZ
480-816-5152
This 12 acre park offers a dog park for off-leash romping. The area is fully fenced with multi-station watering fountains and shade structures. Paws in the Park, an annual dog festival, is held at this park. The park is located on Saguaro Blvd., between Tower Drive and Desert Vista. To get there, head east on Shea Blvd. Turn left onto Saguaro Blvd. Go 1.5 miles and turn right onto Desert Vista. Turn left immediately onto Saguaro Blvd. Go about .2 miles and then turn right onto Tower Drive. The park is on the right. Thanks to ADOG (Association of Dog Owners Group) for the directions. The hours are from sunrise to sunset.

Pecos Park Dog Park
48th Street
Phoenix, AZ
602-262-6862
This two acre dog park is fully fenced with double-gates and a separate area for small and large dogs. Pecos Park is located at 48th Street and Pecos Parkway. Enter from 48th Street via Chandlers Blvd. The dog park is located at the southeast corner of the park.

PetsMart Dog Park
21st Avenue
Phoenix, AZ
602-262-6971
This fully fenced dog park has over 2.5 grassy acres. Amenities include a water fountain and two watering stations for dogs, benches, bag dispensers and garbage cans. This off-leash park is located in Washington Park on 21st Avenue north of Maryland (between Bethany Home and Glendale roads).

Phoenix Area

Saguaro Ranch Dog Park
63rd Avenue
Glendale, AZ

This fully fenced dog park has a large grassy area with trees, fire hydrants, benches and even a doggie drinking fountain. The park is located at 63rd Avenue and Mountain View Road. The off-leash area is just north of the west parking lot and just south of the softball complex. Thanks to one of our readers for recommending this dog park!

Quail Run Park Dog Park
4155 E. Virginia
Mesa, AZ
480-644-2352
This park offers a completely fenced 3 acre dog park. Amenities include separate areas for timid and active dogs, park benches, water fountains for people and dogs, and doggie poop bags. The dog park is closed every Thursday for maintenance. Dogs must be on leash when outside the off-leash area.

Chaparral Park Dog Park
5401 N. Hayden Road
Scottsdale, AZ
480-312-2353
This park offers a two acre fenced designated off-leash area for dogs. The temporary off-leash area is on Hayden Road, north of Jackrabbit. The permanent dog park will be located on the southeast corner of Hayden and McDonald Drives after the water treatment facility is completed. Dogs must be on leash when outside the dog park.

Horizon Park Dog Park
15444 N. 100th Street
Scottsdale, AZ
480-312-2650
This park offers a designated off-leash area for dogs. The park is located at 100th Street and Thompson Peak. Dogs must be on leash when outside the off-leash area.

Vista del Camino Park Dog Park
7700 E. Roosevelt Street
Scottsdale, AZ
480-312-2330
This park offers a designated off-leash area for dogs. The park is located at Hayden and Roosevelt. Dogs must be on leash when outside the off-leash area.

Creamery Park
8th Street and Una Avenue
Tempe, AZ
480-350-5200
This park offers a designated off-leash area for dogs. Dogs must be on leash when outside the off-leash area.

Jaycee Park
5th Street and Hardy Drive
Tempe, AZ
480-350-5200
This park offers a small designated off-leash area for dogs. Dogs must be on leash when outside the off-leash area.

Mitchell Park
Mitchell Drive and 9th Street
Tempe, AZ
480-350-5200
This park offers a designated off-leash area for dogs. Dogs must be on leash when outside the off-leash area.

Papago Park
Curry Road and College Avenue
Tempe, AZ
480-350-5200
This park offers a designated off-leash area for dogs. Dogs must be on leash when outside the off-leash area.

Prescott

Willow Creek Dog Park
Willow Creek Road
Prescott, AZ
928-777-1100
This completely fenced dog park

offers a separate section for small and large dogs. Amenities include picnic tables, benches, water and shade. The dog park is located next to Willow Creek Park. The park is located just north of the junction of Willow Lake and Willow Creek Roads.

Tucson

Gene C. Reid Park Off-Leash Area
900 S. Randolph Way
Tucson, AZ
520-791-3204
This park offers a designated off-leash area. It is located across from the Reid Park Zoo entrance on a converted Little League field. The one acre dog park is lighted and fenced. Amenities include water, picnic tables, trees, and a separate area for small and large dogs. Dog park hours are from 7am to 9pm. Dogs must be on leash when outside the off-leash area.

McDonald District Park Off-Leash Area
4100 N. Harrison Road
Tucson, AZ
520-877-6000
This park offers a designated off-leash area. Dogs must be on leash when outside the off-leash area.

Palo Verde Park Off-Leash Area
300 S. Mann Avenue
Tucson, AZ
520-791-4873
This park offers a designated off-leash area. Amenities of this fenced and double-gated dog park include doggie drinking fountains, picnic tables and pooper scooper dispensers. Dogs must be on leash when outside the off-leash area. The park is located at 300 S. Mann Avenue, south of Broadway, west of Kolb, and directly between Langley and Mann Avenues.

California
Dog Parks

Beach Area

Redondo Beach Dog Park
Flagler Lane

Redondo Beach, CA
310-378-8555
This dog park is located next to Dominguez Park. Local dogs and vacationing dogs are welcome at the dog park. There is a separate section for small dogs and big dogs. It is completely fenced and has pooper scooper bags available.

Memorial Park
1401 Olympic Blvd
Santa Monica, CA
310-450-1121
There is an off-leash dog run located in this park.

Westminster Dog Park
1234 Pacific Ave
Venice, CA
310-392-5566
Thanks to one of our readers who writes: "Spacious (half a block in size), clean (mulched) dog run in dog-friendly Venice.

Fresno

Woodward Park Dog Park
E. Audubon Drive
Fresno, CA

Thanks to one of our readers who writes "Woodward Park now has a wonderful, enclosed area built specifically for dogs to play off-leash. It is located inside the park area and contains toys, water bowls and plastic bags."

Lincoln

Lincoln Dog Park
Third Street
Lincoln, CA
916-624-6808
The amenities at this dog park include 2.5 fenced acres for dogs to run off-leash, potable water, handicap accessible, parking, and limited seating. The park is open from dawn to dusk and is closed Wednesdays until 12pm. To get there, take Highway 65 (City of Lincoln) to Third Street. Go west on Third Street 1.8 miles to Santa Clara (just past the big oak tree).

Long Beach Area

Recreation Park Dog Park
7th St & Federation Dr
Long Beach, CA
562-570-3100
Licensed dogs over four months are

allowed to run leash-free in this area by the casting pond. As usual with all dog parks, owners are responsible for their dogs and must supervise them at all times. The Recreation Park Dog Park is located off 7th Street and Federation Drive behind the Casting Pond. It is open daily until 10 p.m. Thanks to one of our readers for recommending this park.

Los Angeles

Griffith Park Dog Park
North 200 Drive
Los Angeles, CA
323-913-7390
This dog park is located 1/2 mile west of the 134 Fwy.

Laurel Canyon Park
8260 Mulholland Dr.
Los Angeles, CA

This nice dog park is located in the hills of Studio City. It is completely fenced with water and even a hot dog stand. The on-leash hours are 10am-3pm and off-leash hours are 6am to10am and 3pm to dusk. To get there, take Laurel Canyon Blvd and go west on Mulholland Blvd. Go about a 1/4 mile and turn left. There is a parking lot below.

Silverlake Dog Park
2000 West Silverlake Blvd.
Los Angeles, CA

This is one of the best dog parks in the Los Angeles area and it usually averages 30-40 dogs. It is located at approximately 2000 West Silverlake Blvd. It's on the south side of the reservoir in Silverlake, which is between Hollywood and downtown L.A. between Sunset Blvd. and the 5 Freeway. The easiest way to get there is to take the 101 Freeway to Silverlake Blvd. and go east. Be careful about street parking because they ticket in some areas. Thanks to one of our readers for recommending this dog park.

Marin - North Bay

Rocky Memorial Dog Park
W. Casa Grande Road
Petaluma, CA
707-778-4380
Your dog can run leash-free in this 9 acre fenced dog park. To get there, take Lakeville Hwy. (Hwy 116) east,

and turn west on Casa Grande Rd.

Sausalito Dog Park
Bridgeway and Ebbtide Avenues
Sausalito, CA

This fenced dog park is 1.3 acres complete with lighting, picnic tables, benches, a dog drinking water area, and a scooper cleaning station. On some days, this very popular park has over 300 dogs per day.

Napa Valley

Canine Commons Dog Park
Alston Park - Dry Creek Road
Napa, CA
707-257-9529
This fenced 3 acre dog park has water, benches, and pooper scoopers. The dog park is located in Alston Park which has about 100 acres of dog-friendly on-leash trails. Thanks to one of our readers for recommending this park. To get there from Napa, take Hwy 29 North and exit Redwood Rd. Turn left on Redwood Rd and then right on Dry Creek Rd. The park will be on the left.

Shurtleff Park Dog Park
Shetler Avenue
Napa, CA
707-257-9529
This park offers an off-leash exercise area. Dogs must be under voice control at all times. The park is located on Shetler Avenue, east of Shurtleff Avenue.

Oakland - East Bay

Ohlone Dog Park
Hearst Avenue
Berkeley, CA

This is a relatively small dog park. At certain times, there can be lots of dogs here. The hours are 6am-10pm on weekdays and 9am-10pm on weekends. The park is located at Hearst Ave, just west of Martin Luther King Jr. Way. There is limited street parking.

Central Park Dog Park
Stevenson Blvd
Fremont, CA
510-494-4800
Thanks to one of our readers who writes: "Fenced, fresh water on demand, plenty of free parking, easy to find, all grass." The park. located

on one acre, is adjacent to the Central Park Softball Complex with access off of Stevenson Blvd.

Livermore Canine Park
Murdell Lane
Livermore, CA

This dog park is located in Max Baer Park. It has several trees and a lawn. To get there from downtown Livermore, head west on Stanely Blvd. Turn left on Isabel Ave. Then turn left onto Concannon Blvd (if you reach Alden Ln, you've passed Concannon). Turn left on Murdell Lane and the park will be on the right.

Point Isabel Regional Shoreline
Isabel Street
Richmond, CA
510-562-PARK
The park has rules which state "dogs, except pit bulls, may be taken off leash." This 20 plus acre park is a dog park that is not completely fenced, but has paved paths, grass and beach access to the bay. If your pooch likes chasing birds, beware... dogs sometimes run over to the bird sanctuary which is close to the freeway. Other activities at this park include bay fishing, jogging and running trails, birdwatching, kite flying and picnicking. Thanks to one of our readers for providing us with this great information. From I-80 (the Eastshore Freeway) in Richmond, take Central Avenue west to Point Isabel, adjacent to the U.S. Postal Service Bulk Mail Center.

Orange County Beaches

Bark Park Dog Park
Arlington Dr
Costa Mesa, CA
949-73-4101
Located in TeWinkle Park, this two acre dog park is fully fenced. It is open from 7am until dusk every day except for Tuesday, which is clean-up day. The park is located near the Orange County Fairgrounds on Arlington Drive, between Junipero Drive and Newport Blvd.

Huntington Beach Dog Park
Edwards Street
Huntington Beach, CA
949-536-5672
This dog park has a small dog run for pups under 25 pounds and a separate dog run for the larger pooches. It's been open since 1995 and donations are always welcome.

They have a coin meter at the entrance. The money is used to keep the park maintained and for doggie waste bags. If you want to go for a walk with your leashed pup afterwards, there many walking trails at the adjacent Huntington Central Park.

Orange County South

Central Bark
6405 Oak Canyon
Irvine, CA
949-724-7740
Thanks to one of our readers who writes: "Irvine's dog park is open daily from 6:30 am to 9 pm, closed Wednesdays." The dog park is located next to the shelter.

Laguna Beach Dog Park
Laguna Canyon Rd
Laguna Beach, CA

This dog park, known by the locals as Bark Park, is open six days a week and closed on Wednesdays for clean-up. The park is open from dawn to dusk.

Laguna Niguel Pooch Park
Golden Latern
Laguna Niguel, CA

This fully enclosed dog park is located in the city of Laguna Niguel, which is between Laguna Beach and Dana Point. The park is operated by the City of Laguna Niguel's Parks and Recreation Department. It is located on Golden Latern, next to fire station 49. From the Pacific Coast Highway in Dana Point, go up Goldern Latern about 2 miles. Thanks to one of our readers for this information.

Palm Springs

Palm Springs Dog Park
222 Civic Dr North
Palm Springs, CA
760-322-8362
This fenced dog park is complete with green grass, trees, and fire hydrants. The dog park is on 1.6 acres. It's located at 222 Civic Drive North behind City Hall.

Palo Alto - Peninsula

City of Belmont Dog Park
2525 Buena Vista Avenue

Belmont, CA
650-365-3524
This dog park is located at the Cipriani Elementary School.

Bayside Park Dog Park
1125 South Airport Blvd
Burlingame, CA
650-558-7300
This dog park is over 570 feet long. It is in the back of the parking area and then you have to walk about 1/8 mile down a path to the off-leash dog park.

Foster City Dog Run
Foster City Blvd at Bounty
Foster City, CA

There is a separate dog area for small dogs and large dogs at this off leash dog park.

Coastside Dog Park
Wavecrest Road
Half Moon Bay, CA
650-726-8297
This public off-leash dog park is supported by citizen volunteers. The dog park is located at Smith Field, at the western end of Wavecrest Road.

Mountain View Dog Park
Shoreline Blvd at North Rd
Mountain View, CA

This fenced, off leash dog park is located across from Shoreline Ampitheatre at the entrance to Shoreline Park. Dogs are not allowed in Shoreline Park itself.

Hoover Park
2901 Cowper St
Palo Alto, CA
650-329-2261
This is a small off leash dog exercise area. Dogs on leash are allowed in the rest of the park.

Mitchell Park/Dog Run
3800 Middlefield Rd
Palo Alto, CA
650-329-2261
Located in Mitchell Park at 3800 Middlefield Rd (between E. Charleston and E. Meadow) Note: It can be tough to find at first. The dog run is closer to E. Charleston by the baseball fields and over a small hill.

Shores Dog Park
Radio Road
Redwood City, CA

This dog park (opened Nov/Dec 98) was funded by Redwood City residents. To get there from Hwy

101, take Holly/Redwood Shores Parkway Exit. Go east (Redwood Shore Parkway). Turn right on Radio Road (this is almost at the end of the street). The park will be on the right. Thanks to one of our readers for this information.

Sandburg Fields/San Bruno Dog Park
Maywood
San Bruno, CA
650-877-8868
This park offers a fully enclosed dog run located next to two baseball diamonds. The dog park is located at Maywood and Evergreen, behind the Hoover Children's Center.

Heather Dog Exercise Area
2757 Melendy Drive
San Carlos, CA
650-802-4382
This 1.5 acre park offers a small area where dogs can run off-leash as well as an on-leash hiking trail. Access the park through the Heather School parking lot.

Pomona - Ontario

Pooch Park
100 S. College Avenue
Claremont, CA

This park has lots of grass and trees and a ravine for the dogs to climb up and down. There is a 3 foot fence around the park. The Pooch Park is located in College Park, just south of the Metrolink tracks on S. College Avenue.

Riverside

Butterfield Park Dog Park
1886 Butterfield Drive
Corona, CA
909-736-2241
This .8 acre fenced off-leash dog area is located in Butterfield Park. The dog park is well-shaded with benches, a picnic table and a doggie drinking fountain. From the 91 Freeway, take the Maple Street exit and go north. Maple will dead end at Smith Street. Go left on Smith Street about .5 miles to Butterfield Drive. Then turn left to Butterfield Park just across the street from the airport. Thanks to one of our readers for recommending this dog park.

Riverside Off-Leash Area
Mission Inn Ave

Riverside, CA
909-715-3440
This dog park is located near the river. It is also near Mt. Rubidoux Park, which is a good place for hiking before or after your visit to the dog park. To get to the dog park, take the 91 freeway to Mission Inn St. and go west through downtown Riverside past Market St. The park is on the south side just after you cross a large bridge but before you get to the riverbed. Thanks to one of our readers for recommending this dog park.

Sacramento

Carmichael Park and Dog Park
Fair Oaks Blvd & Grant Ave
Carmichael, CA
916-485-5322
This is a one acre off leash dog park. It is located in Carmichael Park which can be accessed from Fair Oaks Blvd in Carmichael. The rest of the park is nice for picnics and other activities. Dogs must be leashed when not inside the dog park.

Marco Dog Park
1800 Sierra Gardens Drive
Roseville, CA
916-774-5950
RDOG (Roseville Dog Owners Group) helped to establish this 2 acre dog park which is Roseville's first off-leash dog park. This park was named Marco Dog Park in memory of a Roseville Police Department canine named Marco who was killed in the line of duty. The park has a large grassy area with a few trees and doggie fire hydrants. It is closed on Wednesdays from dawn until 3:30pm for weekly maintenance. Like other dog parks, it may also be closed some days during the winter due to mud. To get there from Hwy 80, exit Douglas Blvd. heading east. Go about 1/2 mile and turn left on Sierra Gardens Drive. Marco Dog Park will be on the right.

Bannon Creek Dog Park
Bannon Creek Drive near West El Camino
Sacramento, CA
916-264-5200
This off leash dog park is in Bannon Creek Park. Its hours are 5am to 10 pm daily. The park is 0.6 acres in size.

Granite Park Dog Park
Ramona Avenue near Power Inn Rd
Sacramento, CA

916-264-5200
This dog park is in Granite Regional Park. Its hours are 5 am to 10 pm daily. It is 2 acres in size.

Howe Dog Park
2201 Cottage Way
Sacramento, CA
916-927-3802
Howe Dog Park is completely fenced and located in Howe Park. It has grass and several trees. To get there, take Business Route 80 and exit El Camino Ave. Head east on El Camino Ave. Turn right on Howe Ave. Howe Park will be on the left. Turn left onto Cottage Way and park in the lot. From the parking lot, the dog park is located to the right of the tennis courts.

Partner Park Dog Park
5699 South Land Park Drive
Sacramento, CA
916-264-5200
This dog park is located behind the Bell Cooledge Community Center. The park is 2.5 acres and its hours are 5 am to 10 pm daily. There are lights at the park.

San Bernardino

Wildwood Dog Park
536 E. 40th St
San Bernardino, CA

Thanks to one of our readers who writes: "We have 3.5 acres divided into 2 large areas & 1 smaller area just for little and older dogs. The larger areas are rotated to help reduce wear & tear on the turf. Amenities include: Fencing, Benches, Handicapped Access, Lighting, Parking, Poop Bags, Restrooms, Shelter, Trash Cans, Water Available. Current Shots & License Required. We are also double-gated for Safety."

San Diego

Harry Griffen Park
9550 Milden Street
La Mesa, CA
619-667-1307
Thanks to one of our readers who writes: "A leash-free dog area - very nice area of the park and no restrictions on dog size."

Dusty Rhodes Dog Park
Sunset Cliffs Blvd.

Ocean Beach, CA
619-236-5555
This dog park is located in Dusty Rhodes Neighborhood Park. The park is on Sunset Cliffs Blvd. between Nimitz and West Point Loma.

Balboa Park Dog Run
Balboa Dr
San Diego, CA
619-235-1100
The dog-friendly Balboa Park has set aside a portion of land for an off leash dog run. It's not fenced, so make sure your pup listens to voice commands. It is located between Balboa Drive and Hwy 163.

San Diego County North

Encinitas Park
D Street
Encinitas, CA

Thanks to one of our readers who recommends the following two dog parks in Encinitas Park. Encinitas Viewpoint Park, on "D" Street at Cornish Drive, off-leash dogs permitted 6:00-7:30 AM and 4:00-6:00 PM on MWF only. Other days of the week, dogs must be on leash. Orpheus Park, on Orpheus Avenue at Union Street, off-leash dogs permitted 6:00-7:30 AM and 4:00-6:00 PM on MWF only. Other days of the week, dogs must be on leash.

San Diego I-15 Corridor

Mayflower Dog Park
3420 Valley Center Road
Escondido, CA

Mayflower Dog Park is a 1.5 acre fenced area for off-leash dog play.

San Fernando Valley

Sepulveda Basin Dog Park
17550 Victory Blvd.
Encino, CA

This is a large and nice 5 acre off-leash dog park with separate sections for big dogs and little dogs. Features include parking for 100 cars, an on-leash picnic area and public phones. The park is open daily - sunrise to sunset (except on Fridays, 11am to sunset). It isadjacent to Balboa Park in Encino. Park heading south on Victory, just past White Oak. To get there from

Hwy 101, exit White Oak and head north. Then turn right on Victory and the park will be on the right.

San Francisco

Golden Gate Park Dog Run
Fulton Street
San Francisco, CA

This dog run is completely fenced in and has water bowls for thirsty dogs.Located at 38th Ave & Fulton Street.

Mountain Lake Park
8th Avenue
San Francisco, CA

Dogs can run off leash in the designated dog park. The park is near Lake Street and 8th Avenue.

San Jose

City of Milpitas Dog Park
3100 Calveras Blvd.
Milpitas, CA
408-262-6980
This dog park has separate sections for small and large dogs. The dog park is run by the City of Milpitas, but it is located at Ed Levin County Park. The dog park is located off Calaveras Blvd. Turn onto Downing Road and head toward Sandy Wool Lake. Go uphill by the lake until you come to the dog park.

Ed Levin County Park
3100 Calveras Blvd.
Milpitas, CA
408-262-6980
Dogs are allowed on the Bay Area Ridge Trail from Sandy Wool Lake to Mission Peak. They are not allowed on any other trails in the park. Dogs must be leashed, except when in the off-leash dog park.

Hellyer Park/Dog Run
Hellyer Ave
San Jose, CA
408-225-0225
This two acre dog park has a nice lawn and is completely fenced. It is closed Wednesdays for maintenance. The dog park is located at the northeast end of Hellyer Park, near the Shadowbluff group area. There is a minimal fee for parking. To get there, take Hwy 101 to Hellyer Ave. Exit and head west on Hellyer. Continue straight,

pay at the booth and drive to the parking lot where the dog park is located.

Miyuki Dog Park
Santa Teresa Boulevard
San Jose, CA
408-277-4573
This dog park is almost one half acre. There is a rack where dog owners can leave spare toys for other pups to use. All dogs that use this off-leash park must wear a current dog license and proof of the rabies vaccine. The park is open from sunrise to one hour after sunset.

Watson Dog Park
East Jackson and 22nd St.
San Jose, CA
408-277-4661
This dog park opened in August of 2003 and offers a nice grassy area complete with benches. It also has a special puppy and older dog area. Thanks to one of our readers for recommending this park.

Santa Clara Dog Park
3450 Brookdale Drive
Santa Clara, CA
408-615-2260
The Santa Clara Dog Park was originally located on Lochnivar Ave. but has moved to a new location at 3450 Brookdale Drive. This park is completely fenced. Weekday hours are from 7am to a 1/2 hour after sunset and weekend hours are from 9am to a 1/2 hour after sunset.

Las Palmas Park/Dog Park
850 Russett Drive
Sunnyvale, CA
408-730-7506
After your pup finishes playing with other dogs at this dog park, you can both relax by the pond at one of the many picnic tables. It's located at 850 Russett Drive (by Remington Avenue and Saratoga-Sunnyvale Rd).

San Luis Obispo

El Chorro Regional Park and Dog Park
Hwy 1
San Luis Obispo, CA
805-781-5930
This regional park offers hiking trails, a botanical garden, volleyball courts, softball fields, campground and a designated off-leash dog park. The hiking trails offer scenic views on

Eagle Rock and a cool creek walk along Dairy Creek. The Eagle Rock trail is about .7 miles and is rated strenuous. There are two other trails including Dairy Creek that are about 1 to 2 miles long and rated easy. Dogs must be on leash at all times, except in the dog park. To get to the park from Highway 101, head south and then take the Santa Rosa St. exit. Turn left on Santa Rosa which will turn into Highway 1 after Highland Drive. Continue about 5 miles and the park will be on your left, across from Cuesta College.

Santa Cruz

Polo Grounds Dog Park
2255 Huntington Avenue
Aptos, CA
831-454-7900
This one acre off leash dog park is fenced and includes water and benches. The park is open during daylight hours. To get there, take Highway 1 and exit at Rio Del Mar. Go left over the freeway and turn right onto Monroe Avenue (second stop light). After Monroe turns into Wallace Avenue, look for Huntington Drive on the left. Turn left on Huntington and the park entrance will be on the left.

Scotts Valley Dog Park
Bluebonnet Road
Scotts Valley, CA
831-438-3251
This off leash dog park is located in the Skypark complex next to the soccer fields. The dog park offers 1.2 fully enclosed acres which is divided into two sections. One section is for small dogs under 25 pounds, puppies or shy dogs. The other section is for all dogs but primarily for larger and more active dogs. Other amenities include water bowls, wading pools, tennis balls, other dog toys, drinking fountains, shaded seating, plastic bags and pooper scoopers. To get there from Highway 17, take the Mt. Hermon exit and follow Mt. Hermon Road straight. Pass two stoplights and take the second right into the shopping center at the movie theatre sign. Go about .1 miles and turn left on Bluebonnet Road. The dog park is on the left.

Sonoma

Elizabeth Anne Perrone Dog Park
13630 Sonoma Highway
Glen Ellen, CA
707-565-2041
This one acre fenced dog run is located in the dog-friendly Sonoma Valley Regional Park. The dog park has a doggie drinking fountain, and a gazebo which provides shade for both people and dogs.

Dog Park-Deturk Park
819 Donahue Street
Santa Rosa, CA
707-543-3292
This dog park is fully fenced.

Dolye Community Park Dog Park
700 Doyle Park Drive
Santa Rosa, CA
707-543-3292
This dog park is fully fenced.

Galvin Community Park Dog Park
3330 Yulupa Avenue
Santa Rosa, CA
707-543-3292
This dog park is fully fenced.

Northwest Community Dog Park
2620 W. Steele Lane
Santa Rosa, CA
707-543-3292
Thanks to one of our readers who writes "Wonderful dog park. 2 separately fenced areas (one for little dogs too... It's all grassy and some trees and right near the creek. Also a brand new childrens play area (one for big kids and one fenced for toddlers). This dog park is sponsored by the Peanut's comics creator Charles M. Schultz's estate."

Rincon Valley Community Park Dog Park
5108 Badger Road
Santa Rosa, CA
707-543-3292
This dog park is fully fenced.

Thousand Oaks

Calabasas Bark Park
Las Virgines Road
Calabasas, CA

Thanks to one of our readers for recommending this dog park. It is located on Las Virgines Road, south of the Agoura Road and Las Virgines Road intersection.

Thousand Oaks Dog Park

Avenida de las Flores
Thousand Oaks, CA
805-495-6471
This 3.75 acre enclosed dog park
has a separate section for large dogs
and small dogs. Amenities include
picnic tables and three drinking
fountains. The dog park is located at
Avenida de las Flores, at the
northwest quadrant of Conejo Creek.

Ventura - Oxnard

Camarillo Grove Dog Park
off Camarillo Springs Road
East Camarillo, CA
805-482-1996
This fenced dog park is about one
acre and double gated. Amenities
include a water fountain for dogs and
people, benches, and a fire hydrant.
The dog park is located off Camarillo
Springs Road, at the base of the
Conejo Grade.

Colorado Dog Parks

Boulder

East Boulder Park
5660 Sioux Drive
Boulder, CO
303-413-7258
This three acre dog park has
separate fenced areas for small and
large dogs. There is limited water
access to a small lake. The city
warns to be careful as water quality
can vary. People need to pick up
after their pets, especially near the
water because of water quality
issues. The dog park is located near
the East Boulder Community Center.

Howard Hueston Dog Park
34th Street
Boulder, CO
303-413-7258
This 1.25 acre off-leash area (Voice
and Sight area) is not fenced but is
designated by yellow poles. Dogs
must be leashed when outside the
off-leash area. The park is located on
34th Street, south of Iris Avenue and
east of 30th Street.

Valmont Dog Park
5275 Valmont Road
Boulder, CO
303-413-7258

This three acre dog park has
separate fenced areas for small and
large dogs. Water is available
seasonally.

Colorado Springs

Garden of the Gods Park Off-Leash
Area
Gateway Road
Colorado Springs, CO
719-385-2489
This park has a designated off-
leash area which is not fenced. The
area is located east of Rock Ledge
Ranch and south of Gateway Road.
Dogs must be leashed when
outside the off-leash area.

Palmer Park Dog Park
3650 Maizeland Road
Colorado Springs, CO
719-385-2489
This park has a fenced off-leash
area. It is located at the old
baseball field, .3 miles from the
Maizeland entrance. There is also
an off-leash area (Dog Run Area) in
the park which is not fenced. Dogs
must be leashed when outside the
off-leash area.

Rampart Park Dog Park
8270 Lexington Drive
Colorado Springs, CO
719-385-2489
This park has a fenced off-leash
area. It is located just east of the
baseball diamond. Dogs must be
leashed when outside the off-leash
area. The area is located near
Rampart High School, next to the
running track.

Denver

Grandview Park Dog Park
17500 E. Salida Street
Aurora, CO
303-739-7160
This park has a designated off-
leash dog park. The 5 acre dog
park is fenced. It is located at the
west end of Quincy Reservoir,
about a third of a mile east of
Buckley on Quincy. Dogs must be
leashed when outside of the off-
leash area.

Barnum Park Off-Leash Area
Hooker and West 5th
Denver, CO
720-913-0696
This park has a designated off-

leash area which is located in the
northeast area of the park. It borders
the 6th Avenue Freeway. Enter from
the parking lot on 5th. This off-leash
area is part of a pilot program for the
city and county of Denver. It is in
place to test the feasibility of off-
leash areas in Denver parks.
Volunteers observe the conditions at
the parks on a regular basis and the
success and future of the program
will be determined at the end of the
pilot program.

Berkeley Park Dog Park
Sheridan and West 46th
Denver, CO
720-913-0696
This park has a designated fenced
dog park which is located west of the
lake. Enter from lake side. This dog
park is part of a pilot program for the
city and county of Denver. It is in
place to test the feasibility of off-
leash areas in Denver parks.
Volunteers observe the conditions at
the parks on a regular basis and the
success and future of the program
will be determined at the end of the
pilot program.

Denver's Off Leash Dog Park
666 South Jason Street
Denver, CO
303-698-0076
This park is Denver's first off leash
dog park. It is open from sunrise to
sunset, seven days a week. The park
is located directly behind the Denver
Animal Control building.

Fuller Park Dog Park
Franklin and East 29th
Denver, CO
720-913-0696
This park has a designated fenced
dog park which is located at the
northwest part of the park. It is west
of the basketball courts. Enter from
29th Avenue. This dog park is part of
a pilot program for the city and
county of Denver. It is in place to test
the feasibility of off-leash areas in
Denver parks. Volunteers observe
the conditions at the parks on a
regular basis and the success and
future of the program will be
determined at the end of the pilot
program.

Green Valley Ranch East Off-Leash
Area
Jebel and East 45th
Denver, CO
720-913-0696
This park has a designated off-leash

area which is located at the southwest area of the park. This off-leash area is part of a pilot program for the city and county of Denver. It is in place to test the feasibility of off-leash areas in Denver parks. Volunteers observe the conditions at the parks on a regular basis and the success and future of the program will be determined at the end of the pilot program.

Kennedy Soccer Complex Off-Leash Area
Hampden and South Dayton
Denver, CO
720-913-0696
This park has a designated off-leash area which is located at the southwest point of the park. Do not park inside the complex gate as it will be locked. This off-leash area is part of a pilot program for the city and county of Denver. It is in place to test the feasibility of off-leash areas in Denver parks. Volunteers observe the conditions at the parks on a regular basis and the success and future of the program will be determined at the end of the pilot program.

Durango

Durango Dog Park
Highway 160
Durango, CO
970-385-2950
This dog park is located off Highway 160 West, at the base of Smelter Mountain. The designated parking area is located at the first driveway located west of the off-leash area entrance on Highway 160.

Estes Park

Estes Valley Dog Park
off Highway 36
Estes Park, CO
970-586-8191
The dog park is located off Highway 36. It is next to Fishcreek Road. This fenced off-leash area has lake access.

Fort Collins

Fossil Creek Dog Park
5821 South Lemay Avenue
Fort Collins, CO
970-221-6618
This one acre dog park has a separate fenced area for small and

shy dogs. Amenities include a double-gated entry and a drinking fountain. The park is located at the entrance to Fossil Creek Community Park.

Spring Canyon Dog Park
Horsetooth Road
Fort Collins, CO
970-221-6618
This 2 to 3 acre dog park has a separate fenced area for small and shy dogs. Amenities include water fountains, bags and trash cans. The dog park is located at the west end of Horsetooth Road. It is in the undeveloped Spring Canyon Community Park along Spring Creek.

Connecticut Dog Parks

Hamden

Hamden R-Dog Dog Park
Waite St and Ridge Rd
Hamden, CT

This is a fenced dog park located at Bassett Park. The dog park is sponsored by Hamden R-DOG.

Norwich

Pawsitive Park
Asylum Street
Norwich, CT
860-367-7271
This is a fenced dog park that opened in the summer of 2005.

Ridgefield

Bark Park
Governor Street
Ridgefield, CT

There are two fenced parks, one for large dogs and one for small dogs. There is water at the park. From Route 35 take Main Street. Turn right on Governor Street and proceed to the end of Governor Street. The park is on the right.

Florida Dog Parks

Jacksonville

Dogwood Park
7407 Salisbury Rd South
Jacksonville, FL
904-296-3636
This dog park is great for any size canine. It has 25 acres that are fenced in a 42 acre park. Dogs can be off leash in any part of the park. The park offers picnic tables, a pond for small dogs, a pond for large dogs (Lake Bow Wow), shower for dogs, warm water for dog baths, tennis balls and toys for play, a playground with games for your dogs, trails to walk on, and bag stations for cleanup. Locals can become members for the year for about $24.00 per month or out-of-town visitors can pay about $11 for a one time visit.

Largo

Walsingham Park Paw Playground
12615 102nd Avenue North
Largo, FL
727-549-6142
This leash free dog park is fully fenced with amenities like cooling stations complete with showers and dog-level water fountains. People need to clean up after their pets and all dogs must be on a leash when outside of the Paw Playground area. Walsingham Park is located south of Highway 688, on 102nd Avenue N near 125th Street.

Miami

Amelia Earhart Park Bark Park
401 East 65th Street
Miami, FL
305-755-7800
This 5 acre dog park is completely fenced and has a separate area for small dogs. There are paved walkways, benches, shade, and water. The dog park is open from sunrise to sunset. The Bark Park is located in Amelia Earhart Park.

Orlando

Paw Park of Historic Sanford
427 S. French Avenue
Sanford, FL

407-330-5688
This off-leash dog park is located in the historic district of Sanford. The fenced park has a dog water fountain and dog shower. It is located south of State Route 46, off Highway 17-92 at East 5th Street.

Fleet Peoples Park Dog Park
South Lakemont Avenue
Winter Park, FL
407-740-8897
This park is a fenced dog park with a pond for swimming. Dogs are allowed off-leash within the park. There is shade, water, and bags for cleanup. The park is open to Winter Park residents as well as the public at large. The park is located in Fleet Peoples Park on South Lakemont Avenue.

Satellite Beach

Satellite Beach Off-leash Dog Park
Satellite Beach Sports & Rec Park
Satellite Beach, FL
321-777-8004
The dog park is 1.5 acres and fully fenced. The park offers water, tables and benches. There is a separate area for small dogs. The park is open daily from 8 am to 8 pm except for Mondays and Thursdays from 12 - 3 pm for maintenance. The park is next to the Satellite Beach Library which is at 751 Jamaica Blvd.

Seminole

Boca Ciega Park Paw Playground
12410 74th Ave. N
Seminole, FL
727-588-4882
This leash free dog park is fully fenced with amenities like cooling stations complete with showers and dog-level water fountains. People need to clean up after their pets and all dogs must be on a leash when outside of the Paw Playground area. Boca Ciega Park is located south of Park Blvd, on 74th Avenue N. near 125th Street N.

South Florida

Boca Raton Dog Park
751 Banyan Trail
Boca Raton, FL
561-393-7821
The Boca Raton Dog Park is entirely fenced and consists of one acre for large dogs and one acre for smaller dogs. The park is open 7:30 am to

Dusk all days except Wednesday when it opens at 12 noon to allow for maintenance.

Lake Ida Dog Park
2929 Lake Ida Road
Delray Beach, FL
561-966-6664
This 2 1/2 acre fenced dog park is located in Lake Ida Park. There is a section for small dogs as well. Water is available.

Bark Park At Snyder Park
3299 S.W. 4th Avenue
Fort Lauderdale, FL
954-828-3647
This fully fenced dog park has separate areas for small dogs and large dogs. There are benches, water, and pickup bags. Dogs must be on leash when outside the Bark Park. To get to Bark Park from I-95, exit at State Road 84 and head east to S.W. 4th Avenue. Turn right into Snyder Park. The Bark Park will be on your right.

Tampa Bay

Sand Key Park Paw Playground
1060 Gulf Blvd.
Clearwater, FL
727-588-4852
This leash free dog park is fully fenced with amenities like cooling stations complete with showers and dog-level water fountains. People need to clean up after their pets and all dogs must be on a leash when outside of the Paw Playground area. Sand Key Park is located south of Cleveland Street, on Gulf Blvd.

Chestnut Park Paw Playground
2200 East Lake Road
Palm Harbor, FL
727-669-1951
This leash free dog park is fully fenced with amenities like cooling stations complete with showers and dog-level water fountains. People need to clean up after their pets and all dogs must be on a leash when outside of the Paw Playground area. Chestnut Park is located on East Lake Road, between Keystone Road and Highway 580.

Al Lopez Dog Park
4810 North Himes
Tampa, FL
813-274-8615
There is a 1.5 acre fenced dog park for larger dogs and an 8000 square foot park for small dogs. There is a

double gated entry area, benches, water and pickup bags are available. The dog park is located on the west side of Al Lopez Park.

Davis Islands Dog Park
1002 Severn
Tampa, FL
813-274-8615
There are two fenced dog parks at the south end of Davis Islands. One of the parks is entirely fenced and is about one acre. The other park is a 1 1/2 acre beach front park with over 200 feet of waterfront available for dogs. There is water, double gated entry, and pickup bags available.

Palma Ceia
San Miguel & Marti
Tampa, FL
813-274-8615
The dog park is about 3/4 acres and is entirely fenced. It has a double gated entry, water, and pickup bags available. The park is located on the northeast corner of the park at West San Miguel & Marti.

Anderson Park Paw Playground
39699 U.S. Highway 19 North
Tarpon Springs, FL
727-943-4085
This leash free dog park is fully fenced with amenities like cooling stations complete with showers and dog-level water fountains. People need to clean up after their pets and all dogs must be on a leash when outside of the Paw Playground area. Anderson Park is located off Highway 19, north of Klosterman Road.

Tierra Verde

Fort DeSoto Park Paw Playground
3500 Pinellas Bayway South
Tierra Verde, FL
727-582-2267
This leash free dog park is fully fenced with amenities like cooling stations complete with showers and dog-level water fountains. People need to clean up after their pets and all dogs must be on a leash when outside of the Paw Playground area. Fort DeSoto Park is located at the southern end of the Pinellas Bayway.

Georgia Dog Parks

Atlanta

Piedmont Park Off Leash Dog Park
Park Drive
Atlanta, GA
404-875-7275
Dogs can run leash-free only in this designated area of Piedmont Park. The dog park is just over 1.5 acres. To get there, take I-85/75 north and take exit 101 (10th Street). Go straight to the first light, then turn right on 10th Street. Go past Piedmont Park, then turn left onto Monroe Drive. At the first light, turn left onto Park Drive. The dog park is below the bridge on the north side.

Macon

Macon Dog Park
Chestnut and Adams
Macon, GA
478-742-5084
This fully fenced dog park is open from sunrise to sunset. The Dog Park is just off of I-75 at the Forsyth Street exit. It is located one block north of Tatnall Square at the corner of Chestnut Street and Adams Street.

Savannah

Savannah Dog Park
41st and Drayton St
Savannah, GA

This dog park is located in the Starland Area at 41st and Drayton St. The park is shaded and fenced.

Idaho Dog Parks

Boise

Military Reserve Off-Leash Park
Mountain Cove Road and Reserve St
Boise, ID
208-384-4240
Dogs are allowed off-leash in this park. There is some shade and picnic tables.

Illinois Dog Parks

Chicago

Churchill Field Park Dog Park
1825 N. Damen Ave.
Chicago, IL
312-742.PLAY
This is one of a number of official off-leash areas in the city for dogs. There is a fenced off-leash dog area. Beginning in September, 2005 all dogs that use the dog parks are required to have an annual permit. The permits cost $35 for the first dog and $15 for additional dogs. Proof of certain vaccinations are also required.

Coliseum Park Dog Park
1466 S. Wabash Ave.
Chicago, IL
312-742.PLAY
This is one of a number of official off-leash areas in the city for dogs. There is a fenced off-leash dog area. Beginning in September, 2005 all dogs that use the dog parks are required to have an annual permit. The permits cost $35 for the first dog and $15 for additional dogs. Proof of certain vaccinations are also required.

Hamlin Park Dog Park
3035 N. Hoyne Ave.
Chicago, IL
312-742.PLAY
This is one of a number of official off-leash areas in the city for dogs. There is a fenced off-leash dog area. Beginning in September, 2005 all dogs that use the dog parks are required to have an annual permit. The permits cost $35 for the first dog and $15 for additional dogs. Proof of certain vaccinations are also required.

Margate Park Dog Park
4921 N. Marine Drive
Chicago, IL
312-742.PLAY
Also known as Puptown, this is one of a number of official off-leash areas in the city for dogs. There is a fenced off-leash dog area. Beginning in September, 2005 all dogs that use the dog parks are required to have an annual permit. The permits cost $35 for the first dog and $15 for additional dogs. Proof of certain vaccinations are

also required.

Noethling (Grace) Park Dog Park
2645 N. Sheffield Ave.
Chicago, IL
312-742.PLAY
Also known as Wiggly Field, this is one of a number of official off-leash areas in the city for dogs. There is a fenced off-leash dog area. Beginning in September, 2005 all dogs that use the dog parks are required to have an annual permit. The permits cost $35 for the first dog and $15 for additional dogs. Proof of certain vaccinations are also required.

Walsh Park Dog Park
1722 N. Ashland Ave.
Chicago, IL
312-742.PLAY
This is one of a number of official off-leash areas in the city for dogs. There is a fenced off-leash dog area. Beginning in September, 2005 all dogs that use the dog parks are required to have an annual permit. The permits cost $35 for the first dog and $15 for additional dogs. Proof of certain vaccinations are also required.

Wicker Park Dog Park
1425 N. Damen Ave.
Chicago, IL
312-742.PLAY
This is one of a number of official off-leash areas in the city for dogs. There is a fenced off-leash dog area. Beginning in September, 2005 all dogs that use the dog parks are required to have an annual permit. The permits cost $35 for the first dog and $15 for additional dogs. Proof of certain vaccinations are also required.

Indiana Dog Parks

Gary

Dogwood Run at Lemon Lake
County Park
6322 W. 133rd Avenue
Crown Point, IN
219-945-0543
This 14 acre dog park is divided into two 7 acre areas. Only one is open at a time. There is a $35 annual fee or a $2 per day pass. The single day

pass is collected on the honor system. All users must have proof of vaccinations unless you have an annual pass.

Elkhart

Robert Nelson Dog Park
60376 C.R. 13
Goshen, IN

This fenced dog park is open from sunrise to sunset daily. You must be a member in order to use the park. Membership is available at the Animal Aid Clinic South at 3718 Mishawaka Rd, Elkhart, IN. For more information about the membership call 574-875-5102.

Fort Wayne

Pawster Park Pooch Playground
Winchester Road and Bluffton Road
Fort Wayne, IN
260-427-6000
A Pooch Pass is required to use this fenced dog park. The park is open from 6 am to 10 pm daily. The annual Pooch Pass costs $25 for residents and $40 for non-residents. To obtain a Pooch Pass visit the Parks and Rec Dept office at 705 East State Street, Fort Wayne, IN 46805.

Indianapolis

Broad Ripple Park Bark Park
1550 Broad Ripple Avenue
Indianapolis, IN
317-327-7161
This fenced Bark Park requires an annual Pooch Pass. The cost of a pass is $40 annually. You may get the annual pass at the park office during business hours.

Eagle Creek Park Bark Park
7840 W 56th St
Indianapolis, IN
317-327-7110
This fenced Bark Park requires an annual Pooch Pass. The cost of a pass is $40 annually. You may get the annual pass at the park office during business hours.

Kansas Dog Parks

Kansas City

Kill Creek Streamway Park
33460 West 95th St
De Soto, KS
913-831-3355
This park features on leash walking trails and 19 acres of fenced area for off leash dogs. Cleanup and water stations are provided.

Heritage Park
16050 Pflumm
Olathe, KS
913-831-3355
This park features an offleash dog park that is fenced in. Water and cleanup stations are provided.

Shawnee Mission Park
7900 Renner Rd/87th St
Shawnee, KS
913-831-3355
This off leash park provides water and cleanup stations in a fenced area. Open to everyone with no fee. Dogpark is located at the 87th St parkway entrance. In the main park area, pets have to be leashed.

Lawrence

Mutt Run
1330 East 902 Road
Lawrence, KS
785-832-3405
This 30 acre off-leash area has mowed paths through the fields and along wooded areas. Amenities include a drinking fountain and water for dogs, restrooms and a small parking lot. The off-leash area is about 30 minutes east of Topeka. From I-70, take the KS 10 Exit. Turn right on KS 10 and go about 3.5 miles. Take Clinton Parkway west to the Clinton Day road. Turn south on the dam road and take the first left onto 902 Road. Take 902 Road to the first left.

Topeka

Bark Park (Gage Park)
10th and Gage St
Topeka, KS
785-368-3838
Dogs are allowed off leashed in the Bark Park section and leashed in the main park area. The dog park features water fountains, cleanup stations, and running areas in a fenced-in area.

Kentucky Dog Parks

Ashland

Ashland Boyd County Dog Park
Fraley Field
Ashland, KY

This dog park is located near the West Virginia and Kentucky State line in Ashland, KY. The dog park is fully fenced and there are cleanup bags provided. From I-64, take exit 185 at Cannonsburg. Follow US 180 toward Ashland. US 180 will merge with US 60 - stay on US 60. Turn left at West Summit Rd. Turn left onto the road to Fraley Field just past Boyd County Middle School. From Ashland, take US 60 west from town and turn right at West Summit Rd.

Louisiana Dog Parks

Lake Charles

Calcasieu Parish Animal Control Public Dog Park
5500-A Swift Plant Rd.
Lake Charles, LA
337-439-8879
This fenced off-leash dog park is open daily from dawn to dusk.

Maine Dog Parks

Bar Harbor

Little Long Pond Leash-Free Area near Seal Harbor
Bar Harbor, ME
207-288-3338
This leash free area is a privately owned section of land within the Acadia National Park. The off-leash property is located near Seal Harbor. Pets must be leashed when on Acadia National Park property.

Harpswell Road

Pine Grove Park
Harpswell Road
Harpswell Road, ME
207-874-8793
Dogs can be off-leash in this park but
need to be under direct voice control.
People need to make sure they pick
up their dog's waste with a plastic
bag and throw it away in a trash can.

Old Orchard Park

Old Orchard Beach Dog Park
Memorial Park on 1st St.
Old Orchard Park, ME
207-934-0860
This fenced dog park is open 24
hours a day. It is located in Memorial
Park.

Portland

Capisic Pond Park
Capisic Street
Portland, ME
207-874-8793
Dogs can be off-leash in this park but
need to be under direct voice control.
People need to make sure they pick
up their dog's waste with a plastic
bag and throw it away in a trash can.
There is no fenced off-leash area in
the park.

Eastern Promenade Park Off-Leash
Area
Cutter Street
Portland, ME
207-874-8793
Dogs are allowed off-leash under
direct voice control during certain
hours and only within the perimeter
bounded by the Portland House
Property, the water side of the
Eastern Prominade, and Cutter
Street following the curve of the
parking lot. Fort Allen Park is not part
of the off-leash area. Off-leash play
is allowed from April 15 to October
15, from 5am to 9am and from 5pm
to 10pm daily. From October 16
through April 14, the off-leash hours
are from 5am to 10pm daily.

Hall School Woods
23 Orono Road
Portland, ME
207-874-8793
Dogs can be off-leash in the woods
near this school, but need to be
under direct voice control. Dogs
need to be leashed except for when
in this special area. People need to

make sure they pick up their dog's
waste with a plastic bag and throw it
away in a trash can.

Jack School Dog Run
North St. and Washington Ave.
Portland, ME
207-874-8793
Dogs can be off-leash in this area,
but need to be under direct voice
control. The leash free area is
located behind Jack School. Dogs
need to be leashed except for when
in this special area. People need to
make sure they pick up their dog's
waste with a plastic bag and throw it
away in a trash can.

Portland Arts & Technology School
Dog Run
196 Allen Avenue
Portland, ME
207-874-8793
Dogs can be off-leash in the woods
behind this school, but need to be
under direct voice control. Dogs
need to be leashed except for when
in this special area. People need to
make sure they pick up their dog's
waste with a plastic bag and throw it
away in a trash can.

Riverton Park
Riverside Street
Portland, ME
207-874-8793
Dogs can be off-leash in this park
but need to be under direct voice
control. People need to make sure
they pick up their dog's waste with a
plastic bag and throw it away in a
trash can.

University Park
Harvard Street
Portland, ME
207-874-8793
Dogs can be off-leash in this park
but need to be under direct voice
control. People need to make sure
they pick up their dog's waste with a
plastic bag and throw it away in a
trash can.

Valley Street Park
Valley St.
Portland, ME
207-874-8793
Dogs can be off-leash in this park
but need to be under direct voice
control. People need to make sure
they pick up their dog's waste with a
plastic bag and throw it away in a
trash can.

Maryland Dog Parks

Annapolis

Quiet Waters Dog Park
600 Quiet Waters Park Rd
Annapolis, MD
410-222-1777
This fenced off-leash dog park is
located between the South River and
Harness Creek in Quiet Waters Park.
There is a separate fenced dog park
for small and older dogs. The dog
park is next to the dog beach (see
separate listing).

Baltimore

Canton Dog Park
Clinton & Toone Streets
Baltimore, MD
410-396-7900
This fenced dog park has two areas.
One is for small dogs and one is for
larger dogs. Water is provided and
the dog park is open during daylight
hours. To get to the park, take the I-
95 Boston Street Exit, then west to
Clinton Street. Turn right on Clinton
Street.

Bowie

Bowie Dog Park
Northview Drive and Enfield Drive
Bowie, MD

This one acre fenced dog park has
two areas, one for larger dogs and
one for small or shy dogs.

Washington Suburbs

Black Hills Regional Park Dog Park
20930 Lake Ridge Rd
Boyds, MD
301-972-9396
This fenced dog park is located in
the Black Hills Regional Park. The
park also has over ten miles of trails
to hike with your leashed dog.

Green Run Dog Park
Bickerstaff Rd and I-370
Gaithersburg, MD

This dog park is run by the city of
Gaithersburg and charges a $25 fee

for non-residents to use the park.

Ridge Road Recreational Dog Park
21155 Frederick Road
Germantown, MD
301-972-9396
This is a fenced off-leash dog park.

Laurel Dog Park
Brock Bridge Road
Laurel, MD
410-222-7317
This fenced dog park has two areas, one for larger dogs and one for small or shy dogs.

Wheaton Regional Park Dog Exercise Area
11717 Orebaugh Ave
Silver Spring, MD
301-680-3803
This fenced off-leash dog park is located in Wheaton Regional Park. Use the Orebaugh Ave entrance to the park.

Massachusetts Dog Parks

Boston

Charlesgate Dog Run
Massachusetts Ave and Beacon St
Boston, MA

This is a very small dog park but it is fenced in.

Peters Park Dog Run
E. Berkeley and Washington St.
Boston, MA

This off-leash dog park is located in South Boston on East Berkeley Street between Shawmut and Washington Streets.

Cambridge Dog Park
Mt. Auburn and Hawthorne
Cambridge, MA
617-349-4800
This dog park is located at Mount Auburn and Hawthorne Streets. Dogs need to be under voice control. Please remember to clean up after your dog.

Danehy Park
99 Sherman Street
Cambridge, MA
617-349-4800

This park is a 50 acre recreational facility that was built on a former city landfill. There is a unfenced leash free area located with this park. The park is located in North Cambridge, on Sherman Street, adjacent to Garden and New Streets.

Fort Washington Park
Waverly Street
Cambridge, MA

This park offers an off-leash dog run. Dogs need to be under voice control. The park is located on Waverly Street between Erie Street and Putnam Avenue. Please remember to clean up after your dog.

Boston Area

Henry Garnsey Canine Recreation Park
Cottage Street and Village Street
Medway, MA

This fenced off-leash dog park allows your dog to stretch his legs off-leash.

Sharon Dog Park
East Foxboro Street
Sharon, MA

This dog park is fenced, and is about one acre in size. It is free to use and has water, benches and a few trees. The dog park is located on East Foxboro Street about 1/4 mile from Sharon Center near the skateboard park. Park near the skateboard park and follow the walking trail to the dog park.

Michigan Dog Parks

Ann Arbor

Saline Dog Park
W. Bennett St
Saline, MI

This dog park is fenced on 3 sides with a pond on the 4th side. Dogs may swim in the pond. From US-12 in Saline go north on Ann Arbor Street and left on W. Bennett St.

The dog park is located in Mill Pond Park.

Detroit

Clinton Township Dog Park
Romeo Plank Rd
Clinton Township, MI
586-286-9336
This fenced dog park is located at the Clinton Township Civic Center. There is a fee for non-residents to use the park.

E-Z Dog Park and Training Center
230 Norlynn Dr
Howell, MI
810-229-7353
This off-leash dog park is privately owned and includes a fenced dog park and an agility center. The agility center includes indoor facilities. Fees to use the dog park are $25 per month or $5 per visit per dog. The facility is open 24 hours a day every day of the year. The dog park is for dogs larger than about 25 pounds, smaller dogs may use the agility center. From I-96 west take exit 145 (Grand River) and turn right at the exit. Turn right on Hacker in 7/10 mile, and go 3.3 miles to the facility. Hacker will become a gravel road before the facility.

Orion Oaks Bark Park
Clarkston Rd
Lake Orion, MI
248-858-0906
This is a 7-acre fenced dog park with water, benches and picnic tables. There is a swimming area in Lake Sixteen at the Bark Park for dogs only. The park is open from sunrise to sunset. There is a park fee to enter Orion Oaks Park of $5 per car per day or an annual pass is available for local residents.

Lyon Oaks Bark Park
52251 Pontiac Trail
Lyon Township, MI
248-437-7345
This is a 13-acre fenced dog park with water, benches and picnic tables. There is a separate small dog area. The park is open from sunrise to sunset. There is a park fee to enter Lyon Oaks Park of $5 per car per day or an annual pass is available for local residents.

Behnke Memorial Dog Park
300 N Groesbeck Highway
Mount Clemens, MI

This fully fenced dog park is open

from 7 am to 11 pm. There are benches, tables and water.

Cummingston Park Dog Run
Torquay & Leafdale
Royal Oak, MI
248-246-3300
This is an unfenced dog run area located in part of Cummingston Park. Dogs must be on leash in all areas of the park that are not designated as off-leash. Dogs must be cleaned up after throughout the park.

Lockman Park Dog Run
Connecticut and Derby
Royal Oak, MI
248-246-3300
This is an unfenced dog run area located in part of Lockman Park. Dogs must be on leash in all areas of the park that are not designated as off-leash. Dogs must be cleaned up after throughout the park.

Mark Twain Park Dog Run
Campbell Rd, South of 14 Mile
Royal Oak, MI
248-246-3300
This is an unfenced dog run area located in part of Mark Twain Park. Dogs must be on leash in all areas of the park that are not designated as off-leash. Dogs must be cleaned up after throughout the park.

Quickstad Park Dog Run
Marais between Normandy & Lexington
Royal Oak, MI
248-246-3300
This is an unfenced dog run area located in part of Quckstad Park. Dogs must be on leash in all areas of the park that are not designated as off-leash. Dogs must be cleaned up after throughout the park.

Wagner Park Dog Run
Detroit Ave, between Rochester and Main
Royal Oak, MI
248-246-3300
This is an unfenced dog run area located in part of Wagner Park. Dogs must be on leash in all areas of the park that are not designated as off-leash. Dogs must be cleaned up after throughout the park.

Hines Park Dog Park
Hawthorne Ridge west of Merriman
Westland, MI

This 3 acre dog park requires a

registration and that you sign a waiver before using the park. You may register at Wayne County Administrative Offices at 33175 Ann Arbor Trl in Westland. The park is open from dawn to dusk year round.

Grand Rapids

Shaggy Pines Dog Park
3895 Cherry Lane SE
Ada, MI
616-676-9464
This is a 20 acre private dog park featuring a fenced dog park, one mile jogging trail, a large sand pile for climbing, a dog swimming pond, and a small dog area. A membership is required to use the park. These fees are $24 and up per month for the first dog and $5 and up per month for each additional dog. Visitors to the area may use the park on Sundays from 10 to 5 for an $8 per day fee for the first dog and $2.50 per additional dog.

Minnesota Dog Parks

Minneapolis - St Paul

Bloomington Off-leash Recreation Area
111th Street
Bloomington, MN
952-563-8892
This huge fenced 25 acre dog park is located at 111th Street, between Nesbitt and Hampshire Ave. The site features a swimming pond for your dog, hills, trees and grass.

Missouri Dog Parks

Kansas City

Wayside Waifs Bark Park
3901 Martha Truman Rd
Kansas City, MO
816-761-8151
This off leash park provides water and cleanup stations in a fenced area. This a private park that

charges a fee for residents and non-residents.

St Louis

Lister Dog Park
Taylor Rd and Olive St
St Louis, MO

This off leash dog park is located in Central West End for residents only. There are no day passes and there is an annual fee. The dog park offers a fenced in area, water and cleanup stations, and it is lighted in the evenings.

Shaw Neighborhood Dog Park
Thurman and Cleveland Ave
St Louis, MO

This fenced in area is an off-leash park for dogs. Open 6am-10pm with lighting available in the evenings. The dog park offers water and cleanup stations. There are no day passes but there are annual passes for a fee to both residents and nonresidents.

Taylor Dog Park
Taylor Rd
St Louis, MO

This off leash dog park is located in the Central West End for residents only. There is an annual fee to use the park. No day passes are available. The park is fenced and lit in the evenings.

Quail Ridge Park
Quail Ridge Rd
Wentzville, MO

The hours are from dawn until dusk. Dogs to have to be leashed outside of the fenced in area. This park features a six feet high fence, bathrooms, water fountains (for dogs and people), and cleanup stations. It is located in the suburbs of St Louis.

Montana Dog Parks

Missoula

Jacob's Island Park Dog Park
off VanBuren Street

Missoula, MT
406-721-7275
This park has a dog park located at the east end of the park. This six acre fenced off-leash area includes a double-gate.

Nebraska Dog Parks

Holmes Lake Dog Run
70th Street
Lincoln, NE
402-441-7847
This 3 to 4 acre off-leash area is located across the street from Holmes Lake.

Nevada Dog Parks

Desert Breeze Dog Run
8425 W. Spring Mtn. Road
Las Vegas, NV

This dog park is fully enclosed with benches, trees, trash cans and water. There are two runs available, one for small dogs under 30 pounds and one for larger dogs over 30 pounds. Thanks to one of our readers who recommended this park. The park is located approximately 5 miles west of downtown Las Vegas and the Strip. From Flamingo Road/589 in downtown, head west and pass Hwy 15. Turn right on Durango Drive. Then turn right onto Spring Mountain Road. The dog park is located off Spring Mountain Rd., between the Community Center and Desert Breeze County Park.

Dog Fancier's Park
5800 E. Flamingo Rd.
Las Vegas, NV
702-455-8200
Dog Fancier's Park is a 12 acre park that allows canine enthusiasts to train their dogs off leash. Owner's must still have control over their dogs and may be cited if their dogs (while off leash) interfere with other animals

training at the park. This dog park has benches, poop bags and water taps.

Shadow Rock Dog Run
2650 Los Feliz on Sunrise Mountain
Las Vegas, NV
702-455-8200
This is a 1.5 acre dog park with benches, poop bags and water taps.

Sunset Park Dog Run
2601 E. Sunset Rd
Las Vegas, NV
702-455-8200
Located in Sunset Park, this dog park offers about 1.5 acres of land for your pooch to play. The dog park has benches, poop bags and water taps.

Virginia Lake Dog Park
Lakeside Drive
Reno, NV
775-334-2099
This one acre dog park includes mitt dispensers. The park is located at Mountain View and Lakeside Drive, at the north field.

Whitaker Dog Park
550 University Terrace
Reno, NV
775-334-2099
This fenced dog park is about .75 acres. Amenities include mitt dispensers.

New Hampshire Dog Parks

Town of Derry Dog Park
45 Fordway
Derry, NH
603-432-6100
This half acre dog park is adjacent to the Derry Animal Control office. To get there from I-93, take exit #4/Route 102 towards Derry(east). Go about 1.5 miles and turn right onto Fordway. Go about 1/2 mile and arrive at the dog park at 45 Fordway.

Portsmouth Dog Park
South Mill Pond
Portsmouth, NH
603-431-2000
This fenced dog park is located at the South Mill Pond. The South Mill Pond is located near downtown Portsmouth, south of the Pleasant Street and Junkins Avenue intersection. From I-93, take exit #4.

New Jersey Dog Parks

Pooch Park (Cooper River Park)
North Park Drive
Cherry Hill, NJ
856-225-5431
The Pooch Park portion of the park allows dogs to be unleashed in the fenced in area. The dog park offers water and cleanup stations, tables, and lighting. Open 6am-10pm with no fee.

Rocky Top Dog Park
4106 Route 27
Kingston, NJ
732-297-6527
This fenced in area allows dogs to be off leash. There is a fee and dogs must have proof of shots. The dog park features a pond, cleanup and water stations, and has lighting in the evening.

Thompson Park Dog Park
805 Newman Springs Road
Lincroft, NJ
732-842-4000x4256
This fenced off-leash dog park is located in Thompson Park adjacent to the Craft Center. Access the area using the park maintenance entrance which is west of the park gate and follow the road to the end and turn right.

Church Square Dog Run
4th and 5th, between Garden and
Willow
Hoboken, NJ

There are two dog runs in Church
Square Park. One is for larger dogs
and another for small dogs only.

Elysian Park Dog Run
Hudson between 10th and 11th
Hoboken, NJ

There is an off-leash dog run in the
park.

Stevens Park Dog Run
Hudson between 4th and 5th
Hoboken, NJ

There is an off-leash dog run in the
park.

Overpeck County Park Dog Run
Fort Lee Road
Leonia, NJ
201-336-7275
There is an official Bergen County
off-leash dog run area in Overpeck
County Park.

Riverside County Park Dog Run
Riverside Ave
Lyndhurst, NJ
201-336-7275
There is an official Bergen County
off-leash dog run area in Riverside
County Park.

Wood Dale County Park Dog Run
Prospect Avenue
Woodcliff Lake, NJ
201-336-7275
There is an official Bergen County
off-leash dog run area in Wood Dale
County Park.

New Mexico
Dog Parks

Albuquerque

Rio Grande Park Dog Park
Iron Avenue
Albuquerque, NM
505-873-6620
Rio Grande Park offers a designated
off-leash area for dogs. The dog park
is located on Iron Avenue, between
Alcalde Place and 14th Street.

Roosevelt Park Dog Park
Hazeldine Avenue
Albuquerque, NM
505-873-6620
Roosevelt Park offers a designated
off-leash area for dogs. The park is
located off Hazeldine Avenue,
between Cedar and Maple Streets.

Tom Bolack Urban Forest Dog Park
Haines Avenue
Albuquerque, NM
505-873-6620
Tom Bolack Park offers a
designated off-leash area for dogs.
The park is located near Haines
Avenue and San Pedro Drive.

Santa Fe

Frank Ortiz Park Off-Leash Area
Camino Las Crucitas
Santa Fe, NM
505-955-2100
This off-leash area is located in
Frank Ortiz park which used to be
the old landfill. To get there from
town, head west on Paseo De
Paralta towards St. Francis. When
you come to St. Francis, do not turn
left or right, but instead go across to
Camino Las Crucitas Street. Follow
this road which takes you through
the Casa Solana residential
neighborhood. The park has a large
field on the left where the off-leash
area is located.

New York
Dog Parks

NYC Borroughs

All New York City Off-leash Dog
Parks are run by the New York City
Parks Department. They can be
reached at 212-NEW-YORK or by
calling 311 from a phone in the city
of New York. Only some areas of
the parks are designated for off-
leash and dogs must be on-leash
outside of the designated areas.

Ewen Park Dog Run
Riverdale to Johnson Aves., South
of West 232nd St.
Bronx, NY
212-NEW-YORK
This is an official off-leash dog area.

Frank S. Hackett Park Dog Run
Riverdale Ave. and W. 254th Street
Bronx, NY
212-NEW-YORK
This is an official off-leash dog area.

Pelham Bay Park Dog Run
Middletown Rd. & Stadium Ave.,
Northwest of Parking Lot
Bronx, NY
212-NEW-YORK
This is an official off-leash dog area.

Seton Park Dog Run
West 232nd St. & Independence
Ave.
Bronx, NY
212-NEW-YORK
This is an official off-leash dog area.

Van Cortlandt Park Dog Run
West 251st Street & Broadway
Bronx, NY
212-NEW-YORK
This is an official off-leash dog area.

Williamsbridge Oval Dog Run
3225 Reservoir Oval East
Bronx, NY
212-NEW-YORK
This is an official off-leash dog area.

DiMattina Park Dog Run
Hicks, Coles and Woodhull Streets
Brooklyn, NY
212-NEW-YORK
There are two official off-leash dog
areas in DiMattina Park.

Dyker Beach Park Dog Run
86th Street from 7th Ave to 14th Ave
Brooklyn, NY
212-NEW-YORK
This is an official off-leash dog area.

Hillside Park Dog Run
Columbia Heights & Vine Street
Brooklyn, NY
212-NEW-YORK
This is an official off-leash dog area.

J J Byrne Memorial Park Dog Run
3rd to 4th Streets between 4th and
5th Ave
Brooklyn, NY
212-NEW-YORK
This is an official off-leash dog area.

Manhattan Beach Dog Run
East of Ocean Avenue, North Shore
Rockaway inlet

Off-leash Dog Parks - Please always call ahead to make sure an establishment is still dog-friendly.

Brooklyn, NY
212-NEW-YORK
This is an official off-leash dog area.

McCarren Park Dog Run
Nassau Ave, Bayard, Leonard & N.
12th Sts
Brooklyn, NY
212-NEW-YORK
This is an official off-leash dog area.

Owls Head Park Dog Run
Shore Pkwy, Shore Rd, Colonial Rd,
68th Street
Brooklyn, NY
212-NEW-YORK
This is an official off-leash dog area.

Palmetto Playground Dog Run
Atlantic Ave, Furman, Columbia,
State Streets
Brooklyn, NY
212-NEW-YORK
This is an official off-leash dog area.

Prospect Park

Brooklyn, NY
212-NEW-YORK
Prospect Park, in Brooklyn, allows
dogs in much of the park on leash
has a number of large off-leash
areas during specified hours. Dogs
are allowed off-leash before 9 am
and after 9 pm in the summer and
after 5 pm in the winter in the Long
Meadow, Nethermead and the
Peninsula Meadow areas of the park.
Dogs are not allowed in the
children's playground or on the Bridle
paths. Owners must clean up after
their dogs. There's even a man made
dog beach in the park.

Seth Low Playground Dog Run
Avenue P, Bay Parkway, W. 12th
Street
Brooklyn, NY
212-NEW-YORK
This is an official off-leash dog area.

Forest Park Dog Run
Park Lane South & 85th Street
Forest Park, NY
212-NEW-YORK
This is an official off-leash dog area.
Its hours are 8 am to 8 pm seven
days a week.

Alley Pond Park Dog Run
Alley Picnic Field Number 12
Queens, NY
212-NEW-YORK
This is an official off-leash dog area.

Road and Radnor Road
Queens, NY
212-NEW-YORK
This is an official off-leash dog area.

Murray Playground Dog Run
21st Street & 45th Road on the SE
side of park
Queens, NY
212-NEW-YORK
This is an official off-leash dog area.

Underbridge Playground Dog Run
64th Ave and 64th Road on Grand
Central Parkway service road
Queens, NY
212-NEW-YORK
This is an official off-leash dog area.

Veteran's Grove Dog Run
Judge & Whitney on the south side
of the park
Queens, NY
212-NEW-YORK
This is an official off-leash dog area.

Windmuller Park Dog Run
Woodside Ave., 54-56 Sts.
Queens, NY
212-NEW-YORK
This is an official off-leash dog area.

Wolfe's Pond Park Dog Run
End of Huguenot & Chester
Avenues
Staten Island, NY
212-NEW-YORK
This is an official off-leash dog area.

New York
All New York City Off-leash Dog
Parks are run by the New York City
Parks Department. They can be
reached at 212-NEW-YORK or by
calling 311 from a phone in the city
of New York. Only some areas of
the parks are designated for off-
leash and dogs must be on-leash
outside of the designated areas.

Carl Schurz Park Dog Run
East End Ave.between 84th and
89th Street

New York, NY
212-NEW-YORK
This is an official off-leash dog area.

DeWitt Clinton Park Dog Run
Between 10th and 11th Ave at 52nd
and 54th
New York, NY
212-NEW-YORK
This is an official off-leash dog area.

Fish Bridge Park Dog Run
Dover St., between Pearl & Water St.
New York, NY
212-NEW-YORK
This is an official off-leash dog area.

Fort Tryon Park Dog Run
Margaret Corbin Drive, Washington
Heights
New York, NY
212-NEW-YORK
This is an official off-leash dog area.

Inwood Hill Park Dog Run
Dyckman St and Payson Ave
New York, NY
212-NEW-YORK
This is an official off-leash dog area.

J. Hood Wright Dog Run
Fort Washington & Haven Aves.,
West 173rd St.
New York, NY
212-NEW-YORK
This is an official off-leash dog area.

Madison Square Park Dog Run
Madison Ave. To 5th Ave. between
East 23rd St. & East 26th St.
New York, NY
212-NEW-YORK
This is an official off-leash dog area.

Morningside Park Dog Run
Morningside Avenue between 114th
and 119th Streets
New York, NY
212-NEW-YORK
This is an official off-leash dog area.

Peter Detmold Park Dog Run
West Side of FDR Drive between
49th and 51st
New York, NY
212-NEW-YORK
This is an official off-leash dog area.

Riverside Park Dog Runs
Riverside Dr at W 72nd,87th, and
105th
New York, NY
212-NEW-YORK

There are three official off-leash dog areas in Riverside Park.

Robert Moses Park Dog Run
41st Street and 1st Ave.
New York, NY
212-NEW-YORK
This is an official off-leash dog area.

Theodore Roosevelt Park Dog Run
Central Park West and W 81st St.
New York, NY
212-NEW-YORK
This is an official off-leash dog area.

Thomas Smith Park Dog Run
11th Ave and W. 22nd St
New York, NY
212-NEW-YORK
This is an official off-leash dog area.

Tompkins Square Park Dog Run
1st Ave and Ave B between 7th and 10th
New York, NY
212-NEW-YORK
This is an official off-leash dog area.

Union Square Dog Run
Union Square
New York, NY
212-NEW-YORK
This is an official off-leash dog area located on 15th Street at Union Square.

North Carolina Dog Parks

Charlotte

Barkingham Park Dog Park - Reedy Creek
2900 Rocky River Rd.
Charlotte, NC
704-365-0750
Reedy Creek Dog Park opened in the Summer of 2003. It consists of 4 acres. Currently the park has an off-leash dog park. Expected to be added soon are a small dog area and an agility playground. Charlotte Dog Parks require a annual pooch pass which you can get by signing a liability form. Currently the fee is $35 per year for a pooch pass. More information is available from

FidoCarolina at
http://www.fidocarolina.org.

Fetching Meadows Dog Park
McAlpine Park
Charlotte, NC
704-365-0750
Fetching Meadows Dog Park opened in late 2002. Charlotte Dog Parks require a annual pooch pass which you can get by signing a liability form. Currently the fee is $35 per year for a pooch pass. More information is available from FidoCarolina at
http://www.fidocarolina.org.

Raleigh

Millbrook Exchange Off Leash Dog Park
1905 Spring Forest Road
Raleigh, NC
919-872-4156
This park is the home of the fenced Millbrook Exchange Off Leash Dog Park, and it is double-gated to prevent dogs from wandering off. When dogs are not in the off-leash area they must be on lead.

North Dakota Dog Parks

Fargo

Village West Dog Park
45th Street
Fargo, ND

This off-leash dog park has been opened with fenced areas for both small and large dogs. The dog park is located in Village West Park. The park is at 45th Street and 9th Avenue.

Ohio Dog Parks

Cincinnati

Mt. Airy Forest Dog Park
Westwood Northern Blvd.
Cincinnati, OH

513-352-4080
The City of Cincinnati has designated about 2 acres in the Mt. Airy Forest for an off-leash dog park. Dogs may run leash free when accompanied by a person. The area is fenced and the rules are posted on site. The dog park is located at Mt. Airy Forest's Highpoint Picnic Area on Westwood Northern Blvd. between Montana Avenue and North Bend Road.

Oklahoma Dog Parks

Norman

Norman Community Dog Park
Robinson and 12th St NE
Norman, OK
This dog park has separate areas for large and small dogs. It is open 7 days a week from dawn to dusk. The park is located north of the intersection of Robinson and 12th Street NE.

Oklahoma City

Paw Park
Grand Blvd. and Lake Hefner Parkway
Oklahoma City, OK
405-782-4311
This two acre off-leash dog park is fenced and double-gated. Amenities include a small pond where dogs can swim or play in the water, separate areas for small or senior dogs and large dogs, trees, park benches and trash cans. Use of the dog park is free, but donations for keeping the park clean and in good condition are always appreciated. Envelopes and information forms are available at the park. The dog park is located in Lake Hefner Park. It is at the corner of North Grand Blvd. and Hefner Parkway in northwest Oklahoma City. Go north on the paved road east of the Grand Blvd/Hefner Parkway overpass. Continue north and park near the baseball fields. Thanks to PAW OK for the directions. Check out their web site at http://pawok.com for more details including photos of the park.

Pets and People Dog Park

701 Inla
Yukon, OK

This off-leash dog park is located west of Oklahoma City, in Yukon. From I-40, take the OK 92 exit towards Yukon. Turn right on Garth Brooks Blvd./S 11th Street and go about 1.4 miles. Continue on N 11th Street for .2 miles. Turn right on Inla Avenue and go for about .5 miles and you will reach the dog park.

Oregon Dog Parks

Ashland

The Dog Park
Nevada and Helman Streets
Ashland, OR
541-488-6002
This 2 acre fenced dog park has picnic tables and drinking water. It is located behind the Ashland Greenhouse and Nursery, off Nevada, across from Helman Street.

Canby

Molalla River State Park Off-Leash Area
Canby Ferry Road
Canby, OR
800-551-6949
This state park offers a designated off-leash exercise area. Dogs must be leashed in all other areas of the park. The park is located about 2 miles north of Canby.

Corvallis

Bald Hill Park Dog Park
Oak Creek Drive
Corvallis, OR
541-766-6918
There is a designated off-leash area located west of this park. People must clean up after their pets.

Chip Ross Park Dog Park
Lester Avenue
Corvallis, OR
541-766-6918
This park has a designated off-leash area. People must clean up after their pets. The park is located at the end of Lester Avenue.

Crystal Lake Sports Field Dog Park

Crystal Lake Drive
Corvallis, OR
541-766-6918
From March to November only, dogs can play off-leash at the non-improved turf areas. People must clean up after their pets. This sports field area is lcoated off Crystal Lake Drive, adjacent to Williamette Park.

Walnut Park Dog Park
Walnut Boulevard
Corvallis, OR
541-766-6918
This park has a designated off-leash area which is located in the southwest corner of the park. People must clean up after their pets.

Williamette Park Dog Park
SE Goodnight Avenue
Corvallis, OR
541-766-6918
This park has a designated off-leash area. People must clean up after their pets. The park is located southeast of Corvallis, off Highway 99W on southeast Goodnight Avenue.

Woodland Meadow Park Dog Park
Circle and Witham Hill Drive
Corvallis, OR
541-766-6918
This park has a designated off-leash area which is located in the upper portion of the park. People must clean up after their pets.

Estacada

Milo McIver State Park Off-Leash Area
Springwater Road
Estacada, OR
503-630-7150
This state park offers a designated off-leash exercise area. Dogs must be leashed in all other areas of the park. The park is located on Springwater Road, 4 miles west of Estacada.

Eugene

Alton Baker Park Off-Leash Area
Leo Harris Parkway
Eugene, OR
541-682-4800
This park offers a designated off-leash area. The dog park is located off Martin Luther King Jr. Boulevard on Leo Harris Parkway, behind

Autzen Stadium. Park in lot 8.

Amazon Park Off-Leash Area
Amazon Parkway
Eugene, OR
541-682-4800
This park offers a designated off-leash area. The park is located off Amazon Parkway, at 29th Avenue.

Candlelight Park Off-Leash Area
Royal Avenue
Eugene, OR
541-682-4800
This park offers a designated off-leash area. The park is located off Royal Avenue, at Candlelight.

Morse Ranch Park Off-Leash Area
595 Crest Drive
Eugene, OR
541-682-4800
This park offers a designated off-leash area.

Medford

Bear Creek Park Dog Park
Highland Drive
Medford, OR
541-774-2400
This park offers a 2 acre fenced off-leash area. Amenities include water and a picnic table. Dogs must be on leash when not in the dog park. People must clean up after their pets. The park is located at the corner of Highland Drive and Barnett Road, near I-5, exit 27.

Portland

Hazeldale Park Dog Park
Off 196th, N of Farmington
Beaverton, OR

This fenced dog park has a separate section for small dogs and large dogs. Thanks to one of our readers for recommending this dog park.

Chimney Dog Park
9360 N. Columbia Blvd
Portland, OR
503-823-7529
This entire 16-acre park is designated as an off-leash area. The park has meadows and trails but is not fenced and no water is available. The park is open year-round and is located next to the City Archives Building.

Rooster Rock State Park Off-Leash

Area
I-84
Portland, OR
503-695-2261
This state park offers a designated off-leash exercise area. Dogs must be leashed in all other areas of the park. The park is located on I-84, 22 miles east of Portland (exit 25).

Salem

Minto-Brown Island Park
2200 Minto Island Road
Salem, OR
503-588-6336
This park offers a designated area for dogs to play off-leash. The area is not fenced. Dogs must be leashed when outside the off-leash area.

Orchard Heights Park
1165 Orchard Heights Road NW
Salem, OR
503-588-6336
This park has a small designated area where dogs can play off-leash. Dogs must be leashed when outside the off-leash area.

Pennsylvania Dog Parks

Dutch Country

Buchanon Park Dog Park
Buchanan Avenue and Race Avenue
Lancaster, PA

This fenced off-leash dog park is in the 22 acre Buchanon Park. This city owned park is run by Franklin & Marshall University. The park is located at the F&M campus.

Philadelphia

Mondaug Bark Park
1130 Camphill Road
Fort Washington, PA

This park opened in July, 2005. It is a one acre fenced off-leash dog park. There is a separate dog park for small dogs and there is a double entry fence around the dog park. There are also trails around the dog park where you can walk your

leashed dog. There is a stream where your leashed dog can play.

Chester Avenue Dog Park
Chester Ave and 48th
Philadelphia, PA
215-748-3440
This nearly one acre park is a privately run dog park. Membership is required to use the park and runs $50 per year. For membership information, please contact Linda Amsterdam at 215-748-3440.

Eastern State Dog Pen
Corinthian Ave & Brown St
Philadelphia, PA

This is a fenced dog park. Barking in the park is prohibited between 9 pm and 9 am.

Orianna Hill Dog Park
North Orianna St, between Poplar and Wildey
Philadelphia, PA
215-423-4516
This is a privately owned fenced dog run. Dues are required and are $20 per year. To join, please call 215-423-4516.

Pretzel Park Dog Run
Cresson St
Philadelphia, PA

This is a fenced in dog park in the dog-friendly Manayunk region of Philadelphia.

Schuylkill River Park Dog Run
25th St between Pine and Locust
Philadelphia, PA

This fenced dog park is located near the Centre City across the Schuylkill River from the 30th Street Train Station.

Segar Dog Park
11th Street between Lombard and South St.
Philadelphia, PA

Located in Segar Park, this is a fenced dog park with separate areas for small dogs and large dogs.

Pittsburgh

South Park Dog Park
Corrigan Drive at South Park Library, PA

412-350-7275
This fenced dog park has drinking water, pickup bags and benches. Dogs on leash are allowed in most of the rest of this 2000 acre park.

White Oak Dog Park
Route 48
McKeesport, PA
412-350-7275
This fenced dog park in White Oak Park has water, pickup bags and benches. It is about 2 acres in size. The dog park can be accessed from Route 48. Take the White Oak Park entrance. Dogs are allowed on leash in most of the rest of this 810 acre park.

Heritage Park Dog Park
2364 Saunders Station Road
Monroeville, PA
412-350-7275
This fenced dog park has shade, water, and pickup bags. The park is open from sunrise to sunset.

Hartwood County Park Dog Run
215 Saxonburg Blvd
Pittsburgh, PA
412-767-9200
This unfenced dog park is located in Hartwood County Park. Only a section of the park is reserved for off-leash dog exercise. Your leashed dog may accompany you through the rest of this 629 acre park including the Summer Concert Series at the outdoor amphitheatre.

Upper Frick Dog Park
Beechwood and Nicholson
Pittsburgh, PA

This fenced dog park has pickup bags. It is about one acre in size.

Rhode Island Dog Parks

Newport

Newport Dog Park
Connell Highway
Newport, RI
401-845-5800
This dog park is located on Connell Highway in Newport. It is a fenced dog park and is open from 6 am to 9 pm.

South Carolina Dog Parks

Charleston

Hampton Park Off-Leash Dog Park
corner of Rutledge and Grove
Charleston, SC

This park has a fenced dog run for your pet. Dogs must be on leash when not in the dog run area.

James Island County Park Off-leash Dog Area
871 Riverland Drive
Charleston, SC
843-795-7275
James Island County Park has an off-Leash dog area. Dogs must be leashed when entering and exiting the Dog Park and at all times when outside of the designated off-leash area, and dogs must be current on rabies vaccinations and wear current tags.

Hilton Head Island

Best Friends Dog Park
Off Hwy 40
Hilton Head, SC

Dogs are allowed unleashed in the dog park and leashed outside on the beaches. There is a water and cleanup stations for your pets.

South Dakota Dog Parks

Sioux Falls

Lien Park Off-Leash Area
North Cliff Avenue
Sioux Falls, SD
605-367-6076
This off-leash area is being run on a trial basis by the city of Sioux Falls. Amenities at the off-leash area include a picnic table, plastic bag dispenser and a trash can. The park is located on the east side of North

Cliff Ave. at the Big Sioux River, about .25 miles north of the Rice Street and Cliff Avenue intersection. Off-street parking is available.

Spencer Park Off-Leash Area
3501 South Cliff Avenue
Sioux Falls, SD

This fenced off-leash area is being run on a trial basis by the city of Sioux Falls. Amenities at the off-leash area include a picnic table, plastic bag dispenser and a trash can. The park is located at 3501 S. Cliff Avenue, on the west side of Cliff Avenue near I-229. Off-street parking is available.

Texas Dog Parks

Austin

Auditorium Shores Off-Leash Area
920 W. Riverside Drive
Austin, TX
512-974-6700
This designated off-leash area is located between South First and Bouldin Avenue.

Bull Creek District Dog Park
6701 Lakewood Drive
Austin, TX
512-974-6700
This dog park is not fenced. It has access to the creek for water-loving pooches. Well-behaved dogs can roam and play off-leash, but must be under verbal control and within your sight. The off-leash area is located behind the restrooms.

Emma Long Metro Park Off-Leash Area
1600 City Park Rd.
Austin, TX
512-974-6700
This park has a designated off-leash area. It is located between City Park Drive, the west park boundary fence, Turkey Creek and the top ridge of the bluff line overlooking Lake Austin.

Northeast District Park Off-Leash Area
5909 Crystalbrook Drive
Austin, TX
512-974-6700

This park has a designated off-leash area. It is located between Crystalbrook Drive, the railroad right of way and Decker Lake Road.

Norwood Estate Dog Park
I-35 and Riverside Drive
Austin, TX
512-974-6700
This is a fully fenced dog park. Well-behaved dogs can roam and play off-leash, but must be under verbal control and within your sight. The dog park is located on the north end of Travis Heights at the northwest corner of Riverside Drive and I-35.

Onion Creek District Park Off-Leash Area
6900 Onion Creek Drive
Austin, TX
512-974-6700
This off-leash dog park is located at the north end of the greenbelt.

Red Bud Isle Off-Leash Area
3401 Red Bud Trail Unit Circle
Austin, TX
512-974-6700
Dogs can play leash-free in this designated off-leash area.

Shoal Creek Greenbelt Off-Leash Area
2600-2799 Lamar Blvd.
Austin, TX
512-974-6700
This park has a designated off-leash area. It is located between 24th and 29th Streets.

Walnut Creek District Off-Leash Area
12138 North Lamar Blvd.
Austin, TX
512-974-6700
This park has a designated off-leash area. It is located between Old Cedar Lane, Walnut Creek and the east and west park fences.

Zilker Dog Park
2100 Barton Springs Rd.
Austin, TX
512-974-6700
This dog park is not fenced. Well-behaved dogs can roam and play off-leash, but must be under verbal control and within your sight. The dog park is located in Zilker Metropolitan Park at 2100 Barton Springs Road. The leash free area is located near the soccer field area, between Great Northern Blvd. and Shoal Creek Blvd.

Dallas

White Rock Lake Dog Park
8000 Mockingbird Lane
Dallas, TX
214-670-8895
Dogs are welcome to run leash-free at this dog park. The fully enclosed park offers a separate section for large dogs and small dogs. The dog park is closed on Mondays for maintenance. To get there from Central Expressway (75), go East on Mockingbird Lane. After you pass the West Lawther exit, begin looking for the parking lot. If you go to Buckner Blvd., then you have passed the dog park. The dog park is located on Mockingbird Point.

Fort Worth

Fort Woof Dog Park
750 North Beach Street
Fort Worth, TX
817-871-5700
This 5 acre fenced off-leash area is located in Gateway Park. Amenities include a double-gated entry, separate area for small and large dogs, picnic tables, benches, water fountains for dogs and people, dog washing areas, bags and trash cans.

Houston

Ervan Chew Park Dog Park
4502 Dunlavy
Houston, TX
713-845-1000
This park has a designated dog park. The 9,000 square foot off-leash area is fully fenced. The dog park is located adjacent to the picnic area and swimming pool.

Maxey Park Dog Park
601 Maxey Road
Houston, TX

This off-leash park is 12-13 acres with fencing, including an area for smaller dogs and doggie drinking fountains.

Millie Bush Dog Park
Westheimer Parkway
Houston, TX
713-755-6306
This 15 acre dog park was named after Millie, the English Springer Spaniel who shared the White House with George and Barbara Bush. The park was dedicated and opened on April 2, 2004. The off-leash area is

open from 7am to dusk. It is located in George Bush Park, on the south side of Westheimer Parkway, across from the American Shooting Center.

Plano

Jack Carter Park Dog Park
Pleasant Valley Drive
Plano, TX
972-941-7250
This city park has a 2 acre designated dog park. The off-leash area is fenced and double-gated. Amenities include benches, picnic tables, drinking fountains for people and dogs and trash cans. The dog park is located in Jack Carter Park, along Bluebonnet Trail and near the intersection of Chisolm Trail. Parking is available west of the dog park. Go 1/2 block north on Pleasant Valley Drive, from the intersection of Spring Creek Parkway, west of Custer Road.

San Antonio

Pearsall Park Dog Park
4700 Old Pearsall Road
San Antonio, TX
210-207-3000
This city park has a 1.5 acre designated dog park. The fenced in area has picnic tables, trash cans and play features. Dog park hours are from 5am to 11pm every day.

Utah Dog Parks

Salt Lake City

Herman Frank's Park
700 E 1300 S
Salt Lake City, UT

This park has a designated off-leash area. Dogs must be leashed when outside the leash free area.

Jordan Park
1060 South 900 West
Salt Lake City, UT
801-972-7800
This park has a designated off-leash area. Dogs must be leashed when outside the leash free area.

Lindsey Gardens
9th Avenue and M Street
Salt Lake City, UT
801-972-7800
This park has a designated off-leash area. Dogs must be leashed when outside the leash free area.

Memory Grove Park
485 N. Canyon Road
Salt Lake City, UT
801-972-7800
This park has a designated off-leash area which is located in the Freedom Trail area. Dogs must be leashed when outside the leashed area. The park is located east of the Utah State Capitol.

Vermont Dog Parks

Burlington

Starr Farm Dog Park
Starr Farm Rd
Burlington, VT
802-864-0123
This off-leash dog park is fenced and offers separate large and small dogs sections. It is located west of the bike path and adjacent to the Starr Farm Community Garden. Parking is available. The dog park is open 8am to 8pm in April through October and 8am to 6pm in November through March. To get there from I-89, take exit #14w towards Burlington(west). The road becomes Main Street. Turn right on Route 127 and go about a half of a mile. Turn left on Sherman Street. Sherman St. becomes North Avenue. Go about 3 miles and turn left on Starr Farm Road. The park is located off Starr Farm Road, near Lake Champlain and adjacent to the community garden.

Waterfront Dog Park
near Moran Building
Burlington, VT
802-865-7247
This off-leash dog park is fenced and provides access to the lake. It is located about 1,000 feet north of the Moran Building (the old electric generating station). It is a walk-in area with parking at the north end of Waterfront Park or at North Beach. The park is open daily with no hour restrictions. To get there from I-89, take exit #14w towards Burlington

(west). The road becomes Main Street. Main Street turns to the right (north) and becomes Lake Street. Park at the north end of Waterfront Park or at North Beach.

Virginia Dog Parks

Northern Virginia

Ben Brenman Dog Park
at Backlick Creek
Alexandria, VA
703-838-4343
This is an official off-leash dog area. The park is completely fenced. All Alexandria dog parks are controlled by the Alexandria Department of Recreation, Parks and Cultural Activities.

Braddock Road Dog Run Area
SE Corner of Braddock Rd and Commonwealth
Alexandria, VA
703-838-4343
This is an unfenced official off-leash dog area.

Chambliss Street Dog Run Area
Chambliss St
Alexandria, VA
703-838-4343
This is an unfenced official off-leash dog area. It is located south of the tennis courts.

Chinquapin Park Dog Run Area
Chinquapin Park East of Loop
Alexandria, VA
703-838-4343
This is an unfenced official off-leash dog area.

Duke Street Dog Park
5000 block of Duke Street
Alexandria, VA
703-838-4343
This is an official off-leash dog area. The park is completely fenced. The park is located east of the Beatley Library.

Fort Ward Park Offleash Dog Run
East of Park Road
Alexandria, VA
703-838-4343
This is an unfenced official off-leash dog area.

Fort Williams Dog Run Area
Between Ft Wiliams and Ft Williams Parkway
Alexandria, VA
703-838-4343
This is an unfenced official off-leash dog area.

Founders Park Dog Run Area
Oronoco St and Union St
Alexandria, VA
703-838-4343
This is an unfenced official off-leash dog area.

Hooff's Run Dog Run Area
Commonwealth between Oak and Chapman St
Alexandria, VA
703-838-4343
This is an unfenced official off-leash dog area.

Montgomery Park Dog Park
Fairfax and 1st Streets
Alexandria, VA
703-838-4343
This is an official off-leash dog area. The park is completely fenced.

Monticello Park Dog Run Area
Monticello Park
Alexandria, VA
703-838-4343
This is an unfenced official off-leash dog area.

Simpson Stadium Dog Park
Monroe Avenue
Alexandria, VA
703-838-4343
This is an official off-leash dog area. The park is completely fenced.

Tarleton Park Dog Run Area
Old Mill Run west of Gordon St
Alexandria, VA
703-838-4343
This is an unfenced official off-leash dog area.

W&OD Railroad Dog Run Area
Raymond Avenue
Alexandria, VA
703-838-4343
This is an unfenced official off-leash dog area.

Windmill Hill Park Dog Run Area
Gibbon and Union Streets
Alexandria, VA

703-838-4343
This is an unfenced official off-leash dog area.

Mason District
6621 Columbia Pike
Annandale, VA

This fenced dog park is open from dawn to dusk. The park is controlled by the Fairfax County Park Authority and sponsored by the Mason District Dog Opportunity Group.

Benjamin Banneker Park Dog Run
1600 Block North Sycamore
Arlington, VA

This partially fenced off-leash dog park is open during daylight hours. It is over eleven acres. This dog park is maintained by Banneker Dogs.

Fort Barnard Dog Run
Corner of South Pollard St and South Walter Reed Drive
Arlington, VA

This dog run is open from dawn to dusk. It is sponsored by Douglas Dogs.

Glencarlyn Park Dog Run
301 South Harrison St
Arlington, VA

This is an unfenced dog run area in Glencarlyn Park. The area is located near a creek. It is open during daylight hours.

Madison Community Center Dog Park
3829 North Stafford St
Arlington, VA

This 15 acre fully fenced dog park is located at the Madison Community Center. Please note that dogs are not allowed on the adjacent soccer field and that you need to park in the Community Center front lot and not the back lot.

Shirlington Park Dog Run
2601 South Arlington Mill Drive
Arlington, VA

This unfenced dog park is located along the bicycle path between Shirlington Rd and South Walter Reed Dr. It is open during daylight hours.

Towers Park Dog Park

801 South Scott St
Arlington, VA

This fenced dog park is located in Towers Park behind the tennis courts. There is a separate fenced small dog off-leash area.

Chandon Dog Park
900 Palmer Drive
Herndon, VA

This fenced dog park is open from dawn to dusk. The park is controlled by the Fairfax County Park Authority and sponsored by Herndon Dogs, Inc.

Blake Lane Dog Park
10033 Blake Lane
Oakton, VA

This fenced dog park is open from dawn to dusk. The park is controlled by the Fairfax County Park Authority and sponsored by OaktonDogs, Inc.

Baron Cameron Dog Park
11300 Baron Cameron Avenue
Reston, VA

This fenced dog park is open from dawn to dusk. The park is controlled by the Fairfax County Park Authority and sponsored by RestonDogs, Inc. This dog park has a separate area for small dogs and water for your dog.

South Run Dog Park
7550 Reservation Drive
Springfield, VA

This fenced dog park is open from dawn to dusk. The park is controlled by the Fairfax County Park Authority and sponsored by Lorton Dogs, Inc.

Virginia Beach Area

Brambleton Dog Park
Booth Street and Malloy Ave
Norfolk, VA
757-441-2400
This off-leash dog park is not fenced. You must control your dog at all times.

Cambridge Dog Park
Cambridge Place and Cambridge Place
Norfolk, VA
757-441-2400
This off-leash dog park is not fenced. You must control your dog at all times.

Dune Street Dog Park
Dune St & Meadow Brook Lane
Norfolk, VA
757-441-2400
This off-leash dog park is not fenced. You must control your dog at all times.

Red Wing Park Dog Park
1398 General Booth Blvd.
Virginia Beach, VA
757-563-1100
This is a one acre fenced dog park. The park is open from 7:30 am until sunset. There is a $5 annual fee. Dogs must also show proof of license and vaccination. You may get the annual pass at the Maintenance Office at the dog park.

Woodstock Park Dog Park
5709 Providence Rd.
Virginia Beach, VA
757-563-1100
This is a one acre fenced dog park. The park is open from 7:30 am until sunset. There is a $5 annual fee. Dogs must also show proof of license and vaccination. You may get the annual pass at the Maintenance Office at the dog park.

Washington Dog Parks

Seattle

Genesee Park Dog Park
46th Avenue S & S Genesee Street
Seattle, WA
206-684-4075
This fully fenced dog park in Genesee Park has double gates, a drinking fountain for dogs and a kiosk for community notices.

I-90 "Blue Dog Pond" Off-Leash Area
S Massachusetts
Seattle, WA
206-684-4075
This dog park is located at the northwest corner of the intersection of Martin Luther King Jr. Way S and S Massachusetts. The park has a large sculpture of a blue dog.

Jose Rizal Park Off-Leash Area

1008 12th Avenue S
Seattle, WA
206-684-4075
This park offers a designated off-leash area. The park is located at 1008 12th Avenue S on North Beacon Hill. Parking is available on 12th South.

Northacres Park Off-Leash Area
North 130th Street
Seattle, WA
206-684-4075
This park is located west of I-5 at North 130th Street. The park is south of North 130th Street and the off-leash area is in the northeast corner of the park. Parking is available on the west side of the park on 1st NE and on the south side of the park on N 125th.

Regrade Park Off-Leash Area
2251 3rd Avenue
Seattle, WA
206-684-4075
This small off-leash area in Regrade Park is located in downtown at 2251 3rd Avenue at Bell Street.

Sand Point Magnuson Park Dog Off-Leash Area
7400 Sand Point Way NE
Seattle, WA
206-684-4946
This leash free dog park covers about 9 acres and is the biggest fully fenced off-leash park in Seattle. It also offers an access point to the lake where your pooch is welcome to take a dip in the fresh lake water. To find the dog park, take Sand Point Way Northeast and enter the park at Northeast 74th Street. Go straight and park near the playground and sports fields. The main gate to the off-leash area is located at the southeast corner of the main parking lot. Dogs must be leashed until you enter the off-leash area.

Westcrest Park
8806 8th Avenue SW
Seattle, WA
206-684-4075
This dog park in Westcrest Park is over 4 acres in size. It is located in West Seattle.

Woodland Park Off-Leash Area
W Green Lake Way N
Seattle, WA
206-684-4075
This park has a designated off-leash area.

Seattle Area

Golden Gardens Park Dog Park
8498 Seaview Place NW
Ballard, WA
206-684-4075
This fenced dog park is located in the upper park.

Marymoor Park Off-Leash Area
6046 West Lake
Redmond, WA
206-205-3661
This park has a designated off-leash area for dogs. To get to the park from I-5 or I-405, take State Route 520 east to the West Lake Sammamish Parkway exit. At the bottom of the ramp, go right/southbound on W. Lake Sammamish Parkway NE. The park entrance is the next left at the traffic light.

Wisconsin Dog Parks

Cross Plains

Indian Lake Pet Exercise Area
Hwy 19
Cross Plains, WI
608-266-4711
The dog exercise areas in the park are posted on signs in the park. This is a non-fenced dog exercise area. A permit is required to use the off-leash park. The permit allows use of all Madison and Dane County off-leash areas. An annual permit costs $20 per dog or you may opt for a daily fee of $3 per dog per day. Permits may be purchased at the parks department at 4318 Robertson Rd or at many places around the county. The pet exercise area is located north of Cross Plains on Hwy 19 in Indian Lake Park.

Eau-Claire

Eau-Claire Dog Park
4503 House Rd
Eau-Claire, WI
715-839-4923
This dog park requires a permit. You may purchase a day pass by depositing $2 per day in a drop box at the dog park or you may purchase an annual permit for $15 for residents or $20 for non-residents.

Green Bay

Brown County Park Pet Exercise Area
Highway 54
Green Bay, WI
920-448-4466
This fenced dog park is open from 8 am to sunset daily. You must have a permit to use the dog park. Annual permits cost $15 and are available at a number of Green Bay locations. Or you can call 920-448-6242 for an application. Visitors to Green Bay or residents may use the park for $2 for a one day pass. This may be purchased at the dog park. To get to the park from Green Bay take Highway 54 west. The park is located just east of the Brown County Golf Course.

Janesville

Palmer Park Pet Exercise Area
Palmer Park
Janesville, WI

This off-leash dog exercise area is not fenced. Dogs may be off-leash in the area designated as off-leash. Outside of this area dogs must be on leash.

Rock River Parkway Pet Exercise Area
Rock River Parkway
Janesville, WI

This off-leash dog exercise area is not fenced. Dogs may be off-leash in the area designated as off-leash only. Outside of this area dogs must be on leash. The off-leash dog exercise area is located near the boat launch near Center Ave and Rockport Rd.

Johnson Creek

Jefferson County Dog Park
Hwy 26
Johnson Creek, WI

The Jefferson County Dog Park requires a permit in order to use the park. You may pay $2 at the dog park through a self-registration or purchase an annual permit at the Jefferson County Court House, Rm 204, 320 South Main St, Jefferson, WI.

Madison

Brittingham Park Dog Park
401 West Shore Dr
Madison, WI
608-266-4711
The dog exercise areas in the park are posted on signs in the park. This is a non-fenced dog exercise area. A permit is required to use the off-leash park. The permit allows use of all Madison and Dane County off-leash areas. An annual permit costs $20 per dog or you may opt for a daily fee of $3 per dog per day. Permits may be purchased at the parks department at 4318 Robertson Rd or at many places around the county.

Quann Park Dog Park
1802 Expo Drive
Madison, WI
608-266-4711
The dog exercise areas in the park are posted on signs in the park. This is a non-fenced dog exercise area. A permit is required to use the off-leash park. The permit allows use of all Madison and Dane County off-leash areas. An annual permit costs $20 per dog or you may opt for a daily fee of $3 per dog per day. Permits may be purchased at the parks department at 4318 Robertson Rd or at many places around the county.

Sycamore Park Dog Park
4517 Sycamore Park
Madison, WI
608-266-4711
The dog exercise areas in the park are posted on signs in the park. This is a non-fenced dog exercise area. A permit is required to use the off-leash park. The permit allows use of all Madison and Dane County off-leash areas. An annual permit costs $20 per dog or you may opt for a daily fee of $3 per dog per day. Permits may be purchased at the parks department at 4318 Robertson Rd or at many places around the county.

Token Creek Park Pet Exercise Area
Hwy 51
Madison, WI
608-266-4711
The dog exercise areas in the park are posted on signs in the park. This is a non-fenced dog exercise area. A permit is required to use the off-leash park. The permit allows use of all Madison and Dane County off-leash areas. An annual permit costs $20 per dog or you may opt for a daily fee of $3 per dog per day. Permits may be purchased at the parks

department at 4318 Robertson Rd or at many places around the county. The pet exercise area is located north of Madison on Hwy 51 in Token Creek Park.

Warner Park Dog Park
Sheridan Drive
Madison, WI
608-266-4711
The dog exercise areas in the park are posted on signs in the park. This is a non-fenced dog exercise area. A permit is required to use the off-leash park. The permit allows use of all Madison and Dane County off-leash areas. An annual permit costs $20 per dog or you may opt for a daily fee of $3 per dog per day. Permits may be purchased at the parks department at 4318 Robertson Rd or at many places around the county. The park is located on Sheridan Drive along Lagoon at the boat launch auxilary parking lot.

Yahara Heights Pet Exercise Area
5428 State Highway 113
Madison, WI
608-266-4711
The dog exercise areas in the park are posted on signs in the park. This is a non-fenced dog exercise area. A permit is required to use the off-leash park. The permit allows use of all Madison and Dane County off-leash areas. An annual permit costs $20 per dog or you may opt for a daily fee of $3 per dog per day. Permits may be purchased at the parks department at 4318 Robertson Rd or at many places around the county. The pet exercise area is located near the intersection of State Highway 113 and Highway M.

Middleton

Middleton Pet Exercise Area
County Highway Q S of Hwy K
Middleton, WI
608-266-4711
The dog exercise areas in the park are posted on signs in the park. This is a non-fenced dog exercise area. A permit is required to use the off-leash park. The permit allows use of all Madison and Dane County off-leash areas. An annual permit costs $20 per dog or you may opt for a daily fee of $3 per dog per day. Permits may be purchased at the parks department at 4318 Robertson Rd or at many places around the county. The pet exercise area is located north of Middleton on the left side of

County Hwy Q, south of the County Hwy K intersection.

Milwaukee

Brookfield Dog Park
River Rd
Brookfield, WI

This off-leash dog park is not fenced. Dogs must be leashed outside of the off-leash area. The park is located on the north side of River Rd between N. Barker Rd and N. Brookfield Rd.

Muttland Meadows Dog Park
Green Bay Rd
Grafton, WI
262-377-8500
This is a 6.6 acre fenced dog park . It is located southwest of Lime Kiln Park on South Green Bay Road.

Katherin Kearny Carpenter Dog Run
N Katherine Dr
Mequon, WI

This park offers an off-leash dog run area. It is not fenced. Dogs must be on leash outside of the off-leash area. To get to the park from I-43 exit at N Port Washington Rd and head north. When the road curves to go over I-43, merge right on N. Katherine Dr.

Runway Dog Exercise Area
1214 E Rawson Ave
Milwaukee, WI

This dog park opened in August, 2005. It is fully fenced with a double gate. A permit is required to use the dog park. See the website http://www.county.milwaukee.gov/di splay/router.asp?docid=11518 to download a permit application. An annual pass to the dogpark costs $20. You may also pay $5 at the dogpark for a day pass. The park is located on Rawson Avenue between Howell and Nicholson.

Oshkosh

Winnebago County Community Park Dog Park
501 East County Road Y
Oshkosh, WI
920-232-1960
This dog park is located in the Winnebago County Community Park in Oshkosh. The park is open from dawn to dusk daily.

Stevens Point

Standings Rock Park Dog Exercise Area
Standing Rocks Road
Portage, WI
715-346-1433
The dog exercise area is located in Standing Rocks Road between Custer Road and Bear Lake Rd.

Stoughton

Viking Park Pet Exercise Area
Highway N
Stoughton, WI
608-266-4711
The dog exercise areas in the park are posted on signs in the park. This is a non-fenced dog exercise area. A permit is required to use the off-leash park. The permit allows use of all Madison and Dane County off-leash areas. An annual permit costs $20 per dog or you may opt for a daily fee of $3 per dog per day. Permits may be purchased at the parks department at 4318 Robertson Rd or at many places around the county. The pet exercise area is located north of Stoughton on Hwy N.

Sun Prairie

Sun Praire Pet Exercise Area
S. Bird Street
Sun Prairie, WI
608-266-4711
The dog exercise areas in the park are posted on signs in the park. This is a non-fenced dog exercise area. A permit is required to use the off-leash park. The permit allows use of all Madison and Dane County off-leash areas. An annual permit costs $20 per dog or you may opt for a daily fee of $3 per dog per day. Permits may be purchased at the parks department at 4318 Robertson Rd or at many places around the county. The pet exercise area is located south of Sheehan Park on S. Bird Street, over the railroad tracks and hill.

Verona

Praire Moraine Parkway Pet Exercise Area
County Hwy PB
Verona, WI
608-266-4711
The dog exercise areas in the park are posted on signs in the park. This is a non-fenced dog exercise area. A

permit is required to use the off-leash park. The permit allows use of all Madison and Dane County off-leash areas. An annual permit costs $20 per dog or you may opt for a daily fee of $3 per dog per day. Permits may be purchased at the parks department at 4318 Robertson Rd or at many places around the county.

Waupaca

Waupaca County Dog Park
Hwy K
Waupaca, WI
715-258-6243
The dog park is located on Hwy K, south of Waupaca. It is next to the Waupaca Regional Recycling and Composting Center.

British Columbia Dog Parks

Vancouver

Confederation Park Off-Leash Area
Willingdon Avenue
Burnaby, BC
604-294-7450
Dogs are allowed off-leash year-round in a designated area. The area is located north of Penzance Drive, roughly between Willingdon and Gamma Avenues. There will be signs posted indicating the off-leash area. The following off-leash codes apply: clean up after your pet, you must be present and in verbal control of your dog at all times, dogs must wear a valid rabies tag, no aggressive dogs allowed, and dogs must be leashed before and after using the off-leash area. Dogs on leash are allowed throughout Confederation Park.

Burnaby Fraser Foreshore Park Off-Leash Area
Byrne Road
South Burnaby, BC
604-294-7450
From October through March, dogs are allowed off-leash in a designated area near the Fraser River. The area is located near the end of Byrne Road. The following off-leash codes apply: clean up after your pet, you must be present and in verbal control of your dog at all times, dogs must wear a valid rabies tag, no

aggressive dogs allowed, and dogs must be leashed before and after using the off-leash area. Dogs on leash are allowed in the rest of the park, but not on the banks of the Fraser River.

Queen Elizabeth Park Off-Leash Area
37th Avenue and Columbia St.
Vancouver, BC
604-257-8400
Dogs are allowed off-leash from 6am to 10pm only in the designated area. The off-leash area is located at approximately 37th Avenue and Columbia Street.

Ontario Dog Parks

Toronto

Dog Park - High Park
1873 Bloor Street
Toronto, ON
416-397-8186
Dogs can run leash-free at the open area located west of the Dream Site and the allotment Gardens, and northeast of the Grenadier Restaurant. The dog park area is open 24 hours a day, except for 6pm to 10pm during stage productions at the Dream Site. The park is located at Bloor Street and Parkside Drive.

Toronto Area

Totoredaca Leash Free Park
2715 Meadowvale Blvd
Mississauga, ON

This off leash park features a wading pool, tables, and cleanup stations in 3 fenced-in acres. There is a fee for use of the park.

Chapter 5

Dog-Friendly Highway Guides

Interstate 5 Campground Listings

Washington Listings (Interstate 5)   Dogs per Site

Blaine

Birch Bay State Park	360-371-2800	5105 Helwig - Exit Grandview Road Blaine WA	3+

Lynden

Lynden/Bellingham KOA	360-354-4772	8717 Line Road - Exit H 539 Lynden WA	3+

Ferndale

The Cedars RV Resort	360-384-2622	6335 Portal Way Ferndale WA	3+

Bellingham

Bellingham RV Park	360-752-1224	3939 Bennett Drive - Exit 258 Bellingham WA	3+
Larrabee State Park	360-676-2093	245 Chuckanut Drive - Exit 250 Bellingham WA	3+

Anacortes

Fidalgo Bay Resort	360-293-5353	4701 Fidalgo Bay Road Anacortes WA	2
Pioneer Trails RV Resort	360-293-5355	7337 Miller Road - Exit 230 Anacortes WA	2

Burlington

Burlington/Anacortes KOA	360-724-5511	6397 N Green Road - Exit Bow Hill Burlington WA	3+

Everett

Lakeside Park	425-347-2970	12321 H 99S Everett WA	2
Maple Grove RV Resort	425-423-9608	12417 H 99 Everett WA	2

Lynnwood

Twin Cedars RV Park	425-742-5540	17826 H 99N Lynnwood WA	3+

Seattle

Blue Sky RV Park	425-222-7910	9002 302nd Avenue SE Seattle WA	3+

Kent

Seattle/Tacoma KOA	253-872-8652	5801 S 212th Street - Exit 152 Kent WA	3+

Federal Way

Dash Point State Park	253-661-4955	5700 SW Dash Point Road - Exit 320th Federal Way WA	3+

Olympia

Olympic National Forest	360-956-23300	1835 Black Lk Blvd SW - Exit H 101 Olympia WA	3+

Rochester

Outback RV Park	360-273-0585	19100 Huntington - Exit 88 Rochester WA	2

Chehalis

Chehalis/H 12 KOA	360-262-9220	118 h 12 - Exit 68 Chehalis WA	2

Castle Rock

Seaquest State Park	206-274-8633	Spirit Lake H Castle Rock WA	1+

Vancouver

Gifford Pinchot National Forest	360-891-5000	10600 N.E. 51st Circle Vancouver WA	3+
Vancouver RV Park	360-695-1158	7603 NE 13th Avenue - Exit 4 Vancouver WA	2

Woodland

Columbia Riverfront RV Park	360-225-8051	1881Pike Road - Exit 22 Woodland WA	2

Oregon Listings (Interstate 5)   Dogs per Site

Portland

Jantzen Beach RV Park	503-289-7626	1503 N Hayden Island Drive Portland OR	1

Portland Area

Portland Fairview RV Park	503-661-1047	21401 NE Sandy Blvd Fairview OR	3+
Rolling Hills RV Park	503-666-7282	20145 NE Sandy Blvd Fairview OR	3+
RV Park of Portland	503-692-0225	6645 SW Nyberg Road Tualatin OR	1+

Salem

Premier RV Resorts	503-364-7714	4700 H 22 Salem OR	3+
Salem Campground	503-581-6736	3700 Hager's Grove Road - Exit H 22E Salem OR	2

Lebanon

Premier RV Resort	541-259-0070	31958 Bellinger Scale Road - Exit 228 Lebanon OR	3+

Corvallis

Siuslaw National Forest	541-750-7000	4077 SW Research Way Corvallis OR	3+

Albany

Albany/Corvallis KOA	541-967-8521	33775 Oakville Road S - Exit 228/W on H 34 Albany OR	1+

Eugene

Premier RV Resorts	541-686-3152	33022 Van Duyn Road - Exit 199 Eugene OR	3+
Shamrock RV Village	541-747-7473	4531 Franklin Blvd - Exit 189 Eugene OR	3+

Roseburg

Rising River RV Park	541-679-7256	5579 Grange Road - Exit H 42 Roseburg OR	2
Umpqua National Forest	541-750-7000	2900 Stewart Parkway Roseburg OR	3+

Myrtle Creek			
On the River Golf & RV Resort	541-679-3505	111 Whitson Lane Myrtle Creek OR	3+
Central Point			
Medford/Gold Hill KOA	541-855-7710	12297 Blackwell Road - Exit 40/Gold Hill Central Point OR	3+
Grants Pass			
Jack's Landing RV Resort	541-472-1144	247 NE Morgan Lane - Exit 58 Grants Pass OR	3+
Siskiyou National Forest	541-471-6500	2164 NE Spalding Avenue Grants Pass OR	3+
Medford			
Rogue River National Forest	541-858-2200	333 W 8th Street Medford OR	3+
Hornbrook			
Blue Heron RV Park	530-475-3270	6930 Copco Road - Exit 789 Hornbrook OR	3+

California Listings   (Interstate 5)   Dogs per Site

Yreka			
Tree of Heaven Campground, Klamath National Forest	530-468-5351	1312 Fairlane Road Yreka CA	3+
Mount Shasta			
Mount Shasta KOA	530-926-4029	900 N Mt Shasta Blvd Shasta City CA	3+
Redding			
Mountain Gate RV Park	530-283-0769	14161 Holiday Road Redding CA	3+
Sacramento River RV Resort	530-365-6402	6596 Riverland Drive Redding CA	1+
Corning			
Woodson Bridge State Rec Area	530-839-2112	25340 South Avenue Corning CA	3+
Orland			
Buckhorn Recreation Area	530-865-4781	19225 Newville Road Orland CA	3+
Sacramento			
Beals Point Campground	916-988-0205	7806 Folsom-Auburn Road Folsom CA	3+
Cal Expo RV Park	916-263-3000	1600 Exposition Blvd Sacramento CA	2
Sacramento Metropolitan KOA	916-371-6771	3951 Lake Road West Sacramento CA	1+
Lost Hills			
Lost Hills RV Park (formally KOA)	661-797-2719	14831 Warren Street Lost Hills CA	3+
Castaic			
Valencia Travel Resort	661-257-3333	27946 Henry Mayo Drive (H 126) Castaic CA	3+
Anaheim Resort Area			
Canyon RV Park at Featherly	714-637-0210	24001 Santa Ana Canyon Road Anaheim CA	3+
Orangeland RV Park	714-633-0414	1600 W Struck Avenue Orange CA	3+
Orange County South			
Doheny State Beach Park	949-496-6172	25300 Dana Point Harbor Drive Dana Point CA	3+
San Clemente State Beach	949-492-3156	3030 El Avenida Del Presidente San Clemente CA	3+
San Diego County North			
San Elijo State Beach Campground	760-753-5091	2050 Coast H Cardiff CA	2
Guajome County Park	760-724-4489	3000 Guajome Lake Road Oceanside CA	3+
Paradise by the Sea RV Resort	760-439-1376	1537 S Coast H Oceanside CA	3+
San Diego			
San Diego Metro	619-427-3601	111 N 2nd Avenue Chula Vista CA	3+
Sunland RV Resort - San Diego	619-469-4697	7407 Alvarado Road La Mesa CA	2
Campland on the Bay		2211 Pacific Beach Drive San Diego CA	2
Santee Lakes Recreation Preserve	619-596-3141	9310 Fanita Parkway San Diego CA	2

Interstate 10 Campground Listings

California Listings   (Interstate 10)   Dogs per Site

Pomona - Ontario			
East Shore RV Park	909-599-8355	1440 Camper View Road San Dimas CA	3+
Palm Springs			
Palm Springs Oasis RV Resort	800-680-0144	36-100 Date Palm Drive Cathedral City CA	3+
Indian Wells RV Resort	800-789-0895	47-340 Jefferson Street Indio CA	3+

Arizona Listings   (Interstate 10)   Dogs per Site

Quartzsite			
B-10 Campground	928-927-4393	615 Main - Exit 17 Quartzsite AZ	3+
Phoenix			
Covered Wagon RV Park	602-242-2500	6540 N Black Canyon H Phoenix AZ	3+
Desert Sands RV Park	623-869-8186	22036 N 27th Avenue Phoenix AZ	3+

Desert Shadows RV Resort	623-869-8178	19203 N 29th Avenue Phoenix AZ	2
Destiny RV Resort	623-853-0537	416 N Citrus Road - Exit 124 Phoenix AZ	1+
Pioneer RV Resort	800-658-5895	36408 N Black Canyon H Phoenix AZ	2
Tonto National Forest	602-225-5200	2324 E. McDowell Road Phoenix AZ	3+
Phoenix Area			
Mesa Spirit	480-832-1770	3020 E Main Street Mesa AZ	2
Silveridge RV Resort	480-373-7000	8265 E Southern Mesa AZ	3+
Apache Junction			
La Hacienda RV Resort	480-982-2808	1797 W 28th Avenue Apache Junction AZ	1+
Lost Dutchman State Park	480-982-4485	6109 N. Apache Trail Apache Junction AZ	3+
Mesa/Apache Junction KOA	480-982-4015	1540 S Tomahawk Road - Exit H 60E Apache Junction AZ	3+
Superstition Sunrise	480-986-4524	702 S Meridian Apache Junction AZ	3+
Weaver's Needle Travel Trailor Resort	480-982-3683	250 S Tomahawk Road Apache Junction AZ	1+
Casa Grande			
Buena Tierra RV Park and Campground	520-836-3500	1995 S Cox Road Casa Grande AZ	3+
Palm Creek Golf and RV Resort	800-421-7004	1110 N Hennes Road - Exit 194 Casa Grande AZ	2
Tucson			
Catalina State Park	520-628-5798	11570 N Oracle Road Tucson AZ	3+
Coronado National Forest	520-388-8300	5700 N Sabino Canyon Road Tucson AZ	3+
Crazy Horse RV Park	520-574-0157	6660 S Craycroft - Exit S Craycroft Tucson AZ	2
Prince of Tucson RV Park	520-887-3501	3501 N Freeway - Exit Prince Road Tucson AZ	3+
Benson			
Benson KOA	520-586-3977	180 W Four Feathers - Exit 304 N Benson AZ	2
Butterfield RV Resort and Observatory	520-586-4400	251 S Ocotillo - Exit 204 Benson AZ	3+
Kartchner Caverns State Park	520-586-2283	2980 S H 90 - Exit H 90 Benson AZ	3+

New Mexico Listings   (Interstate 10)
Dogs per Site

Deming			
Little Vineyard	505-546-3560	2901 E Pine - Exit 85 Deming NM	3+
Roadrunner RV Park	505-546-6960	2849 E Pine Street - Exit 85 Deming NM	3+
Rockhound State Park	505-546-6182	P. O. Box 1064 Deming NM	3+
Las Cruces			
Hacienda RV and Rally Resort	888-686-9090	740 Stern Drive - Exit 140 Las Cruces NM	3+
The Coachlight Inn and RV Park	505-526-3301	301 S Motel Blvd Las Cruces NM	1+

Texas Listings   (Interstate 10)
Dogs per Site

El Paso			
El Paso Roadrunner RV Park	915-598-4469	1212 LaFayette - Exit 28B El Paso TX	3+
Sampson RV Park	915-859-8383	11300 Gateway Blvd - Exit 351/East Lake El Paso TX	3+
Van Horn			
Van Horn KOA	432-283-2728	10 Kamper's Lane - Exit 140A Van Horn TX	3+
Junction			
Junction KOA	325-446-3138	2145 Main Street - Exit 456 Junction TX	3+
Fredericksburg			
Fredericksburg	830-997-4796	5681 H 290E Fredericksburg TX	1+
Oakwood RV Resort	830-997-9817	#78 FM 2093 - Exit Kerriville to Tivydale Road Fredericksburg TX	1+
Kerrville			
Kerrville KOA	830-895-1665	2950 Goat Creek Road - Exit 501 Kerrville TX	3+
San Antonio			
Admiralty RV Resort	800-999-7872	1485 N Ellison Drive San Antonio TX	3+
Blazing Star RV Resort	210-680-7827	1120 W H 1604N San Antonio TX	2
San Antonio KOA	210-224-9296	602 Gembler Road - Exit 580 San Antonio TX	2
Traveler's World RV Resort	210-532-8310	2617 Roosevelt Avenue San Antonio TX	3+
Brookshire			
Houston West/Brookshire KOA	281-375-5678	35303 Cooper Road - Exit 731 Brookshire TX	3+
Houston			
All Star RV Resort	713-981-6814	10650 SW Plaza Court Houston TX	3+
Houston Central KOA	281-442-3700	1620 Peachleaf Houston TX	3+
Houston Leisure RV Resort	281-426-3576	1601 S Main Street - Exit 787 Houston TX	3+
Trader's Village	281-890-5500	7979 N Eldridge Road Houston TX	3+
Baytown			
Houston East/Baytown KOA	281-383-3618	11810 I-10E - Exit H 146 Baytown TX	3+

Louisiana Listings   (Interstate 10)
Dogs per Site

Sulphur			
Hidden Ponds RV Park	337-583-4709	1207 Ravia Road Sulphur LA	3+
Lake Charles			

			Dogs per Site
Jellystone Park	337-433-1114	4200 Luke Powers Road - Exit 36 Lake Charles LA	3+
Scott			
Lafayette KOA	337-235-2739	537 Apollo Road - Exit 97 Scott LA	3+
Port Allen			
Cajun Country Campground	800-264-8554	4667 Relle Lane - Exit 151 Port Allen LA	3+
New Orleans			
New Orleans/Hammond KOA	985-542-8094	14154 Club Deluxe Road Hammond LA	3+

Alabama Listings (Interstate 10)   Dogs per Site

Mobile			
Magnolia Springs RV Hideaway	800-981-0981	10831 Magnolia Springs H Foley AL	3+
Palm Lake Resort	251-970-3773	15810 H 59 Foley AL	3+
Shady Acres Campground	251-478-0013	2500 Old Military Road - Exit 22 Mobile AL	3+
Gulf Shores			
Gulf Breeze Resort	251-968-8884	19800 Oak Road W - Exit H 59 Gulf Shores AL	3+
Gulf State Park	251-948-6353	22050 Campground Road Gulf Shores AL	3+
Luxury RV Resort	251-948-5444	590 Gulf Shores Parkway Gulf Shores AL	3+

Florida Listings (Interstate 10)   Dogs per Site

Holt			
Blackwater River State Park	850-983-5363	7720 Deaton Bridge Road - Exit 31/H 87N Holt FL	3+
Chipley			
Falling Waters State Rec Area	850-638-6130	1130 State Park Road - Exit 121/H77 Chipley FL	3+
Marianna			
Florida Caverns State Park	850-482-9598	3345 Caverns Road (H 166) Marianna FL	3+
Chattahoochee			
Chattahoochee/Tallahassee W KOA	850-442-6657	2309 Flat Circle Road - Exit 166/H270A Chattahoochee FL	3+
Tallahassee			
Apalachicola National Forest	850-643-2282	11152 NW State Road 20 Tallahassee FL	3+
Big Oak RV Park	850-562-4660	4024 N Monroe Street - Exit 199 Tallahassee FL	3+
Madison			
Jellystone Park	800-347-0174	1051 SW Old St. Augustine Road - Exit 258 Madison FL	3+
Live Oak			
Suwannee River State Park	386-362-2746	20185 County Road 132 - Exit H 90 Live Oak FL	3+
Jacksonville			
Little Talbot Island State Park	904-251-2320	12157 Heckscher Drive Jacksonville FL	3+
Flamingo Lake RV Resort	904-766-0672	3640 Newcomb Road N Jacksonville FL	3+

Interstate 15 Campground Listings

Montana Listings (Interstate 15)   Dogs per Site

Great Falls			
Acklley Lake State Park	406-454-5840	4600 Giant Srings Road Great Falls MT	3+
Dick's RV Park	406-452-0333	1403 11th Street SW - Exit 278 to Exit '0' Great Falls MT	3+
Great Falls KOA	406-727-3191	1500 51st Street S - Exit 278 go E Great Falls MT	3+
Lewis and Clark National Forest	406-791-7700	1101 15th Street N. Great Falls MT	3+
Wolf Creek			
Holter Lake Recreation Area	406-494-5059	Recreation Road - Exit 226 Left on Missouri River Road Wolf Creek MT	3+
Helena			
Helena Campground	406-458-4714	5820 N Montana Avenue Helena MT	2
Helena National Forest	406-449-5201	2880 Skyway Drive - Exit H 12 Helena MT	3+
Butte			
Butte KOA	406-782-8080	1601 Kaw Avenue Butte MT	3+
Dillon			
Bannack State Park	406-834-3413	4200 Bannack Road Dillon MT	3+
Deerlodge (Beaverhead) National Forest	406-683-3900	420 Barrett Street - Exit Barrett Street Dillon MT	3+
Dillon KOA	406-683-2749	735 Park Street - Exit 62 Dillon MT	3+

Idaho Listings (Interstate 15)   Dogs per Site

Idaho Falls			
Caribou-Targhee National Forest	208-524-7500	3659 East Ririe Highway Idaho Falls ID	3+

Targhee-Caribou National Forest	208-524-7500	1405 Hollipark Drive Idaho Falls ID	3+
Pocatello			
Pocatello KOA	208-233-6851	9815 W Pocatello Creek Road - Exit 71 Pocatello ID	3+

Utah Listings   (Interstate 15)

Dogs per Site

Willard			
Willard Bay State Park	435-734-9494	900 West 650 North #A/ On H 315 - Exit 354 for the south marina Willard UT	3+
Syracuse			
Antelope Island State Park	801-773-2941	4528 West 1700 South - Exit 332/Antelope Drive Syracuse UT	3+
Kaysville			
Cherry Hill RV Resort	801-451-5379	1325 S Main - Exit 324/H 89 Kaysville UT	3+
Salt Lake City			
Sunset Campground	877-444-6777	Farmington Canyon Farmington City UT	1+
Salt Lake City KOA	801-355-1214	1400 W North Temple - Exit 311 Salt Lake City UT	3+
Wasatch -Cache National Forest	801-466-6411	3285 East 3800 S Salt Lake City UT	3+
Quail Run RV Park	801-255-9300	9230 S State Street - Exit 295 Sandy UT	3+
Provo			
Lakeside RV Campground	801-373-5267	4000 W Center Street - Exit 265 or 265B Provo UT	3+
Provo KOA	801-375-2994	320N 2050 W - Exit 265 Provo UT	3+
Uinta National Forest	801-377-5780	88 W 100 N - Exit W 100 N Provo UT	3+
Fillmore			
Fillmore KOA	435-743-4420	900 S 410 W - Exit 163 Fillmore UT	1+
Beaver			
Beaver KOA	435-438-2924	1428 Manderfield Road - Exit 112 Beaver UT	3+
Cedar City			
Cedar City KOA	435-586-9872	1121 N Main - Exit 57 Cedar City UT	1+
Dixie National Forest	435-865-3700	1789 N Wedgewood Lane - Exit 57 (H 14-goes into the forest) Cedar City UT	3+
Zion National Park			
Quail Creek State Park	435-879-2378	H 318 M.P. #2 - Exit 16/Hurricane Hurricane UT	3+
Red Cliffs Recreation Area	435-688-3246	4.5 miles from Leeds on I-15 - Exit 6 Leeds UT	3+
Zion Canyon Campground & Resort	435-772-3237	479 Zion Park Blvd - Exit H 9 Springdale UT	2
Hurricane			
Brentwood RV Resort	800-447-2239	15N 3700W - Exit 16 Hurricane UT	1
St George			
Snow Canyon State Park	435-628-2255	1002 Snow Canyon Drive (H 18) St George UT	3+
Templeview RV Resort	800-381-0321	975 S Main - Exit 6 St George UT	2

Nevada Listings   (Interstate 15)

Dogs per Site

Overton			
Valley of Fire State Park	702-397-2088	P. O. Box 515/ Valley of Fire Road Overton NV	3+
Las Vegas			
Las Vegas KOA at Circus Circus	702-733-9707	500 Circus Circus Drive Las Vegas NV	3+
Oasis Las Vegas RV Resort	800-566-4707	2711 W Windmill Lane Las Vegas NV	2

California Listings   (Interstate 15)

Dogs per Site

Baker			
Hole in the Wall Campground	760-928-2562	Black Canyon Road Baker CA	3+
Mohave National Preserve Campgrounds	760-252-6101	Black Canyon Road Baker CA	3+
Victorville			
Victorville/Inland Empire KOA	760-245-6867	16530 Stoddard Wells Road Victorville CA	1+
Temecula			
Pechanga RV Resort	951-587-0484	45000 Pechanga Parkway Temecula CA	2
Vail Lake Wine Country RV Resort	951-303-0173	38000 H 79 S Temecula CA	2
San Diego I-15 Corridor			
Sunland RV Resorts	760-740-5000	1740 Seven Oaks Road Escondido CA	2
San Diego County North			
San Elijo State Beach Campground	760-753-5091	2050 Coast H Cardiff CA	2
Guajome County Park	760-724-4489	3000 Guajome Lake Road Oceanside CA	3+
Paradise by the Sea RV Resort	760-439-1376	1537 S Coast H Oceanside CA	3+
San Diego			
San Diego Metro	619-427-3601	111 N 2nd Avenue Chula Vista CA	3+
Sunland RV Resort - San Diego	619-469-4697	7407 Alvarado Road La Mesa CA	2
Campland on the Bay		2211 Pacific Beach Drive San Diego CA	2
Santee Lakes Recreation Preserve	619-596-3141	9310 Fanita Parkway San Diego CA	2

Interstate 20 Campground Listings

Texas Listings (Interstate 20)   Dogs per Site

Monahans			
Monahans Sandhills State Park	432-943-2092	Park Road 41 - Exit 86 Monahans TX	3+
Odessa			
Midessa Oil Patch RV Park	432-563-2368	4220 S County Road 1290 - Exit 126 Odessa TX	3+
Abilene			
Abilene KOA	915-672-3681	4851 W Stamford Street - Exit 282 Abilene TX	3+
Dallas - Fort Worth Area			
Treetops RV Village	817-467-7943	1901 W Arbrook - Exit H 157 Arlington TX	1+
RV Ranch	888-855-9091	2301 S I 35W Burleson TX	3+

Louisiana Listings (Interstate 20)   Dogs per Site

Shreveport			
Cash Point Landing	318-742-4999	215 Cash Point Landing Bossier City LA	3+
Shreveport/Bossier KOA	318-687-1010	6510 W 70th Street - Exit 10 S to W 70th Shreveport LA	3+
Minden			
Caney Lakes Rec Area	318-927-2061	194 Caney Lake Road Minden LA	3+
Monroe			
Bayou Boeuf RV Park	318-665-2405	11791 H 165 N Sterlington LA	3+

Mississippi Listings (Interstate 20)   Dogs per Site

Vicksburg			
Rivertown Campground	601-630-9995	5900 H 61S - Exit H 61S Vicksburg MS	3+
Vicksburg Battlefield	601-636-2025	4407 N Frontage Road - Exit 4B Vicksburg MS	3+
Jackson			
LeFleur's Bluff State Park	601-987-3923	2140 Riverside Drive Jackson MS	3+
Forest			
Bienville National Forest	601-469-3811	3473 H 35S Forest MS	3+
Meridian			
Nanabe Creek Campground	601-485-4711	1933 Russell Mount Gilliad Road - Exit 160 Meridian MS	3+

Alabama Listings (Interstate 20)   Dogs per Site

Knoxville			
Knox Hill RV Park	205-372-3911	252 Old Patton Road Knoxville AL	3+
Birmingham			
Cherokee Campground	205-428-8339	2800 H 93 Helena AL	3+
Birmingham South Campground	205-664-8832	222 H 33 Pelham AL	3+

Georgia Listings (Interstate 20)   Dogs per Site

Atlanta			
Stone Mountain Park	800-385-9807	H 78E Stone Mountain GA	3+
Atlanta Area			
Brookwood RV Park	877-727-5787	1031 Wylie Road SE Marietta GA	3+
Atlanta South RV Resort	770-957-2610	281 Mount Olive Road McDonough GA	3+

South Carolina Listings (Interstate 20)   Dogs per Site

Columbia			
Sesquicentennial State Park	803-788-2706	9564 Two Notch Road Columbia SC	3+
Barnyard RV Park	803-957-1238	201 Oak Drive - Exit 58 Lexington SC	3+
Florence			
Florence KOA	843-665-7007	1115 E Campground Road Florence SC	3+

Interstate 25 Campground Listings

Wyoming Listings (Interstate 25)   Dogs per Site

Buffalo

Buffalo KOA	307-684-5423	87 H 16E - Exit 299 Buffalo WY	3+
Deer Park RV Park	307-684-5722	Box 568, On H 16E Buffalo WY	3+
Indian Campground	307-684-9601	660 E Hart Street - Exit 299 Buffalo WY	1+

Casper

Casper KOA	307-577-1664	1101 Prairie Lane - Exit 191 Casper WY	3+
Fort Casper Campground	888-243-7709	4205 Fort Caspar Road Casper WY	2

Douglas

Douglas KOA	307-358-2164	168 H 91 - Exit 146 Douglas WY	3+

Glendo

Glendo State Park	307-735-4433	397 Glendo Park Road - Exit 111 Glendo WY	3+

Guernsey

Guernsey State Park	307-836-2334	On H 317 - Exit 92 Guernsey WY	3+
Hawk Springs Recreation Area	307-836-2334	3 miles south of Hawk Springs off H 85 Guernsey WY	3+

Cheyenne

Cheyenne KOA	307-638-8840	8800 Archer Frontage Road Cheyenne WY	3+
Curt Gowdy State Park	307-632-7946	1319 Hynds Lodge Road Cheyenne WY	3+
Terry Bison Ranch	307-634-4171	51 I 25 Service Road E - Exit 2 Cheyenne WY	3+

Colorado Listings (Interstate 25)

Dogs per Site

Wellington

Fort Collins North/Wellington KOA	970-568-7486	4821 E County Road 70/Owl Canyon Road - Exit 281 Wellington CO	3+

Fort Collins

Arapaho Roosevelt National Forest	970-498-2770	2150 Center Avenue, Building E - Exit Prospect Road Fort Collins CO	3+
Heron Lake RV Park	877-254-4063	1910 N Taft Hill - Exit 269B Fort Collins CO	3+

Loveland

Johnson's Corner RV Retreat	970-669-8400	3618 SE Frontage Road - Exit 254 Loveland CO	3+

Longmont

St. Vrain State Park	303-678-9402	3525 H 119 Longmont CO	3+

Denver

Denver Meadows RV Park	303-364-9483	2075 Potomac Street Aurora CO	3+
Dakota Ridge RV Park	800-398-1625	17800 W Colfax Golden CO	3+
Chatfield State Park	303-791-7275	11500 N Roxborough Park Road Littleton CO	3+
Prospect RV Park	303-424-4414	11600 W 44th Avenue Wheat Ridge CO	3+

Castle Rock

Castle Rock Campground	303-681-3169	6527 S I 25 - Exit 174 Castle Rock CO	3+

Colorado Springs

Fountain Creek RV Park	719-633-2192	3023 W Colorado Avenue - Exit 141 Colorado Springs CO	3+
Garden of the Gods Campground	719-475-9450	3704 W Colorado Avenue Colorado Springs CO	3+

Fountain

Colorado Springs South KOA	719-382-7575	8100 Bandley Drive - Exit 132 Fountain CO	3+

Pueblo

Lake Pueblo	719-561-9320	640 Reservoir Road Pueblo CO	3+
Pike and San Isabel National Forests	719-545-8737	2840 Kachina Drive Pueblo CO	3+
Pueblo KOA	719-542-2273	4131 I 25N - Exit 108 Pueblo CO	3+

New Mexico Listings (Interstate 25)

Dogs per Site

Raton

Sugarite Canyon State Park	505-445-5607	HCR 63, Box 386 Raton NM	3+

Las Vegas

Storrie Lake State Park	505-425-7278	HC 33, Box 109 #2 Las Vegas NM	3+

Santa Fe

Hyde Memorial State Park	505-983-7175	740 Hyde Park Road Santa Fe NM	3+
Rancheros de Santa Fe	800-426-9259	736 Old Las Vegas H - Exit 290 Santa Fe NM	3+
Santa Fe National Forest	505-438-7840	1474 Rodeo Road Santa Fe NM	3+
Santa Fe Skies RV Park	505-473-5946	14 Browncastle Ranch - Exit 276 Santa Fe NM	3+
Trailer Ranch RV Resort	505-471-9970	3471 Cerrillos - Exit 278 Santa Fe NM	3+

Bernalillo

Albuquerque N/Bernalillo KOA	505-867-5227	555 S Hill Road - Exit 240 Bernalillo NM	3+

Albuquerque

Albuquerque Central KOA	505-296-2729	12400 Skyline Road NE Albuquerque NM	3+
Enchanted Trails	505-831-6317	14305 Central Albuquerque NM	3+
High Desert RV Park	866-839-9035	13000 W Frontage Road SW Albuquerque NM	3+

Elephant Butte

Elephant Butte Lake	505-744-5421	Box 13; H 195/171 - Exit 83 Elephant Butte NM	3+

Truth or Consequences

Cielo Vista RV Resort	505-894-3738	501 S Broadway - Exit 75 Truth or Consequences NM	3+

Caballo

Caballo Lake State Park	505-743-3942	Box 32; On H 187 - Exit 59 N Caballo NM	3+
Percha Dam State Park	505-743-3942	Box 32; on H 187 - Exit 59 S Caballo NM	3+
Las Cruces			
Hacienda RV and Rally Resort	888-686-9090	740 Stern Drive Las Cruces NM	3+
The Coachlight Inn and RV Park	505-526-3301	301 S Motel Blvd Las Cruces NM	1+

Interstate 35 Campground Listings

Minnesota Listings (Interstate 35)   Dogs per Site

Duluth			
Indian Point Campground	218-628-4977	7500 Pulaski Duluth MN	2
Superior National Forest	218-626-4300	8901 Grand Avenue Place Duluth MN	3+
Hinckley			
St Croix State Park	320-384-6591	30065 St Croix Park Road Hinckley MN	3+
Minneapolis - St Paul			
Greenwood Campground	651-437-5269	13797 190th Street E Hastings MN	2
Minneapolis Northwest KOA	763-420-2255	10410 Brockton Maple Grove MN	2
Dakotah Meadows RV Park	952-445-8800	2341 Park Place Prior Lake MN	3+
St Paul East KOA	651-436-6436	568 Cottage Grove Woodbury MN	3+
Owatonna			
Hope Oak Knoll Campground	507-451-2998	9545 County Road 3 - Exit 32 Owatonna MN	3+

Iowa Listings (Interstate 35)   Dogs per Site

Clear Lake			
Clear Lake State Park	641-357-4212	6490 S Shore Drive Clear Lake IA	3+
Oakwood RV Park	641-357-4019	5419 240th Street - Exit 193 Clear Lake IA	3+
Des Moines			
Adventureland Campground	512-265-7384	2600 Adventureland Drive Altoona IA	2
Kellogg RV Park	641-526-8535	1570 H 224 Kellogg IA	3+
Rolling Acres RV Park	641-792-2428	1601 E 36th Street Newton IA	3+
Osceola			
Terribles Lakeside Casino	541-342-9511	777 Casino Drive Osceola IA	2

Missouri Listings (Interstate 35)   Dogs per Site

Kansas City			
Trailside RV Park	816-229-2267	1000 R.D. Mize Road Grain Valley MO	3+
Basswood Country RV Resort	816-858-5556	15880 Inter Urban Road Platte City MO	3+

Kansas Listings (Interstate 35)   Dogs per Site

Kansas City			
Rutlader Outpost and RV Park	866-888-6779	33565 Metcalf Louisburg KS	3+
Emporia			
Emporia RV Park	620-343-3422	1601 W H 50 Emporia KS	3+
El Dorado			
Deer Grove RV Park	316-321-6272	2873 SE H 54 El Dorado KS	3+
El Dorado State Park	316-321-7180	618 NE Bluestem Road El Dorado KS	3+
Wichita			
USI RV Park	316-838-8699	2920 E 33rd Wichita KS	3+

Oklahoma Listings (Interstate 35)   Dogs per Site

Oklahoma City			
Oklahoma City East KOA	405-391-5000	6200 S Choctaw Road Choctaw OK	3+
Abe's RV Park	405-478-0278	12115 N I 35 Service Road - Exit 137 Oklahoma City OK	3+
Rockwell RV Park	405-787-5992	720 S Rockwell Oklahoma City OK	3+
Davis			
Dreamweaver RV Resort	580-369-3399	110 Kay Star Trail - Exit 51 Davis OK	3+
Ardmore			
Lake Murray State Park	580-223-4044	204 Scenic State H 77 Ardmore OK	3+
Marietta			
Ardmore/Marietta KOA	580-276-2800	Oswalt Road (Rt 1, Box 640) - Exit 21 Marietta OK	3+

Texas Listings (Interstate 35)

Dogs per Site

Dallas - Fort Worth Area

| Treetops RV Village | 817-467-7943 | 1901 W Arbrook   Arlington TX | 1+ |
| RV Ranch | 888-855-9091 | 2301 S I 35W   Burleson TX | 3+ |

Bellmead

| Waco North KOA | 254-826-3869 | 24132 N I 35 - Exit 355 Waco TX | 3+ |
| i 35 RV Park | 254-829-0698 | 1513 N I 35 - Exit 345 or 346 Waco TX | 2 |

Belton

| Belton/Temple/Killeen KOA | 254-939-1961 | 2901 S I 35 - Exit 292 Belton TX | 3+ |

Austin

| Austin Lone Star RV Resort | 512-444-6322 | 7009 S IH 35   Austin TX | 3+ |
| Oak Forest RV Park | 800-478-7275 | 8207 Canoga Avenue - Exit H 290E Austin TX | 3+ |

San Antonio

Admiralty RV Resort	800-999-7872	1485 N Ellison Drive San Antonio TX	3+
Blazing Star RV Resort	210-680-7827	1120 W H 1604N San Antonio TX	2
San Antonio KOA	210-224-9296	602 Gembler Road - Exit 160 San Antonio TX	2
Traveler's World RV Resort	210-532-8310	2617 Roosevelt Avenue - Exit Military Drive San Antonio TX	3+

Interstate 40 Campground Listings

California Listings (Interstate 40)

Dogs per Site

Needles

| Moabi Regional Park Campgrounds | 760-326-3831 | Park Moabi Road   Needles CA | 3+ |
| Needles KOA | 760-326-4207 | 5400 National Old Trails H   Needles CA | 3+ |

Arizona Listings (Interstate 40)

Dogs per Site

Kingman

| Kingman KOA | 928-757-4397 | 3820 N Roosevelt - Exit 51N Kingman AZ | 3+ |

Grand Canyon

Ash Fork RV Park	928-637-2521	783 W Old Route 66 - Exit Old H 66 Ash Fork AZ	3+
Flintstones Bedrock City	928-635-2600	Junction 64 and 180 Williams AZ	3+
Grand Canyon/Williams KOA	928-635-2307	5333 H 64 - Exit 165 N Williams AZ	3+
Kaibab National Forest	928-635-8200	Railroad Blvd Williams AZ	3+
Williams/Circle Pines KOA	928-635-2626	1000 Circle Pines Road - Exit 167 Williams AZ	3+

Flagstaff

Coconino National Forest	928-527-3600	1824 S Thompson Street Flagstaff AZ	3+
Flagstaff KOA	928-526-9926	5803 N H 89 - Exit 201 Flagstaff AZ	3+
Woody Mountain Campground and RV Park	928-774-7727	2727 W H 66 - Exit 191/H 66 Flagstaff AZ	2

Winslow

| Homolovi Ruins State Park | 928-289-4106 | Honahanie Road   Winslow AZ | 3+ |

Holbrook

| Holbrook/Petrified Forest KOA | 928-524-6689 | 102 Hermosa Drive - Exit 289 Holbrook AZ | 3+ |

New Mexico Listings (Interstate 40)

Dogs per Site

Gallup

| USA RV Park | 505-863-5021 | 2925 W H 66 Gallup NM | 3+ |

Prewitt

| Bluewater Lake State Park | 505-876-2391 | Box 3419/ at end of H 412 - Exit 63 Prewitt NM | 3+ |

Albuquerque

Albuquerque Central KOA	505-296-2729	12400 Skyline Road NE - Exit 166 Albuquerque NM	3+
Enchanted Trails	505-831-6317	14305 Central - Exit 149 Albuquerque NM	3+
High Desert RV Park	866-839-9035	13000 W Frontage Road SW - Exit 149 Albuquerque NM	3+

Cedar Crest

| Turquoise Trail Campground | 505-281-2005 | 22 Calvary Road - Exit 175 Cedar Crest NM | 3+ |

Santa Rosa

| Santa Rosa Campground | 505-472-3126 | 2136 Historic H 66 - Exit 277 Santa Rosa NM | 3+ |
| Santa Rosa Lake State Park | 505-472-3110 | P.O. Box 384 Santa Rosa NM | 3+ |

Tucumcari

| Mountain Road RV Park | 505-461-9628 | 1700 Mountain Road - Exit 333 Tucumcari NM | 3+ |

Texas Listings (Interstate 40)

Dogs per Site

Amarillo

Amarillo KOA	806-335-1762	1100 Folsom Road - Exit 75/H60 Amarillo TX	3+
Amarillo Ranch	806-373-4962	1414 Sunrise - Exit 74 Amarillo TX	3+
Fort Amarillo RV Resort	806-331-1700	10101 Amarillo Blvd - Exit Soncy Amarillo TX	3+

Oklahoma Listings (Interstate 40)

Dogs per Site

Elk City

Elk Creek RV Park	580-225-7865	317 E 20th - Exit 38 Elk City OK	3+
Canute			
Elk City/Clinton KOA	580-592-4409	Clinton Lake Road - Exit 50 Canute OK	3+
Calumet			
El Reno West KOA	405-884-2595	301 S Walbaum Road - Exit 108 Calumet OK	3+
Oklahoma City			
Oklahoma City East KOA	405-391-5000	6200 S Choctaw Road - Exit 166 Choctaw OK	3+
Abe's RV Park	405-478-0278	12115 N I 35 Service Road Oklahoma City OK	3+
Rockwell RV Park	405-787-5992	720 S Rockwell - Exit S. Rockwell Oklahoma City OK	3+
Checotah			
Checotah/Henryetta KOA	918-473-6511	On I 40 @Pierce Road (HC 68, Box750) - Exit 255/Pierce Road Checotah OK	3+
Sallisaw			
Sallisaw KOA	918-775-2792	1908 Power Drive - Exit 308/H 59 Sallisaw OK	3+

Arkansas Listings (Interstate 40)

Dogs per Site

Alma

Fort Smith/Alma KOA	479-632-2704	3539 N H 71 - Exit 13/H 71 Alma AR	1+
Russellville			
Ozark-St. Francis National Forest	479-964-7200	605 W Main Street Russellville AR	3+
Morrilton			
Morrilton/Conway KOA	501-354-8262	30 Kamper Lane - Exit 107 N/H 95 Morrilton AR	3+
Petit Jean State Park	501-727-5441	1285 Petit Jean Mountain Road Morrilton AR	3+
Little Rock			
Little Rock North/Jct I 40 KOA	501-758-4598	7820 Crystal Hill Road - Exit 148/Crystal Hill Road N Little Rock AR	3+
Burns Park Campground	501-771-0702	4101 Arlene Laman Drive - Exit 150 North Little Rock AR	3+
West Memphis			
Tom Sawyer's Mississippi River RV Park	870-735-9770	1286 S 8th Street - Exit I 55 West Memphis AR	3+

Tennessee Listings (Interstate 40)

Dogs per Site

Memphis

Memphis Graceland RV Park and Campground	901-396-7125	3691 Elvis Presley Blvd Memphis TN	3+
T. O. Fuller State Park	901-543-7581	1500 W Mitchell Road Memphis TN	3+
Tom Sawyer's Mississippi River RV Park	870-735-9770	1286 S 8th Street - Exit I 55 West Memphis AR	3+
Hurricane Mills			
Buffalo/I-40/Exit 143 KOA	931-296-1306	473 Barren Hollow Road - Exit 143 Hurricane Mills TN	1+
Loretta Lynn's Ranch	931-296-7700	44 Hurricane Mills - Exit 143 Hurricane Mills TN	3+
Nashville			
Brown County State Park	812-988-6406	1450 State Road 46 W Nashville TN	3+
Jellystone Park	615-889-4225	2572 Music Valley Drive - Exit Briley Parkway to exit 12 Nashville TN	3+
Two Rivers Campground	615-883-8559	2616 Music Valley Drive Nashville TN	3+
Lebanon			
Cedars of Lebanon State Park	615-443-2769	328 Cedar Forest Road Lebanon TN	3+
Countryside RV Resort	615-449-5527	2100 Safari Camp Road - Exit 232/L. on H 109 Lebanon TN	3+
Crossville			
Ballyhoo Campground	931-484-0860	256 Werthwyle Drive - Exit 322 Crossville TN	1+
Roam and Roost RV Campground	931-707-1414	255 Fairview Drive - Exit 322 Crossville TN	2
Knoxville			
Southlake RV Park	865-573-1837	3730 Maryville Pike Knoxville TN	3+
Kodak			
Knoxville East KOA	865-933-6393	241 KOA Way - Exit 407 Kodak TN	3+
Sevierville			
River Plantation RV Park	865-429-5267	1004 Parkway Sevierville TN	3+

North Carolina Listings (Interstate 40)   Dogs per Site

Candler			
Asheville West KOA	828-665-7015	309 Wiggins Road - Exit 37 R Candler NC	3+
Asheville			
Bear Creek RV Park	828-253-0798	81 S Bear Creek Road - Exit 47/Farmer's Market Asheville NC	3+
Pisgah National Forest	828-877-3350	1001 Pisgah H (H276) Asheville NC	3+
Swannanoa			
Asheville East KOA	828-686-3121	2708 H 70 E - Exit 59 Swannanoa NC	3+
Mama Gerties Hideaway Campground	828-686-4258	15 Uphill Road - Exit 59 Swannanoa NC	2
Marion			
Buck Creek Campground	828-724-4888	2576 Toms Creek Road - Exit 86 Marion NC	3+
Jellystone Park at Hidden Valley Campground	828-652-7208	1210 Deacon Drive - Exit 86/H 226 Marion NC	3+
Statesville			
Statesville KOA	704-873-5560	162 KOA Lane Statesville NC	3+

Interstate 55 Campground Listings

Illinois Listings (Interstate 55)   Dogs per Site

Chicago Area			
Windy City Campground	708-720-0030	18701 S 80th Avenue Tinley Park IL	2
Hide-A-Way Lakes	630-553-6323	8045 Van Emmons Road Yorkville IL	3+
Springfield			
Springfield KOA	217-498-7002	4320 KOA Road - Exit 94 Rochester IL	1+
St Louis Area			
MGM Lakeside Campground	618-797-2820	3133 W Chain of Rocks Granite City IL	3+

Missouri Listings (Interstate 55)   Dogs per Site

St Louis			
St Louis South KOA	636-479-4449	8000 Metropolitan Blvd - Exit H M or Z to W Outer Road Barnhart MO	3+
St Louis West KOA	636-257-3018	18475 Old H 66 Eureka MO	3+
Sundermeier RV Park	636-940-0111	111 Transit Street St Charles MO	3+
Beacon RV Park	816-279-5417	822 S Belt H St Joseph MO	3+
Pin Oak Creek RV Park	636-451-5656	1302 H 8AT Villa Ridge MO	3+
Perryville			
Perryville/Cape Girardeau KOA	573-547-8303	89 KOA Lane - Exit 129 Perryville MO	2
Jackson			
Trail of Tear State Park	573-334-1711	429 Moccasin Springs Jackson MO	3+

Arkansas Listings (Interstate 55)   Dogs per Site

Marion			
America's Best Campground	870-739-4801	7037 I 55 - Exit 14 Marion AR	3+
West Memphis			
Tom Sawyer's Mississippi River RV Park	870-735-9770	1286 S 8th Street - Exit 4 West Memphis AR	3+

Tennessee Listings (Interstate 55)   Dogs per Site

Memphis			
Memphis Graceland RV Park and Campground	901-396-7125	3691 Elvis Presley Blvd Memphis TN	3+
T. O. Fuller State Park	901-543-7581	1500 W Mitchell Road Memphis TN	3+
Tom Sawyer's Mississippi River RV Park	870-735-9770	1286 S 8th Street - Exit 4 West Memphis AR	3+

Mississippi Listings (Interstate 55)   Dogs per Site

Sardis			
John W Kyle State Park	662-487-1345	4235 State Park Road Sardis MS	3+
John W Kyle State Park	662-487-1345	4235 State Park Road Sardis MS	3+
Canton			

Movietown RV Park	601-859-7990	109 Movietown Drive Canton MS	3+
Jackson			
LeFleur's Bluff State Park	601-987-3923	2140 Riverside Drive Jackson MS	3+
Bryam			
Swinging Bridge RV Park	800-297-9127	100 Holiday Rambler Lane - Exit 85 Bryam MS	3+

Louisiana Listings   (Interstate 55)   Dogs per Site

| **New Orleans** | | | |
| New Orleans/Hammond KOA | 985-542-8094 | 14154 Club Deluxe Road - Exit 28 Hammond LA | 3+ |

Interstate 59 Campground Listings

Georgia Listings   (Interstate 59)   Dogs per Site

| **Trenton** | | | |
| Lookout Mountain/Chattanooga West KOA | 706-657-6815 | 930 Mountain Shadows Drive - Exit 17/Slygo Road Trenton GA | 3+ |

Alabama Listings   (Interstate 59)   Dogs per Site

Fort Payne			
Desoto State Park	256-845-5075	13883 County Road 89 Fort Payne AL	3+
Gadsden			
Noccalula Falls Park and Campground	256-543-7412	1600 Noccalula Road - Exit 188 Gadsden AL	3+
River Country Campground	256-543-7111	1 River Road Gadsden AL	2
Birmingham			
Cherokee Campground	205-428-8339	2800 H 93 Helena AL	3+
Birmingham South Campground	205-664-8832	222 H 33 Pelham AL	3+
Knoxville			
Knox Hill RV Park	205-372-3911	252 Old Patton Road Knoxville AL	3+

Mississippi Listings   (Interstate 59)   Dogs per Site

Meridian			
Nanabe Creek Campground	601-485-4711	1933 Russell Mount Gilliad Road Meridian MS	3+
Hattiesburg			
Paul Johnson State Park	601-582-7721	319 Geiger Lake Road Hattiesburg MS	3+

Interstate 64 Campground Listings

Missouri Listings   (Interstate 64)   Dogs per Site

St Louis			
St Louis South KOA	636-479-4449	8000 Metropolitan Blvd Barnhart MO	3+
St Louis West KOA	636-257-3018	18475 Old H 66 Eureka MO	3+
Sundermeier RV Park	636-940-0111	111 Transit Street St Charles MO	3+
Beacon RV Park	816-279-5417	822 S Belt H St Joseph MO	3+
Pin Oak Creek RV Park	636-451-5656	1302 H 8AT Villa Ridge MO	3+

Illinois Listings   (Interstate 64)   Dogs per Site

| **St Louis Area** | | | |
| MGM Lakeside Campground | 618-797-2820 | 3133 W Chain of Rocks   Granite City IL | 3+ |

Indiana Listings   (Interstate 64)   Dogs per Site

Santa Claus			
Lake Rudolph Campground	877-478-3657	78 N Holiday Blvd - Exit 63 Santa Claus IN	3+
Corydon			
O'Bannon Woods State Park	812-738-8232	7240 Old Forest Road - Exit 105 Corydon IN	3+

Kentucky Listings (Interstate 64)

Dogs per Site

Louisville

Louisville Metro KOA	812-282-4474	900 Marriott Drive - Exit I 65N to Exit 1 Clarksville IN	3+
Grand Trails RV Park	812-738-9077	205 S Mulberry Corydon IN	3+

Lexington

Elkhorn Campground	502-695-9154	165 N Scruggs Lane - Exit 58 Frankfort KY	3+
Kentucky Horse Park Campground	859-259-4257	4089 Iron Works Parkway Lexington KY	3+

Winchester

Daniel Boone National Forest	859-745-3100	1700 Bypass Road Winchester KY	3+

Morehead - Cave Run Lake

Poppy Mountain Campground	606-780-4192	8030 H 60E Morehead KY	3+
Twin Knobs Rec Area	606-784-6428	2375 Kentucky H Morehead KY	3+

West Virginia Listings (Interstate 64)

Dogs per Site

Milton

Fox Fire Resort	304-743-5622	Route 2, Box 655 - Exit 20A Milton WV	2

Charleston

Kanawha State Forest	304-558-3500	Rt 2 Box 285 Charleston WV	3+

Virginia Listings (Interstate 64)

Dogs per Site

Charlottesville

Charlottesville KOA	434-296-9881	3825 Red Hill Lane Charlottesville VA	3+

Williamsburg

Williamsburg KOA	757-565-2907	5210 Newman Road - Exit 234B Williamsburg VA	3+
Williamsburg/Colonial KOA	757-565-2734	4000 Newman Road - exit 234B Williamsburg VA	3+

Virginia Beach Area

First Landing State Park	757-412-2300	2500 Shore Drive Virginia Beach VA	3+
Virginia Beach KOA	757-428-1444	1240 General Booth Blvd Virginia Beach VA	3+

Interstate 65 Campground Listings

Indiana Listings (Interstate 65)

Dogs per Site

Gary

Oak Lake Campground	219-345-3153	5310 E 900N Fair Oaks IN	1+

Remington

Caboose Lake Campground	877-600-CAMP (2267)	3657 H 24 - Exit H 24 Remington IN	3+

Battle Ground

Prophetstown State Park	765-567-4919	4112 E State Road 4 - Exit 178/H 43 Battle Ground IN	3+

Indianapolis

Broadview Lake Campground	765-324-2622	4850 Broadview Road Colfax IN	3+
Heartland Resort	317-326-3181	1613 W 300N Greenfield IN	2
Indianapolis KOA	317-894-1397	5896 W 200 N Greenfield IN	3+
S & H Campground	317-326-3208	2573 W 100N Greenfield IN	3+

Columbus

Woods N Waters Kampground	812-342-1619	8855 S 300 W - Exit 64 Columbus IN	3+

Scottsburg

Jellystone Park	812-752-4062	4577 W H 56 Scottsburg IN	3+

Kentucky Listings (Interstate 65)

Dogs per Site

Louisville

Louisville Metro KOA	812-282-4474	900 Marriott Drive Clarksville IN	3+
Grand Trails RV Park	812-738-9077	205 S Mulberry Corydon IN	3+

Horse Cave

Horse Cave KOA	270-786-2819	109 Knob Hill Road - Exit 58 Horse Cave KY	3+

Cave City

Crystal Onyx Cave and Campground Resort	270-773-2359	363 Prewitts Knob Road Cave City KY	2
Jellystone Park	270-773-3840	1002 Mammoth Cave Road - Exit 53 Cave City KY	3+

Bowling Green

Beech Bend Park & Splash Lagoon Family Campground	270-781-7634	798 Beech Bend Road - Exit 28 Bowling Green KY	3+
Bowling Green KOA	270-843-1919	1960 Three Springs Road - Exit 22 Bowling Green KY	3+
Franklin			
Franklin KOA	270-586-5622	2889 Scottsville Road Franklin KY	3+

Tennessee Listings (Interstate 65)   Dogs per Site

Nashville			
Brown County State Park	812-988-6406	1450 State Road 46 W Nashville TN	3+
Jellystone Park	615-889-4225	2572 Music Valley Drive Nashville TN	3+
Two Rivers Campground	615-883-8559	2616 Music Valley Drive Nashville TN	3+

Alabama Listings (Interstate 65)   Dogs per Site

Decatur			
Point Mallard Campground	256-351-7772	2600-C Point Mallard Drive Decatur AL	3+
Cullman			
Good Hope Campground	256-739-1319	330 Super Saver Road - Exit 304 Cullman AL	3+
Birmingham			
Cherokee Campground	205-428-8339	2800 H 93 Helena AL	3+
Birmingham South Campground	205-664-8832	222 H 33 Pelham AL	3+
Pelham			
Oak Mountain State Park	205-620-2527	200 Terrace Drive Pelham AL	3+
Montgomery			
Capital City RV Park	877-271-8026	4655 Old Wetumpka H (H 231N) Montgomery AL	3+
Mobile			
Magnolia Springs RV Hideaway	800-981-0981	10831 Magnolia Springs H Foley AL	3+
Palm Lake Resort	251-970-3773	15810 H 59 Foley AL	3+
Shady Acres Campground	251-478-0013	2500 Old Military Road Mobile AL	3+

Interstate 70 Campground Listings

Utah Listings (Interstate 70)   Dogs per Site

Richfield			
Fishlake National Forest	435-896-9233	115 East 900 North Richfield UT	3+
Richfield KOA	435-896-6674	600 W 600 S - Exit 37 or 40 Richfield UT	2
Green River			
Green River State Park	435-564-3633	125 Fairway Avenue - Exit Green River Green River UT	3+
United Campground of Green River	435-564-8195	910 E Main Street - Exit 164 Green River UT	3+

Colorado Listings (Interstate 70)   Dogs per Site

Fruita			
Mountain RV Resort	970-858-3155	607 H 340 - Exit 19 Fruita CO	1+
Clifton			
RV Ranch at Grand Junction	970-434-6644	3238 E I 70 Business Loop Clifton CO	1
Rifle			
Rifle Falls State Park	970-625-1607	575 H 325 - Exit H 13 Rifle CO	3+
Glenwood Springs			
Rock Gardens RV Resort and Campground	800-958-6737	1308 County Road 129 - Exit 119 Glenwood Springs CO	3+
White River Naional Forest	970-945-2521	900 Grand Avenue Glenwood Springs CO	3+
Denver			
Denver Meadows RV Park	303-364-9483	2075 Potomac Street Aurora CO	3+
Dakota Ridge RV Park	800-398-1625	17800 W Colfax - Exit 259 Golden CO	3+
Chatfield State Park	303-791-7275	11500 N Roxborough Park Road Littleton CO	3+
Prospect RV Park	303-424-4414	11600 W 44th Avenue - Exit 266 Wheat Ridge CO	3+
Strasburg			
Denver East/Strasburg KOA	303-622-9274	1312 Monroe - Exit 310 Strasburg CO	3+
Limon			
Limon KOA	719-775-2151	575 Colorado Avenue - Exit 361 Limon CO	3+
Burlington			
Bonny Lake State Park	970-354-7306	32300 Yuma County Road 2 - Exit H 385 Burlington CO	3+

Kansas Listings (Interstate 70)

Dogs per Site

Goodland			
Goodland KOA	785-890-5701	1114 E H 24 - Exit 19 Goodland KS	3+
Colby			
Bourquin's RV Park	785-462-3300	155 E Willow - Exit 54 Colby KS	3+
Oakley			
High Plains Camping	785-672-3538	462 H 83 - Exit H 83 Oakley KS	3+
WaKeeney			
WaKeeney KOA	785-743-5612	I 70 S. Frontage Road, Box 170 - Exit 127 WaKeeney KS	3+
Salina			
Salina KOA	785-827-3182	1109 W Diamond Drive - Exit 252 Salina KS	1+
Abilene			
Covered Wagon RV Resort	785-263-2343	803 Buckeye - Exit 275 Abilene KS	3+
Junction City			
Owl's Nest RV Campground	785-238-0778	1912 Old H 40 Junction City KS	3+
Manhattan			
Tuttle Creek State Park	785-539-7941	5800A River Pond Road Manhattan KS	3+
Topeka			
Capital City RV Park	785-862-5267	1949 SW 49th Street Topeka KS	3+
Lawrence			
Lawrence/Kansas City KOA	785-842-3877	1473 H 40 - Exit 204 N Lawrence KS	3+
Kansas City			
Rutlader Outpost and RV Park	866-888-6779	33565 Metcalf Louisburg KS	3+

Missouri Listings (Interstate 70)

Dogs per Site

Kansas City			
Trailside RV Park	816-229-2267	1000 R.D. Mize Road - Exit 24 Grain Valley MO	3+
Basswood Country RV Resort	816-858-5556	15880 Inter Urban Road Platte City MO	3+
Oak Grove			
Kansas City East/Oak Grove KOA	816-690-6660	303 NE 3rd - Exit 28 Oak Grove MO	3+
Higginsville			
Interstate RV Park	800-690-2267	On Old H 40 - Exit 49 Higginsville MO	3+
Columbia			
Cottonwoods RV Park	573-474-2747	5170 Oakland Gravel Road Columbia MO	3+
Finger Lakes State Park	573-443-5315	1505 E Peabody Road Columbia MO	3+
St Louis			
St Louis South KOA	636-479-4449	8000 Metropolitan Blvd Barnhart MO	3+
St Louis West KOA	636-257-3018	18475 Old H 66 Eureka MO	3+
Sundermeier RV Park	636-940-0111	111 Transit Street St Charles MO	3+
Beacon RV Park	816-279-5417	822 S Belt H St Joseph MO	3+
Pin Oak Creek RV Park	636-451-5656	1302 H 8AT Villa Ridge MO	3+

Illinois Listings (Interstate 70)

Dogs per Site

St Louis Area			
MGM Lakeside Campground	618-797-2820	3133 W Chain of Rocks Granite City IL	3+
Effingham			
Camp Lakewood	217-342-6233	1217 W Rickelman Effingham IL	3+
Casey			
Casey KOA	217-932-5319	1248 E 1250th Road - Exit 129 Casey IL	3+
Marshall			
Lincoln Trail State Park	217-826-2222	1685 1350th Road Marshall IL	3+

Indiana Listings (Interstate 70)

Dogs per Site

Terre Haute			
Terre Haute KOA	812-232-2457	5995 E Sony Drive - Exit 11/H46 Terre Haute IN	3+
Indianapolis			
Broadview Lake Campground	765-324-2622	4850 Broadview Road Colfax IN	3+
Heartland Resort	317-326-3181	1613 W 300N - Exit 96 Greenfield IN	2
Indianapolis KOA	317-894-1397	5896 W 200 N - Exit 96 Greenfield IN	3+
S & H Campground	317-326-3208	2573 W 100N - Exit 96 Greenfield IN	3+
Knightstown			
Yogi Bear Campground	765-737-6585	5964 S H 109 - Exit Knightstown/Wilkenson (H 109) Knightstown IN	3+
New Castle			
Summit Lake State Park	765-766-5873	5993 N Messick Road New Castle IN	3+
Walnut Ridge Campground	877-619-2559	408 County Road 300W New Castle IN	3+

Richmond

Richmond KOA	756-962-1219	3101 Cart Road - Exit 151 or 151B Richmond IN	1+

Ohio Listings (Interstate 70)

Dogs per Site

Springfield

Buck Creek State Park	937-322-5284	1901 Buck Creek Lane - Exit 64 Springfield OH	2
Buck Creek State Park Campground	937-322-5284	1901 Buck Creek Lane Springfield OH	1+
Enon Beach Campground	937-882-6431	2401 Enon Road - Exit 48 Springfield OH	3+
Columbus			
Crosscreek Camping Resort	740-549-2267	3190 S Old State Delaware OH	3+
Buckeye Lake			
Buckeye Lake/Columbus East KOA	740-928-0706	4460 Walnut Road Buckeye Lake OH	2
Cambridge			
Hillview Acres Campground	740-439-3348	66271 Wolfs Den Road Cambridge OH	1+
Spring Valley Campground	740-439-9291	8000 Dozer Road - Exit 178 Cambridge OH	3+

West Virginia Listings (Interstate 70)

Dogs per Site

Triadelphia

Wheelings Dallas Pike Campground	304-547-0940	Road 1, Box 231 - Exit 11 Triadelphia WV	3+

Pennsylvania Listings (Interstate 70)

Dogs per Site

Washington

Washington KOA	724-225-7590	7 KOA Road - Exit 20 Washington PA	1+
Pittsburgh			
Bear Run Campground	888-737-2605	184 Badger Hill Road Portersville PA	2
Madison/Pittsburgh SE KOA	724-722-4444	119 Tanglewood Lane - Exit 54 Ruffs Dale PA	3+
Keen Lake Camping and Cottage Resort	570-488-5522	155 Keen Lake Road Waymart PA	2
Somerset			
Kooser State Park	814-445-7725	934 Glades Pike Somerset PA	2

Interstate 75 Campground Listings

Michigan Listings (Interstate 75)

Dogs per Site

Brimley

Brimley State Park	906-248-3422	9200 W 6 Mile Road - Exit H 28 Brimley MI	3+
Mackinaw City			
Mackinaw City/Mackinac Island KOA	231-436-5643	566 Trailsend Road - Exit H 108 Mackinaw City MI	1+
Mackinaw Mill Creek Camping	231-436-5584	9730 H 23 Mackinaw City MI	3+
St. Ignace/Mackinac Island KOA	906-643-9303	1242 H 2 W - Exit H 2W St Ignace MI	3+
Gaylord			
Gaylord KOA	989-939-8723	5101 Campfires Parkway - Exit 279 Gaylord MI	3+
Grayling			
Jellystone Park	989-348-2157	370 W 4 Mile Road - Exit 251 Grayling MI	3+
Roscommon			
Higgins Hills RV Park	989-275-8151	3800 Federal H - Exit 244 Roscommon MI	2
North Higgins Lake State Park	989-821-6125	11747 N Higgins Lake Drive - Exit 244 Roscommon MI	3+
Linwood			
Hoyles Marina and Campground	989-697-3153	135 S Linwood Beach Road - Exit 173/Linwood Linwood MI	3+
Saginaw Area			
Valley Plaza Resort	989-496-2159	5215 Bay City Road Midland MI	1
Frankenmuth			
Frankenmuth Jellystone Park	989-652-6668	1339 Weiss Street - Exit 136 Frankenmuth MI	3+
Detroit			
Wayne County Fairgrounds and RV Park	734-697-7002	10871 Quirk Road Belleville MI	3+
Harbortown RV Resort	734-384-4700	14931 La Plaisance - Exit 11 Monroe MI	3+

Ohio Listings (Interstate 75)

Dogs per Site

Toledo

Name	Phone	Address	Dogs per Site
Maumee Bay State Park Campground	419-836-7758	1400 State Park Road Oregon OH	1+
Toledo East/Stony Ridge KOA	419-837-6848	24787 Luckey Road Perrysburg OH	3+
Findlay			
Pleasant View	419-299-3897	12611 Township Road 218 Van Buren OH	3+
Van Buren State Park Campgrounds	419-832-7662	12259 Township Rd. 218 Van Buren OH	1+
Wapakoneta			
Wapakoneta/Lima S KOA	419-738-6016	14719 Cemetary Road - Exit 111 Wapakoneta OH	3+
Cincinnati			
Miami Whitewater Forest Campground	513-521-PARK	various entrances Crosby OH	1+
Indian Springs Campground	513-353-9244	3306 Stateline Road N Bend OH	2
Winton Woods Campground	513-521-PARK	Winton Road Springfield Township OH	1+

Kentucky Listings (Interstate 75)   Dogs per Site

Name	Phone	Address	Dogs per Site
Crittenden			
Cincinnati South KOA	859-428-2000	3315 Dixie H - Exit 166 Crittenden KY	3+
Lexington			
Elkhorn Campground	502-695-9154	165 N Scruggs Lane Frankfort KY	3+
Kentucky Horse Park Campground	859-259-4257	4089 Iron Works Parkway Lexington KY	3+
Berea			
Old Kentucky RV Park	859-986-1150	1142 Paint Lick Road Berea KY	3+
Renfro Valley			
Renfro Valley KOA	606-256-2474	Red Foley Road, H 25 - Exit 62 Renfro Valley KY	1+
Renfro Valley RV Park	606-256-2638	Renfro Valley Entertainment Center - Exit 62 Renfro Valley KY	3+
Corbin			
Corbin KOA	806-528-1534	171 E City Dam Road - Exit 29 Corbin KY	1+
Cumberland Falls State Resort Park	606-528-4121	7351 H 90 Corbin KY	3+

Tennessee Listings (Interstate 75)   Dogs per Site

Name	Phone	Address	Dogs per Site
Jellico			
Indian Mountain State Park	423-784-7958	143 State Park Circle Jellico TN	3+
Caryville			
Cove Lake State Park	423-566-9701	110 Cove Lake Lane Caryville TN	3+
Royal Blue RV Resort	423-566-4847	305 Luther Seiber Road - Exit 141 Caryville TN	3+
Knoxville			
Southlake RV Park	865-573-1837	3730 Maryville Pike Knoxville TN	3+
McDonald			
Chattanooga North/Cleveland KOA	423-472-8928	648 Pleasant Grove Road - Exit 20 McDonald TN	1+
The Smoky Mountains			
Arrow Creek Campground	865-430-7433	4721 E Parkway Gatlinburg TN	1+
Great Smoky Jellystone	423-487-5534	4946 Hooper H Gatlinburg TN	2
Great Smoky Mountains National Park	865-436-1200	107 Park Headquarters Road Gatlinburg TN	3+
Smoky Bear Campground	865-436-8372	4857 E Parkway Gatlinburg TN	3+
Twin Creek RV Resort	865-436-7081	E Parkway Gatlinburg TN	2
Riveredge RV Park	865-453-5813	4220 Huskey Street Pigeon Forge TN	3+

Georgia Listings (Interstate 75)   Dogs per Site

Name	Phone	Address	Dogs per Site
Calhoun			
Calhoun KOA	706-629-7511	2523 Redbud Road NE - Exit 315/Redbud Road E Calhoun GA	3+
Adairsville			
Harvest Moon RV Park	770-773-7320	1001 Poplar Springs Road - Exit 306 Adairsville GA	2
Cartersville			
Allatoona Landing Marine Resort	770-974-6089	24 Allatoona Landing Road - Exit 283 Cartersville GA	3+
Red Top Mountain State Park	770-975-4226	50 Lodge Road Cartersville GA	3+
Atlanta Area			
Brookwood RV Park	877-727-5787	1031 Wylie Road SE Marietta GA	3+
Atlanta South RV Resort	770-957-2610	281 Mount Olive Road - Exit 222 McDonough GA	3+
Atlanta			
Stone Mountain Park	800-385-9807	H 78E Stone Mountain GA	3+
Forsyth			
Forsyth KOA	478-994-2019	414 S Frontage Road - Exit 186 Forsyth GA	3+
Cordele			
Cordele KOA	229-273-5454	373 Rockhouse Road E - Exit 97 Cordele GA	1+
Veterans Memorial State Park	229-276-2371	2459A H 280W Cordele GA	3+
Tifton			
Agirama RV Park	229-386-3344	1392 Windmill Road - Exit 63b Tifton GA	2

Amy's South Georgia RV Park	229-386-8441	4632 Union Road - Exit 60 Tifton GA	3+
Lake Park			
Eagle's Roost RV Resort	229-559-5192	5465 Mill Store Road - Exit 5 Lake Park GA	3+
Valdosta/Lake Park KOA	229-559-9738	5300 Jewel Futch Road - Exit 5 Lake Park GA	3+

Florida Listings   (Interstate 75)   Dogs per Site

White Springs			
Stephen Foster Folk Culture Center State Park	386-397-2733	P. O. Drawer G/ US 41 N - Exit H 136 White Springs FL	3+
Suwannee Valley Campground	866-397-1667	786 N W Street - Exit 439/H 136 White Springs FL	2
Ocala			
Silver River State Park	352-236-7148	1425 NE 58th Avenue - Exit 352 onto H 40 E Ocala FL	3+
Tampa Bay			
Horseshoe Cove RV Resort	941-758-5335	5100 60th Street & Caruso Road - Exit 217/70th Street Bradenton FL	2
Lake Manatee State Park	941-741-3028	20007 H 64E - Exit 220 Bradenton FL	3+
Sarasota North Resort	800-678-2131	800 K Road - Exit 220 Bradenton FL	3+
Oscar Scherer State Park	941-483-5956	1843 S Tamiami Trail - Exit Laurel Road Osprey FL	3+
Clearwater/Tarpon Springs KOA	727-937-8412	37061 H 19N Palm Harbor FL	3+
Fort Myers			
Indian Creek RV Resort	800-828-6992	17340 San Carlos Blvd - Exit 131 Fort Myers Beach FL	2
Naples			
Collier-Seminole State Park	239-394-3397	20200 E Tamiami Trail Naples FL	3+
Hitching Post RV Resort	239-774-1259	100 Barefoot Williams Road Naples FL	3+
Lake San Marino RV Resort	239-597-4202	1000 Wiggins Pass Naples FL	2
South Florida			
Juno RV Park	561-622-7500	900 Juno Ocean Walk Juno Beach FL	3+
Paradise Island RV Resort	954-485-1150	2121 NW 29th Court Oakland Park FL	3+
Highland Woods	866-340-0649	850/900 NE 48th Street Pompano Beach FL	3+

Interstate 77 Campground Listings

Ohio Listings   (Interstate 77)   Dogs per Site

Cleveland			
Kool Lakes Family RV park	440-548-8436	12990 H 282 Parkman OH	3+
Country Acres Campground	866-813-4321	9850 Minyoung Road Ravenna OH	3+
Akron			
Portage Lakes State Park Campground	330-644-2220	5031 Manchester Road Akron OH	1+
Canton			
Canton/East Sparta KOA	330-484-3901	3232 Downing Street SW East Sparta OH	1+
Cambridge			
Hillview Acres Campground	740-439-3348	66271 Wolfs Den Road Cambridge OH	1+
Spring Valley Campground	740-439-9291	8000 Dozer Road Cambridge OH	3+

West Virginia Listings   (Interstate 77)   Dogs per Site

Charleston			
Kanawha State Forest	304-558-3500	Rt 2 Box 285 Charleston WV	3+
Camp Creek			
Camp Creek State Park	304-425-9481	2390 Camp Creek Road Camp Creek WV	3+

Virginia Listings   (Interstate 77)   Dogs per Site

Wytheville			
Whtheville KOA	276-228-2601	231 KOA Road - Exit Bluesky Drive Wytheville VA	3+

North Carolina Listings   (Interstate 77)   Dogs per Site

Statesville			
Statesville KOA	704-873-5560	162 KOA Lane - Exit 45 Statesville NC	3+
Charlotte			
Charlotte/Fort Mill KOA	803-548-1148	940 Gold Hill Road - Exit 88 Fort Mill NC	3+

South Carolina Listings   (Interstate 77)   Dogs per Site

410

Winnsboro

Lake Wateree State Rec Area	803-482-6401	881 State Park Road Winnsboro SC	3+

Columbia

Sesquicentennial State Park	803-788-2706	9564 Two Notch Road Columbia SC	3+
Barnyard RV Park	803-957-1238	201 Oak Drive Lexington SC	3+

Interstate 80 Campground Listings

California Listings (Interstate 80)   Dogs per Site

San Francisco

Candlestick RV Park	415-822-2299	650 Gilman Avenue San Francisco CA	3+

Vacaville

Midway RV Park	707-446-7679	4933 Midway Road Vacaville CA	3+
Vineyard RV Park	707-693-8797	4985 Midway Road Vacaville CA	2

Sacramento

Beals Point Campground	916-988-0205	7806 Folsom-Auburn Road Folsom CA	3+
Cal Expo RV Park	916-263-3000	1600 Exposition Blvd Sacramento CA	2
Sacramento Metropolitan KOA	916-371-6771	3951 Lake Road West Sacramento CA	1+

Auburn - Gold Country North

Auburn Gold Country RV (formally KOA)	530-885-0990	3550 KOA Way Auburn CA	3+
Rocky Rest Campground	530-288-3231	H 49 Downieville CA	3+
French Meadows Reservoir Campground	530-367-2224	Mosquito Ridge Road Foresthill CA	3+
Robinson Flat Campground	530-367-2224	Foresthill Divide Road Foresthill CA	3+
Lodgepole Campground	916-386-5164	Lake Valley Reservoir Nevada City CA	2
South Yuba Campground	916-985-4474	North Bloomfield Road Nevada City CA	3+
South Yuba Campground	919-985-4474	North Bloomfield Road Nevada City CA	3+

Lake Tahoe

D. L. Bliss State Park	530-525-9529	H 89 South Lake Tahoe CA	3+
Encore Tahoe Valley RV Resort	877-717-8737	1175 Melba Drive South Lake Tahoe CA	3+
Fallen Leaf Campground	530-543-2600	Fallen Leaf Lake Road South Lake Tahoe CA	3+
Lake Tahoe-South Shore KOA	530-577-3693	760 North Highway 50 South Lake Tahoe CA	3+
Meeks Bay Campground	530-543-2600	H 89 Tahoe City CA	3+
General Creek Campground	530-525-7982	West Shore Lake Tahoe Tahoma CA	3+
Lakeside Campground	530-587-3558	Off H 89 Truckee CA	2
Logger Campground, Truckee District	530-587-3558	9646 Donner Pass Road Truckee CA	3+
Camp at the Cove	775-589-4907	760 H 50 Zephyr Cove NV	3+
Zephyr Cove RV Park and Campground	775-589-4922	760 H 50 Zephyr Cove NV	3+

Nevada Listings (Interstate 80)   Dogs per Site

Reno

Bonanza Terrace RV Park	775-329-9624	4800 Stoltz Road Reno NV	3+
Reno KOA	775-789-2147	2500 E 2nd Street Reno NV	3+
Reno RV Park	775-323-3381	735 Mill Street Reno NV	3+
Rivers Edge RV Park	775-358-8533	1405 S Rock Blvd Sparks NV	3+

Lovelock

Rye Patch State Recreation Area	775-538-7321	2505 Rye Patch Reservoir Road Lovelock NV	3+

Winnemucca

Model T RV Park	775-623-2588	1130 W Winnemucca Blvd Winnemucca NV	3+

Elko

Double Dice RV Park	775-738-5642	3730 Idaho Street Elko NV	3+
Wild Horse State Recreation Area	775-758-6493	HC 31, Box 26/H 225 Elko NV	3+

West Wendover

Wendover KOA	775-664-3221	651 N Camper Drive West Wendover NV	3+

Utah Listings (Interstate 80)   Dogs per Site

Salt Lake City

Sunset Campground	877-444-6777	Farmington Canyon Farmington City UT	1+
Salt Lake City KOA	801-355-1214	1400 W North Temple - Exit 115 Salt Lake City UT	3+
Wasatch -Cache National Forest	801-466-6411	3285 East 3800 S Salt Lake City UT	3+
Quail Run RV Park	801-255-9300	9230 S State Street Sandy UT	3+

Wyoming Listings (Interstate 80)   Dogs per Site

Lyman			
Lyman KOA	307-786-2188	1531N H 413 - Exit 41/H 413 Lyman WY	3+
Rock Springs			
Rock Springs KOA	307-362-3063	86 Foothill Blvd - Exit 99 Rock Springs WY	3+
Rawlins			
Rawlins KOA	307-328-2021	205 E H 71 - Exit 214 Rawlins WY	3+
Western Hills Campground	888-568-3040	2500 Wagon Circle Road - Exit 211 Rawlins WY	3+
Laramie			
Laramie KOA	307-742-6553	1271 W Baker Street - Exit 310 Laramie WY	1+
Medicine Bow - Routt National Forests	307-745-2300	2468 Jackson Street Laramie WY	3+
Cheyenne			
Cheyenne KOA	307-638-8840	8800 Archer Frontage Road - Exit 367/Campstool Road Cheyenne WY	3+
Curt Gowdy State Park	307-632-7946	1319 Hynds Lodge Road Cheyenne WY	3+
Terry Bison Ranch	307-634-4171	51 I 25 Service Road E Cheyenne WY	3+
Pine Bluffs			
Pine Bluffs RV Park	800-294-4968	10 Paint Brush Road - Exit 1 or 406 Pine Bluffs WY	3+

Nebraska Listings (Interstate 80)   Dogs per Site

Kimball			
Kimball KOA	308-235-4404	4334 Link 53E Kimball NE	3+
Twin Pines RV Camp	308-235-3231	1508 S H 71 - Exit 20 Kimball NE	3+
Potter			
Buffalo Point RV Park and Motel	308-879-4400	8175 H 30 - Exit 38/Potter to H 30 Potter NE	3+
Brule			
Eagle Canyon Hideaway	866-866-5253	1086 Lakeview W Road - Exit Big Springs Brule NE	3+
Ogallala			
Lake Ogallala State Rec Area	308-284-8800	1475 H 61N Ogallala NE	3+
North Platte			
Holiday Trav-L-Park	308-534-2265	601 Halligan Drive - Exit 177/H 83 North Platte NE	3+
Lake Maloney State Rec Area	308-535-8025	301 E State Farm Road North Platte NE	3+
Maxwell			
Fort McPherson Campground	308-582-4320	12567 Valley View Road - Exit 190 Maxwell NE	3+
Gothenburg			
Gothenburhg KOA	308-537-7387	1102 S Lake Avenue - Exit H 47S Gothenburg NE	3+
Wood River			
Wood River Motel and RV Park	308-583-2256	11774 S H 11 - Exit 300 Wood River NE	3+
Doniphan			
Grand Island KOA	402-886-2249	904 South B Road - Exit 318 Doniphan NE	3+
Mormon Island State Rec Area	308-385-6211	7425 S H 281 Doniphan NE	3+
Waco			
Double Nickel Campground	402-728-5558	905 Road S - Exit 360 Waco NE	1+
Lincoln			
Camp A Way	866-719-2267	200 Camper's Circle - Exit 401 Lincoln NE	3+
Greenwood			
Pine Grove RV Park	402-994-3550	23403 Mynard Road - Exit 420 Greenwood NE	3+

Iowa Listings (Interstate 80)   Dogs per Site

Adel			
Des Moines West KOA	515-834-2729	3418 L Avenue - Exit 106 Adel IA	3+
Des Moines			
Adventureland Campground	512-265-7384	2600 Adventureland Drive - Exit 142 or 142A Altoona IA	2
Kellogg RV Park	641-526-8535	1570 H 224 - Exit 173/Kellogg Kellogg IA	3+
Rolling Acres RV Park	641-792-2428	1601 E 36th Street - Exit 168 Newton IA	3+
Amana Colonies			
Amana Colony RV Park	319-622-7616	#39 38th Avenue - Exit 225 Amana IA	3+
W Liberty			
West Liberty KOA	319-627-2676	1961 Garfield Avenue - Exit W Liberty W Liberty IA	3+
Tipton			
Hunt's Cedar River Campground	563-946-2431	1231 306th Street - Exit 267 Tipton IA	3+
Quad Cities			
Interstate RV Park	563-386-7292	8448 Fairmont - Exit 292 Davenport IA	3+

Illinois Listings (Interstate 80) Dogs per Site

Utica

Hickory Hollow Campground	815-667-4996	757 N 3029 Road - Exit 81 Utica IL	2
LaSalle/Peru KOA	815-667-4988	756 N 3150th Road - Exit 81/H 178 Utica IL	3+

Chicago Area

Windy City Campground	708-720-0030	18701 S 80th Avenue - Exit Harlem Tinley Park IL	2
Hide-A-Way Lakes	630-553-6323	8045 Van Emmons Road Yorkville IL	3+

Indiana Listings (Interstate 80) Dogs per Site

Gary

Oak Lake Campground	219-345-3153	5310 E 900N Fair Oaks IN	1+

Portage

Yogi Bear Campground	219-762-7757	5300 Old Porter Road Portage IN	3+

South Bend

Mini Mountain Campground	574-654-3307	32351 H 2 New Carlisle IN	3+

Granger

South Bend East KOA	574-277-1335	50707 Princess Way - Exit 83 Granger IN	3+

Elkhart

Elkhart Campground	574-264-2914	25608 County Road 4 Elkhart IN	2

Middlebury

Elkhart Co/Middlebury Exit KOA	574-825-5932	52867 H 13 - Exit 107 Middlebury IN	3+

Howe

Twin Mills Camping Resort	260-562-3212	1675 W H 120 Howe IN	1+

Ohio Listings (Interstate 80) Dogs per Site

Toledo

Maumee Bay State Park Campground	419-836-7758	1400 State Park Road Oregon OH	1+
Toledo East/Stony Ridge KOA	419-837-6848	24787 Luckey Road Perrysburg OH	3+

Lake Erie Island Region

Kelleys Island State Park Campground	419-746-2546	Division Street Kelleys Island OH	1+
Cedarlane RV Park	419-797-9907	2926 NE Catawba Road Port Clinton OH	2
East Harbor State Park Campground	419-734-4424	Route 269 Port Clinton OH	1+
Shade Acres RV Campground	419-797-4681	1810 W. Catawba Road Port Clinton OH	1+
Sleepy Hollows Family Camping	419-734-3556	2817 E. Harbor Road Port Clinton OH	1+
Camper Village RV Park	419-627-2106	One Cedar Point Drive Sandusky OH	1+
South Bass Island State Park Campground	419-285-2112	Catawba Avenue South Bass Island OH	1+

Cleveland

Kool Lakes Family RV park	440-548-8436	12990 H 282 Parkman OH	3+
Country Acres Campground	866-813-4321	9850 Minyoung Road - Exit 209/H 209W Ravenna OH	3+

Akron

Portage Lakes State Park Campground	330-644-2220	5031 Manchester Road Akron OH	1+

Pennsylvania Listings (Interstate 80) Dogs per Site

Mercer

Mercer/Grove City KOA	724-748-3160	1337 Butler Pike Mercer PA	3+

Bellefonte

Bellefonte/State College KOA	814-355-7912	2481 Jacksonville Road - Exit 161 Bellefonte PA	3+

New Columbia

Nittany Mountain Campground	570-568-5541	2751 Miller's Bottom Road - Exit 15S New Columbia PA	1+

Poconos

Delaware Water Gap KOA	570-223-8000	233 Hollow Road - Exit 309 E Stroudsburg PA	3+
Mountain Vista Campground	570-223-0111	50 Taylor Drive - Exit 309 E Stroudsburg PA	3+
Otter Lake Camp Resort	570-223-0123	4805 Marshall's Creek Road - Exit 309 E Stroudsburg PA	3+
Tri-State RV Park	800-562-2663	200 Shay Lane Matamoras PA	1+
Hickory Run State Park	570-443-0400	On H 534 - Exit 274 White Haven PA	2

Interstate 81 Campground Listings

New York Listings   (Interstate 81)   Dogs per Site

Clayton

Grass Point State Park	315-686-4472	36661 Cedar Point State Park Drive - Exit 50S/H 12 Clayton NY	3+
Merry Knoll 1000 Islands Campground	315-686-3055	38115 H 12E Clayton NY	3+

Dexter

Black River Bay Campground	315-639-3735	16129 Foster Park Road (Box541) - Exit 46 Dexter NY	1+

Henderson Harbor

Association Island RV Resort & Marina	315-938-5655	Snowshoe Road - Exit 41 to H 3/Adams Henderson Harbor NY	3+

Pulaski

Brennan Beach RV Resort	315-298-2242	80 Brennan's Beach Road Pulaski NY	2
Selkirk Sores State Park	315-298-5737	7101 H 3 - Exit 36 Pulaski NY	3+

Finger Lakes

Hickory Hill Family Camping Resort	607-776-4345	7531 Country Route 13 Bath NY	2
Spruce Row Campsite & RV Park	607-387-9225	2271 Kraft Road Ithaca NY	3+

Pennsylvania Listings   (Interstate 81)   Dogs per Site

Poconos

Delaware Water Gap KOA	570-223-8000	233 Hollow Road E Stroudsburg PA	3+
Mountain Vista Campground	570-223-0111	50 Taylor Drive E Stroudsburg PA	3+
Otter Lake Camp Resort	570-223-0123	4805 Marshall's Creek Road E Stroudsburg PA	3+
Tri-State RV Park	800-562-2663	200 Shay Lane Matamoras PA	1+
Hickory Run State Park	570-443-0400	On H 534 White Haven PA	2

Wyoming

Frances Slocum State Park	570-696-3525	565 Mount Olivet Road - Exit 170B Wyoming PA	2

Jonestown

Jonestown/I-81,78 KOA	717-865-2526	145 Old Route 22 - Exit 90 Jonestown PA	1+

Chambersburg

Twin Bridge Meadow Campground	717-369-2216	1345 Twin Bridges Road Chambersburg PA	2

Maryland Listings   (Interstate 81)   Dogs per Site

Williamsport

KOA Hagerstown/Snug Harbor	301-223-7571	11759 Snug Harbor Lane Williamsport MD	3+
Yogi Bear Jellystone Park	800-421-7116	16519 Lappans Road - Exit 1 in Maryland Williamsport MD	2

Virginia Listings   (Interstate 81)   Dogs per Site

Luray

Jellystone Park	540-743-4002	2250 H 211E - Exit 264/New Market Luray VA	3+

Harrisonburg

Harrisonburg/New Market	540-896-8929	12480 Mountain Valley Road - Exit 257 Broadway VA	1+

Verona

Staunton/Verona KOA	540-248-2746	296 Riner Lane - Exit 227 Verona VA	3+

Natural Bridge

Natural Bridge/Lexington KOA	540-291-2770	214 Killdeer Lane - Exit 180B Natural Bridge VA	1+

Wytheville

Whtheville KOA	276-228-2601	231 KOA Road Wytheville VA	3+

Marion

Hungry Mother State Park	276-781-7400	2854 Park Blvd Marion VA	3+

Tennessee Listings   (Interstate 81)   Dogs per Site

Blountville

Bristol/Kingsport KOA	423-323-7790	425 Rocky Branch Road - Exit 63 Blountville TN	3+

Kingsport

Warriors Path State Park	423-239-8531	490 Hemlock Road Kingsport TN	3+

Morristown

Panther Creek State Park	423-587-7046	2010 Panther Creek Road Morristown TN	3+

Interstate 84 Campground Listings

Oregon Listings (Interstate 84)   Dogs per Site

Portland

Jantzen Beach RV Park	503-289-7626	1503 N Hayden Island Drive Portland OR	1

Portland Area

Portland Fairview RV Park	503-661-1047	21401 NE Sandy Blvd - Exit 14 Fairview OR	3+
Rolling Hills RV Park	503-666-7282	20145 NE Sandy Blvd - Exit 14 Fairview OR	3+
RV Park of Portland	503-692-0225	6645 SW Nyberg Road Tualatin OR	1+

Cascade Locks

Cascade Locks/Portland East KOA	541-374-8668	841 NW Forest Lane - Exit 44 Cascade Locks OR	3+

Pendleton

Umatilla National Forest	541-278-3716	2517 SW Hailey Avenue Pendleton OR	3+

Baker City

Oregon Trails West RV Park	888-523-3236	42534 N Cedar Road - Exit 302 Baker City OR	3+
Wallowa-Whitman National Forest	541-523-6391	1550 Dewey Avenue Baker City OR	3+

Idaho Listings (Interstate 84)   Dogs per Site

Caldwell

Ambassador RV Resort	888-877-8307	615 S Mead Parkway - Exit 29 Caldwell ID	3+

Meridian

Boise Meridian RV Resort	877-894-1357	184 Pennwood - Exit 44 Meridian ID	2
The Playground RV Park	208-887-1022	1680 Overland Road - Exit 44 Meridian ID	3+

Boise

On the River RV Park	208-375-7432	6000 Glenwood - Exit Eagle Road Boise ID	3+

Mountain Home

Bruneau Dunes State Park	208-366-7919	27608 Sand Dunes Road Mountain Home ID	3+
Mountain Home KOA	208-587-5111	220 E 10th N Mountain Home ID	3+
Mountain Home RV Park	208-890-4100	2295 American Legion Blvd - Exit 95 Mountain Home ID	3+

Jerome

Twin Falls/Jerome KOA	208-324-4169	5431 H 93 Jerome ID	3+

Twin Falls

Anderson Camp	888-480-9400	S Tipperary - Exit 182 Eden ID	3+
Sawthooth National Forest	208-737-3200	2647 Kimberly Road E. Twin Falls ID	3+

Utah Listings (Interstate 84)   Dogs per Site

Kaysville

Cherry Hill RV Resort	801-451-5379	1325 S Main Kaysville UT	3+

Interstate 85 Campground Listings

Virginia Listings (Interstate 85)   Dogs per Site

Petersburg

Petersburg KOA	804-732-8345	2809 Cortland Road Petersburg VA	3+

North Carolina Listings (Interstate 85)   Dogs per Site

Henderson

Kerr Lake State Rec Area	252-438-7791	6254 Satterwhite Point Road Henderson NC	3+
Kerr Lake State Rec Area	252-438-7791	6254 Satterwhite Point Road Henderson NC	3+

Concord

Fleetwood RV Racing Camping Resort	704-455-4445	6600 Speedway Blvd - Exit 49 Concord NC	3+

Charlotte

Charlotte/Fort Mill KOA	803-548-1148	940 Gold Hill Road Fort Mill NC	3+

South Carolina Listings (Interstate 85)   Dogs per Site

Blacksburg

Kings Mountain State Park	803-222-3209	1277 Park Road Blacksburg SC	3+

Anderson

Anderson/Lake Hartwell KOA	864-287-3161	200 Wham Road - Exit 14S Anderson SC	3+

Townville

Lake Hartwell Camping and Cabins	888-427-8935	400 Ponderosa Point - Exit 11 Townville SC	3+
Fair Play			
Lake Hartwell State Rec Area	864-972-3352	19138 A H 11S Fair Play SC	3+

Georgia Listings (Interstate 85)   Dogs per Site

Atlanta			
Stone Mountain Park	800-385-9807	H 78E Stone Mountain GA	3+
Atlanta Area			
Brookwood RV Park	877-727-5787	1031 Wylie Road SE Marietta GA	3+
Atlanta South RV Resort	770-957-2610	281 Mount Olive Road McDonough GA	3+

Alabama Listings (Interstate 85)   Dogs per Site

Auburn			
Leisure Time Campground	334-821-2267	2670 S College Street Auburn AL	3+
Tuskegee			
Tuskegee National Forest	334-727-2652	125 National Forest Road, Bldg 949 Tuskegee AL	3+
Montgomery			
Capital City RV Park	877-271-8026	4655 Old Wetumpka H (H 231N) Montgomery AL	3+

Interstate 90 Campground Listings
(From Chicago to Cleveland see Highway 80 Listings)

Washington Listings (Interstate 90)   Dogs per Site

Seattle			
Blue Sky RV Park	425-222-7910	9002 302nd Avenue SE - Exit 22 Seattle WA	3+
Seattle Area			
Issaquah Highlands	425-392-2351	10610 Renton Issaquah Road - Exit Exi t 15 Issaquah WA	2
Eagle Tree RV Park	360-598-5988	16280 H 305 Poulsbo WA	3+
Ellensburg			
Ellensburg KOA	509-925-9319	32 Thorp H S - Exit 106 Ellensburg WA	3+
Ephrata			
Oasis RV Park and Golf	509-754-5102	2541 Basin Street SW - Exit Ephrata Ephrata WA	3+
Spokane			
Alderwood RV Resort	509-467-5320	14007 N Newport H Spokane WA	3+
Spokane Valley			
Trailer Inns RV Park	509-535-1811	6021 E 4th - Exit 285 Spokane Valley WA	3+
Otis Orchards			
Spokane KOA	509-924-4722	N 3025 Barker Road - Exit 293 Otis Orchards WA	3+

Idaho Listings (Interstate 90)   Dogs per Site

Post Falls			
Suntree RV Park	208-773-9982	350 N Idahline Road - Exit 2/Pleasant View Road Post Falls ID	2
Coeur D'Alene			
Coeur D'Alene KOA	208-664-4471	10588 E Wolf Lodge Bay Road - Exit 22 Coeur D'Alene ID	3+
Blackwell Island RV Resort	208-665-1300	800 S Marina Way Coeur d'Alene ID	3+
Idaho Panhandle National Forest	208-765-7223	3815 Schreiber Street Coeur d'Alene ID	3+
Pinehurst			
Kellogg/Silver Valley KOA	208-682-3612	801 N Division Street - Exit 45 Pinehurst ID	2

Montana Listings (Interstate 90)   Dogs per Site

St Regis			
Campground St Regis	406-649-2470	44 Frontage Road - Exit 33 St Regis MT	3+
Nugget Campground	888-800-0125	E of Stop Sign on Main Street - Exit 33/St Regis St Regis MT	3+
Missoula			
Beavertail Hill State Park	406-542-5500	3201 Spurgin Road Missoula MT	3+
Jellystone Park	406-543-9400	9900 Jellystone Drive Missoula MT	2
Lolo National Forest	406-329-3750	Building 24, Fort Missoula - Exit Missoula Missoula MT	3+
Missoula KOA	406-549-0881	3450 Tina Avenue - Exit 101 Missoula MT	3+
Deer Lodge			
Deer Lodge KOA	406-846-1629	330 Park Street - Exit at either end of town Deer Lodge MT	3+
Butte			

Butte KOA	406-782-8080	1601 Kaw Avenue - Exit 126 Butte MT	3+
Whitehall			
Lewis and Clark Caverns State Park	406-287-3541	1455 H 2E - Exit Three Forks to H 2E Whitehall MT	3+
Pipestone RV Park	406-287-5224	41 Bluebird Lane - Exit 241 Whitehall MT	3+
Bozeman			
Bozeman KOA	406-587-3030	81123 Gallatin Road - Exit 298 at Belgrade Bozeman MT	3+
Sunrise Campground	877-437-2095	31842 Frontage Road - Exit 309 Bozeman MT	3+
Livingston			
Livingston/Paradise Valley KOA	406-222-0992	163 Pine Creek Road Livingston MT	3+
East Big Timber			
Big Timber KOA	406-932-6569	693 H 10 - Exit 377 East Big Timber MT	1+
Laurel			
Pelican RV Park	406-628-4324	11360 S Frontage - Exit 437 Laurel MT	3+
Billings			
Billings KOA	406-252-3104	547 Garden Avenue - Exit 447 or 450 Billings MT	3+
Custer National Forest	406-657-6200	1310 Main Street Billings MT	3+
Trailer Village RV Park	406-248-8685	325 S Billings Blvd - Exit 447 Billings MT	2
Yellowstone River Campground	406-259-0878	309 Garden Avenue - Exit 450 Billings MT	3+
Hardin			
Hardin KOA	406-665-1635	RR 1 - Exit 495 Hardin MT	3+

Wyoming Listings   (Interstate 90)   Dogs per Site

Sheridan			
Bighorn National Forest	307-674-2600	2013 Eastside 2nd Street Sheridan WY	3+
Sheridan/Big Horn Mountains KOA	307-674-8766	63 Decker Road - Exit 20 Sheridan WY	3+
Buffalo			
Buffalo KOA	307-684-5423	87 H 16E - Exit 56A or 56B Buffalo WY	3+
Deer Park RV Park	307-684-5722	Box 568, On H 16E Buffalo WY	3+
Indian Campground	307-684-9601	660 E Hart Street - Exit 56b Buffalo WY	1+
Moorcroft			
Keyhole State Park	307-756-3596	353 McKean Road Moorcroft WY	3+

South Dakota Listings   (Interstate 90)   Dogs per Site

Spearfish			
Spearfish KOA	605-642-4633	41 H 14 - Exit 8 or 10W Service Road Spearfish SD	3+
Deadwood			
Deadwood KOA	605-578-3830	1 mile W of Deadwood on H 14A - Exit 30 Deadwood SD	3+
Sturgis			
Bear Butte State Park	605-347-5240	PO Box 688; E Hwy 79 Sturgis SD	3+
Elkview Campground	877-478-5162	13014 Pleasant Valley Road Sturgis SD	3+
Mount Rushmore - Black Hills			
Black Hills National Forest	605-673-9200	25041 N H 16 Custer SD	3+
Custer State Park	605-255-4515	13329 H 16A Custer SD	3+
KOA Campground	605-673-4304	U.S. Highway 16 Custer SD	1+
The Flintstones Bedrock City Campground	605-673-4079	US Highways 16 and 385 Custer SD	1+
The Roost Resort	605-673-2326	12462 H 16 A Custer SD	3+
Crooked Creek Resort	800-252-8486	24184 S H 385/16 Hill City SD	2
Horse Thief Campground	605-574-2668	24391 H 87 Hill City SD	3+
KOA Campground and Resort	605-574-2525	12620 Highway 244 Hill City SD	1+
Rafter J Bar Ranch	605-574-2527	12325 Rafter J Road Hill City SD	3+
Berry Patch Campground	800-658-4566	1860 E North Street - Exit 60 Rapid City SD	3+
Happy Holiday Resort	605-342-7365	8990 H 16S Rapid City SD	3+
Jellystone Park	605-341-8554	7001 S H 16 Rapid City SD	3+
KOA Campground	605-348-2111	P.O. Box 2592 Rapid City SD	1+
Rushmore Shadows	800-231-0425	23645 Clubhouse Drive Rapid City SD	3+
Wall			
Arrow Campground	605-279-2112	PO Box 366 Wall SD	3+
Sleepy Hollow Campground	605-279-2100	116 4th Avenue W - Exit 109 Wall SD	3+
Interior			
Badland National Park	605-433-5361	25216 Ben Reifel Place Interior SD	3+
Badlands/White River KOA	605-433-5337	20720 H 44 - Exit 131 Interior SD	3+
Kennebec			
Kennebec KOA	605-869-2300	311 S H 273 - Exit 235 Kennebec SD	3+
Mitchell			
Dakota Campground	605-996-9432	1800 Spruce - Exit 330 Mitchell SD	3+
Mitchell KOA	605-996-1131	41244 H 38 - Exit 335 N Mitchell SD	3+
Rondees Campground	605-996-0769	911 East K - Exit 332 Mitchell SD	3+
Sioux Falls			
Sioux Falls KOA	605-332-9987	1401 E Robur Drive - Exit 399/Cliff Avenue Sioux Falls SD	3+

Brandon

Yogi Bear Jellystone Park	605-332-2233	26014 478th Avenue - Exit 402 Brandon SD	3+

Minnesota Listings (Interstate 90)   Dogs per Site

Luverne

Blue Mounds State Park	507-283-1307	1410 161st Street Luverne MN	3+

Jackson

Jackson KOA	507-847-3825	2035 H 71N - Exit 73 Jackson MN	3+

Fairmont

Flying Goose Campground	507-235-3458	2521 115th Street - Exit 107 Fairmont MN	3+

Hayward

Albert Lea/Austin KOA	507-373-5170	84259 County Road 46 Hayward MN	3+

Austin

Beaver Trails Campground and RV Park	507-584-6611	21943 630th Avenue - Exit 187 Austin MN	3+

Rochester

Rochester/Marion KOA	507-288-0785	5232 65th Avenue SE Rochester MN	3+

Wisconsin Listings (Interstate 90)   Dogs per Site

La Crosse

Neshonoc Lakeside Camp Resort	608-786-1792	N4668 H 16 West Salem WI	2

Oakdale

Oakdale KOA	608-372-5622	200 J Street - Exit 48 Oakdale WI	3+

Camp Douglas

Mill Bluff State Park	608-427-6692	15819 Funnel Rd. - Exit 48 or 55 Camp Douglas WI	3+

Wisconsin Dells

Wisconsin Dells KOA	608-254-4177	S 235 Stand Rock Road - Exit 87 Wisconsin Dells WI	3+

Baraboo

Baraboo Hill Campground	800-226-7242	E 10545 Terrytown Road Baraboo WI	3+
Devil's Lake State Park	608-356-8301	5975 Park Road - Exit 92 Baraboo WI	3+
Mirror Lake State Park	608-254-2333	E10320 Fern Dell Road - Exit 92 (H 12) Baraboo WI	3+
Natural Bridge State Park	608-356-8301	S5975 Park Road Baraboo WI	3+
Rocky Arbor State Park	608-339-6881	E10320 Fern Dell Road - Exit 85 (H 1216) to Wisconsin Dells Baraboo WI	3+

DeForest

Madison KOA	608-846-4528	4859 CTH-V - Exit 126 DeForest WI	3+

Madison

Crystal Lake Campground	608-592-5607	N550 Gannon Road Lodi WI	3+

Stoughton

Lake Kegonsa State Park	608-873-9695	2405 Door Creek Road - Exit 147 Stoughton WI	3+

Milton

Hidden Valley RV Resort	608-868-4141	872 E State Road 59 - Exit 163/H 59 Milton WI	3+

Illinois Listings (Interstate 90)   Dogs per Site

Loves Park

Rock Cut State Park	815-885-3311	7318 Harlem Road - Exit Riverside to Perryville Road Loves Park IL	3+

Rockford

River's Edge Campground	815-629-2526	12626 N Meridian Rockton IL	3+

Garden Prairie

Holiday Acres Camping Resort	815-547-7846	7050 Epworth - Exit H 20 Garden Prairie IL	1+

Marengo

Lehman's Lakeside RV Resort	815-923-4533	19609 Harmony Road - Exit H 20 Marengo IL	3+

Union

Chicago Northwest KOA	815-923-4206	8404 S Union Road - Exit Marengo-Hampshire to H20 Union IL	3+

Chicago Area

Windy City Campground	708-720-0030	18701 S 80th Avenue Tinley Park IL	2
Hide-A-Way Lakes	630-553-6323	8045 Van Emmons Road Yorkville IL	3+

Ohio Listings (Interstate 90)   Dogs per Site

Cleveland

Kool Lakes Family RV park	440-548-8436	12990 H 282 Parkman OH	3+
Country Acres Campground	866-813-4321	9850 Minyoung Road Ravenna OH	3+

Conneaut

Evergreen Lake Park Campground	440-599-8802	703 Center Road Conneaut OH	1+

Pennsylvania Listings (Interstate 90)

Dogs per Site

McKean

Erie KOA	814-476-7706	6645 West Road - Exit 18 McKean PA	3+

New York Listings (Interstate 90)

Dogs per Site

Westfield

KOA Westfield/Lake Erie	716-326-3573	8001 H 5 Westfield NY	3+

Brocton

Lake Erie State Park	716-792-9214	5905 H 5 - Exit H 5 Brocton NY	3+

Rochester

Genesee Country Campgrounds	585-538-4200	40 Flinthill Road Caledonia NY	2

Austerlitz

Woodland Hills Campground	518-392-3557	386 Foghill Road - Exit B-3 Austerlitz NY	3+

Massachusetts Listings (Interstate 90)

Dogs per Site

Sturbridge

Jellystone Park	508-347-9570	30 River Road Sturbridge MA	3+
Wells State Park	508-347-9257	159 Walker Pond Road Sturbridge MA	3+

Boston Area

Normandy Farms	508-543-7600	72 West Street Foxboro MA	3+
Boston Minuteman Campground	877-677-0042	264 Ayer Road Littleton MA	3+
KOA	508-947-6435	438 Plymouth Street Middleboro MA	3+
Winter Island Park	978-745-9430	50 Winter Island Road Salem MA	2
Rusnik Campground	978-462-9551	115 Lafayette Road Salisbury MA	3+

Interstate 94 Campground Listings

Montana Listings (Interstate 94)

Dogs per Site

Billings

Billings KOA	406-252-3104	547 Garden Avenue Billings MT	3+
Custer National Forest	406-657-6200	1310 Main Street Billings MT	3+
Trailer Village RV Park	406-248-8685	325 S Billings Blvd Billings MT	2
Yellowstone River Campground	406-259-0878	309 Garden Avenue Billings MT	3+

Miles City

Miles City KOA	406-232-3991	1 Palmer Street - Exit 135 Miles City MT	3+

North Dakota Listings (Interstate 94)

Dogs per Site

Mandan

Fort Abraham Lincoln State Park	701-667-6340	4480 Fort Lincoln Road Mandan ND	3+

Bismarck

Bismarck KOA	701-222-2662	3720 Centennial Road - Exit 161 Bismarck ND	3+

Jamestown

Frontier Fort Campground	701-252-7492	1838 3rd Avenue SE - Exit 258 Jamestown ND	3+
Jamestown Campground	701-252-6262	3605 80th Avenue - Exit 256 Jamestown ND	3+

Minnesota Listings (Interstate 94)

Dogs per Site

Moorhead

Moorhead/Fargo KOA	218-233-0671	4396 28th Avenue S - Exit 2 Moorhead MN	3+

St Cloud

St Cloud Campground	320-251-4463	2491 2nd Street SE St Cloud MN	1+

Monticello

River Terrace Park	763-295-2264	1335 River Street W - Exit 195 Monticello MN	3+

Minneapolis - St Paul

Greenwood Campground	651-437-5269	13797 190th Street E Hastings MN	2
Minneapolis Northwest KOA	763-420-2255	10410 Brockton Maple Grove MN	2
Dakotah Meadows RV Park	952-445-8800	2341 Park Place Prior Lake MN	3+
St Paul East KOA	651-436-6436	568 Cottage Grove - Exit 253 Woodbury MN	3+

Wisconsin Listings (Interstate 94)

Dogs per Site

Black River Falls			
Black River State Forest	715-284-4103	10325 H 12 E - Exit H 5 4E Black River Falls WI	3+
Warrens			
Jellystone Park	608-378-4303	1500 Jellystone Park Drive - Exit 135 Warrens WI	2
Madison			
Crystal Lake Campground	608-592-5607	N550 Gannon Road Lodi WI	3+
Delafield			
Lapham Peak Unit, Kettle Moraine State Forest	262-646-3025	W 329 N 846 County Road C - Exit Lapham Peak State Park Delafield WI	3+
Milwaukee			
Wisconsin State Fair RV Park	414-266-7035	601 S 76th Street - Exit 68th or 70th Street Milwaukee WI	3+
Caledonia			
Jellystone Park	262-835-2526	8425 H 38 - Exit 7 Mile Road (H-326) E Caledonia WI	3+

Illinois Listings (Interstate 94)   Dogs per Site

Chicago Area			
Windy City Campground	708-720-0030	18701 S 80th Avenue Tinley Park IL	2
Hide-A-Way Lakes	630-553-6323	8045 Van Emmons Road Yorkville IL	3+

Indiana Listings (Interstate 94)   Dogs per Site

Gary			
Oak Lake Campground	219-345-3153	5310 E 900N Fair Oaks IN	1+
Portage			
Yogi Bear Campground	219-762-7757	5300 Old Porter Road Portage IN	3+
Chesterton			
Indiana Dunes State Park	219-926-1952	1600 North 25 E Chesterton IN	3+
Michigan City			
Michigan City Campground	800-813-2267	601 N H 421 Michigan City IN	2

Michigan Listings (Interstate 94)   Dogs per Site

Benton Harbor			
House of David Travel Trailer Park	269-927-3302	1019 E Empire - Exit 28 Benton Harbor MI	2
Jackson			
Greenwood Campgrounds	517-522-8600	2401 Hilton Road - Exit 147 Jackson MI	3+
Chelsea			
Waterloo Recreation Area	734-475-8307	16345 McClure Road - Exit 153/Clearlake (Sugarloaf) Chelsea MI	3+
Ypsilanti			
Detroit/Greenfield KOA	734-482-7222	6680 Bunton Road - Exit 187 Ypsilanti MI	3+
Detroit			
Wayne County Fairgrounds and RV Park	734-697-7002	10871 Quirk Road - Exit 190 Belleville MI	3+
Harbortown RV Resort	734-384-4700	14931 La Plaisance Monroe MI	3+

Interstate 95 Campground Listings

Maine Listings (Interstate 95)   Dogs per Site

Medway			
Katahdin Shadows Campground and Cabins	207-746-9349	H 157 - Exit 244 Medway ME	3+
Bangor			
Paul Bunyan Campground	207-941-1177	1862 Union Street - Exit 184 Bangor ME	1+
Hermon			
Pumpkin Patch	207-848-2231	149 Billings Road - Exit 180 Hermon ME	3+
Augusta			
Augusta West Lakeside Resort	207-377-9993	183 Holmes Brook Lane Winthrop ME	2
Freeport			
Cedar Haven Campground	207-865-6254	39 Baker Road Freeport ME	1+
Portland			
Bayley's Camping Resort	207-883-6043	275 Pine Point Road Scarborough ME	3+
Wassamki Springs	207-839-4276	56 Soco Street Scarborough ME	2
Old Orchard Beach			
Hid'n Pines Family Campground	207-934-2352	8 Cascade Road Old Orchard Beach ME	1

Powder Horn Family Camping Resort	207-934-4733	48 Cascade Road Old Orchard Beach ME	3+
Wild Acres Family Camping Resort	207-934-2535	179 Saco Avenue - Exit 36 Old Orchard Beach ME	3+
Saco			
KOA Saco/Portland South	207-282-0502	814 Portland Road Saco ME	3+

Massachusetts Listings (Interstate 95)   Dogs per Site

Boston Area			
Normandy Farms	508-543-7600	72 West Street Foxboro MA	3+
Boston Minuteman Campground	877-677-0042	264 Ayer Road Littleton MA	3+
KOA	508-947-6435	438 Plymouth Street Middleboro MA	3+
Winter Island Park	978-745-9430	50 Winter Island Road Salem MA	2
Rusnik Campground	978-462-9551	115 Lafayette Road Salisbury MA	3+

Rhode Island Listings (Interstate 95)   Dogs per Site

Providence			
Bowdish Lake	401-568-8890	40 Safari Road Glocester RI	3+

New Jersey Listings (Interstate 95)   Dogs per Site

Northern New Jersey			
Liberty Harbor RV Park	201-387-7500	11 Marin Blvd - Exit 14C/Jersey City-Grand Street Jersey City NJ	3+

Delaware Listings (Interstate 95)   Dogs per Site

Wilmington Area			
Delaware Motel and RV Park	302-328-3114	235 S. Dupont Highway New Castle DE	3+

Maryland Listings (Interstate 95)   Dogs per Site

Washington Suburbs			
Cherry Hill Park	800-801-6449	9800 Cherry Hill Road - Exit 25 College Park MD	3+
Duncan's Family Campground	410-741-9558	5381 Sands Beach Road Lothian MD	3+

Virginia Listings (Interstate 95)   Dogs per Site

Northern Virginia			
Bull Run Regional Park	703-631-0550	7700 Bull Run Drive Centreville VA	3+
Lake Fairfax Park	703-471-5415	1400 Lake Fairfax Drive Reston VA	3+
Fredericksburg			
Fredericksburg/Washington DC S KOA	540-898-7252	7400 Brookside Lane - Exit H 607 Fredericksburg VA	2
Petersburg			
Petersburg KOA	804-732-8345	2809 Cortland Road - Exit 41 Petersburg VA	3+
Emporia			
Jellystone Park	434-634-3115	2940 Sussex Drive - Exit 17 Emporia VA	3+

North Carolina Listings (Interstate 95)   Dogs per Site

Enfield			
Enfield/Rocky Mount KOA	252-445-5925	101 Bell Acres - Exit 154/Enfield Enfield NC	3+
Wade			
Fayetteville/Wade KOA	910-484-5500	6250 Wade Stedman Road - Exit 61 Wade NC	3+

South Carolina Listings (Interstate 95)   Dogs per Site

Florence			
Florence KOA	843-665-7007	1115 E Campground Road - Exit 169 Florence SC	3+
Yemassee			
Point South KOA	843-726-5733	14 Campground Road - Exit 33 to H 17 Yemassee SC	3+

Georgia Listings (Interstate 95)   Dogs per Site

Savannah			
Brookwood RV Park	888-636-4616	Rt 5, Box 3107; on Pulaski Excelsior Metter GA	3+
Fort McAllister State Historic Park	912-727-2339	3894 Fort McAllister Road Richmond Hill GA	3+
Savannah South KOA	912-765-3396	4915 H 17 - Exit 87 @ Richmond Hill Richmond Hill GA	3+
Waterway RV Park	912-756-2296	70 H 17 Richmond Hill GA	2
Skidaway Island State Park	912-598-2300	52 Diamond Causeway Savannah GA	3+

Brunswick

Blythe Island Regional Park	912-279-2812	6616 Blythe Island H (H 303) Brunswick GA	3+

Jekyll Island

Jekyll Island Campground	866-658-3021	1197 Riverview Drive - Exit 29 Jekyll Island GA	3+

Kingsland

Jacksonville N/Kingsland KOA	912-729-3232	2970 Scrubby Buff Road - Exit 1 Kingsland GA	3+

Florida Listings (Interstate 95)

Dogs per Site

Jacksonville

Little Talbot Island State Park	904-251-2320	12157 Heckscher Drive Jacksonville FL	3+
Flamingo Lake RV Resort	904-766-0672	3640 Newcomb Road N Jacksonville FL	3+

St Augustine

Anastasia State Park	904-461-2033	1340-A A1A South St Augustine FL	3+
Anastasia State Park Campgrounds	904-461-2033	Anastasia Park Drive St Augustine FL	1+
St. Augustine Beach KOA	904-471-3113	525 West Pope Road St Augustine FL	1+
Stagecoach RV Park	904-824-2319	2711 County Road 208 - Exit H 16W St Augustine FL	3+

Flagler Beach

Beverly Beach Campground	800-255-2706	2816 N Ocean Shore Blvd Flagler Beach FL	3+
Gamble Rogers Memorial State Recreation Area	386-517-2086	3100 S A1A (Ocean Shore Blvd) Flagler Beach FL	3+

Daytona Beach

Bulow Plantation RV Resort	800-782-8569	3345 Old Kings Road S - Exit 278 Flagler Beach FL	3+
Daytona North RV Resort	877-277-8737	1701 H 1 - Exit H 1 Ormond Beach FL	3+
Tomoka State Park	386-676-4050	2099 N Beach Street - Exit 268 Ormond Beach FL	3+

Port Orange

Daytona Beach Campground	386-761-2663	4601 Clyde Morris Blvd - Exit 256 Port Orange FL	3+

Melbourne Beach

Sebastian Inlet State Park	321-984-4852	9700 S A1A - Exit State Road 192 Melbourne Beach FL	3+

Hobe Sound

Jonathan Dickinson State Park	772-546-2771	16450 SE Federal H (H 1) - Exit 87A/Indiantown Road Hobe Sound FL	3+

South Florida

Juno RV Park	561-622-7500	900 Juno Ocean Walk Juno Beach FL	3+
Paradise Island RV Resort	954-485-1150	2121 NW 29th Court - Exit 33311 Oakland Park FL	3+
Highland Woods	866-340-0649	850/900 NE 48th Street - Exit 39/Sample Road Pompano Beach FL	3+

Highway 101 Campground Listings

Washington Listings (Highway 101)

Dogs per Site

Olympia

Olympic National Forest	360-956-23300	1835 Black Lk Blvd SW Olympia WA	3+

Sequim

Rainbows End RV Park	360-683-3863	261831 H 101 Sequim WA	2

Port Angeles

Log Cabin Resort	360-928-3325	3183E Beach Road Port Angeles WA	3+
Olympia National Park	360-452-4501	600 East Park Avenue - Exit Race Street Port Angeles WA	3+
Port Angeles/Swquim KOA	360-457-5916	80 O'Brien Road Port Angeles WA	2

Ilwaco

Ilwaco/Long Beach KOA	360-642-3292	1509 H 101 Ilwaco WA	2

Oregon Listings (Highway 101)

Dogs per Site

Cannon Beach

Cannon Beach RV Resort	800-847-2231	340 Elk Creek Road Cannon Beach OR	3+
Sea Ranch RV Park and Stables	503-436-2815	415 1st Street Cannon Beach OR	3+

Tillamook

Cape Lookout State Park	503-842-4981	13000 Whiskey Creek Road W Tillamook OR	3+

Otis

Lincoln City KOA	541-994-2961	5298 NE Park Lane - Exit East Devil's Lake Road Otis OR	3+

Newport

Beverly Beach State Park	541-265-9278	198 NE 123rd Street Newport OR	3+

Florence

Jessie M Honeyman Memorial State Park	541-997-3641	84505 H 101S Florence OR	3+
Mercer Lake Resort	800-355-3633	88875 Bay Berry Lane Florence OR	2

Winchester Bay

The Marina RV Resort	541-271-0287	End of Marina Way - Exit Salmon Harbor Winchester Bay OR	3+

North Bend

Oregon Dunes KOA	541-756-4851	68632 H 101 North Bend OR	3+

Coos Bay

Lucky Loggers RV Park	541-267-6003	250 E Johnson - Exit E Johnson Coos Bay OR	3+
Sunset Bay State Park	541-888-4902	89814 Cape Arago Coos Bay OR	3+

Bandon

Bandon by the Sea RV Park	541-347-5155	49612 H 101 Bandon OR	3+
Bullards Beach State Park	541-347-2209	52470 H 101 Bandon OR	3+

Langlois

Bandon/Port Orford KOA	541-348-2358	46612 H 101 Langlois OR	2

Gold Beach

Four Seasons RV Resort	800-248-4503	96526 N Bank Road - Exit River Road Gold Beach OR	2
Indian Creek Resort	541-247-7704	94680 Jerry's Flat Road - Exit Jerry's Flat Road Gold Beach OR	2
Turtle Rock RV Resort	541-247-9203	28788 Hunter Creek Loop - Exit Hunter Creek Loop Gold Beach OR	3+

Brookings

At Rivers Edge RV Park	541-469-3356	98203 S Bank Chetco River Road Brookings OR	2
Harris Beach State Park	541-469-2021	1655 H 101N Brookings OR	3+

California Listings (Highway 101)   Dogs per Site

Crescent City

Crescent City KOA	707-464-5744	4241 H 101N Crescent City CA	3+
De Norte Coast Redwoods State Park	707-464-6101, ext. 5064	7 miles S of Crescent City off H 101 Crescent City CA	3+
Jedediah Smith Campground	707-464-6101	1440 H 199 Crescent City CA	3+
Jedediah Smith Redwoods State Park	707-464-6101, ext. 5112	9 miles east of Crescent City on Highway 199. Crescent City CA	1+
Mill Creek Campground	707-464-9533	1375 Elk Valley Road Crescent City CA	3+
Panther Flat Campground	707-457-3131	mile post 16.75 on Highway 199 Gasquet CA	3+
Panther Flat Campground	707-442-1721	Mile Post 16.75 H 199 Gasquet CA	3+

Eureka

Eureka KOA	707-822-4243	4050 N H 101 Eureka CA	3+

Sonoma

Cloverdale KOA	707-894-3337	1166 Asti Ridge Road Cloverdale CA	3+
Casini Ranch Family Campground	707-865-2255	22855 Moscow Road Duncan Mills CA	3+
Fifes Guest Ranch	707-869-0656	16467 H 116 Guerneville CA	2
Spring Lake Regional Park Campgrounds	707-785-2377	5585 Newanga Avenue Santa Rosa CA	3+

Marin - North Bay

Bodega Dunes Campground	707-875-3483	3095 H 1 Bodega Bay CA	3+
Doran Regional Park Campgrounds	707-875-3540	201 Doran Beach Road Bodega Bay CA	3+
Westside Regional Park Campground	707-875-3540	2400 Westshore Road Bodega Bay CA	3+
Novato RV Park	415-897-1271	1530 Armstrong Avenue Novato CA	3+
Olema Ranch Campground	415-663-8001	10155 H 1 Olema CA	3+
San Francisco North/Petaluma KOA	707-763-1492	20 Rainsvile Road Petaluma CA	3+

San Francisco

Candlestick RV Park	415-822-2299	650 Gilman Avenue San Francisco CA	3+

Palo Alto - Peninsula

Butano State Park Campground	650-879-2040	Off H 1 4.5 miles SE of Pescadero Pescadero CA	3+

San Juan Bautista

Betabel RV Park	831-623-2202	9664 Betabel Road San Juan Bautista CA	2
Mission Farms RV Park & Campground	831-623-4456	400 San Juan Hollister Road San Juan Bautista CA	3+

Salinas

Laguna Seca Campground	831-755-4895	1025 Monterey H 68 Salinas CA	2

King City

San Lorenzo Campground and RV Park	831-385-5964	1160 Broadway King City CA	2

San Luis Obispo

Lake San Antonio Campground	805-472-2311	2610 San Antonio Road Bradley CA	2
North Beach Campground, Pismo State Beach Park	805-489-1869	555 Pier Avenue Oceano CA	3+
Pacific Dunes RV Resort	760-328-4813	1025 Silver Spur Place Oceano CA	3+
Lake Nacimiento Resort RV and Campgrounds	805-238-3256	10625 Nacimiento Lake Drive Paso Robles CA	3+
Pismo Coast Village RV Park	805-773-1811	165 S Dolliver Street Pismo Beach CA	3+
El Chorro Regional Park Campground	805-781-5930	H 1 San Luis Obispo CA	3+
Santa Margarita KOA	805-438-5618	4765 Santa Margarita Lake Road Santa Margarita CA	2
Santa Margarita Lake Regional Park Camping	805-781-5930	4695 Santa Margarita Lake Road Santa Margarita CA	3+

Solvang

Flying Flags RV Park and Campground	805-688-3716	180 Avenue of the Flags Buellton CA	1+

Santa Barbara

El Capitan State Beach	805-968-1033	10 Refugio Beach Road Goleta CA	2
Cachuma Lake Rec Area	805-686-5054	H 154 Santa Barbara CA	3+

Canadian Highway 1 and 5 (West) and Highway 17 (East) Campground Listings

British Columbia Listings (Trans-Canada)   Dogs per Site

Surrey

Dogwood Campground and RV Park	604-583-5585	15151 112th Avenue - Exit 108E Surrey BC	2
Hazelmere RV Park	877-501-5007	18843 8th Avenue Surrey BC	1+

Hope

Hope Valley Campground	604-869-9857	62280 Flood Hope Road Hope BC	3+

Sicamous

Sicamous KOA	250-836-2507	3250 Oxboro Road Sicamous BC	3+

Revelstoke

Canyon Hot Springs Resort	250-837-2420	35 KM E of Revelstoke on H 1 Revelstoke BC	1
Lamplighter Campground	250-837-3385	1760 Nixon - Exit 23S Revelstoke BC	3+
Revelstoke KOA	250-837-2085	2411 KOA Road Revelstoke BC	2
Williamson's Lake Campground	250-837-5512	1816 Williamson Lake Road Revelstoke BC	3+

Field

Yoho National Park of Canada	250-343-6783	P. O. Box 99/H 1 Field BC	3+

Alberta Listings (Trans-Canada)   Dogs per Site

Banff

Banff National Park of Canada	403-762-1550	224 Banff Avenue Banff AB	1+

Canmore

Spring Creek Mountain Village	403-678-5111	502 3rd Avenue - Exit Town Center Canmore AB	3+

Calgary

Hinton/Jasper KOA	403-288-8351	4720 Vegas Road NW Calgary AB	2
Pine Creek RV Campground	403-256-3002	On McCloud Trail Calgary AB	2
Symon's Valley RV Park	403-274-4574	260011 Symon's Valley Road NW Calgary AB	2

Brooks

Dinosaur Provincial Park	403-378-3700	Prairie Road 30 - Exit Patricia Brooks AB	3+

Medicine Hat

Wild Rose Trailer Park	403-526-2248	28B Camp Drive SW Medicine Hat AB	3+

Saskatchewan Listings (Trans-Canada)   Dogs per Site

Swift Current

Ponderosa Campground	306-773-5000	On H 1 a quarter mile E of Swift Current SK	3+
Trail Campground	306-773-8088	701 11th Avenue NW Swift Current SK	3+

Chaplin

Silver Dollar RV Park and Campground	306-395-2332	Corner of H 1 and H 19 Chaplin SK	3+

Moose Jaw

Besant Trans-Canada Campground	306-756-2700	25 miles W of Moose Jaw on H 1 Moose Jaw SK	3+
Prairie Oasis Campground and Motel	306-693-8888	955 Thatcher Moose Jaw SK	2
River Park Campground	306-692-5474	300 River Drive Moose Jaw SK	3+

Regina

Buffalo Lookout Campground	306-525-1448	2 miles E of Regina on H 1 Regina SK	3+
Kings Acres Campground	306-522-1619	I km E of Regina on H 1, N service road Regina SK	3+
Sherwood Forest Country Club	306-545-0330	RR 2 Box 16 - Exit Grand Clouee Regina SK	3+

Moosomin

Fieldstone Campground	306-435-2677	Box 1524 - Exit H 8N 2 km Moosomin SK	1+

Manitoba Listings (Trans-Canada)   Dogs per Site

Virden

Virden's Lion's Campground	204-748-6393	Corner &th and H 257 Virden MB	3+
Brandon			
Curran Park Campground	204-571-0750	Box 6, 305 RR 3 - Exit Grand Valley Road Brandon MB	3+
Meadowlark Campground	204-728-7205	1629 Middleton Brandon MB	3+
Portage la Prairie			
Miller's Camping Resort	204-857-4255	6 miles E of Portage on H 1 Portage la Prairie MB	3+
Portage Campground	204-267-2191	8 miles E of Portage on H 1 Portage la Prairie MB	2
Shediac			
Wikiwak Campground	506-532-6713	55 S Cove - Exit 31 or 37 Shediac MB	3+
Winnipeg			
Bird's Hill Provincial Park	888-482-2267	On Lagimodiere/H 59 Winnipeg MB	3+
Northgate Trailer Park	204-339-6631	2695 Main - Exit H 52 Winnipeg MB	3+
Traveller's RV Resort	204-256-2186	56001 Murdock Road - Exit Murdock Road Winnipeg MB	3+
Hadashville			
Whitemouth River RV Park and Campground	204-426-5367	On Government Jet Road - Exit H 43N Hadashville MB	1
West Hawk Lake			
Whitelshell Provincial Park	204-349-2245	P. O. Box 119 West Hawk Lake MB	3+

Ontario Listings   (Trans-Canada)   Dogs per Site

Thunder Bay			
Thunder Bay KOA	807-683-6221	162 Spruce River Road Thunder Bay ON	3+
Spragge			
Spragge KOA	705-849-2210	4696 H 17 - Exit H 17W Spragge ON	3+
North Bay			
Champlain Tent and Trailer Park	705-474-4669	1202 Premier Road - Exit 338/Lakeshore Drive North Bay ON	3+
Renfrew			
Renfrew KOA	613-432-6280	2826 Johnston Road Renfrew ON	3+
Ottawa			
Poplar Grove Tourist Camp	613-821-2973	6154 Bank Street Ottawa ON	2
Rec-Land	613-833-2974	1566 Canaan Road - Exit Canaan Road Ottawa ON	3+

Canadian Highway 16
Campground Listings

Alberta Listings   (Highway 16)   Dogs per Site

Hinton			
Best Canadian Motor Inn and RV Park	780-865-5099	386 Smith Street Hinton AB	1+
Edson			
East of Eden Campground and RV Park	780-723-2287	162 Range Road Edson AB	2
Edmonton			
Glowing Embers RV Park	877-785-7275	26309 Acheson Edmonton AB	3+
Whitemud Creek Gold and RV Park	780-988-6800	3428 156th Street SW Edmonton AB	2
Vermilion			
Vermilion Campground	780-853-4372	5301 48th Street Vermilion AB	3+

Saskatchewan Listings   (Highway 16)   Dogs per Site

Lloydminster			
Weaver Park Campground	306-825-3726	On H 16 at Bar Colony Museum Lloydminster SK	3+
North Battleford			
David Laird Campground	306-445-3552	Box 1383 North Battleford SK	3+
Saskatoon			
Gordon Howe Campground	306-975-3328	Avenue P South Saskatoon SK	3+
Saskatoon 16 West RV Park	306-931-8905	Corner of 71st Street and H 16 Saskatoon SK	3+
Yorkton			
Yorkton City Campground	306-786-1757	On H 16 W of Yorkton Yorkton SK	3+

Canadian Highway 401 (Ontario) and Highway 20 (Quebec) Campground Listings

Ontario Listings (Highways 401 and 20)   Dogs per Site

McGregor			
Wildwood Golf and RV Resort	519-726-6176	11112 11 Consession McGregor ON	3+
London			
London/401 KOA	519-644-0222	136 Cromarty Drive London ON	2
Cambridge			
Valens Conservation Area	905-525-2183	1691 Regional Park Road 97 Cambridge ON	3+
Toronto Area			
Indian Line Campground	905-678-1233	7625 Finch Avenue W Brampton ON	3+
Milton Heights Campground	905-878-6781	8690 Tremaine Road Milton ON	3+
Toronto			
Glen Rouge Campground	416-338-2267	7450 Kingston Road - Exit 390 Toronto ON	3+
Cherry Valley			
Quinte's Isle Campark	613-476-6310	237 Salmon Point Road - Exit 566 Cherry Valley ON	3+
Johnstown			
Grenville Park	613-925-2000	2323 County Road 2 RR3 - Exit 721B Johnstown ON	3+
Kingston			
1000 Islands/Kingston KOA	613-546-6140	2039 Cordukes Road Kingston ON	3+
Lake Ontario Park	613-542-6574	1000 King Street W - Exit 615 Kingston ON	3+
Rideau Acres	613-546-2711	1014 Cunningham Road - Exit H 15 Kingston ON	3+
Lans Downe			
1000 Islands Camping Resort	613-659-3058	382 1000 Islands Parkway - Exit 1000 Isalnds Parkway Lans Downe ON	1+
Cardinal			
Cardinal KOA	613-657-4536	609 Pittston Road Cardinal ON	3+

Quebec Listings (Highways 401 and 20)   Dogs per Site

Montreal			
Camping de Compton	800-563-5277	24 Chemin De La Station Compton PQ	3+
Montreal West KOA	450-763-5625	171 H 338 Coteau du Lac PQ	3+
Camping Lac LaFontaine	450-431-7373	110 Boul Grand Heron PQ	2
Camping Alouette	450-464-1661	3449 L'Industrie Saint-Mathieu-de-beloeil PQ	3+
Drummondville			
Camping La Detente	819-478-0651	1580 Fontaine Bleau Drummondville PQ	3+

Chapter 6

United States National Parks

DogFriendly.com's Top 5 National Parks
(Ratings based on sights to see and places to walk or hike with dogs)

1. Grand Canyon National Park, Arizona, 928-638-7888

You and your dog can view the popular Grand Canyon along the South Rim where millions of visitors come every year. Dogs are allowed on the South Rim trails which includes a 2.7 mile scenic walk along the rim. And, well-behaved pooches are allowed on the Geology Walk, a one hour park ranger guided tour which consists of a leisurely walk along a 3/4 mile paved rim trail. The following is the remainder of the doggie regulations. Dogs are not allowed in park lodging, or on park buses. Pets are not permitted at all on North Rim trails with the exception of a bridle path which connects the lodge with the North Kaibab Trail.

2. Acadia National Park, Maine, 207-288-3338

Dogs are allowed on most of the trails and carriage roads. There is even an off-leash area within the park at Little Long Pond. Pets are not allowed on sand beaches or on the steeper hiking trails. Pets must be on a 6 foot or less leash at all times, except for the above mentioned off-leash area.

3. Shenandoah National Park, Virginia, 540-999-3500

This national park, located along a section of the Blue Ridge Parkway, offers miles and miles of dog-friendly hiking trails. There are some trails where dogs are not allowed, but your pooch is allowed on the majority of trails in this park. Pets must be on a 6 foot or less leash at all times, and are allowed in campgrounds, and picnic areas.

4.Yosemite National Park, California, 209-372-0200

Dogs are allowed on the paved trails throughout the Yosemite Valley. The valley is where the majority of tourists visit and you can see most of the popular landmarks and sights from the valley floor, with your pet. Dogs are not allowed on other trails, in wilderness areas, or on the shuttle buses. Owners must clean up after their pets.

5. North Cascades National Park, Washington, 360-856-5700

Dogs are allowed on one of the hiking trails, the Pacific Crest Trail. This scenic hiking trail runs through the park and is rated moderate to difficult. The trail is located off Highway 20, about one mile east of Rainy Pass. At the Bridge Creek Trailhead, park on the north side of the highway and then hike north (uphill) or south (downhill). A Northwest Forest Pass is required to park at the trailhead. The cost is about $5 and can be purchased at the Visitor's Center in Newhalem. For a larger variety of trails, including a less strenuous hike, dogs are also allowed on trails at the adjacent Ross Lake National Recreation Area and the Lake Chelan National Recreation Area. Both recreation areas are managed by the national park.

Author Tara Kain and her dog Java at the Grand Canyon.

Alaska

Copper Center

Wrangell-St Elias National Park and
Preserve
PO Box 439
Copper Center, AK
907-822-5234
Dogs on leash are allowed in the
park. They are not allowed in
buildings. The park features
camping, hiking, auto touring, and
more.

Denali Park

Denali National Park and Preserve
PO Box 9
Denali Park, AK
907-683-2294
Dogs must be on leash and must be
cleaned up after in Denali National
Park. Dogs are only allowed on the
paved roads and dirt roads. One
place to walk is on the road to
Savage after mile 15, which is a dirt
road and only the park buses are
allowed. Access is by car depending
on weather. Dogs on leash are
allowed in the Denali National Park
campgrounds, but they may not be
left unattended in the campgrounds.
The park features auto touring,
camping, and scenery.

Fairbanks

Gates of the Arctic National Park
and Preserve
201 First Avenue
Fairbanks, AK
907-692-5494
Dogs must be on leash and must be
cleaned up after in the park. The
park is accessed by plane, foot and
car depending on weather. Dogs are
allowed in the backcountry of the
park but there are no man-made
trails. It is a wilderness park. The
nearest places to stay when visiting
the park are the towns of Bettles
Field and Wiseman. There are no
campgrounds in the park and there
are no facilities in the park.

Gustabus

Glacier Bay National Park
1 Park Road
Gustabus, AK
907-697-2230
This national park offers coastal
beaches and high mountains. The

way to arrive at this park is by plane,
boat, or ferry, usually from Juneau.
The Glacier Bay Visitor Center is
open daily from May 27 to
September 11, from noon to 8:45
p.m. Dogs are not allowed to be off
the road more than 100 feet, and
they are not allowed on any of the
trails into the back country. They are
also not allowed on the Barlett Trail
or on the Forest Loop Trail, or in any
of the camp buildings. The Visitor
Information Station for boaters and
campers, is open May through June
from 8 to 5 p.m.; June, July, and
August from 7 to 9 p.m., and
September 8 to 5 p.m. Dogs are
allowed at no additional fee, and
they can be in the developed Barlett
Cove area, or on any of the marked
trails. Dogs may not be left
unattended at any time, and they
must be leashed at all times, and
cleaned up after.

King Salmon

Katmai National Park and Preserve
PO Box 7
King Salmon, AK
907-246-3305
Dogs on leash are allowed only in
developed areas. They are not
allowed in the Brooks camping area.
The park is accessed by plane or
dogsled only.

Kotzebue

Kobuk Valley National Park
PO Box 1029
Kotzebue, AK
907-442-3760
Dogs on leash are allowed in the
park. The park is accessed by plane,
foot, or dogsled only.

Western Arctic National Parklands
PO Box 1029
Kotzebue, AK
907-442-3760
Pets are allowed. There is not an
official pet policy. The park is
accessed by plane and dogsledding.

Port Alsworth

Lake Clark National Park and
Preserve
1 Park Place
Port Alsworth, AK
907-781-2218
Dogs on leash are allowed in the
park area. The park is accessed by
plane or dogsled only. The park

features boating, camping, fishing,
hiking, and more.

Seward

Kenai Fjords National Park
PO Box 1727
Seward, AK
907-224-2132
Dogs on leash are only allowed in
the parking lot area and along roads.
They are not allowed in buildings, on
trails, or in the back country.

Arizona

Grand Canyon

Grand Canyon National Park
Hwy 64
Grand Canyon, AZ
928-638-7888
The Grand Canyon, located in the
northwest corner of Arizona, is
considered to be one of the most
impressive natural splendors in the
world. It is 277 miles long, 18 miles
wide, and at its deepest point, is
6000 vertical feet (more than 1 mile)
from rim to river. The Grand Canyon
has several entrance areas, but the
most popular is the South Rim. Dogs
are not allowed on any trails below
the rim, but leashed dogs are
allowed on the paved rim trail. This
dog-friendly trail is about 2.7 miles
each way and offers excellent views
of the Grand Canyon. Remember
that the elevation at the rim is 7,000
feet, so you or your pup may need to
rest more often than usual. Also, the
weather can be very hot during the
summer and can be snowing during
the winter, so plan accordingly. And
be sure you or your pup do not get
too close to the edge! Feel like
taking a tour? Well-behaved dogs
are allowed on the Geology Walk.
This is a one hour park ranger
guided tour and consists of a
leisurely walk along a 3/4 mile paved
rim trail. They discuss how the
Grand Canyon was created and
more. The tour departs at 11am
daily (weather permitting) from the
Yavapai Observation Station. The
Grand Canyon park entrance fee is
currently $20.00 per private vehicle,
payable upon entry to the park.
Admission is for 7 days, includes
both South and North Rims, and
covers the entrance fee only.

Hot Springs

Hot Springs National Park
369 Central Avenue
Hot Springs, AZ
501-624-2701
There are 47 hot springs here, and this reserve was established in 1832 to protect them. That makes this park our oldest national park. The park is open daily from 9:00 a.m. to 5:00 p.m., except in the summer from May 28 to August 12, when they stay open until 6:00 p.m. Dogs are allowed at no additional fee at the park and in the campground, which does not have hookups. Dogs may not be left unattended, they must be leashed, and cleaned up after. Dogs are not allowed on the trails or in the buildings.

Petrified Forest National Park

Petrified Forest National Park
Entrances on Hwy 40 and Hwy 180
Petrified Forest National Park, AZ
928-524-6228
The Petrified Forest is located in northeastern Arizona and features one of the world's largest and most colorful concentrations of petrified wood. Also included in the park's 93,533 acres are the multi-hued badlands of the Painted Desert, archeological sites and displays of 225 million year old fossils. Your leashed dog is welcome on all of the paved trails and scenic overlooks. Take a walk on the self-guided Giant Logs trail or view ancient petroglyphs from an overlook. The entrance fee is $10 per private vehicle.

Tucson

Saguaro National Park
3693 South Old Spanish Trail
Tucson, AZ
520-733-5100
Dogs must be on leash and must be cleaned up after on roadways and picnic areas. They are not allowed on any trails or buildings.

California

Crescent City

Redwood National Park
1112 2nd Street
Crescent City, CA
707-464-6101
The Redwoods Park is home to some of the world's oldest and tallest trees. This park is part of a collective management effort involving 3 other California state parks, making this a World Heritage Site and an International Biosphere Reserve. The Crescent City Information Center is open daily from 9 to 5 p.m. Dogs are allowed, for no additional fee, at the park and in the campgrounds (no hookups). Dogs are not allowed on the main trails or at the beach, but they can be on the dirt trails. Dogs may not be left unattended, they must be leashed, and cleaned up after.

Death Valley

Death Valley National Park
Highway 190
Death Valley, CA
760-786-2331
Death Valley is one of the hottest places on Earth, with summer temperatures averaging well over 100 degrees Fahrenheit. It is also the lowest point on the Western Hemisphere at 282 feet below sea level. Average rainfall here sets yet another record. With an average of only 1.96 inches per year, this valley is the driest place in North America. Because of the high summer heat, the best time to visit the park is during the winter. Even though dogs are not allowed on any trails, you will still be able to see the majority of the sights and attractions from your car. There are several scenic drives that are popular with all visitors, with or without dogs. Dante's View is a 52 mile round trip drive that takes about 2 hours or longer. Some parts of the road are graded dirt roads and no trailers or RVs are allowed. On this drive you will view scenic mudstone hills which are made of 7 to 9 million year old lakebed sediments. You will also get a great view from the top of Dantes View. Another scenic drive is called Badwater. It is located about 18 miles from the Visitor Center and can take about 1.5 to 2 hours or longer. On this drive you will view the Devil's Golf Course where there are almost pure table salt crystals from an ancient lake. You will also drive to Badwater which is the lowest point in the Western Hemisphere at 282 feet below sea level. Dogs are allowed at view points which are about 200 yards or less from roads or parking lots. Pets must be leashed and attended at all times. Please clean up after your pets. While dogs are not allowed on any trails in the park, they can walk along roads. Pets are allowed up to a few hundred yards from the paved and dirt roads. Stop at the Furnace Creek Visitor Center to pick up a brochure and more information. The visitor center is located on Highway 190, north of the lowest point.

Joshua Tree National Park

Joshua Tree National Park
74485 National Park Drive
Twentynine Palms, CA
760-367-5500
Dogs are not allowed on the trails, cannot be left unattended, and must be on leash. However, they are allowed on dirt and paved roads including the Geology Tour Road. This is actually a driving tour, but you'll be able to see the park's most fascinating landscapes from this road. It is an 18 mile tour with 16 stops. The park recommends taking about 2 hours for the round trip. At stop #9, about 5 miles out, there is room to turnaround if you do not want to complete the whole tour.

Lassen Volcanic Area

Lassen Volcanic National Park
PO Box 100
Mineral, CA
530-595-4444
This national park does not really have much to see or do if you bring your pooch, except for staying overnight at the campgrounds. However, the dog-friendly Lassen National Forest surrounds the national park. At the national forest you will be able to find dog-friendly hiking, sightseeing and camping. Pets must be leashed and attended at all times. Please clean up after your pet.

Sequoia National Park

Sequoia and Kings Canyon National Park
47050 General Highway
Three Rivers, CA
559-565-3341
This national park does not really have much to see or do if you bring your pooch, except for driving through a giant redwood forest in your car and staying overnight at the campgrounds. However, located to the west and south of this national park is the dog-friendly Giant

430

National Sequoia Monument. There you will be able to find dog-friendly hiking, sightseeing and camping. Pets must be leashed and attended at all times. Please clean up after your pet.

Ventura - Oxnard

Channel Islands National Park
1901 Spinnaker Drive
Ventura, CA
805-658-5730
Dogs are not allowed in Channel Islands National Park.

Yosemite

Yosemite National Park
PO Box 577
Yosemite National Park, CA
209-372-0200
This 750,000 acre park is one of the most popular national parks in the country. Yosemite's geology is world famous for its granite cliffs, tall waterfalls and giant sequoia groves. As with most national parks, pets have limited access within the park. Pets are not allowed on unpaved or poorly paved trails, in wilderness areas including hiking trails, in park lodging (except for some campgrounds) and on shuttle buses. However, there are still several nice areas to walk with your pooch and you will be able to see the majority of sights and points of interest that most visitors see. Dogs are allowed in developed areas and on fully paved trails, include Yosemite Valley which offers about 2 miles of paved trails. From these trails you can view El Capitan, Half Dome and Yosemite Falls. You can also take the .5 mile paved trail right up to the base of Bridalveil Fall which is a 620 foot year round waterfall. The best time to view this waterfall is in the spring or early summer. The water thunders down and almost creates a nice rain at the base. Water-loving dogs will be sure to like this attraction. In general dogs are not allowed on unpaved trails, but this park does make the following exceptions. Dogs are allowed on the Meadow Loop and Four Mile fire roads in Wawona. They are also allowed on the Carlon Road and on the Old Big Oak Flat Road between Hodgdon Meadow and Hazel Green Creek. Dogs must be on a 6 foot or less leash and attended at all times. People must also clean up after their pets. For a detailed map of Yosemite, visit their

web site at http://www.nps.gov/yose/pphtml/maps.html. The green dots show the paved trails. There are four main entrances to the park and all four lead to the Yosemite Valley. The park entrance fees are as follows: $20 per vehicle, $40 annual pass or $10 per individual on foot. The pass is good for 7 days. Prices are subject to change. Yosemite Valley is open year round and may be reached via Highway 41 from Fresno, Highway 140 from Merced, Highway 120 from Manteca and in late spring through late fall via the Tioga Road (Highway 120 East) from Lee Vining. From November through March, all park roads are subject to snow chain control (including 4x4s) or temporary closure at any time due to hazardous winter driving conditions. For updated 24 hour road and weather conditions call (209) 372-0200.

Colorado

Estes Park

Rocky Mountain National Park
1000 Highway 36
Estes Park, CO
970-586-1206
Dogs cannot really do much in this park, but as you drive through the park, you will find some spectacular scenery and possibly some sightings of wildlife. Pets are not allowed on trails, or in the backcountry. Pets are allowed in your car, along the road, in parking lots, at picnic areas and campgrounds. Dogs must be on a 6 foot or less leash. You can still take your dog for a hike, not in the national park, but in the adjacent Arapaho-Roosevelt National Forest.

Gunnison

Black Canyon of the Gunnison National Park
102 Elk Creek
Gunnison, CO
970-641-2337
This unique canyon in the Rockies is narrow and deep. Dogs may view the Canyon with you from the Rim Rock Trail. Dogs on leash are allowed on roads, campgrounds, overlooks, the Rim Rock trail, Cedar Point Nature trail, and North Rim Chasm View Nature trail. They are not allowed on other hiking trails, inner canyon routes, or in the

wilderness area within the park. Dogs on leash are permitted throughout the Curecanti National Recreation Area nearby.

Mesa Verde

Mesa Verde National Park
PO Box 8
Mesa Verde, CO
970-529-4465
Dogs on leash are allowed in the campgrounds and parking lots only. Dogs are not allowed on hiking trails or archaeological sites. Pets cannot be left alone or in vehicles.

Mosca

Great Sand Dunes National Park and Preserve
11999 Highway 150
Mosca, CO
719-378-6300
The dunes of Great Sand Dunes National Park rise over 750 feet high. Dogs are allowed throughout the park and must be on leash. You must clean up after your dog and dogs may not be left unattended in the park. Leashed dogs are also welcome in the campgrounds. The park features auto touring, camping fishing, hiking, and more.

Florida

Key West

Dry Tortugas National Park
PO Box 6208
Key West, FL
305-242-7700
This set of Islands is 70 miles west of Key West in the Gulf of Mexico. Dogs must be on leash and must be cleaned up after on this island. Dogs are not allowed on the ferry but they can come over by private boat or charter from Key West. The park features picnicking, camping, fishing, swimming and more. Open year round.

Miami

Biscayne National Park
9700 SW 328 Street
Homestead, FL
305-230-7275
Biscayne National Park displays the coral reefs that thrive in the Miami

area. Dogs are allowed in the developed areas of Elliott Key and Convoy Point on the mainland. They must be leashed and attended at all times and are not allowed in the buildings or swimming area. Pets are not allowed at all on the islands of Boca Chita Key or Adams Key or even in boats docked at the islands. Dogs may camp with you at Elliott Key.

Everglades National Park
40001 State Road 9336
Homestead, FL
305-242-7700
Dogs on leash are allowed in the parking lot and campgrounds of Everglades National park. They are not allowed on trails or wilderness areas. Open year round this is the only subtropical preserve in North America. In the campgrounds and anywhere throughout this region where pets are allowed, pay close attention to them as alligators and snakes are always a danger. For more freedom to hike with your pet, try the Big Cypress National Preserve nearby.

Hawaii

Hawaii

Haleakala National Park
It is located off Hana Highway
Hawaii, HI
808-572-4400
Dogs are not allowed on the trails or in any wilderness area. Dogs are allowed in the campgrounds. There are no water or bathroom facilities at this park, so be sure to bring enough for you and your pet.

Hawaii National Park

Hawaii Volcanoes National Park
MM 31.5 H 11
Hawaii National Park, HI
808-985-6000
This park covers the top of earth's most massive volcano the Mauna Loa at almost 14,000 feet. The park is open 7 days a week year round. Dogs are allowed at no additional fee, but they may only be on paved roads, the developed areas, and the campgrounds. They are not allowed on any of the trails or off the roads. Dogs may not be left unattended at any time, and they must be leashed and cleaned up after.

Kentucky

Mammoth Cave National Park

Mammoth Cave National Park
off Interstate 65
Mammoth Cave, KY
270-758-2251
At this national park, leashed dogs are allowed on hiking trails and in campgrounds. There are over 70 miles of hiking trails which go through valleys, up into hills, and next to rivers, lakes and waterfalls. However, dogs are not allowed in the cave, which is the main attraction at this park. The park does offer kennels that are located near the Mammoth Cave Hotel. The kennels are outdoor and not heated or air-conditioned. If you want to try the kennels at Mammoth Cave, be sure to check them out first. You will need to make a reservation for the kennels and there is a $5 key deposit fee for the cage lock and a $2.50 fee for half a day or a $5.00 fee for the entire day. To make kennel reservations, call the Mammoth Cave Hotel directly at 270-758-2225.

Maine

Bar Harbor

Acadia National Park
Eagle Lake Road
Bar Harbor, ME
207-288-3338
This national park ranks high on the tail wagging meter. Dogs are allowed on most of the hiking trails, which is unusual for a national park. There are miles and miles of both hiking trails and carriage roads. Pets are also allowed at the campgrounds, but must be attended at all times. They are not allowed on sand beaches or on the steeper hiking trails. Pets must be on a 6 foot or less leash at all times. There is one exception to the leash rule. There is an area in the park that is privately owned where dogs are allowed to run leash-free. It is called Little Long Pond and is located near Seal Harbor. Overall, this is a pretty popular national park for dogs and their dog-loving owners. There is a $10 entrance fee into the park, which is good for 7 days. You can

also purchase an audio tape tour of the Park Loop Road which is a self-guided auto tour. The driving tour is about 27 miles and takes 3 to 4 hours including stops. Audio tapes are available at the Hulls Cove Visitor Center.

Michigan

Houghton

Isle Royale National Park
800 East Lakeshore Drive
Houghton, MI
906) 482-0984
No dogs are allowed within the park.

Minnesota

International Falls

Voyageurs National Park
3131 H 53S
International Falls, MN
218-283-9821
Voyageurs is a water based park located on the northern edge of Minnesota, and has some of the oldest exposed rock formations in the world. The park can also be accessed on Highway 11 from the west. There is camping, but a boat is required to access the trailheads to get there. There is another camping area just outside of the park as well. Dogs are allowed in developed areas of the park, outside visitor centers, at boat ramps, picnic areas, at tent camping areas, houseboats, and day use sites on the four main lakes. There are no additional pet fees. Dogs may not be left unattended at any time, they must be on no more than a 6 foot leash, and be cleaned up after. Pets are not allowed on park trails or in the backcountry.

Montana

West Glacier

Glacier National Park
PO Box 128
West Glacier, MT
406-888-7800
Dogs must be on leash and must be cleaned up after in the park area. Dogs are not allowed on the hiking trails. They are allowed in the camping, picnic areas and along

roadways and parking lots.

Nevada

Baker

Great Basin National Park
100 Great Basin
Baker, NV
775-234-7331
The Great Basin Park rises to over 13,000 feet and hosts the Lehman Caves and an abundant variety of wildlife, plants, and waterways. They are open year round for tent and RV camping with no hook ups. There is no additional fee for dogs, but they may not be left unattended, they must be on no more than a 6 foot leash, and be cleaned up after. Dogs are not allowed on any of the trails.

New Mexico

Carlsbad

Carlsbad Canyon National Park
727 Carlsbad Canyon H 62/180
Carlsbad, NM
505-785-2232
This national park was established to preserve the Carlsbad Caverns, and over 100 other caves housed within a fossil reef. It is also home to America's deepest and 4th longest limestone cave. Dogs are not allowed at the park, except in the parking lot and at the kennel that is on site, and they must be on leash and cleaned up after.

North Dakota

Medora

Theodore Roosevelt National Park
On I 94 at Exits 25 or 27 (South Unit)
Medora, ND
701-623-4466
This Park is located in the North Dakota Badlands. It is named after the 26th president, Theodore Roosevelt. He was a great conservationist who, out of concern for the future of our lands, established the National Forest

Service in 1906. The park is open all year although some roads close at times due to snow. The campgrounds are also open all year (no hookups). Dogs are allowed in the park and the campgrounds at no additional fee, but dogs may not be left unattended at any time, and they are not allowed in any of the buildings, or on any of the trails. However, there are trails just outside the park where dogs are allowed. One of the trails is the Maahdaahhey Trail.

Ohio

Cleveland

Cuyahoga Valley National Park
Canal Road
Brecksville, OH
216-524-1497
This national park consists of 33,000 acres along the banks of the Cuyahoga River. Scenery and terrain varies from a rolling floodplain to steep valley walls, ravines and lush upland forests. Popular activities at this park include hiking, bicycling, birdwatching and picnicking. Dogs are allowed at the park including the hiking trails. Pets must be leashed and cleaned up after. Pets are not allowed inside any buildings. The park is open daily and can be accessed by many different highways, including I-77, I-271, I-80/Ohio Turnpike, and State Route 8. To get to Canal Visitor Center, exit I-77 at Rockside Road. Go approximately 1 mile east to Canal Road and turn right. The visitor center is about 1.5 miles on the right. To get to Happy Days Visitor Center, take State Route 8 to west State Route 303. The visitor center is about 1 mile on the left. There is no park entrance fee.

Oregon

Crater Lake

Crater Lake National Park
PO Box 7
Crater Lake, OR
541-594-3100
Dogs must be on leash and must be

cleaned up after in park. Dogs must remain in the developed portions of the park and are not allowed on the dirt trails or in the backcountry. They are allowed on the roads and the sidewalks. There is a road and sidewalk surrounding Crater Lake so you and your dog may view the lake and walk quite a ways around it. Dogs are not allowed in any buildings. Dogs are allowed in the campgrounds on leash in the park.

South Carolina

Columbia

Congaree National Park
48 Old Bluff Road
Columbia, SC
803-776-4396
This 22,200-acre park protects the largest contiguous tract of old-growth bottomland hardwood forest still in the US. The park's floodplain forest has one of the highest canopies and some of the tallest trees in the eastern US. Enjoy hiking, primitive camping, birdwatching, picnicking, canoeing, kayaking, Ranger guided interpretive walks, canoe tours, nature study, and environmental education programs. Open all year; Monday to Thursday from 8:30 am to 5 pm, and Friday to Sunday from 8 am to 7 pm. To walk the trails after hours park outside the gate. Well behaved dogs on leash are allowed on the trails and the outside guided tours, but they are not allowed on the Boardwalk or in the buildings.

South Dakota

Hot Springs

Wind Cave National Park
26611 H 385
Hot Springs, SD
605-745-4600
This park is home to one of the world's longest and most complex caves. The park is open year round from 8 to 5 pm during summer hours and until 4:30 pm winter hours. Dogs are allowed at the park and at the campground (no hookups) for no additional fee, but basically they can only go where your car can go. The campground is open year round except when it snows and they have to close the roads to the camping areas. Dogs are not allowed on the trails, they may not be left

unattended, they must be leashed at all times, and cleaned up after.

Interior

Badlands National Park
25216 Ben Reifel Rd
Interior, SD
605-433-5361
This park covers 160 square acres, has America's largest mixed grass prairies, and is home to the Badlands National Monument. Highway 240 is the Badlands Loop Scenic Byway and is 31 1/2 miles long with 14 lookouts. Dogs are not allowed on any of the trails in the park. They are allowed only at the campground or the parking lots. The contact station for the Cedar Pass Campground is on Highway 240, and this campground has an amphitheater. The other campground, White River, has a visitor's center on Highway 27. The campgrounds are open year round, and there are no hook-ups at either camp. Dogs of all sizes are allowed in the campgrounds. There are no additional fees. Dogs may not be left unattended outside, and only inside if it creates no danger to the pet. Dog must be leashed and cleaned up after.

Tennessee

The Smoky Mountains

Great Smoky Mountains National Park
107 Park Headquarters Road
Gatlinburg, TN
865-436-1200
Pets must be leashed or restrained at all times and are not allowed on hiking trails. They can accompany you in your car and at lookouts and stops near the road. However, there is one trail from the park headquarters to the city of Gatlinburg that allows leashed dogs. It is a nice 2 mile long dirt trail that follows a creek. There are spots along the way where your dog can take a dip in the water. If you want a longer hike, try the nearby dog-friendly Pisgah National Forest or the Nantahala National Forest. Both are in North Caorlina, and they are located about a two hour drive from the national park.

Texas

Big Bend National Park

Big Bend National Park
P.O. Box 129
Big Bend National Park, TX
432-477-2251
This park is at the big bend of the Rio Grande, and there are 2 entrances; in the North on Highway 118, and in the West on Highway 385. Dogs are not allowed anywhere in the back country, on any of the trails, at the river, or off any of the roads.There are 3 campgrounds, and an RV park. The RV park is the only camp area with full hookups. It is concession operated, sites are on a first come/first served basis, and full hookup capability is required. Dogs may not be left unattended at any time, they must be leashed or crated at all times, and be cleaned up after.

Pine Springs

Guadalupe Mountains National Park
H 62/180
Pine Springs, TX
915-828-3251
This parks hosts an extensive Permisan Limestone fossil reef. The park is open year-round; visitor center hours are from 8:00 a.m. to 4:30 p.m., and a bit longer in summer. Dogs on lead are allowed to go to the Sitting Bull Falls and the Last Chance Canyon. Dogs are not allowed on any of the other trails, but they are allowed on the trails in the neighboring Lincoln National Forest. This forest is very rugged, and pets must be watched very closely that they do not step on the plant called Letchigia Cactus. It may even go through tires and must be removed only by surgical means. Dogs are allowed at no additional fee at either of the campgrounds, and the campsites do not have hookups. Dogs may not be left unattended, they must be leashed, and cleaned up after. This park can also be accessed from the New Mexico side on Highway 137.

Utah

Bryce Canyon

Bryce Canyon National Park
PO Box 640201/ On H 63
Bryce, UT
435-834-5322
This park is famous for it's unique geology, creating vast and unusual limestone formations throughout the region. Dogs are not allowed on any of the trails, the shuttle, the viewpoints, or the visitor's center. The park is open 24 hours a day year round. There are 2 campgrounds; Loop A, the north campground, is open all year, and the Sunset campground is only open for the season. There are no hookups at either campground. Dogs can walk along the road in the campground. There are no additional fees for the dogs. Dogs may not be left unattended, they must be leashed at all times, and cleaned up after.

Moab

Arches National Park
PO Box 907
Moab, UT
435-719-2299
Pets on leash with cleanup are allowed in the campsites and paved areas of the parks. Dogs are not allowed on any trails or backcountry. They are allowed unattended if well-behaved in the Devil's Garden campground.

Canyonlands National Park
2282 SW Resource Blvd
Moab, UT
435-719-2313
Pets on leash are allowed in developed areas, such as campgrounds, paved roads, and the Potash/Shafer Canyon road between Moab and the Island in the Sky. They are not allowed on hiking trails or in the backcountry.

Torrey

Capitol Reef National Park
HC 70 Box 15
Torrey, UT
435-425-3791
Dogs on leash are allowed in campsites and on paved road areas. Dogs are not allowed on hiking trails or in the backcountry.

Zion National Park

Zion National Park
State Route 9
Springdale, UT
435-772-3256
Dogs are allowed on one walking trail at this national park. Dogs on a 6 foot or less leash are allowed on the Pa'rus Trail which is a 1.5 mile long trail that runs from the South Campground to Canyon Junction. You and your pooch can also enjoy a 10-12 mile scenic drive on the Zion-Mount Carmel Highway which goes through the park. If you are there from November through March, you can also take your car on the Zion Canyon Scenic Drive. If you arrive during the summer months, the Zion Canyon Scenic Drive is closed and only allows park shuttle buses. Other pet rules include no pets on shuttle buses, in the backcountry, or in public buildings. Pets are allowed in the campgrounds and along roadways.

Virginia

Luray

Shenandoah National Park
3655 U.S. Highway 211 East
Luray, VA
540-999-3500
This national park, located along a section of the Blue Ridge Parkway, offers miles and miles of dog-friendly hiking trails. There are some trails where dogs are not allowed, but your pooch is allowed on the majority of trails in this park. Pets must be on a 6 foot or less leash at all times, and are allowed in campgrounds, and picnic areas.

Washington

Ashford

Mount Rainer National Park
Tahoma Woods State Route
Ashford, WA
360-569-2211
Dogs must be on leash where they are allowed. Dogs are only allowed on roads, parking lots, and campgrounds. They are not allowed on trails, snow, in buildings, or any

wilderness areas. There is a small portion of Pacific Crest Trail near the park's eastern boundary that allows pets on leash.

North Cascades National Park

North Cascades National Park
State Route 20
Newhalem, WA
360-856-5700
Dogs are allowed on one of the hiking trails, the Pacific Crest Trail. This scenic hiking trail runs through the park and is rated moderate to difficult. The trail is located off Highway 20, about one mile east of Rainy Pass. At the Bridge Creek Trailhead, park on the north side of the highway and then hike north (uphill) or south (downhill). A Northwest Forest Pass is required to park at the trailhead. The cost is about $5 and can be purchased at the Visitor's Center in Newhalem. For a larger variety of trails, including a less strenuous hike, dogs are also allowed on trails at the adjacent Ross Lake National Recreation Area and the Lake Chelan National Recreation Area. Both recreation areas are managed by the national park.

Olympic National Park

Olympic National Park
600 East Park Avenue
Port Angeles, WA
360-565-3130
Pets are not permitted on park trails, meadows, beaches or in any undeveloped area of the park. There is one exception. Dogs are allowed on leash, during daytime hours only, on Kalaloch Beach along the Pacific Ocean and from Rialto Beach north to Ellen Creek. For those folks and dogs who want to hike on a trail, try the adjacent dog-friendly Olympic National Forest.

Wyoming

Yellowstone - Grand Teton

Grand Teton National Park

Moose, WY
307-739-3300
Pets are only allowed in your car,

on roads and road shoulders, campgrounds, picnic areas, parking lots, etc. Dogs must be leashed. Dogs are not allowed on any park trails or in the backcountry. For trails that are dog-friendly try the Bridger-Teton National Forest next door.

Yellowstone National Park
various
Yellowstone National Park, WY
307-344-7381
While this national park is not particularly dog-friendly, you will still be able to see some of the major attractions. Dogs are allowed in parking areas, campgrounds and within 100 feet of roads. Pets must be on a 6 foot or less leash or crated or caged at all times. Pets are not allowed on the trails, boardwalks, or in thermal areas where the geysers, including Old Faithful, are located. While dogs are not allowed next to the Old Faithful Geyser, you and your pooch will be able to view its large eruptions from about 200 feet back. And if you drive the Grand Loop Road, you will be able to view some points of interest and perhaps see some wildlife including black bears, grizzly bears, bison and elk. If you are looking for some hiking trails, there are numerous dog-friendly trails in the nearby Shoshone National Forest, located between the town of Cody and Yellowstone National Park.